Contents in Brief

GIVE YOUR STUDENTS EXPERIENCE WITH OUR RICH "BEST OF THE WEB" RESOURCES

GLANCE AT THIS SAMPLING OF OUR 55 LETTER-, MEMO-, AND E-MAIL REAL COMPANY CASES

Business Communication Today

SEVENTH EDITION

COURTLAND L. BOVÉE

Professor of Business Communication
C. Allen Paul Distinguished Chair
Grossmont College

JOHN V. THILL

Chief Executive Officer
Communication Specialists of America

BARBARA E. SCHATZMAN

Keller Graduate School of Management
President
Summit One Global Business Solutions

Upper Saddle River, NJ 07458

Library of Congress Cataloging-in-Publication Data
Bovée, Courtland L.
Business communication today/Courtland L. Bovée, John V. Thill, Barbara E. Schatzman—7th ed.
p. cm.
Includes bibliographical references and index.
ISBN 0-13-092858-5
1. Business communication—United States—Case studies. 2. Communication in organizations—United States—Case studies. I. Thill, John V. II. Schatzman, Barbara E. III. Title.

HF5718.B66 2002
658.4'5--dc21 2002017097

Acquisitions Editor: David Parker
Editor-in-Chief: Jeff Shelstad
Assistant Editor/Editorial Assistant: Ashley Keim
Media Project Manager: Anthony Palmiotto
Executive Marketing Manager: Debbie Clare
Marketing Assistant: Amanda Fisher
Managing Editor (Production): Judy Leale
Production Editor: Michele Foresta
Production Assistant: Dianne Falcone
Permissions Coordinator: Suzanne Grappi
Associate Director, Manufacturing: Vincent Scelta
Production Manager: Arnold Vila
Manufacturing Buyer: Arnold Vila
Design Manager: Patricia Smythe
Art Director: Janet Slowik
Interior Design: Liz Harasymczuk
Cover Design: Joan O'Connor
Cover Illustration/Photo: George B. Diebold
Illustrator (Interior): Electragraphics
Manager, Print Production: Christy Mahon
Composition: Carlisle Communications
Full-Service Project Management: Carlisle Communications
Printer/Binder: Courier/Kendallville

Credits and acknowledgments borrowed from other sources and reproduced, with permission, in this textbook appear on page R1.

Pearson Education LTD.
Pearson Education Australia PTY, Limited
Pearson Education Singapore, Pte. Ltd
Pearson Education North Asia Ltd
Pearson Education, Canada, Ltd
Pearson Educación de Mexico, S.A. de C.V.
Pearson Education–Japan
Pearson Education Malaysia, Pte. Ltd

10 9 8 7 6 5 4 3 2 1
ISBN 0-13-092858-5

Contents

PART 3 Writing Letters, Memos, E-Mail, and Other Brief Messages 183

Preface

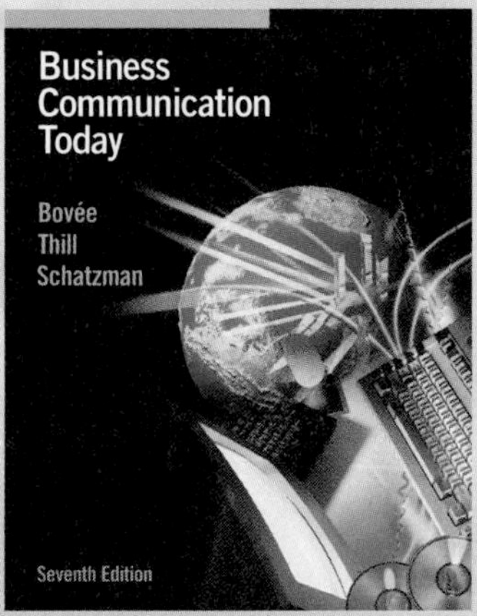

With its vivid insights into real-world communication situations and lively, conversational writing style, this text holds the interest of students and teachers alike. In the 17 years since the first edition was published, millions of students have learned about business communication from ***Business Communication Today****. In 2000 the text was awarded the prestigious Award for Excellence by the Text and Academic Authors Association.*

Business Communication Today Wins Textbook Excellence Award

Business Communication Today was accorded the prestigious Textbook Excellence Award (a "Texty") in 2000 by the Text and Academic Authors Association (TAA). The selection was made by a distinguished panel of judges who are themselves noted textbook authors.

The purpose of the award is to identify and honor outstanding books and learning materials that enhance the quality of what is available to students and scholars for teaching, education, and research. The text received the highest ranking for being interesting, informative, well organized, well prepared, up to date, appealing, and teachable.

We welcome our new co-author, Barbara Schatzman, to the seventh edition of this text. With over 20 years of managerial and consulting experience and outstanding academic credentials, Barbara brings new insights and real-world perspectives to this text that will help keep it at the forefront of its field.

This seventh edition of ***Business Communication Today*** is the centerpiece of a comprehensive teaching and learning package. The text covers all the basic principles and goals as recommended by the Association of Collegiate Business Schools and Programs and the American Assembly of Collegiate Schools of Business (AACSB), the International Association for Management Education. Moreover, it fully integrates issues critical to successful business communication. Take this opportunity to explore the new edition of ***Business Communication Today, Seventh Edition***.

New CONTENTS

This chapter discusses techniques for writing for the Web.

This chapter explains how companies today use the Internet and other technologies to communicate information, as well as the challenges created by these technology advances.

This chapter discusses preparing, designing, and using visual aids in presentations and emphasizes electronic presentations such as PowerPoint.

This appendix provides tips for composing and sending e-mails, plus provides strategies for making electronic communication more readable and effective.

New FEATURES IN THIS EDITION

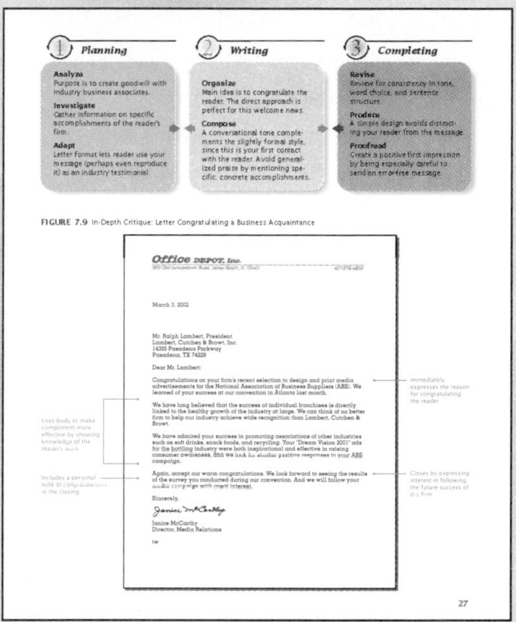

1 **Planning**

Analyze
Purpose is to create goodwill with industry business associates.

Investigate
Gather information on specific accomplishments of the reader's firm.

Adapt
Letter format lets reader use your message (perhaps even reproduce it) as an industry testimonial.

2 **Writing**

Organize
Main idea is to congratulate the reader. The direct approach is perfect for this welcome news.

Compose
A conversational tone complements the slightly formal style, since this is your first contact with the reader. Avoid generalized praise by mentioning specific, concrete accomplishments.

3 **Completing**

Revise
Review for consistency in tone, word choice, and sentence structure.

Produce
A simple design avoids distracting your reader from the message.

Proofread
Create a positive first impression by being especially careful to send an error-free message.

FIGURE 7.9 In-Depth Critique: Letter Congratulating a Business Acquaintance

Office DEPOT, Inc.

March 3, 2002

Mr. Ralph Lambert, President
Lambert, Cutchen & Browt, Inc.
14355 Pasadena Parkway
Pasadena, TX 74229

Dear Mr. Lambert:

Congratulations on your firm's recent selection to design and print media advertisements for the National Association of Business Suppliers (ABS). We learned of your success at our convention in Atlanta last month.

We have long believed that the success of individual franchises is directly linked to the healthy growth of the industry at large. We can think of no better firm to help our industry achieve wide recognition than Lambert, Cutchen & Browt.

We have admired your success in promoting associations of other industries such as soft drinks, snack foods, and recycling. Your "Dream Vision 2001" ads for the bottling industry were both inspirational and effective in raising consumer awareness, and we look for similar positive responses to your ABS campaign.

Again, accept our warm congratulations. We look forward to seeing the results of the survey you conducted during our convention. And we will follow your media campaign with great interest.

Sincerely,

Janice McCarthy
Director, Media Relations

tw

Immediately expresses the reason for congratulating the reader

Uses body to make compliment more effective by showing knowledge of the reader's work

Includes a personal note of congratulations in the closing

Closes by expressing interest in following the future success of the firm

27

GREATER EMPHASIS ON PROCESS AND PRODUCT

We reorganized the text material into a series of **three easy-to-follow steps** to offer students a practical strategy to solve communication problems. The three-step process includes:

- **planning business messages**
- **writing business messages**
- **completing business messages**

The process is thoroughly integrated and applied throughout the text.

EMPHASIS ON TEAMS

Communicating effectively through teamwork is covered extensively in Chapter 2. Throughout the text, teamwork exercises are included in the **"Communication Challenges"** feature at the conclusion of each chapter and in the **"Practice Your Knowledge"** section in the end-of-chapter exercises. Topics include characteristics of effective teams, collaborative writing, cultural diversity in teams, group dynamics, groupthink, role playing, group decision making, use of technology to enhance decisions made in groups, conflict resolution in groups, and group interviewing.

CHAPTER 7 Writing Routine, Good-News, and Goodwill Messages 31

6 **Describe the importance of goodwill messages, and describe how to make them effective.** Goodwill messages are important for building relationships with customers, colleagues, and other businesspeople. These friendly, unexpected notes have no direct business purpose, but they make people feel good about doing business with the sender. To make goodwill messages effective, make them honest and sincere. Avoid exaggerating, back up compliments with specific points, and give restrained praise.

TEST YOUR KNOWLEDGE

1. When is a request routine?
2. What are some of the guidelines for asking a series of questions in a routine request?
3. What information should be included in an order request?
4. Should you use the direct or indirect approach for most routine messages? Why?
5. Where in a routine message should you state your actual request?
6. How does a claim differ from an adjustment?
7. How does the question of fault affect what you say in a message granting a claim?
8. What is the appropriate strategy for responding to a request for a recommendation about a job candidate whose performance was poor?
9. How can you avoid sounding insincere when writing a goodwill message?
10. What are some of the guidelines for writing condolence messages?

APPLY YOUR KNOWLEDGE

1. When organizing request messages, why is it important to know whether any cultural differences exist between you and your audience? Explain.
2. Your company's error cost an important business customer a new client; you know it and your customer knows it. Do you apologize, or do you refer to the incident in a positive light without admitting any responsibility? Briefly explain.
3. You've been asked to write a letter of recommendation for an employee who is disabled and uses a wheelchair. The disability has no effect on the employee's ability to do the job, and you feel confident about writing the best recommendation possible. Nevertheless, you know the prospective company and its facilities aren't well suited to wheelchair access. Do you mention the employee's disability in your letter? Explain.
4. Every time you send a direct-request memo to Ted Jackson, he delays or refuses to comply. You're beginning to get impatient. Should you send Jackson a memo to ask what's wrong? Complain to your supervisor about Jackson's uncooperative attitude? Arrange a face-to-face meeting with Jackson? Bring up the problem at the next staff meeting? Explain.
5. Ethical Choices You have a complaint against one of your suppliers, but you have no documentation to back it up. Should you request an adjustment anyway? Why or why not?

PRACTICE YOUR KNOWLEDGE

Documents for Analysis

Read the following documents; then (1) analyze the strengths and weaknesses of each sentence and (2) revise each document so that it follows this chapter's guidelines.

Document 7.A: Requesting Routine Information from a Business

Our college is closing its dining hall for financial reasons, so we want to do something to help the students prepare their own food in their dorm rooms if they so choose. Your colorful ad in *Collegiate Magazine* caught our eye. We need the following information before we make our decision.

- Would you be able to ship the microwaves by August 15th? I realize this is short notice, but our board of trustees just made the decision to close the dining hall last week and we're scrambling around trying to figure out what to do.
- Do they have any kind of a warranty? College students can be pretty hard on things, as you know, so we will need a good warranty.
- How much does it cost? Do you give a discount for a big order?
- Do we have to provide a special outlet?
- Will students know how to use them, or will we need to provide instructions?

As I said before, we're on a tight time frame and need good information from you as soon as possible to help us make our decision about ordering. You never know what the board might come up with next. I'm looking at several other companies, also, so please let us know ASAP.

Document 7.B: Making Claims and Requests for Adjustment

At a local business-supply store, I recently purchased your "Negotiator Pro" for my computer. I bought the CD because I saw your ad for it in *MacWorld* magazine, and it looked as if it might be an effective tool for use in my corporate seminar on negotiation.

Unfortunately, when I inserted it in my office computer, it wouldn't work. I returned it to the store, but since I had already opened it, they refused to exchange it for a CD that would work or give me a refund. They told me to contact you and that you might be able to send me a version that would work with my computer.

You can send the information to me at the letterhead address. If you cannot send me the correct disk, please refund my $79.95. Thanks in advance for any help you can give me in this matter.

Integrated Approach to Technology

Business Communication Today reinforces the importance of using technology effectively in business communication throughout the text.

1. **Full-chapter coverage.** See the annotated Contents in this preface for more details.

2. **In-text discussion.** The text includes extensive coverage of e-mail, voice mail, faxes, communication software, the Internet, chat, instant messaging, multimedia, and more.

3. **"Keeping Pace with Technology" boxes.** Special boxes highlight how to use technology in business communication to achieve a competitive advantage.

4. **Focus on e-business.** Chapter vignettes, In-Depth Critiques, photos, and letter-, memo-, and report-writing and e-mail cases feature communication challenges students are likely to encounter in the world of e-business.

5. **Internet resources.**
   - ***Internet exercises tied to the book.*** Students become acquainted with the wealth of business communication information on the web by visiting the text's **"Best of the Web"** websites and by completing the **"Exploring the Best of the Web"** end-of-chapter Internet exercises.
   - ***Grammar diagnostic tests.*** Students can reinforce their grammar and language skills by taking four online diagnostic tests offered at this text's website, **www.prenhall.com/bovee**. The tests cover a variety of topics, including spelling, verbs, adjectives, adverbs, pronouns, capitalization, punctuation, word choice, sentence structure, clarity, style, proofreading, and more. Once a test is submitted, it's automatically scored, the correct answers are provided, and students can improve areas where they are weak.
   - ***"My Companion Website."*** This powerful website offers chapter-specific current events articles called *"In the News,"* Internet exercises, and an interactive study guide. The study guide includes multiple-choice, true/false, and essay questions. For faculty, downloadable supplements are included.

6. **Online course resources. The 60 Keys to Mastering Effective Business Communication** is a first-of-its-kind instructional tool, available as an online course on the web or on a CD-ROM. We personally introduce each chapter with a video presentation. Students learn about three key concepts and practice applying them with interactive exercises.

Hallmark Features

UPDATED FOR THIS EDITION

Chapter 7

Writing Routine, Good-News, and Goodwill Messages

After studying this chapter, you will be able to

1. *Apply the three-step writing process to routine positive messages*
2. *Illustrate the strategy for writing routine requests*
3. *Discuss the differences among four types of routine requests*
4. *Explain the main [illegible] granting a claim when the company, the customer, or a third party is at fault*
5. *Outline how best to protect yourself when referring to a candidate's shortcoming in a recommendation letter*
6. *Describe the importance of goodwill messages, and describe how to make them effective*

COMMUNICATION CLOSE-UP AT UNUMPROVIDENT CORPORATION

www.unumprovident.com

No one wants to think about the chance of disability from illness or injury. But UnumProvident has to. It's the nation's largest disability insurer, aiming to protect individuals' paychecks, assets, and lifestyles. Through programs such as LifeBalance, the company emphasizes return to work, offers highly responsive service, and addresses many of the life and work challenges facing people with a long-term disability or terminal illness. To succeed, the company must communicate effectively not only externally with brokers, benefit managers, and insured employees but also internally with its own people. UnumProvident must be sure that its internal messages are understandable to everyone, from CEO to newest [illegible] in every location, from Toronto to Los Angeles—and that's where Becky Bumgardner comes in.

As senior corporate writer in the corporate relations department, Bumgardner is responsible for writing and sending internal messages to more than 10,000 UnumProvident employees in nearly 60 offices across the United States and Canada. Many of these messages are routine and are sent by e-mail to employees in various states, countries, and time zones. Bumgardner writes on topics ranging from departmental meeting announcements to incentive programs for managers. She writes about departmental reorganizations, virus alerts, corporate earnings, and promotions. She also composes feature articles for the monthly newsletter and prepares daily updates for the company intranet.

But whether she's requesting routine information for the company newsletter or reminding employees about an upcoming deadline, Bumgardner is always careful to compose messages that are both concise and clear. Before writing anything, she makes sure that she fully understands the information she needs to communicate. As Bumgardner says, "I ask lots of questions before I begin to write. The old adage is true: The only dumb question is the one you don't ask. So don't be afraid to verify your information and make sure you understand a topic."

Clarity also depends on how much information you provide. For example, when preparing a routine request, "it helps your readers to know why you're making the request," explains Bumgardner. "It gives them an incentive to act. So I explain what needs to be done, why it needs to be done, and how the request affects the audience." To be as clear as possible, she tries to imagine all the ways a request might be misunderstood and then carefully chooses her words to avoid those pitfalls. For instance, knowing that Canadian insurance regulations often differ from U.S. regulations, Bumgardner is careful to address the needs of both U.S. and Canadian employees when sending mass e-mail messages to "all employees." That way, she eliminates any confusion.

Bumgardner keeps her messages brief and to the point. "With too much extra information," she advises, "your audience will stop reading your message." And to make it easier for audiences to absorb her messages, Bumgardner emphasizes important deadlines with bold or italic type and draws attention to important facts with bullet points. To close, she summarizes her message and includes any necessary deadlines, reminders, or contact information.

2

COMMUNICATION CLOSE-UPS

Each chapter begins with an instructive **"Communication Close-Up"** featuring a communication expert who, in his or her own words, applies the chapter's concepts to common business situations. That expert reappears from time to time throughout the chapter to dramatize the connection between the chapter's contents and life on the job.

COMMUNICATION CHALLENGES

Projects called **"Communication Challenges"** conclude each chapter and are related to the situations described in the Communication Close-Ups. Each chapter has one **individual challenge** and one **team challenge.** These challenges are exclusive to ***Business Communication Today***, providing a dimension of reality unmatched by any other textbook in the field.

All internal company information was gathered through personal interviews with our business associates, friends, and contacts, and it gives ***Business Communication Today*** the real-world applications for which students are so eager.

COMMUNICATION CHALLENGES AT UNUMPROVIDENT CORPORATION

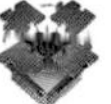

Business is booming at UnumProvident Corporation. Quarterly sales of group disability insurance plans have increased by 20 percent, and the company is hiring new personnel to keep up with the growth. As the company expands, Becky Bumgardner's projects keep mounting, and she has asked for your help writing several routine messages.

Individual Challenge: Bumgardner wants to hire Jim Moody as a new staff member in the corporate relations department. She's impressed with his résumé and interview. Bumgardner thinks Moody may be a "good fit" for her department, and she'd like to know whether he responds well under pressure. As public relations coordinator for Brentwell Insurance in Snohomish, Washington, Moody may have dealt with stressful situations. Write a letter to Moody's

30 PART VII Letters, Memos, E-Mail, and Other Brief Messages

Brentwell supervisor, requesting information about Moody, especially about his behavior under pressure. Make up any necessary details, and address the letter to Henry Watrous, Brentwell Insurance, 1552 10th Avenue, Snohomish, WA 98290.

Team Challenge: Managers at UnumProvident Corporation participate in incentive programs, receiving rewards for achieving or exceeding their sales quotas. This quarter, the number of managers entitled to rewards has increased by 20 percent. Winners of incentive programs can select (1) four tickets to a Seattle Mariner's major league baseball home game, (2) a DVD player, or (3) a gift basket of gourmet foods. Bumgardner asks your team to develop a form letter to be sent to the winners, congratulating them on their outstanding performance and requesting winners to notify Bumgardner via e-mail of their prize selection. Be sure to state in your form letter how prizes will be distributed to winners.

Communication Across Cultures

Tested techniques help students communicate successfully in the global arena and in the culturally diverse business world at home. Some examples include

- Communicating with a Global Audience on the Web
- Actions Speak Louder Than Words All Around the World
- Test Your Intercultural Knowledge

Communicating Across Cultures

How Direct Is Too Direct?

Being direct is civil, considerate, and honest—or so say people in the United States. Other folks view that same directness as being abrupt, rude, and intrusive—even dishonest and offensive. Countries such as France, Mexico, Japan, Saudi Arabia, Italy, and the Philippines all tend toward high-context cultures (see discussion in Chapter 3). That is, the people in these countries depend on shared knowledge and inferred messages to communicate; they gather meaning more from context and less from direct statement.

Offering a little constructive criticism may actually hurt your Mexican assistant's dignity. In fact, in high-context cultures, avoid saying outright, "You are wrong." You could cause the other person to lose face. When making requests, determine whether to use a direct or an implied approach by considering audience attitudes toward destiny, time, authority, and logic:

- **Destiny.** Do audience members believe they can control events themselves? Or do they see events as predetermined and uncontrollable? If you're supervising employees who believe that fate controls a construction deadline, your crisp e-mail message requesting them to stay on schedule may be hard for them to understand; it may even be insulting.
- **Time.** Do audience members view time as exact, precise, and not to be wasted? Or do they see time as relative, relaxed, and necessary for developing interpersonal relationships? If you see time as money and you get straight to business in your memo to your Mexican manager, your message may be overlooked in the confusion over your disregard for social propriety.
- **Authority.** Do audience members conduct business more autocratically or more democratically? In Mexico, rank and status are highly valued, so when communicating downward, you may need to be even more direct than you're used to being in the United States. And when communicating upward, you may need to be much less direct than usual.
- **Logic.** Do audience members pursue logic in a straight line, from point A to point B? Or do they communicate in circular or spiral patterns of logic? If you organize a speech or letter in a straightforward and direct manner, your message may be considered illogical, unclear, and disorganized.

You may want to decide not only how direct to be in written messages but also whether to write at all; perhaps a phone call or a visit would be more appropriate. By finding out how much or how little a culture tends toward high-context communication, you'll know whether to be direct or to rely on nuance when communicating with the people of that culture.

Career Applications

1. Research a high-context culture such as that of Japan, Korea, or China, and write a one- or two-paragraph summary of how someone in that culture would go about requesting information.
2. When you are writing in American English to someone in a high-context culture, would it be better to (a) make the request directly in the interest of clarity or (b) try to match your audience's unfamiliar logic and make your request indirectly? Explain your answer.

Focusing on Ethics

Recommendation Letters: What's Right to Write?

You were Frank Walker's supervisor for four years. When he left the company recently, he asked you to write a letter of recommendation for him. However, your company's legal experts said no.

Why Not Give Recommendations?

Thousands of lawsuits have been filed (and won) by employees, charging former employers with making slanderous (oral) and libelous (written) statements in job recommendations. During one seven-year period in California, employees won 72 percent of the libel and related suits they brought against employers, and their average award was $582,000. One employer lost for saying an employee had "suddenly resigned," which implied the employee had resigned under "a veil of suspicion," said the court. Another employer lost for saying an employee was fired "for causes." Plus, when employees prove actual malice, damage awards skyrocket.

To complicate matters, one court ruling held an employer liable for *omitting* information about a former employee. So what sort of information should or should not be included in a recommendation? Even though some states have passed laws protecting companies against lawsuits when the employer acts in good faith, legal and human resources experts often advise companies to control what's being said by centralizing all recommendations. The cautious approach is to supply only dates of employment and titles of positions held—and to give that information only to people who have written authorization from former employees.

But What If You Want to Give a Recommendation?

Even so, Frank Walker was a terrific employee—a good friend—and you believe he really deserves a recommendation. You have two options. The first is to write the letter with Walker so that the contents satisfy you both and then to discuss the letter with your human resources department before releasing it. The second option is to ask Walker to list you as a *personal* reference, which removes your company from any responsibility for statements you make. But be careful—you can still be held personally responsible for your comments.

Of course, if it had been Sharon Brown who had asked for your recommendation, you'd be facing a different dilemma. Brown wasn't the greatest employee. So would you owe her potential employer the whole story? Including negative information could get you sued by Brown, and omitting negative information could get you sued by the hiring company for "failure to disclose" or "negligent referral."

Regardless of the circumstances, consult your human resources or legal department, and be sure to (1) comment only on your own experience working with a former employee, (2) make all comments in writing, and (3) limit your remarks to provable facts (don't exaggerate).

Career Applications

1. A former employee was often late for work but was an excellent and fast worker who got along well with everyone. Do you think it's important to mention the tardiness to potential employers? If so, how will you handle it?
2. Step outside yourself for a moment and write a letter of recommendation about you from a former employer's perspective. Practice honesty, integrity, and prudence.

Focusing on Ethics

By examining critical ethical issues that face business communicators in today's workplace, students gain insight into how to identify areas of ethical vulnerability, how to steer clear of ethical perils, and when to seek ethical advice. The wide range of topics include

- Should Employers Use E-Mail to Deliver Negative Employment Messages?
- Spin Cycle: Deciphering Corporate Doublespeak
- Résumé Deception: Risky or Fatal?

Sharpening Your Career Skills

Practical pointers and confidence-building guidelines help students improve their writing and speaking skills. This feature helps students strengthen their career skills by exploring such topics as

- Ordinary or Extraordinary? Using the Web to Produce Better PowerPoint Presentations
- Beating Writer's Block: Nine Ideas to Get Words Flowing
- Interview Strategies: Answering the 16 Toughest Questions

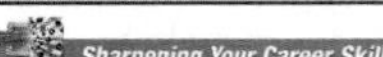

Sharpening Your Career Skills

How to Proofread Like a Pro: Tips for Creating the Perfect Document

You've carefully revised and polished your document, and it's been sent off to the word-processing department or a designer to be put into final form. You can breathe a sigh of relief, but only for the moment: You'll still be proofreading what comes out of the printer. To ensure that any document is error-free, always proofread the final version. Following are some hints to help make your proofreading more effective.

- **Multiple passes.** Go through the document several times, focusing on a different aspect each time. The first pass might be to look for omissions and errors in content; the second pass could be for layout, spacing, and other aesthetic features; a final pass might be to check for typographical, grammatical, and spelling errors.
- **Perceptual tricks.** Your brain has been trained to ignore transposed letters, improper capitalization, and misplaced punctuation. Try (1) reading each page from the bottom to the top (starting at the last word in each line), (2) placing your finger under each word and reading it silently, (3) making a slit in a sheet of paper that reveals only one line of type at a time, and (4) reading the document aloud and pronouncing each word carefully.
- **Impartial reviews.** Have a friend or colleague proofread the document for you. Others are likely to catch mistakes that you continually fail to notice. (All of us have blind spots when it comes to reviewing our own work.)
- **Typos.** Look for the most common typographical errors (typos): transposition (such as *teh*), substitution (such as *ecomonic*), and omission (such as *productvity*).
- **Mechanics.** When looking for errors in spelling, grammar, punctuation, and capitalization, if you're unsure about something, look it up in a dictionary, a usage book, or another reference work.
- **Accuracy.** Double-check the spelling of names and the accuracy of dates, addresses, and all numbers (quantities ordered, prices, and so on). It would not do to order 500 staplers when you want only 50.
- **Distance.** If you have time, set the document aside and proofread it the next day.
- **Vigilance.** Avoid reading large amounts of material in one sitting, and try not to proofread when you're tired.
- **Focus.** Concentrate on what you're doing. Try to block out distractions, and focus as completely as possible on your proofreading task.
- **Caution.** Take your time. Quick proofreading is not careful proofreading.

Proofreading may require patience, but it adds credibility to your document.

Career Applications

1. What qualities does a person need to be a good proofreader? Are such qualities inborn, or can they be learned?
2. Proofread the following sentence:
   aplication of thse methods in stores in San Deigo nd Cinncinati have resultted in a 30 drop in roberies an a 50 precent decling in violnce there, acording ot thedevelpers if the security sytem, Hanover brothrs, Inc.

Keeping Pace with Technology

Warding Off Digital Disaster

Today's data are being threatened. Some 20 percent of the information carefully collected on Jet Propulsion Laboratory computers during NASA's 1976 Viking mission to Mars has been lost. Defense Department computers can no longer read some POW and MIA records from the Vietnam War. And malicious computer viruses are erasing computer files and locking up computer systems all over the globe. Not only can computer viruses turn detailed records into electronic confetti, but the very media carrying our precious bits of information aren't lasting as long as we had expected. Moreover, chances are good that the software (or even the hardware) needed to get at today's data might not be readily available in 10 years. Anyone who has tried wresting information from a 5 1/4-inch floppy disk knows that.

You can help prevent your digits from turning to dust by taking these precautions:

- **Keep your computer clean.** Keep food and drink away from your equipment.
- **Maintain your hard drive.** Scan your drive for errors often, and correct them. Defragment your hard drive once a year (but only after performing a complete system backup).
- **Install surge protectors.** Make sure your protectors have a UL1449 rating of 330 volts or less, and install a backup power supply.
- **Exit your system correctly.** Close all applications before you turn off your computer; then shut down your computer in proper sequence.
- **Register your hardware and software.** Send in registration cards so that you are eligible for customer support and are notified about major problems or upgrades.
- **Install antivirus programs.** Use a good virus-scanning program, and update it at least quarterly. Run a virus scan on everything that comes into your computer: new software, new floppy disks, and Internet downloads. Don't open e-mail attachments from strangers.
- **Back up your system regularly.** Make sure you flag all important files and keep a regular backup schedule. Back up your entire system before installing any new software.
- **Store your backups properly.** Store your backup media off-site in a cool, dry cabinet away from heat, humidity, light, dust, and smoke. Keep them away from electric motors, speakers, phone handsets, monitors, TV screens, and transformers (which can cause electromagnetic radiation and erasure). Serious PC users may want to consider online backup services, a safe and inexpensive option.
- **Keep your copies clean and organized.** Label your backup media clearly. Twice a year buy and use new backup media, and clean the magnetic heads on your backup hardware. Do a "test restore" monthly to make sure your backups are usable.

By taking these steps, you can substantially reduce your risk should a data disaster strike.

Career Applications

1. Your office has just decided to electronically store all written communications, reports, policies, and so on. Express your concerns about this policy in a brief memo to the president of the company.
2. E-mail has increasingly become a vehicle for spreading computer viruses that destroy computer files and programs. What cautions can you take to protect your computer from being infected by a deadly virus?

Keeping Pace with Technology

Specific techniques offer students guidance for using technological applications to improve business communication. Some examples include

- Beware of the Mischievous Webmaster
- Caution: E-Mail Can Bite
- Netting a Job on the Web

Real-World Competencies

SCANS—Secretary's Commission on Achieving Necessary Skills

Like no other business communication text, this edition emphasizes the skills and competencies necessary for students to make the transition from school to the workplace. As described in the SCANS report from the Department of Labor, it is essential that students meet national standards of academic and occupational skill. To help accomplish the SCANS goal, this text offers a wide variety of interactive pedagogy (much of which is grounded in real-world situations).

Checklists

To help students organize their thinking when they begin a communication project, make decisions as they write, and check their own work, we've included checklists throughout the book. In the seventh edition, we've streamlined these checklists to increase their usefulness. These checklists are reminders, not "recipes." They provide useful guidelines for writing, without limiting creativity.

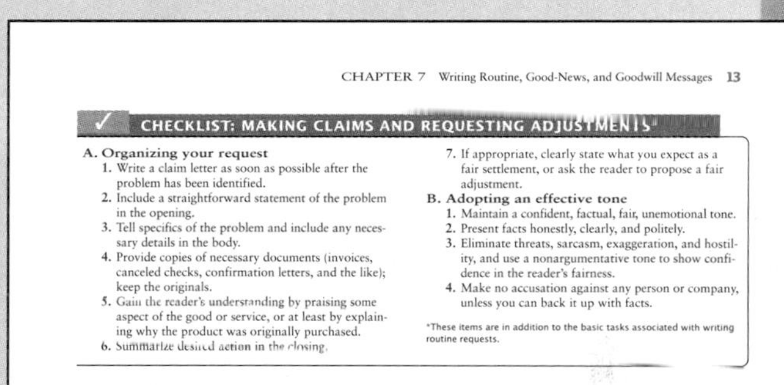

CHAPTER 7 Writing Routine, Good-News, and Goodwill Messages 13

✓ CHECKLIST: MAKING CLAIMS AND REQUESTING ADJUSTMENTS*

A. Organizing your request
1. Write a claim letter as soon as possible after the problem has been identified.
2. Include a straightforward statement of the problem in the opening.
3. Tell specifics of the problem and include any necessary details in the body.
4. Provide copies of necessary documents (invoices, canceled checks, confirmation letters, and the like); keep the originals.
5. Gain the reader's understanding by praising some aspect of the good or service, or at least by explaining why the product was originally purchased.
6. Summarize desired action in the closing.
7. If appropriate, clearly state what you expect as a fair settlement, or ask the reader to propose a fair adjustment.

B. Adopting an effective tone
1. Maintain a confident, factual, fair, unemotional tone.
2. Present facts honestly, clearly, and politely.
3. Eliminate threats, sarcasm, exaggeration, and hostility, and use a nonargumentative tone to show confidence in the reader's fairness.
4. Make no accusation against any person or company, unless you can back it up with facts.

*These items are in addition to the basic tasks associated with writing routine requests.

In-Depth Critiques

You will find a variety of up-to-date sample documents, many collected by us in our consulting work, that focus on real companies. All In-Depth Critiques are introduced in the text (identifying the particular business situation being illustrated) and are accompanied by focused comments that point to specific sections to help students see precisely how to apply the principles being discussed. Many samples are also accompanied by a three-step-writing-process graphic that gives students important insights into planning, writing, and completing the specific document shown. Additional documents are displayed within the text, **many including poor and improved examples,** to illustrate common errors and effective techniques for correcting them.

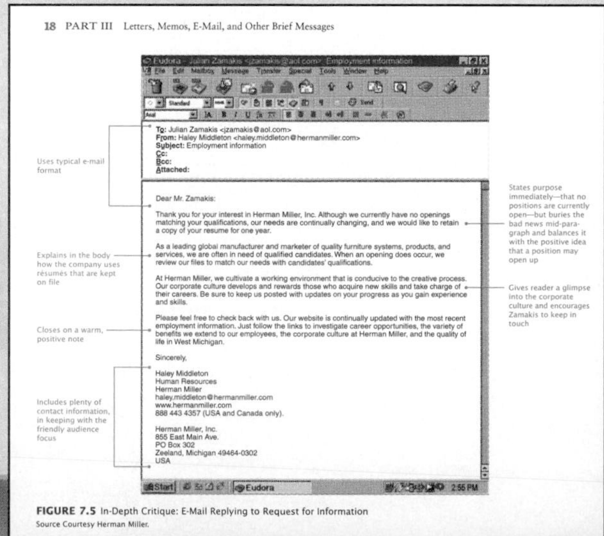

18 PART III Letters, Memos, E-Mail, and Other Brief Messages

Eudora - Julian Zamakis <jzamakis@aol.com>, Employment information

To: Julian Zamakis <jzamakis@aol.com>
From: Haley Middleton <haley.middleton@hermanmiller.com>
Subject: Employment information
Cc:
Bcc:
Attached:

Dear Mr. Zamakis:

Thank you for your interest in Herman Miller, Inc. Although we currently have no openings matching your qualifications, our needs are continually changing, and we would like to retain a copy of your resume for one year.

As a leading global manufacturer and marketer of quality furniture systems, products, and services, we are often in need of qualified candidates. When an opening does occur, we review our files to match our needs with candidates' qualifications.

At Herman Miller, we cultivate a working environment that is conducive to the creative process. Our corporate culture develops and rewards those who acquire new skills and take charge of their careers. Be sure to keep us posted with updates on your progress as you gain experience and skills.

Please feel free to check back with us. Our website is continually updated with the most recent employment information. Just follow the links to investigate career opportunities, the variety of benefits we extend to our employees, the corporate culture at Herman Miller, and the quality of life in West Michigan.

Sincerely,

Haley Middleton
Human Resources
Herman Miller
haley.middleton@hermanmiller.com
www.hermanmiller.com
888 443 4357 (USA and Canada only).

Herman Miller, Inc.
855 East Main Ave.
PO Box 302
Zeeland, Michigan 49464-0302
USA

Uses typical e-mail format

Explains in the body how the company uses résumés that are kept on file

Closes on a warm, positive note

Includes plenty of contact information, in keeping with the friendly audience focus

States purpose immediately—that no positions are currently open—but buries the bad news mid-paragraph and balances it with the positive idea that a position may open up

Gives reader a glimpse into the corporate culture and encourages Zamakis to keep in touch

FIGURE 7.5 In-Depth Critique: E-Mail Replying to Request for Information
Source Courtesy Herman Miller.

Documents for Analysis

This textbook provides a wide selection of documents that students can critique and revise. Documents include letters, memos, e-mail messages, a letter of application, and a résumé. Hands-on experience in analyzing and improving sample documents will help students revise their own business messages.

EXERCISES

With the dozens of new exercises and cases (almost all companies featured are real), we have placed an even greater emphasis in this edition on providing practical assignments like those that students will most often face at work. Many of them are memo-writing and e-mail tasks. New in the seventh edition, each exercise is labeled as to its type, such as **"Team," "Ethical Choices," "Self-Assessment,"** or **"Internet."**

32 PART III Writing Letters, Memos, E-Mail, and Other Brief Messages

Document 7.C: Responding to Claims and Adjustment Requests When the Customer Is at Fault

We read your letter requesting your deposit refund. We couldn't figure out why you hadn't received it, so we talked to our maintenance engineer as you suggested. He said you had left one of the doors off the hinges in your apartment in order to get a large sofa through the door. He also confirmed that you had paid him $5.00 to replace the door since you had to turn in the U-Haul trailer and were in a big hurry.

This entire situation really was caused by a lack of communication between our housekeeping inspector and the maintenance engineer. All we knew was that the door was off the hinges when it was inspected by Sally Tarnley. You know that our policy states that if anything is wrong with the apartment, we keep the deposit. We had no way of knowing that George just hadn't gotten around to replacing the door.

But we have good news. We approved the deposit refund, which will be mailed to you from our home office in Teaneck, New Jersey. I'm not sure how long that will take, however. If you don't receive the check by the end of next month, give me a call.

Next time, it's really a good idea to stay with your apartment until it's inspected as stipulated in your lease agreement. That way, you'll be sure to receive your refund when you expect it. Hope you have a good summer.

Document 7.D: Letter of Recommendation

Your letter to Tanaka Asata, President of SONY, was forwarded to me because I am the human resources director. In my job as head of HR, I have access to performance reviews for all of the SONY employees in the United States. This means, of course, that I would be the person best qualified to answer your request for information on Nick Oshinski.

In your letter of the 15th, you asked about Nick Oshinski's employment record with us because he has applied to work for your company. Mr. Oshinski was employed with us from January 5, 1995, until March 1, 2001. During that time, Mr. Oshinski received ratings ranging from 2.5 up to 9.6, with 10 being the top score. As you can see, he must have done better reporting to some managers than to others. In addition, he took all vacation days, which is a bit unusual. Although I did not know Mr. Oshinski personally, I know that our best workers seldom use all the vacation time they earn. I do not know if that applies in this case.

In summary, Nick Oshinski performed his tasks well depending on who managed him.

Exercises

For live links to all websites discussed in this chapter, visit this text's website at www.prenhall.com/bovee. Just log on and select Chapter 7, and click on "Student Resources." Locate the name of the site or the URL related to the material in the text. For "Exploring the Best of the Web" exercises, you'll also find navigational directions. Click on the live link to the site.

7.1 **Revising Messages: Directness and Conciseness** Revise the following short e-mail messages so that they are more direct and concise; develop a subject line for each revised message.

a. I'm contacting you about your recent order for a High Country backpack. You didn't tell us which backpack you wanted, and you know we make a lot of different ones. We have the canvas models with the plastic frames and vinyl trim and we have the canvas models with leather trim, and we have the ones that have more pockets than the other ones. Plus they come in lots of different colors. Also they make the ones that are large for a big-boned person and the smaller versions for little women or kids.

b. Thank you for contacting us about the difficulty you had collecting your luggage at the Denver airport. We are very sorry for the inconvenience this has caused you. As you know, traveling can create problems of this sort regardless of how careful the airline personnel might be. To receive compensation, please send us a detailed list of the items that you lost and complete the following questionnaire. You can e-mail it back to us.

c. Sorry it took us so long to get back to you. We were flooded with résumés. Anyway, your résumé made the final ten, and after meeting three hours yesterday, we've decided we'd like to meet with you. What is your schedule like for next week? Can you come in for an interview on June 15 at 3:00 p.m.? Please get back to us by the end of this work week and let us know if you will be able to attend. As you can imagine, this is our busy season.

d. We're letting you know that because we use over a ton of paper a year and because so much of that paper goes into the wastebasket to become so much more environmental waste, starting Monday, we're placing white plastic bins outside the elevators on every floor to recycle that paper and in the process, minimize pollution.

7.2 **Revising Messages: Directness and Conciseness** Rewrite the following sentences so that they are direct and concise.

a. We wanted to invite you to our special 40% off by-invitation-only sale. The sale is taking place on November 9.

b. We wanted to let you know that we are giving a tote bag and a free Phish CD with every $50 donation you make to our radio station.

c. The director planned to go to the meeting that will be held on Monday at a little before 11:00 A.M.

d. In today's meeting, we were happy to have the opportunity to welcome Paul Eccelson. He reviewed some of the newest types of order forms. If you have any questions about these new forms, feel free to call him at his office.

7.3 **Internet** Visit the business section of the Blue Mountain site at www.bluemountain.com/eng3/business/ and analyze one of the electronic greeting cards bearing a goodwill message of appreciation for good performance. Under what circumstances would you send this electronic message? How could you person-

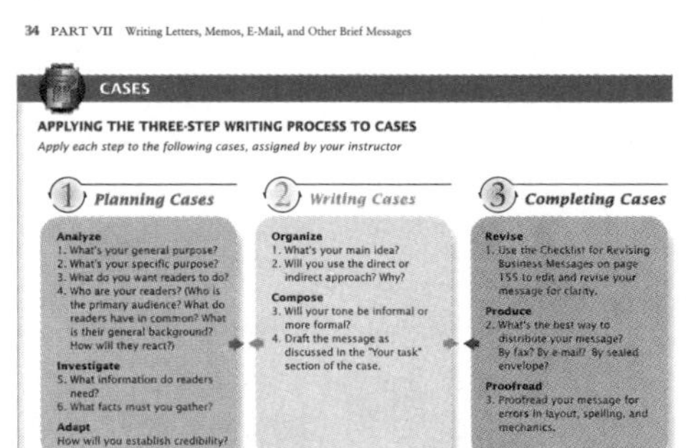

34 PART VII Writing Letters, Memos, E-Mail, and Other Brief Messages

CASES

APPLYING THE THREE-STEP WRITING PROCESS TO CASES

Apply each step to the following cases, assigned by your instructor

1 Planning Cases

Analyze
1. What's your general purpose?
2. What's your specific purpose?
3. What do you want readers to do?
4. Who are your readers? (Who is the primary audience? What do readers have in common? What is their general background? How will they react?)

Investigate
5. What information do readers need?
6. What facts must you gather?

Adapt
How will you establish credibility?

2 Writing Cases

Organize
1. What's your main idea?
2. Will you use the direct or indirect approach? Why?

Compose
3. Will your tone be informal or more formal?
4. Draft the message as discussed in the "Your task" section of the case.

3 Completing Cases

Revise
1. Use the Checklist for Revising Business Messages on page 155 to edit and revise your message for clarity.

Produce
2. What's the best way to distribute your message? By fax? By e-mail? By sealed envelope?

Proofread
3. Proofread your message for errors in layout, spelling, and mechanics.

ROUTINE REQUESTS

1. Step on it: Letter to Floorgraphics requesting information about underfoot advertising As the small-town owner of Better Bike and Ski Shop, you're used to receiving promotional displays, giveaway gadgets, and flashy posters from major manufacturers. The old ones clutter your back room, where employees fight over the used ski posters. But now a manufacturer wants to buy a piece of your floor!

Your Schwinn rep, Marva Beeker, approached you with the idea. Schwinn wants to put floor ads in your store. But first you have to sign up with the company that invented and sells them. Floorgraphics, Inc., leases floor space from retail stores and sells it to advertisers in 4-, 8-, or 12-week cycles.

"Floorgraphics has been doing this for years in thousands of Kmart and chain supermarkets all over the country," Beeker assures you, "and now it's trying to sign up smaller retailers to sell a wider variety of products. If floor ads work for Spaghetti-Os, why not for bicycles?"

Beeker goes on to explain how surprised everyone was by the success of strategically placing decals at the point of consumer decision making: on the floor beneath the product's shelf space. After the first placements, product sales went up anywhere from 25 to 75 percent. One survey showed that Oreo cookie sales went up by 72 percent in the two months after decals were installed on Kmart floors.

"Floorgraphics will want to lease your entire floor for advertisers other than Schwinn," Beeker explains. "And these people know what they're doing. They limit ads to two per aisle and to one company per category. Best of all, in addition to leasing fees, you get a commission on whatever Floorgraphics makes selling your space to advertisers. I think it's about 25 percent, but you should ask Richard yourself."

That's Richard Rebh, CEO of Floorgraphics, whose business card Beeker hands to you.

"We're the first bike manufacturer to sign up," she says, grinning. "We're going to get a big jump on the other guys . . . if we can get storeowners like you to agree. And keep in mind, the retailers that are already in the Floorgraphics network will get first crack at the new animated floor ads! Can't you just see it? The bicycle will start to move as customers crowd in for a look!"

Long after Beeker leaves, you find yourself staring at the dusty linoleum in front of the bike racks, marveling that manufacturers want to pay hard cash to put their names down there where customers are going to track dirt and melting snow all over them. But if what Beeker says is true, you could gain three new ways of earning money: the leasing fee, the increased sales, and the share in ad revenues.

Your task: Write to CEO Richard Rebh at Floorgraphics, Inc. (5 Vaughn Drive, Princeton, NJ 08540). You want to find out whether Beeker has been exaggerating. You'll need all the financial details, but you also want some practical information about the ads themselves: Who installs and removes them? What will your cleaning solutions do to them? What are the risks of floor damage? Is there a way to terminate the lease if you don't like them? Your questions are endless. Put as many as you deem reasonable in your letter, and be sure to justify your request for a speedy reply.[7]

CASES

The cases are yet another tool for demonstrating the role of communication in the real business world. Examples include:

- Got It Covered? Letter from American Express about SUV rentals
- Betting the Company: Letter from Boeing replying to questions about new aircraft plans
- Boomerang Back to Us: E-Mail from EDS to dot-com deserters
- More Layoffs: Memo to Motorola employees
- No Choking Matter: Persuasive letter from the Consumer Product Safety Commission about fast-food giveaways

Both the exercises and cases deal with all types and sizes of organizations, both domestic and international. Each chapter also includes exercises and cases that require access to the World Wide Web, giving students practice with this fast-growing communication technology.

Bumgardner strives to establish a feeling of partnership with her fellow employees by using a polite tone and by projecting enthusiasm into her writing. However, even though her tone is friendly and conversational, she carefully avoids using irony and sarcasm, especially in e-mail. "Don't joke about serious matters," she cautions. "Too often, your messages are interpreted differently from what you intend."

Bumgardner believes that clear, direct messages get positive results. As she puts it, "Effective communication creates a positive impression—and a positive impression will get more positive responses to your requests." [1] ■

USING THE THREE-STEP WRITING PROCESS FOR ROUTINE MESSAGES

Whether you're reminding employees about meetings or upcoming deadlines, like UnumProvident's Becky Bumgardner, congratulating an employee on a job well done, or requesting information from another firm, chances are that in the course of everyday business, you'll compose a lot of routine, good-news, and goodwill messages. In fact, most of a typical employee's communication is about routine matters: orders, information, company policies, claims, credit, employees, products, operations, and so on. Such messages are rarely long or complex. Even so, to produce the best messages possible, you'll want to apply the three-step writing process.

Learning Objective 1

Apply the three-step writing process to routine positive messages

Step 1: Planning Routine Messages

As with longer, complex messages, you need to analyze your purpose and audience, investigate audience needs, and adapt your message to your readers. However, for routine messages, this planning step may take only a few moments. First, analyze your purpose to make sure that it's specific and it's worth pursuing at this time. Also, think a moment about your readers. Are you sure they'll receive your message positively (or at least neutrally)? Most routine messages are of interest to your readers because they contain information necessary to conduct day-to-day business. Even so, you may need to discover more about audience attitudes or needs in order to gauge your audience's probable reaction.

Even for routine situations, you need to analyze, investigate, and adapt your messages.

Learning Objectives

Chapter-opening learning objectives are clearly stated to signal important concepts that students are expected to master. In addition, the numbered objectives reappear in the text margins, close to the relevant material. Finally, the end-of-chapter "Summary of Learning Objectives" reinforces basic concepts by capsulizing chapter highlights for students.

End-of-Chapter Questions

The end-of-chapter questions are divided into two types:

- **Test Your Knowledge** (review questions)
- **Apply Your Knowledge** (application questions)

The end-of-chapter questions are designed to get students thinking about the concepts introduced in each chapter. The questions may also prompt students to stretch their learning beyond the chapter content. Not only will students find the questions useful in studying for examinations, but the instructor may also draw on them to promote classroom discussion of issues that have no easy answers.

CHAPTER 7 Writing Routine, Good-News, and Goodwill Messages 31

6 **Describe the importance of goodwill messages, and describe how to make them effective.** Goodwill messages are important for building relationships with customers, colleagues, and other businesspeople. These friendly, unexpected notes have no direct business purpose, but they make people feel good about doing business with the sender. To make goodwill messages effective, make them honest and sincere. Avoid exaggerating, back up compliments with specific points, and give restrained praise.

TEST YOUR KNOWLEDGE

1. When is a request routine?
2. What are some of the guidelines for asking a series of questions in a routine request?
3. What information should be included in an order request?
4. Should you use the direct or indirect approach for most routine messages? Why?
5. Where in a routine message should you state your actual request?
6. How does a claim differ from an adjustment?
7. How does the question of fault affect what you say in a message granting a claim?
8. What is the appropriate strategy for responding to a request for a recommendation about a job candidate whose performance was poor?
9. How can you avoid sounding insincere when writing a goodwill message?
10. What are some of the guidelines for writing condolence messages?

APPLY YOUR KNOWLEDGE

1. When organizing request messages, why is it important to know whether any cultural differences exist between you and your audience? Explain.
2. Your company's error cost an important business customer a new client; you know it and your customer knows it. Do you apologize, or do you refer to the incident in a positive light without admitting any responsibility? Briefly explain.
3. You've been asked to write a letter of recommendation for an employee who is disabled and uses a wheelchair. The disability has no effect on the employee's ability to do the job, and you feel confident about writing the best recommendation possible. Nevertheless, you know the prospective company and its facilities aren't well suited to wheelchair access. Do you mention the employee's disability in your letter? Explain.
4. Every time you send a direct-request memo to Ted Jackson, he delays or refuses to comply. You're beginning to get impatient. Should you send Jackson a memo to ask what's wrong? Complain to your supervisor about Jackson's uncooperative attitude? Arrange a face-to-face meeting with Jackson? Bring up the problem at the next staff meeting? Explain.
5. **Ethical Choices** You have a complaint against one of your suppliers, but you have no documentation to back it up. Should you request an adjustment anyway? Why or why not?

PRACTICE YOUR KNOWLEDGE

Documents for Analysis

Read the following documents; then (1) analyze the strengths and weaknesses of each sentence and (2) revise each document so that it follows this chapter's guidelines.

Document 7.A: Requesting Routine Information from a Business

Our college is closing its dining hall for financial reasons, so we want to do something to help the students prepare their own food in their dorm rooms if they so choose. Your colorful ad in *Collegiate Magazine* caught our eye. We need the following information before we make our decision.

- Would you be able to ship the microwaves by August 15th? I realize this is short notice, but our board of trustees just made the decision to close the dining hall last week and we're scrambling around trying to figure out what to do.
- Do they have any kind of a warranty? College students can be pretty hard on things, as you know, so we will need a good warranty.
- How much does it cost? Do you give a discount for a big order?
- Do we have to provide a special outlet?
- Will students know how to use them, or will we need to provide instructions?

As I said before, we're on a tight time frame and need good information from you as soon as possible to help us make our decision about ordering. You never know what the board might come up with next. I'm looking at several other companies, also, so please let us know ASAP.

Document 7.B: Making Claims and Requests for Adjustment

At a local business-supply store, I recently purchased your "Negotiator Pro" for my computer. I bought the CD because I saw your ad for it in *MacWorld* magazine, and it looked as if it might be an effective tool for use in my corporate seminar on negotiation.

Unfortunately, when I inserted it in my office computer, it wouldn't work. I returned it to the store, but since I had already opened it, they refused to exchange it for a CD that would work or give me a refund. They told me to contact you and that you might be able to send me a version that would work with my computer.

You can send the information to me at the letterhead address. If you cannot send me the correct disk, please refund my $79.95. Thanks in advance for any help you can give me in this matter.

Margin Notes

Making Claims and Requesting Adjustments

When you're dissatisfied with a company's product or service, you make a **claim** (a formal complaint) or request an **adjustment** (a claim settlement). Although a phone call or visit may solve the problem, a written claim letter is better because it documents your dissatisfaction. Moreover, even though your first reaction to a clumsy mistake or a defective product is likely to be anger or frustration, the person reading your letter probably had nothing to do with the problem. So a courteous, clear, concise explanation will impress your reader much more favorably than an abusive, angry letter.

Putting your claim in writing
- Documents your dissatisfaction
- Requires courtesy, clarity, and conciseness

In most cases, and especially in your first letter, assume that a fair adjustment will be made, and follow the plan for direct requests. Begin with a straightforward statement of the problem. In the middle section, give a complete, specific explanation of the details. Provide any information an adjuster would need to verify your complaint about faulty merchandise or unsatisfactory service. In your closing, politely request specific action or convey a sincere desire to find a solution. And don't forget to suggest that the business relationship will continue if the problem is solved satisfactorily.

In your claim letter
- Explain the problem and give details
- Provide backup information
- Request specific action

Companies usually accept the customer's explanation of what's wrong, so ethically it's important to be entirely honest when filing claims. Also, be prepared to back up your claim with invoices, sales receipts, canceled checks, dated correspondence, catalog descriptions, and any other relevant documents. Send copies and keep the originals for your files.

Be prepared to document your claim. Send copies and keep the original documents.

If the remedy is obvious, tell your reader exactly what will return the company to your good graces—for example, an exchange of merchandise for the right item or a refund if the item is out of stock. In some cases you might ask the reader to resolve the problem. However, if you're uncertain about the precise nature of the trouble, you could ask the company to make an assessment. But be sure to supply your contact information and the best time to call, so that the company can discuss the situation with you if necessary.

Be as specific as possible about what you want to happen next.

The following letter was written to a gas and electric company. As you read it, compare its tone with the tone of the letter in Figure 7.3. If you were the person receiving the complaint, which version would you respond to more favorably?

To reinforce learning, the book's margins contain short summary statements that highlight key points in the text. These notes are no substitute for reading the chapters, but they can help students quickly get the gist of a section, review a chapter, and locate areas of greatest concern.

Real-World Issues

The boundaries of business communication are always expanding. So in addition to covering all the traditional subjects, ***Business Communication Today, Seventh Edition***, provides material to help students manage these important current issues in business communication:

- **Ethics.** Taking an ethical position in the face of pressures and temptations requires more than courage—it requires strong communication skills.
- **Communication Barriers.** The shift toward a service economy means that more and more careers will depend on interpersonal skills, making it vital for people to overcome communication barriers.
- **Cultural Diversity.** The changing nature of the domestic workforce requires strong communication skills to relate to workers of various ages, genders, socioeconomic status, ethnic backgrounds, and so on. Also, strong skills are needed to communicate effectively with people from other countries.
- **Communication Technology.** More and more face-to-face interactions are giving way to interactions with and through computers. And this trend will continue. To survive in today's business world, students must master high-tech communication skills.
- **Law.** The increasing tendency of people to sue makes it important to understand the legal implications of written and oral communication.
- **Employment Search.** More and more people are making radical mid-career job changes, whether by choice or because their companies are downsizing and flattening hierarchies. These people need to master new communication skills to compete in today's job market.
- **Communication Versatility.** Small businesses create most of the new jobs and employ more people than large corporations do. Because these businesses are unable to support communication specialists for specific jobs, people working for them need to be versatile in their communication skills.

An Unparalleled Supplements Package

OFFERING A FULLY INTEGRATED TEACHING SYSTEM

Instructor's Resource Manual

This comprehensive supplement is an instructor's tool kit. Among its many teaching aids, this manual provides a section about collaborative writing, suggested solutions to exercises, suggested solutions and fully formatted letters for every case in the letter-writing chapters, and a grammar pretest and posttest. This comprehensive manual contains a set of completely integrated support materials. It is designed to assist instructors in quickly finding and assembling the resources available for each chapter of the text and includes the following new material:

- Course planning guide
- Collaborative writing guide
- Diagnostic tests of English skills
- Changes to the new edition
- Chapter outline
- Lecture notes
- Answers to all end-of-chapter questions and assignments
- Solutions to all cases and exercises

Test Item File

The Test Item File contains approximately 1,500 questions, all of which have been carefully reviewed to provide a fair, structured program of evaluation. The questions for each chapter consist of a comprehensive set of multiple-choice, true/false, and fill-in questions. The Test Item File reinforces students' understanding of key terms and concepts and requires them to apply their critical-thinking and analytical skills.

Prentice Hall's Computerized Test Manager (Windows Version)

This user-friendly software allows you to generate error-free tests quickly and easily by previewing questions individually on the screen and then selecting them randomly by query or by number. The Computerized Test Manager allows you to generate random tests with the extensive bank of questions. You can also edit the questions/answers and even add some of your own. You can create an exam, administer it traditionally or online, and analyze your success with the simple click of the mouse. The newest version of our Computerized Test Manager, ESATEST 2000, has been improved to provide users with a vast array of new options.

Telephone Test Preparation

For those instructors who prefer not to use the *Computerized Test Manager*, Prentice Hall provides a special 800 call-in service. All you need to do is call the **800 Testing Help Desk** to have a customized test created. The test can then be delivered by e-mail, U.S. mail, or overnight carrier.

Color Acetate Transparency Programs

A set of 150+ large-type transparency acetates is available to instructors on request. These visuals help bring concepts alive in the classroom and provide a starting point for discussing communication techniques. All transparencies are keyed to the *Instructor's Resource Manual.* **Many contrast poor and improved solutions to featured cases** from the textbook.

PowerPoint Presentation

An exciting, high-quality PowerPoint package created by Myles Hassell, University of New Orleans, is the best in the field. It comes in two versions:

1. Instructor version: an enhanced PowerPoint package for instructors to use for class, with colorful text-specific electronic slides that highlight and reinforce important concepts in the text. Free to adopters, these PowerPoint slides are available on CD or can be downloaded from the instructor's resource section of the "My Companion Website" at **www.prenhall.com/bovee**.
2. Student version: a special PowerPoint version for students to use for review purposes, or which can be conveniently printed three to a page for in-class note taking. These slides can be accessed in the student's resource section of this text's website.

Study Guide

A *Study Guide for Business Communication Today* by William Peirce, Prince Georges Community College, is designed to increase your students' comprehension of the concepts presented in this text. The guide provides chapter-by-chapter explanations and exercises designed to reinforce comprehension of key terms and concepts and to promote concept-application skills.

Online Course Resources

The "60 Keys to Mastering Effective Business Communication," available as an online course on the Web or on a CD, presents three key concepts in each chapter in an enhanced, interactive lecture outline. Depth is added to the outline with a video introduction by the authors and with interactive elements and exercises to reinforce learning. Each lesson is concluded with a chapter summary writing assignment to strengthen students' understanding.

Video series and Video Guide

In early 2003, a series of thematically driven business communications videos will be launched. The first installment of four will include **"Challenge of Using Technology to Communicate Effectively," "Challenge of Working Effectively in Teams," "Challenge of Committing to Ethical Communication," and "Challenge of Choosing a Career and the Job Search."**

Business Communication Update Newsletter for Faculty

Delivered exclusively by e-mail every month, this newsletter provides interesting materials that can be used in class and offers a wealth of practical ideas about teaching methods. To receive a complimentary subscription, send an e-mail to bovee@leadingtexts.com. In the subject line, type "BCU Subscription Request." In the message area, please list your name and institutional affiliation. You can also subscribe at the author's website at **www.leadingtexts.com.**

Authors' E-Mail Hotline for Faculty

Integrity, excellence, and responsiveness are our hallmarks. That means providing you with textbooks that are academically sound, creative, timely, and sensitive to instructor and student needs. As an adopter of ***Business Communication Today***, you are invited to use our E-Mail Hotline: bovee@leadingtexts.com. You can also access the hotline at **www.leadingtexts.com.** We want to be sure you're completely satisfied, so if you ever have a question or concern related to the text or its supplements, please contact us. We'll get back to you as quickly as possible.

Introducing "My Companion Website" for

BUSINESS COMMUNICATION TODAY, SEVENTH EDITION

"My Companion Website" is your personal tool for the free online resources for this book, located at **www.prenhall.com/bovee.**

The website features one-click access to all of the resources created by an award-winning team of educators. Here is a preview of its exciting features.

For the Student

- **"My Companion Website" pages.** Unite all of your texts with this personal access page.
- **Notes.** Add personal notes to website resources for personal reminders and references.
- **Study guide.** Test your knowledge with the interactive study guide that offers a wide variety of self-assessment questions for every chapter. Results from the automatically graded questions provide immediate feedback that can serve as practice or be e-mailed to the instructor for extra credit.
- **Student resources.** Access the websites featured in this text by using the hotlinks provided and updated by the authors of this text, review chapter content by viewing the student version of the PowerPoint slides, see videos, or use the special materials developed for this course.
- **Internet resources.** New Internet exercises, in addition to those offered in the text, have been created by the website team of professors and are continually being added to the website. These exercises are designed to promote students' critical thinking skills as they use the Internet to explore current issues.
- **Research area.** Save time finding the most valuable and relevant material available on the web. The research area provides a resource library that includes links to tutorials, virtual libraries, Internet resources, and more. Each link is annotated to expedite your research.
- **Talk to the Tutor.** Take advantage of the virtual office hours that allow you to post questions from any supported discipline and receive responses from the dedicated website faculty team.
- **Writing Resources Center.** Use the writing center's links to directories, thesauruses, writing tutors, style and grammar guides, and additional tools.
- **Career Resource Center.** Get career information, view sample résumés, even apply for jobs online.

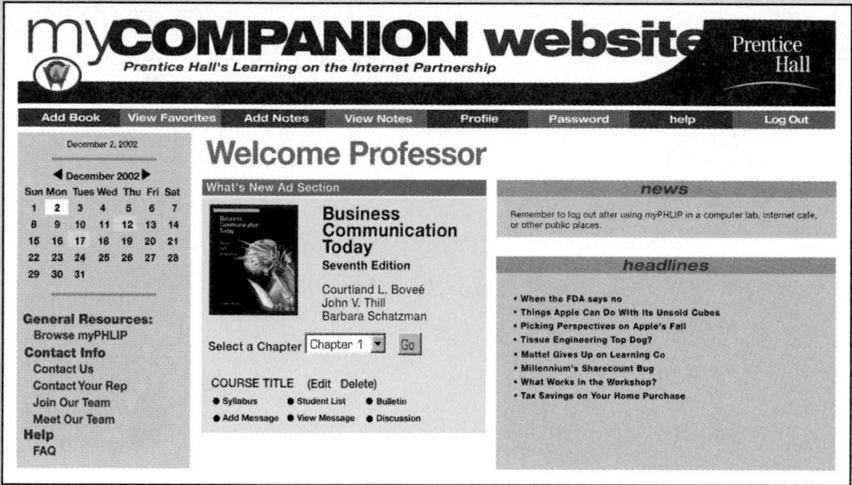

- **Business Headlines.** Check out links to articles in today's business news.
- **Search.** Search all websites' resources for relevant articles and exercises.

For the Instructor

- **Online faculty support.** In this password-protected area, get the most current and advanced support materials that are available, including downloadable supplements, such as the instructor's manual, PowerPoints, articles, links, and suggested answers to current events activities offered on the website.
- **Syllabus manager.** Follow the easy steps for creating and revising a syllabus, with direct links to companion websites and other online content. Changes you make to your syllabus are immediately available to your students at their next login.
- **Messages.** Send messages to individual students or to all students linked to a course.
- **Faculty resources.** Take advantage of the teaching tips, techniques, academic papers, and sample syllabuses contributed by professors throughout the world.
- **What's New.** Get one-click access to all newly posted website resources.
- **Talk to the Team.** Participate in a moderated faculty chat room.

Offering Business Communication Today,

SEVENTH EDITION, AS AN ONLINE COURSE

Now you have the freedom to personalize your own online course materials. Prentice Hall Business Publishing provides the content and support you need to create and manage your own online course materials with WebCT, Blackboard, and CourseCompass.

WEBCT **www.prenhall.com/webct**

Gold Level Support, available exclusively to adopters of Prentice Hall courses, is awarded free of charge on adoption and provides you with priority assistance, training discounts, and dedicated technical support from WebCT.

BLACKBOARD **www.prenhall.com/blackboard**

Take your courses to new heights in student interaction and learning. Prentice Hall's class-tested online course content is now available with Blackboard's products and easy-to-use interface.

COURSECOMPASS **www.coursecompass.com**

CourseCompass™ is a dynamic, interactive course management tool powered by Blackboard. This exciting product allows you to teach with market-leading Pearson Education content in an easy-to-use customizable format.

Personal Acknowledgments

Business Communication Today, Seventh Edition, is the product of the concerted efforts of a number of people. A heartfelt thanks to our many friends, acquaintances, and business associates who agreed to be interviewed so that this textbook could feature real people at actual companies, including LivePerson, SEI Investments, Sheraton Hotels Hawaii, Home Depot, Weather.com, Turner Broadcasting System, UnumProvident, Caponigro Public Relations, AT&T Language Line, Gosh Enterprises, Black Entertainment Television, Dell Computer, San Diego Wild Animal Park, Corporate Dynamics, Anderson Business Resources, Allbee Green, Recreational Equipment Incorporated, and Microsoft.

We are also indebted to Krispy Kreme Doughnuts, Ace Hardware, Swiss Army Brands, Target, Office Depot, Qantas, Petsmart, General Nutrition, Discovery Communications, Host Marriott Services, Carnival Cruise Lines, National Geographic Society, Greyhound Lines, Herman Miller Inc., and Kelly Services for granting us permission to use materials from their companies. The model memos and letters that are shown in this textbook on company stationery have been included to provide realistic examples of company documents for educational purposes. They do not always represent actual business documents created by these companies.

Our thanks also to Terry Anderson, whose outstanding communication skills, breadth of knowledge, and organizational ability assured this project of clarity and completeness. We are also grateful to Jackie Estrada for her remarkable talents and special skills; to Susan Sawyer for her dedication and valuable contributions; to Lianne Downey for her unique insights and valuable experience; to Stef Gould for her artistry and exceptional abilities; to Joe Glidden for his research efforts and database supervision; to John Cutchen for his wise counsel and sound judgment; and to Chad Bailey for his persistence and expertise.

We also feel it is important to acknowledge and thank the Association for Business Communication, an organization whose meetings and publications provide a valuable forum for the exchange of ideas and for professional growth.

Thanks to the many individuals whose valuable suggestions and constructive comments contributed to the success of this book. The authors are deeply grateful for the efforts of Robert Allen, Northwest Connecticut Community College; Lois J. Bachman, Community College of Philadelphia; Jane Bennett, Dekalb College; Mary Bresnahan, Michigan State University; Julian Caplan, Borough of Manhattan Community College; Donald Crawford, West Georgia College; Susan Currier, California Polytechnic State University; David P. Dauwalder, California State University, Los Angeles; Carol David, Iowa State University; Rod Davis, Ball State University; Earl A. Dvorak, Indiana University—Bloomington; Norma J. Gross, Houston Community College; Florence Grunkemeyer, Ball State University; Maxine Hart, Baylor University; Susan Hilligoss, Clemson University; Louise C. Holcomb, Gainesville Junior College; J. Kenneth Horn, Southwestern Missouri State University; Randolph H. Hudson, Northeastern Illinois University; Edna Jellesed, Lane Community College; Betty Johnson, Stephen F. Austin State University; Paul J. Killorin, Portland Community College; Lorraine Krajewski, Louisiana State University; Patricia Kuriscak, Niagara County Community College; Reva Leeman, Portland Community College; Ethel A. Martin, Glendale Community College; Kenneth R. Mayer, Cleveland State University; Gertrude M. McGuire, University of Montevallo; Willie Minor, Phoenix College; Evelyn P. Morris, Mesa Community College; Linda Munilla, Georgia Southern College; Tom Musial, Saint Mary's University; Alexa North, Georgia State University; Devern Perry, Brigham Young University; Paul Preston, University of Texas, San Antonio; Thomas P. Proietti, Monroe Community College; Nelda Pugh, Jefferson

State College; Richard David Ramsey, Southeastern Louisiana University; Lillian E. Rollins, Dekalb College; W. J. Salem, Central Michigan University; Grant T. Savage, Texas Tech University; Dorothy Sibley, Brevard Community College; Roberta M. Supnick, Western Michigan University; Sumner B. Tapper, Northeastern University; Vincent Trofi, Providence College; Linda N. Ulman, University of Miami; Dona Vasa, University of Nebraska; Ruth A. Walsh, University of South Florida; John L. Waltman, Eastern Michigan University; Kathryn Jensen White, University of Oklahoma; and Mimi Will, Foothill College; J. Douglas Andrews, University of Southern California; Jane Beamish, North Country Community College; Pauline Ann Buss, William R. Harper College; James L. Godell, North Michigan University; Kenneth Gorman, Winona State University; Francis N. Hamlet, Longwood College; William Hendricks, Temple University; Elizabeth Jenkins, Pennsylvania State University; Barbara Jewell, Pierce College; Elaine Krajewski, Louisiana State University; Reeva Leeman, Portland Community College; Virgil R. Pufahl, University of Wisconsin—Platteville; Jim Rucker, Fort Hays State University; Carla L. Sloan, Liberty University; Jeremiah J. Sullivan, University of Washington; Rose Ann Swartz, Ferris State University; Janet Adams, Mankato State University; Sauny Dills, California Polytechnic State University; and Claudia Rawlins, California State University—Chico; Janet Adams, Mankato State University; Bill Hendricks, California University, Pennsylvania; Carol Lutz, University of Texas at Austin; Glynna Morse, Georgia College, Georgia; and David Victor, East Michigan University; Lillie Anderton-Lewis, North Carolina A&T State University; Dr. Colleen Vawdrey, Utah Valley State College; Nanette Clinch Gilson, College of Business, San Jose State University; and Susan Eisner, Ramapo College.

A special debt is owed to the following individuals who reviewed the sixth edition in preparation for the seventh edition: Sheryll Roeber, University of Nebraska; James Dubinsky, Virginia Tech; William Wardrope, Southwest Texas State University; Mary Meredith, University of Louisiana; Marianna Larsen, Utah State University; Vivian Brown, Laredo Community College; and John Lammers, University of Illinois.

We want to extend our warmest appreciation to the devoted professionals at Prentice Hall. They include Jerome Grant, president; Jeff Shelstad, editor-in-chief; David Parker, acquisitions editor; Debbie Clare, executive marketing manager; Ashley Keim, editorial assistant; all of Prentice Hall Business Publishing; and the outstanding Prentice Hall sales representatives. Finally, we thank Judy Leale, managing editor of production; Michele Foresta, production editor; and Janet Slowik, art director; for their dedication; and we are grateful to Lynn Steines, project manager at Carlisle Communications; Deborah Dwyer, copy editor; Suzanne Grappi, permissions supervisor; Melinda Alexander, photo researcher; and Liz Harasymczuk, designer; for their superb work.

Courtland L. Bovée

John V. Thill

Barbara E. Schatzman

Dedication

To the millions of students throughout the world who have
learned about business communication from *Business Communication Today,*
and
to the Text and Academic Authors Association, which awarded
Business Communication Today its prestigious Award for Excellence.

PART 1

Understanding the Foundations of Business Communication

Achieving Success Through Effective Business Communication

After studying this chapter, you will be able to

1 *Explain what effective communication is and highlight five characteristics of effective business messages*

2 *Discuss three developments in the workplace that are intensifying the need to communicate effectively*

3 *Describe how organizations share information internally and externally*

4 *List and briefly define the six phases of the communication process*

5 *Identify and briefly discuss five types of communication barriers*

6 *Discuss four guidelines for overcoming communication barriers*

7 *Discuss the attributes of ethical communication and differentiate between an ethical dilemma and an ethical lapse*

COMMUNICATION CLOSE-UP AT LIVEPERSON

www.liveperson.com

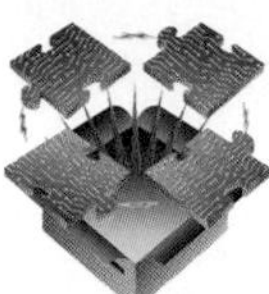

You're shopping online, but you'd like some more information. Does that sweater come in red? Will you get free shipping? Wouldn't it be great to have the help of a real, live person? That's the idea behind Robert LoCascio's LivePerson, a New York service that adds the human touch to online shopping at a variety of sites.

LoCascio knows that many businesses depend on their websites as their chief form of interaction with customers. But LoCascio sees many websites that are ineffective. Companies create communication barriers by jamming too much information on their webpages. Moreover, many websites have weak content, poor writing, and cluttered design elements. These oversights confuse and frustrate shoppers, forcing them to sift through page after page of detail to find the information they need.

All too often, online customers with unanswered questions abandon their shopping carts in the checkout line. So to help Internet companies communicate effectively with customers, LoCascio's LivePerson software allows companies to communicate with customers in a real-time environment. Shoppers simply click on the LivePerson icon, and a pop-up window appears on the screen. Type in your name, and you're greeted by a LivePerson rep who types, "What can I do for you?" Customers can then type their questions. The reps provide immediate assistance and facilitate feedback by encouraging shoppers to ask additional questions.

Through LivePerson's real-time, two-way chat sessions, customer reps can focus on each shopper's needs. LivePerson operators suggest alternatives to customers by clicking on various webpages to show similar products. Some reps even guide customers through the process of making selections. As LoCascio explains, "We embrace the customers and help them through the process of shopping."

Offering instant, two-way communication and one-on-one connections with a company rep are just some of the ways LivePerson helps Internet companies foster an open communication climate with customers. LoCascio's company also teaches website reps how to communicate with customers and supplies valuable information about each shopper's past purchases and previous visits to the site. Responses to common questions are prepared in advance so that customer service reps can chat with four or five customers at once by calling up the prescripted messages during live chat sessions.

LoCascio believes LivePerson helps Internet companies foster an open communication climate by creating a warm, welcoming shopping environment that eliminates barriers to communication and cultivates a wealth of loyal, satisfied customers. "If you walk into a store, and there's no person there to help you, the experience is pretty bad. The same thing is true online," says LoCascio. But with LivePerson's instant communication tools, Internet companies can "convert the people with problems into happy customers."[1] ■

LivePerson helps companies communicate effectively on the web with their customers—a much needed service as more and more companies transact e-commerce.

COMMUNICATION, BUSINESS, AND YOU

Communication enables organizations to function.

Organizations such as LivePerson understand that achieving success in today's workplace is closely tied to the ability of employees and managers to communicate effectively with each other and with people outside the organization. **Communication** is the process of sending and receiving messages. However, communication is *effective* only when the message is understood and when it stimulates action or encourages the receiver to think in new ways.

Learning Objective 1

Explain what effective communication is and highlight five characteristics of effective business messages

Your ability to communicate effectively increases productivity, both yours and your organization's (see Figure 1.1). With good communication skills, you can anticipate

FIGURE 1.1 The Benefits of Effective Communication

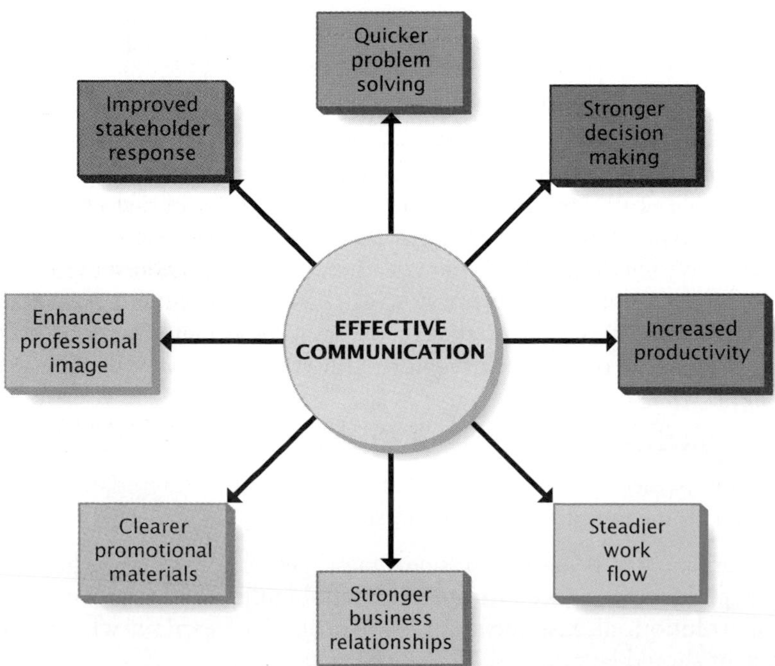

FIGURE 1.2 In-Depth Critique: Ineffective Business Communication

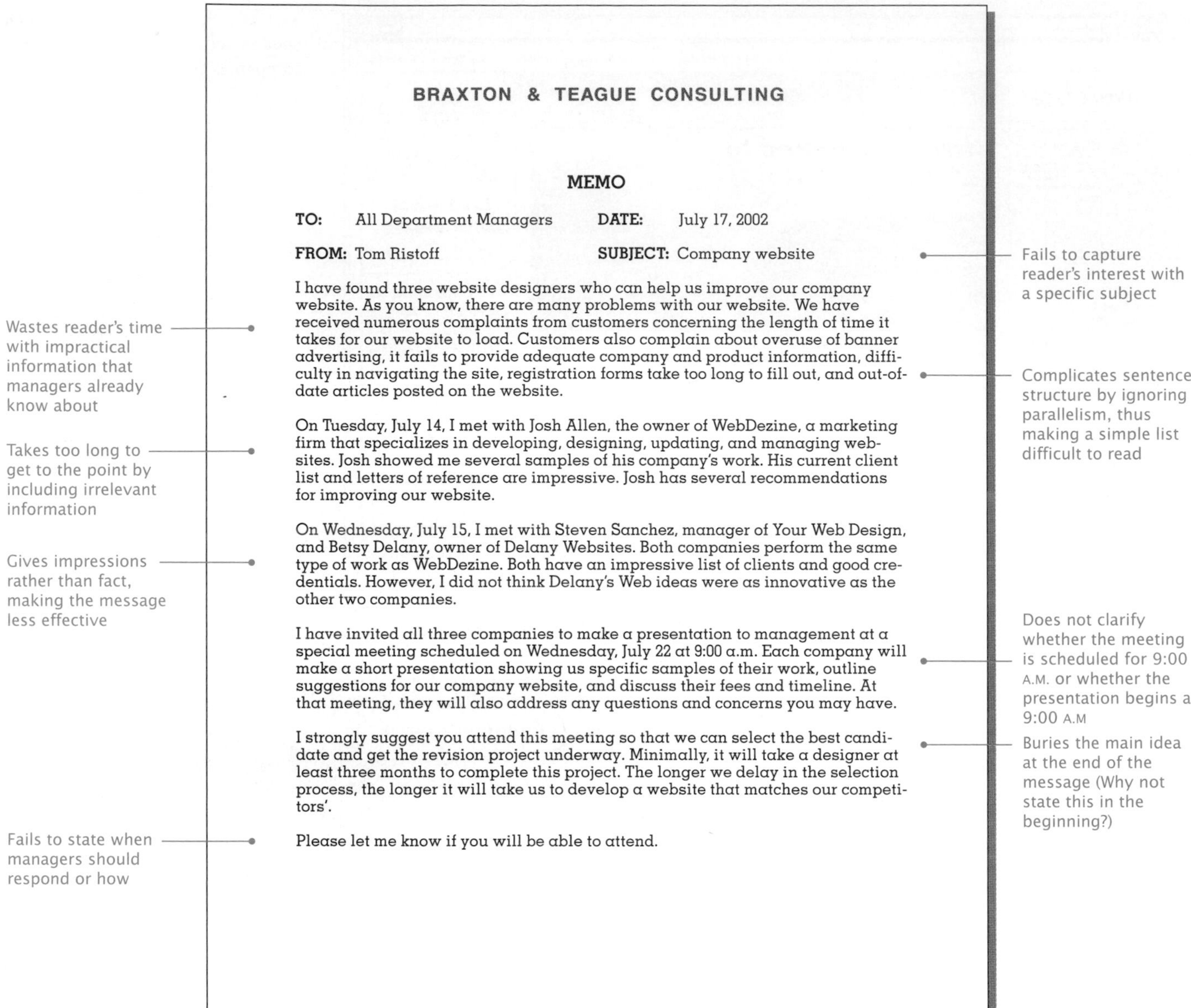

BRAXTON & TEAGUE CONSULTING

MEMO

TO: All Department Managers DATE: July 17, 2002

FROM: Tom Ristoff SUBJECT: Company website

I have found three website designers who can help us improve our company website. As you know, there are many problems with our website. We have received numerous complaints from customers concerning the length of time it takes for our website to load. Customers also complain about overuse of banner advertising, it fails to provide adequate company and product information, difficulty in navigating the site, registration forms take too long to fill out, and out-of-date articles posted on the website.

On Tuesday, July 14, I met with Josh Allen, the owner of WebDezine, a marketing firm that specializes in developing, designing, updating, and managing websites. Josh showed me several samples of his company's work. His current client list and letters of reference are impressive. Josh has several recommendations for improving our website.

On Wednesday, July 15, I met with Steven Sanchez, manager of Your Web Design, and Betsy Delany, owner of Delany Websites. Both companies perform the same type of work as WebDezine. Both have an impressive list of clients and good credentials. However, I did not think Delany's Web ideas were as innovative as the other two companies.

I have invited all three companies to make a presentation to management at a special meeting scheduled on Wednesday, July 22 at 9:00 a.m. Each company will make a short presentation showing us specific samples of their work, outline suggestions for our company website, and discuss their fees and timeline. At that meeting, they will also address any questions and concerns you may have.

I strongly suggest you attend this meeting so that we can select the best candidate and get the revision project underway. Minimally, it will take a designer at least three months to complete this project. The longer we delay in the selection process, the longer it will take us to develop a website that matches our competitors'.

Please let me know if you will be able to attend.

Effective communication helps you and your organization succeed.

problems, make decisions, coordinate work flow, supervise others, develop relationships, and promote products and services. You can shape the impressions you and your company make on colleagues, employees, supervisors, investors, and customers in addition to perceiving and responding to the needs of these **stakeholders** (the various groups you interact with).[2] Without effective communication, people misunderstand each other and misinterpret information. Ideas misfire or fail to gain attention, and people and companies flounder. In fact, studies show that on average, 14 percent of each 40-hour workweek is wasted because of poor communication between staff and management.[3]

Characteristics of Effective Business Messages

Business communication differs from communication in other settings.

Effective business messages have a number of common characteristics. As you study the communication examples in this book, see how they[4]

- **Provide practical information.** Business messages usually describe how to do something, explain why a procedure was changed, highlight the cause of a problem or a possible solution, discuss the status of a project, or explain why a new piece of equipment should be purchased.

FIGURE 1.3 In-Depth Critique: Effective Business Communication

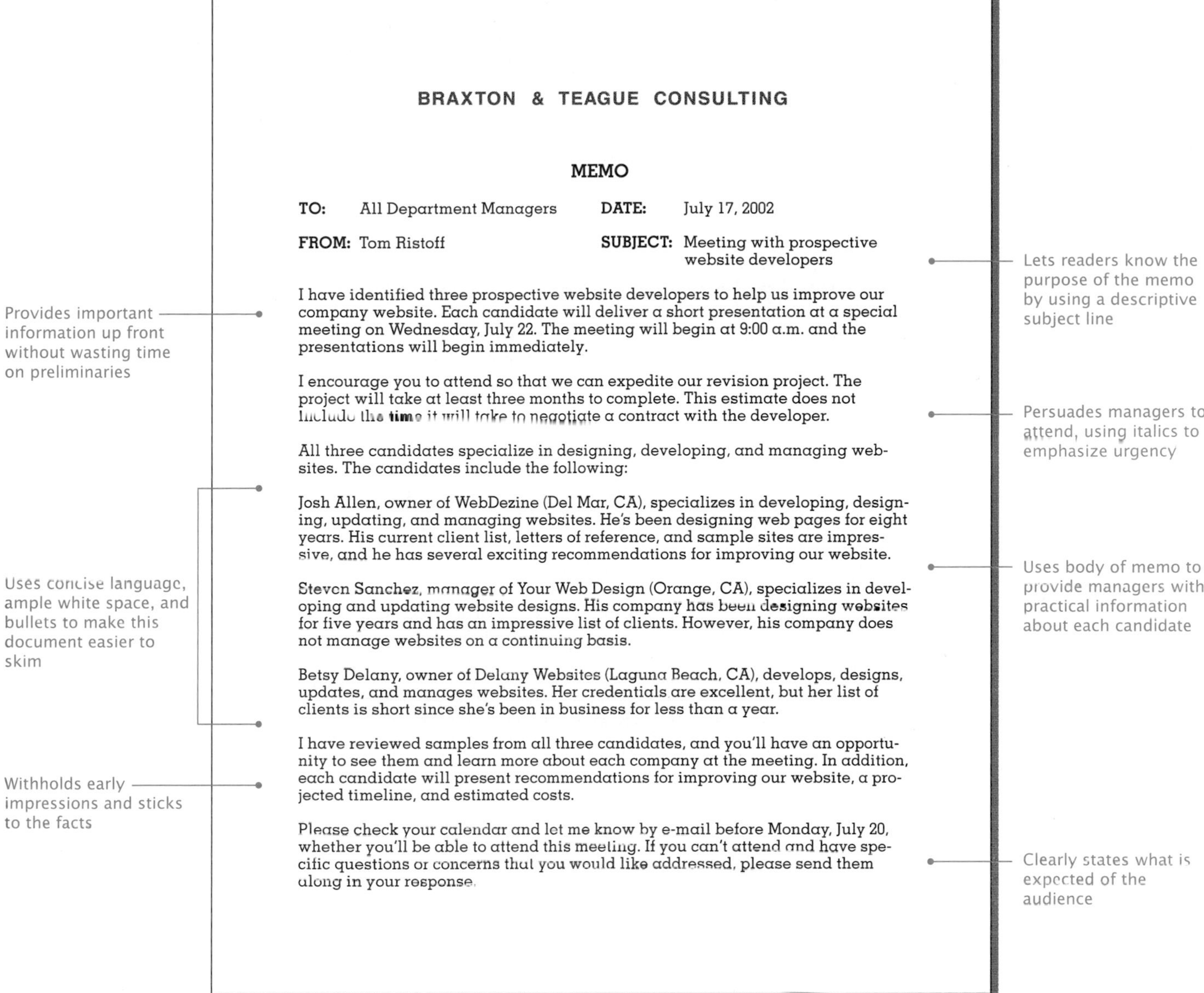

BRAXTON & TEAGUE CONSULTING

MEMO

TO: All Department Managers DATE: July 17, 2002

FROM: Tom Ristoff SUBJECT: Meeting with prospective website developers

I have identified three prospective website developers to help us improve our company website. Each candidate will deliver a short presentation at a special meeting on Wednesday, July 22. The meeting will begin at 9:00 a.m. and the presentations will begin immediately.

I encourage you to attend so that we can expedite our revision project. The project will take at least three months to complete. This estimate does not *include the time it will take to negotiate* a contract with the developer.

All three candidates specialize in designing, developing, and managing websites. The candidates include the following:

Josh Allen, owner of WebDezine (Del Mar, CA), specializes in developing, designing, updating, and managing websites. He's been designing web pages for eight years. His current client list, letters of reference, and sample sites are impressive, and he has several exciting recommendations for improving our website.

Steven Sanchez, manager of Your Web Design (Orange, CA), specializes in developing and updating website designs. His company has been designing websites for five years and has an impressive list of clients. However, his company does not manage websites on a continuing basis.

Betsy Delany, owner of Delany Websites (Laguna Beach, CA), develops, designs, updates, and manages websites. Her credentials are excellent, but her list of clients is short since she's been in business for less than a year.

I have reviewed samples from all three candidates, and you'll have an opportunity to see them and learn more about each company at the meeting. In addition, each candidate will present recommendations for improving our website, a projected timeline, and estimated costs.

Please check your calendar and let me know by e-mail before Monday, July 20, whether you'll be able to attend this meeting. If you can't attend and have specific questions or concerns that you would like addressed, please send them along in your response.

- **Give facts rather than impressions.** Business messages use concrete language and specific details. Information must be clear, convincing, accurate, and ethical. You must present hard evidence (not just opinion) and present all sides of an argument before you commit to a conclusion.
- **Clarify and condense information.** Business messages frequently use tables, charts, photos, or diagrams to clarify or condense information, to explain a process, or to emphasize important information.
- **State precise responsibilities.** Business messages are directed to a specific audience. Therefore, you must clearly state what is expected of, or what you can do for, that particular audience.
- **Persuade others and offer recommendations.** Business messages frequently persuade employers, customers, or clients to purchase a product or service or adopt a plan of action. To be effective, persuasive messages must show readers just how a product, service, or idea will benefit them specifically.

Keep these five characteristics in mind as you review Figures 1.2 and 1.3. Although Figure 1.2 *appears* to be a well-constructed message, Figure 1.3 is more effective, as explained in the document's margins. Furthermore, Figure 1.2 shows that you can have the greatest ideas in the world, but they're no good to your company, or your career, if you can't express them clearly and persuasively. As one project manager at NASA's Marshall Space Flight Center put it, "Knowledge may be power, but communication skills are the primary raw materials of good client relationships." Every job description for a new position on this manager's staff includes the following line: "Required—effective organization skills and mastery of the English language in written and oral forms."[5]

The ability to find and communicate information is a requirement for most jobs.

In this course you will learn how to create effective messages such as the one shown in Figure 1.3. But first you must understand some of the basic forms of communication and become aware of the communication challenges you'll face in today's workplace.

The Basic Forms of Communication

In this course, you will learn how to select the best form of communication for your message.

Communication occurs in many forms. You can pick up the phone and have a conversation with your supervisor or leave her a voice-mail message if she's unavailable. You can choose, instead, to write her a memo and send it by e-mail. In turn, she can respond to your message in the form of her choice. Your supervisor may decide to forward your message to other employees or managers, and they may communicate it to customers and other outsiders. The process is fluid; the form in which a message is communicated changes constantly. Communication can be internal or external, formal or informal, spoken or written. In fact, it can even be a simple smile.

Nonverbal Communication

Nonverbal communication is the process of communicating without words.

The most basic form of communication is **nonverbal communication**: all the cues, gestures, facial expressions, spatial relationships, and attitudes toward time that enable people to communicate without words. Anthropologists theorize that long before human beings used words to talk things over, our ancestors communicated with one another by using their bodies. They gritted their teeth to show anger; they smiled and touched one another to indicate affection. Although we have come a long way since those primitive times, we still use nonverbal cues to express superiority, dependence, dislike, respect, love, and other feelings.[6]

Nonverbal communication differs from verbal communication in fundamental ways. For one thing, it's less structured, so it's more difficult to study. You can't pick up a book on nonverbal language and master the vocabulary of gestures, expressions, and inflections that are common in our culture. Even experts don't really know how people learn nonverbal behavior. No one teaches a baby to cry or smile, yet these forms of self-expression are almost universal. Other types of nonverbal communication, such as the meaning of colors and certain gestures, vary from culture to culture.

Nonverbal communication also differs from verbal communication in terms of intent and spontaneity. You generally plan your words. When you say, "Please get back to me on that order by Friday," you have a conscious purpose; you think about the message, if only for a moment. However, when you communicate nonverbally, you sometimes do so unconsciously. You don't mean to raise an eyebrow or to blush. Those actions come naturally. Without your consent, your emotions are written all over your face. As Chapter 2 discusses in greater detail, good communicators recognize the value of nonverbal communication and use it to maximize the effectiveness of their messages.

Actions speak louder than words.

Verbal Communication

Although you can express many things nonverbally, there are limits to what you can communicate without the help of language. If you want to discuss past events, ideas, or abstractions, you need symbols that stand for your thoughts. **Verbal communication** consists of words arranged in meaningful patterns. The ever-growing

Keeping Pace with Technology

Business Writing—A Craft Under Siege?

Watch out! An assault on the English language is intensifying in the American workplace—from executive suites to cubicle seats. According to Lynn Agress, founder of Business Writing at Its Best (BWB), the culprits are television, the informality of the Internet, and schools that sometimes emphasize teaching computer skills over reading. But Agress and other guardians of grammar have one consolation: The age of technology has brought them full employment.

Agress and other writing consultants teach lawyers, doctors, and corporate executives what they should have learned in public school for free. Now dozens of companies pay Agress fees ranging from $5,500 plus travel expenses for two half-day workshops to $66,000 for a series of 13 sessions—to improve their writing skills. Workshop participants submit writing samples to BWB instructors, who pinpoint trouble spots and tailor a training course based on the organization's writing needs. BWB clients have included AT&T, Citibank, PricewaterhouseCoopers, Johns Hopkins Medical Center, and more.

Wordiness, use of technical jargon, and poor mechanics are the most common weaknesses in business writing. "As technology improves and expands, literacy declines . . . And with e-mail, writing just keeps deteriorating," says Agress. "There is no question that business writing is a craft under siege," adds Peter Post, co-author of *The Etiquette Advantage of Business.* "In our so-called Information Age, no skill is more important than the ability to organize and convey information with clarity and coherence." Still, the working vocabulary of the average 14-year-old has declined over the past 50 years, dropping from 25,000 to 10,000 words. In addition, more and more U.S. children are becoming dependent on word-processing aids such as spell checkers. As a result, 20 years from now, those children will likely end up in similar writing workshops.

Career Applications

1. How is e-mail and Internet informality encouraging poor business writing?
2. Why is the ability to organize and convey information with clarity and coherence an important skill in the Information Age?

English language currently contains about 750,000 words, although most people in the United States recognize only about 20,000 of them.[7] (And vocabularies are shrinking—see "Keeping Pace with Technology: Business Writing—A Craft Under Siege?") To create a thought with these words, you arrange them according to the rules of grammar, putting the various parts of speech in the proper sequence. You then transmit the message in spoken or written form, anticipating that someone will hear or read what you have to say.

Language is composed of words and grammar.

Given a choice, people would rather talk to each other than write to each other (see Figure 1.4). Talking takes less time and needs no composing, keyboarding, rewriting, duplicating, or distributing. Even more important, oral communication provides the opportunity for feedback. When people communicate orally, they can ask questions and test their understanding of the message; they can share ideas and work together to solve problems.

Most people would rather talk than write.

Nonetheless, oral communication has its drawbacks. You have far less opportunity to revise your spoken words than to revise your written words. You can't cross out what you just said and start all over. Furthermore, at times written forms, such as letters, memos, reports, and proposals, are more appropriate and effective: when the information you are conveying is very complex, when a permanent record is needed for future reference, when the audience is large and geographically dispersed, and when immediate interaction with the audience is either unimportant or undesirable.

Spoken words are more difficult to revise than written ones.

Now look again at Figure 1.4. In addition to underscoring the importance of oral communication, it illustrates that people spend more time *receiving* information than transmitting it. Listening and reading are every bit as important as speaking and writing. But as Chapter 2 points out, most of us aren't very good listeners. A major reason is that we are distracted by a number of challenges in the workplace.

The ability to listen is a vital skill in business.

FIGURE 1.4 The Percentage of Communication Time Businesspeople Spend on Various Communication Channels

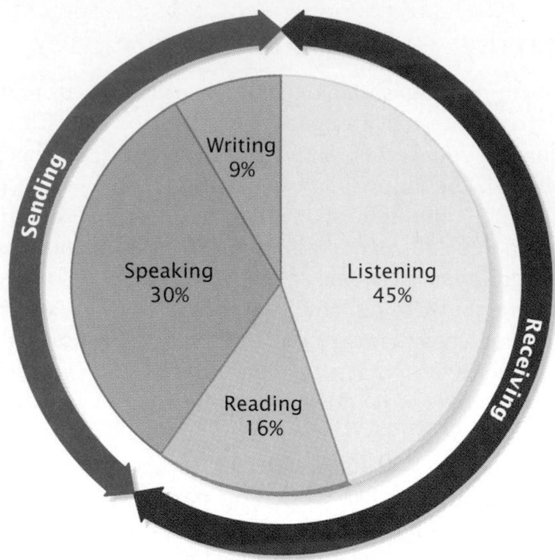

Communication Challenges in Today's Workplace

Learning Objective 2

Discuss three developments in the workplace that are intensifying the need to communicate effectively

Good communication skills have always been important in the workplace. They are even more vital today, when the changing workplace has brought these communication challenges: advances in technology, globalization, an increasing culturally diverse workforce, and the adoption of team-based organizational structures.

As you proceed through this book, you'll meet a cross section of real people—men and women who work for some of the world's most fascinating organizations. Chapter-opening slice-of-life vignettes titled "Communication Close-Up" give you an opportunity to read about these and other communication challenges faced by people such as Robert LoCascio. At the end of each chapter, you'll take part in solving the company's "Communication Challenges" by playing the role of a person working in that organization (both as an individual and as a member of a team). You will face a situation you might encounter in that organization, and it's up to you or your team to recommend a course of action by using the various communication ideas, concepts, and techniques discussed in the chapter.

Advances in Technology

The Internet, e-mail, voice mail, faxes, pagers, and other wireless devices have revolutionized the way people communicate. Such technological advances not only bring new and better tools to the workplace but also increase the speed, frequency, and reach of communication. People from opposite ends of the world can work together seamlessly, 24 hours a day. Moreover, advances in technology make it possible for more and more people to work away from the office—in cars, airports, hotels, and at home.

Using technology showcases your communication skills.

This increased use of new technology requires employees to communicate more effectively and efficiently. Technology showcases your communication skills—your writing skills are revealed in every e-mail message, and your verbal skills are revealed in audio and video teleconferences.[8] Furthermore, *intranets* (private corporate networks based on Internet technology), and *extranets* (the extension of private networks to certain outsiders such as suppliers) facilitate communication among employees, managers, customers, suppliers, and investors. The challenges of communicating effectively with people inside and outside the organization are magnified as more

Electronic commerce intensifies the need to communicate effectively.

businesses install such networks and as they increasingly engage in **electronic commerce (e-commerce)**, the buying and selling of goods and services over the Internet.

As Robert LoCascio knows, each form of electronic communication has its limitations, and individuals must learn when it's appropriate to use each form.[9] You have to think not only about what you are going to say and how you are going to say it but also about which technological tools you'll use to do so. Throughout this book we present numerous examples of the types of technological tools you'll encounter on the job and how to use those tools effectively and wisely. We've also included a special appendix (Appendix IV) to give you practical advice when communicating via e-mail, voice mail, instant messaging, and other electronic formats.

At Staples, managers must communicate clearly with the employees they supervise, regardless of differences in their age, gender, culture, or ethnic background.

Globalization and a Culturally Diverse Workforce

More and more businesses today are crossing national boundaries to compete on a global scale. Over 2 million North Americans now work for multinational employers, and the number of foreign companies that have built plants in the United States is increasing.[10] In addition, a growing percentage of the U.S. workforce is made up of people with diverse cultural and ethnic backgrounds, a trend that will continue in the years ahead. In the United States, for example, ethnic minorities are entering the workforce in record numbers (see Figure 1.5). By 2010, Hispanic Americans will become the largest minority group, and by 2050 the number of minority workers will almost equal that of white workers.[11]

The increases in international business dealings and in the diversity of the workforce create communication challenges.

Increased globalization and workforce diversity mean that employees must understand the laws, customs, and business practices of many countries and be able to communicate with people who speak other languages. Look at 3Com's sprawling modem factory in Chicago. The plant employs 1,200 people, the vast majority of whom are immigrants. Urban Asians with multiple college degrees work alongside people only recently arrived from Central American villages. Serbs work with Bosnian Muslims and with Iraqis, Peruvians, and South Africans. The employees speak more than 20 different languages, including Tagalog, Gujarati, and Chinese. English of varying degrees ties them together.[12]

Today's employees must communicate with people who speak English as a second language.

FIGURE 1.5 Ethnic Composition of the U.S. Workforce

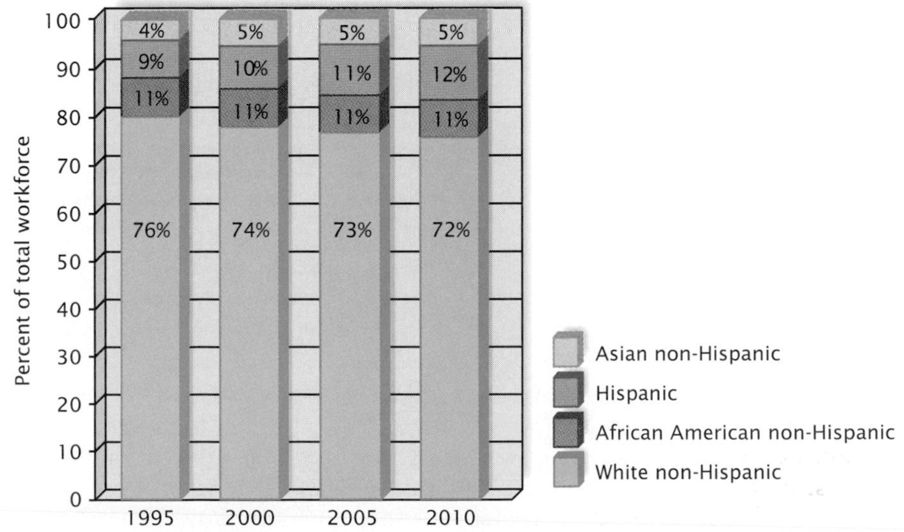

Earth and Environmental Services in San Francisco encourages its employees to work collaboratively so that they can benefit from the knowledge of other team members.

Chapter 3 discusses intercultural communication in detail and explains how understanding other backgrounds, personalities, and perceptions helps you become a more effective communicator. Moreover, special "Communicating Across Cultures" boxes throughout this text explore cultural issues you will likely encounter in the global workplace.

Team-Based Organizations

The command-and-control style of traditional management structures is ineffective in today's fast-paced, e-commerce environment.[13] Successful companies like LivePerson no longer limit decisions to a few managers at the top of a formal hierarchy. Instead, organizations use teams and collaborative work groups to make the fast decisions required to succeed in a global and competitive marketplace. Although working in teams has many advantages, it also offers many challenges, as team members often come from different departments, perform different functions, and come from diverse cultural backgrounds. As Chapter 2 discusses in detail, to function in a team-based organization, you must understand how groups interact, reach decisions, work collaboratively, and resolve conflict. Moreover, you must be able listen to and understand others, give balanced feedback, explore ideas, keep everyone involved, and credit others' work.[14] Doing so requires a basic understanding of the communication process in organizational settings.

When working in teams, you should be able to clarify, confirm, give feedback, explore ideas, and credit others.

COMMUNICATION IN ORGANIZATIONAL SETTINGS

Learning Objective 3

Describe how organizations share information internally and externally

Whether an organization is large, small, or virtual, sharing information among its parts and with the outside world is the glue that binds the organization together. When you join a company, you become a link in its information chain. Whether you're a top manager or an entry-level employee, you have information that others need in order to perform their jobs, and others have information that is crucial to you. In fact, communication is the lifeblood of an organization. It includes the internal and external structure through which messages pass and the way information is presented, as well as the actual content of the messages themselves. As you exchange information with people inside and outside the organization, you use a variety of formal and informal forms of communication (see Figure 1.6).

To succeed, organizations must share information with people both inside and outside the company.

FIGURE 1.6 Forms of Communication

	Internal	External
Formal	Planned communication among insiders (letters, reports, memos, e-mail) that follows the company's chain of command	Planned communication with outsiders (letters, reports, memos, speeches, websites, and news release)
Informal	Casual communication among employees (e-mail, face-to-face conversations, and phone calls that do not follow the company's chain of command)	Casual communication with suppliers, customers investors, and other outsiders (face-to-face conversations, e-mail, and phone calls)

FIGURE 1.7 In-Depth Critique: Internal Communication by E-Mail

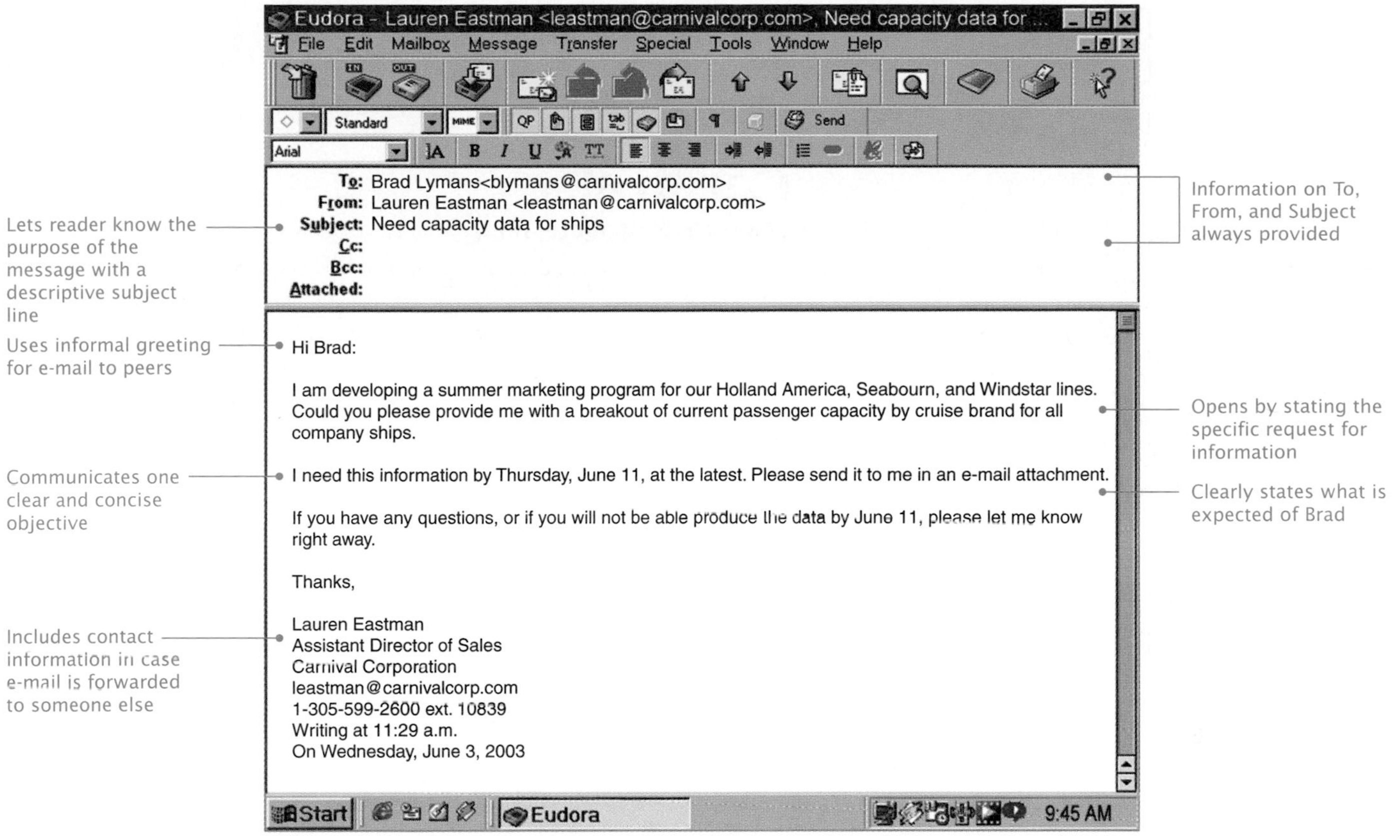

Eudora - Lauren Eastman <leastman@carnivalcorp.com>, Need capacity data for ...

File Edit Mailbox Message Transfer Special Tools Window Help

To: Brad Lymans<blymans@carnivalcorp.com>
From: Lauren Eastman <leastman@carnivalcorp.com>
Subject: Need capacity data for ships
Cc:
Bcc:
Attached:

Hi Brad:

I am developing a summer marketing program for our Holland America, Seabourn, and Windstar lines. Could you please provide me with a breakout of current passenger capacity by cruise brand for all company ships.

I need this information by Thursday, June 11, at the latest. Please send it to me in an e-mail attachment.

If you have any questions, or if you will not be able produce the data by June 11, please let me know right away.

Thanks,

Lauren Eastman
Assistant Director of Sales
Carnival Corporation
leastman@carnivalcorp.com
1-305-599-2600 ext. 10839
Writing at 11:29 a.m.
On Wednesday, June 3, 2003

Start Eudora 9:45 AM

Lets reader know the purpose of the message with a descriptive subject line

Uses informal greeting for e-mail to peers

Communicates one clear and concise objective

Includes contact information in case e-mail is forwarded to someone else

Information on To, From, and Subject always provided

Opens by stating the specific request for information

Clearly states what is expected of Brad

Internal Communication

Internal communication refers to the exchange of information and ideas within an organization. As an employee, you are in a position to observe things that your supervisors and co-workers cannot see: a customer's first reaction to a product display, a supplier's brief hesitation before agreeing to a delivery date, an odd whirring noise in a piece of equipment, or a slowdown in the flow of customers. Managers and co-workers need these little gems of information in order to do their jobs. If you don't pass that information along, nobody will—because nobody else knows.

You are a contact point in both the external and internal communication networks.

In most businesses, much information can be exchanged internally by phone, e-mail, fax, interoffice memo, or company intranet. For example, at Carnival Corporation, the world's largest multiple-night cruise company, assistant director of sales Lauren Eastman used e-mail to request capacity information from the company's operations manager, Brad Lymans (see Figure 1.7). To reply, Lymans used an internal memo (see Figure 1.8). As these examples show, communicating freely among the members of an organization is essential for effective functioning.

Internal communication helps employees do their jobs, develop a clear sense of the organization's mission, and identify and react quickly to potential problems. To maintain a healthy flow of information within the organization, effective communicators use both formal and informal channels.

Formal Communication Network

The **formal communication network** is typically shown as an organization chart like the one in Figure 1.9 on page 13. Such charts summarize the lines of authority; each box represents a link in the chain of command, and each line represents a formal channel for the transmission of official messages. Information may travel down, up, and across an organization's formal hierarchy.

The formal flow of information follows the official chain of command.

FIGURE 1.8 In-Depth Critique: Internal Communication by Memo

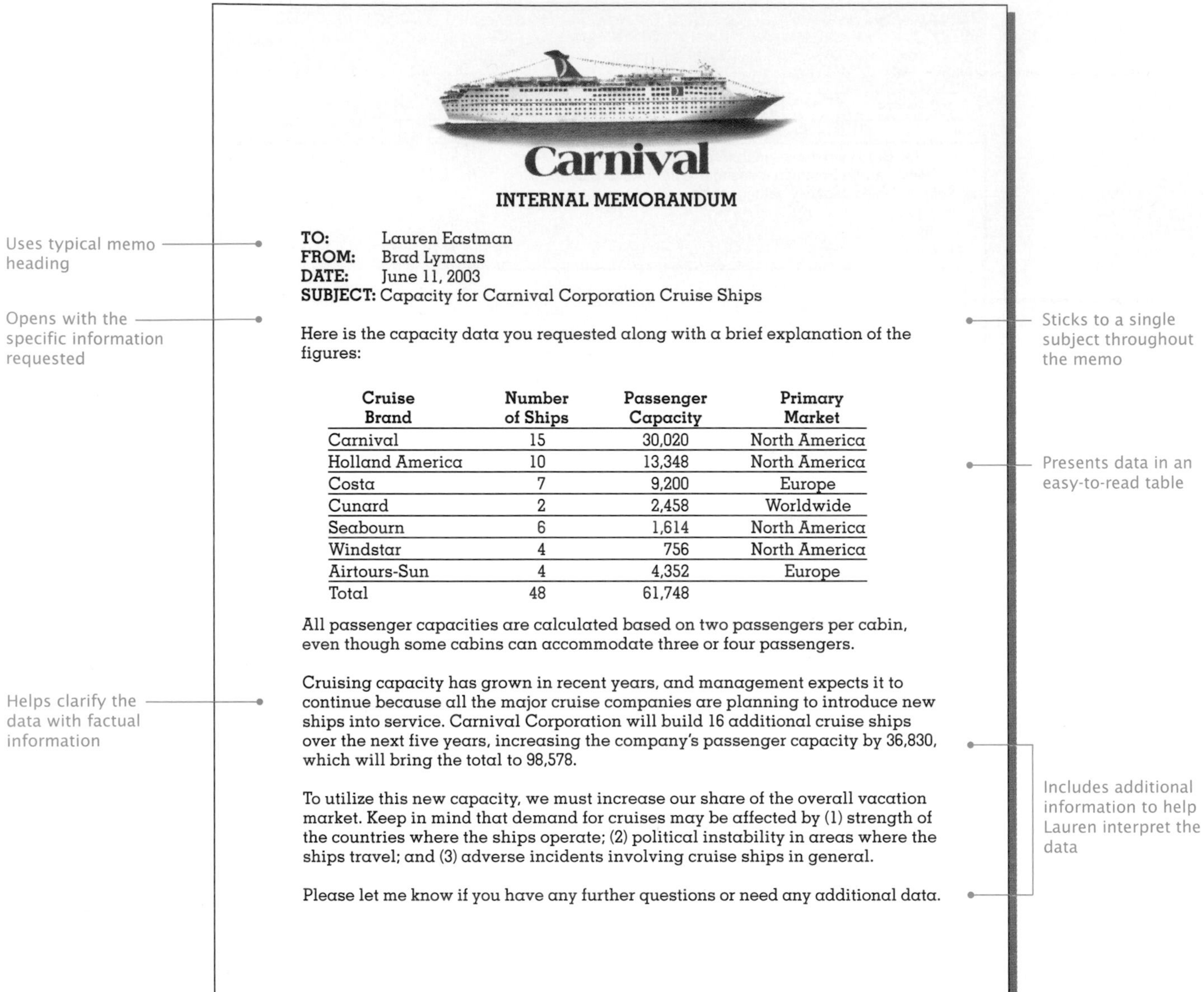

Carnival

INTERNAL MEMORANDUM

TO: Lauren Eastman
FROM: Brad Lymans
DATE: June 11, 2003
SUBJECT: Capacity for Carnival Corporation Cruise Ships

Here is the capacity data you requested along with a brief explanation of the figures:

Cruise Brand	Number of Ships	Passenger Capacity	Primary Market
Carnival	15	30,020	North America
Holland America	10	13,348	North America
Costa	7	9,200	Europe
Cunard	2	2,458	Worldwide
Seabourn	6	1,614	North America
Windstar	4	756	North America
Airtours-Sun	4	4,352	Europe
Total	48	61,748	

All passenger capacities are calculated based on two passengers per cabin, even though some cabins can accommodate three or four passengers.

Cruising capacity has grown in recent years, and management expects it to continue because all the major cruise companies are planning to introduce new ships into service. Carnival Corporation will build 16 additional cruise ships over the next five years, increasing the company's passenger capacity by 36,830, which will bring the total to 98,578.

To utilize this new capacity, we must increase our share of the overall vacation market. Keep in mind that demand for cruises may be affected by (1) strength of the countries where the ships operate; (2) political instability in areas where the ships travel; and (3) adverse incidents involving cruise ships in general.

Please let me know if you have any further questions or need any additional data.

Information flows down, up, and across the formal hierarchy.

- **Downward flow.** Organizational decisions are usually made at the top and then flow down to the people who will carry them out. Most of what filters downward is geared toward helping employees do their jobs. From top to bottom, each person must understand each message, apply it, and pass it along.
- **Upward flow.** To solve problems and make intelligent decisions, managers must learn what's going on in the organization. Because they can't be everywhere at once, executives depend on lower-level employees to furnish them with accurate, timely reports on problems, emerging trends, opportunities for improvement, grievances, and performance.
- **Horizontal flow.** Communication also flows from one department to another, either laterally or diagonally. This horizontal communication helps employees share information and coordinate tasks, and it is especially useful for solving complex and difficult problems.[15]

Formal organization charts illustrate how information is supposed to flow. In actual practice, however, lines and boxes on a piece of paper cannot prevent people from talking with one another.

FIGURE 1.9 Formal Communication Network

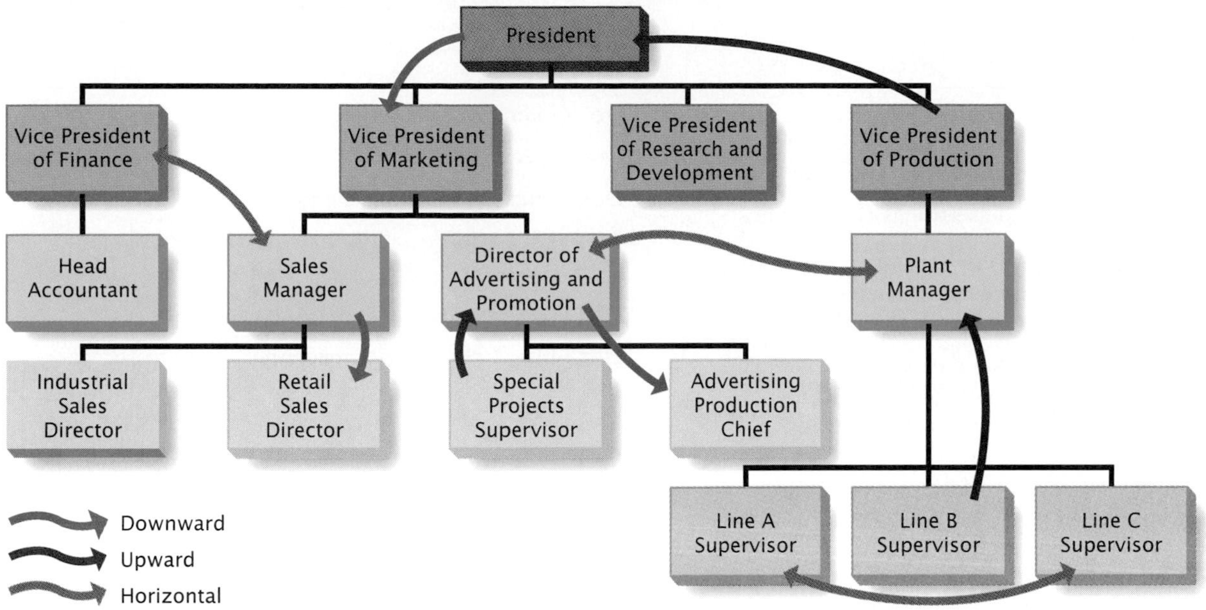

Informal Communication Network

Every organization has an **informal communication network**—a *grapevine*—that supplements official channels. As people go about their work, they have casual conversations with their friends in the office. Although many of these conversations deal with personal matters, about 80 percent of the information that travels along the grapevine pertains to business.[16]

The informal communication network carries information along the organization's unofficial lines of activity and power.

Some executives are wary of the informal communication network, possibly because it threatens their power to control the flow of information. However, savvy managers tap into the grapevine, using it to spread and receive informal messages.[17] Because eliminating the grapevine is virtually impossible, sophisticated companies minimize its importance by making certain that the official word gets out.

The grapevine is an important source of information in most organizations.

External Communication

Just as internal communication carries information up, down, and across the organization, **external communication** carries it into and out of the organization. Companies constantly exchange messages with customers, vendors, distributors, competitors, investors, journalists, and community representatives. Sometimes this external communication is carefully orchestrated—especially during a crisis. At other times it occurs informally as part of routine business operations.

The external communication network links the organization with the outside world of customers, suppliers, competitors, and investors.

Formal External Communication

Whether by letter, website, phone, fax, Internet, or videotape, good communication is the first step in creating a favorable impression. Carefully constructed letters, reports, memos, oral presentations, and websites convey an important message to outsiders about the quality of your organization, as Robert LoCascio can attest. Messages such as statements to the press, letters to investors, advertisements, price increase announcements, and litigation updates require special care because of their delicate nature. Therefore, such documents are often drafted by a marketing or public relations team—a group of individuals whose sole job is creating and managing the flow of formal messages to outsiders.

Companies use external communication to create a favorable impression.

The public relations team is also responsible for helping management plan for and respond to crises—which can range from environmental accidents or sabotage situations to strikes, massive product failure, major litigation, or even an abrupt change in

The way a company handles a crisis can have a profound effect on the organization's subsequent performance.

TABLE 1.1 What To Do in a Crisis

When a Crisis Hits:

Do	***Don't***
Do prepare for trouble ahead of time by identifying potential problems, appointing and training a response team, and preparing and testing a crisis management plan.	Don't blame anyone for anything.
Do get top management involved as soon as the crisis hits.	Don't speculate in public.
Do set up a news center for company representatives and the media, equipped with phones, computers, and other electronic tools for preparing news releases. ■ Issue at least two news updates a day, and have trained personnel to respond to questions around the clock. ■ Provide complete information packets to the media as soon as possible. ■ Prevent conflicting statements and provide continuity, appointing a single person, trained in advance, to speak for the company. ■ Tell receptionists to direct all calls to the news center.	Don't refuse to answer questions.
Do tell the whole story—openly, completely, and honestly. If you are at fault, apologize.	Don't release information that will violate anyone's right to privacy.
Do demonstrate the company's concern by your statements and your actions.	Don't use the crisis to pitch products or services.
	Don't play favorites with media representatives.

When evidence surfaced that Ford and Firestone knew about peeling-tire-tread problems years before they recalled the faulty Firestone tires, both companies were forced to swing into full crisis-control mode. Here former Ford CEO Jacques Nasser defends Ford's safety record and explains how his company is handling the Firestone tire recall for the Ford Explorer.

management. To minimize the impact of any crisis, expert communicators advise managers to communicate honestly, openly, and often (see Table 1.1).[18] If handled improperly, a crisis can destroy a company's reputation, drain its financial strength, erode employee morale, and result in negative publicity.

Ford and Bridgestone/Firestone learned this lesson the hard way. Both companies failed to communicate to the public in a timely and effective manner the seriousness of malfunctioning tires fitted on Ford Explorer sport utility vehicles. When the vehicles were driven at high speed (and especially in warm climates), the treads separated from the tires, causing the car to roll over and injuring—even killing—passengers.[19] Now both companies are suffering the consequences. Sales of Firestone tires have plunged, Bridgestone/Firestone has dropped Ford as a customer, and some experts question whether the Firestone tire brand can make a comeback.[20]

Informal External Communication

Although companies usually communicate with outsiders in a formal manner, informal contacts with outsiders are important for learning about customer needs. As a member of an organization, you are an important informal conduit for communicating with the outside world. In the course of your daily activities, you unconsciously absorb bits and pieces of information that add to the collective knowledge of your company. Moreover, every time you speak for or about your company, you send a message. Many outsiders may form their impression of your organization on the basis of the subtle, unconscious clues you transmit through your tone of voice, facial expression, and general appearance.

Top managers rely heavily on informal contacts with outsiders to gather information that might be useful to their companies. Much of their networking involves interaction with fellow executives. However, plenty of high-level managers recognize the value of keeping in touch with "the real world" by creating opportunities to talk with and get feedback from customers and frontline employees. Receiving feedback is a key phase of the communication process.

Every employee informally accumulates facts and impressions that contribute to the organization's collective understanding of the outside world.

The Communication Process

Communication doesn't occur haphazardly in organizations. Nor does it happen all at once. It is more than a single act. Communication is a dynamic, transactional (two-way) process that can be broken into six phases (see Figure 1.10).

Learning Objective 4

List and briefly define the six phases of the communication process

The communication process consists of six phases linking sender and receiver.

1. **The sender has an idea.** You conceive an idea and want to share it.
2. **The sender encodes the idea.** When you put your idea into a message that your receiver will understand, you are **encoding** it. You decide on the message's form (word, facial expression, gesture), length, organization, tone, and style—all of which depend on your idea, your audience, and your personal style or mood.
3. **The sender transmits the message.** To physically transmit your message to your receiver, you select a **communication channel** (verbal or nonverbal, spoken or written) and a **medium** (telephone, letter, memo, e-mail, report, face-to-face exchange). This choice depends on your message, your audience's location, your need for speed, and the formality required.
4. **The receiver gets the message.** For communication to occur, your receiver must first get the message. If you send a letter, your receiver has to read it before understanding it. If you're giving a speech, your listeners have to be able to hear you, and they have to be paying attention.
5. **The receiver decodes the message.** Your receiver must **decode** (absorb and understand) your message. The decoded message must then be stored in the receiver's mind. If all goes well, the receiver interprets your message correctly, assigning the same meaning to your words as you intended and responding in the desired way.

FIGURE 1.10 The Communication Process

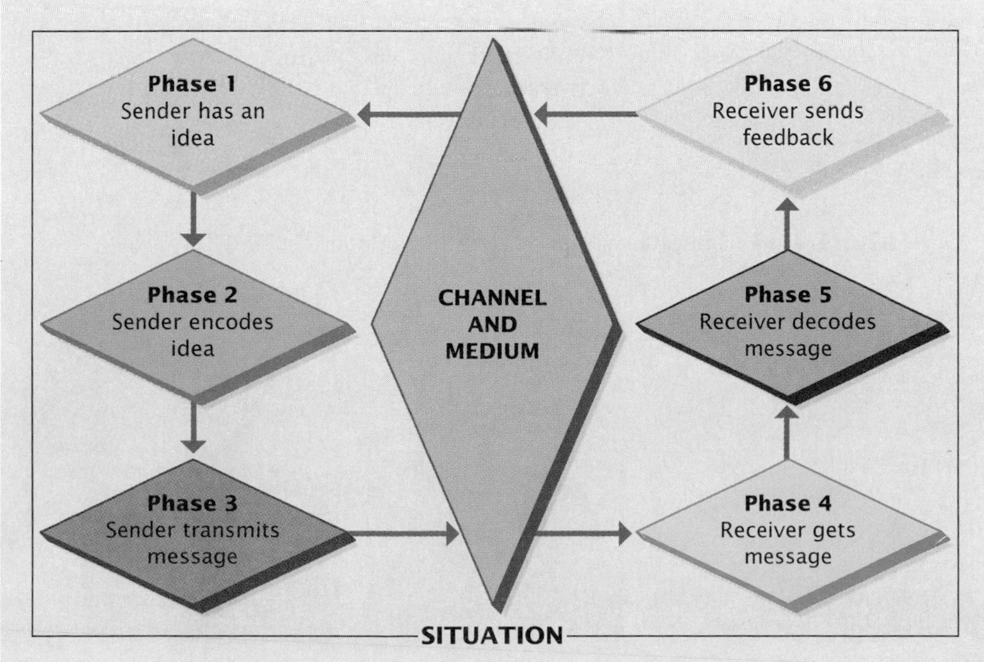

Feedback is your audience's response; it enables you to evaluate your message's effectiveness.

6. **The receiver sends feedback.** After decoding your message, the receiver responds in some way and signals that response to you. This **feedback** enables you to evaluate the effectiveness of your message: If your audience doesn't understand what you mean, you can tell by the response and refine your message.

As Figure 1.10 illustrates, the communication process is repeated until both parties have finished expressing themselves.[21] Moreover, effective business communicators don't cram too much information into one message. Instead, they limit the content of a message to a specific subject and use this back-and-forth exchange to provide additional information or details in subsequent messages.

COMMUNICATION BARRIERS

Learning Objective 5

Identify and briefly discuss five types of communication barriers

Communication barriers block the communication process.

Communication is successful only when the receiver understands the message intended by the sender. If any step in the communication process is blocked by some sort of interference, the message will be garbled or lost. Interference in the communication process that distorts or obscures the sender's meaning is called *noise*. Such noise can be caused by a variety of **communication barriers.** Common barriers to effective communication include perceptual and language differences, restrictive environments, distractions, deceptive communication tactics, and information overload.

Perceptual and Language Differences

Perception is people's individual interpretation of the sensory world around them.

The world constantly bombards us with sights, sounds, scents, and so on. Our minds organize this stream of sensation into a mental map that represents our **perception** of reality. Even when two people have experienced the same event, their mental images of that event will not be identical. Because your perceptions are unique, the ideas you want to express differ from other people's. As a sender, you choose the details that seem important to you, a process known as **selective perception.** As a receiver, you try to fit new details into your existing pattern. If a detail doesn't quite fit, you are inclined to distort the information rather than rearrange the pattern.

Language is an arbitrary code that depends on shared definitions. However, there's a limit to how completely any two people can share the same meaning for a given word. Take the simple word *cookie*, for example. You might think of oatmeal, chocolate chip, and sugar cookies. However, others might think of *cookie* in its technological context—that is, a text file stored on a visitor's computer to identify each time the user visits a website. As the cookie example shows, the more experiences you share with another person, the more likely you are to share perception and thus share meaning (see Figure 1.11). Still, even when two people experience the same event, their mental images are not identical.

The more experiences people share, the more likely they will be to understand each other.

FIGURE 1.11 How Shared Experience Affects Understanding

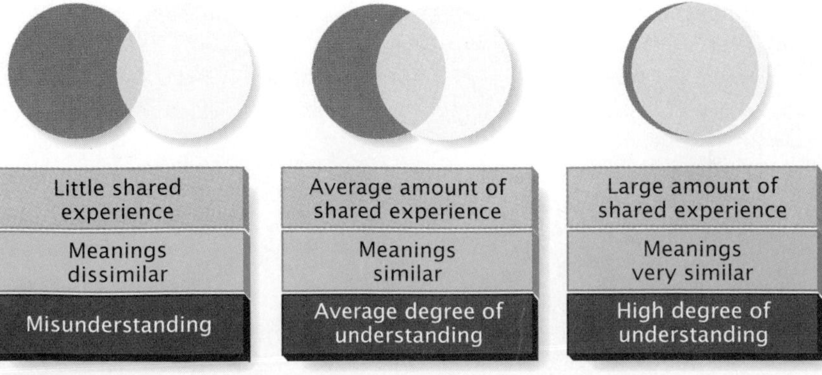

Restrictive Environments

Every link in the communication chain is open to error. So by the time a message travels all the way up or down the chain, it may bear little resemblance to the original idea. If a company's formal communication network limits the flow of information in any direction (upward, downward, or horizontal), communication becomes fragmented. Lower-level employees may obtain only enough information to perform their own isolated tasks, learning little about other areas; thus, only the people at the very top of the organization can see "the big picture."

The communication climate suffers when information is distorted, fragmented, or blocked by an authoritarian style of management.

When managers use a directive and authoritarian leadership style, information moves down the chain of command, but not up. In a recent poll of 638 employees, 90 percent said they had good ideas on how their companies could run more successfully. Yet more than 50 percent said they were prevented from communicating these thoughts because of a lack of management interest and a lack of effective means for sharing their ideas.[22]

Distractions

Physical distractions such as bad connections, poor acoustics, or illegible copy may seem trivial, but they can block an otherwise effective message. Your receiver might be distracted by an uncomfortable chair, poor lighting, health problems, or some other irritating condition.

Your audience is more likely to receive your message accurately if nothing physical interrupts or distorts the message.

Emotional distractions can also get in the way of your message. When you are upset, hostile, or fearful, you have a hard time shaping a message objectively. If your receivers are emotional, they may ignore or distort your message. It's practically impossible to avoid all communication in which emotions are involved, but you must recognize that emotional messages have a greater potential for misunderstanding.

Emotions block the communication process.

Deceptive Tactics

Language itself is made up of words that carry values. So merely by saying things a certain way, you influence how others perceive your message, and you shape expectations and behaviors.[23] An organization cannot create illegal or unethical messages and still be credible or successful in the long run. Still, some business communicators try to manipulate their receivers by using deceptive tactics.

Deceptive communicators may exaggerate benefits, quote inaccurate statistics, or hide negative information behind an optimistic attitude. They may state opinions as facts, leave out crucial information, or portray graphic data unfairly. Unscrupulous communicators may seek personal gain by making others look better or worse than they are. And they may allow personal preferences to influence their own perception and the perception of others.

Using deceptive tactics to manipulate receivers blocks communication and ultimately leads to failure.

Information Overload

Every day, the number of documents on the Internet increases by 7.5 million. In addition to these documents, people receive more and more messages via e-mail, overnight express couriers, fax machines, voice mail, websites, regular mail, pagers, and cell phones.[24] A recent study by office-equipment maker Pitney Bowes found that, on a typical day, the average office worker sends and receives over 200 messages (see Figure 1.12).[25]

Today's businesspeople are plagued by message overload.

The content of the messages ranges from crucial news and information to chitchat and jokes. The sheer number of messages can be distracting, making it difficult to discriminate between useful and useless information. Some companies are dealing with this information overload by encouraging employees to send fewer messages and by discouraging the use of the word *urgent*. Others are encouraging employees to tune out and disconnect. Still others are taking more extreme measures. The CEO of Computer Associates, for example, ordered the company's e-mail system to be shut down for two hours a day. "When it first

FIGURE 1.12 Message Mania

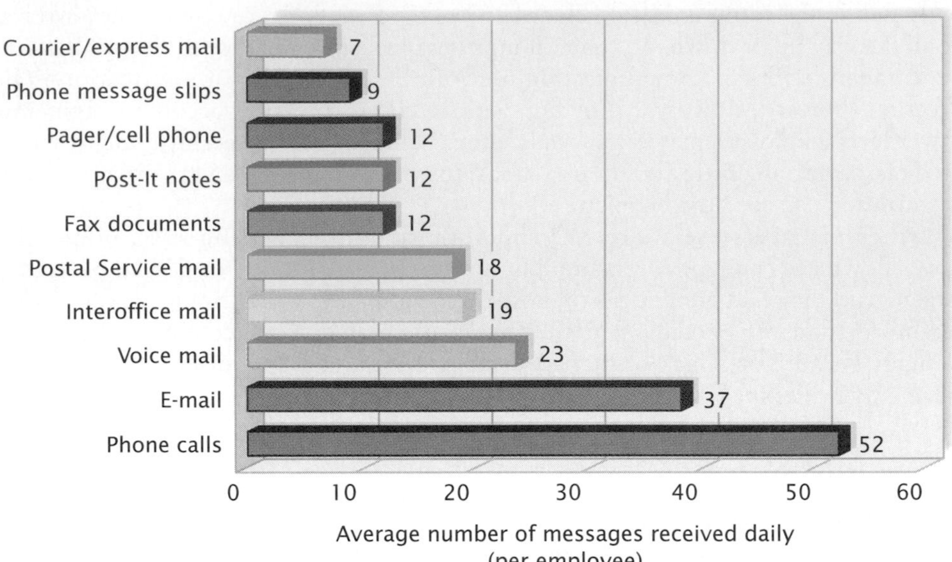

happened, it was like quitting cigarettes," notes one company manager. "We had 9,000 very edgy employees. But we got used to it. People found that they had time to think."[26]

Nonetheless, the realities of today's workplace make tuning out a virtual impossibility. Technology has created an expectation for instant answers. Not only is it unrealistic for employees to ignore a crucial project or a spate of e-mail messages asking for additional information, but it's quite common for professionals to find themselves constantly tied to work.[27] They make calls on their cell phones as they commute. They check their pagers and voice mail at business meetings, in their kitchens, and at the grocery store. They take work home and plug into their company intranet in the evening. Even when they are on vacation, some find it easier to take an hour out of their day to check e-mail and quickly respond than to return to work and tackle over 1,000 e-mail messages. "I'd be lost on Monday," notes one manager, "if I didn't spend an hour or so on Sunday evening cleaning up my e-mail."[28]

GUIDELINES FOR OVERCOMING COMMUNICATION BARRIERS

Learning Objective 6

Discuss four guidelines for overcoming communication barriers

Effective communicators work hard at perfecting the messages they deliver. When they make mistakes, they learn from them. If a memo they've written doesn't get the response they had hoped for, they change their approach the next time. If a meeting they're running gets out of control or proves unproductive, they do things differently at the next one. If they find that they have to explain themselves over and over again, they reevaluate their choice of words or rework their messages.

In the coming chapters, we present real-life examples of both good and bad communication and explain what's good or bad about them. After a while you'll begin to see a pattern. You'll notice that four themes keep surfacing: (1) adopting an audience-centered approach, (2) fostering an open communication climate, (3) committing to ethical communication, and (4) creating lean, efficient messages. These guidelines will help you overcome barriers and improve your communication.

Guideline 1: Adopt an Audience-Centered Approach

Using an audience-centered approach means keeping your audience in mind at all times when communicating.

Adopting an **audience-centered approach** means focusing on and caring about your audience, making every effort to get your message across in a way that is meaningful to them. As Robert LoCascio knows, you need to learn as much as possible about the biases, education, age, status, and style of your receiver to create an effective message. When you address strangers, try to find out more about them; if that's impossible, try to project yourself into their position by using your common sense and imagination. By writing and speaking from your audience's point of view, you can help them understand and accept your message.

At Amy's ice cream parlors, the corporate culture of "fun" leads to an open communication climate and makes it easy for all employees to speak up.

Guideline 2: Foster an Open Communication Climate

An organization's communication climate is a reflection of its **corporate culture**: the mixture of values, traditions, and habits that give a company its atmosphere or personality. Successful companies such as LivePerson encourage employee contributions by making sure that communication flows freely down, up, and across the organization chart. They encourage candor and honesty, and their employees feel free to confess their mistakes, disagree with the boss, and express their opinions. These companies create an open climate in two ways: by modifying the number of organizational levels and by facilitating feedback.

Modify the Number of Organizational Levels

The organization's communication climate affects the quantity and quality of the information exchanged.

One way to foster an open communication climate is to reduce the number of levels in the organization's structure. The fewer the links in the communication chain, the less likely it is that misunderstandings will occur.[29] In other words, having a flat structure (fewer levels) and a wide span of control (more people reporting to each supervisor) is less likely to introduce distortion than having a tall structure and a narrow span of control. Moreover, flatter organizations enable managers to share information with colleagues and employees and to include employees in decision making, goal setting, and problem solving.[30] Still, designing too few formal channels and having too many people report to a single individual can block effective communication by overburdening that key individual.

Adjusting organizational levels can improve the communication climate.

Facilitate Feedback

Giving your audience a chance to provide feedback is crucial to maintaining an open communication climate. According to a recent American Express survey, what employees want the most from employers is personal feedback (money was rated second). But many managers are eager to avoid conflict, so they avoid giving frank feedback to underperforming employees until it's too late.[31]

Best of the Web

Check Out These Resources at the Business Writer's Free Library

The Business Writer's Free Library is a terrific resource for business communication material. Categories of information include basic composition skills, basic writing skills, correspondence, reference material, and general resources and advice. Log on and read about the most common errors in English, become a word detective, ask Miss Grammar, review samples of common forms of correspondence, fine-tune your interpersonal skills, join a newsgroup, and more. Follow the links and improve your effectiveness as a business communicator.

www.mapnp.org/library/commskls/cmm_writ.htm

TABLE 1.2 Giving Constructive Feedback

To Give Constructive Feedback

- **Focus on particular behaviors.** Feedback should be specific rather than general.
- **Keep feedback impersonal.** No matter how upset you are, keep feedback job related, and never criticize someone personally.
- **Use "I" statements.** Instead of saying, "You are absent from work too often," say, "I feel annoyed when you miss work so frequently."
- **Keep feedback goal oriented.** If you have to say something negative, make sure it's directed toward the recipient's goals. Ask yourself whom the feedback is supposed to help. If the answer is essentially you, bite your tongue.
- **Make feedback well timed.** Feedback is most meaningful when there is a short interval between the recipient's behavior and the receipt of feedback about that behavior.
- **Ensure understanding.** If feedback is to be effective, you need to make sure the recipient understands it.
- **Direct negative feedback toward behavior that is controllable by the recipient.** There's little value reminding a person of some shortcoming over which he or she has no control.

Encourage feedback by
- Asking specific questions
- Encouraging your audience to express general reactions
- Being receptive to your audience's response

Knowing how to give constructive criticism or feedback is an important communication skill, as Table 1.2 highlights. To encourage feedback, many companies use techniques such as employee surveys, open-door policies, company newsletters, memos, e-mail, task forces, and even real-time two-way chat, as this chapter's opening vignette demonstrates. Still, feedback isn't always easy to get. You may have to draw out the other person by asking specific questions. You can also gain useful information by encouraging your audience to express general reactions. Longtime General Electric CEO Jack Welch used this process successfully. A fierce believer in the power of his people, Welch encouraged near-brutal candor in meetings. He ensured that GE's triumphs and failures were shared openly.[32]

Guideline 3: Commit to Ethical Communication

Learning Objective 7

Discuss the attributes of ethical communication and differentiate between an ethical dilemma and an ethical lapse

Ethics are the principles of conduct that govern a person or a group.

Ethical communication is truthful and relevant.

Ethics are the principles of conduct that govern a person or a group. Unethical people say or do whatever it takes to achieve an end. Ethical people are generally trustworthy, fair, and impartial, respecting the rights of others and concerned about the impact of their actions on society. Former Supreme Court Justice Potter Stewart defined ethics as "knowing the difference between what you have a right to do and what is the right thing to do."[33]

Ethical communication includes all relevant information, is true in every sense, and is not deceptive in any way. By contrast, unethical communication can include falsehoods and misleading information (or withhold important information). Some examples of unethical communication include:[34]

- *Plagiarism.* Stealing someone else's words or work and claiming it as your own
- *Selective misquoting.* Deliberately omitting damaging or unflattering comments to paint a better (but untruthful) picture of you or your company
- *Misrepresenting numbers.* Increasing or decreasing numbers, exaggerating, altering statistics, or omitting numerical data
- *Distorting visuals.* Making a product look bigger or changing the scale of graphs and charts to exaggerate or conceal differences

An ethical message is accurate and sincere. It avoids language that manipulates, discriminates, or exaggerates. When communicating ethically, you do not hide negative information behind an optimistic attitude, you don't state opinions as facts,

Focusing on Ethics

Ethical Boundaries: Where Would You Draw the Line?

At the very least, you owe your employer an honest day's work for an honest day's pay: your best efforts, obedience to the rules, a good attitude, respect for your employer's property, and a professional appearance. Such duties and considerations seem clear-cut, but where does your obligation to your employer end? For instance, where would you draw the line in communication situations such as the following?

- Writing your résumé so that an embarrassing two-year lapse won't be obvious
- Telling your best friend about your company's upcoming merger right after mailing the formal announcement to your shareholders
- Hinting to a co-worker (who's a close friend) that it's time to look around for something new, when you've already been told confidentially that she's scheduled to be fired at the end of the month
- Saying nothing when you witness one employee taking credit for another's successful idea
- Preserving your position by presenting yourself to supervisors as the only person capable of achieving an objective
- Buying one software package for use by three computer operators
- Making up an excuse when (for the fourth time this month) you have to pick up your child from school early and miss an important business meeting
- Calling in sick because you're taking a few days off and you want to use up some of the sick leave you've accumulated.

The ethics involved in these situations may seem perfectly clear . . . until you think about them. But wherever you are, whatever the circumstances, you owe your employer your best efforts. And time and again, it will be up to you to decide whether those efforts are ethical.

Career Applications

1. List ethical behaviors you would expect from your employees, and compare your list with those of your classmates.
2. As the supervisor of the office typing pool, you must deal with several typists who have a tendency to gossip about their co-workers. List five things you might do to resolve the situation.

and you portray graphic data fairly. You are honest with employers, co-workers, and clients, never seeking personal gain by making others look better or worse than they are. You don't allow personal preferences to influence your perception or the perception of others, and you act in good faith. On the surface, such ethical practices appear fairly easy to recognize. But deciding what is ethical can be quite complex—see "Focusing on Ethics: Ethical Boundaries: Where Would You Draw the Line?"

Recognize Ethical Choices

Every company has responsibilities to various groups: customers, employees, shareholders, suppliers, neighbors, the community, and the nation. Unfortunately, what's right for one group may be wrong for another.[35] Moreover, as you attempt to satisfy the needs of one group, you may be presented with an option that seems right on the surface but somehow feels wrong. When people must choose between conflicting loyalties and weigh difficult trade-offs, they are facing a dilemma.

Conflicting priorities and the vast gray areas between right and wrong create ethical dilemmas for an organization's communicators.

An **ethical dilemma** involves choosing among alternatives that aren't clear-cut (perhaps two conflicting alternatives are both ethical and valid, or perhaps the alternatives lie somewhere in the vast gray area between right and wrong). Suppose you are president of a company that's losing money. You have a duty to your shareholders to try to cut your losses and to your employees to be fair and honest. After looking at various options, you conclude that you'll have to lay off 500 people immediately. You suspect you may have to lay off another 100 people later on, but right now you need those 100 workers to finish a project. What do you tell them? If you confess that their jobs are shaky, many of them may quit just when you need them most. However, if you tell them that the future is rosy, you'll be stretching the truth.

Unlike a dilemma, an **ethical lapse** is making a clearly unethical or illegal choice. Suppose you have decided to change jobs and have discreetly landed an interview with your boss's largest competitor. You get along great with the interviewer, who is impressed enough with you to offer you a position on the spot. Not only is the new position a step up from your current job, but the pay is double what you're getting now. You accept the job and agree to start next month. Then as you're shaking hands with the interviewer, she asks you to bring along profiles of your current company's ten largest customers when you report for work. Do you comply with her request? How do you decide between what's ethical and what is not?

Make Ethical Choices

Laws provide ethical guidelines for certain types of messages.

One place to look for guidance is the law. If saying or writing something is clearly illegal, you have no dilemma: You obey the law. However, even though legal considerations will resolve some ethical questions, you'll often have to rely on your own judgment and principles. If your intent is honest, the statement is ethical, even though it may be factually incorrect; if your intent is to mislead or manipulate the audience, the message is unethical, regardless of whether it is true. You might look at the consequences of your message and opt for the solution that provides the greatest good to the greatest number of people.[36] You might also ask yourself:[37]

Asking the right questions can help you decide what is ethical.

- **Is this message legal?** Does it violate civil law or company policy?
- **Is this message balanced?** Does it do the most good and the least harm? Is it fair to all concerned in the short term as well as the long term? Does it promote positive win-win relationships? Did you weigh all sides before drawing a conclusion?
- **Is it a message you can live with?** Does it make you feel good about yourself? Does it make you proud? Would you feel good about your message if a newspaper published it? If your family knew about it?
- **Is this message feasible?** Can it work in the real world? Have you considered your position in the company? Your company's competition? Its financial and political strength? The likely costs or risks of your message? The time available?

Motivate Ethical Choices

Organizations can foster ethical behavior

- By formalizing a written code of ethics
- By using ethics audits
- By setting a good ethical example

Some companies lay out an explicit ethical policy by using a written **code of ethics** to help employees determine what is acceptable. In addition, many managers use **ethics audits** to monitor ethical progress and to point out any weaknesses that need to be addressed. They know that being ethical is simply the right thing to do. Plus, it's contagious. Others will follow your example when they observe you being ethical and see the success you experience both in your interpersonal relationships and in your career.[38]

Guideline 4: Create Lean, Efficient Messages

You must distinguish between necessary and unnecessary information.

Too much information is as bad as too little; it reduces the audience's ability to concentrate on the most important data. You need to determine which information is unnecessary and make necessary information easily available. Try to give information meaning, rather than just passing it on, and set priorities for dealing with the overall message flow. Successful communicators overcome information overload and other communication barriers by reducing the number of messages, minimizing distractions, and fine-tuning their business communication skills.

Reduce the Number of Messages

Organizations save time and money by sending only necessary messages.

A good way to make your messages more effective is to send fewer of them. Think twice before sending one. For example, if a written message merely adds to the information overload, it's probably better left unsent or handled some other way—for example, by a quick telephone call or a face-to-face chat. Holding down the number of messages reduces the chance of information overload.

Minimize Distractions

Although you don't have power over every eventuality, the key to overcoming distractions is control. To overcome physical barriers, exercise as much control as possible over the physical transmission link: If you're preparing a written document, make sure its appearance doesn't detract from your message. If you're delivering an oral presentation, choose a setting that permits the audience to see and hear you without straining. When you're the audience, learn to concentrate on the message rather than on any distractions.

Eliminate physical distractions such as the messy appearance of a written message or poor acoustics in an oral presentation.

Overcome emotional barriers by recognizing the feelings that arise in yourself and in others as you communicate and by attempting to control these emotions. For example, choose neutral words to avoid arousing strong feelings unduly. Avoid placing blame and generally reacting subjectively. Most important, be aware of the greater potential for misunderstanding that accompanies emotional messages.

Do your best to control emotions before they block the communication process.

As a listener, overcome listening barriers by paraphrasing what you've heard. Try to view the situation through the speaker's eyes, and resist jumping to conclusions. Listen without interrupting, and clarify meaning by asking nonthreatening questions. As a speaker, help listeners by connecting your subject to their needs, using language that is clear and vivid, and relating your subject to familiar ideas.

Overcome listening barriers by doing everything you can to understand and provide feedback.

Fine-Tune Your Business Communication Skills

Improving your business communication skills is the key to creating lean, efficient messages. Many companies provide employees a variety of opportunities for communication skills training. Some companies offer seminars and workshops on handling common oral communication situations (dealing with customers, managing subordinates, getting along with co-workers); some offer training in computers and other electronic means of communication. But even though you may ultimately receive training on the job, don't wait. Start mastering business communication skills right now, in this course. People with good communication skills have an advantage in today's workplace.

Don't wait for communication training on the job.

Lack of experience may be the only obstacle between you and effective messages, whether written or spoken. Perhaps you have a limited vocabulary, or maybe you're uncertain about questions of grammar, punctuation, and style. Perhaps you're simply frightened by the idea of writing something or appearing before a group. People aren't "born" writers or speakers. Their skills improve the more they speak and write. Someone who has written ten reports is usually better at it than someone who has written only two.

Practice helps you improve your communication skills.

One of the great advantages of taking a course in business communication is that you get to practice in an environment that provides honest and constructive criticism. For instance, this course gives you an understanding of acceptable and unacceptable techniques so that you can avoid making costly mistakes on the job. It provides the kind of communication practice that will help you get the job you want, boost your chances for a promotion, start your own business, or succeed at whatever you choose to do in the future. You'll learn how to collaborate in teams, listen well, master nonverbal communication, ensure successful meetings, and communicate across cultures and through the Internet. This book presents a three-step process for composing business messages. It gives tips for writing letters, memos, e-mail messages, reports, and oral presentations, and it provides a collection of good and bad communication examples with annotated comments to guide you with your own communication efforts. Finally, it explains how to write effective résumés and application letters and how to handle employment interviews.

Constructive criticism also helps you improve your communication skills.

Perhaps the best place to begin strengthening your communication skills is with an honest assessment of where you stand. In the next few days, watch how you handle the communication situations that arise. Try to figure out what you're doing right and what you're doing wrong. Then, as you progress through this course in the months ahead, focus on those areas in which you need the most work.

Focus on building skills in the areas where you've been weak.

COMMUNICATION CHALLENGES AT LIVEPERSON

Although you've been with LivePerson as a member of the training staff from the beginning, you've never felt as disconnected as you do now. Every day, you find 30 new e-mail messages waiting for you, a stack of unopened mail on your desk, and several unread company bulletins in your in-basket. But all you can think about is the five new e-commerce sites that have signed up to use LivePerson. All those customer service reps are waiting to be trained on LivePerson software, and it's your job to develop training programs for each website. You know you should be glad that business is booming, but the thought brings you no pleasure. It seems that all the fun is gone.

You go back a long way with your good friend, CEO Robert LoCascio. He took a chance on hiring you, and you've always given him 150 percent. In fact, he popped into your office last week to ask how the training programs were shaping up. Although you said everything was "great," you later kicked yourself for not mentioning something about the information overload. The stress of not keeping up with the flow of communication is beginning to take its toll on you in lost productivity. You vow that next time Robert gives you the opportunity, you'll speak up.

Individual Challenge: "How's it going, Terry?" Startled, you raise your head to see that Robert has dropped in. He drapes himself across a chair. You take a deep breath. What will you tell him?

Team Challenge: Robert LoCascio takes your information about communication overload as a serious threat to both the harmony and the future profitability of LivePerson. He asks you to hold a series of meetings with the training staff to generate ideas on ways to pare down the enormous amounts of information and yet make sure that key people have everything they need to work well together. Assuming the role of the training staff, discuss the problem and possible solutions with your classmates. Prepare a list of key issues and suggestions to present to CEO Robert LoCascio. ■

SUMMARY OF LEARNING OBJECTIVES

1 **Explain what effective communication is and highlight five characteristics of effective business messages.** Communication is effective when it helps people understand each other, stimulates others to take action, and encourages others to think in new ways. Effective business messages provide practical information such as instructions, explanations, problems, solutions, and status reports; give facts and hard evidence rather than impressions or opinions; clarify and condense information and use visual aids to help explain a process or highlight important information; clearly state what is expected of a specific audience; and offer recommendations or persuade others to do something by showing how the audience will benefit from a specific product or service.

2 **Discuss three developments in the workplace that are intensifying the need to communicate effectively.** Technological advances such as the Internet and portable communication devices make it possible for employees to work from remote places, but using such devices also taxes their ability to write and speak clearly. Increased cultural diversity in the workforce requires employees to adapt their communication so that they can be understood by other cultures. Increased use of teams requires mastery of interpersonal skills such as listening, giving feedback, working collaboratively, and resolving conflict.

3 **Describe how organizations share information internally and externally.** Within an organization, communication occurs formally or informally. The formal communication network can be depicted as an organization chart, with information flowing downward from managers to employees, upward from employees to managers, and horizontally between departments. The informal communication network, or grapevine, follows the path of casual conversation and has no set flow pattern. Communication between organizations and the outside world can be as formal as a news release carefully prepared by a marketing or public relations team. Other outside communication can be as informal as talking with a customer or letting your appearance transmit an impression of your organization.

4 **List and briefly define the six phases of the communication process.** The communication process occurs in six phases. First, the sender has an idea (conceives a thought and wants to share it). Second, the sender encodes the idea (puts it into message form). Third, the sender transmits the message (sends the message using a specific channel and medium). Fourth, the receiver gets the message (receives the physical message by hearing or reading it). Fifth, the receiver decodes the message (absorbs and understands the meaning). And

sixth, the receiver sends feedback (responds to your message and signals that response to you).

5 **Identify and briefly discuss five types of communication barriers.** First, perceptual differences affect how people see the world; no two people perceive things exactly the same way. Perception also influences how people develop language, which depends on shared definitions for meaning, and is shaped by their culture. Second, restrictive structures and management block effective communication. Formal channels tend to cause distortion, as each link in the communication channel holds the potential for misinterpretation. If managers aren't diligent in their efforts to communicate down the formal network, their messages can become fragmented so that employees never get the "big picture." Third, communication can be hampered by distractions, whether physical (from poor acoustics to illegible copy) or emotional, or the result of information overload. Fourth, unethical communicators can use deceptive communication tactics to manipulate their receivers. And fifth, as the number of messages increases it becomes more difficult to discriminate between useful and useless information.

6 **Discuss four guidelines for overcoming communication barriers.** The first guideline is to adopt an audience-centered approach—to focus on and care about the audience's needs. Doing so means finding out as much as you can about audience members, especially if your audience is from a different culture. The second guideline is to foster an open communication climate, which means encouraging employee contributions, candor, and honesty. You can create an open climate by modifying the number of organizational levels and by facilitating feedback. The third guideline is to commit to ethical communication, making your message true in every sense and not deceptive in any way. The fourth guideline is to create lean and efficient messages, which is accomplished by reducing the number of messages you send, minimizing distractions, and improving your business communication skills.

7 **Discuss the attributes of ethical communication and differentiate between an ethical dilemma and an ethical lapse.** Ethical communication is not deceiving and is true in every sense. It avoids language that manipulates, discriminates, or exaggerates. It does not conceal negative information by misrepresenting numbers or distorting visual aids. It states facts rather than opinions and it is not influenced by personal preferences. An ethical dilemma involves choosing between two or more alternatives that are neither clearly ethical nor clearly unethical, such as alternatives that are all ethical but conflicting or alternatives that lie somewhere in the gray area between right and wrong. An ethical lapse involves choosing an alternative that is clearly unethical or illegal, perhaps placing your own desire or ambition above the welfare of others.

TEST YOUR KNOWLEDGE

1. What is the main objective of any business communication?
2. How is technology changing communication in the workplace?
3. How does internal communication differ from external communication?
4. In what directions can information travel within an organization's formal hierarchy?
5. What is the grapevine, and why should managers know how it works?
6. In which of the six phases of the communication process do messages get encoded and decoded?
7. Why should communicators take an audience-centered approach to communication?
8. How can information overload affect communication?
9. How does corporate culture affect the communication climate within an organization?
10. Define ethics, and explain what ethical communication covers.

APPLY YOUR KNOWLEDGE

1. Why do you think good communication in an organization improves employees' attitudes and performance? Explain briefly.
2. Under what circumstances might you want to limit the feedback you receive from an audience of readers or listeners? Explain briefly.
3. Would written or spoken messages be more susceptible to noise? Why?
4. As a manager, how can you impress on your employees the importance of including both negative and positive information in messages?
5. **Ethical Choices** Because of your excellent communication skills, your boss always asks you to write his reports for him. When you overhear the CEO complimenting him on his logical organization and clear writing style, he responds as if he'd written all those reports himself. What kind of ethical choice does this response represent? What can you do in this situation? Briefly explain your solution and your reasoning.

PRACTICE YOUR KNOWLEDGE

Document for Analysis

Read the following document, then (1) analyze whether the document is effective or ineffective communication (be sure to explain why); and (2) revise the document so that it follows this chapter's guidelines.

It has come to my attention that many of you are lying on your time cards. If you come in late, you should not put 8:00 on your card. If you take a long lunch, you should not put 1:00 on your time card. I will not stand for this type of cheating. I simply have no choice but to institute a time-clock system. Beginning next Monday, all employees will have to punch in and punch out whenever they come and go from the work area.

The time clock will be right by the entrance to each work area, so you have no excuse for not punching in. Anyone who is late for work or late coming back from lunch more than three times will have to answer to me. I don't care if you had to take a nap or if you girls had to shop. This is a place of business, and we do not want to be taken advantage of by slackers who are cheaters to boot.

It is too bad that a few bad apples always have to spoil things for everyone.

Exercises

For live links to all websites discussed in this chapter, visit this text's website at www.prenhall.com/bovee. Just log on, select Chapter 1, and click on "Student Resources." Locate the name of the site or the URL related to the material in the text. For the "Exploring the Best of the Web" exercises, you'll also find navigational directions. Click on the live link to the site.

1.1 **Effective Business Communication: Understanding the Difference** Bring to class a memo or a sales letter that you received in the mail. Comment on how well the communication

a. Provides practical information
b. Gives facts rather than impressions
c. Clarifies and condenses information
d. States precise responsibilities
e. Persuades others and offers recommendations

1.2 **Internal Communication: Planning the Flow** For the following tasks, identify the necessary direction of communication (downward, upward, horizontal), suggest an appropriate type of communication (casual conversation, formal interview, meeting, workshop, videotape, newsletter, memo, bulletin board notice, and so on), and briefly explain your suggestion.

a. As personnel manager, you want to announce details about this year's company picnic.
b. As director of internal communication, you want to convince top management of the need for a company newsletter.
c. As production manager, you want to make sure that both the sales manager and the finance manager receive your scheduling estimates.
d. As marketing manager, you want to help employees understand the company's goals and its attitudes toward workers.

1.3 **Communication Networks: Formal or Informal?** An old college friend phoned you out of the blue to say, "Truth is, I had to call you. You'd better keep this under your hat, but when I heard my company was buying you guys out, I was dumbfounded. I had no idea that a company as large as yours could sink so fast. Your group must be in pretty bad shape over there!" Your stomach suddenly turned queasy, and you felt a chill go up your spine. You'd heard nothing about any buyout, and before you could even get your college friend off the phone, you were wondering what you should do. Of the following, choose one course of action and briefly explain your choice.

a. Contact your CEO directly and relate what you've heard.
b. Ask co-workers whether they've heard anything about a buyout.
c. Discuss the phone call confidentially with your immediate supervisor.
d. Keep quiet about the whole thing (there's nothing you can do about the situation anyway).

1.4 **Ethical Choices** In less than a page, explain why you think each of the following is or is not ethical.

a. Deemphasizing negative test results in a report on your product idea
b. Taking a computer home to finish a work-related assignment
c. Telling an associate and close friend that she'd better pay more attention to her work responsibilities or management will fire her
d. Recommending the purchase of excess equipment to use up your allocated funds before the end of the fiscal year so that your budget won't be cut next year

1.5 **The Changing Workplace: Always in Touch** Technological devices such as faxes, cellular phones, electronic mail, and voice mail are making businesspeople easily accessible at any time of day or night, at work and at home. What kind of impact might frequent intrusions have on their professional and personal lives? Please explain your answer in less than a page.

1.6 **Internet** As a manufacturer of aerospace, energy, and environmental equipment, Lockheed Martin has developed a code of ethics that it expects employees to abide by. Visit Lockheed Martin's website at www.lockheedmartin.com/about/ethics/standards/print.html and review the six important virtues and the company's code of ethics (scroll down). In a brief paragraph, describe three specific examples of things you could do that would violate these provisions. Now scroll down and study the list of "Warning Signs" of ethics violations and take the "Quick Quiz." In another brief paragraph, describe how you could use this advice to avoid ethical problems as you write business letters, memos, and reports. Submit both paragraphs to your instructor.

1.7 **Communication Process: Know Your Audience** Top management has asked you to speak at an upcoming executive meeting to present your arguments for a more open communication climate. Which of the following would be most important for you to know about your audience before giving your presentation? (Briefly explain your choice.)

a. How many top managers will be attending
b. Your audience's preferred management style
c. How firmly these managers are set in their ways

1.8 **Ethical Choices** Your boss often uses you as a sounding board for her ideas. Now she seems to want you to act as an unofficial messenger, passing her ideas along to the staff without mentioning her involvement and informing her of what staff members say without telling them you're going to repeat their responses. What questions should you ask yourself as you consider the ethical implications of this situation? Write a short paragraph explaining the ethical choice you will make in this situation.[39]

1.9 **Formal Communication: Self-Introduction** Write a memo or prepare an oral presentation introducing yourself to your instructor and your class. Include such things as your background, interests, achievements, and goals. If you write a memo, keep it under one page, and use Figure 1.8 as a model for the format. If you prepare an oral presentation, plan to speak for no more than two minutes.

1.10 **Teamwork** Your boss has asked your work group to research and report on corporate child-care facilities. Of course, you'll want to know who (besides your boss) will be reading your report. Working with two team members, list four or five other things you'll want to know about the situation and about your audience before starting your research. Briefly explain why each of the items on your list is important.

1.11 **Communication Process: Analyzing Miscommunication** Use the six phases of the communication process to analyze a miscommunication you've recently had with a coworker, supervisor, classmate, teacher, friend, or family member. What idea were you trying to share? How did you encode and transmit it? Did the receiver get the message? Did the receiver correctly decode the message? How do you know? Based on your analysis, identify and explain the barriers that prevented your successful communication in this instance.

1.12 **Ethical Choices** You've been given the critical assignment of selecting the site for your company's new plant. After months of negotiations with landowners, numerous cost calculations, and investments in ecological, social, and community impact studies, you are about to recommend building the new plant on the Lansing River site. Now, just 15 minutes before your big presentation to top management, you discover a possible mistake in your calculations: Site-purchase costs appear to be $50,000 more than you calculated, nearly 10 percent over budget. You don't have time to recheck all your figures, so you're tempted to just go ahead with your recommendation and ignore any discrepancies. You're worried that management won't approve this purchase if you can't present a clean, unqualified solution. You also know that many projects run over their original estimates, so you can probably work the extra cost into the budget later. On your way to the meeting room, you make your final decision. In a few paragraphs, explain the decision you made.

1.13 **Communication Barriers: Eliminating Noise** Whenever you report negative information to your boss, she never passes it along to her colleagues or supervisors, even though you think the information is important and should be shared. What barriers to communication are operating in this situation? What can you do to encourage more sharing of this kind of information?

EXPAND YOUR KNOWLEDGE

Exploring the Best of the Web:

Check Out These Resources at the Business Writer's Free Library, p. 19

It takes plenty of practice and hard work to become an effective communicator. Start now by logging on to the Business Writer's Free Library and expand your knowledge of the topics discussed in this chapter.

1. How do the objectives of professional writing differ from the objectives of composition and literature?
2. What is the purpose of feedback?
3. What are some basic guidelines for giving feedback?

Exploring the Web on Your Own

Review these chapter-related websites on your own to learn more about achieving communication success in the workplace.

1. Netiquette Home Page, www.albion.com/netiquette/index.html. Learn the do's and don'ts of online communication at this site, then take the Netiquette Quiz.
2. You Can Work from Anywhere, www.youcanworkfromanywhere.com. Click on this site's Info and Tech Center and follow the links. Review the tips, tools, articles, ideas, and other helpful resources to improve your productivity as a telecommuter, mobile, or home-based worker.
3. Internet Help, www.city.grande-prairie.ab.ca/h_email.htm. Learn the ins and outs of e-mail at this comprehensive site so that your e-mail will stand out from the crowd.

LEARN INTERACTIVELY

Interactive Study Guide

Visit "My Companion Website" at www.prenhall.com/bovee. For Chapter 1, take advantage of the interactive "Study Guide" to test your chapter knowledge. Get instant feedback on whether you need additional studying. Read the "Current Events" articles to get the latest on chapter topics, and complete the exercises as specified by your instructor.

This site's "Study Hall" helps you succeed in this course. "Talk in the Hall" lets you leave messages and meet new friends online. If you have a question, you can "Ask the Tutor." And to get a better grade in this course, you can find more help at "Writing Skills," "Study Skills," and "Study Tips."

Grammar Diagnostic Tests

Review and reinforce your grammar and language skills by taking one of the four online diagnostic tests offered at our companion website, www.prenhall/bovee.com. The four tests cover a variety of topics, including spelling, capitals, punctuation, verbs, pronouns, adjectives, adverbs, sentence structure, sentence punctuation, clarity, word choice, style, organization skills, proofreading, and more. Submit your test and assess your competency. Then focus on improving areas where you are weak as you complete the exercises in this chapter.

Communicating in Teams and Mastering Listening and Nonverbal Communication Skills

After studying this chapter, you will be able to

1 *Highlight the advantages and disadvantages of working in teams*

2 *Identify the characteristics of effective teams*

3 *Discuss the tasks involved in preparing team messages and list nine guidelines for improvement*

4 *Explain how you can improve meeting productivity through preparation, leadership, and participation*

5 *Describe the listening process and discuss three barriers that interfere with this process*

6 *Clarify the importance of nonverbal communication and briefly describe six categories of nonverbal expression*

COMMUNICATION CLOSE-UP AT SEI INVESTMENTS

www.seiinvestments.com

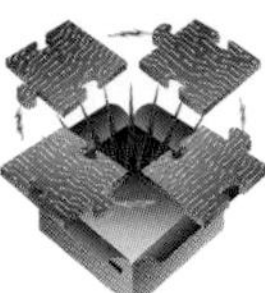

Named by *Fortune* magazine as one of the "100 Best Companies to Work For," SEI Investments helps corporations, financial institutions, financial advisers, and affluent families manage and create wealth. The company's success and high ratings with employees can be attributed in part to its defiance of commonplace organizational structures. Like many of today's companies, SEI relies entirely on teams. It has organized all 1,500 employees into 140 self-managed teams.

Most SEI employees belong to one "base" team and to three or four additional teams. At SEI, teams range in size from 2 members to as many as 30, and they are structured according to project. Some teams are permanent, designed to serve big customers or important markets. Other teams are temporary, bringing employees together to solve a problem and disbanding after the solution is achieved.

SEI has fashioned its physical environment to foster the use of employee work teams. The company designed its 600,000-square-foot building in Oaks, Pennsylvania, to resemble an aircraft hangar—with exposed steel beams and wide-open work spaces. No one, including the CEO, has an office. Cables dangle like vines from the vaulted ceilings, providing instant connections to electricity, phone lines, and the Internet from any location. All office furniture and workstations are equipped with wheels so that employees can easily move their desks to collaborate with other team members and serve as effective members of several different teams. In fact, employees move their desks so often that the company created special computer software to map everyone's location.

It's up to team leaders like Bob Aller to assemble teams with strong group dynamics and keep them producing. Aller identifies prospective team members and then recruits them by describing the project in an enthusiastic way. "The hard part is marshaling the resources," he says. "You have to convince people to get involved." Ultimately, Aller wants people to say, "That sounds like a team I'd like to be on."

Once a team is up and running, Aller serves as a coach, pointing team members in the right direction to complete their projects successfully. He listens carefully to their needs, and he steers them toward solutions without dominating their actions or decisions. "I step in when a team needs tools to be productive," he says. "Otherwise, I don't have to interfere."

To keep team projects on track, Aller pays careful attention to the nonverbal signals of his team members. "You build a sixth sense that tells you whether a team is making progress or not," he says. "You can read people's expressions. And you can tell a lot from the informal updates you get in the halls."

Aller believes the team concept not only makes work more effective and efficient, but stimulates creativity and energy among employees. Team members draw on each other's knowledge and freely share information as they strive to reach individual and team goals. Moreover, teams respond to change more quickly and serve clients more effectively, as compared to the efforts of an individual employee. In fact, since SEI adopted the team concept, both employee and company performance have improved dramatically. Today, SEI is a leader in its field, processing over $1.5 trillion in investment transactions daily and managing nearly $140 billion in client assets.[1] ■

Working in teams is a way of life at companies such as SEI Investments. Functioning in a team requires that all employees communicate effectively so that they can make decisions efficiently, solve problems quickly, and achieve their respective goals.

WORKING IN TEAMS

SEI's Bob Aller knows that working in teams and small groups puts everyone's communication skills to the test. A **team** is a unit of two or more people who work together to achieve a goal. Team members share a mission and the responsibility for working to achieve it.[2]

Team members have a shared mission and are collectively responsible for their work.

Whether the task is to write reports, give oral presentations, produce a product, solve a problem, or investigate an opportunity, team members must communicate effectively among themselves and with people outside their team. Thus, companies are looking for people who can interact successfully in teams and make useful contributions while working together. Some companies even base pay raises and promotions on an employee's effectiveness as a team player.

Companies like to hire people who work effectively in teams.

In a recent survey of Fortune 1000 executives, 83 percent said their firms are working in teams or moving in that direction.[3] Why are teams so important in today's workplace? One reason is performance. A recent study of 232 organizations across 16 countries and more than eight industries revealed that organizations working in teams experience the highest improvement in performance.[4] Creativity is another reason that teams are important. Teams encourage creativity in workers through **participative management**—involving employees in the company's decision making. At Kodak, for example, using teams has allowed the company to halve the amount of time it takes to move a new product from the drawing board to store shelves.[5]

Studies show that teams contribute to an organization's performance.

Types of Teams

The type, structure, and composition of individual teams vary within an organization. Companies can create *formal teams* that become part of the organization's structure, or they can establish *informal teams,* which aren't part of the formal organization but are formed to solve a problem, work on a specific activity, or encourage employee participation.

Problem-solving teams and **task forces** are informal teams that assemble to resolve specific issues and then disband once their goal has been accomplished. Team members often include representatives of many departments so that those who have a stake in the outcome are allowed to provide input.[6] When Saint Francis Hospital in Tulsa, Oklahoma, established a task force to find ways to reduce the cost of supplies, team members came from departments such as surgery, laboratory, nursing, financial planning, administration, and food service. This cross-department team not only helped the hospital save money by curbing supply waste but also generated excitement among hospital employees about working together toward common goals.[7]

Two popular types of informal teams are problem-solving teams and task forces.

Committees are long-term teams.

In contrast to problem-solving teams and task forces, a **committee** usually has a long life span and can become a permanent part of the organizational structure. Committees typically deal with regularly recurring tasks. For example, a grievance committee may be formed as a permanent resource for handling employee complaints and concerns.

Virtual teams conduct their business by using advanced communication technology.

Virtual teams bring together geographically distant employees to interact, share information, and accomplish goals. At Texas Instruments, for instance, microchip engineers in India, Texas, and Japan are able to pool ideas, design new chips, and collaboratively debug them—even though they're 8,000 miles and 12 time zones apart.[8] Virtual teams can use computer networks, teleconferencing, e-mail, videoconferencing, and web technology to build teams that are as effective as those in organizations functioning under a single roof.

Web technology allows companies to develop large-scale work spaces on the Internet for online discussions and data sharing. Using a virtual whiteboard, for example, virtual teammates can simultaneously annotate, edit, or view documents, slides, videos, or webpages. At KPMG Consulting, eight employees scattered around the globe wrote, edited, and commented on a report, using WebFlow Corp.'s SamePage. This software allows users to draft various sections of a document while editing other sections and participating in a web-based discussion—all at the same time.[9]

Web-based collaboration offers definite benefits: It's easy, it's cost-effective, and it allows companies to do multiple activities in a seamless fashion. But virtual teams are not without disadvantages. For one thing, virtual teams must function with less direct interaction among members. So virtual team members require excellent project-management skills, strong time-management skills, and heightened interpersonal awareness. In addition, they must be able to use electronic communication and collaboration technologies, and they need to be able to work across cultures.[10]

Advantages and Disadvantages of Teams

Learning Objective 1

Highlight the advantages and disadvantages of working in teams

Teams can play a vital role in helping an organization reach its goals, as SEI Investments can attest. However, teams are not appropriate for every situation. When deciding whether to use teams, managers must weigh both the advantages and disadvantages of doing so.[11]

The combined knowledge and skills of team members can lead to high performance and good decisions.

At their best, teams can be an extremely useful forum for making key decisions. For one thing, the interaction of the participants and the combined intelligence of the group produce better decisions than what would have been achieved had the members worked independently. In short, team decision making can benefit an organization by delivering[12]

- **Increased information and knowledge.** By pooling the resources of several individuals, teams bring more information to the decision-making process.
- **Increased diversity of views.** Team members bring a variety of perspectives to the decision-making process.
- **Increased acceptance of a solution.** Those who participate in making a decision are more likely to support the decision enthusiastically and encourage others to

Best of the Web

Building Teams in the Cyber Age

If You want to learn more about building effective teams, you can read many excellent books on the subject. But you might be surprised by just how much information on team building you can find on the Internet. One good starting point is the Self Directed Work Team page. This site's designers are passionate about teamwork, and they want to make it easier for people to work effectively in teams. Read the Frequently Asked Questions (FAQs) to better understand the site's purpose. Then explore some of the links to discover more about teams and teamwork.

users.ids.net/~brim/sdwth.html

accept it. Because they share in the final product, they are committed to seeing it succeed.

- **Higher performance levels.** Working in teams can unleash vast amounts of creativity and energy in workers who share a sense of purpose and mutual accountability. Furthermore, teams fill the individual worker's need to belong to a group, reduce employee boredom, increase feelings of dignity and self-worth, and reduce stress and tension between workers.

Although teamwork has many advantages, it also has a number of potential disadvantages. At their worst, teams are unproductive and frustrating, and they waste everyone's time. Some may actually be counterproductive, because they may arrive at bad decisions. For instance, when individuals are pressured to conform, they may abandon their sense of personal responsibility and agree to ill-founded plans. Similarly, a team may develop **groupthink,** the willingness of individual members to set aside their personal opinions and go along with everyone else, simply because belonging to the team is more important to them than making the right decision. Groupthink can lead to poor decisions and ill-advised actions, even inducing people to act unethically.

The advantages of teams outweigh the disadvantages.

Because they feel pressured to conform, members of a group may agree to unwise decisions.

Some team members may have a **hidden agenda**—private motives that affect the group's interaction. Sam might want to prove that he's more powerful than Laura, Laura might be trying to share the risk of making a decision, and Don might be looking for a chance to postpone doing "real" work. Each person's hidden agenda can detract from the team's effectiveness. Other team members may be **free riders**—those who don't contribute their fair share to the group's activities because they aren't being held individually accountable for their work. The free-ride attitude can lead to certain tasks going unfulfilled.

Group members' personal motives can interfere with the group's efforts to accomplish its mission.

Still another drawback to teamwork is the high cost of coordinating group activities. Aligning schedules, arranging meetings, and coordinating individual parts of a project can eat up a lot of time and money. The fact is that teams simply aren't effective for all situations. As management guru Peter Drucker puts it, "When the ship goes down, you don't call a meeting. The captain gives an order or everybody drowns."[13]

Some situations aren't appropriate for teams.

Group Dynamics

The interactions and processes that take place in a team are called **group dynamics.** Some teams are more effective than others simply because the dynamics of the group facilitate member input and the resolution of differences. To keep things moving forward, productive teams also tend to develop rules that are conducive to business. Often these rules are unstated; they just become standard group practice, or **norms**—informal standards of conduct that members share and that guide member behavior. For example, members may have an unspoken agreement that it's okay to be 10 minutes late for meetings but not 15 minutes late, or that it's preferable to use e-mail to communicate with other team members rather than using the phone.

Group dynamics are the interactions and processes that take place in a team.

When a team has a strong identity, the members observe team rules religiously: They're upset by any deviation and feel a great deal of pressure to conform. This loyalty can be positive, giving members a strong commitment to one another and highly motivating them to see that the team succeeds. However, an overly strong identity could lead to negative conditions such as groupthink.

Team Roles

Members of a team can play various roles, which fall into three categories (see Table 2.1). Members who assume **self-oriented roles** are motivated mainly to fulfill personal needs, so they tend to be less productive than other members. Far more likely to contribute to team goals are those members who assume **team-maintenance roles,** to help everyone work well together, and those members who assume **task-facilitating roles,** to help solve problems or make decisions.

Each member of a group plays a role that affects the outcome of the group's activities.

TABLE 2.1 Team Roles People Play

Self-Oriented Roles	*Team-Maintenance Roles*	*Task-Facilitating Roles*
Controlling: dominating others by exhibiting superiority or authority	**Encouraging:** drawing out other members by showing verbal and nonverbal support, praise, or agreement	**Initiating:** getting the team started on a line of inquiry
Withdrawing: retiring from the team either by becoming silent or by refusing to deal with a particular aspect of the team's work	**Harmonizing:** reconciling differences among team members through mediation or by using humor to relieve tension	**Information giving or seeking:** offering (or seeking) information relevant to questions facing the team
Attention seeking: calling attention to oneself and demanding recognition from others	**Compromising:** offering to yield on a point in the interest of reaching a mutually acceptable decision	**Coordinating:** showing relationships among ideas, clarifying issues, summarizing what the team has done
Diverting: focusing the team's discussion on topics of interest to the individual rather than on those relevant to the task		**Procedure setting:** suggesting decision-making procedures that will move the team toward a goal

Roles are often determined by status, which can vary from team to team.

To a great extent, the roles that individuals assume in a group depend on whether they joined the group voluntarily or involuntarily and their status in that group. Status depends on many variables, including personal attractiveness, competence in a particular field, past successes, education, age, social background, and organizational position. A person's status also varies from team to team. In most teams, as people try to establish their relative status, an undercurrent of tension can get in the way of the real work. Until roles and status have stabilized, a team may have trouble accomplishing its goals.

Five Phases of Team Decisions

Whenever teams tackle decision-making tasks, they typically pass through five phases:[14]

Group decision making passes through five phases: orientation, conflict, brainstorming, emergence, and reinforcement.

- **Orientation.** Team members socialize, establish their roles, and begin to define their task or purpose.
- **Conflict.** Team members begin to discuss their positions and become more assertive in establishing their roles. If members have been carefully selected to represent a variety of viewpoints and expertise, disagreements are a natural part of this phase.
- **Brainstorming.** Team members air all the options and discuss the pros and cons fully. At the end of this phase, members begin to settle on a single solution to the problem.
- **Emergence.** Team members reach a decision. Consensus is reached when the team finds a solution that is acceptable enough for all members to support (even if they have reservations). This consensus happens only after all members have had an opportunity to communicate their positions and feel that they have been listened to.
- **Reinforcement.** Group feeling is rebuilt and the solution is summarized. Members receive their assignments for carrying out the group's decision, and they make arrangements for following up on those assignments.

These five phases almost always occur regardless of what task or what type of decision is being considered. Moreover, team members naturally use this process, even when they lack experience or training in team communication.

Characteristics of Effective Teams

Learning Objective 2

Identify the characteristics of effective teams

In effective collaborative relationships, all team members recognize that each individual brings valuable assets, knowledge, and skills to the team. They are willing to exchange information, examine issues, and work through conflicts that arise. They trust each other, looking toward the greater good of the team and organization rather than focusing on personal agendas, making unilateral decisions, or pulling power plays.[15] In short, effective teams[16]

Effective teams
- understand their purpose
- communicate openly
- build consensus
- think creatively
- stay focused
- resolve conflict

- **Have a clear sense of purpose.** Team members clearly understand the task at hand, what is expected of them, and their role on the team.
- **Communicate openly and honestly.** The team culture encourages discussion and debate. Team members speak openly and honestly, without the threat of anger, resentment, or retribution. They listen to and value feedback from others. As a result, all team members participate.
- **Reach decisions by consensus.** All decisions are arrived at by consensus. No easy, quick votes are taken. Instead, all members express their opinions and engage in debate. The decision that emerges is generally supported by all team members.
- **Think creatively.** Effective teams encourage original thinking, considering options beyond the usual.
- **Remain focused.** Team members get to the core issues of the problem and stay focused on key issues.
- **Resolve conflict effectively.** The ability to handle conflict—clashes over ideas, opinions, goals, or procedures—is a key contributing factor to a team's overall effectiveness.

Learning these team skills takes time and practice, so many companies now offer employees training in building their team skills. At Saturn, for example, every team member goes through a minimum of 92 hours of training in problem-solving and people skills. Saturn teaches team members how to reach a consensus point they call "70 percent comfortable but 100 percent supportive." At that level of consensus, everybody supports the solution.[17] For a brief review of the characteristics that make an effective team, see this chapter's "Checklist: Developing an Effective Team."

Employees can learn effective team skills on the job.

Doug Jaeger, interactive creative director of TBWA/Chiat/Day ad agency, stimulates this team of advertising people to think creatively by walking on the conference room table.

Conflict in Teams

Conflict can arise for any number of reasons. Teams and individuals may believe they are competing for scarce or declining resources, such as money, information, and supplies. Team members may disagree about who is responsible for a specific task (usually the result of poorly defined responsibilities and job boundaries). Poor communication can lead to misunderstandings and misperceptions about other team members, and intentionally withholding information can undermine member trust. Basic differences in values, attitudes, and personalities may lead to arguments. Power struggles may result when one party questions the authority of another or when people or teams with limited authority attempt to increase their power or exert more influence. And conflict can also arise because individuals or teams are pursuing different goals.[18]

Conflict can be both constructive and destructive to a team's effectiveness. Conflict is constructive if it forces important issues into the open, increases the involvement of team members, and generates creative ideas for the solution to a problem. Conflict is destructive if it diverts energy from more important issues, destroys the morale of teams or individual team members, or polarizes or divides the team.[19] For instance, if you believe that the only solution is for one party to win and the other party to lose (win-lose strategy), the outcome of the conflict will surely make someone unhappy. Unfortunately, some conflicts degenerate to the point that both parties would rather lose than see the other party win (lose-lose strategy).

Conflict is not necessarily bad, as long as it is handled in a constructive fashion.

On the other hand, if you approach conflict with the idea that both parties can satisfy their goals at least to some extent (win-win strategy), no one loses. The principle behind the win-win strategy is that parties in conflict can better solve their

✓ CHECKLIST: DEVELOPING AN EFFECTIVE TEAM

A. Build a sense of fairness in decision making
1. Encourage debate and disagreement without fear of reprisal.
2. Allow members to communicate openly and honestly.
3. Consider all proposals.
4. Build consensus by allowing team members to examine, compare, and reconcile differences.
5. Avoid quick votes.
6. Keep everyone informed.
7. Present all the facts.

B. Select team members wisely
1. Involve stakeholders.
2. Limit size to no more than 12 to 15 members.
3. Select members with a diversity of views.
4. Select creative thinkers.

C. Make working in teams a top management priority
1. Recognize and reward individual and group performance.
2. Provide ample training opportunities for employees to develop interpersonal, decision-making, and problem-solving skills.
3. Allow enough time for the team to develop and learn how to work together.

D. Manage conflict constructively
1. Share leadership.
2. Encourage equal participation.
3. Discuss disagreements.
4. Focus on the issues, not the people.
5. Don't let things get out of hand.

E. Stay on track
1. Make sure everyone understands the team's purpose.
2. Communicate what is expected of team members.
3. Don't deviate from the core assignment.
4. Develop and adhere to a schedule.
5. Develop rules and obey norms.

problems by working together than by waging war. However, for the win-win strategy to work, everybody must believe that it's possible to find a solution both parties can accept, that cooperation is better for the organization than competition, that the other party can be trusted, and that higher status doesn't entitle one party to impose a solution.

Resolving Conflict

One of the first steps to finding a win-win solution is to preserve the "you" attitude by considering the other person's needs. Before you meet, try to find out what might be acceptable to the other party. Keep your eyes and ears open; ask questions that will help you understand the other person's wants. Search for mutually satisfactory solutions or compromises that result in joint gain.[20] And remember, both parties can usually get what they want if both are willing to work together. In many cases, the resolution process is chiefly an exchange of opinions and information that gradually leads to a mutually acceptable solution.[21]

The important thing to remember about resolving conflict is that people can usually get what they want if they are willing to work together. In many cases, the resolution process is an exchange of opinions and information that gradually leads to a mutually acceptable solution.

Here are seven measures that can help team members successfully resolve conflict:

- **Proaction.** Deal with minor conflict before it becomes major conflict.
- **Communication.** Get those directly involved in the conflict to participate in resolving it.
- **Openness.** Get feelings out in the open before dealing with the main issues.
- **Research.** Seek factual reasons for the problem before seeking solutions.
- **Flexibility.** Don't let anyone lock into a position before considering other solutions.
- **Fair play.** Don't let anyone avoid a fair solution by hiding behind the rules.
- **Alliance.** Get parties to fight together against an "outside force" instead of against each other.

Overcoming Resistance

Part of dealing with conflict is learning how to persuade other people to accept your point of view. In a business situation, reason usually prevails. However, you sometimes encounter people who react emotionally. When you face irrational resistance, try to remain calm and detached so that you can avoid destructive confrontations and present your position in a convincing manner.

When you encounter resistance or hostility, try to maintain your composure and address the other person's emotional needs.

- **Express understanding.** Most people are ashamed of reacting emotionally in business situations. Show that you sympathize. You might say, "I can understand that this change might be difficult, and if I were in your position, I might be reluctant myself." Help the other person relax and talk about his or her anxiety so that you have a chance to offer reassurance.[22]
- **Make people aware of their resistance.** When people are noncommittal and silent, they may be tuning you out without even knowing why. Continuing with your argument is futile. Deal directly with the resistance, without being accusing. You might say, "You seem cool to this idea. Have I made some faulty assumptions?" Such questions force people to face and define their resistance.[23]
- **Evaluate others' objections fairly.** Don't simply repeat yourself. Focus on what the other person is expressing, both the words and the feelings. Get the person to open up so that you can understand the basis for the resistance. Others' objections may raise legitimate points that you'll need to discuss, or they may reveal problems that you'll need to minimize.[24]
- **Hold your arguments until the other person is ready for them.** Getting your point across depends as much on the other person's frame of mind as it does on your arguments. You can't assume that a strong argument will speak for itself. By becoming more audience-centered, you will learn to address the other person's emotional needs first.

The whole purpose of developing a team that's effective is to get members to collaborate on necessary tasks. A team's ability to collaborate is put to the test on a number of tasks, which include writing collaborative messages and running productive meetings.

Hewlett-Packard's Industrial Lab investigative team collaborated to write a major report on research-and-development (R&D) contributions to the company. Their team effort produced a document that assessed the impact and value of all future R&D.

WRITING COLLABORATIVE MESSAGES

In addition to working together during meetings, team members often jointly produce a single document or presentation known as a **collaborative message**. For instance, team members might participate in an all-out group effort to write a company's business plan or draft and deliver a major sales presentation. Such collaborative messages can involve a project manager, researchers, writers, typists, graphic artists, and editors.

Because team messages bring multiple perspectives and various skills to a project, the result is often better than could have been produced by an individual working alone. For instance, team presentations and reports can give an organization the opportunity to show off its brightest talent while capitalizing on each person's unique presentation and writing skills. In other words, you can take the collective energy and expertise of the team and create something that transcends what you could do otherwise.[25]

Collaborative writing is common in many organizations.

Still, collaborative messages have their challenges. To begin with, team members often come from different backgrounds and have different work habits or concerns: A technical expert may focus on accuracy and scientific standards, an editor on organization and coherence, and a manager on schedules, cost, and corporate goals. Team members also differ in writing styles and personality traits.

Collaborative messages benefit from multiple perspectives and various skills; however, team members may have to work hard to overcome differences in background and working habits.

Guidelines for Composing Effective Collaborative Messages

To compose effective collaborative messages, you must be flexible and open to the opinions of others—focusing on your team's objectives instead of your own.[26] You must

Learning Objective 3

Discuss the tasks involved in preparing team messages and list nine guidelines for improvement

also get organized, select a leader, and clarify goals.[27] Before anyone begins to write, team members must agree on the purpose of the project and the audience. Your team must also plan the organization, format, and style of the document—after all, the final message must look and sound as if one writer prepared it. The following nine guidelines will help you produce team messages that are clear, seamless, and successful:[28]

- **Select team members wisely.** Choose team members who have strong interpersonal skills, understand team dynamics, and care about the project.
- **Select a responsible leader.** Identify a group leader who will keep members informed and intervene when necessary.
- **Promote cooperation.** Establish communication standards that motivate accuracy, openness, and trust.
- **Clarify goals.** Make sure team goals are aligned with individual expectations.
- **Elicit commitment.** Create a sense of ownership and shared responsibility for the document.
- **Clarify responsibilities.** Assign specific roles and establish clear lines of reporting.
- **Foster prompt action.** Establish a timeline and deadlines for every part of the project.
- **Ensure technological compatibility.** Use the same word-processing program to facilitate combining files.
- **Apply technology wisely.** Use electronic tools to communicate quickly and effectively with other team members.

Guidelines for Critiquing the Writing of Others

When critiquing someone else, provide specific, constructive comments.

Whether you're writing in teams or reviewing a document prepared by someone else for your signature, you will sometimes need to critique the writing of another. When you do, be sure to provide specific, constructive comments. To help the writer make meaningful changes, you need to say more than simply "This doesn't work" or "This isn't what I wanted" or "I don't see what you're trying to say."[29] When critiquing a document, concentrate on four elements:[30]

- **Are the assignment instructions clear?** Be sure to determine whether the directions given with the initial assignment were clear and complete.
- **Does the document accomplish the intended purpose?** Is the purpose clearly stated? Does the body support the stated purpose? Is the conclusion supported by the data? Are the arguments presented logically?
- **Is the factual material correct?** A proposal to provide nationwide computer-training services for $15 million would be disastrous if your intention was to provide those services for $150 million.
- **Does the document use unambiguous language?** If you interpret a message differently from what a writer intended, the document must be revised.

Once these elements are deemed satisfactory, the question is whether to request other changes. Minor changes can be made at any time in the critiquing process. But if these criteria are in fact met, consider these additional points before requesting a major revision: (1) Can the document truly be improved? (2) Can you justify the time needed for a rewrite or revision? (3) Will your request have a negative impact on morale?[31]

MAKING YOUR TEAM MEETINGS MORE PRODUCTIVE

Learning Objective 4

Explain how you can improve meeting productivity through preparation, leadership, and participation

Meetings are a prime tool for solving problems, developing ideas through giving and getting feedback, identifying opportunities, and deciding how to maximize the company's resources. Whether you're meeting virtually or in person, much of the oral communication you'll do in the workplace will take place in small-group meetings. Your ability to contribute to the group and the organization as a whole will depend on how well you have mastered oral communication skills. As more and more companies increase their use of teams to solve problems and work collaboratively on projects, chances are that the number of meetings you'll attend will also increase. Already, more than 25 million meetings take place worldwide every day.[32]

Unfortunately, many meetings are unproductive. In a recent study, senior and middle managers reported that only 56 percent of their meetings were actually productive and that 25 percent of them could have been replaced by a phone call or a memo.[33] Given these demoralizing statistics, no wonder companies today are focusing on making their meetings more productive. The three most frequently reported problems with meetings are getting off the subject, not having an agenda, and meeting for too long.[34]

Preparing for Team Meetings

The biggest mistake in holding meetings is not having a specific goal. So before you call a meeting, satisfy yourself that one is truly needed. Perhaps you could communicate more effectively in a memo or through individual conversations. If you do require the interaction of a group, you want to bring the right people together in the right place for just enough time to accomplish your goals. The key to productive meetings is careful planning of purpose, participants, location, and agenda.

The best preparation for a meeting is having a specific goal that would be best handled in a face-to-face situation.

Decide on Your Purpose

Although many meetings combine purposes, most are either informational or decision making. Informational meetings allow participants to share information and perhaps coordinate action. Briefings may come from each participant or from the leader, who then answers questions from attendees. Decision-making meetings mainly involve persuasion, analysis, and problem solving. They often include a brainstorming session, followed by a debate on the alternatives, and they require that each participant be aware of the nature of the problem and the criteria for its solution.

Select Participants

Being invited to a specific meeting can be a mark of status, so you may be reluctant to leave anyone out. Nevertheless, try to invite only those people whose presence is essential. If the session is purely informational and one person will be doing most of the talking, you can include a relatively large group. However, if you're trying to solve a problem, develop a plan, or reach a decision, try to limit participation to between 6 and 12 people.[35] The more participants, the more comments and confusion you're likely to get, and the longer the meeting will take. But even as you try to limit participation, be sure to include key decision makers and those who can contribute. Holding a meeting is pointless if the people with necessary information aren't there.

A meeting's purpose can determine its size.

Choose an Appropriate Location

Decide where you'll hold the meeting, and reserve the location. For work sessions, morning meetings are usually more productive than afternoon sessions. Also, consider the seating arrangements. Are rows of chairs suitable, or do you need a conference table? Plus, give some attention to details such as room temperature, lighting, ventilation, acoustics, and refreshments. These things may seem trivial, but they can make or break a meeting.

Set and Follow an Agenda

The success of any meeting depends on the preparation of the participants. Meeting agendas aid this process by putting the meeting plan into a permanent, written form. Although small, informal meetings may not require a formal agenda, even they benefit if you prepare at least a list of matters to be discussed. Distribute the agenda to participants several days before the meeting so that they will know what to expect and can come prepared to respond to the issues at hand.

Distribute the agenda ahead of time.

A typical agenda format (shown in Figure 2.1) may seem stiff and formal, but it helps you start and end your meetings on time and stay on track once the meeting begins. Starting and ending on time and sticking to the agenda send a signal of good organization and allow attendees to meet other commitments.

A productive agenda answers three key questions: (1) What do we need to do in this meeting to accomplish our goals? (2) What issues will be of greatest importance to all the participants? (3) What information must be available in order to discuss these

FIGURE 2.1 Typical Meeting Agenda

AGENDA

PLANNING COMMITTEE MEETING

Monday, October 21, 2002
10.00 A.M. to 11:00 A.M.

Executive Conference Room

		Person	Proposed Time
I.	Call to Order		
II.	Roll Call		
III.	Approval of Agenda		
IV.	Approval of Minutes from Previous Meeting		
V.	Chairperson's Report on Site Selection Progress		
VI.	Subcommittee Reports		
	a. New Markets	Alan	5 minutes
	b. New Products	Jennifer	5 minutes
	c. Finance	Craig	5 minutes
VII.	Old Business—Pricing Policy for New Products	Terry	10 minutes
VIII.	New Business		
	a. Carson and Canfield Data on New Product Sales	Sarah	10 minutes
	b. Restructuring of Product Territories due to New Product Introductions	Edith	10 minutes
IX.	Announcements		
X.	Adjournment		

issues?[36] Agendas also include the names of the participants, the time, the place, and the order of business. Make sure agenda items are specific. For example, the phrase "development budget" doesn't reveal much, whereas the longer explanation "Discussion: Proposed reduction of 2002–2003 development budget due to new product postponement" helps all committee members prepare in advance with facts and figures.

Conducting and Participating in Meetings

A meeting's success depends largely on the effectiveness of its leader. If the leader is prepared and has selected participants carefully, notes SEI's Bob Aller, the meeting will generally be productive, especially if the leader has good listening skills.

Keep the Meeting on Track

Don't be so rigid that you cut off discussion too quickly.

A good meeting is not a series of dialogues between individual members and the leader. Rather, it's a cross-flow of discussion and debate. Good leaders occasionally guide, mediate, probe, stimulate, and summarize, but mostly they let others thrash out their ideas. That's why it's important for leaders such as Bob Aller to avoid being so domineering that they close off suggestions. Of course, they must also avoid leaning too far the other way and being so passive that they lose control of the group.

As leader, you're responsible for keeping the meeting moving along. If the discussion lags, call on those who haven't been heard. Pace the presentation and discussion so that you'll have time to complete the agenda. As time begins to run out, interrupt the discussion and summarize what has been accomplished. However, don't be too rigid. Allow enough time for all the main ideas to be heard, and give people a chance to raise related issues. If you cut off discussion too quickly or limit the subject too narrowly, no real consensus can emerge.

Follow Parliamentary Procedure

One way you can improve the productivity of a meeting is by using **parliamentary procedure**, a time-tested method for planning and running effective meetings. Anyone belonging to a team should understand the basic principles of parliamentary procedure. Used correctly, it can help teams[37]

- Transact business efficiently
- Protect individual rights
- Maintain order
- Preserve a spirit of harmony
- Accomplish team and organizational goals

The most common guide to parliamentary procedure is *Robert's Rules of Order*, available in various editions and revisions. Also available are less technical guides based on *Robert's Rules*. You can determine how strictly you want to adhere to parliamentary procedure. For small groups you may be quite flexible, but for larger groups you'll want to use a more formal approach.

Robert's Rules of Order is the most common guide to parliamentary procedure.

Encourage Participation

As the meeting gets under way, you'll discover that some participants are too quiet and others are too talkative. To draw out the shy types, ask for their input on issues that particularly pertain to them. You might say something like "Roberto, you've done a lot of work in this area. What do you think?" For the overly talkative, simply say that time is limited and others need to be heard from. The best meetings are those in which everyone participates, so don't let one or two people dominate your meeting while others doodle on their notepads. As you move through your agenda, stop at the end of each item, summarize what you understand to be the feelings of the group, and state the important points made during the discussion.

Don't let one or two members dominate the meeting.

If you're a meeting participant, try to contribute to both the subject of the meeting and the smooth interaction of the participants. Use your listening skills and powers of observation to size up the interpersonal dynamics of the people; then adapt your behavior to help the group achieve its goals. Speak up if you have something useful to say, but don't monopolize the discussion.

Close Effectively

At the conclusion of the meeting, tie up the loose ends. Either summarize the general conclusion of the discussion or list the actions to be taken. Wrapping things up ensures that all participants agree on the outcome and gives people a chance to clear up any misunderstandings. Before the meeting breaks up, briefly review who has agreed to do what by what date.

Following Up

As soon as possible after the meeting, make sure all participants receive a copy of the minutes or notes, showing recommended actions, schedules, and responsibilities. Generally, the secretary who attends the meeting prepares a set of minutes for distribution to all attendees and other interested parties. An informal meeting may not require minutes. Instead, attendees simply make their own notes on their copies of the agenda.

Following up with minutes of the meeting allows you to remind everyone of what happened and who needs to take action.

✓ CHECKLIST: IMPROVING MEETING PRODUCTIVITY

A. Prepare carefully
1. Determine the meeting's objectives.
2. Work out an agenda that will achieve your objectives.
3. Select participants.
4. Determine the location, and reserve a room.
5. Arrange for light refreshments, if appropriate.
6. Determine whether the lighting, ventilation, acoustics, and temperature of the room are adequate.
7. Determine seating needs: chairs only or table and chairs.

B. Be an effective leader
1. Begin and end the meeting on time.
2. Control the meeting by following the announced agenda.
3. Encourage full participation, and either confront or ignore those who seem to be working at cross-purposes with the group.
4. Sum up decisions, actions, and recommendations as you move through the agenda, and restate main points at the end.

C. Remember to follow up
1. Distribute the meeting's notes or minutes on a timely basis.
2. Take the follow-up action agreed to.

Follow-up is then their responsibility, although the meeting leader may need to remind them to do so through an e-mail or phone call.

Meeting minutes are prepared in much the same format as a memo or letter, except for the heading, which takes this form:

Minutes
Planning Committee Meeting
Monday, October 21, 2002

Present: [All invited attendees who were present are listed here, generally by rank, in alphabetical order, or in some combination.]

Absent: [All invited attendees who were not present are listed here, in similar order.]

The body of the minutes follows the heading: It notes the times the meeting started and ended, all major decisions reached at the meeting, all assignments of tasks to meeting participants, and all subjects that were deferred to a later meeting. In addition, the minutes objectively summarize important discussions, noting the names of those who contributed major points. Outlines, subheadings, and lists help organize the minutes, and additional documentation (such as tables or charts submitted by meeting participants) are noted in the minutes and attached.

At the end of the minutes, the words *Submitted by* should be added, followed by a couple of blank lines for a signature and then the signer's printed (or typed) name and title (if appropriate). If the minutes have been written by one person and prepared by another, the preparer's initials should be added, just as reference initials are added to a letter or memo. Well-constructed minutes will remind everyone of what took place, provide a reference for future actions, and make meetings more productive. To review the tasks that contribute to productive meetings, see this chapter's "Checklist: Improving Meeting Productivity."

Using Electronic Meeting and Videoconferencing Alternatives

New technology has made electronic meeting systems and videoconferencing systems popular alternatives to face-to-face meetings.

Electronic meetings and videoconferences are two increasingly popular alternatives to traditional face-to-face meetings.

Electronic meetings are led by trained facilitators and held in specially equipped conference rooms with large viewing screens. During an electronic meeting session, participants brainstorm via keyboards while special electronic meeting software (EMS) organizes, records, analyzes, and ranks the ideas submitted, but without attaching names to

Working with team members in different locations is less of a challenge when you bridge the distances using interactive websites such as WebEx (www.webex.com). Following the site's prompts, you simply enter the meeting date and time and send e-mail announcements to attendees. Then, at meeting time, participants log onto WebEx, enter a special code, and join the meeting.

the submissions. Such anonymity allows employees to share opinions candidly without fear of retribution from supervisors. Electronic meetings have several advantages.[38] They

- Encourage participation
- Allow participants to contribute and vote at the same time
- Stimulate candor and debate
- Engender a true sense of shared decision making
- Accelerate the pace of meetings

Still, electronic meetings are not without drawbacks. For instance, people who offer the best ideas may not get credit for them. Moreover, brutal honesty may damage participants' feelings. Furthermore, the process lacks the rich nonverbal feedback of face-to-face communication. These drawbacks are minimized with videoconferencing equipment.

Videoconferencing is an effective way for people at diverse locations to meet and talk to each other. Unlike EMS, these systems are not designed to preserve anonymity. In fact, because of continually improving video capabilities, videoconferencing is increasingly being used as an alternative to face-to-face meetings (see "Keeping Pace with Technology: What You Should Know About Videoconferencing vs. Face-to-Face Meetings").

Two types of videoconferencing equipment exist. *Room systems* are permanently set up in a dedicated room equipped with phone lines, high-speed data networks, video cameras, and a large video screen that shows the participants in the other location(s). *Desktop systems* are much less sophisticated versions in which individual computers are equipped with videoconferencing software and a web camera. In both cases, the quality of the video and sound transmission depends on the quality of the network. Video and sound sent over a high-speed data network are far superior to transmissions via telephone lines and modems.

Keeping Pace with Technology

What You Should Know About Videoconferencing vs. Face-to-Face Meetings

Ever since AT&T unveiled a videophone at the 1964 World's Fair, two-way TV has been touted as the next revolution in communication. Videoconferencing has always been a good idea, but its high costs and technical complexity had put off widespread acceptance—until now.

Today's videoconferencing equipment is better, faster, and more user friendly than that of just a few years ago. The quality of the systems makes participants feel like they are in the same room. Furthermore, the costs of installing videoconferencing systems have dropped dramatically in the last few years. Installations range from $10,000 for a portable, TV-monitor videoconferencing unit to $250,000 for a fully outfitted conference room with a giant screen and remote-control video camera. In some cases, the time and cost savings from reduced corporate travel could pay for these systems in less than one year.

Spurred by such savings and by a heightened fear of flying, canceled flights, and long airport delays following the September 11, 2001, terrorist attacks, sales of videoconferencing equipment are expected to top $40 billion soon. Companies that have considered videoconferencing for years are now being pressured by customers and suppliers to install such systems. In fact, the hottest first-class seat is no longer on an airplane; instead, it's in front of a videoconferencing camera.

Will videoconferencing make the face-to-face meetings obsolete? Probably not. You still need to seal important deals with personal handshakes—especially when conflicts or emotions are involved or when a relationship requires personal interaction to flourish. But videoconferencing will likely change the way people meet. For instance, low-priority meetings and even details of merger talks could take place without participants having to leave their hometown offices. "There's been far too much traveling around the country for 30-minute meetings," says one corporate executive. "It's foolish to have 15 people from different places fly thousands of miles to sit opposite each other at a conference table . . . It doesn't make any sense. It never made any sense." As one frequent business traveler put it, with videoconferencing, "there is no reason to get on a plane unless you absolutely need to."

Career Applications

1. Is videoconferencing appropriate for all business meetings? Explain your answer.
2. What are the advantages and disadvantages of videoconferencing?

Whether interacting with customers or with fellow employees, workers at Harley Davidson's Kansas City plant must know how to listen. Developing good listening skills helps team members overcome distractions so that they can work together successfully and respond to customers' needs.

IMPROVING YOUR LISTENING SKILLS

Your ability to listen effectively is directly related to your success in team relationships. Unfortunately, most people aren't very good listeners. Most of us face so many distractions that we often give speakers less than our full attention. We listen at or below a 25 percent efficiency rate, remember only about half of what's said during a 10-minute conversation, and forget half of that within 48 hours.[39] Furthermore, when questioned about material we've just heard, we are likely to get the facts mixed up. That's because although we tend to listen to words, we don't necessarily listen to the message.[40]

Effective listening requires a conscious effort and a willing mind. Effective listeners welcome new information and new ideas. Effective listening strengthens organizational relationships, enhances product delivery, alerts the organization to innovation from both internal and external sources, and allows the organization to manage growing diversity both in the workforce and in the customers it serves.[41] Companies that listen effectively stay informed, up to date, and out of trouble. Those that don't lose millions of dollars each year.[42]

Because listening is such a routine, everyday activity, few people think of developing their listening skills. Learning to listen effectively can be difficult indeed, but it's one of the best ways to improve your communication skills. Good listening gives you an edge and increases your impact when you speak (see Table 2.2). Furthermore, it enhances your performance, which leads to raises, promotions, status, and power.[43]

Most people need to improve their listening skills.

TABLE 2.2 Distinguishing Good Listeners from Bad Listeners

The Bad Listener	*The Good Listener*	*To Listen Effectively*
Tunes out dry subjects	Opportunizes; asks, "What's in it for me?"	1. Find areas of interest
Tunes out if delivery is poor	Judges content; skips over delivery errors	2. Judge content, not delivery
Tends to enter into argument	Doesn't judge until comprehension is complete; interrupts only to clarify	3. Hold your fire
Listens for facts	Listens for central themes	4. Listen for ideas
Takes extensive notes	Takes fewer notes	5. Take selective notes
Fakes attention	Works hard; exhibits active body state	6. Work at listening
Is distracted easily	Fights or avoids distractions; knows how to concentrate	7. Block out competing thoughts
Resists difficult expository material	Uses heavier material as exercise for the mind	8. Paraphrase the speaker's ideas
Reacts to emotional words	Interprets emotional words; does not get hung up on them	9. Stay open-minded
Tends to daydream with slow speakers	Listens between the lines; weighs the evidence; mentally summarizes	10. Capitalize on the fact that thought is faster than speech

Types of Listening

Different situations call for different listening skills. When you attend a briefing on the company's new medical insurance, you listen mainly for content. You want to know what the policy is. As the speaker describes the prescription drug plan, you begin to listen more critically, assessing the benefits of the new plan relative to your own needs. Later, as a friend talks to you about his medical problems, you listen empathically, trying to understand his feelings.

These types of listening differ not only in purpose but also in the amount of feedback or interaction that occurs. You can improve relationships and productivity by matching your listening style to the speaker's purpose.[44] For example, the goal of **content listening** is to understand and retain the speaker's message. You may ask questions, but basically information flows from the speaker to you. It doesn't matter that you agree or disagree, approve or disapprove—only that you understand.[45] When you listen to a regional sales manager's monthly report on how many of your products sold that month, you are listening for content.

To be a good listener, vary the way you listen to suit the situation.

The goal of **critical listening** is to understand and evaluate the meaning of the speaker's message on several levels: the logic of the argument, the strength of the evidence, the validity of the conclusions, the implications of the message for you and your organization, the speaker's intentions and motives, and the omission of any important or relevant points. Critical listening generally involves interaction as you try to uncover the speaker's point of view and credibility.[46] When the regional sales manager presents sales projections for the next few months, you listen critically, evaluating whether the estimates are valid and what the implications are for your manufacturing department.

The goal of **empathic listening** is to understand the speaker's feelings, needs, and wants so that you can appreciate his or her point of view, regardless of whether you share that perspective. By listening in an empathic way, you help the individual vent the emotions that prevent a dispassionate approach to the subject. Avoid the temptation to give advice. Try not to judge the individual's feelings. Just let the other person talk.[47] You listen empathically when your regional sales manager tells you about the problems he had with his recreational vehicle while vacationing with his family.

Each type of listening is most effective in particular situations. To gain better control of your listening skill, examine what happens when you listen.

The Listening Process

Learning Objective 5

Describe the listening process and discuss three barriers that interfere with this process

Listening involves five steps: receiving, interpreting, remembering, evaluating, and responding.

By understanding the process of listening, you begin to understand why oral messages are so often lost. Listening involves five related activities, which usually occur in sequence:[48]

- **Receiving:** Physically hearing the message and taking note of it. Physical reception can be blocked by noise, impaired hearing, or inattention.
- **Interpreting:** Assigning meaning to sounds according to your own values, beliefs, ideas, expectations, roles, needs, and personal history. The speaker's frame of reference may be quite different from yours, so you may need to determine what the speaker really means.
- **Remembering:** Storing a message for future reference. As you listen, you retain what you hear by taking notes or by making a mental outline of the speaker's key points.
- **Evaluating:** Applying critical thinking skills to weigh the speaker's remarks. You separate fact from opinion and evaluate the quality of the evidence.
- **Responding:** Reacting once you've evaluated the speaker's message. If you're communicating one-on-one or in a small group, the initial response generally takes the form of verbal feedback. If you're one of many in an audience, your initial response may take the form of applause, laughter, or silence. Later on, you may act on what you have heard.

Because listening requires a mix of physical and mental activities, it is subject to a variety of physical and mental barriers. A large part of becoming a good listener is the ability to recognize and overcome these barriers.

Barriers to Effective Listening

Listeners who jump to conclusions close their minds to additional information.

Prejudgment is one of the most common barriers to listening. It can be difficult to overcome because it is an automatic process. To operate in life, people must hold some assumptions. However, in new situations, these assumptions can often be incorrect. Moreover, some people listen defensively, viewing every comment as a personal attack. To protect their self-esteem, they distort messages by tuning out anything that doesn't confirm their view of themselves.

Self-centered listeners shift their attention from the speaker to themselves.

Self-centeredness causes some people to take control of conversations, rather than listen to what's being said. For example, if a speaker mentions a problem (perhaps a manager is trying to deal with conflict between team members), self-centered listeners eagerly relate their own problems with team conflict. They trivialize the speaker's concerns by pointing out that their own difficulties are twice as great. And they can top positive experiences as well. No matter what subject is being discussed, they know more than the speaker does—and they're determined to prove it.

Selective listeners tune the speaker out.

Another common problem is selective listening. When you listen selectively (also known as *out-listening*), you let your mind wander to things such as whether you brought your dry-cleaning ticket to work. You stay tuned out until you hear a word or phrase that gets your attention once more. The result is that you don't remember what the speaker *actually* said; instead, you remember what you *think* the speaker probably said.[49]

Your mind can process information more than four times faster than the rate of speech.

One reason people's minds tend to wander is that they think faster than they speak. Most people speak at about 120 to 150 words per minute. However, studies indicate that, depending on the subject and the individual, people can process information at 500 to 800 words per minute.[50] This disparity between rate of speech and rate of thought can be used to pull your arguments together, but some listeners let their minds wander and just tune out.

The important thing is to recognize these counterproductive tendencies as barriers and to work on overcoming them. Becoming a good listener will help you in many business situations—especially those that are emotion laden and difficult. You can assess your listening skills by paying attention to how you listen. Are you really hear-

CHECKLIST: IMPROVING YOUR LISTENING SKILLS

A. Look beyond the speaker's style
1. Don't judge the message by the speaker but by the argument.
2. Ask yourself what the speaker knows that you don't.
3. Depersonalize your listening.
4. Decrease the emotional impact of what's being said.

B. Fight distractions
1. Close doors.
2. Turn off radios or televisions.
3. Move closer to the speaker.
4. Stay ahead of the speaker by anticipating what will be said next and summarizing what's already been said.
5. Don't interrupt—avoid sidetracking solutions and throwing the speaker off course.
6. Hold your rebuttal until you've heard the entire message.

C. Provide feedback
1. Let the speaker know you're paying attention.
2. Maintain eye contact.
3. Offer appropriate facial expressions.
4. Paraphrase what you've heard when the speaker reaches a stopping point.
5. Keep all criticism and feedback positive.

D. Listen actively
1. Listen for concepts, key ideas, and facts.
2. Be able to distinguish between evidence and argument, idea and example, fact and principle.
3. Analyze the key points—whether they make sense and are supported by facts.
4. Look for unspoken messages in the speaker's tone of voice or expressions.
5. Keep an open mind.
6. Ask questions that clarify.
7. Reserve judgment until the speaker has finished.
8. Take meaningful notes that are brief and to the point.

ing what is said? Or are you mentally rehearsing how you will respond? For a summary of how to listen better, see this chapter's "Checklist: Improving Your Listening Skills."

IMPROVING YOUR NONVERBAL COMMUNICATION SKILLS

Learning Objective 6

Clarify the importance of nonverbal communication and briefly describe six categories of nonverbal expression

The old maxim is true: People's actions often do speak louder than their words. In fact, most people can deceive others much more easily with words than they can with their bodies. Words are relatively easy to control; body language, facial expressions, and vocal characteristics are not. By paying attention to these nonverbal cues, you can detect deception or affirm a speaker's honesty.

Nonverbal communication is more reliable and more efficient than verbal communication.

Because nonverbal communication is so reliable, people generally have more faith in nonverbal cues than they do in verbal messages. If a person says one thing but transmits a conflicting message nonverbally, listeners almost invariably believe the nonverbal signal.[51] Chances are, if you can read other people's nonverbal messages correctly, you can interpret their underlying attitudes and intentions and respond appropriately.

People use nonverbal signals to support and clarify verbal communication.

Nonverbal communication is also important because it is efficient. You can transmit a nonverbal message without even thinking about it, and your audience can register the meaning unconsciously. At the same time, when you have a conscious purpose, you can often achieve it more economically with a gesture than with words. A wave of the hand, a pat on the back, a wink—all are streamlined expressions of thought. However, nonverbal communication usually blends with speech to carry part of the message—to augment, reinforce, and clarify that message.

Types of Nonverbal Communication

According to one estimate, there are more than 700,000 forms of nonverbal communication.[52] For discussion purposes, however, these forms can be grouped into the following general categories: facial expression, gesture and posture, vocal characteristics, personal appearance, touching behavior, and use of time and space.

Facial Expression

The face, especially the eyes, commands particular attention as a source of nonverbal messages.

Your face is the primary site for expressing your emotions; it reveals both the type and the intensity of your feelings.[53] Your eyes are especially effective for indicating attention and interest, influencing others, regulating interaction, and establishing dominance.

In fact, eye contact is so important in the United States that even when your words send a positive message, averting your gaze can lead your audience to perceive a negative one.[54] Of course, people sometimes manipulate their expressions to simulate an emotion they do not feel or to mask their true feelings. Of course, the interpretation of facial expressions, and of all nonverbal signals, varies from culture to culture (as discussed in Chapter 3). However, even though many nonverbal gestures and expressions are interpreted differently in different cultures, six fundamental facial expressions are understood around the globe (see Figure 2.2).

Gesture and Posture

Body language and tone of voice reveal a lot about a person's emotions and attitudes.

By moving your body, you can express both specific and general messages, some voluntary and some involuntary. Many gestures—a wave of the hand, for example—have a specific and intentional meaning, such as "hello" or "good-bye." Other types of body movement are unintentional and express a more general message. Slouching, leaning forward, fidgeting, and walking briskly are all unconscious signals that reveal whether you feel confident or nervous, friendly or hostile, assertive or passive, powerful or powerless (see "Communicating Across Cultures: Actions Speak Louder Than Words All Around the World").

Vocal Characteristics

Like body language, your voice carries both intentional and unintentional messages. On a conscious level, you can use your voice to create various impressions. Consider the sentence "What have you been up to?" If you repeat that question four or five times, changing your tone of voice and stressing various words, you can convey quite different messages. However, your vocal characteristics also reveal many things of which you are unaware. The tone and volume of your voice, your accent and speaking pace, and all the little *um*'s and *ah*'s that creep into your speech say a lot about who you are, your relationship with the audience, and the emotions underlying your words.

Personal Appearance

Physical appearance and personal style contribute to one's identity.

People respond to others on the basis of their physical appearance. Because you see yourself as others see you, their expectations are often a self-fulfilling prophecy; that is, when people think you're capable and attractive, you feel good about yourself, and that feeling affects your behavior, which in turn affects other people's perceptions of you. Although an individual's body type and facial features impose limitations, most people are able to control their attractiveness to some degree. Grooming, clothing,

FIGURE 2.2 Facial Expressions Around the World

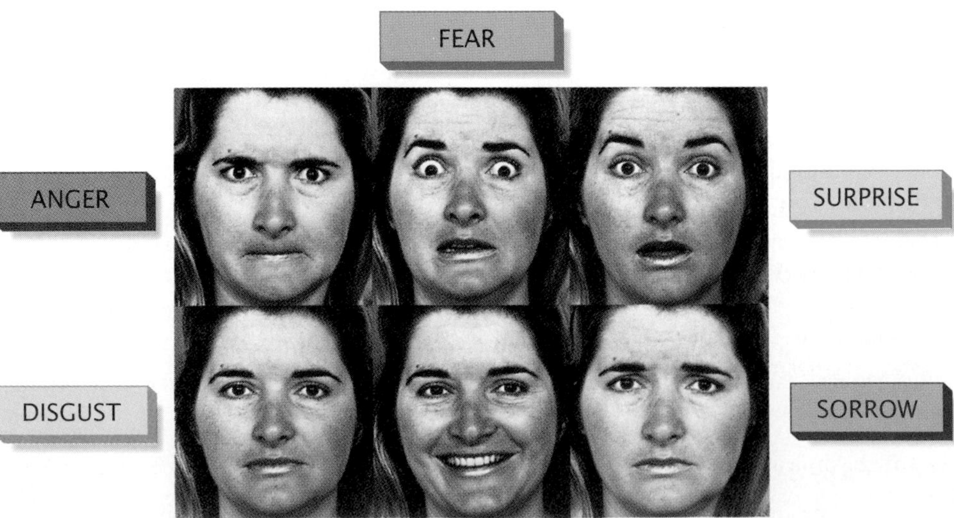

Communicating Across Cultures

Actions Speak Louder Than Words All Around the World

"He wouldn't look me in the eye. I found it disconcerting that he kept looking all over the room but rarely at me," said Barbara Walters after her interview with Libya's Colonel Muammar al-Qadhafi. Like many people in the United States, Walters was associating eye contact with trustworthiness, so when Qadhafi withheld eye contact, she felt uncomfortable. In fact, Qadhafi was paying Walters a compliment. In Libya, *not* looking conveys respect, and looking straight at a woman is considered nearly as serious as physical assault.

Nonverbal communication varies widely between cultures, even between subcultures, and the differences strongly affect communication in the workplace. Whether you're trying to communicate with your new Asian American assistant, the Swedish managers who recently bought out your company, the African American college student who won a summer internship with your firm, or representatives from the French company you hope will buy your firm's new designs, your efforts will depend as much on physical cues as on verbal ones. Most Americans aren't usually aware of their own nonverbal behavior, so they have trouble understanding the body language of people from other cultures. The list of differences is endless:

- In Thailand it's rude to place your arm over the back of a chair in which another person is sitting.
- Finnish female students are horrified by Arab girls who want to walk hand in hand with them.
- Canadian listeners nod to signal agreement.
- Japanese listeners nod to indicate only that they have understood.
- British listeners stare at the speaker, blinking their eyes to indicate understanding.
- People in the United States are taught that it's impolite to stare.
- Saudis accept foreigners in Western business attire but are offended by tight-fitting clothing and by short sleeves.
- Spaniards indicate a receptive friendly handshake by clasping the other person's forearm to form a double handshake.
- Canadians consider touching any part of the arm above the hand intrusive, except in intimate relationships.

It may take years to adjust your nonverbal communication to other cultures, but you can choose from many options to help you prepare. Books and seminars on cultural differences are readily available, as are motion pictures showing a wide range of cultures. You can always rent videos of films and TV shows from other countries. Examining the illustrations in news and business magazines can give you an idea of expected business dress and personal space. Finally, remaining flexible and interacting with people from other cultures who are visiting or living in your country will go a long way toward lowering the barriers presented by nonverbal communication.

Career Applications

1. Explain how watching a movie from another country might help you prepare to interpret nonverbal behavior from that culture correctly.
2. One of your co-workers is originally from Saudi Arabia. You like him, and the two of you work well together. However, he stands so close when you speak with him that it makes you very uncomfortable. Do you tell him of your discomfort, or do you try to cover it up?

accessories, "style"—all modify a person's appearance. If your goal is to make a good impression, adopt the style of the people you want to impress.

Touching Behavior

Touch is an important way to convey warmth, comfort, and reassurance. Perhaps because it implies intimacy, touching behavior is governed by relatively strict customs that establish who can touch whom and how in various circumstances. The accepted norms vary, depending on the gender, age, relative status, and cultural background of the persons involved. In business situations, touching suggests dominance, so a higher-status person is more likely to touch a lower-status person than the other way around. Touching has become controversial, however, because it can sometimes be interpreted as sexual harassment.

Touching behavior depends on many variables.

Use of Time and Space

Like touch, time and space can be used to assert authority. Some people demonstrate their importance by making other people wait; others show respect by being on time. People can also assert their status by occupying the best space. In U.S. companies, the chief executive usually has the corner office and the prettiest view. Apart from serving as a symbol of status, space can determine how comfortable people feel talking with each other. When

Punctuality and comfort zones vary by culture and authority.

✓ CHECKLIST: IMPROVING NONVERBAL COMMUNICATION SKILLS

A. Pay close attention to nonverbal signals

1. Avoid giving conflicting signals.
2. Try to be as honest as possible in communicating your emotions.
3. Smile genuinely. Faking a smile is obvious to observers.
4. Maintain the eye contact your audience expects.
5. Be aware of your posture and of the gestures you use.
6. Try to use appropriate vocal signals while minimizing unintentional messages.
7. Imitate the appearance of the people you want to impress.
8. Respect your audience's comfort zone.
9. Adopt a handshake that matches your personality and intention.
10. Be aware of varying attitudes toward time.
11. Use touch only when appropriate.

B. Interpret nonverbal signals carefully

1. Be aware that people may give false nonverbal cues.
2. Remember, few gestures convey meaning in and of themselves.
3. Consider nonverbal signals in the context of situation and culture.

others stand too close or too far away, we are likely to feel ill at ease. Again, attitudes toward punctuality and comfort zones vary from culture to culture (see Chapter 3).

Tips for Maximizing Your Nonverbal Communication Skills

You can improve your nonverbal skills by paying more attention to cues, both yours and those of others.

When communicating orally, pay attention to your nonverbal cues. Avoid giving others conflicting signals. For instance, if you tell an employee that you are free to talk to her about her raise but your nonverbal signals suggest that this is not the best time to discuss the subject, she will be confused. So try to be as honest as possible in communicating your emotions. Here are some additional tips for honing your nonverbal skills:[55]

- Smile genuinely. A fake smile is obvious because the timing isn't right and the wrinkles don't follow.
- Be aware that people may give false nonverbal cues.
- Keep an appropriate distance between you and others, and use touch only when appropriate.
- Respect status with your eye contact.
- Adopt a handshake that matches your personality and intention.

Few gestures convey meaning in and of themselves; they have to be interpreted in clusters, and they should reinforce your words. To improve your nonverbal skills, pay more attention to the kinds of signals discussed in this chapter and review this chapter's "Checklist: Improving Nonverbal Communication Skills."

COMMUNICATION CHALLENGES AT SEI INVESTMENTS

Whether communicating through one-on-one interviews, meetings, and phone calls, Bob Aller always strives to achieve a balanced and fair conclusion that meets everyone's needs. The all-for-one, one-for-all team environment at SEI requires every member of Aller's team to be a good listener and a good speaker.

Individual Challenge: Several members of your team have been confused by Aller's way of doing things, which is slightly different from his predecessor's. A fellow team member explains to you that when Aller's predecessor retired, he was a "well-loved man throughout the company. They all miss him." Aller wants to clear the air and establish his own way of doing things. As Aller's assistant, you have been asked to advise him whether to (1) write a memo clarifying new procedures, (2) call each of the team members to his desk for a one-on-one discussion, or (3) hold a meeting of the entire team. Decide on the best approach and explain your reasoning in a brief memo to Aller.

Team Challenge: Most members of Aller's team make vital contributions to the group's efforts—except Greg and Jane. During meetings, Greg disagrees with everyone's suggestions, often reacting with a sneer on his face and a belligerent tone of voice. Jane remains silent most of the time, doodling on her notepad instead of taking constructive notes. When she finally speaks up, she jumps ahead of topic or interrupts a speaker's train of thought. As team leader, how can Aller overcome Greg's resistance and help Jane to improve her meeting skills? Working as a team with several classmates, discuss Aller's options for keeping his team members on track during meetings. Be prepared to share your team's recommendations in class. ■

SUMMARY OF LEARNING OBJECTIVES

1 **Highlight the advantages and disadvantages of working in teams.** Teams can achieve a higher level of performance than individuals because of the combined intelligence and energy of the group. Motivation and creativity flourish in team settings. Moreover, individuals tend to perform better because they achieve a sense of purpose by belonging to a group. Teams also bring more input and a greater diversity of views, which tends to result in better decisions. And because team members participate in the decision process, they are committed to seeing the results succeed. Teams are not without disadvantages, however. If poorly managed, teams can be a waste of everyone's time. If members are pressured to conform, they may develop groupthink, which can lead to poor-quality decisions and ill-advised actions; some members may let their private motives get in the way. Others may not contribute their fair share, so certain tasks may not be completed.

2 **Identify the characteristics of effective teams.** Effective team members interact openly and recognize the value that others bring to the group. Members are willing to exchange information, examine issues, and work though conflicts. They focus on the greater good of the team instead of personal agendas. As a group, they understand what is expected of them, stick to the task at hand, and reach decisions by consensus after open, honest debate. All members are encouraged to think creatively and participate. They listen to and value feedback from others, they don't feel threatened by taking an unpopular stance, and they resolve conflict effectively.

3 **Discuss the tasks involved in preparing effective team messages, and list nine guidelines for improvement.** Effective team messages require team members to be flexible and open-minded so that they can focus on the team's objectives rather than their own. Team members need to get organized, select a leader, and clarify goals. They must agree on the purpose of their project and on who their audience is. Members must plan how the document will be organized and formatted, and they must choose a writing style. To prepare effective messages, team members can use guidelines such as the following: (1) Select team members wisely, (2) select a responsible leader, (3) promote cooperation, (4) clarify goals, (5) elicit commitment, (6) clarify responsibilities, (7) foster prompt action, (8) ensure technological compatibility, (9) apply technology wisely.

4 **Explain how you can improve meeting productivity through preparation, leadership, and participation.** When preparing to have a meeting, be sure that your purpose cannot be accomplished better by some other means (e-mail, phone calls, etc.). Plan effectively by deciding on your purpose, selecting participants who really need to be there, choosing a location and time that are conducive to your goals, and developing an agenda that is specific and thorough. Conduct productive meetings by guiding, mediating, and summarizing. Pace the discussion, and encourage everyone to participate. Before the end, summarize conclusions and review who has agreed to do what by what deadline. Follow up with minutes that show recommended actions, schedules, and responsibilities. As a participant in any meeting, do everything you can to contribute to the smooth interaction of attendees as well as to the subject.

5 **Describe the listening process, and list three barriers that interfere with this process.** The listening process involves five activities: (1) receiving (physically hearing the message), (2) interpreting (assigning meaning to what you hear), (3) remembering (storing the message for future reference), (4) evaluating (thinking about the message), and (5) responding (reacting to the message, taking action, or giving feedback). Three barriers can interfere with the listening process. Prejudgment involves holding assumptions, right or wrong, sometimes even distorting messages if they don't conform with what you want to hear. Self-centeredness involves people monopolizing a conversation with their own experience rather than listening to what someone else has to say. And, finally, selective listening (or out-listening) involves letting your mind wander away from the speaker and not paying close attention.

6 **Clarify the importance of nonverbal communication, and briefly describe six categories of nonverbal expression.** Nonverbal communication is important because actions speak louder than words. Body language is more difficult to control than words and may reveal a person's true feelings, motivation, or character. Because of this, people believe nonverbal signals over words. In addition, nonverbal communication is more efficient; with a wave of your hand or a wink, you can streamline your thoughts and do so without much thought. Types of nonverbal expression include facial expression, gesture and posture, vocal characteristics, personal appearance, touching behavior, and use of time and space.

TEST YOUR KNOWLEDGE

1. What are three ways in which an organization's decision making can benefit from teams?
2. What role does the leader play in helping a team produce effective messages?
3. How do self-oriented team roles differ from team-maintenance roles and task-facilitating roles?
4. What is groupthink, and how can it affect an organization?
5. How can organizations help team members successfully resolve conflict?

6. What is the purpose of using parliamentary procedure?
7. What questions should an effective agenda answer?
8. What are the main activities that make up the listening process?
9. How does content listening differ from critical listening and empathic listening?
10. In what six ways can an individual communicate nonverbally?

APPLY YOUR KNOWLEDGE

1. How can nonverbal communication help you run a meeting? How can it help you call a meeting to order, emphasize important topics, show approval, express reservations, regulate the flow of conversation, and invite a colleague to continue with a comment?
2. Whenever your boss asks for feedback, she blasts anyone offering criticism, which causes people to agree with everything she says. You want to talk to her about it, but what should you say? List some of the points you want to make when you discuss this issue with your boss.
3. Is conflict in a team good or bad? Explain your answer.
4. At your last department meeting, three people monopolized the entire discussion. What might you do at the next meeting to encourage other department members to voluntarily participate?
5. **Ethical Choices** You've just come from a meeting of your project team, where the marketing representative kept raising objections to points of style in a rough draft of your group's report. Instead of focusing on recommendations, the team spent precious time debating individual words and even punctuation. After the meeting, two members asked you to join them in going to management to request that the marketing rep be removed from the team. You don't want to make this member look bad, nor do you want to stifle constructive comments and participation. On the other hand, you're concerned about completing the project on time. What should you do? Explain your choice.

PRACTICE YOUR KNOWLEDGE

 *Document for Analysis*

A project leader has made notes about covering the following items at the quarterly budget meeting. Prepare a formal agenda by putting these items into a logical order and rewriting, where necessary, to give phrases a more consistent sound.

Budget Committee Meeting to be held on December 12, 2003, at 9:30 A.M.

- I will call the meeting to order.
- Site director's report: A closer look at cost overruns on Greentree site.
- The group will review and approve the minutes from last quarter's meeting.
- I will ask the finance director to report on actual vs. projected quarterly revenues and expenses.
- I will distribute copies of the overall divisional budget and announce the date of the next budget meeting.
- Discussion: How can we do a better job of anticipating and preventing cost overruns?
- Meeting will take place in Conference Room 3.
- What additional budget issues must be considered during this quarter?

Exercises

For live links to all websites discussed in this chapter, visit this text's website at www.prenhall.com/bovee. Just log on and select Chapter 2, and click on "Student Resources." Locate the name of the site or the URL related to the material in the text. For the Exploring the Best of the Web exercises, you'll also find navigational directions. Click on the live link to the site.

2.1 **Teamwork** With a classmate, attend a local community or campus meeting where you can observe group discussion as well as voting or another group action. Take notes individually during the meeting and then work together to answer the following questions.
  a. What is your evaluation of this meeting? In your answer, consider (1) the leader's ability to articulate the meeting's goals clearly, (2) the leader's ability to engage members in a meaningful discussion, (3) the group's dynamics, and (4) the group's listening skills.
  b. How did group members make decisions? Did they vote? Did they reach decisions by consensus? Did the naysayers get an opportunity to voice their objections?
  c. How well did the individual participants listen? How could you tell?
  d. Did any participants change their expressed views or their votes during the meeting? Why might that have happened?
  e. Did you observe any of the communication barriers discussed in Chapter 1? Identify them.
  f. Compare the notes you took during the meeting with those of your classmate. What differences do you notice? How do you account for these differences?

2.2 **Team Communication: Overcoming Barriers** Every month, each employee in your department is expected to give a brief oral presentation on the status of his or her project. However, your department has recently hired an employee with a severe speech impediment that prevents people from understanding most of what he has to say. As department manager, how will you resolve this dilemma? Please explain.

2.3 **Team Development: Resolving Conflict** Describe a recent conflict you had with a team member at work or at school, and explain how you resolved it. Did you find a solution that was acceptable to both of you and to the team?

2.4 **Ethical Choices** During team meetings, one member constantly calls for votes before all the members have voiced their views. As the leader, you asked this member privately about his behavior. He replied that he was trying to move the team toward its goals, but you are concerned that he is really trying to take control. How can you deal with this situation without removing the member from the group?

2.5 **Meeting Productivity: Analyzing Agendas** Obtain a copy of the agenda from a recent campus or work meeting. Does this agenda show a start time or end time? Is it specific enough that you, as an outsider, would be able to understand what was to be discussed? If not, how would you improve the agenda?

2.6  **Internet** Visit the PolyVision website at www.pixid.com and read about electronic whiteboards. What advantages do you see in using this kind of whiteboard during a meeting? Draft a short internal memo to your boss outlining the product's advantages, using the memo format in Figure 1.3 on page 5.

2.7 **Listening Skills: Overcoming Barriers** Identify some of your bad listening habits and make a list of some ways you could correct them. For the next 30 days, review your list and jot down any improvements you've noticed as a result of your effort.

2.8 **Listening Skills: Self-Assessment** How good are your listening skills? Rate yourself on each of the following elements of good listening; then examine your ratings to identify where you are strongest and where you can improve, using the tips in this chapter.

2.9 **Nonverbal Communication: Analyzing Written Messages** Select a business letter and envelope that you have received at work or home. Analyze their appearance. What nonverbal messages do they send? Are these messages consistent with the content of the letter? If not, what could the sender have done to make the nonverbal communication consistent with the verbal communication?

2.10 **Nonverbal Communication: Analyzing Body Language** Describe what the following body movements suggest when they are exhibited by someone during a conversation. How do such movements influence your interpretation of spoken words?
a. Shifting one's body continuously while seated
b. Twirling and playing with one's hair
c. Sitting in a sprawled position
d. Rolling one's eyes
e. Extending a weak handshake

Element of Listening	Always	Frequently	Occasionally	Never
1. I look for areas of interest when people speak.	______	______	______	______
2. I focus on content rather than delivery.	______	______	______	______
3. I wait to respond until I understand the content.	______	______	______	______
4. I listen for ideas and themes, not isolated facts.	______	______	______	______
5. I take notes only when needed.	______	______	______	______
6. I really concentrate on what speakers are saying.	______	______	______	______
7. I stay focused even when the ideas are complex.	______	______	______	______
8. I keep an open mind despite emotionally charged language.	______	______	______	______

EXPAND YOUR KNOWLEDGE

Exploring the Best of the Web:

Building Teams in the Cyber Age, p. 30

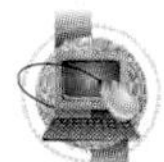

The wealth of information on the Internet makes it convenient to learn more about almost any topic, and teamwork is no exception. Visit the Self Directed Work Team homepage and click through the links to get a feel for the many resources available. Then answer the following questions.

1. Do high-performing teams prefer dialogue or debate?
2. Which three major issues facing teams are most important to the assigned in-class teams in which you've participated?
3. What aspects of teamwork are the team assessment questions measuring? Take this test (using your experience on a school or work team) and submit your answers. What response do you get? Which areas do you think are most important for your team to focus on?

Exploring the Web on Your Own

Review these chapter-related websites on your own to learn more about achieving communication success in the workplace.

1. Teamworks: The Virtual Team Assistant, www.vta.spcomm.uiuc.edu, is a website dedicated to providing support for group communication processes and teams.
2. The Center for the Study of Work Teams, www.workteams.unt.edu, has many links, articles, and research reports on the subject matter of teams.
3. 3M Meeting Network, www.3m.com/meetingnetwork, has dozens of articles and tips on how to run effective meetings—from the basics to advanced facilitation skills.

LEARN INTERACTIVELY

Interactive Study Guide

Visit "My Companion Website" at www.prenhall.com/bovee. For Chapter 2, take advantage of the interactive "Study Guide" to test your chapter knowledge. Get instant feedback on whether you need additional studying. Read the "Current Events" articles to get the latest on chapter topics, and complete the exercises as specified by your instructor.

This site's "Study Hall" helps you succeed in this course. "Talk in the Hall" lets you leave messages and meet new friends online. If you have a question, you can "Ask the Tutor." And to get a better grade in this course, you can find more help at "Writing Skills," "Study Skills," and "Study Tips."

Grammar Diagnostic Tests

Review and reinforce your grammar and language skills by taking one of the four online diagnostic tests offered at our companion website, www.prenhall/bovee.com. The four tests cover a variety of topics including spelling, capitals, punctuation, verbs, pronouns, adjectives, adverbs, sentence structure, sentence punctuation, clarity, word choice, style, organization skills, proofreading, and more. Submit your test and assess your competency. Then focus on improving areas where you are weak as you complete the exercises in this chapter.

Communicating Interculturally

After studying this chapter, you will be able to

1. *Discuss two trends that have made intercultural business communication so important*
2. *Define* culture *and* subculture, *and explain how culture is learned*
3. *Explain the importance of recognizing cultural differences, and list four categories of cultural differences*
4. *Define* ethnocentrism *and* stereotyping, *then give three suggestions for overcoming these limiting mind-sets*
5. *Discuss four ways to improve communication with people who speak English as a second language and three ways to improve communication with people who don't speak your language at all*
6. *List eight recommendations for writing more effectively*
7. *List 12 guidelines for speaking across cultures more effectively*

COMMUNICATION CLOSE-UP AT SHERATON HOTELS HAWAII

www.sheraton-hawaii.com

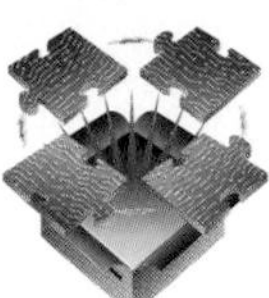

Michiru Tamanai and Kayomi Kaneda love bringing together people from different cultures. Tamanai is the director of training and Kaneda is the training administrator for Sheraton Hotels Hawaii. Together, they've taught thousands of Sheraton employees how to improve customer satisfaction by being sensitive to cultural differences. As Tamanai sees it, having a broad cultural perspective is a necessary skill for businesspeople today. "The business world is becoming more global," she says. "Distance- and time-wise, we are closer than ever . . . But we are still learning to understand each other's mind-set. We need to develop cultural awareness in order to be successful."

That's especially true in the hospitality industry, where success depends on satisfying customers from a variety of cultural backgrounds. In Hawaii, the number of Japanese tourists alone doubled in the past decade, and today they account for over 60 percent of Sheraton's guests. But as business has soared, language and cultural barriers have made it increasingly difficult for employees to meet guests' needs, creating frustration and job dissatisfaction among employees. In response, Sheraton started a program providing all guest-contact employees with six hours of Japanese language training and two hours of cultural sensitivity training. In the past few years, over 3,500 employees have been trained, and the satisfaction of both employee and customer has increased as a result. Management is so pleased with the success of the program that plans are under way to offer employee training in additional languages and cultures.

According to Kaneda, a common mistake employees make is assuming that international guests have the same behavior and communication patterns as themselves. For instance, guests from the United States usually complain right away when they are unhappy about the hotel service, because the United States is a low-context culture; that is, its members rely mostly on verbal communication to convey their messages. On the other hand, guests from high-context cultures, such as Japan, rely less on verbal communication and more on circumstances and nonverbal actions to communicate their messages. So rather than complain directly to the employees, Japanese guests expect employees to anticipate their needs. Other behavioral differences are more overt. For example, when a hotel receptionist pulls out a chair for a Japanese woman, the woman's husband will typically sit down first, thinking the receptionist has pulled it out for him.

Gestures are another big difference. In fact, Japanese guests find some Western forms of nonverbal communication offensive, including leaning on a wall, using an index finger to summon someone, and moving things with one's feet. So Tamanai and Kaneda instruct employees to avoid these offensive behaviors and to communicate in ways that guests are accustomed to. After all, making guests feel comfortable is an important part of Sheraton Hotels Hawaii's cultural sensitivity training program.

But the program has other goals, too. For instance, Tamanai and Kaneda strive to improve communication among Sheraton's diverse employees, who come from many cultural backgrounds, including Chinese, Korean, Japanese, Native Hawaiian, Filipino, and American. Their goal is for all employees to treat each other as *ohana,* or extended

Because over 60 percent of the guests of Sheraton Hotels Hawaii come from Japan, all hotel employees receive extensive training in the Japanese culture as part of the hotel's intercultural training program.

family, even though the cultural differences are numerous. Achieving this goal is no easy task, but as Tamanai sees it, "Businesses need to promote a multicultural work environment for global competitiveness. This means respecting different cultures, values, work styles, and backgrounds." To be successful, Kaneda adds, you must also have patience and a "sincere desire for understanding others," no matter what business you're in.[1] ■

Learning Objective 1

Discuss two trends that have made intercultural business communication so important

UNDERSTANDING THE IMPORTANCE OF COMMUNICATING ACROSS CULTURES

Like Sheraton Hotels Hawaii, more and more companies are facing the challenges of communicating across cultures. **Intercultural communication** is the process of sending and receiving messages between people whose cultural background leads them to interpret verbal and nonverbal signs differently. Two trends contributing to the rapidly increasing importance of intercultural communication in the workplace are market globalization and the multicultural workforce.

Intercultural communication allows the transfer of information between people whose cultural backgrounds lead them to interpret verbal and nonverbal signals differently.

The Global Marketplace

Market globalization is the increasing tendency of the world to act as one market. Technological advances in travel and telecommunications are the driving force behind market globalization. For instance, new communication technologies allow teams from all over the world to work on projects and share information without leaving their desks. At the same time, advanced technologies allow manufacturers to produce their goods in foreign locations that offer an abundant supply of low-cost labor.[2]

Advances in technology help companies cross national borders to find customers, materials, and money, leading to market globalization.

In the global marketplace, natural boundaries and national borders have disappeared, for the most part, as more and more domestic markets open to worldwide competition and as businesses look for new growth opportunities for their goods and services. Even firms that once thought they were too tiny to expand into a neighboring city have discovered that they can tap the sales potential of overseas markets with the help of fax machines, overnight delivery services, e-mail, and the Internet. Look at Trek Bicycle of Waterloo, Wisconsin. This small farming town seems an unlikely place for the headquarters of an international bicycle business, yet Trek Bicycle sells more than half a million bikes annually in more than 70 countries. Over 40 percent of the company's sales come from international business.[3]

FIGURE 3.1 Going Global Has Its Barriers

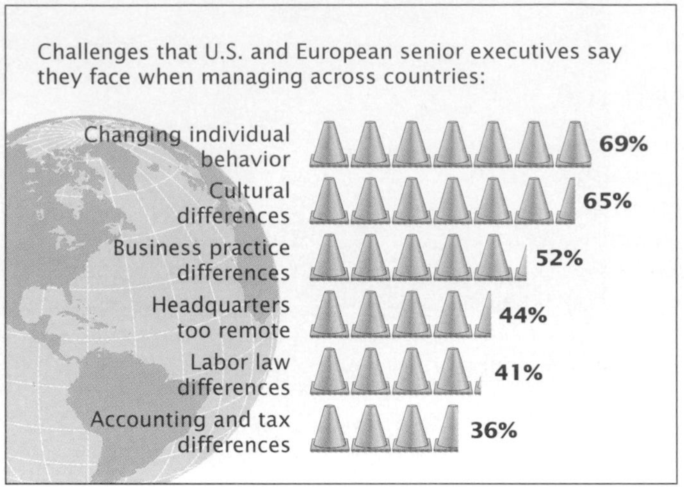

To be successful in the global marketplace, cultural and language barriers must be minimized.

Companies such as Trek Bicycle, Sheraton Hotels Hawaii, and others know that to be successful in the global marketplace, they must minimize cultural and language barriers among customers and employees (see Figure 3.1). Outdoor-equipment retailer REI, for example, uses custom-designed international websites to recognize and accommodate cultural differences in the global marketplace. Similarly, UPS has expanded its web-based tracking services so that customers in 13 European countries can check—in their own language—to see whether packages have reached their destinations around the world.

But you need not "go global" or launch a website to interact with someone who speaks another language or who thinks, acts, or transacts business differently than you

When Recreational Equipment Inc. (REI) noticed many orders were coming from Japan, the company hired native speakers to develop a site for that country that adjusts the graphics as well as the words. For example, when an item is out of stock, the site displays a graphic of someone politely bowing.

do.[4] Even if your company transacts business locally, chances are you will be communicating at work with people who come from various national, religious, and ethnic backgrounds.

The Multicultural Workforce

The U.S. workforce is partly composed of immigrants (new arrivals from Europe, Canada, Latin America, India, Africa, and Asia) and people from various ethnic backgrounds (such as African Americans, Hispanic Americans, and Asian Americans), all of whom bring their own language and culture to the workplace. As a result, today's workforce is increasingly made up of people who differ in race, gender, age, culture, family structure, religion, and educational background. Such **cultural diversity** is the second trend contributing to the importance of intercultural communication. It affects how business messages are conceived, planned, sent, received, and interpreted in the workplace.

A company's cultural diversity affects how its business messages are conceived, composed, delivered, received, and interpreted.

It is estimated that by 2010, minorities will account for 50 percent of the U.S. population. Hispanics will make up about 24 percent; African Americans, 14 percent; Asian Americans, 8 percent; and Native Americans, 1 percent. Moreover, immigrants will account for half of all new U.S. workers.[5] Managing this changing mix of ages, faces, values, and views is becoming increasingly difficult. A diverse workforce brings with it a wide range of skills, traditions, backgrounds, experiences, outlooks, and attitudes toward work that can affect employee behavior on the job. Supervisors must be able to communicate with and motivate these diverse employees while fostering cooperation and harmony among them.

The experiences of Rafael Rodriquez, a stock clerk supervisor at a Target store in Pasadena, California, typifies the diversity challenges today's employees face. Rodriguez is Hispanic, his manager is African American, and the employees that Rodriguez supervises have cultural backgrounds that are as diverse as the communities served by the nearly 700 Target retail outlets across the United States. Rodriguez finds that basic language barriers often prevent employees from understanding each other, but the potential for problems goes beyond differences in language. In one case, a recently immigrated employee was inadvertently making some female coworkers uncomfortable by asking personal questions about hairstyles and nose piercing. His questions were innocent, but because of his cultural background, he couldn't see the invisible boundary that his colleagues had built around their personal lives. Experiences like these are just one of the reasons that Target, Sheraton Hotels Hawaii, Allstate Insurance, Marriott Marquis Hotel in New York, and many other companies offer their employees classes that help them understand and accept cultural differences.[6]

Like Target's Rafael Rodriguez and Sheraton's Tamanai and Kaneda, you will be exchanging business messages with co-workers, customers, suppliers, investors, and competitors who come from culturally diverse backgrounds. To be successful, you must be sensitive to cultural differences as you communicate with people around the world and within your organization. Glance at the job ads in newspapers, and you will find that employment opportunities are everywhere if you have good intercultural communication skills. In fact, you will be left behind if you do not develop these skills. However, to do so, you must first understand some basics about culture.

Be sensitive to cultural differences as you communicate with people throughout the world.

Learning Objective 2

Define culture *and* subculture, *and explain how culture is learned*

IMPROVING INTERCULTURAL SENSITIVITY

Culture is a shared system of symbols, beliefs, attitudes, values, expectations, and norms for behavior. You belong to several cultures. The most obvious is the culture you share with all the people who live in your own country. In addition, you belong to other cultural groups, including an ethnic group, probably a religious group, and perhaps a profession that has its own special language and customs. All members of

Culture is a shared system of symbols, beliefs, attitudes, values, expectations, and norms for behavior.

To better understand culture, remember that culture is learned and that it varies in stability, complexity, and tolerance.

a culture have similar assumptions about how people should think, behave, and communicate, and they all tend to act on those assumptions in much the same way. Cultures differ widely from group to group and may vary in a number of ways, including their rate of change, degree of complexity, and tolerance toward outsiders. These differences can affect the level of trust and open communication that you can achieve with people of other cultures.

Subcultures are distinct groups that exist within a major culture.

Ethnocentrism is the tendency to judge all other groups according to one's own group's standards, behaviors, and customs and to see other groups as inferior by comparison.

People learn culture directly and indirectly from other members of their group. As you grow up in a culture, you are taught who you are and how best to function in that culture by the group's members. Sometimes you are explicitly told which behaviors are acceptable, while at other times you learn by observing which values work best in a particular group. This multiple learning format ensures that culture is passed on from person to person and from generation to generation.[7]

Distinct groups that exist within a major culture are referred to as **subcultures**. For example, Indonesia is home to a wide variety of ethnic and religious subcultures, whereas Japan is much more homogeneous, having only a few subcultures.[8] Groups that might be considered subcultures in the United States are Mexican Americans, Mormons, wrestling fans, Russian immigrants, disabled individuals, and Harvard graduates. As you can imagine, communication is strongly affected by culture. You can improve your ability to communicate effectively across cultures by recognizing cultural differences and then overcoming your own **ethnocentrism**—the tendency to judge all other groups according to your own group's standards, behaviors, and customs. When making such comparisons, people too often decide that their group is superior.[9]

Putting more people of various ethnicities on the floor—and in executive positions—is commonplace for Wal-Mart, which was recently ranked by *Fortune* magazine as one of America's 50 best companies for Asian, black, and Hispanic Americans. This diverse group of Wal-Mart managers clearly understands the importance of being sensitive to others' cultures.

Recognize Cultural Differences

When you write to or speak with someone from another culture, you encode your message using the assumptions of your own culture. However, members of your audience decode your message according to the assumptions of their culture, so your meaning may be misunderstood. The greater the difference between cultures, the greater the chance for misunderstanding.[10] Consider these cultural mishaps:

Learning Objective 3

Explain the importance of recognizing cultural differences, and list four categories of cultural differences

Effective intercultural communication depends on recognizing ways in which people differ.

Clients from different cultures can interpret a company's best intentions negatively.

- When Hewlett-Packard (HP) brought its U.S. engineers together with its French engineers to design software, cultural differences got in the way. The U.S. engineers sent long, detailed e-mails to their counterparts in France. But the engineers in France viewed the lengthy messages as patronizing and replied with quick, concise e-mails. That response made the U.S. engineers believe that French engineers were withholding information. The process spiraled out of control until HP hired a consulting firm to provide cultural training so that both sides could learn to work through their differences.[11]
- When Japanese auto manufacturer Mazda opened a plant in the United States, officials passed out company baseball caps and told U.S. employees that they could wear the caps at work, along with their mandatory company uniform (blue pants and khaki shirts). The employees assumed that the caps were a *voluntary* accessory, and many decided not to wear them. Japanese managers were upset, regarding the decision as a sign of disrespect and believing that employees who really cared about the company would want to wear the caps. However, the U.S. employees resented being told what they should want to do.[12]
- Exhibitors at a trade show could not understand why Chinese visitors were not stopping by their booth. The exhibitors were wearing green hats and giving them away as promotional items. They soon discovered that for many Chinese people, green hats are associated with infidelity; the Chinese expression "He wears a green hat" indicates that a man's wife has been cheating on him. As soon as the

Communicating Across Cultures

Test Your Intercultural Knowledge

Never take anything for granted when you're doing business in a foreign country. All sorts of assumptions that are valid in one place can trip you up elsewhere if you fail to consider that customs may vary. Here are several examples based on true stories about businesspeople who blundered by overlooking some simple but important cultural differences. Can you spot the erroneous assumptions in each situation?

1. You're tired of the discussion and you want to move on to a new topic. You ask your Australian business associate, "Can we table this for a while?" To your dismay, your colleague keeps right on discussing just what you want to put aside. Are Australians that inconsiderate?
2. You finally made the long trip overseas to meet the new German director of your division. Despite slow traffic, you arrive only four minutes late. His door is shut, so you knock on it and walk in. The chair is too far away from the desk, so you pick it up and move it closer. Then you lean over the desk, stick out your hand and say, "Good morning, Hans, it's nice to meet you." Of course, you're baffled by his chilly reaction. Why?
3. Your meeting went better than you'd ever expected. In fact, you found the Japanese representative for your new advertising agency to be very agreeable; she said yes to just about everything. When you share your enthusiasm with your boss, he doesn't appear very excited. Why?
4. You've finally closed the deal, after exhausting both your patience and your company's travel budget. Now, two weeks later, your Chinese customers are asking for special considerations that change the terms of the agreement. How could they do this? Why are they doing it? And, most important, what should you do?

In each case, the problems have resulted from inaccurate assumptions. Here are the explanations of what went wrong:

1. To "table" something in Australia means to bring it forward for discussion. This is the opposite of what Americans usually mean. The English that's spoken in Australia is closer to British than to American English. If you are doing business in Australia, become familiar with the local vocabulary. Note the tendency to shorten just about any word whenever possible, and adding "ie" to it is a form of familiar slang: for example, *brolly* (umbrella) and *lollie* (candy). And yes, it's true: "G'day" is the standard greeting. Use it.
2. You've just broken four rules of German polite behavior: punctuality, privacy, personal space, and proper greetings. In time-conscious Germany, you should never arrive even a few minutes late. Also, Germans like their privacy and space, and they adhere to formal greetings of "Frau" and "Herr," even if the business association has lasted for years.
3. The word *yes* may not always mean "yes" in the Western sense. Japanese people may say *yes* to confirm they have heard or understood something but not necessarily to indicate that they agree with it. You'll seldom get a direct no. Some of the ways that Japanese people say no indirectly include "It will be difficult," "I will ask my supervisor," "I'm not sure," "We will think about it," and "I see."
4. For most U.S. businesspeople, the contract represents the end of the negotiation. For Chinese businesspeople, however, it's just the beginning. Once a deal is made, Chinese negotiators view their counterparts as trustworthy partners who can be relied on for special favors—such as new terms in the contract.

exhibitors discarded the green hats (giving out T-shirts instead), the Chinese attendees began visiting the booth.[13]

Problems such as these arise when we assume, wrongly, that other people's attitudes and lives are like ours (see "Communicating Across Cultures: Test Your Intercultural Knowledge"). As a graduate of one intercultural training program said, "I used to think it was enough to treat people the way I wanted to be treated. But [after taking the course] . . . I realized you have to treat people the way *they* want to be treated."[14] You can improve intercultural sensitivity by recognizing and accommodating four main types of cultural differences: contextual, ethical, social, and nonverbal.

It's best to treat people the way they expect to be treated.

Contextual Differences

One of the ways people assign meaning to a message is according to **cultural context**, the pattern of physical cues, environmental stimuli, and implicit understanding that convey meaning between two members of the same culture. However, from culture to

Cultural context is the pattern of physical cues, environmental stimuli, and implicit understanding that conveys meaning between members of the same culture.

TABLE 3.1 How Cultural Context Affects Business

In Low-Context Companies	*In High-Context Companies*
Executive offices are separate with controlled access.	Executive offices are shared and open to all.
Workers rely on detailed background information.	Workers do not expect or want detailed information.
Information is highly centralized and controlled.	Information is shared with everyone.
Objective data are valued over subjective relationships.	Subjective relationships are valued over objective data.
Business and social relationships are discrete.	Business and social relationships overlap.
Competence is valued as much as position and status.	Position and status are valued much more than competence.
Meetings have fixed agendas and plenty of advance notice.	Meetings are often called on short notice, and key people always accept.

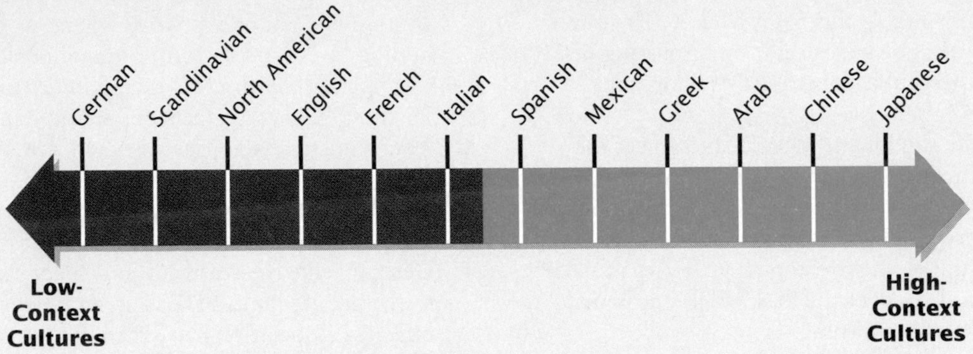

German, Scandinavian, North American, English, French, Italian, Spanish, Mexican, Greek, Arab, Chinese, Japanese

Low-Context Cultures ← → **High-Context Cultures**

culture, people convey contextual meaning differently. In fact, correct social behavior and effective communication can be defined by how much a culture depends on contextual cues (see Table 3.1).

High-context cultures rely on implicit nonverbal actions and environmental setting to convey meaning, unlike low-context cultures, which rely heavily on explicit verbal communication.

In a **high-context culture** such as South Korea or Taiwan, people rely less on verbal communication and more on the context of nonverbal actions and environmental setting to convey meaning. A Chinese speaker expects the receiver to discover the essence of a message and uses indirectness and metaphor to provide a web of meaning.[15] In high-context cultures, the rules of everyday life are rarely explicit; instead, as individuals grow up, they learn how to recognize situational cues (such as gestures and tone of voice) and how to respond as expected.[16]

In a **low-context culture** such as the United States or Germany, people rely more on verbal communication and less on circumstances and cues to convey meaning. An English speaker feels responsible for transmitting the meaning of the message and often places sentences in chronological sequence to establish a cause-and-effect pattern.[17] In a low-context culture, rules and expectations are usually spelled out through explicit statements such as "Please wait until I'm finished" or "You're welcome to browse."[18] Contextual differences are apparent in the way cultures approach situations such as decision making, problem solving, and negotiating.

High-context cultures encourage lengthy decision making, concentrating on every detail, whereas low-context cultures emphasize quick, efficient decisions on major points while leaving the details to be worked out later.

Decision-Making Practices In lower-context cultures, businesspeople try to reach decisions as quickly and efficiently as possible. They are concerned with reaching an agreement on the main points, leaving the details to be worked out later by others. However, this approach would backfire in higher-context cultures such as Greece, because there executives assume that anyone who ignores the details is being evasive and untrustworthy. Spending time on each little point is considered a mark of good faith.

Problem-Solving Techniques Cultures differ in their tolerance for open disagreement. Low-context U.S. businesspeople typically enjoy confrontation and debate, but high-context Japanese executives shun such tactics. To avoid the unpleasant feelings that might result from open conflict, Japanese companies may use a go-between or third party. Chinese businesspeople also try to prevent public conflict, making concessions slowly and staying away from proposal-counterproposal methods. If you try to get members of a Chinese team to back down from their position, you will cause them to lose face—very likely ruining the relationship.

High-context cultures avoid confrontation and debate, whereas low-context cultures encourage open disagreement.

Negotiating Styles Canadian, German, and U.S. negotiators tend to take a relatively impersonal view of negotiations. Members of these low-context cultures see their goals in economic terms and usually presume the other party is trustworthy, at least at the outset. In contrast, high-context Japanese negotiators prefer a more sociable negotiating atmosphere that is conducive to forging personal ties as the basis for trust. To high-context negotiators, achieving immediate economic gains is secondary to establishing and maintaining a long-term relationship.[19]

High-context cultures emphasize relationships and a sociable atmosphere when negotiating, whereas low-context cultures view negotiations impersonally and focus on economic goals.

Legal and Ethical Differences

Cultural context also influences legal and ethical behavior. For example, because low-context cultures value the written word, they consider written agreements binding. But high-context cultures put less emphasis on the written word and consider personal pledges more important than contracts. They also have a tendency to view law with flexibility, whereas low-context cultures would adhere to the law strictly.[20]

High-context cultures view laws as being more flexible, whereas low-context cultures tend to value written agreements and interpret laws strictly.

As you conduct business around the world, you'll find that legal systems differ from culture to culture. In the United Kingdom and the United States, someone is presumed innocent until proved guilty, a principle rooted in English common law. However, in Mexico and Turkey, someone is presumed guilty until proved innocent, a principle rooted in the Napoleonic code.[21] These distinctions can be particularly important if your firm must communicate about a legal dispute in another country.

Legal systems differ from culture to culture.

As discussed in Chapter 1, making ethical choices can be difficult, even within your own culture. When communicating across cultures, ethics can be even more complicated. What does it mean for a business to do the right thing in Thailand? In Africa? In Norway? What happens when a certain behavior is unethical in the United States but an accepted practice in another culture? For example, in the United States, bribing officials is illegal, but Kenyans consider paying such bribes a part of life. To get something done right, they pay *kitu kidogo* (or "something small"). In China businesses pay *huilu,* in Russia they pay *vzyatka,* in the Middle East it's *baksheesh,* and in Mexico it's *una mordida* ("a small bite").[22] The United States has lobbied other nations for 20 years to outlaw bribery, and at last the industrialized nations have signed a treaty that makes payoffs to foreign officials a criminal offense. Of course, bribery won't end just because a treaty has been signed, but supporters are optimistic that countries will ratify the treaty, pass legislation, and enforce the new laws stringently.[23] Making ethical choices across cultures can seem incredibly complicated, but doing so actually differs little from the way you choose the most ethical path in your own culture (see Chapter 1).

Ethical choices can be even more complicated when communicating across cultures; for example, bribing officials is viewed differently from culture to culture.

When communicating across cultures, keep your messages ethical by applying four basic principles:[24]

Keep your messages ethical by actively seeking mutual ground, exchanging messages without judgment, sending messages that are honest, and showing respect for cultural differences.

- **Actively seek mutual ground.** To allow the clearest possible exchange of information, both parties must be flexible and avoid insisting that an interaction take place strictly in terms of one culture or another.
- **Send and receive messages without judgment.** To allow information to flow freely, both parties must recognize that values vary from culture to culture, and they must trust each other.
- **Send messages that are honest.** To ensure that the information is true, both parties must see things as they are—not as they would like them to be. Both parties must be fully aware of their personal and cultural biases.
- **Show respect for cultural differences.** To protect the basic human rights of both parties, each must understand and acknowledge the other's needs and preserve each other's dignity by communicating without deception.

Social Differences

Formal rules of etiquette are explicit and well defined, but informal rules are learned through observation and imitation.

Social behavior is another distinguishing factor among cultures. In any culture, rules of social etiquette may be formal or informal. Formal rules are the specifically taught dos and don'ts of how to behave in common social situations, such as table manners at meals. When formal rules are violated, members of a culture can explain why they feel upset. In contrast, informal social rules are more difficult to identify and are usually learned by watching how people behave and then imitating that behavior. Informal rules govern how males and females are supposed to behave, when it is appropriate to use a person's first name, and so on. When informal rules are violated, members of a culture are likely to feel uncomfortable, although they may not be able to say exactly why.[25] Such informal rules are apparent in the way members value wealth, recognize status, define manners, and think about time.

People from the United States emphasize hard work, material success, and efficiency more than many people in other countries do.

Attitudes Toward Materialism Although the United States is home to millions of people having different religions and values, the major social influence is the Puritan work ethic. The predominant U.S. view is that money solves many problems, that material comfort (earned by individual effort) is a sign of superiority, and that people who work hard are better than those who don't. By and large, people in the United States assume that people from other cultures also dislike poverty and value hard work. However, many societies condemn materialism, and some prize a more carefree lifestyle. For example, U.S. workers annually put in almost 300 more hours at work than West Germans and 60 more hours than their Japanese peers (see Figure 3.2).

Roles and Status Culture dictates the roles people play, including who communicates with whom, what they communicate, and in what way. For example, in many countries women still don't play a prominent role in business, so female executives who visit these countries may find that they're not taken seriously as businesspeople. When they're in modern western Europe, women can usually behave as they would in the United States, but they should be more cautious in Latin American and eastern European countries, and they should be extremely cautious in the Middle East and East Asia.[26]

Respect and rank are reflected differently from culture to culture in the way people are addressed and in their working environment.

Culture also dictates how people show respect and signify rank. For example, people in the United States show respect by addressing top managers as "Mr. Roberts" or "Ms. Gutierrez." However, people in China address businesspeople according to their official titles, such as "President" or "Manager."[27] In addition, a U.S. executive's rank may be reflected by a large corner office, deep carpets, an expensive desk, and handsome accessories. But the highest-ranking executives in France sit in the middle of an open area, surrounded by lower-level employees. And in the Middle East, fine possessions are reserved for the home, while business is conducted in cramped and modest quarters.

FIGURE 3.2 Working Hours Vary from Culture to Culture

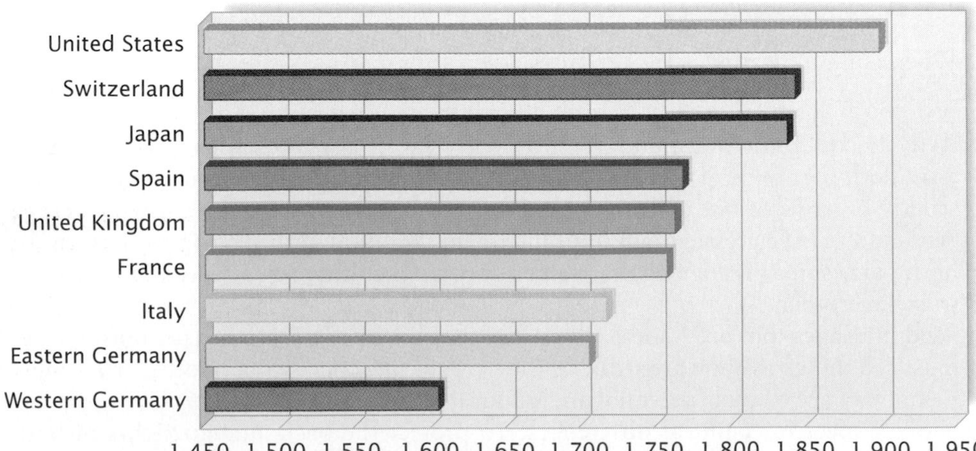

Use of Manners What is polite in one culture may be considered rude in another. For instance, asking an employee "How was your weekend?" is a common way of making small talk in the United States, but the question sounds intrusive to people in cultures where business and private lives are seen as totally separate. In Arab countries it's impolite to take gifts to a man's wife, but it's acceptable to take gifts to his children. In Germany giving a woman a red rose is considered a romantic invitation—inappropriate if you're trying to establish a business relationship with her. In India, if you're invited to visit someone's home "any time," you should make an unexpected visit without waiting for a definite invitation. Failure to take the "any time" invitation literally would be an insult, a sign that you don't care to develop the friendship.

The rules of polite behavior vary from country to country.

Concepts of Time Conducting business entails schedules, deadlines, and appointments, but these matters are regarded differently from culture to culture. German and U.S. executives see time as a way to plan the business day efficiently, focusing on only one task during each scheduled period and viewing time as limited. However, executives from Latin America and Asia see time as more flexible. Meeting a deadline is less important than building a business relationship. So the workday isn't expected to follow a rigid, preset schedule.[28]

Although businesspeople in the United States, Germany, and some other nations see time as a way to organize the business day efficiently, other cultures see time as more flexible.

Nonverbal Differences

As discussed in Chapter 2, nonverbal communication is extremely reliable when determining meaning, but that reliability is valid only when the communicators belong to the same culture. The simplest hand gestures change meaning from culture to culture, so interpreting nonverbal elements according to your own culture can be dangerous. Nonverbal elements are apparent in attitudes toward personal space and in body language.

Concepts of Personal Space People in Canada and the United States usually stand about five feet apart during a business conversation. However, this distance is uncomfortably close for people from Germany or Japan and uncomfortably far for Arabs and Latin Americans. Because of these differing concepts of personal space, a Canadian manager may react negatively (without knowing exactly why) when an Arab colleague moves closer during their conversation. And the Arab colleague may react negatively (again, without knowing why) when the Canadian manager backs away.

Use of Body Language Gestures help members of a culture clarify confusing messages, but differences in body language can be a major source of misunderstanding during intercultural communication. Don't assume that someone from another culture who speaks your language has mastered your culture's body language. For example, people in the United States and Canada say no by shaking their heads back and forth, people in Bulgaria nod up and down, people in Japan move their right hand, and people in Sicily raise their chin. Similarly, U.S. businesspeople assume that a person who won't meet their gaze is evasive and dishonest. However, in many parts of Asia, keeping one's eyes lowered is a sign of respect.[29]

People from different cultures may misread an intentional nonverbal signal, may overlook the signal entirely, or may assume that a meaningless gesture is significant. For example, an Arab man indicates a romantic interest in a woman by

As pictured here at Anspach International in Chicago, U.S. executives commonly maintain a five-foot comfort zone during business discussions. However, senior businessmen in Tunisia are more comfortable conducting business up close.

running a hand backward across his hair, but most Westerners would not see the gesture as significant. Conversely, an Egyptian might mistakenly assume that a Westerner who exposes the sole of his or her shoe is offering a grave insult.[30] Calling someone by raising your hand, then taking your index finger and wiggling it toward you is considered rude in places like China, Japan, South Korea, and the Philippines. There, if you want to get someone's attention, you put your arm out with your palm down, and then make scratching motions with your fingers.[31]

Recognizing cultural differences must be followed by the sincere attempt to accommodate those differences.

Recognizing cultural differences helps you avoid sending inappropriate signals and helps you correctly interpret the signals from others—an important step toward improving intercultural sensitivity. But simple recognition isn't the whole story. Being aware of cultural differences is only the first step in improving your intercultural communication. To achieve intercultural sensitivity, you need to balance cultural awareness with cultural flexibility. The diagram in Figure 3.3 shows the relationship of language, exposure, and technique to communication skill (all of which are covered in detail in this chapter). To communicate across cultures successfully, you must be able to accommodate these differences without judging them, which means you must be able to overcome the human tendency toward ethnocentrism.

Learning Objective 4

Define ethnocentrism *and* stereotyping, *then give three suggestions for overcoming these limiting mind-sets*

Overcome Ethnocentrism

When communicating across cultures, your effectiveness depends on maintaining an open mind. Unfortunately, many people lapse into ethnocentrism. They lose sight of the possibility that their words and actions can be misunderstood, and they forget that they are likely to misinterpret the actions of others.

Stereotyping is the attempt to categorize individuals by trying to predict their behavior or character on the basis of their membership in a particular group.

When you first begin to investigate the culture of another group, you may attempt to understand the common tendencies of that group's members by **stereotyping**—predicting individuals' behavior or character on the basis of their membership in a particular group or class. For example, Japanese visitors often

FIGURE 3.3 Components of Successful Intercultural Communication

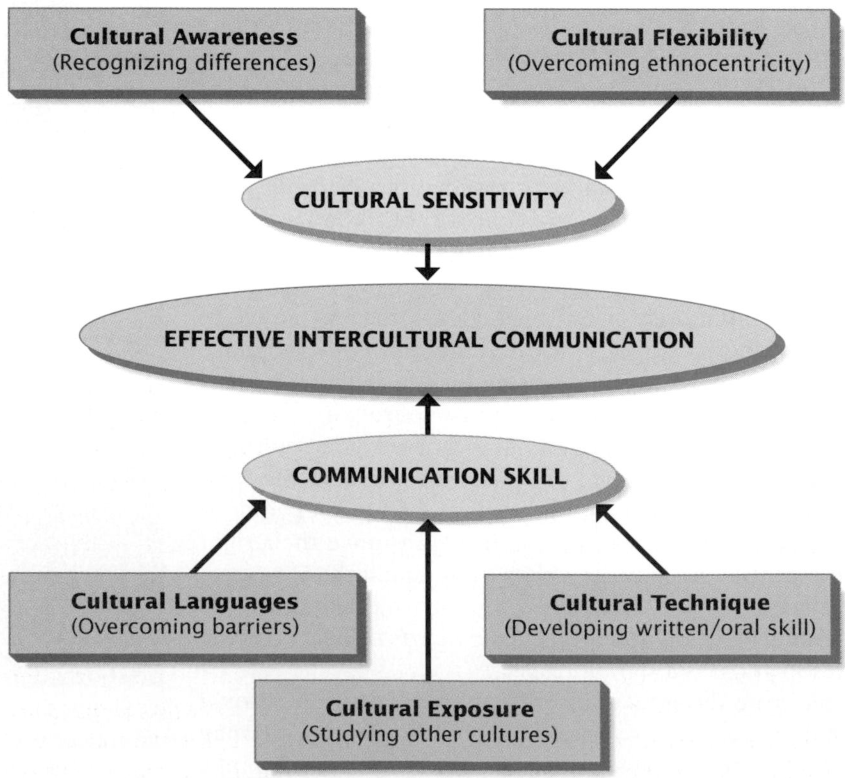

stereotype Americans as people who walk fast, are wasteful in utilizing space, speak directly, ask too many questions in the classroom and don't respect professors, are disrespectful of age and status, lack discipline, and are extravagant.[32]

Although stereotyping may be useful in the beginning, your next step is to move beyond the stereotypes to relationships with real people. Unfortunately, when ethnocentric people stereotype, they tend to do so on the basis of limited, general, or inaccurate evidence. They frequently develop biased attitudes toward the group, and they fail to move beyond that initial step.[33] So instead of talking with Abdul Karhum, unique human being, ethnocentric people are talking to "an Arab." They may believe that all Arabs are, say, hagglers, so Abdul Karhum's personal qualities cannot alter such preconceptions. His every action is forced to fit the preconceived image, even if that image is wrong.

Move beyond stereotypes to relationships with real people.

To overcome ethnocentrism, follow a few simple suggestions:

- **Acknowledge distinctions.** Don't ignore the differences between another person's culture and your own.
- **Avoid assumptions.** Don't assume that others will act the same way you do, that they will operate from the same assumptions, or that they will use language and symbols the same way you do.
- **Avoid judgments.** When people act differently, don't conclude that they are in error, that their way is invalid, or that their customs are inferior to your own.

You can overcome ethnocentrism by acknowledging distinctions, avoiding assumptions, and avoiding judgments.

At Sheraton Hotels Hawaii, Tamanai and Kaneda work hard to move employees away from ethnocentrism and toward understanding and tolerance. Too often, both parties in an intercultural exchange are guilty of ethnocentrism and prejudice. Little wonder, then, that misunderstandings arise when communicating across cultures.

IMPROVING COMMUNICATION ACROSS CULTURES

Once you can recognize cultural elements and overcome ethnocentrism, you're ready to focus directly on your intercultural communication skills. To communicate more effectively with people from other cultures, you need to study other cultures, overcome language barriers, and develop effective intercultural communication skills, both written and oral.

Study Other Cultures

Learning all you can about a particular culture is a good way to figure out how to send and receive intercultural messages effectively. Read books and articles about these cultures, and talk to people who have done business with members of these cultures. Concentrate on learning something about each culture's history, religion, politics, values, and customs. Find out about a country's subcultures, especially its business subculture, and any special rules or protocol. Studying culture is especially important if you interact with people from a variety of cultures or subcultures, like Sheraton's Tamanai and Koneda.

Learning as much as possible about another culture will enhance your ability to communicate with its members.

"In dealing with American businesspeople," says Y. A. Cho, chief operating officer of Korean Airlines, "I'm amazed at how naive most are about other cultures and the way that others do business."[34] Something as simple as a handshake differs from culture to culture. For example, in Spain a proper handshake must last five to seven strokes, and pulling away too soon may be interpreted as rejection. However, in France the preferred handshake is only a single stroke. In Arab countries, you'll insult your hosts if you turn down food, drink, or hospitality of any kind. But don't accept too quickly, either. A polite refusal (such as "I don't want to put you to any trouble") is expected before you finally accept.

People from the United States are often uninformed about the customs of other cultures.

This chapter's "Checklist: Doing Business Abroad" can help you start your investigation of another culture. However, don't expect to ever understand another culture completely. No matter how much you study German culture, for example, you'll never be a German or share the experiences of having grown up in Germany. The trick is to

You can't expect to understand another culture as completely as someone born to that culture.

✓ CHECKLIST: DOING BUSINESS ABROAD

A. Understand social customs

1. How do people react to strangers? Are they friendly? Hostile? Reserved?
2. How do people greet each other? Should you bow? Nod? Shake hands?
3. How are names used for introductions?
4. What are the attitudes toward touching people?
5. How do you express appreciation for an invitation to lunch or dinner or to someone's home? Should you bring a gift? Send flowers? Write a thank-you note?
6. How, when, and where are people expected to sit in social and business situations?
7. Are any phrases, facial expressions, or hand gestures considered rude?
8. How close do people stand when talking?
9. How do you attract the attention of a waiter? Do you tip the waiter?
10. When is it rude to refuse an invitation? How do you refuse politely?
11. What are the acceptable patterns of eye contact?
12. What gestures indicate agreement? Disagreement? Respect?
13. What topics may or may not be discussed in a social setting? In a business setting?
14. How is time perceived?
15. What are the generally accepted working hours?
16. How do people view scheduled appointments?

B. Learn about clothing and food preferences

1. What occasions require special clothing? What colors are associated with mourning? Love? Joy?
2. Are some types of clothing considered taboo for one sex or the other?
3. What are the attitudes toward human body odors? Are deodorants or perfumes used?
4. How many times a day do people eat?
5. How are hands or utensils used when eating?
6. What types of places, food, and drink are appropriate for business entertainment?
7. Where is the seat of honor at a table?

C. Assess political patterns

1. How stable is the political situation? Does it affect businesses in and out of the country?
2. How is political power manifested? Military power? Economic strength?
3. What are the traditional government institutions?
4. What channels are used for expressing official and unofficial political opinion?
5. What information media are important? Who controls them?
6. Is it appropriate to talk politics in social or business situations?

D. Understand religious and folk beliefs

1. To which religious groups do people belong?
2. How do religious beliefs influence daily activities?
3. Which places, objects, and events are sacred?
4. Is there a tolerance for minority religions?
5. How do religious holidays affect business and government activities?
6. Does religion affect attitudes toward smoking? Drinking? Gambling?
7. Does religion require or prohibit eating specific foods? At specific times?
8. Which objects or actions portend good luck? Bad luck?

E. Learn about economic and business institutions

1. Is the society homogeneous?
2. What minority groups are represented?
3. What languages are spoken?
4. Do immigration patterns influence workforce composition?
5. What are the primary resources and principal products?
6. What vocational/technological training is offered?
7. What are the attitudes toward education?
8. Are businesses generally large? Family controlled? Government controlled?
9. Is it appropriate to do business by telephone? By fax? By e-mail?
10. Do managers make business decisions unilaterally, or do they involve employees?
11. How are status and seniority shown in an organization? In a business meeting?
12. Must people socialize before conducting business?

F. Appraise the nature of ethics, values, and laws

1. Is money or a gift expected in exchange for arranging business transactions?
2. What ethical or legal issues might affect business transactions?
3. Do people value competitiveness or cooperation?
4. What are the attitudes toward work? Toward money?
5. Is politeness more important than factual honesty?
6. What qualities are admired in a business associate?

learn useful general information while remaining aware of and open to variations and individual differences. You can communicate more effectively if you follow these tips from successful intercultural businesspeople:[35]

- **Assume differences until similarity is proved.** Don't assume that others are more similar to you than they actually are.
- **Take responsibility for communication.** Don't assume it's the other person's job to communicate with you.

Best of the Web

Improve Your Cultural Savvy

Do you understand the importance of improving your cultural savvy? It's the secret to an international competitive advantage. Log on to Joyce Millet & Associates' Cultural Savvy website, where you'll find country reports, cross-cultural training programs, business and cultural tips, and links to interviews, profiles, articles, books, and more learning resources. Avoid culture shock by developing your ability to understand the traditions, assumptions, etiquette, and values of other cultures as well as your own. This site is your business and cultural guide to Asia and the Western world.

www.culturalsavvy.com

- **Withhold judgment.** Learn to listen to the whole story and accept differences in others without judging them.
- **Show respect.** Learn how respect is communicated in various cultures (through gestures, eye contact, and so on).
- **Empathize.** Before sending a message, put yourself in the receiver's shoes. Imagine the receiver's feelings and point of view.
- **Tolerate ambiguity.** Learn to control your frustration when placed in an unfamiliar or confusing situation.
- **Look beyond the superficial.** Don't be distracted by things such as dress, appearance, or environmental discomforts.
- **Be patient and persistent.** If you want to communicate with someone from another culture, don't give up easily.
- **Recognize your own cultural biases.** Learn to identify when your assumptions are different from the other person's.
- **Be flexible.** Be prepared to change your habits and attitudes when communicating with someone from another culture.
- **Emphasize common ground.** Look for similarities to work from.
- **Send clear messages.** Make both your verbal and nonverbal signals clear and consistent.
- **Deal with the individual.** Communicate with each person as an individual, not as a stereotypical representative of another group.
- **Learn when to be direct.** Investigate each culture so that you'll know when to send your message in a straightforward manner and when to be indirect.
- **Treat your interpretation as a working hypothesis.** Once you think you understand a foreign culture, carefully assess the feedback provided by recipients of your communication to see if it confirms your hypothesis.

This advice will help you communicate with anybody, regardless of culture, but it isn't enough. Overcoming language barriers is another good way to improve your communication across cultures.

Overcome Language Barriers

By choosing specific words to communicate, you signal that you are a member of a particular culture or subculture and that you know the code. The nature of your code—your language and vocabulary—imposes its own barriers on your message. For example, the language of a lawyer differs from that of an accountant or a doctor, and the difference in their vocabularies affects their ability to recognize and express ideas. Barriers also exist because words can be interpreted in more than one way. In fact, it's often said that the United States and the United Kingdom are two countries divided by a common language (see Table 3.2). The barriers become greater still when you're communicating across cultures. To someone from France, for example, the word *catastrophe* can be used in casual exaggeration to describe a relatively small problem.

Language barriers can result from your choice of words and from the fact that words can be interpreted in more than one way.

TABLE 3.2 U.S. Versus British English

U.S. English	British English
apartment	flat
eggplant	auberg
cleaning lady	charwoman
elevator	lift
first floor	ground level
long-distance call	trunk call
organization	organisation
pharmacist	chemist
rare	underdone
roast	joint
string bean	French bean
sweater	pullover

But in Germany, the word is often taken literally as an earth-shaking event. You must be able to communicate effectively both with people who speak English as a second language (ESL) and with people who don't speak your language at all.

Breaking Through ESL Barriers

Learning Objective 5

Discuss four ways to improve communication with people who speak English as a second language and three ways to improve communication with people who don't speak your language at all

As the U.S. workforce becomes more culturally diverse, the number of people who speak English as a second language grows proportionately. One out of every seven people in the United States now speaks a language other than English when at home. After English, Spanish is by far the most common spoken language, followed by French, German, Italian, and Chinese.[36] When U.S. businesspeople deal with individuals who use English as a second language, misunderstandings are likely to involve vocabulary, pronunciation, or usage.

Of the many millions of people who use English as a second language, some are extremely fluent, and others have only an elementary command. When dealing with those less fluent in your own language, you can expect your audience to miss a few subtleties, but you are still able to communicate. Even so, don't assume that the other person understands everything you say. Your message can be mangled by slang and idioms, by local accents, and by vocal variations.

Slang and idioms, local accents and pronunciation, and vocal variations can pose problems when you're speaking to people from other cultures.

Avoid Using Slang and Idioms Languages never translate word for word. They are **idiomatic**—constructed with phrases that mean more than the sum of their literal parts. For example, if a U.S. executive tells an Egyptian executive that a certain product "doesn't cut the mustard" or that making the monthly sales quota will be "a piece of cake," chances are that the communication will fail. When speaking to people less fluent in your language, try to choose words carefully to convey only their most specific denotative meaning. Use words that have singular rather than multiple meanings. The word *high* has 20 meanings; the word *expensive* has one.[37]

Pay Attention to Local Accents and Pronunciation Even when people speak your language, you may have a hard time understanding their pronunciation. After transferring to Toyota's U.S. office, some English-speaking Japanese employees had to enroll in a special course to learn that "Jeat yet?" means "Did you eat yet?" and that "Cannahepya?" means "Can I help you?" Some nonnative English speakers don't distinguish between the

English sounds *v* and *w*, so they say "wery" for "very." At the same time, many people from the United States are unable to pronounce the French *r* or the German *ch*.

Be Aware of Vocal Variations Some people use their voices differently from culture to culture. Russian speakers tend to use a flat, level tone, so to some U.S. listeners they sound bored or rude. Middle Easterners tend to speak more loudly than Westerners and may therefore mistakenly be considered more emotional. On the other hand, people from Japan are soft-spoken, a characteristic that implies politeness or humility to Western listeners.

When speaking to people from another culture, take time to research their preferences for the direct or indirect approach to communication.

Respect Preferences for Communication Styles U.S. workers typically prefer an open and direct communication style and consider anything else to be dishonest or insincere. In Sweden, a direct approach is also valued as a sign of efficiency, but unlike discussions in the United States, heated debates and confrontations are unusual. Swedish business culture strongly favors compromise. Workers from other cultures, such as Japan or China, tend to be more indirect. Finnish and German workers tend to prefer written communication instead of face-to-face interaction. A letter recognizing employee accomplishments would be most effective in these cultures. Moreover, Italians, Germans, and French executives don't soften up colleagues with praise before they criticize. Doing so seems manipulative to Europeans.[38]

In general, U.S. businesspeople will also want to be somewhat more formal in their international correspondence than they would be when writing to people in their own country. In many cultures, writers use a more elaborate style, so your audience will expect more formal language in your letter. The letter in Figure 3.4 was written by a supplier in Germany to a nearby retailer. The tone is more formal than would be used in the United States, but the writer clearly focuses on his audience. In Germany, business letters usually open with a reference to the business relationship and close with a compliment to the recipient. Of course, if you carry formality to extremes, you'll sound unnatural.

International business letters generally have a formal tone and a relatively elaborate style.

Breaking Through Foreign Language Barriers

To compete globally, many European businesses are making English their official language. Look through the listings for professional and managerial jobs in French newspapers and recruitment websites and you'll find that those that don't require *anglais courant* (fluent English) are few and far between. Moreover, as more and more European companies become entwined with each other politically and economically, they rely on English as their common tongue. The European Commission, with 11 official languages, recently switched to English as its official working language.[39]

English is the most prevalent language in international business, but it's a mistake to assume that everyone understands it.

Some multinational companies ask all their employees to use English when writing to employees in other countries, regardless of where they're located. Nissan employees, for example, use English for internal memos to colleagues around the world, even though the corporation is based in Japan.[40] But requiring employees to use a specific language when they're on the job may be considered discriminatory and can create tension.

Consider Air France's decision to do what was once unthinkable—make its pilots speak English to the control towers. Rather than having bilingual airwaves that frequently confuse and infuriate pilots from other countries, France put aside linguistic pride for safety considerations and decided to adopt English as the official communication language of the tower (as is commonplace in many European airports). But the government had underestimated the pilots' resistance and rescinded the order after only 15 days. Some pilots were shocked by the symbolism of being asked to speak English in their own country. Others didn't have sufficient English-speaking skills yet.[41] Still others saw the move as conflicting with the nation's drive over the last decade to protect the French language and French industries.

FIGURE 3.4 In-Depth Critique: Translated German Business Letter

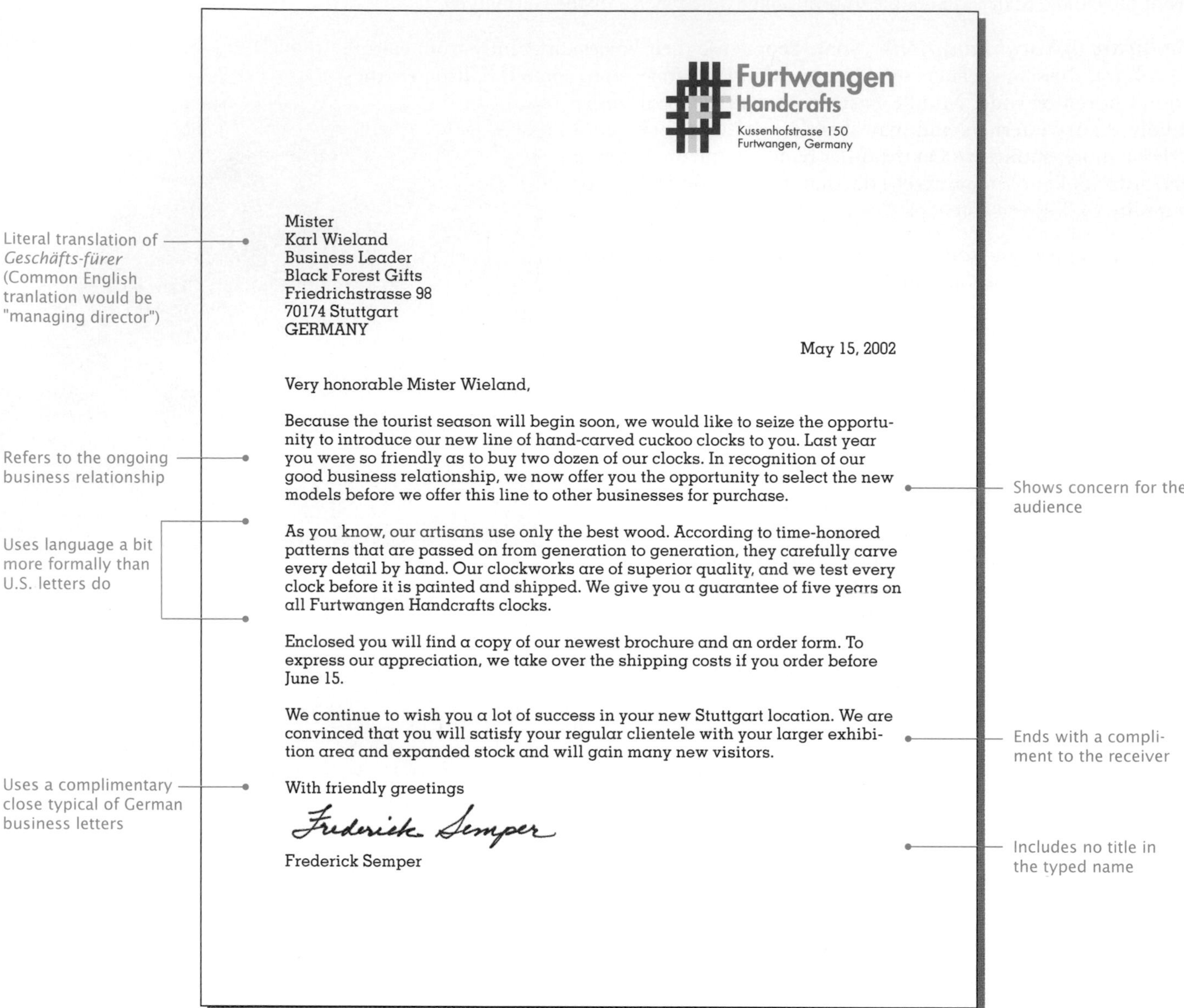

Furtwangen Handcrafts
Kussenhofstrasse 150
Furtwangen, Germany

Mister
Karl Wieland
Business Leader
Black Forest Gifts
Friedrichstrasse 98
70174 Stuttgart
GERMANY

May 15, 2002

Very honorable Mister Wieland,

Because the tourist season will begin soon, we would like to seize the opportunity to introduce our new line of hand-carved cuckoo clocks to you. Last year you were so friendly as to buy two dozen of our clocks. In recognition of our good business relationship, we now offer you the opportunity to select the new models before we offer this line to other businesses for purchase.

As you know, our artisans use only the best wood. According to time-honored patterns that are passed on from generation to generation, they carefully carve every detail by hand. Our clockworks are of superior quality, and we test every clock before it is painted and shipped. We give you a guarantee of five yerrs on all Furtwangen Handcrafts clocks.

Enclosed you will find a copy of our newest brochure and an order form. To express our appreciation, we take over the shipping costs if you order before June 15.

We continue to wish you a lot of success in your new Stuttgart location. We are convinced that you will satisfy your regular clientele with your larger exhibition area and expanded stock and will gain many new visitors.

With friendly greetings

Frederick Semper

Frederick Semper

Many companies recognize that they must be able to conduct business in languages other than English.

Even though English is widely spoken in the global business marketplace, the language of business is the language of the customer. And increasingly, that language may not be English.[42] So U.S. companies are realizing that they can no longer get by speaking only English, even in their own country. When communicating with people who don't speak your language at all, you have three options: You can learn their language, use an intermediary or a translator, or teach them your language. However you choose to overcome language barriers, remember that effective communication requires a major commitment—even on the web (see "Communicating Across Cultures: Communicating with a Global Audience on the Web").

If you have a long-term business relationship with people of another culture, it is helpful to learn their language.

Learn a Foreign Language If you're planning to live in another country or to do business there repeatedly, you might want to learn the language. The same holds true if you'll be working closely with a subculture that has its own language, such as Vietnamese Americans. Even if you're doing business in your own language, you show respect by making the effort to learn the subculture's language, or at least to learn a few words. One problem is that language courses may take more time and more money than you can afford.

Communicating Across Cultures

Communicating with a Global Audience on the Web

With growing global access to the World Wide Web, some U.S. corporate sites are already reporting that foreign visitors account for as much as 30 percent of their traffic and 10 percent of their commerce. Nevertheless, reaching an international audience on the web involves more than simply offering translations of the English language. Successful global sites address the needs of international customers in five ways:

1. **Consider the reader's viewpoint.** Assume your audience is unfamiliar with common U.S. phrases and references. To avoid confusion, provide both U.S. units and metric equivalents for weights, measures, sizes, and temperatures. Also, use universal terms for times, dates, and geographical names. For example, consider expressing time in military format ("16:00" for 4 P.M.). Because Europeans read "10/04/2002" as April 10, 2002, be sure you spell out the month and year. And offer complete location descriptions, such as "Kansas City, MO, USA."
2. **Take cultural differences into account.** Since humor is rooted in cultural norms, a touch of U.S. humor may not be so funny to Asian or European readers. Don't risk offending or slighting your audience with cultural stereotypes or expressions. Avoid idioms and references that aren't universally recognized, such as "putting all your eggs in one basket" or "jumping out of the frying pan into the fire."
3. **Keep the message clear.** Use simple words and write in the active voice. Avoid complicated sentence structure to achieve a simple, straightforward tone. And don't forget to define abbreviations and acronyms.
4. **Break through language barriers with graphics.** Clarify written concepts with graphics. However, even though most graphical icons are internationally recognized, some images are more widely accepted than others. In some countries, for example, a mailbox doesn't necessarily convey the idea of sending mail. So an envelope might be a more appropriate symbol to reinforce the message "Contact us." Keep in mind that the colors you select for your graphics are equally as important. Red works well in China, where it conveys good fortune. But it's the color of death in Turkey.
5. **Consult local experts.** Work with local experts and webmasters to develop native-language keywords that will direct international customers to your site. Also seek the advice of local experts about customary phrases and references. Even terms as simple as *homepage* differ from country to country. Spanish readers refer to the "first page," or *pagina inicial,* whereas the French term is "welcome page," or *page d'accuei.*

For additional tips on writing for the web's global audience, see Component Chapter A.

Career Applications

1. Visit the World of Sony Music Entertainment at www.sonymusic.com/world and examine Sony's sites for Argentina, France, and Germany. How does Sony "localize" each country's site?
2. Compare Sony Music's international sites to IBM's global webpages at ww.ibm.com. How does Sony's approach differ from IBM's? Do both corporations successfully address the needs of a global audience? Write a two-paragraph summary that compares the international sites of both companies.

Use an Intermediary or a Translator Because so many international business letters are written in English, U.S. firms don't always worry about translating their correspondence. However, many other forms of written communication must be translated. Advertisements are almost always translated into the customer's language. Warranties, repair and maintenance manuals, and product labels also require translation. For example, the warranty for a Hewlett-Packard laser jet printer cartridge is written in English, French, Spanish, Italian, and Japanese. In addition, many multinational companies translate policy and procedure manuals for use in overseas offices. Reports from foreign branches to the home office may be written in one language and then translated into another. One multinational company, E. I. Du Pont de Nemours & Company, translates roughly 70,000 pages of documents each year.[43]

Many companies use translators to help them communicate with people who don't speak English.

An experienced translator can analyze a message, understand its meaning in the cultural context, consider how to convey the meaning in another language, and then use verbal and nonverbal signals to encode or decode the message for someone from another culture. If you use translators, you should meet with them ahead of time to give them a sense of what you are presenting and to discuss specific words or concepts that could be confusing.[44] Some companies use *back-translation* to ensure accuracy.

Back-translation helps ensure accuracy by allowing translators to check a second translation against the original message.

Once a translator encodes a message into another language, a different translator retranslates the same message into the original language. This back-translation is then compared with the original message to discover any errors or discrepancies.

Some companies find it useful to teach their employees to speak English.

Offer English-Language Training Programs for Employees The option of teaching other people to speak your language doesn't appear to be practical at first glance. However, many companies find it beneficial to offer language training programs. For example, Tenneco instituted an English-language training program in New Jersey for its Spanish-speaking employees. The training concentrated on practical English for use on the job, and thanks to the classes, accidents and grievances declined and productivity improved.[45]

Develop Effective Intercultural Communication Skills

Whether you choose written or oral channels to communicate your message across cultures, you must adapt your style and approach.

Once you understand what sort of cultural differences you'll be facing, and once you discover which language barriers must be overcome, you must decide whether using written or oral channels would be best. Then you must adapt your style and approach to make the right impression.

Improve Your Writing Skills

Learning Objective 6

List eight recommendations for writing more effectively

Be aware of various cultures' tendency to organize thoughts differently.

Letter writers in other countries use various techniques to organize their thoughts. If you are aware of some of these practices, you'll be able to concentrate on the message without passing judgment on the writers. Letters from Japanese businesspeople, for example, are slow to come to the point. They typically begin with a remark about the season or weather, which is followed by an inquiry about your health or congratulations on your success. A note of thanks for your patronage might come next. After these preliminaries, the main idea is introduced.

When sending written communication to businesspeople from another culture, familiarize yourself with their written communication preferences and adapt your approach, style, and tone to meet their expectations. To help you prepare effective written communications for multicultural audiences, follow these recommendations:[46]

- **Use plain English.** Use short, precise words that say exactly what you mean: For example, use *climb* instead of *walk up, maintain* instead of *keep up,* and *return* instead of *bring back.*
- **Be clear.** Rely on specific terms and concrete examples to explain your points.
- **Address international correspondence properly.** Refer to Table 1.2 in Appendix I for an explanation of different address elements and salutations commonly used in certain foreign countries.
- **Cite numbers carefully.** Use figures (27) instead of spelling them out (twenty-seven).
- **Avoid slang and idioms.** Avoid using slang, idioms, jargon, and buzzwords. Abbreviations, acronyms (such as CAD/CAM), and unfamiliar product names may also lead to confusion.
- **Be brief.** Construct sentences that are shorter and simpler than those you might use when writing to someone fluent in your own language.
- **Use short paragraphs.** Each paragraph should stick to one topic and be no more than eight to ten lines long.
- **Use transitional elements.** Help readers follow your train of thought by using transitional words and phrases. Precede related points with expressions such as *in addition* and *first, second, third.*

Take a look at Figure 3.5. Then review the corrected version (Figure 3.6) to see how the original letter is improved by paying close attention to this chapter's guidelines.

Improve Your Oral Skills

Learning Objective 7

List 12 guidelines for speaking across cultures more effectively

If you've ever studied another language, you know it's easier to write in that language than to conduct a conversation. However, some transactions simply cannot be handled without face-to-face contact. In many countries, business relationships are based on personal relationships, and until you establish rapport, nothing happens. When speaking in English to people who speak English as a second language, you may find these guidelines helpful:

FIGURE 3.5 In-Depth Critique: Poor Example of an Intercultural Letter

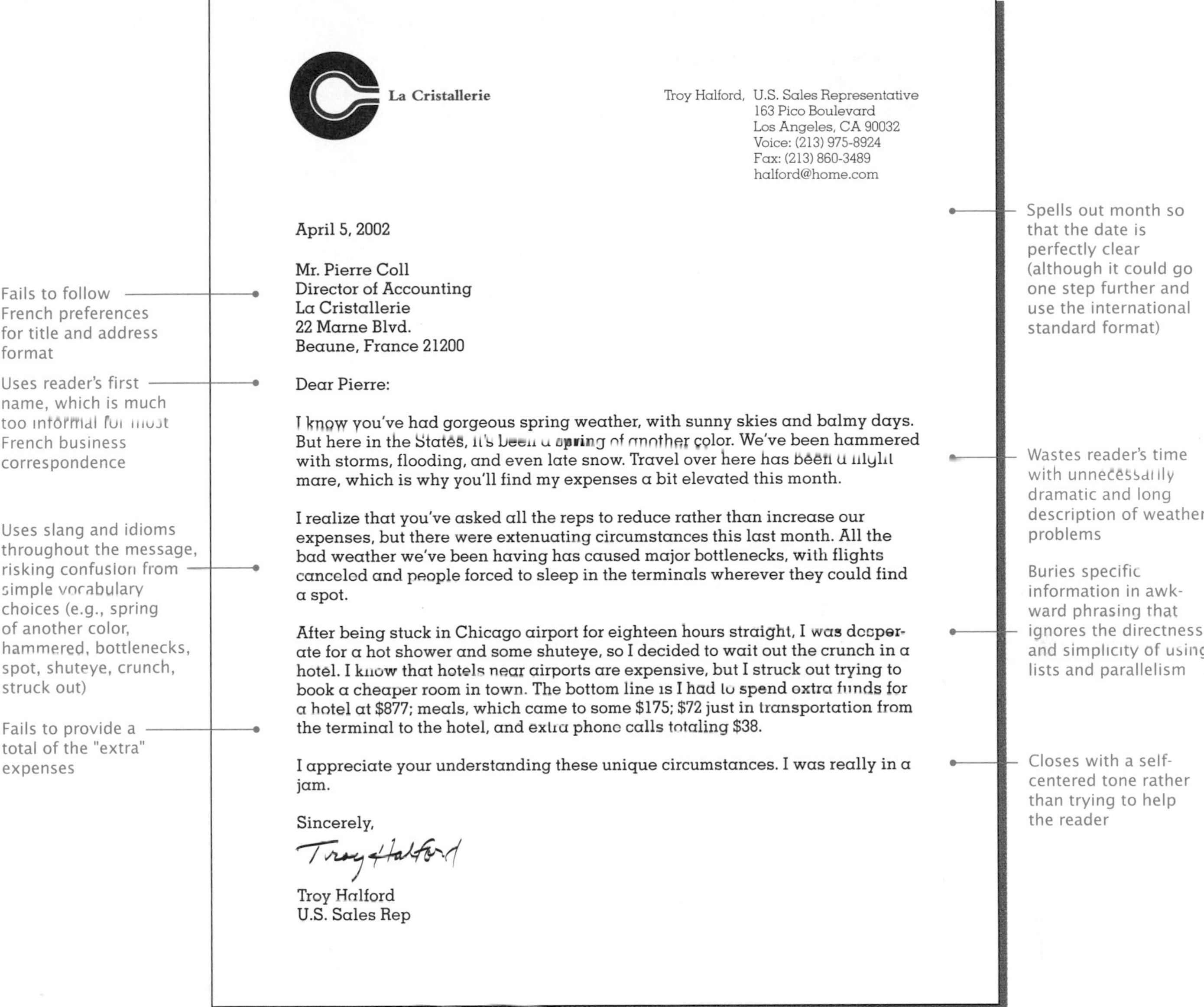

La Cristallerie

Troy Halford, U.S. Sales Representative
163 Pico Boulevard
Los Angeles, CA 90032
Voice: (213) 975-8924
Fax: (213) 860-3489
halford@home.com

April 5, 2002

Mr. Pierre Coll
Director of Accounting
La Cristallerie
22 Marne Blvd.
Beaune, France 21200

Dear Pierre:

I know you've had gorgeous spring weather, with sunny skies and balmy days. But here in the States, it's been a spring of another color. We've been hammered with storms, flooding, and even late snow. Travel over here has been a night-mare, which is why you'll find my expenses a bit elevated this month.

I realize that you've asked all the reps to reduce rather than increase our expenses, but there were extenuating circumstances this last month. All the bad weather we've been having has caused major bottlenecks, with flights canceled and people forced to sleep in the terminals wherever they could find a spot.

After being stuck in Chicago airport for eighteen hours straight, I was desperate for a hot shower and some shuteye, so I decided to wait out the crunch in a hotel. I know that hotels near airports are expensive, but I struck out trying to book a cheaper room in town. The bottom line is I had to spend extra funds for a hotel at $877; meals, which came to some $175; $72 just in transportation from the terminal to the hotel, and extra phone calls totaling $38.

I appreciate your understanding these unique circumstances. I was really in a jam.

Sincerely,

Troy Halford

Troy Halford
U.S. Sales Rep

- **Try to eliminate noise.** Pronounce words clearly, stop at distinct punctuation points, and make one point at a time.
- **Look for feedback.** Be alert to signs of confusion in your listener. Realize that nods and smiles don't necessarily mean understanding. Recognize that gestures and expressions mean different things in different cultures. If the other person's body language seems at odds with the message, take time to clarify the meaning.
- **Speak slowly and rephrase your sentence when necessary.** If someone doesn't seem to understand you, choose simpler words; don't just repeat the sentence in a louder voice.
- **Clarify your true intent with repetition and examples.** Try to be aware of unintentional meanings that may be read into your message.
- **Don't talk down to the other person.** Try not to overenunciate, and don't "blame" the listener for not understanding. Use phrases such as "Am I going too fast?" rather than "Is this too difficult for you?"
- **Use objective, accurate language.** Avoid throwing around adjectives such as *fantastic* and *fabulous,* which people from other cultures might consider unreal and overly dramatic.

Face-to-face communication lets you establish a personal relationship with people from other cultures and gives you the benefit of immediate feedback.

FIGURE 3.6 In-Depth Critique: Good Example of an Intercultural Letter

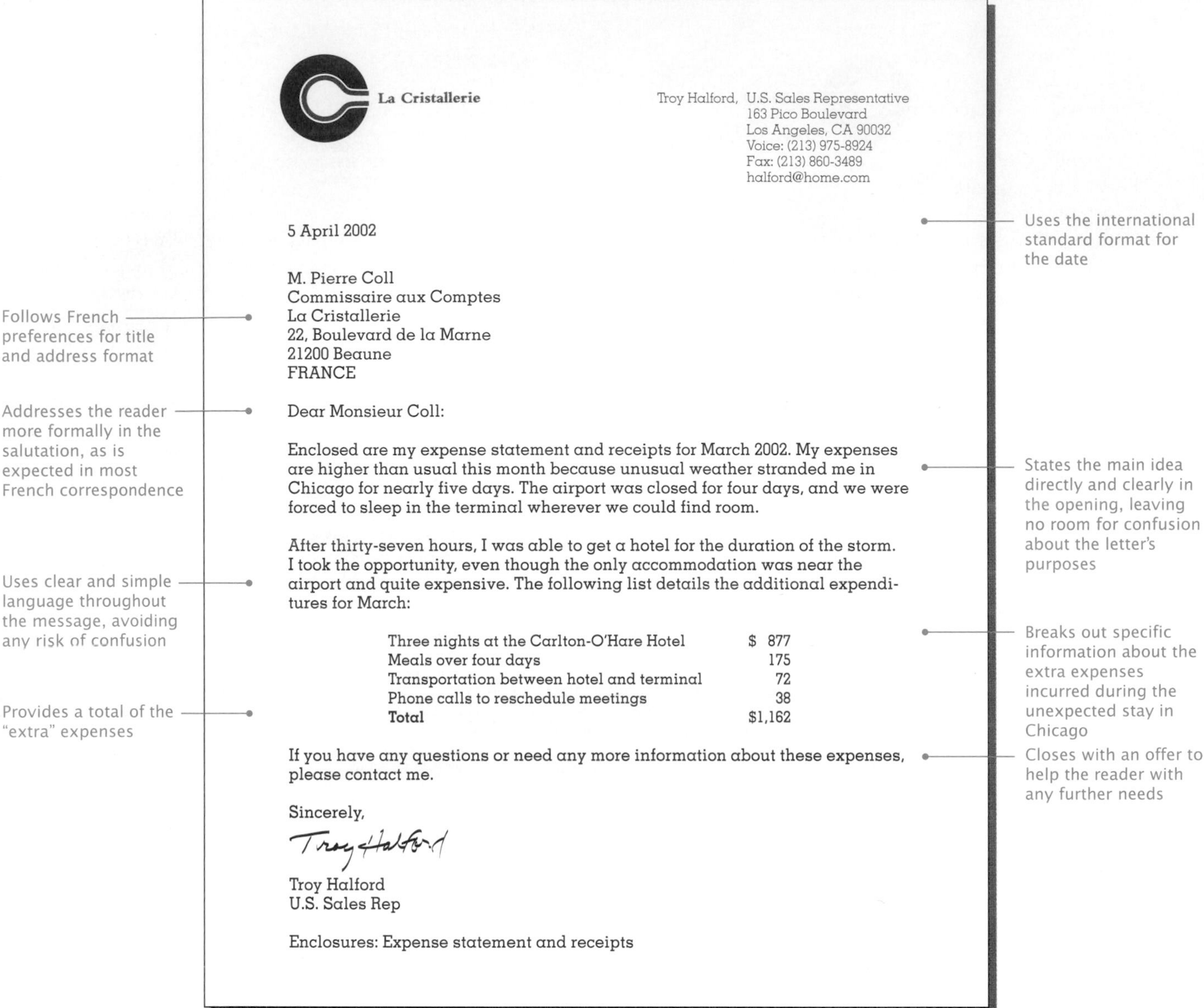

La Cristallerie

Troy Halford, U.S. Sales Representative
163 Pico Boulevard
Los Angeles, CA 90032
Voice: (213) 975-8924
Fax: (213) 860-3489
halford@home.com

5 April 2002

M. Pierre Coll
Commissaire aux Comptes
La Cristallerie
22, Boulevard de la Marne
21200 Beaune
FRANCE

Dear Monsieur Coll:

Enclosed are my expense statement and receipts for March 2002. My expenses are higher than usual this month because unusual weather stranded me in Chicago for nearly five days. The airport was closed for four days, and we were forced to sleep in the terminal wherever we could find room.

After thirty-seven hours, I was able to get a hotel for the duration of the storm. I took the opportunity, even though the only accommodation was near the airport and quite expensive. The following list details the additional expenditures for March:

Three nights at the Carlton-O'Hare Hotel	$ 877
Meals over four days	175
Transportation between hotel and terminal	72
Phone calls to reschedule meetings	38
Total	$1,162

If you have any questions or need any more information about these expenses, please contact me.

Sincerely,

Troy Halford

Troy Halford
U.S. Sales Rep

Enclosures: Expense statement and receipts

- **Learn foreign phrases.** Learn common greetings and a few simple phrases in the other person's native language. Key phrases are usually listed in travel books and in a separate section of most travel dictionaries.
- **Listen carefully and patiently.** Let other people finish what they have to say. If you interrupt, you may miss something important. You'll also show a lack of respect. If you do not understand a comment, ask the person to repeat it.
- **Adapt your conversation style to the other person's.** For instance, if the other person appears to be direct and straightforward, follow suit.
- **Check frequently for comprehension.** Make one point at a time and pause to check for comprehension before moving on.
- **Clarify what will happen next.** At the end of the conversation, be sure that you and the other person agree on what has been said and decided. If appropriate, follow up by writing a letter or a memo summarizing the conversation and thanking the person for meeting with you.
- **Observe body language.** Be alert to roving eyes, glazed looks, and other facial expressions that signal the listener is lost or confused.

CHECKLIST: COMMUNICATING WITH A CULTURALLY DIVERSE WORKFORCE

A. Accept cultural differences

1. Study your own culture.
2. Learn about other cultures through books, articles, videos, and other resources.
3. Encourage employees to discuss their culture's customs.
4. Avoid being judgmental.
5. Create a formal forum to teach employees about the customs of all cultures represented in the firm.
6. Train employees to see and overcome ethnocentric stereotyping.
7. Stamp out negative labels by observing how people identify their own groups.

B. Improve oral and written communications

1. Define the terms people need to know on the job.
2. Emphasize major points with repetition and recap.
3. Use familiar words whenever possible.
4. Be concise.
5. Don't cover too much information at one time.
6. Adjust your message to employees' education level.
7. Be specific and explicit—using descriptive words, exact measurements, and examples when possible.
8. Give the reason for asking employees to follow a certain procedure and explain what will happen if the procedure is not followed.
9. Use written summaries and visual aids (when appropriate) to clarify your points.
10. Demonstrate and encourage the right way to complete a task, use a tool, and so on.
11. Reduce language barriers: Train managers in the language of their employees, train employees in the language of most customers and of most people in the company, ask bilingual employees to serve as translators, print important health and safety instructions in as many languages as necessary.

C. Assess how well you've been understood

1. Research the nonverbal reactions of other cultures; then be alert to facial expressions and other nonverbal signs that indicate confusion or embarrassment.
2. Probe for comprehension.
3. Encourage employees to ask questions in private and in writing.
4. Observe how employees use the information you've provided, and review any misunderstood points.

D. Offer feedback to improve communication

1. Focus on the positive by explaining what *should* be done rather than what *shouldn't* be done.
2. Discuss a person's behaviors and the situation, rather than making a judgment about the person.
3. Be supportive as you offer feedback, and reassure individuals that their skills and contributions are important.

In short, take advantage of the other person's presence to make sure that your message is getting across and that you understand his or her message too. For more ideas on how to improve communication in the workplace, see this chapter's "Checklist: Communicating with a Culturally Diverse Workforce."

COMMUNICATION CHALLENGES AT SHERATON HOTELS HAWAII

Employee diversity at Sheraton Hotels Hawaii helps to create a rich and dynamic working environment. However, it can also lead to communication difficulties between employees on an interpersonal level as well as between management and employees on a companywide level. Different employees, depending on the cultural context they are most familiar with, may interpret a single message several ways.

Individual Challenge: As a member of Michiru Tamanai's training staff, you have been asked to deliver a brief oral presentation to a group of 20 new employees on the importance of respecting cultural differences. These employees come from many cultural backgrounds, including Korean, Japanese, Filipino, Iranian, Kenyan, and American. Drawing on what you have learned in this chapter, develop an outline for your presentation. List the topics that you feel are most important to address, and jot down some ideas about how to deliver your message to such a diverse group. Keep in mind that you'll want to ensure smooth communication and a productive work environment.

Team Challenge: Michiru Tamanai has just received a fax from the hotel manager confirming that the entire hotel has been reserved for IBM's annual international sales meeting, to take place in three months. During the meeting, individuals of practically every nationality, culture, and language will be staying at the hotel. As members of Tamanai's training staff, you are responsible for developing a plan to make sure the hotel is ready for this big event. Your first job is to brainstorm every conceivable thing that will help this diverse cultural group feel welcome at Sheraton Hotels Hawaii. Don't worry about costs for now. Rather, think about the things you might want if you were staying at a hotel in a country whose customs and language were unfamiliar to you.[47] ■

SUMMARY OF LEARNING OBJECTIVES

1 **Discuss two trends that have made intercultural business communication so important.** *Market globalization,* the first trend, is brought about by improvements in communication and transportation technology. Such technological advancements allow companies to sell and produce goods all over the world. As a result, more people are working in companies whose employees come from various national, ethnic, racial, and religious backgrounds. This, of course, affects a company's *cultural diversity,* the second trend contributing to the importance of intercultural business communication. The U.S. workforce includes recent immigrants (from Europe, Canada, Latin America, India, Africa, and Asia), people from various ethnic backgrounds (such as African Americans, Hispanic Americans, and Asian Americans), and people who differ from each other in other characteristics (such as gender, age, family status, and educational background). Thus, to be successful in today's workplace, you must be sensitive to cultural differences and possess good intercultural skills.

2 **Define *culture* and *subculture,* and explain how culture is learned.** *Culture* is a shared system of symbols, beliefs, attitudes, values, expectations, and norms for behavior. A *subculture* is a distinct group existing within a major culture, such as Russian immigrants or disabled individuals existing within the United States. Culture is learned by listening to other members' advice and observing their behaviors. These direct and indirect methods of learning ensure that culture is passed from person to person and from generation to generation.

3 **Explain the importance of recognizing cultural differences, and list four categories of cultural differences.** People from different cultures encode and decode messages differently, increasing the chances of misunderstanding. By recognizing cultural differences, we don't automatically assume that everyone's thoughts and actions are just like ours. The four categories of cultural differences are contextual differences (the degree to which culture relies on verbal or nonverbal actions to convey meaning), legal and ethical differences (the degree to which laws and ethics are regarded and obeyed), social differences (how members value wealth, recognize status, define manners, and think about time), and nonverbal differences (differing attitudes toward personal space and body language).

4 **Define *ethnocentrism* and *stereotyping*; then give three suggestions for overcoming these limiting mind-sets.** *Ethnocentrism* is the tendency to judge all other groups according to one's own standards, behaviors, and customs. *Stereotyping* is predicting individuals' behavior or character on the basis of their membership in a particular group or class. To overcome ethnocentrism, follow three suggestions: (1) acknowledge distinctions, (2) avoid assumptions, and (3) avoid judgments.

5 **Discuss four ways to improve communication with people who speak English as a second language; then discuss three ways to improve communication with people who don't speak your language at all.** When communicating with people who speak English as a second language, clarify your meaning in three ways. First, since language never translates word for word, avoid using slang and idioms. Choose words that will convey only the most specific denotative meaning. Second, listen carefully and pay close attention to local accents and pronunciation. Third, don't assume that people from different cultures use their voice the same way you do. Be aware of vocal variations across cultures. Fourth, respect preferences for communication styles (direct or indirect) and formalities. When communicating with someone who doesn't speak your language at all, you have three choices. First, you can learn a foreign language or at least show respect by learning a few words. Second, you can use an intermediary or a translator to analyze a message, understand its cultural context, and convey its meaning in another language. Back-translation helps ensure accuracy and avoid embarrassing mistakes. Third, you can teach others your language. Many companies offer language training programs to employees who speak little or no English.

6 **List eight recommendations for writing more effectively.** Word choice reflects the relationship between you and your audience; for example, the appropriate level of formality is achieved by word choice. To write more effectively, follow eight recommendations: (1) use plain English, (2) be clear, (3) address international correspondence properly, (4) cite numbers carefully, (5) avoid slang and idioms, (6) be brief, (7) use short paragraphs, and (8) use transitional elements.

7 **List 12 guidelines for speaking across cultures more effectively.** To speak across cultures more effectively, follow these 12 guidelines: (1) try to eliminate noise, (2) look for feedback, (3) speak slowly and rephrase your sentence when necessary, (4) clarify your true intent with repetition and examples, (5) don't talk down to the other person, (6) use objective and accurate language, (7) learn foreign phrases, (8) listen carefully and patiently, (9) adapt your conversation style to the other person's, (10) check frequently for comprehension, (11) clarify what will happen next, and (12) observe body language.

TEST YOUR KNOWLEDGE

1. How have market globalization and cultural diversity contributed to the increased importance of intercultural communication?
2. What is the relationship between culture and subculture?
3. How do high-context cultures differ from low-context cultures?
4. In addition to contextual differences, what other categories of cultural differences exist?
5. What four principles apply to ethical intercultural communication?
6. What is ethnocentrism, and how can it be overcome in communication?
7. Why is it a good idea to avoid slang and idioms when addressing a multicultural audience?
8. What are some ways to improve oral skills when communicating with people of other cultures?
9. What are some ways to improve written skills when communicating with people of other cultures?
10. What is the purpose of back-translation when preparing a message in another language?

APPLY YOUR KNOWLEDGE

1. What are some of the intercultural differences that managers of a U.S.-based firm might encounter during a series of business meetings with a China-based company whose managers speak English fairly well?
2. What are some of the intercultural communication issues to consider when deciding whether to accept an overseas job with a firm whose headquarters are in the United States? A job in the United States with a local branch of a foreign-owned firm? Explain.
3. How do you think company managers from a country that has a relatively homogeneous culture might react when they do business with the culturally diverse staff of a company based in a less homogeneous country? Explain your answer.
4. You company has relocated to a U.S. city where a Vietnamese subculture is strongly established. Many of your employees will be from this subculture. What can you do to improve communication between your management and the Vietnamese Americans you are currently hiring?
5. **Ethical Choices** Your office in Turkey desperately needs the supplies that have been sitting in Turkish customs for a month. Should you bribe a customs official to speed up delivery? Explain your decision.

PRACTICE YOUR KNOWLEDGE

 *Document for Analysis*

Your boss wants to send a brief e-mail message welcoming employees recently transferred to your department from your Hong Kong branch. They all speak English, but your boss asks you to review his message for clarity. What would you suggest your boss change in the following e-mail message—and why? Would you consider this message to be audience centered? Why or why not?

I wanted to welcome you ASAP to our little family here in the States. It's high time we shook hands in person and not just across the sea. I'm pleased as punch about getting to know you all, and I for one will do my level best to sell you on America.

Exercises

For live links to all websites discussed in this chapter, visit this text's website at www.prenhall.com/bovee. Just log on and select Chapter 3, and click on "Student Resources." Locate the name of the site or the URL related to the material in the text. For the "Exploring the Best of the Web" exercises, you'll also find navigational directions. Click on the live link to the site.

3.1 **Intercultural Sensitivity: Recognizing Differences** You represent a Canadian toy company that's negotiating to buy miniature truck wheels from a manufacturer in Osaka, Japan. In your first meeting, you explain that your company expects to control the design of the wheels as well as the materials that are used to make them. The manufacturer's representative looks down and says softly, "Perhaps that will be difficult." You press for agreement, and to emphasize your willingness to buy, you show the prepared contract you've brought with you. However, the manufacturer seems increasingly vague and uninterested. What cultural differences may be interfering with effective communication in this situation? Explain.

3.2 **Ethical Choices** A U.S. manager wants to export T-shirts to a West African country, but a West African official expects a special payment before allowing the shipment into his country. How can the two sides resolve their different approaches without violating U.S. rules against bribing foreign officials? On the basis of the information presented in Chapter 1, would you consider this situation an ethical dilemma or an ethical lapse? Please explain.

3.3 **Teamwork** Working with two other students, prepare a list of 10 examples of slang (in your own language) that would probably be misinterpreted or misunderstood during a business conversation with someone from another culture. Next to each example, suggest other words you might use to convey the same message. Do the alternatives mean *exactly* the same as the original slang or idiom?

3.4 **Intercultural Communication: Studying Cultures** Choose a specific country, such as India, Portugal, Bolivia, Thailand, or Nigeria, with which you are not familiar. Research the culture and write a brief summary of what a U.S. manager would need to know about concepts of personal space and rules of social behavior in order to conduct business successfully in that country.

3.5 **Multicultural Workforce: Bridging Differences** Differences in gender, age, and physical abilities contribute to the diversity of today's workforce. Working with a classmate, role-play a conversation in which

a. A woman is being interviewed for a job by a male personnel manager
b. An older person is being interviewed for a job by a younger personnel manager
c. A person using a wheelchair is being interviewed for a job by a person who can walk

How did differences between the applicant and the interviewer shape the communication? What can you do to improve communication in such situations?

3.6 **Intercultural Sensitivity: Understanding Attitudes** As the director of marketing for a telecommunications firm based in Germany, you're negotiating with an official in

Guangzhou, China, who's in charge of selecting a new telephone system for the city. You insist that the specifications be spelled out in detail in the contract. However, your Chinese counterpart argues that in developing a long-term business relationship, such minor details are unimportant. What can you do or say to break this intercultural deadlock and obtain the contract so that both parties are comfortable?

3.7 **Culture and Language: Understanding Differences** Germany is a low-context culture; by comparison, France and England are high-context cultures. These three translations of the same message were posted on a lawn in Switzerland: The German sign read, "Walking on the grass is forbidden"; the English sign read, "Please do not walk on the grass"; and the French sign read, "Those who respect their environment will avoid walking on the grass."[48] How does the language of each sign reflect the way information is conveyed in the cultural context of each nation? Write a brief (two- to three-paragraph) explanation.

3.8 **Culture and Time: Dealing with Differences** When a company knows that a scheduled delivery time given by an overseas firm is likely to be flexible, managers may buy in larger quantities or may order more often to avoid running out of product before the next delivery. Identify three other management decisions that may be influenced by differing cultural concepts of time, and make notes for a short (two-minute) presentation to your class.

3.9 **Intercultural Communication: Using Translators** Imagine that you're the lead negotiator for a company that's trying to buy a factory in Prague, capital of the Czech Republic. Your parents grew up near Prague, so you understand and speak the language fairly well. However, you wonder about the advantages and disadvantages of using a translator anyway. For example, you may have more time to think if you wait for an intermediary to translate the other side's position. Decide whether to hire a translator, and then write a brief (two- or three-paragraph) explanation of your decision.

3.10 **Internet** Some companies are experimenting with software that automatically translates business messages. To see how this works, go to the AltaVista site at www.altavista.com. Click on "translate" and enter a sentence such as "We are enclosing a purchase order for four dozen computer monitors." Select "English to Spanish" and click to complete the translation. Once you've read the Spanish version, cut and paste it into the "text for translation" box, select "Spanish to English," and click to translate. Try translating the same English sentence into German, French, or Italian and then back into English. How do the results of each translation differ? What are the implications for the use of automated translation services and back-translation? How could you use this website to sharpen your intercultural communication skills?

3.11 **Intercultural Communication: Improving Skills** You've been assigned to host a group of Swedish college students who are visiting your college for the next two weeks. They've all studied English but this is their first trip to your area. Make a list of at least eight slang terms and idioms they are likely to hear on campus. How will you explain each phrase? When speaking with the Swedish students, what word or words might you substitute for each slang term or idiom?

EXPAND YOUR KNOWLEDGE

Exploring the Best of the Web:

Improve Your Cultural Savvy, p. 64

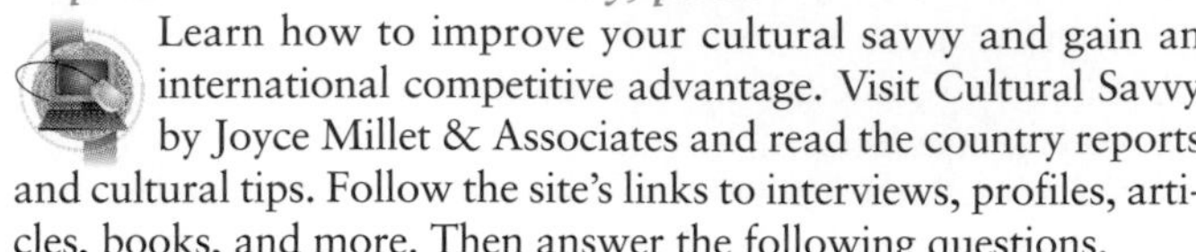

Learn how to improve your cultural savvy and gain an international competitive advantage. Visit Cultural Savvy by Joyce Millet & Associates and read the country reports and cultural tips. Follow the site's links to interviews, profiles, articles, books, and more. Then answer the following questions.

1. Why should you avoid humor when communicating with people of a different culture?
2. Every culture has its own business protocol. What should you know about a culture's business protocol before you transact business with that culture?
3. What are some examples of cultural gift-giving taboos?

Exploring the Web on Your Own

Review these chapter-related websites on your own to learn more about intercultural communication.

1. Country Commercial Guides, at www.usatradc.gov, contains helpful information on foreign marketing practices, trade regulations, investment climate, and business travel for a number of countries.
2. Window on the World, http://windowontheworldinc.com, has many tips on conducting business around the world, including resourceful country profiles.
3. Travlang, www3.travlang.com, can help you learn a foreign language. Check out the site's translating dictionaries and learn a new word in a foreign language every day.

LEARN INTERACTIVELY

Interactive Study Guide

Visit "My Companion Website" at www.prenhall.com/bovee. For Chapter 3, take advantage of the interactive "Study Guide" to test your chapter knowledge. Get instant feedback on whether you need additional studying. Read the "Current Events" articles to get the latest on chapter topics, and complete the exercises as specified by your instructor.

This site's "Study Hall" helps you succeed in this course. "Talk in the Hall" lets you leave messages and meet new friends online. If you have a question, you can "Ask the Tutor." And to get a better grade in this course, you can find more help at "Writing Skills," "Study Skills," and "Study Tips."

Grammar Diagnostic Tests

Review and reinforce your grammar and language skills by taking one of the four online diagnostic tests offered at our companion website, www.prenhall/bovee.com. The four tests cover a variety of topics, including spelling, capitals, punctuation, verbs, pronouns, adjectives, adverbs, sentence structure, sentence punctuation, clarity, word choice, style, organization skills, proofreading, and more. Submit your test and assess your competency. Then focus on improving areas where you are weak as you complete the exercises in this chapter.

PART 2

Applying the Three-Step Writing Process

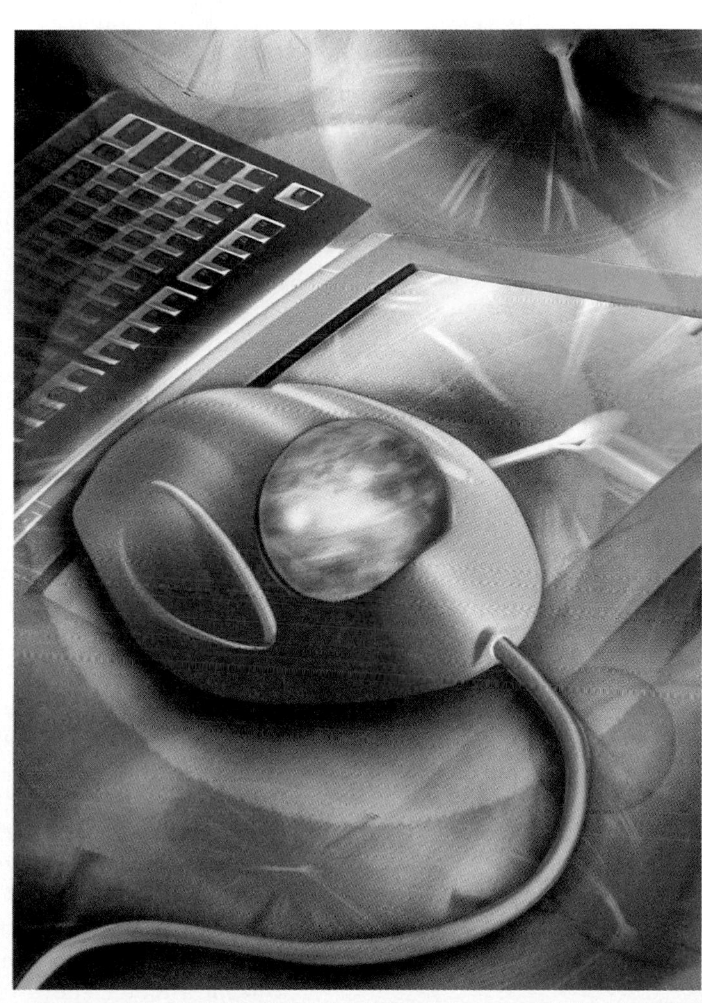

CHAPTER 4
Planning Business Messages

CHAPTER 5
Writing Business Messages

CHAPTER 6
Completing Business Messages

COMPONENT CHAPTER A
Writing for the Web

Planning Business Messages

After studying this chapter, you will be able to

1 *Describe the three-step writing process*

2 *Explain why it's important to define your purpose carefully and then list four questions that can help you test that purpose*

3 *Justify the importance of analyzing your audience, and then list six ways of developing an audience profile*

4 *Name five ways to satisfy your audience's information needs*

5 *List factors to consider when choosing the most appropriate channel and medium for your message*

6 *Discuss six ways you can establish a good relationship with your audience*

COMMUNICATION CLOSE-UP AT HOME DEPOT

www.homedepot.com

Whether you need a few tips on installing curtain rods or some expert guidance on kitchen remodeling, Home Depot wants to lend a helping hand. Since launching Home Depot in 1979, co-founders Bernie Marcus and Arthur Blank have worked hard to create a retail culture that encourages homeowners to tackle their own home improvement and repair projects without hiring contractors. Together, they have opened more than 900 stores throughout the United States, Canada, Puerto Rico, and Chile. And plans exist to open 900 more, doubling the size of Home Depot in the near future.

But Home Depot's future success depends on management's ability to communicate effectively with employees, customers, and suppliers. To keep operations running smoothly, managers need to establish good working relationships with all three audiences. They must find out what each audience needs to know, and they must determine the right way to communicate that information. For example, before Home Depot can stock a new product, managers must analyze the needs of their audiences and plan appropriate messages for each one. They must assess customer demand, educate employees about product use, and seek vendors that can deliver the right amount of merchandise in a timely manner.

Gathering this kind of information wasn't as difficult when Marcus and Blank opened their first four stores in Atlanta. Working in the stores, the two co-founders communicated with customers face-to-face, helping them find the right tools and supplies for their projects, and they personally trained every employee. But today Home Depot stocks 40,000 to 50,000 products in each store. So the company must establish relationships with 200,000 employees, 25,000 suppliers, and millions of customers, which means managers can no longer rely on communicating face-to-face with their various audiences. Instead they must select the right channel and medium for each message they send.

For instance, the company uses a variety of media to educate their customers about various repair techniques. They invite customers to attend small-group in-store meetings, known as "how-to clinics," where live presentations demonstrate repair techniques and product installations. They also distribute free product literature, installation instructions, and informational brochures throughout the stores. Plus they offer a toll-free customer service number, staffed by home improvement experts and company managers who answer questions and handle customer complaints immediately. Customers can also review how-to articles either in Home Depot's magazine, *Weekend,* or on a Home Depot CD-ROM. Home Depot's television program, *House Smart,* is a regular feature on the Discovery Channel, showing viewers how to handle home improvement projects and problems.

Home Depot uses a different approach with its 25,000 North American suppliers. Twice each year, the company sponsors weeklong vendor conferences, holding the events in large arenas throughout the country. During these conferences, managers interact in small groups to become better acquainted with new suppliers and to learn about new product offerings from current suppliers. They also make presentations to large audiences, informing suppliers about which products customers want, which ones aren't selling, and which need to be changed or dropped.

As the world's largest home improvement retailer, Home Depot keeps its operations running smoothly by carefully planning its communications and adapting its messages to meet the needs of its customers, suppliers, and employees.

Regardless of how Home Depot communicates with customers and suppliers, the company understands that each channel and medium has its advantages and disadvantages. The important thing is to find out what the audience wants to know and then select the best way to deliver that information.[1] ■

UNDERSTANDING THE THREE-STEP WRITING PROCESS

Like Home Depot's managers, you'll face a variety of communication assignments in your career, both oral and written. Some of your tasks will be routine, requiring little more than jotting down a few sentences on paper or keyboarding a brief e-mail message; others will be more complex, requiring reflection, research, and careful document preparation. Because your audience is exposed to an increasing number of business messages each day, your messages must be livelier, easier to read, more concise, and more interesting than ever before.

To compete for attention, business messages must be purposeful, audience-centered, and concise.

Of course, making your business messages interesting doesn't mean using the dramatic techniques of creative writing. Your purpose is not to dazzle your readers with your extensive knowledge or powerful vocabulary. Instead, your messages must be

- **Purposeful.** Business messages provide information, solve a problem, or request the resources necessary to accomplish a goal. Every message you prepare will have a specific purpose.
- **Audience-centered.** Business messages help audiences understand an issue, ask them to collaborate on accomplishing a goal, or persuade them to take some action. So every message you prepare must consider the audience's background, point of view, and needs.
- **Concise.** Business messages respect everyone's time by presenting information clearly and efficiently. Every message you prepare will be as short as it can be without detracting from the subject.

The goal of effective business writing is to express your ideas rather than to impress your audience. One of the best ways to do so is to follow a systematic writing process.

What Is the Three-Step Process?

Learning Objective 1

Describe the three-step writing process

The specific actions you take to write business messages will vary with each situation, audience, and purpose. However, following a process of generalized steps will help you write more effective messages. As Figure 4.1 shows, this **writing process** may be viewed

FIGURE 4.1 The Three-Step Writing Process

Planning

Analyze
Study your purpose, lay out your writing schedule, and then profile your audience.

Investigate
Satisfy your audience's information needs through formal and informal research methods.

Adapt
Choose the right channel and medium; then establish a good relationship with your audience.

Writing

Organize
Define your main idea, limit the scope, group your points, and choose the direct or indirect approach.

Compose
Control your style through level of formality and conversational tone. Choose your words carefully so that you can create effective sentences and paragraphs.

Completing

Revise
Evaluate content and review readability, editing, and rewriting for clarity and conciseness.

Produce
Use effective design elements and suitable delivery methods.

Proofread
Review for errors in layout, spelling, and mechanics.

as comprising three simple steps: (1) planning, (2) writing, and (3) completing your business messages.

- **Planning.** Think about the fundamentals of your message. Clarify your purpose in communicating, and analyze audience members so that you can tailor your message to their needs and expectations. Gather the information that will inform, persuade, or motivate your audience. Then adapt your message by selecting the channel and medium that suit both your needs and those of your audience's. And finally, establish a good relationship with your audience. Planning business messages is the focus of this chapter.
- **Writing.** Once you've planned your message, organize your ideas and begin composing your first draft. This is the stage when you commit your thoughts to words, create sentences and paragraphs, and select illustrations and details to support your main idea. Writing business messages is discussed in Chapter 5.
- **Completing.** After writing your first draft, step back to review the content and organization for overall style, structure, and readability. Revise and rewrite until your message comes across clearly and effectively; then edit your message for details such as grammar, punctuation, and format. Next produce your message, putting it into the form that your audience will receive. Finally, proof the final draft for typos, spelling errors, and other mechanical problems. Completing business messages is discussed in Chapter 6.

How Does the Three-Step Process Work?

Because so many of today's business messages are composed under pressure and on a schedule that is anything but realistic, allocating your time among these three steps can be a challenge. In some cases, your audience may expect you to get your message out in record time—sometimes only minutes after speaking with a client or attending a meeting. But whether you have 30 minutes or two days, try to give yourself enough time to plan, write, and complete your message.

As a general rule, try using roughly half of your time for planning—for deciding on your purpose, getting to know your audience, and immersing yourself in your subject matter. Use less than a quarter of your time for writing your document. Then use more than a quarter of your time for completing the project (so that you don't shortchange important final steps such as revising and proofing).[2]

Home Depot's managers understand that there is no right or best way to write all business messages. As you work through the writing process presented in Chapters 4,

FIGURE 4.2 The Relation Between the General Purpose of a Business Message and Communicator Control

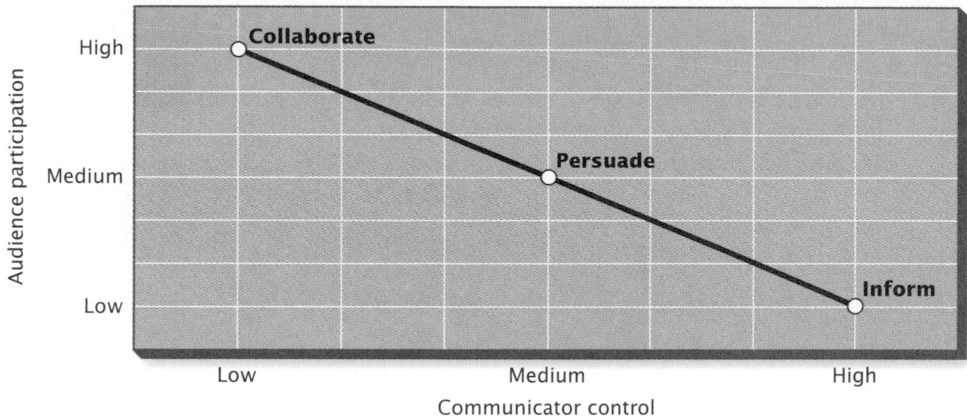

5, and 6, try not to view it as a list of how-to directives but as a way to understand the various tasks involved in effective business writing.[3] The three-step process will help you avoid the risky "rush in and start writing" routine.

ANALYZING YOUR PURPOSE AND AUDIENCE

When planning a business message, the first thing you need to think about is your purpose. For a business message to be effective, its purpose and its audience must complement each other.

Define Your Purpose

Learning Objective 2

Explain why it's important to define your purpose carefully, and list four questions that can help you test that purpose

All business messages have a **general purpose**: to inform, to persuade, or to collaborate with your audience. This overall purpose determines both the amount of audience participation you need and the amount of control you have over your message. As Figure 4.2 shows, to inform your audience, you need little interaction. Audience members absorb the information and accept or reject it, but they don't contribute to message content; you control the message. To persuade your audience, you require a moderate amount of participation, and you need to retain a moderate amount of message control. Finally, to collaborate with audience members, you need maximum participation. Your control of the message is minimal because you must adjust to new input and unexpected reactions.

Your general purpose may be to inform, to persuade, or to collaborate.

Business messages also have a **specific purpose**. That purpose may be clear and straightforward (such as placing an order or communicating survey responses), or it may be more encompassing (such as convincing management to hire more part-time employees during the holiday season). To help you define the specific purpose of your message, ask yourself what you hope to accomplish with your message and what your audience should do or think after receiving your message. For instance, is your goal simply to update your audience on an event, or do you want them to take immediate action? State your specific purpose as precisely as possible, even identifying which audience members should respond.

To determine the specific purpose, think of how the audience's ideas or behavior should be affected by the message.

You must also consider whether your purpose is worth pursuing at this time. Too many business messages serve no practical purpose, and writing useless memos can destroy your credibility. If you suspect that your ideas will have little impact, wait until you have a more practical purpose. To help you decide whether to proceed, ask yourself four questions:

Defer a message, or do not send it at all, if

- The purpose is not realistic
- The timing is not right
- You are not the right person to deliver the message
- The purpose is not acceptable to your organization

- **Is your purpose realistic?** If your purpose involves a radical shift in action or attitude, go slowly. Consider proposing the first step and using your message as the beginning of a learning process.

- **Is this the right time?** If an organization is undergoing changes of some sort, you may want to defer your message until things stabilize and people can concentrate on your ideas.
- **Is the right person delivering your message?** Even though you may have done all the work, achieving your objective is more important than taking the credit. You may want to play a supporting role in delivering your message if, for example, your boss's higher status could get better results.
- **Is your purpose acceptable to your organization?** If you receive an abusive letter that unfairly attacks your company, you might feel like firing back an angry reply. But your supervisors might prefer that you regain the customer's goodwill. Your response must reflect the organization's priorities.

Once you are satisfied that you have a legitimate purpose in communicating, you must take a good look at your intended audience.

Learning Objective 3

Justify the importance of analyzing your audience, and then list six ways of developing an audience profile

Ask yourself some key questions about your audience:

- Who are they?
- What is their probable reaction to your message?
- How much do they already know about the subject?
- What is their relationship to you?

Focus on the common interests of the audience, but be alert to their individual concerns.

Develop an Audience Profile

Who are your audience members? What are their attitudes? What do they need to know? And why should they care about your message? The answers to such questions will indicate which material you'll need to cover and how to cover it.

If you're communicating with someone you know well, perhaps your boss or a co-worker, audience analysis is relatively easy. You can predict this person's reaction pretty well, without a lot of research. On the other hand, your audience could be made up of strangers—customers or suppliers you've never met, a new boss, or new employees. So just like Home Depot's Marcus and Blank, you'll have to learn about the members of your audience before you can adjust your message to serve them (see Figure 4.3).

- **Identify the primary audience.** If you can reach the decision makers or opinion molders in your audience, other audience members will fall into place. Key people ordinarily have the most organizational clout, but occasionally a person of relatively low status may have influence in one or two particular areas.
- **Determine audience size.** A report for wide distribution requires a more formal style, organization, and format than one directed to three or four people in your department. Also, be sure to respond to the particular concerns of key individuals. The head of marketing would need different facts than the head of production or finance would need.
- **Determine audience composition.** Look for common denominators that tie audience members together across differences in culture, education, status, or attitude. Include evidence that touches on everyone's area of interest. To be understood across cultural barriers, consider how audience members think and learn, as well as what style they expect.[4]
- **Gauge your audience's level of understanding.** If audience members share your general background, they'll understand your material without difficulty. If not, you must educate them. But deciding how much information to include can be a challenge. As a guideline, include only enough information to accomplish your objective. Everything else is irrelevant and must be eliminated; otherwise it will overwhelm your audience and divert attention from the important points. If audience members do not have the same level of understanding, gear your coverage to your primary audience (the key decision makers).
- **Project your audience's expectations and preferences.** Will members of your audience expect complete details or will a summary of the main points suffice? Do they want an e-mail or will they expect a formal memo? Should the memo be short or a comprehensive 10- to 15-page report?

Nicola Shirley uses her Jamaican background and West Indian cooking talent to entice customers to eat at her restaurant or try her JaHut food products. But savory cooking is only one of her strengths. When it comes to communicating with customers, suppliers, or investors, Shirley gets results by making sure her message has a clear purpose and addresses her audience's information needs.

FIGURE 4.3 Audience Analysis Helps You Plan Your Message

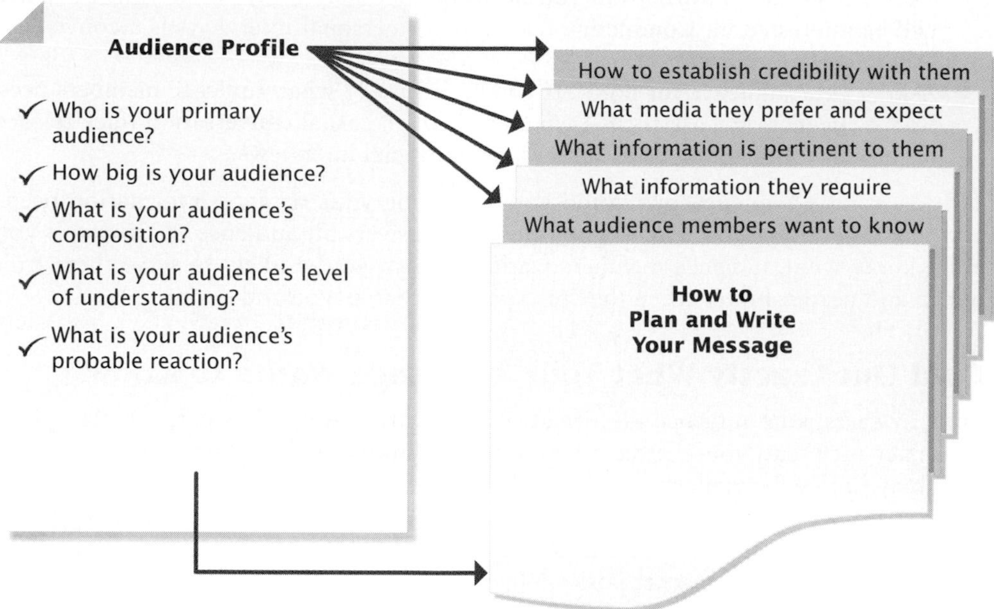

- **Estimate your audience's probable reaction.** Chapter 5 discusses how audience reaction affects message organization. If you expect a favorable response, you can state conclusions and recommendations up front and offer minimal supporting evidence. If you expect skepticism, you can introduce conclusions gradually, with more proof. By anticipating the primary audience's response to certain points, you can include evidence to address those issues.

A gradual approach and plenty of evidence are required to win over a skeptical audience.

SATISFYING YOUR AUDIENCE'S INFORMATION NEEDS

Before you compose your message, you'll most likely need to gather some information to communicate to your audience. When writing long, formal reports, you'll conduct formal research to locate and analyze all the information relevant to your purpose and your audience. Formal techniques for finding, evaluating, and processing information are discussed in Chapter 10. Other kinds of business messages, however, require less-formal information gathering.

Whether you're preparing for an informational interview with your supervisor, writing an e-mail message to a close colleague, or gathering opinions for an article to appear in your organization's monthly newsletter, you can gather information to satisfy your audience's needs by using these informal methods:

Gathering information from co-workers in conversations or informal interviews helps Levi Strauss editors determine how much detail about a project their audience expects in the company newsletter.

- **Considering others' viewpoints.** You might put yourself in others' positions to consider what they might be thinking, feeling, or planning.
- **Reading reports and other company documents.** Your company's files may be a rich source of the information you need for a particular memo or e-mail message. Consider company annual reports, financial statements, news releases, memos, marketing reports, and customer surveys for helpful information.

- **Chatting with supervisors, colleagues, or customers.** Fellow workers and customers may have information you need, or they may know what your audience will be interested in. Conducting telephone or personal interviews is a convenient way to gather information.
- **Asking your audience for input.** If you're unsure of what audience members need from your message, ask them—whether through casual conversation (face-to-face or over the phone), informal surveys, or unofficial interviews.

Learning Objective 4

Name five ways to satisfy your audience's information needs

The key to effective communication is determining your reader's information needs and then responding to them. A good message answers all audience questions. If you don't know what audience members want to know, you're likely to serve them fruit punch and peanut butter when they're expecting champagne and caviar.

Find Out Exactly What Your Audience Wants to Know

By restating a vague request in more specific terms, you can get the requester to define his or her needs more precisely.

In many cases your audience's information needs are readily apparent; for example, a consumer may send you a letter asking a specific question. In other cases, your audience may not be particularly good at telling you what's needed. When your audience makes a vague request, try restating the request in more specific terms. If your boss says, "Find out everything you can about Polaroid," you might respond, "You want me to track down their market position by product line and get sales and profit figures by division for the past five years, right?" Another way to handle a vague request is to get a fix on its priority. You might ask, "Should I drop everything else and devote myself to this for the next week?" Asking a question or two forces the person to think through the request and define more precisely what is required.

Include any additional information that might be helpful, even though the requester didn't specifically ask for it.

Also, try to think of information needs that your audience may not even be aware of. Suppose your company has just hired a new employee from out of town, and you've been assigned to coordinate this person's relocation. At a minimum, you would write a welcoming letter describing your company's procedures for relocating employees. With a little extra thought, however, you might include some information about the city: perhaps a guide to residential areas, a map or two, brochures about cultural activities, or information on schools and transportation facilities. In some cases, you may be able to tell your audience something they consider important but wouldn't have thought to ask. Although adding information of this sort lengthens your message, doing so creates goodwill.

Provide All Required Information

Test the completeness of your document by making sure it answers all the important questions: who, what, when, where, why, and how.

Once you've defined your audience's information needs, be sure you satisfy those needs completely. One good way to test the thoroughness of your message is to use the **journalistic approach**: Check to see whether your message answers *who, what, when, where, why,* and *how*. Many messages fail to pass the test—such as this letter requesting information from a large hotel:

Dear Ms. Hill:

I just got back from a great vacation in Hawaii. However, this morning I discovered that my favorite black leather shoes are missing. Since I wore them in Hawaii, I assume I left them at the Hawaii Sands Hotel. Please check the items in your "lost and found" and let me know whether you have the missing shoes.

The letter fails to tell Hill everything she needs to know. The *what* could be improved by a detailed description of the missing shoes (size, brand, distinguishable style or trim). Hill doesn't know *when* the writer stayed at the Hawaii Sands, *where* (in what room) the writer stayed, or *how* to return the shoes. Hill will have to write or call the writer to get the missing details, and the inconvenience may be just enough to prevent her from complying with the request.

Be Sure the Information Is Accurate

There's no point in answering all your audience's questions if the answers are wrong. Your organization is legally bound by any promises you make, so be sure your company is able to follow through. Whether you're promising delivery by a given date or agreeing to purchase an item, if you have any doubt about the organization's ability or willingness to back up your promises, check with the appropriate people *before* you make the commitment.

Be certain that the information you provide is accurate and that the commitments you make can be kept.

You can minimize mistakes by double-checking everything you write or say. If you are using outside sources, ask yourself whether they are current and reliable. If your sources are international, remember that various cultures can view accuracy differently. A German bank may insist on balancing the books to the last penny, whereas an Italian bank may be more lenient.[5] Be sure to review any mathematical or financial calculations. Check all dates and schedules, and examine your own assumptions and conclusions to be certain they are valid.

Double-check everything.

Be Sure the Information is Ethical

Honest mistakes are certainly possible. You may sincerely believe that you have answered someone's questions correctly and then later realize that your information was incorrect. If that happens, the most ethical thing for you to do is to contact the person immediately and correct the error. Most people will respect you for your honesty.

Messages can be unethical simply because information is omitted. Of course, as a business professional, you may have legal or other sound business reasons for not including every detail about every matter. So just how much detail should you include? Even though most people don't want to be buried in an avalanche of paperwork, include enough detail to avoid misleading your audience. If you're unsure about how much information your audience needs, offer as much as you believe best fits your definition of complete, and then offer to provide more upon request.

Good ethics will help you determine how much detail to include in your message.

Be Sure the Information is Pertinent

When deciding how to respond to your audience's information needs, remember that some points will be of greater interest and importance than others. If you're summarizing a recent conversation you had with one of your company's oldest and best customers, the emphasis you give each point of the conversation will depend on your audience's concerns. The head of engineering might be most interested in the customer's reaction to your product's new design features. The shipping manager might be most concerned about the customer's comments on recent delivery schedules. In other words, you must choose and emphasize the points that will have the most impact on your audience.

Try to figure out what points will especially interest your audience; then give those points the most attention.

If you don't know your audience, or if you're communicating with a large group of people, use your common sense to identify points of particular interest. Audience factors such as age, job, location, income, and education can give you a clue. If you're trying to sell memberships in the Book-of-the-Month Club, you would adjust your message for college students, suburban homemakers, retired people, traveling sales representatives, and auto mechanics. All these people would need to know the same facts about membership, but each group would be more interested in some facts than in others. Economy might be important to college students or retired people, and convenience might attract sales reps or homemakers. As Figure 4.4 shows, your main goal is to tell audience members what they need to know.

Your knowledge of your audience members can help you figure out what will most interest them.

ADAPTING YOUR MESSAGE TO SERVE YOUR AUDIENCE AND PURPOSE

By now you know why you're writing, you know the audience you're writing to, and you have most of the information you need. But before actually beginning to write your message, you need to figure out how to make it serve both your audience and your purpose. To adapt your message, you may need to decide matters as detailed as whether to

FIGURE 4.4 In-Depth Critique: An Audience-Centered Letter

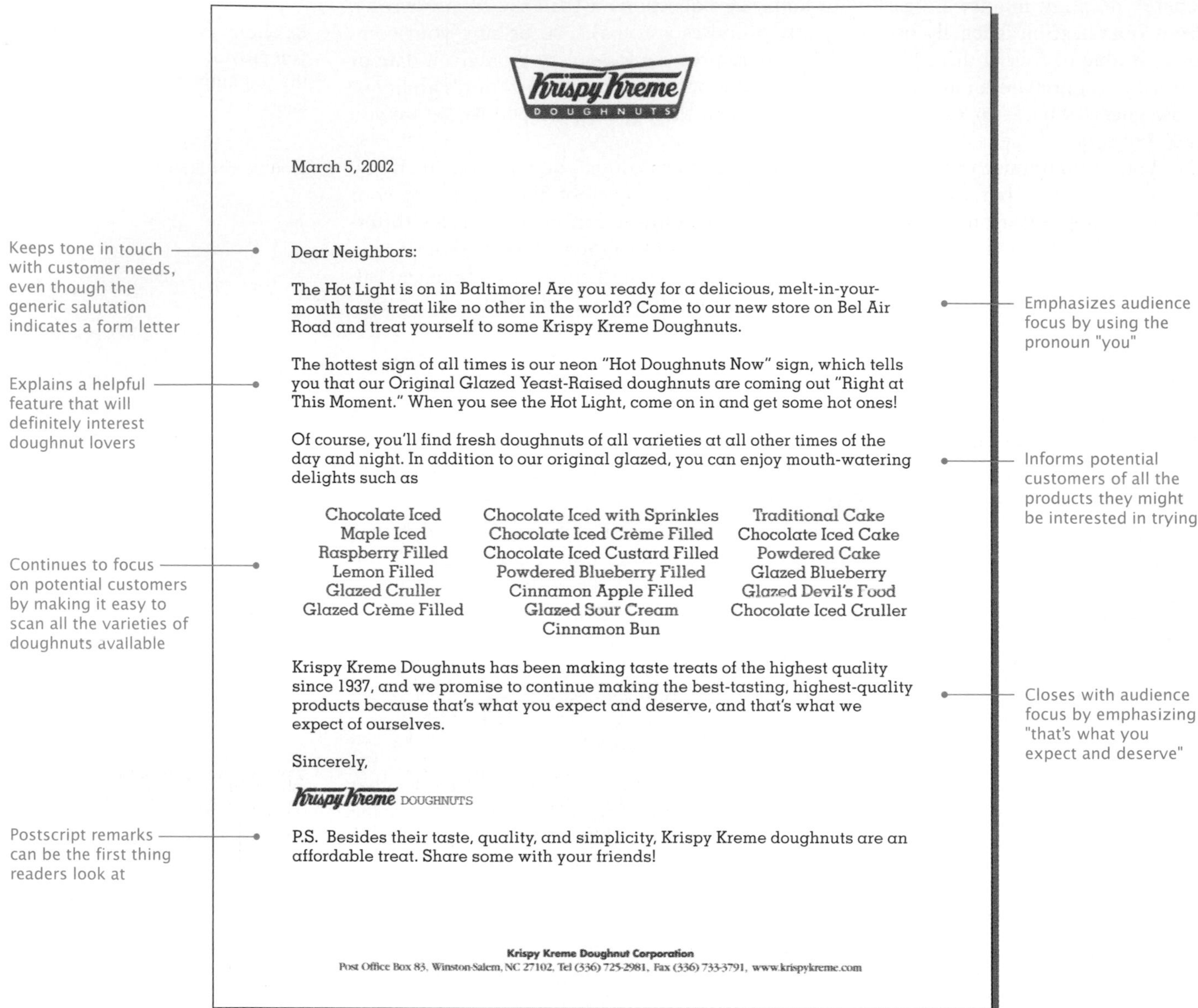

include a date on your website materials. Mainly, you need to select a channel and a medium that fit your purpose and satisfy your audience's expectations. In addition, you need to make plans for establishing a good relationship with your audience.

Select the Appropriate Channel and Medium

Learning Objective 5

List factors to consider when choosing the most appropriate channel and medium for your message

Different types of messages require different communication channels and media.

Selecting the best channel and medium for your message can make the difference between effective and ineffective communication.[6] When selecting a channel, you must choose between the oral and the written channel, and you must consider the media within each channel. For example, the oral channel includes media such as face-to-face conversations, speeches, videotapes, voice mail, phone conversations, and so on. The written channel includes media such as letters, reports, e-mail, faxes, flyers, and so on. No matter what channel and medium you choose, do your best to match your selection to your message and your intention.

Your channel and medium choices also govern the style and tone of your message. For instance, you wouldn't write an e-mail message with the same level of formality that you would use in a letter. Thus, if your purpose were to notify employees of a new

FIGURE 4.5 Media Richness

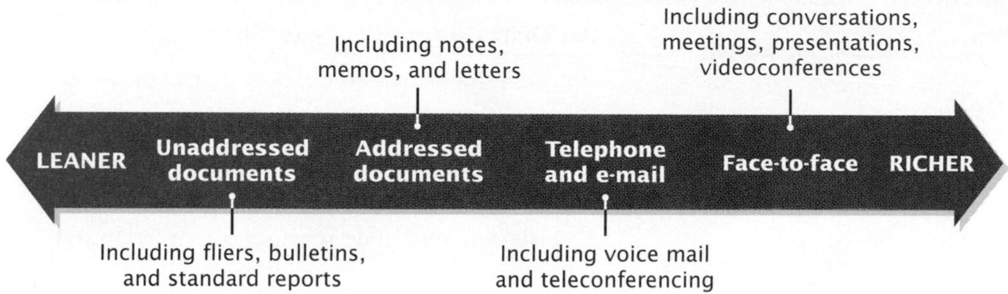

procedure, you would probably send an e-mail message rather than write a formal letter or make a lengthy face-to-face presentation. Similarly, drafting a few notes for a conversation with an employee would be less formal than drafting a letter of reprimand. So before you begin writing, make sure your channel and medium match your purpose and your audience, and then tailor your message accordingly.

Prior to writing, make sure your channel and medium match your purpose and your audience.

Media richness is the value of a medium in a given communication situation. Richness is determined by a medium's ability to

- Convey a message by means of more than one informational cue (visual, verbal, vocal)
- Facilitate feedback
- Establish personal focus

Face-to-face communication is the richest medium because it is personal, it provides both immediate verbal and nonverbal feedback, and it conveys the emotion behind the message. But it's also one of the most restrictive media because you and your audience must be in the same place at the same time.[7] Unaddressed documents, such as fliers, are the leanest media. Choose the richest media for nonroutine, complex messages (see Figure 4.5). Use rich media to extend and humanize your presence throughout the organization, to communicate caring to employees, and to gain employee commitment to organizational goals. Home Depot uses satellite video broadcasts to educate employees and to introduce new hires to the company's culture. Use leaner media to communicate simple, routine messages.

The more complicated the message, the richer the medium required.

Keep in mind that every medium has limitations that filter out parts of the message. For example, fliers may be ineffective for communicating complex messages, but they're perfect for simple ones. Moreover, every medium influences your audience's perception of your intentions. If you want to emphasize the formality of your message, use a more formal medium, such as a memo or a letter. If you want to emphasize the confidentiality of your message, use voice mail rather than a fax, send a letter rather than a memo, or address the matter in a private conversation rather than during a meeting. If you want to instill an emotional commitment to corporate values, consider a visual medium (videotape or videoconference). If you require immediate feedback, face-to-face conversation is your best choice.[8] However, if you'll need a written record, you'll probably want to write a memo or a letter.

Your intentions heavily influence your choice of medium.

Time is another factor to consider when selecting a medium. If your message is urgent, you'll probably choose the phone, fax, or next-day mail. You'll also need to consider cost. For instance, you wouldn't think twice about telephoning an important customer overseas if you just discovered your company had erroneously sent the customer the wrong shipment, but you'd probably choose to fax or e-mail a routine order acknowledgment to your customer in Australia.

Time and cost also affect medium selection.

Finally, you'll need to consider which media your audience expects or prefers.[9] What would you think if your college tried to deliver your diploma by fax? It would seem a bit strange, wouldn't it? You'd expect the college to hand it to you at graduation or mail it to you. In addition, some cultures tend to favor one channel over another. For example, the United States, Canada, and Germany emphasize written

When choosing the appropriate medium, don't forget to consider your audience's expectations.

TABLE 4.1 Choosing the Most Appropriate Channel and Medium

A Written Channel Is Best When	*An Oral Channel Is Best When*
You need no immediate feedback	You want immediate feedback from the audience
Your message is detailed and complex, and it requires careful planning	Your message is relatively simple and easy to accept
You need a permanent, verifiable record	You need no permanent record
Your audience is large and geographically dispersed	You can assemble your audience conveniently and economically
You want to minimize the distortion that can occur when a message passes orally from person to person	You want to encourage interaction to solve a problem or reach a decision
Written Media Include	***Oral Media Include***
• Letters and memos • Reports and proposals • Electronic mail • Faxes	• Face-to-face conversation, speeches, meetings • Telephone and voice mail • Audiotape and videotape • Teleconferences and videoconferences

messages, whereas Japan emphasizes oral messages—perhaps because its high-context culture carries so much of the message in nonverbal cues and "between the lines" interpretation.[10]

Oral Media

Primary oral communication media include face-to-face conversations, telephone calls, speeches, presentations, and meetings. Your choice between a face-to-face conversation and a telephone call would depend on audience location, message importance, and your need for the sort of nonverbal feedback that only body language can reveal.

In general, use an oral channel if your purpose is to collaborate with the audience.

The chief advantage of oral communication is the opportunity it provides for immediate feedback. This is the channel to use when you want the audience to ask questions and make comments or when you're trying to reach a group decision. It's also the best channel if your message has an emotional component and you want to read the audience's body language or hear the tone of their response (see Table 4.1).[11]

Written Media

A written channel increases the sender's control but eliminates the possibility of immediate feedback.

Written messages take many forms. At one end are the scribbled notes people use to jog their own memories; at the other are elaborate, formal reports that rival magazines in graphic quality. Regardless of the form, written messages have one big advantage: They let you plan and control the message. A written format is appropriate when the information is complex, when a permanent record is needed for future reference, when the audience is large and geographically dispersed, and when immediate interaction with the audience is either unimportant or undesirable.

Although many types of written communication are specialized, the most common are letters, memos, and reports. Appendix I discusses accepted formats for business documents.

Letters and memos are organized according to their purpose; the relationship between writer and reader dictates their style and tone.

Letters and Memos Most letters and memos are relatively brief documents, generally one or two pages. Memos are the workhorses of business communication, used for the routine, day-to-day exchange of information within an organization. In general, memos lack a salutation. They use "To," "From," "Date," and "Subject" headings to emphasize the needs of readers who usually have time only to skim messages. Good memos discuss only one topic, and their tone is conversational. Because of their open construction and informal method of delivery (e-mail or interoffice mail), memos are less private than letters.

Letters frequently go to outsiders, and they perform an important public relations function in addition to conveying a particular message. Many organizations rely on form letters (and sometimes form memos) to save time and money on routine communication. Form letters are particularly handy for such one-time mass mailings as sales messages about products, explanations of policies and procedures, information about organizational activities, goodwill messages such as seasonal greetings, and acknowledgments of job applications.

Letters to outsiders perform an important public relations function.

Both letters and memos can be classified by function into three categories: (1) routine, good-news, and goodwill messages; (2) bad-news messages; and (3) persuasive messages. Chapters 7–9 elaborate on the function and nature of each of these message types.

Reports and Proposals Reports and proposals are factual, objective documents that may be distributed to insiders or outsiders, depending on their purpose and subject. They come in many formats, including preprinted forms, letters, memos, and manuscripts. In length, they range from a few to several hundred pages, and they are generally more formal in tone than a typical business letter or memo. Chapters 12–14 discuss reports and proposals in detail.

Reports are generally longer and more formal than letters and memos, and they have more components.

Electronic Media

The availability of a variety of electronic media increases your options as a communicator. In addition to the traditional forms of oral communication, oral media also include electronic forms such as voice mail, audiotape and videotape, teleconferencing and videoconferencing, closed-circuit television, instant messaging, and many more. Written media also include such electronic forms as e-mail, faxing, computer conferencing (with groupware), websites, and more.

The trick is to pick the tool that does the best overall job in each situation. Electronic media are useful when you need speed, when you're physically separated from your audience, when time zones differ, when you must reach a dispersed audience personally, and when you're unconcerned about confidentiality. Although no hard rules dictate which tool to use in each case, here are a few pointers that will help you determine when to select electronic over more traditional forms:[12]

In general, use electronic forms of communication for speed, to overcome time-zone barriers, and to reach a widely dispersed audience personally.

- **Voice mail** can be used to replace short memos and phone calls that need no response. It is most effective for short, unambiguous messages. It solves time-zone difficulties and reduces a substantial amount of interoffice paperwork.[13] Voice mail is a powerful tool when you need to communicate your emotion or tone. It is especially useful for goodwill and other positive messages.
- **Teleconferencing** is best for informational meetings, although ineffective for negotiation. It's an efficient alternative to a face-to-face meeting, but it discourages the "secondary" conversations that occur during a meeting of more than four or five people—which helps participants focus on a topic but prevents them from sharing valuable information.
- **Videotape** is often effective for getting a motivational message out to a large number of people. By communicating nonverbal cues, it can strengthen the sender's image of sincerity and trustworthiness; however, it offers no opportunity for immediate feedback.
- **Computer conferencing** allows users to meet and collaborate in real time while viewing and sharing documents electronically. It offers democracy because more attention is focused on ideas than on who communicates them. But overemphasizing a message (to the neglect of the person communicating it) can threaten corporate culture, which needs a richer medium.
- **Faxing** can be used to overcome time-zone barriers when a hard copy is required. It has all the characteristics of a written message, except that (1) it may lack the privacy of a letter, and (2) the message may appear less crisp, even less professional, depending on the quality of the audience's machine.
- **E-mail** offers speed, low cost, increased access to other employees, portability, and convenience (not just overcoming time-zone problems but carrying a message

FIGURE 4.6 In-Depth Critique: A Brief E-Mail Message Conveying Time-Sensitive Material

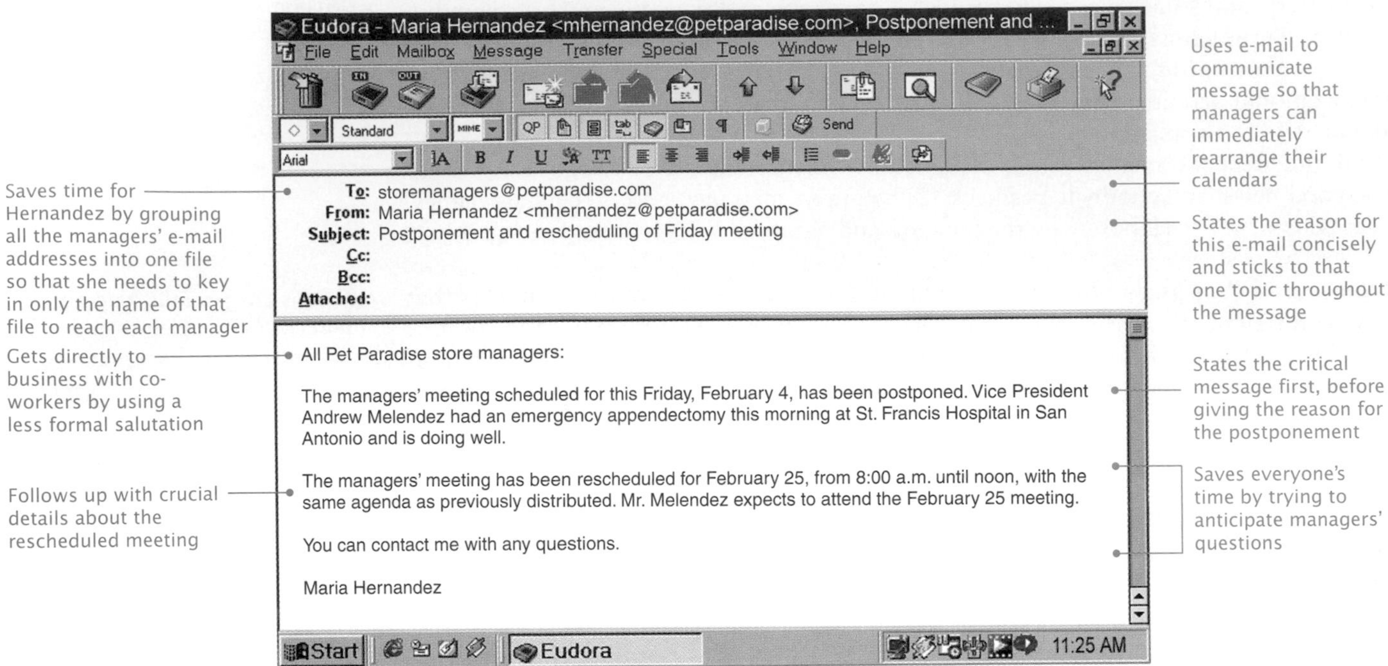

to many receivers at once). It's best for communicating brief, noncomplex information that is time sensitive, but its effectiveness depends on user skill (see Figure 4.6). Because the turnaround time can be quite fast, e-mail tends to be more conversational than traditional paper-based media.

- **Instant messaging** (IM) allows people to carry on real-time, one-on-one, and small-group text conversations. More versatile than a phone call and quicker than e-mail, IM is becoming a valuable business tool. You can send your boss a text message that is immediately displayed on her or his computer screen, and you can have your response within seconds. Similarly, co-workers in different branch offices can use IM to exchange documents or hold a virtual meeting online in a private chat area. Because messages generated via instant messaging aren't recorded or saved, they don't clog the company's network system, and they don't create a permanent record.[14]
- **Websites** offer interactive communication through hyperlinks, allowing readers to absorb information nonsequentially: They can take what they need and skip everything else. A website can tailor the same information for numerous readers by breaking up the information into linked pages. Writing for the web can be a specialized skill (see Component Chapter A).

Best of the Web

Learn How Instant Messaging Works

No doubt the Internet has changed the way we communicate. But do you understand how all this electronic stuff works? Fret no more. Log on to Marshall Brain's How Stuff Works website and learn all about instant messaging and why the future of this form of communication is bright indeed. In fact, try using it next time you want to hold a virtual conference or collaborate on a project with teammates. You'll see why instant messaging is becoming a valuable tool in the workplace.

www.howstuffworks.com/instant-messaging.htm

Even though electronic messages offer innumerable advantages, they aren't problem-free. Consider e-mail, for example. People sometimes include things in e-mail messages that they wouldn't dream of saying in person or typing in a document. So although this new openness can help companies get input from a wider variety of people, it can also create tension and interpersonal conflict. Furthermore, because e-mail is so cheap and easy to send, people tend to overuse it, distributing messages more widely than necessary and contributing to the hundreds of junk-mail messages that some executives receive every day. Overusing e-mail can also overload company networks, resulting in lost messages or even system crashes.

Electronic forms also have disadvantages: Tactless remarks may cause tension, and overuse leads to information overload.

Another drawback is lack of privacy. Some people negate their own privacy by being careless about screening their electronic distribution lists and sending information to receivers who shouldn't have it or don't need it. Of course, even if your message goes only where you originally intended, any recipient can easily forward it to someone else. In addition, e-mail and voice mail can legally be monitored by employers, and both can be subpoenaed for court cases (see "Keeping Pace with Technology: Caution! E-Mail Can Bite" and Appendix IV).

Electronic forms lack privacy.

Finally, employee productivity is constantly interrupted by e-mail, voice mail, conference calls, and faxes. Chat or real-time conversation windows can pop up on computer screens and demand immediate conversation. Employees can also diminish their productivity by surfing the web and visiting non-business-related websites during working hours. In one report, 31 percent of the businesses surveyed cited financial losses from reduced employee productivity as a result of Internet misuse alone.[15]

Electronic forms can reduce productivity.

Still, the advantages of electronic media often outweigh the drawbacks, so businesses are selecting electronic forms over traditional ones more and more often (see this chapter's "Checklist: Observing High-Tech Etiquette").

Keeping Pace with Technology

Caution! E-Mail Can Bite

Gone are the days when memos were dictated, typed, revised, retyped, photocopied, and circulated by interoffice "snail" mail. Today, e-mail messages are created, sent, received, and forwarded in the blink of an eye and at the stroke of a key. But this quick and efficient method of communication can cause a great deal of trouble for companies.

One of the greatest features—and dangers—of e-mail is that people tend to treat it far more informally than other forms of business communication. They think of e-mail as casual conversation and routinely make unguarded comments. Moreover, they are led to believe that "deleting" e-mail destroys it permanently. But that's a dangerous misunderstanding of technology.

Even after you delete an e-mail message, it can still exist on the system's hard drive and backup storage devices at both the sender's and the recipient's locations. Deleting files only signals the computer that the space required to store the message is no longer needed. The space is so marked, but the data that occupy it continue to exist until the computer overwrites the space with new data. Thus, deleted messages are recoverable—even though data recovery is an involved and expensive process—and they can be used as court evidence against you. Embarrassing e-mail has played a big role in corporate battles. In the high-profile court battle between the U.S. Justice Department and Microsoft, for instance, e-mail emerged as the star witness.

So how can companies guard against potential e-mail embarrassment and resulting litigation? Besides restricting the use of e-mail by employees, monitoring employees' e-mail, developing company e-mail policies, and reprimanding or terminating offenders, they can train employees to treat e-mail as any other form of written communication. Perhaps one of the best ways to ensure that employees' messages won't come back to haunt the company is to teach employees that e-mail messages are at least as permanent as, if not more so than, letters and memos.

Career Applications

1. Why do most people treat e-mail so casually?
2. What kinds of things should a company address in an e-mail policy?

✓ CHECKLIST: OBSERVING HIGH-TECH ETIQUETTE

A. Be clear and concise when leaving answering-machine and voice-mail messages

1. State whom you are calling, your first and last name, your company and title, the reason for your call, and your phone number (with area code and extension).
2. Be brief when stating your message, and indicate specific callback times.
3. Speak slowly.
4. Deliver bad news personally.
5. Follow up on important messages to make sure they were received.

B. Focus on your audience's needs when recording outgoing answering-machine and voice-mail messages

1. Limit menus and options.
2. Give callers an easy way to reach a live person.
3. Test your message.
4. Update greetings frequently, and change your message when going on vacation.

C. Keep your audience in mind when faxing messages

1. Fax nonpersonal messages only.
2. Use a cover sheet stating the date, number of pages, recipient's name, sender's name, and a phone number to call if there is a transmission error.
3. Sign your fax for a more personal message.
4. Call before faxing urgent messages or long documents.
5. Check your fax machine regularly to make sure it has adequate paper and cartridges.

D. Make your e-mail easy to read

1. Use the subject line of your e-mail to tell the recipient the purpose of the message.
2. Use short paragraphs.
3. Refrain from using all capital letters ("shouting").
4. Quote a previous e-mail when responding to questions or requests.
5. Don't send large files (including large attachments) without prior notice.
6. Proofread every message.

E. Use good judgment before sending or responding to e-mail messages

1. Respect other people's electronic space by sending messages only when necessary.
2. Respond to messages quickly.
3. Avoid overusing the label "urgent."
4. Be careful about using the "reply all" button.
5. Remember that e-mail isn't always private.

Establish a Good Relationship with Your Audience

Once you've chosen an appropriate channel and medium, you're still not ready to start writing yet. Effective communicators do more than convey information. They make sure that they establish a good relationship with their audience.

Learning Objective 6

Discuss six ways you can establish a good relationship with your audience

The first step toward establishing a good relationship with your audience is to think about who you are and who your audience is. Are you friends with common interests, or are you total strangers? Are you equal in status, experience, and education, or are you clearly unequal? Your answers to these questions will help you give the right impression in your message.

To establish a good relationship, be yourself.

Perhaps the most important thing you can do to establish a good relationship with your audience is to avoid trying to be someone you're not. People can spot falseness very quickly, so just be yourself and be sincere. Home Depot's managers will tell you that as in any undertaking, a good relationship is based on respect and courtesy. So when trying to establish good relationships in your business messages, remember to use the "you" attitude, emphasize the positive, establish your credibility, be polite, use bias-free language, and project the company's image.

Use the "You" Attitude

The "you" attitude is best implemented by expressing your message in terms of the audience's interests and needs.

You are already becoming familiar with the audience-centered approach, trying to see a subject through your audience's eyes. Now you want to project this approach in your messages by adopting a **"you" attitude**–that is, by speaking and writing in terms of your audience's wishes, interests, hopes, and preferences. When you talk about the other person, you're talking about the thing that most interests him or her.

On the simplest level, you can adopt the "you" attitude by replacing terms that refer to yourself and your company with terms that refer to your audience. In other words, use *you* and *yours* instead of *I, me, mine, we, us,* and *ours:*

Instead of This	Use This
To help us process this order, we must ask for another copy of the requisition.	So that your order can be filled promptly, please send another copy of the requisition.
We are pleased to announce our new flight schedule from Atlanta to New York, which is any hour on the hour.	Now you can take a plane from Atlanta to New York any hour on the hour.
We offer the printer cartridges in three colors: black, blue, and green.	Select your printer cartridge from three colors: black, blue, and green.

Too many business business messages have an "I" or "we" attitude, which sounds selfish and uninterested in the audience. The message tells what the sender wants, and the audience is expected to go along with it. However, using *you* and *yours* requires finesse. If you overdo it, you're likely to create some rather awkward sentences, and you run the risk of sounding like a high-pressure carnival barker.[16] The "you" attitude is not intended to be manipulative or insincere. It's an extension of the audience-centered approach. In fact, the best way to implement the "you" attitude is to be sincere in thinking about your audience.

The "you" attitude isn't just a matter of using one pronoun rather than another; it's a matter of genuine empathy. You can use *you* 25 times in a single page and still ignore your audience's true concerns. In other words, it's the thought and sincerity that count, not the pronoun. If you're talking to a retailer, try to think like a retailer; if you're dealing with a production supervisor, put yourself in that position; if you're writing to a dissatisfied customer, imagine how you would feel at the other end of the transaction. The important thing is your attitude toward audience members and your appreciation of their position.

In fact, on some occasions you'll do better to avoid using *you*. For instance, using *you* in a way that sounds dictatorial is impolite. Or, when someone makes a mistake, you may want to minimize ill will by pointing out the error impersonally. You might say, "We have a problem," instead of "You caused a problem."

Jenny J. Ming, president of Old Navy, oversees everything from store operations to marketing and advertising. Her passion for fashion has helped drive the company's record growth. So has her ability to communicate effectively with others. Ming recognizes that people's needs change as quickly as the latest fashion trend. So when communicating with others, she takes extra care to focus on her audience's changing needs.

Instead of This	Use This
You should never use that type of paper in the copy machine.	That type of paper doesn't work very well in the copy machine.
You must correct all five copies by noon.	All five copies must be corrected by noon.

As you practice using the "you" attitude, be sure to consider the attitudes and policies of your organization and those of other cultures. In some cultures, it is improper to single out one person's achievements because the whole team is responsible for the outcome; using the pronoun *we* or *our* is more appropriate. Similarly, some companies have a tradition of avoiding references to *you* and *I* in their memos and formal reports. If you work for a company that expects a formal, impersonal style, confine your use of personal pronouns to informal letters and memos.

Avoid using *you* and *yours* when doing so
- Makes you sound dictatorial
- Make someone else feel guilty
- Goes against your organization's style

Emphasize the Positive

Another way of establishing a good relationship with your audience is to emphasize the positive side of your message.[17] Focus on the silver lining, not on the cloud. Stress what is or will be instead of what isn't or won't be. Most information, even bad news, has some redeeming feature. If you can make your audience aware of that feature, your message will be more acceptable.

Explain what you have done, what you can do, and what you will do—not what you haven't done, can't do, or won't do.

Instead of This	Use This
It is impossible to repair your vacuum cleaner today.	Your vacuum cleaner will be ready by Tuesday.
We apologize for inconveniencing you during our remodeling.	The renovations now under way will help us serve you better.
We never exchange damaged goods.	We are happy to exchange merchandise that is returned to us in good condition.

When you are offering criticism or advice, focus on what the person can do to improve.

In addition, when you're criticizing or correcting, don't hammer on the other person's mistakes. Avoid referring to failures, problems, or shortcomings. Focus instead on what the person can do to improve:

Instead of This	Use This
The problem with this department is a failure to control costs.	The performance of this department can be improved by tightening up cost controls.
You filled out the order form wrong. We can't send you the paint until you tell us what color you want.	So that your order can be processed properly, please check your color preferences on the enclosed card.

Show your audience how they will benefit from complying with your message.

If you're trying to persuade the audience to buy a product, pay a bill, or perform a service for you, emphasize what's in it for them. Don't focus on why *you* want them to do something. An individual who sees the possibility for personal benefit is more likely to respond positively to your appeal.

Instead of Saying	Say
Please buy this book so that I can make my sales quota.	The plot of this novel will keep you in suspense to the last page.
We need your contribution to the Boys and Girls Club.	You can help a child make friends and build self-confidence through your donation to the Boys and Girls Club.

Avoid words with negative connotations; use meaningful euphemisms instead.

In general, try to state your message without using words that might hurt or offend your audience. Substitute *euphemisms* (mild terms) for those that have unpleasant connotations. You can be honest without being harsh. Gentle language won't change the facts, but it will make them more acceptable:

Instead of This	Use This
cheap merchandise	bargain prices
toilet paper	bathroom tissue
used cars	resale cars
high-calorie food	high-energy food
elderly	senior citizen
pimples and zits	complexion problems

On the other hand, don't carry euphemisms to extremes. If you're too subtle, people won't know what you're talking about. "Derecruiting" workers to the "mobility pool" instead of telling them that they have six weeks to find another job isn't really very helpful. When using euphemisms, you walk a fine line between softening the blow and hiding the facts. It would be unethical to speak to your community about relocating refuse when you're really talking about your plans for disposing of toxic waste. Such an attempt to hide the facts would very likely backfire, damaging your business image

Focusing on Ethics

Spin Cycle: Deciphering Corporate Doublespeak

If there's one product U.S. businesses can produce in large amounts, it's doublespeak. Doublespeak is language that only pretends to say something but that in reality hides, evades, or misleads. Like most products, doublespeak comes in many forms, from the popular buzzwords that everyone uses but no one really understands—such as *competitive dynamics* and *empowerment*—to words that try to hide meaning, such as *reengineering, synergy,* and *restructure.*

With doublespeak, bribes and kickbacks are called *rebates* or *fees for product testing,* used-car-parts dealers have become *auto dismantlers and recyclers,* and travel agents are called *vacation specialists, destination counselors,* or *reservation specialists.* Plus, just about everyone's job title has the word *chief* in it: Chief Nuclear Officer, Chief Learning Officer, Chief Cultural Officer, Chief Ethics Officer, Chief Turnaround Officer, and Chief Creative Officer. After all the "operations improvement" that corporations have undergone, you have to wonder who all those "chiefs" are leading. Never before have so many led so few.

With doublespeak, banks don't have *bad loans* or *bad debts*; they have *nonperforming credits* that are *rolled over* or *rescheduled.* And corporations never lose money; they just experience *negative cash flow, deficit enhancement,* or *negative contributions to profits.*

Of course, no one gets fired these days. If you're high enough in the corporate pecking order, you *resign for personal reasons.* But for those below the lofty heights of corporate power, you're *involuntarily terminated* as the result of *downsizing, workforce adjustments,* and *headcount reductions.* Some companies even *implement a skills mix adjustment* or *eliminate redundancies in the human resources area.* One automobile company (which closed an entire assembly plant and eliminated over 8,000 jobs) calls it *a volume-related production schedule adjustment.*

But don't worry, if you're *dehired, deselected, surplused,* or *uninstalled,* corporations will offer you a *career change opportunity* or *vocational relocation.* In fact, hardly anyone is laid off these days. "We don't characterize it as a layoff," said one corporate doublespeaker (sometimes called a spin doctor). "We're managing our staff resources. Sometimes you manage them up, and sometimes you manage them down."

Career Applications

1. The president of one company just learned that some of his employees have been playing a popular game called "buzzword bingo," in which participants ridicule doublespeak by tracking the jargon their bosses use during staff meetings on bingo-like cards. Some managers are complaining that it's getting out of control. In fact, as one meeting dragged on, employees tried to steer the conversation to use all the buzzwords on their cards. What can managers do to avoid these silly games?
2. Visit one of the following buzzword bingo websites and print out a card or two. Read the current business section of your favorite newspaper. How many buzzwords did you find?
   http://fooz.com/bingo
   http://funnies.paco.to/bingo
   www.esc3.net/wm/bbbingo

and reputation. In the end, people respond better to an honest message delivered with integrity than they do to sugar-coated double-talk (see "Focusing on Ethics: Spin Cycle: Deciphering Corporate Doublespeak").

Establish Your Credibility

People are more likely to react positively to your message when they have confidence in you.

If you're unknown to your audience members, you'll have to earn their confidence before you can win them to your point of view. Their belief in your competence and integrity is important. You want people to trust that your word is dependable and that you know what you're doing.

Credibility (or your believability) is based on how reliable you are and how much trust you evoke in others. If you're communicating with a familiar group, your credibility has already been established, so you can get right down to business. Of course, even in this case some audience members may have preconceptions about you and may have trouble separating your arguments from your personality or your field. If they think of you as, say, a "numbers person," they may question your competence in other areas. You can overcome these prejudices as you develop your message by providing ample evidence for any material outside your usual area of expertise.

But what if audience members are complete strangers? Or worse, what if they start off with doubts about you? In a new or hostile situation, devote the initial portion of your message to gaining credibility. First, show an understanding of your audience's situation

To enhance your credibility
- Show that you understand the other person's situation
- Explain your own credentials or ally yourself with a credible source
- Back up your claims with evidence, not exaggerations
- Use words that express confidence
- Believe in yourself and your message

by calling attention to the things you have in common. If you're communicating with someone who shares your professional background, you might say, "As a fellow engineer [lawyer, doctor, teacher, or whatever], I'm sure you can appreciate this situation." Another approach is to use technical or professional terms that identify you as a peer.

You can also gain your audience's confidence by explaining your credentials, but be careful not to sound pompous. Mentioning one or two aspects of your background is enough. Your title or the name of your organization might be enough to impress your audience with your abilities. If not, you might mention the name of someone who carries some weight with your audience. You might begin a letter with "Professor Goldberg suggested that I contact you," or you could quote a recognized authority on your subject, even if you don't know the authority personally. The fact that your ideas are shared by a credible source adds prestige to your message.

Your credibility is enhanced by the quality of the information you provide. If you support your points with evidence that can be confirmed through observation, research, experimentation, or measurement, audience members will recognize that you have the facts, and they'll respect you. On the other hand, exaggerated claims are unethical and do more harm than good. A mail-order catalog promised: "You'll be absolutely amazed at the remarkable blooms on this healthy plant. Gorgeous flowers with brilliant color and an intoxicating aroma will delight you week after week." Terms such as *amazing, incredible, extraordinary, sensational,* and *revolutionary* exceed the limits of believability, unless they're supported with some sort of proof.

You also risk losing credibility if you seem to be currying favor with insincere compliments. So support compliments with specific points:

Instead of This	Use This
My deepest heartfelt thanks for the excellent job you did. It's hard these days to find workers like you. You are just fantastic! I can't stress enough how happy you have made us with your outstanding performance.	Thanks for the fantastic job you did filling in for Gladys at the convention with just an hour's notice. Despite the difficult circumstances, you managed to attract several new orders with your demonstration of the new line of coffeemakers. Your dedication and sales ability are truly appreciated.

Another threat to credibility is too much modesty and not enough confidence. You express a lack of confidence when you use words such as *if, hope,* and *trust.* Try not to undermine your credibility with vague sentiments:

Instead of This	Use This
We hope this recommendation will be helpful.	We're glad to make this recommendation.
If you'd like to order, mail us the reply card.	To order, mail the reply card.
We trust that you'll extend your service contract.	By extending your service contract, you can continue to enjoy top-notch performance from your equipment.

If you lack faith in yourself, you're likely to communicate an uncertain attitude that undermines your credibility. The key to being believable is to believe in yourself. If you are convinced that your message is sound, you can state your case with authority so that your audience has no doubts.

Be Polite

Being polite is another good way to earn your audience's respect. By being courteous to members of your audience, you show consideration for their needs and feelings. Express yourself with kindness and tact.

You will undoubtedly be frustrated and exasperated by other people many times in your career. When that happens, you'll be tempted to say what you think in blunt terms. But venting your emotions rarely improves the situation and can jeopardize your audience's goodwill. Instead, be gentle when expressing yourself:

Although you may be tempted now and then to be brutally frank, try to express the facts in a kind and thoughtful manner.

Instead of This	Use This
You really fouled things up with that last computer run.	Lets go over what went wrong with the last computer run so that the next run goes smoothly.
You've been sitting on my order for two weeks, and we need it now!	We are eager to receive our order. When can we expect delivery?

Of course, some situations require more diplomacy than others. If you know your audience well, you can get away with being less formal. However, when you are communicating with people who outrank you or with people outside your organization, an added measure of courtesy is usually needed.

Use extra tact when writing and when communicating with higher-ups and outsiders.

In general, written communication requires more tact than oral communication. When you're speaking, your words are softened by your tone of voice and facial expression. Plus, you can adjust your approach according to the feedback you get. But written communication is stark and self-contained. If you hurt a person's feelings in writing, you can't soothe them right away. In fact, you may not even know that you have hurt the other person, because the lack of feedback prevents you from seeing his or her reaction. Keep these points in mind as you review Figures 4.7 and 4.8. Because of a death in the family, a restaurant owner closed his doors for three days over Labor Day weekend. Unfortunately, someone left the freezer door ajar, which burned out the motor and spoiled all the food stored there. The total cost to replace the motor and food was over $2,000. The customer requested that Eppler Appliances cover these costs, but Eppler had to refuse. Compare the two letters for diplomacy.

Another simple but effective courtesy is to be prompt in your correspondence. If possible, answer your mail within two or three days. If you need more time to prepare a reply, call or write a brief note to say that you're working on an answer. Most people are willing to wait if they know how long the wait will be. What annoys them is the suspense.

Promptness is a form of courtesy.

Use Bias-Free Language

Most of us think of ourselves as being sensitive, unbiased, ethical, and fair. But being fair and objective isn't enough; to establish a good relationship with your audience, you must also *appear* to be fair.[18] **Bias-free language** avoids unethical, embarrassing blunders in language related to gender, race, ethnicity, age, and disability. Good communicators make every effort to change biased language (see Table 4.2 on page 100).

Avoid biased language that might offend your audience.

- **Gender bias.** Avoid sexist language by using the same label for everyone (don't call a woman *chairperson* and then call a man *chairman*). Reword sentences to use *they* or to use no pronoun at all. Vary traditional patterns by sometimes putting women first (*women and men, she and he, her and his*). And finally, the preferred title for women in business is *Ms.*, unless the individual asks to be addressed as *Miss* or *Mrs.* or has some other title, such as *Dr.*

Replace words that inaccurately exclude women or men.

- **Racial and ethnic bias.** The central principle is to avoid language suggesting that members of a racial or an ethnic group have stereotypical characteristics. The best solution is to avoid identifying people by race or ethnic origin unless such a label is relevant.

Eliminate references that reinforce racial or ethnic stereotypes.

- **Age bias.** As with gender, race, and ethnic background, mention the age of a person only when it is relevant. When referring to older people, avoid such stereotyped adjectives as *spry* and *frail.*

Avoid references to an individual's age or physical limitations.

FIGURE 4.7 In-Depth Critique: Ineffective Business Communication

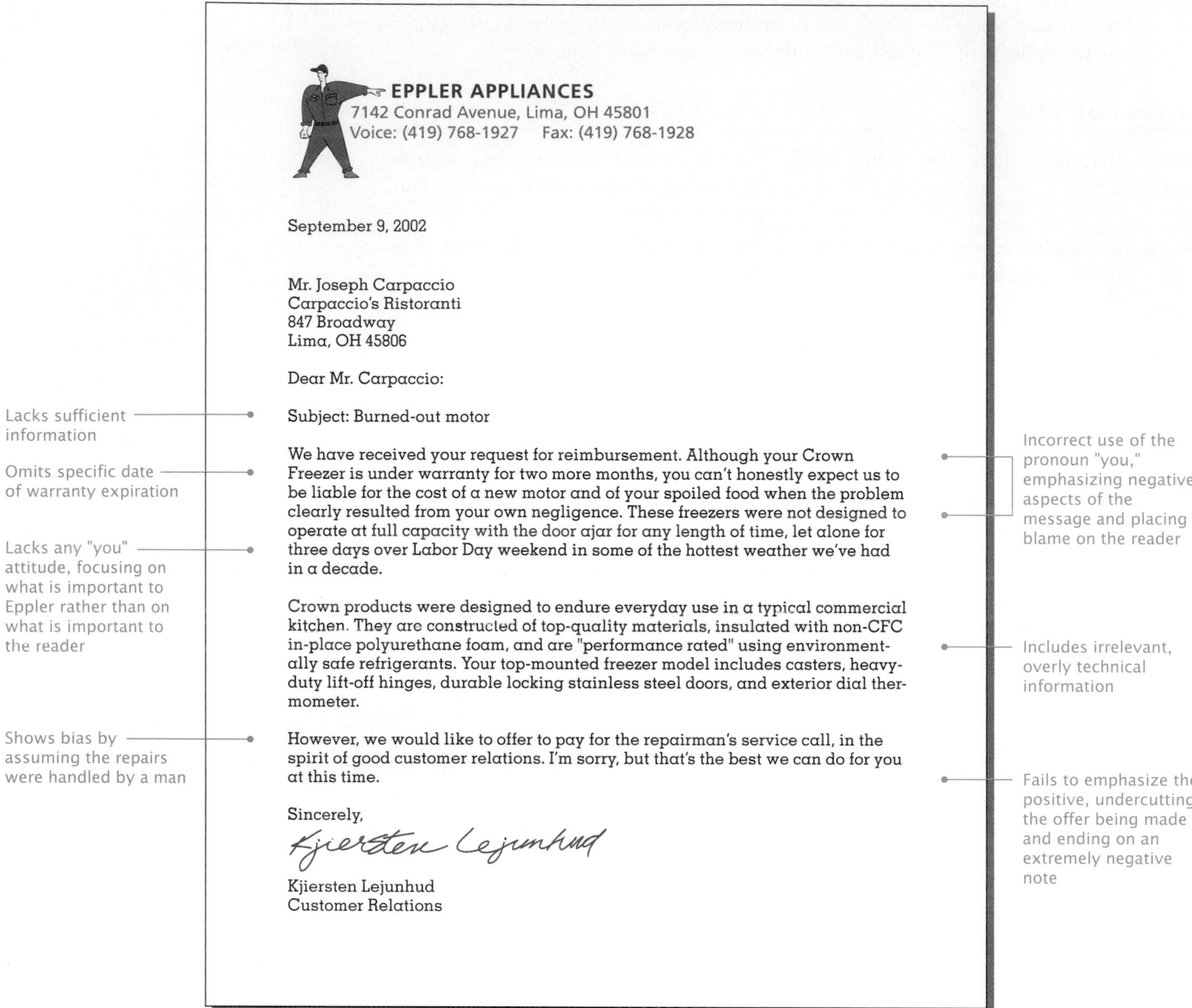

September 9, 2002

Mr. Joseph Carpaccio
Carpaccio's Ristoranti
847 Broadway
Lima, OH 45806

Dear Mr. Carpaccio:

Subject: Burned-out motor

We have received your request for reimbursement. Although your Crown Freezer is under warranty for two more months, you can't honestly expect us to be liable for the cost of a new motor and of your spoiled food when the problem clearly resulted from your own negligence. These freezers were not designed to operate at full capacity with the door ajar for any length of time, let alone for three days over Labor Day weekend in some of the hottest weather we've had in a decade.

Crown products were designed to endure everyday use in a typical commercial kitchen. They are constructed of top-quality materials, insulated with non-CFC in-place polyurethane foam, and are "performance rated" using environmentally safe refrigerants. Your top-mounted freezer model includes casters, heavy-duty lift-off hinges, durable locking stainless steel doors, and exterior dial thermometer.

However, we would like to offer to pay for the repairman's service call, in the spirit of good customer relations. I'm sorry, but that's the best we can do for you at this time.

Sincerely,

Kjiersten Lejunhud

Kjiersten Lejunhud
Customer Relations

Always refer to people first and their disabilities second.

- **Disability bias.** No painless label exists for people with a physical, mental, sensory, or emotional impairment. Avoid mentioning a disability unless it is pertinent. However, if you must refer to someone's disability, avoid terms such as *handicapped, crippled*, or *retarded*. Put the person first and the disability second.[19] Present the whole person, not just the disability, by showing the limitation in an unobtrusive manner.

Project the Company's Image

Subordinate your own style to that of the company.

Even though establishing a good relationship with the audience is your main goal, give some thought to projecting the right image for your company. When you communicate with outsiders, on even the most routine matter, you serve as the spokesperson for your organization. The impression you make can enhance or damage the reputation of the entire company. Thus, your own views and personality must be subordinated, at least to some extent, to the interests and style of your company.

Say you've just taken a job with a hip, young retail organization called Rappers. One of your first assignments is to write a letter canceling additional orders for clothing items that haven't been selling well.

FIGURE 4.8 In-Depth Critique: Effective Business Communication

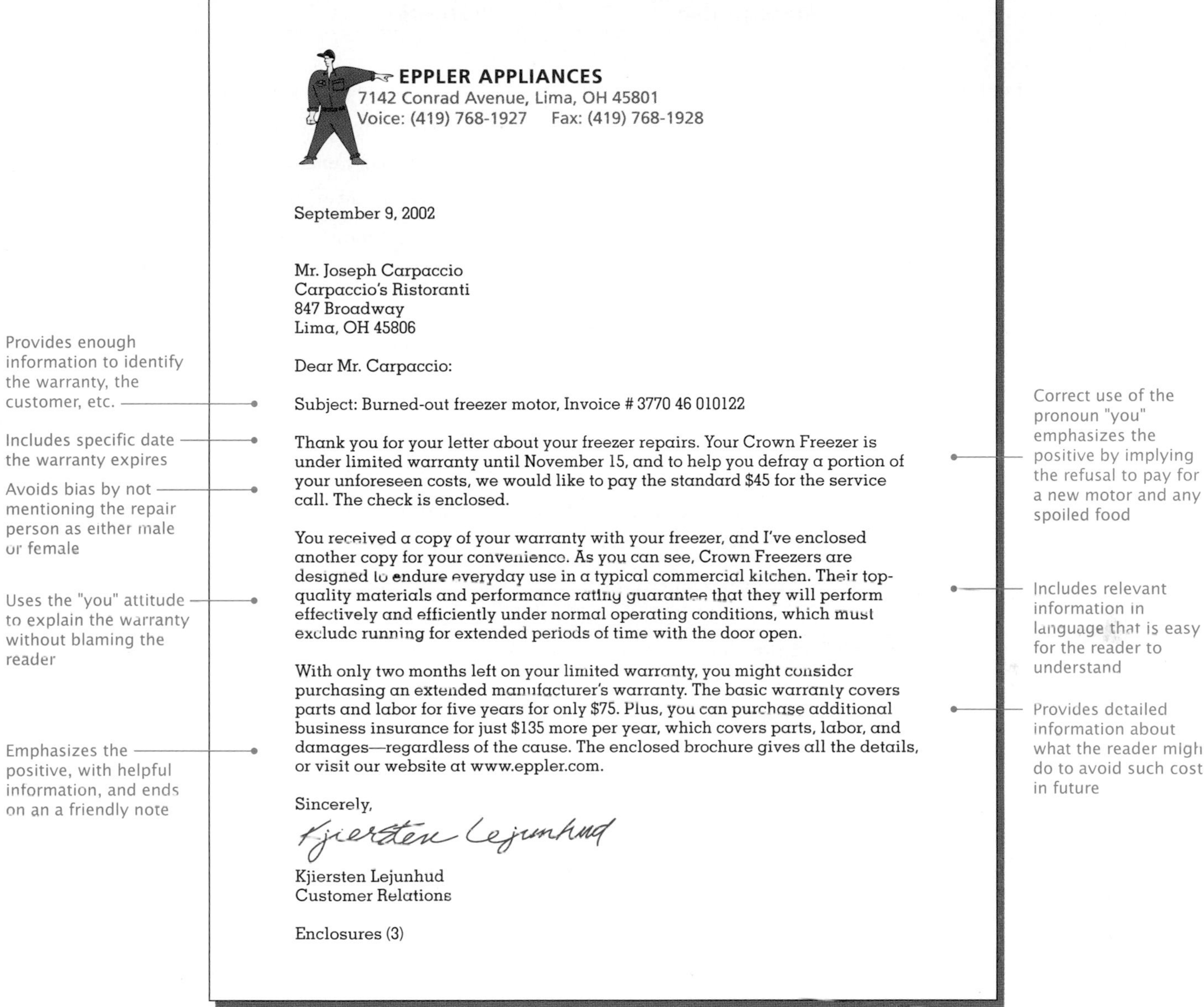

September 9, 2002

Mr. Joseph Carpaccio
Carpaccio's Ristoranti
847 Broadway
Lima, OH 45806

Dear Mr. Carpaccio:

Subject: Burned-out freezer motor, Invoice # 3770 46 010122

Thank you for your letter about your freezer repairs. Your Crown Freezer is under limited warranty until November 15, and to help you defray a portion of your unforeseen costs, we would like to pay the standard $45 for the service call. The check is enclosed.

You received a copy of your warranty with your freezer, and I've enclosed another copy for your convenience. As you can see, Crown Freezers are designed to endure everyday use in a typical commercial kitchen. Their top-quality materials and performance rating guarantee that they will perform effectively and efficiently under normal operating conditions, which must exclude running for extended periods of time with the door open.

With only two months left on your limited warranty, you might consider purchasing an extended manufacturer's warranty. The basic warranty covers parts and labor for five years for only $75. Plus, you can purchase additional business insurance for just $135 more per year, which covers parts, labor, and damages—regardless of the cause. The enclosed brochure gives all the details, or visit our website at www.eppler.com.

Sincerely,

Kjiersten Lejunhud

Kjiersten Lejunhud
Customer Relations

Enclosures (3)

Dear Ms. Bataglia:

Please cancel our purchase order 092397AA for the amount of $12,349. Our contract with your organization specifies that we have a 30-day cancellation clause, which we wish to invoke. If any shipments went out before you received this notification, they will be returned; however, we will remunerate freight charges as specified in the contract.

I am told we have ordered from you since our inception in 1993. Your previous service to us has been quite satisfactory; however, recent sales of the "Colored Denim" line have been less than forecast. We realize that our cancellation may have a negative impact, and we pledge to more accurately predict our needs in the future.

We maintain positive alliances with all our vendors and look forward to doing further business with you. Please keep us informed of new products as they appear.

TABLE 4.2 Overcoming Bias in Language

Examples	*Unacceptable*	*Preferable*
GENDER BIAS		
Using words containing "man"	Mankind	Humanity, human beings, human race, people
	Man-made	Artificial, synthetic, manufactured, constructed
	Manpower	Human power, human energy, workers, workforce
	Businessman	Executive, business manager, businessperson
	Salesman	Sales representative, salesperson, clerk, sales agent
	Foreman	Supervisor
Using female-gender words	Authoress, actress, stewardess	Author, actor, cabin attendant
Using special designations	Woman doctor, male nurse	Doctor, nurse
Using "he" to refer to "everyone"	The average worker . . . he	The average worker . . . he or she
Identifying roles with gender	The typical executive spends four hours of his day in meetings.	Most executives spend four hours a day in meetings.
	the consumer . . . she	Consumers . . . they
	the nurse/teacher . . . she	nurses/teachers . . . they
Identifying women by marital status	Phil Donahue and Marlo	Phil Donahue and Marlo Thomas
	Phil Donahue and Ms. Thomas	Mr. Donahue and Ms. Thomas
RACIAL/ETHNIC BIAS		
Assigning stereotypes	My black assistant speaks more articulately than I do.	My assistant speaks more articulately than I do.
	Jim Wong is an unusually tall Asian.	Jim Wong is tall.
Identifying people by race or ethnicity	Mario M. Cuomo, Italian American politician and ex-governor of New York	Mario M. Cuomo, politician and ex-governor of New York
AGE BIAS		
Including age when irrelevant	Mary Kirazy, 58, has just joined our trust department.	Mary Kirazy has just joined our trust department.
DISABILITY BIAS		
Putting the disability before the person	Crippled workers face many barriers on the job.	Workers with physical disabilities face many barriers on the job.
	An epileptic, Tracy has no trouble doing her job.	Tracy's epilepsy has no effect on her job performance.

After reading your draft, you realize that its formal tone may leave a feeling of ill will. Moreover, it certainly doesn't reflect the corporate culture of your new employer. You try again.

Dear Ms. Bataglia:

We appreciate the relationship we've had with you since 1993. Your shipments have always arrived on time and in good order.

However, our recent store reports show a decline in sales for your "Colored Denim" line. Therefore, we're canceling our purchase order 092397AA for $12,349. If you'll let us know the amounts, we'll pay the shipping charges on anything that has already gone out.

We're making a lot of changes at Rappers, but one thing remains the same—the positive relationship we have with vendors such as you. Please keep us informed of your new lines as they appear. We look forward to doing business with you in the future.

This version reflects the more relaxed image of your new company. You can save yourself a great deal of time and frustration if you master your company's style early in your career.

The three stages of planning help you get ready to write business messages. This chapter's "Checklist: Planning Business Messages" is a reminder of the tasks and choices you address during the planning process.

Before writing a letter or an e-mail message on behalf of your company, think about how you project the company image, says Elizabeth Taris (center), manager of consumer affairs at Sara Lee Bakery. "We want everyone to understand about the high quality and high standards at Sara Lee—that's how we made our good name, and that's how we're going to keep it."

✓ CHECKLIST: PLANNING BUSINESS MESSAGES

A. Analyze your purpose and audience

1. Determine whether the purpose of your message is to inform, persuade, or collaborate.
2. Identify the specific behavior you hope to induce in the audience.
3. Make sure that your purpose is worthwhile and realistic.
4. Make sure that the time is right for your purpose.
5. Make sure the right person is delivering your message.
6. Make sure your purpose is acceptable to your organization.
7. Identify the primary audience.
8. Determine the size of your audience.
9. Determine the composition of your audience.
10. Determine your audience's level of understanding.
11. Estimate your audience's probable reaction to your message.

B. Satisfy your audience's information needs

1. Decide whether to use formal or informal techniques for gathering information.
2. Find out what your audience wants to know.
3. Provide all required information and make sure it's accurate, ethical, and pertinent.

C. Adapt your message to serve your audience and your purpose

1. Select a channel and medium for your message by matching media richness to your audience and purpose.
2. Select the right medium for your message by considering factors such as urgency, formality, complexity, confidentiality, emotional content, cost, audience expectation, and your need for a permanent record.
3. Consider the problems as well as the advantages of using electronic forms.
4. Adopt an audience-centered approach by using the "you" attitude.
5. Emphasize the positive aspects of your message.
6. Gain audience confidence by establishing your credibility.
7. Show respect for your audience by using a polite tone.
8. Show your sensitivity and fairness by using bias-free language.
9. Project your company's image to make sure your audience understands that you are speaking for your organization.

COMMUNICATION CHALLENGES AT HOME DEPOT

You have recently joined Home Depot's community relations department in the company's Atlanta headquarters, known as the Store Support Center. Two of your major functions in this position are (1) helping store managers and other company executives plan effective business messages for a variety of audiences, and (2) responding to press inquiries about Home Depot.

Individual Challenge: You have received a phone call from Ann Mason, a reporter for an Idaho newspaper. She is planning to write an article about Home Depot's recent decision to open a store in her community, a small town in a rural area of Idaho. Mason has asked you for information about the economic impact of Home Depot stores in other small communities across the nation. When responding to Mason's request, what should the purpose of your letter be?

Team Challenge: A lightbulb manufacturer is unable to keep up with consumer demand for lightbulbs in Home Depot stores. Customers and store managers are complaining about the shortage of lightbulbs on the shelves. Home Depot's merchandising manager decides that the manufacturer must correct the supply problem within 30 days or Home Depot will have to find another, more reliable supplier that can meet the high demand. The merchandising manager asks the community relations department to suggest the best method of communicating this message to the lightbulb manufacturer. Which communication medium will your department recommend? Why? ■

SUMMARY OF LEARNING OBJECTIVES

1 **Describe the three-step writing process.** (1) Planning consists of analyzing your purpose and your audience, investigating necessary information (whether formally or informally), and adapting your message by selecting the appropriate channel and medium and by establishing a good relationship with your audience. (2) Writing consists of organizing your ideas and actually composing words, sentences, paragraphs, and visual graphics. (3) Completing your message consists of revising your message by evaluating content and then rewriting and editing for clarity, producing your message by using effective design elements and suitable delivery methods, and proofreading your message for typos and errors in spelling and mechanics.

2 **Explain why it's important to define your purpose carefully, and list four questions that can help you test that purpose.** You must know enough about the purpose of your message to shape that message in a way that will achieve your goal. To decide whether you should proceed with your message, ask four questions: (1) Is my message realistic? (2) Is my message acceptable to my organization? (3) Is my message being delivered by the right person? (4) Is my message being delivered at the right time?

3 **Justify the importance of analyzing your audience, and then list six ways of developing an audience profile.** Analyzing your audience helps you discover who the members of your audience are, what their attitudes are, what they need to know, and why they should care about your purpose in communicating. An effective profile helps you predict how your audience will react to your message. It also helps you know what to include in your message and how to include it. To develop an audience profile, you need to determine your primary audience (key decision makers), the size of your audience, the makeup of your audience, the level of your audience's understanding, your audience's expectations, and their probable reaction.

4 **Name five ways to satisfy your audience's information needs.** To satisfy your audience's information needs: find out what they want to know; provide all required information; make sure all information is accurate; communicate ethically; and emphasize ideas of greatest interest to them.

5 **List factors to consider when choosing the most appropriate channel and medium for your message.** The first factor to consider is media richness. Richness is determined by the medium's ability to (1) convey a message using more than one informational cue (visual, verbal, vocal), (2) facilitate feedback, and (3) establish personal focus. Other factors to consider when selecting media include complexity, formality, confidentiality, emotional commitment, feedback needs, whether a written record is needed, urgency, cost, and audience expectation. Electronic forms are best for speed, to overcome physical separation and differing time zones, to reach a dispersed audience personally, and when confidentiality is not an issue.

6 **Discuss six ways you can establish a good relationship with your audience.** An important way to establish a good relationship with your audience is to use the "you" attitude to empathize with your audience. Emphasize the positive by talking about what is possible, by not focusing on another person's mistakes, and by using euphemisms when appropriate. Establish your credibility by providing ample evidence for material outside your expertise, calling attention to what you have in common with your audience, explaining your credentials when necessary, and always providing

the highest-quality information. Be polite by expressing yourself with courtesy, kindness, and tact and by being prompt in your correspondence. Use bias-free language to avoid blunders with respect to gender, race and ethnicity, age, and disability. And finally, be sure that you establish the right relationship with your audience by projecting your company's image.

TEST YOUR KNOWLEDGE

1. What are the three steps in the writing process?
2. What two types of purposes do all business messages have?
3. What do you need to know in order to develop an audience profile?
4. How can you test the thoroughness of the information you include in a message?
5. What is media richness and how is it determined?
6. What are the main advantages of oral communication? Of written media?
7. What are the advantages and disadvantages of e-mail?
8. What is the "you" attitude and how does it differ from an "I" attitude?
9. Why is it important to establish your credibility when communicating with an audience of strangers?
10. How does using bias-free language help communicators to establish a good relationship with their audiences?

APPLY YOUR KNOWLEDGE

1. Some writers argue that planning messages wastes time because they inevitably change their plans as they go along. How would you respond to this argument? Briefly explain.
2. As a member of the public relations department, what medium would you recommend using to inform the local community that your toxic-waste cleanup program has been successful? Why?
3. When composing business messages, how can you be yourself and project your company's image at the same time?
4. Considering how fast and easy it is, should e-mail replace meetings and other face-to-face communication in your company? Why or why not?
5. **Ethical Choices** The company president has asked you to draft a memo to the board of directors informing them that sales in the newly acquired line of gourmet fruit jams have far exceeded anyone's expectations. As purchasing director, you happen to know that sales of moderately priced jams have declined substantially (many customers have switched to the more expensive jams). You were not directed to add that tidbit of information. What should you do?

PRACTICE YOUR KNOWLEDGE

 *Document for Analysis*

Read the following document; then (1) analyze the strengths and weaknesses of each sentence and (2) revise the document so that it follows this chapter's guidelines.

I am a new publisher with some really great books to sell. I saw your announcement in *Publishers Weekly* about the bookseller's show you're having this summer, and I think it's a great idea. Count me in, folks! I would like to get some space to show my books. I thought it would be a neat thing if I could do some airbrushing on T-shirts live to help promote my hot new title, *T-Shirt Art*. Before I got into publishing, I was an airbrush artist, and I could demonstrate my techniques. I've done hundreds of advertising illustrations and have been a sign painter all my life, so I'll also be promoting my other book, hot off the presses, *How to Make Money in the Sign Painting Business*.

I will be starting my PR campaign about May 2003 with ads in *PW* and some art trade papers, so my books should be well known by the time the show comes around in August. In case you would like to use my appearance there as part of your publicity, I have enclosed a biography and photo of myself.

P.S. Please let me know what it costs for booth space as soon as possible so that I can figure out whether I can afford to attend. Being a new publisher is mighty expensive!

Exercises

For live links to all websites discussed in this chapter, visit this text's website at www.prenhall.com/bovee. Just log on and select Chapter 4, and click on "Student Resources." Locate the name of the site or the URL related to the material in the text. For the "Exploring the Best of the Web" exercises, you'll also find navigational directions. Click on the live link to the site.

4.1 **Message Planning Skills: Self-Assessment** How good are you at planning business messages? Use the following chart to rate yourself on each of the following elements of planning an audience-centered business message. Then examine your ratings to identify where you are strongest and where you can improve, using the tips in this chapter.

Element of Planning	Always	Frequently	Occasionally	Never
1. I start by defining my purpose.	______	______	______	______
2. I analyze my audience before writing a message.	______	______	______	______
3. I investigate what my audience wants to know.	______	______	______	______
4. I check that my information is accurate, ethical, and pertinent.	______	______	______	______
5. I consider my audience and purpose when selecting media.	______	______	______	______
6. I adopt the "you" attitude in my messages.	______	______	______	______
7. I emphasize the positive aspects of my message.	______	______	______	______
8. I establish my credibility with audiences of strangers.	______	______	______	______
9. I express myself politely and tactfully.	______	______	______	______
10. I use bias-free language.	______	______	______	______
11. I am careful to project my company's image.	______	______	______	______

4.2 **Planning Messages: General and Specific Purpose** Make a list of communication tasks you'll need to accomplish in the next week or so (for example, a job application, a letter of complaint, a speech to a class, an order for some merchandise). For each, determine a general and a specific purpose.

4.3 **Planning Messages: Specific Purpose** For each of the following communication tasks, state a specific purpose (if you have trouble, try beginning with "I want to . . .").

a. A report to your boss, the store manager, about the outdated items in the warehouse
b. A memo to clients about your booth at the upcoming trade show
c. A letter to a customer who hasn't made a payment for three months
d. A memo to employees about the office's high water bills
e. A phone call to a supplier checking on an overdue parts shipment
f. A report to future users of the computer program you have chosen to handle the company's mailing list

4.4 **Planning Messages: Audience Profile** For each communication task below, write brief answers to three questions: Who is my audience? What is my audience's general attitude toward my subject? What does my audience need to know?

a. A final-notice collection letter from an appliance manufacturer to an appliance dealer, sent 10 days before initiating legal collection procedures
b. An unsolicited sales letter asking readers to purchase computer disks at near-wholesale prices
c. An advertisement for peanut butter
d. Fliers to be attached to doorknobs in the neighborhood, announcing reduced rates for chimney lining or repairs
e. A cover letter sent along with your résumé to a potential employer
f. A request (to the seller) for a price adjustment on a piano that incurred $150 in damage during delivery to a banquet room in the hotel you manage

4.5 **Meeting Audience Needs: Necessary Information** Choose an electronic device (videocassette recorder, personal computer, telephone answering machine) that you know how to operate well. Write two sets of instructions for operating the device: one set for a reader who has never used that type of machine and one set for someone who is generally familiar with that type of machine but has never operated the specific model. Briefly explain how your two audiences affect your instructions.

4.6 **Adapting Messages: Media and Purpose** List five messages you have received lately, such as direct-mail promotions, letters, e-mail messages, phone solicitations, and lectures. For each, determine the general and the specific purpose; then answer the following questions: (a) Was the message well timed? (b) Did the sender choose an appropriate medium for the message? (c) Did the appropriate person deliver the message? (d) Was the sender's purpose realistic?

4.7 **Adapting Messages: Media Selection** Barbara Marquardt is in charge of public relations for a cruise line that operates out of Miami. She is shocked to read a letter in a local newspaper from a disgruntled passenger, complaining about the service and entertainment on a recent cruise. Marquardt will have to respond to these publicized criticisms in some way. What audiences will she need to consider in her response? What medium should she choose? If the letter had been published in a travel publication widely read by travel agents and cruise travelers, how might her course of action differ?

4.8 **Teamwork** Your team has been studying a new method for testing the durability of your company's electric hand tools. Now the team needs to prepare three separate reports on the findings: first, a report for the administrator who will decide whether to purchase the equipment needed for this new testing method; second, a report for the company's engineers who design and develop the hand tools; and third, a report for the trainers who will be showing workers how to use the new equipment. To determine the audience's needs for each of these reports, the team has listed the following questions: (1) Who are the readers? (2) Why will they read my report? (3) Do they need introductory or background material? (4) Do they need definitions of terms? (5) What level or type of language is needed? (6) What level of detail is needed? (7) What result does my report aim for? Working with two other students, answer the questions for each of these audiences:

a. The administrator
b. The engineers
c. The trainers

4.9 **Internet** More companies are reaching out to audiences through their websites. Go to the PepsiCo website at www.pepsico.com and follow the link to the latest annual report. Then locate and read the chairman's letter. Who is the audience for this message? What is the general purpose of the message? What do you think this audience wants to know from the chairman of PepsiCo? How does the chairman emphasize the positive in this letter? Summarize your answers in a brief (one page) memo or oral presentation.

4.10 **Audience Relationship: Courteous Communication** Substitute a better phrase for each of the following:

a. You claim that
b. It is not our policy to
c. You neglected to
d. In which you assert
e. We are sorry you are dissatisfied
f. You failed to enclose
g. We request that you send us
h. Apparently you overlooked our terms
i. We have been very patient
j. We are at a loss to understand

4.11 **Audience Relationship: The "You" Attitude** Rewrite these sentences to reflect your audience's viewpoint.

a. We request that you use the order form supplied in the back of our catalog.
b. We insist that you always bring your credit card to the store.
c. We want to get rid of all our 15-inch monitors to make room in our warehouse for the 19-inch screens. Thus we are offering a 25 percent discount on all sales this week.
d. I am applying for the position of bookkeeper in your office. I feel that my grades prove that I am bright and capable, and I think I can do a good job for you.
e. As requested, we are sending the refund for $25.

4.12 Audience Relationship: Emphasize the Positive Revise these sentences to be positive rather than negative.

a. To avoid the loss of your credit rating, please remit payment within 10 days.
b. We don't make refunds on returned merchandise that is soiled.
c. Because we are temporarily out of Baby Cry dolls, we won't be able to ship your order for 10 days.
d. You failed to specify the color of the blouse that you ordered.
e. You should have realized that waterbeds will freeze in unheated houses during winter. Therefore, our guarantee does not cover the valve damage and you must pay the $9.50 valve-replacement fee (plus postage).

4.13 Audience Relationship: Emphasize the Positive Provide euphemisms for the following words and phrases:

a. Stubborn
b. Wrong
c. Stupid
d. Incompetent
e. Loudmouth

4.14 Audience Relationship: Bias-Free Language Rewrite each of the following to eliminate bias:

a. For an Indian, Maggie certainly is outgoing.
b. He needs a wheelchair, but he doesn't let his handicap affect his job performance.
c. A pilot must have the ability to stay calm under pressure, and then he must be trained to cope with any problem that arises.
d. Candidate Renata Parsons, married and the mother of a teenager, will attend the debate.
e. Senior citizen Sam Nugent is still an active salesman.

4.15 Ethical Choices Your supervisor, whom you respect, has asked you to withhold important information that you think should be included in a report you are preparing. Disobeying him could be disastrous for your relationship and your career. Obeying him could violate your personal code of ethics. What should you do? On the basis of the discussion in Chapter 1, would you consider this situation to be an ethical dilemma or an ethical lapse? Please explain.

4.16 Three-Step Process: Other Applications How can the material discussed in this chapter also apply to meetings as discussed in Chapter 2? (Hint: Review the section headings in Chapter 4 and think about making your meetings more productive.)

EXPAND YOUR KNOWLEDGE

Exploring the Best of the Web:

Learn How Instant Messaging Works, p. 90

No doubt the Internet has changed the way we communicate. But do you understand how all this electronic stuff works? Log on to Marshall Brain's How Stuff Works website and learn all about instant messaging, then answer these questions.

1. What are the key advantages of instant messaging?
2. What is the difference between a chat room and instant messaging?
3. Is instant messaging a secure way to communicate?

Exploring the Web on Your Own

Review these chapter-related websites on your own to learn more about achieving communication success in the workplace:

1. Learn more about the writing process, English grammar, style and usage, words, and active writing at Garbl's Writing Resources Online, www.garbl.com./.
2. Plan your messages well, improve your organization, and learn how to write better with the sound advice and writing help at Bull's Eye Business Writing Tips, www.basic-learning.com/wbwt/tips-index.htm.
3. Discover how e-mail works and how to improve your e-mail communications by following the steps at About Internet for Beginners—Harness E-Mail, www.learnthenet.com/english/section/email.html.

LEARN INTERACTIVELY

Interactive Study Guide

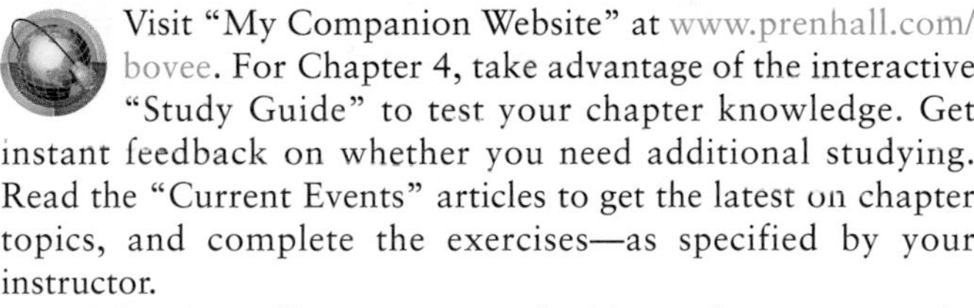

Visit "My Companion Website" at www.prenhall.com/bovee. For Chapter 4, take advantage of the interactive "Study Guide" to test your chapter knowledge. Get instant feedback on whether you need additional studying. Read the "Current Events" articles to get the latest on chapter topics, and complete the exercises—as specified by your instructor.

This site offers a variety of additional resources: The "Research Area" helps you locate a wealth of information to use in course assignments. You can even send a message to online research experts, who will help you find exactly the information you need. The "Study Hall" helps you succeed in this course. "Talk in the Hall" lets you leave messages and meet new friends online. If you have a question, you can "Ask the Tutor." And to get a better grade in this course, you can find more help at "Writing Skills," "Study Skills," and "Study Tips."

Grammar Diagnostic Tests

Review and reinforce your grammar and language skills by taking one of the four online diagnostic tests offered at our companion website, www.prenhall/bovee.com. The four tests cover a variety of topics, including spelling, capitals, punctuation, verbs, pronouns, adjectives, adverbs, sentence structure, sentence punctuation, clarity, word choice, style, organization skills, proofreading, and more. Submit your test and assess your competency. Then focus on improving areas where you are weak as you complete the exercises in this chapter.

Writing Business Messages

After studying this chapter, you will be able to

1 *Cite four of the most common organization mistakes made by communicators*

2 *Explain why good organization is important to both the communicator and the audience*

3 *Summarize the process for organizing business messages effectively*

4 *Discuss three ways of achieving a businesslike tone with a style that is clear and concise*

5 *Briefly describe how to select words that are not only correct but also effective*

6 *List five ways to develop a paragraph and discuss three factors that increase paragraph readability*

COMMUNICATION CLOSE-UP AT WEATHER.COM

www.weather.com

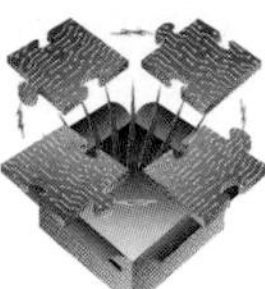

As the official website of The Weather Channel, weather.com has become one of the Internet's most trusted sources for news and information about the constantly changing forces of Mother Nature. About 12 million people click on weather.com each day to find the latest weather forecasts and information—and it's up to writer/producer Julie Galle to organize and compose clear, concise messages that every site visitor can understand.

On a typical day, Galle writes three to five news stories for weather.com. She also composes longer, in-depth articles about weather-related topics for the site's archives. But whether Galle is writing a short news item about a flood in Missouri or a lengthy report on the effects of global warming, she must structure her messages so that her audience can easily understand the information, believe it, and quickly apply it to their own lives.

After a morning briefing from meteorologists, Galle brainstorms with fellow writers about ideas for articles. "Brainstorming makes you think about topics that you might not have considered by yourself," she says. Based on input from her colleagues about breaking news and research findings, Galle limits the scope of her articles by choosing the topics that are the most interesting and compelling for her audience.

Before she writes the first draft, Galle carefully organizes her messages, spending at least 10 percent of her writing time on organization. Although short news stories may require only a brief sketch of a few facts, Galle outlines long pieces by using a technique she learned in college. "Once I've gathered the facts, I place a circle beside the most important information, a triangle beside the second most important, and a square beside the least important," she explains. "If I have to leave anything out, I do not include the items with squares beside them."

Galle strives to present the most important information in the first two paragraphs of a story. To write the first line, she follows the advice of one of her college professors. "He said to take what you know, close your eyes, and pretend you're running home, opening the door, and saying, 'Hey, Mom, guess what?' The next words will be your first line," she explains. "I spend a lot of time at my computer with my eyes closed, following that process. It simplifies what you're trying to say."

To be clearly understood, Galle chooses short words that everyone can understand quickly. "Our users may be weather enthusiasts, but they're not all scientists. So we try to avoid meteorological 'techno-babble,'" she says. When Galle uses a weather term, she defines it in her article. She also tries to hold the reader's interest by making creative use of words and by devising new ways of describing routine weather events such as "hail pounded" and "it rained again."

Galle drafts short news items as quickly as possible, using the active voice. "Active voice and the noun-verb format help you to use small words," she advises. For non-news items and long reports, Galle usually writes three drafts: the first for style, the second for covering meteorological points, and a third for proofing grammar and punctuation. Between drafts, she sets the piece aside for several days. Taking a fresh look gives her the opportunity to tighten up phrases and eliminate unnecessary words—with the ultimate goal of helping her audience clearly understand how the weather affects their daily lives.[1] ■

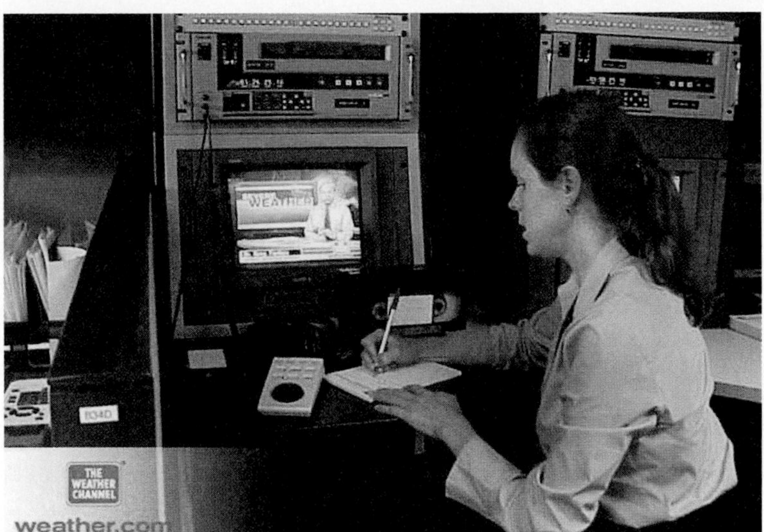

When Julie Galle writes news stories and articles for weather.com, she makes sure that the content, style, and tone of her messages are appropriate for a global Internet audience.

ORGANIZING YOUR MESSAGE

As Julie Galle knows, all business communicators face the challenge of composing messages that their audiences can easily understand. People tend not to remember isolated facts and figures, so successful communicators rely on good organization to make their messages meaningful.[2] But what exactly makes a particular organization "good"? Here's a closer look at what constitutes good organization and why it is important.

What Good Organization Means

Various cultures define good organization differently.

Although the definition of good organization varies from country to country, in the United States and Canada, it generally means creating a linear message that proceeds point by point. If you've ever received a disorganized message, you're familiar with the frustration of trying to sort through a muddle of ideas. Consider this letter from Jill Saunders, the accounting manager at General Nutrition Corporation (GNC), manufacturer of health-food products and nutritional supplements:

> General Nutrition Corporation has been doing business with ComputerTime since I was hired six years ago. Your building was smaller then, and it was located on the corner of Federal Avenue and 2nd N.W. Jared Mallory, our controller, was one of your first customers. I still remember the day. It was the biggest check I'd ever written. Of course, over the years, I've gotten used to larger purchases.
>
> Our department now has 15 employees. As accountants, we need to have our computers working so that we can do our jobs. The CD-RW drive we bought for my assistant, Suzanne, has been a problem. We've taken it in for repairs three times in three months to the authorized service center, and Suzanne is very careful with the machine and hasn't abused it. She does like playing interactive adventure games on lunch breaks. Anyway, it still doesn't work right, and she's tired of hauling it back and forth. We're all putting in longer hours because it is our busy season, and none of us has a lot of spare time.
>
> This is the first time we've returned anything to your store, and I hope you'll agree that we deserve a better deal.

This letter displays a lack of organization that U.S. and Canadian readers find frustrating. By taking a closer look at what's wrong, you can distinguish four of the most common organization mistakes made by communicators:

Learning Objective 1

Cite four of the most common organization mistakes made by communicators

Most disorganized communication suffers from problems with clarity, relevance, grouping, and completeness.

- **Taking too long to get to the point.** Saunders didn't introduce her topic, the faulty CD-RW drive, until the third paragraph. Then she waited until the final paragraph to state her purpose: requesting an adjustment. *Solution:* Make the subject and purpose clear.
- **Including irrelevant material.** Does it matter that ComputerTime used to be smaller or that it was in a different location? Is it important that Saunders's department has 15 employees or that her assistant likes playing computer games during lunch? *Solution:* Include only information that is related to the subject and purpose.
- **Getting ideas mixed up.** Saunders tries to make five points: (1) Her company has money to spend, (2) it's an old customer, (3) it has purchased numerous items at ComputerTime, (4) the CD-RW drive doesn't work, and (5) Saunders wants an adjustment. However, the ideas are mixed up and located in the wrong places. *Solution:* Group the ideas and present them in a logical way. For example, begin with the fact that the drive doesn't work, and group some ideas to show that the company is a valuable customer.
- **Leaving out necessary information.** ComputerTime may want to know the make, model, and price of the CD-RW drive; the date of purchase; the specific problems the machine has had; and whether the repairs were covered by the warranty. Saunders also failed to say what she wants the store to do: send her a new CD-RW drive of the same type, send her a different model, or simply refund her money. *Solution:* Include all the necessary information.

A message is well organized when all the pieces fit together in a coherent pattern.

Achieving good organization can be a challenge. However, solving these common problems can help you communicate clearly. Saunders can make her letter more effective by organizing all the necessary information in a sequence that helps ComputerTime understand the message (see Figure 5.1).

Why Good Organization Is Important

Learning Objective 2

Explain why good organization is important to both the communicator and the audience

Poor organization costs time, efficiency, and relationships.

Does it matter whether a message is well organized as long as its point is eventually made? Why not just let your ideas flow naturally and trust your audience to grasp your meaning? For one thing, misinterpreted messages lead to wasted time reading and rereading, poor decision making, and shattered business relationships. When you consider such costs, you begin to realize the value of clear writing and good organization.[3]

In business, the objective is to get work done, not to produce messages. When chief executives were asked what they would most like to improve about their own business writing, they mentioned speed of composition more often than any other factor.[4] Being well organized helps you compose your messages more quickly and efficiently.

Good organization saves time, strengthens relationships, and improves efficiency.

So before you begin to write, think about what you're going to say and how you're going to say it. Good organization will save you time. Your draft will go more quickly because you won't waste time putting ideas in the wrong places or composing material you don't need. In addition, you can use your organizational plan to get some advance input from your audience. That way, you can be sure you're on the right track *before* you spend hours working on your draft. If you're working on a large, complex project, you can use your organization plan to divide the writing job among co-workers.

Good organization helps audience members understand your message, accept your message, and save time.

In addition to helping you, good organization also helps your audience in three ways:

1. **Good organization helps your audience understand your message.** As Julie Galle points out, successful organization is the key to communicating effectively with audiences. By making your main point clear at the outset, and by stating your needs precisely, your well-organized message will satisfy your audience's need for information.
2. **Good organization helps your audience accept your message.** Even when your message is logical, you need to select and organize your points in a diplomatic way. By softening refusals and leaving a good impression, you enhance your credibility and add authority to your messages. When ComputerTime responds to the GNC

FIGURE 5.1 In-Depth Critique: Letter with Improved Organization

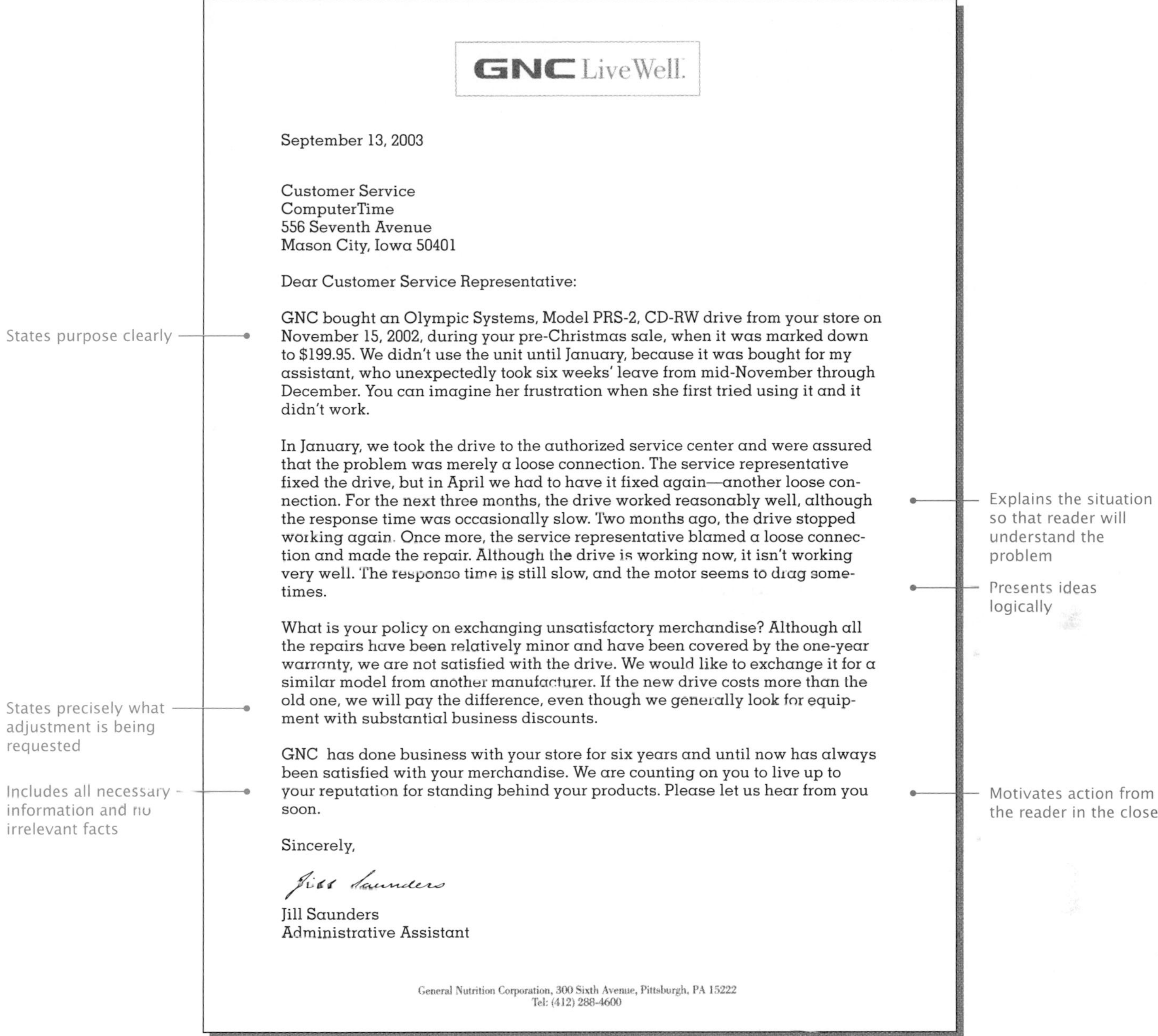

September 13, 2003

Customer Service
ComputerTime
556 Seventh Avenue
Mason City, Iowa 50401

Dear Customer Service Representative:

GNC bought an Olympic Systems, Model PRS-2, CD-RW drive from your store on November 15, 2002, during your pre-Christmas sale, when it was marked down to $199.95. We didn't use the unit until January, because it was bought for my assistant, who unexpectedly took six weeks' leave from mid-November through December. You can imagine her frustration when she first tried using it and it didn't work.

In January, we took the drive to the authorized service center and were assured that the problem was merely a loose connection. The service representative fixed the drive, but in April we had to have it fixed again—another loose connection. For the next three months, the drive worked reasonably well, although the response time was occasionally slow. Two months ago, the drive stopped working again. Once more, the service representative blamed a loose connection and made the repair. Although the drive is working now, it isn't working very well. The response time is still slow, and the motor seems to drag sometimes.

What is your policy on exchanging unsatisfactory merchandise? Although all the repairs have been relatively minor and have been covered by the one-year warranty, we are not satisfied with the drive. We would like to exchange it for a similar model from another manufacturer. If the new drive costs more than the old one, we will pay the difference, even though we generally look for equipment with substantial business discounts.

GNC has done business with your store for six years and until now has always been satisfied with your merchandise. We are counting on you to live up to your reputation for standing behind your products. Please let us hear from you soon.

Sincerely,

Jill Saunders

Jill Saunders
Administrative Assistant

General Nutrition Corporation, 300 Sixth Avenue, Pittsburgh, PA 15222
Tel: (412) 288-4600

inquiry, the message is negative, but the letter is diplomatic and positive (see Figure 5.2).

3. **Good organization saves your audience time.** Well-organized messages are efficient. They contain only relevant ideas, and they are brief. Moreover, all the information in a well-organized message is in a logical place. Audience members receive only the information they need, and because that information is presented as accessibly and succinctly as possible, audience members can follow the thought pattern without a struggle.

How Good Organization Is Achieved

Learning Objective 3

Summarize the process for organizing business messages effectively

Understanding the *need* for good organization is half the battle. Knowing *how* to organize your messages well is the other half. When writing messages at weather.com, Julie Galle achieves good organization by defining the main idea, limiting the scope,

FIGURE 5.2 In-Depth Critique: Letter Demonstrating a Diplomatic Organization Plan

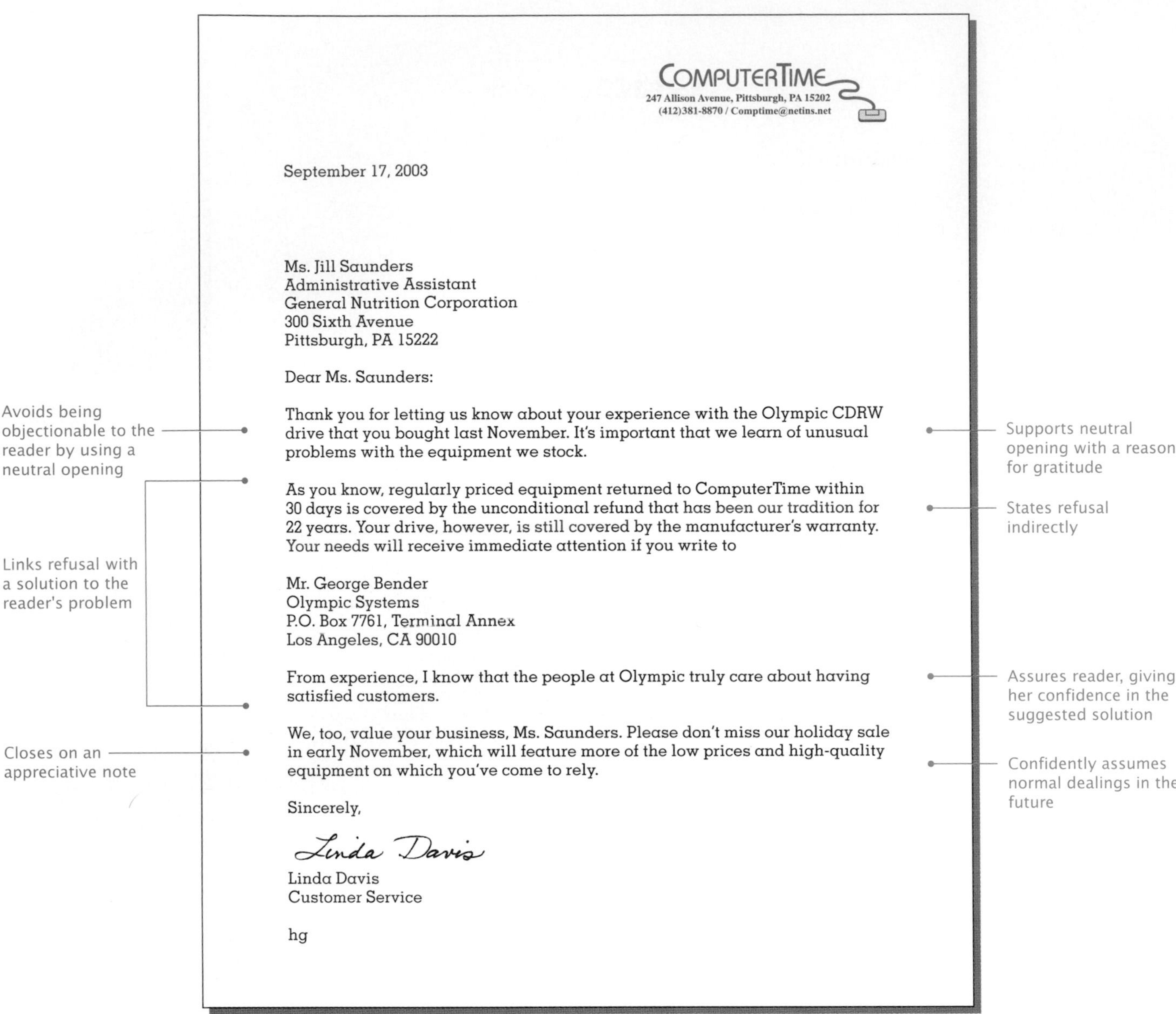

To organize a message
- Define your main idea
- Limit the scope
- Group your points
- Choose the direct or indirect approach

grouping supporting points, and establishing their sequence by selecting either a direct or an indirect approach.

Define the Main Idea

The topic is the broad subject; the main idea makes a statement about the topic.

In addition to having a general purpose and a specific purpose, all business messages can be boiled down to one main idea—one central point that sums up everything. The rest of your message supports, explains, or demonstrates this point. Your main idea is not the same as your topic. The broad subject of your message is the **topic**, and your **main idea** makes a statement about that topic. Consider the examples in Table 5.1.

Defining your main idea is more difficult when you're trying to persuade someone or convey disappointing information.

Your main idea may be obvious when you're preparing a brief message with simple facts that have little emotional impact on your audience. If you're responding to a request for information, your main idea may be simply, "Here is what you wanted." However, defining your main idea is more complicated when you're trying to persuade someone or when you have disappointing information to convey. In these situations, try to define a main idea that will establish a good relationship between you and your audience. For example, you may choose a main idea that highlights a common interest

TABLE 5.1 Defining Business Messages

General Purpose	Specific Purpose	Topic	Main Idea
To inform	Teach customer service reps how to file insurance claims	Insurance claims	Proper filing by reps saves the company time and money.
To persuade	Get top managers to approve increased spending on research and development	Funding for research and development	Competitors spend more than we do on research and development.
To collaborate	Solicit ideas for a companywide incentive system that ties wages to profits	Incentive pay	Tying wages to profits motivates employees and reduces compensation in tough years.

you share with your audience or that emphasizes a point that you and your audience can agree on.

In longer documents and presentations, you'll need to unify a mass of material, so you'll need to define a main idea that encompasses all the individual points you want to make. For tough assignments like these, you may want to take special measures to define your main idea. Figure 5.3 describes six techniques you can use to generate your main idea and key points.

As chairman and CEO of Living Omnimedia, Martha Stewart publishes two magazines, numerous books, and a newspaper column. Her creative, practical ideas on cooking, gardening, crafts, holidays, and home improvement have made Stewart a trusted guide to stylish living. Stewart's messages are a prime example of good organization: The subject and purpose are clear, information relates to the subject and purpose, and good organization allows the audience to receive only the information they need.

Limit the Scope

The scope of your message (its length and detail) must match your main idea. Whether your audience expects a one-page memo or a one-hour speech, you must develop your main idea with major points and supporting evidence within that framework. Once you have a tentative statement of your main idea, test it against the length limitations that have been imposed for your message. If you lack the time and space to develop your main idea fully, or if your main idea won't fill up the time and space allotted, you'll need to redefine it.

As you adjust your message to fit the time or space available, don't change the number of major points. Regardless of how long the message will be, stick with three or four major points—five at the very most. According to communication researchers, that's all your audience will remember.[5] Instead of introducing additional points, you can more fully develop complex issues by supporting your points with a variety of evidence.

Deal with three or four major points (not more than five), regardless of message length.

If your message is brief (four minutes or one page), you'll have only a minute or a paragraph each for the introduction, conclusion, and major points. Because the amount of evidence you can present is limited, your main idea will have to be both easy to understand and easy to accept. However, if you're delivering a long message (say, a 60-minute presentation or a 20-page report), you can develop the major points in considerable detail. You can spend about 10 minutes or 10 paragraphs (more than three pages of double-spaced, typewritten text) on each of your key points, and you'll still have room for your introduction and conclusion.

How much you can communicate in a given number of words depends on the nature of your subject, your audience members' familiarity with the topic, their receptivity to your conclusions, and your credibility. You'll need fewer words to present routine information to a knowledgeable audience that already knows and respects you. You'll need more time to build consensus about a complex and controversial subject, especially if the audience is composed of skeptical or hostile strangers.

FIGURE 5.3 Idea Generation Techniques

Idea Generation Techniques

Brainstorming: Generate as many possibilities as you can think of by letting your mind wander and by being completely uncensored. Then develop criteria to test your ideas against your purpose, your audience, and the facts you've gathered. Eliminate ideas that fail to meet your criteria.

Random List: On a computer screen or a clean sheet of paper, list everything you can think of that pertains to your message. Once you begin your list, your thoughts will start to flow. When you've exhausted the possibilities, study the list for relationships. Sort the items into groups, as you would sort a deck of cards into suits. Look for common denominators; the connection might be geographic, sequential, spatial, chronological, or topical. Part of the list might break down into problems, cases, and solutions; another part, into pros and cons. Regardless of what categories finally emerge, the sorting process will help you sift through your thoughts and decide what's important—thus clarifying what you need to include in your communication. Of course, the best way to decide importance is to concentrate on the points that will benefit your audience most.

FCR Worksheet: If your subject involves the solution to a problem, you might try an FCR worksheet to help you visualize the relationships among your findings (F), your conclusions (C), and your recommendations (R). For example, you might find that you're losing sales to a competitor who offers lower prices than you do (F). From this information, you might conclude that your loss of sales is due to your pricing policy (C). This conclusion would lead you to recommend a price cut (R). To make an FCR worksheet, divide a computer screen or a sheet of paper into three columns. List the major findings in the first column, then extrapolate conclusions and write them in the second column. These conclusions form the basis for the recommendations, which are listed in the third column. An analysis of the three columns should help you define the information you need to include in your communication.

Journalistic Approach: For informational messages, the journalistic approach may provide a good point of departure. Find the answers to six questions—who, what, when, where, why, and how. The answers you come up with should help guide you into providing all the required information in your message.

Question-and-Answer Chain: Perhaps the best approach is to look at the subject of your message from your audience's point of view. Ask yourself: "What are the audience's main questions? What do audience members need to know?" Write down and examine your answers. As additional questions emerge, write down and examine those answers. Follow the chain of questions and answers until you have replied to every conceivable question that might occur to your audience. By assuming your audience's perspective, you will include the information of greatest value to your audience in your communication.

Storyteller's Tour: Turn on your tape recorder and pretend that you've just run into an old friend on the street. Give an overview of your message, focusing on your reasons for communicating, your major points, your rationale, and the implications for your audience. Listen critically to the tape; then repeat the exercise until you are able to give a smooth, two-minute summary that conveys the gist of your message. Be sure to include the key points you've defined in your communication.

Moreover, the scope of your message determines the amount and depth of investigation you can conduct. You may need only to glance at your calendar to confirm a meeting, or you may need to spend weeks conducting formal research for a complicated report. Gathering information for reports and proposals is thoroughly discussed in Chapter 10.

Structure Your Message

A good way to visualize how all the points will fit together is to construct an outline.

Once you have narrowed the scope of your message, you must provide your supporting details in the most logical and effective way. Constructing an outline of your message, as Julie Galle does, is one good way to visualize how all the points will fit together. Whether you use the outlining features provided with word-processing soft-

FIGURE 5.4 Two Common Outline Forms

ALPHANUMERIC OUTLINE	DECIMAL OUTLINE
I. First Major Part	1.0 First Major Part
A. First subpoint	1.1 First subpoint
B. Second subpoint	1.2 Second subpoint
1. Evidence	1.2.1 Evidence
2. Evidence	1.2.2 Evidence
a. Detail	1.2.2.1 Detail
b. Detail	1.2.2.2 Detail
3. Evidence	1.2.3 Evidence
C. Third subpoint	2.0 Third subpoint
II. Second Major Point	2.0 Second Major Point
A. First subpoint	2.1 First subpoint
1. Evidence	2.1.1 Evidence
2. Evidence	2.1.2 Evidence
B. Second subpoint	2.2 Second subpoint

ware or simply jot down three or four points on the back of an envelope, making a plan and sticking to it will help you cover the important details.

When you're preparing a longer, more complex message, an outline is indispensable because it helps you visualize the relationships among the various parts. Without an outline, you may be inclined to ramble. As you're describing one point, another point may occur to you, so you describe it. One detour leads to another, and before you know it, you've forgotten the original point. With an outline to guide you, however, you can communicate in a more systematic way. Following an outline also helps you insert transitions so that your message is coherent and your audience can understand the relationships among your ideas.

An outline or a schematic diagram will help you visualize the relationship among parts of a message.

You're no doubt familiar with the basic outline formats, which (1) use numbers—or letters and numbers—to identify each point and (2) indent points to show which ideas are of equal status. A good outline divides a topic into at least two parts, restricts each subdivision to one category, and ensures that each group is separate and distinct (see Figure 5.4).

Outlines can appear in various formats.

Another way to visualize the structure of your message is by creating a message "organization chart" similar to the charts used to show a company's management structure (see Figure 5.5). The main idea is shown in the highest-level box and, like a top executive, establishes the big picture. The lower-level ideas, like lower-level employees, provide the details. All the ideas are logically organized into divisions of thought, just as a company is organized into divisions and departments.[6] Using a visual chart instead of a traditional outline has many benefits. Charts help you (1) see the various levels of ideas and how the parts fit together, (2) develop new ideas, and (3) restructure your information flow.

Whether you use an outline format or an organization chart to structure your message, your message begins with the main idea, follows with major supporting points, and then illustrates these points with evidence.

When Terry and Donna Plunkett investigated franchise opportunities with Critter Care of America, they began the process by sending an inquiry letter to the franchisor. Now, as successful owners of this Colorado pet-sitting franchise, they know that well-organized communications can expedite the entire franchising process.

Start with the Main Idea The main idea helps you establish the goals and general strategy of the message and summarizes two things: (1) what you want your audience to do or think and (2) why they should do so. Everything in the message should either support the main idea or explain its implications.

FIGURE 5.5 "Organization Chart" for Organizing a Message

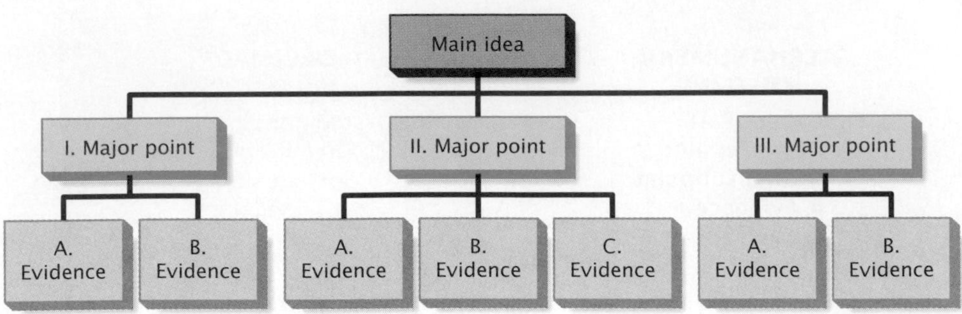

Major supporting points clarify your main idea.

State the Major Points Once you've determined the main idea, identify between three and five major points that support and clarify your message in more concrete terms. If you come up with more, go back and look for opportunities to combine some of your ideas.

The division of major points may be based on physical relationships, the description of a process, the components of an object, or a historical chronology.

If your purpose is to inform and the material is factual, your major points might be based on something physical—something you can visualize or measure, such as activities to be performed, functional units, spatial or chronological relationships, or parts of a whole. When you're describing a process, the major points are almost inevitably steps in the process. When you're describing an object, the major points correspond to the components of the object. When you're giving a historical account, major points represent events in the chronological chain. If your purpose is to persuade or to collaborate, select major points that develop a line of reasoning or logical argument that proves your central message and motivates your audience to act.

Illustrate with Evidence After you've defined the main idea and identified three to five major points to support that idea, you're ready to illustrate your major points with specific evidence. This evidence is the flesh and blood that helps your audience understand and remember the more abstract concepts you're presenting. For example, if you're advocating that your company increase its advertising budget, you can support your major point by providing evidence that your most successful competitors spend more on advertising than you do. You can also describe a case in which a particular competitor increased its ad budget and achieved an impressive sales gain. Then you can show that over the past five years, your firm's sales have gone up and down in response to the amount spent on advertising.

If you're developing a long, complex message, you may need to carry the organization chart (or outline) down several levels. Remember that every level is a step along the chain from the abstract to the concrete, from the general to the specific. The lowest level contains the individual facts and figures that tie the generalizations to the observable, measurable world. The higher levels are the concepts that reveal why those facts are significant.

The more evidence you provide, the more conclusive your case will be. If your subject is complex and unfamiliar or if your audience is skeptical, you'll need a lot of facts and figures to demonstrate your points. On the other hand, if your subject is routine and the audience is positively inclined, you can be more sparing with the evidence. You want to provide enough support to be convincing but not so much that your message becomes boring or inefficient.

Each major point must be supported with enough specific evidence to be convincing, but not so much that it's boring.

Another way to keep the audience interested is to vary the type of detail. As you draft your message, try to incorporate the methods described in Table 5.2. Switch from facts and figures to narration; add a dash of description; throw in some examples or a reference to authority. Be sure to reinforce all these details with visual aids. Think of your message as a stew: a mixture of ingredients seasoned with a blend of spices. Each separate flavor adds to the richness of the whole.

TABLE 5.2 Six Types of Detail

Type of Detail	*Example*	*Comment*
Facts and figures	Sales are strong this month. We have received two new contracts worth $5 million and have a good chance of winning another with an annual value of $2.5 million.	Most common form of detail in business messages. Adds more credibility than any other form of development. May become boring if used in excess.
Example or illustration	We've spent the past four months trying to hire recent accounting graduates for our internal audit staff, and, so far, only one person has agreed to join our firm. One woman told me that she would love to work for us, but she can get $5,000 more a year elsewhere.	Adds life to a message, but one example does not prove a point. Idea must be supported by other evidence as well.
Description	Upscale hamburger restaurants are designed for McDonald's graduates who still love the taste of a Big Mac but who want more than convenience and low prices. The adult hamburger establishments feature attractive waitresses, wine and beer, half-pound burgers, and substantial side dishes, such as nachos and potato skins. "Atmosphere" is a key ingredient in the formula for success.	Useful when you need to explain how something looks or functions. Helps audience visualize the subject by creating a sensory impression. Does not prove a point, but clarifies points and makes them memorable. Begins with overview of object's function; defines its purpose, lists major parts, and explains how it operates; relies on words that appeal to senses.
Narration	Under former management, the company operated in a casual style. Executives came to work in blue jeans, meetings rarely started on time, and lunch rarely ended on time. When Mr. Wilson took over as CEO, however, the company got religion—financial religion. A Harvard M.B.A. who favors Brooks Brothers suits, Mr. Wilson has embarked on a complete overhaul of the operation. He has cut the product line from 6,000 items to 1,200 and has chopped $12 million off expenses.	Good for attracting attention and explaining ideas, but lacks statistical validity.
Reference to authority	I talked with Jackie Lohman in the Cleveland plant about this idea, and she was very supportive. As you know, Jackie has been in charge of that plant for the past six years. She is confident that we can speed up the number 2 line by 150 units per hour if we add another worker.	Bolsters a case and adds variety and credibility. Works only if "authority" is recognized and respected by audience.
Visual aids	Graphs, charts, tables	Essential when presenting specific information. Used more often in memos and reports than in letters.

Choose Between the Direct and Indirect Approaches

Once you've defined your ideas and outlined or diagrammed the structure of your message, you're ready to decide on the sequence you will use to present your points. When you're addressing a U.S. or Canadian audience with minimal cultural differences, you have two basic options:

- **Direct approach (deductive).** The main idea (such as a recommendation, conclusion, or request) comes first, followed by the evidence. Use this approach when your audience will be neutral about your message or pleased to hear from you.
- **Indirect approach (inductive).** The evidence comes first, and the main idea comes later. Use this approach when your audience may be displeased about or may resist what you have to say.

Use the direct approach if the audience's reaction is likely to be positive and the indirect approach if it is likely to be negative.

FIGURE 5.6 Audience Reaction Affects Organizational Approach

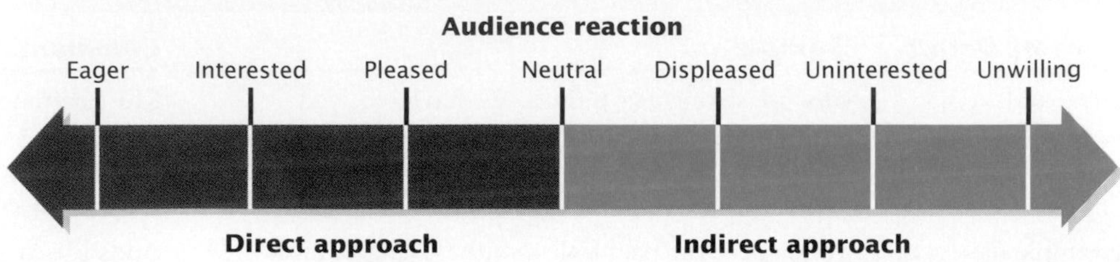

Audience reaction can range from eager to unwilling.

To choose between these two alternatives, you must analyze your audience's likely reaction to your purpose and message. Audience reaction will fall somewhere between being eager to accept your message and being unwilling to accept your message (see Figure 5.6). The direct approach is generally fine when audience members will be receptive—if they are eager, interested, pleased, or even neutral. But you may have better results with the indirect approach if audience members are likely to resist your message—if they are displeased, uninterested, or unwilling.

Analyze each communication situation to determine the best approach.

Bear in mind, however, that each message is unique. No simple formula will solve all your communication problems. For example, if you're sending bad news to outsiders, an indirect approach may be best. On the other hand, if you're writing a memo to an associate, you may want to get directly to the point, even if your message is unpleasant. The direct approach might also be a good choice for long messages, regardless of your audience's attitude, because delaying the main idea could cause confusion and frustration. To summarize, your choice of a direct or an indirect approach depends on the following factors:

Choice of approach depends on audience reaction, message length, and type.

- **Audience reaction:** positive, neutral, or negative
- **Message length:** short (memos and letters—discussed in Part 3 of this text) or long (reports, proposals, and presentations—discussed in Part 5)
- **Message type:** (1) routine, good-news, and goodwill messages; (2) bad-news messages; or (3) persuasive messages (all three of which are discussed in Part 3)

Table 5.3 summarizes how your approach may differ depending on the message type and likely audience reaction. When used with good judgment, the three basic types of business messages can be powerful tools of communication.[7] Just remember, your first priority is to make your message clear. In the following brief discussions, note how the

TABLE 5.3 Choosing Between the Direct and Indirect Approaches

Message Type	*Audience Reaction*	*Approach*	*Opening*	*Body*	*Close*
Routine, good news, goodwill	Pleased or neutral	**Direct**	Begin with the main idea, the request, or the good news.	Provide necessary details.	Close with a cordial comment, a reference to the good news, or a statement about the specific action desired.
Bad news	Displeased	**Indirect**	Begin with a neutral statement that acts as a transition to the reasons for the bad news.	Give reasons to justify a negative answer. State or imply the bad news, and make a positive suggestion.	Close cordially.
Persuasive	Uninterested or unwilling	**Indirect**	Begin with a statement or question that captures attention.	Arouse the audience's interest in the subject. Build the audience's desire to comply.	Request action.

opening, body, and close all play an important role in getting your message across, regardless of message type.

Routine, Good-News, and Goodwill Messages The most straightforward business messages are routine, good-news, and goodwill messages. If you're inquiring about products or placing an order, your audience will usually want to comply. If you're announcing a price cut, granting an adjustment, accepting an invitation, or congratulating a colleague, your audience will most likely be pleased to hear from you. If you're providing routine information as part of your regular business, your audience will probably be neutral, neither pleased nor displeased.

Aside from being easy to understand, these kinds of messages are easy to prepare. In most cases you get right down to business. In the opening, you state your main idea directly, without searching for some creative introduction. The body of your message can then provide all necessary details. The close is cordial and emphasizes your good news or makes a statement about the specific action desired.

By starting off with your positive idea, you put your audience in a good frame of mind and encourage them to be receptive to whatever else you have to say. This approach also emphasizes the pleasing aspect of your message by putting it right up front, where it's the first thing recipients see. Routine, good-news, and goodwill messages are discussed in greater detail in Chapter 7.

When Ralph Congers takes orders from phone customers, he asks for the same information that a writer would need to include in an order letter: contact information (name, address, phone, e-mail), payment information (credit card type and number), and item information (item description, quantity, etc.). Because such orders are routine, the information is presented in a direct and straightforward manner.

Bad-News Messages If you're turning down a job applicant, refusing credit, or denying a request for an adjustment, your audience will be disappointed. In such cases, it may be best to use the indirect approach—putting the evidence first and the main idea later. For example, by blurting out an unpleasant message, you may think that you're just being businesslike or that your audience is too far away or too unimportant to matter. However, astute businesspeople know that every person they encounter could be a potential customer, supplier, or contributor or could influence someone who is a customer, supplier, or contributor.

If you have bad news, try to put it somewhere in the middle, cushioned by other, more positive ideas.

Successful communicators take a little extra care with their bad-news messages. They open with a neutral statement that acts as a transition to the reasons for the bad news. In the body, they give the reasons that justify a negative answer before stating or implying the bad news. And they are always careful to close cordially.

The challenge lies in being honest but kind. You don't want to sacrifice ethics and mislead your audience; nor do you want to be overly blunt. To achieve a good mix of candor and kindness, focus on some aspect of the situation that makes the bad news a little easier to take.

The indirect approach should not be used to manipulate.

Keep in mind that the indirect approach is neither manipulative nor unethical. As long as you can be honest and reasonably brief, you're better off opening a bad-news message with a neutral point and putting the negative information after the explanation. Then if you can close with something fairly positive, you're likely to leave the audience feeling okay—not great, but not hostile either (which is often about all you can hope for when you must deliver negative messages). Bad-news messages are discussed further in Chapter 8.

Using the indirect approach gives you an opportunity to get your message across to an uninterested or skeptical audience.

Persuasive Messages The indirect approach is also useful when you know that your audience will resist your message (will be uninterested in your request or unwilling to comply without extra coaxing). You might find an audience resistant to a sales letter, a collection letter, an unsolicited job application, or a request for a favor of some kind. In such cases, you have a better chance of getting through to the person if you lead off

✓ CHECKLIST: ORGANIZING BUSINESS MESSAGES

A. Recognize good organization
1. Subject and purpose are clear.
2. Information is directly related to subject and purpose.
3. Ideas are grouped and presented logically.
4. All necessary information is included.

B. Define the main idea
1. Develop a global statement that sums up the central point of your message.
2. Make your global statement audience centered.
3. Evaluate whether the main idea is realistic, given the imposed length limitations.

C. Decide what to say
1. Start with the main idea.
2. State the major points.
3. Illustrate with evidence.

D. Organize the message to respond to the audience's probable reaction
1. Use the direct approach when your audience will be neutral, pleased, interested, or eager.
2. Use the indirect approach when your audience will be displeased, uninterested, or unwilling.

with something catchy. This doesn't mean that you should go in for gimmicks, but try to think of something that will make your audience receptive to what you have to say.

You have to capture people's attention before you can persuade them to do something. You have to get your audience to consider with an open mind what you have to say. So you have to make an interesting point and provide supporting facts that encourage the audience to continue paying attention.

Persuasive messages have their own indirect pattern.

The opening begins by mentioning a possible benefit, referring to a problem that the recipient might have, posing a question, or mentioning an interesting statistic. Then the body builds interest in the subject and arouses your audience members' desire to comply. Once you have them thinking, you can introduce your main idea. The close is cordial and requests the desired action. Persuasive messages are discussed at greater length in Chapter 9. For a reminder of the organization tasks involved in preparing your messages, see "Checklist: Organizing Business Messages."

COMPOSING AND SHAPING YOUR MESSAGE

Once you've completed the planning process and organized your message, you're ready to begin composing your first draft. If your schedule permits, put aside your outline or organization chart for a day or two. Then review it with a fresh eye, looking for opportunities to improve the flow of ideas.

Composition is easiest if you've already figured out what to say and in what order, although you may need to pause now and then to find the right word. You may also discover as you go along that you can improve on your outline. Feel free to rearrange, delete, and add ideas, as long as you don't lose sight of your purpose.

Composition is the process of drafting your message; polishing it is a later step.

As you compose your first draft, try to let your creativity flow. Don't try to draft and edit at the same time or worry about getting everything perfect. Just put down your ideas as quickly as you can. You'll have time to revise and refine the material later. If you get stuck, try to overcome writer's block—the temporary inability to write—by following some of the techniques presented in "Sharpening Your Career Skills: Beating Writer's Block: Nine Workable Ideas to Get Words Flowing."

Once you have all your thoughts and ideas jotted down, begin shaping your message. Start by paying attention to your style and tone. Try to select words that match the tone you want to achieve. Next, create effective sentences and develop coherent paragraphs. The following sections discuss each of these elements.

Learning Objective 4

Discuss three ways of achieving a businesslike tone with a style that is clear and concise

Controlling Your Style and Tone

Style is the way you use words to achieve a certain **tone**, or overall impression. You can vary your style—your sentence structure and vocabulary—to sound forceful or objective, personal or formal, colorful or dry. The right choice depends on the nature of your

Sharpening Your Career Skills

Beating Writer's Block: Nine Workable Ideas to Get Words Flowing

Putting words on a page or on screen can be a real struggle. Some people get stuck so often that they develop a mental block. If you get writer's block, here are some ways to get those words flowing again:

- **Use positive self-talk.** Stop worrying about how well or easily you write, and stop thinking of writing as difficult, time-consuming, or complicated. Tell yourself that you're capable and that you can do the job. Also, recall past examples of your writing that were successful.
- **Know your purpose.** Be specific about what you want to accomplish with this particular piece of writing. Without a clear purpose, writing can indeed be impossible.
- **Visualize your audience.** Picture audience backgrounds, interests, subject knowledge, and vocabulary (including the technical jargon they use). Such visualization can help you choose an appropriate style and tone for your writing.
- **Create a productive environment.** Write in a place that's for writing only, and make that place pleasant. Set up "writing appointments." Scheduling a session from 9:30 to noon is less intimidating than an indefinite session. Also, keep your mind fresh with scheduled breaks.
- **Make an outline or a list.** Even if you don't create a formal outline, at least jot down a few notes about how your ideas fit together. As you go along, you can revise your notes, as long as you end up with a plan that gives direction and coherence.
- **Just start.** Put aside all worries, fears, distractions—anything that gives you an excuse to postpone writing. Then start putting down any thoughts you have about your topic. Don't worry about whether these ideas can actually be used; just let your mind range freely.
- **Write the middle first.** Start wherever your interest is greatest and your ideas are most developed. You can follow new directions, but note ideas to revisit later. When you finish one section, choose another without worrying about sequence. Just get your thoughts down.
- **Push obstacles aside.** If you get stuck at some point, don't worry. Move past the thought, sentence, or paragraph, and come back to it later. Prime the pump simply by writing or talking about why you're stuck: "I'm stuck because . . ." Also try brainstorming. Before you know it, you'll be writing about your topic.
- **Read a newspaper or magazine.** Try reading an article that uses a style similar to yours. Choose one you'll enjoy so that you'll read it more closely.
- **Work on nontext segments.** Work on a different part of the project, such as formatting or creating graphics or verifying facts and references.

When deadlines loom, don't freeze in panic. Concentrate on the major ideas first, and save the details for later, after you have something on the page. If you keep things in perspective, you'll succeed.

Career Applications

1. List the ways you procrastinate, and discuss what you can do to break these habits.
2. Analyze your own writing experiences. What negative self-talk do you use? What might you do to overcome this tendency?

message and your relationship with the reader. Although style can be refined during the revision phase (see Chapter 6), you'll save time and a lot of rewriting if you use a style that allows you to achieve the desired tone from the start.

When composing your message, you can vary the style to create a tone that suits the occasion.

Use a Conversational Tone

The tone of your business messages may span a continuum from informal to conversational to formal. Most business messages aim for a conversational tone, using plain language that sounds businesslike without being stuffy, stiff, wordy, or full of jargon. Rather than trying to impress audiences with an extensive vocabulary, good communicators focus on being sensible, logical, and objective; they provide supporting facts and a rationale. To achieve such a conversational tone in your messages, try to avoid obsolete and pompous language, intimacy, humor, and preaching or bragging:

Your composition style says a lot about you.

Most business messages aim for a conversational style. To achieve a warm but businesslike tone
- Don't use obsolete language
- Don't use pompous phrases
- Don't be too familiar
- Use humor only with great care
- Don't preach
- Don't brag

- **Avoid obsolete and pompous language.** Business language used to be much more formal than it is today, and some out-of-date phrases still remain. You can avoid using such language if you ask yourself, "Would I say this if I were talking with someone face-to-face?" Similarly, avoid using big words, trite expressions, and overly complicated sentences to impress others. Such pompous language sounds puffed up and roundabout (see Table 5.4).

Best of the Web

Compose a Better Business Message

At Purdue's Online Writing Lab (OWL) you'll find tools to help you improve your business messages. For advice on composing written messages, for help with grammar, and for referrals to other information sources, you'd be wise to visit this site. Purdue's OWL offers online services and an introduction to Internet search tools. You can also download a variety of handouts on writing skills. Check out the resources at the OWL homepage and learn how to write a professional business message.

owl.english.purdue.edu

- **Avoid intimacy.** Don't mention anything about anyone's personal life unless you know the individual well. Avoid phrases that imply intimacy, such as "just between you and me" and "as you and I are well aware." Be careful about sounding too folksy or chatty; such a familiar tone may be seen as an attempt to seem like an old friend when, in fact, you're not.
- **Avoid humor.** Using humor can backfire, especially if you don't know your audience very well. What seems humorous to you may be deadly serious to others. And when you're communicating across cultures, chances are slim that your audience will appreciate your humor or even realize that you're trying to be funny.[8] Also, humor changes too quickly. What's funny today may not be in a week or a month from now.

TABLE 5.4 Staying Up to Date and Down to Earth

Obsolete	***Up to Date***
in due course	today, tomorrow (or a specific time)
permit me to say that	(permission is not necessary)
we are in receipt of	we have received
pursuant to	(omit)
in closing, I'd like to say	(omit)
the undersigned	I; me
kindly advise	please let us know
we wish to inform you	(just say it)
attached please find	enclosed is
it has come to my attention	I have just learned; or, Ms. Garza has just told me
our Mr. Lydell	Mr. Lydell, our credit manager
please be advised that	(omit)
Pompous	***Down to Earth***
Upon procurement of additional supplies, I will initiate fulfillment of your order.	I will fill your order when I receive more supplies.
Perusal of the records indicates a substantial deficit for the preceding accounting period due to the utilization of antiquated mechanisms.	The records show a company loss last year due to the use of old equipment.

- **Avoid preaching and bragging.** Few things are more irritating than people who think that they know everything and others know nothing. If you must tell your audience something obvious, place the information in the middle of a paragraph, where it will sound like a casual comment rather than a major revelation. Also, avoid bragging about your accomplishments or about the size or profitability of your organization (unless your audience is a part of your organization).

Your conversational tone may become less or more formal, depending on the situation. If you're in a large organization and you're communicating with your superiors or if you're communicating to customers, your conversational tone would tend to be more formal and respectful.

You can adjust the formality of your conversational tone.

What do you think of the formality and tone of this letter?[9]

Dear Ms. Navarro:

Enclosed please find the information that was requested in our telephone communication on May 14. As was mentioned at that time, Midville Hospital has significantly more doctors of exceptional quality than any other health facility in the state.

As you were also informed, our organization has offices located throughout the state. In the event that you need a specialist, our professionals will refer you to the most appropriate party. You are also entitled to utilize one of our numerous programs that will assist you and your family in achieving the highest level of health possible.

Please contact me in the event that you have questions or would like additional information.

Most sincerely yours,

Samuel G. Berenz

A little pompous, isn't it? Now review Figure 5.7 to see how the letter can be rewritten in both a professional and informal tone.

FIGURE 5.7 Professional Versus Informal Tone

PROFESSIONAL TONE (RECOMMENDED FOR MOST BUSINESS COMMUNICATION)	INFORMAL TONE (USE ONLY WITH FRIENDS AND CLOSE BUSINESS ASSOCIATES)
Dear Ms. Navarro: I am sending along the information you requested on Friday. As I mentioned, Midville Hospital has more doctors than any hospital in the state. In addition, we have a vast network of doctors and other health professionals with offices throughout Massachusetts and in parts of New Hampshire and Rhode Island. If you need a specialist, they can refer you to the right one. You and your family can also participate in numerous programs, such as smoking-cessation classes, a 24-hour hotline with a registered nurse to answer your questions seven days a week, health fairs, and more. Feel free to call anytime between 9:00 and 5:00 Monday through Friday if you would like more information. Sincerely, Samuel G. Berenz	Dear Gabriella: Just sending along the information we talked about on Friday. As I said, Midville Hospital has more doctors than any hospital in the state. We also have an impressive network of doctors and other professionals with offices near your work or home. Need a specialist? They'll refer you to the right one. You and your family can also get health-wise, thanks to our numerous programs, such as health fairs and classes to improve your overall fitness. We even have a health hotline designed to answer your health questions all day, every day. Want to know more? Just call. I'm at the office between 9:00 and 5:00, Monday through Friday. Take care, Sam

These two business letters to Gabriella Navarro deliver the same information included in the letter above, but they omit the formal tone.

Sharpening Your Career Skills

No Need to Explain It, Just Say It in Plain English

The goal of good writing is to communicate, not to confuse; to be understood, not to hide behind words. Look at this confusing excerpt from an investment document:

> *The applicability of the general information and administrative procedures set forth below accordingly will vary depending on the investor and the record-keeping system established for a shareholder's investment in the Fund. Participants in 401(k) and other plans should first consult with the appropriate persons at their employer or refer to the plan materials before following any of the procedures below.*

No wonder investors turn to brokers, accountants, and lawyers for help. Even Arthur Levitt, Jr., past chairman of the Securities and Exchange Commission (SEC), found that he couldn't understand some investment documents: "I realized the SEC did a good job requiring disclosure, but not enough to make sure documents were in a form most investors could understand."

Today's consumers want to understand the investments and the insurance policies they purchase, as well as the leases, mortgages, and sales contracts they sign. And in January 1998, the SEC began requiring companies to write all investment documents in plain English, following six basic writing principles:

- Use active voice
- Use lists to present complex material
- Use short sentences
- Avoid legal jargon
- Use everyday words
- Avoid multiple negatives

Restating our excerpt in plain English reveals one simple thought: "If you are investing through a large retirement plan or other special program, follow the instructions in your program material."

Some companies are concerned that writing documents in plain English will increase their liability, but many companies are finding just the opposite. "In many ways," notes one Bell Atlantic employee, "we reduced our liability because we have created a document that is much clearer and less ambiguous." Similarly, when Citibank introduced promissory notes written in plain English, the number of collection lawsuits fell dramatically. The clearer writing simply made it easier for borrowers to understand their obligations.

Some lawyers may purposely choose obscure language to control vital information, to take advantage of those who don't know what they're signing, or to profit from people who call them to interpret the gobbledygook. But many legal professionals strongly endorse the plain-English movement. The State Bar of Texas offers sarcastic "legaldygook" awards for especially atrocious writing. And law schools are investing in programs designed to teach students how to write in plain English.

The plain-English movement has generated such momentum that in 1998, President Clinton signed an executive order requiring federal agencies to communicate in language that is "clearer and easier to understand." Agencies must now use plain English in any new document explaining how to get a benefit or comply with a requirement, and all new regulations must use simple wording. Clearly, confusing language is becoming obsolete.

Career Applications

1. How does writing in plain English affect a company's image?
2. Why don't more companies draft their documents using plain English?

Use Plain English

Plain English is close to spoken English and can be easily understood.

Plain English is a way of writing and arranging technical materials so that your audience can understand your meaning. Because it's close to the way people normally speak, plain English is easily understood by anyone with an eighth- or ninth-grade education. If you've ever tried to make sense of an overwritten or murky passage in a legal document or credit agreement, you can understand why governments and corporations today are endorsing the plain-English movement.[10]

Plain English is already being used in many areas.

This movement has already led to the use of plain English in loan and credit card application forms, insurance policies, investment documents, and real estate contracts (see "Sharpening Your Career Skills: No Need to Explain It, Just Say It in Plain English"). Even software programmers are trying to simplify their language. They need to communicate clearly with product users who may not understand what it means to "pop out to DOS."[11]

Not every application is appropriate for plain English.

Of course, plain English has some limitations. It lacks the precision necessary for scientific research, intense feeling, and personal insight. Moreover, it fails to embrace

TABLE 5.5 Choosing Active or Passive Voice

Avoid Passive Voice in General	Use Active Voice in General
The new procedure is thought by the president to be superior.	The president thinks the new procedure is superior.
There are problems with this contract.	This contract has problems.
It is necessary that the report be finished by next week.	The report must be finished by next week.
Sometimes Avoid Active Voice	***Sometimes Use Passive Voice***
You lost the shipment.	The shipment was lost.
I am analyzing the production line to determine the problem.	The production line is being analyzed to determine the problem.
We have established criteria to evaluate capital expenditures.	Criteria have been established to evaluate capital expenditures.

all cultures and dialects equally. But even though it's intended for audiences who speak English as their primary language, plain English can also help you simplify the messages you prepare for audiences who speak English only as a second or even third language. For example, by choosing words that have only one interpretation, you will surely communicate more clearly with your intercultural audience.[12]

Select Active or Passive Voice

Your choice of active or passive voice also affects the tone of your message. You're using **active voice** when the subject (the "actor") comes before the verb and the object of the sentence (the "acted upon") follows the verb: "John rented the office." You're using **passive voice** when the subject follows the verb and the object precedes it: "The office was rented by John." As you can see, the passive voice combines the helping verb *to be* with a form of the verb that is usually similar to the past tense. Active sentences generally sound less formal and make it easier for the reader to figure out who performed the action (see Table 5.5). Passive voice, by contrast, de-emphasizes the subject and implies action done by something or someone.

Using the active voice produces shorter, stronger sentences and makes your writing more vigorous, concise, and generally easier to understand.[13] Using the passive voice, while not wrong grammatically, is cumbersome, wordy, and often unnecessarily vague, and it can make sentences longer. Nevertheless, using the passive voice makes sense in some situations because it can help you focus on your audience and demonstrate the "you" attitude:

Active sentences are stronger than passive ones.

Use passive sentences to soften bad news, to put yourself in the background, or to create an impersonal tone.

- When you want to be diplomatic about pointing out a problem or error of some kind (the passive version seems less like an accusation)
- When you want to point out what's being done without taking or attributing either the credit or the blame (the passive version leaves the actor completely out of the sentence)
- When you want to avoid personal pronouns in order to create an objective tone (the passive version may be used in a formal report, for example)

Learning Objective 5

Briefly describe how to select words that are not only correct but also effective

Selecting the Best Words

To compose effective messages, you must choose your words carefully.[14] First, pay close attention to correctness. The "rules" of grammar and usage are constantly changing to reflect changes in the way people speak. Even editors and grammarians occasionally have questions about correct usage, and they sometimes disagree about the answers. For

Correctness is the first consideration when choosing words.

example, the word *data* is the plural form of *datum,* yet some experts now prefer to treat *data* as a singular noun when it's used in nonscientific material to refer to a body of information. You be the judge: Which of the following sentences sounds better?

> The data on our market share is consistent from region to region.
> The data on our market share are consistent from region to region.

Correct grammar enhances your image.

Although debating the finer points of usage may seem like nitpicking, using words correctly is important. If you make grammatical or usage errors, you lose credibility with your audience. Poor grammar implies that you're unaware or uninformed, and audiences put little faith in an uninformed source. Even if an audience is broad-minded enough to withhold such a judgment, grammatical errors are distracting.

If in doubt, check it out.

If you have doubts about what is correct, don't be lazy. Look up the answer, and use the proper form of expression. Check the grammar and usage guide in Appendix III, or consult any number of special reference books and resources available in libraries, in bookstores, and on the Internet. Most authorities agree on the basic conventions.

Effectiveness is the second consideration when choosing words.

Just as important as selecting the correct word is selecting the most suitable word for the job at hand. Word effectiveness is generally more difficult to achieve than correctness, particularly in written communication. Writers such as Julie Galle have to work at their craft, using functional and content words correctly and finding the words that communicate.

Use Functional and Content Words Correctly

Functional words (conjunctions, prepositions, articles, and pronouns) express relationships among content words (nouns, verbs, adjectives, and adverbs).

Words can be divided into two main categories. **Functional words** express relationships and have only one unchanging meaning in any given context. They include conjunctions, prepositions, articles, and pronouns. Your main concern with functional words is to use them correctly. **Content words** are multidimensional and therefore subject to various interpretations. They include nouns, verbs, adjectives, and adverbs. These words carry the meaning of a sentence. In your sentences, content words are the building blocks, and functional words are the mortar that holds them together. In the following sentence, all the content words are underlined:

> <u>Some objective observers</u> of the <u>cookie market give Nabisco</u> the <u>edge</u> in <u>quality</u>, but <u>Frito-Lay is lauded</u> for <u>superior distribution</u>.

Both functional words and content words are necessary, but your effectiveness as a communicator depends largely on your ability to choose the right content words for your message.

Content words have both a denotative (explicit, specific) meaning and a connotative (implicit, associative) meaning.

Denotation and Connotation Content words have both a denotative and a connotative meaning. The **denotative meaning** is the literal, or dictionary, meaning. The **connotative meaning** includes all the associations and feelings evoked by the word.

The denotative meaning of *desk* is "a table used for writing." Some desks may have drawers or compartments, and others may have a flat top or a sloping top, but the literal meaning is generally well understood. The connotative meaning of *desk* may include thoughts associated with work or study, but the word *desk* has fairly neutral connotations—neither strong nor emotional. However, some words have much stronger connotations than others. For example, if you say that a student *failed* to pass a test, the connotative meaning suggests that the person is inferior, incompetent, below some standard of performance. The connotations of the word *fail* are negative and can carry strong emotional meaning.

Business communicators avoid words with negative connotations.

In business communication, avoid using terms that are high in connotative meaning. By saying that a student achieved a score of 65 percent, you communicate the facts and avoid a heavy load of negative connotations. If you use words that have relatively few possible interpretations, you are less likely to be misunderstood. In addition, because you are trying to communicate in an objective, rational manner, you want to avoid emotion-laden comments.

Abstraction and Concreteness An **abstract word** expresses a concept, quality, or characteristic. Abstractions are usually broad, encompassing a category of ideas. They are often intellectual, academic, or philosophical. *Love, honor, progress, tradition,* and *beauty* are abstractions.

A **concrete word** stands for something you can touch or see. Concrete terms are anchored in the tangible, material world. *Chair, table, horse, rose, kick, kiss, red, green,* and *two* are concrete words; they are direct, clear, and exact.

The more abstract a word, the more it is removed from the tangible, objective world of things that can be perceived with the senses.

You might assume that concrete words are better than abstract words, because they are more precise, but you would sometimes be wrong. For example, try to rewrite this sentence without using the underlined abstract words:

> We hold these truths to be self-evident, that all men are created equal, that they are endowed by their Creator with certain unalienable Rights, that among these are Life, Liberty, and the Pursuit of Happiness.

As you can see, the Declaration of Independence needs abstractions, and so do business messages. Abstractions permit us to rise above the common and tangible. They allow us to refer to concepts such as *morale, productivity, profits, quality, motivation,* and *guarantees.*

Even though they're indispensable, abstractions can be troublesome. They tend to be fuzzy and subject to many interpretations. They also tend to be boring. It isn't always easy to get excited about ideas, especially if they're unrelated to concrete experience. The best way to minimize such problems is to blend abstract terms with concrete ones, the general with the specific. State the concept, then pin it down with details expressed in more concrete terms. Save the abstractions for ideas that cannot be expressed any other way.

In business communication, use concrete, specific terms whenever possible; use abstractions only when necessary.

Because words such as *small, numerous, sizable, near, soon, good,* and *fine* are imprecise, try to replace them with terms that are more accurate. Instead of referring to a *sizable loss,* talk about a *loss of $32 million.*

Find Words That Communicate

Anyone who earns a living by crafting words is a *wordsmith*—including journalists, public relations specialists, editors, and letter and report writers. Unlike poets, novelists, or dramatists, wordsmiths don't strive for dramatic effects. Instead, they are concerned with using language to be clear, concise, and accurate. To reach their goal, they emphasize words that are strong and familiar. When you compose your business messages, do your best to think like a wordsmith (see Table 5.6).

Business communicators aim for clarity and accuracy rather than dramatic effect.

Wordsmiths choose strong words, choose familiar words, avoid clichés, and use jargon carefully.

- **Choose strong words.** Choose words that express your thoughts most clearly, specifically, and dynamically. Nouns and verbs are the most concrete, so use them as much as you can. Adjectives and adverbs have obvious roles, but use them sparingly—they often evoke subjective judgments. Verbs are especially powerful because they tell what's happening in the sentence, so make them dynamic and specific (replace *rise* or *fall* with *soar* or *plummet*).
- **Choose familiar words.** You'll communicate best with words that are familiar to your readers. However, keep in mind that words familiar to one reader might be unfamiliar to another.
- **Avoid clichés.** Although familiar words are generally the best choice, beware of terms and phrases so common that they have become virtually meaningless. Because clichés are used so often, readers tend to slide right by them to whatever is coming next. Most people use these phrases not because they think it makes their message more vivid and inviting but because they don't know how to express themselves otherwise.[15]
- **Use jargon carefully.** Handle technical or professional terms with care. As Julie Galle puts it, meteorological techno-babble and jargon can add precision and authority

It's fine to use jargon on the job with your peers, but when communicating with outsiders you must be careful to put technical information into words your audience can understand.

TABLE 5.6 Thinking Like a Wordsmith

Avoid Weak Phrases	***Use Strong Terms***
Wealthy businessperson	Tycoon
Business prosperity	Boom
Hard times	Slump
Avoid Unfamiliar Words	***Use Familiar Words***
Ascertain	Find out, learn
Consummate	Close, bring about
Peruse	Read, study
Circumvent	Avoid
Increment	Growth, increase
Unequivocal	Certain
Avoid Clichés	***Use Plain Language***
Scrape the bottom of the barrel	Strain shrinking resources
An uphill battle	A challenge
Writing on the wall	Prediction
Call the shots	Be in charge
Take by storm	Attack
Cost an arm and a leg	Expensive
A new ballgame	Fresh start
Worst nightmare	Strong competitor; disaster
Fall through the cracks	Be overlooked

to a weather message, but many people don't understand jargon. When deciding whether to use technical jargon, let your audience's knowledge guide you. For example, when addressing a group of engineers or scientists, it's probably fine to refer to *meteorological effects on microwave propagation;* otherwise, refer to the *effects of weather on radio waves.*

Remember, good business writing is learned by imitation and practice. As you read business journals, newspapers, and even novels, make a note of the words you think are effective and keep them in a file. Then look through them before you draft your next letter or report. Try using some of these words in your document. You may be surprised how they can strengthen your writing.

Creating Effective Sentences

Every sentence contains a subject (noun or noun equivalent) and a predicate (verb and related words).

In English, words don't make much sense until they're combined in a sentence to express a complete thought. Thus the words *Jill, receptionist, the, smiles,* and *at* can be organized into "Jill smiles at the receptionist." Now that you've constructed the sentence, you can begin exploring the possibilities for improvement, looking at how well each word performs its particular function. Nouns and noun equivalents are the topics (or subjects) you're communicating about, and verbs and related words (or predicates) make statements about those subjects. In a complicated sentence, adjectives and adverbs modify the subject and the statement, and various connectors hold the words together.

The Four Types of Sentences

Sentences come in four basic varieties: simple, compound, complex, and compound-complex. A **simple sentence** has one main clause (a single subject and a single predicate), although it may be expanded by nouns and pronouns serving as objects of the action and by modifying phrases. Here's a typical example (with the subject underlined once and the predicate verb underlined twice):

A simple sentence has one main clause.

> Profits have increased in the past year.

A **compound sentence** has two main clauses that express two or more independent but related thoughts of equal importance, usually joined by *and, but,* or *or*. In effect, a compound sentence is a merger of two or more simple sentences (independent clauses) that are related. For example:

A compound sentence has two main clauses.

> Wage rates have declined by 5 percent, and employee turnover has been high.

The independent clauses in a compound sentence are always separated by a comma or by a semicolon (in which case the conjunction—*and, but, or*—is dropped).

A **complex sentence** expresses one main thought (the independent clause) and one or more subordinate thoughts (dependent clauses) related to it, often separated by a comma. The subordinate thought, which comes first in the following sentence, could not stand alone:

A complex sentence has one main clause and one subordinate clause.

> Although you may question Gerald's conclusions, you must admit that his research is thorough.

A **compound-complex sentence** has two main clauses, at least one of which contains a subordinate clause:

A compound-complex sentence has two main clauses and at least one dependent clause.

> Profits have increased in the past year, and although you may question Gerald's conclusions, you must admit that his research is thorough.

When constructing a sentence, choose the form that matches the relationship of the ideas you want to express. If you have two ideas of equal importance, express them as two simple sentences or as one compound sentence. However, if one of the ideas is less important than the other, place it in a dependent clause to form a complex sentence. For example, although the following compound sentence uses a conjunction to join two ideas, they aren't truly equal:

> The chemical products division is the strongest in the company, and its management techniques should be adopted by the other divisions.

By making the first thought subordinate to the second, you establish a cause-and-effect relationship. So the following complex sentence is much more effective:

> Because the chemical products division is the strongest in the company, its management techniques should be adopted by the other divisions.

To make your writing as effective as possible, balance all four sentence types. If you use too many simple sentences, you won't be able to properly express the relationships among your ideas. If you use too many long, compound sentences, your writing will sound monotonous. On the other hand, an uninterrupted series of complex or compound-complex sentences is hard to follow.

Writing is more effective if it balances all four sentence types.

Use Sentence Style to Emphasize Key Thoughts

Sentence style varies from culture to culture. German sentences are extremely complex, with lots of modifiers and appositives; Japanese and Chinese languages don't even have sentences in the same sense that Western languages do.[16] However, in

English try to make your sentences grammatically correct, efficient, readable, interesting, and appropriate for your audience. In general, strive for straightforward simplicity. For most business audiences, clarity and efficiency take precedence over literary style.

Emphasize parts of a sentence by
- Giving them more space
- Putting them at the beginning or at the end of the sentence
- Making them the subject of the sentence

In every message, some ideas are more important than others. You can emphasize these key ideas through your sentence style. One obvious technique is to give important points the most space. When you want to call attention to a thought, use extra words to describe it. Consider this sentence:

> The chairperson of the board called for a vote of the shareholders.

To emphasize the importance of the chairperson, you might describe her more fully:

> Having considerable experience in corporate takeover battles, the chairperson of the board called for a vote of the shareholders.

You can increase the emphasis even more by adding a separate, short sentence to augment the first:

> The chairperson of the board called for a vote of the shareholders. She has considerable experience in corporate takeover battles.

You can also call attention to a thought by making it the subject of the sentence. In the following example, the emphasis is on the person:

> *I* can write letters much more quickly using a computer.

However, by changing the subject, the computer takes center stage:

> The *computer* enables me to write letters much more quickly.

Another way to emphasize an idea is to place it at either the beginning or the end of a sentence:

> **Less Emphatic:** We are cutting the *price* to stimulate demand.
> **More Emphatic:** To stimulate demand, we are cutting the *price*.

Dependent clauses can determine emphasis.

In complex sentences, the placement of the dependent clause hinges on the relationship between the ideas expressed. If you want to emphasize the idea, put the dependent clause at the end of the sentence (the most emphatic position) or at the beginning (the second most emphatic position). If you want to downplay the idea, bury the dependent clause within the sentence.

> **Most Emphatic:** The electronic parts are manufactured in Mexico, *which has lower wage rates than the United States.*
> **Emphatic:** *Because wage rates are lower there,* the electronic parts are manufactured in Mexico.
> **Least Emphatic:** Mexico, *which has lower wage rates,* was selected as the production point for the electronic parts.

Techniques like these give you a great deal of control over the way your audience interprets what you have to say.

Developing Coherent Paragraphs

Paragraphs are functional units that revolve around a single thought.

A *paragraph* is a cluster of sentences all related to the same general topic. It is a unit of thought, separated from other units by skipping a line or indenting the first line. A series of paragraphs makes up an entire composition. Each paragraph is an important part of the whole, a key link in the train of thought. As you compose your message, think about the paragraphs and their relationship to one another.

Elements of the Paragraph

Paragraphs vary widely in length and form. You can communicate effectively in one short paragraph or in pages of lengthy paragraphs, depending on your purpose, your audience, and your message. The typical paragraph contains three basic elements: a topic sentence, related sentences that develop the topic, and transitional words and phrases.

Most paragraphs consist of a topic sentence, related sentences, and transitional elements.

Topic Sentence Every properly constructed paragraph is *unified;* it deals with a single topic. The sentence that introduces that topic is called the **topic sentence.** In informal and creative writing, the topic sentence may be implied rather than stated. In business writing, the topic sentence is generally explicit and is often the first sentence in the paragraph. The topic sentence gives readers a summary of the general idea that will be covered in the rest of the paragraph. The following examples show how a topic sentence can introduce the subject and can suggest the way that subject will be developed:

The topic sentence
- Reveals the subject of the paragraph
- Indicates how the subject will be developed

> The medical products division has been troubled for many years by public relations problems. [In the rest of the paragraph, readers will learn the details of the problems.]
>
> Relocating the plant in New York has two main disadvantages. [The disadvantages will be explained in subsequent sentences.]
>
> To get a refund, you must supply us with some additional information. [The details of the necessary information will be described in the rest of the paragraph.]

Related Sentences The sentences that explain the topic sentence round out the paragraph. These related sentences must all have a bearing on the general subject and must provide enough specific details to make the topic clear:

Paragraphs are developed through a series of related sentences that provide details about the topic sentence.

> The medical products division has been troubled for many years by public relations problems. Since 1997 the local newspaper has published 15 articles that portray the division in a negative light. We have been accused of everything from mistreating laboratory animals to polluting the local groundwater. Our facility has been described as a health hazard. Our scientists are referred to as "Frankensteins," and our profits are considered "obscene."

The developmental sentences are all more specific than the topic sentence. Each one provides another piece of evidence to demonstrate the general truth of the main thought. Also, each sentence is clearly related to the general idea being developed; the relation between the sentences and the idea is what gives the paragraph its unity. A paragraph is well developed when it contains enough information to make the topic sentence convincing and interesting.

Transitional Elements In addition to being unified and well developed, effective paragraphs are *coherent;* that is, they are arranged in a logical order so that the audience can understand the train of thought. When you complete a paragraph, your readers automatically assume that you've finished with a particular idea. You achieve coherence by using transitions that show the relationship between paragraphs and among sentences within paragraphs. **Transitions,** words or phrases that tie ideas together, show how one thought is related to another; they help readers understand the connections you're trying to make. You can establish transitions in various ways:

Because each paragraph covers a single idea, use transitional words and phrases to show readers how paragraphs relate to each other.

- Use connecting words: *and, but, or, nevertheless, however, in addition,* and so on.
- Echo a word or phrase from a previous paragraph or sentence: "A system should be established for monitoring inventory levels. *This system* will provide . . ."
- Use a pronoun that refers to a noun used previously: "Ms. Arthur is the leading candidate for the president's position. *She* has excellent qualifications."
- Use words that are frequently paired: "The machine has a *minimum* output of . . . Its *maximum* output is . . ."

Some transitional devices include
- Connecting words (conjunctions)
- Repeated words or phrases
- Pronouns
- Words that are frequently paired

Some transitional elements serve as mood changers; that is, they alert the reader to a change in mood from the previous paragraph. Some announce a total contrast with

Transitions move readers between sentences and paragraphs.

what's gone on before, some announce a causal relationship, and some signal a change in time. They prepare your reader for the change. Here is a list of transitions frequently used to move readers smoothly between sentences and paragraphs:

Additional detail:	moreover, furthermore, in addition, besides, first, second, third, finally
Causal relationship:	therefore, because, accordingly, thus, consequently, hence, as a result, so
Comparison:	similarly, here again, likewise, in comparison, still
Contrast:	yet, conversely, whereas, nevertheless, on the other hand, however, but, nonetheless
Condition:	although, if
Illustration:	for example, in particular, in this case, for instance
Time sequence:	formerly, after, when, meanwhile, sometimes
Intensification:	indeed, in fact, in any event
Summary:	in brief, in short, to sum up
Repetition:	that is, in other words, as I mentioned earlier

Although transitional words and phrases are useful, they're not sufficient in themselves to overcome poor organization. Your goal is first to put your ideas in a strong framework and then to use transitions to link them together even more strongly.

Consider using a transition device whenever it might help the reader understand your ideas and follow you from point to point. You can use transitions inside paragraphs to tie related points together and between paragraphs to ease the shift from one distinct thought to another. In longer reports, transitions that link major sections or chapters are often complete paragraphs that serve as mini-introductions to the next section or as summaries of the ideas presented in the section just ending. Here's an example:

> Given the nature of this product, the alternatives are limited. As the previous section indicates, we can stop making it altogether, improve it, or continue with the current model. Each of these alternatives has advantages and disadvantages, which are discussed in the following section.

Five Ways to Develop a Paragraph

Learning Objective 6

List five ways to develop a paragraph and discuss three factors that increase paragraph readability

Five ways to develop paragraphs:

- Illustration
- Comparison or contrast
- Cause and effect
- Classification
- Problem and solution

Paragraphs can be developed in many ways. Five of the most common techniques are illustration; comparison or contrast; cause and effect; classification; and problem and solution (see Table 5.7). Your choice of technique depends on your subject, your intended audience, and your purpose.

In practice, you'll often combine two or more methods of development in a single paragraph. To add interest, you might begin by using illustration, shift to comparison or contrast, and then shift to problem and solution. However, before settling for the first approach that comes to mind, consider the alternatives. Think through various methods before committing yourself. If you fall into the easy habit of repeating the same old paragraph pattern time after time, your writing will be boring.

Using Technology to Compose and Shape Your Messages

Word processing makes composing and shaping as painless as possible, automating many of the text entry and revision tasks. For example, when you compose a numbered list, the software will automatically renumber the remaining segments if an entry is removed. Computers can also help you keep track of footnotes or endnotes, renumbering them every time you add or delete references. For report indexes and tables of con-

TABLE 5.7 Five Techniques for Developing Paragraphs

Technique	*Description*	*Sample*
Illustration	Giving examples that demonstrate the general idea	Some of our most popular products are available through local distributors. For example, Everett & Lemmings carries our frozen soups and entrees. The J. B. Green Company carries our complete line of seasonings, as well as the frozen soups. Wilmont Foods, also a major distributor, now carries our new line of frozen desserts.
Comparison or Contrast	Using similarities or differences to develop the topic	In previous years, when the company was small, the recruiting function could be handled informally. The need for new employees was limited, and each manager could comfortably screen and hire her or his own staff. Today, however, Gambit Products must undertake a major recruiting effort. Our successful bid on the Owens contract means that we will be doubling our labor force over the next six months. To hire that many people without disrupting our ongoing activities, we will create a separate recruiting group within the human resources department.
Cause and Effect	Focusing on the reasons for something	The heavy-duty fabric of your Wanderer tent probably broke down for one of two reasons: (1) a sharp object punctured the fabric, and without reinforcement, the hole was enlarged by the stress of erecting the tent daily for a week or (2) the fibers gradually rotted because the tent was folded and stored while still wet.
Classification	Showing how a general idea is broken into specific categories	Successful candidates for our supervisor trainee program generally come from one of several groups. The largest group, by far, consists of recent graduates of accredited data-processing programs. The next largest group comes from within our own company, as we try to promote promising clerical workers to positions of greater responsibility. Finally, we do occasionally accept candidates with outstanding supervisory experience in related industries.
Problem and Solution	Presenting a problem and then discussing the solution	Selling handmade toys by mail is a challenge because consumers are accustomed to buying heavily advertised toys from major chains. However, if we develop an appealing catalog, we can compete on the basis of product novelty and quality. In addition, we can provide craftsmanship at a competitive price: a rocking horse of birch, with a hand-knit tail and mane; a music box with the child's name painted on the top; a real Indian teepee, made by Native American artisans.

tents, you simply flag the items you want to include, and the software assembles the lists for you. Other helpful features include automatic page numbering and dating. When you insert a date code into a document, the software automatically fills in the day's date each time you open or print that document. This feature is especially handy if you use form letters.

Some of the text that business communicators use in their documents is "prewritten." For example, say that you want to announce to the media that you've developed a new product or hired an executive. Such announcements—called press releases—usually end with a standard paragraph about the company and its line of business. Any standard block of text that is used in various documents without being changed is called a **boilerplate**. With a good word processor, you simply store the paragraph the first time you write it and then pop it into a document whenever you need it. Using boilerplates saves time and reduces mistakes because you're not retyping the paragraph every time you use it. A related concept applies to manipulating existing text. If you're a national sales manager compiling a report that includes summaries from your four regional managers, you can use your word processor's *file*

A boilerplate is any standard block of text used in various documents without being changed.

CHECKLIST: COMPOSING AND SHAPING BUSINESS MESSAGES

A. Generate ideas

1. Get ideas down as quickly as you can.
2. Rearrange, delete, and add ideas without losing sight of your purpose.

B. Vary the style to create a tone that suits the occasion

1. Use the appropriate level of formality.
2. Avoid being overly familiar, using inappropriate humor (including obvious flattery), sounding preachy, bragging, or trying to be something you're not.
3. Avoid obsolete and pompous language.
4. Use plain English.
5. Write mainly in the active voice, but use the passive voice to achieve specific effects.

C. Select the best words

1. Use concrete words that avoid negative connotations.
2. Rely on nouns, verbs, and specific adjectives and adverbs.
3. Choose words that are strong and familiar while avoiding clichés.

D. Create effective sentences and paragraphs

1. Use simple, compound, and complex sentences, choosing the form that best fits the thought you want to express.
2. Emphasize key points through sentence style; give important points the most space.
3. Be sure each paragraph contains a topic sentence, related sentences, and transitional elements.
4. Choose a method of development that suits the subject: illustration, comparison or contrast, cause and effect, classification, problem and solution.

merge capability to combine the four documents into one, saving yourself the trouble of retyping all four.

For a reminder of the tasks involved in composing and shaping your messages, see "Checklist: Composing and Shaping Business Messages."

WRITING EFFECTIVE E-MAIL MESSAGES

E-mail messages need as much care and attention as other business messages.

Even though e-mail seems transitory, organization and style are just as important for these messages as for any other type of business message. In addition to the principles and techniques already discussed in this chapter, consider the following when writing e-mail messages.

Organizing Your E-Mail Messages

The usual way to mark quoted text in e-mail messages is with a greater-than sign (>) at the beginning of each line.

Use the first few lines to tell the reader what you need, what you're providing, or what you want him or her to do. If you are responding to a question or a request for information, be sure to start your e-mail by inserting the original question into your reply. You can preprogram most e-mail software packages to automatically include the sender's original message in your e-mail replies and forwards. Or you can cut and paste the message yourself. Either way, use this feature with care. You can save the reader time by editing the original message to include only the information that is directly applicable to your reply. In other words, include only enough to refresh your audience's memory as to why you are sending the e-mail and how it addresses their specific needs.

Make responding easy.

If you are initiating a request for information, be sure to clearly state the type of response you need and ask for that response early in your message—perhaps even in your subject line. Then make it easy for your audience to respond by stating your request in a series of organized and perhaps numbered questions. Keep your questions or requests simple by restating compound requests into several single topics. If possible, word your requests so that your audience can respond with a simple yes or no answer.

Number your questions if you seek a series of replies.

Finally, make your e-mail easy to follow. Avoid lines that run off screen or wrap oddly by using the Enter key to limit lines to 80 characters (60 if e-mail will be forwarded). Avoid styled text (boldface, italics), unless your receiver's system can read it.[17] Write short, focused, logically organized paragraphs, using the composition tips discussed throughout this chapter. And try to limit e-mail to one screen; otherwise, write like a reporter—starting with the "headline" and adding detail in descending order of importance.[18] That way you'll be sure to get your point across as early as possible, in case your reader doesn't have the time or interest to finish reading your message.

Consider how your message will appear on your audience's screen.

Composing Your E-Mail Messages

E-mail can be as informal and casual as a conversation between old friends. But it can also emulate "snail mail" by using conventional business language, a respectful style, and a more formal format—such as a traditional greeting, formalized headings, and a formal closing and signature.[19] As with any business communication, how formal you make your message depends on your audience and your purpose.

The formality of an e-mail message depends upon your audience and your purpose.

Be sure to use correct spelling and proper grammar in these electronic messages. Some e-mail old-timers insist that spelling, grammar, capitalization, and punctuation take a backseat in cyberspace.[20] But in business communication, e-mail needs to be as clear and as easy to understand as possible. In addition to organizing your e-mail in a logical format, be sure to include an informative subject line and to make your message personal.

Creating Effective E-Mail Subject Lines

Effective e-mail subject lines grab the audience's attention. When e-mail receivers are deciding which messages to read first, they look at who sent each message, they check the subject line, and then they may scan the first screen. A message with a blank subject line or a general subject line such as "Question" will probably go unread and will perhaps be deleted.[21]

Make your e-mail interesting by making your subject line informative, personalizing your message, and making it easy to follow.

To capture your audience's attention, make your subject line informative. Do more than just describe or classify message content. You have 25 to 40 characters to build interest with key words, quotations, directions, or questions:[22]

Ineffective Subject Line	Effective Subject Line
July sales figures	Send figures for July sales
Tomorrow's meeting	Bring consultant's report to Friday's meeting
Marketing report	Need budget for marketing report
Employee parking	Revised resurfacing schedule for parking lot
Status report	Warehouse remodeling is on schedule

If you are exchanging multiple e-mails with someone on the same topic, be sure to periodically modify the subject line of your message to reflect the revised message content. Most e-mail programs will copy the subject line when you press the Reply key. Multiple messages in your e-mail electronic files with the same subject line can be confusing. Moreover, they may have absolutely nothing to do with the original topic. Modifying the subject line with each new response can make it easier to locate a message at a later date.

Personalizing Your E-Mail Messages

Adding a greeting to your e-mail message makes it more personal. Naturally, whether you use a formal greeting (*Dear Professor Ingersol*) or a more casual one (*Hi Marty*) depends on your audience and your purpose. Your closing and signature also personalize your e-mail message. In most cases, use simple closings, such as *Thanks* or *Regards,*

Use a greeting to make your e-mail more personal.

FIGURE 5.8 In-Depth Critique: Poor Example of On-Screen E-Mail Message

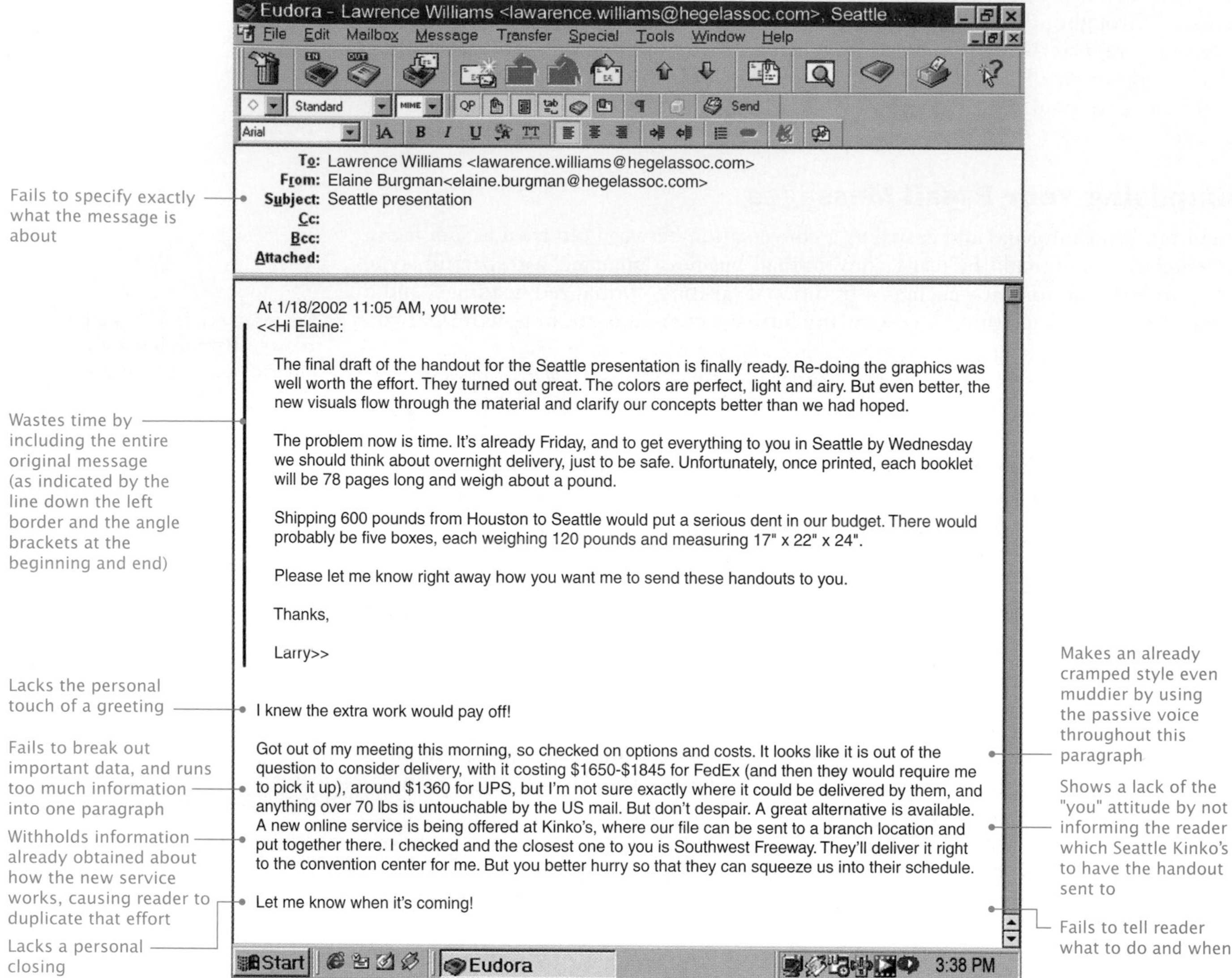

rather than more traditional business closings such as *Sincerely yours*. However, you may want to use a more formal closing for international e-mail.

After a simple closing, you can include a signature in several ways.

For your signature, you can simply type your name on a separate line. Or you may want to use a *signature file,* a short identifier that can include your name, company, postal address, fax number, other e-mail addresses, and sometimes even a short quotation or thought. Some business writers believe you should include only your contact information. Once you create a signature file, you can save it in your mail program and add it to e-mail messages without retyping it. You can also use a digital copy of your handwritten signature, which is becoming acceptable as legal proof in business transactions, especially when accompanied by a date stamp, which is automatically inserted by your mail program.

For an in-depth discussion of additional e-mail strategies and etiquette, see Chapter 4, "Checklist: Observing High-Tech Etiquette" and Appendix IV. Finally, compare and contrast Figures 5.8 and 5.9. Pay close attention to the subject line, organization, word choice, tone, and sentence structure used in each e-mail message.

FIGURE 5.9 In-Depth Critique: Good Example of On-Screen E-Mail Message

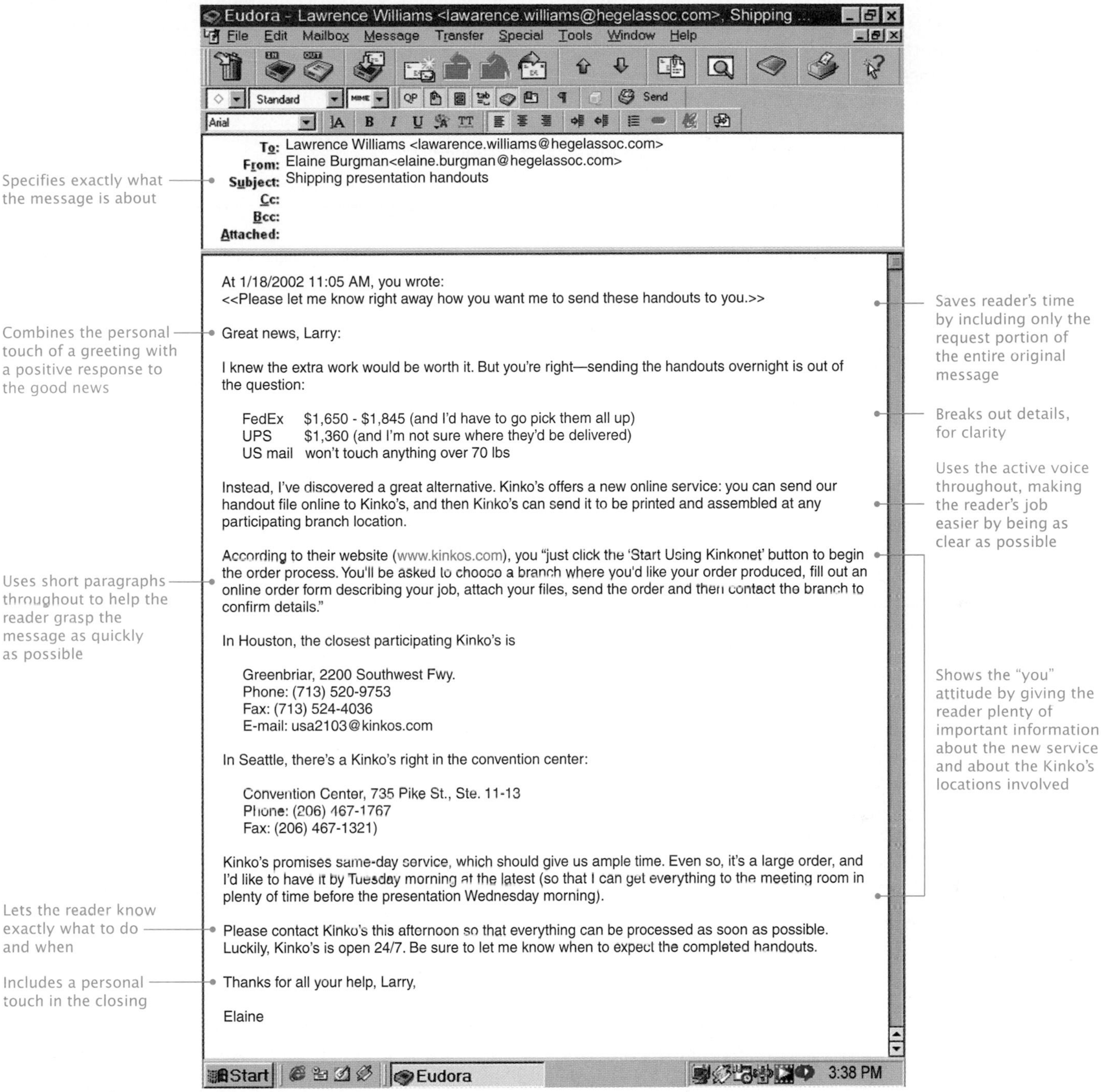

Eudora - Lawrence Williams <lawarence.williams@hegelassoc.com>, Shipping ...

File Edit Mailbox Message Transfer Special Tools Window Help

Standard Send

Arial

To: Lawrence Williams <lawarence.williams@hegelassoc.com>
From: Elaine Burgman<elaine.burgman@hegelassoc.com>
Subject: Shipping presentation handouts
Cc:
Bcc:
Attached:

Specifies exactly what the message is about

At 1/18/2002 11:05 AM, you wrote:
<<Please let me know right away how you want me to send these handouts to you.>>

Saves reader's time by including only the request portion of the entire original message

Great news, Larry:

Combines the personal touch of a greeting with a positive response to the good news

I knew the extra work would be worth it. But you're right—sending the handouts overnight is out of the question:

FedEx $1,650 - $1,845 (and I'd have to go pick them all up)
UPS $1,360 (and I'm not sure where they'd be delivered)
US mail won't touch anything over 70 lbs

Breaks out details, for clarity

Instead, I've discovered a great alternative. Kinko's offers a new online service: you can send our handout file online to Kinko's, and then Kinko's can send it to be printed and assembled at any participating branch location.

Uses the active voice throughout, making the reader's job easier by being as clear as possible

According to their website (www.kinkos.com), you "just click the 'Start Using Kinkonet' button to begin the order process. You'll be asked to choose a branch where you'd like your order produced, fill out an online order form describing your job, attach your files, send the order and then contact the branch to confirm details."

Uses short paragraphs throughout to help the reader grasp the message as quickly as possible

In Houston, the closest participating Kinko's is

Greenbriar, 2200 Southwest Fwy.
Phone: (713) 520-9753
Fax: (713) 524-4036
E-mail: usa2103@kinkos.com

In Seattle, there's a Kinko's right in the convention center:

Convention Center, 735 Pike St., Ste. 11-13
Phone: (206) 467-1767
Fax: (206) 467-1321)

Kinko's promises same-day service, which should give us ample time. Even so, it's a large order, and I'd like to have it by Tuesday morning at the latest (so that I can get everything to the meeting room in plenty of time before the presentation Wednesday morning).

Shows the "you" attitude by giving the reader plenty of important information about the new service and about the Kinko's locations involved

Please contact Kinko's this afternoon so that everything can be processed as soon as possible. Luckily, Kinko's is open 24/7. Be sure to let me know when to expect the completed handouts.

Lets the reader know exactly what to do and when

Thanks for all your help, Larry,

Includes a personal touch in the closing

Elaine

Start Eudora 3:38 PM

COMMUNICATION CHALLENGES AT WEATHER.COM

Writing special reports about weather-related topics is one of Julie Galle's primary responsibilities as a writer and producer for weather.com. Covering topics that range from global warming to deadly hurricanes, these special reports appear on weather.com's archives for indefinite periods.

To write the special reports, Galle must translate reams of scientific weather information into language that clearly explains how weather events work and how those events affect everyone's lives. She must take special care to organize the reports so that her audience can understand the information, and she must select words that users can comprehend quickly as they scroll through weather.com's website. Because millions of people read the reports, Galle wants to organize and compose her messages so that the information can be clearly understood by all of weather.com's users—whether they're rocket scientists interested in the long-term effects of global warming or retail sales clerks with a slight interest in learning more about tornadoes.

Team Challenge: Go to www.weather.com and click on "Special Reports." Then select one of the reports to discuss with several of your classmates. What is the main idea? Does the report use the direct approach or the indirect approach? How? What facts are included in the report? Does the report define technical terms? How does the report gain and hold the audience's interest? How is the report concluded? Once you've answered these questions, diagram the report by following the format shown in Figure 5.5 on page 114.

Individual Challenge: Write an e-mail message to Julie Galle at julie@weather.com, telling her how much you enjoyed the special report. Explain why the report was easy to understand, how the information was clearly presented to the users of weather.com, and how you benefited from learning about the topic. Be sure to choose the proper style and level of formality to use when composing your message. ■

SUMMARY OF LEARNING OBJECTIVES

1 **Cite four of the most common organization mistakes made by communicators.** Taking too long to get to the point, including irrelevant material, getting ideas mixed up, and leaving out necessary information are the most common organization mistakes made by communicators.

2 **Explain why good organization is important to both the communicator and the audience.** Audiences benefit from good organization in several ways. When audience members receive a message that is well organized, they don't have to read and reread a message to make sense of it, so they save time. They are also better able to understand the content, so they can accept the message more easily and can make better decisions based on its information. Communicators also benefit from good organization. When a message is well organized, communicators save time because preparing the message is quicker. Communicators can also use their organization plan to get advance input from their audience members, making sure they're on the right track. Finally, good organization allows communicators to divide portions of the writing assignment among co-workers.

3 **Summarize the process for organizing business messages effectively.** The process for organizing messages effectively involves defining the main idea of the message by making a specific statement about the topic; limiting the scope of the message by adjusting the space and detail you allocate to major points (which should number three to five, regardless of message length); grouping the points by constructing an outline to visualize the relationship between the ideas and the supporting material; and choosing either a direct or an indirect approach by anticipating the audience's reaction to the message (positive, neutral, or negative) and by matching the approach to message length (short or long) and message type (routine, good-news, and goodwill; bad-news; or persuasive).

4 **Discuss three ways of achieving a businesslike tone with a style that is clear and concise.** To ensure that messages are businesslike, clear, and concise, start by using a conversational tone: (1) focus on the facts, (2) construct rational arguments, and (3) try to avoid obsolete and pompous language, intimacy, humor, and preaching and bragging. Support this conversational tone by using plain English, which is easily understood by anyone with an eighth- or ninth-grade education. Then select the best voice for your message. Use the active voice to emphasize the subject of the message and to produce shorter, stronger sentences; use the passive voice to be diplomatic, to avoid taking credit or placing blame, or to create an objective tone.

5 **Briefly describe how to select words that are not only correct but also effective.** To select the best words, first make sure they are correct by checking grammar and usage guides. Next, make sure the words you select are effective by knowing how to use functional and content words. Choose words that have fewer connotations and no negative connotations. Blend abstract words with concrete ones, narrowing from the general to the specific, and select words that communicate clearly, specifically, and dynamically. Choose words that are strong, choose words that are familiar, avoid clichés, and use jargon only when your audience will understand it.

6 **List five ways to develop a paragraph and discuss three factors that increase paragraph readability.** Paragraphs can be developed by illustration (giving examples), by comparison and contrast (pointing out similarities or differences), by focusing on cause and effect (giving reasons), by classification (discussing categories), and by focusing on the solution to a problem (stating a problem and showing how to solve it). Paragraphs are easier to read when they are short (100 words or fewer), when they are broken up by headings (which highlight and summarize the material covered), and when they occasionally contain questions (which engage reader interest).

TEST YOUR KNOWLEDGE

1. What is the process for organizing messages?
2. How does the denotative meaning of a word differ from its connotative meaning?
3. What three elements do you consider when choosing between a direct and an indirect approach?
4. How does the audience benefit from a well-organized message?

5. What is style, and how do you decide on the appropriate style for a message?
6. How does an abstract word differ from a concrete word?
7. In what three situations is passive voice appropriate?
8. What is the purpose of the topic sentence?
9. What functions do transitions serve?
10. How do you use the subject line in an e-mail?

APPLY YOUR KNOWLEDGE

1. When organizing the ideas for your business message, how can you be sure that what seems logical to you will also seem logical to your audience?
2. Would you use a direct or an indirect approach to ask employees to work overtime to meet an important deadline? Please explain.
3. Which approach would you use to let your boss know that you'll be out half a day this week to attend your father's funeral—direct or indirect? Why?
4. Is it ever okay to use an indirect approach when writing e-mail? How can you put off the bad news when you have to state your purpose in the subject line? Explain.
5. **Ethical Choices** Do you think that using an indirect approach to cushion bad news is manipulative? Discuss the ethical issues in your answer.

PRACTICE YOUR KNOWLEDGE

Document for Analysis

A writer is working on an insurance information brochure and is having trouble grouping the ideas logically into an outline. Prepare the outline, paying attention to appropriate subordination of ideas. If necessary, rewrite phrases to give them a more consistent sound.

Accident Protection Insurance Plan

- Coverage is only pennies a day
- Benefit is $100,000 for accidental death on common carrier
- Benefit is $100 a day for hospitalization as result of motor vehicle or common carrier accident
- Benefit is $20,000 for accidental death in motor vehicle accident
- Individual coverage is only $17.85 per quarter; family coverage is just $26.85 per quarter
- No physical exam or health questions
- Convenient payment—billed quarterly
- Guaranteed acceptance for all applicants
- No individual rate increases
- Free, no-obligation examination period
- Cash paid in addition to any other insurance carried
- Covers accidental death when riding as fare-paying passenger on public transportation, including buses, trains, jets, ships, trolleys, subways, or any other common carrier
- Covers accidental death in motor vehicle accidents occurring while driving or riding in or on automobile, truck, camper, motor home, or nonmotorized bicycle

Exercises

For live links to all websites discussed in this chapter, visit this text's website at www.prenhall.com/bovee. Just log on and select Chapter 5, and click on "Student Resources." Locate the name of the site or the URL related to the material in the text. For "Exploring the Best of the Web" exercises, you'll also find navigational directions. Click on the live link to the site.

5.1 **Message Organization: Structuring Your Message** Using the GNC letter on page 109 (Figure 5.1), draw an organizational chart similar to the one shown in Figure 5.5 (see page 114). Fill in the main idea, the major points, and the evidence provided in this letter. (Note: Your diagram may be smaller than the one provided in Figure 5.5).

5.2 **Message Organization: Limiting Scope** Suppose you are preparing to recommend that top management install a new heating system (using the cogeneration process). The following information is in your files. Eliminate topics that aren't essential; then arrange the other topics so that your report will give top managers a clear understanding of the heating system and a balanced, concise justification for installing it.

- History of the development of the cogeneration heating process
- Scientific credentials of the developers of the process
- Risks assumed in using this process
- Your plan for installing the equipment in your building
- Stories about its successful use in comparable facilities
- Specifications of the equipment that would be installed
- Plans for disposing of the old heating equipment
- Costs of installing and running the new equipment
- Advantages and disadvantages of using the new process
- Detailed 10-year cost projections
- Estimates of the time needed to phase in the new system
- Alternative systems that management might wish to consider

5.3 **Message Organization: Choosing the Approach** Indicate whether the direct or the indirect approach would be best in each of the following situations; then briefly explain why. Would any of these messages be inappropriate for e-mail? Explain.

a. A letter asking when next year's automobiles will be put on sale locally
b. A letter from a recent college graduate requesting a letter of recommendation from a former instructor
c. A letter turning down a job applicant
d. An announcement that because of high air-conditioning costs, the plant temperature will be held at 78 degrees during the summer
e. A final request to settle a delinquent debt

5.4 **Message Organization: Drafting Persuasive Messages** If you were trying to persuade people to take the following actions, how would you organize your argument?

a. You want your boss to approve your plan for hiring two new people.
b. You want to be hired for a job.
c. You want to be granted a business loan.
d. You want to collect a small amount from a regular customer whose account is slightly past due.
e. You want to collect a large amount from a customer whose account is seriously past due.

5.5 **Message Composition: Controlling Style** Rewrite the following letter to Mrs. Betty Crandall (1597 Church Street, Grants Pass, OR 97526) so that it conveys a helpful, personal, and interested tone:

> We have your letter of recent date to our Ms. Dobson. Owing to the fact that you neglected to include the size of the dress you ordered, please be advised that no shipment of your order was made, but the aforementioned

shipment will occur at such time as we are in receipt of the aforementioned information.

5.6 **Message Composition: Selecting Words** Write a concrete phrase for each of these vague phrases:

a. Sometime this spring
b. A substantial saving
c. A large number attended
d. Increased efficiency
e. Expanded the work area

5.7 **Message Composition: Selecting Words** List terms that are stronger than the following:

a. Ran after
b. Seasonal ups and downs
c. Bright
d. Suddenly rises
e. Moves forward

5.8 **Message Composition: Selecting Words** As you rewrite these sentences, replace the clichés with fresh, personal expressions:

a. Being a jack-of-all-trades, Dave worked well in his new selling job.
b. Moving Leslie into the accounting department, where she was literally a fish out of water, was like putting a square peg into a round hole, if you get my drift.
c. I knew she was at death's door, but I thought the doctor would pull her through.
d. Movies aren't really my cup of tea; as far as I am concerned, they can't hold a candle to a good book.
e. It's a dog-eat-dog world out there in the rat race of the asphalt jungle.

5.9 **Message Composition: Selecting Words** Suggest short, simple words to replace each of the following:

a. Inaugurate
b. Terminate
c. Utilize
d. Anticipate
e. Assistance
f. Endeavor
g. Ascertain
h. Procure
i. Consummate
j. Advise
k. Alteration
l. Forwarded
m. Fabricate
n. Nevertheless
o. Substantial

5.10 **Message Composition: Selecting Words** Write up-to-date versions of these phrases; write *none* if you think there is no appropriate substitute:

a. As per your instructions
b. Attached herewith
c. In lieu of
d. In reply I wish to state
e. Please be advised that

5.11 **Message Composition: Creating Sentences** Suppose that end-of-term frustrations have produced this e-mail message to Professor Anne Brewer from a student who believes he should have received a B in his accounting class. If this message were recast into three or four clear sentences, the teacher might be more receptive to the student's argument. Rewrite the message to show how you would improve it:

> I think that I was unfairly awarded a C in your accounting class this term, and I am asking you to change the grade to a B. It was a difficult term. I don't get any money from home, and I have to work mornings at the Pancake House (as a cook), so I had to rush to make your class, and those two times that I missed class were because they wouldn't let me off work because of special events at the Pancake House (unlike some other students who just take off when they choose). On the midterm examination, I originally got a 75 percent, but you said in class that there were two different ways to answer the third question and that you would change the grades of students who used the "optimal cost" method and had been counted off 6 points for doing this. I don't think that you took this into account, because I got 80 percent on the final, which is clearly a B. Anyway, whatever you decide, I just want to tell you that I really enjoyed this class, and I thank you for making accounting so interesting.

5.12 **Message Composition: Creating Sentences** Rewrite each sentence so that it is active rather than passive:

a. The raw data are submitted to the data processing division by the sales representative each Friday.
b. High profits are publicized by management.
c. The policies announced in the directive were implemented by the staff.
d. Our computers are serviced by the Santee Company.
e. The employees were represented by Janet Hogan.

5.13 **Message Composition: Writing Paragraphs** In the following paragraph, identify the topic sentence and the related sentences (those that support the idea of the topic sentence):

> Each year, McDonald's sponsors the All-American Band, made up of two high school students from each state. The band marches in Macy's Thanksgiving Day parade in New York City and the Rose Bowl Parade in Pasadena. Franchisees are urged to join their local Chamber of Commerce, United Way, American Legion, and other bastions of All-Americana. McDonald's tries hard to project an image of almost a charitable organization. Local outlets sponsor campaigns on fire prevention, bicycle safety, and litter cleanup, with advice from Hamburger Central on how to extract the most publicity from their efforts.[23]

Now add a topic sentence to this paragraph:

> Your company's image includes what a person sees, hears, and experiences in relation to your firm. Every business letter you write is therefore important. The quality of the letterhead and typing, the position of the copy on the page, the format, the kind of typeface used, and the color of the typewriter ribbon—all these factors play a part in creating an impression of you and your company in the mind of the person you are writing to.[24]

5.14 **Teamwork** Working with four other students, divide the following five topics among yourselves and each write one paragraph on his or her selected topic. Be sure each student uses a different technique when writing his or her paragraph: One student should use the illustration technique, one the comparison or contrast technique, one a discussion of cause and effect, one the classification technique, and one a discussion of problem and solution. Then exchange paragraphs within the team and pick out the main idea and general purpose of the paragraph one of your teammates wrote. Was everyone able to correctly identify the main idea and purpose? If not, suggest how the paragraph might be rewritten for clarity.

a. Types of cameras (or dogs or automobiles) available for sale

b. Advantages and disadvantages of eating at fast-food restaurants
c. Finding that first full-time job
d. Good qualities of my car (or house, or apartment, or neighborhood)
e. How to make a dessert recipe (or barbecue a steak or make coffee)

5.15 **Internet** Visit the Security Exchange Commission's (SEC) plain-English website at www.sec.gov, click on "Online Publications," and review the online handbook. In one or two sentences, summarize what the SEC means by the phrase "plain English." Now read the SEC's online advice about how to invest in mutual funds. Does this document follow the SEC's plain-English guidelines? Can you suggest any improvements to organization, words, sentences, or paragraphs?

5.16 **Message Organization: Transitional Elements** Add transitional elements to the following sentences to improve the flow of ideas. (Note: You may need to eliminate or add some words to smooth out your sentences.)

a. Steve Case saw infinite possibilities in cyberspace. Steve Case was determined to turn his vision into reality. The techies scoffed at his strategy of building a simple Internet service for ordinary people. Case doggedly pursued his dream. He analyzed other online services. He assessed the needs of his customers. He responded to their desires for an easier way to access information over the Internet. In 1992, Steve Case named his company America Online (AOL). Critics predicted the company's demise. By the end of the century, AOL was a profitable powerhouse.
b. Facing some of the toughest competitors in the world, Harley-Davidson had to make some changes. The company introduced new products. Harley's management team set out to rebuild the company's production process. New products were coming to market and the company was turning a profit. Harley's quality standards were not on par with those of its foreign competitors. Harley's costs were still among the highest in the industry. Harley made a U-turn and restructured the company's organizational structure. Harley's efforts have paid off.
c. Whether you're indulging in a doughnut in New York or California, Krispy Kreme wants you to enjoy the same delicious taste with every bite. The company maintains consistent product quality by carefully controlling every step of the production process. Krispy Kreme tests all raw ingredients against established quality standards. Every delivery of wheat flour is sampled and measured for its moisture content and protein levels. Krispy Kreme blends the ingredients. Krispy Kreme tests the doughnut mix for quality. Krispy Kreme delivers the mix to its stores. Krispy Kreme knows that it takes more than a quality mix to produce perfect doughnuts all the time. The company supplies its stores with everything they need to produce premium doughnuts—mix, icings, fillings, equipment—you name it.

5.17 **Ethical Choices** Under what circumstances would you consider the use of terms that are high in connotative meaning to be ethical? When would you consider it to be unethical? Explain your reasoning.

EXPAND YOUR KNOWLEDGE

Exploring the Best of the Web:

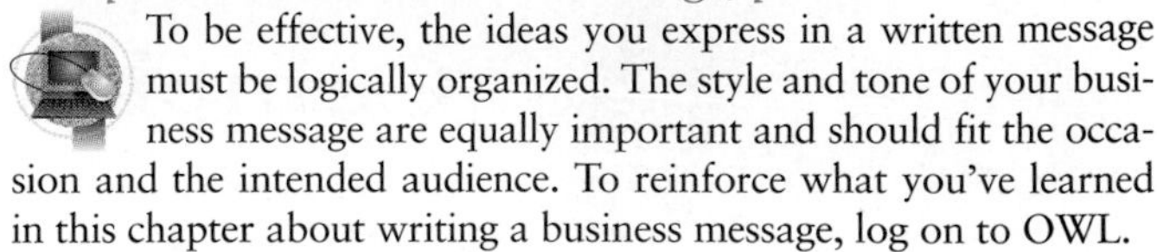

Compose a Better Business Message, p. 120

To be effective, the ideas you express in a written message must be logically organized. The style and tone of your business message are equally important and should fit the occasion and the intended audience. To reinforce what you've learned in this chapter about writing a business message, log on to OWL.

1. Explain why positive wording in a message is more effective than negative wording. Why should you be concerned about the position of good news or bad news in your written message?
2. What six factors of tone should you consider when conveying your message to your audience?
3. What points should you include in the close of your business message? Why?

Exploring the Web on Your Own

Review these chapter-related websites on your own to learn more about writing business messages.

1. Write it right by paying attention to these writing tips, grammar pointers, style suggestions, and reference sources at www.webgrammar.com.
2. Looking for the perfect word? Try Word Play at www.wolinskyweb.com/word.htm, where you'll find links to more than 30 helpful sites, including Acronym Finder, Book of Clichés, Oxymorons, Rhyming Dictionary, and Word Frequency Indexer.
3. Maximize your e-mail effectiveness by visiting A Beginner's Guide to Effective E-Mail, www.webfoot.com/advice/email.top.html.

LEARN INTERACTIVELY

Interactive Study Guide

Visit "My Companion Website" at www.prenhall.com/bovee. For Chapter 5, take advantage of the interactive "Study Guide" to test your chapter knowledge. Get instant feedback on whether you need additional studying. Read the "Current Events" articles to get the latest on chapter topics, and complete the exercises as specified by your instructor.

This site offers a variety of additional resources: The "Research Area" helps you locate a wealth of information to use in course assignments. You can even send a message to online research experts, who will help you find exactly the information you need. The "Study Hall" helps you succeed in this course. "Talk in the Hall" lets you leave messages and meet new friends online. If you have a question, you can "Ask the Tutor." And to get a better grade in this course, you can find more help at "Writing Skills," "Study Skills," and "Study Tips."

Grammar Diagnostic Tests

Review and reinforce your grammar and language skills by taking one of the four online diagnostic tests offered at our companion website, www.prenhall/bovee.com. The four tests cover a variety of topics, including spelling, capitals, punctuation, verbs, pronouns, adjectives, adverbs, sentence structure, sentence punctuation, clarity, word choice, style, organization skills, proofreading, and more. Submit your test and assess your competency. Then focus on improving areas where you are weak as you complete the exercises in this chapter.

Completing Business Messages

After studying this chapter, you will be able to

1 *Discuss when revision is performed, and list the main tasks involved in completing a business message*

2 *List four writing techniques you can use to improve the readability of your messages*

3 *List nine tips for making your writing clear*

4 *Discuss why it's important to make your message more concise and give four tips on how to do so*

5 *Describe four design elements, explain how they can change a document's appearance, and tell how to use them effectively*

6 *Highlight the types of errors to look for when proofreading*

COMMUNICATION CLOSE-UP AT TURNER BROADCASTING SYSTEM

www.turner.com

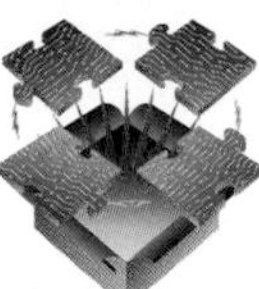

"Make sure that it's *Turner Broadcasting System* and not *Systems*," coaches corporate communications manager Adrianne Proeller when asked to talk about her work at the Atlanta-based media giant (now owned by AOL Time Warner). According to the company's corporate style manual, *TBS* or *Turner* is okay for subsequent references. "That's one of the first things you do when editing," says Proeller. "You make sure you get the name of the company right."

Not only does Proeller write speeches and statements for TBS president R. E. (Ted) Turner, she has enough other public relations duties to keep her busy during frequent 10-hour days. She enjoys her job, even when she's revising a document for the second or third time, weeding out weak verbs, simplifying complicated sentences, and eliminating unnecessary facts. She revises everything she writes, a task that she says "just comes with the territory."

The "territory" Proeller covers on a daily basis includes writing letters, memos, speeches, press releases, executive biographies, corporate fact sheets, and company histories. She also writes sample questions and answers for corporate executives before media interviews. "The Q & A prepares the executive for just about every possible question that might be asked," explains Proeller. Company founder Ted Turner is a favorite media topic, and so are the conglomerate's highly visible international divisions, which include Cable News Network (CNN), CNN Headline News, TBS Superstation, Turner Network Television (TNT), Turner Classic Movies (TCM), Hanna-Barbera Productions, TNT Latin America, TNT & Cartoon Asia, New Line Cinema, and Castle Rock Entertainment. TBS also owns the Atlanta Braves baseball team, the Atlanta Hawks basketball team, and other sports and entertainment ventures. Reporters are always asking questions, and the answers executives give could turn up on tomorrow's front page or today's broadcast news. So Proeller has to be certain her memos and press releases are clear and accurate.

That doesn't mean she always has time to let her writing "cool off" before she takes a second look—which is the ideal way to approach revision. "If I have the luxury of printing it out instead of just looking at it on my computer screen, then I'm doing well," Proeller says with a laugh. Whether the document is on screen or in hard copy, however, she rereads it through completely, asking herself: "What am I trying to say? Is it getting across? Is there anything that could make this better? Could anything make it stronger? Is there anything missing?"

For clarity, Proeller often narrows her communication to one primary message; then, to gain her readers' attention, she makes sure that this key idea is mentioned in the first paragraph. Because TBS is an international company, she also checks her copy for any cultural references that could be considered narrow-minded or biased. For instance, did she mistakenly assume a U.S. perspective? *Domestic sales* would confuse European readers, so Proeller replaces it with *U.S.-based sales* when sending memos overseas.

"Mr. Turner is very much an internationalist," Proeller explains. "A few years ago he sent around a memo to all of CNN, saying that because we're an international network, he didn't want any use of the word *foreign*. In fact, I could be fined for saying that—literally fined money (about $50). Most newsrooms have a national desk and a foreign desk; Turner

Communication is the profession of many employees of Turner Broadcasting System (owned by AOL Time Warner) and its international divisions, such as CNN. Whether writing press releases for the Atlanta Braves or working with Adrianne Proeller at TBS, these professionals understand the importance of careful revision.

has a national desk and an international desk." Of course, employees have poked a little fun at the rule, joking, "Excuse me, I have an international substance in my eye." However, they don't laugh at Turner's international success.

During her revision, Proeller checks the corporate style book for the proper formats and for company updates (for example, *TBS Superstation* used to be *TBS SuperStation*, and before that it was *Superstation TBS*). She also reconsiders her word choices. "I'm always trying to cut out unnecessary words, and I'm a big believer in strong verbs." She simplifies sentences that are too cumbersome and eliminates secondary messages if a document is too long. Overall, she makes sure the writing is positive, even when referring to TBS's competitors. That is company policy, Proeller says, because competitors of one division are often customers of another.

"Every document that passes your desk is a reflection on you," Proeller believes. "Your reputation, both internally and externally, is built one little bit at a time. I think typos are unforgivable, but beyond that, you want every document to be the best it can be. If you're not putting 100 percent of your thought into looking at it once it has been drafted—for all of the different aspects of style and content and accuracy—you're risking your professional image."[1] ■

MOVING BEYOND YOUR FIRST DRAFT

Learning Objective 1

Discuss when revision is performed, and list the main tasks involved in completing a business message

Once you've completed the first draft of your message, you may be tempted to breathe a sigh of relief and go on to the next project. Resist the temptation. Professional communicators like Adrianne Proeller are aware that the first draft is rarely good enough. In a first attempt, most writers don't say what they want to say—or don't say it as well as they could. You owe it to yourself and to your audience to review and refine your messages before sending them. In fact, many writing authorities suggest that you go over a document several times: one pass for content, organization, style, and tone; one for readability; and one for clarity and conciseness.

You might wonder whether all this effort to fine-tune a message is worthwhile. But successful businesspeople care very much about saying precisely the right thing in precisely the right way. Their willingness to go over the same document several times shows just how important it is to communicate effectively. As Ernest Hemingway once said, "There's no such thing as writing—only rewriting." Yet, once most businesspeople have a first draft, they make one of two mistakes: They shuffle words around on the page rather than actually making improvements, or they think rewriting is too time-consuming and send the document out the moment that last period hits the page.[2]

FIGURE 6.1 Completing Business Messages

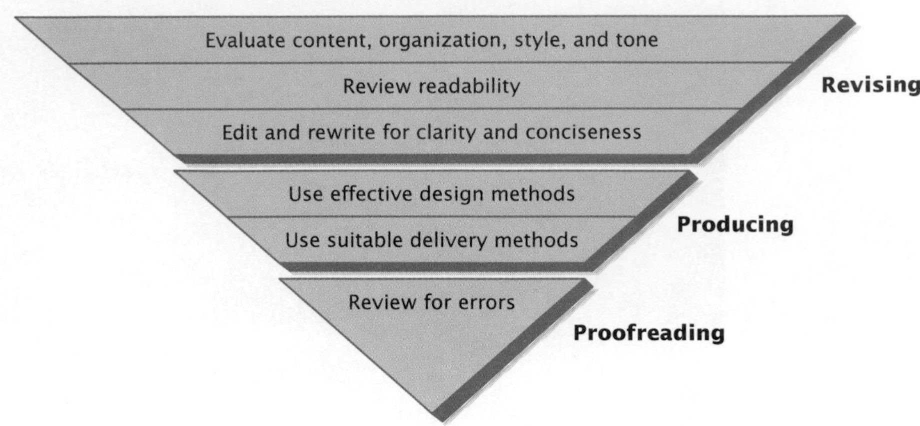

After revising, producing, and proofreading a message, you must also check its design and mechanics.

Even after you've fine-tuned your written message, your work is still not finished. Look back at the diagram of the three-step writing process (Figure 4.1 on page 80). You will see that completing your message consists of three tasks: revising, producing, and proofreading your message. Thus, to complete your business message, you must also check its design and mechanics. As Figure 6.1 shows, you perform these steps from the top down—addressing the document as a whole before looking at details. Focusing on big picture first is more efficient, since you won't be wasting time perfecting sections that you may eventually eliminate or change substantially.

REVISING YOUR MESSAGE

Revision takes place during and after preparation of the first draft.

After a day or two, review your message for content and organization.

Although the tendency is to separate revision from composition, revision is an ongoing activity that occurs throughout the writing process. You revise as you go along; then you revise again after you've completed the first draft. You constantly search for the best way to say something, probing for the right words, testing alternative sentences, reshaping, tightening, and juggling elements that already exist. Ideally, you should let your draft age a day or two before you begin the revision process so that you can approach the material with a fresh eye. Then read through the document quickly to evaluate its overall effectiveness before moving to finer points such as word choice, conciseness, and grammar.

As you complete the tasks shown in Figure 6.1, you'll find yourself rewriting sentences, passages, and even whole sections to improve their effectiveness. Of course, you're probably also facing a deadline, so try to stick to the schedule you set during the planning stage of the project. Do your best to revise and rewrite thoroughly but also economically. With a minimal amount of rewriting, you'll end up with a stronger document. Look closely at the draft in Figure 6.2 responding to Louise Wilson's request for information about the frequent-guest program at Commerce Hotel. It has been edited using the proofreading marks shown in Appendix V. Now review the letter in Figure 6.3 (on page 144), the result of incorporating all the revisions. As you can see, Figure 6.3 provides the requested information in a more organized fashion, in a friendlier style, and with clearer mechanics.

Evaluating Your Content, Organization, Style, and Tone

When you begin the revision process, you're mainly concerned with content, organization, style, and tone. To evaluate the content, ask yourself these questions:

- Is the information accurate?
- Is the information relevant to your audience?
- Have you provided enough information to satisfy your reader's needs?
- Is there a good balance between the general and the specific?

FIGURE 6.2 In-Depth Critique: Sample Edited Letter

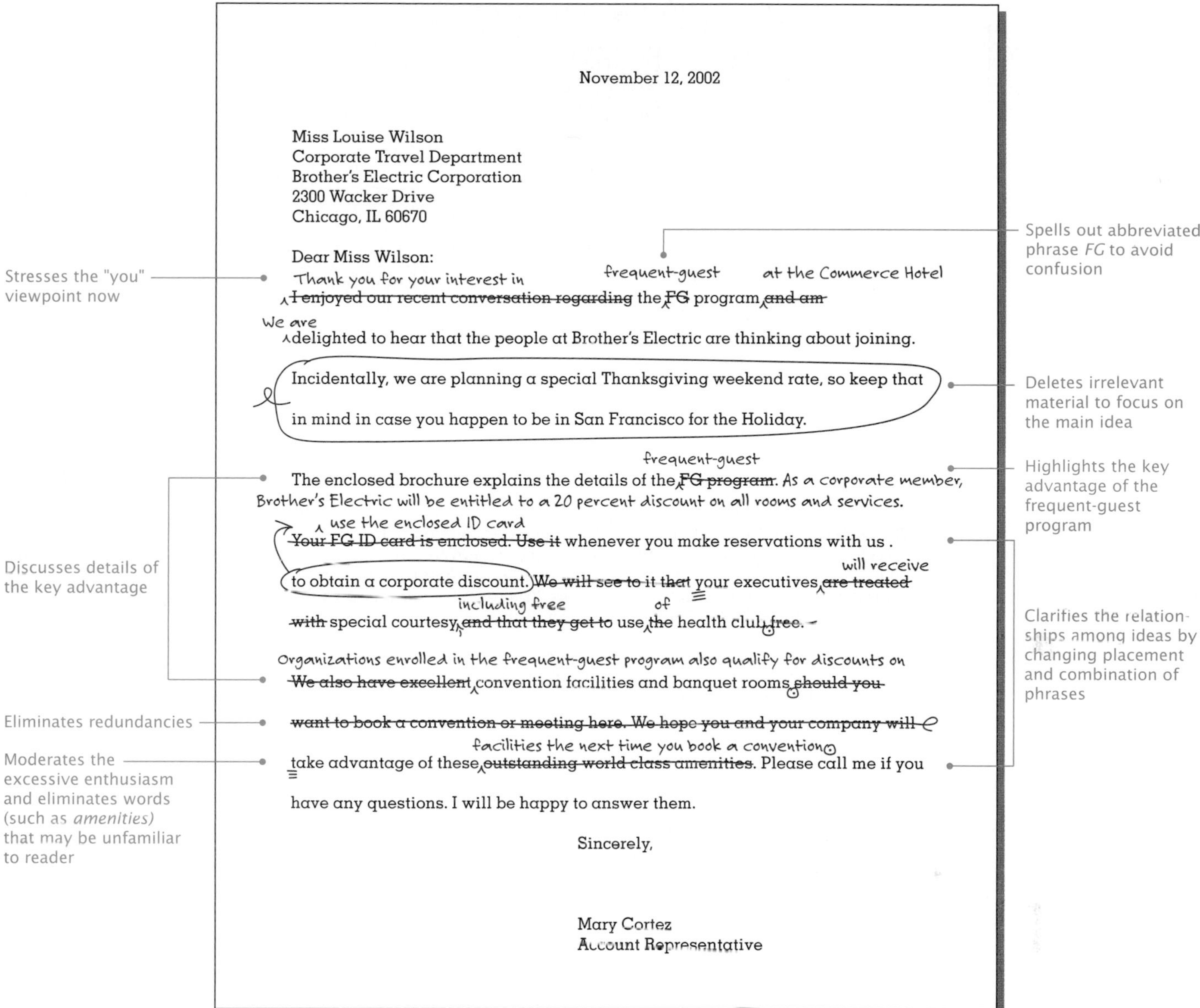

November 12, 2002

Miss Louise Wilson
Corporate Travel Department
Brother's Electric Corporation
2300 Wacker Drive
Chicago, IL 60670

Dear Miss Wilson:

I enjoyed our recent conversation regarding the FG program and am delighted to hear that the people at Brother's Electric are thinking about joining.

Incidentally, we are planning a special Thanksgiving weekend rate, so keep that in mind in case you happen to be in San Francisco for the Holiday.

The enclosed brochure explains the details of the FG program.

Your FG ID card is enclosed. Use it whenever you make reservations with us to obtain a corporate discount. We will see to it that your executives are treated with special courtesy and that they get to use the health club free.

We also have excellent convention facilities and banquet rooms should you want to book a convention or meeting here. We hope you and your company will take advantage of these outstanding world class amenities. Please call me if you have any questions. I will be happy to answer them.

Sincerely,

Mary Cortez
Account Representative

Once you are satisfied with the content of your message, you can review its organization. Ask yourself:

- Have you covered all your points in the most logical order?
- Do the most important ideas receive the most space, and are they placed in the most prominent positions?
- Would the message be more convincing if it were arranged in another sequence?
- Do you repeat yourself?
- Are details scattered that need to be grouped together?

Finally, consider the effect that your words will actually have on readers, and ask yourself whether you have achieved the right style and tone for your audience.

Make sure you achieve the right tone and interest level.

In this first pass, spend a few extra moments on the beginning and ending of the message. These are the sections that have the greatest impact on the audience. Be sure that the opening of a letter or memo is relevant, interesting, and geared to the reader's probable reaction. In longer messages, check to see that the first few paragraphs establish the subject, purpose, and organization of the material. Review the conclusion to be sure that it summarizes the main idea and leaves the audience with a positive impression.

The beginning and end of a message have the greatest impact on readers.

FIGURE 6.3 In-Depth Critique: Final Revised Letter

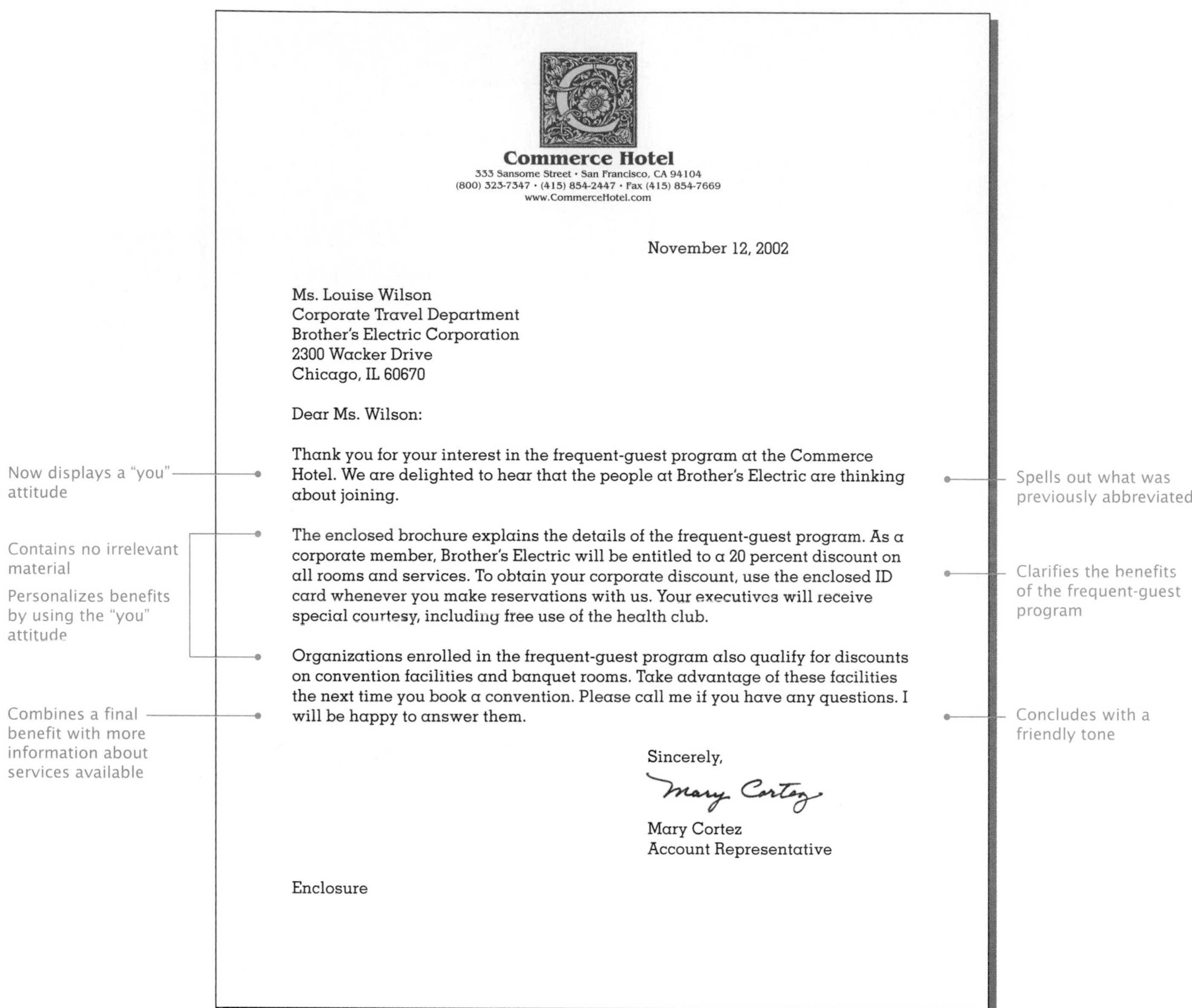

November 12, 2002

Ms. Louise Wilson
Corporate Travel Department
Brother's Electric Corporation
2300 Wacker Drive
Chicago, IL 60670

Dear Ms. Wilson:

Thank you for your interest in the frequent-guest program at the Commerce Hotel. We are delighted to hear that the people at Brother's Electric are thinking about joining.

The enclosed brochure explains the details of the frequent-guest program. As a corporate member, Brother's Electric will be entitled to a 20 percent discount on all rooms and services. To obtain your corporate discount, use the enclosed ID card whenever you make reservations with us. Your executives will receive special courtesy, including free use of the health club.

Organizations enrolled in the frequent-guest program also qualify for discounts on convention facilities and banquet rooms. Take advantage of these facilities the next time you book a convention. Please call me if you have any questions. I will be happy to answer them.

Sincerely,

Mary Cortez
Account Representative

Enclosure

Reviewing for Readability

Readability formulas gauge reading level.

Once you're satisfied with the content, organization, style, and tone of your message, make a second pass to look at its readability. You might even apply a readability formula to gauge the difficulty of your writing. The most common readability formulas measure the length of words and sentences to give you a rough idea of how well educated your audience must be to understand your message. Figure 6.4 shows how one readability formula, the Fog Index, has been applied to an excerpt from a memo. (For more on this topic, visit www.profusion.com and enter "Fog Index" in the search box.) As the calculation shows, anyone who reads at a 9th-grade level should be able to read this passage with ease. For technical documents, you can aim for an audience that reads at a 12th- to 14th-grade level; for general business messages, your writing should be geared to readers at the 8th- to 11th-grade level. The Fog Index of popular business publications such as the *Wall Street Journal* and *Forbes* magazine is somewhere between 10 and 11.

Readability formulas are easy to apply; many are commonly done by computer. However, they tend to overvalue condensed prose, and they ignore some important

FIGURE 6.4 The Fog Index

EXCERPT

I called Global Corporation to ask when we will receive copies of its insurance policies and engineering reports. Cindy Turner of Global said that they are putting the documents together and will send them by Express Mail next week. She told me that they are late because most of the information is in the hands of Global's attorneys in Boston. I asked why it was in Boston; we had understood that the account is serviced by the carrier's Dallas branch. Turner explained that the account originally was sold to Global's Boston division, so all paperwork stays there. She promised to phone us when the package is ready to ship.

1. SELECT WRITING SAMPLE
Keep the sample between 100 and 125 words long. (See excerpt.)

2. DETERMINE AVERAGE SENTENCE LENGTH
Count the number of words in each sentence. Treat independent clauses (stand-alone word groups containing subject and predicate) as separate sentences. For example, "In school we studied; we learned; we improved" counts as three sentences. Then add all word counts for each sentence to get the total word count, and divide that by the number of sentences. This excerpt has an average sentence length of 14:

18 + 21 + 21 + 7 + 13 + 12 + 5 + 12 = 109 words ÷ 8 sentences = 14

3. DETERMINE PERCENTAGE OF LONG WORDS
Count the number of long words—that is, all words that have three or more syllables (underlined in the excerpt). Omit proper nouns, combinations of short words (such as *butterfly* and *anyway*), and verbs that gain a third syllable by adding -es or -ed (as in *trepasses* and *created*). Divide the number of long words by the total number of words in the sample. The percentage of long words in this excerpt is 10 percent:

11 long words ÷ 109 total words = 10 percent

4. DETERMINE GRADE LEVEL REQUIRED TO READ EXCERPT
Add the numbers for average sentence length and percentage of long words. Multiply the sum by 0.4, and drop the number after the decimal point. The number of years of schooling required to easily read this excerpt is 9:

14 words per sentence + 10 percent long words =
24 × 0.4 = 9.6 – 0.6 = 9 (Fog Index)

variables that contribute to reading ease, such as sentence structure, the organization of ideas, and the appearance of the message on the page.[3] Moreover, readability indexes can't be applied to languages other than English. Counting syllables makes no sense in other languages. For example, compare the English *forklift driver* with the German *Gabelstaplerfahrer*. Also, Chinese and Japanese characters don't lend themselves to syllable counting at all.[4]

Readability depends on word choice, sentence length, sentence structure, organization, and the message's physical appearance.

Of course, most business writers know that busy readers seldom read every word of a message on their first pass. Instead, they typically skim a message, reading only certain sections carefully to assess the worthiness of the document. If they determine that the document contains valuable information or requires a response, they will read it more carefully when time permits. You can adopt a number of techniques to make your message easier to skim through and help move your readers through the material more quickly. Varying sentence length, using shorter paragraphs, using lists and bullets instead of narrative, and adding effective headings and subheadings ensure that your readers will notice key points if they do skim messages. These techniques will also make your message more appealing.

Learning Objective 2

List four writing techniques you can use to improve the readability of your messages

Vary the Sentence Length

Variety is the key to making your message interesting and readable. With your words and sentence structure, you create a rhythm that emphasizes important points, enlivens your writing style, and makes your information appealing to your reader. Although good business writers use short sentences most of the time, too many short sentences in a row can make your writing choppy. Conversely, if all your sentences move at the same plodding gait, you're likely to lull your reader to sleep. So to be interesting, use a variety of both short and long sentences.

To keep readers' interest, use both long and short sentences.

Keep in mind that long sentences are usually harder to understand than short sentences because they are packed with information that must all be absorbed at once. Longer sentences are also more difficult to skim. Readers can absorb only a few words per glance. Thus, the longer your sentence is, the greater the possibility that the reader who skims will not read enough words to process the full meaning of your sentence.

On the other hand, long sentences are especially well suited for grouping or combining ideas, listing points, and summarizing or previewing information. Medium-length sentences (those with about 20 words) are useful for showing the relationships among ideas. Short sentences emphasize important information. Most good business writing has an average sentence length of 20 words or fewer. (For audiences abroad, varying sentence length can create translation problems for the reader, so stick to short sentences in international messages.)[5]

Average sentence length for most good business writing is 20 words or fewer.

Keep Paragraphs Short

Most business readers are put off by large blocks of text. Unless you break up your thoughts somehow, you'll end up with a three-page paragraph that's guaranteed to intimidate even the most dedicated reader. Short paragraphs (of 100 words or fewer) are easier to read than long ones, and they make your writing look inviting. Direct-mail letters almost always use very short paragraphs because the writers know that their letters will be read more carefully that way. Even in memos, letters, and reports, you may want to emphasize an idea from time to time by isolating it in a short, forceful paragraph.

Short paragraphs are easier to read than long ones.

As you write your message, try to use a variety of paragraph lengths. But be careful to use one-sentence paragraphs only occasionally and only for emphasis. When you want to package a big idea in short paragraphs, break the idea into subtopics and treat each subtopic in a separate paragraph—being careful to provide plenty of transitional elements. By breaking a large single paragraph into several shorter ones, you can make material more readable. Of course, many other approaches might be as effective. As we saw in Chapter 5, there is no "right" way to develop a paragraph.

Use Lists and Bullets for Emphasis and Clarity

An effective alternative to using straight sentences is to set off important ideas in a **list**—a series of words, names, or items. Lists can show the sequence of your ideas, heighten their impact visually, and increase the likelihood that a reader will find your key points. In addition, lists provide readers with clues, simplify complex subjects, highlight the main point, break up the page visually, ease the skimming process for busy readers, and give the reader a breather. Consider the difference between the following two approaches to the same information:

Lists are effective tools for highlighting and simplifying material.

Narrative	List
Owning your own business has many advantages. One is the ease of establishment. Another advantage is the satisfaction of working for yourself. As a sole proprietor, you also have the advantage of privacy because you do not have to reveal your information or plans to anyone.	Owning your own business has three advantages: ■ Ease of establishment ■ Satisfaction of working for yourself ■ Privacy of information

When creating a list, you can separate items with numbers, letters, or bullets (a general term for any kind of graphical element that precedes each item). Of course, for shorter lists such as this one, graphic elements aren't required. Nonetheless, when using graphic elements, bullets are generally preferred over numbers, unless the sequence of events is critical (if the steps in a process must be completed in a specific order, for example). The following three steps need to be performed in the order indicated, and the numbers make that clear:

1. Find out how many employees would like on-site day-care facilities.
2. Determine how much space the day-care center would require.
3. Estimate the cost of converting a conference room for the on-site facility.

One thing that Jerry Blount depends on when making a sale is contract clarity. He doesn't want his customers to feel confused about what services they're purchasing from his home security company. That's why Blount's contracts break out specific security services in bulleted lists that are easy to locate, read, and understand.

Lists are easier to read if the entire numbered or bullet-pointed section is indented, as the preceding examples demonstrate. Furthermore, when using lists, make sure to introduce them clearly so that people know what they're about to read. One way to introduce lists is to make them a part of the introductory sentence:

The board of directors met to discuss the revised annual budget. To keep expenses in line with declining sales, the directors voted to

- Cut everyone's salary by 10 percent
- Close the employee cafeteria
- Reduce travel expenses

If necessary, add further discussion after the lists to complete your thought. Another way to introduce a list is to use a complete introductory sentence, followed by a colon:

The decline in company profit is attributable to these factors:

- Slower holiday sales
- Increased transportation and fuel costs
- Higher employee wages
- Slower inventory turnover

Use the same grammatical form for each heading.

Regardless of the format you choose, the items in the lists should be phrased in parallel form. For example, if one list item begins with a verb, all list items should begin with a verb. If one is a noun phrase, all should be noun phrases. Parallel construction shows that the ideas are related, of similar importance, and on the same level of generality.

Nonparallel List Items	**Parallel List Items**
■ Improve our bottom line	■ Improving our bottom line
■ Identification of new foreign markets for our products	■ Identifying new foreign markets for our products
■ Global market strategies	■ Developing our global market strategies
■ Issues regarding pricing and packaging size	■ Resolving pricing and packaging issues

For additional discussion of parallelism, see "Editing for Clarity and Conciseness" later in this chapter, and look at Table 6.2 on page 150.

Add Headings and Subheadings

Use headings to grab the reader's attention and divide material into short sections.

A **heading** is a brief title that cues readers about the content of the section that follows. Headings are similar to the subject line in memos and e-mail correspondence. However, subject lines merely identify the purpose of the memo or e-mail, whereas headings also advise the reader about the material included in the paragraph.

Headings serve these important functions:

- **Organization.** Headings show your reader at a glance how the document is organized. They act as labels to group related paragraphs together and effectively organize your material into short sections.
- **Attention.** Informative, inviting, and in some cases intriguing headings grab the reader's attention, make the copy easier to read, and help the reader find the parts he or she needs to read—or skip.
- **Connection.** Using headings and subheadings together helps readers see the relationship between subordinate and main ideas so that they can understand your message more easily. Moreover, headings and subheadings visually indicate shifts from one idea to the next.

Headings fall into two categories. **Descriptive headings**, such as "Cost Considerations," identify a topic but do little more. **Informative headings**, such as "A New Way to Cut Costs," put your reader right into the context of your message.

Informative headings are generally more helpful than descriptive ones.

Informative headings guide readers to think in a certain way about the topic. They are also helpful in guiding your work as a writer, especially if written in terms of questions you plan to address in your document. However, informative headings are more difficult to create. A well-written informative heading is self-contained. In other words, readers should be able to read your headings and subheadings and understand them without reading the rest of the document. For example, "Introduction" does not make sense by itself, whereas the heading "An Insight into the Need for Better Communication" makes sense by itself, catches the reader's attention, and sparks interest. Whatever types you choose, keep your headings brief, and use parallel construction as you would for an outline, lists, or a series of words.

Editing for Clarity and Conciseness

Learning Objective 3

List nine tips for making your writing clear

Clarity prevents confusion.

Once you've reviewed and revised your message for readability, you'll want to make sure that your message is clear. Perhaps a sentence is so cluttered that the reader can't unravel it, or it's constructed in a way that the reader can interpret it in several ways; perhaps pronouns or tenses switch midsentence so that the reader loses track of who is talking or when an event took place; perhaps sentence B is not a logical sequel to sentence A; or perhaps an important word is used incorrectly.[6]

Writing is hard work and takes actual practice. The more you write (whether on the job or for pleasure), the better writer you'll become. Ask yourself whether your sentences are easy to decipher. Do your paragraphs have clear topic sentences? Are the transitions between ideas obvious? Are your statements simple and direct? Remember, a clear sentence is no accident. Few sentences come out right the first time, or even the third time. See Table 6.1 for examples of the following tips:

In many cases, the parts of a compound sentence should be separated into two sentences.

Don't be afraid to present your opinions without qualification.

When you use the same grammatical pattern to express two or more ideas, you show that they are comparable thoughts.

Make sure that modifier phrases are really related to the subject of the sentence.

- **Break up overly long sentences.** Don't connect too many clauses with *and*. If you find yourself stuck in a long sentence, you're probably trying to make the sentence do more than it can reasonably do, such as express two dissimilar thoughts. You can often clarify your writing style by separating a string into individual sentences.
- **Rewrite hedging sentences.** Sometimes you have to write *may* or *seems* to avoid stating a judgment as a fact. Nevertheless, when you have too many such hedges, you aren't really saying anything.
- **Impose parallelism.** When you have two or more similar (parallel) ideas to express, use the same grammatical pattern for each related idea—parallel construction. Repeating the pattern makes your message more readable: It tells readers that the ideas are comparable, and it adds rhythm. Parallelism can be achieved by repeating the pattern in words, phrases, clauses, or entire sentences (see Table 6.2).
- **Correct dangling modifiers.** Sometimes a modifier is not just an adjective or an adverb but an entire phrase modifying a noun or a verb. Be careful not to leave this type of modifier dangling with no connection to the subject of the sentence. The first unacceptable example under "Dangling Modifiers" in Table 6.1 implies that the red sports car has both an office and the legs to walk there. The second example shows one frequent cause of dangling modifiers: passive construction.

TABLE 6.1 Revising for Clarity

Examples	***Unacceptable***	***Preferable***
OVERLY LONG SENTENCES		
Taking compound sentences too far	The magazine will be published January 1, and I'd better meet the deadline if I want my article included.	The magazine will be published January 1. I'd better meet the deadline if I want my article included.
HEDGING SENTENCES		
Overqualifying sentences	I believe that Mr. Johnson's employment record seems to show that he may be capable of handling the position.	Mr. Johnson's employment record shows that he is capable of handling the position.
UNPARALLEL SENTENCES		
Using dissimilar construction for similar ideas	Miss Simms had been drenched with rain, bombarded with telephone calls, and her boss shouted at her.	Miss Sims had been drenched with rain, bombarded with telephone calls, and shouted at by her boss.
	Ms. Reynolds dictated the letter, and next she signed it and left the office.	Ms. Reynolds dictated the letter, signed it, and left the office.
	To waste time and missing deadlines are bad habits.	Wasting time and missing deadlines are bad habits.
	Interviews are a matter of acting confident and to stay relaxed.	Interviews are a matter of acting confident and staying relaxed.
DANGLING MODIFIERS		
Placing modifiers close to the wrong nouns and verbs	Walking to the office, a red sports car passed her.	A red sports car passed her while she was walking to the office.
	Working as fast as possible, the budget was soon ready.	Working as fast as possible, the committee soon had the budget ready.
	After a 3-week slump, we increased sales.	After a 3-week slump, sales increased.
LONG NOUN SEQUENCES		
Stringing too many nouns together	The window sash installation company will give us an estimate on Friday.	The company that installs window sashes will give us an estimate on Friday.
CAMOUFLAGED VERBS		
Changing verbs and nouns into adjectives	The manager undertook implementation of the rules.	The manager implemented the rules.
	Verification of the shipments occurs weekly.	Shipments are verified weekly.
Changing verbs into nouns	reach a conclusion about make a discovery of give consideration to	conclude discover consider
SENTENCE STRUCTURE		
Separating subject and predicate	A 10 percent decline in market share, which resulted from quality problems and an aggressive sales campaign by Armitage, the market leader in the Northeast, was the major problem in 2001.	The major problem in 2001 was a 10 percent loss of market share, which resulted from both quality problems and an aggressive sales campaign by Armitage, the market leader in the Northeast.
Separating adjectives, adverbs, or prepositional phrases from the words they modify	Our antique desk is suitable for busy executives with thick legs and large drawers.	With its thick legs and large drawers, our antique desk is suitable for busy executives.
AWKWARD REFERENCES	The Law Office and the Accounting Office distribute computer supplies for legal secretaries and beginning accountants, respectively.	The Law Office distributes computer supplies for legal secretaries; the Accounting Office distributes those for beginning accountants.
TOO MUCH ENTHUSIASM	We are extremely pleased to offer you a position on our staff of exceptionally skilled and highly educated employees. The work offers extraordinary challenges and a very large salary.	We are pleased to offer you a position on our staff of skilled and well-educated employees. The work offers challenges and an attractive salary.

TABLE 6.2 Achieving Parallelism

Method	*Example*
Parallel words:	The letter was approved by Clausen, Whittaker, Merlin, and Carlucci.
Parallel phrases:	We have beaten the competition in supermarkets, in department stores, and in specialty stores.
Parallel clauses:	I'd like to discuss the issue after Vicki gives her presentation but before Marvin shows his slides.
Parallel sentences:	In 2000 we exported 30 percent of our production. In 2001 we exported 50 percent.

Stringing together a series of nouns may save a little space, but it causes confusion.

- **Reword long noun sequences.** When nouns are strung together as modifiers, the resulting sentence is hard to read. You can clarify the sentence by putting some of the nouns in a modifying phrase. Although you add a few more words, your audience won't have to work as hard to understand the sentence.

Turning verbs into nouns or adjectives weakens your writing style.

- **Replace camouflaged verbs.** Watch for word endings such as *-ion, -tion, -ing, -ment, -ant, -ent, -ence, -ance,* and *-ency*. Most of them change verbs into nouns and adjectives. Get rid of them. Also, try not to transform verbs into nouns (writing "we performed an analysis of" rather than "we analyzed"). To prune and enliven your messages, use verbs instead of noun phrases.

Subject and predicate should be placed as close together as possible, as should modifiers and the words they modify.

- **Clarify sentence structure.** Keep the subject and predicate of a sentence as close together as possible. When subject and predicate are far apart, readers have to read the sentence twice to figure out who did what. Similarly, adjectives, adverbs, and prepositional phrases usually make the most sense when they're placed as close as possible to the words they modify.

Be specific in your references.

- **Clarify awkward references.** To save words, business writers sometimes use expressions such as *the above-mentioned, as mentioned above, the aforementioned, the former, the latter,* and *respectively*. These words cause readers to jump from point to point, which hinders effective communication. Use specific references, even if you must add a few more words.

Business writing shouldn't be gushy.

- **Moderate your enthusiasm.** An occasional adjective or adverb intensifies and emphasizes your meaning, but too many can ruin your writing.

Once you have edited your sentences for clarity, you're ready to focus on conciseness. Many business documents today are swollen with words and phrases that do no new work. In fact, three-fourths of the executives who participated in one survey complained that most written messages are too long.[7] Because executives are more likely to

Best of the Web

Write It Right: Rethink and Revise

Are you sure that readers perceive your written message as you intended? If you want help revising a message that you're completing, use the Paradigm Online Writing Assistant (POWA). With this interactive writer's guide, you can select topics to get tips on how to edit your work, reshape your thoughts, and rewrite for clarity. Read discussions about perfecting your writing skills, and for practice, complete one of the many online activities provided to reinforce what you've learned. Or select the Forum to "talk" about writing. At POWA's website, you'll learn how to improve the final draft of your message.

www.powa.org

read documents that efficiently say what needs to be said, it's especially important to weed out unnecessary material.

Conciseness means efficiency.

Learning Objective 4

Discuss why it's important to make your message more concise and give four tips on how to do so

Most first drafts can be cut by 50 percent.[8] By reorganizing your content, improving the readability of your document, and correcting your sentence structure for clarity, you will have already eliminated most of the excess. Now it is time to examine every word you put on paper. When you edit for conciseness, you eliminate every word that serves no function, replace every long word that could be a short word, and remove every adverb that adds nothing to the meaning already carried in the verb. To test whether every word counts, try removing a phrase or words that don't appear to be essential. If the meaning doesn't change, leave them out. For instance, *very* can be a useful word to achieve emphasis, but more often it's clutter. There's no need to call someone "very methodical." The person is either methodical or not. As you begin your editing task, simplify, prune, and strive for order. See Table 6.3 for examples of the following tips:

Be on the lookout for inefficient phrases and excessive or confusing relative pronouns and articles.

Short words and infinitives are generally more vivid than long words and phrases, and they improve the readability of a document.

Remove unneeded repetition.

Avoid starting sentences with *it* and *there*.

- **Delete unnecessary words and phrases.** Some combinations of words have more efficient, one-word equivalents. In addition, avoid the clutter of too many or poorly placed relative pronouns (*who, that, which*). Even articles can be excessive (mostly too many *the*'s). However, well-placed relative pronouns and articles prevent confusion.
- **Shorten long words and phrases.** Short words are generally more vivid and easier to read than long ones are. The idea is to use short, simple words, *not* simple concepts.[9] Plus, by using infinitives in place of some phrases, you not only shorten your sentences but also make them clearer.
- **Eliminate redundancies.** In some word combinations, the words tend to say the same thing. For instance, "visible to the eye" is redundant because *visible* is enough; nothing can be visible to the ear.
- **Recast "It is/There are" starters.** If you start a sentence with an indefinite pronoun (an expletive) such as *it* or *there,* odds are that the sentence could be shorter.

As you rewrite, concentrate on how each word contributes to an effective sentence and how that sentence develops a coherent paragraph. Be sure to consider the effect your words will actually have on readers (not just the effect you *plan* for them to have). Look for opportunities to make the material more interesting through the use of strong, lively words and phrases (as discussed in Chapter 5). For a reminder of the tasks involved in revision, see this chapter's "Checklist: Revising Business Messages."

Sometimes you'll find that the most difficult problem in a sentence can be solved by simply removing the problem itself. When you come upon a troublesome element, ask yourself, "Do I need it at all?" Probably not. In fact, you may find that it was giving you so much grief because it was trying to do an unnecessary job.[10] Once you remove the troublesome element, the afflicted sentence will spring to life and breathe normally. Of course, before you delete anything, you'll probably want to keep copies of your previous versions. Professional communicators such as TBS's Adrianne Proeller know how important it is to keep a paper trail for future reference.

When Starbucks Coffee Company Chairman and CEO Howard Schultz announced that Starbucks would expand beyond the coffee business, his message got the attention of customers and analysts alike. But Schultz has more than one message. He's launched a program to support literacy in children, and he's written a book (*Pour Your Heart into It*) about the motivation for his ambition. In interviews, Schultz's excitement shows through, but in writing, he moderates his enthusiasm. He knows that using too many adjectives and adverbs spoils good writing, so he uses just a few to intensify the meaning.

Using Technology to Revise Your Message

When it's time to revise and polish your message, your word processor helps you add, delete, and move text with functions such as *cut and paste* (taking a block of text out of one section of a document and pasting it in somewhere else) and *search and replace* (tracking down words or phrases and changing them if you need to). Be careful, though; choosing the "replace all" option can result in some unintended errors. For example,

TABLE 6.3 Revising for Conciseness

Examples	***Unacceptable***	***Preferable***
UNNECESSARY WORDS AND PHRASES		
Using wordy phrases	for the sum of	for
	in the event that	if
	on the occasion of	on
	prior to the start of	before
	in the near future	soon
	have the capability of	can
	at this point in time	now
	due to the fact that	because
	in view of the fact that	because
	until such time as	when
	with reference to	about
Using too many relative pronouns	Cars that are sold after January will not have a six-month warranty.	Cars sold after January will not have a six-month warranty.
	Employees who are driving to work should park in the underground garage.	Employees driving to work should park in the underground garage.
Using too few relative pronouns	The project manager told the engineers last week the specifications were changed.	The project manager told the engineers last week that the specifications were changed.
		The project manager told the engineers that last week the specifications were changed.
LONG WORDS AND PHRASES		
Using overly long words	During the preceding year, the company accelerated productive operations.	Last year the company sped up operations.
	The action was predicated on the assumption that the company was operating at a financial deficit.	The action was based on the belief that the company was losing money.
Using wordy phrases rather than infinitives	If you want success as a writer, you must work hard.	To be a successful writer, you must work hard.
	He went to the library for the purpose of studying.	He went to the library to study.
	The employer increased salaries so that she could improve morale.	The employer increased salaries to improve morale.
REDUNDANCIES		
Repeating meanings	absolutely complete	complete
	basic fundamentals	fundamentals
	follows after	follows
	reduce down	reduce
	free and clear	free
	refer back	refer
	repeat again	repeat
	collect together	collect
	future plans	plans
	return back	return
	important essentials	essentials
	midway between	between
	end result	result
	actual truth	truth
	final outcome	outcome
	uniquely unusual	unique
	surrounded on all sides	surrounded
Using double modifiers	modern, up-to-date equipment	modern equipment
IT IS/THERE ARE STARTERS		
Starting sentences with *it* or *there*	It would be appreciated if you would sign the lease today.	Please sign the lease today.
	There are five employees in this division who were late to work today.	Five employees in this division were late to work today.

Keeping Pace with Technology

Warding Off Digital Disaster

Today's data are being threatened. Some 20 percent of the information carefully collected on Jet Propulsion Laboratory computers during NASA's 1976 Viking mission to Mars has been lost. Defense Department computers can no longer read some POW and MIA records from the Vietnam War. And malicious computer viruses are erasing computer files and locking up computer systems all over the globe. Not only can computer viruses turn detailed records into electronic confetti, but the very media carrying our precious bits of information aren't lasting as long as we had expected. Moreover, chances are good that the software (or even the hardware) needed to get at today's data might not be readily available in 10 years. Anyone who has tried wresting information from a 5¼-inch floppy disk knows that.

You can help prevent your digits from turning to dust by taking these precautions:

- **Keep your computer clean.** Keep food and drink away from your equipment.
- **Maintain your hard drive.** Scan your drive for errors often, and correct them. Defragment your hard drive once a year (but only after performing a complete system backup).
- **Install surge protectors.** Make sure your protectors have a UL1449 rating of 330 volts or less, and install a backup power supply.
- **Exit your system correctly.** Close all applications before you turn off your computer; then shut down your computer in proper sequence.
- **Register your hardware and software.** Send in registration cards so that you are eligible for customer support and are notified about major problems or upgrades.
- **Install antivirus programs.** Use a good virus-scanning program, and update it at least quarterly. Run a virus scan on everything that comes into your computer: new software, new floppy disks, and Internet downloads. Don't open e-mail attachments from strangers.
- **Back up your system regularly.** Make sure you flag all important files and keep a regular backup schedule. Back up your entire system before installing any new software.
- **Store your backups properly.** Store your backup media off-site in a cool, dry cabinet away from heat, humidity, light, dust, and smoke. Keep them away from electric motors, speakers, phone handsets, monitors, TV screens, and transformers (which can cause electromagnetic radiation and erasure). Serious PC users may want to consider online backup services, a safe and inexpensive option.
- **Keep your copies clean and organized.** Label your backup media clearly. Twice a year buy and use new backup media, and clean the magnetic heads on your backup hardware. Do a "test restore" monthly to make sure your backups are usable.

By taking these steps, you can substantially reduce your risk should a data disaster strike.

Career Applications

1. Your office has just decided to electronically store all written communications, reports, policies, and so on. Express your concerns about this policy in a brief memo to the president of the company.
2. E-mail has increasingly become a vehicle for spreading computer viruses that destroy computer files and programs. What cautions can you take to protect your computer from being infected by a deadly virus?

finding *power* and replacing all occurrences with *strength* will also change the word *powerful* to *strengthful*. In addition, the AutoCorrect feature of many word-processing programs allows you to store words you commonly misspell or mistype, along with their correct spelling. So if you frequently type *teh* instead of *the*, AutoCorrect will automatically correct your typo for you.

Software tools such as revision marks keep track of proposed editing changes electronically and provide a history of a document's revisions. The revisions appear in a different font color than the original text (see Figure 6.5), giving you a chance to review changes before accepting or rejecting them. Besides adding, deleting, and moving text, you can use revision marks to attach electronic notes and keep track of editing changes made by team members. This feature is especially helpful if you are writing collaborative messages.

In addition to the many revision tools, three advanced software functions can help bring out the best in your documents. First, a *spell checker* compares your document with an electronic dictionary, highlights unrecognized words, and suggests correct spelling. Spell checkers are a wonderful way to weed major typos out of your documents, but they are no substitute for good spelling skills. For example, if you use

Spell checkers, grammar checkers, and computerized thesauruses can all help with the revision process, but they can't take the place of good writing and editing skills.

FIGURE 6.5 Revision Marks

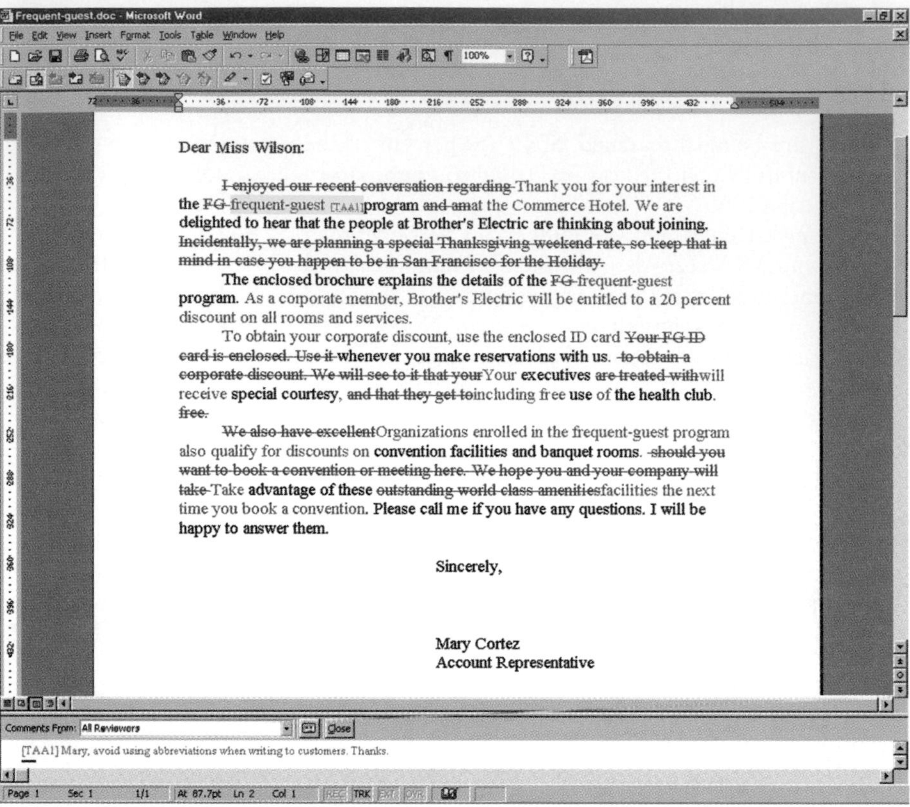

Dear Miss Wilson:

~~I enjoyed our recent conversation regarding~~ Thank you for your interest in the ~~FG~~ frequent-guest [TAA1]program ~~and am~~at the Commerce Hotel. We are delighted to hear that the people at Brother's Electric are thinking about joining. ~~Incidentally, we are planning a special Thanksgiving weekend rate, so keep that in mind in case you happen to be in San Francisco for the Holiday.~~

The enclosed brochure explains the details of the ~~FG~~ frequent-guest program. As a corporate member, Brother's Electric will be entitled to a 20 percent discount on all rooms and services.

To obtain your corporate discount, use the enclosed ID card ~~Your FG ID card is enclosed. Use it~~ whenever you make reservations with us. ~~to obtain a corporate discount. We will see to it that your~~Your executives ~~are treated with~~will receive special courtesy, ~~and that they get to~~including free use of the health club. ~~free.~~

~~We also have excellent~~Organizations enrolled in the frequent-guest program also qualify for discounts on convention facilities and banquet rooms. ~~should you want to book a convention or meeting here. We hope you and your company will take~~ Take advantage of these ~~outstanding world-class amenities~~facilities the next time you book a convention. Please call me if you have any questions. I will be happy to answer them.

Sincerely,

Mary Cortez
Account Representative

[TAA1] Mary, avoid using abbreviations when writing to customers. Thanks.

their when you mean to use *there,* your spell checker can't notice, because *their* is spelled correctly. If you're in a hurry and accidentally omit the *p* at the end of *top,* your spell checker will read *to* as correct. Or if you mistakenly type a semicolon instead of *p,* your spell checker will read *to;* as a correctly spelled word. Plus, some of the "errors" that the spell checker notes may actually be proper names, technical words, words that you misspelled on purpose, or simply words that weren't included in the spell checker's dictionary. It's up to you to decide whether each flagged word should be corrected or left alone, and it's up to you to find the errors that your spell checker has overlooked.

Second, a computer *thesaurus* gives you alternative words, just as your printed thesaurus does. Not only can a computer thesaurus give you answers faster and more easily than a printed thesaurus, it may be able to do things that your printed thesaurus could never do. The electronic version of the *American Heritage Dictionary* provides a thesaurus and a special WordHunter function that gives you a term when all you know is part of the definition. If you're racking your brain to remember the word that means a certain quantity of paper, you simply type *quantity AND paper* and then WordHunter searches for every definition in the dictionary that includes those two terms. In a few seconds, the word *ream* pops into view—"Aha! That's the word I was looking for."

Third, the *grammar checker* tries to do for your grammar what a spell checker does for your spelling. The catch is that checking your spelling is much easier than checking your grammar. A spell checker simply compares each word in your document with a list of correctly spelled words. A grammar checker has to determine whether you're using words correctly and constructing sentences according to the complex rules of composition.

Because the program doesn't have a clue about what you're trying to say, it can't tell whether you've said it correctly. Moreover, even if you've used all the rules correctly, a grammar checker still can't tell whether your document communicates clearly. However, grammar checkers can perform some helpful review tasks and point out

FIGURE 6.6 Readability Indexes Using a Grammar Checker

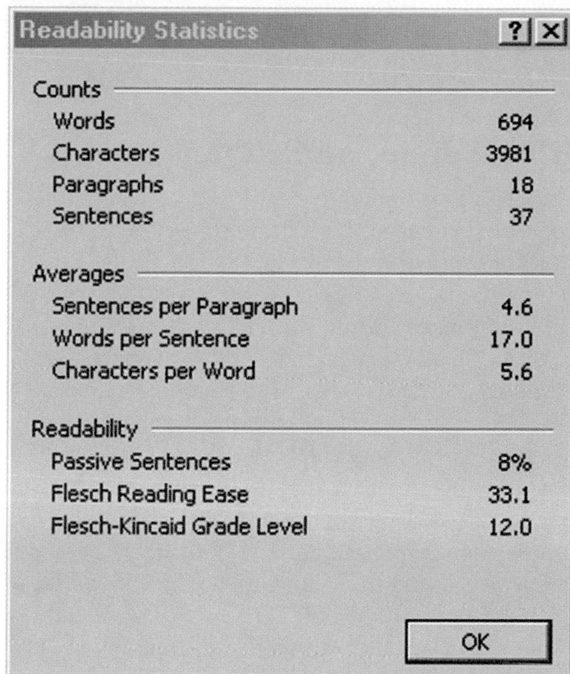

things you should consider changing, such as passive voice, long sentences, and words that tend to be misused or overused. Some programs even run readability formulas for you. Figure 6.6 shows the readability statistics that Grammatik computed for a paragraph in one document.

By all means, use any software that you find helpful when revising your documents. Just remember that it's unwise to rely on grammar checkers or spell checkers to do all your revision work. What these programs can do is identify "mistakes" you may overlook on your own. It's up to you to decide what, if anything, needs to be done, and it's up to you to catch the mistakes that these computer programs can't.[11]

Spelling and grammar checkers have their limitations.

✓ CHECKLIST: REVISING BUSINESS MESSAGES

A. Evaluate content, organization, style, and tone

1. Review your draft against the message plan.
2. Check that all necessary points appear in logical order.
3. Make sure your message is organized according to the audience's probable reaction.
4. Verify that you present enough support to make the main idea convincing and interesting.
5. Eliminate unnecessary material, and add useful material.
6. Be sure the beginning and ending are effective.
7. Make sure you've achieved the right tone.

B. Review for readability

1. Check vocabulary and sentence structure for readability.
2. Consider using a readability index.
3. Use a mix of short and long sentences.
4. Keep paragraphs short.
5. Use bulleted and numbered lists to set off key points.
6. Use headings and subheadings.
7. Use questions and punctuation marks.

C. Edit for clarity

1. Break up overly long sentences.
2. Rewrite hedging sentences.
3. Impose parallelism.
4. Correct dangling modifiers.
5. Reword long noun sequences.
6. Replace camouflaged verbs.
7. Clarify sentence structure.
8. Clarify awkward references.
9. Moderate your enthusiasm.

D. Edit for conciseness

1. Delete unnecessary words and phrases.
2. Shorten long words and phrases.
3. Eliminate redundancies.
4. Recast "It is/There are" starters.

PRODUCING YOUR MESSAGE

Even after you have revised and refined your message from start to finish, you're not done yet. Now you need to produce your message, which involves adding elements such as graphics or hypertext and designing a page layout to give your message an attractive, contemporary appearance.

Adding Graphics, Sound, and Hypertext

You can use graphics software to add visual elements to your message.

Your document can have live links to other documents and to the Internet.

With the recent advances in computer technology, it's becoming easier and easier to illustrate and enliven your text with full-color pictures, sound recordings, and hypertext links. The software for creating business visuals falls into two basic groups: *Presentation software* helps you create overhead transparencies and computerized slide shows (electronic presentations are discussed in Chapter 16). *Graphics software* ranges from products that can create simple diagrams and flowcharts (see Chapter 11) to comprehensive tools geared to artists and graphic designers. You can create your pictures from scratch, use *clip art* (collections of uncopyrighted images), or scan in drawings or photographs.

Adding sound bites to your documents is an exciting new way to get your message across. Several systems now allow you to record a brief message or other sound and attach it to particular places in a document. For instance, you can add sound annotations, instead of written ones. Then, clicking on the special speaker icon plays a recorded comment, such as "Please convert this paragraph to a bulleted list." To actually hear the sound, the person receiving the memo has to load the memo into his or her computer and have a sound card installed.

You can also use hypertext markup language (HTML) to insert hyperlinks into your message. Readers can easily jump from one document to another by clicking on such a link. They can go directly to a website (provided they have an active Internet hookup), jump to another section of your document, or go to a different document altogether. For example, say you're preparing a report on this year's budget. Rather than include pages and pages of budget details from prior years, you can submit your report on disk and include a hyperlink in the file. Then, when readers click on the hyperlink, they can access a document containing details of the prior years' budgets. By using hyperlinks, you can customize your documents to meet the individual information needs of your readers—just as you can on a webpage. Of course, you'll have to make sure that the file, or the software program used to open that file, is either included with your electronic document or installed on the recipient's computer.

Paying attention to appeal is one way Michael Wood, founder of educational toy-maker LeapFrog Enterprises, turned his ideas into a huge success. Every new toy is reviewed by a battery of experts and skeptics. Only the heartiest ideas—one in ten—make it to the retailers' shelves. You should focus on appeal when writing a business message. Adding sound bites, graphics, and hypertext to a business message can increase its overall appeal and give it a contemporary appearance.

Designing Page Layout

The way you package your ideas has a lot to do with how successful your communication will be. The first thing your readers will notice about your message is its appearance. If your document looks tired and out of date, it will give that impression to your readers—even if your ideas are innovative. Good looks can help you get your message across, especially to busy readers. Consider the memo in Figure 6.7. The bar chart in this memo is centered to give a formal impression, and the color used in the graphic is balanced by the letterhead logo.

Design affects the impression your message makes.

Effective design guides your readers through your message, so be sure your document's design has these elements:

For effective design, pay attention to
- Consistency
- Balance
- Restraint
- Detail

- **Consistency.** Throughout a message (and sometimes even from message to message), be consistent in your use of margins, typeface, type size, and spacing (for example, in paragraph indents, between columns, and around photographs). Also be consistent when using recurring design elements, such as vertical lines, columns, and borders.

FIGURE 6.7 In-Depth Critique: The Importance of Appearance

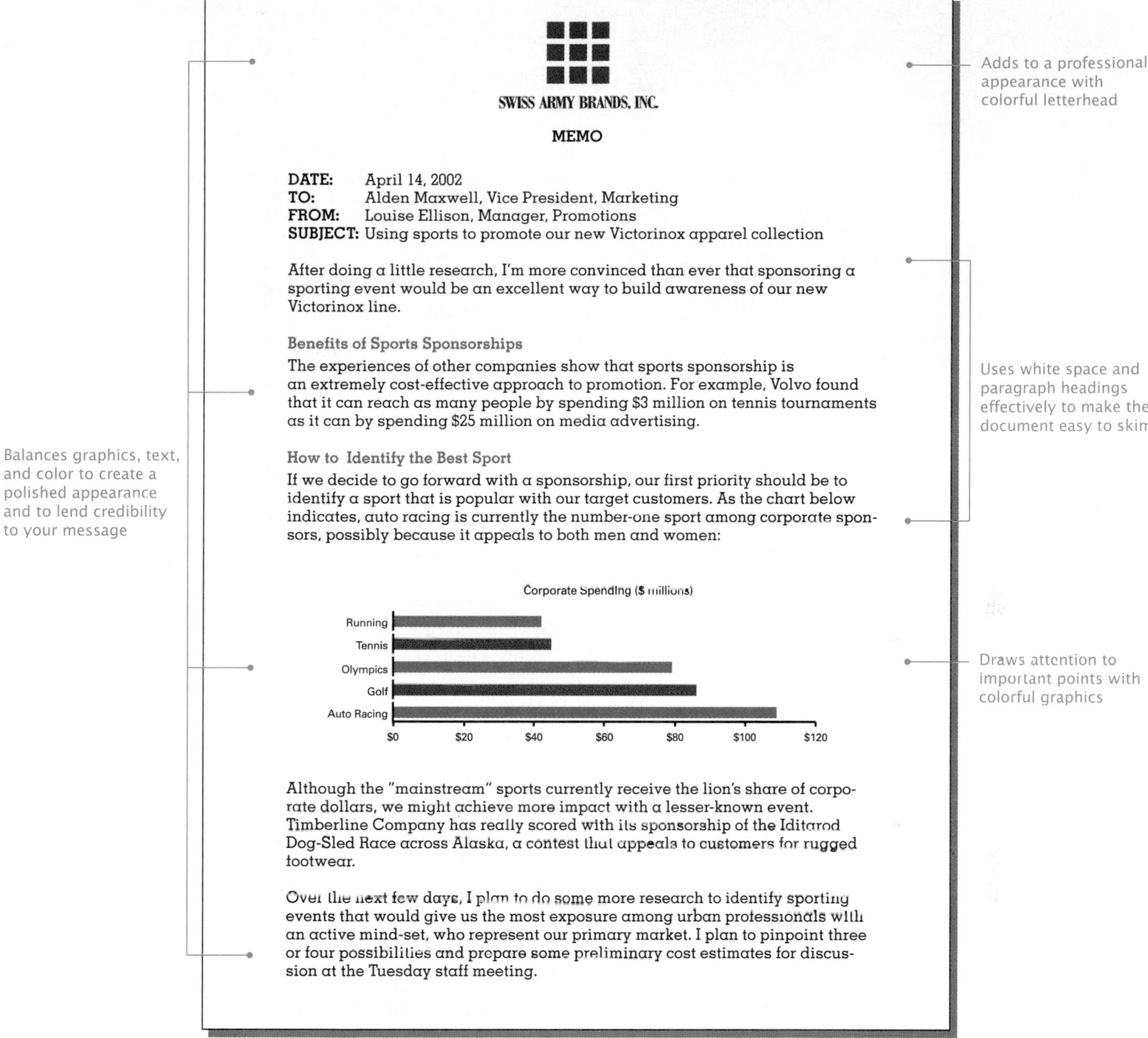

SWISS ARMY BRANDS, INC.

MEMO

DATE: April 14, 2002
TO: Alden Maxwell, Vice President, Marketing
FROM: Louise Ellison, Manager, Promotions
SUBJECT: Using sports to promote our new Victorinox apparel collection

After doing a little research, I'm more convinced than ever that sponsoring a sporting event would be an excellent way to build awareness of our new Victorinox line.

Benefits of Sports Sponsorships

The experiences of other companies show that sports sponsorship is an extremely cost-effective approach to promotion. For example, Volvo found that it can reach as many people by spending $3 million on tennis tournaments as it can by spending $25 million on media advertising.

How to Identify the Best Sport

If we decide to go forward with a sponsorship, our first priority should be to identify a sport that is popular with our target customers. As the chart below indicates, auto racing is currently the number-one sport among corporate sponsors, possibly because it appeals to both men and women:

Although the "mainstream" sports currently receive the lion's share of corporate dollars, we might achieve more impact with a lesser-known event. Timberline Company has really scored with its sponsorship of the Iditarod Dog-Sled Race across Alaska, a contest that appeals to customers for rugged footwear.

Over the next few days, I plan to do some more research to identify sporting events that would give us the most exposure among urban professionals with an active mind-set, who represent our primary market. I plan to pinpoint three or four possibilities and prepare some preliminary cost estimates for discussion at the Tuesday staff meeting.

- **Balance.** To create a pleasing design, balance the space devoted to text, artwork, and white space.
- **Restraint.** Strive for simplicity in design. Don't clutter your message with too many design elements, too much highlighting, or too many decorative touches.
- **Detail.** Pay attention to details that affect your design and thus your message. For instance, headings and subheadings that appear at the bottom of a column or a page can offend readers when the promised information doesn't appear until the next column or page. And narrow columns with too much space between words can be distracting.

Learning Objective 5

Describe four design elements, explain how they can change a document's appearance, and tell how to use them effectively

You can use a variety of design elements, such as white space, margins and line justification, typefaces, and type styles to make your message look professional, interesting, and up to date. But be careful, too many design elements will confuse your audience. If you will be designing a lot of documents that contain a variety of elements, you would be wise to take a course in page layout or to at least read further about effective design techniques.

When creating these appealing sculptures, Monita Somers and Ann Carlson pay careful attention to detail, use decorative touches tastefully, and strive for visual contrast. You should use these same guidelines to create successful business messages and give them a professional look.

White Space

White space is free of text and artwork.

White space, or space free of text or artwork, provides visual contrast for your readers, and perhaps even more important, it gives them a resting point. White space includes the open area surrounding headings, margin areas, the vertical space between columns, the space created by ragged line endings, the paragraph indents or extra space between unindented paragraphs, and the horizontal space between lines of text.

Heading Placement When placing headings and subheadings into your documents, remember that their purpose is to invite readers to become involved in your message. Centered heads should contain no more than two lines, as multiple lines will slow your readers as they search for the beginning of each line. To improve readability, position your headings "flush left" (aligned with the left-hand margin). You may even want to set them in a type size larger than the type used for text and use a different typeface. Because headings and subheadings clue readers in to the organization of your message's content, link them as closely as possible to the text they introduce. You can do so by putting more space above the heading than below it.

Caption Placement Captions are the most widely read part of a document. They tie photographs and illustrations into the rest of your message. Although usually placed below the exhibits they describe, captions can also be placed beside or above their exhibits. Make sure that the width of your captions is pleasing in proportion to the width of the exhibit, the surrounding white space, and the text.

Margins and Line Justification

Margins frame your text.

Margins define the space around your text and between text columns. They're influenced by the way you place lines of type, which can be set (1) justified (flush on the left and flush on the right), (2) flush left with a ragged right margin, (3) flush right with a ragged left margin, or (4) centered.

Justified type makes messages look more like form letters.

Justified type "darkens" your message's appearance, because the uniform line lengths lack the white space created by ragged margins. It also tends to make your message look more like a form letter and less like a customized message. Justified type is often considered more difficult to read, because large gaps can appear between words and because more words are hyphenated. Excessive hyphenation is distracting and hard to follow. Even so, many magazines and newspapers use justified type because it accommodates more text.

Flush-left–ragged-right type gives your message an open feeling.

Flush-left, ragged-right type "lightens" your message's appearance. It gives a document an informal, contemporary feeling of openness. Spacing between words is the same, and only long words that fall at the ends of lines are hyphenated.

Centered type lends a formal tone to your message. However, centering long blocks of type slows reading because your audience has to search for the beginning of each line. The same problem is true of flush-right, ragged-left type. These two approaches are usually avoided for long passages of text.

Typefaces

Typeface refers to the physical design of letters, numbers, and other text characters. Most computers offer innumerable choices of fonts or typefaces. Each typeface influences the tone of your message, making it look authoritative or friendly, businesslike or casual, classic or modern, and so on. So choose fonts that are appropriate for your message.

TABLE 6.4 Common Typefaces

Sample Serif Typeface	*Sample Sans Serif Typeface*
Times Roman is often used for text.	Helvetica is often used for headings.
TIMES ROMAN IS HARDER TO READ IN ALL CAPS.	HELVETICA IS A CLEANER FACE, EVEN IN ALL CAPS.

Serif typefaces have small crosslines (called serifs) at the ends of each letter stroke (see Table 6.4). Serif faces such as Times Roman (packaged with most laser printers) are commonly used for text; they can look busy and cluttered when set in large sizes for headings or other display treatments. Typefaces with rounded serifs can look friendly; those with squared serifs can look official.

Serif typefaces are commonly used for text.

Sans serif typefaces have no serifs. Faces such as Helvetica are ideal for display treatments that use larger type. Sans serif faces can be difficult to read in long blocks of text. They look best when surrounded by plenty of white space—as in headings or in widely spaced lines of text.

Sans serif typefaces are commonly used for headings.

Limit the number of typefaces in a single document.[12] In general, avoid using more than two typefaces on a page. Many great-looking documents are based on a single sans serif typeface for heads and subheads, with a second serif typeface for text and captions. Using too many typefaces clutters the document and reduces your audience's comprehension.

Type Styles

Type style refers to any modification that lends contrast or emphasis to type. Most computers offer boldface, italic, underlining, and other highlighting and decorative styles. Using boldface type for subheads breaks up long expanses of text. Just remember that too much boldfacing will darken the appearance of your message and make it look heavy. You can set isolated words in boldface type in the middle of a text block to draw more attention to them. If you boldface too many words, however, you might create a "checkerboard" appearance in a paragraph.

Avoid using type styles that slow your readers down.

Use italic type for emphasis. Although italics are sometimes used when irony or humor is intended, quotation marks are usually best for that purpose. Italics can also be used to set off a quote and are often used in captions. Boldfaced type and italics are most effective when reserved for key words—those that help readers understand the main point of the text. A good example of using boldface type effectively is found in the document-revision tips listed under the heading "Editing for Clarity and Conciseness" on pages 148–151 of this chapter. Here the boldfaced type draws attention to the key tips, followed by a short, regular typeface explanation of each tip.

Use italic type for emphasis.

As a general rule, avoid using any style that slows your audience's progress through your message. For instance, underlining or using all-uppercase letters can interfere with your reader's ability to recognize the shapes of words, improperly placed boldface or italicized type can slow down your reader, and shadowed or outlined type can seriously hinder legibility. So use these styles judiciously.

Generally avoid using any type styles that inhibit your audience's ability to read your messages.

Make sure the size of your type is proportionate to the importance of your message and the space allotted. For most business messages, use a type size of 10 to 12 points (a point is approximately 1/72 of an inch). Resist the temptation to reduce your type size to squeeze in text or to enlarge it to fill up space. Smaller type is hard to read, whereas larger type looks unprofessional and, if squeezed into a small area, is hard to read and visually claustrophobic.

Giving Your Message a Professional Look

Most word-processing programs include several elements to help you assemble your finished pages, combining text and graphics so that the appearance is both professional and inviting. But if you want a first-class report with photos and drawings, consider

In general, the software most appropriate for assembling finished pages with graphics elements is desktop publishing (DTP), although word-processing software can handle graphics to a limited extent.

Computer software can help you add a first-class look to your most important business documents.

desktop publishing (DTP) software, which includes additional specialized tools for formatting, drawing, design, and layout. Desktop publishing software such as Quark XPress and Adobe Pagemaker, can make it easy for anyone to produce great-looking documents in two ways:

- **Adding a first-class finish.** You can use DTP to select attractive typefaces and add color graphics, turning a plain piece of text into a dazzling and persuasive document. Used improperly, however, the same technology can turn your document into garish, high-tech rubbish. Knowing how to use technological tools is critical for business communicators.
- **Managing document style.** To maintain consistent style in your document, most word processors and DTP packages use *styles,* formatting commands that you can save and apply as needed. High-end packages collect these commands into *style sheets* that save formatting effort, ensure consistency in each section you add to your report, and ensure a consistent look for all documents created in a department or even in an entire company.

PROOFREADING YOUR MESSAGE

Your credibility is affected by your attention to the details of mechanics and form.

Although spelling, punctuation, and typographical errors seem trivial to some people, most readers view your attention to detail as a sign of your professionalism (see Figure 6.8). Adrianne Proeller of TBS says, "When I get a college résumé and I see a typo on it, I instantly disregard that résumé." Whether you're writing a one-paragraph memo or a 500-page report, if you let mechanical errors slip through, your readers wonder whether you're unreliable in more important ways. Companies such as *The New Yorker* magazine take great pride in their editorial standards: When *The New Yorker* misspelled *Tucson* as 'Tuscon,' it gave Arizona $66,000 worth of free advertising to set things right.[13]

FIGURE 6.8 Why Accuracy in Proofreading Is Important

If you believe that 99.9% accuracy is acceptable, then

Every hour:
18,322 pieces of mail would be mishandled
22,000 checks would be deducted from the wrong bank account

Every day:
12 newborn babies would be given to wrong parents
55 incorrect drug prescriptions would be written

Every week:
500 incorrect surgical procedures would be performed
48,000 books would be shipped with the wrong cover

Every year:
81,000 faulty rolls of 35mm film would be loaded
2 million documents would be lost by the IRS

In addition:
320 entries in Webster's Third New International Dictionary of the English Language would be misspelled

Sharpening Your Career Skills

How to Proofread Like a Pro: Tips for Creating the Perfect Document

You've carefully revised and polished your document, and it's been sent off to the word-processing department or a designer to be put into final form. You can breathe a sigh of relief, but only for the moment: You'll still be proofreading what comes out of the printer. To ensure that any document is error-free, always proofread the final version. Following are some hints to help make your proofreading more effective.

- **Multiple passes.** Go through the document several times, focusing on a different aspect each time. The first pass might be to look for omissions and errors in content; the second pass could be for layout, spacing, and other aesthetic features; a final pass might be to check for typographical, grammatical, and spelling errors.
- **Perceptual tricks.** Your brain has been trained to ignore transposed letters, improper capitalization, and misplaced punctuation. Try (1) reading each page from the bottom to the top (starting at the last word in each line), (2) placing your finger under each word and reading it silently, (3) making a slit in a sheet of paper that reveals only one line of type at a time, and (4) reading the document aloud and pronouncing each word carefully.
- **Impartial reviews.** Have a friend or colleague proofread the document for you. Others are likely to catch mistakes that you continually fail to notice. (All of us have blind spots when it comes to reviewing our own work.)
- **Typos.** Look for the most common typographical errors (typos): transposition (such as *teh*), substitution (such as *ecomonic*), and omission (such as *productvity*).
- **Mechanics.** When looking for errors in spelling, grammar, punctuation, and capitalization, if you're unsure about something, look it up in a dictionary, a usage book, or another reference work.
- **Accuracy.** Double-check the spelling of names and the accuracy of dates, addresses, and all numbers (quantities ordered, prices, and so on). It would not do to order 500 staplers when you want only 50.
- **Distance.** If you have time, set the document aside and proofread it the next day.
- **Vigilance.** Avoid reading large amounts of material in one sitting, and try not to proofread when you're tired.
- **Focus.** Concentrate on what you're doing. Try to block out distractions, and focus as completely as possible on your proofreading task.
- **Caution.** Take your time. Quick proofreading is not careful proofreading.

Proofreading may require patience, but it adds credibility to your document.

Career Applications

1. What qualities does a person need to be a good proofreader? Are such qualities inborn, or can they be learned?
2. Proofread the following sentence:
   aplication of thse methods in stores in San Deigo nd Cinncinati have resultted in a 30 drop in roberies an a 50 precent decling in violnce there, acording ot thedevelpers if the securty sytem, Hanover brothrs, Inc.

What to Look for When Proofreading

Learning Objective 6

Highlight the types of errors to look for when proofreading

Proofread your message to ensure that it's letter-perfect. You'll want to check it for correct grammar, usage, and punctuation (for a quick review, see Appendix III). You'll also want to be on the lookout for common spelling errors and typos. Check too for missing material: a missing source note, a missing exhibit, or even a missing paragraph. Look for design errors. For example, some headings and text might appear in the wrong typeface (Helvetica rather than Times New Roman, or Arial Black rather than Arial Narrow). One or two special elements may appear in the wrong type style (boldface instead of italic, or italic instead of underlined). Columns within tables and exhibits on a page might be misaligned. Graphic characters such as ampersands and percent signs may appear when they should be spelled out, and numerical symbols might be incorrect. Look closely at the type to spot problems, such as extra spacing between lines or between words, crowded type, a short line of type ending a paragraph at the top of a new page, a heading left hanging at the bottom of a page, or incorrect hyphenation. (See "Sharpening Your Career Skills: How to Proofread Like a Pro: Tips for Creating the Perfect Document.")

The types of details to look for when proofreading include language errors, missing material, design errors, and typographical errors.

Also, give some attention to your overall format. Have you followed accepted conventions and company guidelines for laying out the document on the page (margin

FIGURE 6.9 In-Depth Critique: The Importance of Revision (Ineffective Letter)

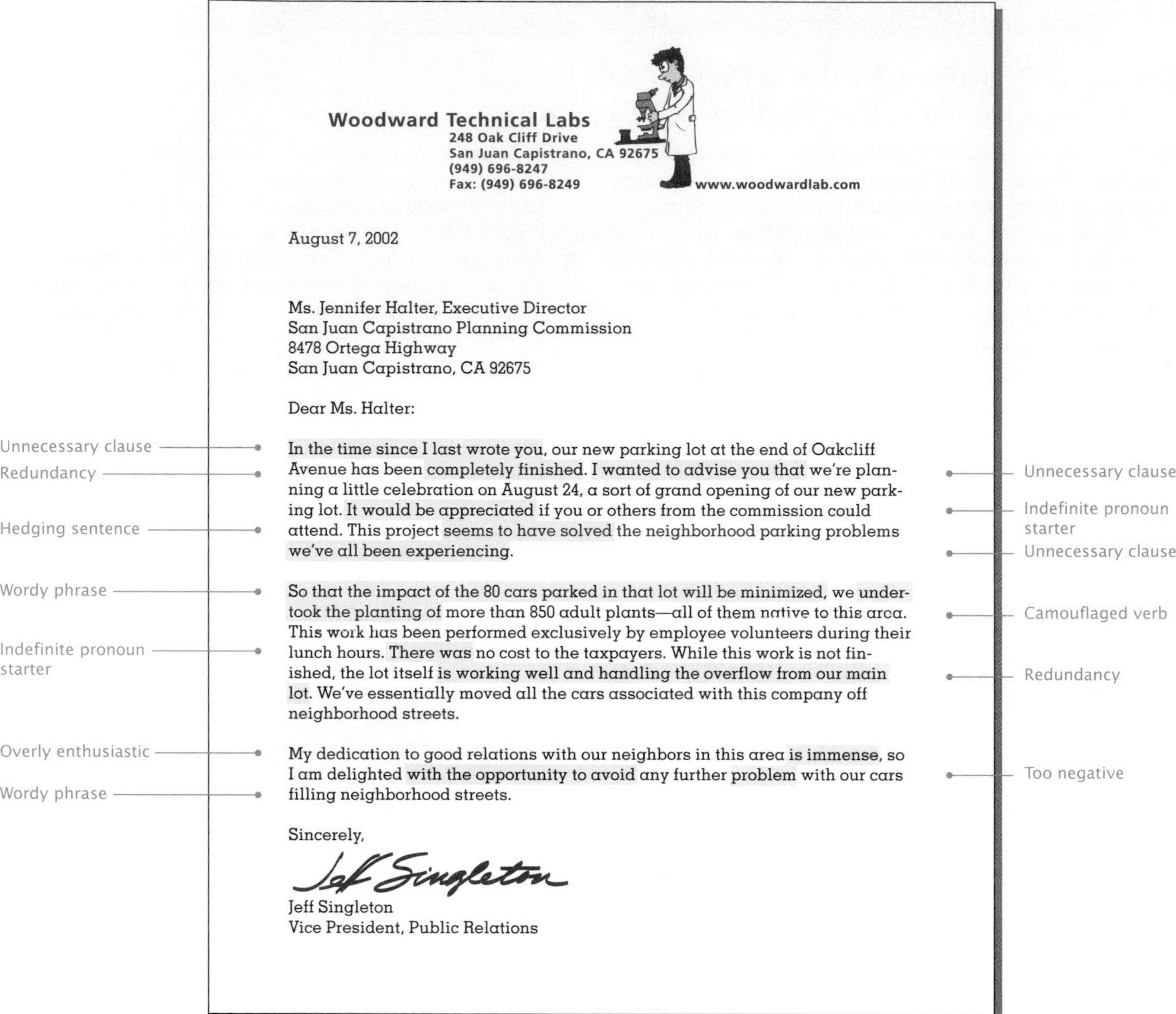

Woodward Technical Labs
248 Oak Cliff Drive
San Juan Capistrano, CA 92675
(949) 696-8247
Fax: (949) 696-8249
www.woodwardlab.com

August 7, 2002

Ms. Jennifer Halter, Executive Director
San Juan Capistrano Planning Commission
8478 Ortega Highway
San Juan Capistrano, CA 92675

Dear Ms. Halter:

In the time since I last wrote you, our new parking lot at the end of Oakcliff Avenue has been completely finished. I wanted to advise you that we're planning a little celebration on August 24, a sort of grand opening of our new parking lot. It would be appreciated if you or others from the commission could attend. This project seems to have solved the neighborhood parking problems we've all been experiencing.

So that the impact of the 80 cars parked in that lot will be minimized, we undertook the planting of more than 850 adult plants—all of them native to this area. This work has been performed exclusively by employee volunteers during their lunch hours. There was no cost to the taxpayers. While this work is not finished, the lot itself is working well and handling the overflow from our main lot. We've essentially moved all the cars associated with this company off neighborhood streets.

My dedication to good relations with our neighbors in this area is immense, so I am delighted with the opportunity to avoid any further problem with our cars filling neighborhood streets.

Sincerely,

Jeff Singleton
Vice President, Public Relations

width, number of columns, running heads)? Have you included all the traditional elements that belong in documents of the type you're creating? Have you been consistent in handling page numbers, heading styles, exhibits titles, source notes, and other details? (To resolve questions about format and layout, see Appendix I.)

How to Adapt the Proofreading Process

How many and what sort of errors you catch when proofreading depends on how much time you have and what sort of document you are preparing. The more routine your document, the less time you'll need to spend. Routine documents have fewer elements to check. Moreover, the more often you prepare one type of document, the more you'll know about what sorts of errors to look for.

Even when you're pressed for time, try to maintain the schedule you laid out during the planning step of the writing process.

Longer, more complex documents can have many more components that need checking. For complicated documents, you may feel pressed for enough time to do a good proofreading job. But back in step one of the writing process (look back at Figure 4.1),

FIGURE 6.10 In-Depth Critique: The Importance of Revision (Effective Letter)

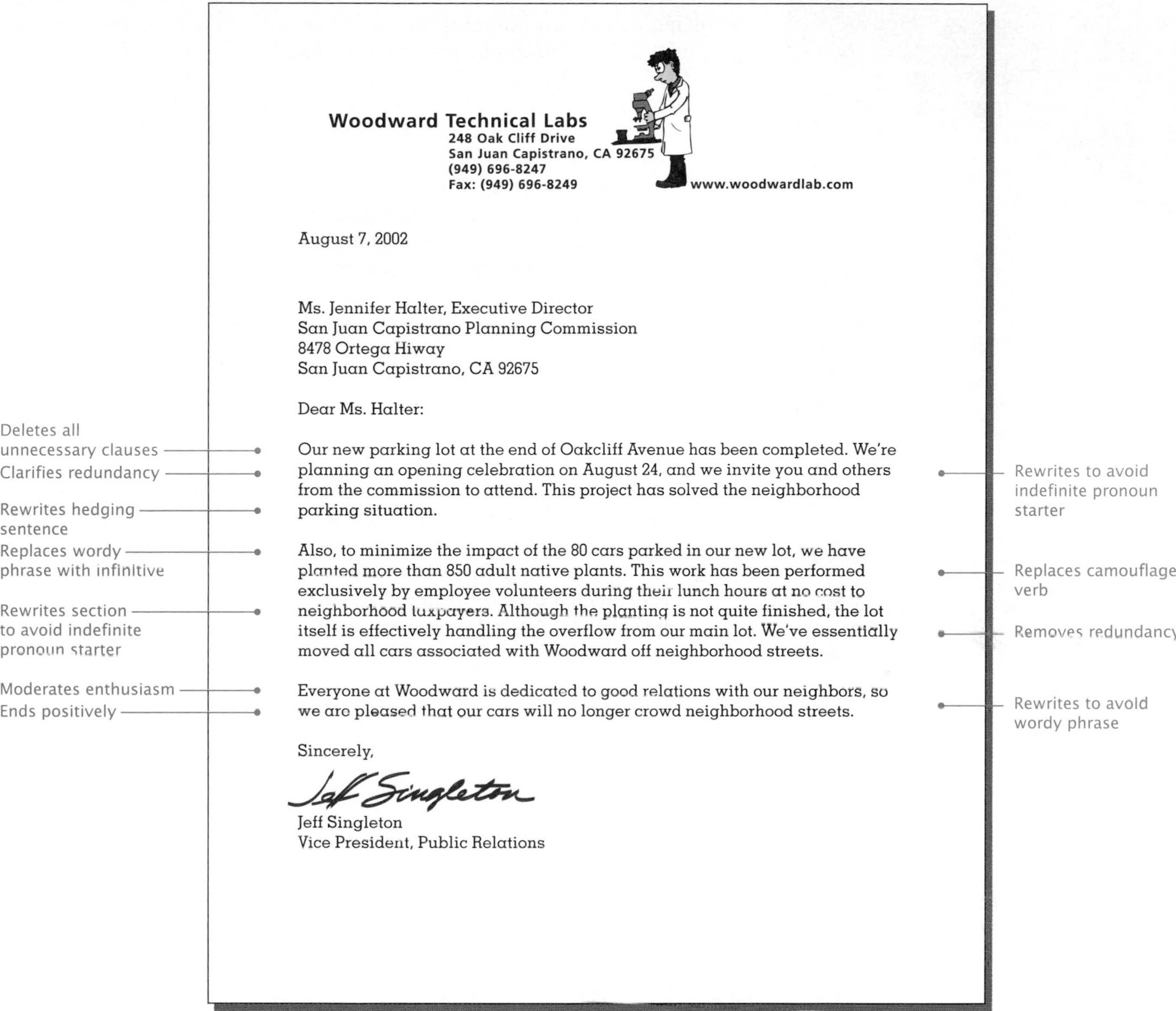

Woodward Technical Labs
248 Oak Cliff Drive
San Juan Capistrano, CA 92675
(949) 696-8247
Fax: (949) 696-8249
www.woodwardlab.com

August 7, 2002

Ms. Jennifer Halter, Executive Director
San Juan Capistrano Planning Commission
8478 Ortega Hiway
San Juan Capistrano, CA 92675

Dear Ms. Halter:

Our new parking lot at the end of Oakcliff Avenue has been completed. We're planning an opening celebration on August 24, and we invite you and others from the commission to attend. This project has solved the neighborhood parking situation.

Also, to minimize the impact of the 80 cars parked in our new lot, we have planted more than 850 adult native plants. This work has been performed exclusively by employee volunteers during their lunch hours at no cost to neighborhood taxpayers. Although the planting is not quite finished, the lot itself is effectively handling the overflow from our main lot. We've essentially moved all cars associated with Woodward off neighborhood streets.

Everyone at Woodward is dedicated to good relations with our neighbors, so we are pleased that our cars will no longer crowd neighborhood streets.

Sincerely,

Jeff Singleton
Vice President, Public Relations

you planned out how you would approach this message and you allotted a certain amount of time for each task. Try to stick to your schedule. You want to do your best to create a perfect document, but you also want to meet your deadline and turn your work in promptly. As with every task in the writing process, practice helps—you not only become more familiar with what errors to look for but also become more skilled in identifying those errors. Look at the letter in Figure 6.9. The organization is basically sound, and the content is more or less satisfactory. However, the overall readability is poor. The message is filled with awkward language that is wordy and redundant. The letter in Figure 6.10 is much improved.

DISTRIBUTING YOUR MESSAGE

Technology can also help you distribute your message in the most appropriate fashion.

Once you have revised, produced, and proofread your message, you are ready to distribute it. For multiple copies of your document, you can print as many as you

Cushcity.com owners Gwen and Willie Richardson are e-tailers, selling Afrocentric books, videos, calendars, collectibles, toys, and educational items over the Internet. They also distribute business documents over the Internet, routinely sending e-mail messages and attachments of all sizes to employees and often to customers. This method of distribution is popular because of the speed. Mrs. Richardson says, "We have a very responsive e-mail system." Customers are especially impressed with the two-hour response time from Cushcity.

like on an inkjet or laser printer, or you can print a single copy and reproduce it with a *photocopier*. For high-volume and complex reproduction (involving colors or photographs, for instance), you'll want to take your document to a *print shop*, a company that has the special equipment needed for such jobs.

When you need to send the same document (sales letter, invoice, or other customer communication) to a large number of people, *mail merge* automatically combines a standard version of the document with a list of names and addresses. It will produce one copy for each person on your mailing list, saving you the trouble of inserting the name and address each time. The names and addresses can come from your own customer databases or from mailing lists you rent from firms that specialize in collecting names and addresses.

Similarly, *broadcast faxing* allows you to enter mailing lists into your fax machine and transmit your document to the fax machines of all members on the list. Fax machines are indispensable for international business, particularly because they overcome the delay problems of regular mail and the time-zone problems of trying to contact someone by telephone.[14]

Many companies now distribute information on CD-ROM or computer disk rather than on paper. For instance, several of Hewlett-Packard's product catalogs are available either on CD-ROM or in printed form. CD-ROMs hold a large amount of information, they're inexpensive, and their small size saves money in postage and shipping.

Of course, one of the most popular methods for distributing documents is over the Internet. Most Internet browser software allows you to attach documents of all sizes and types to e-mail messages. If you are sending multiple documents or long documents over the Internet, you can use special software to encode or compress your message, reducing the file size so that it can be transmitted faster. Before doing that, however, make sure your recipients have similar software so that they can decode or uncompress the message and convert it back into its original file format.

COMMUNICATION CHALLENGES AT TURNER BROADCASTING SYSTEM

One of Adrianne Proeller's tasks is to send out internal memos announcing new employees hired by TBS. You're one of the newest—hired right out of college—and Proeller has asked you to provide the information she needs to write the official announcement.

Individual Challenge: Decide which job you've been hired for (communications assistant, sales trainee, technical engineer, marketing associate, or any other you choose) and determine what qualifications you'll bring to the position (you may need to invent some). For help, consult library references such as *Dictionary of Occupational Titles,* which describes positions and qualifications. Then draft a routine memo to Proeller that supplies her with everything she needs to write her announcement. This is one of your first on-the-job tasks, so you want your memo to look good. Scrutinize your first draft for content, organization, style, and readability. Then produce a second draft.

Team Challenge: In a small group, exchange copies of your memos so that everyone can mark suggestions for revision on each group member's memo. Then compare your efforts. Did everyone spot the same errors? Where did you disagree? Is it a good idea to let others review your work?[15] ■

SUMMARY OF LEARNING OBJECTIVES

1 **Discuss when revision is performed, and list the main tasks involved in completing a business message.** Revision is an ongoing activity. It occurs throughout the writing process, again after you complete the first draft of your business message, and again after you produce the final version. Revision consists of three main tasks: (1) evaluating content, organization, style, and tone, (2) reviewing for readability and scannability, and (3) editing for clarity and conciseness. After you revise your message, you complete it by using design elements to give your message a professional look, and by proofreading the final version after it has been produced.

2 **List four writing techniques you can use to improve the readability of your messages.** The four techniques that improve readability are varying sentence length, keeping paragraphs short, using lists and bullets, and adding headings and subheadings.

3 **List nine tips for making your writing clear.** Clear writing doesn't happen the first time, so you need to revise your work. As you try to clarify your message, (1) break up overly long sentences, (2) rewrite hedging sentences, (3) impose parallelism, (4) correct dangling modifiers, (5) reword long noun sequences, (6) replace camouflaged verbs, (7) clarify sentence structure, (8) clarify awkward references, and (9) moderate your enthusiasm.

4 **Discuss why it's important to make your message more concise, and give four tips on how to do so.** Businesspeople are more likely to read documents that give information efficiently. So to make business messages more concise, try to include only necessary material and write clean sentences by (1) deleting unnecessary words and phrases, (2) shortening overly long words and phrases, (3) eliminating redundancies, and (4) recasting "It is" and "There are" starters.

5 **Describe four design elements, explain how they can change a document's appearance, and tell how to use them effectively.** White space provides contrast and gives readers a resting point. Margins define the space around the text and contribute to the amount of white space. Typefaces influence the tone of the message. Type styles provide contrast or emphasis. When selecting and applying design elements, you can ensure their effectiveness by being consistent throughout your document; balancing your space between text, art, and white space; showing restraint in the number of elements you use; and paying attention to every detail.

6 **Highlight the types of errors to look for when proofreading.** When proofreading the final version of your document, always keep an eye out for errors in grammar, usage, and punctuation. In addition, watch for spelling errors and typos. Make sure that nothing is missing (whether a source note, an exhibit, or text). Correct design errors such as elements that appear in the wrong typeface, elements that appear in the wrong type style, misaligned elements (columns in a table, exhibits on a page, etc.), and graphic characters (such as ampersands and percent signs) that appear in both symbol and spelled-out form. Look for typographical errors such as uneven spacing between lines and words, a short line of type at the top of a page, a heading at the bottom of a page, or incorrect hyphenation. In addition, make sure your layout conforms to company guidelines.

TEST YOUR KNOWLEDGE

1. What are the three main tasks involved in revising a business message?
2. How can you increase the readability of your paragraphs?
3. What is the purpose of the Fog Index and similar formulas?
4. What functions do headings serve?
5. What are some ways you can make a document more concise?
6. What computer tools can you use when revising messages?
7. What is parallel construction, and why is it important?
8. Why is it a good idea to use verbs instead of noun phrases?
9. How do readers benefit from white space?
10. Why is proofreading an important part of the writing process?

APPLY YOUR KNOWLEDGE

1. Why is it important to let your draft "age" a day before you begin the editing process?
2. Given the choice of only one, would you prefer to use a grammar checker or a spell checker? Why?
3. When you are designing a formal business letter, which design elements do you have to consider and which are optional?
4. How does design contribute to a document's overall effectiveness?
5. **Ethical Choices** What are the ethical implications of using underlining, all capitals, and other hard-to-read type styles in a document explaining how customers can appeal the result of a decision made in the company's favor during a dispute?

PRACTICE YOUR KNOWLEDGE

 ***Documents for Analysis***

Read the following documents; then (1) analyze the strengths and weaknesses of each sentence and (2) revise each document so that it follows the guidelines in Chapters 4 through 6.

Document 6.A

The move to our new offices will take place over this coming weekend. For everything to run smooth, everyone will have to clean out their own desk and pack up the contents in boxes that will be provided. You will need to take everything off the walls too, and please pack it along with the boxes.

If you have alot of personal belongings, you should bring them home with you. Likewise with anything valuable. I do not mean to infer that items will be stolen, irregardless it is better to be safe than sorry.

On Monday, we will be unpacking, putting things away, and then get back to work. The least amount of disruption is anticipated by us, if everyone does their part. Hopefully, there will be no negative affects on production schedules, and current deadlines will be met.

Document 6.B

Dear Ms. Giraud:

Enclosed herewith please find the manuscript for your book, *Careers in Woolgathering*. After perusing the first two chapters of your 1,500-page manuscript, I was forced to conclude that the subject matter, handicrafts and artwork using wool fibers, is not coincident with the publishing program of Framingham Press, which to this date has issued only works on business endeavors, avoiding all other topics completely.

Although our firm is unable to consider your impressive work at the present time, I have taken the liberty of recording some comments on some of the pages. I am of the opinion that any feedback that a writer can obtain from those well versed in the publishing realm can only serve to improve the writer's authorial skills.

In view of the fact that your residence is in the Boston area, might I suggest that you secure an appointment with someone of high editorial stature at the Cambridge Heritage Press, which I believe might have something of an interest in works of the nature you have produced.

Wishing you the best of luck in your literary endeavors, I remain

Arthur J. Cogswell
Editor

Document 6.C

For delicious, air-popped popcorn, please read the following instructions: The popper is designed to pop 1/2 cup of popcorn kernels at one time. Never add more than 1/2 cup. A half cup of corn will produce three to four quarts of popcorn. More batches may be made separately after completion of the first batch. Popcorn is popped by hot air. Oil or shortening is not needed for popping corn. Add only popcorn kernels to the popping chamber. Standard grades of popcorn are recommended for use. Premium or gourmet type popping corns may be used. Ingredients such as oil, shortening, butter, margarine, or salt should never be added to the popping chamber. The popper, with popping chute in position, may be preheated for two minutes before adding the corn. Turn the popper off before adding the corn. Use electricity safely and wisely. Observe safety precautions when using the popper. Do not touch the popper when it is hot. The popper should not be left unattended when it is plugged into an outlet. Do not use the popper if it or its cord has been damaged. Do not use the popper if it is not working properly. Before using the first time, wash the chute and butter/measuring cup in hot soapy water. Use a dishcloth or sponge. Wipe the outside of the popper base. Use a damp cloth. Dry the base. Do not immerse the popper base in water or other liquid. Replace the chute and butter/measuring cup. The popper is ready to use.

Exercises

For live links to all websites discussed in this chapter, visit this text's website at www.prenhall.com/bovee. Just log on and select Chapter 6, and click on "Student Resources." Locate the name of the site or the URL related to the material in the text. For "Exploring the Best of the Web" exercises, you'll also find navigational directions. Click on the live link to the site.

6.1 **Message Readability: Writing Paragraphs** Rewrite the following paragraph to vary the length of the sentences and to shorten the paragraph so it looks more inviting to readers.

> Although major league baseball remains popular, more people are attending minor league baseball games because they can spend less on admission, snacks, and parking and still enjoy the excitement of America's pastime. Connecticut, for example, has three AA minor league teams, including the New Haven Ravens, who are affiliated with the St. Louis Cardinals; the Norwich Navigators, who are affiliated with the New York Yankees; and the New Britain Rock Cats, who are affiliated with the Minnesota Twins. These teams play in relatively small stadiums, so fans are close enough to see and hear everything, from the swing of the bat connecting with the ball to the thud of the ball landing in the outfielder's glove. Best of all, the cost of a family outing to see rising stars play in a local minor league game is just a fraction of what the family would spend to attend a major league game in a much larger, more crowded stadium.

6.2 **Message Readability: Using Bullets** Rewrite the following paragraph using a bulleted list:

> With our alarm system, you'll have a 24-hour security guard who signals the police at the suggestion of an intruder. You'll also appreciate the computerized scanning device that determines exactly where and when the intrusion occurred. No need to worry about electrical failure, either, thanks to our backup response unit.[16]

6.3 **Revising Messages: Clarity** Break these sentences into shorter ones by adding more periods:

a. The next time you write something, check your average sentence length in a 100-word passage, and if your sentences average more than 16 to 20 words, see whether you can break up some of the sentences.

b. Don't do what the village blacksmith did when he instructed his apprentice as follows: "When I take the shoe out of the fire, I'll lay it on the anvil, and when I nod my head, you hit it with the hammer." The apprentice did just as he was told, and now he's the village blacksmith.

c. Unfortunately, no gadget will produce excellent writing, but using a yardstick like the Fog Index gives us some guideposts to follow for making writing easier to read because its two factors remind us to use short sentences and simple words.

d. Know the flexibility of the written word and its power to convey an idea, and know how to make your words behave so that your readers will understand.

e. Words mean different things to different people, and a word such as *block* may mean city block, butcher block, engine block, auction block, or several other things.

6.4 **Revising Messages: Conciseness** Cross out unnecessary words in the following phrases:

a. Consensus of opinion
b. New innovations
c. Long period of time
d. At a price of $50
e. Still remains

6.5 **Revising Messages: Conciseness** Revise the following sentences, using shorter, simpler words:

a. The antiquated calculator is ineffectual for solving sophisticated problems.

b. It is imperative that the pay increments be terminated before an inordinate deficit is accumulated.

c. There was unanimity among the executives that Ms. Jackson's idiosyncrasies were cause for a mandatory meeting with the company's personnel director.

d. The impending liquidation of the company's assets was cause for jubilation among the company's competitors.

e. The expectations of the president for a stock dividend were accentuated by the preponderance of evidence that the company was in good financial condition.

6.6 **Revising Messages: Conciseness** Use infinitives as substitutes for the overly long phrases in these sentences:

a. For living, I require money.

b. They did not find sufficient evidence for believing in the future.

c. Bringing about the destruction of a dream is tragic.

6.7 **Revising Messages: Conciseness** Rephrase the following in fewer words:

a. In the near future
b. In the event that
c. In order that
d. For the purpose of
e. With regard to
f. It may be that
g. In very few cases
h. With reference to
i. At the present time
j. There is no doubt that

6.8 **Revising Messages: Conciseness** Condense these sentences to as few words as possible:

a. We are of the conviction that writing is important.

b. In all probability, we're likely to have a price increase.

c. Our goals include making a determination about that in the near future.

d. When all is said and done at the conclusion of this experiment, I'd like to summarize the final windup.

e. After a trial period of three weeks, during which time she worked for a total of 15 full working days, we found her work was sufficiently satisfactory so that we offered her full-time work.

6.9 **Revising Messages: Modifiers** Remove all the unnecessary modifiers from these sentences:

a. Tremendously high pay increases were given to the extraordinarily skilled and extremely conscientious employees.

b. The union's proposals were highly inflationary, extremely demanding, and exceptionally bold.

6.10 **Revising Messages: Hedging** Rewrite these sentences so that they no longer contain any hedging:

a. It would appear that someone apparently entered illegally.

b. It may be possible that sometime in the near future the situation is likely to improve.

c. Your report seems to suggest that we might be losing money.

d. I believe Nancy apparently has somewhat greater influence over employees in the word-processing department.

e. It seems as if this letter of resignation means you might be leaving us.

6.11 **Revising Messages: Indefinite Starters** Rewrite these sentences to eliminate the indefinite starters:

a. There are several examples here to show that Elaine can't hold a position very long.

b. It would be greatly appreciated if every employee would make a generous contribution to Mildred Cook's retirement party.

c. It has been learned in Washington today from generally reliable sources that an important announcement will be made shortly by the White House.

d. There is a rule that states that we cannot work overtime without permission.

e. It would be great if you could work late for the next three Saturdays.

6.12 Revising Messages: Parallelism Present the ideas in these sentences in parallel form:

a. Mr. Hill is expected to lecture three days a week, to counsel two days a week, and must write for publication in his spare time.
b. She knows not only accounting, but she also reads Latin.
c. Both applicants had families, college degrees, and were in their thirties, with considerable accounting experience but few social connections.
d. This book was exciting, well written, and held my interest.
e. Don is both a hard worker and he knows bookkeeping.

6.13 Revising Messages: Awkward Pointers Revise the following sentences to delete the awkward pointers:

a. The vice president in charge of sales and the production manager are responsible for the keys to 34A and 35A, respectively.
b. The keys to 34A and 35A are in executive hands, with the former belonging to the vice president in charge of sales and the latter belonging to the production manager.
c. The keys to 34A and 35A have been given to the production manager, with the aforementioned keys being gold embossed.
d. A laser printer and a dot-matrix printer were delivered to John and Megan, respectively.
e. The walnut desk is more expensive than the oak desk, the former costing $300 more than the latter.

6.14 Revising Messages: Dangling Modifiers Rewrite these sentences to clarify the dangling modifiers:

a. Running down the railroad tracks in a cloud of smoke, we watched the countryside glide by.
b. Lying on the shelf, Ruby saw the seashell.
c. Based on the information, I think we should buy the property.
d. Being cluttered and filthy, Sandy took the whole afternoon to clean up her desk.
e. After proofreading every word, the memo was ready to be signed.

6.15 Revising Messages: Noun Sequences Rewrite the following sentences to eliminate the long strings of nouns:

a. The focus of the meeting was a discussion of the bank interest rate deregulation issue.
b. Following the government task force report recommendations, we are revising our job applicant evaluation procedures.
c. The production department quality assurance program components include employee training, supplier cooperation, and computerized detection equipment.
d. The supermarket warehouse inventory reduction plan will be implemented next month.
e. The State University business school graduate placement program is one of the best in the country.

6.16 Revising Messages: Sentence Structure Rearrange the following sentences to bring the subjects closer to their verbs:

a. Trudy, when she first saw the bull pawing the ground, ran.
b. It was Terri who, according to Ted, who is probably the worst gossip in the office (Tom excepted), mailed the wrong order.
c. William Oberstreet, in his book *Investment Capital Reconsidered,* writes of the mistakes that bankers through the decades have made.
d. Judy Schimmel, after passing up several sensible investment opportunities, despite the warnings of her friends and family, invested her inheritance in a jojoba plantation.
e. The president of U-Stor-It, which was on the brink of bankruptcy after the warehouse fire, the worst tragedy in the history of the company, prepared a press announcement.

6.17 Revising Messages: Camouflaged Verbs Rewrite each sentence so that the verbs are no longer camouflaged:

a. Adaptation to the new rules was performed easily by the employees.
b. The assessor will make a determination of the tax due.
c. Verification of the identity of the employees must be made daily.
d. The board of directors made a recommendation that Mr. Ronson be assigned to a new division.
e. The auditing procedure on the books was performed by the vice president.

6.18 Producing Messages: Design Elements Look back at your revised version of Document 6.C (see exercise under "Documents for Analysis"). Which design elements could you use to make this document more readable? Produce your revision of Document 6.C using your selected design elements. Then experiment by changing one of the design elements. How does the change affect readability? Exchange documents with another student and critique each other's work.

6.19 Internet Visit the stock market page of Bloomberg's website at www.bloomberg.com and evaluate the use of design in presenting the latest news. What design improvements can you suggest to enhance readability of the information posted on this page?

6.20 Teamwork Team up with another student and exchange your revised versions of Document 6.A, 6.B, or 6.C (see exercises under "Documents for Analysis"). Review the assignment to be sure the instructions are clear. Then read and critique your teammate's revision to see whether it can be improved. After you have critiqued each other's work, take a moment to examine the way you expressed your comments and the way you felt listening to the other student's comments. Can you identify ways to improve the critiquing process in situations such as this?

6.21 Proofreading Messages: E-Mail Proofread the following e-mail message and revise it to correct any problems you find:

> Our final company orrientation of the year will be held on Dec. 20. In preparation for this sesssion, please order 20 copies of the Policy handbook, the confindentiality agreenemt, the employee benefits Manual, please let me know if you anticipate any delays in obtaining these materials.

6.22 Ethical Choices Three of your company's five plants exceeded their expense budgets last month. You want all the plants to operate within their budgets from now on. You were thinking of using broadcast faxing to let all five plants see the memo you are sending to the managers of the three over-budget plants. Is this a good idea? Why or why not?

EXPAND YOUR KNOWLEDGE

Exploring the Best of the Web:

Write it Right: Rethink and Revise, p. 150

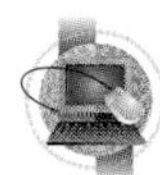

Before completing a message, go to www.powa.org for advice on organizing ideas, choosing the best word and appropriate style, and placing each paragraph effectively so that your message achieves its purpose.

1. Why is it better to write out ideas in a rough format and later reread your message to revise its content? When revising your message, what questions can you ask about your writing?
2. Name the four elements of the "writing context." Imagine that you're the reader of your message. What questions might you ask?
3. When you revise a written message, what is the purpose of "tightening"? What is one way to tighten your writing as you complete a message?

Exploring the Web on Your Own

Review these chapter-related websites on your own to learn more about writing business messages.

1. Take the fog out of your documents by visiting the Training Post, trainingpost.org/3-2-res.htm, and following the hotlinks to the Gunning Fog Index.
2. Produce flawless messages by reviewing the material at the Guide to Grammar and Writing, http://ccc.commnet.edu/grammar
3. Need help with grammar? Visit the Grammar Slammer at englishplus.com/grammar and find out why it promotes itself as the complete English Grammar Resource.

LEARN INTERACTIVELY

Interactive Study Guide

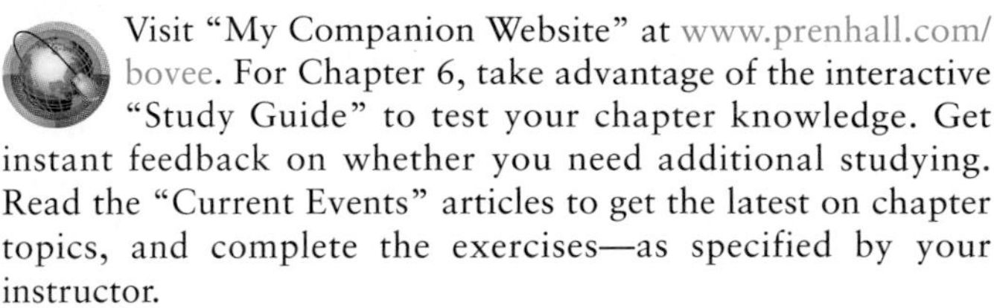

Visit "My Companion Website" at www.prenhall.com/bovee. For Chapter 6, take advantage of the interactive "Study Guide" to test your chapter knowledge. Get instant feedback on whether you need additional studying. Read the "Current Events" articles to get the latest on chapter topics, and complete the exercises—as specified by your instructor.

This site offers a variety of additional resources: The "Research Area" helps you locate a wealth of information to use in course assignments. You can even send a message to online research experts, who will help you find exactly the information you need. The "Study Hall" helps you succeed in this course. "Talk in the Hall" lets you leave messages and meet new friends online. If you have a question, you can "Ask the Tutor." And to get a better grade in this course, you can find more help at "Writing Skills," "Study Skills," and "Study Tips."

Grammar Diagnostic Tests

Review and reinforce your grammar and language skills by taking one of the four online diagnostic tests offered at our companion website, www.prenhall/bovee.com. The four tests cover a variety of topics, including spelling, capitals, punctuation, verbs, pronouns, adjectives, adverbs, sentence structure, sentence punctuation, clarity, word choice, style, organization skills, proofreading, and more. Submit your test and assess your competency. Then focus on improving areas where you are weak as you complete the exercises in this chapter.

Writing for the Web

CONSIDER HOW WRITING FOR THE WEB IS UNIQUE

In cyberspace, "you are what you write," says Charles Rubin, author of 30 books about technology. "People's opinion of you is determined to a large extent by your command of the written word." But don't think you can simply apply the lessons you learned in English class to creating effective web documents. The web is unlike any other medium you may be required to write for. People go on the web because they want to get information efficiently. So you need to grab the reader's attention and make your main points immediately.[1]

In this chapter we explain how writing for the web is different from writing for traditional print, and we explore some of the techniques that effective web writers use. Keep in mind that when writing for the web, you still follow all the business-writing guidelines discussed throughout this textbook. For instance, you continue to use a three-step writing process, you focus on making your writing more coherent and concise, and you adapt your message to your audience. But in addition to paying attention to these guidelines, you need to address some new challenges: understanding how web audiences differ from other readers; analyzing the difficulties of reading online; modifying your writing style to accommodate the nonlinear, interactive nature of the web; and adapting to its three-dimensional format.

Web Readers Have Unique Needs and Expectations

The web is a reader-driven environment. So the first step in effective web writing is to understand what web readers need and expect.

Most readers on the web are impatient. The pace of business today and the sheer amount of information available on the web have made readers hungry for instant gratification. They want the information they are looking for in the blink of an eye. Because their time is limited, readers tend to move between webpages, searching for the most appealing segments of each page instead of spending a lot of time on a single page. "I like to get into a website and then get out," said one participant in a web-user study.[2] In fact, 79 percent of web users said they scan text on the web rather than read it.[3]

Complicating this scenario, of course, is the fact that web users have hundreds of millions of pages to choose from—each competing for the user's attention.[4] Furthermore, people don't pay money to view most websites, so they have less incentive to stick around. The skim-and-scan style of today's online reader demands extreme brevity. Web writers must take extra care to hook their readers quickly, write concisely, and get directly to the point. But catering to the reader's short attention span is only part of the challenge you face as a web writer.

Reading Online Is Difficult

For most people, reading on a computer monitor is more difficult than reading from the printed page. In fact, studies show that reading speeds are about 25 percent slower on a monitor than on paper.[5] Two factors contribute to this slower reading speed: First, text is not easy to read on-screen. Monitor screen settings and quality vary. The size of the type depends on the size of the monitor and on each monitor's screen settings, regardless of how a webpage was designed. For instance, a monitor that displays graphics at 640 by 480 pixels will produce larger type than a monitor set to higher settings such as 800 by 600 pixels or 1024 by 768 pixels. Second, reading from computer screens is tiring on the eyes. Screens are typically in landscape orientation (horizontal), but most traditional documents are in portrait orientation (vertical). Thus, one page of written information scanned onto a webpage can take up multiple screens, forcing readers to scroll through the document. Successful web writers help their readers by breaking information into smaller screen-sized chunks that may be accessed in any order.

The Web Is a Nonlinear, Interactive Medium

Traditional writing follows straight lines; writers provide directions for readers by organizing information into a logical flow and by ordering that flow into progressive paragraphs and pages. Most readers move through a printed document in a fairly linear path, perhaps skipping over a few sections here and there, but generally moving from the beginning of the document to the end. With traditional print, the most interactive thing readers can do is to turn the pages.

But on the web, readers move about a document and its related screens in any order they please. Readers may choose to follow a linear path, but they are not obligated to do so. The tool that makes such interactivity possible is the **hyperlink**—the in-text tag that allows readers to click

FIGURE A.1 The Three-Dimensional Nature of the Web

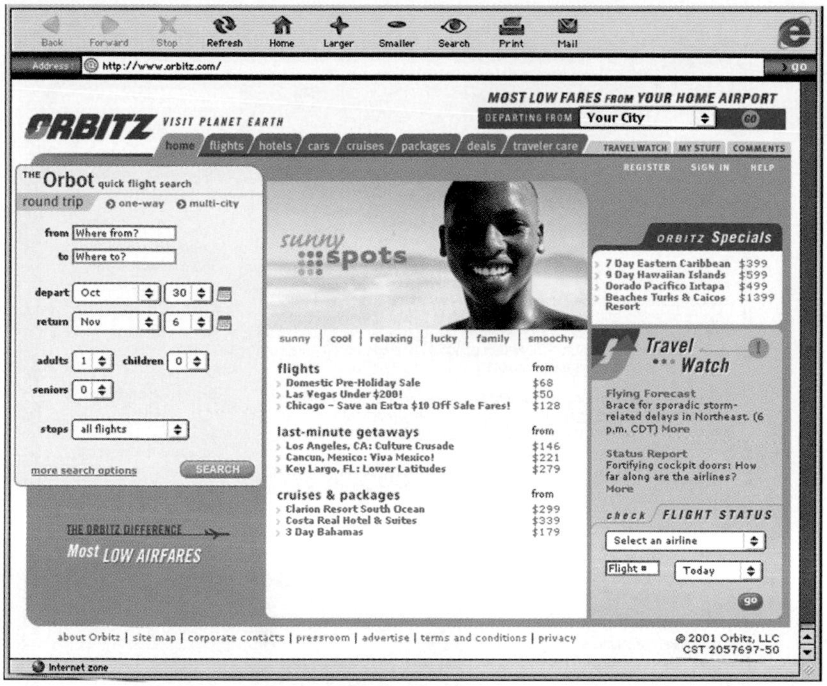

Regardless of how or why visitors arrive at the Orbitz homepage, they will decide whether to explore further or go somewhere else based on their initial evaluation of the site's content, depth, presentation of material, and navigational structure.
www.orbitz.com

on a screen element and be instantly transported to information on the same webpage, to related information on a different webpage in the same website, to related information on a webpage in a different website, or to just about anywhere on the web. Using hyperlinks, web writers can minutely tailor their messages to various members of their audience. Web readers expect a certain level of involvement, so when writing for the web, you either create three-dimensional documents by using hyperlinks or lose readers.

The Web Is Three-Dimensional

In the online world, there is no beginning, middle, or end. In most cases, readers access a website from another site's link. This ability to jump into, out of, and all around a document gives the web its three-dimensional format. Consider the Orbitz website, for example (see Figure A.1). Some visitors arrive at this website from search engines; others come from the sites of Orbitz alliance partners (such as United Airlines, American Airlines, or Northwest Airlines); still others arrive from online newspaper articles, financial sites, travel sites, and so on. Once these visitors arrive, they decide whether to navigate other pages at this website, return to the site at a later time, or go somewhere else. They make that decision based on their initial experience with the first page they see—which may or may not be the site's homepage. And if their initial experience with a website is displeasing, they're less likely to return.[6]

Being able to access information from all directions is a powerful benefit for readers. But it also makes it difficult for them to judge the depth and scope of a website. In the world of traditional print, a reader can thumb through a 300-page book in a few seconds to gauge its depth, scope, organizational structure, and layout. Getting the same overview of a website of similar volume could take hours, requiring readers to click on every page of the site. Moreover, linking to external websites can increase the scope of a document to the entire cyberworld. Finally, because cyber content is constantly changing, readers find it nearly impossible to quantify or gauge the depth of a site's material. Therefore, it is your job as a web writer to help readers along. You can do so by developing a hyperlink structure that is well organized.

DEVELOP A WELL-ORGANIZED HYPERLINK STRUCTURE

By now you can see how the nonlinear, interactive, three-dimensional nature of the web can pose additional challenges for web writers, requiring them to think differently about the material they are preparing for the web.

FIGURE A.2 SAS Institute Community Relations Webpage

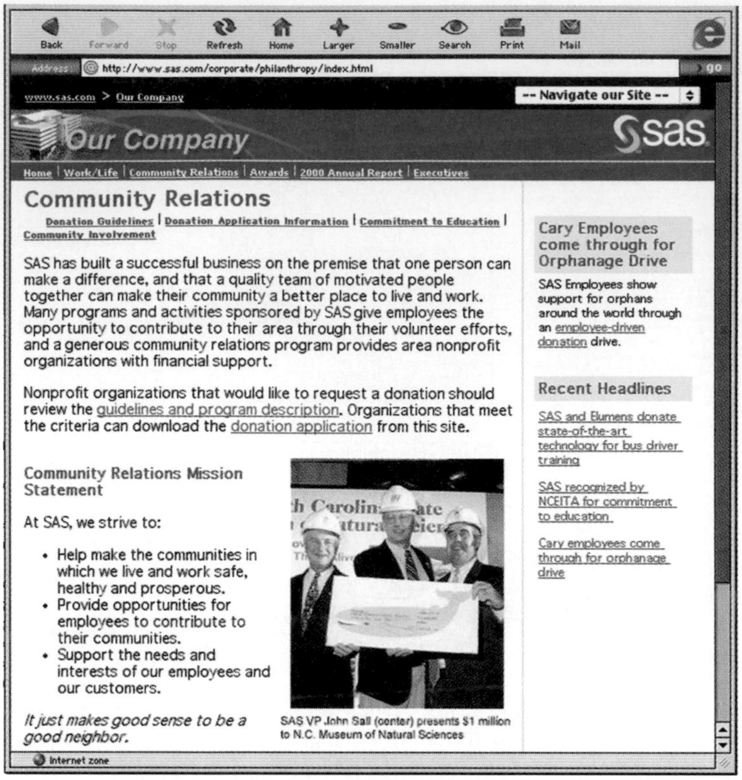

Developing a well-organized hyperlink structure is the first step to writing effective web messages. At this SAS webpage, readers can follow links to read additional information about employee-driven donations, donation guidelines, application information, the company's commitment to education, and the company's most recent community-involvement projects.

www.sas.com/corporate/community

Accommodating readers who can begin a document from multiple locations is one of the most difficult tasks.[7] When writing for the web, you must not only incorporate the effective business-writing skills discussed in this textbook but also modify the structure and style of your writing for this medium. You must think in terms of the words that will appear in your webpages and coordinate them with your navigational elements. Such attention to detail will help readers either find the information they want or bypass the information that is of no interest to them.

Plan Your Navigation First

Unfortunately, too many writers make the same mistake when writing for the web: They write a document as if they were writing for traditional print, then reduce it to smaller segments, and finally connect the segments with hyperlinks. In other words, they establish a design that is geared toward traditional print, and they worry about navigation last.[8] One of the best ways to ensure that readers will be able to navigate your document effectively and efficiently is to plan your navigation before you write.[9]

Look at Figure A.2, the Community Relations webpage for SAS Institute (maker of statistical analysis software). By planning ahead, SAS leaves certain details off this page, such as its sponsored volunteer programs. Instead, the page includes strategically placed navigational links to webpages discussing this information for those readers who want more detail. Like SAS, you must incorporate navigation as an integral part of your written material, not as an afterthought or an element to be left to a designer or developer.[10]

Planning your navigation before you write forces you to think about who your readers are and what paths they will follow to get key information.[11] It helps you decide up front how much information you will actually write and how much information your readers will access via links to other sites. This knowledge saves you time, since you won't have to write information that your readers can obtain elsewhere (via links). By planning the navigation of your material first, you will produce a higher-quality, easier-to-navigate document.

FIGURE A.3 Burpee Garden School

The table of contents provided at the Burpee Garden School webpage gives readers an overview of the structure and depth of the company's free online learning material. The table is placed in the side margin so that readers can easily navigate the many online vegetable and flower classes offered at this site.
www.burpee.com/Burpee/GardenSchool/school1/class1/c1p1.asp?uid=

Let Your Readers Be in Control

Many business writers believe that navigation is a simple matter of providing a few links: one to the top level of the document, another to the site's homepage, and some others to take the reader forward and backward through the document. However, the best navigational tools help readers move about the document in a smooth, intuitive fashion without forcing them to follow a specific direction.

Most readers want to navigate webpages using paths they establish themselves. After all, the web is a user-driven medium. So when linking your information, be sure that each step on your navigational path makes sense and leads naturally to the next step, or else you will frustrate your readers. Also, avoid forcing readers into following only one path. Let them explore on their own. Even if some documents (such as a tutorial or instructions) should be followed linearly, give readers an option for jumping around. As a web writer, you need to find a good balance between directing your readers and giving them the freedom to choose their own path.

Including a search engine in your document is one good way to let readers control their own navigation. Another helpful tool is similar to an organizational chart or outline of your message. A site map (or image map) is a hyperlinked, graphical representation of a site's layout that helps readers understand the structure and depth of the website. You can also let readers know how many links are involved in a document by including an index or a table of contents similar to the one shown in Figure A.3. These links to navigational tools should be placed at the top or on the side or bottom margin of your webpage, where they are easy to find.

MODIFY YOUR MESSAGE STYLE AND FORMAT

Once you have established a navigational structure for your message, begin composing it in a style and format suitable for the web. Even though solid design is important for effective web messages, substantive content is what drives a site's success. According to John Oatis, editor of Reuters Internet Report, one of the most common errors found on corporate websites is lackluster copy—messages written without interesting and specific details.[12]

Modify Your Message for Global Audiences

Writing for the global community means writing material that speaks to customers who may not speak English or who speak English as a second language. For web writing, you should generally use a lighter, less formal tone but without being chatty. Also, infuse as much of your organization's or your own personality into your text as possible. But be careful. The web is a global medium, so avoid clever, humorous, or jargon-filled phrases that can be misunderstood by readers from other cultures (see Chapter 3 for tips on communicating with global audiences).

You should also keep in mind that English is the official language in only seven countries (Australia, Canada, Ireland, New Zealand, South Africa, the United Kingdom, and the United States), composing little more than 5 percent of the world's population.[13] Yet the majority of online content is in English. Although many businesspeople speak English as a second language, more prefer to communicate in their native tongue. If many of your customers are overseas, it may pay to have your site and material "localized," so that it reflects not only the native language of your customers but their local norms, weights, measures, time, currency, and so on.

Localization involves much more than simply translating your material into another language. Localization makes your site and material appear as if it were originally developed in that language. This process demands a keen understanding of your target audience. You must adapt your style and tone, translate your text, include appropriate design elements (colors, icons, imagery), and design a navigation system that works for your target culture. For instance, in the United States, the picture of a raised flag on a mailbox indicates mail waiting, but the same picture has no meaning for many European and Asian nations.

Yahoo! is a perfect example of a company that has chosen to localize its website for global markets (see Figure A.4). In target countries, the company employs local teams of web producers, editors, and engineers. "This is the only way to get it right," says one Yahoo! spokesperson. For instance, in the United States, we sort names in address books alphabetically. But in some Asian countries, the names must be sorted according to the number of keystrokes.[14]

FIGURE A.4 Yahoo! Sweden

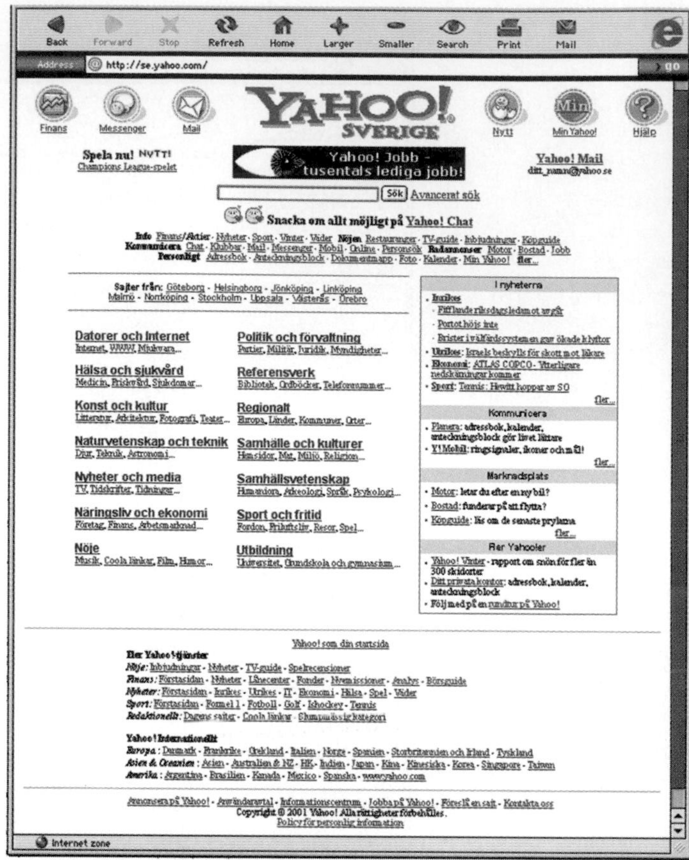

This Yahoo! Sweden website typifies the company's commitment to global audiences. Yahoo's localized sites such as this one include much more than foreign language translations. Here the links feature local information, weather, news, and business and cultural events.
http://se.yahoo.com

Break Your Information into Chunks

Whether you are writing for local or global audiences, remember to adjust the format of your writing for the web. In traditional print, your document forms a whole, and readers focus on the complete set of information. On the web, however, you need to help online readers scan and absorb information by breaking it into self-contained, readable chunks (or pages) of information. Each chunk is composed of several paragraphs that are brief, that are focused, and that stick to a single theme. The theme-related chunks make up one webpage that may not be viewable all at once on your computer screen (you must often scroll the screen to see the entire message).

In most cases, the chunks of information you write will be linked to other chunks both inside and outside your website. Breaking information into manageable chunks and then linking them to other chunks allows you to provide comprehensive coverage in a concise way. After all, as one web expert puts it, "Web surfers may be in a hurry, but if they like what they see, they'll want as much of it as they can get."[15]

As you "chunk" your information, consider these tips:

- **Make the content of each webpage independent.** Explain your material so that readers can understand the subject matter of a webpage regardless of the navigational path they followed to arrive at that page. Don't assume that readers approached your material in a linear order, as they might in a book. Frustration mounts if readers must click backward through your website to gain understanding by reading previous pages.
- **Don't force subdivisions.** Be careful not to subdivide your information into too many linked layers. For instance, don't use hypertext links if the information can be succinctly presented in a short paragraph or on a single webpage. Forcing readers to tunnel through too many links will anger them, and they will click away.
- **Reduce the length of your stories.** Recognized as an expert on web usability, Dr. Jakob Nielsen says that online text should be at least 50 percent shorter than print.[16] Try to limit your web articles to one computer screen. But if doing so is impossible, try not to exceed three full screens of text. Most readers are willing to punch their "page down" or "scroll" key twice. If they haven't found what they are seeking by the third full screen of text, they are likely to give up in frustration.
- **Handle longer documents with care.** If your written material is longer than three screens, try breaking the concept down further. If possible, note key information on one page, and offer links to detail and background on another. That way, each link will focus on a specific topic within a larger concept. However, if you cannot break down your concept any further, do not randomly divide it into several webpages. Illogical interruptions in a single piece of linear material can irritate readers.[17]
- **Provide a printable version of longer documents.** Because long documents are difficult to read online, most readers prefer to download a printable copy to read offline. Help readers by providing a print-ready version of your document and by providing a link to it. Be sure to indicate the file size so that readers can gauge the amount of time your document will take to download. Also, put your URL in the document title so that the source of the document will print on the page. That way readers can return to your website at a later date.

Being an effective web writer means knowing what works and what doesn't for this medium. Keep in mind that not everything is well suited to on-screen presentation. For instance, pages of text that simply mimic pages of print will fall below the minimum degree of interactivity readers expect to find on the web.[18]

Adopt an Inverted Pyramid Style

Effective web writers know that most people go to the web for information; they want to find what they're looking for fast, or they will click away. So your goal as a web writer is to make sure your online messages get right to the point. Make sure your readers get all the information they need in as little time as possible.

One way to get straight to the point is to write your material using an inverted pyramid style. Journalists have long used this inverse approach—writing the conclusion first and providing the detail later (see Figure A.5). This style is useful for newspapers because readers can stop at any time and will still get the most important parts of the article.

The inverted pyramid becomes even more important on the web, since users don't like to scroll and frequently read only the top portion of an article. Using an inverted pyramid style allows you to place your most important information above the scroll—equivalent to placing your material "above the fold" in a newspaper (which is what you see when the newspaper is folded on the news rack). As with newspapers, this top-level space is prime property, so use it economically. *The Wall Street Journal*, for example, reserves its front page for short summaries of articles that are discussed in detail on interior pages.

Present Your Information in a Concise and Scannable Format

On the web, every sentence, every phrase, every word has to fight for its life. This means that your job as a writer is to pack the maximum meaning into the minimum text so that your readers get the message in the shortest time possible. You can achieve this goal by writing short sentences, limiting paragraphs to one point and clearly making that point in the first sentence, editing paragraphs to between 55 and 75 words, and covering a topic in two to three short paragraphs.[19] In addition to tightening your writing, use techniques for producing your message such as those discussed in Chapter 6 (see pages 156–159). Here's how some of those techniques apply to web writing.

Use Lists

Lists are useful devices for presenting key points on the web. They slow down roving eyes and draw attention to important points. They also facilitate the skimming process for busy readers, simplify complex subjects, highlight the main point, and break up the page visually (see Figure A.6 on page 177). Number your lists when the order of entries is important, and use bullets when it is not. To keep your lists easy to skim, be concise: Up to five words is best; between two and four words is even better. But don't get carried away. Too many lists will make your website read like a sales presentation.

FIGURE A.5 Inverted Pyramid Style

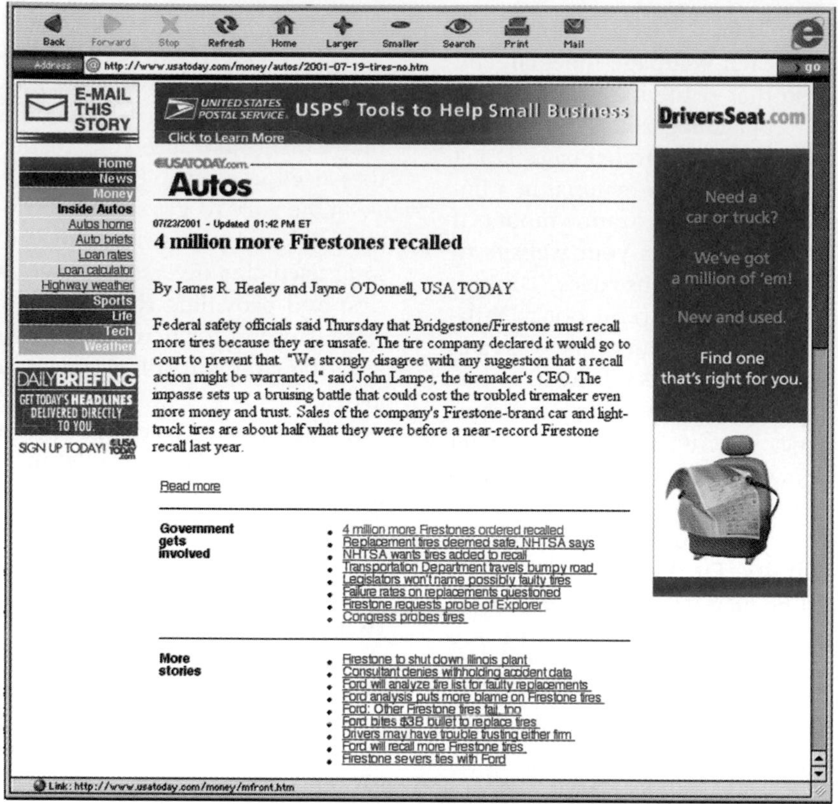

Back Forward Stop Refresh Home Larger Smaller Search Print Mail

Address: http://www.usatoday.com/money/autos/2001-07-19-tires-no.htm

E-MAIL THIS STORY

UNITED STATES POSTAL SERVICE. USPS® Tools to Help Small Business
Click to Learn More

DriversSeat.com
Need a car or truck?
We've got a million of 'em!
New and used.
Find one that's right for you.

Home
News
Money
Inside Autos
Autos home
Auto briefs
Loan rates
Loan calculator
Highway weather
Sports
Life
Tech
Weather

DAILYBRIEFING
GET TODAY'S HEADLINES DELIVERED DIRECTLY TO YOU.
SIGN UP TODAY! USA TODAY.com

USATODAY.com
Autos

07/23/2001 - Updated 01:42 PM ET

4 million more Firestones recalled

By James R. Healey and Jayne O'Donnell, USA TODAY

Federal safety officials said Thursday that Bridgestone/Firestone must recall more tires because they are unsafe. The tire company declared it would go to court to prevent that. "We strongly disagree with any suggestion that a recall action might be warranted," said John Lampe, the tiremaker's CEO. The impasse sets up a bruising battle that could cost the troubled tiremaker even more money and trust. Sales of the company's Firestone-brand car and light-truck tires are about half what they were before a near-record Firestone recall last year.

Read more

Government gets involved

- 4 million more Firestones ordered recalled
- Replacement tires deemed safe, NHTSA says
- NHTSA wants tires added to recall
- Transportation Department travels bumpy road
- Legislators won't name possibly faulty tires
- Failure rates on replacements questioned
- Firestone requests probe of Explorer
- Congress probes tires

More stories

- Firestone to shut down Illinois plant
- Consultant denies withholding accident data
- Ford will analyze tire list for faulty replacements
- Ford analysis puts more blame on Firestone tires
- Ford: Other Firestone tires fail, too
- Ford bites $3B bullet to replace tires
- Drivers may have trouble trusting either firm
- Ford will recall more Firestone tires
- Firestone severs ties with Ford

Link: http://www.usatoday.com/money/mfront.htm

This *USA Today* online article gets right to the point. It immediately states the decision rendered by U.S. safety officials, presents Firestone's position, and offers supporting facts. When writing longer articles for the web, use the top-down pyramid style to grab the readers' attention. Provide an initial summary along with links to the full story and links to additional related material for those readers who want more detail.
www.usatoday.com/money/autos/2001-07-19-tires-no.htm

Use Color and Boldface

Color and boldface help your readers skim text. Both are used for hyperlinks and are most effective when reserved for words that express the most important elements in your document. Avoid highlighting entire sentences or phrases, since a scanning eye can pick up only two or three words at a time. In fact, if you highlight too many words, you risk making your documents even harder to read.[20]

> See **how hard** it is to read this paragraph with **all the boldfaced words** and other emphasis techniques cluttering the space. The boldfacing is **"crying wolf"** (pretending that something is important when it really **isn't**). The change from bold to normal type **slows down the eye,** and the change from normal to bold type **speeds it up** by attracting the eye forward to the next bold word and skipping over the middle text, which is nearly as important as the rest. Also, bold type **detracts from the value** of the boldfacing used in the subheadings **on a page.**

One format that works well on-screen is a list of short, bold headings, each a few words long and each followed by a sentence or two of summary in normal font. Look at the following information from a health-care website:

> The five most common types of health insurance policies sold by our company are
>
> - **Basic medical.** Pays for most inpatient and some outpatient hospital costs
> - **Major medical.** Protects the insured against catastrophic financial losses by covering medical expenses that exceed the coverage limits of the basic policies
> - **Disability income.** Protects against the loss of short-term or long-term income while the insured is disabled due to an illness or accident
> - **Medicare supplemental.** Supplements benefits provided under the Medicare program
> - **Long-term care.** Covers stays in long-term care facilities

FIGURE A.6 Access Vanguard

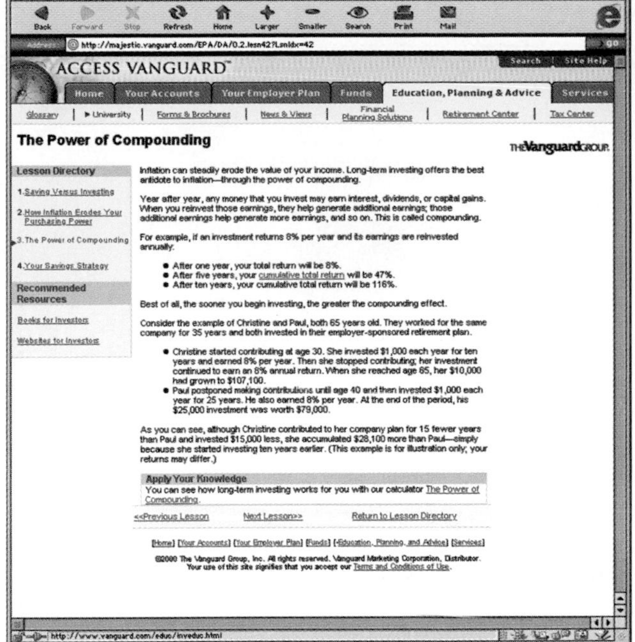

Access Vanguard Group, a mutual fund company, uses a bulleted list to present information about compound interest. The lists make the webpage easy to skim and helps simplify the complex material in addition to highlighting key points.
www.vanguard.com

This approach eases skimming by boldfacing the list item and providing more information whenever a reader's eye stops on an item.

Write Effective Headings

Some writers have the document title and major headings serve as links to relevant sections of their web document. If you choose to follow that path, keep in mind that in print, headings are usually displayed in context. That is, the heading appears first, followed by the body of the article, associated photos, and subheads—all of which can be read in context.

In the online environment, however, a much smaller amount of information is visible. So headings are often displayed out of context: as a list of articles, a series of steps, and so on. That's why your web headings should be able to stand on their own; they must make sense without reading the rest of the article. Even when a heading is displayed together with related content, the reduced amount of information that can be seen at a glance makes it harder for readers to infer meaning from the surrounding information.[21]

Cute newspaper-style headings are inappropriate. In most cases a newspaper has already won the readers' attention and trust, while chances are you have not. You may have only a few seconds to impress your readers. So don't waste their time with fluff. Write your titles and headings using an informative style (see Chapter 6). And reserve your headings for making key points. Readers should be able to scroll down the webpage and read titles and headings to obtain an overview of the main ideas presented in the article. You might even combine your headings with a short summary and turn your headings into hotlinks:

> Acme/Zenith lawsuit settled: Acme Industries dropped its patent infringement suit against Zenith Associates and the two companies signed a mutual licensing pact.

Clicking on the links (blue words) in this example will take you to the details of the article. Combining hotlinked headings and short summaries saves your readers time because they aren't being forced to follow a link just to find out a small amount of information.

Write Summaries

Summaries are an effective way to help readers decide whether they should continue reading or follow a link. For example, you can give a general overview and provide links to a wide range of supporting details, as demonstrated by the AT&T Foundation webpage (see Figure A.7).

FIGURE A.7 AT&T Foundation

Writing summaries with accompanying links to details is one way the AT&T Foundation helps readers determine whether they should read further.
www.att.com/foundation

Summaries let the document serve a wider range of people—those who want only the highlights, and those who want all the details.

Also, providing short summaries of the content of your webpage gives web surfers and those using search engines a quick insight into the main idea of your message. Your summaries may be only one sentence or a short paragraph. A paragraph summary gives you a few more lines to influence a reader whose interest in your topic may be relatively small.

When writing a one-paragraph summary, be concise. Use only a few short sentences to give people an insight into the information that follows. Don't slow down the skimmer. Save the details and flowing language for the linked information. That way only those readers who want the details will have to read them.

Write Effective Links

As a web writer, your job is to write effective links and strategically place them in your web documents so that your readers can easily navigate your material. Links can be words, graphics, phrases, or even complete sentences. You will most likely use a mixture of textual and graphical hyperlinks. Most text hyperlinks are emphasized with either underlining or a different text color (often blue). Once a viewer has followed a text hyperlink on a web browser, the default hyperlink color changes so that users can keep track of which links they've tried. Graphical images used as links can vary from smaller images of your products to custom designs. If you choose to use graphical links, be careful not to overdo it. Overloading your document with too many images can slow down the loading time of your webpages. Furthermore, you need to accommodate those readers who conserve downloading time by turning off the graphic capabilities in their web browsers. Simply include a short textual caption near your graphic links, just as the Breadworld webpage does (see Figure A.8).

FIGURE A.8 Graphical Links

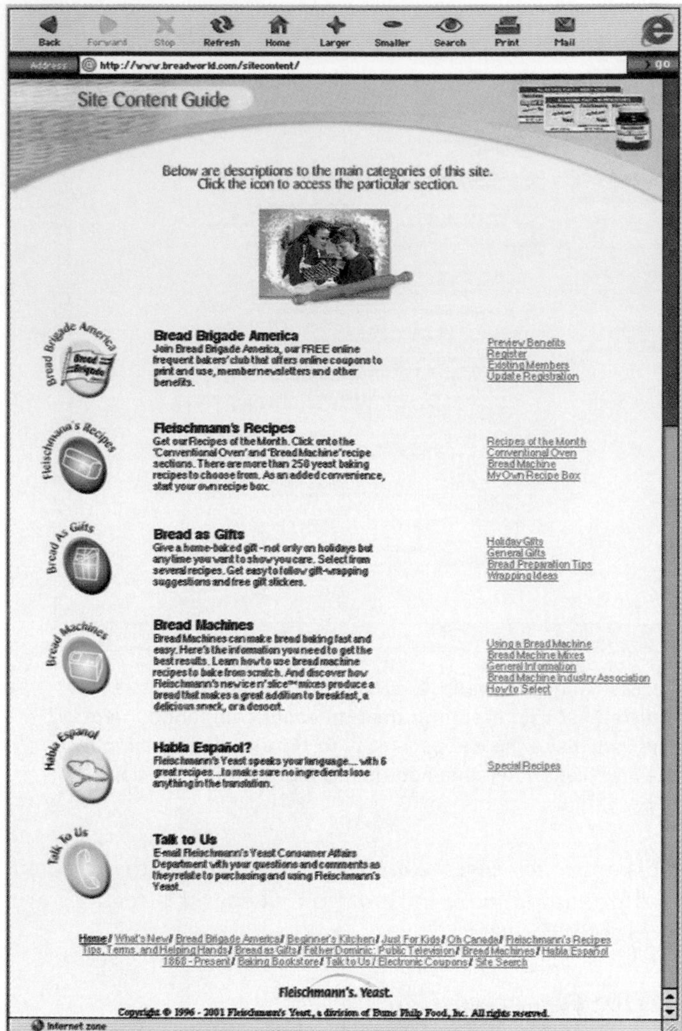

Using graphics as navigational links can liven up a webpage. But resist the temptation to overuse them. Graphics and photos take time to load on computer screens—time that your readers may not have. Some readers of online text turn graphics off to minimize loading time. So when using graphics, be sure to accompany them with text labels and, if possible, descriptions, as the Breadworld webpage does.
www.breadworld.com/sitecontent

As with any written material, when writing hypertext links, you need to observe the effective business-writing techniques and standards discussed in Chapters 5 and 6 and throughout this text. For instance, you'll need to write concisely, use strong words, and use parallel construction. In addition you'll need to pay attention to the following details:

- **Avoid self-referential terms.** Take advantage of the options the web has to offer, without calling attention to the web. Avoid using self-referential terms such as *click here, follow this link,* or *this website.* Generally, if words or phrases are specific to the web, they can probably be omitted. You can safely assume that a web user will be able to find and follow your links by looking for different colored or formatted text or by finding graphical elements. Once readers find a link, they will know to click on it. Of course, if your site has an unusual layout or design, then help your readers navigate your site by giving them a short tutorial or providing separate navigational instructions.[22]
- **Use absolute directions.** A well-written link tells readers where they are going. Avoid directional words such as *back, forward, next, above, below bottom,* or *top.* Such words are meaningful in a linear document, but not necessarily in a hypertext document, where visitors can enter your site at many places and from many directions. Instead, use absolute directions such as *Return to Tables, Next Learning Step,* or *Beginning of Tutorial.*[23]

FIGURE A.9 Providing Context for Your Links

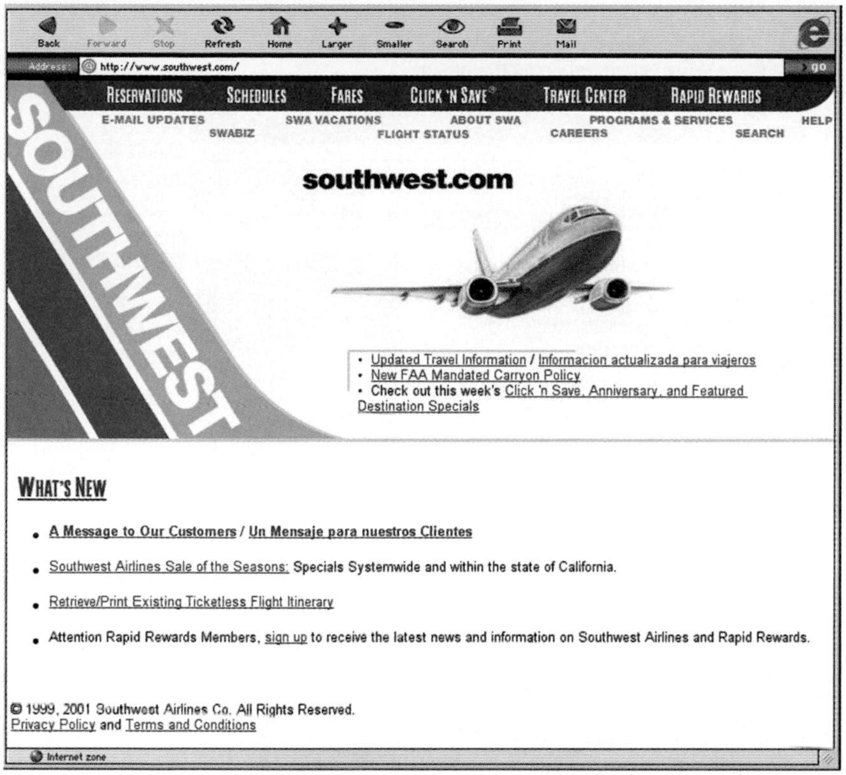

Embedding your navigational links in sentences, phrases, lists, and summaries, as this Southwest Airlines webpage does, helps your readers identify what they will find by clicking.
www.southwest.com

- **Tell readers what they will find.** A well-written link tells readers what they will find once they click on the link. For instance, to link to a company performance announcement, you could state, "Southwest Airlines announced **improved financial results.**" Or to link to a broker's security report, you could say, "Our **conclusion** is that the stock is a good investment." Both of these links do a good job of letting the reader know what they will find by clicking on the hotlink.
- **Provide context for your links.** As Figure A.9 shows, writing a one-sentence summary and embedding your link within the sentence provides readers with context to help them determine the specific content of the link and gauge their level of interest. Providing this one-sentence description also makes it easy for others to write links to your articles. They can simply copy and paste your actual sentence, giving you some control over how they word their links to your material. In addition to sentences, you can include hypertext words in lists, headings, summaries, and other written elements of your webpage.
- **Place your links strategically.** Position relevant links in prime locations. Position less relevant, but meaningful links in the margins of your webpage or at the end of the document.

Even if you present your information in a concise and scannable format and use a perfect style, the material you write for the web won't be effective unless you can gain the trust of web readers.

ESTABLISH YOUR CREDIBILITY

Establishing your credibility is especially important on the web because anyone can post material on a website and much of that material is not edited or verified by professionals. Thus, you have to work extra hard to earn a reader's trust. And that trust is rapidly lost if you use exaggerated claims or overly boastful language. To improve your credibility, be sure to include these elements in your web documents:

- **Sponsor.** List the institution, organization, department, or business unit that owns the information or is accountable for it.
- **Author's name.** Include the name of the author on every printable webpage. Include contact information (either a phone number or an e-mail address) and

FIGURE A.10 Playing the Dating Game

Because currency is an issue for the material at this website, CNN.com shows the dates and time the information was posted and updated.
www.cnn.com

affiliations along with mentions of other works written by the author and, if possible, links to such material.

- **Dates.** Dating your online messages is one of the best ways to reassure readers that the information is still accurate and pertinent (see Figure A.10). Documents without posting and revision dates are among the most suspect online. Furthermore, there is no way for readers to be certain that the information is current.
- **Content.** Be sure that your content is current, complete, and accurate.

Of course, one of the best ways to enhance your credibility is to make sure that your online writing is error-free. Accuracy is of the utmost importance everywhere, but it takes on a little extra meaning on the web. Visitors are testing you and have millions of other sites to choose from. "If I see an inaccuracy in a print story, I won't necessarily stop reading the magazine. But on the web, if the first story I see has an inaccuracy in it, you've lost me forever," says Doug Himerson, vice president and editor-in-chief of Garden.com.[24]

For a quick review of the concepts presented in this chapter, see. "Checklist: Writing for the Web."

TEST YOUR KNOWLEDGE

1. How is writing for the web different from writing for print media?
2. Why is the web considered a three-dimensional medium?
3. When writing for the web, why is it important to plan the navigation of your material first?
4. When developing your navigational structure, why is it important to let your readers be in control?
5. What does it mean to localize a website?
6. Why is it important to break written web material into chunks? What guidelines should you follow when doing so?
7. Why do effective web writers organize their material in an inverted pyramid style?
8. How can you make your web material easier to skim?
9. Why aren't cute, newspaper-style headings effective for web material?
10. What are five things to keep in mind when writing navigational links?

✓ CHECKLIST: WRITING FOR THE WEB

A. Develop a well-organized hyperlink structure

1. Plan your navigation first.
2. Let readers decide how they will access the information on your site—how much they will read, in what order, and when.
3. Provide search engines.
4. Show your outline, or diagram it with a hyperlinked site map or table of contents at the top or bottom of your page.

B. Modify your message style

1. Use a lighter, less formal writing style.
2. Avoid clever, humorous, or jargon-filled phrases that could be misunderstood by readers from other cultures.
3. Modify your messages for global audiences.

C. Modify your message format

1. Break information into independent chunks and connect them with hyperlinks.
2. Don't repeat information; instead, link your reader to the page where that information already resides.
3. Don't burden others with unwanted detail. Place specific details on subsequent pages.
4. Try to keep longer stories to a maximum of three scrollable screens if possible.
5. Avoid randomly breaking a single, linear article (even a lengthy one) into a series of pages once you've determined its concept cannot be further subdivided.
6. Include a downloadable, printable version of longer documents for offline reading.
7. Adopt an inverted pyramid style so that readers can quickly see your topic, main idea, and conclusion.
8. Put your most important concept in the first 50 words, in case search engines pick up those words to describe your site.

D. Help readers skim text for the information they need

1. Write shorter sentences and paragraphs to ease the reading process and to fit in narrow columns.
2. Cut traditional print by 40 percent or more and try to keep chunks to 75 words or less.
   a. Tighten your writing by avoiding passive voice, needless prepositional phrases, and wordiness.
   b. Avoid tightening your prose to the point that it's choppy and abrupt.
   c. Delete superfluous details, and stick to what's relevant.
3. Use bulleted and numbered lists.
4. Use boldface, color, and other typographical elements conservatively.
5. Write informative headings that stand on their own and are consistent in their wording.
6. Write concise summaries and descriptions that are informative and crystal clear.

E. Write effective links and place them strategically

1. Use a combination of text and graphical hyperlinks, but don't overdo graphics since they slow down document loading time.
2. Avoid self-referential terms such as *click here* or *follow this link*.
3. Use absolute directions.
4. Write informative hyperlinks so that the content of subsequent pages is obvious.
5. Place your links strategically and carefully.

F. Establish your credibility

1. Include your name and the name of your sponsor (if applicable) on every webpage.
2. Provide contact information (at least an e-mail address) so that readers can get in touch with you or your sponsor easily.
3. Include posting and revision dates for your information.
4. Make sure your content is error-free.

APPLY YOUR KNOWLEDGE

1. Select any webpage and assess its effectiveness for these criteria:
   a. Scannability
   b. Readability
   c. Navigational effectiveness
2. Select any webpage and critique the headings. Do they make sense on their own? Do they include hyperlinks? Does the author use color or boldface effectively? What changes, if any, would you recommend?
3. Select any webpage and critique the effectiveness of the written hyperlinks. Does the author use self-referential terms or absolute directions? Is the writing concise? Are linked words embedded in a sentence or paragraph to provide the reader with context? Are the hyperlinks placed effectively?
4. Select a short article from any print magazine or newspaper. Now rewrite the article in a format suitable for the web, using the techniques discussed in this chapter. Focus on writing only one webpage. Include some hyperlinks on that page and in your article, but you need not develop material for the linked page.
5. **Ethical Choices.** More and more unhappy employees and customers are launching websites to write negative information about companies. Log on to Untied.com at www.untied.com, for example, and read what some customers and employees have to say about United Airlines. Do you think it is ethical for employees to criticize their employers in a public venue such as the web?

PART 3

Writing Letters, Memos, E-Mail, and Other Brief Messages

Writing Routine, Good-News, and Goodwill Messages

After studying this chapter, you will be able to

1. *Apply the three-step writing process to routine positive messages*
2. *Illustrate the strategy for writing routine requests*
3. *Discuss the differences among four types of routine requests*
4. *Explain the main differences in messages granting a claim when the company, the customer, or a third party is at fault*
5. *Outline how best to protect yourself when referring to a candidate's shortcoming in a recommendation letter*
6. *Describe the importance of goodwill messages, and describe how to make them effective*

COMMUNICATION CLOSE-UP AT UNUMPROVIDENT CORPORATION

www.unumprovident.com

No one wants to think about the chance of disability from illness or injury. But UnumProvident has to. It's the nation's largest disability insurer, aiming to protect individuals' paychecks, assets, and lifestyles. Through programs such as LifeBalance, the company emphasizes return to work, offers highly responsive service, and addresses many of the life and work challenges facing people with a long-term disability or terminal illness. To succeed, the company must communicate effectively not only externally with brokers, benefit managers, and insured employees but also internally with its own people. UnumProvident must be sure that its internal messages are understandable to everyone, from CEO to newest employee, in every location, from Toronto to Los Angeles—and that's where Becky Bumgardner comes in.

As senior corporate writer in the corporate relations department, Bumgardner is responsible for writing and sending internal messages to more than 10,000 Unum-Provident employees in nearly 60 offices across the United States and Canada. Many of these messages are routine and are sent by e-mail to employees in various states, countries, and time zones. Bumgardner writes on topics ranging from departmental meeting announcements to incentive programs for managers. She writes about departmental reorganizations, virus alerts, corporate earnings, and promotions. She also composes feature articles for the monthly newsletter and prepares daily updates for the company intranet.

But whether she's requesting routine information for the company newsletter or reminding employees about an upcoming deadline, Bumgardner is always careful to compose messages that are both concise and clear. Before writing anything, she makes sure that she fully understands the information she needs to communicate. As Bumgardner says, "I ask lots of questions before I begin to write. The old adage is true: The only dumb question is the one you don't ask. So don't be afraid to verify your information and make sure you understand a topic."

Clarity also depends on how much information you provide. For example, when preparing a routine request, "it helps your readers to know why you're making the request," explains Bumgardner. "It gives them an incentive to act. So I explain what needs to be done, why it needs to be done, and how the request affects the audience." To be as clear as possible, she tries to imagine all the ways a request might be misunderstood and then carefully chooses her words to avoid those pitfalls. For instance, knowing that Canadian insurance regulations often differ from U.S. regulations, Bumgardner is careful to address the needs of both U.S. and Canadian employees when sending mass e-mail messages to "all employees." That way, she eliminates any confusion.

Bumgardner keeps her messages brief and to the point. "With too much extra information," she advises, "your audience will stop reading your message." And to make it easier for audiences to absorb her messages, Bumgardner emphasizes important deadlines with bold or italic type and draws attention to important facts with bullet points. To close, she summarizes her message and includes any necessary deadlines, reminders, or contact information.

Each day some 24,000 workers are injured on the job, and each one of them must communicate with companies such as UnumProvident to receive disability payments. All claim requests must contain necessary details and a clear statement of the request before the claim can be processed.

Bumgardner strives to establish a feeling of partnership with her fellow employees by using a polite tone and by projecting enthusiasm into her writing. However, even though her tone is friendly and conversational, she carefully avoids using irony and sarcasm, especially in e-mail. "Don't joke about serious matters," she cautions. "Too often, your messages are interpreted differently from what you intend."

Bumgardner believes that clear, direct messages get positive results. As she puts it, "Effective communication creates a positive impression—and a positive impression will get more positive responses to your requests."[1] ■

USING THE THREE-STEP WRITING PROCESS FOR ROUTINE MESSAGES

Learning Objective 1

Apply the three-step writing process to routine positive messages

Whether you're reminding employees about meetings or upcoming deadlines, like UnumProvident's Becky Bumgardner, congratulating an employee on a job well done, or requesting information from another firm, chances are that in the course of everyday business, you'll compose a lot of routine, good-news, and goodwill messages. In fact, most of a typical employee's communication is about routine matters: orders, information, company policies, claims, credit, employees, products, operations, and so on. Such messages are rarely long or complex. Even so, to produce the best messages possible, you'll want to apply the three-step writing process.

Step 1: Planning Routine Messages

Even for routine situations, you need to analyze, investigate, and adapt your messages.

As with longer, complex messages, you need to analyze your purpose and audience, investigate audience needs, and adapt your message to your readers. However, for routine messages, this planning step may take only a few moments. First, analyze your purpose to make sure that it's specific and it's worth pursuing at this time. Also, think a moment about your readers. Are you sure they'll receive your message positively (or at least neutrally)? Most routine messages are of interest to your readers because they contain information necessary to conduct day-to-day business. Even so, you may need to discover more about audience attitudes or needs in order to gauge your audience's probable reaction.

Second, investigate to learn exactly what your audience needs to know. Do you have all the relevant information? Do you need to take a little time to gather more?

Organize your routine messages according to the direct approach.

Third, adapt your routine messages to your readers. Consider whether your message should be written, rather than handled in a quick phone call or by walking down

Perry Klebahn's company, Atlas Snowshoe, sells high-end showshoes in more than 1,000 stores across the United States, ringing up annual sales of about $12 million. Klebahn tells his employees to establish a good relationship with their audience by learning what they need to know and by using language that is positive and polite.

the hall for a brief chat. If written, select the most appropriate format (memo, letter, e-mail). Finally, you'll want to establish or maintain a good relationship with your audience, so be sure to use the "you" attitude and keep your language positive and polite.

Step 2: Writing Routine Messages

Organizing and composing routine messages can go rather quickly. Your main idea may already be fairly well defined. Just be sure you stick to it by limiting the scope of your message. Cover only relevant points, grouping them in the most logical fashion. Because your readers will be interested or neutral, you can usually adopt the direct approach for routine messages: Open with a clear statement of the main idea, include all necessary details in the body, and then close cordially.

However, even though these messages are the least complicated to write, communicating across cultural boundaries can be a challenge, especially if you're not familiar with the cultural differences involved. So before selecting the direct approach for your message, verify the customs of your audience, making sure your readers prefer direct organization. (See "Communicating Across Cultures: How Direct Is Too Direct?") When you're addressing an audience with minimal cultural differences, keep your tone conversational and use plain English.

Step 3: Completing Routine Messages

Just as you do for other messages, you need to revise, produce, and proofread routine messages.

No matter how short or straightforward your message, make it professional by allowing plenty of time to revise, produce, and proofread it. First, revise your routine message for overall effect. Evaluate your content and organization to make sure you've said what you want to in the order you want to say it. Review your message's readability. Edit and rewrite routine messages for conciseness and clarity. Second, design your document to suit your audience. Choose effective design elements and appropriate delivery methods. Finally, proofread the final version of your routine message. Look for typos, errors in spelling and mechanics, alignment problems, poor print quality, and so on.

MAKING ROUTINE REQUESTS

Whenever you ask for something—information, action, products, adjustments, references—you are making a request. A request is routine if it's part of the normal course of business and you anticipate that your audience will want to comply. Be careful not to make unnecessary requests. If you can find information yourself, don't burden others and risk your credibility by asking someone else to find it for you. But when you must make a routine request, make sure it's efficient and effective.

Learning Objective 2

Illustrate the strategy for writing routine requests

Strategy for Routine Requests

For routine requests and positive messages
- State the request or main idea
- Give necessary details
- Close with a cordial request for specific action

Like all routine messages, routine requests may be thought of as having three parts: an opening, a body, and a close. Using the direct approach, you place your main idea (a clear statement of the request) in the opening. You use the middle to give details and justify your request. Then you close by requesting specific action and concluding cordially (see Figure 7.1 on page 188). As you prepare your routine requests, keep in mind that despite their simple organization, they can still cause ill will through ambiguous wording or a discourteous tone. In fact, even the briefest note can create confusion and hard feelings. As with any business message, keep your purpose in mind. Ask yourself what you want readers to do or to understand as a result of reading your message.

Exactly what do you want your audience to understand or to do as a result of reading your request?

Communicating Across Cultures

How Direct Is Too Direct?

Being direct is civil, considerate, and honest—or so say people in the United States. Other folks view that same directness as being abrupt, rude, and intrusive—even dishonest and offensive. Countries such as France, Mexico, Japan, Saudi Arabia, Italy, and the Philippines all tend toward high-context cultures (see discussion in Chapter 3). That is, the people in these countries depend on shared knowledge and inferred messages to communicate; they gather meaning more from context and less from direct statement.

Offering a little constructive criticism may actually hurt your Mexican assistant's dignity. In fact, in high-context cultures, avoid saying outright, "You are wrong." You could cause the other person to lose face. When making requests, determine whether to use a direct or an implied approach by considering audience attitudes toward destiny, time, authority, and logic:

- **Destiny.** Do audience members believe they can control events themselves? Or do they see events as predetermined and uncontrollable? If you're supervising employees who believe that fate controls a construction deadline, your crisp e-mail message requesting them to stay on schedule may be hard for them to understand; it may even be insulting.
- **Time.** Do audience members view time as exact, precise, and not to be wasted? Or do they see time as relative, relaxed, and necessary for developing interpersonal relationships? If you see time as money and you get straight to business in your memo to your Mexican manager, your message may be overlooked in the confusion over your disregard for social propriety.
- **Authority.** Do audience members conduct business more autocratically or more democratically? In Mexico, rank and status are highly valued, so when communicating downward, you may need to be even more direct than you're used to being in the United States. And when communicating upward, you may need to be much less direct than usual.
- **Logic.** Do audience members pursue logic in a straight line, from point A to point B? Or do they communicate in circular or spiral patterns of logic? If you organize a speech or letter in a straightforward and direct manner, your message may be considered illogical, unclear, and disorganized.

You may want to decide not only how direct to be in written messages but also whether to write at all; perhaps a phone call or a visit would be more appropriate. By finding out how much or how little a culture tends toward high-context communication, you'll know whether to be direct or to rely on nuance when communicating with the people of that culture.

Career Applications

1. Research a high-context culture such as that of Japan, Korea, or China, and write a one- or two-paragraph summary of how someone in that culture would go about requesting information.
2. When you are writing in American English to someone in a high-context culture, would it be better to (a) make the request directly in the interest of clarity or (b) try to match your audience's unfamiliar logic and make your request indirectly? Explain your answer.

State Your Request Up Front

Begin routine requests by placing your request first—up front is where it stands out and gets the most attention. Of course, getting right to the point should not be interpreted as a license to be abrupt or tactless:

Keep your direct approach from being abrupt or tactless.

- **Pay attention to tone.** Even though you expect a favorable response, the **tone** of your initial request is important. Instead of demanding action ("Send me your catalog no. 33A"), soften your request with words such as *please* and *I would appreciate.*
- **Assume your audience will comply.** An impatient demand for rapid service isn't necessary. Generally make the assumption that your audience will comply with your request once the reason for it is clearly understood.
- **Avoid beginning with personal introductions.** Don't be tempted to begin your request with a personal introduction such as "I am the senior corporate writer in the corporate relations department of UnumProvident, and I am looking for information that . . ." Becky Bumgardner knows that this type of beginning buries the main idea, so the request may get lost.

FIGURE 7.1 The Parts of Routine, Good-News, and Goodwill Messages

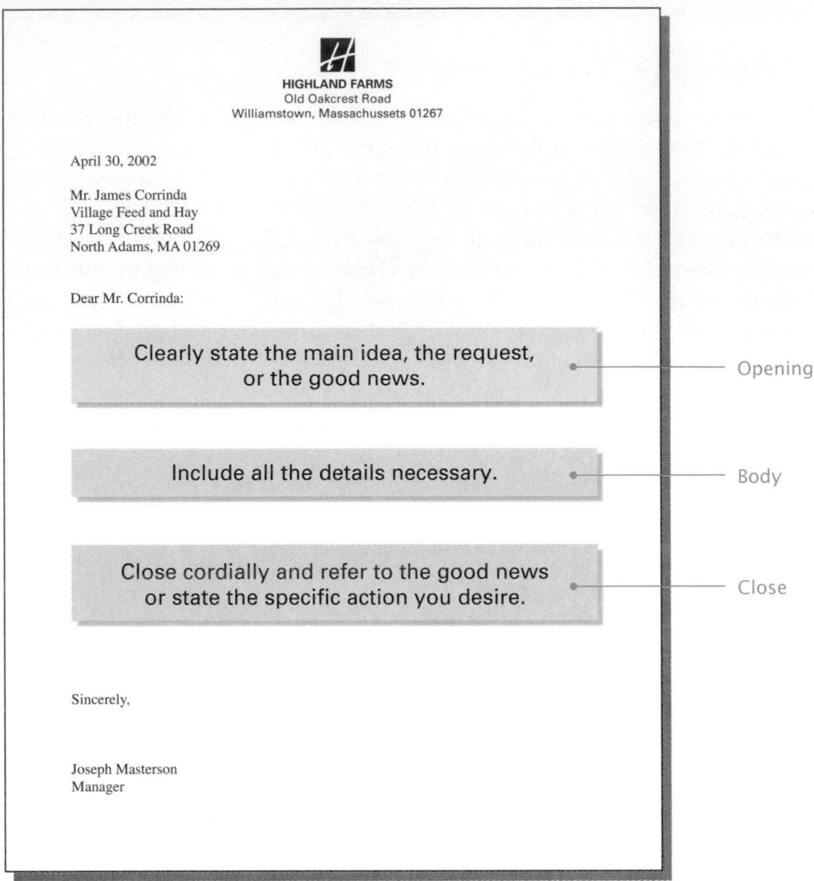
HIGHLAND FARMS
Old Oakcrest Road
Williamstown, Massachussets 01267

April 30, 2002

Mr. James Corrinda
Village Feed and Hay
37 Long Creek Road
North Adams, MA 01269

Dear Mr. Corrinda:

Sincerely,

Joseph Masterson
Manager

- **Punctuate questions and polite requests differently.** A polite request in question form requires no question mark: "Would you please help us determine whether Kate Kingsley is a suitable applicant for this position." A direct question within your message does require a question mark: "Did Kate Kingsley demonstrate an ability to work smoothly with clients?"
- **Be specific.** State precisely what you want. For example, if you request the latest census figures from a government agency, be sure to say whether you want a page or two of summary figures or a detailed report running several thousand pages.

Explain and Justify Your Request

In the middle section of the request, give the details of your request.

Use the middle section of your message to explain your initial request. Make the explanation a smooth and logical outgrowth of your opening remarks. For example, you might show how your readers could benefit from complying. When Becky Bumgardner writes e-mail messages to managers, she's looking for information, but she's also telling them why she needs the information and explaining how they might benefit from granting the request. For instance, Bumgardner might write, "By participating in the quarterly incentive program for managers, you will become eligible to receive valuable incentive awards."

Whether you're writing a formal letter or a simple e-mail, you can use the middle section of your routine request to list a series of questions. This method is particularly useful if your inquiry concerns machinery or complex equipment. For instance, you might ask about technical specifications, exact dimensions, and the precise use of the equipment. Be sure to break down multiple requests, and when requesting several items or answers, number them and list them in logical order or in descending order of importance. When using a series of questions, just keep a few basics in mind:

Numbered lists help readers sort through multiple related items or multiple requests.

- **Ask the most important questions first.** If cost is your main concern, you might begin with a question such as "What is the cost for shipping the merchandise by air versus truck?" Then you may want to ask more specific but related questions about, say, the cost of shipping partial orders.
- **Ask only relevant questions.** So that your request can be handled quickly, ask only questions central to your main request. If your questions require simple yes-or-no answers, you might provide readers with a form or with boxes to check. If you need more elaborate answers, pose open-ended questions. "How fast can you ship the merchandise?" is more likely to elicit the information you want than "Can you ship the merchandise?"
- **Deal with only one topic per question.** If you have an unusual or complex request, list the request and provide supporting details in a separate, short paragraph. You may even use paragraph headings to make your reader's job easier.

Request Specific Action in a Courteous Close

Close your message with three important elements: (1) a specific request, (2) information about how you can be reached, and (3) an expression of appreciation or goodwill. Use the closing to request a specific action and to ask that readers respond by a specific and appropriate time ("Please send the figures by April 5 so that I can return first-quarter results to you before the May 20 conference"). Help your reader respond easily by including your phone number, office hours, and other contact information.

Close with
- A request for some specific action
- Information about how you can be reached
- An expression of appreciation

Conclude your message by sincerely expressing your goodwill and appreciation. However, don't thank the reader "in advance" for cooperating. If the reader's reply warrants a word of thanks, send it after you've received the reply. To review, see this chapter's "Checklist: Writing Routine Requests."

Types of Routine Requests

The various types of routine requests are innumerable, from asking favors to requesting credit. However, many of the routine messages that you'll be writing will likely fall into major categories. The following sections discuss four of these categories: placing orders, requesting information and action, making claims and requesting adjustments, and requesting recommendations and references.

Learning Objective 3

Discuss the differences among four types of routine requests

✓ CHECKLIST: WRITING ROUTINE REQUESTS

A. Direct statement of the request
1. Use the direct approach, since your audience will respond favorably to your request.
2. Phrase the opening clearly and simply so that the main idea cannot be misunderstood.
3. Write in a polite, undemanding, personal tone.
4. Preface complex requests with a sentence or two of explanation.

B. Justification, explanation, and details
1. Justify the request, or explain its importance.
2. Explain the benefit of responding.
3. State desired actions in a positive and supportive (not negative or dictatorial) manner.
4. Itemize parts of a complex request in a logical or numbered series.
5. List specific questions that you can't answer through your own efforts.
6. Limit any question to one topic.
7. Word any questions to get the type of answers you need.

C. Courteous close with request for specific action
1. Courteously request a specific action.
2. Make it easy to comply by including your contact information: name, address, phone and fax numbers (with area code), and e-mail address.
3. Indicate gratitude.
4. Clearly state any important deadline or time frame for the request.

Best of the Web

The Medium and the Message

Explore About.com's numerous links to sources of information on a variety of subjects. You can find tips on business writing with examples of letters, memos, and press releases. You'll find web-design ideas and help from numerous guides on many business-related topics. You can even get online help with setting standards for a company's online communication.

www.about.com

Placing Orders

Messages placing orders are considered some of the simplest types of routine messages. When placing an order, you need not excite your reader's interest; just state your needs clearly and directly. Most orders refer to a product that the reader knows about, so these messages are usually processed without objection.

Most companies today use computer-generated order forms.

Most companies today are moving toward paperless ordering by using computer-generated order forms. The forms provide a list of products with a description of each item and information such as the catalog number, name or trade name, color, size, and unit price. Your job is simple: Fill in the quantity, compute the total amount due, and provide the shipping address. Still, if you need to draft an order letter, follow the same format as you would on an order blank. Open with the general request. In the middle, include specific information about the items you want. Present this information in column form, double-space between the items, and total the price at the end. In the close, be sure to specify the delivery address, since it may differ from the billing address. Also indicate how the merchandise is to be shipped: by air or ground, by a specific delivery service, and so on. Otherwise, the seller chooses the mode of transportation. Finally, in any letter including a payment, mention the amount enclosed, explain how the amount was calculated, and if necessary, explain to what account the amount should be charged. Here's an example:

When placing orders, be thorough and clear.

States general request first →

Please send the following items from your current spring–summer catalog:

Provides all necessary details in a format similar to an order form

Count	Stock I.D.	Description	Item Price	Total Price
3	139-24	Daily appointment books (black)	$ 8.95	$ 26.85
50	289-90	Mechanical pencils (0.5 mm/black)	1.69	84.50
5	905-18	Wrist pads (gray)	6.99	34.95
10	472-67	Bulk IBM-format 3 1/2" diskettes (50/box)	17.99	179.90
		TOTAL SALE		$326.20
		SHIPPING		FREE
		AMOUNT DUE		**$326.20**

Includes additional important information in the close →

My check #1738 for $326.20 is enclosed. Please ship these supplies UPS ground to the address in the letterhead.

When placing international orders, use the transposed format: day/month/year.

When placing orders with international companies, remember that in most countries, the day is placed before the month: 15 March 2002 (15.3.02) rather than March 15, 2002 (3/15/02).

Requesting Information and Action

When making a routine request, say
- What you want to know
- Why you want to know
- Why it is in the reader's interest to help you

When you need to know about something, to elicit an opinion from someone, or to suggest a simple action, you usually need only ask. In essence, simple requests say, "This is what I want to know or what I want you to do, why I'm making the request, and why it may be in your interest to help me." If your reader can do what you want, such a straightforward request gets the job done with a minimum of fuss. Follow the direct approach: Start with a clear statement of your reason for writing. In the middle, provide whatever explanation is needed to justify your request. Then close with a specific account of what you expect, and include a deadline if appropriate. In more complex situations, readers might be unwilling to respond unless they understand how the request benefits them, so be sure to include this information in your explanation.

Jyoti Gupta, owner of Jyoti Cuisine India, doesn't spend her entire day making specialty frozen meals for passengers of British Airways and US Airways. Most of the time she's running her business and communicating with her suppliers, customers, and employees. Gupta routinely sends memos to these parties requesting information and action or responding to their information requests. For routine communications, Gupta uses a direct approach and a cordial tone.

Asking Company Insiders Requests to fellow employees are often oral and rather casual. However, as long as you avoid writing frequent, long, or unneeded messages, sending a clear, thoughtfully written memo or e-mail message can save time and questions by helping readers understand precisely what you want. But "don't try to be fancy in your e-mail messages or impress your boss with five-syllable words," advises UnumProvident's Becky Bumgardner.

The memo in Figure 7.2 was sent to all employees of Ace Hardware. It seeks employee input about a new wellness and benefits program and about a new fee. The tone is matter-of-fact, and the memo assumes some shared background, which is appropriate when communicating about a routine matter to someone in the same company. Both memos and e-mail messages have efficient headings that spell out who the message is for ("To:"), who wrote it ("From:"), when it was written ("Date:"), and what it's about ("Subject:"). For more information on formatting memos and other business messages, see Appendix I.

Asking Company Outsiders Business writers often ask businesses, customers, or others outside their organization to provide information or to take some simple action: attend a meeting, return an information card, endorse a document, confirm an address, or supplement information on an order. Such requests are often in letter form, although some are sent via e-mail. These messages are usually short and simple, like this request for information:

Would you please supply me with information about the lawn services you provide. Pralle Realty owns approximately 27 pieces of rental property in College Station, and we're looking for a lawn service to handle all of them. We are making a commitment to provide quality housing in this college town, and we are looking for an outstanding firm to work with us.

> Makes overall request in polite question form (no question mark)
>
> Keeps reader's interest by hinting at possibility of future business

1. **Lawn care:** What is your annual charge for each location for lawn maintenance, including mowing, fertilizing, and weed control?
2. **Shrubbery:** What is your annual charge for each location for the care of deciduous and evergreen bushes, including pruning, fertilizing, and replacing as necessary?
3. **Contract:** How does Agri-Lawn Service structure such large contracts? What additional information do you need from us?

> Avoids making an overly broad request by using a series of specific questions
>
> Itemizes questions in a logical sequence
>
> Avoids useless yes-or-no answers by including open-ended questions

Please let us hear from you by February 15. We want to have a lawn-care firm in place by March 15.

> Specifies a time limit in the courteous close

A more complex request might require not only greater detail but information on how responding will benefit the reader.

Planning

Analyze
Purpose is to request feedback from fellow employees.

Investigate
Gather accurate, complete information on program benefits and local gym.

Adapt
Office memo or e-mail is appropriate medium. Use "you" attitude, and make responding easy.

Writing

Organize
Main idea is saving money while staying healthy. Save time and meet audience expectations using the direct aproach.

Compose
Keep style informal but business-like. Using a "we" attitude includes readers in the decision-making process.

Completing

Revise
Keep it brief—weed out overly long words and phrases. Avoid unnecessary details.

Produce
No need for fancy design elements in this memo. Include a response form.

Proofread
Review carefully for both content and typographical errors.

FIGURE 7.2 In-Depth Critique: Memo Requesting Action from Company Insiders

ACE — Ace Hardware Corporation

INTERNAL MEMORANDUM

TO: All Employees
FROM: Tony Ramirez, Human Resources
DATE: October 15, 2002
SUBJ: New Wellness Program Opportunity

Routes message efficiently, with all needed information

The benefits package committee has asked me to contact everyone about an opportunity to save money and stay healthier in the bargain. As you know, we've been meeting to decide on changes in our benefits package. Last week, we sent you a memo detailing the Synergy Wellness Program.

States purpose in opening to avoid wasting busy readers' time

In addition to the package as described in the memo (life, major medical, dental, hospitalization), Synergy has sweetened the pot by offering IDD a 10 percent discount. To meet the requirements for the discount, we have to show proof that at least 25 percent of our employees participate in aerobic exercise at least three times a week for at least 20 minutes. (Their actuarial tables show a resulting 10 percent reduction in claims.)

After looking around, we discovered a gymnasium just a few blocks south on Haley Boulevard. Sports Midwest will give our employees unlimited daytime access to their indoor track, gym, and pool for a group fee that comes to approximately $4.50 per month per employee if at least half of us sign up.

Presents the situation that makes the inquiry necessary

In addition to using the track and pools, we can play volleyball, jazzercise, form our own intramural basketball teams, and much more. Our spouses and children can also participate at a deeply discounted monthly fee. If you have questions, please e-mail or call me (or any member of the committee). Let us know your wishes on the following form.

Lists reader benefits and requests action

Sign and return the following no later than Friday, October 29.

= =

______ Yes, I will participate in the Synergy Wellness program and pay $4.50 a month.
______ Yes, I am interested in a discounted family membership.
______ No, I prefer not to participate.

Provides an easy-to-use response form

Signature ______________________________

Employee ID Number ______________________________

Sometimes businesses need to reestablish a relationship with former customers or suppliers. In many cases, when customers are unhappy about some purchase or about the way they were treated, they don't complain; they simply stay away from the offending business. Thus, a letter of inquiry might encourage customers to use idle credit accounts, offering them an opportunity to register their displeasure and then move on to a good relationship. In addition, a customer's response to such an inquiry may provide the company with insights into ways to improve its products and customer service. Even if they have no complaint, customers still welcome the personal attention. Such an inquiry to a customer might begin this way:

The purpose of some routine requests to customers is to reestablish communication.

When a good charge customer like you has not bought anything from us in six months, we wonder why. Is there something we can do to serve you better?

Similar inquiry letters are sent from one business to another. For example, a sales representative of a housewares distributor might send the same type of letter to a retailer.

Making Claims and Requesting Adjustments

When you're dissatisfied with a company's product or service, you make a **claim** (a formal complaint) or request an **adjustment** (a claim settlement). Although a phone call or visit may solve the problem, a written claim letter is better because it documents your dissatisfaction. Moreover, even though your first reaction to a clumsy mistake or a defective product is likely to be anger or frustration, the person reading your letter probably had nothing to do with the problem. So a courteous, clear, concise explanation will impress your reader much more favorably than an abusive, angry letter.

Putting your claim in writing
- Documents your dissatisfaction
- Requires courtesy, clarity, and conciseness

In most cases, and especially in your first letter, assume that a fair adjustment will be made, and follow the plan for direct requests. Begin with a straightforward statement of the problem. In the middle section, give a complete, specific explanation of the details. Provide any information an adjuster would need to verify your complaint about faulty merchandise or unsatisfactory service. In your closing, politely request specific action or convey a sincere desire to find a solution. And don't forget to suggest that the business relationship will continue if the problem is solved satisfactorily.

In your claim letter
- Explain the problem and give details
- Provide backup information
- Request specific action

Companies usually accept the customer's explanation of what's wrong, so ethically it's important to be entirely honest when filing claims. Also, be prepared to back up your claim with invoices, sales receipts, canceled checks, dated correspondence, catalog descriptions, and any other relevant documents. Send copies and keep the originals for your files.

Be prepared to document your claim. Send copies and keep the original documents.

If the remedy is obvious, tell your reader exactly what will return the company to your good graces—for example, an exchange of merchandise for the right item or a refund if the item is out of stock. In some cases you might ask the reader to resolve the problem. However, if you're uncertain about the precise nature of the trouble, you could ask the company to make an assessment. But be sure to supply your contact information and the best time to call, so that the company can discuss the situation with you if necessary.

Be as specific as possible about what you want to happen next.

The following letter was written to a gas and electric company. As you read it, compare its tone with the tone of the letter in Figure 7.3. If you were the person receiving the complaint, which version would you respond to more favorably?

First Draft

We have been at our present location only three months, and we don't understand why our December utility bill is $815.00 and our January bill is $817.50. Businesses on both sides of us, in offices just like ours, are paying only $543.50 and $545.67 for the same months. We all have similar computer and office equipment, so something must be wrong.

Small businesses are helpless against big utility companies. How can we prove that you read the meter wrong or that the November bill from before we even moved in here got added to our December bill? We want someone to check this meter right away. We can't afford to pay these big bills.

FIGURE 7.3 In-Depth Critique: Claim Letter

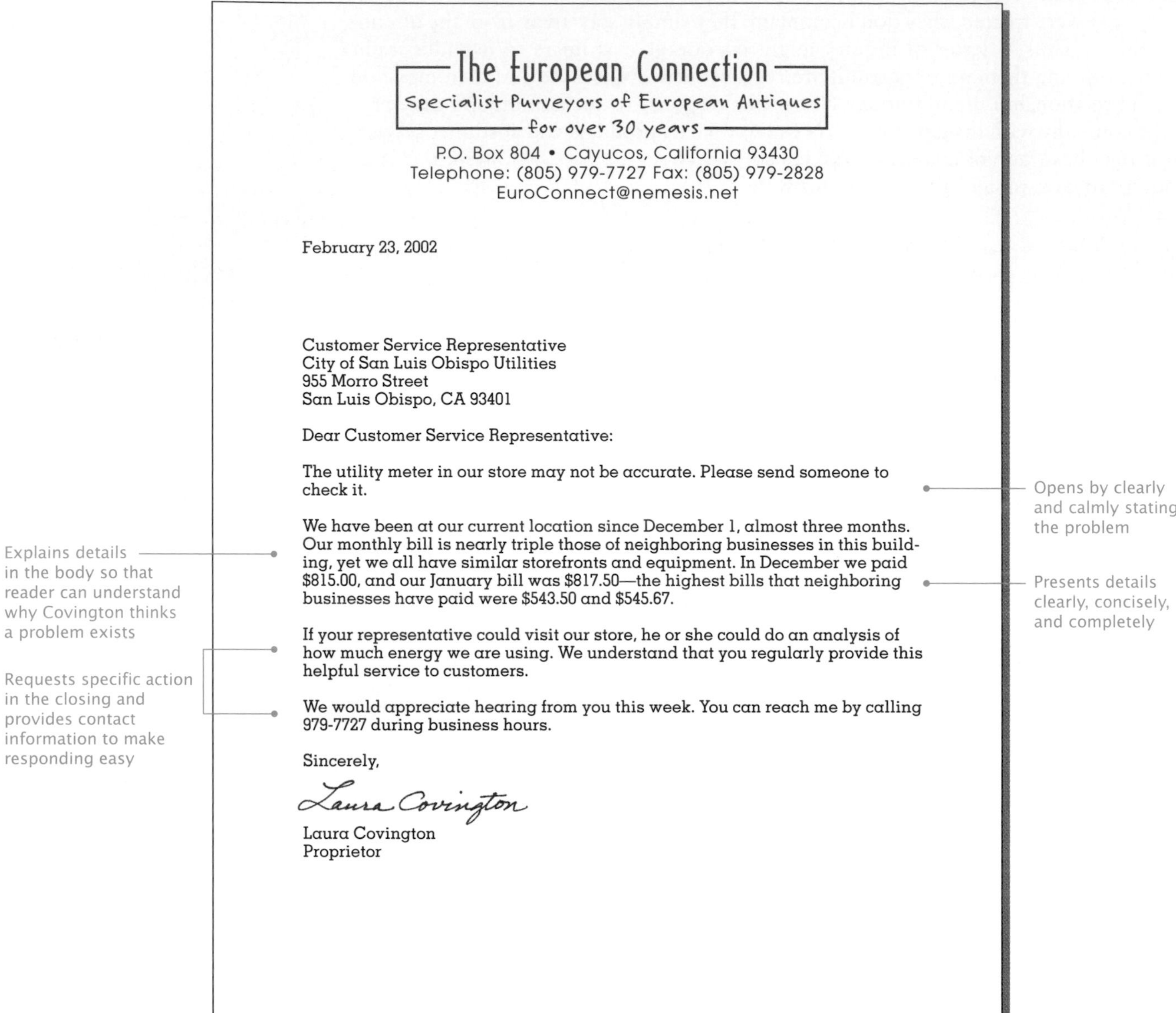

The European Connection
Specialist Purveyors of European Antiques
for over 30 years
P.O. Box 804 • Cayucos, California 93430
Telephone: (805) 979-7727 Fax: (805) 979-2828
EuroConnect@nemesis.net

February 23, 2002

Customer Service Representative
City of San Luis Obispo Utilities
955 Morro Street
San Luis Obispo, CA 93401

Dear Customer Service Representative:

The utility meter in our store may not be accurate. Please send someone to check it.

We have been at our current location since December 1, almost three months. Our monthly bill is nearly triple those of neighboring businesses in this building, yet we all have similar storefronts and equipment. In December we paid $815.00, and our January bill was $817.50—the highest bills that neighboring businesses have paid were $543.50 and $545.67.

If your representative could visit our store, he or she could do an analysis of how much energy we are using. We understand that you regularly provide this helpful service to customers.

We would appreciate hearing from you this week. You can reach me by calling 979-7727 during business hours.

Sincerely,

Laura Covington
Proprietor

Most people would react much more favorably to the version in Figure 7.3. A rational, clear, and courteous approach is best for any routine request. To review the tasks involved in making claims and requesting adjustments, see this chapter's "Checklist: Making Claims and Requesting Adjustments."

Requesting Recommendations and References

The need to inquire about people arises often in business. For example, before awarding credit, contracts, jobs, promotions, scholarships, and so on, some companies ask applicants to supply references. If you're applying for a job and your potential employer asks for references, you may want to ask a close personal or professional associate to write a letter of recommendation. Or, if you're an employer considering whether to hire an applicant, you may want to write directly to the person the applicant named as a reference.

Always ask for permission before using someone's name as a reference.

Companies ask applicants to supply references who can vouch for their ability, skills, integrity, character, and fitness for the job. Before you volunteer someone's name as a reference, ask that person's permission. Some people won't let you use their names, perhaps because they don't know enough about you to feel comfortable writing a letter or because they have a policy of not providing recommendations. In any event, you are

✓ CHECKLIST: MAKING CLAIMS AND REQUESTING ADJUSTMENTS*

A. Organizing your request

1. Write a claim letter as soon as possible after the problem has been identified.
2. Include a straightforward statement of the problem in the opening.
3. Tell specifics of the problem and include any necessary details in the body.
4. Provide copies of necessary documents (invoices, canceled checks, confirmation letters, and the like); keep the originals.
5. Gain the reader's understanding by praising some aspect of the good or service, or at least by explaining why the product was originally purchased.
6. Summarize desired action in the closing.
7. If appropriate, clearly state what you expect as a fair settlement, or ask the reader to propose a fair adjustment.

B. Adopting an effective tone

1. Maintain a confident, factual, fair, unemotional tone.
2. Present facts honestly, clearly, and politely.
3. Eliminate threats, sarcasm, exaggeration, and hostility, and use a nonargumentative tone to show confidence in the reader's fairness.
4. Make no accusation against any person or company, unless you can back it up with facts.

*These items are in addition to the basic tasks associated with writing routine requests.

likely to receive the best recommendation from people who agree to write about you, so check first.

Because requests for recommendations and references are routine, you can assume your reader will honor your request, and you can organize your inquiry using the direct approach. Begin your message by clearly stating that you're applying for a position and that you would like your reader to write a letter of recommendation. If you haven't had contact with the person for some time, use the opening to recall the nature of the relationship you had, the dates of association, and any special events that might bring a clear, favorable picture of you to mind.

Refresh the memory of any potential reference you haven't been in touch with for a while.

If you're applying for a job, a scholarship, or the like, include a copy of your résumé to give the reader an idea of the direction your life has taken. After reading the résumé, your reader will know what favorable qualities to emphasize and will be able to write the recommendation that best supports your application. If you don't have a résumé, use the middle of your letter to include any information about yourself that the reader might use to support a recommendation, such as a description of related jobs you've held.

Provide your reader with as much information as possible about your qualifications.

Close your letter with an expression of appreciation and the full name and address of the person to whom the letter should be sent. When asking for an immediate recommendation, you should also mention the deadline. You'll make a response more likely if you enclose a stamped, preaddressed envelope. The letter from Joanne Tucker in Figure 7.4 covers all these points and adds important information about some qualifications that might be of special interest to her potential employer.

SENDING ROUTINE ANNOUNCEMENTS, REPLIES, AND POSITIVE MESSAGES

When sending routine announcements, responding positively to a request, or sending a good-news or goodwill message, you have several goals: to communicate the information or good news, answer all questions, provide all required details, and leave your reader with a good impression of you and your firm. Routine messages can be quite brief and to the point. And even though you may be doing someone a favor by responding to a request, you want to be courteous and upbeat and maintain a you-oriented tone.

Strategy for Routine Announcements, Replies, and Positive Messages

Like requests, routine announcements, replies, and positive messages have an opening, a body, and a close. Readers receiving these messages will generally be interested in

Use the direct organizational plan for positive messages.

Planning

Analyze
Purpose is to request a recommendation letter from your college professor.

Investigate
Gather information to help the reader recall you and to clarify the position you want.

Adapt
A letter format will give your message the formality you need. Be polite.

Writing

Organize
Main idea is to convince your professor to send a glowing recommendation to a potential employer. Use the direct approach.

Compose
Make message friendly but businesslike and slightly more formal than usual. Use plain English and an active voice.

Completing

Revise
Be concise but thorough. Make sure that concrete detail flows logically.

Produce
Use simple typeface with ample margins and spacing between text. Enclose SASE and perhaps your résumé.

Proofread
Review letter and enclosures for errors.

FIGURE 7.4 In-Depth Critique: Letter Requesting a Recommendation

1181 Ashport Drive
Tate Springs, TN 38101
March 14, 2002

Professor Lyndon Kenton
School of Business
University of Tennessee, Knoxville
Knoxville, TN 37916

Dear Professor Kenton:

May I have a letter of recommendation from you? I recently interviewed with Strategic Investments and have been called for a second interview for their Analyst Training Program (ATP). They have requested at least one recommendation from a professor, and I immediately thought of you.

Opens with the request, assumes the reader will honor the request, and names the potential employer

As you may recall, I took BUS 485, Financial Analysis, from you in the fall of 2000. I enjoyed the class and finished the term with an "A." Professor Kenton, your comments on assertiveness and cold-calling impressed me beyond the scope of the actual course material. In fact, taking your course helped me decide on a future as a financial analyst.

Includes information in the opening to refresh reader's memory about this former student

My enclosed résumé includes all my relevant work experience and volunteer activities. But I'd also like to add that I've handled the financial planning for our family since my father passed away several years ago. Although initially, I learned by trial and error, I have increasingly applied my business training in deciding what stocks or bonds to trade. This, I believe, has given me a practical edge over others who may be applying for the same job.

Refers to résumé in the body and mentions experience that could set applicant apart from other candidates

If possible, Ms. Blackmon in Human Resources needs to receive your letter by March 30. For your convenience, I've enclosed a preaddressed, stamped envelope.

Gives a deadline for response in the closing and includes information about the person expecting the recommendation

I appreciate your time and effort in writing this letter of recommendation for me. It will be great to put my education to work, and I'll keep you informed of my progress.

Sincerely,

Joanne Tucker

Joanne Tucker

Enclosure

what you have to say, so you'll usually use the direct approach. Place your main idea (the positive reply or the good news) in the opening. Use the middle to explain all the relevant details, and close cordially, perhaps highlighting a benefit to your reader.

Start with the Main Idea

By beginning your positive message with the main idea or good news, you're preparing your audience for the detail that follows. Try to make your opening clear and concise. Although the following introductory statements make the same point, one is cluttered with unnecessary information that buries the purpose, whereas the other is brief and to the point:

Prepare your audience for the detail that follows by beginning your positive message with the main idea or good news.

Instead of This	Write This
I am pleased to inform you that after deliberating the matter carefully, our human resources committee has recommended you for appointment as a staff accountant	Congratulations. You've been selected to join our firm as a staff accountant, beginning March 20.

The best way to write a clear opening is to have a clear idea of what you want to say. Before you put one word on paper, ask yourself, "What is the single most important message I have for the audience?"

Before you begin, have a clear idea of what you want to say.

Provide Necessary Details and Explanation

The middle part of a positive message is typically the longest. You need the space to explain your point completely so that the audience will experience no confusion or lingering doubt. In addition to providing details in the middle section, maintain the supportive tone established at the beginning. This tone is easy to continue when your message is purely good news, as in this example:

> Your educational background and internship have impressed us, and we believe you would be a valuable addition to Green Valley Properties. As discussed during your interview, your salary will be $3,300 per month, plus benefits. In that regard, you will meet with our benefits manager, Paula Sanchez, at 8:00 a.m. on Monday, March 20. She will assist you with all the paperwork necessary to tailor our benefit package to your family situation. She will also arrange various orientation activities to help you acclimate to our company.

However, if your routine message is mixed and must convey mildly disappointing information, put the negative portion of your message into as favorable a context as possible:

Embed negative information in a positive context.

Instead of This	Write This
No, we no longer carry the Sportsgirl line of sweaters.	The new Olympic line has replaced the Sportsgirl sweaters that you asked about. Olympic features a wider range of colors and sizes and more contemporary styling.

The more complete description is less negative and emphasizes how the audience can benefit from the change. Be careful, though: You can use negative information in this type of message *only* if you're reasonably sure the audience will respond positively. Otherwise, use the indirect approach (discussed in Chapter 8).

If you are communicating to customers, you might also want to use the body of your message to assure the customer of the wisdom of his or her purchase selection.

Use resale material to assure customers of the wisdom of their purchases.

Talking favorably about something the customer has bought even though it may not have been delivered is a good way to build customer relationships. Such favorable comments, or **resale,** is commonly included in order acknowledgments and routine announcements to customers and is most effective when it is relatively short and specific:

The zipper on the carrying case you purchased is double-stitched and guaranteed for the life of the product.

The Kitchen Aid mixer you ordered is our best-selling model. It should service your cooking needs for many years.

Use sales promotion material to build sales and to show your company wants to be of further service.

Keep in mind that the purpose of resale is to increase the buyer's faith in goods or services already purchased or ordered. **Sales promotion** material is similar to resale, but it seeks to promote interest in goods or services where a purchase commitment does not already exist.

End with a Courteous Close

Make sure the audience understands what to do next and how that action will benefit them.

Your message is most likely to succeed if your readers are left feeling that you have their personal welfare in mind. You accomplish this task either by highlighting a benefit to the audience or by expressing appreciation or goodwill. If follow-up action is required, clearly state who will do what next. See this chapter's "Checklist: Writing Routine Replies and Positive Messages" to review the primary tasks involved in this type of business message.

Types of Routine Announcements, Replies, and Positive Messages

Innumerable types of routine announcements, replies, and positive messages are used in business every day. Most of these messages fall into six main categories: informative

✓ CHECKLIST: WRITING ROUTINE REPLIES AND POSITIVE MESSAGES

A. Initial statement of the good news or main idea

1. If message is mixed, present the good news first.
2. Respond promptly.
3. Avoid trite and obvious statements such as "I am pleased to," "We have received," "This is in response to," or "Enclosed please find."
4. Convey an upbeat, courteous, you-oriented tone.

B. Middle, informational section

1. Imply or express interest in the request, or provide details of the good news.
2. List all information in an orderly manner.
3. If possible, answer all questions and requests in the order posed.
4. Adapt replies to the reader's needs.
5. Indicate what you have done and what you will do.
6. Include any necessary details or interpretations that the reader may need in order to understand your answers.
7. If you cannot comply with part of the request (perhaps because the information is unavailable or confidential), tell the reader why and then offer other assistance
8. Embed negative statements in positive contexts or balance them with positive alternatives.
9. Inform or remind the reader of the general benefits of doing business with your firm. Avoid exaggerations and flamboyant language.

C. Warm, courteous close

1. If further action is required, tell the reader how to proceed and encourage the reader to act promptly.
2. Avoid clichés (such as "Please feel free to").
3. Offer additional service but avoid implying that your answer is inadequate (by using doubtful statements such as "I trust that" or "I hope").
4. Express goodwill or take an optimistic look into the future, if appropriate.

messages, grants of requests for information and action, grants of claims and requests for adjustments, recommendations and references, good-news announcements, and goodwill messages.

Sending Informative Messages

All companies send routine informative messages such as reminder notices and policy statements. Employees must be informed of organizational changes, upcoming events, new procedures, and changing policies. Customers and suppliers must be informed of shipping and return policies, sales discount procedures, and company developments that might be helpful when doing business with the company or when using the company's products. When writing informative messages, use the beginning of the message to state the purpose (to inform) and briefly mention the nature of the information you are providing; use the body to provide the necessary details; and end with a courtesy close.

When writing informative messages:
- State the purpose at the beginning and briefly mention the nature of the information you are providing
- Provide the necessary details
- End with a courtesy note

Most informative communications are neutral. That is, they stimulate neither a positive nor a negative response from readers. Becky Bumgardner's departmental meeting announcements and reminder notices, for example, generally receive a neutral response from employees. Bumgardner simply presents the factual information in the body of the message and does not care about the reader's attitude toward the information.

Some informative messages, however, require additional care. Policy statements or procedural changes, for instance, may be good news for both the company and employees—the company can save money, which will provide additional resources and even raises for employees— but such benefits may not be obvious to employees. In instances where the reader may not initially view the information positively, use the body of the message to highlight the benefits from the reader's perspective. In other words, show the reader exactly how the policy or procedure will enhance their work or personal life.

Patrick Byrne, CEO of Overstock.com, is one of the few people cashing in on the surplus of high-tech equipment from manufacturers—and dead dot.coms. But finding the equipment at liquidation prices and selling it to consumers at a substantial discount means Byrne must answer numerous daily requests for information and action. Moreover, because a potential sale is usually involved, Byrne uses his letters to explain how customers will benefit by purchasing from Overstock.com.

Granting Requests for Information and Action

If your answer to a request is yes or is straightforward information, the direct plan is appropriate. Your prompt, gracious, and thorough response will positively influence how people think about your company, its products, your department, and you. Readers' perceptions are the reason that UnumProvident's Becky Bumgardner is so sensitive to the tone of her memos, letters, and other messages. Bumgardner makes it a point to adopt the "you" attitude in all her business correspondence.

Many requests are similar. For example, a human resources department gets numerous routine inquiries about job openings. To handle repetitive queries like these, companies usually develop form responses. Although these messages are often criticized as being cold and impersonal, you can put a great deal of thought into wording them, and you can use computers to personalize and mix paragraphs. Thus, a computerized form letter prepared with care may actually be more personal and sincere than a quickly dictated, hastily typed "personal" reply. E-mail messages may be standardized as well. For Example, Julian Zamakis sent an e-mail to Herman Miller asking for information about employment opportunities and received the encouraging e-mail reply in Figure 7.5.

When you're answering requests and a potential sale is involved, you have three main goals: (1) to respond to the inquiry and answer all questions, (2) to leave your reader with a good impression of you and your firm, and (3) to encourage the future sale. The following letter succeeds in meeting all three objectives:

FIGURE 7.5 In-Depth Critique: E-mail Replying to Request for Information

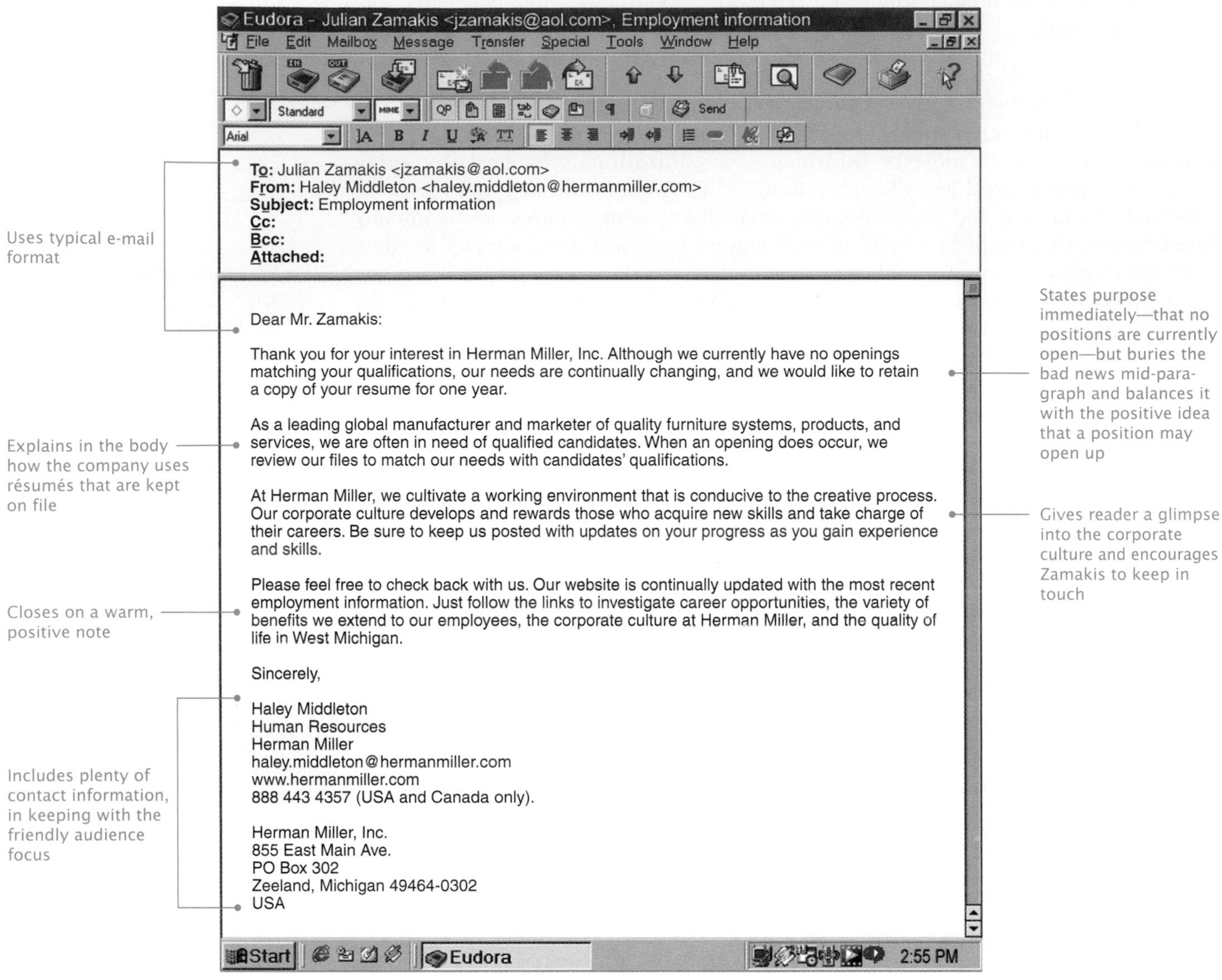

To: Julian Zamakis <jzamakis@aol.com>
From: Haley Middleton <haley.middleton@hermanmiller.com>
Subject: Employment information
Cc:
Bcc:
Attached:

Dear Mr. Zamakis:

Thank you for your interest in Herman Miller, Inc. Although we currently have no openings matching your qualifications, our needs are continually changing, and we would like to retain a copy of your resume for one year.

As a leading global manufacturer and marketer of quality furniture systems, products, and services, we are often in need of qualified candidates. When an opening does occur, we review our files to match our needs with candidates' qualifications.

At Herman Miller, we cultivate a working environment that is conducive to the creative process. Our corporate culture develops and rewards those who acquire new skills and take charge of their careers. Be sure to keep us posted with updates on your progress as you gain experience and skills.

Please feel free to check back with us. Our website is continually updated with the most recent employment information. Just follow the links to investigate career opportunities, the variety of benefits we extend to our employees, the corporate culture at Herman Miller, and the quality of life in West Michigan.

Sincerely,

Haley Middleton
Human Resources
Herman Miller
haley.middleton@hermanmiller.com
www.hermanmiller.com
888 443 4357 (USA and Canada only).

Herman Miller, Inc.
855 East Main Ave.
PO Box 302
Zeeland, Michigan 49464-0302
USA

Starts with a clear statement of the main point — Here is the brochure "Entertainment Unlimited" that you requested. This booklet describes the vast array of entertainment options available to you with an Ocean Satellite Device (OSD).

Presents key information immediately, along with resale and sales promotion — On page 12 of "Entertainment Unlimited" you'll find a list of the 338 channels that the OSD brings into your home. You'll have access to movie, sport, and music channels; 24-hour news channels; local channels; and all the major television networks. OSD gives you a clearer picture and more precise sound than those old-fashioned dishes that took up most of your yard—and OSD uses only a small dish that mounts easily on your roof.

Encourage readers to take one more step toward a purchase by highlighting product benefits — More music, more cartoons, more experts, more news, and more sports are available to you with OSD than with any other cable or satellite connection in this region. Yes, it's all there, right at your fingertips.

Points toward the sale confidently — Just call us at 1-800-786-4331, and an OSD representative will come to your home to answer your questions. You'll love the programming and the low monthly cost. Call us today!

Granting Claims and Requests for Adjustment

Satisfied customers bring additional business to a firm; angry or dissatisfied customers do not. In addition, angry customers complain to anyone who will listen, creating poor public relations. So even though claims and adjustments may seem unpleasant, progressive businesspeople treat claims and requests for adjustment as golden opportunities to build customer loyalty.[2]

Few people go to the trouble of requesting an adjustment unless they actually have a problem. So the most sensible reaction to a routine claim is to assume that the claimant's account of the transaction is an honest statement of what happened—unless the same customer repeatedly submits dubious claims or the dollar amount is very large. When you receive a complaint, you'll want to investigate the problem first to determine what went wrong and why. You'll also want to determine whether your company, your customer, or a third party is at fault.

Learning Objective 4

Explain the main differences in messages granting a claim when the company, the customer, or a third party is at fault

When Your Company Is at Fault The usual human response to a bad situation is to say, "It wasn't my fault!" However, businesspeople can't take that stance. When your company is at fault and your response to a claim is positive, you must protect your company's image and try to regain the customer's goodwill by referring to company errors carefully. Don't blame an individual or a specific department. And avoid lame excuses such as "Nobody's perfect" or "Mistakes will happen." Don't promise that problems will never happen again; such guarantees are unrealistic and often beyond your control. Instead, explain your company's efforts to do a good job, implying that the error was an unusual incident.

An ungracious adjustment may increase customer dissatisfaction.

For example, a large mail-order clothing company has created the following form letter to respond to customers who claim they haven't received exactly what was ordered. The form letter can be customized through word processing and then individually signed:

> Your letter concerning your recent Klondike order has arrived and has been forwarded to our director of order fulfillment. Your complete satisfaction is our goal; when you are satisfied, we are satisfied. Our customer service representative will contact you soon to assist with the issues raised in your letter.
>
> Whether you're skiing or driving a snowmobile, Klondike Gear offers you the best protection from wind, snow, and cold—and Klondike has been taking care of customers' outdoor needs for over 27 years! Because you're a loyal customer, enclosed is a $5 gift certificate. You may wish to consider our new line of quality snow goggles.
>
> Thank you for taking the time to write to us. Your input helps us better serve you and all our customers.

Starts with a "good attitude" statement (not the usual good-news statement) because it's going to people with various complaints

Puts customer at ease with "you" attitude

Avoids suggesting that customer was wrong to write to Klondike

Includes resale and sales promotion

Closes with statement of company's concern for all its customers

In contrast, a response letter written as a personal answer to a unique claim would start with a clear statement of the good news: the settling of the claim according to the customer's request. Here is a more personal response from Klondike Gear:

> Here is your heather-blue wool-and-mohair sweater (size large) to replace the one returned to us with a defect in the knitting on the left sleeve. Thanks for giving us the opportunity to correct this situation. Customers' needs have come first at Klondike Gear for 27 years. Our sweaters are handmade by the finest knitters in this area.
>
> Our newest catalog is enclosed. Browse through it, and you'll see what wonderful new colors and patterns we have for you. Whether you are skiing or driving a snowmobile, Klondike Gear offers you the best protection available from wind, snow, and cold. Let us know how we may continue to serve you and your sporting needs.

When the Customer Is at Fault When your customer is at fault (perhaps washing a dry-clean-only sweater in hot water), you can (1) refuse the claim and attempt to justify your refusal or (2) simply do what the customer asks. But remember, if you refuse the claim, you may lose your customer—as well as many of the customer's friends, who will hear only one side of the dispute. You must weigh the cost of making the adjustment against the cost of losing future business from one or more customers.

When complying with an unjustified claim, let the customer know that the merchandise was mistreated, but maintain a respectful and positive tone.

If you choose to grant the claim, you can start off with the good news: You're replacing the merchandise or refunding the purchase price. However, the middle section needs more attention. Your job is to make the customer realize that the merchandise was mistreated, but you want to avoid being condescending ("Perhaps you failed to read the instructions carefully") or preachy ("You should know that wool shrinks in hot water"). The dilemma is this: If the customer fails to realize what went wrong, you may commit your firm to an endless procession of returned merchandise; but if you insult the customer, your cash refund will have been wasted because you'll lose your customer anyway. Without being offensive, the letter in Figure 7.6 educates a customer about how to treat his in-line skates.

When a Third Party Is at Fault Sometimes neither you nor the claimant is at fault. Perhaps the carrier damaged merchandise in transit. Or perhaps the original manufacturer is responsible for some product defect. When a third party is at fault, you have three options:

You have three options when a third party is at fault.

- **Simply honor the claim.** This option is the most attractive. You can satisfy your customer with the standard good-news letter and no additional explanation. This way you maintain your reputation for fair dealing and bear no cost (because the carrier, manufacturer, or other third party will reimburse you for the damage).
- **Honor the claim, but explain you're not at fault.** This option corrects any impression that the damage was caused by your *negligence*. You can still write the standard good-news letter, but stress the explanation.
- **Refer the claimant to the third party.** This option is almost always a bad choice. When you suggest filing a claim with the firm that caused the defect or damage, you fail to satisfy the claimant's needs. The exception is when you're trying to dissociate yourself from any legal responsibility for the damaged merchandise, especially if it has caused a personal injury, in which case you would send a bad-news message (see Chapter 8).

This chapter's "Checklist: Granting Claims and Adjustment Requests" reviews the tasks involved in these kinds of business messages.

Providing Recommendations and References

When writing a letter of recommendation, your goal is to convince readers that the person being recommended has the characteristics necessary for the job or benefit being sought. Your letter must contain all the relevant details:

- Candidate's full name
- Job or benefit being sought
- Nature of your relationship with the candidate
- Whether you're answering a request or taking the initiative
- Facts relevant to the position or benefit sought
- Your overall evaluation of the candidate's suitability for the job or benefit

Learning Objective 5

Outline how best to protect yourself when referring to a candidate's shortcoming in a recommendation letter

Oddly enough, the most difficult recommendation letters to write are those for truly outstanding candidates. Your audience will have trouble believing uninterrupted praise for someone's talents and accomplishments. So illustrate your general points with a specific example or two that point out the candidate's abilities. Be sure to discuss the candidate's abilities in relation to the "competition."

Most candidates aren't perfect, however. Omitting reference to a candidate's shortcomings may be tempting, especially if the shortcomings are irrelevant to the demands of the job in question. Even so, you have an obligation to refer to any shortcoming that is serious and related to job performance. You owe it to your audience, to your own conscience, and even to the better-qualified candidate who's relying on honest references.

A serious shortcoming cannot be ignored, but beware of being libelous:

- Include only relevant, factual information
- Avoid value judgments
- Balance criticisms with favorable points

Of course, the danger in writing a critical letter is that you might engage in libel (making a false and malicious written statement that injures the candidate's reputation). On the other hand, if that negative information is truthful and relevant, it may be unethical and illegal to omit it from your recommendation. So if you must refer to a

1 Planning

Analyze
Purpose is to grant a customer's claim, gently educate him, and encourage further business.

Investigate
Gather information on product care, warranties, and resale information.

Adapt
Use letter format to reinforce businesslike tone. Give customer relationship utmost attention.

2 Writing

Organize
Main idea is that you're replacing the wheel assembly—even though you are not required to do so.

Compose
Use an upbeat conversational style, but remain businesslike. Choose words carefully, especially when educating the customer. Include resale information to reinforce future business.

3 Completing

Revise
Revise for tone, focusing on conciseness, clarity, and the "you" attitude.

Produce
Avoid confusing your positive message with fussy design elements. Keep it simple.

Proofread
Review for the usual errors, and include all promised enclosures.

FIGURE 7.6 In-Depth Critique: Letter Responding to a Claim When the Buyer Is at Fault

Skates Alive!

20901 El Dorado Hills
Laguna Niguel, CA 92677
(714) 332-7474 • Fax: (714) 336-5297
skates@speed.net

February 7, 2002

Mr. Steven Cox
1172 Amber Court
Jacksonville, FL 32073

Dear Mr. Cox:

Thank you for contacting us about your in-line skates. Even though your six-month warranty has expired, Skates Alive! is mailing you a complete wheel assembly replacement free of charge. The enclosed instructions make removing the damaged wheel line and installing the new one relatively easy.

Acknowledges reader communication, keeps opening positive by avoiding words such as "problem," and conveys the good news right away

The "Fastrax" (model NL 562) you purchased is our best selling and most reliable skate. However, wheel jams may occur when fine particles of sand block the smooth rotating action of the wheels. These skates perform best when used on roadways and tracks that are relatively free of sand. We suggest that you remove and clean the wheel assemblies (see enclosed directions) once a month and have them checked by your dealer about every six months.

Explains the problem without blaming the customer by avoiding the pronoun "you" and by suggesting ways to avoid future problems

Because of your Florida location, you may want to consider our more advanced "Glisto" (model NL 988) when you decide to purchase new skates. Although more expensive than the Fastrax, the Glisto design helps shed sand and dirt quite efficiently and should provide years of carefree skating.

Includes sales promotion in the body, encouraging the customer to "trade up"

Enjoy the enclosed copy of "Rock & Roll," with our compliments. Inside, you'll read about new products, hear from other skaters, and have an opportunity to respond to our customer questionnaire.

Adds value by enclosing a newsletter that invites future response from customer

We love hearing from our skaters, so keep in touch. All of us at Skates Alive! wish you good times and miles of healthy skating.

Closes positively, ending on a "feel good" note that conveys an attitude of excellent customer service

Sincerely,

Candace Parker

Candace Parker
Customer Service Representative

Enclosure

✓ CHECKLIST: GRANTING CLAIMS AND ADJUSTMENT REQUESTS*

1. In the opening, state your willingness to honor the reader's claim, without negative comment.
2. Thank the claimant for taking the time to write.
3. In the body, explain how you will remedy the problem.
4. Minimize or, if possible, omit any disagreements with your reader's interpretation of events.
5. Make your explanation objective, nonvindictive, and impersonal.
6. Apologize only when appropriate; then do so crisply and without an overly dramatic tone.
7. Maintain a supportive tone: "Thank you for," "May we ask," and "We are glad to work with you."
8. Admit your firm's faults carefully: Don't shift blame, imply inefficiency, or make unrealistic promises.
9. Be careful when discussing the claimant's role in creating the problem.
10. In the closing, remind the reader how you are honoring the claim.
11. Encourage the claimant to look favorably on your company or the product in question.
12. Clarify any actions that your reader must take.

*These items are in addition to the basic tasks associated with writing positive responses.

shortcoming, you can best protect yourself by sticking to the facts, avoiding value judgments, and placing your criticism in the context of a generally favorable recommendation, as in Figure 7.7. In this letter, the writer supports all statements with facts and steers clear of vague, critical judgments.

Recommendation letters are usually confidential; that is, they're sent directly to the person or committee who requested them and are not shown to the candidate. However, recent litigation has made it advisable in some situations to prepare a carefully worded letter that satisfies both parties. To explore the topic further, see "Focusing on Ethics—Recommendation Letters: What's Right to Write?" You can also avoid trouble by asking yourself the following questions before mailing a recommendation letter:

A recommendation letter presenting negatives can be carefully worded to satisfy both the candidate and the person or company requesting information.

- Does the person receiving this personal information have a legitimate right to it?
- Does all the information I've presented relate directly to the job/benefit being sought?
- Have I put the candidate's case as strongly and as honestly as I can?
- Have I avoided overstating the candidate's abilities or otherwise misleading the reader?
- Have I based all my statements on firsthand knowledge and provable facts?

Announcing Good News

To develop and maintain good relationships, savvy companies such as UnumProvident recognize that it's good business to spread the word about positive developments, whether the company is opening new facilities, appointing a new executive, introducing new products or services, or sponsoring community events. Because good news is always welcome, use the direct approach.

About Employment Writing a letter to the successful job applicant is a pleasure. Such a letter is eagerly awaited, so the direct approach is appropriate:

Announces news in a friendly, welcoming tone

Welcome to Lake Valley Rehabilitation Center. A number of excellent candidates were interviewed, but your educational background and recent experience at Memorial Hospital make you the best person for the position of medical records coordinator.

Explains all necessary details

As we discussed, your salary is $26,200 a year. We would like you to begin on Monday, February 1. Please come to my office at 8:00 a.m. I will give you an in-depth orientation to Lake Valley and discuss the various company benefits available to you. You can also sign all the necessary employment documents.

Explains first day's routine to ease new employee's uncertainty

After lunch, Vanessa Jackson will take you to the medical records department and help you settle into your new responsibilities at Lake Valley Rehabilitation Center. I look forward to seeing you first thing on February 1.

FIGURE 7.7 In-Depth Critique: Recommendation Letter

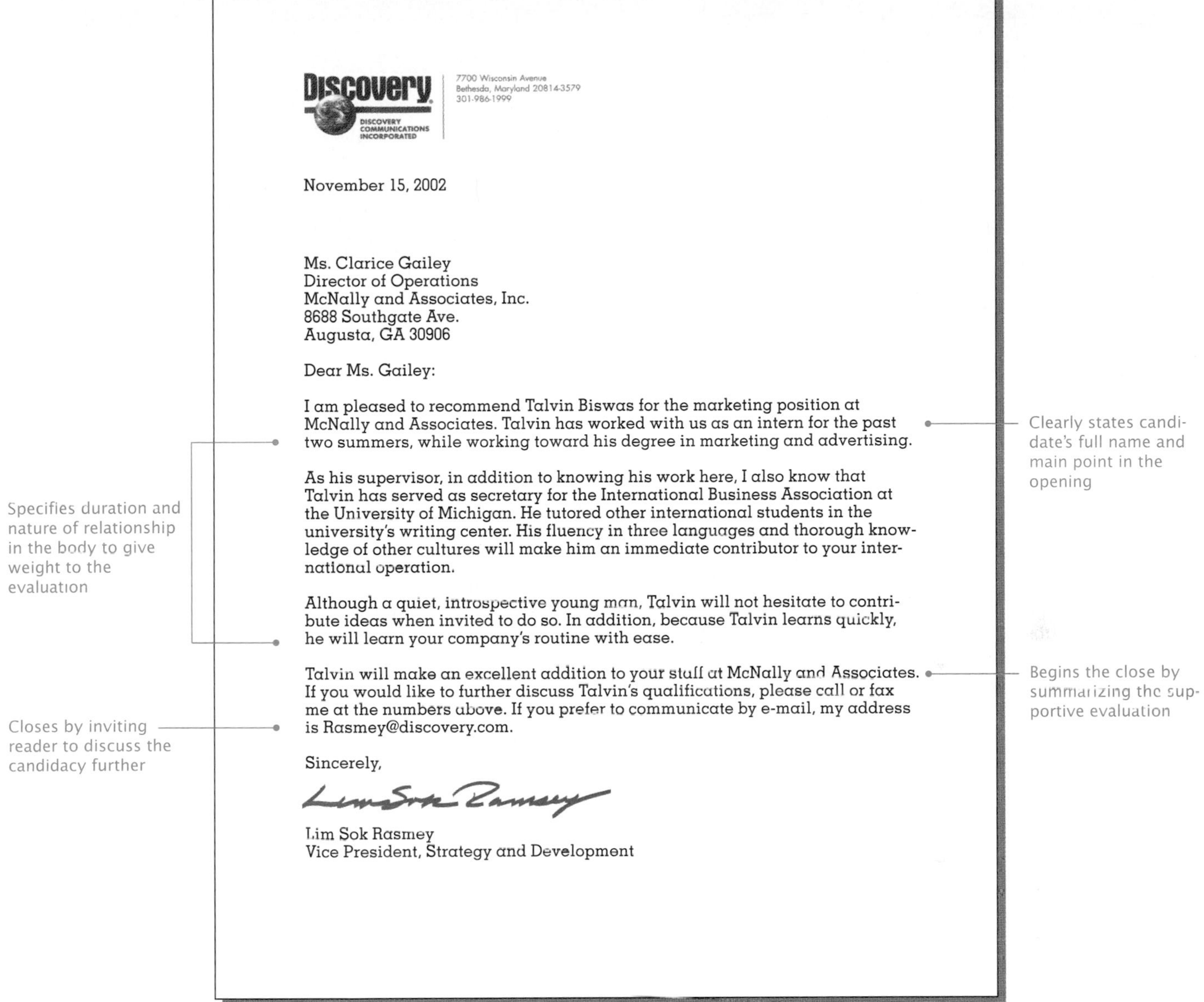

Discovery
DISCOVERY COMMUNICATIONS INCORPORATED
7700 Wisconsin Avenue
Bethesda, Maryland 20814-3579
301-986-1999

November 15, 2002

Ms. Clarice Gailey
Director of Operations
McNally and Associates, Inc.
8688 Southgate Ave.
Augusta, GA 30906

Dear Ms. Gailey:

I am pleased to recommend Talvin Biswas for the marketing position at McNally and Associates. Talvin has worked with us as an intern for the past two summers, while working toward his degree in marketing and advertising.

As his supervisor, in addition to knowing his work here, I also know that Talvin has served as secretary for the International Business Association at the University of Michigan. He tutored other international students in the university's writing center. His fluency in three languages and thorough knowledge of other cultures will make him an immediate contributor to your international operation.

Although a quiet, introspective young man, Talvin will not hesitate to contribute ideas when invited to do so. In addition, because Talvin learns quickly, he will learn your company's routine with ease.

Talvin will make an excellent addition to your staff at McNally and Associates. If you would like to further discuss Talvin's qualifications, please call or fax me at the numbers above. If you prefer to communicate by e-mail, my address is Rasmey@discovery.com.

Sincerely,

Lim Sok Rasmey
Vice President, Strategy and Development

Although letters like these are pleasant to write, they constitute a legal job offer. You and your company may be held to any promises you make. So attorneys sometimes recommend stating salary as a monthly amount and keeping the timing of performance evaluations and raises vague; you want to avoid implying that the newly hired employee will be kept on, no matter what, for a whole year or until the next scheduled evaluation.[3]

A letter telling someone that she or he got the job is a legal document, so make sure all statements are accurate.

About Products and Operations A company announcing a new discount program to customers would begin the letter by trumpeting the news. The middle section would fill in the details of the discount program, and the close would include a bit of resale information and a confident prediction of a profitable business relationship.

However, when the audience for a good-news message is large and scattered, companies often communicate through the mass media. When McDonald's opened its first restaurant in Moscow, it sent announcements to newspapers, magazines, radio stations, and television networks. The specialized documents used to convey such information to the media are called **news releases.** Written to match the style of the medium they are intended for, news releases are typed on plain $8^1/2$-by-11-inch paper or on special letterhead (not on regular letterhead). They are double spaced for print media or triple spaced for electronic media.

Specially formatted news releases convey good news to the media, which in turn disseminate it to the public.

Focusing on Ethics

Recommendation Letters: What's Right to Write?

You were Frank Walker's supervisor for four years. When he left the company recently, he asked you to write a letter of recommendation for him. However, your company's legal experts said no.

Why Not Give Recommendations?

Thousands of lawsuits have been filed (and won) by employees, charging former employers with making slanderous (oral) and libelous (written) statements in job recommendations. During one seven-year period in California, employees won 72 percent of the libel and related suits they brought against employers, and their average award was $582,000. One employer lost for saying an employee had "suddenly resigned," which implied the employee had resigned under "a veil of suspicion," said the court. Another employer lost for saying an employee was fired "for causes." Plus, when employees prove actual malice, damage awards skyrocket.

To complicate matters, one court ruling held an employer liable for *omitting* information about a former employee. So what sort of information should or should not be included in a recommendation? Even though some states have passed laws protecting companies against lawsuits when the employer acts in good faith, legal and human resources experts often advise companies to control what's being said by centralizing all recommendations. The cautious approach is to supply only dates of employment and titles of positions held—and to give that information only to people who have written authorization from former employees.

But What If You Want to Give a Recommendation?

Even so, Frank Walker was a terrific employee—a good friend—and you believe he really deserves a recommendation. You have two options. The first is to write the letter with Walker so that the contents satisfy you both and then to discuss the letter with your human resources department before releasing it. The second option is to ask Walker to list you as a *personal* reference, which removes your company from any responsibility for statements you make. But be careful—you can still be held personally responsible for your comments.

Of course, if it had been Sharon Brown who had asked for your recommendation, you'd be facing a different dilemma. Brown wasn't the greatest employee. So would you owe her potential employer the whole story? Including negative information could get you sued by Brown, and omitting negative information could get you sued by the hiring company for "failure to disclose" or "negligent referral."

Regardless of the circumstances, consult your human resources or legal department, and be sure to (1) comment only on your own experience working with a former employee, (2) make all comments in writing, and (3) limit your remarks to provable facts (don't exaggerate).

Career Applications

1. A former employee was often late for work but was an excellent and fast worker who got along well with everyone. Do you think it's important to mention the tardiness to potential employers? If so, how will you handle it?
2. Step outside yourself for a moment and write a letter of recommendation about you from a former employer's perspective. Practice honesty, integrity, and prudence.

Figure 7.8 illustrates the correct format for print media. The content follows the customary pattern for a good-news message: good news, followed by details and a positive close. However, it avoids explicit references to any reader and displays the "you" attitude by presenting information presumed to be of interest to all readers. To write a successful news release, keep the following points in mind:[4]

- Include no marketing or sales material in your news release.
- Put your most important idea first. (Don't say "Calco's president James Grall announced today that the company will move its headquarters to the Main Street office." Instead, start with the news: "Calco will move its headquarters to the Main Street office, President James Grall announced today.")
- Be brief: Break up long sentences and keep paragraphs short.
- Eliminate clutter such as redundancy and extraneous facts.
- Be as specific as possible.
- Avoid adjectives and adverbs (understatement goes a long way with the media).

In addition to issuing written news releases, many large companies hold news conferences or create their own videotapes, which are sent to television stations and networks.

FIGURE 7.8 In-Depth Critique: News Release Format

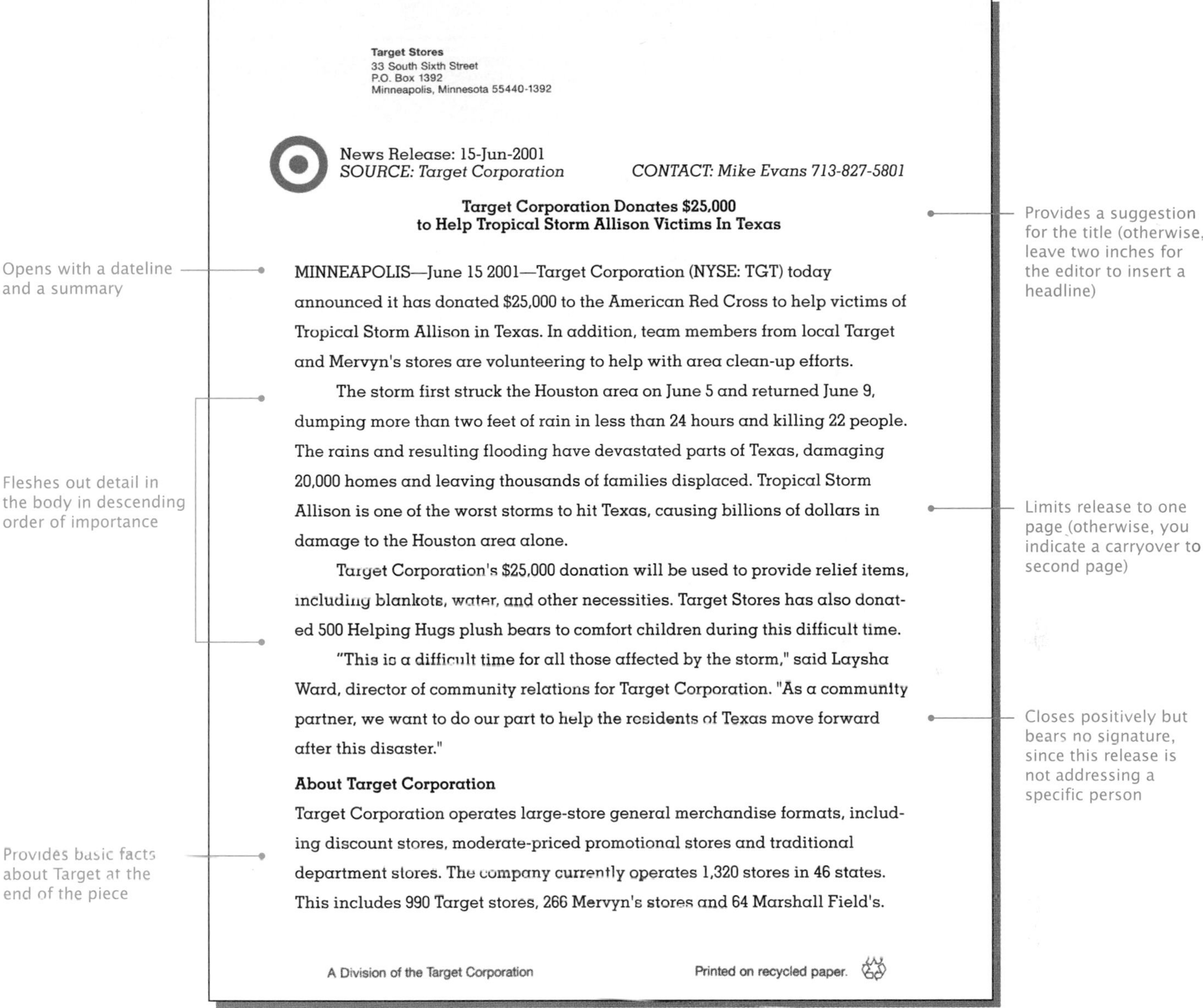

Target Stores
33 South Sixth Street
P.O. Box 1392
Minneapolis, Minnesota 55440-1392

News Release: 15-Jun-2001
SOURCE: Target Corporation *CONTACT: Mike Evans 713-827-5801*

Target Corporation Donates $25,000 to Help Tropical Storm Allison Victims In Texas

MINNEAPOLIS—June 15 2001—Target Corporation (NYSE: TGT) today announced it has donated $25,000 to the American Red Cross to help victims of Tropical Storm Allison in Texas. In addition, team members from local Target and Mervyn's stores are volunteering to help with area clean-up efforts.

The storm first struck the Houston area on June 5 and returned June 9, dumping more than two feet of rain in less than 24 hours and killing 22 people. The rains and resulting flooding have devastated parts of Texas, damaging 20,000 homes and leaving thousands of families displaced. Tropical Storm Allison is one of the worst storms to hit Texas, causing billions of dollars in damage to the Houston area alone.

Target Corporation's $25,000 donation will be used to provide relief items, including blankets, water, and other necessities. Target Stores has also donated 500 Helping Hugs plush bears to comfort children during this difficult time.

"This is a difficult time for all those affected by the storm," said Laysha Ward, director of community relations for Target Corporation. "As a community partner, we want to do our part to help the residents of Texas move forward after this disaster."

About Target Corporation

Target Corporation operates large-store general merchandise formats, including discount stores, moderate-priced promotional stores and traditional department stores. The company currently operates 1,320 stores in 46 states. This includes 990 Target stores, 266 Mervyn's stores and 64 Marshall Field's.

A Division of the Target Corporation Printed on recycled paper.

Sending Goodwill Messages

Learning Objective 6

Describe the importance of goodwill messages, and describe how to make them effective

You can enhance your relationships with customers, colleagues, and other businesspeople by sending friendly, unexpected notes with no direct business purpose. Jack Welch, former CEO of General Electric, is known for his handwritten notes to all employees, from managers to hourly workers. He once wrote a congratulatory note to one manager who had turned down a promotion because he didn't want to move his teenager to a different school: "Bill," wrote Welch, "we like you for a lot of reasons—one of them is that you are a very special person. You proved it again this morning. Good for you and your lucky family . . ."[5]

Goodwill is the positive feeling that encourages people to maintain a business relationship.

Effective goodwill messages must be sincere and honest. Otherwise, the writer appears interested in personal gain rather than in benefiting customers or fellow workers. To come across as sincere, avoid exaggeration and back up any compliments with specific points. In addition, readers often regard more restrained praise as being more sincere:

Make sure your compliments are grounded in reality.

When writing an online news release, be sure to include lots of links so those interested can get additional information with just a click or two.

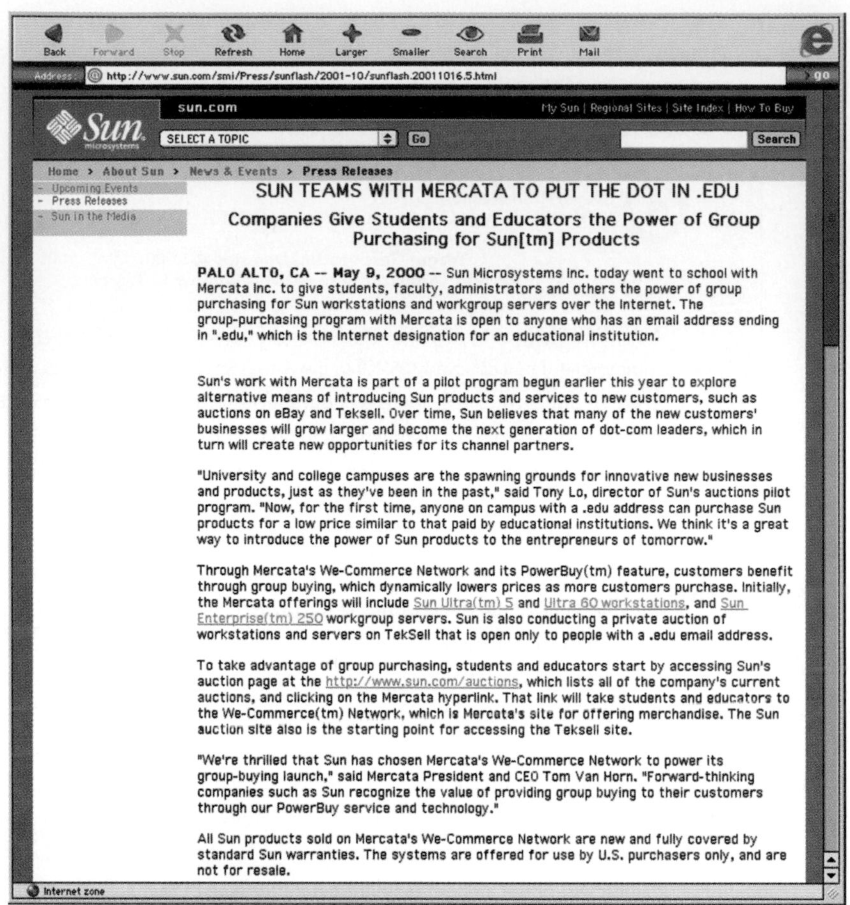

SUN TEAMS WITH MERCATA TO PUT THE DOT IN .EDU

Companies Give Students and Educators the Power of Group Purchasing for Sun[tm] Products

PALO ALTO, CA -- May 9, 2000 -- Sun Microsystems Inc. today went to school with Mercata Inc. to give students, faculty, administrators and others the power of group purchasing for Sun workstations and workgroup servers over the Internet. The group-purchasing program with Mercata is open to anyone who has an email address ending in ".edu," which is the Internet designation for an educational institution.

Sun's work with Mercata is part of a pilot program begun earlier this year to explore alternative means of introducing Sun products and services to new customers, such as auctions on eBay and Teksell. Over time, Sun believes that many of the new customers' businesses will grow larger and become the next generation of dot-com leaders, which in turn will create new opportunities for its channel partners.

"University and college campuses are the spawning grounds for innovative new businesses and products, just as they've been in the past," said Tony Lo, director of Sun's auctions pilot program. "Now, for the first time, anyone on campus with a .edu address can purchase Sun products for a low price similar to that paid by educational institutions. We think it's a great way to introduce the power of Sun products to the entrepreneurs of tomorrow."

Through Mercata's We-Commerce Network and its PowerBuy(tm) feature, customers benefit through group buying, which dynamically lowers prices as more customers purchase. Initially, the Mercata offerings will include Sun Ultra(tm) 5 and Ultra 60 workstations, and Sun Enterprise(tm) 250 workgroup servers. Sun is also conducting a private auction of workstations and servers on TekSell that is open only to people with a .edu email address.

To take advantage of group purchasing, students and educators start by accessing Sun's auction page at the http://www.sun.com/auctions, which lists all of the company's current auctions, and clicking on the Mercata hyperlink. That link will take students and educators to the We-Commerce(tm) Network, which is Mercata's site for offering merchandise. The Sun auction site also is the starting point for accessing the Teksell site.

"We're thrilled that Sun has chosen Mercata's We-Commerce Network to power its group-buying launch," said Mercata President and CEO Tom Van Horn. "Forward-thinking companies such as Sun recognize the value of providing group buying to their customers through our PowerBuy service and technology."

All Sun products sold on Mercata's We-Commerce Network are new and fully covered by standard Sun warranties. The systems are offered for use by U.S. purchasers only, and are not for resale.

Instead of This	Write This
Words cannot express my appreciation for the great job you did. Thanks. No one could have done it better. You're terrific! You've made the whole firm sit up and take notice, and we are ecstatic to have you working here.	Thanks again for taking charge of the meeting in my absence. You did an excellent job. With just an hour's notice, you managed to pull the legal and public relations departments together so that we could present a united front in the negotiations. Your dedication and communication abilities have been noted and are truly appreciated.

Congratulations One prime opportunity for sending goodwill messages is to congratulate someone for a significant business achievement—perhaps for being promoted or for attaining an important civic position. The congratulatory note in Figure 7.9 moves swiftly to the subject: the good news. It gives reasons for expecting success and avoids extravagances such as "Only you can do the job!"

Taking note of significant events in someone's personal life helps cement the business relationship.

Other reasons for sending congratulations include the highlights in people's personal lives—weddings, births, graduations, success in nonbusiness competitions. You may congratulate business acquaintances on their own achievements or on the accomplishments of a spouse or child. You may also take note of personal events, even if you don't know the reader well. Of course, if you're already friendly with the reader, you can get away with a more personal tone.

Some companies even develop a mailing list of potential customers by assigning an employee to clip newspaper announcements of births, engagements, weddings, and graduations or to obtain information on real estate transactions in the local

Planning

Analyze
Purpose is to create goodwill with industry business associates.

Investigate
Gather information on specific accomplishments of the reader's firm.

Adapt
Letter format lets reader use your message (perhaps even reproduce it) as an industry testimonial.

Writing

Organize
Main idea is to congratulate the reader. The direct approach is perfect for this welcome news.

Compose
A conversational tone complements the slightly formal style, since this is your first contact with the reader. Avoid generalized praise by mentioning specific, concrete accomplishments.

Completing

Revise
Review for consistency in tone, word choice, and sentence structure.

Produce
A simple design avoids distracting your reader from the message.

Proofread
Create a positive first impression by being especially careful to send an error-free message.

FIGURE 7.9 In-Depth Critique: Letter Congratulating a Business Acquaintance

Office DEPOT, Inc.
2200 Old Germantown Road, Delray Beach, FL 33445 407/278-4800

March 3, 2002

Mr. Ralph Lambert, President
Lambert, Cutchen & Browt, Inc.
14355 Pasadena Parkway
Pasadena, TX 74229

Dear Mr. Lambert:

Congratulations on your firm's recent selection to design print media advertisements for the National Association of Business Suppliers (ABS). We learned of your success at our convention in Atlanta last month.

Immediately expresses the reason for congratulating the reader

We have long believed that the success of individual franchises is directly linked to the healthy growth of the industry at large. We can think of no better firm to help our industry achieve wide recognition than Lambert, Cutchen & Browt.

Uses body to make compliment more effective by showing knowledge of the reader's work

We have admired your success in promoting associations of other industries such as soft drinks, snack foods, and recycling. Your "Dream Vision 2001" ads for the bottling industry were both inspirational and effective in raising consumer awareness, and we look for similar positive responses to your ABS campaign.

Includes a personal note of congratulations in the closing

Closes by expressing interest in following the future success of the firm

We look forward to seeing the results of the survey you conducted during our convention. You can be sure we will follow your media campaign with great interest.

Sincerely,

Janice McCarthy

Janice McCarthy
Director, Media Relations

tw

community. Then they introduce themselves by sending out a form letter that might read like this:

> Congratulations on your new home! Our wish is that it brings you much happiness.
>
> To help you commemorate the occasion, we've enclosed a key chain with your new address engraved on the leather tab. Please accept this with our best wishes.

In this case, the company's letterhead and address are enough of a sales pitch. This simple message has a natural, friendly tone, even though the sender has never met the recipient.

A message of appreciation documents a person's contributions.

Messages of Appreciation An important business quality is the ability to recognize the contributions of employees, colleagues, suppliers, and other associates. Your praise does more than just make the person feel good; it encourages further excellence. Moreover, a message of appreciation may become an important part of someone's personnel file. So when you write a message of appreciation, try to specifically mention the person or people you want to praise. The brief message that follows expresses gratitude and reveals the happy result:

> Thank you for sending the air-conditioning components by overnight delivery. You allowed us to satisfy the needs of two customers who were getting very impatient with the heat.
>
> Special thanks to Susan Brown, who took our initial call and never said, "It can't be done." Her initiative on our behalf is greatly appreciated.

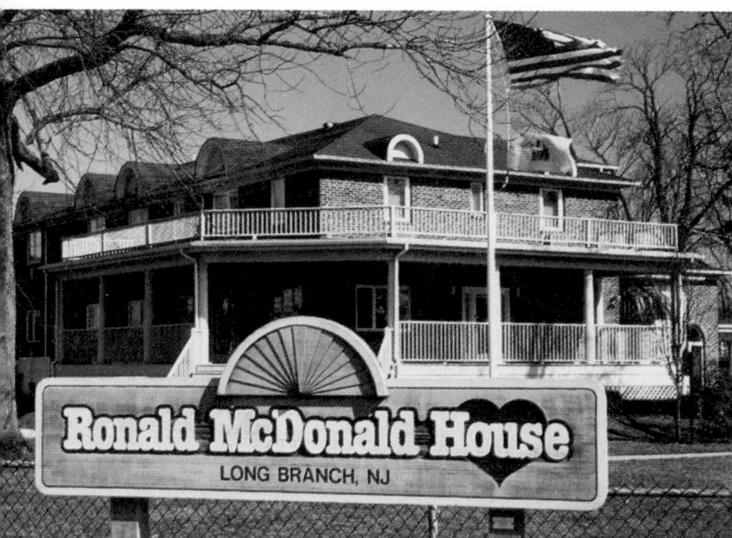

Both oral and written messages from organizations can promote good relationships with colleagues, customers, and the community. For example, Ronald McDonald House has become known worldwide as a home away from home for the families of seriously ill children. But when employees of the global office send congratulations, thank-you notes, or condolences to associates inside or outside the organization, they don't boast about all the good their organization accomplishes; they focus on the situation of the person receiving the message.

Condolences In times of serious trouble and deep sadness, written condolences and expressions of sympathy leave their mark. Granted, this type of message is difficult to write, but don't let the difficulty of the task keep you from responding promptly. Those who have experienced a health problem, the death of a loved one, or a business misfortune like to know that they're not alone.

Begin condolences with a brief statement of sympathy, such as "I was deeply sorry to hear of your loss." In the middle, mention the good qualities or the positive contributions made by the deceased. State what the person or business meant to you. In closing, you can offer your condolences and your best wishes. One considerate way to end this type of message is to say something that will give the reader a little lift, such as a reference to a brighter future. Here are a few general suggestions for writing condolence messages:

In condolence messages, try to find a middle path between being superficial and causing additional distress.

- **Keep reminiscences brief.** Recount a memory or an anecdote (even a humorous one), but don't dwell on the details of the loss, lest you add to the reader's anguish.
- **Write in your own words.** Write as if you were speaking privately to the person. Don't quote "poetic" passages or use stilted or formal phrases. If the loss is a death, refer to it as such rather than as "passing away" or "departing."
- **Be tactful.** Mention your shock and dismay, but remember that bereaved and distressed loved ones take little comfort in lines such as "Richard was too young to

✓ CHECKLIST: SENDING GOODWILL MESSAGES*

1. Be prompt when sending out goodwill messages so that they lose none of their impact.
2. Send a written message whenever possible (it can be savored more than once), but a telephone call is better than no message at all.
3. Use letter format for all condolences and any other goodwill message sent to outsiders or mailed to an employee's home.
4. Except for condolences, use the memo format for any goodwill messages sent through interoffice mail.
5. Hand-write condolences and replies to handwritten invitations.
6. Use special stationery, if available.
7. For added impact, present congratulations in a folder with a clipping or photo commemorating the special event.
8. In the beginning, incorporate a friendly statement that builds goodwill.
9. Focus on the good qualities of the person or situation.
10. In the middle, express personalized details in sincere, not gushy, language.
11. Be warm but concise.
12. Make the reader the focus of all comments.
13. Close with a positive or forward-looking statement.
14. Restate the important idea in the close, when appropriate.

*These items are in addition to the basic tasks associated with writing positive responses.

die" or "Starting all over again will be so difficult." Try to strike a balance between superficial expressions of sympathy and heart-rending references to a happier past or the likelihood of a bleak future.

- **Take special care.** Be sure to spell names correctly and to be accurate in your review of facts. Try to be prompt.
- **Write about special qualities of the deceased.** You may have to rely on reputation to do this, but let the grieving person know you valued his or her loved one.
- **Write about special qualities of the bereaved person.** A pat on the back helps a bereaved family member feel more confident about handling things during such a traumatic time.[6]

Supervisor George Bigalow sent the following condolence letter to his administrative assistant, Janice Case, after learning of the death of Janice's husband:

My sympathy to you and your children. All your friends at Carter Electric were so very sorry to learn of John's death. Although I never had the opportunity to meet him, I do know how very special he was to you. Your tales of your family's camping trips and his rafting expeditions were always memorable.

To review the tasks involved in writing goodwill messages, see "Checklist: Sending Goodwill Messages."

COMMUNICATION CHALLENGES AT UNUMPROVIDENT CORPORATION

Business is booming at UnumProvident Corporation. Quarterly sales of group disability insurance plans have increased by 20 percent, and the company is hiring new personnel to keep up with the growth. As the company expands, Becky Bumgardner's projects keep mounting, and she has asked for your help writing several routine messages.

Individual Challenge: Bumgardner wants to hire Jim Moody as a new staff member in the corporate relations department. She's impressed with his résumé and interview. Bumgardner thinks Moody may be a "good fit" for her department, and she'd like to know whether he responds well under pressure. As public relations coordinator for Brentwell Insurance in Snohomish, Washington, Moody may have dealt with stressful situations. Write a letter to Moody's

Brentwell supervisor, requesting information about Moody, especially about his behavior under pressure. Make up any necessary details, and address the letter to Henry Watrous, Brentwell Insurance, 1552 10th Avenue, Snohomish, WA 98290.

Team Challenge: Managers at UnumProvident Corporation participate in incentive programs, receiving rewards for achieving or exceeding their sales quotas. This quarter, the number of managers entitled to rewards has increased by 20 percent. Winners of incentive programs can select (1) four tickets to a Seattle Mariner's major league baseball home game, (2) a DVD player, or (3) a gift basket of gourmet foods. Bumgardner asks your team to develop a form letter to be sent to the winners, congratulating them on their outstanding performance and requesting winners to notify Bumgardner via e-mail of their prize selection. Be sure to state in your form letter how prizes will be distributed to winners. ■

SUMMARY OF LEARNING OBJECTIVES

1 **Apply the three-step writing process to routine positive messages.** Even though routine messages are usually short and simple, they benefit from the three-step writing process. Planning routine messages may take only a few moments to (1) analyze your purpose and audience, (2) investigate your readers' needs and make sure that you have all the facts to satisfy them, and (3) adapt your message to your audience through your choice of medium and your use of the "you" attitude. When writing routine messages, use the direct approach, as long as your readers will be positive (or neutral) and have minimal cultural differences. Completing routine messages means making them as professional as possible by (1) revising for clarity and conciseness, (2) selecting appropriate design elements and delivery methods, and (3) careful proofreading.

2 **Illustrate the strategy for writing routine requests.** When writing a routine request, open by stating your specific request. At the same time, avoid being abrupt or tactless: pay attention to tone, assume your audience will comply, avoid personal introductions, end polite requests with a period, and be specific. Use the middle of a routine request to justify your request and explain its importance. Close routine requests by asking for specific action (including a deadline as often as possible), and expressing goodwill. Be sure to include all contact information so that your reader can respond easily.

3 **Discuss the differences among four types of routine requests.** Each type of routine request has distinguishing features. All start with a statement of the main idea. But in letters placing orders, the body includes columns for product information, just like any good order blank. The close includes the delivery address, the preferred method of shipment, and information about any enclosed payment. When the request is for information or action, the middle explains or justifies your request, and the close specifies what you need and when you need it. When the message is a claim or request for adjustment, the middle includes whatever facts your reader needs to verify your complaint. The close requests a specific solution or conveys a sincere desire to find one, and it suggests that future business depends on a satisfactory resolution. In a request for recommendation, the opening states the position or award being applied for and, if necessary, recalls the nature and dates of your relationship with the reader. The middle refers to your résumé or includes information that would support a recommendation, and the appreciative close includes the name and address of the person to whom the recommendation will be sent.

4 **Explain the main differences in messages granting a claim when the company, the customer, or a third party is at fault.** In messages granting a claim, the explanatory section differs depending on who is at fault. If your company is at fault, avoid reacting defensively, and be careful when referring to company errors. Rather than placing blame, explain your company's efforts to do a good job. Remember not to make any unrealistic promises or guarantees. If your customer is at fault, you must help your reader realize what went wrong so that it won't happen again and again. However, you don't want to sound condescending, preachy, or insulting. If a third party is at fault, you can honor the claim with no explanation, or you can honor the claim and explain that the problem was not your fault.

5 **Outline how best to protect yourself when referring to a candidate's shortcoming in a recommendation letter.** When you find that you must refer to a candidate's shortcoming, stick to the facts. Try to give your criticism in the context of a generally favorable recommendation. Also ask yourself the following questions: Does the person receiving this personal information have a legitimate right to it? Does all the information I've presented relate directly to the job/benefit being sought? Have I put the candidate's case as strongly and as I honestly can? Have I avoided overstating the candidate's abilities or otherwise misleading the reader? Have I based all my statements on firsthand knowledge and provable facts?

6 Describe the importance of goodwill messages, and describe how to make them effective. Goodwill messages are important for building relationships with customers, colleagues, and other businesspeople. These friendly, unexpected notes have no direct business purpose, but they make people feel good about doing business with the sender. To make goodwill messages effective, make them honest and sincere. Avoid exaggerating, back up compliments with specific points, and give restrained praise.

TEST YOUR KNOWLEDGE

1. When is a request routine?
2. What are some of the guidelines for asking a series of questions in a routine request?
3. What information should be included in an order request?
4. Should you use the direct or indirect approach for most routine messages? Why?
5. Where in a routine message should you state your actual request?
6. How does a claim differ from an adjustment?
7. How does the question of fault affect what you say in a message granting a claim?
8. What is the appropriate strategy for responding to a request for a recommendation about a job candidate whose performance was poor?
9. How can you avoid sounding insincere when writing a goodwill message?
10. What are some of the guidelines for writing condolence messages?

APPLY YOUR KNOWLEDGE

1. When organizing request messages, why is it important to know whether any cultural differences exist between you and your audience? Explain.
2. Your company's error cost an important business customer a new client; you know it and your customer knows it. Do you apologize, or do you refer to the incident in a positive light without admitting any responsibility? Briefly explain.
3. You've been asked to write a letter of recommendation for an employee who is disabled and uses a wheelchair. The disability has no effect on the employee's ability to do the job, and you feel confident about writing the best recommendation possible. Nevertheless, you know the prospective company and its facilities aren't well suited to wheelchair access. Do you mention the employee's disability in your letter? Explain.
4. Every time you send a direct-request memo to Ted Jackson, he delays or refuses to comply. You're beginning to get impatient. Should you send Jackson a memo to ask what's wrong? Complain to your supervisor about Jackson's uncooperative attitude? Arrange a face-to-face meeting with Jackson? Bring up the problem at the next staff meeting? Explain.
5. **Ethical Choices** You have a complaint against one of your suppliers, but you have no documentation to back it up. Should you request an adjustment anyway? Why or why not?

PRACTICE YOUR KNOWLEDGE

 *Documents for Analysis*

Read the following documents; then (1) analyze the strengths and weaknesses of each sentence and (2) revise each document so that it follows this chapter's guidelines.

Document 7.A: Requesting Routine Information from a Business

Our college is closing its dining hall for financial reasons, so we want to do something to help the students prepare their own food in their dorm rooms if they so choose. Your colorful ad in *Collegiate Magazine* caught our eye. We need the following information before we make our decision.

- Would you be able to ship the microwaves by August 15th? I realize this is short notice, but our board of trustees just made the decision to close the dining hall last week and we're scrambling around trying to figure out what to do.
- Do they have any kind of a warranty? College students can be pretty hard on things, as you know, so we will need a good warranty.
- How much does it cost? Do you give a discount for a big order?
- Do we have to provide a special outlet?
- Will students know how to use them, or will we need to provide instructions?

As I said before, we're on a tight time frame and need good information from you as soon as possible to help us make our decision about ordering. You never know what the board might come up with next. I'm looking at several other companies, also, so please let us know ASAP.

Document 7.B: Making Claims and Requests for Adjustment

At a local business-supply store, I recently purchased your "Negotiator Pro" for my computer. I bought the CD because I saw your ad for it in *MacWorld* magazine, and it looked as if it might be an effective tool for use in my corporate seminar on negotiation.

Unfortunately, when I inserted it in my office computer, it wouldn't work. I returned it to the store, but since I had already opened it, they refused to exchange it for a CD that would work or give me a refund. They told me to contact you and that you might be able to send me a version that would work with my computer.

You can send the information to me at the letterhead address. If you cannot send me the correct disk, please refund my $79.95. Thanks in advance for any help you can give me in this matter.

Document 7.C: Responding to Claims and Adjustment Requests When the Customer Is at Fault

We read your letter requesting your deposit refund. We couldn't figure out why you hadn't received it, so we talked to our maintenance engineer as you suggested. He said you had left one of the doors off the hinges in your apartment in order to get a large sofa through the door. He also confirmed that you had paid him $5.00 to replace the door since you had to turn in the U-Haul trailer and were in a big hurry.

This entire situation really was caused by a lack of communication between our housekeeping inspector and the maintenance engineer. All we knew was that the door was off the hinges when it was inspected by Sally Tarnley. You know that our policy states that if anything is wrong with the apartment, we keep the deposit. We had no way of knowing that George just hadn't gotten around to replacing the door.

But we have good news. We approved the deposit refund, which will be mailed to you from our home office in Teaneck, New Jersey. I'm not sure how long that will take, however. If you don't receive the check by the end of next month, give me a call.

Next time, it's really a good idea to stay with your apartment until it's inspected as stipulated in your lease agreement. That way, you'll be sure to receive your refund when you expect it. Hope you have a good summer.

Document 7.D: Letter of Recommendation

Your letter to Tanaka Asata, President of SONY, was forwarded to me because I am the human resources director. In my job as head of HR, I have access to performance reviews for all of the SONY employees in the United States. This means, of course, that I would be the person best qualified to answer your request for information on Nick Oshinski.

In your letter of the 15th, you asked about Nick Oshinski's employment record with us because he has applied to work for your company. Mr. Oshinski was employed with us from January 5, 1995, until March 1, 2001. During that time, Mr. Oshinski received ratings ranging from 2.5 up to 9.6, with 10 being the top score. As you can see, he must have done better reporting to some managers than to others. In addition, he took all vacation days, which is a bit unusual. Although I did not know Mr. Oshinski personally, I know that our best workers seldom use all the vacation time they earn. I do not know if that applies in this case.

In summary, Nick Oshinski performed his tasks well depending on who managed him.

Exercises

For live links to all websites discussed in this chapter, visit this text's website at www.prenhall.com/bovee. Just log on and select Chapter 7, and click on "Student Resources." Locate the name of the site or the URL related to the material in the text. For "Exploring the Best of the Web" exercises, you'll also find navigational directions. Click on the live link to the site.

7.1 **Revising Messages: Directness and Conciseness** Revise the following short e-mail messages so that they are more direct and concise; develop a subject line for each revised message.

a. I'm contacting you about your recent order for a High Country backpack. You didn't tell us which backpack you wanted, and you know we make a lot of different ones. We have the canvas models with the plastic frames and vinyl trim and we have the canvas models with leather trim, and we have the ones that have more pockets than the other ones. Plus they come in lots of different colors. Also they make the ones that are large for a big-boned person and the smaller versions for little women or kids.

b. Thank you for contacting us about the difficulty you had collecting your luggage at the Denver airport. We are very sorry for the inconvenience this has caused you. As you know, traveling can create problems of this sort regardless of how careful the airline personnel might be. To receive compensation, please send us a detailed list of the items that you lost and complete the following questionnaire. You can e-mail it back to us.

c. Sorry it took us so long to get back to you. We were flooded with résumés. Anyway, your résumé made the final ten, and after meeting three hours yesterday, we've decided we'd like to meet with you. What is your schedule like for next week? Can you come in for an interview on June 15 at 3:00 p.m.? Please get back to us by the end of this work week and let us know if you will be able to attend. As you can imagine, this is our busy season.

d. We're letting you know that because we use over a ton of paper a year and because so much of that paper goes into the wastebasket to become so much more environmental waste, starting Monday, we're placing white plastic bins outside the elevators on every floor to recycle that paper and in the process, minimize pollution.

7.2 **Revising Messages: Directness and Conciseness** Rewrite the following sentences so that they are direct and concise.

a. We wanted to invite you to our special 40% off by-invitation-only sale. The sale is taking place on November 9.

b. We wanted to let you know that we are giving a tote bag and a free Phish CD with every $50 donation you make to our radio station.

c. The director planned to go to the meeting that will be held on Monday at a little before 11:00 A.M.

d. In today's meeting, we were happy to have the opportunity to welcome Paul Eccelson. He reviewed some of the newest types of order forms. If you have any questions about these new forms, feel free to call him at his office.

7.3 **Internet** Visit the business section of the Blue Mountain site at www.bluemountain.com/eng3/business/ and analyze one of the electronic greeting cards bearing a goodwill message of appreciation for good performance. Under what circumstances would you send this electronic message? How could you personalize it for the recipient and the occasion? What would be an appropriate close for this message?

7.4 **Teamwork** With another student, identify the purpose and select the most appropriate format for communicating these written messages. Next, consider how the audience is likely to respond to each message. Based on this audience analysis, determine whether the direct or indirect approach would be effective for each message, and explain your reasoning.

a. A notice to all employees about the placement of recycling bins by the elevator doors
b. The first late-payment notice to a good customer who usually pays his bills on time

7.5 **Revising Messages: Conciseness, Courteousness, and Specificity** Critique the following closing paragraphs. How would you rewrite each to be concise, courteous, and specific?

a. I need your response sometime soon so I can order the parts in time for your service appointment. Otherwise your air-conditioning system may not be in tip-top condition for the start of the summer season.
b. Thank you in advance for sending me as much information as you can about your products. I look forward to receiving your package in the very near future.
c. To schedule an appointment with one of our knowledgeable mortgage specialists in your area, you can always call our hotline at 1-800-555-8765. This is also the number to call if you have more questions about mortgage rates, closing procedures, or any other aspect of the mortgage process. Remember, we're here to make the home-buying experience as painless as possible.

7.6 **Ethical Choices** Your small supermarket chain has received dozens of complaints about the watery consistency of the ketchup sold under the chain's brand name. You don't want your customers to stop buying other store-brand foods, which are made and packaged for your chain by various suppliers, but you do want to address their concerns about the ketchup. In responding to these complaints, should you explain that the ketchup is actually manufactured by a local supplier and then name the supplier, who has already started bottling a thicker ketchup?

EXPAND YOUR KNOWLEDGE

Exploring the Best of the Web:

The Medium and the Message, p. 190

Choosing what to include in a message, deciding how to effectively express it, and selecting an appropriate format are all important considerations when you write. Go to About.com and add to what you've already learned in this chapter about writing requests and other messages.

1. Both the chapter and this site offer guidelines for writing effective messages. List the "Seven C's" that characterize good letters and memos. If you use clear language in a routine message, is it still important to restrict yourself to one topic? Why or why not?
2. Even the best-run businesses sometimes disappoint their customers. Imagine that you have been asked to write a response to an angrily worded e-mail message that charges your company with fraud because a product ordered through the web has not arrived. Which of the ten "secrets" of writing business letters do you think would be most useful in shaping your reply?
3. Describe some similarities and differences between a memo and a letter.

Exploring the Web on Your Own

1. Learn how to write effective thank-you notes by reviewing the steps at this Learn2 webpage, www.learn2.com/05/0547/0547.asp.
2. Polish your press release writing by following the steps at this Learn2 webpage, www.learn2.com/06/0622/0622.asp.
3. Turn praise into prose when writing letters of recommendation by following the steps at this Learn2 webpage, www.learn2.com/06/0600/0600.asp.

LEARN INTERACTIVELY

Interactive Study Guide

Visit "My Companion Website" at www.prenhall.com/bovee. For Chapter 7, take advantage of the interactive "Study Guide" to test your chapter knowledge. Get instant feedback on whether you need additional studying. Read the "Current Events" articles to get the latest on chapter topics, and complete the exercises—as specified by your instructor.

This site offers a variety of additional resources: The "Research Area" helps you locate a wealth of information to use in course assignments. You can even send a message to online research experts, who will help you find exactly the information you need. The "Study Hall" helps you succeed in this course. "Talk in the Hall" lets you leave messages and meet new friends online. If you have a question, you can "Ask the Tutor." And to get a better grade in this course, you can find more help at "Writing Skills," "Study Skills," and "Study Tips."

Grammar Diagnostic Tests

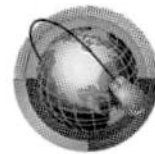

Review and reinforce your grammar and language skills by taking one of the four online diagnostic tests offered at our companion website, www.prenhall/bovee.com. The four tests cover a variety of topics, including spelling, capitals, punctuation, verbs, pronouns, adjectives, adverbs, sentence structure, sentence punctuation, clarity, word choice, style, organization skills, proofreading, and more. Submit your test and assess your competency. Then focus on improving areas where you are weak as you complete the exercises in this chapter.

CASES

APPLYING THE THREE-STEP WRITING PROCESS TO CASES

Apply each step to the following cases, assigned by your instructor

Planning Cases

Analyze

1. What's your general purpose?
2. What's your specific purpose?
3. What do you want readers to do?
4. Who are your readers? (Who is the primary audience? What do readers have in common? What is their general background? How will they react?)

Investigate

5. What information do readers need?
6. What facts must you gather?

Adapt

How will you establish credibility?

Writing Cases

Organize

1. What's your main idea?
2. Will you use the direct or indirect approach? Why?

Compose

3. Will your tone be informal or more formal?
4. Draft the message as discussed in the "Your task" section of the case.

Completing Cases

Revise

1. Use the Checklist for Revising Business Messages on page 155 to edit and revise your message for clarity.

Produce

2. What's the best way to distribute your message? By fax? By e-mail? By sealed envelope?

Proofread

3. Proofread your message for errors in layout, spelling, and mechanics.

ROUTINE REQUESTS

1. Step on it: Letter to Floorgraphics requesting information about underfoot advertising As the small-town owner of Better Bike and Ski Shop, you're used to receiving promotional displays, giveaway gadgets, and flashy posters from major manufacturers. The old ones clutter your back room, where employees fight over the used ski posters. But now a manufacturer wants to buy a piece of your floor!

Your Schwinn rep, Marva Beeker, approached you with the idea. Schwinn wants to put floor ads in your store. But first you have to sign up with the company that invented and sells them. Floorgraphics, Inc., leases floor space from retail stores and sells it to advertisers in 4-, 8-, or 12-week cycles.

"Floorgraphics has been doing this for years in thousands of Kmart and chain supermarkets all over the country," Beeker assures you, "and now it's trying to sign up smaller retailers to sell a wider variety of products. If floor ads work for Spaghetti-Os, why not for bicycles?"

Beeker goes on to explain how surprised everyone was by the success of strategically placing decals at the point of consumer decision making: on the floor beneath the product's shelf space. After the first placements, product sales went up anywhere from 25 to 75 percent. One survey showed that Oreo cookie sales went up by 72 percent in the two months after decals were installed on Kmart floors.

"Floorgraphics will want to lease your entire floor for advertisers other than Schwinn," Beeker explains. "And these people know what they're doing. They limit ads to two per aisle and to one company per category. Best of all, in addition to leasing fees, you get a commission on whatever Floorgraphics makes selling your space to advertisers. I think it's about 25 percent, but you should ask Richard yourself."

That's Richard Rebh, CEO of Floorgraphics, whose business card Beeker hands to you.

"We're the first bike manufacturer to sign up," she says, grinning. "We're going to get a big jump on the other guys . . . if we can get storeowners like you to agree. And keep in mind, the retailers that are already in the Floorgraphics network will get first crack at the new animated floor ads! Can't you just see it? The bicycle will start to move as customers crowd in for a look!"

Long after Beeker leaves, you find yourself staring at the dusty linoleum in front of the bike racks, marveling that manufacturers want to pay hard cash to put their names down there where customers are going to track dirt and melting snow all over them. But if what Beeker says is true, you could gain three new ways of earning money: the leasing fee, the increased sales, and the share in ad revenues.

Your task: Write to CEO Richard Rebh at Floorgraphics, Inc. (5 Vaughn Drive, Princeton, NJ 08540). You want to find out whether Beeker has been exaggerating. You'll need all the financial details, but you also want some practical information about the ads themselves: Who installs and removes them? What will your cleaning solutions do to them? What are the risks of floor damage? Is there a way to terminate the lease if you don't like them? Your questions are endless. Put as many as you deem reasonable in your letter, and be sure to justify your request for a speedy reply.[7]

2. Reverse migration: Letter requesting letter of recommendation for "dot-com" dropout You really wanted to join the so-called "Great Migration" of executive talent to online companies. You'd seen colleagues become overnight millionaires by abandoning their jobs at big companies and plunging into the world of Internet commerce. Employee stock options and inflated IPOs offered a lure they couldn't resist, and neither could you. So you contacted Michele James, a headhunter specializing in finding executives for online start-ups. James went to work and quickly landed you a lucrative offer at a well-funded dot-com company in your industry (travel services). You took it.

The first week as creative services director wasn't so bad. You learned tons of new things and adapted readily to the seat-of-the-pants work style. You discovered with delight that at your new company, creativity and vision weren't considered terrifying traits of overachievers who had to be kept on a short leash; instead, these traits were cultivated prerequisites. The more "out there" your ideas, the more attention they merited. That's because e-business moves fast and everybody needs to move fast with it.

You just didn't realize how long and how often you'd be expected to keep moving. That first week was only 50 hours. The second was 60. By the third week, 70 hours wasn't considered outlandish. Anyone who went home before 7 P.M. or who didn't show up on Saturday or Sunday was considered a loser and quickly disappeared from your workscape.

Your spouse was soon complaining about not recognizing you anymore; your children told people at school functions that you were in the hospital; and you couldn't remember the last time you ate a meal without a computer screen, cell phone, or beeper a few inches from your plate. You love the fast decision making, and your CEO loves your exemplary work, but you are exhausted. One day you pick up your briefcase and leave at 5 P.M. Horror registers on the few faces that lift to see you go. Then their weary eyes shift back to their computer screens.

Money is nice, you muse. But when will you enjoy the things it can buy? When will you live your life?

You've read about others who have taken the Internet plunge but quit after experiencing similar job stress. "Reverse migration" was the term the newspapers used to describe people like you who leave dot-com jobs to return to the "normalcy" of the traditional workplace.

Your task: You've already resigned. Now write a hard-copy letter to Glenna Evans, CEO of Yourtravel.com, asking for a letter of recommendation.[8]

3. Fortune or folly: Request for information from a Subway franchise operator Even before you heard Jared Fogle's story, you were thinking about buying into a franchise. Reading about the young man who lost 245 pounds while eating two Subway sandwiches a day has inspired your choice. If Jared can reach his goal by sheer determination, so can you. Maybe you should invest in a Subway franchise.

You do have some misgivings. From popular books such as Robert Kiyosaki's *Rich Dad, Poor Dad*, you know that franchises can be a smart first move for aspiring business owners. But you've also read that they demand long hours, steep investments, and rigid rule-following. What you'd like to know is exactly how long those hours will be, what unforeseen costs might suddenly arise, and whether it's hard for a would-be entrepreneur to fit into the franchise mold, where everything from the signage to the size of the ham slices is dictated by the company.

You decide to ask someone who's already taken the plunge, signed that 20-year agreement, and doled out the necessary $65,000 to $184,000 (depending on store size and location). That money covers franchise fees, leasehold improvements, equipment, outdoor signs, supplies, and inventory, but what isn't covered?

You also have questions you're embarrassed to ask Subway because you think maybe you should already know the answers. For instance, do you get any say-so in that range of 500 to 1,500 square feet, standard sizes for Subway outlets? Does Subway insist on choosing its own locations, or will you get to specify Bartlesville, Oklahoma, which you've determined to be an untapped market for the sandwich franchise? How long before you'll see any profit?

When you called Subway's headquarters and asked for references, you were told about Tharita Jones, who operates a Subway store in Tulsa, about 30 miles from Bartlesville. "She's been with us for about five years now," said the woman as she gave you Jones's name and number. Trouble is, you can't bring yourself to call her.

You have an image in your mind of a fast-food-franchise owner watching employees, doing paperwork, ordering supplies, talking to customers, and checking restrooms. She won't have the time to take a call from someone like you. You have so many questions: how to calculate the 8 percent royalties on gross sales and the 3.5 percent advertising fees charged weekly by the Subway franchise, whether franchise owners can switch suppliers if they find a better price, and what happens if royalty payments arrive late. You're also dying to find out whether Jones is happy with Subway's advertising programs and how much help she got from Subway in the beginning. You're even wondering whether you could drop by and observe Jones's operation for a day—sort of a behind-the-scenes look. How can you ask all this by phone?

You decide that a letter would be more considerate. You hate to impose, but you need to investigate before you sign a contract. With 14,700 stores worldwide, Subway *seems* like a good investment, but you need to be certain.

Your task: Write a letter to Tharita Jones (Owner, Subway restaurant, 120 W. Greenfield Street, Tulsa, OK 74133), requesting permission to visit her operation for a day (at her convenience) so that you can learn more about investing in a Subway franchise. Let her know how you got her name, and reassure her that you will need only about an hour of her time to address your specific questions. To make your meeting more productive, list your questions in the letter. You'll need to make your decision soon, so politely suggest a time limit for her reply.[9]

4. A juicy position: E-mail requesting information on management careers at Jamba Juice Working as a personal trainer at 24-Hour Fitness wasn't your college goal, but your love for sports made the gym an ideal place for an undergrad internship. When they offered you a full-time position as a trainer, you took it.

But now that you've earned your business degree, you're sick of Cybex machines and working from 5 A.M. to 9 P.M. to meet clients' schedules. And unlike many of your co-workers (of both genders), you don't dream of becoming a TV fitness guru or landing a celebrity client who'll pay all your bills. What you really want is to use what you've learned about business in a job with more responsibility—and better pay!

Last week you heard an intriguing rumor about the manager of the Jamba Juice bar located inside the gym. You wanted to ask her about it, but decided it would be more discreet to log on to www.jambajuice.com. There you discovered that the truth is even better than the rumor.

Jamba Juice is actively recruiting new managers by offering impressive incentives. It turns out that the chain is an up-and-comer in the health, fitness, and nutrition industry. That's a customer base you understand well, after long hours talking to clients sweating on treadmills. You love Jamba's smoothies, and now you discover that you can make more money working for the company.

The information at the Jamba Juice website was vague. It mentioned a "General Manager J.U.I.C.E. Plan"—some sort of profit sharing—but it never explained what J.U.I.C.E. stands for. Everything else sounded good, such as an average 7.5 percent of the store's profit as a take-home bonus every eight weeks for general managers, 1.5 percent for assistant general managers, with a "minimum guaranteed bonus" every eight weeks based on meeting "customer service goals." No explanation was given of what those goals are or how much the minimum is, but the site promised health benefits, paid time off for community service, and "private stock options" (Jamba Juice is a privately owned company).

You were most impressed by the "retention bonus for general managers." Again, how it's calculated is unclear, but the promise is a bonus based on the manager's ability to "build sales" over time. You earn the bonus from day one, but you don't actually get paid the accumulated bonus until you've been in the store or in a position of greater responsibility for three years. The website states the bonus could be as high as $50,000; one manager has already collected $10,000.

If you sign on for another three years, you're given a three-week paid sabbatical, in addition to accrued vacation or personal time! That, and a $1,000 bonus for every assistant you promote to general manager. All this after a five-week management training program.

Your task: The website suggests sending an e-mail to careers@jambajuice.com for more information. Draft such a message, asking for clarification on each of the vague points and for information about qualifications and application procedures. You'll also want to know whether the training would require traveling to the company's San Francisco headquarters. Plus, you're curious about which locations currently have openings. You wonder whether you might have to move. Decide whether or not to mention your familiarity with the company's customer base, your business education, and so on; for instance, you might mention these special qualifications in your closing to encourage a speedy reply.[10]

ROUTINE ANNOUNCEMENTS

5. Temper, temper: E-mail reminder to employees about technology failures This is the third time in two months your company, Metro Power, has had to escort an employee from the building after a violent episode. Frankly, everyone is a little frightened by this development, and as a human resources administrator, you have the unhappy task of trying to quell the storm.

Metro Power rarely fires employees, preferring to transfer them to new responsibilities, which may either draw out their finer points (and prove better for everyone in the long run) or help them decide to seek greener pastures. But in three cases, you had no choice. One man punched out his computer screen after the system failed. Another threw his keyboard across the room when he couldn't get access to the company's intranet. And in the third incident a woman kicked a printer while screaming obscenities.

In all three cases, co-workers were terrified by these sudden outbursts. Too many disgruntled workers have committed too many violent acts against others in recent years, and whenever workers lose their temper on the job these days, it causes great fear—not to mention financial losses from the destruction of property and the disruption of work flow.

People are on edge at Metro Power right now. Rising energy costs, public and government scrutiny, and cries of price gouging are causing additional work and stress for all your employees. Plus, too much overtime, unrealistic expectations for overworked departments, and high demands on sensitive equipment are contributing to the problem. Tempers are frayed and nerves strained. You're concerned that these three incidents are just the tip of the iceberg.

"Why don't you write a reminder to all employees about controlling tempers in the workplace?" your department head suggests. "Tell them that technology glitches are commonplace and not some unholy disaster. And remind them to report routine computer failures to Bart Stone. He'll get to them in due course."

You don't say anything to contradict her idea, but how can you do what she asks without sounding trite or condescending? You don't want to sound like some nagging parent—no one will pay attention to your message. You sigh deeply as your boss strolls calmly back to her office. You're fairly certain that every employee already knows about reporting computer failures to Bart Stone, assistant director of information services.

Even so, you can think of a few suggestions that might be helpful, such as taking a walk to cool down, or recognizing that machines, like humans, are not infallible. You want cooler heads to prevail, and that's just the sort of cliché you'd like to avoid in your message.

Your task: Write the e-mail message to all employees. Instead of uttering platitudes or wagging your finger, include preventive maintenance tips for office equipment, such as turning systems off at night, keeping food and liquids away from keyboards, making use of dusting sprays and special cloths, and so on. Your boss also asked you to make it clear that abusive behavior will be reprimanded, so include that point in a tactful way.[11]

6. Skimmers beware: Warning letter to Capital One customers about credit card fraud "Isn't there anything consumers can do?" you ask in disbelief.

Capital One vice president Shauna Perkins has just concluded a presentation to gathered executives on the latest twist in credit card fraud. At her side is agent Tim Raymond from the Secret Service financial crimes division.

"All they can do is take precautionary measures," replies Perkins. "And we all know what those are: Check your statements, check your statements online during the month or call automated account services to review charges, and report any discrepancies as soon as possible. Unfortunately, that might be 30 to 60 days after the crime."

One of your co-workers pipes up, "But what if you're on vacation and don't get your mail, or you don't have computer or phone access?"

"Well," Perkins hesitates, "obviously using cash is an option, but that's not the option we want our customers to take.

Of course, they're not liable for any spurious charges on their account, but they'll have to prove fraud." She turns back to you and you know what's coming. "As our director of consumer fraud, you will need to inform our customers about this new scam as soon as possible."

"Yes, of course," you mumble. You're stunned by the overwhelming advantage carved out by the bad guys this time. They're more organized and more technologically sophisticated than most credit card customers. Worse, they're stealing millions at a time to finance even more serious crimes.

Perkins did a good job of explaining everything during the meeting. The crooks are using small devices, about the size of a pager, to "skim" vital information from a credit card's magnetic strip, including cardholder name, account number, expiration date, and the invisible verification codes introduced in the early 1990s to foil counterfeit cards. These algorithms, based on account numbers, are normally transmitted from merchants to the credit card company to validate the card at the point of sale. But with that code, an electronically indistinguishable duplicate card can be created.

The actual "skimming" is done by a dishonest waiter or store clerk who has been paid to conceal the skimming device in a coat pocket, inside a jacket, or under a counter. The data are stored and later downloaded into a computer. From there, the stolen codes can be transmitted anywhere in the world via the Internet, often to Europe, Asia (where the practice originated), or Latin America. Phony cards are embedded with the stolen codes, and purchases can be made within hours.

All your customers can do is report any discrepancies in their statements to your customer services department and try to cope with the ensuing hassle of proving the fraud, discontinuing their old cards, and getting new ones.

"If it's any consolation," agent Raymond adds, "new technologies are beginning to help. Visa has already begun using a higher-coercivity tape with a higher magnetic pull, and MasterCard is experimenting with embedding the last three digits of the account number in the plastic, not the mag stripe. In the future, fingerprinting may become a routine part of the card validation process."

Your task: Write a letter to Capital One consumers, warning them about skimming. Advise them of the precautionary measures, and suggest that they keep a close watch on their cards when handing them over for transactions. Try to encourage customers to continue using their cards, despite the risks.[12]

7. Got it covered? Letter from American Express about SUV rentals You can always tell when fall arrives at American Express—you are deluged with complaints from customers who've just received their summer vacation bills. Often these angry calls are about a shock-inducing damage repair bill from a car rental agency. Vacation car rentals can be a lot more complicated than most people think. Here's what happens.

Your credit card customers are standing at the Hertz or Avis counter, ready to drive away, when the agent suggests an upgrade to, say, a Ford Excursion or another of those monstrous gas-eaters that families love to drive on city streets. Feeling happy-go-lucky on vacation, your customers say, "Why not?" and hand over their American Express card.

As they drive off in the lumbering, unfamiliar, supersize SUV, 9 out of 10 are unaware that the most common accidents among rental cars take place at low speeds in parking lots. Plus, the upgraded vehicle they're driving is no longer fully covered either by their regular auto insurance or by the secondary car rental insurance they expect from American Express. If they've agreed to pay the additional $10 to $25 a day for the car rental agency's "collision and liability damage wavier fee," they will be able to walk away from any accident with no liability. Otherwise, they're running a costly risk.

Soon they pull into a shopping mall with the kids to pick up the forgotten sunscreen and sodas, where they discover that this luxury van is not so easy to park in stalls designed when compact cars were all the rage. *Thwack*—there goes the door panel. *Crunch*—a rear bumper into a light post. *Wham!* There goes the family bank account, but they don't realize it yet—not until they receive the bill from the rental agency, the one that comes *after* their auto insurance and credit card companies have already paid as much as they're going to pay for damages.

Auto insurers typically provide the same coverage for rentals as you carry on your own car. When customers use their credit card to pay for car rentals, American Express offers secondary protection that generally covers any remaining, unpaid damages. But there are important exceptions.

Neither insurance nor credit card companies will pay the "loss of vehicle use fees" that car rental agencies always tack on. These fees can run into thousands of dollars, based on the agency's revenue losses while their car is in the repair shop. When your customers are billed for this fee, they invariably call you, angrily demanding to know why American Express won't pay it. And if they've rented an SUV, they're even angrier.

American Express Green and Gold cards provide secondary coverage up to $55,000, and the Platinum card extends that to $75,000. But large SUVs such as the Ford Expedition, GMC Yukon, and Chevrolet Suburban are not covered at all. Such exclusions are common. For instance, Diners Club specifically excludes "high-value, special interest or exotic cars"—such as the Ferraris, Maseratis, and even Rolls Royces that are urged on customers by rental agencies.

Your task: As assistant vice president of customer service, you'd like to keep the phone lines cooler this summer. It's April, so there's still time. Write a form letter to be sent to all American Express customers, urging them to check their rental car coverages, warning them to rent no vehicles larger than they require, and encouraging them to consider paying the rental agency's daily loss waiver fees. [13]

8. Mind your own e-mail: Memo stating electronic privacy policy at the *Los Angeles Times* When you stepped into your office at the *Los Angeles Times* this morning, the place was buzzing with gossip about a reporter in the paper's Moscow bureau. Apparently he'd been snooping into his fellow reporters' e-mail. To catch him, supervisors there set up a "sting" operation, planting an exchange of phony e-mail messages with the Jerusalem bureau, which cooperated in catching the snoop. The bogus e-mail referred to "shrinking travel allowances."

The suspect took the bait, apparently using a co-worker's password to view the e-mail. When he later mentioned the new travel rules, he was slapped with a reassignment back to Los Angeles, to an as-yet-undesignated job—probably writing obituaries, or so the rumormongers in your office have decided.

The *Los Angeles Times* has always observed strict discipline with regard to journalistic ethics. But because journalists traditionally hold "confidentiality" in high regard, management assumed that e-mail privacy needed no special rules or enforcement policies. Clearly, that assumption was wrong. In the past, the company casually conveyed a list of commonsense e-mail guidelines, such as not using the system for personal business; being aware that your e-mail is not invisible to computer system administrators or even managers; not using derogatory language, obscenity, or copyrighted material; and so on. Now, a strict "privacy policy" will be added to the list, which will be sent out to bureau managers in an official memo.

As an employee of the newspaper's legal department, you've been handed the task of writing the memo to managers. Outline the company's policy for handling e-mail privacy violations. Management has already decided the penalties: reassignment, suspension without pay, or termination of employment. What you'll be communicating is how the new penalties are to be implemented. You will also suggest that managers immediately introduce these new rules to employees in a special meeting and that they routinely explain all the rules and guidelines to new hires.

For a first offense, the penalty will be a verbal warning in a personal meeting with a direct supervisor, which will also be entered in writing in the employee's human resources file. For a second offense, reassignment or suspension without pay, for a period to be determined by the employee's supervisor (who will know best the most appropriate length of time). A third offense will result in immediate termination without severance pay.

Your task: Address your memo to news bureau managers (who oversee editorial offices around the globe). Outline the company's policy for handling employees who violate e-mail privacy rules. Explain that a more detailed company-issued policy memo covering all issues will be in their hands in a few weeks and must be posted at each bureau in an area visible to employees. For managerial reference in the meantime, list the penalties for privacy violations, and the appropriate sequence for applying them.[14]

ROUTINE REPLIES

9. Satellite farming: Letter granting credit from Deere & Company This is the best part of your job with Deere & Company in Moline, Illinois: saying yes to a farmer. In this case, it's Arlen Ruestman in Toluca, Illinois. Ruestman wants to take advantage of new farming technology. Your company's new GreenStar system uses satellite technology originally developed by the defense department: the Global Positioning System (GPS). By using a series of satellites orbiting Earth, the system can pinpoint (to the meter) exactly where a farmer is positioned at any given moment as he drives his GreenStar-equipped combine over a field. For farmers like Ruestman, that means a new ability to micromanage even 10,000 acres of corn or soybeans.

For instance, using the GreenStar system, farmers can map and analyze characteristics such as acidity, soil type, or crop yields from a given area. Using this information, they know exactly how much herbicide or fertilizer to spread over precisely which spot, thereby eliminating waste and achieving better results. With cross-referencing and accumulated data, farmers can analyze why crops are performing well in some areas and not so well in others. Then they can program farm equipment to treat only the problem area—for example, spraying a new insect infestation two meters wide, 300 yards down the row.

Some farms have already saved as much as $10 an acre on fertilizers alone. For 10,000 acres, that's $100,000 a year. Once Ruestman retrofits your GreenStar precision package on his old combine and learns all its applications, he should have no problem saving enough to pay off the $7,350 credit account you're about to grant him.

Your task: Write a letter to Mr. Ruestman (P.O. Box 4067, Toluca, IL 61369), informing him of the good news.[15]

10. Online expertise: Letter of recommendation for LifeSketch.com executive Mike Smith is founder, president, and CEO of LifeSketch.com (www.lifesketch.com). As his assistant, you've seen a lot of people come and go—but no one you'd rather see stay than Creative Director Becky Sharp. When you overheard her ask Smith for a letter of recommendation, you sat up and took notice. Was Becky leaving?

"She just wants to be prepared," Smith assures you. "You know how start-ups go: work hard, attract investors, make a good showing with your IPO—and then it's up to the world to find you and embrace you or send you off to another job as fast as you can say 'e-business.'"

LifeSketch is a good concept—good enough to attract Smith. As former president and CEO of apparel retailer Lands' End (www.landsend.com), Smith succeeded in building Landsend.com into one of the only retail sites on the web to actually make a profit. Smith brought Becky Sharp with him from Lands' End, where she had been creative director and had done a terrific job revamping the Landsend.com site.

But now Sharp's challenge is even more difficult. The Lands' End consumers had been accustomed to buying clothes from the retailer. Now Sharp must develop a market for an entirely new product. LifeSketch.com must convince visitors to preserve their memories in digital format. By becoming members, visitors can upload their family photographs and store them online (20 MB free, 100 MB at $29.95 per year, 250 MB at $49.95 per year). Members can also turn these photos into a multimedia digital photo album, the Sketchbook, using free art, backgrounds, audio clips, and text. Plus, for just $19.95, members can buy a CD of the finished product. So far, Sharp has designed a site that's entertaining and easy to navigate. She's been working long, hard hours to do it, and Smith is thrilled by the results.

Smith has every intention of fulfilling Sharp's request for a letter of recommendation, but his schedule is packed, so he asks you to write the first draft. "She's wise to keep her résumé polished at all times," he explains to you, "and we owe her at least that much. She's already made us look good at two companies!

"You know her work as well as I do," he continues. "Just don't forget to mention the way she collected 3,000 photos and then featured online those few that convey exactly the 'nostalgic hip family' feeling that LifeSketch needs to evoke." He sighs as he turns back to his office, "What would we do without her?"

Your task: Try to capture Smith's appreciation in your recommendation draft, but make sure it's believable.[16]

11. Betting the company: Letter from Boeing replying to questions about new aircraft plans The moment Boeing chairman Phil Condit made the announcement, the questions started pouring in by letter, fax, and e-mail. Why wasn't Boeing following the lead of its competitor, Airbus Industrie, in developing a new superjumbo jet?

For decades, Boeing aircraft company reigned supreme in the market for supersize commercial airplanes, selling its popular 416-seat 747 jumbo jets to airlines around the world. But shortly after you took a job in corporate communications for Seattle-based Boeing in 1999, the company took a big hit from its overseas rival, Airbus. That year, Airbus sold twice as many planes as Boeing.

Airbus has always approached manufacturing differently. Founded by a group of partners in Great Britain, Germany, France, and Spain, Airbus assembles its planes in Toulouse, France, using parts manufactured all over the world. Boeing traditionally manufactured everything in-house, until competition from Airbus and a financial crisis in the mid-1990s brought about a corporate restructuring. Now Boeing also uses subcontractors. But that's where the imitation is going to stop, according to chairman Condit.

With huge fanfare, Airbus announced its vision of commercial air travel in the future: more people wanting to fly to the major terminals, with airports unable to handle more planes. So Airbus is spending $12 billion to create a superjumbo jet that will carry 555 to 650 passengers in a double-decker design, using the latest technology and lightweight materials. The company claims that its A380 will cost 21 cents less per "seat mile" to operate than a 747, but it won't fly any faster.

Boeing sees a different future: airlines wanting smaller, faster jets to reach smaller, less-congested airports in the suburbs. So Boeing is designing the Sonic Cruiser, which will save one hour of traditional flying time for every 3,000 miles flown by traveling at Mach .95 (or 95 percent of the speed of sound). That's 20 percent faster than today's jets.

The Sonic Cruiser will cost $10 billion to design, but Boeing is betting that new, smaller airports will be built and that its sleek, swept-back "delta wing" jet, which will also fly at longer ranges, will become the ideal vehicle for reaching them.

Older airports may have to spend hundreds of millions of dollars to upgrade facilities to service the two-level Airbus A380. And it will be useful only for heavily traveled routes, since airlines will need to fill all 550 seats. On the other hand, the Sonic Cruiser's faster flights will let airlines charge premium prices while costing less to operate because of reduced flying time. Moreover, designing a new aircraft will allow Boeing to develop more efficient manufacturing, using outside suppliers for parts so that Boeing's engineers can focus on the more sophisticated systems.

Boeing is betting that airlines will choose its Sonic Cruiser over the huge A380s, but it will be years before either company knows who'll win the market. Both planes aren't due out until 2006 or later.

Your task: Draft a form reply letter to be sent to the customers, suppliers, and general public who have contacted Boeing to learn why the company is not manufacturing a superjumbo. In your letter, focus on what Boeing is doing, rather than what it's not doing.[17]

12. Lighten up: E-mail reply to a website designer at Organizers Unlimited Designing your Superclean Organizer was comparatively easy. It's a clever device for organizing bathroom items that families accumulate under sinks and in drawers—shampoo bottles, soaps, sponges, deodorants, cosmetics, antiseptics, sunscreens, hairbrushes, loofahs, cotton balls, toothbrushes, toothpaste, and so on. You've created the perfect organizer to handle it all. Setting up your company—Organizers Unlimited—and getting your product into retail stores wasn't much more difficult. But designing a website—now that's a headache.

At first you thought you'd do it all yourself. You did your homework, reading all about website design for small businesses. You learned a lot, but realized you needed to hire a professional. You chose Pete Womack, whose résumé impressed you. Now he's e-mailed his first design proposal and you're stunned.

He's loaded up the homepage with graphics and animation—what you've heard others describe as "dancing baloney"—at least 500 kilobytes (K) worth of bouncing cotton balls, swishing hairbrushes, and jogging soap bars. Clever, it may be, but over your dead body! It was your hatred of clutter that inspired you to design the Superclean Organizer in the first place, and you dislike cluttered websites even more. They take forever to load, especially with your 56-kilobytes-per-second (K bps) dial-up modem.

During your research, you learned that creating "heavy homepages" is an Internet no-no. Experts suggest no more than 40 to 50 K of data for the first page your visitors will see. That takes about 8 to 10 seconds to load on modems like yours. If visitors don't see your homepage by then, most will "bail out," clicking off in frustration to find the same product elsewhere. And you suspect that most of your customers will be home computer users, with slower modem connections like yours.

At first you're amazed that Womack doesn't know this. But on second thought, you realize he's not alone. You read in a survey conducted by Byte Level Research that business homepages on the web average about 150 K. Some of the heaviest the survey found were for Revlon (522 K), General Motors (547 K), Nickelodeon (638 K), and Hugo Boss (646 K), companies that can afford to hire the best design talent on the Internet. According to Zona Research, this mistake costs online businesses about $362 million in lost income each month from customer bail-out.

If Womack is banking on high-speed connections such as cable or DSL being common, he shouldn't. Research indicates that the so-called "broadband revolution" hasn't happened yet.

Your task: Womack asked for your feedback on his initial design proposal. Give it to him straight, using the facts you've gathered to explain your reasons for rejecting his ideas. His e-mail address is pwomack @designsite.com. Fortunately, the design process is still in its infancy, so he won't be too shocked by your routine reply, even though it's going to suggest that he try a new angle.[18]

POSITIVE MESSAGES

13. Cold comfort: E-mail offering a regional sales position with Golight Winter in Nebraska ranch country is something to sneeze at—and to shiver over. That's why rancher Jerry Gohl invented the Golight, a portable spotlight that can be mounted on a car or truck roof and rotated 360 degrees horizontally and 70 degrees vertically *by remote control*. No more getting out of the truck in freezing, predawn temperatures to adjust a manual spotlight in order to check on his livestock in the dark. In fact, for Gohl, there's hardly any time left to check the livestock at all these days: His invention has become so popular that Golight, Inc., expects to sell more than $2 million worth of the remote-controlled lights next year.

The company expanded fast, with Golights becoming popular all over the world among hunters, boaters, commuters who fear dark-of-night roadside tire changes, and early-morning fishing enthusiasts who can scope out the best shoreline sites by controlling the spotlight from inside their warm and cozy vehicles. Sales reps have been hired for every part of the country and overseas, but Gohl has been holding out for just the right person to replace him in the Nebraska territory. After all, the company president knows better than anyone what the local ranchers need and how they think—that's why his invention was such a success there. He doesn't want to jinx his good fortune by choosing the wrong replacement.

Finally, last week he met a young man who seems a likely candidate. His name is Robert Victor, and he grew up on a Nebraska ranch, helping his dad with those 4 A.M. chores. He's young, but he's felt the bite of Nebraska's cold, he knows the rancher mind, and best of all, he's been bringing in top dollar selling agricultural equipment in Montana for the past few years. Now he wants to return to his home state. Gohl liked him from the first moment they shook hands. "He's got the job if he wants it," the boss tells you. "Better send him some e-mail before someone else grabs him. He can start as soon as he's settled."

Your task: Compose the message communicating Gohl's offer to Robert Victor: salary plus commission as discussed, full benefits (paid vacation, health and dental insurance) if he's still around in six months. His e-mail address is rvictor@ism.net. Sign with your name, as Gohl's personnel manager.[19]

14. Midnight mission: Thank-you letter at the Blue Marble bookstore As owner of the Blue Marble bookstore in Fort Thomas, Kentucky, Tina Moore won't be outdone this time. You are store manager, and along with the rest of the staff, you've been working hard to prepare for the biggest book sales party your store has ever hosted. Tonight's the night.

Last time you blew it with the popular *Harry Potter* series (about a boy who discovers he's not only a wizard-in-training, but a famous one). Book number four was to be released at 12:01 A.M. on Saturday, July 8, a "strict on sale" date in the United States and Britain. Like thousands of other adults, you've enjoyed the cleverly written stories of Harry and his friends at Hogwarts school of wizardry. But you and Moore agreed that customers would probably be content to come in for a copy on Saturday morning. Who would let their kids stay up past midnight for a book party?

Apparently, tens of thousands of parents did—all grateful to see their kids reading so avidly. On Friday night, bookstores all over the country opened up at midnight—especially the chains, your biggest competitors. By morning, very few copies of "HP4" were left, and within days the entire, record-breaking first U.S. press run of 3.8 million copies was gone. British author J. K. Rowling had done it again. Even well-known adult critics loved the new book. Rowling's U.S. publisher, Scholastic, called it a "phenomenon" in publishing history, "beyond anything we imagined."

Of course, that morning you still had copies available, but your customers felt cheated. "Why didn't you have a pajama party last night?" they complained. "My kids saw the crowds on TV and wanted to go—but the nearest chain store is miles from here!" Some fans even called your staff "clueless muggles" (non-wizards—usually the last to know about anything truly interesting). But that was last time.

This time, when the clock chimes midnight and you're allowed to sell Harry Potter number 5, your customers will be ushered in by staff members in costume. A local trainer will stroll the store with a pet owl (favorite messengers in Harry's

world). From the big black cauldrons your staff built, you'll serve oatmeal and Harry's favorite "butter beer" (apple juice and ginger ale over dry ice). The first kids in line will get free lightning-bolt stickers to create forehead scars like Harry's, and some will receive black, round-rimmed imitation "Harry Potter spectacles." It's going to be great fun.

Your task: Your staff has been working on their own time sewing costumes, making hats, and inventing butter-beer recipes. Write a thank-you letter to them from both you and Moore, and enclose a $25 gift certificate in each one. You plan to distribute the letters before tonight's party.[20]

15. On a course for Harvard: Reply to a request for a recommendation letter After working for several years for Zoe Coulson in Campbell Soup Company's department of consumer affairs, one of your co-workers, Angela Cavanaugh, has decided to apply for admission to the Harvard Business School's M.B.A. program. She has asked Coulson, a Harvard graduate, to write a letter of recommendation for her. Here are the facts about Angela Cavanaugh:

1. She has an undergraduate degree in journalism from the University of Iowa, where she was an honors student.
2. She joined Campbell directly after graduating and has worked for the firm for the past five years.
3. Her primary responsibility has been to answer letters from consumers; she has done an outstanding job.
4. Her most noteworthy achievement has been to analyze a year's worth of incoming mail, categorize the letters by type and frequency, and create a series of standardized replies. The department now uses Cavanaugh's form letters to handle approximately 75 percent of its mail.
5. Although Cavanaugh has outstanding work habits and is an excellent writer, she lacks confidence as a speaker. Her

reluctance to present her ideas orally has prevented her from advancing more rapidly at Campbell. This could be a problem for her at Harvard Business School, where skill in classroom discussion influences a student's chances of success.

Your task: Because you have worked closely with Cavanaugh, Zoe Coulson has asked you to draft the letter, which Coulson will sign.[21]

16. Boomerang back to us: E-mail from EDS to dot-com deserters "Now's our chance to get them back," announces Tom Templeton as he pounces on you after a staff meeting. The director of human resources at EDS is known to be forthright, but you're startled.

"Get who back?" you inquire calmly.

"Everyone we lost to dot-com mania! You work in human resources; you should know what kind of talent drain we suffered when stock options and overnight millionaires allowed the dot-coms to steal us blind! But now that their days are numbered, it's our turn."

You could swear that's an evil gleam in his eye. "What are you proposing?"

He rubs his chin. "Well, we could do like Deloitte Consulting. Did you see their full-page ad in the *Wall Street Journal*? They invited Internet consulting firm employees to leave their roller-coaster stock options—stocks now falling like snowflakes—for an 'innovative firm with a rock-solid foundation.' I love that phrase. I'm tempted to steal it." He winks.

"You mean invite back the 550 employees we lost to dot-coms in recent years?"

"Exactly. Recruiters are all over the sinking dot-coms these days, plucking back the talent stolen years ago from companies like ours. Well, let's put out our own call! Surely our alumni must be shaking in their boots. I read that some 12,000 dot-com jobs were cut in one nine-month period last year. That number is probably higher now. Online companies are crashing like cymbals!"

You manage a smile.

"Think how much we can save if we catch these former employees on the rebound," he adds, and you begin to see his point. No training required. Rapid orientation periods. They already know the business. And you can see on Templeton's face the pride gleaming. He's thinking that each employee who comes back will prove that stability and prudence can beat dot-com flash and dazzle any day. Plus, he'll save EDS considerable money and hassle, because finding and keeping good employees is one of the greatest costs of running any business.

"You know, I think you're right. They just might be willing to give us a second chance," you concede.

"Darn right they will. Especially after you send them an e-mail encouraging them! You have the list, don't you?"

Fortunately, you do. With commendable foresight, Templeton insisted two years ago that you keep contact records for every employee who took a dot-com job. He even invited them to company events after they left. Now he's going to reap his reward for clear thinking—with your help.

"Some of our best employees are out there looking for new jobs. Are we going to let our competitors snag them? They didn't hate us—and they weren't traitors. They were merely seeking opportunity like any intelligent person. That only proves they're good people. Well, guess whose pasture is greener now?" he says with a grin.

Your task: Tempelton has asked you, his assistant, to write an encouraging e-mail message, announcing to ex-employees that EDS will welcome them back if their "flashy" new jobs have turned into dead ends. Try to echo Templeton's sense of pride in EDS. You're not begging, exactly, just letting these former employees know that the company's rehire policy is open and liberal.[22]

17. Stargazing: News release announcing new life for Mount Wilson Observatory Today, gazing at

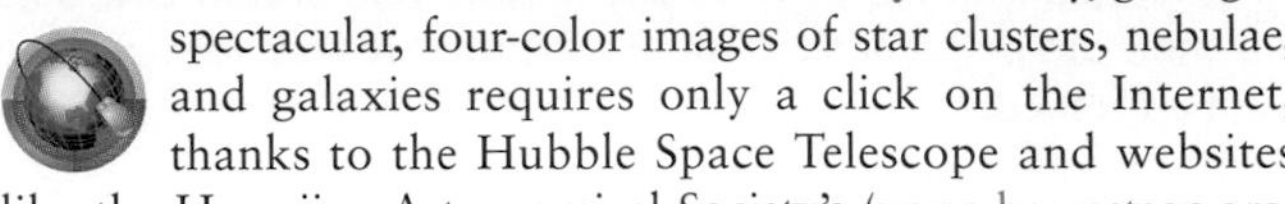

spectacular, four-color images of star clusters, nebulae, and galaxies requires only a click on the Internet, thanks to the Hubble Space Telescope and websites like the Hawaiian Astronomical Society's (www.hawastsoc.org/deepsky/index.html). But in 1929, Edwin P. Hubble searched the stars night after night, climbing up to a chilly wooden platform high in the dome housing the 100-inch Hooker telescope at the Mount Wilson Observatory on the outskirts of Los Angeles. His computer-bereft studies of light from distant galaxies required endless analysis of crude photographic plates taken with the help of his assistant, a former mule skinner named Milton Humason. Their hard work paid off, however, and Hubble is credited with discovering the redshift that is the basis for the Big Bang theory of an expanding universe.

With the famous new space-based telescope named in his honor, we won't forget Hubble. But Mount Wilson and the Hooker telescope faded from importance as scientists rushed to larger scopes on bigger, darker mountains. In the 1980s, the Hooker was closed for eight years. Its 4.5- ton, green-glass mirror (built by a French wine-bottle manufacturer) became no more than a relic to curious visitors to the site in the San Gabriel Mountains, outside Pasadena.

Now the organization you work for, the Mount Wilson Institute in Pasadena, California, administers a reborn observatory, playing host to scientists from all over the map. And the Hooker telescope is once again making history.

For example, a team led by Dr. Laird Thompson of the University of Illinois is using the Hooker to test a computerized system of "laser adaptive optics." Adaptive optics have long been used to cancel the blur caused by atmospheric distortions, relying on natural guide stars to give computers a standard for making optical adjustments. But certain areas of space lack sufficient guide stars. Dr. Thompson's team is testing a 12-mile-high ultraviolet laser beam, sent into space at 333 pulses a second, as an artificial guide for adjustments. The resulting views are clearer than anything Hubble ever saw.

Mount Wilson also features an older, 60-inch telescope, a 60-foot solar tower operated by the University of Southern California for NASA, and a 150-foot solar tower run by the University of California at Los Angeles. A group headed by Dr. Harold A. McAlister (from Georgia State University) and another led by Nobel Prize–winning physicist Dr. Charles Townes (from the University of California at Berkeley) are both at the observatory conducting tests with "interferometry," using arrays of small telescopes to collect starlight simultaneously.

McAlister's team combines six small telescopes to mimic the effect of a single scope with an 1,100-foot mirror—

impossible to build, but capable of detecting stellar details 200 times finer than the Hubble Space Telescope. Townes's group is using an array to make star surfaces visible beneath dust clouds.

Your task: Targeting science journalists, write a news release from the Mount Wilson Institute, a non-profit, tax-exempt consortium of astronomers, educators, and private donors, which is directed by Dr. Robert Jastrow, former NASA scientist and author of astronomy books. You're hoping for news coverage of the observatory's new activities, which may attract donors. At the close of your release, invite journalists to sign up for a night tour with Dr. Jastrow and the scientists mentioned. Journalists can request a detailed science data sheet now or at the tour.[23]

Writing Bad-News Messages

After studying this chapter, you will be able to

1. *Apply the three-step writing process to bad-news messages*
2. *Show how to achieve an audience-centered tone and explain why it helps readers*
3. *Differentiate between the direct and indirect organizational approaches to bad-news messages and discuss when it's appropriate to use each one*
4. *Discuss the three techniques for saying no as clearly and kindly as possible*
5. *Define* defamation *and explain how to avoid it in bad-news messages*
6. *List three guidelines for delivering bad news to job applicants and give a brief explanation of each one*
7. *Outline the main purpose of performance reviews, give three ways to accomplish that purpose, and list five guidelines to follow when giving negative reviews*

COMMUNICATION CLOSE-UP AT CAPONIGRO PUBLIC RELATIONS

www.caponigro.com

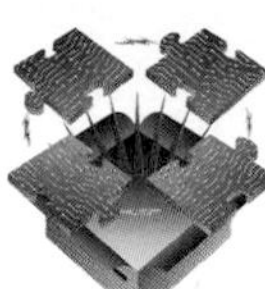

Employee layoffs, product recalls, tainted fast food—bad news in the business world comes in all shapes and sizes. But even though bad news may be commonplace, Jeffrey Caponigro has observed that most businesspeople don't know how to communicate this type of news effectively. "They convince themselves that it's far better to bury their heads in the sand and hope the problem won't be exposed," says Caponigro, president and CEO of Caponigro Public Relations in Detroit, Michigan. "Also, they're fearful of the damage bad news can cause—poor employee morale, lost customers, reduced revenues, litigation, and other unpleasant effects."

But hiding from bad news doesn't make it go away, Caponigro cautions. Working in public relations for over 20 years, Caponigro has helped dozens of companies communicate bad news on such topics as plant closings, product-related lawsuits, criminal investigations, and other unfavorable situations. "The worst mistake is the tendency to clam up and pull back from communicating, rather than recognizing the need to communicate with even greater efficiency and effectiveness," he explains.

To establish an effective tone for bad-news messages, Caponigro first considers the audience. "Put yourself in the shoes of those who will receive the bad news," he advises. "How does this news affect them? What will they be concerned about? What will they want to know? What questions can we answer in advance? Thinking it through will help organize the presentation of the bad news and make it more effective to communicate and to understand."

When planning bad-news messages, Caponigro focuses on keeping the audience informed by developing a small number of key messages to communicate first. "Show your audience that you have the situation under control and recognize their need to know the facts as soon as possible. If it's a decision that you know will be seen as bad news—such as laying off a large number of people in your company—describe how you arrived at the difficult decision," he says. Caponigro often advises clients to explain the options that they considered, how they attempted to avoid the bad-news decision, their concern and sensitivity for the situation, and why they believe they've acted in the company's best interest. "In many cases," he explains, "it's important for the customer to know how the bad news occurred, what lessons were learned from it, and what is being done to ensure it won't occur again."

To maintain goodwill with an audience, Caponigro sticks with the facts and avoids speculation in bad-news communication. "First and foremost, a company needs to be seen as honest, trustworthy, and credible. A great deal of damage can be caused by misleading someone—even if it was done unintentionally," he says. Which means you should carefully consider your choice of words for bad-news messages. In written messages, "you have a better opportunity to carefully wordsmith what you are saying and how you are saying it." Still, Caponigro cautions clients to use "the same principles and thought process when communicating bad news to someone in person."

Jeffrey Caponigro, president of Caponigro Public Relations, advises clients to focus on the audience's information needs and concerns when delivering bad news.

Of course, communicating bad news isn't always easy, but the proper tone and approach can help people accept and understand your message. As Caponigro advises clients, "Most people will forgive just about anything if you admit to it, take responsibility for it, explain how it happened, and tell what you're doing to ensure it won't occur again."[1] ■

USING THE THREE-STEP WRITING PROCESS FOR BAD-NEWS MESSAGES

Learning Objective 1

Apply the three-step writing process to bad-news messages

As Jeffrey Caponigro can attest, nobody likes bad news. People don't like to get it, and they don't like to give it. Saying no to an idea from an employee, a proposal from a shareholder, a request from a customer, or even a suggestion from your boss can put knots in your stomach and cost you hours of sleep.

The word *no* is terse and abrupt, so negative that a lot of people have difficulty saying it. And for most, it's the toughest word to hear or understand. The delivery can be far more damaging than the answer itself. But the most damaging *no* is usually the one you don't explain.[2] That's why you must be careful whenever you deliver bad news. The three-step process can help you write bad-news messages that are more effective and less damaging.

Step 1: Planning Your Bad-News Messages

Analysis, investigation, and adaptation help you avoid alienating your readers.

When your message is a negative one, analysis becomes extremely important. If your purpose is specific, you are able to word it in the best possible way. You want to be sure that a bad-news message should indeed be sent and should definitely be sent in writing (versus communicating it face-to-face or in a quick phone call). And more than ever, you need to know how your audience will receive your message. Do readers prefer to receive negative news up front, without delay? Or would they accept the news more readily if you explained your reasons first?

Any investigation or research must yield reliable, unmistakable facts that will support your negative decision. You'll want to be sure that you have all the facts your audience will need. After sending your bad news, you don't want to face a barrage of questions from confused readers.

Finally, you'll want to pay particular attention to maintaining a good relationship with your audience. Be sure to adapt your medium and tone to your audience. Careful attention to adaptation can help you avoid alienating your readers.

Step 2: Writing Your Bad-News Messages

The appropriate organization helps readers accept your negative news.

In a bad-news message, your main idea is a refusal, a rejection, or a negative announcement, so you want to be careful to define that main idea and to cover relevant points thoroughly and logically. Choosing between the direct and indirect approaches takes on added importance in bad-news messages. You need to know whether it will be better to open with the bad news or to prepare your readers with a cogent explanation before giving them the negative bits. You also need to pay special attention to word choice so that you can create sentences and paragraphs that are tactful and diplomatic.

Step 3: Completing Your Bad-News Messages

Revision is as important as the other steps in the writing process; it helps you make sure that your bad-news messages are organized properly, that they say what you want them to say, and that they do so concisely and clearly. You'll want to make sure that your design is appropriate for the bad news and contributes to your efforts to be sensitive. And as always, proofreading bad-news messages guarantees that misunderstandings won't arise from typos, errors in spelling, or problems with mechanics.

DEVELOPING STRATEGIES FOR BAD-NEWS MESSAGES

It's bad news when you refuse to grant a claim, encounter problems filling an order, announce that quarter profits are down, or give an employee a negative performance review. Whatever the details of your particular message, when you have bad news, you want your readers to feel that they have been taken seriously and to agree that your news is fair and reasonable.

Five goals of bad-news messages:

- Give the bad news
- Ensure its acceptance
- Maintain reader's goodwill
- Maintain organization's good image
- Reduce future correspondence on the matter

When delivering bad news, you have five main goals: (1) to convey the bad news, (2) to gain acceptance for it, (3) to maintain as much goodwill as possible with your audience, (4) to maintain a good image for your organization, and (5) to reduce or eliminate the need for future correspondence on the matter. Accomplishing so many goals in a single message is not easy. But you can make your bad-news messages effective by following these guidelines: First, adopt an audience-centered tone. Second, organize your message to meet your audience's needs and expectations by using either the direct approach, which presents the main idea before the supporting data (fully described in Chapter 7), or the indirect approach, which presents the supporting data before the main idea.

Creating an Audience-Centered Tone

Learning Objective 2

Show how to achieve an audience-centered tone and explain why it helps readers

When establishing tone, strive for

- Firmness
- Fairness
- Goodwill
- Respect

You've heard it before: It's not *what* you say but *how* you say it that counts. That adage couldn't be truer with bad-news messages. Your tone contributes to your message's effectiveness by helping your readers

- Accept that your bad-news represents a firm decision
- Understand that, under the circumstances, your decision was fair and reasonable
- Remain well disposed toward your business
- Preserve their pride

Dr. Robert Buckman, a breast cancer specialist, has delivered more than his share of bad news. Now Buckman teaches doctors and other business executives how to deliver bad news effectively. Communicators can adopt an audience-centered tone by listening to the audience first instead of talking, advises Buckman. "You can

TABLE 8.1 Choosing Positive Words

Avoid a Negative Tone	***Use a Positive Tone***
I *cannot understand* what you mean.	Please clarify your request.
The *damage* won't be fixed for a week.	The item will be repaired next week.
There will be a *delay* in your order.	We will ship your order as soon as possible.
You are clearly *dissatisfied.*	We are doing what we can to make things right.
Your account is in *error.*	Corrections have been made to your account.
The breakage was not our *fault.*	The merchandise was broken during shipping.
Sorry for your inconvenience.	The enclosed coupon will save you $5 next time.
We *regret* the misunderstanding.	I'll try my best to be more clear from now on.
I was *shocked* to learn that you're unhappy.	Your letter reached me yesterday.
Unfortunately, we haven't received it.	It hasn't arrived yet.
The enclosed statement is *wrong.*	Please recheck the enclosed statement.

build trust by letting people say what they feel first," says Buckman. "Eventually it will be time for you to talk." Buckman emphasizes that because bad news involves emotions, you must acknowledge these emotions in your communication. A good empathic response acknowledges someone's feelings. But, notes Buckman, "you can't let those emotions interfere with your message. If you've got to fire somebody, you can't *not* fire him because he's crying."[3]

Of course, if you are delivering bad news in writing versus communicating it orally, you may not be able to "listen" to your audience first. But you can certainly do your research up front and learn as much as possible about your audience so that you can demonstrate in your written communication that you are aware of your audience's needs, concerns, and feelings. Experts suggest that you adopt an audience-centered tone by paying attention to these techniques:

Carly Fiorina, CEO of Hewlett-Packard, builds and maintains strong relationships with customers, employees, and investors by focusing on audience feelings. She explains the reasons for any bad news and tries to focus on the positive aspects of a negative situation.

- **Use the "you" attitude.** Using the "you" attitude is crucial to every message you write, but it's especially important in bad-news messages. For example, point out how your decision might actually further your audience's goals. Convey concern by looking for the best in your audience. And assume that your audience is interested in being fair, even when they are at fault.
- **Choose positive words.** As Jeffrey Caponigro can tell you, wording and tone conspire to make a letter either offensive or acceptable. You can ease disappointment by using positive words rather than negative, counterproductive ones (see Table 8.1). Just be sure that your positive tone doesn't hide the bad news behind difficult language.[4] Remember, you want to convey the bad news, not cover it up.
- **Use respectful language.** When you use language that conveys respect and avoids an accusing tone, you protect your audience's pride. For instance, when refusing an adjustment or a claim, try using third-person, impersonal, passive language to explain your audience's mistakes in an inoffensive way. This approach downplays the doer of the action because the doer is not specified. Say, "The appliance won't work after being immersed in water" instead of "You shouldn't have immersed the appliance in water." When your audience is at fault, the "you" attitude is better observed by avoiding the word *you*.

The "you" attitude is especially important in bad-news messages.

Use positive rather than negative phrasing in bad-news messages.

Sometimes the "you" attitude is best observed by avoiding the word *you*.

FIGURE 8.1 Differences Between the Indirect and Direct Organizational Plans for Bad-News Messages

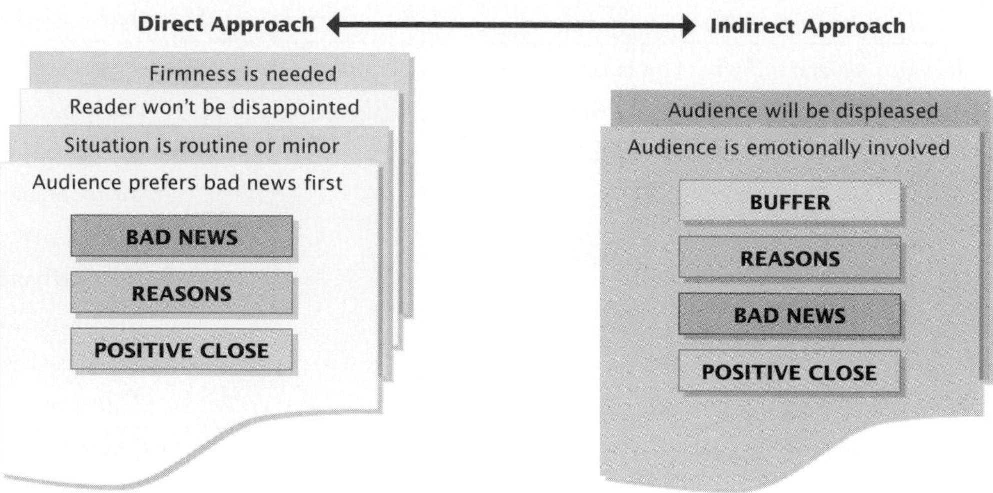

Using the Direct Approach

Learning Objective 3

Differentiate between the direct and indirect organizational approaches to bad-news messages and discuss when it's appropriate to use each one

Audience analysis is crucial for determining organization of bad-news messages.

As with most business messages, the key to choosing the best approach for bad-news messages is to analyze audience members first. Try to put yourself in their shoes. What is their likely reaction to the news? How important is the message? How well do you know them? Some people like to know the bad news right away. Similarly, some situations are more appropriate for directness than others. If you know that your audience is likely to prefer the bad news first, or if the situation is minor and the news will cause your audience little pain or disappointment, use the direct approach.

A bad-news message organized using the direct approach starts with a clear statement of the bad news, proceeds to the reasons for the decision (perhaps offering alternatives), and ends with a positive statement aimed at maintaining a good relationship with the audience (see Figure 8.1). Stating the bad news at the beginning can have two advantages: (1) It makes a shorter message possible, and (2) the audience needs less time to reach the main idea of the message, the bad news itself.

When the City of New York (property owner) informed vendors of New York City's Mart 125 in Harlem that the property was being redeveloped for more "profitable" uses, the letter got right to the point. Omar Fall (vendor) received the eviction notice and immediately began packing up his merchandise for sale.

Memos are often organized so that the bad news comes before the reasons. Some managers expect all internal correspondence to be brief and direct, regardless of whether the message is positive or negative. Routine bad-news messages to other companies often follow the direct approach, especially if they relay decisions that have little or no personal impact. The indirect approach can actually cause ill will in people who see bad news frequently (such as people searching for employment).[5] In addition, you'll sometimes know from experience that your audience simply prefers reading the bad news first in any message. The direct approach is also appropriate when you want to present an image of firmness and strength; for example, the last message in a debt collection series (just before the matter is turned over to an attorney) usually gets right to the point.

You may want to use the direct approach in a variety of circumstances, saving your positive comments for the close. Even so, remember that a tactful tone and a focus on reasons will help make any bad-news message easier to accept.

Use the direct approach when your negative answer or information will have little personal impact.

Using the Indirect Approach

Beginning a bad-news message with a blunt "no" could well prevent people who prefer an explanation first from reading or listening to your reasons. For such audiences, the indirect approach is appropriate. This approach eases the audience into your message by explaining your reasons before delivering the bad news. Presenting the reasons first increases your chances of gaining audience acceptance by gradually preparing readers for the negative news to come. The indirect approach follows a four-part sequence (as shown in Figure 8.1): (1) Open with a buffer, (2) continue with a logical, neutral explanation of the reasons for the bad news, (3) follow with a clear but diplomatic statement of the bad news (emphasizing any good news and de-emphasizing the bad), and (4) close with a positive, forward-looking statement that is helpful and friendly.

Use the indirect approach when some preparation will help your audience accept your bad news.

Begin with a Buffer

The first step in using the indirect approach is to make a neutral, noncontroversial statement that is closely related to the point of the message; this statement is called a **buffer**. A good buffer is tricky to write. Some critics believe that using a buffer is manipulative, dishonest, and thus unethical. In fact, buffers are unethical only if they're insincere. Breaking bad news with kindness and courtesy is the humane way. Consideration for the feelings of others is never dishonest, and that consideration helps your audience accept your message.

A buffer is a neutral lead-in to bad news.

A good buffer expresses your appreciation for being thought of, assures the reader of your attention to the request, compliments the reader, or indicates your understanding of the reader's needs. A buffer must not insult the audience with insincere flattery or self-promoting blather. Because it sets the stage for the bad news to follow, it must be both sincere and relevant so that readers don't feel they are being set up or "snowed." For example, in a memo telling another supervisor that you can't spare anyone from your staff for a temporary assignment to the order fulfillment department, you might begin with a sentence like this:

Use a buffer that is
- Neutral
- Relevant
- Not misleading
- Assertive
- Succinct

Our department shares your goal of processing orders quickly and efficiently.

If possible, base your buffer on statements made by the person you're responding to. This type of buffer shows the person that you have listened well. If you use an unrelated buffer, you will seem to be avoiding the issue; that is, you'll appear manipulative and unethical, and you'll lose your audience's respect.

Another goal when composing your buffer is to avoid giving the impression that good news will follow. Building up your audience's expectations at the beginning only makes the actual bad news even more surprising. Imagine your reaction to the following openings:

To write an effective buffer, avoid giving the impression that good news will follow.

Your résumé indicates that you would be well suited for a management trainee position with our company.

Your résumé shows very clearly why you are interested in becoming a management trainee with our company.

The second opening emphasizes the applicant's interpretation of her qualifications rather than the company's evaluation, so it's less misleading but still positive. Here are some other things to avoid when writing a buffer:

- **Avoid saying no.** An audience encountering the blunt refusal right at the beginning usually reacts negatively to the rest of the message, no matter how reasonable and well phrased it is.
- **Avoid using a know-it-all tone.** When you use phrases such as "you should be aware that," readers expect your lecture to lead to a negative response, so they resist the rest of your message.
- **Avoid wordy and irrelevant phrases and sentences.** Sentences such as "We have received your letter," "This letter is in reply to your request," and "We are writing in response to your request" are irrelevant. Make better use of the space by referring directly to the subject of the letter.

TABLE 8.2 Types of Buffers

Buffer	*Strategy*	*Example*
Agreement	Find a point on which you and the reader share similar views.	We both know how hard it is to make a profit in this industry.
Appreciation	Express sincere thanks for receiving something.	Your check for $127.17 arrived yesterday. Thank you.
Cooperation	Convey your willingness to help in any way you realistically can.	Employee Services is here to smooth the way for all of you who work to achieve company goals.
Fairness	Assure the reader that you've closely examined and carefully considered the problem, or mention an appropriate action that has already been taken.	For the past week, we have carefully monitored those using the photocopying machine to see whether we can detect any pattern of use that might explain its frequent breakdowns.
Good news	Start with the part of your message that is favorable.	A replacement knob for your range is on its way, shipped February 10 via UPS.
Praise	Find an attribute or an achievement to compliment.	Your résumé shows an admirable breadth of experience, which should serve you well as you progress in your career.
Resale	Favorably discuss the product or company related to the subject of the letter.	With their heavy-duty, full-suspension hardware and fine veneers, the desks and file cabinets in our Montclair line have become a hit with value-conscious professionals.
Understanding	Demonstrate that you understand the reader's goals and needs.	So that you can more easily find the printer with the features you need, we are enclosing a brochure that describes all the Panasonic printers currently available.

- **Avoid apologizing.** Unless warranted by extreme circumstances, an apology only weakens the explanation of your unfavorable news that follows.
- **Avoid writing a buffer that is too long.** Be brief. Identify something that both you and your audience are interested in and agree on before proceeding in a businesslike way.

Table 8.2 shows several types of buffers you could use to open a bad-news message tactfully.

After you've composed a buffer, evaluate it by asking yourself four questions: Is it pleasant? Is it relevant? Is it neutral, saying neither yes nor no? Does it provide for a smooth transition to the reasons that follow? If you can answer yes to every question, you can proceed confidently to the next section of your message.

Follow with Reasons

Present reasons to show that your decision is reasonable and fair.

If you've done a good job of composing the buffer, the reasons will follow naturally. Cover the more positive points first; then move to the less positive ones. Provide enough detail for the audience to understand your reasons, but be concise; a long, roundabout explanation may make your audience impatient. Your goal is to explain *why* you have reached your decision before you explain *what* that decision is. If you present your reasons effectively, they should convince your audience that your decision is justified, fair, and logical.

Focus on how the audience might benefit from your negative message.

One way to be tactful when giving your reasons is to highlight how your negative decision benefits your readers (rather than focusing on why the decision is good for you or your company). For example, when denying a credit request, you can show how your decision will keep the person from becoming overextended financially. Facts and figures are often helpful in convincing members of your audience that you're acting in their best interests.

Avoid hiding behind company policy to cushion the bad news. If you say, "Company policy forbids our hiring anyone who does not have two years' management experience," you seem to imply that you haven't considered the person on her or his own merits. Skilled and sympathetic communicators explain company policy (without referring to it as "policy") so that the audience can try to meet the requirements at a later time.

Similarly, avoid apologizing when giving your reasons. Apologies are appropriate only when someone in your company has made a severe mistake or has done something terribly wrong. If no one in the company is at fault, an apology gives the wrong impression. For example, suppose you're refusing the application of a management trainee. A tactfully worded letter might give these reasons for the decision not to hire:

Because these management trainee positions are quite challenging, our human relations department has researched the qualifications needed to succeed in them. The findings show that the two most important qualifications are a bachelor's degree in business administration and two years' supervisory experience.

The paragraph does a good job of stating the reasons for the refusal:

- It provides enough detail to make the reason for the refusal logically acceptable.
- It implies that the applicant is better off avoiding a program in which he or she would probably fail, given the background of potential co-workers.
- It explains the company's policy as logical rather than rigid.
- It offers no apology for the decision.
- It avoids negative personal expressions ("You do not meet our requirements").

Well-written reasons are
- Detailed
- Tactful
- Individualized
- Unapologetic
- Positive

Jeffrey Caponigro has learned that even though specific reasons help audiences accept bad news, reasons cannot always be given. Don't include reasons when they involve confidential, excessively complicated, or purely negative information or when they benefit only you or your firm (by enhancing the company's profits, for example). Instead, move directly to the next section.

Sometimes detailed reasons should not be provided.

State the Bad News

Learning Objective 4

Discuss the three techniques for saying no as clearly and kindly as possible

When the bad news is a logical outcome of the reasons that come before it, the audience is psychologically prepared to receive it. However, the audience may still reject your message if the bad news is handled carelessly. Three techniques are especially useful for saying no as clearly and as kindly as possible. First, de-emphasize the bad news:

- Minimize the space or time devoted to the bad news.
- Subordinate bad news in a complex or compound sentence ("My department is already shorthanded, so I'll need all my staff for at least the next two months"). This construction pushes the bad news into the middle of the sentence, the point of least emphasis.
- Embed bad news in the middle of a paragraph or use parenthetical expressions ("Our profits, which are down, are only part of the picture").

To handle bad news carefully
- De-emphasize the bad news visually and grammatically
- Use a conditional statement
- Tell what you did do, not what you didn't do

Second, use a conditional (*if* or *when*) statement to imply that the audience could have received, or might someday receive, a favorable answer ("When you have more managerial experience, you are welcome to reapply"). Such a statement could motivate applicants to improve their qualifications.

Third, tell the audience what you did do, can do, or will do rather than what you did not do, cannot do, or will not do. Say,"We sell exclusively through retailers, and the one nearest you that carries our merchandise is . . . " rather than "We are unable to serve you, so please call your nearest dealer." By implying the bad news, you may not need to actually state it ("The five positions currently open have been filled with people whose qualifications match those uncovered in our research"). By focusing on the positive and implying the bad news, you soften the blow.

Don't let the bad news get lost by overemphasizing the positive.

When implying bad news, be sure your audience understands the entire message—including the bad news. It would be unethical to overemphasize the positive. So if an implied message might leave doubt, state your decision in direct terms. Just be sure to avoid overly blunt statements that are likely to cause pain and anger:

Instead of This	Use This
I *must refuse* your request.	I will be out of town on the day you need me.
We *must deny* your application.	The position has been filled.
I *am unable* to grant your request.	Contact us again when you have established . . .
We *cannot afford to* continue the program.	The program will conclude on May 1.
Much as I would like to attend . . .	Our budget meeting ends too late for me to attend.
We *must reject* your proposal.	We've accepted the proposal from AAA Builders.
We *must turn down* your extension request.	Please send in your payment by June 14.

End with a Positive Close

An upbeat, positive close
- Builds goodwill
- Offers a suggestion for action
- Provides a look toward the future

After giving your audience the bad news, your job is to end your message on an upbeat note. You might propose an attainable solution to the audience's problem ("The human resources department has offered to bring in temporary workers when I need them, and they would probably consider doing the same for you"). In a message to a customer or potential customer, an off-the-subject ending that includes resale information or sales promotion may also be appropriate. If you've asked readers to decide between alternatives or to take some action, make sure that they know what to do, when to do it, and how to do it with ease. Whatever type of close you choose, follow these guidelines:

- **Keep it positive.** Don't refer to, repeat, or apologize for the bad news, and refrain from expressing any doubt that your reasons will be accepted (avoid statements such as "I trust our decision is satisfactory").
- **Limit future correspondence.** Encourage additional communication *only* if you're willing to discuss your decision further (avoid wording such as "If you have further questions, please write").
- **Be optimistic about the future.** Don't anticipate problems (avoid statements such as "Should you have further problems, please let us know").
- **Be sincere.** Steer clear of clichés that are insincere in view of the bad news (avoid saying, "If we can be of any help, please contact us").
- **Be confident.** Don't show any doubt about keeping the person as a customer (avoid phrases such as "We hope you will continue to do business with us").

If you are the one who has to reject the applicant for the management trainee position, you can observe these guidelines by writing a close like this:

> Many companies seek other qualifications in management trainees, so I urge you to continue your job search. You'll certainly find an opening in which your skills and aspirations match the job requirements exactly.

Keep in mind that the close is the last thing the audience has to remember you by. Try to make the memory a positive one.

Modifying Your Approach for Cultural Differences

Even though bad news is unwelcome in any language, the conventions for passing it on to business associates can vary considerably from country to country. For instance, all French business letters are very formal and writer-oriented (without reference to audience needs or benefits). Moreover, when the news is bad, French writers take a direct approach. They open with a reference to the problem or previous correspondence and then state the bad news clearly. While they don't refer to the audience's needs, they often do apologize and express regret for the problem.[6]

In contrast, Japanese letters traditionally open with remarks about the season, business prosperity, or health. When the news is bad, these opening formalities serve as a buffer. Explanations and apologies follow, and then comes the bad news or refusal. Japanese writers protect their reader's feelings by wording the bad news ambiguously. Western readers may even misinterpret this vague language as a condition of acceptance rather than as the refusal it truly is.[7] In short, if you are communicating across cultures, you'll want to use the tone, organization, and other cultural conventions that your audience expects. Only then can you avoid the inappropriate or even offensive approaches that could jeopardize your business relationship.[8] For a reminder of the strategies for delivering bad-news messages, see this chapter's "Checklist: Bad-News Messages."

WRITING BAD-NEWS MESSAGES

In the course of your business career, you will write various types of bad-news messages, from refusing credit to giving negative performance reviews. Many of the messages that you'll be writing will probably fall into three major categories: negative answers to routine requests, negative organizational news, and negative employment messages.

✓ CHECKLIST: BAD-NEWS MESSAGES

A. Overall strategy

1. Use the direct approach when the situation is routine (between employees of the same company), when the reader is not emotionally involved in the message, when you know that the reader would prefer the bad news first, or when you know that firmness is necessary.
2. Use the indirect approach in all other cases.
3. Adopt an audience-centered tone by being sincere, using the "you" attitude, choosing positive words, and using respectful language.
4. Modify your strategy for cultural differences.

B. Buffer

1. Express appreciation, cooperation, fairness, good news, praise, resale, or understanding.
2. Introduce a topic that is relevant to the subject and that both you and the reader can agree on.
3. Avoid apologies and negative-sounding words *(won't, can't, unable to)*.
4. Be brief and to the point.
5. Maintain a confident, positive, supportive tone.

C. Reasons

1. Check the lead-in from the buffer for a smooth transition from the favorable to the unfavorable.
2. Show how the decision benefits your audience.
3. Avoid apologies and expressions of sorrow or regret.
4. Offer enough detail to show the logic of your position.
5. Include only factual information.
6. Include only business reasons, not personal ones.
7. Carefully word the reasons so that readers can anticipate the bad news.
8. Work from the general to the specific.

D. Bad News

1. State the bad news as positively as possible, using tactful wording.
2. De-emphasize bad news by minimizing the space devoted to it, subordinating it, or embedding it.
3. Emphasize what the firm did do or is doing rather than what it can't or won't do.

E. Positive, friendly, helpful close

1. Remind the reader of how his or her needs are being met.
2. Keep the close as positive as possible by eliminating any reference to the bad news, avoiding apologies and words of regret, and eliminating words suggesting uncertainty.
3. Suggest actions the reader might take.
4. Keep a positive outlook on the future.
5. Be confident about keeping the person as a customer.

Sending Negative Answers to Routine Requests

The businessperson who tries to say yes to everyone probably won't win many promotions or stay in business for long. Occasionally, your response to routine requests must simply be "no." It's a mark of your skill as a communicator to be able to say no clearly yet not cut yourself off from future dealings with other people.

Refusing Requests for Information

Use either the direct or the indirect approach to tell someone you cannot provide what has been requested.

When people ask you for information and you can't honor the request, you may answer with either the direct approach or the indirect approach. Say that you've asked a company to participate in your research project concerning sales promotion. However, that company has a policy against disseminating any information about projected sales figures. You receive the following letter, which uses the direct approach even though you are outside the company and may be emotionally involved in the response. This letter would offend most readers:

First Draft

The writer hides behind the blanket "company policy," a policy that the reader may find questionable

Our company policy prohibits us from participating in research projects where disclosure of discretionary information might be necessary. Therefore, we decline your invitation to our sales staff to fill out questionnaires for your study.

Tone is unnecessarily negative and abrupt

The offer to help is an unpleasant irony, given the writer's unwillingness to help in this instance

Thank you for trying to include Qualcomm Corporation in your research. If we can be of further assistance, please let us know.

As Jeffrey Caponigro can tell you, wording and tone conspire to make a letter either offensive or acceptable. The letter that follows conveys the same negative message as the previous letter but without sounding offensive:

Buffer is supportive and appreciative.

Bad news is implied, not stated explicitly.

We at Qualcomm Corporation appreciate and benefit from the research of companies such as yours. Your study sounds interesting.

Body fully explains reason for decision without falling back on a blanket reference to company policy.

Our board requires strict confidentiality of all sales information until quarterly reports are mailed to stockholders. We release press reports at the same time the quarterly reports go out, and we'll be sure to include you in all our future mailings.

Close is friendly, positive, and helpful.

Although we cannot release projected figures, we are more than willing to share information that is part of the public record. I've enclosed several of our past earnings reports for your inspection. We look forward to seeing the results of your study. Please let us know if there is any additional way we can help.

As you think about the different impact those two letters might have on you, you can see why effective business writers take the time and the effort to give negative messages the attention they deserve.

Refusing Invitations and Requests for Favors

When turning down an invitation or a request for a favor, consider your relationship to the reader.

When you must say no to an invitation or a requested favor, your use of the direct or the indirect approach depends on your relationship with the reader. For example, suppose the president of the local community college asks your company to host graduation on your corporate grounds, but your sales meetings will be taking place at the same time. If you don't know the president well, you'll probably use the indirect approach. See Figure 8.2, in which May Yee Kwan delivers this bad news in a helpful and supportive way. If you are friends with the president and work frequently on projects for the college, you might use the direct approach:

Sandra, thanks for asking us to host your graduation. You know we've always supported the college and would love to do this for you. During this same time, though, our annual

Planning

Analyze
Gauge audience's reaction to refusal; gear level of formality to reader familiarity.

Investigate
Collect information on possible alternatives.

Adapt
For a more formal response, letterhead is best. Maintain the relationship with the "you" attitude, and focus on the reader's problem.

Writing

Organize
Main idea is to refuse a request. Respect your reader by showing that the request received serious consideration. Use an indirect approach.

Compose
Make your style conversational but keep it businesslike. Keep the letter brief, clear, and helpful.

Completing

Revise
Maintain a friendly tone by eliminating overly formal words and phrases. Ensure your tone is positive.

Produce
Use letterhead with a straightforward format.

Proofread
Be careful to review for accuracy, spelling, and mechanics.

FIGURE 8.2 In-Depth Critique: Letter Declining a Favor

927 Dawson Valley Road, Tulsa, Oklahoma 74151
Voice: (918) 669-4428 Fax: (918) 669-4429
www.infotech.com

March 5, 2002

Dr. Sandra Wofford, President
Whittier Community College
333 Whittier Avenue
Tulsa, OK 74150

Dear Dr. Wofford:

Because we appreciate Whittier Community College and the many opportunities you have provided to deserving students over the years, we at Infotech have supported the college in many ways. Thank you for considering our grounds for your graduation ceremony.

Buffers bad news by demonstrating respect and recapping request

Our company-wide sales meetings will be held during the weeks of May 29 and June 5. We will host over 200 sales representatives and their families, and activities will take place at both our corporate campus and the Ramada Renaissance. Therefore, we will be unable to devote an adequate support staff for your graduation.

States reason for the bad news explicitly and in detail

My assistant, Roberta Seagers, suggests you contact the Municipal Botanical Gardens as a possible graduation site. She recommends calling Jerry Kane, director of public relations. If we can help in any other way with graduation, please let us know.

Suggests an alternative—showing that Kwan cares about the college and has given the matter some thought

Even though our annual meeting will most likely prevent us from ever hosting graduation, we remain firm in our commitment to you, President Wofford, and to the fine students you represent. We will continue to be a corporate partner to Whittier College and will support your efforts as you move forward.

Closes by renewing the corporation's future support

Sincerely,

May Yee Kwan

May Yee Kwan
Public Relations Director

lc

company sales meeting will be taking place. Our special events staff will be devoting all of their time to logistics pertaining to the meeting.

Have you called Jerry Kane over at the Botanical Gardens? I can't think of a prettier site for graduation. Roberta in my office volunteers over there and knows Jerry. She can fill you in on the details, if you'd like to talk to her first.

Thanks again for considering us. Let's have lunch in mid-June to plan our involvement with the college for the next school year. You can think of all kinds of ways to make me sorry I had to say no! I'll look forward to seeing you and catching up on family news.

This letter gets right to the point but still uses some blow-softening techniques: It compliments the person and organization making the request, suggests an alternative, and looks toward future opportunities for cooperation.

Handling Bad News About Orders

The basic goal of a bad-news letter about orders is to protect or make a sale.

For several reasons, businesses must sometimes convey bad news concerning orders. Also, when delivering bad news to existing or would-be customers, you have an additional challenge—resale. To make readers feel good about continuing to do business with your firm, you want to

- Work toward an eventual sale along the lines of the original order
- Keep instructions or additional information as clear as possible
- Maintain an optimistic, confident tone so that your reader won't lose interest

Reinforcing the customer's confidence in your service or product is an effective way to meet the resale challenge. Just don't overdo it.

When you must back-order for a customer, you have one of two types of bad news to convey: (1) You're able to send only part of the order, or (2) you're able to send none of the order. When sending only part of the order, you actually have both good news and bad news. In such situations, the indirect approach works very well.

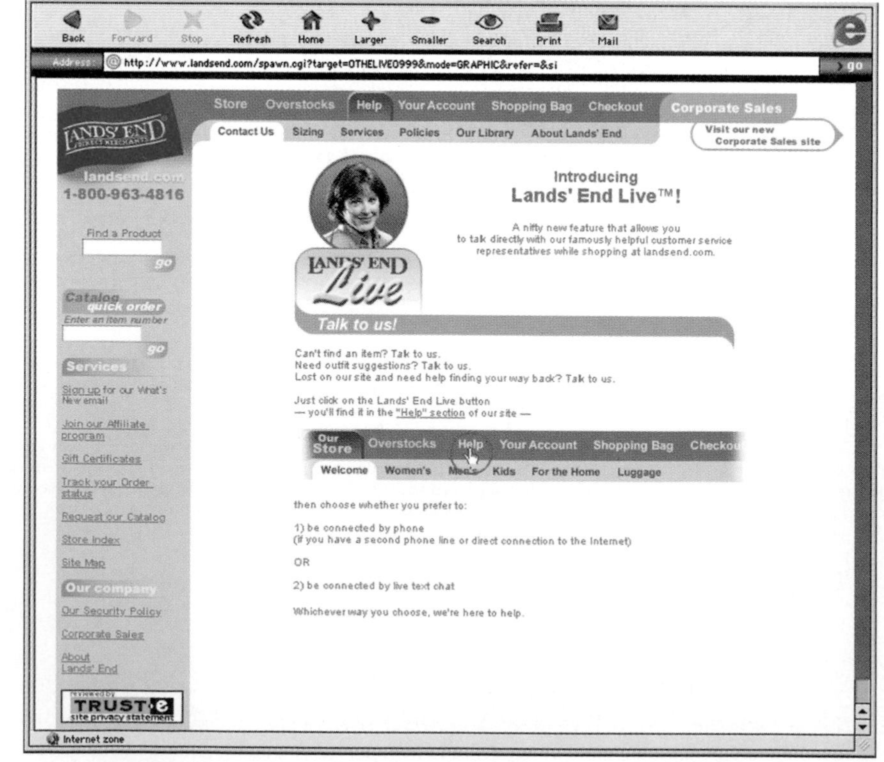

Problems are opportunities in disguise—at least that's how Lands' End sees it. Whether the customer is being notified about an out-of-stock item, a partial shipment, or a delivery delay, Lands' End uses the communication to strengthen customer loyalty. The company does so by clearly stating the facts, by letting the customer know that it intends to make things right, and by responding promptly.

FIGURE 8.3 In-Depth Critique: E-Mail Advising of a Back Order

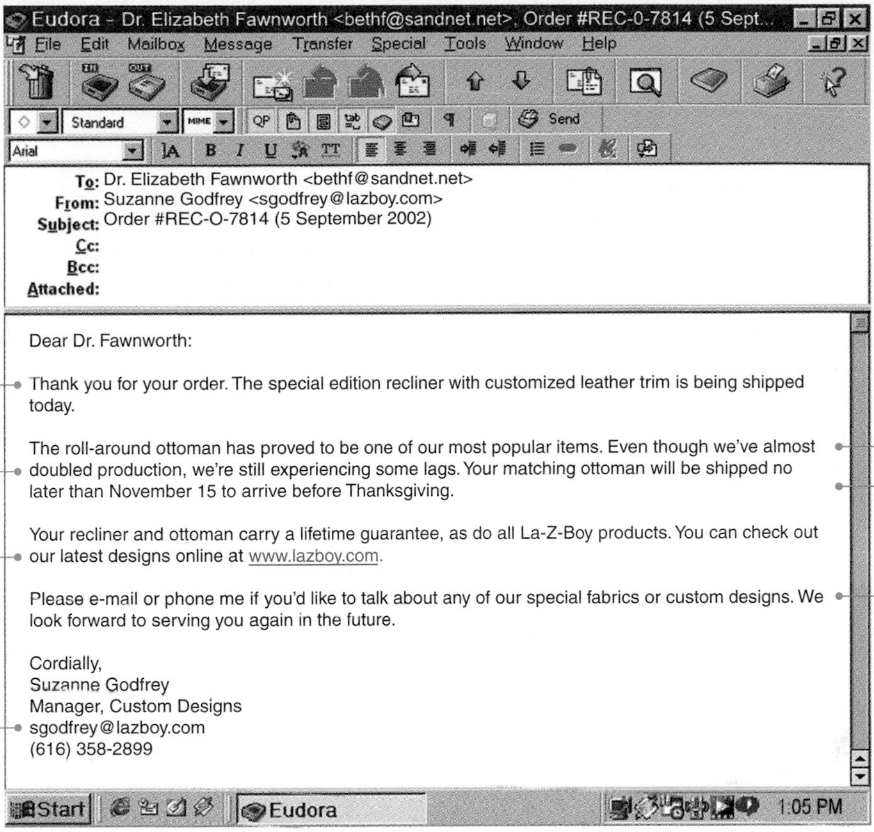

Eudora - Dr. Elizabeth Fawnworth <bethf@sandnet.net>, Order #REC-0-7814 (5 Sept...

File Edit Mailbox Message Transfer Special Tools Window Help

Standard | Send | Arial

To: Dr. Elizabeth Fawnworth <bethf@sandnet.net>
From: Suzanne Godfrey <sgodfrey@lazboy.com>
Subject: Order #REC-O-7814 (5 September 2002)
Cc:
Bcc:
Attached:

Dear Dr. Fawnworth:

Thank you for your order. The special edition recliner with customized leather trim is being shipped today.

The roll-around ottoman has proved to be one of our most popular items. Even though we've almost doubled production, we're still experiencing some lags. Your matching ottoman will be shipped no later than November 15 to arrive before Thanksgiving.

Your recliner and ottoman carry a lifetime guarantee, as do all La-Z-Boy products. You can check out our latest designs online at www.lazboy.com.

Please e-mail or phone me if you'd like to talk about any of our special fabrics or custom designs. We look forward to serving you again in the future.

Cordially,
Suzanne Godfrey
Manager, Custom Designs
sgodfrey@lazboy.com
(616) 358-2899

Start | Eudora | 1:05 PM

Conveys the good news first in the buffer

Implies the actual bad news by telling the reader what's being done, not what can't be done

Includes resale information in a simple statement of a consumer benefit

Includes relevant contact information

States reasons for the delay by indicating that the ottoman is a popular choice

Cushions bad news with a pledge to ship by a definite time

Opens the door to future business in this positive close

The buffer contains the good news (that part of the order is en route) along with a resale reminder of the product's attractiveness. After the buffer come the reasons for the delay of the remainder of the shipment. A strong close encourages a favorable attitude toward the entire transaction. For a customer whose order for a recliner and ottoman will be only partially filled, your e-mail message might read like the one in Figure 8.3.

When you're unable to send the customer any portion of an order, you still use the indirect approach. However, because you have no good news to give, your buffer only confirms the sale, and the explanation section states your reasons for not filling the order promptly. For a brief outline of back-order tasks, see this chapter's "Checklist: Bad News About Orders."

Use the indirect approach for both types of bad news about orders.

Refusing Claims and Requests for Adjustment

Almost every customer who makes a claim is emotionally involved; therefore, the indirect method is usually the best approach for a refusal. Your job as a writer is to avoid accepting responsibility for the unfortunate situation and yet avoid blaming or accusing the customer. To steer clear of these pitfalls, pay special attention to the tone of your letter. Keep in mind that a tactful and courteous letter can build goodwill even while denying the claim. For example, Village Electronics recently received a letter from Daniel Lindmeier, who purchased a digital video camera a year ago. He wrote to say that the unit doesn't work correctly and to inquire about the warranty. Lindmeier believes that the warranty covers one year, when it actually covers only three months (see Figure 8.4).

Use the indirect approach in most cases of refusing a claim.

When refusing a claim, avoid language that might have a negative impact on the reader. Instead, demonstrate that you understand and have considered the complaint. Then, even if the claim is unreasonable, rationally explain why you are refusing the

When refusing a claim
- Demonstrate your understanding of the complaint
- Explain your refusal
- Suggest alternative action

✓ CHECKLIST: BAD NEWS ABOUT ORDERS*

A. Buffer

1. Include any details identifying the order.
2. Extend a welcome to a new customer.
3. Use resale information on the ordered merchandise to build the customer's confidence in the original choice (except for unfillable orders).
4. For partial shipments, include the good news about the fulfilled part.

B. Reasons

1. State the facts without laying blame.
2. Specify shipping dates.
3. Explain why the item is out of stock, such as high popularity or exceptional demand, which may stimulate the customer's desire for the item.
4. Reinforce the customer's confidence (for consumers, emphasize resale information such as personal attention, credit, repair services, free delivery, special discounts, telephone shopping, and other services; for dealers, emphasize free counter and window displays, advertising materials, sales manuals, factory guarantees, and nearby warehousing).
5. Refer to sales promotion material, if desirable.

C. The bad news

1. Stress the reader benefit of the decision to buy.
2. Offer a substitute product, if available.

D. Positive, friendly, helpful close

1. Adopt a tone that shows you remain in control of the situation and will continue to give customers' orders personal attention.
2. Use resale information to clinch the sale, especially for back orders.

*These items are in addition to the material included in the "Checklist: Bad-News Messages."

request. Remember, don't apologize and don't rely on company policy. End the letter on a respectful and action-oriented note.

Learning Objective 5

Define defamation *and explain how to avoid it in bad-news messages*

You may be tempted to respond to something particularly outrageous by calling the person responsible a crook, a swindler, or an incompetent. Resist! If you don't, you could be sued for **defamation**, a false statement that tends to damage someone's character or reputation. (Written defamation is called *libel;* spoken defamation is called *slander*.) Someone suing for defamation must prove (1) that the statement is false, (2) that the language is injurious to the person's reputation, and (3) that the statement has been "published."

Avoid defamation by not responding emotionally.

If you can prove that your accusations are true, you haven't defamed the person. The courts are likely to give you the benefit of the doubt because our society believes that ordinary business communication should not be hampered by fear of lawsuits. However, beware of the irate letter intended to let off steam: If the message has no necessary business purpose and is expressed in abusive language that hints of malice, you'll lose the case. To avoid being accused of defamation, follow these guidelines:

- Avoid using any kind of abusive language or terms that could be considered defamatory.
- If you wish to express your own personal opinions about a sensitive matter, use your own stationery (not company letterhead), and don't include your job title or position. Take responsibility for your own actions without involving your company.
- Provide accurate information and stick to the facts.
- Never let anger or malice motivate your messages.
- Consult your company's legal department or an attorney whenever you think a message might have legal consequences.
- Communicate honestly, and make sure that what you're saying is what you believe to be true.

For a brief review of the tasks involved when refusing claims, see this chapter's "Checklist: Refusing Claims."

Refusing to Extend Credit

Be aware that credit is a legally sensitive subject.

Credit is refused for a variety of reasons, all involving sensitive personal or legal considerations. When denying credit to the applicant with a proven record of delinquent payments and to the applicant with an unstable background, you would probably be

Planning

Analyze
Purpose is to explain that the warranty has expired and to offer repairs that the reader can pay for.

Investigate
Briefly gather information on product warranties, terms for repair, and resale information.

Adapt
Use letter format and focus on customer relationship.

Writing

Organize
Main idea is that you're offering repairs, even though the warranty has expired. Use the indirect approach to help reader accept your message.

Compose
Make the style conversational. Choose your words carefully, and enclose a catalog to encourage future business.

Completing

Revise
Review for logical order and tone. Be clear but friendly.

Produce
Use a clean letter format on letterhead.

Proofread
Review for accuracy and correctness. Be sure to include promised enclosures.

FIGURE 8.4 In-Depth Critique: Letter Refusing a Claim

NUMBER ONE IN ENTERTAINMENT
Village Electronics
68 Lake Itasca Boulevard • Hannover, MN 55341
Voice: (612) 878-1312 • Fax: (612) 878-1316

May 3, 2002

Mr. Daniel Lindmeier
849 Cedar Street
Lake Elmo, MN 55042

Dear Mr. Lindmeier:

Thank you for your letter about the battery release switch on your JVC digital camera. We believe, as you do, that electronic equipment should be built to last. That's why we stand behind our products with a 90-day warranty.

Buffers the bad news by emphasizing a point that reader and writer both agree on

Even though your JVC camera is a year old and therefore out of warranty, we can still help. Please package your camera carefully and ship it to our store in Hannover. Include your complete name, address, phone number, and a brief description of the malfunction, along with a check for $35. After examining the unit, we will give you a written estimate of the needed parts and labor. Then just let us know whether you want us to make the repairs—either by phone or by filling out the prepaid card we'll send you with the estimate.

States bad news indirectly, tactfully leaving the repair decision to the customer

Puts company's policy in a favorable light

If you choose to repair the unit, the $35 will be applied toward your bill, the balance of which is payable by check or credit card. If you decide not to repair the unit, the $35 will pay for the technician's time examining the unit. JVC also has service centers available in your area. If you would prefer to take the unit to one of them, please see the enclosed list.

Helps soothe the reader with a positive alternative action

Thanks again for inquiring about our service. I've enclosed a catalog of our latest cameras and accessories. In June JVC is offering a "Trade-Up Special," at which time you can receive trade-in credit for your digital camera when you purchase a newer model. Come and visit Village Electronics soon.

Closes by blending sales promotion with an acknowledgment of customer's interests

Sincerely,

Walter Brodie

Walter Brodie
President

mk

Enclosures: List of service centers
Catalog

✓ CHECKLIST: REFUSING CLAIMS*

A. Buffer
1. Indicate your full understanding of the nature of the complaint.
2. Avoid all areas of disagreement.
3. Avoid any hint of your final decision.

B. Reasons
1. Provide an accurate, factual account of the transaction.
2. Emphasize ways things should have been handled, rather than dwelling on reader's negligence.
3. Avoid using a know-it-all tone.
4. Use impersonal, passive language.
5. Avoid accusing, preaching (*you should have*), blaming, or scolding the reader.
6. Do not make the reader appear or feel stupid.

C. The bad news
1. Make the refusal clear, using tactful wording.
2. Avoid any hint that your decision is less than final.
3. Avoid words such as *reject* and *claim*.
4. Make a counterproposal, offer a compromise, or make a partial adjustment (if desirable).
5. Make your tone willing, not begrudging, in a spirit of honest cooperation.
6. Include resale information for the company or product.
7. Emphasize a desire for a good relationship in the future.
8. Extend an offer to replace the product or to provide a replacement part at the regular price.

D. Positive, friendly, helpful close
1. Make no reference to your refusal.
2. Refer to enclosed sales material.
3. Make any suggested action easy for readers to comply with.

*These items are in addition to the material included in the "Checklist: Bad-News Messages."

justified in offering little hope for future credit approval. You could be more encouraging to other types of applicants. You most certainly would like their current cash business, and you may want their future credit business.

In a letter denying credit to a business
- Be more factual and less personal than in a letter to an individual
- Suggest ways to continue doing business

Denials of business credit, as opposed to denials of individual credit, are less personally sensitive but more financially significant. Businesses have failed because major suppliers have suspended credit at inconvenient times. When refusing to extend credit to a business, explain your reasons as factually and as impersonally as possible (perhaps the firm's latest financial statements don't meet your criteria, or its credit rating has fallen below an acceptable minimum). Also, explain the steps that must be taken to restore credit. Emphasize the benefits of continued dealings on a cash basis until the firm's creditworthiness has been established or restored. You might offer discounts for cash purchases or assistance in cooperative merchandising to reduce the firm's inventory and increase its cash flow. Third-party loans are another possibility you might suggest.

Whether denying credit to consumers or to business customers, you need to exercise good judgment to avoid legal action. A faulty decision may unfairly damage a person's reputation, which in turn may provoke a lawsuit and other bad publicity for your company. Handling credit denials over the phone instead of in writing is no guarantee of avoiding trouble; companies that orally refuse credit must still proceed with caution. For a summary of the tasks involved in this type of message, see this chapter's "Checklist: Credit Refusals."

Sending Negative Organizational News

Refusing a request isn't the only type of bad news. At times, you may have bad news about your company's products or about its operations. Whether you're reporting to a supervisor or announcing your news to the media, the particular situation dictates whether you will use the direct or the indirect approach.

Providing Bad News About Products

Use either the direct or the indirect approach when providing bad news about a product.

Suppose you have to provide bad news about a product. If you were writing to tell your company's bookkeeping department about increasing product prices, you'd use the direct approach. Your audience would have to make some arithmetical adjustments once the increases are put into effect, but readers would presumably be unemotional about the matter. On the other hand, if you were writing to convey the same information to customers or even to your own sales department, you would probably use the indirect

✓ CHECKLIST: CREDIT REFUSALS*

A. Buffer
1. Express appreciation for the credit request.
2. Phrase buffer to avoid misleading reader.

B. Reasons
1. Explain your general credit criteria.
2. Carefully present reasons for the refusal.
3. Avoid a condescending lecture about how credit is earned.
4. Avoid relying on unexplained company policy.
5. Stress the benefits of not being overextended.

C. The bad news
1. Make the refusal clear to the reader.
2. Offer only honest encouragement about considering the credit application at a later date, if future approval is realistic.
3. Avoid negative words, such as *must decline.*
4. For consumers, suggest positive alternatives, such as cash and layaway purchases.
5. For businesses, describe cash discounts or offer promotional and marketing aid.

D. Positive, friendly, helpful close
1. Encourage the reader to look to the future, when the application may be approved.
2. Suggest alternative financing sources.

*These items are in addition to the material included in the "Checklist: Bad-News Messages."

approach. Customers never like to pay more, and your sales reps would see the change as weakening your product's competitive edge, thereby threatening their incomes and possibly even their jobs.

When Webvan closed up shop, management had the difficult task of informing customers of the bad news. In these delicate situations, it's best to stick to the facts, state them clearly, and provide the audience with all the details they might need to know—such as, how their outstanding orders will be handled or how to process a claim.

Handling Bad News About Company Operations

At least three situations require bad-news letters about company operations or performance: (1) a change in company policy or future plans that will have a negative effect on the reader, (2) problems with company performance, and (3) controversial or unpopular company operations. In trying situations, apologies may be in order. If an apology is appropriate, good writers usually make it brief and bury it somewhere in the middle of the letter. Moreover, they try to leave readers with a favorable impression by closing on a positive note.

Companies that produce unpopular products or have controversial operations can find themselves caught in a political crossfire. In such cases, your general strategy might be to explain the reasons your company is manufacturing the controversial item or providing the unpopular service. You want to show that reason and need are behind your operation (not villainy, carelessness, or greed).

When conveying bad news about your company, focus on the reasons and on possible benefits.

When a change in company policy will have a negative effect on your audience, state the reasons for the change clearly and carefully. The explanation section of the message convinces readers that the change was necessary and, if possible, explains how the change will benefit them. For example, if your company decided to drop orthodontic coverage from its employee dental plan, you could explain the decision this way:

> By eliminating this infrequently used benefit we will not have to increase the monthly amount withheld from your paycheck for insurance coverage.

If your company is having serious performance problems, your customers and shareholders want to learn of the difficulty from you, not from newspaper accounts or from rumors. Even if the news leaks out before you announce it, counter with your own explanation as soon as possible. Business is based on mutual trust; if your customers and shareholders can't trust you to inform them of your problems, they may choose to work with someone they *can* trust. When you do inform stakeholders, use your common business sense and present the bad news in as favorable a light as possible.

FIGURE 8.5 In-Depth Critique: E-Mail Message Providing Bad News About Products

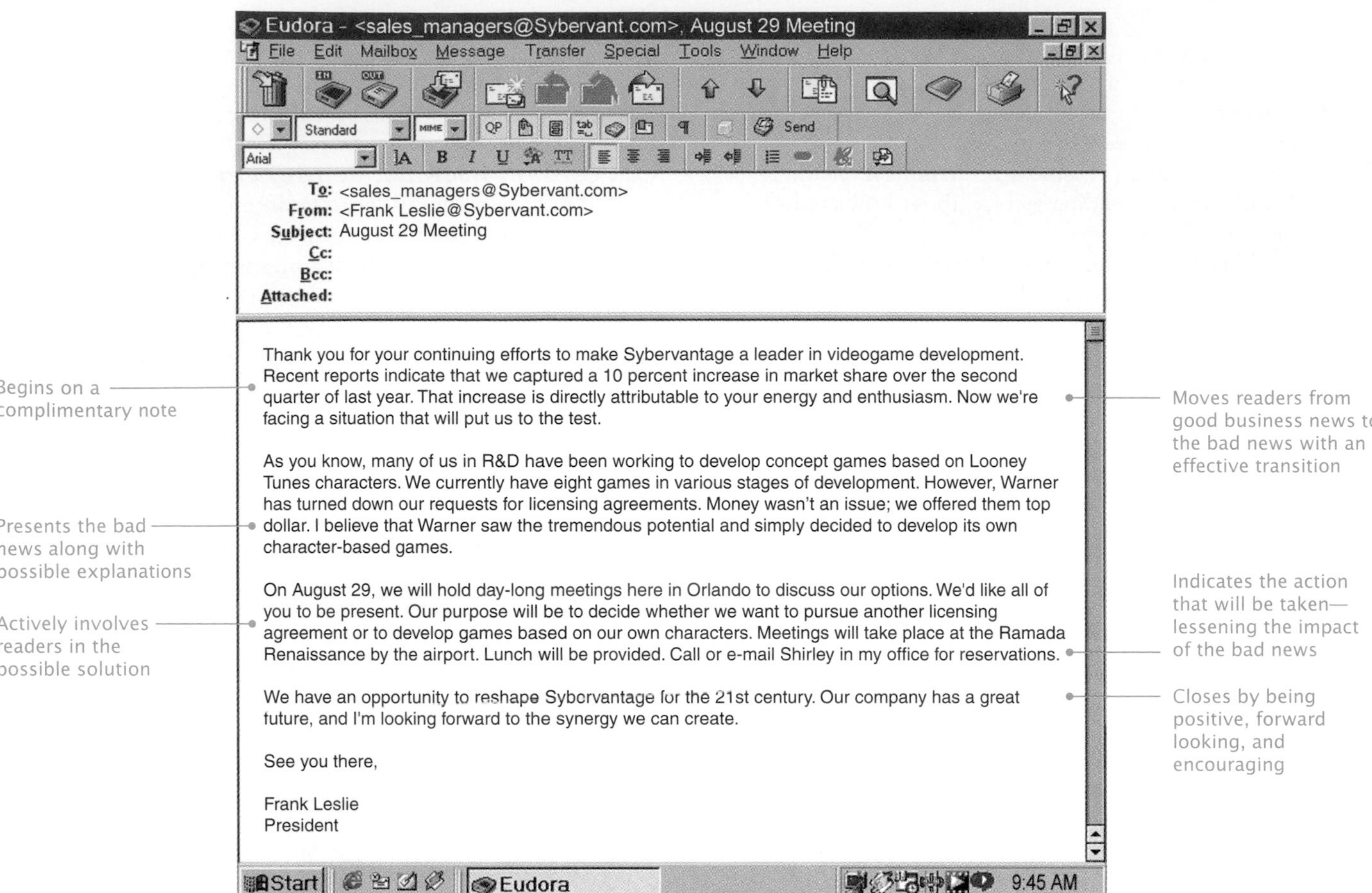

If your company lost a major business customer or if an important deal fell through, you could present the bad news as an opportunity to focus on smaller, growing businesses or on new products, as the e-mail in Figure 8.5 does. In this example, Sybervantage pursued licensing agreements with Warner and expected to enter into a mutually profitable arrangement. But when Warner rejected the deal, Sybervantage had to notify its sales force. Rather then dwell on the bad news, the company focuses on possible options for the future. The upbeat close diminishes the effect of the bad news.

Sending Negative Employment Messages

Use the direct approach when giving readers bad news about someone else's job; use the indirect approach when giving readers bad news about their own jobs.

Most managers must convey bad news about people from time to time. You can use the direct approach when communicating with other companies, sending a negative reference to a prospective employer, or writing to job applicants. But it's best to use the indirect approach when giving negative performance reviews to employees, because they will most certainly be emotionally involved. In addition, choose the media you use for these messages with care. (See "Focusing on Ethics: Should Employers Use E-Mail to Deliver Negative Employment Messages?")

Refusing Requests for Recommendation Letters

Even though many states have passed laws to protect employers who provide open and honest job references for former employees, legal hazards persist.[9] That's why many former employers still refuse to write recommendation letters—especially for people

Focusing on Ethics

Should Employers Use E-Mail to Deliver Negative Employment Messages?

Most people are more comfortable delivering bad news via e-mail than in person or on the phone. But is it appropriate to avoid the dreaded task of explaining layoffs and spending cuts in person by using e-mail to break such bad news? Some think it is.

Few executives advise using e-mail in extremely personal situations such as firing an employee, but some think using e-mail is perfectly fine for other uncomfortable scenarios such as job cuts, travel restrictions, hiring freezes, and significant spending changes. Consider these examples:

- Amazon.com called an in-person meeting to announce job cuts, but telecommuters who couldn't attend the meeting were informed via e-mail. "I want you to know that this was a very difficult decision for the company to make . . . we know this must be very painful to hear," the e-mail read.
- Discovery Communications used e-mail to alert Discover.com workers that staffing changes would take place before announcing layoffs of some of its dot-com full-time employees.
- Motorola sent e-mail to employees in its semiconductor sector explaining layoffs and other cost-cutting steps. Workers being let go were told in person, but word of what was happening went out electronically.
- Ameritrade online brokerage notified more than 2,000 call-center workers of layoffs via e-mail.

Employers who use e-mail to deliver bad news claim that it's a quick and effective way to get information to all employees—especially those in remote locations or home offices. With face-to-face or even voice-to-voice communication, people have a tendency to tune out the worst and sugarcoat the bad news. But delivering bad news via e-mail lets people be more honest. E-mail facilitates straight talk because senders don't see the discomfort of their recipients.

However, critics cry foul when companies break job-related bad news via e-mail. As they see it, e-mail is too impersonal. "The only advantage is that it gives management an opportunity to duck and dodge angry employees," says one communications expert. If you want to maintain good relationships with your employees, "these kinds of things should be done in person."

Career Applications

1. Do you think employers should deliver negative employment messages via e-mail? Explain your answer.
2. Why does e-mail facilitate straight talk?

whose job performance has been unsatisfactory. When sending refusals to prospective employers, your message may be brief and direct:

In letters informing prospective employers that you will not provide a recommendation, be direct, brief, and factual (to avoid legal pitfalls).

According to guidelines from our human resources department, we are authorized to confirm only that Yolanda Johnson worked for Tandy, Inc., for three years, from June 1999 to July 2001. Best of luck as you interview the administrative applicants.

This message doesn't need to say, "We cannot comply with your request." It simply gets down to the business of giving readers the information that is allowable.

Letters to the applicants themselves are another matter. Any refusal to cooperate may seem a personal slight and a threat to the applicant's future. Diplomacy and preparation help readers accept your refusal:

In letters telling job applicants that you will not write a recommendation, use the utmost tact.

Thank you for letting me know about your job opportunity with Coca-Cola. Your internship there and the MBA you've worked so hard to earn should place you in an excellent position to land the marketing job.

Although we send out no formal recommendations here at PepsiCo, I can certainly send Coke a confirmation of your employment dates. For more in-depth recommendations, be sure to ask the people you worked with during your internship to write evaluations of your work performance, and don't forget to ask several of your professors to write evaluations of your marketing skills. Best of luck to you in your career.

This letter deftly and tactfully avoids hurting the reader's feelings, because it makes positive comments about the reader's recent activities, implies the refusal, suggests an alternative, and uses a polite close.

Rejecting Job Applications

Learning Objective 6

List three guidelines for delivering bad news to job applicants and give a brief explanation of each one

In a letter turning down a job applicant, treat the reader with respect; by applying for a job, he or she has complimented your company.

It's also difficult to tactfully tell job applicants that you won't be offering them employment. But don't let the difficulty stop you from communicating the bad news. Rejecting an applicant with silence is unacceptable. At the same time, poorly written rejection letters do have negative consequences, ranging from the loss of qualified candidates for future openings to the loss of potential customers (not only the rejected applicants but also their friends and family).[10] When delivering bad news to job applicants, follow three guidelines:[11]

- **Open with the direct approach.** A recent study by the *Journal of Business and Technical Communication* shows businesses fare better when they reject applicants up front.[12] Job applicants know that good news will most likely come by phone and that bad news will most likely come by letter. If you try to buffer the bad news that your reader is expecting, you will seem manipulative and insincere.
- **Clearly state why the applicant was not selected.** Make your rejection less personal by stating that you hired someone with more experience or whose qualifications match the position requirements more closely.
- **Close by suggesting alternatives.** If you believe the applicant is qualified, mention other openings within your company. You might suggest professional organizations that could help the applicant find employment. Or you might simply mention that the applicant's résumé will be considered for future openings. Any of these positive suggestions may help the applicant be less disappointed and view your company more positively.

A rejection letter need not be long. Remember, sending a well-written form letter that follows these three guidelines is better than not sending one at all. After all, the applicant wants to know only one thing: Did I land the job? Your brief message conveys the information clearly and with tactful consideration for the applicant's feelings. After Carol DeCicco interviewed with Bradley & Jackson, she was hopeful about receiving a job offer. Everything went well, and her résumé was in good shape. The e-mail in Figure 8.6 was drafted by Marvin Fichter to communicate the bad news to DeCicco. After reviewing the first draft, Ficher made several changes to improve the communication (see Figure 8.7). The revised e-mail helps DeCicco understand that (1) she would have been hired if she'd had more tax experience and (2) she shouldn't be discouraged.

Giving Negative Performance Reviews

Learning Objective 7

Outline the main purpose of performance reviews, give three ways to accomplish that purpose, and list five guidelines to follow when giving negative reviews

In performance reviews, say what's right as well as what's wrong, and explain how the employee can improve performance.

A performance review is a manager's formal or informal evaluation of an employee. Few other communication tasks require such a broad range of skills and strategy as those needed for performance reviews, whether positive or negative. The main purpose of these reviews is to improve employee performance by (1) emphasizing and clarifying job requirements, (2) giving employees feedback on their efforts toward fulfilling those requirements, and (3) guiding continued efforts by developing a plan of action, along with its rewards and opportunities. (See "Sharpening Your Career Skills: Mastering the Art of Constructive Criticism.") In addition to improving employee performance, performance reviews help companies set organizational standards and communicate organizational values.[13]

Positive and negative performance reviews share several characteristics: The tone is objective and unbiased, the language is nonjudgmental, and the focus is problem resolution.[14] Also, to increase objectivity, more organizations are giving their employees feedback from multiple sources. In these "360-degree reviews," employees get feedback from all directions in the organization: above, below, and horizontally.[15]

FIGURE 8.6 In-Depth Critique: Ineffective E-Mail Rejecting a Job Application

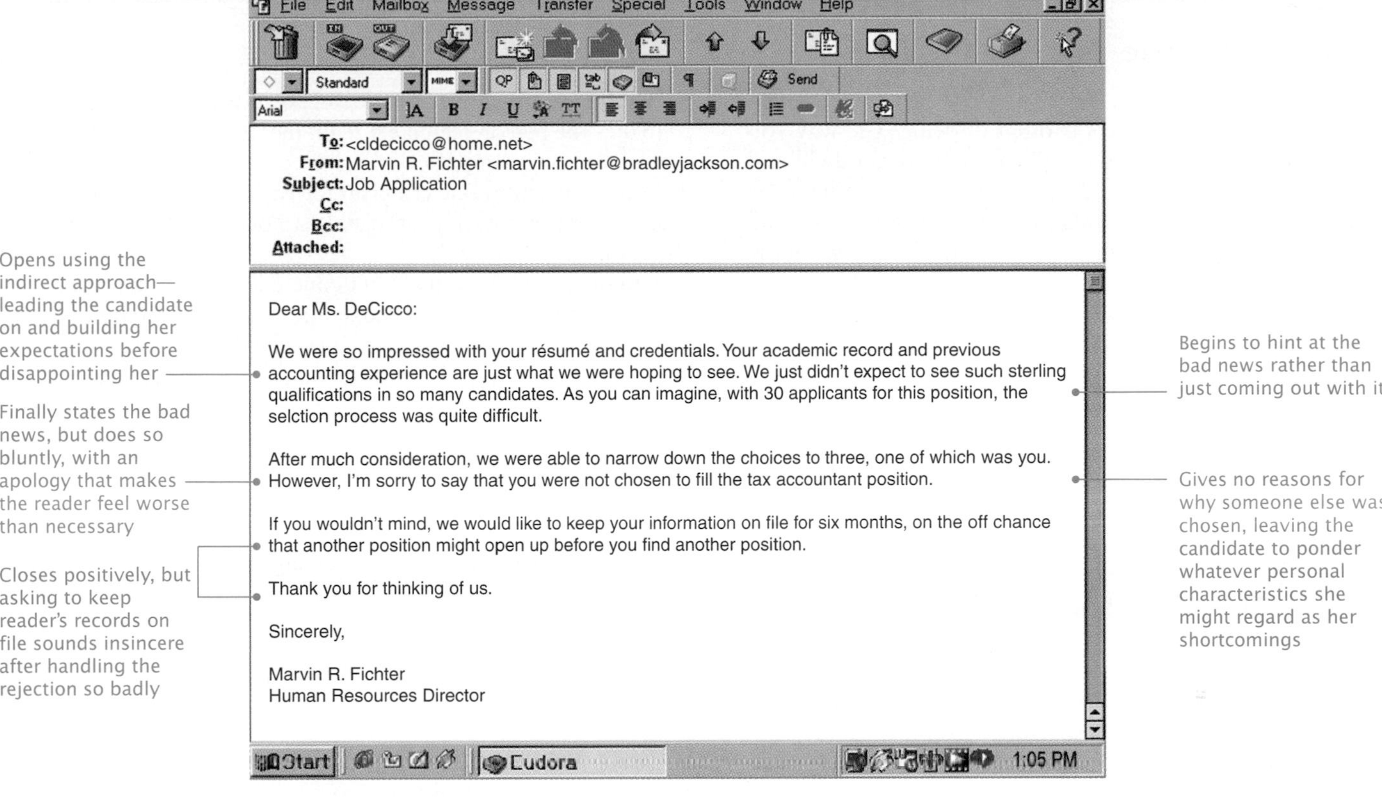

To: <cldecicco@home.net>
From: Marvin R. Fichter <marvin.fichter@bradleyjackson.com>
Subject: Job Application
Cc:
Bcc:
Attached:

Dear Ms. DeCicco:

We were so impressed with your résumé and credentials. Your academic record and previous accounting experience are just what we were hoping to see. We just didn't expect to see such sterling qualifications in so many candidates. As you can imagine, with 30 applicants for this position, the selction process was quite difficult.

After much consideration, we were able to narrow down the choices to three, one of which was you. However, I'm sorry to say that you were not chosen to fill the tax accountant position.

If you wouldn't mind, we would like to keep your information on file for six months, on the off chance that another position might open up before you find another position.

Thank you for thinking of us.

Sincerely,

Marvin R. Fichter
Human Resources Director

FIGURE 8.7 In-Depth Critique: Effective E-Mail Rejecting a Job Application

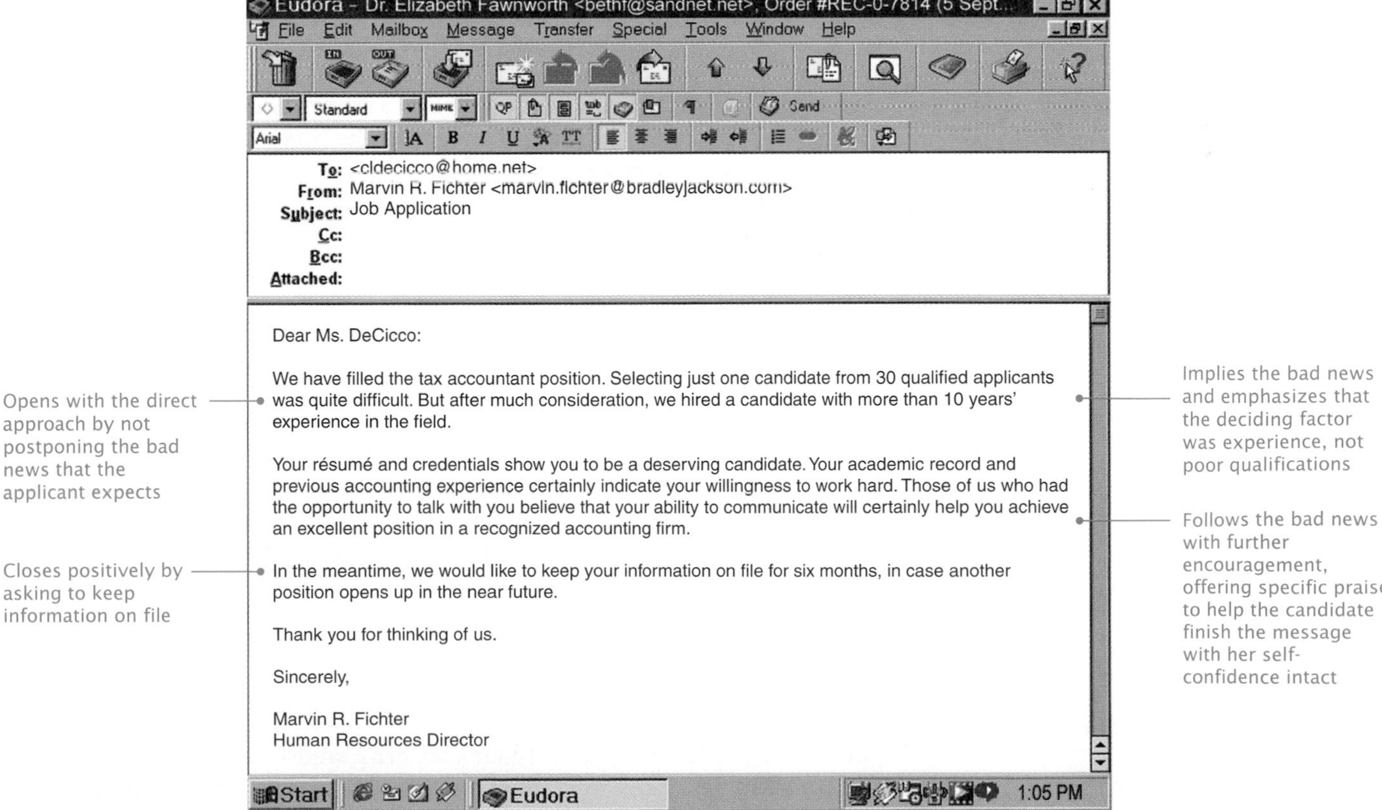

To: <cldecicco@home.net>
From: Marvin R. Fichter <marvin.fichter@bradleyjackson.com>
Subject: Job Application
Cc:
Bcc:
Attached:

Dear Ms. DeCicco:

We have filled the tax accountant position. Selecting just one candidate from 30 qualified applicants was quite difficult. But after much consideration, we hired a candidate with more than 10 years' experience in the field.

Your résumé and credentials show you to be a deserving candidate. Your academic record and previous accounting experience certainly indicate your willingness to work hard. Those of us who had the opportunity to talk with you believe that your ability to communicate will certainly help you achieve an excellent position in a recognized accounting firm.

In the meantime, we would like to keep your information on file for six months, in case another position opens up in the near future.

Thank you for thinking of us.

Sincerely,

Marvin R. Fichter
Human Resources Director

Sharpening Your Career Skills

Mastering the Art of Constructive Criticism

To become better writers, people need to be evaluated, but taking criticism from others is often difficult. The way you tell someone "You did it wrong" can destroy goodwill and cooperation, or it can build the relationship and help the person learn from the mistake, improve performance, and retain self-esteem. To criticize more constructively, follow these suggestions:

- **Get all the facts first.** Don't accept hearsay or rumors. Find out specifically who did or said what, when, where, why, and how.
- **Don't act in haste.** Never act while you're angry. Think things out before you write or speak, and then explain your criticism calmly, rationally, and objectively.
- **Phrase your remarks impersonally.** Criticize the mistake, not the person. Focus your remarks on the action only, and analyze it thoughtfully.
- **Never criticize in an offhand manner.** Treat the situation seriously. Take the time to state the problem in detail, explaining what was wrong and why.
- **Avoid an abusive tone.** Ridiculing someone, talking down to a person, or using sarcasm prevents people from accepting what you have to say.
- **Make the offense clear.** Don't talk in generalities. Be specific about exactly what was done wrong.
- **Preface the criticism with a kind word or a compliment.** Start with a few words of praise or admiration, saying how much you value the person. First the good news, then the bad.
- **Supply the answer.** Explain how to do things right. Don't dwell on the mistake; emphasize how to correct it and how to avoid repeating it.
- **Ask for cooperation.** Don't demand cooperation. Asking makes the person feel like a team member and provides an incentive to improve.
- **Limit yourself to one criticism for each offense.** Don't dredge up or rehash past mistakes. Focus on the current problem.
- **End on a friendly note.** Don't conclude by leaving things up in the air, to be discussed again later. Settle them now, and make the close friendly. Give the other person a pat on the back. Let the last memory of the matter be a good one.
- **Forgive and forget.** Once the criticism has been made, let the person start with a clean slate. Avoid looking for more mistakes, and give the person a chance to improve.
- **Take steps to prevent a recurrence.** Follow up to make sure the person is acting on your suggestions and doing things right.

If you follow these guidelines, constructive criticism can benefit you, your company, and—most important—the person you're criticizing.

Career Applications

1. Think back over the lessons you've learned in life. How did you benefit from someone telling you the truth about something you were doing wrong?
2. With a partner, role-play a situation in which one of you is the boss and the other an employee. The boss is angry because the employee repeatedly arrives late for work, takes long lunches, and leaves 5 to 10 minutes early. However, the employee's work is always excellent. After the role-play, analyze what the boss did right and what could be improved.

Be aware that employee performance reviews can play an important role in lawsuits. It's difficult to criticize employees face-to-face, and it's just as hard to include criticism in written performance evaluations. Nevertheless, if you fire an employee for incompetence and the performance evaluations are all positive, the employee can sue your company, maintaining you had no cause to terminate employment.[16] Also, your company could be sued for negligence if an injury is caused by an employee who received a negative evaluation but received no corrective action (such as retraining).[17] So, as difficult as it may be, make sure your performance evaluations are well balanced and honest.

When you need to give a negative performance review, follow these guidelines:[18]

- **Confront the problem right away.** Avoiding performance problems only makes them worse. The one acceptable reason to wait is to allow you time to calm down and regain your objectivity.
- **Plan your message.** Be clear about your concerns, and include examples of the employee's specific actions. Think about any possible biases you may have, and get

feedback from others. Collect and verify all relevant facts (both strengths and weaknesses).

- **Deliver the message in private.** Whether in writing or in person, be sure to address the performance problem privately. Don't send performance reviews by e-mail or fax. If you're reviewing an employee's performance face-to-face, conduct that review in a meeting arranged expressly for that purpose, and consider holding that meeting in a conference room, the employee's office, or some other neutral area.
- **Focus on the problem.** Discuss the problems caused by the employee's behavior (without attacking the employee). Compare the employee's performance with what's expected, with company goals, or with job requirements (not with the performance of other employees). Identify the consequences of continuing poor performance, and show that you're committed to helping solve the problem.
- **Ask for a commitment from the employee.** Help the employee understand that planning for and making improvements are the employee's responsibility. However, finalize decisions jointly so that you can be sure any action to be taken is achievable. Set a schedule for improvement and for following up with evaluations of that improvement.

Even if your employee's performance has been disappointing, you would do well to mention some good points in your performance review. Then you must clearly and tactfully state how the employee can better meet the responsibilities of the job. If the performance review is to be effective, be sure to suggest ways that the employee can improve.[19] For example, instead of only telling an employee that he damaged some expensive machinery, suggest that he take a refresher course in the correct operation of that machinery. The goal is to help the employee succeed.

Terminating Employment

Carefully word a termination letter to avoid creating undue ill will and grounds for legal action.

When writing a termination letter, you have three goals: (1) present the reasons for this difficult action, (2) avoid statements that might involve the company in legal action, and (3) leave the relationship between the terminated employee and the firm as favorable as possible. For both legal and personal reasons, present specific justification for asking the employee to leave.[20]

Make sure that all your reasons are accurate and verifiable. Avoid words that are open to interpretation, such as *untidy* and *difficult.* Make sure the employee leaves with feelings that are as positive as the circumstances allow. You can do so by telling the truth about the termination and by helping as much as you can to make the employee's transition as smooth as possible.[21] To review the tasks involved in this type of message, see this chapter's "Checklist: Negative Employment Messages."

Best of the Web

Protect Yourself When Sending Negative Employment Messages

A visit to CCH's Business Owner's Toolkit can help you reduce your legal liability, whether you are laying off an employee, firing an employee, or contemplating a company-wide reduction in your workforce. Find out the safest way to fire someone from a legal standpoint before it's too late. Learn why it's important to document disciplinary actions. Discover why some bad news should be given face-to-face and never by a letter or over the phone.

www.toolkit.cch.com/scripts/sohotoc.asp

✓ CHECKLIST: NEGATIVE EMPLOYMENT MESSAGES*

A. Buffer

1. Identify the applicant or employee clearly when writing to a third party.
2. Express the reasons for writing—clearly, completely, and objectively.
3. Avoid insincere expressions of regret.
4. Avoid impersonal business clichés.

B. Reasons

1. Avoid terms with legal definitions (*slanderous, criminal*).
2. Avoid negative terms with imprecise definitions (*lazy, sloppy*).
3. Whenever possible, embed negative comments in favorable or semifavorable passages.
4. Avoid generalities, and explain the limits of your observations about the applicant's or employee's shortcomings.
5. Eliminate secondhand information.
6. Stress the confidentiality of your letter.
7. Avoid negative personal judgments.
8. For letters refusing to supply a recommendation to job seekers, suggest another avenue for getting a recommendation.
9. For rejection letters, emphasize the positive qualities of the person hired rather than the shortcomings of the rejected applicant.
10. For performance reviews, describe the employee's limitations and suggest methods for improving performance.

C. The bad news

1. Imply negative decisions whenever possible.
2. Avoid statements that might involve the company in legal action.

D. Positive, friendly, helpful close

1. For refusals to supply recommendations and for rejection letters, extend good wishes.
2. For performance reviews, express a willingness to help further.
3. For termination letters, make suggestions for finding another job, if applicable.

*These items are in addition to the material included in the "Checklist: Bad-News Messages."

COMMUNICATION CHALLENGES AT CAPONIGRO PUBLIC RELATIONS

Since founding Caponigro Public Relations, President and CEO Jeff Caponigro has helped dozens of companies convey bad news to employees, shareholders, the general public, and the media. As each challenge arises, he relies on well-trained and loyal employees to develop strategies and to provide solutions for clients who are faced with the task of delivering bad news.

Individual Challenge: Ten customers who picked up their dry cleaning in the last two days have complained to Mason Dry Cleaners about experiencing skin irritations after wearing their newly cleaned garments. Now owner Mark Mason has discovered that a new employee mixed the wrong combination of chemicals when making the cleaning solution for the garments. Mason has hired Jeff Caponigro's firm to draft a bad-news form letter to his customers to explain the situation and to emphasize that the problem has been addressed and corrected. Caponigro has asked you to compose the first draft for his review. The letter will convey an offer to reclean the garments for free and include a coupon for another free cleaning. But before you draft your bad-news letter, list your objectives and major points, then plan how you will open your communication. How will you end on a strong, positive note?

Team Challenge: Drawing on recent events from newspapers or from your own experience, think about some instances in which you thought bad news was delivered improperly and discuss these situations with your classmates. As a group, decide how you would have improved each situation. Be sure to consider the following elements of the message:

- Organizational approach
- Adequacy of actual information and detail
- Positive close
- Choice of words and tone

SUMMARY OF LEARNING OBJECTIVES

1 **Apply the three-step writing process to bad-news messages.** Because the way you say no can be far more damaging than the fact that you're saying it, planning your bad-news messages is crucial. Make sure your purpose is specific, necessary, and appropriate for written media. Find out how your audience prefers to receive bad news. Collect all the facts necessary to support your negative decision, and adapt your tone to the situation as well as to your audience. Bad-news messages may be organized according to

the direct or the indirect approach, and your choice depends on audience preference as well as on the situation. In addition, carefully choose positive words to construct diplomatic sentences. Finally, revision, design, and proofreading are necessary to ensure that you are saying exactly what you want to say in the best possible way.

2 **Show how to achieve an audience-centered tone, and explain why it helps readers.** To create an audience-centered tone, be a good listener, do your research, and acknowledge your readers' feelings and concerns. Use the "you" attitude, choose positive words, and use language that is respectful in your communications. Adopting this tone helps your readers accept that your decision is firm, understand that your decision is fair and reasonable, remain well disposed toward your company, and preserve their pride.

3 **Differentiate between the direct and indirect organizational approaches to bad-news messages, and discuss when it's appropriate to use each one.** The direct approach to bad-news messages puts the bad news up front, follows with the reasons (and perhaps offers an alternative), and closes with a positive statement. On the other hand, the indirect approach begins with a buffer (a neutral or positive statement), explains the reasons, clearly states the bad news (de-emphasizing it as much as possible), and closes with a positive statement. It's best to use the direct approach when you know your audience prefers receiving bad news up front or if the bad news will cause readers little pain or disappointment. Otherwise, the indirect approach is best. Be sure to modify your approach for cultural differences.

4 **Discuss the three techniques for saying no as clearly and kindly as possible.** To say no and still be diplomatic, use three techniques. First, de-emphasize the bad news by minimizing the space (or time) devoted to it, subordinating it in a complex or compound sentence, or embedding it mid-paragraph. Second, relate the bad news in a conditional (*if* or *when*) statement to imply that readers could have received or might someday receive a favorable answer. Third, imply the bad news by saying what you will do, not what you won't do.

5 **Define *defamation,* and explain how to avoid it in bad-news messages.** Defamation is a false statement that is damaging to a person's character or reputation. When written, defamation is called libel. When spoken, it's called slander. To avoid being accused of defamation, (1) never use abusive language, (2) express personal opinions without involving your company (using your own personal letterhead and excluding your title or position), (3) stick to the facts, (4) never write a message in anger, (5) seek legal advice about questionable messages, and (6) communicate honestly.

6 **List three guidelines for delivering bad news to job applicants, and give a brief explanation of each one.** When rejecting job applicants, follow three guidelines: (1) Use the direct approach. Your readers probably assume that a letter from you is bad news, so don't build their suspense. (2) State clearly why your reader was not selected. This explanation can be specific without being personal if you explain that you hired someone with more experience or with qualifications that more closely match position requirements. (3) Suggest alternatives. Perhaps your company has other openings or you would be willing to consider the applicant for future openings.

7 **Outline the main purpose of performance reviews, give three ways to accomplish that purpose, and list five guidelines to follow when giving negative reviews.** The main purpose of a performance review is to improve employee performance. To accomplish this purpose, be sure to emphasize and clarify job requirements, give feedback on employee efforts, and develop a plan of action to guide continuing efforts. When giving negative reviews, confront the problem immediately, plan your message carefully, deliver your message in private, focus on the problem (not on the employee), and ask for a commitment from the employee.

TEST YOUR KNOWLEDGE

1. What are the five main goals in delivering bad news?
2. Why is it particularly important to adapt your medium and tone to your audience's needs and preferences when writing a bad-news message?
3. What are the advantages of using the direct approach to deliver the bad news at the beginning of a message?
4. What is the sequence of elements in a bad-news message organized using the indirect approach?
5. What is a buffer, and why do some critics consider it unethical?
6. When using an indirect approach to announce a negative decision, what is the purpose of presenting your reasons before explaining the decision itself?
7. What are three techniques for de-emphasizing bad news?
8. What is defamation, and how does libel differ from slander?
9. What are three guidelines for writing rejection letters to job applicants?
10. When giving a negative review to an employee, what five steps should you follow?

APPLY YOUR KNOWLEDGE

1. Why is it important to end your bad-news message on a positive note? Explain.
2. If company policy changes, should you explain those changes to employees and customers at about the same time, or should you explain them to employees first? Why?
3. If the purpose of your letter is to convey bad news, should you take the time to suggest alternatives to your reader? Why or why not?

4. When a company suffers a setback, should you soften the impact by letting out the bad news a little at a time? Why or why not?
5. **Ethical Choices** Is intentionally de-emphasizing bad news the same as distorting graphs and charts to de-emphasize unfavorable data? Why or why not?

PRACTICE YOUR KNOWLEDGE

 *Documents for Analysis*

Read the following documents; then (1) analyze the strengths and weaknesses of each sentence and (2) revise each document so that it follows this chapter's guidelines.

Document 8.A: Providing Bad News About Products

Your spring fraternity party sounds like fun. We're glad you've again chosen us as your caterer. Unfortunately, we have changed a few of our policies, and I wanted you to know about these changes in advance so that we won't have any misunderstandings on the day of the party.

We will arrange the delivery of tables and chairs as usual the evening before the party. However, if you want us to set up, there is now a $100 charge for that service. Of course, you might want to get some of the brothers and pledges to do it, which would save you money. We've also added a small charge for cleanup. This is only $3 per person (you can estimate because I know a lot of people come and go later in the evening).

Other than that, all the arrangements will be the same. We'll provide the skirt for the band stage, tablecloths, bar setup, and, of course, the barbecue. Will you have the tubs of ice with soft drinks again? We can do that for you as well, but there will be a fee.

Please let me know if you have any problems with these changes and we'll try to work them out. I know it's going to be a great party.

Document 8.B: Refusing Requests for Claims and Adjustments

I am responding to your letter of about six weeks ago asking for an adjustment on your fax/modem, model FM39Z. We test all our products before they leave the factory; therefore, it could not have been our fault that your fax/modem didn't work.

If you or someone in your office dropped the unit, it might have caused the damage. Or the damage could have been caused by the shipper if he dropped it. If so, you should file a claim with the shipper. At any rate, it wasn't our fault. The parts are already covered by warranty. However, we will provide labor for the repairs for $50, which is less than our cost, since you are a valued customer.

We will have a booth at the upcoming trade fair there and hope to see you or someone from your office. We have many new models of office machines that we're sure you'll want to see. I've enclosed our latest catalog. Hope to see you there.

Document 8.C: Rejecting Job Applications

I regret to inform you that you were not selected for our summer intern program at Equifax. We had over a thousand résumés and cover letters to go through and simply could not get to them all. We have been asked to notify everyone that we have already selected students for the 25 positions based on those who applied early and were qualified.

We're sure you will be able to find a suitable position for summer work in your field and wish you the best of luck. We deeply regret any inconvenience associated with our reply.

Exercises

For live links to all websites discussed in this chapter, visit this text's website at www.prenhall.com/bovee. Just log on and select Chapter 8, and click on "Student Resources." Locate the name of the site or the URL related to the material in the text. For the "Exploring the Best of the Web" exercises, you'll also find navigational directions. Click on the live link to the site.

8.1 **Selecting the Approach** Select which approach you would use (direct or indirect) for the following bad-news messages:

a. A memo to your boss informing her that one of your key clients is taking its business to a different accounting firm
b. An e-mail message to a customer informing her that one of the books she ordered over the Internet is temporarily out of stock
c. A letter to a customer explaining that the tape backup unit he ordered for his new custom computer is on back order and that, as a consequence, the shipping of the entire order will be delayed
d. A letter from the telephone company rejecting a customer's claim that the phone company should reimburse the customer for the costs of a new high-speed modem (apparently, the phone lines will carry data at only half the modem's speed)
e. A memo to all employees notifying them that the company parking lot will be repaved during the first week of June and that the company will provide a shuttle service from a remote parking lot during that period
f. A letter from a travel agent to a customer stating that the airline will not refund her money for the flight she missed but that her tickets are valid for one year
g. A form letter from a U.S. airline to a customer explaining that they cannot extend the expiration date of the customer's frequent flyer miles even though the customer was living overseas for the past three years
h. A letter from an insurance company to a policyholder denying a claim for reimbursement for a special medical procedure that is not covered under the terms of the customer's policy
i. A letter from an electronics store stating that the customer will not be reimbursed for a malfunctioning cell phone still under warranty (the terms of the warranty do not cover damages to phones that were accidentally placed in the freezer overnight)
j. An announcement to the repairs department listing parts that are on back order and will be three weeks late

8.2 **Teamwork** Working alone, revise the following statements to de-emphasize the bad news. (*Hint:* Minimize the space devoted to the bad news, subordinate it, embed it, or use the passive voice.) Then team up with a classmate and read each other's revisions. Did you both use the same approach in every case? Which approach seems to be most effective for each of the revised statements?

a. The airline can't refund your money. The "Conditions" segment on the back of your ticket states that there are no refunds for missed flights. Sometimes the airline makes exceptions, but only when life and death are involved. Of course, your ticket is still valid and can be used on a flight to the same destination.

b. I'm sorry to tell you, we can't supply the custom decorations you requested. We called every supplier and none of them can do what you want on such short notice. You can, however, get a standard decorative package on the same theme in time. I found a supplier that stocks these. Of course, it won't have quite the flair you originally requested.

c. We can't refund your money for the malfunctioning lamp. You shouldn't have placed a 250-watt bulb in the fixture socket; it's guaranteed for a maximum of 75 watts.

8.3 **Using Buffers** Answer the following questions pertaining to buffers:

a. You have to tell a local restaurant owner that your plans have changed and you have to cancel the 90-person banquet scheduled for next month. Do you need to use a buffer? Why or why not?

b. Write a buffer for a letter declining an invitation to speak at the association's annual fundraising event. Show your appreciation for being asked.

c. Write a buffer for a letter rejecting a job applicant who speaks three foreign languages fluently. Include praise for the applicant's accomplishments.

8.4 **Internet** Public companies sometimes have to issue news releases announcing or explaining downturns in sales, profits, demand, or other business factors. Search the Web to locate a company that has issued a press release that recently reported lower earnings or other bad news, and access the news release on that firm's website. Alternatively, find the type of press release you're seeking by reviewing press releases at www.prnewswire.com or www.businesswire.com. How does the headline relate to the main message of the release? Is the release organized according to the direct or the indirect approach? What does the company do to present the bad news in a favorable light?

8.5 **Ethical Choices** The insurance company where you work is planning to raise all premiums for health-care coverage. Your boss has asked you to read a draft of her letter to customers announcing the new, higher rates. The first two paragraphs discuss some exciting medical advances and the expanded coverage offered by your company. Only in the final paragraph do customers learn that they will have to pay more for coverage starting next year. What are the ethical implications of this draft? What changes would you suggest?

EXPAND YOUR KNOWLEDGE

Exploring the Best of the Web:

Protect Yourself When Sending Negative Employment Messages, p. 249

Reduce your legal liability before you discipline or fire an employee for misconduct by paying attention to the advice at the CCH Business Owner's Toolkit. Log on, read, and then answer these questions.

1. What should a manager communicate to an employee during a termination meeting?
2. Why is it important to document employee disciplinary actions?
3. What steps should you take before firing an employee for misconduct or poor work?

Exploring the Web on Your Own

Review these chapter-related websites on your own to learn more about the bad-news issues human resources departments are facing today.

1. Workforce magazine online, www.workforce.com, has the basics and the latest on human resource issues such as recruiting, laws, managing the workforce, incentives, strategies, and more. Read the current edition online.
2. HR.com, www.hr.com, is the place to go to read about workplace trends, legislation affecting employers, recruiting, compensation, benefits, staffing, and more. Log on and learn.
3. BusinessTown.com, www.businesstown.com/people/Reviews.asp, has the latest lowdown on how to conduct a performance review.

LEARN INTERACTIVELY

Interactive Study Guide

Visit "My Companion Website" at www.prenhall.com/bovee. For Chapter 8, take advantage of the interactive "Study Guide" to test your chapter knowledge. Get instant feedback on whether you need additional studying. Read the "Current Events" articles to get the latest on chapter topics, and complete the exercises—as specified by your instructor.

This site offers a variety of additional resources: The "Research Area" helps you locate a wealth of information to use in course assignments. You can even send a message to online research experts, who will help you find exactly the information you need. The "Study Hall" helps you succeed in this course. "Talk in the Hall" lets you leave messages and meet new friends online. If you have a question, you can "Ask the Tutor." And to get a better grade in this course, you can find more help at "Writing Skills," "Study Skills," and "Study Tips."

Grammar Diagnostic Tests

Review and reinforce your grammar and language skills by taking one of the four online diagnostic tests offered at our companion website, www.prenhall/bovee.com. The four tests cover a variety of topics, including spelling, capitals, punctuation, verbs, pronouns, adjectives, adverbs, sentence structure, sentence punctuation, clarity, word choice, style, organization skills, proofreading, and more. Submit your test and assess your competency. Then focus on improving areas where you are weak as you complete the exercises in this chapter.

CASES

APPLYING THE THREE-STEP WRITING PROCESS TO CASES

Apply each step to the following cases, as assigned by your instructor

Planning Cases

Analyze
1. What's your general purpose?
2. What's your specific purpose?
3. What do you want readers to do?
4. Who are your readers? (Who is the primary audience? What do readers have in common? What is their general background? How will they react?)

Investigate
5. What information do readers need?
6. What facts must you gather?

Adapt
How will you establish credibility?

Writing Cases

Organize
1. What's your main idea?
2. Will you use the direct or indirect approach? Why?

Compose
3. Will your tone be informal or more formal?
4. Draft the message as discussed in the "Your task" section of the case.

Completing Cases

Revise
1. Use the "Checklist for Revising Business Messages" on page 155 to edit and revise your message for clarity.

Produce
2. What's the best way to distribute your message? By fax? By e-mail? By sealed envelope?

Proofread
3. Proofread your message for errors in layout, spelling, and mechanics.

NEGATIVE ANSWERS TO ROUTINE REQUESTS

1. No deal: Letter from Home Depot to new faucet manufacturer At least this year there were indoor bathrooms! You remember a time when vendor hopefuls at Home Depot's biannual product-line review weren't granted that amenity in their quest to become one of the huge retail chain's 25,303 North American suppliers. That year the manufacturers' representatives were herded into a cavernous, unheated, metal barn in Fort Worth, Texas. Still, they did their best to win, keep, or expand their spot in the Home Depot product lineup, in individual meetings with a panel of regional and national merchandisers for the chain.

As assistant to the vice president of sales for Atlanta-based Home Depot, you were grateful that last week's review was held at Tropicana Field in St. Petersburg, Florida. The 45,000-seat indoor baseball stadium not only had bathrooms, it smelled better than the reviews you attended at the Kansas City Stockyards immediately after a rodeo, where the flies hadn't yet settled and the odor was *not* of fresh paint and plywood. You often wonder if these offbeat locations aren't chosen to keep vendors off guard during negotiations. But wherever they're held, the weeklong product review sessions are heavily attended.

Product suppliers know that Home Depot holds all the cards, so if they want to play, they have to follow its rules, offering low wholesale prices and swift delivery. Once chosen, they're constantly re-evaluated—and quickly dropped for infractions such as requesting a price increase or planning to sell directly to consumers via the Internet. They'll also hear sharp critiques of their past performance. These are not to be taken lightly.

A decade ago, General Electric failed to keep Home Depot stores supplied with lightbulbs, causing shortages. Co-founder Bernard Marcus immediately stripped GE of its exclusive, 80-foot shelf-space and flew off to negotiate with its Netherlands competitor, Phillips. Two years later, after high-level negotiations, GE bulbs were back on Home Depot shelves—but in a position inferior to Phillips's.

Such cautionary tales aren't lost on vendors. But they know that despite tough negotiating, Home Depot is always looking for variety to please its customers' changing tastes and demands. The sales potential is so enormous, the compromises and concessions are worthwhile. If selected, they get immediate distribution in more than 1,000 stores (a number Home Depot plans to double in the next few years).

Still, you've seen the stress on reps' faces as they explain product enhancements and on-time delivery ideas in the review sessions. Their only consolation for this grueling process is that, although merchandisers won't say yes or no on the spot, they do let manufacturers know where they stand within a day or two. And the company is always willing to reconsider at the next product-line review—wherever it's held.

Your task: You're drafting some of the rejection letters, and the next one on your stack is to a faucet manufacturer, Brightway Manufacturing, 133 Industrial Avenue, Gary, IN 46406. "Too expensive," "substandard plastic handles," and "a design not likely to appeal to Home Depot customers," say the panel's notes. (And knowing what its customers want has put Home Depot in the top 10 of the Fortune 500 list, with $40 billion in annual sales.) Find a way to soften the blow in your rejection letter to Brightway. After all, consumer tastes do change. Direct your letter to Pamela Wilson, operations manager.[22]

2. Bad timing: Letter from AFM Ventures denying an e-commerce firm start-up financing WebTaggers had all the right ingredients for start-up success:

- Three young graduates of New Mexico Tech University who put their heads together and came up with a plan for an e-commerce start-up, based on software they designed
- An experienced chief executive whose presentations to investors were skilled, professional, and convincing
- An initial investment of $1 million from AVLabs to get the ball rolling
- A top law firm investigating patents
- A feature story about their capital-raising efforts in *The New York Times*
- An accountant from Virtualcfo, a financial advising firm, who claims WebTaggers was generating revenue and was expected to turn a profit within a few months

The only thing WebTaggers didn't have was good timing.

The venture capital firm you preside over, AFM Ventures based in Austin, Texas, was impressed by the 10-minute presentation WebTaggers' chief executive, 45-year-old David Chevalier, made at the Texas Venture Capitalist Conference in May. Your investor group liked his style and confidence. Moreover, they liked WebTaggers' product, a software application developed by company co-founders Rudy Rouhana, 24, and Sean McCullough, 25. The program allowed online retailers to track customers' movements around their websites and record their preferences, automatically changing the product information presented to them to reflect their personal interests. Brilliant, your investors agreed. And six months previously, you'd have laid down some of the $10 million WebTaggers was seeking.

But now AFM has qualms. Online retailers have been disappearing from the Internet like dandelion puffs all year long, and WebTaggers caters to that e-commerce crowd. Who will be left to buy WebTaggers' product?

Despite their olive-drab trousers, T-shirts, and nose studs, you genuinely admire the talents of Rouhana, McCullough, and his twin brother, Craig, founders of WebTaggers. And with his history as a vice president for Dell Computers who led six other start-ups to success, the business-suited Chevalier seemed an excellent choice to run the company. You know they've got a deadline to raise the $10 million or their doors will shut, and you've heard rumors that other investment companies are turning them down as well. But you just can't argue with the economic realities. After all, your investment group has to look out for its own interests.

This is a tough year for tech talent, but you're pretty certain these young inventors will turn up again with a new idea before too long. They had such a good beginning! As Travis Fuller, their accountant at Virtualcfo, told you, "Sometimes you can do all the right things, and it still doesn't work."

Your task: As president of AFM Ventures, you're the one who must write to WebTaggers, 6120 Lamar Boulevard, Suite 3, Austin, TX 78704, denying their request for funding. Use whatever positive elements you can offer to buffer the bad news. Reflect their own informality in your style, addressing the letter, "Dear Rudy, Sean, Craig, and David."[23]

3. Disappearing soaps: E-mail from Craftopia.com At Craftopia.com, based in West Chester, Pennsylvania, orders for the Seaside Soaps kit have been flying in faster than you can fill them. Consumers are ordering the kit over your 800 line and from your website, through the SSL (Secure Socket Layering) encrypted ordering service. The frenzy started with a national magazine ad campaign—Craftopia's first.

The print ad for the "soap-making" kits featured a luscious summer beach scene with a sun-drenched little girl playing in the surf. Next to this warm image, an inset photo displayed the translucent blue, yellow, and green "sea-life" soaps spilling from a bucket onto the sand like colored ice cubes. The kit includes molds (for conch and scallop shells, bubbles, starfish, and a porpoise), a two-pound block of glycerine soap (enough for 52 soaps), lavender scent, color dyes, and eyedroppers. Although your site sells some 75,000 products for creative crafts projects, the soap kit is the biggest seller the company has had since its springtime launch by former QVC executive Harold Poliskin.

With deep-pocketed funding from an impressive array of investors, Craftopia.com offers an extensive variety of products for the growing number of crafters now shopping online. "We're seeing people order 50 of something at once," Poliskin proudly told *The Philadelphia Inquirer* shortly after Craftopia's debut. "A lot of stores wouldn't have that much in stock."

At www.craftopia.com, consumers can read Craftopia's online magazine, share tips and ideas with others on the bulletin board, search for projects by level of skill required, and read instructions and tips for using the products they order. If they're reluctant to transmit credit card information over the Internet, they can call 1-800-373-0343, Monday through Friday, 9 A.M. to 5 P.M. ET, and speak to an operator.

Yarn, ribbon, candles, stencils—you name it, Craftopia.com can deliver it to your door. Everything a creative dabbler could ask for—except for those cool Seaside Soap kits so enticingly displayed on your website "for the hot price of just $39.01." You've just been informed by your supplier, which drop-ships the merchandise directly, that the stock has run out. Regardless of the scramble to speed up production, the new kits won't be ready to ship until six weeks from today.

Your task: As customer service supervisor (www.hsn.com/customer_service), you've been asked to break the bad news in an e-mail message notifying customers of the delay. Craftopia will offer refunds or merchandise credit to customers who make such a request. Also, because the soap kits are hitting the kind of numbers that investors want to see, your message will be reviewed by CEO Poliskin before it's released. Better make it your best work.[24]

4. Cyber-surveillance: Memo refusing claim from Silent Watch victim Next week you're going to write a thank-you letter to Roy Young of Adavi, Inc., makers of Silent Watch software, for solving an impossible management task. But right now you've got an employee's claim on your desk, and you're trying to calm yourself before you reply.

Your business is called Advertising Inflatables, and your specialty is designing and building the huge balloon replicas used for advertising atop retail stores, tire outlets, used-car lots, fast-food outlets, fitness clubs, etc. You've built balloon re-creations of everything from a 50-foot King Kong to a "small" 10-foot pizza. When your business grew from 2 employees to 25, you thought your biggest concern would be finding enough work to support them.

Your fame spread after local newspapers wrote about your company building giant soft drink "cans" for a Pepsi Superbowl commercial, set in outer space with real cosmonauts. The commercial never aired, but your business boomed. You hired more designers, salespeople, customer service reps, and additional painters and builders to work in the shop. Today, even design work is done on computers, and it turns out the hardest part of your job is managing the people who run them.

As business increased, you started spending your days outside the office, attending business events and making presentations. That's when productivity began to slip. If you showed up at the office unexpectedly, you noticed computer screens suddenly switching to something else. You got suspicious.

You decided to install the "cyber-surveillance" software, Silent Watch, to record your employees' every keystroke. You sent around a memo informing your staff that their computer use should be limited to work projects only and that their e-mail should not include personal messages. You also informed them that their work would be monitored. You didn't tell them that Silent Watch would record their work while you were gone or that you could now monitor them from a screen in your office.

Sure enough, Silent Watch caught two of your sales staff spending between 50 and 70 percent of their time surfing Internet sites unrelated to their jobs. You docked their pay accordingly, without warning. You notified them that they were not fired but were on probation. You considered this extremely generous, but also wise. When they work, both of them are very good at what they do, and talent is hard to find.

Now salesman Jarod Harkington is demanding reinstatement of his pay because he claims you "spied on him illegally." On the contrary, your attorneys have assured you that the courts almost always side with employers on this issue, particularly after employees receive a warning such as the one you gave your workers. The computer equipment is yours, and you're paying a fair price for your employees' time.

Your task: Write a memo refusing Mr. Harkington's claim.[25]

5. No nukes: Letter from SDG&E refusing adjustment request "I will not support nuclear power and I demand that you remove this 'nuclear decommissioning' charge from my bill," wrote Walter Wittgen to the president of San Diego Gas and Electric Company (SDG&E). The president has turned the letter over to you.

As a supervisor in customer service, your life has recently been filled with stress, overtime, and pressure from above. Between angry customers on overloaded phone lines and company directors under pressure from the news media, Mr. Wittgen is a minor problem. But he's part of your job. And his letter came to you all the way from President Edwin A. Guiles.

The larger crisis began when summer heat struck California. As the first former power monopoly in the country to fulfill deregulation requirements, SDG&E was required by law to pass on actual electricity costs to its customers. SDG&E no longer produces or prices electricity but purchases it from a new, open-market Power Exchange (PX). Prices fluctuate with supply and demand, and they had doubled with the heat wave. Customer bills doubled and just kept climbing. Even worse, SDG&E had failed to warn the public, so customers were stunned and angry.

The media descended, and politicians responded. With similar deregulation planned throughout the country, the governor and even the president of the United States have gotten involved, but no solution has emerged yet. Too late, SDG&E's marketing department tried to publicize that the utility's operations are still controlled by a government agency, the California Public Utilities Commission (CPUC). The new laws meant that SDG&E became only an "energy delivery service provider," selling off its generating plants. It passes on but does not set prices. Nevertheless, people saw SDG&E's name on huge bills, and a few started attacking employees and destroying property.

Then Mr. Wittgen called. Your phone operators pointed out the explanation for "nuclear decommissioning" charges on the back of his bill: "This charge pays for the retirement of nuclear power plants." The wording, like the fee itself, was ordered by the CPUC. When Wittgen called again, he was told that SDG&E bills more than a million customers every month, using a sophisticated software system. It would take a highly paid specialist more than an hour to hand-calculate Wittgen's bill every month, given all the complex line items and formulas involved. For a 50-cent charge, that's unreasonable; plus, it could introduce errors that would cost him more. And the PUC requires that you charge him this fee.

How you handle the smallest customer problem in this volatile atmosphere could easily make tonight's news. It wouldn't be the first time.

Your task: Write a polite refusal to Mr. Walter Wittgen (732 La Cresta Boulevard, El Cajon, CA 92021), explaining why his bill will not be adjusted. SDG&E asks employees to word and sign their letters personally. Your contact number is 1-800-411-SDG&E (7343).[26]

6. Not this time: Letter to Union Bank of California customer denying ATM debit adjustments The ATM Error Resolution Department at Union Bank of California (where you work as an operations officer) often adjusts customer accounts for multiple ATM debit errors. It's usually an honest mistake: A merchant will run a customer's check debit card two or three times through the credit-card machine, thinking the first few times didn't "take," when in fact the machine *was* working. Problem is, customers don't discover they've paid multiple times for one purchase until they receive a bank statement at the end of the month. And then they hit the roof.

The bank's teleservices operators calmly take their information, give them a claim number, and explain that they must send your department a signed, dated claim letter, describing the situation and enclosing receipt copies if they have them. They'll be notified of your decision within 10 to 20 business days.

The routine is usually a credit to their account to correct the error. But this time, your experience and your intuition have made you suspicious about a letter from a Margaret Caldwell. She maintains several hefty joint accounts with her husband at Union Bank of California.

It is true that three debits indicated on her checking account statement were processed on the same day, using her card (not her husband's), and were credited to the same market, Wilson's Gourmet. The debits even carry the same transaction reference number, 1440022-22839837109, which is what got her attention. While that number does indicate time, it changes daily, not hourly. So purchases made on the same day but from different stores can carry the same number, as can different purchases from the same store.

Mrs. Caldwell's statement indicates debits for different amounts: $23.02, $110.95, and $47.50. That doesn't strike you as a multiple-card-swipe situation. And no receipts are enclosed. Mrs. Caldwell writes that the store must have been trying to steal from her by reusing her card numbers, but you doubt it.

You've contacted Wilson's Gourmet, and their statements corroborate your suspicions. The manager, Ronson Tibbits, claims that he's had no problems with his equipment, so it was unlikely that either customer or clerk was able to run a card more than once. He also mentioned that it's common for food shoppers to return at different times during the day to make additional purchases, particularly for highly consumable products, such as beverages, or to pick up merchandise they forgot the first time, perhaps to complete a recipe. Some will stop in during a work break to buy a deli lunch, then return after work to do their shopping. And so on.

You're convinced this was neither a bank error nor an error on the part of Wilson's Gourmet. Whether Mrs. Caldwell is trying to commit an intentional fraud is not going to concern you. It could be that she is merely mistaken or has a memory problem. She might even be an elderly woman on medication. In a situation like this, bank rules are clear: Deny the request politely.

Your task: Write to Margaret Caldwell, 2789 Aviara Parkway, Carlsbad, CA 92008, explaining your denial of her claim #7899. Remember, you don't want to lose this wealthy customer's business.[27]

7. Too anomalous: E-mail declining an invitation from the Disclosure Project As president of the Mid-State Flying Club, your job is to entice pilots to join your organization, which offers discounts on flying lessons and small plane rentals. Like most pilots, you're interested in anomalous aerial phenomena. But two Mid-State members who've become volunteers for the Disclosure Project are now pressuring you to sponsor the nonprofit research organization's free public "Campaign for Disclosure" event in Phoenix next week. You're worried about the club's reputation. Last thing you want to hear is airport scuttlebutt about "those kooks over in Hangar 5."

The Disclosure Project is a high-profile endeavor founded by Dr. Steven Greer, an emergency room physician who gave up his doctor's salary to pursue a course he believes to be vital to our future. Greer and volunteers have documented more than 400 "top-secret military, government, and other witnesses to UFO and extraterrestrial events," from the United States, Britain, Russia, and other countries, and from the armed services, the CIA, NASA, and other agencies, according to the book of transcripts your two members showed you. They also sent the club's name to Greer's Virginia headquarters, so now you've received an e-mail from him, inviting Mid-State to sponsor next week's local event.

Your members, both retired military pilots, insisted that you watch the Disclosure Project videotape. You had to admit it was intriguing to see witnesses with impressive titles and affiliations discuss UFOs they've encountered, secret government "black projects" they know about, and amazing technologies they've witnessed. Their mutual goal is to convince Congress to hold open hearings on the subject. They also want to encourage legislation banning space-based weapons in favor of peaceful cooperation with all cultures, since they say previous encounters prove that "ETs are not hostile." And they want a release of all information on "extraterrestrial technologies" allegedly captured and duplicated by the "black projects." They say these technologies could save the environment and provide new energy sources, and therefore should belong to the public, not private interests.

You watched military and civilian pilots, astronauts, FAA investigation chiefs, air traffic controllers, Air Force intelligence officers, and even a space missile defense consultant and former spokesperson for Werhner von Braun on the tape. Some say they're speaking out despite death threats to remain silent. No wonder your two members sympathize! You've heard them telling their own tales of UFO encounters during airborne military maneuvers—events they were also advised to forget.

In private meetings, congressional representatives, presidential advisers, and military officials have all professed sympathy but concluded with the same statement: They cannot instigate disclosure hearings without an overwhelming public mandate. Considering that Greer's news conference at the National Press Club attracted 250,000 viewers to its simultaneous webcast (the NPC's largest ever), Greer might be closer to achieving that mandate than they suspect.

Your task: You're impressed by this businesslike effort to treat anomalous aerial phenomena seriously, but you know how people are. You don't want your business to become a laughingstock. Keeping your personal views private, write a courteous, appropriate e-mail to Dr. Steven Greer, inquiries@disclosureproject.org, refusing the sponsorship invitation.[28]

NEGATIVE ORGANIZATIONAL NEWS

8. More layoffs: Memo to Motorola employees "Success is a journey, not a destination," Motorola chairman and chief executive Christopher B. Galvin said famously a few years ago. That was when the battered company his grandfather started in 1928 first began its yo-yo pattern of rises and falls in profitability, reflecting big upsets in the markets it serves as manufacturer of semiconductors, cellular telephones, and other communications equipment.

Galvin turned the company upside down to keep it alive. You weren't a vice president at the Schaumburg, Illinois, headquarters at the time, but you are now—the result of much restructuring, plant closings, layoffs, and determined analysis of the world markets for high-tech communications in the late 1990s. You were one of the lucky ones. Instead of being laid off, you rose to become director of technology and manufacturing. Others weren't so lucky. In one year alone, Galvin's company cut more than 30,000 jobs in its quest to modernize, streamline, and bring inventories down to realistic levels.

Galvin's first move was to reinvent Motorola's corporate culture. To keep up with competitors and respond quickly to changing consumer demand, he saw a need to transform the company's notoriously cutthroat internal rivalry among executives working in separate departments. He eliminated, combined, and laid down the law, molding a new internal culture by rewarding what might be called "cooperation for survival."

But when consumers stopped buying cell phones in record numbers in late 2000, Motorola, as well as its competitors and business partners in the high-technology industry (companies like Nokia, Cisco Systems, 3Com, and others) all felt the crunch. They'd overestimated demand and the market was flooded with semiconductors. Profits fell again as consumer demand slowed—and Motorola's designs weren't first choice to begin with (Nokia and Samsung were winning in the cell phone markets). Galvin's urgent quest now is to cut production, cut operating budgets, reduce inventory, close and consolidate plant operations, make fewer but better products, and ultimately, eliminate jobs.

The good news is that it appears Galvin's strategies are working. More promisingly, the cell phone business has begun to rebound, a sign that indicates Motorola may return to profitability soon. With Motorola striving to improve its market responsiveness, especially with cell phones designed for Internet access, financial analysts are hopeful. It may still be a roller-coaster ride for a while, but bets are on that Motorola will rise again.

Your immediate task, however, is unenviable. You must announce another round of closings: two wafer fabrication lines at the Mesa, Arizona, plant. The phase-out will take place over the next two years, shutting down the MOS-6 line and Bipolar Manufacturing Center and affecting 1,200 employees. Many of them will be offered positions at other Motorola plants in the Phoenix area—but not all. It's all part of the continuing "manufacturing renewal process to improve asset management by investing in advanced technologies and consolidating older production facilities." That's what you're planning to tell the financial media.

Your task: Write the memo to employees in the Mesa, Arizona, plant. Use all the good communication techniques you can muster to make this difficult reality more palatable. Unfortunately, decisions about who will lose their jobs and who won't aren't currently available. Such details will be released slowly over the next few months, on a case-by-case basis.[29]

9. Goodbye, Four Seasons: E-mail about budgetary cutbacks at Black & Decker "They aren't going to like this at all, are they, Boss?" you say to Peter Buchheit, director of travel and meeting services for Black & Decker Corp. He's watching you read a memo from upper management.

He nods, "And that 50 percent cut in the travel budget is twice as deep as the one I helped to engineer back in '94, and much worse than the one that got us through the recession in '91."

It was 1998 when you went to work in Buchheit's department for the power tool and home-improvement product manufacturer. The economy was booming, revenues were high, and companies were fighting over talented employees. Black & Decker encouraged its executives to enjoy their travel duties. So they booked costly flights at the last minute, upgraded their lodgings from an ordinary Hilton to a premium Four Seasons, and returned with fat wads of receipts, which your department processed without question. Lavish dining, client entertainment—whatever they wanted to get the job done. Now you quail at the thought of telling these pampered travelers that the gravy days are over.

On the other hand, who knows better than they that the company is enduring hard economic times? As profits slip, salaries, employee benefits, and travel budgets are where most companies start cutting corners.

"So how do we meet these numbers? And who's going to tell them?" you ask Buchheit.

He says nothing, but winks at you and disappears into his office. Two hours later he emerges with a hand-scribbled list of brainstormed ideas about things to cut and things to try, in no particular order:

- Four-star hotels
- Gourmet dining
- Cheaper fares (coach class vs. business), weekend flights, suburban airports

- Hit hotel chains for discounts, based on our repeat business volume
- Buy nonrefundable airline tickets (cheaper)
- Consider company's videoconferencing facility
- Compose e-mail offline/save hotel surcharges on phone usage
- Gas up rental cars at cheaper stations before returning them
- Use imagination to save, save, save

"And this is just the beginning," Buchheit says as he plops these scrambled notes on your desk.

Your task: Buchheit says you'd better send out an e-mail message warning executives about the budget cuts. He asked you to write it so that they feel as if finding cheaper options—such as choosing video over face-to-face meetings—will be voluntary sacrifices they'll make for the company's financial health. Be sure to ask them to get creative.[30]

10. Proud goodbye: Letter to customers from Internet grocer Webvan Group Inc. The only vans you see around Webvan headquarters these days are moving vans. You're surrounded by fast-emptying offices and stacks of moving boxes—the debris of a dying dot-com experiment. Your office is littered with clippings trumpeting your company's demise.

"Webvan Checks Out," announced the *San Francisco Chronicle*. "Traditional Grocers Feel Vindicated," said *The Wall Street Journal*. And worst of all, *Business Week*'s analysis of your failure, "Webvan Left the Basics on the Shelf," and *The Wall Street Journal*'s cautionary tale for managers, "Why Webvan Went Bust."

"The failure was the most spectacular dotcom disaster so far," crowed *Internetweek*.

Not so long ago Wall Street loved you and investors leaped on board. You took a job as assistant to CEO Robert Swan late in the game, but you were also caught up in the Webvan excitement. Hailed as the biggest online retail venture yet, Webvan spent some $1.2 billion in investment capital to carve out a new niche in the grocery business. The concept was to sell groceries over the Internet to consumers too busy to shop in brick-and-mortar stores. As polls indicated, 41 percent of consumers said they hate supermarket shopping.

With traditional supermarket chains watching nervously but skeptically, Webvan spent three years building an expensive infrastructure of high-tech warehouses and distribution centers, served by custom-built Unix software for online ordering, warehousing, and delivery logistics. The service was rolled out ambitiously in several major cities, but sales never met Webvan's projections and a slowing economy dried up potential cash rescues from new investors. Too bad those polls hadn't asked if consumers wanted to *change* their shopping habits.

In San Francisco, 7 percent of the population gave the new service a try—once. It's not that Webvan didn't deliver the goods; it was that consumers too busy to shop were also too busy to wait for the delivery van. And waiting for webpages to display products for selection apparently did not have the same appeal as the social and sensual pleasures of shopping in a bustling market.

Webvan also erred by absorbing a $30–$35 cost per order for something consumers willingly did for free: picking and delivering their own groceries. With a typically thin, 1 percent profit margin in the grocery industry, that was a killer. The company also ignored a history lesson: Consumers gave up home deliveries offered by mom-and-pop grocers back in the 1960s because lifestyles had changed. Working women could easily swing by a market after work as men had always done—but no one was home anymore to receive perishable deliveries.

So now you're one of the last company survivors, helping Swan wrap things up. One of the CEO's biggest regrets publicly admitted was that customers took a backseat in the last days of Webvan. For instance, the company switched to lower-quality produce suppliers to cut expenses. Swan says the least he can do for them now is to express a gracious farewell.

Your task: You're to draft a courtesy letter to customers announcing Webvan's closure, which Swan will sign. Most already know, so use a direct approach and focus on thanking them for their loyalty and their pioneering spirit. As Swan says, "In a different climate, I believe that our business model would prove successful . . . however, the clock has run out on us."[31]

11. The check's in the mail—almost: Letter from Sun Microsystems explaining late payments You'd think that a computer company could install a new management information system without a hitch, wouldn't you? The people at Sun Microsystems thought so too, but they were wrong. When they installed their own new computerized system for getting information to management, a few things, such as payments to vendors, fell through the cracks.

It was embarrassing when Sun's suppliers started clamoring for payment. Terence Lenaghan, the corporate controller, found himself in the unfortunate position of having to tell 6,000 vendors why Sun Microsystems had failed to pay its bills on time—and why it might be late with payments again. "Until we get these bugs ironed out," Lenaghan confessed, "we're going to have to finish some of the accounting work by hand. That means that some of our payments to vendors will probably be late next month too. We'd better write to our suppliers and let them know that there's nothing wrong with the company's financial performance. The last thing we want is for our vendors to think our business is going down the tubes."

Your task: Write a form letter to Sun Microsystem's 6,000 vendors explaining that bugs in their new management information system are responsible for the delays in payment.[32]

12. Everything old is new again: E-mail message reporting polyester findings Polyester got a bad rap in the 1980s. Now it's making a comeback in both fashion and food. What? Eat and drink from polyester containers? It's an idea whose time has come, according to chemical companies ranging from Dow to Amoco. An ice-cold Coke sipped from a polyester container may be tough for some Americans to swallow, but experts predict that a new generation of plastic may solve many of the problems, such as carbonation loss and heat sensitivity, caused by the containers now being used.

Today's drink bottles use a plastic called PET (polyethylene terephthalate). When stressed by heat, PET is too porous to contain the "fizz." But PET can now be mixed with a recently developed polyester called PEN (polyethylene naphthalate) to create a new generation of tougher plastic. Shell Chemical's director of polyester research and development, David Richardson, believes in the product. "In a few years, I'll be able to fix you a nice meal, and everything in it will come out of a polyester container."

Why make the switch from aluminum or glass to plastic? "Plastic is less deadly than glass when you throw it at a soccer match," says Richard Marion, an executive at Amoco Corporation's Amoco Chemical Company. Airlines like it because it's lightweight. Their little jelly containers used in first class will weigh less. Consumers like it because it's clear, resealable, lightweight, and easily recycled. Polyester is definitely making a comeback. But one segment of the population is proving resistant to the trend: young adults. In a market research study, students preferred aluminum cans: Of all the container materials, aluminum ranked highest, achieving an 84 percent acceptance rate.

According to the study, students like the feel of the aluminum cans (plastic feels slippery and is harder to hold) and believe that aluminum keeps drinks colder. They also believe that aluminum keeps the carbonation longer, creating a "mouth buzz," whereas plastic lets the fizz out. And finally, they think that aluminum cans look "cool" and that plastic containers look "dorky."

Your market research team has come up with a couple of ways to deal with these perceptions. One approach would be an ad campaign showing "cool" young adults drinking from plastic bottles. Another would be ads showing that new technology is helping the plastic containers to hold in the "fizz."

Your task: As assistant director of marketing for Coca-Cola, write an e-mail message to your boss, Tom Ruffenbach, TomRuf@marketing.coca-cola.com, in which you report your findings and suggest ways to overcome this consumer bias.[33]

13. Product recall: Letter from Perrigo Company to retailers about children's painkiller Discovering that a batch of your company's cherry-flavored children's painkiller contains more than the label-indicated amount of acetaminophen was not a happy occasion around Perrigo Company. But such errors do happen, and the best move is immediate, direct, and complete honesty with retailers and the public—so say your superiors in the Customer Support and Service Department. Full and prompt disclosure is especially crucial when consumers' health is involved, as it always is in your line of business.

Perrigo is the leading manufacturer of store-brand, over-the-counter (OTC) pharmaceuticals and nutritional products, producing more than 900 products. These are the items found beside brand-name products such as Tylenol, Motrin, Aleve, Benadryl, NyQuil, Centrum, or Ex-Lax, but they're packaged under the name of the store customers are shopping in. They're priced a bit lower and offer "comparable quality and effectiveness," as your sales literature proclaims.

For retailers, selling Perrigo products yields a higher profit margin than name brands. For consumers, buying the store brands can mean significant savings.

As of this morning, your marketing department calculates that 6,500 four-ounce bottles of the "children's nonaspirin elixir" (a Tylenol look-alike) are already in the hands of consumers. That leaves some 1,288 bottles still on store shelves. The problem is that the acetaminophen contained in the painkilling liquid is up to 29 percent more than labels state, enough to cause an overdose in the young children the product is designed for. Such overdoses can cause liver failure. No one is telling you how this error happened, and it's only been found in lot number 1AD0228, but frankly, finding a guilty party is not so important to your job. You're more concerned about getting the word out fast.

The painkiller has been sold under the Kroger label at stores in Alabama, Arkansas, Georgia, Illinois, Indiana, Kentucky, Louisiana, Michigan, Mississippi, Missouri, North Carolina, Ohio, South Carolina, Tennessee, Texas, Virginia, and West Virginia. It was sold under the Hy-Vee label in Illinois, Iowa, Kansas, Minnesota, Missouri, Nebraska, and South Dakota, and under the Good Sense label at independent retail chains throughout the United States. Perrigo needs to notify consumers throughout the United States that they should not give the product to children, but check the lot number and return the bottle to the store they bought it from for a refund if it's from the affected batch.

Your task: Perrigo's corporate communications department is sending out immediate news releases announcing the product recall to all media, but as customer service supervisor, you must notify retailers. They've already been told verbally, but legal requirements mandate a written notification. That's good, because a form letter to your retail customers can also include follow-up instructions. Explain the circumstances behind the recall, and instruct stores to pull bottles from the shelves immediately for return to your company. Refunds they provide to consumers will, of course, be reimbursed by Perrigo. Questions should be directed to Perrigo at 1-800-321-0105—and it's okay if they give that number to consumers. Be sure to mention all that your company is doing, and use resale information.[34]

14. Safe selling: Memo from The Sports Authority headquarters about dangerous scooters You're not surprised that the Consumer Product Safety Commission (CPSC) has issued a consumer advisory on the dangers of motorized scooters. You've tried them yourself, as a merchandiser for The Sports Authority's 198-store chain. You've still got the scars to prove it! You made a mistake too many parents are making: You skipped the elbow pads.

The electric or gas-powered scooters, which feature two wheels similar to in-line skates, travel 9 to 14 miles per hour. Sales have been growing steadily—with a comparable rise in statistics for broken arms and legs, scraped faces, and bumped heads. Over a six-month period, the CPSC says 2,250 motorized scooter injuries were reported by emergency rooms around the country, as well as three deaths.

It's that last figure that disturbs you most. Your stores sell a wide selection of both the foot-powered ($25 to $150) and motorized scooters ($350 to $1,000). Children and adults alike are hopping on to try them out, get from here to there, or learn new tricks. Unlike a motorcycle or bicycle, a scooter can be mastered by first-timers almost immediately, so the temptation is to jump on and go. For you, it was only while you were in that slow-motion moment before hitting the cement that you thought about safety gear, with serious regret.

What's bothering you now is that all three of the fatal accidents could have been prevented. In each case, the rider died from a head injury. None of them were wearing helmets, a $26 item for adults, $24 for children. One victim was 6 years old (fell off), one was 11 (ran into a truck), and one

was 46 (hit by a car). You've decided that if Sports Authority is to continue selling scooters, you've got to address the safety issue. Embrace the bad news and turn it into a public campaign. And as merchandise manager, you have the authority to get things rolling.

Some states already require helmets, or restrict motorized scooters to children over 16. The CPSC advisory urges helmets, knee and elbow pads, sturdy, closed-toe shoes, riding only during daylight, and avoiding public roads or elaborate stunts. The commission also suggests that children under 12 shouldn't ride the motorized scooters at all, and children under 8 should only ride foot-powered scooters with adult supervision. Your plan is for The Sports Authority, largest full line sporting goods retailer in the United States, to publicly support the CPSC safety guidelines. It's not only the right thing to do—helping to make scooters safe to enjoy will also support future sales.

First, you compose a "Scooter Safety Rules" brochure to be given to customers and posted on The Sports Authority website. Now you must educate your 12,000 employees, starting with news about the negative consumer advisory and the three preventable fatalities. You will mandate a staff meetings to teach employees to include safety issues in their sales pitch. Contented, safe customers are your best business. You want to see increased sales of reflective gear ($6–$15), helmets ($24), and elbow and knee pads ($19)—not to improve on your $1.5 billion annual revenue, but to save lives.

Your task: Draft a bad-news memo to store managers, informing them of the CPSC advisory and the steps you expect them to take. Ample copies of "Scooter Safety Rules" will be sent to stores in two weeks.[35]

NEGATIVE EMPLOYMENT MESSAGES

15. Reverse hiring: Form e-mail breaking bad news to Intel's campus recruits When a company stops hiring to fill vacancies, starts closing plants, defers payment of management raises for six months, and splits the rank-and-file raises into "half now, half in six months," you know times are tough. That's what Intel has done, while human resources strives to hit the numbers management has targeted for a large and immediate reduction in staff and salary expenses. But others' sacrifices are going to be small consolation to the talented college graduates Intel recruited last winter. They're about to become the latest victims of a soft economy.

As a human resources manager at Intel, you truly despise certain aspects of your job. De-hiring college recruits is one of the worst. The only consolation is that it's happening everywhere, particularly among your high-tech partners and competitors. A short time ago, recruiting new talent was so crucial to your success that companies were competing to hire the best college graduates in hot-and-heavy, on-campus recruiting sessions—and then figuring out later what jobs to place them in. Now you'll be gently rescinding job offers you made to campus recruits while they were in the last half of their last semester. It's too late for them to take other offers or to re-experience the job-fair atmosphere. They'll have to go out on the streets looking for something new on their own.

Worst of all, they'll be competing with hundreds of thousands of newly unemployed, but more experienced workers laid off from nearly every segment of industry during the economic slump. Add the retirees trying to get back into the workplace after a sliding stock market devalued their retirement funds and the moms returning to work to help the family budget, plus last year's college graduates who fell under "last-in, first-out" layoff policies, and you would not be in these grads' shoes for anything. But of course, you might be, if things don't pick up soon.

At least Intel plans to offer the grads a "reverse hiring bonus" of two months' salary for the jobs they'd been promised if they agree not to come to work now. They can also retain any signing bonuses they were granted. By making this offer, Intel is trying avoid legal problems while hitting its job-reduction goals. Meanwhile, the company wants to preserve its reputation on campuses as an excellent employer, which will be as important as ever when the economy rebounds (it always does). Since company recruiters thought enough of these graduates to offer them jobs in the first place, you will do so again when you're able. You want them to maintain a good opinion of Intel.

If the recruits don't accept the offer to dismiss all claims against the company in exchange for the bonus, they can still come to work at Intel now, but you can't promise they'll have the jobs they were originally offered. The new job will likely be much further down the employment ladder than they were expecting, and that job could soon be "redeployed" as other Intel positions have been in recent weeks. Then they'll wind up in a waiting pool with other workers whose jobs were eliminated, waiting their turn for another position.

Your task: Write a form e-mail to break the news to Intel's college recruits. Explain the options, and give them an address for reply and a time limit of two weeks.[36]

16. Survive this: Recommendation refusal at Bank of America Rogan Halliwell is highly intelligent, quick with his work, handsome, accurate, and one of the most conceited individuals you've ever met. As manager of a Bank of America branch office, you've never had an employee irritate you like Halliwell. But he charmed his way through the interview with agile diplomacy, and you made the mistake of hiring him.

You were dazzled at first, like his co-workers. But in the eight months he worked for you, you had to call him in three times and remind him of new harassment laws, which prohibit any behavior that distracts or irritates others. Among the complaints about him was one from a woman who said he kept calling her "Babe."

"But a 60-year-old woman should be flattered!" he argued.

Most of his co-workers complained as well: His overbearing ego disgusted them and his steady chatter about his personal life ruined their days. He made jokes about customers behind their backs, and he amused himself by stirring up conflicts among employees. Morale was rapidly disintegrating.

The problem was that, despite his abysmal interpersonal skills, Halliwell was a good teller. His cash drawer almost always balanced perfectly. He was fast, he was charming to customers while they were present, and he learned quickly. You got so many compliments about that "nice young man" from older customers that you couldn't believe they were talking about the same Rogan Halliwell. How could you fire him?

One bright morning, Halliwell solved your problem. "I've decided to move to Hollywood," he announced, loudly enough for his co-workers to hear. "I think they're ready for me." You said a silent "Thank you" as you accepted his notice.

Today you received a letter from Halliwell. He writes that he expects to be hired by one of those *Survivor*-type reality TV shows. He wants a character reference.

You blanch. He may have the right qualities to make reality TV interesting, but listing them would sound slanderous coming from a bank manager. Moreover, you can't in good conscience recommend that anyone work with him. Yet his demonstrated skills make it risky for you to refuse.

Your task: Using techniques you've learned in this chapter, write a refusal that won't expose you or Bank of America to legal repercussions. Send it to Rogan Halliwell, 2388 Pitt Avenue, Apt. 4, Hollywood, CA 90028.[37]

17. Cost sharing: Memo to Bright Manufacturing employees announcing additional employee costs for health insurance benefits As benefits manager in the human resources department of Bright Manufacturing in Tustin, California, you've never before asked employees to share the cost of their health-care coverage. But those costs have been skyrocketing for years. You've seen statistics saying that, nationwide, employer-sponsored medical plan costs are rising 10 to 20 percent per year.

Your provider, Blue Cross of California, has announced a monthly cost increase of 40 percent next year. They say the increase is necessary because, in addition to the rising costs of medical care, claims from your workers and their dependents have been high. Although Bright has paid its employees' health-care expenses since its founding in 1946 as a manufacturer of architectural hardware, this is more than the company can afford.

Last year you were able to juggle costs by working with Blue Cross to modify benefits and raise office visit copayments, or "copays" (the amount employees and dependents pay at each appointment, which rose last year from $5 to $8). This time, you'll have to further modify benefits, raise the office copay to $10, raise emergency room copays from $35 to $50, in addition to collecting 20 percent of the cost of their health insurance from employees' paychecks each month. Bright will pay the remainder, including 10 percent of the cost increase. This year, you will absorb prescription drug increases (23 percent); next year, maybe not.

In light of these escalating costs, you've been working long hours to develop an alternative for employees. If they opt to switch to a new Blue Cross HMO plan (assigned doctors) instead of their former, pick-your-own-doctor Blue Cross Plus plan, Bright will pay the entire cost. That's because the HMO plan costs much less.

Employees can make this change during the Open Enrollment period, the only time during the year that they can make alterations to their health coverage. This year, that will be between November 20 and December 1. Forms to fill out are available in your office. If employees submit no changes, their coverage will remain Blue Cross Plus, and the 20 percent will be deducted monthly from their paychecks, beginning January 1.

How much will that be in dollars? That depends on the number of dependents and other factors. You're setting up a benefits information line to answer these and other questions. You expect to be deluged with calls about this confusing subject, so you're assigning extra staff to handle the phones. Employees will also find more information on the company's intranet. Plus, you're going to give them the Blue Cross website address, www.bluecrossca.com, for general information on health-care coverage.

All in all, your workers aren't so bad off. Many companies have required health-care contributions for years; with the recent increases, those companies are now asking employees to pay an even larger portion of the expense.

Your task: Write a memo to all employees informing them of the increased health plan copay costs and the new payroll deduction for health insurance. Be sure to explain the reasons for these changes. Then inform employees of the HMO option at no cost to them, remind them of the Open Enrollment period, and highlight the ways they can obtain more information. You'll also be sending them a company-produced booklet with charts and tables detailing health insurance costs, options, and alternatives. Soften the blow by emphasizing what Bright has done in the past and present for its employees.[38]

18. Too much *teléfono:* Negative performance review letter to Pacific Bell employee Because doing business in San Diego is a multicultural proposition, Pacific Bell tries to be savvy about its diverse workforce. For example, the company does not condone behaviors that interfere with the tasks at hand, no matter who commits them or why. That the offender in this case happens to be your 22-year-old nephew, and that his offense is likely due to his Mexican American heritage, is not going to get him off the hook, even though you may understand it better than anyone. You long ago joined your culture to his, via marriage to his mother's sibling.

You are supervisor of the billing adjustments department for Pacific Bell, where you and your staff make certain that the millions of phone bills sent out are calculated correctly by your computer programs and fulfill changing government tariffs (written regulations and requirements) imposed on phone companies. You didn't personally hire Jorge Gutierrez. That was done by a man one level below you, who found Gutierrez working as a temporary in another department and gave him a try, with your approval.

You were both amazed and pleased by his fast learning skills and innate understanding of the customer accounts associate job that's been almost impossible to fill. Few employees could enter, verify price changes, and test computerized price calculation formulas with the accuracy and speed that Gutierrez, an extremely intelligent and skilled mathematician, could. With over 1 million customers, even tiny mistakes can be costly. Gutierrez was a real find—except for one problem he hasn't been able to surmount.

The man who hired him, now his supervisor, tells you that every morning your nephew receives a phone call from his Mexican American mother, who wants to be sure he's made it to work safely. Often his father also calls. Afternoon calls are from his baseball buddies—the ones he plays with in the Mexican league on weekends—and other family members. Then it's his girlfriend, also Mexican American. In one month's time, he asked permission to leave for "family emergencies" to (1) change his girlfriend's flat tire on the freeway, (2) deliver an extra car key because she locked herself out, and (3) defend her from an aggressive and unsavory boss at a job she quit that afternoon.

Gutierrez is fully aware of the problem these calls are causing at work and has asked friends and family not to call his office number—so they dial his cell phone instead. He still lives with his parents, which may be why they seem insensitive to his appeals.

Both you and his supervisor have given Gutierrez verbal warnings. You really can't afford to lose him, so you're hoping that stepping up the pressure with a written, negative review will give him greater incentive to persuade friends and relatives. You'll deliver the letter in a meeting and help him find ways to resolve the issue within a mutually agreed-upon time frame.

As an "adopted" member, you fully understand that Mexican American families tend to remain close-knit. Still, after six months on the job, Gutierrez should be doing better at balancing his family with his career.

Your task: Write the letter, using suggestions in this chapter and details in this case to help you put the bad news in a constructive light. Avoid culturally biased remarks or innuendo. Culture isn't really the issue; maturity is.

19. Cell phone violations: E-mail message to associates at Wilkes Artis law firm "Our policy is that personnel are not to conduct business using cell phones while on the road unless they pull over and stop or use a hands-free device," David Fuss reminds you. He's a partner at the law firm where you supervise human resource issues, Wilkes Artis in Washington, D.C.

"Yes, I know that," you say, wondering why he's quoting to you a policy you yourself drafted, posted, and personally issued to everyone in the firm after that horrible incident involving another Washington law firm.

But he insists again that you need to be sure the new policy is enforced. Apparently, one of the associates used a cell phone to issue orders to his secretary while driving back from a client meeting. He reminds you of what happened to that 15-year-old girl a couple of years ago.

You shudder. "Yes, sir. I'll see to it."

"It's a commonsense safety concern," he adds. Finally, he leaves you to brood.

The incident he mentioned reverberated throughout the business community. As a result, more companies are adopting no cell phone policies for employees who drive, and several states have passed laws banning their use by drivers. Statistics support the move. The National Highway Transportation Safety Administration has issued figures indicating that 20 to 30 percent of all driving accidents can be related to cell phone usage, whether handheld or not. With an expected 1.26 billion cell phones in use worldwide by 2005, it's no wonder that states are considering bans and that Japan, Israel, Portugal, and Singapore are just a few of more than two dozen countries restricting drivers' use of cell phones.

But statistics pale beside the story of 15-year-old Naeun Yoon and attorney Jane Wagner from the Washington firm of Cooley Godward. Wagner was driving back from a meeting in Tysons Corner, Virginia, late one spring night, talking on her cell phone. She felt her car hit something, thought it was a deer, and kept driving. The next morning she heard news reports of a hit-and-run driver who'd killed the teenaged Yoon. With horror, Wagner realized she was the driver. She turned herself in, eventually serving a year's sentence at a work-release program. She and her firm were sued by Yoon's family in a $30-million wrongful death action.

The lawsuit definitely played a role in forging "no cell phone" policies at many companies, but it was Yoon's death that drove the issue home: Someone could die or be seriously injured, simply because a business call "couldn't wait."

The National Safety Council says talking on the phone causes driver distraction because of the cognitive engagement it requires. Even a dropped phone can be lethal. A broker with Salomon Smith Barney ran a red light and killed a motorcyclist while leaning down to find his phone. His firm, Salomon Smith Barney, admitted no guilt in a subsequent lawsuit but settled out of court with the victim's family for $500,000.

No one knows if the new no-use policies will shield employers from legal liability—but everyone knows they will protect human beings from harmful accidents.

Your task: Fuss insists that you write an e-mail message to all employees, announcing a new penalty for a *first* violation of the cell phone policy: suspension without pay, unless the call was a genuine traffic or health emergency.[39]

Writing Persuasive Messages

After studying this chapter, you will be able to

1 *Discuss the planning tasks that need extra attention when preparing persuasive messages*

2 *Describe the AIDA plan for persuasive messages*

3 *Distinguish between emotional and logical appeals, and discuss how to balance them*

4 *Explain the best way to overcome resistance to your persuasive message, and list four common mistakes in writing persuasive messages*

5 *Compare sales messages with fundraising messages*

6 *List eight guidelines that will help you strengthen your fundraising messages*

COMMUNICATION CLOSE-UP AT AT&T'S LANGUAGE LINE SERVICES

www.languageline.com

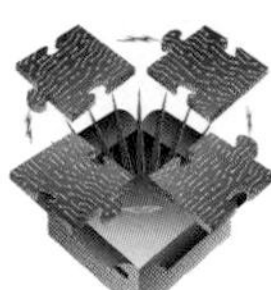

His wife was giving birth, and he didn't know what to do, so the anxious father-to-be dialed 911. Trouble was, he spoke no English, and the operator couldn't understand what the emergency was. Neither party panicked, however; the 911 operator simply dialed an 800 number that connected her to AT&T's Language Line Services. In minutes, the AT&T operator set up a three-way call with a Spanish interpreter who helped talk the worried husband through the delivery of his first child.

As sales director for Language Line Services, Jeanne Anderson has collected dozens of true-life stories like this, and they all illustrate the same thing: the benefits of dialing a toll-free number from any telephone and being connected at a moment's notice with an interpreter in any of 140 languages—24 hours a day. Over the phone, AT&T interpreters have closed a $12 million business deal in Taiwan, handled a marriage proposal in Russia, located a missing parent in Germany, and helped hundreds of nurses, doctors, police officers, and business executives communicate with the diverse populations in their own local communities.

After years of experience writing persuasive messages to help sell Language Line Services, Anderson has developed a few principles she always follows: She is selective with the information she includes in her messages—just enumerating all the languages offered would fill up a page—and she targets a persuasive message directly to her audience's needs. Her goal is not to manipulate readers but to help them make an intelligent, informed decision about her message. Of course, she also makes sure she highlights specific benefits she knows her audience will find attractive.

For every persuasive message, Anderson starts by answering two questions: "Who is my audience, and what are they going to be interested in?" Once she knows the answers, she starts her message with what she calls a "grabber," or attention-getter, designed specifically for this particular audience. Her next paragraphs build her credibility, create interest, and encourage desire by emphasizing benefits she knows her readers care about.

Anderson follows the same principles whether writing persuasive memos to her staff or composing persuasive e-mail messages to clients. She says the only difference is in the language and tone. "When I write an internal memo, I try to make sure that my personality comes out. Otherwise, I think all the same principles apply, because you really are competing for everyone's time." Overall, you want to make your message interesting, and "you really do want to keep it simple," Anderson says. "Even if the first paragraph is interesting, your reader may think, 'Gee, there's just too much detail here. I'll just read this later when I have more time,' and unfortunately, it gets put on that pile—that 'To Do' pile that never gets done!"

To keep it simple, Anderson avoids showy language, unfamiliar words, and AT&T lingo. She chooses active words and phrases that are "crisp and succinct," using the terminology of her audience's own industry when appropriate. Moreover, she always stresses the positive—for example, saying to a potential customer, "This service will save you

To persuade potential customers to try Language Line Services, Jeanne Anderson finds out who her audience is and what they're interested in. Then she crafts her letters to get attention, create interest, encourage desire, and motivate action.

time," instead of saying, "We know you don't have a lot of time." In short, Anderson uses her own skills with language to help others discover a new way to conquer language barriers—if not to save a life, then to make life simpler for everyone.[1] ■

USING THE THREE-STEP WRITING PROCESS FOR PERSUASIVE MESSAGES

Savvy businesspeople such as Jeanne Anderson know that people today ask not only "What should I do?" but also "Why should I do it?" To accomplish her goals, Anderson often uses techniques of **persuasion**—the attempt to change an audience's attitudes, beliefs, or actions.[2] "Quite simply, effective persuasion is the ability to present a message in a way that will lead others to support it," says Jay Conger, author of *Winning 'Em Over.* "It makes audiences feel they have a choice, and they choose to agree."[3]

Persuasion is the attempt to change someone's attitudes, beliefs, or actions.

The most effective business leaders have a knack for putting together a persuasive argument. They know how to take the pulse of a group and communicate with people in terms they can both understand and embrace.[4] So whether you're selling real estate or just trying to sell your idea to your boss, writing effective persuasive messages is indeed an important skill. In today's competitive marketplace, applying the three-step writing process to your persuasive messages will help you make them as effective as possible.

Step 1: Planning Persuasive Messages

Learning Objective 1

Discuss the planning tasks that need extra attention when preparing persuasive messages

Unlike routine positive messages (discussed in Chapter 7), persuasive messages aim to influence audiences who are inclined to resist. Therefore, persuasive messages are generally longer, are usually more detailed, and often depend heavily on strategic planning—like that carried out by Jeanne Anderson of AT&T's Language Line Services. Persuasive messages require that you pay particular attention to several planning tasks. For example, because your purpose is to persuade, making sure of your purpose is perhaps the most important planning task. When analyzing your audience for a persuasive message, you may want to delve more deeply than you would for other messages. Your credibility takes on extra importance in a persuasive message. So whenever you're trying to persuade someone, you must make sure your ethics are above reproach.

For a persuasive message, some planning tasks require more effort.

Analyze Your Purpose

Writing an external persuasive message is one of the most difficult tasks you could undertake. For one thing, your purpose is to persuade people to do something different or to try something new. But people are busy, so they're reluctant to act, especially if it takes time and offers no guarantee of any reward in return. For another, competing

Persuasive requests encounter two problems:
- Audiences are busy.
- Audiences receive many competing requests.

requests are plentiful. The public relations departments of many large corporations receive so many persuasive requests for donations that they must sometimes use lotteries to decide which worthy cause to support. Given the complexity and sensitivity of persuasive messages, you must be absolutely sure that your purpose is clear, necessary, and appropriate for written media.

Analyze Your Audience

You must appeal to the specific needs of your audience, especially in persuasive messages.

Chapter 4 discusses the basics of audience analysis, but the process can become much more involved for persuasive messages. To write an effective persuasive argument, you need to search for common ground, points of agreement on which to build. That means you must shape your argument so that others believe your proposal will satisfy their concerns and bring them rewards. But learning about your audience's needs or concerns can take weeks—even months. Why? Because everyone's needs differ, so everyone responds differently to any given message. For instance, not every reader is interested in economy or even in fair play; you may even find that satisfying someone's need for status or appealing to someone's greed may at times be much more effective than emphasizing human generosity or civic duty.

The questions you ask before writing a persuasive message go beyond those you would ask for other types of messages.

Gauging Audience Needs The best persuasive messages are closely connected to your audience's existing desires and interests.[5] Consider these important questions: Who is my audience? What are their needs? What do I want them to do? How might they resist? Are there alternative positions I need to examine? What does the decision maker consider the most important issue? How might the organization's culture influence my strategy?

It may be necessary to satisfy some needs before others.

Some theorists believe that certain needs have priority. Figure 9.1 represents psychologist Abraham Maslow's hierarchy of needs, with the most basic needs appearing at the bottom of the figure. Maslow suggests that only after lower-level needs have been met will a person seek to fulfill needs on higher levels.[6] For example, suppose you supervise someone who consistently arrives late for work. You must either persuade him to change or fire him. First, find out why he's coming in late. Is he oversleeping because he has a second job to support his family (a safety and security need)? Is he coming in late because of a misguided desire to have people notice his arrival (an esteem and status need)? Once you've analyzed the need motivating him to arrive late, you can craft an appeal, a "hook" that will interest him in your message about changing his behavior. If the need for safety and security is behind his tardiness, you might say, "Your job is very important to you, I know." If he craves esteem and status, you could say, "You've always seemed interested in being given more responsibility, perhaps even a promotion."

FIGURE 9.1 Maslow's Hierarchy of Needs

To assess various individual needs, you can refer to specific information such as **demographics** (the age, gender, occupation, income, education, and other quantifiable characteristics of the people you're trying to persuade) and **psychographics** (the personality, attitudes, lifestyle, and other psychological characteristics of an individual). Both types of information are strongly influenced by culture. When analyzing your audience, take into account their cultural expectations and practices so that you don't undermine your persuasive message by using an inappropriate appeal or by organizing your message in a way that seems unfamiliar or uncomfortable to your audience.

Demographics include characteristics such as age, gender, occupation, income, and education.

Psychographics include characteristics such as personality, attitudes, and lifestyle.

Considering Cultural Differences Your understanding and respect for cultural differences will help you satisfy the needs of your audience and will help your audience respect you. That's because persuasion is different in different cultures. In France, using an aggressive, hard-sell technique is no way to win respect. Such an approach would probably antagonize your audience. In Germany, where people tend to focus on technical matters, plan on verifying any figures you use for support, and make sure they are exact. In Sweden, audiences tend to focus on theoretical questions and strategic implications, whereas U.S. audiences are usually concerned with more practical matters.[7]

Cultural differences influence your persuasion attempts.

As with individuals, an organization's culture or subculture heavily influences the effectiveness of messages. All the previous messages in an organization have established a tradition that defines persuasive writing within that culture. When you accept and use these traditions, you establish one type of common ground with your audience. If you reject or never learn these traditions, you'll have difficulty achieving that common ground, which damages both your credibility and your persuasion attempts.

Every message written for a corporation adds to the corporate tradition.

Establish Your Credibility

To persuade a skeptical or hostile audience, you must convince people that you know what you're talking about and that you're not trying to mislead them. Your *credibility* is your capability of being believed because you're reliable and worthy of confidence. Without such credibility, your efforts to persuade will seem manipulative. Research strongly suggests that most managers overestimate their own credibility—considerably.[8] Establishing your credibility is a process—one that takes time to earn your audience's respect. Some of the best ways to gain credibility are to

Your credibility is defined by how reliable, believable, and trustworthy you are.

- **Support your message with facts.** Testimonials, documents, guarantees, statistics, and research results all provide seemingly objective evidence for what you have to say, which adds to your credibility. The more specific and relevant your proof, the better.
- **Name your sources.** Telling your audience where your information comes from and who agrees with you always improves your credibility, especially if your sources are already respected by your audience.
- **Be an expert.** Your knowledge of your message's subject area (or even of some other area) helps you give your audience the quality information necessary to make a decision.
- **Establish common ground.** Those beliefs, attitudes, and background experiences that you have in common with members of your audience will help them identify with you.
- **Be enthusiastic.** Your excitement about your subject can infect your audience.
- **Be objective.** Your ability to understand and acknowledge all sides of an issue helps you present fair and logical arguments in your persuasive message.
- **Be sincere.** Your concern, genuineness, good faith, and truthfulness help you focus on your audience's needs.
- **Be trustworthy.** Your honesty and dependability help you earn your audience's respect.
- **Have good intentions.** Your willingness to keep your audience's best interests at heart helps you create persuasive messages that are ethical.

Gain credibility by supporting your argument with facts such as testimonials, documents, guarantees, statistics, and research results.

Your credibility is improved if you are an expert, enthusiastic, objective, sincere, and trustworthy and if your intentions are good and you establish common ground.

Your credibility will also be enhanced if you maintain high ethical standards.

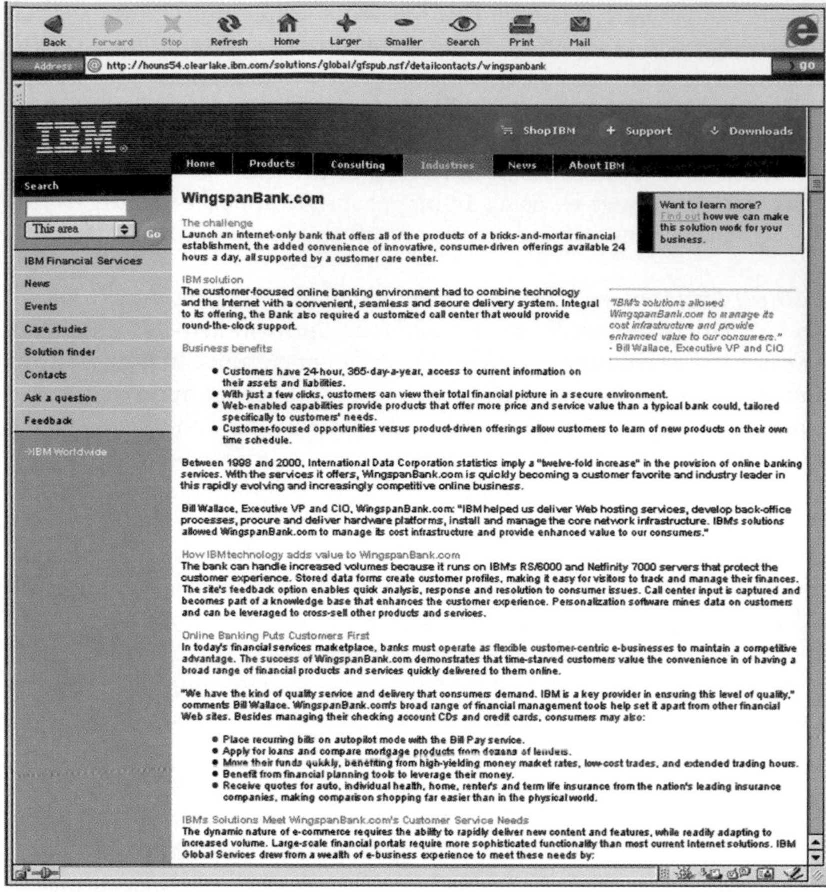

When you use printed messages to build credibility, you generally have limited space for testimonials and other persuasive evidence. On the Internet, however, space is not a problem—you can easily add pages of evidence to convince your audience of your expertise and reliability. You can build credibility by including samples of your work, adding links to third-party supporting documentation, and posting copies of testimonials from satisfied customers.

Strive for High Ethical Standards

Positive persuasion leaves your audience free to choose.

The word *persuasion* is viewed by some as negative. They associate persuasion with dishonest and unethical practices, such as coaxing, urging, and sometimes even tricking people into accepting an idea, buying a product, or taking an unwanted or unneeded action. However, the best businesspeople make persuasion positive. They influence audience members by providing information and aiding understanding, which allows audiences the freedom to choose.[9] Ethical businesspeople inform audiences of the benefits of an idea, an organization, a product, a donation, or an action so that these audiences can recognize just how well the idea, organization, product, donation, or action will satisfy a need they truly have.

To maintain the highest ethics, try to persuade without manipulating.

For anyone trying to influence people's actions, knowing the law is crucial. However, merely avoiding what is illegal may not always be enough. To maintain the highest standards of business ethics, make every attempt to persuade without manipulating. Choose words that won't be misinterpreted, and be sure you don't distort the truth. Adopt the "you" attitude by showing honest concern for your audience's needs and interests. Your consideration of audience needs is more than ethical; it's the proper use of persuasion. That consideration is likely to achieve the response you intend and to satisfy your audience's needs.

Step 2: Writing Persuasive Messages

When applying Step 2 to your persuasive messages, you will define your main idea, limit the scope of your message, and group your points in a meaningful way. But you must focus even more effort on choosing the direct or indirect approach.

As with routine and bad-news messages, the best organizational approach is based on your audience's likely reaction to your message. However, because the nature of persuasion is to convince your audience or to change their attitudes, beliefs, or actions, most persuasive messages use the indirect approach. That means you'll want to explain

FIGURE 9.2 In-Depth Critique: E-Mail Message Selling an Idea to a Boss

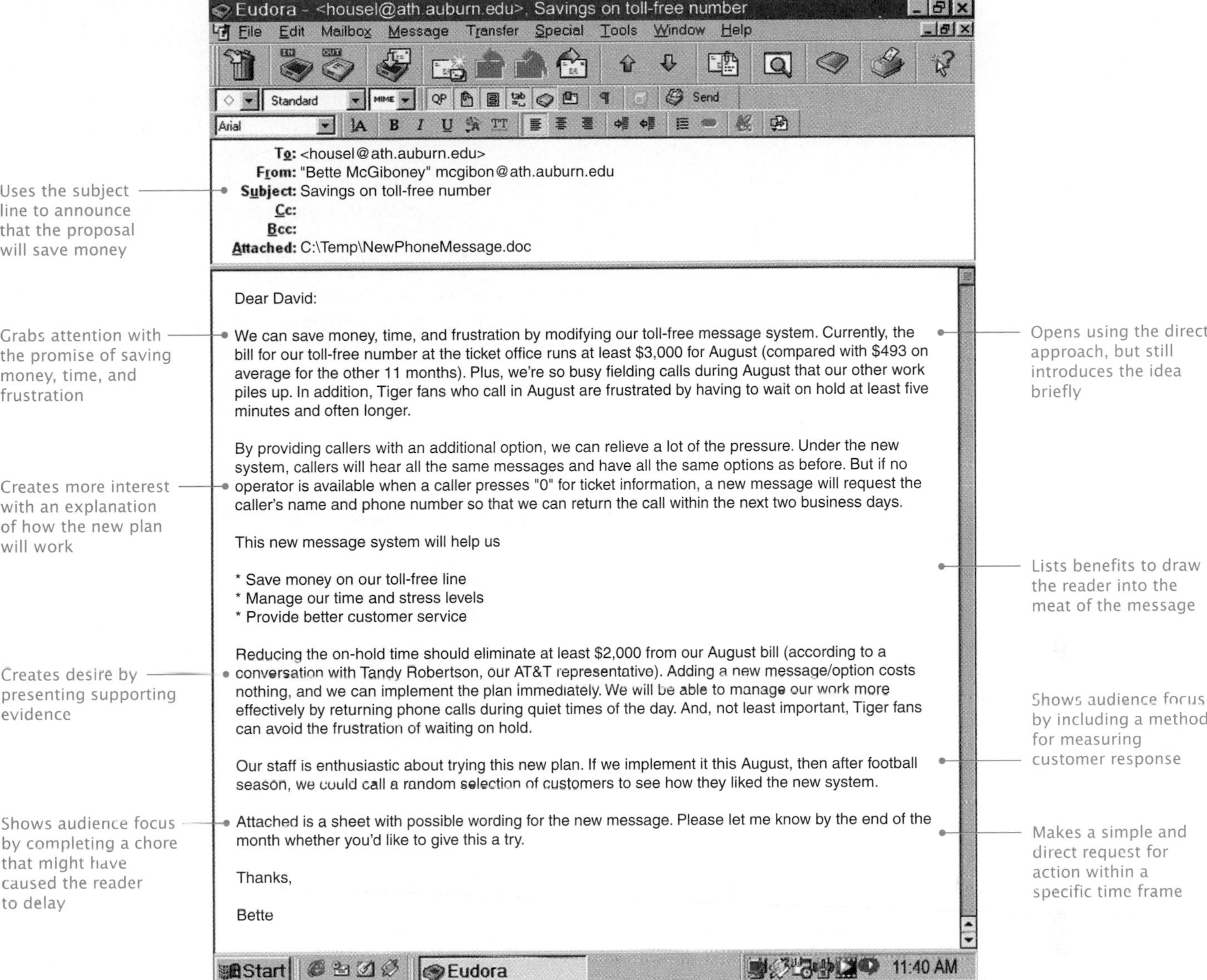

To: <housel@ath.auburn.edu>
From: "Bette McGiboney" mcgibon@ath.auburn.edu
Subject: Savings on toll-free number
Cc:
Bcc:
Attached: C:\Temp\NewPhoneMessage.doc

Dear David:

We can save money, time, and frustration by modifying our toll-free message system. Currently, the bill for our toll-free number at the ticket office runs at least $3,000 for August (compared with $493 on average for the other 11 months). Plus, we're so busy fielding calls during August that our other work piles up. In addition, Tiger fans who call in August are frustrated by having to wait on hold at least five minutes and often longer.

By providing callers with an additional option, we can relieve a lot of the pressure. Under the new system, callers will hear all the same messages and have all the same options as before. But if no operator is available when a caller presses "0" for ticket information, a new message will request the caller's name and phone number so that we can return the call within the next two business days.

This new message system will help us

* Save money on our toll-free line
* Manage our time and stress levels
* Provide better customer service

Reducing the on-hold time should eliminate at least $2,000 from our August bill (according to a conversation with Tandy Robertson, our AT&T representative). Adding a new message/option costs nothing, and we can implement the plan immediately. We will be able to manage our work more effectively by returning phone calls during quiet times of the day. And, not least important, Tiger fans can avoid the frustration of waiting on hold.

Our staff is enthusiastic about trying this new plan. If we implement it this August, then after football season, we could call a random selection of customers to see how they liked the new system.

Attached is a sheet with possible wording for the new message. Please let me know by the end of the month whether you'd like to give this a try.

Thanks,

Bette

your reasons and build interest before revealing your purpose. Nevertheless, many situations do call for the direct approach.

Use the indirect approach when your audience will react unfavorably to your message. Use the direct approach when your message is long or complex, or when your reader prefers directness.

If audience members are objective, or if you know they prefer the "bottom line" first (perhaps because it saves them time), the direct approach might be the better choice. You'll also want to use the direct approach when your corporate culture encourages directness. In addition, when a message is long or complex, your readers may become impatient if the main idea is buried seven pages in, so you may want to choose the direct approach for these messages as well.

Bette McGiboney is administrative assistant to the athletic director of Auburn University. Each year, after season tickets have been mailed, the cost of the athletic department's toll-free phone number skyrockets as fans call with questions about their seats, complaints about receiving the wrong number of tickets, or orders for last-minute tickets. The August phone bill is usually over $3,000, in part because each customer is put on hold while operators serve others. McGiboney came up with an idea that could save the company money and save ticket holders time, so she composed an e-mail message that uses the direct approach (see Figure 9.2).

If you use the direct approach as Betty McGiboney does in Figure 9.2, keep in mind that even though your audience may be easy to convince, you'll still want to include at least a brief justification or explanation. Don't expect your reader to accept your idea on blind faith. For example, consider the following two openers:

Poor	Improved
I recommend building our new retail outlet on the West Main Street site.	After comparing the four possible sites for our new retail outlet, I recommend West Main Street as the only site that fulfills our criteria for visibility, proximity to mass transportation, and square footage.

Choice of approach is also influenced by your position (or authority within the organization) relative to your audience's.

Your choice between the direct and indirect approaches is also influenced by the extent of your authority, expertise, or power in an organization. As a first-line manager writing a persuasive message to top management, you may try to be diplomatic and use an indirect approach. But your choice could backfire if some managers perceive your indirectness as manipulative and time wasting. On the other hand, you may try to save your supervisors time by using a direct approach, which might be perceived as brash and presumptuous. Similarly, when writing a persuasive message to employees, you may use the indirect approach to ease into a major change, but your audience might see your message as weak, even wishy-washy. You need to think carefully about your corporate culture and what your audience expects before selecting your approach.

Step 3: Completing Persuasive Messages

As with other business messages, Step 3 of the writing process helps guarantee the success of your persuasive messages.

The length and complexity of persuasive messages make applying Step 3 even more crucial to your success. When you evaluate your content, try to judge your argument objectively and seriously appraise your credibility. When revising for clarity and conciseness, carefully match the purpose and organization to audience needs.

Your design elements must complement, not detract from, your argument. In addition, make sure your delivery methods fit your audience's expectations as well as your purpose. Finally, meticulous proofreading will identify any mechanical or spelling errors that would weaken your persuasive message.

DEVELOPING PERSUASIVE MESSAGES

Your success as a businessperson is closely tied to your ability to convince others to accept or act on your recommendations. Minimally, you want them to pay close attention to your ideas and value your contributions. Of course, for years you have been doing this informally. Perhaps you persuaded your coach to let you play a position on a team or you convinced students to vote for you in a school election. You may even have persuaded your professor to change a grade. Regardless, being able to persuade others in a written letter or memo is vital in today's competitive workplace. In the following section, we discuss some formal strategies you can use to strengthen your persuasive skills.

Strategies for Persuasive Messages

Four essential persuasion strategies:
- Framing your arguments
- Balancing your appeals
- Reinforcing your position
- Overcoming audience resistance

Whether you use a direct or an indirect approach, you must convince your reader that your request or idea is reasonable. Effective persuasion involves four distinct and essential strategies: framing your arguments, balancing emotional and logical appeals, reinforcing your position, and dealing with resistance. The amount of detail you pursue in each of these strategies varies according to the complexity of your idea or request.

Framing Your Arguments

Learning Objective 2

Describe the AIDA plan for persuasive messages

To effectively persuade your audience, you need to frame your argument in the most effective way. Most persuasive messages follow an organizational plan that goes beyond the indirect approach used for negative messages. The opening does more than serve as a buffer; it grabs your audience's attention. The explanation section does more

TABLE 9.1 The AIDA Organizational Plan

Phase	***Objective***
Attention	Get the reader's attention with a benefit that is of real interest or value.
Interest	Build the reader's interest by further explaining benefits and appealing to his or her logic or emotions.
Desire	Build desire by showing how your offer can really help the reader.
Action	Give a strong and simple call to action and provide a convenient means for the reader to take the next step.

than present reasons, and it's expanded to two sections. The first incites your audience's interest, and the second changes your audience's attitude. Finally, your close does more than end on a positive note with a statement of what action is needed; it emphasizes reader benefits and motivates readers to take specific action. Although similar to the indirect approach of negative messages, this persuasive approach, called the **AIDA plan**, pushes the envelope in each of four phases: (1) attention, (2) interest, (3) desire, and (4) action (see Table 9.1).

Organize persuasive messages using the AIDA plan:
- Attention
- Interest
- Desire
- Action

- **Attention.** Make your audience want to hear about your problem or idea. Write a brief and engaging opening sentence, with no extravagant claims or irrelevant points. And be sure to find some common ground on which to build your case. In the letter in Figure 9.3, Randy Thumwolt uses the AIDA plan in a persuasive memo about his program to reduce Host Marriott's annual plastics costs and to curtail consumer complaints about the company's recycling record.
- **Interest.** Explain the relevance of your message to your audience. Continuing the theme you started with, paint a more detailed picture with words. Get your audience thinking. In Figure 9.3, Thumwolt's interest section introduces an additional, unforeseen problem with plastic product containers. Also, Thumwolt breaks out his suggestions into an easy-to-read list.
- **Desire.** Make audience members want to change by explaining how the change will benefit them. Reduce resistance by thinking up and answering in advance any questions the audience might have. If your idea is complex, explain how you would implement it. Back up your claims in order to increase audience willingness to take the action that you suggest in the next section. Just remember to make sure that all evidence is directly relevant to your point.
- **Action.** Suggest the action you want readers to take. Make it more than a statement such as "Please institute this program soon" or "Send me a refund." This is the opportunity to remind readers of the benefits of taking action. The secret of a successful action phase is making the action easy. In sales letters, AT&T's Jeanne Anderson might ask readers to call a toll-free number for more information. You might ask your audience to use an enclosed order form, or to use a prepaid envelope for donations. Include a deadline when applicable.

Begin every persuasive message with an attention-getting statement that is
- Personalized
- You-oriented
- Straightforward
- Relevant

In the interest section
- Continue the opening theme in greater detail
- Relate benefits specifically to the attention-getter

In the desire section
- Provide evidence to prove your claim
- Draw attention to any enclosures

End by
- Suggesting a specific step the audience can take
- Restating how the audience will benefit by acting as you wish
- Making action easy

The AIDA plan is tailor-made for using the indirect approach, allowing you to save your main idea for the action phase. However, it can also be used for the direct approach, in which case you use your main idea as an attention-getter, build interest with your argument, create desire with your evidence, and emphasize your main idea in the action phase with the specific action you want your audience to take.

Using AIDA with the indirect approach allows you to save your idea for the action phase; using it with the direct approach allows you to use your main idea as your attention-getter.

When your AIDA message uses an indirect approach and is delivered by memo or e-mail, keep in mind that your subject line usually catches your readers' eye first. Your challenge is to make it interesting and relevant enough to capture reader attention without revealing your main idea. If you put your request in the subject line, you're likely to get a quick "no" before you've had a chance to present your arguments.

When using the indirect approach, make subject lines interesting without revealing your purpose.

Planning

Analyze
The purpose is to help solve an ongoing problem. The audience will be receptive.

Investigate
Gather data on recycling problem areas.

Adapt
Use a memo, and strengthen the point by reviewing the bulk-purchase idea, which has already been instituted.

Writing

Organize
Follow the indirect approach by using background information to introduce the continuing problems. Then list the new recycling ideas.

Compose
Make your style businesslike and your appeal logical. Use a conversational tone, and respect the reader's time by avoiding wordiness.

Completing

Revise
Be sure the flow of this memo is logical. Edit and rewrite for conciseness and clarity.

Produce
Minimal design is needed for an internal memo. Send the message either as a printed memo or via e-mail.

Proofread
Review for accuracy and typos.

FIGURE 9.3 In-Depth Critique: Persuasive Letter Using the AIDA Plan

INTERNAL MEMORANDUM

TO: Eleanor Tran, Comptroller
FROM: Randy Thumwolt, Purchasing Director
DATE: May 7, 2002
SUBJECT: Cost Cutting in Plastics

In spite of our recent switch to purchasing plastic product containers in bulk, our costs for these containers are exorbitant. In my January 5 memo, I included all the figures showing that

- We purchase five tons of plastic product containers each year
- The price of the polyethylene terephthalate (PET) tends to rise and fall as petroleum costs fluctuate

In January I suggested that we purchase plastic containers in bulk during winter months, when petroleum prices tend to be lower. Because you approved that suggestion, we should realize a 10 percent saving this year. However, our costs are still out of line, around $2 million a year.

In addition to the cost in dollars of these plastic containers is the cost in image. We have recently been receiving an increasing number of consumer letters complaining about our lack of a recycling program for PET plastic containers, both on the airplanes and in the airport restaurants.

After conducting some preliminary research, I have come up with the following ideas:

- Provide recycling containers at all Host Marriott airport restaurants
- Offer financial incentives for the airlines to collect and separate PET containers
- Set up a specially designated dumpster at each airport for recycling plastics
- Contract with A-Batt Waste Management for collection

I've attached a detailed report of the costs involved. As you can see, our net savings the first year should run about $500,000. I've spoken to Ted Macy in marketing. If we adopt the recycling plan, he wants to build a PR campaign around it.

The PET recycling plan will help build our public image while improving our bottom line. If you agree, let's meet with Ted next week to get things started.

Grabs attention by clearly stating an ongoing problem and briefly providing background information that includes specific numbers

Reminds reader of important facts that have already been established by breaking them out into a list

Builds interest by introducing an additional problem with the plastic product containers

Makes suggestions in an easy-to-read list, providing detailed support in an attachment

Creates desire by providing another reader benefit

Urges action within a specific time frame

Instead of This	Try This
Proposal to Install New Phone Message System	Savings on Toll-Free Number

Another thing to keep in mind when using the AIDA plan is to narrow your objectives. Focus on your primary goal when presenting your case, and concentrate your efforts on accomplishing that one goal. For example, if your main idea is to convince your company to install a new phone-messaging system, leave discussions about switching long-distance carriers until another day—unless it's relevant to your argument.

To make the AIDA plan more successful, focus closely on one goal only.

Balancing Emotional and Logical Appeals

Learning Objective 3

Distinguish between emotional and logical appeals, and discuss how to balance them

How do you actually convince an audience that your position is the right one, that your plan will work, or that your company will do the most with readers' donations? One way is to appeal to the audience's minds and hearts. Most persuasive messages include both emotional and logical appeals. Together, these two elements have a good chance of persuading your audience to act.

Both emotional and logical appeals are needed to write successful persuasive messages.

Finding the right balance between the two types of appeals depends on four factors: (1) the actions you wish to motivate, (2) your reader's expectations, (3) the degree of resistance you must overcome, and (4) how far you feel empowered to go in selling your point of view.[10] When you're persuading someone to accept a complex idea, take a serious step, or make a large and important decision, lean toward logic and make your emotional appeal subtle. However, when you're persuading someone to purchase a product, join a cause, or make a donation, you'll rely a bit more heavily on emotion.

Emotional appeals are best if subtle.

Emotional Appeals An **emotional appeal** calls on human feelings, basing the argument on audience needs or sympathies; however, such an appeal must be subtle.[11] For instance, you can make use of the emotion surrounding certain words. The word *freedom* evokes strong feelings, as do words such as *success, prestige, credit record, savings, free, value,* and *comfort.* Such words put your audience in a certain frame of mind and help them accept your message. However, emotional appeals aren't necessarily effective by themselves. Emotion works with logic in a unique way: People need to find rational support for an attitude they've already embraced emotionally.

Logical Appeals A **logical appeal** calls on human reason. In any argument you might use to persuade an audience, you make a claim and then support your claim with reasons or evidence. When appealing to your audience's logic, you might use three types of reasoning:

- **Analogy.** With analogy, you reason from specific evidence to specific evidence. For instance, to persuade employees to attend a planning session, you might use a town meeting analogy, comparing your company to a small community and your employees to valued members of that community.
- **Induction.** With induction, you reason from specific evidence to a general conclusion. To convince potential customers that your product is best, you might report the results of test marketing in which individuals preferred your product over others. After all, if some individuals prefer it, so will others.
- **Deduction.** With deduction, you might reason from a generalization to a specific conclusion. To persuade your boss to hire additional employees, you might point to industry-wide projections and explain that industry activity (and thus your company's business) will be increasing rapidly over the next three months, so you'll need more employees to handle increased business.

Patagonia, leading designer and distributor of outdoor gear, does its best to persuade customers not only to buy its environmentally safe clothing but to actively protect and support the earth's environment. The company uses words and pictures in its persuasive messages to help people make an emotional connection with the environment.

Logical appeals can use
- Analogy
- Induction
- Deduction

No matter what reasoning method you use, any argument or statement can easily appear to be true when it's actually false. Whenever you appeal to your audience's reason, do everything you can to strengthen your argument by finding common ground (basing your major argument on points that your audience already accepts) and by stating your points clearly. Finally, keep your arguments relevant, well grounded, and systematic. To avoid faulty logic, practice the following guidelines:[12]

Avoid faulty logic such as hasty generalizations, begging the question, attacking your opponent, oversimplifying, assuming a false cause, using faulty analogies, and using illogical support.

- **Avoid hasty generalizations.** Make sure you have plenty of evidence before drawing conclusions.
- **Avoid begging the question.** Make sure you can support your claim without simply restating it in different words.
- **Avoid attacking your opponent.** Be careful to address the real question. Attack the argument your opponent is making, not your opponent's character.
- **Avoid oversimplifying a complex issue.** Make sure you present all the factors rather than relying on an "either/or" statement that makes it look as if only two choices are possible.
- **Avoid assuming a false cause.** Use cause-and-effect reasoning correctly; do not assume that one event caused another just because it happened first.
- **Avoid faulty analogies.** Be sure that the two objects or situations being compared are similar enough for the analogy to hold. Even if A resembles B in one respect, it may not hold true in other important respects.
- **Avoid illogical support.** Make sure the connection between your claim and your support is truly logical and not based on a leap of faith, a missing premise, or irrelevant evidence.

Reinforcing Your Position

Your language helps reinforce your position.

Once you have framed your arguments and chosen your appeal, you can concentrate on strengthening your message with some important persuasive tools. Effective persuaders such as Jeanne Anderson know that the facts alone may not be enough to persuade your audience. So they supplement numerical data with examples, stories, metaphors, and analogies to make their position come alive. They use language to paint a vivid picture of the persuader's point of view.[13]

Semantics is the meaning of words and other symbols.

Semantics Say that you're trying to build your credibility. How do you let your audience know that you're enthusiastic and trustworthy? Simply making an outright claim that you have these traits is sure to raise suspicion. However, you can use *semantics* (the meaning of words and other symbols) to do much of the job for you. The words you choose to state your message say much more than their dictionary definition.[14]

Instead of This	Say This
I think we should attempt to get approval on this before it's too late.	Let's get immediate approval on this.
It seems to me that . . .	I believe . . .
I've been thinking lately that maybe someone could . . .	After careful thought over the past two months, I've decided that . . .
This plan could work if we really push it.	With our support, this plan will work.

Two ways of using semantics are choosing your words carefully and using abstractions to enhance emotional content.

Another way semantics can affect persuasive messages is in the variety of meanings that people attribute to certain words. As discussed in Chapter 5, abstract words are subject to interpretation because they refer to things that people cannot experience with their senses. So you can use abstractions to enhance the emotional content of a persuasive message. For example, you may be able to sell more flags by appealing to your audience's patriotism than by describing the color and size of the flags. You may have better luck collecting an overdue bill by mentioning honesty and fair play than by repeating the sum owed and the date it was due. However, be sure to include the details along with the abstractions; the very fact that you're using abstract words leaves room for misinterpretation.

Other Tools Using semantics skillfully isn't your only persuasive tool. Here are some additional techniques you can use to strengthen your persuasive messages:[15]

In addition to semantics, you have other persuasive tools at your disposal.

- **Be moderate.** Asking your audience to make major changes in attitudes or beliefs will most likely evoke a negative response. However, asking audience members to take one step toward that change may be a more reasonable goal.
- **Focus on your goal.** Your message will be clearest if you shift your focus away from changing minds and emphasize the action you want your audience to take.
- **Use simple language.** In most persuasive situations, your audience will be cautious, watching for fantastic claims, insupportable descriptions, and emotional manipulation. So speak plainly and simply.
- **Anticipate opposition.** Think of every possible objection in advance. In your message, you might raise and answer some of these counterarguments.
- **Provide sufficient support.** It is up to you to prove that the change you seek is necessary.
- **Be specific.** Back up your claims with evidence, and when necessary cite actual facts and figures. Let your audience know that you've done your homework.
- **Create a win-win situation.** Make it possible for both you and your audience to gain something. Audience members will find it easier to deal with change if they stand to benefit.
- **Time your messages appropriately.** The time to sell roofs is right after the tornado. Timing is crucial in persuasive messages.
- **Speak metaphorically.** Metaphors create powerful pictures. One metaphor can convey a lifetime of experience or a head full of logic.
- **Use anecdotes and stories to make your points.** Anecdotes tie it all together—the logic and the emotions. Don't tell your audience what kinds of problems they can have if their system crashes. Tell them what happened to Jeff Porte when his hard drive crashed in the middle of his annual sales presentation.

All these tools will help your persuasive message be accepted, but none of them will actually overcome your audience's resistance. Whether based on emotion or logic, your argument must be strong enough to persuade people to act.

Dealing with Resistance

Learning Objective 4

Explain the best way to overcome resistance to your persuasive message, and list four common mistakes in writing persuasive messages

The best way to deal with audience resistance is to eliminate it. If you expect a hostile audience, one biased against your plan from the beginning, present all sides—cover all options, explaining the pros and cons of each. You'll gain additional credibility if you present these options before presenting the decision.[16]

You can overcome resistance by presenting the pros and cons of all sides of your argument.

To uncover audience objections, try some "What if?" scenarios. Poke holes in your own theories and ideas before your audience does. Then find solutions to the problems you've uncovered. Recognize that people support what they help create, and ask your audience for their thoughts on the subject before you put your argument together. Let your audience recommend some solutions. With enough thought and effort, you may even be able to turn problems into opportunities; for example, you may show how your proposal will be more economical in the long run, even though it may cost more now. Just be sure to be thorough, open, and objective about all the facts and alternatives. When putting together persuasive arguments, avoid common mistakes such as these:[17]

Avoiding common mistakes helps you overcome resistance.

- **Using an up-front hard sell.** Setting out a strong position at the start of a persuasive message gives potential opponents something to grab onto—and fight against.
- **Resisting compromise.** Persuasion is a process of give and take. As one expert points out, a persuader rarely changes another person's behavior or viewpoint without altering his or her own in the process.

✓ CHECKLIST: DEVELOPING PERSUASIVE MESSAGES

A. Get your reader's attention
1. Open with a reader benefit, a stimulating question, a problem, or an unexpected statement.
2. Discuss something your audience can agree with (establishing common ground).
3. Demonstrate that you understand the audience's concerns.

B. Build your reader's interest
1. Elaborate on the main benefit.
2. Explain the relevance of your message to your audience.

C. Increase your reader's desire
1. Make audience members want to change by explaining how the change will benefit them.
2. Back up your claims with relevant evidence.

D. Motivate your reader to take action
1. Confidently ask for the audience's cooperation.
2. Stress the positive results of the action.
3. Include the due date (if any) for a response, and tie it in with audience benefits.
4. Include one last reminder of the audience benefit.
5. Make the desired action clear and easy.

E. Balance emotional and logical appeals
1. Use emotional appeals to help the audience accept your message.
2. Use logical appeals when presenting facts and evidence for complex ideas or recommendations.
3. Avoid faulty logic.

F. Reinforce your position
1. Use semantics to build credibility and enhance the emotional content of your message.
2. Use a variety of critical thinking and effective writing tools to strengthen your case.

G. Deal with resistance
1. Anticipate and answer possible objections. Turn them into opportunities when possible. Otherwise, give assurance that you will handle them as best you can.
2. Try "What if?" scenarios to poke holes in your theories and then find solutions.
3. Let others help you find solutions to problems that you uncover.
4. Present the pros and cons of all options.
5. Avoid common mistakes such as using a hard sell up front, resisting compromise, relying solely on great arguments, and assuming persuasion is a one-shot effort.

H. Increase the effectiveness of your AIDA plan
1. Use the AIDA plan for both direct and indirect approaches.
2. Be careful not to give your message away in the subject line.
3. Limit your objectives by focusing on your primary goal.

- **Relying solely on great arguments.** In persuading people to change their minds, great arguments matter, but they are only one part of the equation. Your ability to create a mutually beneficial framework for your position, to connect with your audience on the right emotional level, and to communicate through vivid language are all just as important; they bring your argument to life.
- **Assuming persuasion is a one-shot effort.** Persuasion is a process, not a one-time event. More often than not, persuasion involves listening to people, testing a position, developing a new position that reflects new input, more testing, more compromise, and so on.

Successful persuasive messages depend on your ability to frame your argument, balance emotional and logical appeals, reinforce your position, and overcome resistance. Using these strategies will help you craft strong persuasive messages, no matter what the situation. To review the steps involved in developing persuasive messages, see this chapter's "Checklist: Developing Persuasive Messages."

Types of Persuasive Requests

Persuasive requests are used both inside and outside the organization.

People write innumerable persuasive messages within an organization: selling a supervisor on an idea for cutting costs, suggesting more efficient operating procedures, eliciting cooperation from competing departments, winning employee support for a new benefits package, requesting money for new equipment or funding for a special project. Similarly, people may send a variety of persuasive messages to people outside the organization: requesting favors, demanding adjustments, asking for information, soliciting funds and cooperation, or collecting an overdue debt. (For some tips in this last area, see "Focusing on Ethics: Writing Effective Collection Messages.")

Focusing on Ethics

Writing Effective Collection Messages

The purpose of the collection message is to collect past-due accounts. Effective writers recognize that collection is a sensitive issue; not only must you maintain goodwill while persuading customers to make the payment, but you must be careful not to embarrass them. In fact, your job is to neutralize customers' feelings by accentuating the benefits of complying with your request for payment. If that strategy fails, you may have to stress the unpleasant consequences of not acting. But stay within the boundaries of the law.

Illegal Practices

The Fair Debt Collection Practices Act of 1978 outlines a number of restrictions on collection procedures. Chief among them are falsely implying that a lawsuit has been filed; contacting the debtor's employer or relatives about the debt; communicating to other persons that the person is in debt; harassing the debtor; using abusive, obscene, or defamatory language; intentionally causing mental distress; or threatening violence.

The law also delineates when you may contact a debtor, how many times you may call, and what information you must provide to the debtor (timely responses, accurate records, and understandable documents). However, that doesn't mean you can't be tough in collection letters. As long as what you state is true and lawful, it can't be construed as harassment or misrepresentation. Collection is a process, not just a single demand. As the past-due period lengthens, a series of collection letters reflecting the increasing seriousness of the problem is sent to the customer at predetermined intervals.

Notification and Reminder Stages

A standard notification notice is generally a form letter or statement, often computerized, clearly stating the amount due, the date due, the penalties for late payment, and the total amount remaining to be paid. If the payment has not been received within a few days after the due date, most creditors send out a gentle reminder. The tone for both of these standardized letters is reassuring, conveying the company's assumption that some minor problem has delayed payment. In other words, the firm still believes that the customer has every intention of paying what is due and need only be reminded.

Inquiry Stage

As frustrating as it may be to send out a reminder and still get no response, don't assume that your customer plans to ignore the debt, especially if the customer has paid bills promptly in the past. So avoid accusations in your inquiry message. However, the time has passed for assuming that the delay is merely an oversight, so you may assume that some unusual circumstance is preventing payment. Personalization at this stage is appropriate because you're asking your customer to work out an individualized solution.

Appeal Stage

The appeal stage represents a significant escalation. Convey your desire to collect the overdue payment immediately and your willingness to get serious, but avoid any overt threats. To communicate a sense of urgency, you might resort to a letter signed by a top official in the company or to a negative appeal. However, an urgent notice still leaves an opening for the debtor to make a payment without losing face.

Ultimatum Stage

Some people's finances are in such disorder that you won't get their attention until you send an ultimatum. Even then, maintain a polite, businesslike manner and avoid defaming or harassing the debtor. Itemize the precise consequences of not paying the bill so that you can encourage debtors to reevaluate their priorities. Remember, you're no longer interested in hearing why it has taken them so long to respond; you're interested in putting your claim at the top of their list. The tone of the ultimatum need not be so personal or individualized as the inquiry or appeal.

If the ultimatum doesn't yield results, the only remaining remedy is to actually begin legal collection procedures. As a final courtesy, you may wish to send the debtor a notice of the action you're about to take. By maintaining until the bitter end your respect for the customer, you may still salvage some goodwill.

Career Applications

1. Why is it important to maintain goodwill in your collection letter?
2. What should you assume about the customer when writing a collection letter? Why?

The most important thing to remember when preparing a persuasive request is to keep your request within bounds. Nothing is as distressing as a request so general, so all-encompassing, or so inconsiderate that it seems impossible to grant, no matter how worthy the cause. Therefore, when making a persuasive request, take special care to highlight both the direct and the indirect benefits of fulfilling it.

Make only reasonable requests.

For example, if you want to persuade your supervisor to institute flextime, a direct benefit for that person might be the reduced workload or the enhanced prestige. An

Highlight the direct and indirect benefits of complying with your request.

indirect benefit might be better employee morale once flextime is instituted. If you are asking someone to respond to a survey, you might offer a premium as the direct benefit and a chance to make a meaningful contribution as the indirect benefit. As examples of persuasive requests, let's look at two specific types: persuasive requests for action and persuasive claims and requests for adjustments.

Persuasive Requests for Action

When making a persuasive request for action, be sure to use the AIDA plan to frame your argument.

Whether you're requesting a favor or a budget increase, remember to use the AIDA plan to frame your message. Begin with an attention-getting device. Show readers that you know something about their concerns and that you have some reason for making such a request. In this type of persuasive message, more than in most others, a flattering comment about your reader is acceptable, as long as it's sincere.

Use the interest and desire sections of your message to cover what you know about the situation you're requesting action on: the facts and figures, the benefits of helping, and any history or experience that will enhance your appeal. Your goals are (1) to gain credibility for you and your request and (2) to make your readers believe that helping you will indeed help solve a significant problem. Be careful not to doom your request to failure by asking your reader to do all your work for you. For example, don't ask your readers to

- Provide information that you were too lazy to seek
- Take action that will save you from embarrassment or inconvenience
- Provide total financial support for a cause that nobody else is supporting

Once you've demonstrated that your message is relevant to your reader, you can close with a request for some specific action. Be aware, however, that a persuasive memo to a colleague is somewhat more subdued than a persuasive letter to an outsider would be. Leslie Jorgensen wrote the memo in Figure 9.4. She's excited about the new Airbus A380 and thinks that purchasing this plane for appropriate markets could help Qantas meet its growth needs while at the same time lower its operating costs. She now needs her boss's approval for a study of the plane's market potential.

When requesting a favor that is routine (such as asking someone to attend a meeting in your absence), use the direct approach and the format for routine messages (see Chapter 7). However, when asking for a special favor (such as asking someone to chair an event or to serve as the team leader because you can no longer fill that role), use persuasive techniques to convince your reader of the value of the project. Include all necessary information about the project and any facts and figures that will convince your reader that his or her contribution will be enjoyable, easy, important, and of personal benefit.

Persuasive Claims and Requests for Adjustments

The goal of a persuasive claim or request for adjustment is to convince someone to make an adjustment in your favor.

Although persuasive claims and adjustment requests are sometimes referred to as complaint letters, your goal is to persuade someone to make an adjustment in your favor; you're not merely getting a complaint off your chest. You reach your goal by demonstrating the difference between what you expected and what you actually got.

Most claim letters are routine messages and use the direct approach discussed in Chapter 7. However, suppose you purchase something and, after the warranty expires, you discover that the item was defective. You write the company a routine request asking for a replacement, but your request is denied. You're not satisfied, and you still believe you have a strong case. Perhaps you just didn't communicate it well enough the first time. Persuasion is necessary in such cases.

You can't threaten to withhold payment, so try to convey the essentially negative information in a way that will get positive results. Fortunately, most people in business are open to settling your claim fairly. It's to their advantage to maintain your goodwill and to resolve your problem quickly.

Make your persuasive claims
- Complete and specific when reviewing the facts
- Confident and positive in tone

The key ingredients of a good persuasive claim are a complete and specific review of the facts and a confident and positive tone. Assume that the other person is not trying to cheat you but that you also have the right to be satisfied with the transaction.

FIGURE 9.4 In-Depth Critique: Persuasive Memo Requesting Action

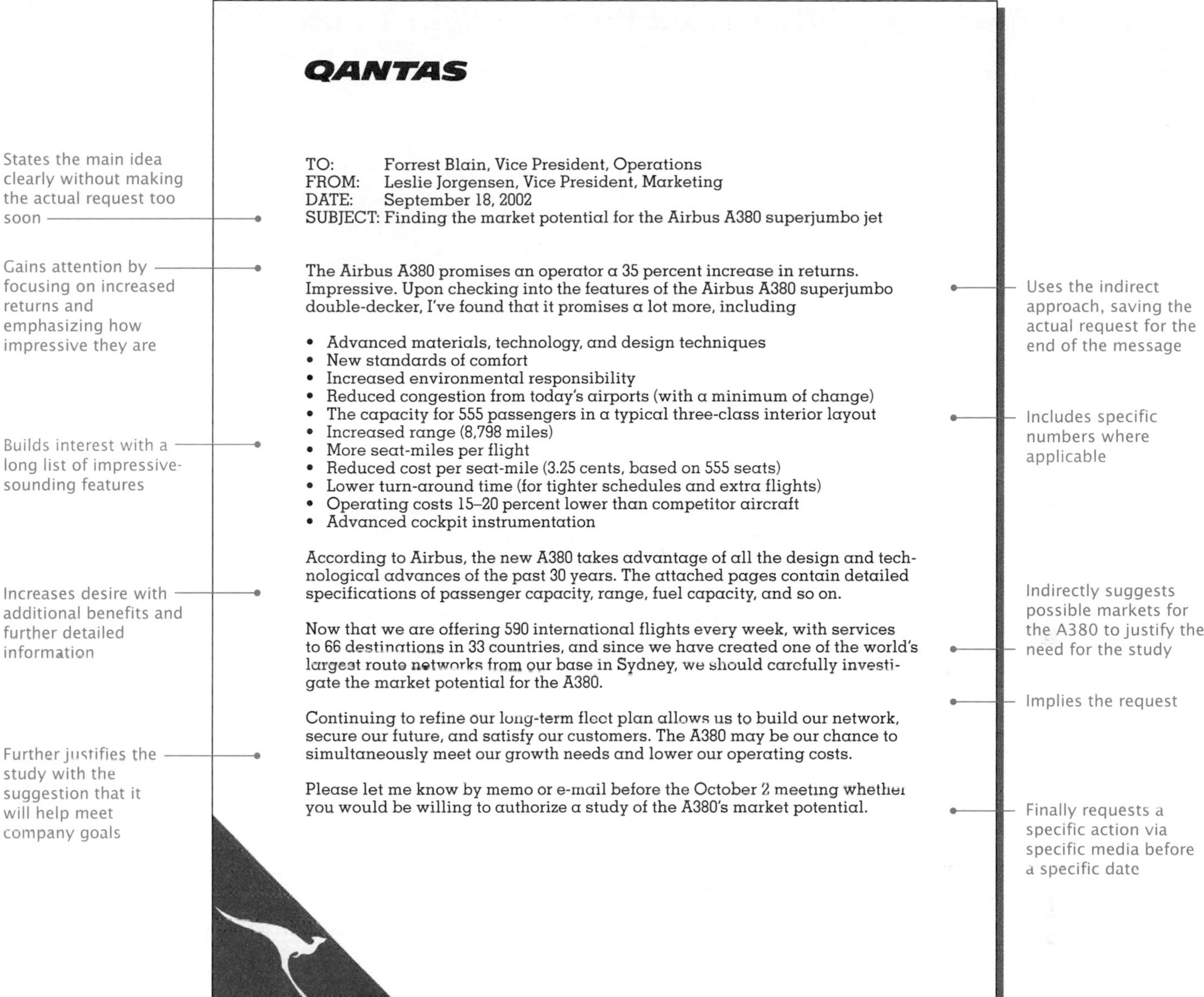

QANTAS

TO: Forrest Blain, Vice President, Operations
FROM: Leslie Jorgensen, Vice President, Marketing
DATE: September 18, 2002
SUBJECT: Finding the market potential for the Airbus A380 superjumbo jet

The Airbus A380 promises an operator a 35 percent increase in returns. Impressive. Upon checking into the features of the Airbus A380 superjumbo double-decker, I've found that it promises a lot more, including

- Advanced materials, technology, and design techniques
- New standards of comfort
- Increased environmental responsibility
- Reduced congestion from today's airports (with a minimum of change)
- The capacity for 555 passengers in a typical three-class interior layout
- Increased range (8,798 miles)
- More seat-miles per flight
- Reduced cost per seat-mile (3.25 cents, based on 555 seats)
- Lower turn-around time (for tighter schedules and extra flights)
- Operating costs 15–20 percent lower than competitor aircraft
- Advanced cockpit instrumentation

According to Airbus, the new A380 takes advantage of all the design and technological advances of the past 30 years. The attached pages contain detailed specifications of passenger capacity, range, fuel capacity, and so on.

Now that we are offering 590 international flights every week, with services to 66 destinations in 33 countries, and since we have created one of the world's largest route networks from our base in Sydney, we should carefully investigate the market potential for the A380.

Continuing to refine our long-term fleet plan allows us to build our network, secure our future, and satisfy our customers. The A380 may be our chance to simultaneously meet our growth needs and lower our operating costs.

Please let me know by memo or e-mail before the October 2 meeting whether you would be willing to authorize a study of the A380's market potential.

Talk only about the complaint at hand, not about other issues involving similar products or other complaints about the company. Your goal is to solve a particular problem, and your audience is most likely to help if you focus on the audience benefits of doing so (rather than focusing on the disadvantages of neglecting your complaint).

Begin persuasive claims by stating the basic problem (or with a sincere compliment, rhetorical question, agreeable assertion, or brief review of what's been done about the problem). Include a statement that both you and your audience can agree with or that clarifies what you wish to convince your audience about. Be as specific as possible about what you want to happen.

Next, give your reader a good reason for granting your claim. Show how your audience is responsible for the problem, and appeal to your reader's sense of fair play, goodwill, or moral responsibility. Explain how you feel about the problem, but don't get carried away, don't complain too much, and don't make threats. Make sure your request is calm and reasonable.

Best of the Web

Influence an Official and Promote Your Cause

At the Thomas site compiled by the Library of Congress, you'll discover voluminous information about federal legislation, congressional members, and committee reports. You can also access committee homepages and numerous links to government agencies, current issues, and historical documents. You can review all kinds of regulatory information, including laws and relevant issues that might affect you in the business world. Visit the site and stay informed. Maybe you'll want to convince a government official to support a business-related issue that affects you.

thomas.loc.gov

Finally, state your request specifically and confidently. Make sure your request proceeds logically from the problem and the facts you've explained. Remember to specify a deadline for action (when necessary or desirable). And don't forget to remind your audience of the main benefit of granting your claim. For a review of the tasks involved in writing persuasive claims and requests for adjustments, see this chapter's "Checklist: Persuasive Claims and Requests for Adjustments."

After you review this checklist, look at the letter in Figure 9.5, and note the improvements that could be made. Figure 9.6 is a revised version of this letter that should yield much more favorable results. As Figure 9.6 illustrates, the best approach to resolving problems is to engage in a reasonable exchange rather than an adversarial struggle.

DEVELOPING SALES AND FUNDRAISING MESSAGES

Learning Objective 5

Compare sales messages with fundraising messages

Sales and fundraising letters are distinctive types of persuasive messages that often come in special direct-mail packages.

Two distinctive types of persuasive messages are sales and fundraising messages. These messages are often sent in special direct-mail packages that can include brochures, reply forms, or other special inserts. Both types of messages are often written by specialized and highly skilled professionals, such as Jeanne Anderson of AT&T's Language Line Services.

How do sales messages differ from fundraising messages? Sales messages are usually sent by for-profit organizations persuading readers to spend money on products for themselves. However, fundraising messages are usually sent by nonprofit organizations persuading readers to donate money or time to help others. Aside from these dif-

✓ CHECKLIST: PERSUASIVE CLAIMS AND REQUESTS FOR ADJUSTMENTS

A. Attention

1. For your opening, use one of the following: sincere compliment, rhetorical question, agreeable comment or assertion, statement of the basic problem, or brief review of what has been done about the problem.
2. At the beginning, state something that you and the audience can agree on or that you wish to convince the audience about.

B. Interest and desire

1. Provide a description that shows the members of your audience that their firm is responsible for the problem.
2. Make your request factual, logical, and reasonable.
3. Appeal to the audience's sense of fair play, desire for customer goodwill, need for a good reputation, or sense of legal or moral responsibility.
4. Emphasize your goal of having the adjustment granted.
5. Present your case in a calm, logical manner.
6. Tell the audience how you feel; your disappointment with the products, policies, or services provided may well be the most important part of your argument.

C. Action

1. Make sure the action request is a logical conclusion based on the problem and the stated facts.
2. State the request specifically and confidently.
3. Specify a due date for action (when desirable).
4. State the main audience benefit as a reminder of benefits in earlier statements.

FIGURE 9.5 In-Depth Critique: Ineffective Letter Making a Persuasive Claim

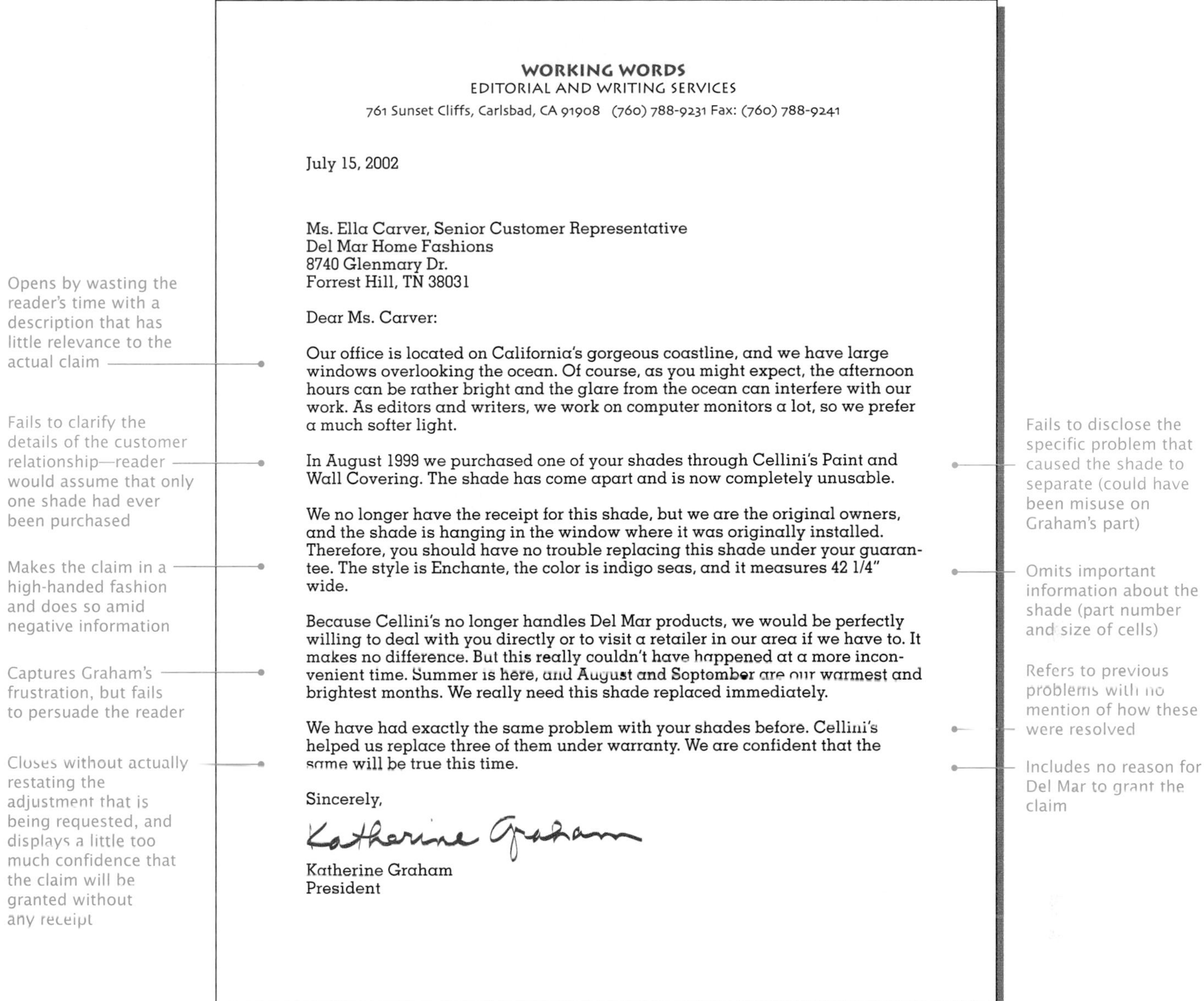

WORKING WORDS
EDITORIAL AND WRITING SERVICES
761 Sunset Cliffs, Carlsbad, CA 91908 (760) 788-9231 Fax: (760) 788-9241

July 15, 2002

Ms. Ella Carver, Senior Customer Representative
Del Mar Home Fashions
8740 Glenmary Dr.
Forrest Hill, TN 38031

Dear Ms. Carver:

Our office is located on California's gorgeous coastline, and we have large windows overlooking the ocean. Of course, as you might expect, the afternoon hours can be rather bright and the glare from the ocean can interfere with our work. As editors and writers, we work on computer monitors a lot, so we prefer a much softer light.

In August 1999 we purchased one of your shades through Cellini's Paint and Wall Covering. The shade has come apart and is now completely unusable.

We no longer have the receipt for this shade, but we are the original owners, and the shade is hanging in the window where it was originally installed. Therefore, you should have no trouble replacing this shade under your guarantee. The style is Enchante, the color is indigo seas, and it measures 42 1/4" wide.

Because Cellini's no longer handles Del Mar products, we would be perfectly willing to deal with you directly or to visit a retailer in our area if we have to. It makes no difference. But this really couldn't have happened at a more inconvenient time. Summer is here, and August and September are our warmest and brightest months. We really need this shade replaced immediately.

We have had exactly the same problem with your shades before. Cellini's helped us replace three of them under warranty. We are confident that the same will be true this time.

Sincerely,

Katherine Graham

Katherine Graham
President

ferences, sales and fundraising messages are quite similar: Both compete for their audience's attention, time, and dollars.[18] Both attempt to persuade readers to spend their time or money on the value being offered—whether that value is the convenience of a more efficient vacuum cleaner or the satisfaction of helping save children's lives. Both require a few more steps than other types of persuasive messages, and both generally use the AIDA sequence to deliver their message.

Sales and fundraising messages compete for readers' attention, time, and dollars.

Strategies for Sales Messages

Your purpose in writing a sales message is to sell a product. One of the first things to do is gain a thorough understanding of that product. What does it look like? How does it work? How is it priced? Are there any discounts? How is it packaged? How is it delivered?

When planning a sales message, know your product.

You'll also need to think about the type of sales campaign you'll conduct. Will you send a letter only, or will you include brochures, samples, response cards, and the like? If you send a brochure, how many pages will it run? Will you conduct a multistage

Before writing your sales message, decide what sort of campaign you'll conduct.

FIGURE 9.6 In-Depth Critique: Effective Letter Making a Persuasive Claim

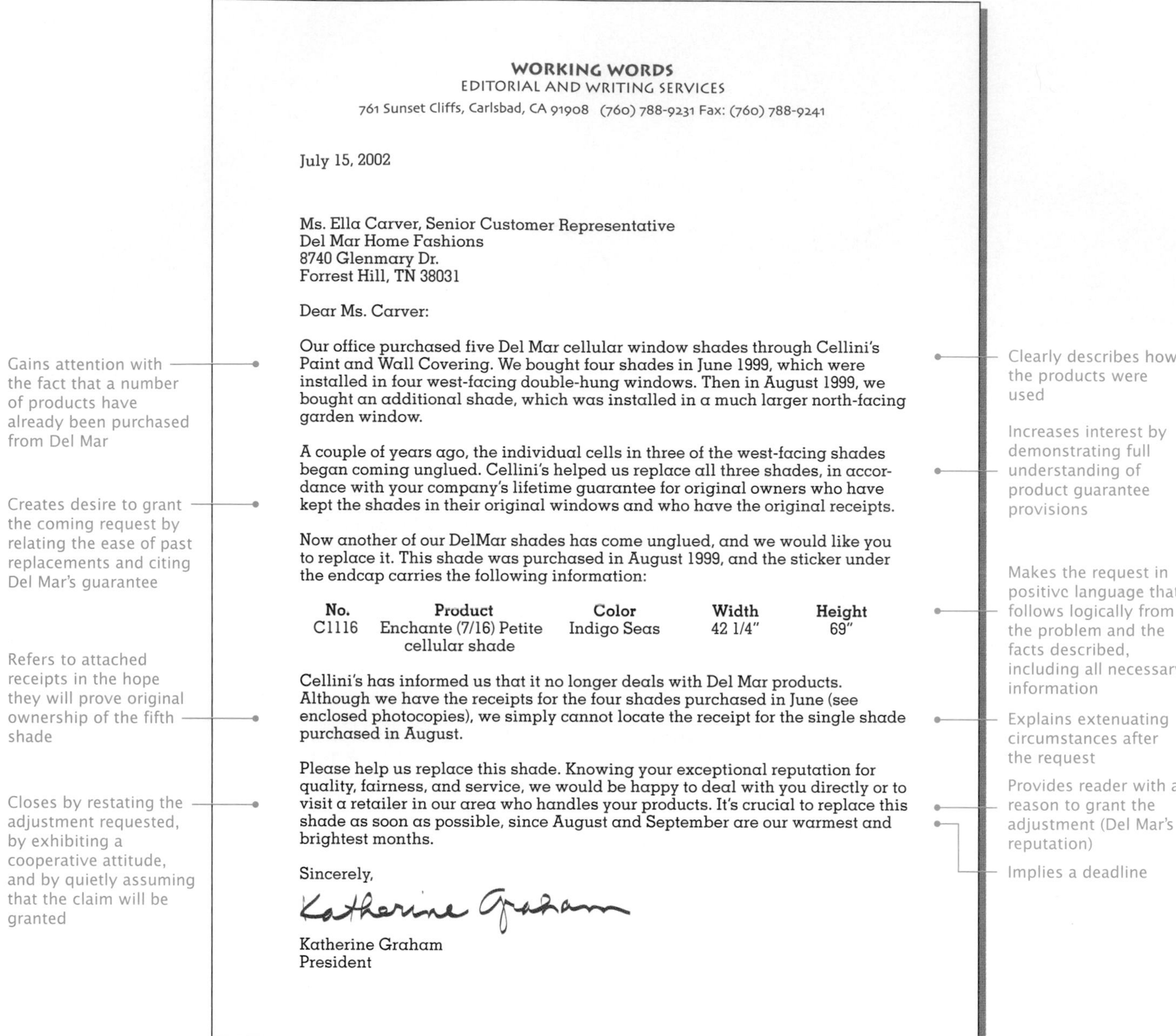

WORKING WORDS
EDITORIAL AND WRITING SERVICES
761 Sunset Cliffs, Carlsbad, CA 91908 (760) 788-9231 Fax: (760) 788-9241

July 15, 2002

Ms. Ella Carver, Senior Customer Representative
Del Mar Home Fashions
8740 Glenmary Dr.
Forrest Hill, TN 38031

Dear Ms. Carver:

Our office purchased five Del Mar cellular window shades through Cellini's Paint and Wall Covering. We bought four shades in June 1999, which were installed in four west-facing double-hung windows. Then in August 1999, we bought an additional shade, which was installed in a much larger north-facing garden window.

A couple of years ago, the individual cells in three of the west-facing shades began coming unglued. Cellini's helped us replace all three shades, in accordance with your company's lifetime guarantee for original owners who have kept the shades in their original windows and who have the original receipts.

Now another of our DelMar shades has come unglued, and we would like you to replace it. This shade was purchased in August 1999, and the sticker under the endcap carries the following information:

No.	Product	Color	Width	Height
C1116	Enchante (7/16) Petite cellular shade	Indigo Seas	42 1/4"	69"

Cellini's has informed us that it no longer deals with Del Mar products. Although we have the receipts for the four shades purchased in June (see enclosed photocopies), we simply cannot locate the receipt for the single shade purchased in August.

Please help us replace this shade. Knowing your exceptional reputation for quality, fairness, and service, we would be happy to deal with you directly or to visit a retailer in our area who handles your products. It's crucial to replace this shade as soon as possible, since August and September are our warmest and brightest months.

Sincerely,

Katherine Graham
President

campaign, with several mailings and some sort of telephone or in-person follow-up? Or will you rely on a single hard-hitting mailing? Expensive items and hard-to-accept propositions call for a more elaborate campaign than low-cost products and simple actions.

All these decisions depend on the audience you're trying to reach—their characteristics and their likely acceptance of or resistance to your message. You must analyze your audience and focus on their needs, interests, and emotional concerns—just as you would for any persuasive message. Try to form a mental image of the typical buyer for the product you wish to sell. But besides the usual questions, also ask yourself: What might audience members want to know about this product? How can your product help them? Are they driven by bottom-line pricing, or is quality more important to them?

In order to make campaign decisions, you need to know your audience.

Determining Selling Points and Benefits

Sales letters require you to know your product's selling points and how each one benefits your particular audience. You'll need to highlight these points when you compose your persuasive message. For example, at AT&T's Language Line Services, Jeanne

TABLE 9.2 Features Versus Benefits

Product Feature (Selling Point)	*Consumer Benefit*
No money down, no interest payments for 24 months.	You can buy what you want right now at no additional costs.
This printer prints 17 pages a minute.	This printer can turn out one of your 100-page proposals in six minutes.
Our shelter provides 100 adult beds and 50 children's beds for the needy.	Your donation will provide temporary housing for 100 women who don't want to return to abusive husbands.
Your corporate sponsorship of the seminar will pay for the keynote speaker's travel and lodging.	Your corporate sponsorship of the seminar will allow your site manager a five-minute introduction at the beginning of the program to summarize your services.

Anderson emphasizes the ease and cost-effectiveness of dialing up one of the 140 languages 24 hours a day.

Selling points focus on the product; benefits focus on the user.

As Table 9.2 shows, **selling points** are the most attractive features of an idea or product; **benefits** are the particular advantages that readers will realize from those features. Selling points focus on the product. Benefits focus on the user. For example, if you say that your shovel has "an ergonomically designed handle," you've described a good feature. But to persuade someone to buy that shovel, say "the ergonomically designed handle will reduce your risk of back injury." That's a benefit. For your letter and your overall sales efforts to be successful, your product's distinguishing benefit must correspond to your readers' primary needs or emotional concerns.

For your sales letter to succeed, your product's benefits must match your audience's needs.

Take a look at Figure 9.7. The sales letter for SecureAbel Alarms uses the AIDA plan to persuade students to buy its dorm-room alarm system. The features of the system are that it can be installed with a screwdriver, it has an activator that hooks to your key chain or belt loop, and it has a blinking red light to warn intruders to stay away. The benefits are ease of installation, ease of activation, and a feeling of safety and security—all obtainable without investing in a full-blown permanently installed alarm system. When composing sales messages, be sure to focus on relatively few product benefits. Ultimately, you'll single out one benefit, which will become the hallmark of your campaign. Safety seems to be the key benefit emphasized by SecureAbel Alarms.

Are cookies or direct flights the key selling point of Midwest Express Airlines? Perhaps both. So when Midwest Express sends persuasive sales messages to customers, the company carefully points out how business travelers will benefit from such amenities as wide leather seats, direct routes between small cities, and, of course, the fresh-baked gooey cookies.

Staying Within the Law

Whether you're selling a good, a service, or your company's image, knowing the law can help you avoid serious legal problems (see "Focusing on Ethics: What You May Legally Say in a Sales Letter"). The laws governing sales letters are quite specific:

- Sales letters are considered binding contracts in many states. So avoid even implying offers or promises that you can't deliver.
- Making a false statement in a sales letter is fraud if the recipient can prove that (1) you intended to deceive, (2) you made a statement regarding a fact rather than an opinion or a speculation, (3) the recipient was justified in relying on the statement, and (4) the recipient was damaged by it (in a legal sense). Misrepresenting the price, quality, or performance of a product in a sales letter is fraud. So is a testimonial by a person misrepresented to be an expert.
- Using a person's name, photograph, or other identity in a sales letter without permission constitutes invasion of privacy—with some exceptions. Using a photo of members of a local softball team in a chamber of commerce mailer may be perfectly legal if team members are public figures in the community and if using the

You can avoid both legal and ethical pitfalls by being genuinely concerned about your audience's needs, but you must also know the law.

Planning

Analyze
The purpose here is to persuade readers to buy the portable alarm system. The audience will be neutral—or even resistant.

Investigate
Gather information on product's features and benefits, as well as on audience needs.

Adapt
Use a typical sales letter format.

Writing

Organize
Make safety the central selling point. Follow the indirect AIDA approach. Get the reader's attention right away.

Compose
Use both logical and emotional appeals. Use a friendly, conversational tone. Include a response card to make reader action easy.

Completing

Revise
Don't emphasize emotional appeals. The point is to help readers, not threaten them. Edit for focus and clarity.

Produce
Use a simple design for the letter and any brochures (in line with reasonable pricing).

Proofread
Be accurate. Remove all typographical distractions.

FIGURE 9.7 In-Depth Critique: Letter Selling a Product

SecureAbel Alarms, Inc.
5654 Lakemont Drive • Altoona, PA 16602 • Voice: (814) 983-4424 • Fax: (814) 983-4422 • http://www.secure.com

October 14, 2002

Mr. Samuel Zolezzi
Penn State University, North Halls
104 Warnock Commons
State College, PA 16802

Dear Mr. Zolezzi:

Did you know that one out of four college students becomes a victim of theft? How would you feel if you returned to your dorm and discovered that your hard-earned stereo, computer, or microwave had been stolen? Remember, locked doors won't stop a determined thief.

Draws the reader into the letter with a provocative question

Raises reader's awareness of a need

My dorm room was burgularized when I was in college. That's why I've developed a portable security system for your dormitory room. This system works like an auto alarm and can be installed with an ordinary screwdriver. The small activator hooks to your key chain or belt loop. Just press the "lock" key. A "beep" tells you your room is secure, and a blinking red light warns intruders to stay away.

Seeks to establish a common bond with the reader

Explains how product works by comparing it to something familiar—a car alarm

If a thief tries to break in, a loud alarm sounds. Your possessions will be safe. And, even more important, you can activate the system from your bedside, so you're safe while you sleep.

Mentions an additional threat (to personal safety), implying another benefit of the security system

Uses both a logical appeal (protecting possessions) and an emotional appeal (personal safety)

You'd expect this peace of mind to cost a fortune—something most college students don't have. But we're offering the SecureAbel Dorm Alarm System for only $75. Here's what you'll receive by return mail:

- The patented alarm unit
- Two battery-operated programmable remote units
- A one-year warranty on all parts
- Complete and easy-to-follow installation instructions

Order additional alarm boxes to install on your window or bathroom door for only $50. Act now. Fill out the response card, and mail it along with your choice of payment method in the enclosed envelope. Don't give thieves and criminals a chance. Protect yourself and your belongings. Send in your card today.

Creates the sense of added value

Urges quick action

Sincerely,

Dan Abel

Dan Abel, President

Enclosures

Focusing on Ethics

What You May Legally Say in a Sales Letter

As you prepare to write your sales letter, think carefully about your choice of words. False or misleading statements could land you in court, so make sure your language complies with legal and ethical standards. To keep your sales letters within the limits of the law, review the legal considerations of these typical sales phrases:

- **"Our product is the best on the market."** This statement is acceptable for a sales letter because the law permits you to express an opinion about your product. In the process of merchandising a product, statements of opinion are known as "puffery," which is perfectly legal as long as you make no deceptive or fraudulent claims.
- **"Our product will serve you well for many years to come."** This statement from a sales brochure triggered a lawsuit by a disgruntled customer who claimed the manufacturer's product lasted only a few years. The courts ruled that the statement was an acceptable form of puffery because the manufacturer did not promise that the product would last for a specific number of years.
- **"We're so confident you'll enjoy our products that we've enclosed a sample of our most popular line. This sample can be yours for only $5.00! Please send your payment in the enclosed, prepaid envelope."** If you include a product sample with your sales letter, your readers may keep the merchandise without paying for it. Under the law, consumers may consider unordered goods as gifts. They are not obligated to return the items to you or submit payments for unsolicited merchandise.
- **"Thousands of high school students—just like you—are already enjoying this fantastic CD collection! Order before March 1 and save!"** If your sales letter appeals to minors, you are legally obligated to honor their contracts. At the same time, however, the law permits minors to cancel their contracts and return the merchandise to you. Sellers are legally obligated to accept contracts voided by minors and any goods returned by them. Legal adult status is defined differently from state to state, ranging from age 18 to age 21.
- **"You'll find hundreds of bargains at our annual 'scratch and dent' sale! All sales are final on merchandise marked 'as is.'"** When you use the term *as is* in your sales letter, you are not misleading customers about the quality of your products. By warning consumers that the condition of sales items is less than perfect, you are not legally obligated to issue refunds to customers who complain about defects later on.

Career Applications

1. Review two sales letters for content. List the "puffery" statements in each letter.
2. Note any statements in these sales letters that appear questionable to you. Rewrite one of the statements, carefully choosing words that won't be misleading to consumers.

photo doesn't falsely imply their endorsement. On the other hand, using a photo of your governor, without consent, on a letter about the profits to be made in worm farming could be deemed an invasion of privacy.

- Publicizing a person's private life in a sales letter can also result in legal problems. Stating that the president of a local bank (mentioned by name) served six months in prison for income tax evasion is a potentially damaging fact that may be considered an invasion of privacy. You would also risk a lawsuit by publicizing another person's past-due debts or by publishing without consent another person's medical records, x-rays, or photograph.

As with other persuasive messages, following the letter of the law isn't always enough. You'll also want to write sales letters of the highest ethical character. One way to do so is to focus on solving your reader's problem rather than selling your product. When you're genuinely concerned about your audience's needs and interests, you'll find it easier to avoid legal or ethical pitfalls.

To keep your sales letters ethical, focus on your reader's problem rather than selling your product.

Using the AIDA Plan in Sales Messages

Most sales letters are prepared according to the AIDA plan. You begin with an attention-getting device, generate interest by describing some of the product's unique features, increase the desire for your product by highlighting the benefits that are most appealing to your audience, and close by suggesting the action you want the audience to take.

Getting Attention Like other persuasive messages, sales letters start with an attention-getting device; however, the emphasis of the attention phase is slightly different. Sales-letter professionals use some common techniques to attract their audience's attention. One popular technique is opening with a provocative question. Look closely at the following three examples. Which seems most interesting to you?

Certain tried-and-true attention-getting devices are used in sales letters for a wide variety of products.

How would you like straight A's this semester?

Get straight A's this semester!

Now you can get straight A's this semester, with . . .

If you're like most people, you'll find the first option the most enticing. The question invites your response—a positive response designed to encourage you to read on. The second option is fairly interesting too, but its commanding tone may make you wary of the claim. The third option is acceptable, but it certainly conveys no sense of excitement. Its quick introduction of the product may lead you to a snap decision against reading further.

Other techniques can also help you open your sales letters with excitement. You can grab your audience's attention by emphasizing

- **A piece of genuine news.** "In the past 60 days, mortgage rates have fallen to a 30-year low."
- **A personal appeal to the reader's emotions and values.** "The only thing worse than paying taxes is paying taxes when you don't have to."
- **Your product's most attractive feature along with the associated benefit.** "New control device ends problems with employee pilferage!"
- **An intriguing number.** "Here are three great secrets of the world's most-loved entertainers."
- **A sample of the product.** "Here's your free sample of the new Romalite packing sheet."
- **A concrete illustration with story appeal.** "In 1985, Earl Colbert set out to find a better way to process credit applications. After 10 years of trial and error, he finally developed a procedure so simple and yet thorough that he was cited for service to the industry by the American Creditors Association."
- **A specific trait shared by the audience.** "Busy executives need another complicated 'time-saving' device like they need a hole in the head!"
- **A challenge.** "Don't waste another day wondering how you're going to become the success you've always wanted to be!"
- **A solution to a problem.** "Tired of arctic air rushing through the cracks around your windows? Stay warm and save energy with StormSeal Weather-stripping."

Look at your own mail to see how many sales messages use these few techniques. Such attention-getting devices will give your sales letters added impact. Look back at Figure 9.7 for a typical example.

Sales-message professionals know that textual openings aren't the only way to get attention. In ads and catalogs, companies capture attention and heighten emotional desire by using a variety of formatting devices. You can grab your audience by using special sizes or styles of type, underlining, bullets, color, indentions, and so on. Even so, not all attention-getting devices are equally effective, and using too many can have the reverse effect. In short, the best attention-getter is the one that makes your audience read the rest of your message.

Choose an attention-getter that encourages the reader to read more.

To determine your product's central selling point, ask
- What does the competition offer?
- What is special about my product?
- What are potential buyers really looking for?

Building Interest In the interest section of your message, highlight your product's key selling point. Say that your company's alarm device is relatively inexpensive, durable, and tamperproof. Although these are all attractive features, you want to focus on only one. Ask what the competition has to offer, what most distinguishes your product, and what most concerns potential buyers. The answers to these questions will help you select the **central selling point**, the single point around which to build your sales message. Build your audience's interest by highlighting this point, and make it stand out through typography, design, or high-impact writing.[19]

Determining the central selling point will also help you define the benefits to potential buyers. Perhaps your company built its new alarm to overcome competing products' susceptibility to tampering. Being tamperproof is the feature you choose as your central selling point, and its benefit to readers is that burglars won't be able to break in so easily.

With a $10,000 loan and a cargo of beachware ordered from a trade show in California, Joni Boldt Ridgway and Kyrle Boldt created "Splash"—five Splashes actually—in St. Louis. The owners know that producing effective sales messages is just as important to the stores' success as the creative merchandise they stock—some 70 kinds of snowboards, fluorescent bikinis, and lime-green nail polish. Both must get the customer's attention, build interest, increase desire, and motivate action.

Increasing Desire In the desire section, mention your main benefit repeatedly, expanding and explaining as you go. Use both words and pictures, if possible. This main benefit is what will entice recipients to read on and take further action.

As you continue to stress your main benefit, weave in references to other benefits. ("You can get this worry-free protection for much less than you might think," and "The same technology that makes it difficult for burglars to crack your alarm system makes the device durable, even when it must be exposed to the elements.") Remember, sales letters reflect the "you" attitude through references to benefits, so always phrase the selling points in terms of what your product's features can do for potential customers.

Keep in mind that most readers are pressed for time and are interested only in what matters most to them.[20] Therefore, refrain from providing every last detail as you explain product benefits. The best letters are short (preferably one but no more than two pages) and use bullet points to highlight important benefits. They include enough detail to spur the reader's interest, but they don't try to be the sole source of information. And to keep readers interested, they use action terms, talk about price, and support any claims.

To increase desire, expand your main benefit while adding others.

Using Action Terms Action words give strength to any business message, but they are especially important in sales letters. Compare the following:

To give force to a message
- Use action terms
- Use colorful verbs and adjectives

Instead of This	Write This
The NuForm desk chair is designed to support your lower back and relieve pressure on your legs.	The NuForm desk chair supports your lower back and relieves pressure on your legs.

The second version says the same thing in fewer words and emphasizes what the chair does for the user ("supports") rather than the intentions of the design team ("is designed to support").

Use colorful verbs and adjectives that convey a dynamic image to keep readers interested. Be careful, however, not to overdo it: "Your factory floors will sparkle like diamonds" is hard to believe and may prevent your audience from believing the rest of your message.

Talking About Price The price that people are willing to pay for a product depends on several factors: the prices of similar products, the general state of the economy, and the psychology of the buyer. Price is a complicated issue and often a sensitive one. So you need to be careful whenever you talk about price in your sales messages.

Whether you highlight or downplay the price of your product, prepare your readers for it. Words such as *luxurious* and *economical* provide unmistakable clues about how your price compares with that of competitors. Such words help your readers accept your price when you finally state it. Here's an example from a sales letter offering a product at a bargain price:

You can prepare readers for your product's price by subtle choice and arrangement of words.

All the Features of Name-Brand Pantyhose at Half the Price!

Why pay for fancy packaging or for that little tag with a famous name on it when you can enjoy cotton lining, reinforced toes, and matchless durability for only $1.99?

If the price is an attractive feature, emphasize it by displaying it prominently.

In this excerpt the price falls right at the end of the paragraph, where it stands out. In addition, the price issue is featured in a bold headline. This technique may even be used as the opening of a letter, if (1) the price is the most important feature and (2) the audience for the letter is value-conscious.

To de-emphasize price
- Bury actual figures in the middle of a paragraph near the end
- Mention benefits and favorable money matters before the actual price
- Break a quantity price into units
- Compare the price with the cost of some other product or activity

If price is not a major selling point, you can handle it in several ways. You could leave the price out altogether or mention it only in an accompanying brochure. You could de-emphasize the price by putting the actual figures in the middle of a paragraph that comes close to the end of your sales letter, well after you've presented the benefits and selling points.

Emphasizes the rarity of the edition to signal value and thus prepare the reader for the big-ticket price that follows

Buries the actual price in the middle of a sentence and ties it in with another reminder of the exclusivity of the offer

Only 100 prints of this exclusive, limited-edition lithograph will be created. On June 15, they will be made available to the general public, but you can reserve one now for only $350, the special advance reservation price. Simply rush the enclosed reservation card back today so that your order is in before the June 15 publication date.

The pros also use two other techniques for minimizing price. One technique is to break a quantity price into units. Instead of saying that a case of wine costs $144, you might say that each bottle costs $12. The other technique is to compare your product's price with the cost of some other product or activity: "The cost of owning your own exercise equipment is less than you'd pay for a health-club membership." Your aim is to make the cost seem as small and affordable as possible, thereby eliminating price as a possible objection.

Supporting Your Claims Providing support for your claims boosts your credibility and increases desire for your product. You can't assume that people will believe what you say about your product just because you've said it in writing. You'll have to prove your claims. Support is especially important if your product is complicated, costs a lot, or represents some unusual approach.

Types of support for product claims:
- Samples
- Brochures
- Examples
- Testimonials
- Statistics
- Guarantees

Support for your claims may take several forms. Samples and brochures, often with photographs, are enclosed in a sales package and are referred to in the letter. The letter also describes or typographically highlights examples of how the product has benefited others. It includes testimonials (quotations from satisfied customers) or cites statistics from scientific studies of the product's performance. Guarantees of exchange or return privileges may be woven into the letter or set off in a special way, indicating that you have faith in your product and are willing to back it up.

It's almost impossible to provide too much support. Try to anticipate every question your audience may want to ask. Put yourself in your audience's place so that you can discover, and solve, all the "what if" scenarios.[21]

Motivating Action After you have raised enough interest and built the reader's desire for your product, you'll want to clearly explain how to take the next step. After all, the overriding purpose of a sales letter is to get your reader to do something. Many consumer products sold through the mail simply ask for a check—in other words, an immediate decision to buy. On the other hand, companies selling big-ticket and more complex items frequently ask for just a small step toward the final buying decision, such as sending for more information or authorizing a call by a sales representative.

Aim to get the reader to act as soon as possible.

Whatever you ask readers to do, try to persuade them to do it right away. Convince them that they must act now, perhaps to guarantee a specific delivery date. If there's no particular reason to act quickly, many sales letters offer discounts for orders placed by a certain date or prizes or special offers to, say, the first 500 people to respond. Others suggest that purchases be charged to a credit card or be paid off over time. Still others offer a free trial, an unconditional guarantee, or a no-strings request card for information—all in an effort to overcome readers' natural inertia.

Of course, adding a postscript (P.S.) is one of the most effective ways to boost audience response. This is the place to make your final impression, so be sure the information is noteworthy. Use the P.S. to reiterate your primary benefit, make an additional offer, or compel the reader to act quickly by emphasizing a deadline.[22]

Finally, use good judgment when distributing your messages to would-be customers. Do not send electronic junk mail (spam). Doing so only irritates consumers, and it can be illegal, depending on the state in which you reside. Laws against spam on the federal level are pending.

Strategies for Fundraising Messages

Motivating action is a challenge for the best sales letters. Even more of a challenge is motivating action when you're trying to raise funds. Most of the techniques used to write sales letters can also be used to write fundraising letters, as long as your techniques match your audience, your goals, and the cause or organization you're representing. Be careful to establish value in the minds of your donors. Above all, don't forget to include the "what's in it for me?" information—for example, telling your readers how good they'll feel by making a donation.[23]

Fundraising letters use many of the same techniques that are used in sales letters.

To make sure that your fundraising letters outshine the competition's letters, take some time to get ready before you actually begin writing.[24] You can begin by reading the mail you receive from donors. Learn as much as you can about your audience by noting the tone of these letters, the language used, and the concerns raised. This exercise will help you write letters that donors will both understand and relate to.

You might also keep a file of competing fundraising letters. Study these samples to find out what other fundraisers are doing and what new approaches they're taking. Most important, find out what works and what doesn't. Then you can continue with your other research efforts, such as conducting interviews, holding focus groups, and reading trade journals to find out what people are concerned about, what they're interested in, and what gets their attention.

Finally, before you start writing, know whose benefits to emphasize. Make a two-column list; on one side list what your organization does, and on the other side list what your donors want. You'll discover that the two columns are quite different. Make sure that the benefits you emphasize are related to what your donors want, not to what your organization does. Then you can work on stating those donor benefits in specific detail. For example: "Your donation of $100 will provide 15 people with a Christmas dinner."

Be sure to focus on the concerns of your readers, not on the concerns of your organization.

Personalizing Fundraising Messages

Because fundraising letters depend so heavily on emotional appeals, keep your message personal. A natural, real-life lead-in is usually the best. People seem to respond best to slice-of-life stories. Storytelling is perfect when your narrative is unforced and goes straight to the heart of the matter.[25] Professional fundraiser Conrad Squires advises you to "find and use relevant human-interest stories," to "show donors the faces of the people they are helping," and to "make the act of sending a contribution as real and memorable and personal" as you can.[26] Such techniques make people feel the warmth of other lives.[27]

Human interest stories are the best way to interest your readers in fundraising letters.

So that your letters remain personal, immediate, and effective, steer clear of three common mistakes:[28]

- Letting your letter sound like a business communication of any kind
- Wasting space on warm-up (the things you write while you're working up to your real argument)
- Assuming that the goals of your organization are more important than your readers' concerns (a deadly mistake)

Personalize fundraising letters by
- Writing about your readers
- Helping your readers identify with recipients

The last caution is crucial when writing fundraising letters. Squires suggests that "the more space you spend writing about the reader, the better response you're likely to get."[29] Here are some examples:

You've proven you are somebody who really cares about what happens to children, Mr. Jones.

Ms. Smith, your company's kindness can change the world for Meta Singh and his family.

It's also up to you to help your donors identify with recipients. A busy company executive may not be able to identify with the homeless man she passes on the street every day. But every human being understands pain; we've all felt it. So do your best to portray that homeless man's pain using words that the busy executive can understand.[30]

Strengthening Fundraising Messages

Learning Objective 6

List eight guidelines that will help you strengthen your fundraising messages

Strong fundraising letters
- Explain a specific need thoroughly
- Show how important it is for readers to help
- Spell out exactly what amount of help is being requested
- Describe in detail the benefits of helping

The best fundraising letters do four things: (1) thoroughly explain a specific need, (2) show how important it is for readers to help, (3) spell out exactly what amount of help is being requested, and (4) describe in detail the benefits of helping.[31] To help you accomplish these four major tasks, here are some fundraising guidelines:[32]

- **Interest your readers immediately.** If you don't catch your readers' interest at the absolute beginning of your letter, you never will.
- **Use simple language.** Tell your story with simple, warm, and personal language. Nothing else is as effective in getting people to empathize.
- **Give readers an opportunity to accomplish something important.** Donors want to feel needed. They want the excitement of coming to your rescue.
- **Make it hard to say no.** Make the need so urgent and strong that your readers will find it difficult to turn you down. "Won't you send a gift now, knowing that children's lives are on the line?"
- **Make your needs clear.** Leave no doubt about the amount of money that you want. Be absolutely clear, and be sure the amount requested is appropriate for your audience. Explain why the money is needed as soon as possible. Also, make it extremely easy to respond by asking for a small gift.
- **Write no longer than you have to.** If you use a telegram-type format, keep your message short. However, longer messages are usually best for fundraising. Just keep sentences and paragraphs short, maximize content, and minimize wordiness.
- **Make your reply form complete and thorough.** Include all the basics: your name, address, and telephone number; a restatement of your request and the gift amount; your donor's name and address (or space enough for a label); information on how to make out the check; and information on tax deductibility.
- **Use interesting enclosures.** Enclosures that simply give more information will decrease returns. Instead, use enclosures that are fun or that give the donor something to do, sign, return, or keep.

These guidelines should help you reach the humanity and compassion of your readers by focusing on specific reader benefits, detailing the unique need, emphasizing the urgency of the situation, and spelling out the exact help needed. As director of PETsMART Charities, Rita Gomez has the task of raising millions of dollars to help save the lives of and find families for thousands upon thousands of homeless pets. Her letter, in Figure 9.8, makes a compelling case for donations.

Like sales letters, fundraising letters are simply particular types of persuasive messages. Both categories have their unique requirements, some of which only professional writers can master. (See this chapter's "Checklist: Composing Sales and Fundraising Letters" as a reminder of the tasks involved in writing these messages.)

FIGURE 9.8 In-Depth Critique: Letter to Raise Funds

PETsMART
Where pets are family™

19601 North 27th Avenue • Phoenix, Arizona 85027 • 623•580•6100

June 17, 2002

Mr. William Hanover, President
Hanover, Jude, and Larson
12785 Sunnyslope Dr.
Phoenix, AZ 85020

Ernie needs your help!

Includes a photo to further personalize the message and strengthen the emotional appeal

Dear Mr. Hanover:

Gains attention by personalizing the message with a real-life story

Ernie deserves a loving home. When Sheila Jenkins found him in the alley behind her apartment, the poor little guy was weak from hunger, infested with fleas, and dragging a broken leg. Under skillful care at the local animal shelter, Ernie recovered fully and won the hearts of all with his indomitable spirit, his quick intelligence, and his perky devotion.

Avoids sounding like a business communication while getting right to the point

Increases interest by providing hard (even painful) numbers and details of just what PETsMART Charities does

Ernie has been waiting patiently for a family to love, but sometimes homes are hard to find. More than 7 million pets are euthanized every year, simply because they have no family or home to call their own. So in 1992 PETsMART decided not to sell cats and dogs. Instead, the company created PETsMART Charities' Adoption Centers—in-store space that is donated to help local animal welfare organizations make homeless pets available for adoption.

Creates a desire to be involved by sharing specific successes of the program

Over the past decade, PETsMART Charities has donated $15 million to animal welfare programs, and through our in-store adoption programs, we've helped save the lives of more than 1 million pets, one by one. These accomplishments are the result of devotion, hard work, and contributions from our own associates and from companies like yours. That's right, we haven't done all this alone. And to continue saving lives, we need your help more than ever.

Uses a carefully constructed transition to move reader from what PETsMART has done to what the reader can do

Makes the request by stating the benefits of the reader's donation to others as well as to the reader

Mr. Hanover, you and your associates have proved that you care about your community. You know business is about more than merely selling a product or service. Now, with a one-time donation of $100, your company can save the lives of many faithful pet companions. With a yearly or a scheduled monthly donation, you can do even more to rescue these loving family members. Your gift saves lives, makes you feel great, and strengthens your firm's reputation as a caring and responsible company.

Takes special pains to focus on the reader and his company

Closes by echoing the real-life story that opened the message and repeating the request for specific action

Please help Ernie find a good home. Just fill out the enclosed reply form and send it along with your donation in the envelope provided. Ernie can't make it without you, and neither can we.

Sincerely,

Rita E. Gomez

Rita E. Gomez
Director

Enclosure

Reply form is complete and thorough

TO HELP PETsMART CHARITIES SAVE LIVES

_______________________________ **(company)**

_______________________________ **(address)**

WISHES TO DONATE

- ❑ **$100**
- ❑ **$____ each year**
- ❑ **$____ a month (for 12 mos.)**

- ❑ **By check (enclosed)**
- ❑ **By credit card:**

____Visa ____Mastercard ____Discover

Card no.: ____________________

Signature: ____________________

Position: ____________________

✓ CHECKLIST: COMPOSING SALES AND FUNDRAISING LETTERS

A. Attention

1. Design a positive opening that awakens a favorable association with the product, need, or cause.
2. Write the opening so that it's appropriate, fresh, honest, interesting, specific, and relevant.
3. Promise a benefit to the reader.
4. Keep the first paragraph short, preferably two to five lines, and sometimes only one.
5. For sales letters, get attention with a provocative question, a significant/startling fact, a solution to a problem, a special offer/gift, a testimonial, a current event, an illustration, a comparison, an event in the reader's life, a problem the reader may face, or a quotation.
6. For fundraising letters, design an attention-getter that uses a human-interest story.

B. Interest

1. State information clearly, vividly, and persuasively, relating it to the reader's concerns.
2. Develop the central selling point.
3. Feature the product or charitable need in two ways: physical description and reader benefits.
4. Place benefits first, or interweave them with a physical description.
5. Describe objective details of the need or product (size, shape, color, scent, sound, texture, etc.).
6. Use psychological appeals to present the sensation, satisfaction, or pleasure readers will gain.
7. Blend cold facts with warm feelings.

C. Desire

1. Enlist one or more appeals to support the central idea (selling point or fundraising goal).
2. If the product is valued mainly because of its appearance, describe its physical details.
3. If the product is machinery or technical equipment, describe its sturdy construction, fine crafting, and other technical details in terms that help readers visualize themselves using it.
4. Include technical sketches and meaningful pictures, charts, and graphs, if necessary.
5. For sales letters, provide test results from recognized experts, laboratories, or authoritative agencies.
6. To raise funds, detail how donations are spent, using recognized accounting/auditing firms.
7. To elicit donations, use strong visual details, good narrative, active verbs, and limited adjectives.
8. Emphasize reader benefits.
9. Anticipate and answer the reader's questions.
10. Use an appropriate form of proof.
11. Include verifiable reports/statistics about users' experience with the product or organization.
12. Provide names (with permission only) of satisfied buyers, users, or donors.
13. Present unexaggerated testimonials from persons or firms whose judgment readers respect.
14. In sales letters, offer a free trial or a guarantee, and refer to samples if they are included.
15. Note any enclosures in conjunction with a selling point or a reader benefit.

D. Action

1. Clearly state the action you desire.
2. Provide specific details on how to order the product, donate money, or reach your organization.
3. Ease action with reply cards, preaddressed envelopes, phone numbers, follow-up phone calls.
4. Offer a special inducement to act now: time limit or situation urgency, special price for a limited time, premium for acting before a certain date, gift for acting, free trial, no obligation to buy with more information or demonstration, easy payments with no money down, credit-card payments.
5. Supply a final reader benefit.
6. In a postscript, convey important donation information or an important sales point (if desired).

COMMUNICATION CHALLENGES AT AT&T'S LANGUAGE LINE SERVICES

The word about AT&T's Language Line Services has spread quickly among hospitals, police departments, city agencies, and businesses looking to expand into overseas markets. Jeanne Anderson's sales and marketing department is busy prospecting for new subscribers, and her staff keeps growing and growing. Anderson has her hands full, and she recently began delegating some of her responsibilities to keep up with the work load.

Individual Challenge: Every December, the sales and marketing department hosts a Holiday Open House Toy and Food Drive for all Language Line employees. Anderson sees the event as a way of bringing old and new members of her department closer together and of helping local charity organizations. But she realizes it's going to take a little persuasion to get her staff to participate; the holidays are a busy time for everyone, and this affair is strictly voluntary. Moreover, she's asking them, as they do every year, to bring finger food and desserts for a potluck buffet, plus a new toy or canned food to donate to the needy. The party will last from 2:00 to 4:00, with music, talk, and maybe even a little dancing.

Anderson has asked you to write a memo to the staff, serving more as a persuasive request for action than as an invitation to a party. She hopes staff members will decide to attend, will bring a toy or food gift, and will contact Laura and Judy (party organizers) to let them know what potluck dish to expect. (Make up any other names or details you need in order to write a convincing memo.)

Team Challenge: Language Line Services became so popular so quickly among certain industries that Anderson has had little time to brainstorm ideas about applications for new markets. She has asked your group to help out. Sooner or later, AT&T's current markets will be saturated; before that happens, Anderson wants her staff ready to target new industries. This goal will require special sales training and new sales literature targeted to each industry—which means she'll need a budget increase.

First, she has asked you to brainstorm ways Language Line Services might be used by government agencies, service organizations, or any untapped industry you can identify. List the applications and benefits for each industry, then decide which three sound most promising. Anderson wants you to write a persuasive memo to convince upper management that these three markets are so promising that the added expenditures for staff training and industry-specific sales literature will bring profitable returns. She's going to ask for a $50,000 total budget increase to start the three-industry campaign. "Don't worry about financial justification; I'll supply a detailed budget breakdown as an attachment to the memo," she tells you. "You just need to convince them this is an idea they can't refuse."[33] ■

SUMMARY OF LEARNING OBJECTIVES

1 **Discuss the planning tasks that need extra attention when preparing persuasive messages.** Because persuasive messages can be complicated and sensitive, several planning tasks need extra attention. You'll be persuading people to take action that they probably wouldn't have taken without your message, so analyzing your purpose is crucial. In addition, audience analysis may be more detailed for persuasive messages, gauging psychological and social needs in addition to cultural differences. Also, when persuading a skeptical audience, your credibility must be unquestionable, so you may need to spend some extra effort to establish it. Since your attempts to persuade could be viewed by some as manipulative, you need to strive for the highest ethical standards.

2 **Describe the AIDA plan for persuasive messages.** When using the AIDA plan, you open your message by getting *attention* with a reader benefit, a problem, a stimulating question, a piece of news, or an unexpected statement. You build *interest* with facts, details, and additional reader benefits. You increase *desire* by providing more evidence and reader benefits and by anticipating and answering possible objections. You conclude by motivating a specific *action*, emphasizing the positive results of that action, and making it easy for the reader to respond.

3 **Distinguish between emotional and logical appeals, and discuss how to balance them.** Emotional appeals call on human feelings, using arguments that are based on audience needs or sympathies. However, these appeals aren't effective by themselves. Logical appeals call on human reason (whether using analogy, induction, or deduction). If you're careful to avoid faulty logic, you can use logic together with emotion, thereby supplying rational support for an idea that readers have already embraced emotionally. In general, logic will be your strongest appeal, with only subtle emotion. However, when persuading someone to purchase a product, join a cause, or make a donation, you can heighten emotional appeals a bit.

4 **Explain the best way to overcome resistance to your persuasive message, and list four common mistakes in writing persuasive messages.** The best way to overcome resistance is to think of all the objections your audience could possibly have and then explain the pros and cons of all sides. Provide solutions to all the problems your audience might perceive. In addition, make sure you do not (1) use an up-front hard sell, (2) rule out compromise, (3) rely solely on great arguments while ignoring how you present them, and (4) assume your persuasive attempt is a one-time effort.

5 **Compare sales messages with fundraising messages.** Sales messages are used by for-profit companies to persuade readers to make a purchase for themselves. In contrast, fundraising messages are used by nonprofit organizations to persuade readers to donate their time or their money to help others. However, these two types of persuasive messages have a lot in common. Primarily, they both try to persuade readers to "buy" (with time or money) the value that is being offered (the product or the cause). In addition, both types of persuasive message generally use the AIDA plan.

6 **List eight guidelines that will help you strengthen your fundraising messages.** To strengthen your fundraising messages, follow these guidelines: (1) interest your readers immediately, (2) use simple language, (3) give your readers the chance to do something important, (4) make it hard to say no, (5) make your needs clear, (6) write no longer than you have to, (7) make your reply form complete and thorough, (8) use interesting enclosures.

TEST YOUR KNOWLEDGE

1. What are some questions to ask when gauging the audience's needs during the planning of a persuasive message?
2. What role do demographics and psychographics play in audience analysis during the planning of a persuasive message?
3. What are four of the ways you can build credibility with an audience when planning a persuasive message?
4. What is the AIDA plan, and how does it apply to persuasive messages?
5. How do emotional appeals differ from logical appeals?
6. What three types of reasoning can you use in logical appeals?
7. How can semantics affect a persuasive message?
8. What are four common mistakes to avoid when developing a persuasive message to overcome resistance?
9. What are the similarities and differences between sales messages and fundraising messages?
10. How do benefits differ from features?

APPLY YOUR KNOWLEDGE

1. Why is it important to present both sides of an argument when writing a persuasive message to a potentially hostile audience?
2. How are persuasive messages different from routine messages?
3. When is it appropriate to use the direct organizational approach in persuasive messages?
4. As an employee, how many of your daily tasks require persuasion? List as many as you can think of. Who are your audiences, and how do their needs and characteristics affect the way you develop your persuasive messages at work?
5. **Ethical Choices** Are emotional appeals ethical? Why or why not?

PRACTICE YOUR KNOWLEDGE

 *Documents for Analysis*

Read the following documents, then (1) analyze the strengths and weaknesses of each sentence and (2) revise each document so that it follows this chapter's guidelines.

Document 9.A: Writing Persuasive Requests for Action

At Tolson Auto Repair, we have been in business for over 25 years. We stay in business by always taking into account what the customer wants. That's why we are writing. We want to know your opinions to be able to better conduct our business.

Take a moment right now and fill out the enclosed questionnaire. We know everyone is busy, but this is just one way we have of making sure our people do their job correctly. Use the enclosed envelope to return the questionnaire.

And again, we're happy you chose Tolson Auto Repair. We want to take care of all your auto needs.

Document 9.B: Writing Persuasive Claims and Requests for Adjustment

Dear Gateway:

I'm writing to you because of my disappointment with my new TelePath x2 Faxmodem. The modem works all right, but the volume is set too high and the volume knob doesn't turn it down. It's driving us crazy. The volume knob doesn't seem to be connected to anything but simply spins around. I can't believe you would put out a product like this without testing it first.

I depend on the modem to run my small business and want to know what you are going to do about it. This reminds me of every time I buy electronic equipment from what seems like any company. Something is always wrong. I thought quality was supposed to be important, but I guess not.

Anyway, I need this fixed right away. Please tell me what you want me to do.

Document 9.C: Writing Sales and Fundraising Letters

We know how awful dining hall food can be, and that's why we've developed the "Mealaweek Club." Once a week, we'll deliver food to your dormitory or apartment. Our meals taste great. We have pizza, buffalo wings, hamburgers and curly fries, veggie roll-ups, and more!

When you sign up for just six months, we will ask what day you want your delivery. We'll ask you to fill out your selection of meals. And the rest is up to us. At "Mealaweek," we deliver! And payment is easy. We accept MasterCard and VISA or a personal check. It will save money especially when compared with eating out.

Just fill out the enclosed card and indicate your method of payment. As soon as we approve your credit or check, we'll begin delivery. Tell all your friends about Mealaweek. We're the best idea since sliced bread!

Exercises

For live links to all websites discussed in this chapter, visit this text's website at www.prenhall.com/bovee. Just log on, select Chapter 9, and click on "Student Resources." Locate the name of the site or the URL related to the material in the text. For the "Exploring the Best of the Web" exercises, you'll also find navigational directions. Click on the live link to the site.

9.1 **Teamwork** With another student, analyze the persuasive memo at Host Marriott (Figure 9.3 on page 272) by answering the following questions:
   a. What techniques are used to capture the reader's attention?
   b. Does the writer use the direct or the indirect organizational approach? Why?
   c. Is the subject line effective? Why or why not?
   d. Does the writer use an emotional or a logical appeal? Why?
   e. What reader benefits are included?

f. How does the writer establish credibility?
g. What tools does the writer use to reinforce his position?

9.2 **Composing Subject Lines** Compose effective subject lines for the following persuasive memos:

a. A request to your supervisor to purchase a new high-speed laser printer for your office. You've been outsourcing quite a bit of your printing to AlphaGraphics, and you're certain this printer will pay for itself in six months.
b. A direct mailing to area residents soliciting customers for your new business, "Meals à la Car," a carryout dining service that delivers from most of the local restaurants. All local restaurant menus are on the Internet. Mom and Dad can dine on egg rolls and chow mein while the kids munch on pepperoni pizza.
c. A special request to the company president to allow managers to carry over their unused vacation days to the following year. Apparently, many managers canceled their fourth-quarter vacation plans to work on the installation of a new company computer system. Under their current contract, vacation days not used by December 31 aren't accruable.

9.3 **Ethical Choices** Your boss has asked you to draft a memo requesting that everyone in your department donate money to the company's favorite charity, an organization that operates a special summer camp for physically challenged children. You wind up writing a three-page memo packed with facts and heartwarming anecdotes about the camp and the children's experiences. When you must work that hard to persuade your audience to take an action such as donating money to a charity, aren't you being manipulative and unethical? Explain.

9.4 **Focusing on Benefits** Determine whether the following sentences focus on features or benefits; rewrite as necessary to focus all the sentences on benefits.

a. All-Cook skillets are coated with a durable, patented nonstick surface.
b. You can call anyone and talk as long as you like on Saturdays and Sundays with this new wireless telephone service.
c. We need to raise $25 to provide each needy child with a backpack filled with school supplies.

9.5 **Internet** Visit the Federal Trade Commission website and read the "Catch the Bandit in Your Mailbox" consumer warning at www.ftc.gov/bcp/conline/pubs/tmarkg/bandit.htm. Select one or two sales or fundraising letters you've recently received and see whether they contain any of the suspicious content mentioned in the FTC warning. What does the FTC suggest you do with any materials that don't sound legitimate?

EXPAND YOUR KNOWLEDGE

Exploring the Best of the Web:

Influence an Official and Promote Your Cause, p. 278

The strategies you use to lobby a government representative and to seal a business transaction are similar. Both tasks require the art of persuasion to convince someone to take action on your behalf. Explore the data at the Thomas site, and find an issue you can use to practice your skills at writing a persuasive message.

1. What key ideas would you include in an e-mail message to persuade your congressional representative to support an issue important to you?
2. In a letter to a senator or member of Congress, what information would you include to convince the reader to vote for an issue supporting small business?
3. When sending a message to someone who daily receives hundreds of written appeals, what attention-getting techniques can you use? How can you get support for a cause that concerns you as a businessperson?

Exploring the Web on Your Own

Review these chapter-related websites on your own to learn more about writing persuasive messages.

1. Visit the Federal Trade Commission website, www.ftc.gov, to find out how consumers can cut down on the number of unsolicited mailings, calls, and e-mails they receive.
2. Check out the how-to and reference articles at the Sales Marketing Network (SMN), www.info-now.com/SMN/home.asp, and learn what the FTC requirements are when using the word *free* in sales and marketing messages.
3. Learn some aggressive sales strategies without going overboard from Guerrilla Marketing at www.gmarketing.com.

LEARN INTERACTIVELY

Interactive Study Guide

Visit "My Companion Website" at www.prenhall.com/bovee. For Chapter 9, take advantage of the interactive "Study Guide" to test your chapter knowledge. Get instant feedback on whether you need additional studying. Read the "Current Events" articles to get the latest on chapter topics, and complete the exercises—as specified by your instructor.

This site offers a variety of additional resources: The "Research Area" helps you locate a wealth of information to use in course assignments. You can even send a message to online research experts, who will help you find exactly the information you need. The "Study Hall" helps you succeed in this course. "Talk in the Hall" lets you leave messages and meet new friends online. If you have a question, you can "Ask the Tutor." And to get a better grade in this course, you can find more help at "Writing Skills," "Study Skills," and "Study Tips."

Grammar Diagnostic Tests

Review and reinforce your grammar and language skills by taking one of the four online diagnostic tests offered at our companion website, www.prenhall/bovee.com. The four tests cover a variety of topics, including spelling, capitals, punctuation, verbs, pronouns, adjectives, adverbs, sentence structure, sentence punctuation, clarity, word choice, style, organization skills, proofreading, and more. Submit your test and assess your competency. Then focus on improving areas where you are weak as you complete the exercises in this chapter.

CASES

APPLYING THE THREE-STEP WRITING PROCESS TO CASES

Apply each step to the following cases, as assigned by your instructor

Planning Cases

Analyze

1. What's your general purpose?
2. What's your specific purpose?
3. What do you want readers to do?
4. Who are your readers? (Who is the primary audience? What do readers have in common? What is their general background? How will they react?)

Investigate

5. What information do readers need?
6. What facts must you gather?

Adapt

How will you establish credibility?

Writing Cases

Organize

1. What's your main idea?
2. Will you use the direct or indirect approach? Why?

Compose

3. Will your tone be informal or more formal?
4. Draft the message as discussed in the "Your task" section of the case.

Completing Cases

Revise

1. Use the "Checklist for Revising Business Messages" on page 155 to edit and revise your message for clarity.

Produce

2. What's the best way to distribute your message? By fax? By e-mail? By sealed envelope?

Proofread

3. Proofread your message for errors in layout, spelling, and mechanics.

PERSUASIVE REQUESTS FOR ACTION

1. Ouch, that hurts! Persuasive memo at Technology One requesting equipment retrofit Mike Andrews leaves your office, shutting the door behind him. The pain in his arm is reflected on his face. He's about to file a worker's compensation claim—your third this month. As human resources director for Technology One, a major software development firm, you're worried not only about costs but also about the well-being of your employees.

Mike's complaints are much the same as those already reported by two other computer technicians: sharp pains in the wrist, numbness, and decreased range of motion. You know that the average technician spends at least six hours a day working on the computer, yet you've never had this many complaints in a short time, and the severity of the symptoms seems to be increasing.

You decide to seek the advice of experts. A local sports and orthopedic medicine clinic gives you a detailed description of repetitive strain injuries, or RSIs. The symptoms they describe are virtually identical to those exhibited by your technicians. You're distressed to learn that, if the cause of these injuries is not found and corrected, your technicians could require surgery or could even become permanently disabled.

The physical therapist at the clinic believes that exercises and wrist splints may help relieve symptoms and could even prevent new injuries. However, she also recommends that you consult an ergonomic analyst who can evaluate the furniture and equipment your technicians are using.

On her advice, you bring in an analyst, who spends an entire day at your facility. After measuring desk and chair height, watching technicians at work, and conducting a detailed analysis of all your equipment, he makes two recommendations: (1) Throw out all your computer keyboards and replace them with ergonomic keyboards, and (2) replace every mouse with a trackball. Suddenly you realize that the RSI complaints began shortly after your controller and purchasing manager bought a truckload of new computer equipment at a local merchant's going-out-of-business sale. You begin to wonder about the quality and design of that equipment, and you ask the analyst what benefits the changes will provide.

The ergonomic keyboard actually splits the traditional rows of keys in half and places the rows of keys at different angles, allowing the wrists to stay straight and relieving pressure on the forearm. The repetitive motions involved in using a mouse further aggravate the symptoms created by use of the traditional keyboard. Using a trackball does not require the repetitive clicking motion of the forefinger.

Your task: You know that replacing peripheral equipment on more than 50 computers will be costly, especially when the existing equipment is nearly new. However, increasing RSIs and disability claims could be even more costly. Write a persuasive memo to Katherine Wilson, your controller, and convince her of the immediate need to retrofit the technicians' computer equipment.[34]

2. Life's little hassles: Request for satisfaction It's hard to go through life without becoming annoyed at the way some things work. You have undoubtedly been dissatisfied with a product you've bought, a service you've received, or an action of some elected official or government agency.

Your task: Write a three- to five-paragraph persuasive e-mail request expressing your dissatisfaction in a particular case. Specify the action you want the reader to take.

3. Let's not swim with the sharks: Memo persuading MBC Mortgage Company to relocate its annual sales event Every year, MBC Mortgage Company runs an "incentive" contest among its salespeople from January through December, awarding the top seller in each of its 25 offices a "Weekend Adventure in Paradise." The trip includes all food, travel, and accommodations for your employee and a guest. They attend one sales meeting, but otherwise it's a well-earned vacation.

As director of meeting planning, you and your staff make the travel arrangements, but management chooses the incentive destination from your recommendations. Next year, winners are going to an exclusive resort in West Palm Beach, Florida. The posters featuring contest rules and picturing Florida palms and gleaming sand are ready to send to your branch offices in January. But it's September now, and last month's news from Florida has bothered you for two reasons: shark attacks and hurricanes.

First, a young boy lost an arm to a shark on Florida's west coast. Surgeons reattached the limb pulled from the eight-foot shark's jaws, but the boy's prognosis is uncertain. Then on Labor Day weekend, a 10-year-old Virginia boy died from massive blood loss after his father beat off a shark. The same weekend, a woman lost her foot and her companion died after sharks attacked them off North Carolina. Up and down Florida's east coast, bathers and surfers were bitten last month in shallow waters. Beaches closed, then reopened, then closed again. Swarms of sharks have been spotted swimming close to shore, in waters usually full of vacationers. Apparently, Florida leads the world in shark attacks (220 in the last decade). By comparison, California recorded only 33 attacks during the same period, according to the International Shark Attack Files, posted on the Internet by the Florida Museum of Natural History in Gainesville, a website intended to be reassuring. It's not.

In addition to shark attacks, you're also worried about hurricanes. Although hurricanes are more common in late summer and early fall, in recent years, climate changes have made hurricanes less seasonal. High winds, heavy rains, and flooding have unpredictably devastated parts of Florida during unusual times of the year. You'd hate for your people to be caught in the wake of a hurricane.

What if employees arrive for their hard-earned weekend—and the beaches of "paradise" are closed? Or open and deadly dangerous? What if hurricanes force employees to evacuate their hotel rooms in the middle of the night? Wouldn't sunny, shark-free California be a better location?

You've heard about the classy Hotel del Coronado in Coronado, California. Located on an island in San Diego bay, the Hotel Del has hosted presidents, diplomats, movie stars, and other wealthy travelers. Those 26 acres of shark-scarce beaches, ocean-view pools, dining terraces, elegant spas, shops, and restaurants are beginning to look very enticing—and safe—as an alternate destination for your top employees.

Your task: Write a memo persuading MBC management to reprint the posters and relocate the incentive weekend to Coronado's Hotel Del. You could log on to the resort's website for juicy details to augment your argument, www.hoteldel.com, but remember that the shark attacks are your primary reason for suggesting the change of venue. Use emotional and logical appeals. If you need them, current statistics are at www.flmnh.ufl.edu/fish/Sharks/Statistics/statsus.htm.[35]

4. I'll be cheaper: Persuasive letter to Miramax Films from a "downsized" publicist Working as a film publicist for Miramax Films was a dream come true—until you got laid off during a Hollywood slowdown. That was a week ago. Not one to let the grass grow, you've been reading business publications, looking for inspiration. You finally found it in the story of Harold Jackson and the Coca-Cola Company.

Like you, Jackson worked for Hill & Knowlton, one of the country's major PR firms, before he was hired as Coca-Cola's manager of media relations in Atlanta. Miramax hired you away from Hill & Knowlton two years ago to become a media relations representative.

Your special task was to cultivate relationships with the countless small and alternative print publications in the western United States. While they don't pull in as many readers as, say, *The Los Angeles Times*, collectively they command a large readership, and a blurb from a small paper's review is almost as effective in movie ads as one from a major critic. You discovered that, if handled politely and with some deference, the small-publication critics treated Miramax films more kindly.

In fact, you attribute the early word-of-mouth success of eventual Academy Award favorites such as *Shakespeare in Love* and *Chocolat* to your personal efforts to get these writers tickets to special previews, and press kits without delay. You returned their phone calls immediately, cultivated personal relationships, and now know them all on a first-name basis.

Back to Jackson's story: After helping Coke open The World of Coca-Cola entertainment center in Atlanta, Jackson launched his own company, JacksonHeath Public Relations International. His first client? His previous employer, Coca-Cola.

"Knowledge of Coke and how it functioned helped me do the job," he told an interviewer. But he also immediately hired employees so that he could spend his time cultivating new clients. "Business is built on relationships," he said, "and you have to take the relationship you have when you leave a company and run very fast."

In his first six months, Jackson's firm made $100,000, nearly 100 percent of it from Coke. The company liked the professionalism of his business plan and the fact that he knew how Coke operated, and they knew his work. Also, he cost less to hire as a consultant than as an employee. Today, Coke accounts for only 7 percent of Jackson's business; his other clients have kept JacksonHeath profitable.

You know that Miramax shaved its promotional staff down to a few and there's no one left who'll be handling your former territory. That's a shame, because those small-publication reviews can do so much to promote a film's most vital asset: word of mouth among moviegoers.

Your task: Borrowing Jackson's ideas, write a letter persuading Miramax co-chairmen Harvey and Bob Weinstein to grant you a Hollywood-style meeting, in which you'll pitch your services as a consultant. Name your company, as Jackson did, and build interest and desire to meet with you by presenting your argument professionally. (At the meeting, you will elaborate on specific promotional ideas you have for films currently in production, since you know Miramax's business so well.)[36]

5. No more driving: Persuasive memo about telecommuting to Bachman, Trinity, and Smith Sitting in your Dallas office at the accounting firm of Bachman, Trinity, and Smith, pouring over financial statements and clacking away on your calculator, it seems as though you could be doing this work from your home. After all, it's been two hours since lunch and you haven't spoken a word to anyone. Would they notice if you weren't here, as long as your work was completed on time? You've been an accountant here for five years; surely they can trust you by now.

During lunch breaks, you've been reading about telecommuting. With three kids at home and your commute time nearly an hour each way, the idea sounds incredibly appealing. Here are some notes you've made:

- Teleworking is environmentally friendly—reducing air pollution, for one thing.
- BellSouth has 1,200 telecommuters among 68,000 employees in a nine-state region.
- Texas Instruments paid a telecommuter for a second home phone line and gave her access to the company's intranet.
- International Telework Association and Council (ITAC), in Washington, D.C., says the number of teleworkers in the United States now tops 25 million and is rising.
- Employers save on overhead by eliminating office space, while employees are more relaxed and productive when commuting time becomes family time.
- Dallas commuters spend 46 hours a year stalled in traffic—fifth worst in the United States, according to a study by the Texas Transportation Institute.
- The same study says Dallas employers lost $1.9 billion last year in fuel costs and lost productivity from those traffic delays.
- New technology—such as Internet accessibility, better laptops, handheld computers, web-enabled cellular phones, and so on—has improved worker mobility.
- Teleworker productivity is improved by as much as 22 percent, and employee turnover and operating costs are reduced, says ITAC.
- Employers who encourage teleworking have reduced absenteeism by 63 percent, saving an average of $2,086 per worker per year, says Telework America, a Washington, D.C., research firm.

While experts debate the economic benefits of telecommuting, you've decided to propose the idea to your employer. You've read that other accounting firms in your area are experimenting with it. Maybe you could convince your boss, Marjorie Bachman, to let you work from home for a six-month trial.

There are good precedents. Some of the early and successful pioneers of teleworking are federal and state government agencies, and companies such as IBM, Cisco Systems, Symantec, AT&T, and American Express. The U.S. General Services Administration (GSA) has nearly 14,000 employees; 7 percent of them are telecommuters. IBM has 60,000 telecommuters worldwide. About half of these organizations provide their employees with equipment and furnishings for home offices; you already have a home office with a PC and fax machine.

You'll have to overcome some drawbacks, including:

- Not being able to be "away" from work; hearing business and fax lines ringing after hours
- Losing the social benefits of interaction with co-workers
- Lacking visibility when it's time for promotions or new assignments
- Missing the opportunity to brainstorm with others (although you'll have e-mail and other tools for this)
- Feeling isolated
- Provoking anxiety in managers who can't handle supervising "invisible" employees

Your task: Using some of the foregoing facts to bolster your argument and counter objections, write a memo to senior partner Marjorie Bachman persuading her to give you a six-month trial as a telecommuter.[37]

6. A laughing matter: Persuasive e-mail to Kinko's manager about making work more fun Working at Kinko's has always been a little tense. After you'd been there awhile, you decided that it's the customers with urgent projects they are trying to finish who bring the stress in the door with them. By design, the round-the-clock copy and business service center attracts people under deadlines. But then employees pick up that tension, and by the end of the day, your shoulders are aching and your head hurts. Fun? Who has time? The people you see all day are in a hurry, hurry, hurry.

During a recent economic slowdown, things got worse. Customers started bringing in résumés for copying and renting time to surf the Internet for jobs. People got testy, customers and employees alike. Mistakes were made, co-workers called in sick whether they were or not, you ran out of pain relievers, your manager got frustrated, and morale sank. Work became a miserable experience.

But you have an idea: You read somewhere about people using laughter to relieve stress. One man watched comedies until his cancer went into remission. While you can't exactly roll out the VCR during working hours, you and your co-workers could bring more fun into the workplace. You've found impressive support for this idea.

"Laughter is a great way to release stress," says Dr. Tracy Gaudet, a women's physician and consultant to the Oprah Winfrey show, website, and magazine. She says researchers have found that laughter helps the immune system. It lowers blood pressure, decreases heart strain, and lowers blood levels of the stress hormone cortisol. In one study, heart attack sufferers cut their risk of a second attack by 20 percent after watching 30 minutes of comedy videos per day. In fact, laughter therapy reduces average hospital stays by two days; it releases endorphins, which are the body's pain relievers. The very process of producing a belly laugh gives the lungs and heart an aerobic workout, and reduces stress by relaxing muscles.

Matt Weinstein owns a consulting company that helps corporations restructure their culture to "support laughter, play, and human values in the workplace—at the same time increasing productivity, teamwork, and physical well-being." At Charleton Memorial Hospital the staff let off steam by holding a contest to match pictures of pets with their employee owners. Sprint has sponsored "fun days" where employees wear clothes backwards, or go on photo safaris with disposable cameras, taking pictures of unsuspecting co-workers. Other companies have held costume parties, hung funny signs and posters, held messy-desk contests, hosted ice cream socials, and created weekend events to help employees relax and have fun.

Companies who've used these tactics say they release creativity, reduce absenteeism, and increase enthusiasm. Having fun on the job doesn't mean workers are slacking off—it could mean they won't come down with a stress-related illness or injury. And think how much better customers are treated by employees who are enjoying their jobs!

Your task: On one of your breaks, send a persuasive e-mail to your manager, Brad Attlebury, convincing him to try some laugh therapy at Kinko's. Suggest the pet-matching contest, or any other tactic you think you can sell. Be sure to address the usual employer concern: that employees having fun can't be working hard enough. Prove that Kinko's will benefit from having workers who enjoy coming to work.[38]

7. Point, click, recruit: Persuasive memo about e-cruiting at Boulder Construction More than 60 percent of computer-related companies are doing it, but only 2 percent of the companies in the building industry have tried it. You think Boulder Construction should join those "e-cruiting" pioneers. After all, you've got projects all over the state needing skilled workers, both in the field and behind the desk. As vice president, you're responsible for keeping costs down, and you're convinced that e-cruiting could save a bundle, while snatching talent out from under your competitors' noses.

Display ads in the Sunday newspapers have always been the standby for your human resources director, Sheila Young. They typically cost $1,000 and up per job. On the other hand, major Internet career sites such as monster.com, hotjobs.com, or careermosaic.com may charge only $100 to $300 a month to list openings. And while the amount of information you can put in a newspaper ad is limited (since you pay by the word), online space is not. You can fully describe Boulder Construction's appeal to talented workers: its status as a major builder in the state of Colorado, its longevity, and its reputation for good benefits, safe working conditions, and upward mobility. *Air Conditioning, Heating, and Refrigeration News* says that in one survey, the average cost per hire via the web was $183, compared to $1,383 for traditional hiring.

Creating a website with a careers page is another good recruiting tactic, but you want to wait until you've tried the job boards. You've read that there are between 30,000 and 100,000 Internet sites devoted to recruiting, with 148.8 million Internet users in the United States. Last year, 74 percent of those over the age of 18 used the Internet to look for a job. That means your pool of potential candidates could be huge, certainly much larger than the local newspaper can attract. And there are no geographical limitations online. If they're willing to relocate, you might land good employees you'd never have met otherwise.

Some companies claim they've started receiving résumés within moments of posting an opening. Hiring decisions that once took six weeks are now being made within the hour, these companies report. No more waiting for snail mail. Using available software, you can search through online résumés using keywords to prescreen candidates for certain qualifications or experience.

Of course, you won't totally abandon traditional hiring. E-cruiting can't do everything. For instance, you won't see online applicants in person. Fulfilling diversity goals could be more difficult, which might lead to legal issues. And you could miss "passive" candidates, the type who are happily employed, highly qualified, and fought over by recruiters because they're often willing to take a good offer. But they rarely post résumés online. On the other hand, passive candidates might respond to an online job posting.

Overall, you think e-cruiting offers advantages that will make the effort worthwhile. Bank of Montreal says it's saving more than $1 million by e-cruiting this year; other large companies claim they've even hired executives using Internet tools.

Your task: Write a memo to Sheila Young persuading her to try e-cruiting for Boulder's next job openings. You don't want this to be an order, so use the AIDA plan to convince her that the advantages outweigh the drawbacks.[39]

8. No choking matter: Persuasive letter from the Consumer Product Safety Commission about fast-food giveaways When two babies died in 1999 after suffocating on plastic Pokemon balls their parents got from Burger King, the fast-food industry took notice. Some restaurants implemented safety tests on the billions of free toys being distributed with kids' meals. But Ann W. Brown, chairman of the Consumer Product Safety Commission (and your boss), isn't convinced they're doing enough.

Brown wants better quality control over the giveaways, most of which are manufactured in China, at a cost of about 30 to 50 cents apiece. "Just because a toy is inexpensive and is given away doesn't mean it shouldn't be as safe as the safest toys," your boss believes. She's afraid toys designed for older children are being given to toddlers. Manufacturing defects are also a problem, and the only way to catch those is to test large numbers of toys as they come off the assembly line. She thinks restaurants should be responsible for such tests.

Fast-food giveaways are a major source of inexpensive playthings for young children, but they also benefit the donors. Kids often influence a family's dining decision—not for the food, but for the toys. A popular giveaway can increase a restaurant's sales by about 4 percent; a really big hit, by 15 percent.

As director of the safety commission's Office of Compliance, you applaud recent safety efforts by Burger King and McDonald's. Burger King has hired independent testers, strengthened safety standards, and conducted tests before, during, and after manufacturing. McDonald's also developed a testing doll, "McBaby," with artificial lungs to check suffocation risks. (They've loaned McBaby to your department so that other restaurants can copy the design.) Both companies recognize that it's to their advantage to protect child safety.

In addition to legal liabilities and damage to their reputations if children are injured or die from playing with toys they've given away, restaurants can lose millions in promotional dollars. A restaurant may spend as much as $25 million advertising a tie-in with a popular film. They may also pay licensing fees of $250,000 to $1 million to movie studios for the right to produce a tie-in toy. Even when fees are reversed, and a manufacturer or entertainment company pays the restaurant to promote its products through a giveaway, the cost of injuries or fatalities from faulty toys could be staggering. And of course, no one wants children hurt.

The problem is growing. In one recent year, four fast-food companies voluntarily recalled five different toys. After receiving reports of "Hourglass Space Sprout" and "Look for Me Bumblebee" toys releasing small beads on which toddlers might choke, Burger King recalled 2.6 million toys, urging parents to bring them back for replacement toys. Prior to that, Burger King recalled 400,000 "Rattling, Paddling Riverboat" toys after reports of metal pins coming loose from the paddle wheel. McDonald's recalled 234,000 "Scooter Bugs" after three children choked on the toys. Fortunately, none were seriously injured.

Burger King gives away nearly 100 million toys annually; McDonald's distributes 1.5 billion worldwide. They are the most vigilant members in a large industry, which accounts for one-third of all toys distributed in the United States. The potential for harm is huge.

Your task: Develop a letter to be sent to fast-food vendors in the United States, urging them to follow McDonald's and Burger King's lead in pretesting giveaway toys. Use facts, anecdotes, and benefits to bolster your position.[40]

PERSUASIVE CLAIMS AND REQUESTS FOR ADJUSTMENTS

9. Too good to be true: E-mail to Page South requesting adjustment Page South offered its pager services for a mere $5 a month. You purchased an inexpensive pager and signed a contract for two years. You thought your pager phone number was up and running for two weeks, but your co-workers and clients say they repeatedly get a busy signal when dialing your pager number. You call Page South and get the problem resolved, but this takes an additional week. You don't want to be charged for the time the pager wasn't in service. After discussing the situation with the local manager, she asks you to contact Judy Hinkley at the company's regional business office.

Your task: Send an e-mail message to Hinkley at Judy@pgsouth.com and request an adjustment to your account. Request credit or partial credit for one month of service. Remember to write a summary of events in chronological order, supplying exact dates for maximum effectiveness.

10. Endless trouble: Claim letter to Abe's Pool Installations As chief administrator, you worked hard to convince the board of directors of Westlake Therapy and Rehabilitation Center that a small, 8-by-15-foot Endless Pool would be a wonderful addition to the facility. Because the pool produces an adjustable current flow, a swimmer can swim "endlessly" against it, never reaching the pool's edge. With this new invention by a Philadelphia manufacturer, your patients could experience a complete range of water therapy in a year-round, indoor pool small enough to fit in a standard living room!

The board agreed, choosing the optional six-foot depth, which would allow for additional therapeutic uses but would require (1) a special platform and (2) installation in a room with a high ceiling. The old gymnasium would become your new Water Therapy Pavilion. Total cost with custom features: $20,080, plus $8,000 budgeted for installation.

According to the manufacturer, "The Endless Pool has been designed as a kit for bolt-together assembly. It can be assembled by two reasonably handy people with no prior installation experience following detailed procedural videos." You can do it yourself, they proclaim, or hire a local contractor.

You've hired Abe's Pool Installation, which will build the special access platform and install the pool. You passed along the instructional videos, along with the manufacturer's hotline numbers. They've offered a preinstallation engineering consultation for your customized pool, without additional charge, as you told Abe. They'll also be glad to help determine whether the planned site can handle the pool's 10-ton filled weight. Abe nodded and told you not to worry.

Finally, Abe's crew completed the platform and amid much excitement from your staff, assembled the galvanized steel pool. At a grand, ribbon-cutting dedication ceremony, you personally flipped the switch.

Immediately the hydraulic motor began moving 5,000 gallons of water a minute through a grill at the front, which smoothes and straightens the current. Everyone's excitement grew as the first wave of water washed down the center of the pool. But instead of entering the turning vane arrays (which were supposed to recirculate the water through hidden channels back to the front of the pool), the water kept going, splashing out the back of the pool and onto the platform and the gathered onlookers . . . at 5,000 gallons a minute. Panic and shouts erupted as you fumbled quickly to turn the thing off.

Final damage included a collapsed platform, a ruined floor, an incorrectly installed pool, and numerous dry-cleaning bills from onlookers. Fortunately, no one was hurt. Estimated cost with floor repair: $10,000. Abe is not returning your phone calls. But local reporters are coming to film the damage tomorrow, and it's your job to conduct their tour.

Your task: Write a claim letter to Abe Hanson, Owner, Abe's Pool Installation, 2525 Rocket Lane, Manchester, MD 21088.[41]

11. Secondhand smoke: Letter requesting rent refund from Kuykendahl Joint, Inc. Last January in Harris County, Texas, your branch of Contract Management Services, Inc., (CMSI) signed a lease with Kuykendahl Joint, Inc., for new office space at 3638 University Boulevard, Suite 302, Houston, TX 77005-3396. No one anticipated the nightmare that would follow. You have been assistant manager since before the move. But after relocating, you've threatened to quit many times—and so has your manager, Kathleen Thomas.

The problem is secondhand smoke invading your offices from other tenants. The Environmental Protection Agency (EPA) calls this ETS (environmental tobacco smoke) and classifies it as a Group A (known human) carcinogen. There is no safe level of exposure to Group A toxins. The Surgeon General says the 4,600 chemicals in ETS (including cyanide, arsenic, formaldehyde, carbon monoxide, and ammonia) are "a cause of disease, including lung cancer, in healthy nonsmokers."

The smoke wafts in the front door of your office and seeps through openings in hollow walls shared with tenants on either side of CMSI. You and others have suffered bronchitis, migraines, and respiratory infections since the move. One of your most valuable employees, a star performer responsible for landing many new contracts, quit last week. "I can't risk this," she said. "I've had asthma since I was little, and it's getting worse."

Another employee is worried about his heart; he's in the high-risk category and there's evidence ETS can trigger heart attacks. Pneumonia, allergies, ear infections, other forms of cancer (including breast, cervical, endocrine, etc.)—all are "causally associated" with ETS, according to the EPA. In fact, secondhand smoke is more dangerous than what smokers inhale. That's because the heat of the draw burns off some of the toxins, which are also filtered by the cigarette or cigar.

Last month CMSI spent $3,000 hiring contractors to weather-strip around vents, electrical outlets, and other built-in fixtures—even to spray polyurethane foam around the pipes that are under sinks and behind toilets. But you're still choking and gagging on smelly carcinogens. By the end of the day, you've got red eyes, a runny nose, often a headache—and you smell like a poker game.

Thomas says it's no use talking to the offending smokers. She's collected a list (from Americans for Nonsmokers' Rights) that cites legal precedents around the country, in which courts have held landlords responsible both for eliminating ETS and for compensating tenants.

Your task: Thomas has asked you to write a persuasive letter for her signature to Robert Bechtold, Manager, Kuykendahl Joint, Inc. (88 North Park Road, Houston, TX 77005). Insist that the landlord (1) improve the air quality immediately, (2) refund lease payments totaling $9,000 from January 1, and (3) reimburse CMSI for the improvements made in an attempt to solve the problem. "If this doesn't work, we're moving," she says grimly. "And then we'll sue."[42]

12. Broadband blues: Persuasive claim letter to ZippieNet about cable modem failures When your cable company offered ZippieNet—high-speed, cable modem Internet access—you signed up right away. You figured $49.95 a month wasn't too much to pay for speed online when your business as a freelance journalist depends on getting access to information as soon as it's available.

Sometimes you have to wade through a dozen websites just to find one vital piece of information, whether a statistic or a quote or a historical fact to support a story you're working on. If you're going to compete with staff writers at the various publications that buy your work as an independent contractor, you need to deliver stories as fast as anyone to meet short deadlines. So having a "broadband" Internet connection that's "always on" and "five times faster" than a dial-up line could be a lifesaver. Imagine—no more busy signals!

At first you were very pleased. When the system worked, it worked beautifully. You were dazzled by the speed, and happy about not having to dial up to check your e-mail. With the always-on connection, your software alerted you as soon as mail arrived. Yes, that first day was quite wonderful.

Then the problems began. Three days a week for four weeks, the system failed and you were stuck offline. When you called ZippieNet's support lines, you were put on hold for 30 minutes, and when someone finally answered, they seemed ill trained and overworked. Finally, a ZippieNet repairman came to check your cable modem. He said he hadn't seen that model in years; the installation subcontractors had apparently supplied ancient equipment. When he installed a newer-model replacement, the service seemed at first to improve.

That was three months ago. Since then, you've experienced total shutdowns at least twice a month. During periods of high usage, the zippy speeds ZippieNet promised you slow down considerably—to levels not much better than your old dial-up connection. At $49.95 per month, that's unacceptable. You've heard about this problem with other providers, where they've oversold their capacity and too many users are trying to access the same network at the same time. So far your latest complaints to ZippieNet via phone have brought no solution or helpful response. Only vague promises that the service will be better soon and urgings to be patient.

And now the unthinkable has happened. Twice last week the system went down for more than 24 hours. Fate being unkind, those 48 hours were smack in the middle of your work on an article that you had contracted to sell for $1,000—except that you were unable to access critical information, unable to deliver the story on time, and not only lost the sale, but your editor who had been counting on it to fill a space was so angry he vowed never to work with you again.

Your task: Write a letter to ZippieNet, 1203 West Barber Avenue, Nashville, TN 37214, demanding a refund for your four months of service, plus $1,000 for lost income on the foiled article sale to *Arete Magazine* (include a copy of your article contract), and $3,000 toward the loss of future sales to the same publication. (If they pay the $1,000, you'll be content, but don't tell them that.) Do suggest that you will remain a customer if they can deliver improved service within three weeks. When it works, you love broadband.[43]

13. Not too late for others: Letter to the U.S. Food Safety and Inspection Service requesting recall of Hillshire Farm meat products All you wanted was to make a big impression on managers at TriTech, Inc., coming to your area for a team meeting on productivity issues yesterday, January 23. The meeting included two managers each from four departments: marketing, administration, manufacturing, and purchasing. The full Productivity Team includes seven departments, but it was decided that smaller group meetings would be a good way to get the ball rolling. Thank goodness.

As marketing manager, you dipped into the departmental budget to finance a buffet luncheon for participants. You decided you could do better than a caterer by buying the food yourself the night before from Bob and Jill's Gourmet Market in Baltimore. As the meeting wound down, members of your staff laid out an attractive array of breads, cheeses, sandwich meats, vegetables, condiments, salads, and desserts pulled from the department's refrigerator.

"Brilliant idea," said a colleague from manufacturing as he dove in hungrily.

"It not only looks great, but you've saved money by doing it yourself. Why don't you come to work in our department?" said the purchasing manager between bites.

Now the only thing you're grateful for is the fact that the entire team wasn't present. This way, TriTech only lost the services of 8 managers at once, not 14. So much for productivity! By 8 P.M., six of you were in the emergency room, lunch coming out, intravenous fluids going in. The other two toughed it out at home, but swore they'd never eat at another company buffet. None of you are at work today.

According to the Baltimore City Hospital emergency room staff, the timing of your reactions and your collective symptoms—nausea, vomiting, diarrhea, intense abdominal cramps, high fever, and screaming headaches—are consistent with salmonellosis, a fairly common form of food poisoning from the *salmonella* bacteria, or it might have been staphylococcal food poisoning. Although you're all home now, feeling miserable, you were lucky. People sometimes die from these forms of poisoning, nurses told you.

After talking with hospital staff, you've decided the culprit was the Hillshire Farms cooked, sliced beef and ham. You kept everything strictly cold until the last minute, and you remember checking the freshness date, which said "Sell Before February 1." It must have been contaminated at the plant. The hospital suggested that you alert the store where you bought the meat. Then, if you wished, you could contact the U.S. Department of Agriculture's Food Safety and Inspection Service.

"They're the ones who issue recalls of tainted meat and other foods," Dr. Samuel Hill told you. "If consumers complain, they'll do laboratory tests if they can find the products. You might save someone from what you've been through or worse, if you hurry."

You decide it's the only humanitarian thing to do. Normally for a faulty product, you'd demand a refund, but $20 from Hillshire Farms won't make up for the horrors of last night. Using your persuasive talents to have this dangerous product recalled is the best compensation you can think of.

Your task: Your complaint should be addressed to Elijah Walker, associate deputy administrator for the Office of Public Health and Science, Food Safety and Inspection Service, U.S. Department of Agriculture, Washington, DC 20250-3700. Persuade him that the meat you bought should be tested for a possible recall. Sending a copy of this letter to Hillshire Farms will constitute your claim to them, so make it thorough.[44]

14. Tangled Web: Persuasive e-mail to PurelySoftware regarding an online order duplication

What a mess. As if running a small business didn't have enough challenges, now your cost-saving tactic is costing you more in lost time than you saved by trying to order products through an online vendor.

Your art consulting business, ArtAlive, has been doing so well you hired a new employee. Your company finds, installs, and often commissions art, sculpture, and signage for corporations, hospitals, universities, and foundations. It's an odd niche, but one you've worked hard to develop. Your new graphic designer, Monica Soderburgh, will be a tremendous help as she produces presentation materials to promote your services.

In hindsight, it would have been easier to send your assistant out to buy Adobe InDesign, Version 1.5, and Adobe Photoshop, Version 6.0, from a brick-and-mortar store. But to save money, you decided to shop on CNET.com, which lists and rates vendors and will send price-drop alerts via e-mail. You chose online vendor PurelySoftware because their price was low and they were offering a "free shipping weekend."

You clicked through to purelysoftware.com, found the products, numbered PN#27510216 and PN#32101335 respectively, hit the "buy" buttons for both, filled out the order forms, including your credit card number and expiration date, and clicked "submit." Nothing happened. Usually after submitting an online order, a "thank you" screen appears, and most vendors send a confirmation e-mail message. You received nothing.

Worried, you called the customer service number (1-888-555-4250). You explained what happened to an operator named Sylvia. "Just a moment," she said and put you on hold. She came back in a moment and said that your order came through, but all it showed was your name, company, and credit card information, with no products listed.

"With the free shipping weekend, it's been very busy and we've been having a little trouble with the website," Sylvia admitted. "You're not the first to call." She said she'd cancel that order and submit a new one, taken from you over the phone. While you were at it, you decided to order the latest version of Norton Antivirus for an additional $20, since shipping was free for the next two days. That was on May 3.

On May 6, you received the products you ordered on the phone. You filed the shipping invoice and credit card receipt ($649 for Adobe InDesign, $564 for Adobe Photoshop, $20 for Norton Antivirus, totaling $1,233) and gave the software to Monica.

Three weeks have passed and today (May 24) you received a second shipment. The shipping invoice listed May 3 as the order date and inside was exactly what you'd ordered online, two software programs only, with a receipt saying your credit card was charged $1,213.00. Coming so much later, you wonder if some technician "unclogged" the website, causing the missing orders to surface. Yours must have been shipped automatically with the rest.

Your task: Technically, you did place the first order. But you also called and canceled, although you have no written proof. Send an e-mail message to customerservice@purelysoftware.com, using persuasive tactics to convince them that the error was theirs, not yours. You want an immediate credit to your Visa account and a postage-paid shipping label to return the products. For security, don't include your credit card number in this first message, but provide your telephone and fax numbers, e-mail address, shipping address, and order number from the latest shipping invoice: AARGS 2287 89 1. (The phone order was AARGT 3928 88 3.)[45]

15. Cow-spotty text: E-mail to Gateway from Words Unlimited requesting warranty extension

Every Gateway computer sold provides a 30-day period during which you can upgrade, downgrade, make exchanges, and change your mind without paying full, stand-alone price for components you wish to add. That's good, because the first thing you discovered when you opened the cow-spotted boxes a week after they were delivered to your offices via UPS was that the salesman who sold you this small-business "Professional S1300" system (Chris Swanson) apparently thought you didn't need Internet access.

You thought every computer in the world came with a built-in modem. Since it wasn't specified, you didn't get it. You made this embarrassing discovery after you tried for half an hour to insert a phone line into the network receptacle. The plug went in fine but you kept getting error messages saying there was no modem. You finally agreed.

All Gateways are shipped direct from the factory, whether ordered online or at a store. You'd ordered yours at the Lincoln, Nebraska, store. You called and Swanson apologized profusely for the mix-up. He ordered a modem for you, charging your credit card the low, add-on price because you were still within the 30-day grace period.

Ten days later, the package arrived. (Modems had been temporarily out of stock.) You were busy with work (still being conducted on your five-year-old Pentium), but when you could get away, you dismantled the unused computer and lugged it to the store, where the modem was installed for free. You had to wait two days because the technician was out sick. It took another day before you could pick it up and, after the weekend, you started connecting the new system again. That took two days because of work interruptions again. Finally, a month after you received it, the new system is assembled.

Your company, Words Unlimited, provides editing and typesetting services to small publishers. You and your partner keep two computers humming all day while you work with text on-screen. You explained this to Swanson and he suggested a Mitsubishi "flat-screen" monitor using "Diamondtron technology" for outstanding imagery. You paid an extra $70 for the upgraded, 17-inch monitor.

Now you can't believe your eyes. Thinking back, you realize that the showroom demos that looked so good involved mostly graphics. You never tested a page of text, much to your regret. You're staring at broken letters—collections of disconnected dots. "It's barely readable!" you exclaim. Your partner agrees, "Our old CRT looks so much better." After a day of eyestrain and a terrible headache, you realize this will never do.

Back at the Gateway store, you discover: (1) No matter what brand, "flat-screen" means liquid crystal display (LCD)—bad for text, although no one here will admit it; and (2) your grace period ended yesterday.

You also find an impressive, 19-inch, CRT monitor with a fast refresh-rate that no one showed you the first time. Text looks great on it! It costs $20 more than the Mitsubishi as an exchange, but if you don't get your warranty extended, it's going to cost a lot more. You'll have to pay the stand-alone price, and you'll have to sell or discard the Mitsubishi monitor because Gateway won't take it as a return.

Your task: Write a persuasive letter to store manager Ann Cameron, Gateway Country Store, 2900 Pine Lake Road, Lincoln, NE 68516, who Swanson says has leeway to extend your 30-day grace period. Use semantics, facts, anecdotes, emotions, and logic to support your argument. So far every Gateway employee has been courteous, quick, and eager to help, despite the mix-ups. You have high hopes.[46]

SALES AND FUNDRAISING MESSAGES

16. Quotesmith.com: E-mail extolling a better way to buy insurance The great thing about Quotesmith.com is that no one is obligated to buy a thing. Consumers can log on to your website, ask for dozens of free insurance quotes, and then go off and buy elsewhere. They can look at instant price-comparison quotes (from more than 300 insurers) for term life, dental, individual and family medical insurance, small group medical insurance, workers' compensation, short-term medical insurance, Medicare supplement insurance, "no-exam" whole life insurance, fixed-annuity insurance, and (in a click-through arrangement with Progressive) private passenger automobile insurance. All rates are up-to-the-day accurate, and Quotesmith is the largest single source for comprehensive insurance price comparisons in the United States.

Once consumers see your price-comparison charts, many choose to fill out an easy insurance application request right on your site. Why deal with an insurance salesperson when you can see the price differences for yourself—especially over such a broad range of companies? Quotesmith backs up this application with toll-free customer-service lines operated by salaried representatives. They're not working on commission, but they know about insurance. And Quotesmith has based its new online service on a long history of serving the insurance industry.

The product pretty much sells itself, and that's what you love about your marketing job with Quotesmith. Consumers and computers do most of the work—and the results are at lightning speed, especially compared with what the insurance business was like just a few years ago. During peak periods, the site has been processing one quote request every four seconds, which leads, ultimately, to increased policy sales without an agent or intermediary.

Quotesmith advertises both in print and on TV, saying that it provides "the lowest term life rates in America or we'll overnight you $500." Your company also guarantees the accuracy of quotes against a $500 reward. Final rates depend on variables such as age, sex, state availability, hazardous activities, personal and family health history, driving records, and so on.

You're proud of the fact that Quotesmith has received positive press from *Nation's Business, Kiplinger's Personal Finance, Good Housekeeping, The Los Angeles Times, Money, U.S. News & World Report,* and *Forbes* ("Quotesmith.com provides rock-bottom quotes")—your favorite. For every term-life quote, you even provide consumers with a look at how each insurer's ability to pay claims is rated by A.M. Best, Duff & Phelps, Moody's, Standard & Poor's, and Weiss Ratings, Inc.

And all of this is free. Too bad more people don't know about your services.

Your task: It's your job to lure more insurance customers to Quotesmith. You've decided to use direct e-mail marketing (like cold-calling without the telephone). Write a pitch extolling the benefits of Quotesmith's services, and focus on consumers who are unfamiliar with the site. Be sure your message is suited to an e-mail format, with an appropriate subject heading.[47]

17. Buses for seniors: Fundraising letter from Morris County Senior Center The Morris County Senior Center is one of New Jersey's oldest nonprofit institutions for the elderly. Over the past 50 years, it has relied on financial support from government, businesses, and individuals.

Unfortunately, recent state and federal cutbacks have dug into the organization's budget. In addition, in the last five years two of the county's largest companies, Hardwick Industries and McCarthy Electrical Motors, have moved offshore and shut down local operations. Both businesses were supporters of the center, as were many of the workers who lost jobs.

However, the needs of the center keep growing. For many of the county's roughly 1,000 seniors who live alone, it's the only place where they can meet their peers, use a special library, avoid extreme weather, or get a well-balanced meal. The center is not a nursing home and has no overnight facilities. Most individuals get to the facility on one of the three shuttle type buses belonging to the center. The buses are also used for various day trips to museums, plays, and similar functions. Occasionally, they are used to help the temporarily disabled get to doctors' offices or pharmacists.

Each bus is more than eight years old. Although not quite unsafe, the buses are showing their age. The constant repairs are stopgap measures at best, and most weeks at least one of the vehicles is inoperable. Monthly repairs are averaging a total of $300 for the three vehicles. In addition, when the vans aren't working, the clients, staff, and budget all suffer. Seniors can't get to the center, trips are canceled, and drivers are sometimes paid for coming to work even though they aren't able to drive.

Conservatively, it would cost about $28,000 to replace each van with a new one: $84,000 total. This includes estimates on how much the center could gain from selling the old vans. It's a fair amount of money, but in the opinion of your board of directors, buying new vans would be better than continuously repairing the old ones or risking the purchase of used ones.

Your task: As director of the center, draft a fundraising letter to send to all of the businesses in the county. Stress the good work the center does and the fact that this is a special fundraising effort. Mention that all the money collected will go directly toward the purchase of the vans.

18. A clean deal: Sales letter from ScrubaDub about its Car Care Club When Bob and Dan Paisner opened 11 ScrubaDub car washes in Massachusetts and Rhode

Island, they applied high-tech solutions to the traditional business, and ScrubaDub emerged as the most innovative car wash in the industry. At ScrubaDub, computers track everything from a customer's name to the date and type of their last wash. They even "sense" what kind of wheels a car has. These are just a few of the reasons your job in ScrubaDub's marketing department is so easy.

When customers arrive, a "touchless system" sizes up their cars—literally—then prescribes exactly how much of the chain's secret-formula "Superglo" detergent to dispense and how much water pressure to use. This process eliminates dull soap residues and handling marks or nicks from abrasive equipment. Special sensors automatically prescribe scrubbing for white walls, pressure spray for wire wheels, or buffing for chrome. Using softened, heated well water eliminates spots, and recycling that water for scrubbing wheels and undercarriages helps the environment. A soft cloth adds a final gloss.

A human "Satisfaction Supervisor" is present to handle special requests, such as towel drying or gas stain removal. Your Bumper to Bumper Guarantee lets dissatisfied customers go through the wash until they're happy, or they get a refund. With a driver's license for proof, people get a free wash on their birthdays.

You're like thousands of others who haven't found a more "personalized" automated car wash. That may sound like an oxymoron, but the Paisners make sure it's not. They say they're New England drivers' "best defense against a dirty world," offering relief from salt, snow, rain, mud, sleet, dust, and pigeons, since clean cars last longer and look newer. And now they have a new brainstorm for you to promote: the ScrubaDub Car Care Club.

By signing up for a $5.95 "lifetime membership" (good for as long as you own the car), drivers can combat whatever Mother Nature or a nearby construction site dishes out. Whether they join at your locations or online at www.scrubadub.com/club.htm, members receive by mail a bar-coded sticker to place in the driver's-side window. When they drive in for a wash, the bar code is scanned and linked to a central database via the Internet. Customer information flashes on a screen, so a well-trained attendant can greet them by name and glance over their washing history, perhaps suggesting it's time for a wax.

This system not only improves customer relations while increasing sales, but club members get exclusive deals designed for Northeastern drivers. The 48-Hour Express Guarantee allows the same exterior wash for free within 48 hours if their car gets dirty—great for inclement weather. The 4-Day Clean Car Guarantee extends that to four days for purchasers of the premium Super Wash, Luxury Wash, Special Wash, or Works Wash. The Frequent Wash Bonus Program awards one free exterior Works Wash ("our best wash for our best customers") after every 10 washes purchased. Members don't have to collect stickers or hole punches—the computer tracks it. They also get an instant $5 rebate on any foam car wax. ScrubaDub offers three types: Turtle Wax (lasts 10 days), Simonize (20 days), or Blue Coral (30 days). And there'll be additional members-only specials from time to time.

Your task: Write a sales letter promoting the Car Care Club. Since most customers are busy people, use techniques for quick-scan communications while following the AIDA plan.[48]

19. Always urgent: Memo pleading case for hosting a Red Cross blood drive Not many people realize that donated blood lasts for only 72 hours. Some components are processed to last longer, but the mainstay of emergency blood supplies must be replenished in an ongoing effort. No one is more skilled, dedicated, or efficient about handling blood than the American Red Cross, which is responsible for half the nation's supply of blood and blood products. Its Jerome H. Holland Laboratory has helped pioneer the blood-collecting and blood-processing methods that make blood banks possible.

This morning before heading off to your job as food service manager at the Pechanga Casino Entertainment Center in Temecula, California, you were concerned to see on TV news that the Red Cross had put out a call for blood—national supplies have fallen dangerously low. When people are moved by a highly publicized disaster, they're emotionally eager to help out by donating blood. But in calm times, only 5 percent of eligible donors think of giving blood. You're one of those few. And today, you're going to do more than just roll up your own sleeve.

Donated blood helps victims of accidents and diseases such as cancer or heart disease, as well as surgery patients. You remember reading about Melissa, who was diagnosed with multiple congenital heart defects and underwent her first open-heart surgery at one week old. She's five now and has used well over 50 units of donated blood, and she wouldn't be alive without them. In a thank-you letter, her mother lauded the many total strangers who had "given a piece of themselves" to save her precious daughter—and countless others. A donor's pint of blood benefits up to four people.

You know the local Red Cross chapter takes its Blood Mobile to corporations, restaurants—even beauty salons—willing to host public blood drives. Wouldn't it be wonderful if the board of directors agreed to support a blood drive at the casino? The slot machines and gaming tables are usually full, hundreds of employees are on hand, and people who've never visited might come down to donate blood. The positive publicity certainly couldn't hurt Pechanga's community image. With materials from the Red Cross, you're confident you can organize Pechanga's hosting effort and handle the promotion. (Last year you headed the casino's successful Toys for Tots drive.)

To give blood, one must be healthy, be at least 17 years old (with no upper age limit), and weigh at least 110 pounds. Donors can give every 56 days. You'll be urging Pechanga donors to eat well, drink water, and be rested before the Blood Mobile arrives.

You like the local chapter's mission statement. It says in part, the Red Cross is "a humanitarian organization led by volunteers and guided by the Fundamental Principles of the International Red Cross Movement" which will "prevent and alleviate human suffering wherever it may be found." All assistance is given free of charge, made possible by "contributions of people's time, money, and skills."

And in the case of you and your co-workers, a piece of yourselves.

Your task: Write a memorandum persuading the Pechanga board of directors to host a public Red Cross blood drive. Ask the board to donate bottled water, orange juice, and snacks for donors. (You'll organize food service workers to handle the distribution.) To support your request, use a variety of appeals, mentioning both tangible and intangible benefits. To donate blood, call 1-800-GIVE-LIFE.[49]

PART 4

Finding and Communicating Information

Finding, Evaluating, and Processing Information

After studying this chapter, you will be able to

1 *Highlight six tasks you should complete when doing business research*

2 *Name seven types of secondary resources you might use to find business information*

3 *Explain how to conduct an effective database search*

4 *Highlight five methods of collecting primary data*

5 *Define information interviews, and list four types of interview questions*

6 *Name nine criteria for evaluating the credibility of an information source*

7 *Discuss the difference between quoting and paraphrasing, and explain the appropriate uses of each*

8 *Explain the difference between drawing a conclusion and developing a recommendation*

COMMUNICATION CLOSE-UP AT GOSH ENTERPRISES

www.charleyssteakery.com

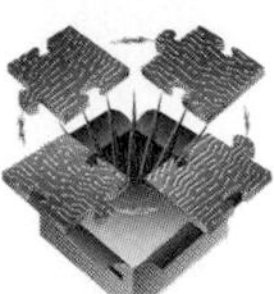

Charley Shin opened his first Philly cheesesteak restaurant—Charley's Steakery—when he was a junior at Ohio State. Today he is the millionaire owner of Gosh Enterprises, franchisor of over 50 Charley's Steakery restaurants. How did he reach this pinnacle of achievement so early in life? Through hard work and vision—backed up by lots of accurate and up-to-date business information.

Shin and his older sister had come to the United States from South Korea in 1979—when he was 13. One year later, Shin's mother bought a small Japanese restaurant, and Shin started washing dishes there (reading *Forbes* in his spare time). By age 17 he was thinking big. It was time to make his move—and that's how the first Charley's Steakery began.

A year after it opened, Shin graduated, and a year after that, he opened the second Charley's Steakery, followed by a third, and then a fourth and fifth with partners. "At that point, I had to decide on the venue for growth: whether to continue with company-owned restaurants, pursue equity-interested partnerships, or start franchising," explains Shin. Before drafting a new plan for the future, he knew he needed to find some information.

"Franchising was very interesting to me because it does not require a lot of capital but it has a venue for quick expansion. So I read a lot of articles," says Shin. "I went to the library almost every day for over a month, and I read everything I could about franchising and the Philly cheesesteak concept." He studied newspaper articles on microfiche, read magazines and books, looked at statistics and trends, and learned what everyone else was doing in the field.

Shin also interviewed a fellow restaurant owner who had many years of experience. The man advised Shin to stick with the "fresh food" concept (instead of precooked or prepackaged sandwiches) and to concentrate on the "captive audience" in shopping-center food courts. Shin now credits this advice as some of the best he ever followed.

After weeks of conducting research, Shin put his information to work and started writing a formal business plan. He wrote an overview, a description of the concept, and a summary of his plans for the future—all based on the business information he had gathered. He hired professionals to help him develop a marketing strategy to include in the plan, but his research enabled him to prepare all the financial statements and projections himself.

Because of Shin's careful research and planning, Gosh Enterprises has done well. In fact, Shin places such importance on finding and evaluating information and then shaping it into a business plan that today he requires all his franchise owners to research and prepare a written business plan during their training. They aren't certified until they complete at least a rough draft.[1] ■

Before writing the business plan for Charley's Steakery, founder Charley Shin did a considerable amount of research to develop the company's marketing strategy, franchising policy, location preference, and financial projections.

ORGANIZING THE RESEARCH PROCESS

Like Charley Shin, you may someday need to gather information on specific companies, industries, trends, issues, or people. This may seem like an overwhelming task, considering the amount of information available today. But if you take time to get organized, define the purpose of your research, identify the right questions, and locate the best resources, you'll find that looking for business information can be a rewarding experience.

This chapter explains a research strategy you can use for your college business studies (including this course), on the job, or whenever you're looking for information. In addition, this chapter introduces you to some popular resources you'll need in business, and it explains where to find these resources, how to use them, and how to evaluate them.

Sharpening your research strategy will help you find all the business information you need.

Learning Objective 1

Highlight six tasks you should complete when doing business research

When it comes to finding information, many people make the mistake of rushing into the research process without developing a plan. They go to the library, log on to a database or the Internet, type in some key words, produce almost endless resources, and immediately begin taking notes on whatever comes up under their topic. Resist the temptation. If your research strategy is weak, any business decisions based on your research will also be weak. Adopt an organized approach to research by completing six tasks: (1) Identify the right questions; (2) find and access secondary and primary information; (3) evaluate and finalize your sources; (4) process your information; (5) analyze your data; and (6) interpret your findings. In most cases you'll perform tasks in order; however, the amount of time you spend on a single task will depend on the nature and volume of information you need, as well as on the purpose of your research. Conducting research often requires jumping around, branching off, or looping back; that is, your discoveries may lead you to additional questions, which require further research, and so on. What's important is to become competent in each task and to complete all six of them as illustrated in Figure 10.1.

Complete six tasks to find, evaluate, and process information effectively and efficiently.

UNDERSTANDING YOUR TOPIC AND ASSIGNMENT

Why are you looking for information? Do you need to solve a problem? Are you thinking about hiring some salespeople and you'd like to gather some information on managing a sales force? Are you researching a company prior to a job interview? Writing your company's annual marketing report? Investigating a new business opportunity?

Businesspeople conduct research for any number of reasons. Sometimes they're only looking for an answer to a simple question or just trying to learn something new.

FIGURE 10.1 The Research Process

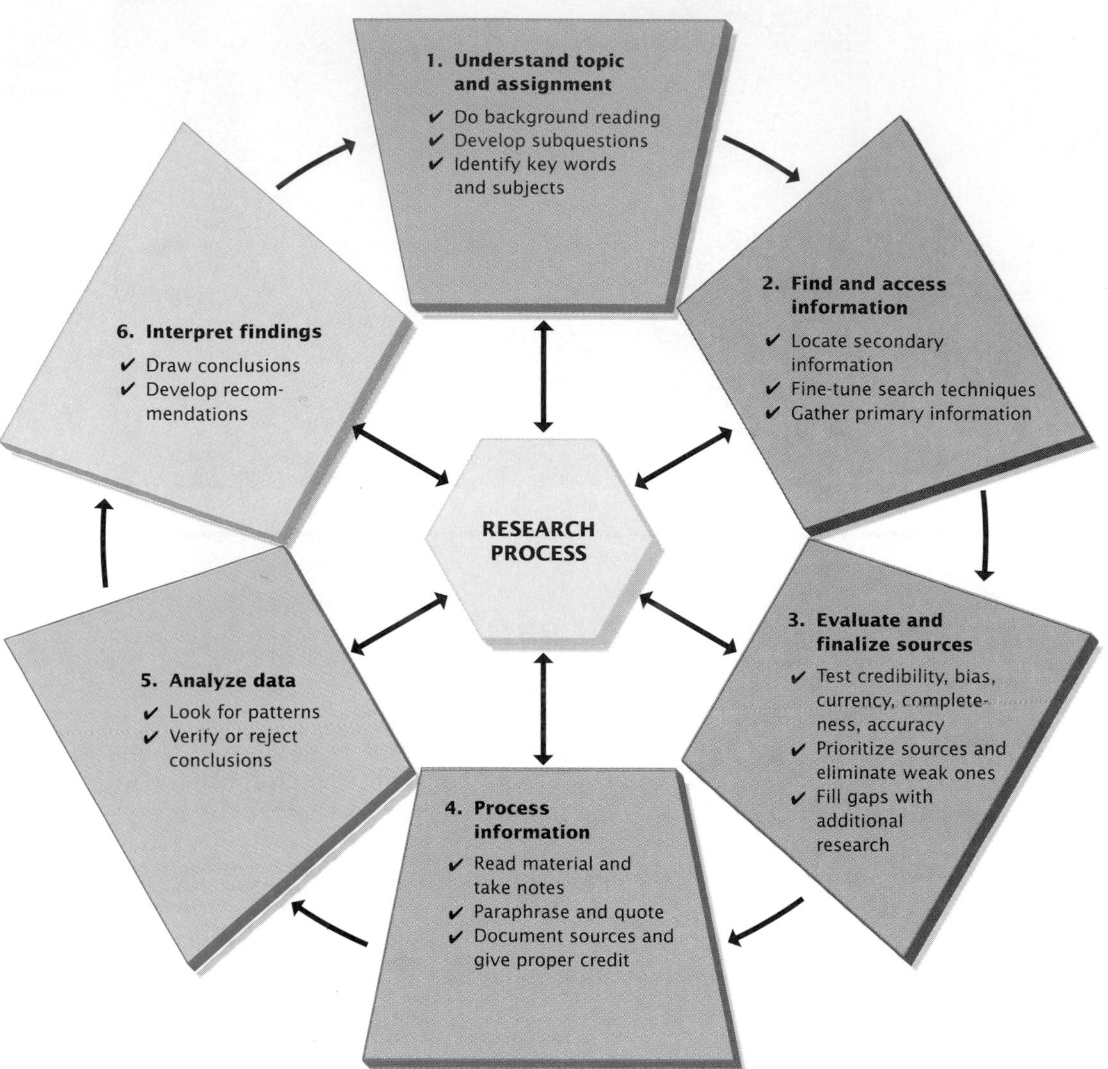

Other times they need to solve a problem or prepare a formal report on a process, product, company, or industry. In the classroom, you have generally been able to select your favorite topic for a research project; in the business world, you will not be given that option. If your boss says, "I need you to investigate how we can grow this business," you won't be able to raise your hand and request a different topic—at least not if you want to keep your job. As a result, in most cases you will be unfamiliar with the subject matter you are investigating, so first you'll need to gather some preliminary information.

Begin your research effort by becoming familiar with your topic.

Gather Preliminary Information

Become familiar with your topic by browsing and gathering preliminary information.

The best way to learn about something new is to browse through materials on your topic. Leaf through some books and periodicals, conduct some loosely structured interviews, or log on to a database (either at the library or on the Internet) and see what comes up. You may even want to visit your favorite bookstore (whether physical or online) and find some business books on your topic, then scan their table of contents.

Say, for example, you're Charley Shin and you want to explore ways to expand Charley's Steakery. By browsing through some business materials, you might discover that franchising is one way to expand your business. You might even begin to uncover related issues, problems, opportunities, or trends in the franchising industry. As you browse, be sure to keep a written bibliographical list of the helpful resources you find.

In addition, start a list of phrases, terms, and key words that recur. You'll use them later to locate and access information.

Once you have gathered some preliminary information, use what you have learned to clarify your assignment. If you're conducting research at the request of someone else, make sure you're both on the same page. If you're conducting research for reasons of your own, use your preliminary information to make your purpose as clear and specific as possible. Develop a **problem statement**, a statement that defines the problem or purpose of your research—even if it's a simple one. Finally, restate the problem as a question. For example, if Charley Shin's original problem statement was "Find a way to expand Charley's Steakery," then he could have rephrased it as "How can Charley's Steakery expand?" Shaping your purpose in question form will help you focus on exactly the information you need to complete your research.

Narrow the focus of your investigation by defining your problem and restating it as a question.

Develop Subquestions

If the problem you must solve is a complex one, such as researching the franchise industry, you'll want to organize your research efforts by dividing your main question into subquestions. Look back at Chapter 5 and review the techniques used to help define the main idea of a message: Brainstorming, generating random lists, using the journalistic approach, and developing a question-and-answer chain are techniques you can use to rephrase your main questions into a series of subquestions you must answer.

For example, Charley Shin might take his main question "How can Charley's Steakery expand?" and develop the subquestion "Is franchising a good way to expand Charely's Steakery?" Then he might break down this subquestion into additional subquestions such as "What are the advantages and disadvantages of franchising?" "Is my product franchisable?" "What are the costs?" and so on. This process focuses on answering one small question at a time. If you don't subdivide your main question into subquestions, your research efforts will likely end in frustration and perhaps failure.

You can shape your investigation by breaking down your problem into subquestions.

If you are researching a complex problem, you'll also probably want to prepare a research outline to guide your information-gathering efforts. Outlines can be useful, especially if you're working in a team, if your investigation involves many subquestions, or if you need to submit a research proposal to your boss. See Chapter 5 for a discussion of outline formats. Informal outlines are a good way to record and organize your ideas during the research process. Later on, you can convert your research outline into a formal outline used for writing a report (see Chapter 12).

FINDING AND ACCESSING INFORMATION

Once you have a better understanding of your topic and assignment, you're ready to begin your research in earnest: identifying the *best* sources of information and gathering the details you'll need to answer your questions. In most cases you'll begin your research by looking for sources of secondary information—information on your subject that already exists and has already been collected, usually in the form of books, periodicals, newspapers, and websites. If secondary information doesn't exist or isn't helpful, then you'll need to collect firsthand, primary information for your specific needs.

Locate Sources of Secondary Information

Many sources of secondary information are easily accessible in print and online.[2] Your challenge as a business researcher is to identify and prioritize the best sources for your needs. Knowing what to look for first, understanding the types of information available in the library or online, and learning how to access it efficiently will make you a more proficient researcher.

Knowing What to Look for First

If you're looking for information about a specific company, one of the first things you'll need to know is whether the company is public (sells shares of stock to the general public) or private. Public companies generally have more information available

FIGURE 10.2 Major Business Resources

COMPANY, INDUSTRY, AND PRODUCT RESOURCES (PRINT)

- ***Brands and Their Companies/Companies and Their Brands.*** Data on over 281,000 consumer products and 51,000 manufacturers, importers, marketers, and distributors.
- ***Corporate and Industry Research Reports (CIRR).*** Collection of industry reports produced by industry analysts for investment purposes. Unique coverage includes industry profitability, comparative company sales, market share, profits, and forecasts.
- ***Directory of Companies Required to File Annual Reports with the Securities and Exchange Commission.*** Listing of U.S. publicly held firms.
- ***Dun's Directory of Service Companies.*** Information on 205,000 U.S. service companies.
- ***Forbes.*** Annual Report on American Industry published in first January issue of each year.
- ***Hoover's Handbook of American Business.*** Profiles of over 500 public and private corporations.
- ***Manufacturing USA.*** Data series listing nearly 25,000 companies, including detailed information on over 450 manufacturing industries.
- ***Market Share Report.*** Data covering products and service categories originating from trade journals, newsletters, and magazines.
- ***Moody's Industry Review.*** Data on 4,000 companies in about 150 industries. Ranks companies within industry by five financial statistics (revenue, net income, total assets, cash and marketable securities, and long-term debt) and includes key performance ratios.
- ***Moody's Manuals.*** Weekly manual of financial data in each of six business areas: industrials, transportation, public utilities, banks, finance, and over-the-counter (OTC) industrials.
- ***Service Industries USA.*** Comprehensive data on 2,100 services grouped into over 150 industries.
- ***Standard & Poor's Industry Surveys.*** Concise investment profiles for a broad range of industries. Coverage is extensive, with a focus on current situation and outlook. Includes some summary data on major companies in each industry.
- ***Standard & Poor's Register of Corporations, Directors and Executives.*** Index of major U.S. and international corporations. Lists officers, products, sales volume, and number of employees.
- ***Thomas's Register of American Manufacturers.*** Information on thousands of U.S. manufacturers indexed by company name and product.
- **U.S. Industrial Outlook.** Annual profiles of several hundred key U.S. industries. Each industry report covers several pages and includes tables, graphs, and charts that visually demonstrate how an industry compares with similar industries, including important component growth factors and other economic measures.

COMPANY, INDUSTRY, AND PRODUCT RESOURCES (ONLINE)

- ***Hoover's Online*** **www.hoovers.com.** Profiles of publicly listed U.S. companies traded on major stock exchanges and more than 1,200 large private companies. Search by ticker symbol, company name, location, industry, or sales.
- ***NAICS Codes*** **www.census.gov/epcd/naics/naicstb2.txt.** North American Industry Classification System.
- ***SEC filings*** **www.sec.gov.edgarhp.htm.** SEC filings including 10Ks, 10Qs, annual reports, and prospectuses for 35,000 U.S. public firms.
- ***Fortune.com*** **www.fortune.com.** Brief profiles of the 500 leading companies in the U.S.
- ***Yahoo!*** **dir.yahoo.com/Business.** More than 50 categories of information with dozens of links.

DIRECTORIES AND INDEXES (PRINT)

- ***Books in Print.*** Index of 425,000 books in 62,000 subject categories currently available from U.S. publishers. Indexed by author and title.
- ***Directories in Print.*** Information on over 16,000 business and industrial directories.
- ***Encyclopedia of Associations.*** Index of thousands of associations listed by broad subject category, specific subject, association, and location.
- ***Reader's Guide to Periodical Literature.*** Periodical index categorized by subject and author.
- ***Ulrich's International Periodicals Directory.*** Listings by title, publisher, editor, phone, and address of over 140,000 publications such as popular magazines, trade journals, government documents, and newspapers. Great for locating hard-to-find trade publications.

PEOPLE (PRINT)

- ***Dun & Bradstreet's Reference Book of Corporate Management.*** Professional histories of people serving as the principal officers and directors of more than 12,000 U.S. companies.
- ***Who's Who in America.*** Biographies of living U.S. citizens who have gained prominence in their fields. Related book, *Who's Who in the World*, covers global achievers.

(continued)

FIGURE 10.2 (Continued)

TRADEMARKS (PRINT/ONLINE)

- ***Official Gazette of the United States Patent and Trademark Office.*** Weekly publication (one for trademarks and one for patents) providing official record of newly assigned trademarks and patents, product descriptions, and product names.
- ***United States Patent and Trademark Office*** **www.uspto.gov.** Trademark and patent information records.

STATISTICS AND FACTS (PRINT)

- ***Industry Norms and Key Business Ratios (Dun & Bradstreet).*** Industry, financial, and performance ratios.
- ***Information Please Almanac.*** Compilation of broad-range statistical data with strong focus on labor force.
- ***Robert Morris Associates' Annual Statement Studies.*** Industry, financial, and performance ratios.
- ***Statistical Abstract of the United States.*** U.S. economic, social, political, and industrial statistics.
- ***The World Almanac and Book of Facts.*** Facts on economic, social, educational, and political events for major countries.

STATISTICS AND FACTS (ONLINE)

- **Bureau of Economic Analysis www.bea.doc.gov.** Large collection of economic and government data.
- **FedStats www.fedstats.gov.** Access to full range of statistics and information from over 70 U.S. government agencies.
- **STAT-USA www.stat-usa.gov.** Large collection of economic and government data.
- **U.S. Census Bureau www.census.gov.** Demographic data on both consumers and businesses based on 1990 census.
- **U.S. Bureau of Labor Statistics www.bls.gov.** Extensive national and regional information on labor and business, including employment, industry growth, productivity, Consumer Price Index (CPI), and overall U.S. economy.

COMMERCIAL DATABASES (REQUIRE SUBSCRIPTIONS)

- **ABI Inform.** Database of over 1,500 scholarly and trade journals in business, management, industry, and economics (full text and abstracts).
- **Dialog.** Over 900 main databases that include areas such as business and finance, news and media, medicine, pharmaceuticals, reference, social sciences, government and regulation, science and technology, and more.
- **Electric Library.** Hundreds of full-text newspaper, magazine, newswire and articles, plus maps and photographs.
- **LEXIS-NEXIS.** More than 1.4 billion documents in more than 8,000 databases.
- **UMI ProQuest Direct.** More than 5,000 journals, magazines, newspapers, and other information sources.

than private companies. You can find a list of public companies in the *Directory of Companies Required to File Annual Reports with the Securities and Exchange Commission,* available in most public libraries.

To research a company, first find out whether it's public or private. You can also look up the company's NAICS code to find information related to the industry.

If you're looking for industry information, you'll need to know the North American Industry Classification System (NAICS) code of that particular industry. The U.S. government requires all companies, from sole proprietorships to corporations, to assign themselves a six-digit industry number that classifies their business by the type of product or service they make available. This six-digit NAICS replaced the four-digit Standard Industrial Classification (SIC) in 1997.

You may need to find information on company and industry statistics, economic forecasts, business concerns, legal issues, competition, and industry performance ratios and averages. Figure 10.2 lists some of the more popular resources for company and industry information (many of which are available in both print and electronic database format). One of the best places to begin your search for secondary information is the nearest public or university library.

Finding Information in the Library

Libraries are where you'll find business books, electronic databases, newspapers, periodicals, directories, almanacs, and government publications. In additon, you'll find your most important resource: librarians. Reference librarians are trained in research techniques and spend their days managing information and helping people find materials. They can show you how to use the library's many databases, and they can help you

Reference librarians are there to assist you with your research efforts.

You can search this library's card catalog by accessing its homepage on the Internet. Of course, you'll have to visit the library to actually check out the book, but checking the Internet first guarantees you won't go home empty-handed.

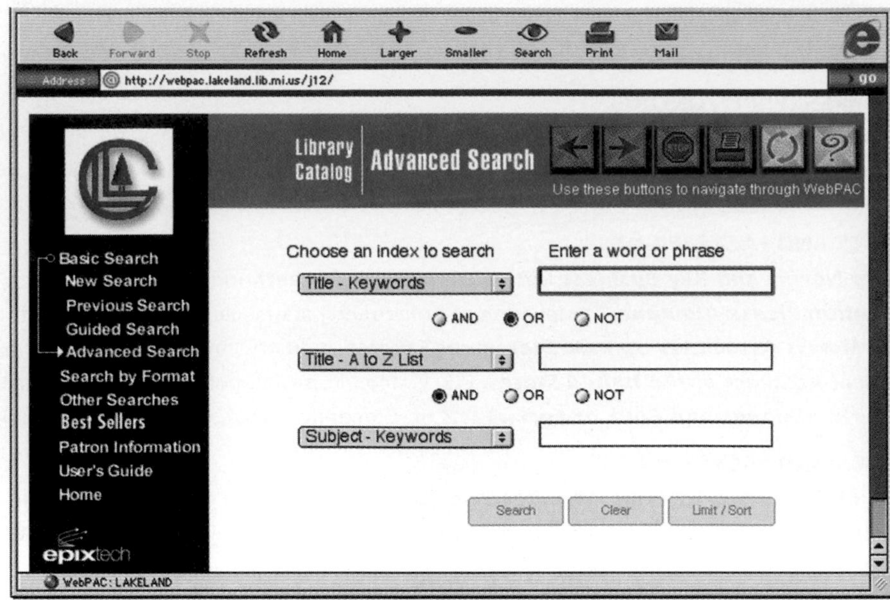

Learning Objective 2

Name seven types of secondary resources you might use to find business information

find obscure information. Whether you're trying to locate information in printed materials, on databases, or on microfilm, each type of resource serves a special function.

Business Books Although less timely than journal articles, business books provide in-depth coverage of a variety of business topics. Because of budgetary constraints, public libraries must be selective about the books they put on their shelves, so you may have better luck finding specialized information at company libraries or at a college library (assuming the college offers courses in those subjects).

Electronic databases contain journal articles that are more timely than books.

Electronic Databases An **electronic database** is a computer-searchable collection of information, often categorized by subject areas such as business, law, science, technology, and education. Electronic databases can be stored on CD-ROM or online (which means they are stored on a computer accessible to other computers—generally via a modem). The main advantages of electronic databases over print-based sources are:

- Instant access to billions of records of the world's published literature
- Reduced time to perform a keyword and subject search (compared with a manual search)
- Current material
- Quick turnaround from request to results
- Convenient reproduction (being able to print out documents—many in full text—for later use in the research process).

When using an electronic database, try to get a list of the periodicals or publications it includes, as well as the time period it covers. Then fill in the gaps for any important resources not in the database.

Newspapers can be one of the more up-to-date resources.

Newspapers Libraries subscribe to only a select number of newspapers and store a limited number of back issues in print. However, they frequently subscribe to databases containing newspaper articles in full text (available online, on CD-ROM, or on microfilm). In addition, most newspapers today offer full-text or limited editions of their papers on the Internet.

Periodicals are another timely resource for business information.

Periodicals Most periodicals fall into one of four categories: (1) popular magazines, (not intended for business, professional, or academic use), (2) trade journals (providing news and other facts about particular professions, industries, and occupations),

(3) business magazines (covering all major industries and professions), and (4) academic journals (publishing data from professional researchers and educators). To locate a certain periodical, check your library's database.

Directories More than 14,000 directories are published in the United States—covering everything from accountants to zoos. Many include membership information for all kinds of special-interest groups. For instance, business directories provide entries for companies, products, and individuals, and they include the name of key contact persons. Directories are considered invaluable for marketers, job seekers, and others who need to establish a prospect list.

Directories offer basic information on organizations and companies.

Almanacs and Statistical Resources Almanacs are handy guides to factual and statistical information about countries, politics, the labor force, and so on. Also check out the *Statistical Abstract of the United States* (published annually by the U.S. Department of Commerce). This resource contains statistics about life, work, government, population patterns, health issues, business, crime, and the environment.

Almanacs offer statistics about countries, politics, the labor force, and more.

Government Publications For information on a law, a court decision, or current population patterns and business trends, consult government documents. A librarian can direct you to the information you want. You'll need the name of the government agency you're interested in, such as U.S. Congress, Ninth Circuit Court of Appeals, or Department of Labor, and some identification for the specific information you need (Safe Drinking Water Act of 1974, *Price v. Shell Oil,* or the latest census). If you know the date and name of a publication, the search will be easier.

The government tracks legal, population, and business trends.

Finding Business Information on the Internet

When doing research on the Internet, you need to be selective because anyone can publish anything.

Today's most popular source of company and industry information is the Internet, with information ranging from current news and industry trends to company-related data on financial performance, products, goals, and employment. You must remember that anyone (including you) can post anything on a website. In many cases information on the web has not been validated by an independent party, which means that it may be biased, inaccurate, or exaggerated. Thus, it's best to refrain from seriously surfing the web for business information until you've had a chance to learn a bit about your topic from journals, books, and commercial databases. You'll be able to detect skewed or erroneous information, and you can be more selective about which websites and documents you choose to use as resources.

One good place to start on the web is the Internet Public Library at www.ipl.org. Modeled after a real library, this site will provide you with a carefully selected collection of links to high-quality business resources that offer such information as company profiles, trade data, business news, corporate tax and legal advice, small-business information, prepared forms and documents, biographies of executives, financial reports, job postings, online publications, and so on.

Finding business information on the Internet is relatively easy, but separating the good from the bad takes patience, skill, and practice.

If you're looking for specific company information, your best source may be the company's website (if it maintains one). These websites generally include detailed information about the firm's products, services, history, mission, strategy, financial performance, and employment needs. Many sites provide links to related company information, such as SEC filings, news releases, and more.

You can find all kinds of information about a company on its website.

You can obtain news releases and general company news from news-release sites such as PRNewswire (www.prnewswire.com) and Business Wire (www.businesswire.com). These two sites offer free databases of news releases from companies subscribing to their services. News-release sites are also good places to look for announcements of new products, management changes, earnings, dividends, mergers, acquisitions, and other company

News releases and general news about companies are also available at news-release sites and through online databases.

Best of the Web

Check Out Materials at This Library 24 Hours a Day

Start your business research by visiting the Internet Public Library. Visit the reference center and explore the many online references available. These cover topics such as business, economics, law, government, science, technology, computers, education, and more. Got a question? There's even a librarian on staff to help you. After all, librarians are one of your most important resources when conducting research.

www.ipl.org

information. If you subscribe to a commercial online database system (such as those listed in Figure 10.2), you can also use the Internet to access information from the provider's database.

Small companies and privately held companies generally don't have much public information written about them.

Keep in mind that the web doesn't have everything. You may find nothing about small organizations, or perhaps just their address and phone number. And even if the information exists on the web, you may not be able to find it. The Internet holds more than 800 million webpages, with hundreds of pages being added every day, and even the best Internet search engines manage to index only about one-third of the pages on the web.[3]

Fine-Tune Your Search Techniques

You can get the most dependable search results from well-known, commercially backed search engines, which are likely to be well maintained and upgraded. Most have simple or advanced search features, plus extras such as interactive maps, weather information, travel information, phone and e-mail directories, and company financial information.

Fine-tune your search techniques until you get the results you want.

Although search engines will often turn up what you're looking for, they're also likely to turn up a mountain of stuff you don't need. Suppose you're looking for information about available jobs for writers. The search engine may turn up information on being an accountant at an insurance company. Why? Because the insurance company described itself on the web as one of the largest *writers* of insurance policies. You can improve your search techniques by understanding what search engines can and can't do and by learning how to conduct an effective database search.

Understanding Search Engines

When you search for webpages using a search engine, you actually search the engine's index, not the entire web.

Search engines are Internet tools that identify and screen resources. Also called spiders or crawlers, the engines travel the web automatically, find new sites, and place a copy of these webpages in their database (commonly called an index or a catalog). Sometimes it can take a while for the spider to find and add new pages to its index. Until a page is indexed, however, it is not available to those searching the web with this particular search engine. In addition to finding new sites, every month or two the spider returns to previously indexed websites to look for changes and to update its index. When a web surfer enters key search words, the search engine scans its index and returns the webpage addresses of all documents that match those words. Keep in mind that the engine does not actually go out to the web each time a search is requested; rather, it only searches the engine's current index.[4]

Each search engine has qualities that distinguish it from the others, and not all search engines operate in the same way. For instance, some engines index all the pages they find; others index only the most popular pages. Many engines also search Usenet newsgroups if you specify a newsgroup search in your search query. Furthermore, each search engine has its own schedule for updating its index. These differences create significant variations in search results. To maximize your search results, read the engine's help page and learn how the search engine works.

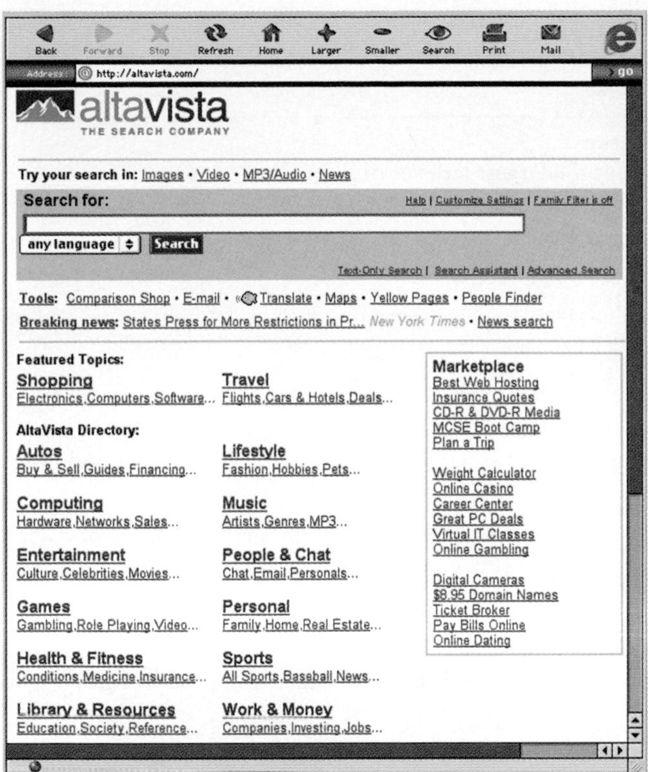

Internet search engines such as AltaVista provide surfers immediate access to webpages, multimedia files, up-to-the minute news, products, and services. During your preliminary research effort, try to identify some keywords and search strategies to maximize your search engine results.

Table 10.1 lists some of the more popular search engines available. Regardless of which search engine you use, getting to know each engine's strengths and weaknesses at the start of your search can save you a lot of time and frustration down the road.

Directories Keep in mind that the term *search engine* is often used to describe both search engines and *directories*. They are not the same. The main difference is in how webpages are added to the database or index. Whereas a search engine uses an automated robot (software) to find and index websites, a **directory** uses humans to do this job. In other words, someone must actually submit a website to the directory, after which humans review the website and assign the site to an appropriate category in the directory's index. Because of this key difference, when you use a search engine, you often find more websites than when you use a directory. However, directories often yield more-precise results than search engines do.[5]

Directory indexes are prepared by humans, whereas search engine indexes are compiled by automated software.

Portals Both search engines and directories can also become **portals** by adding features to their websites. Portals are Internet gateways—your everyday first stop on the web—that offer some means for navigating the chaos of information that exists on the Internet. Websites such America Online, Yahoo!, Lycos, Infoseek, Microsoft Service Network, and Netscape are portals.

Users were initially attracted to portals because of their excellent search engines. Now, rather than pass surfers along, portals try to keep users at their website in order to build a big audience for advertisers—similar to television networks. To hold users' attention, they load their site with free e-mail, weather forecasts, stock reports, news, sports scores, horoscopes, links to other websites, and much more.[6]

Conducting an Effective Database Search

Learning Objective 3

Explain how to conduct an effective database search

Whether you are using a library database or an Internet search engine, follow these search strategies and tips to improve your search results:[7]

- **Select appropriate databases.** You'll want a good business database. However, journals on your topic may be in a database that also includes journals on psychology, computers, or medicine.

TABLE 10.1 Best of Internet Searching

Major Search Engines

AllTheWeb	www.alltheweb.com Consistently one of the largest indexes of the web.
Alta Vista	www.altavista.com Indexes data from millions of webpages and articles from thousands of Usenet newsgroups.
Ask Jeeves	www.ask.com Finds answers to natural-language questions such as "Who won Super Bowl XXV?"
Excite	www.excite.com All-purpose site loaded with options.
Fedstats	www.fedstats.gov/search.html Simultaneously queries 14 federal agencies for specified statistics and numerical data.
Google	www.google.com A simple directory that is especially useful for finding homepages of companies and organizations.
HotBot	www.hotbot.com Wired magazine packs all kinds of searching possibilities into this site.
LookSmart	www.looksmart.com Closest rival to Yahoo! in terms of being a human-compiled directory. Choose "Your Town" for local directories.
Lycos	www.lycos.com One of the oldest of the major search engines; provides short abstracts for each match.
Open Directory	http://dmoz.org This is the largest, most comprehensive human-edited directory of the Web. It is maintained by a vast, global community of volunteer editors.
WebCrawler	www.webcrawler.com Allows you to either search the entire site or browse any of the preselected categories.
Yahoo!	www.yahoo.com The oldest major website directory, listing over 500,000 sites.

Multiple Search Engine Sites—Metacrawlers

C4 Total Search	www.c4.com Search up to 20 search engines at the same time. Customized search options are available.
Dogpile	www.dogpile.com Despite the silly name, just enter one query and this hound sniffs through FTP files, Usenet message boards, and websites.
Infozoid	www.infozoid.com Search up to 15 popular search engines at the same time. Infozoid has been designed for simplicity of use by novices and casual users, and for functionality and flexibility for seasoned researchers.
IXQuick	www.ixquick.com Search up to 14 search engines at the same time. Results are ranked by relevancy.
Mamma	www.mamma.com Claiming to be the "Mother of All Search Engines," this multilegged spider queries the major search engines for fast results.
ProFusion	www.profusion.com The University of Kansas spider retrieves only the "best" results from selected search engines.
Vivisimo	www.vivisimo.com The results are organized with document clustering technology, which provides users with lists of documents in meaningful groups.
Zworks	www.zworks.com Results are ranked based on the cumulative score of all the engines used in the search. Duplicate results are eliminated.

By following a few guidelines, you can improve your database search results.

- **Use multiple search engines.** Don't limit yourself to a single search engine, especially if you are looking for less popular topics. Try your search on several engines by using **metacrawlers**, special engines that search several search engines at once.
- **Translate concepts into keywords and phrases.** For instance, if you want to determine the "effect of TQM on company profits," you should select the keywords *TQM, total quality management, profits, sales, companies,* and *corporations.* Remember, use synonyms or word equivalents whenever possible, and use quotation marks around phrases to look for the entire phrase instead of separate words.
- **Use a short phrase or single term rather than a long phrase.** Search engines look for the words exactly as you key them in. If the words occur, but not in the same order, you may miss relevant hits.
- **Do not use stopwords.** Stopwords are those words the computer disregards and will not search for. Database documentation will identify any stopwords in addition to the common ones: *a, an, the, of, by, with, for,* and *to.*
- **Do not use words contained in the name of the database.** Using words such as *business* or *finance* in the ABI Inform database (see Figure 10.2) will work, but they appear so often that searching for them slows the processing time and adds no precision to your results.
- **Use variations of your terms.** Use abbreviations (*CEO, CPA*), synonyms (*man, male*), related terms (*child, adolescent, youth*), different spellings (*dialog, dialogue*), singular and plural forms (w*oman, women*), nouns and adjectives (*manager, management, managerial*), and open and compound forms (*online, on line, on-line*).
- **Specify a logical relationship between the keywords.** Must the document contain both *companies* and *corporations,* or is either fine? Must it contain both *profits* and *companies,* or should it contain *TQM* or *total quality management* and *profits* or *sales?*
- **Use Boolean operators.** Narrow or broaden your search by including AND, OR, and NOT. As Table 10.2 shows, such Boolean operators can help you create complex, precise search strategies. For example you could create a search strategy such as "(marketing OR advertising) AND (organizations OR associations) AND NOT consultants." This means that qualifying documents or websites must have either the word *marketing* or *advertising* and must have either the word *organizations* or *associations,* but they can't have the word *consultants.* Many search engines automatically include Boolean operators in their strategies even though you can't see them on the screen. Either insert your own (which should override automatic operators) or review the instructions for your search engine.
- **Use proximity operators.** To specify how close one of your keywords should be to another, use a proximity operator such as NEAR. For example, the search phrase "marketing NEAR/2 organizations" means that *marketing* must be within two words of *organizations.*
- **Use wildcards.** Wildcard characters help you find plurals and alternate spellings of your keywords. For example, by using a question mark in the word *organi?ations,* you'll find documents with both *organisations* (British spelling) and *organizations.* Similarly, by using an asterisk at the end of the stem *chair**, you'll find *chairman, chairperson, chairs,* and *chairlift.*
- **Evaluate the precision and quality of your search results to refine your search if necessary.** If you end up with more than 60 to 100 links to sort through, refine your search. If your first page of results doesn't have something of interest, you've entered the wrong words or too few words. Also, pay attention to whether you are searching in the title, subject, or document field of the database. Each will return different results.

Pushing Versus Pulling Information

Push technology automatically delivers information from the Internet to your desktop.

When you obtain information from the Internet by using a search engine or directory, you pull information from the Internet. Another way to obtain information from the Internet is to have it pushed or delivered to you. When "push" technology first hit the Internet scene years ago, it promised Internet users that they would no longer have to

TABLE 10.2 Improving Your Search Results

Search Operator	*Effect*	*Strategy*	*Results*
AND	Narrows the results. Searches for records containing both of the words it separates. Words separated by AND may be anywhere in the document—and far away from each other.	Rock AND roll	Music
OR	Broadens the results. This is a scattergun search that will turn up lots of matches and is not particularly precise. Searches for records containing either of the words it separates.	Rock OR roll	Igneous rocks, gemstones, crescent rolls, music
NOT, AND NOT	Limits the results. Searches for records containing the first word(s) but not the second one. Depending on the database, AND is not always included in combination with NOT.	Snow skiing NOT water skiing; snow skiing AND NOT water skiing	Snow skiing, cross-country skiing
WITHIN or NEAR	Proximity operators. Searches for words that all appear in a specified word range.	Snow WITHIN/ 2 skiing	Terms in which *skiing* is within 2 words of *snow*
ADJ	Adjacency operator. Searches for records in which second word immediately follows first word (two words are next to each other).	Ski ADJ patrol	Ski patrol
?	Wildcard operator for single character; matches any one character.	Ski?	Skit, skid, skin, skip
*	Wildcard operator for string of characters.	Ski*	Ski, skiing, skies, skill, skirt, skit, skinny, skimpy
" "	Exact match. Searches for string of words placed within quotation marks.	"2002 budget deficit"	2002 budget deficit

spend time scouring websites for interesting news and desired information. Instead, users could subscribe to theme-related information channels (such as sports, news, and hobbies), and vendors would push this category of information right to their desktops—all day long.[8] But the concept of push technology soon fell short of its promise because channels pushed too much irrelevant information to subscribers' desktops. Subscribers were forced to dig through mounds of data, which glutted computer networks, slowing them down.[9]

A personal agent is similar to a private search engine that combs the Internet for your specific interests and delivers the results to your desktop.

Push technology was eventually superseded by such personal agents as My Yahoo! that mold desktop information to your personal interests and exclude the types of generic information previously delivered by push channels. But the process is not automatic. First, users must register with a personal agent website (most are free). Next, users must create a detailed profile by entering their individual preferences from a long list of subject categories (these include news, weather forecasts, sports scores and schedules, stock quotations, horoscopes, movie show times, travel alerts, calendar reminders, and even state lottery results). Once a user has completed this process, a personal agent scans a wide range of websites, finds information that matches the user's preferences, and delivers it to her or his desktop (or tells the user where to go get it).[10] Eventually the information gets more and more targeted as the user instructs the personal agent to "find more of this" or to "eliminate that."

Some personal agents specialize in gathering specific types of information. Company Sleuth, at www.companysleuth.com, scours the Internet while you sleep, gathering news releases, trademark applications, stock-trading information, and newsgroup postings for companies you specify. Each day, this detective delivers its findings to your desktop in time for your morning coffee.

Keeping Track of Your Progress

As you find and review source materials, take some brief notes to keep track of your progress. These are not the detailed notes you'll be taking later, but you'll need enough to evaluate and finalize your sources. For instance, write down enough information to distinguish one source from the next. Identify the main idea or theme of each source, and perhaps write a comment about which subquestion the article addresses and whether the information was helpful. For example: "Discusses current franchise trends with statistics on number of new franchises started each year," or "Chapter 3 gives itemized steps for investigating franchise opportunities."

The goal of your initial note taking is to keep track of your sources so that you can select the best ones to use.

When using the Internet, note relevant websites by bookmarking them and keeping them in a separate bookmark folder. Alternatively, you can download or print out the actual webpages. If the library database you're using includes material in full text, print out helpful articles; otherwise print out a copy of your search results and ask the librarian for assistance in finding the articles listed.

To record your comments, use note cards or Post-it notes, or write on copies of the material itself. Develop a system that works for you. In addition, prepare a detailed bibliography of each source you intend to use later. Adopt one of the systems explained in Appendix II, "Documentation of Report Sources." If you photocopy an article, be sure to record on the photocopy all the bibliographic material you'll need to properly cite that source later on.

Collect Primary Information

As Charley Shin can tell you, sometimes what you need is not available from sources of secondary information, or you need something beyond what is covered in secondary information. In that case, you go out into the real world to gather data yourself. Five methods of collecting primary information are examining documents, making observations, conducting experiments, surveying people, and conducting interviews.

Conduct primary research by collecting basic information yourself.

Learning Objective 4

Highlight five methods of collecting primary data

Documents, Observation, and Experiments

Often the most useful method of collecting primary information is examining internal documents, such as company sales reports, memos, balance sheets, income statements, policy statements, brochures, newsletters, annual reports, correspondence with customers or suppliers, and contracts. You can often find a great deal of information in company databases, and by scouring a company's files, you can often piece together an accurate, factual, historical record from the tidbits of evidence revealed in various letters, memos, and reports.

Documentary evidence and historical records are sources of primary data.

A single document may be a source of both secondary and primary information. For example, when citing summaries of financial and operations data from an annual report, you're using the report as secondary information; that is, somebody has already summarized the data for you. However, the same annual report would be considered a primary source if you were analyzing its design features, comparing it with annual reports from other years, or comparing it with reports from other companies.

Another common method of collecting primary business information is making formal observations. For instance, you can observe people performing their jobs or customers interacting with a product. Observation is a useful technique when you're studying objects, physical activities, processes, the environment, or human behavior. However, it can be expensive and time-consuming, and the value of the observation depends on the reliability of the observer.

Observation applies your five senses and your judgment to the investigation.

Conducting experiments is another method of collecting primary information, but this method is far more common in technical fields than in general business. An experiment requires extensive, accurate, and measurable manipulation of the factors

Experiments can be effective, but they are expensive.

Marketing surveys are a common way of gathering data directly from customers.

involved—not only tweaking those variables being tested but also controlling those variables that aren't being tested. This sort of experiment management is usually very expensive.

Surveys

One of the best methods of collecting primary information is to ask people with relevant experience and opinions. Surveys include everything from the one-time, one-on-one interview to the distribution of thousands of questionnaires. When prepared and conducted properly, surveys can tell you what a cross section of people think about a given topic. For instance, Charley Shin may want to survey fast-food customers to keep up with their dining preferences. Surveys are useful only when they're reliable and valid. A survey is *reliable* if it produces identical results when repeated. A survey is *valid* if it measures what it's intended to measure.

Developing an effective survey questionnaire requires care and skill.

One of the most crucial elements of a survey is the questionnaire. To develop a questionnaire, begin by making a list of the points you need to determine. Then break these points into specific questions, choosing an appropriate type of question for each point (Figure 10.3 shows various types of survey questions). The following guidelines will help you produce results that are both valid and reliable:[11]

- **Provide clear instructions.** Respondents need to know exactly how to fill out your questionnaire.
- **Keep the questionnaire short and easy to answer.** Ask only questions that are relevant to your research. Remember that people are most likely to respond if they can complete your questionnaire within 10 to 15 minutes.
- **Formulate questions that provide easily tabulated or analyzed answers.** Remember, numbers and facts are easier to summarize than opinions.
- **Avoid leading questions.** Questions that lead to a particular answer bias your survey. If you ask, "Do you prefer that we stay open in the evenings for customer convenience?" you'll no doubt get a "yes." Instead, ask, "What time of day do you normally do your shopping?"
- **Ask only one thing at a time.** A compound question such as "Do you read books and magazines regularly?" doesn't allow for the respondent who reads one but not the other.
- **Pretest the questionnaire.** Have a sample group identify questions that are subject to misinterpretation.

If you're mailing your questionnaire rather than administering it in person, include a return postage-paid envelope along with a persuasive cover letter that explains why you're conducting the research. Your letter must convince your readers that responding is important. Remember that even under the best of circumstances, you may get no more than a 10 to 20 percent response.

An increasingly popular vehicle for conducting surveys or polling customers is the Internet. Spending on web-based surveys by the 24 biggest U.S. market-research firms is expected to soon reach $200 million.[12] Internet surveys offer many benefits: They are cheaper to conduct, can reach large numbers of people instantly and economically, and can improve survey response rates. For example, Harris Interactive recently conducted an e-commerce online survey of 100,000 people concerning their online shopping habits. The survey took only 17 days to complete and cost $150,000. Harris estimates that the same survey by phone could have taken one year and cost about $5 million.

Learning Objective 5

Define information interviews, and list four types of interview questions

Interviews

Getting information straight from an expert can be another effective method for collecting primary information. **Interviews** are planned conversations with a predetermined purpose that involve asking and answering questions. Before you decide to do

FIGURE 10.3 Types of Survey Questions

QUESTION TYPE	EXAMPLE
Open-ended	How would you describe the flavor of this ice cream?
Either-or	Do you think this ice cream is too rich? _____ Yes _____ No
Multiple choice	Which description best fits the taste of this ice cream? (Choose only one.) a. Delicious b. Too fruity c. Too sweet d. Too intensely flavored e. Bland f. Stale
Scale	Please mark an X on the scale to indicate how you perceive the texture of this ice cream. ←——————————————→ Too light Light Creamy Too creamy
Checklist	Which flavors of ice cream have you had in the past 12 months? (Check all that apply.) _____ Vanilla _____ Chocolate _____ Strawberry _____ Chocolate chip _____ Coffee
Ranking	Rank these flavors in order of your preference, from 1 (most preferred) to 5 (least preferred): _____ Vanilla _____ Cherry _____ Maple nut _____ Chocolate ripple _____ Coconut
Short-answer	In the past month how many times did you buy ice cream in the supermarket? __________ In the past month how many times did you buy ice cream in ice cream shops? __________

one, ask yourself whether an interview is really the best way to get the information you need. Although they are relatively easy to conduct, interviews require careful planning and a lot of time.

An interview is any planned conversation that has a specific purpose and involves two or more people.

In a typical information interview, the interviewer seeks facts that bear on a decision or that contribute to basic understanding. The action is controlled by the interviewer, who asks a list of questions designed to elicit information from the interviewee. When you are conducting an interview, it's important to decide in advance what kind of information you want and how you will use it. This planning will save you time and build goodwill with the people you interview.

Planning the Interview Planning an interview is similar to planning any other form of communication. You begin by analyzing your purpose, learning about the other per-

Effective interviewers develop a communication plan.

Organize an interview much as you would organize a written message.

son, and formulating your main idea. Then you decide on the length, style, and organization of the interview.

Good interviews have an opening, a body, and a close. The opening establishes rapport and orients the interviewee to the remainder of the session. You might begin by introducing yourself, asking a few polite questions, and then explaining the purpose and ground rules of the interview. The body of the interview is used for asking questions. In the close of the interview, you summarize the outcome, preview what will come next, and underscore the rapport that has been established.

A successful interview requires careful planning and organization to ensure you get the information you really need.

Preparing the Interview Questions The answers you receive are influenced by the types of questions you ask, by the way you ask them, and by your subject's cultural and language background. Race, gender, age, educational level, and social status are all influential factors, so know your subject before you start writing questions.[13] In addition, be aware of ethical implications. For example, asking someone to divulge personal information about a co-worker may be asking that person to make an unethical choice. Always be careful about confidentiality, politics, and other sensitive issues.

Sometimes you'll want to provide a list of questions days before the interview.

Consider providing a list of questions a day or two before the interview, especially if you'd like to quote your subject in writing or if your questions might require your subject to conduct research or think extensively about the answers. Receiving your questions early will give your subject time to prepare more complete (and therefore more helpful) answers. Consider tape-recording the interview if the topic is complex or if you plan to quote or paraphrase the interviewee in a written document.

Four basic types of interview questions:

- Open-ended questions
- Direct open-ended questions
- Closed-ended questions
- Restatement questions

As Figure 10.4 suggests, most questions fall along a continuum of openness. **Open-ended questions** invite the interviewee to offer an opinion, not just a yes, no, or one-word answer: "What do you think your company wants most from suppliers?" Such questions help you learn the reasons behind a decision rather than just the facts. However, they diminish your control of the interview.

Direct open-ended questions suggest a response: "What have you done about smoothing out intercultural clashes in your department?" These questions give you more control while still giving the interviewee some freedom in framing a response.

Closed-ended questions require yes-or-no answers or call for short responses: "Did you meet your sales quota?" Such questions produce specific information, save time, require less effort from the interviewee, and eliminate bias and prejudice in answers. On the other hand, they also limit the respondent's initiative and may prevent important information from being revealed.

Restatement questions mirror a respondent's previous answer and invite the respondent to expand on that answer: "You said you dislike sales quotas. Is that correct?" They also signal to the interviewee that you're paying attention.

FIGURE 10.4 Choosing Questions with the Appropriate Degree of Openness

Open-Ended Questions			Closed-Ended Questions		
Explore the breadth and depth of potential information	Require the interviewer to be skilled	Provide the opportunity for interviewee to reveal feelings and information	Yield an economical use of time	Allow the interviewer control over questions and responses	Elicit precise, reproducible, reliable data

The following guidelines will help you come up with a great set of interview questions:[14]

- **Think about sequence.** Arrange your questions in a way that helps uncover layers of information or that helps the subject tell you a complete story.
- **Rate your questions and highlight the ones you really need answers to.** If you start to run out of time during the interview, you may have to skip less important questions.
- **Ask smart questions.** If you ask a question that your subject perceives to be less than intelligent, the interview could go downhill in a hurry.
- **Use a mix of question types.** Vary the pacing of your interview by using open-ended, direct open-ended, closed-ended, and restatement questions.
- **Limit the number of questions.** Don't try to cover more questions than you have time for. People can speak at a rate of about 125 to 150 words (about one paragraph) per minute. If you're using a mix of question types, you can probably handle about 20 questions in a half-hour. Remember that open-ended questions take longer to answer than other types do.
- **Edit your questions.** Try to make your questions as neutral and as easy to understand as possible. Then practice them several times to make sure you're ready for the interview.

Processing Interview Information When you've concluded the interview, take a few moments to write down your thoughts, go over your notes, and organize your material. Look for important themes, helpful facts or statistics, and direct quotes. Fill in any blanks while the interview is fresh in your mind. If you made a tape recording, *transcribe* it (take down word for word what the person said) or take notes from the tape just as you would while listening to someone in person.

Carefully review your interview notes immediately after the interview and fill in the gaps before you forget.

Interviews don't necessarily have to take place in person. As more and more people come online, e-mail interviews are becoming more common. Perhaps one of the biggest advantages of an e-mail interview is that it gives subjects a chance to think through their responses thoroughly, rather than rushing to fit the time constraints of an in-person interview.[15] (As a reminder of the tasks involved in interviews, see this chapter's "Checklist: Conducting Effective Information Interviews.")

Conducting interviews by e-mail is becoming increasingly popular.

✓ CHECKLIST: CONDUCTING EFFECTIVE INFORMATION INTERVIEWS

A. Preparing for the interview

1. Analyze your purpose, goals, and audience.
2. Determine the needs of your interviewee, and gather background information.
3. Outline your interview on the basis of your goals, audience, and interview category.
4. Set the level of formality.
5. Choose a structured or an unstructured approach.
6. Formulate questions as clearly and concisely as possible.
7. Ask questions in an order that helps your subject tell you a complete story.
8. Ask intelligent questions that show you've done your homework.
9. Use a mix of question types.
10. Select a time and a site.
11. Inform the interviewee of the nature of the interview and the agenda to be covered.
12. Provide a list of questions in advance if the interviewee will need time to research and formulate quality answers.

B. Conducting the interview

1. Be on time for the interview appointment.
2. Remind the interviewee of the purpose and format.
3. Clear the taking of notes or the use of a tape recorder with the interviewee.
4. Use your ears and eyes to pick up verbal and nonverbal cues.
5. Follow the stated agenda but be willing to explore relevant subtopics.
6. Close the interview by restating the interviewee's key ideas and by reviewing the actions, goals, and tasks that each of you has agreed to.

C. Following up

1. Write a thank-you memo or letter that provides the interviewee with a record of the meeting.
2. Review notes and revise them while the interview is fresh in your mind.
3. Transcribe tape recordings.
4. Monitor progress by keeping in touch with your interviewee.

EVALUATING AND FINALIZING YOUR SOURCES

Learning Objective 6

Name nine criteria for evaluating the credibility of an information source

Ask questions about the reference works you use, such as

- Who collected the data? How?
- What are the authors' qualifications and reputations?
- Is the source up to date?
- Is the information objective?

Once you've gathered your sources of primary and secondary information, you'll want to review them carefully to select the best ones for your information needs. Common sense will help you judge the credibility of the sources you plan to use. Ask yourself the following questions about each piece of material:

- **Does the source have a reputation for honesty and reliability?** Naturally, you'll feel more comfortable using information from a publication that has a reputation for accuracy. But don't let your guard down completely; even the finest reporters and editors make mistakes. Find out how the publication accepts articles and whether it has an editorial board.
- **Is the source potentially biased?** Depending on what an organization stands for, its messages may be written with a certain bias—which is neither bad nor unethical. The Tobacco Institute and the American Association of Retired Persons have different points of view. In order to interpret an organization's information, you need to know its point of view. An organization's source of funding may also influence its information output.
- **What is the purpose of the material?** Was the material designed to inform others of new research, summarize existing research, advocate for a position, or stimulate discussion? Was it designed to promote or sell a product? Be sure to distinguish between advertising and informing.
- **Is the author credible?** Find out whether the person or the publisher is well known in the field. Is the author an amateur? Merely someone with an opinion to air?
- **Where did the source get its information?** Many sources of secondary information get their material from other sources, removing you even further from the original data. If a newspaper article says that pollutants in a local river dropped by 50 per-

The Bureau of Labor Statistics is an excellent resource for current economic and job-related data.

cent since last year, the reporter probably didn't measure those pollutants directly. That information was obtained from someone else. If possible, check on who collected the data, the methods they used, their qualifications, and their professional reputation.

- **Can you verify the material independently?** A good way to uncover bias or a mistake is to search for the same information from another source. Verification can be particularly important when the information goes beyond simple facts to include projections, interpretations, and estimates.
- **Is the material current?** Make sure you are using the most current information available by checking the publication date of a source. Timeliness is especially important if you are using statistics or citing law.
- **Is the material complete?** Determine whether the information you have is the entire text or a selection from another document. If it's a selection, which parts were excluded? Do you need more detail?
- **Do the source's claims stand up to scrutiny?** Step back and ask yourself whether the information makes sense. If a researcher claims that the market for a particular product will triple in the next five years, ask yourself what would have to happen for that prediction to come true. Will three times as many customers buy the product? Will existing customers buy three times more than they currently buy? Why? Is this information relevant to your needs?

You probably won't have time to conduct a thorough background check on all your sources, so focus your efforts on the most important or most suspicious pieces of information. If the material is from a website, take extra care to verify its accuracy and reliability (see "Keeping Pace with Technology: Beware of the Mischievous Webmaster").

At the end of your evaluation, you should have two piles of information: those sources you want to use and those you have eliminated. Now review the pile of information you intend to use and ask yourself several questions: Do I have enough of the right kind of information to answer all my questions? Do I need more? What type of information am I missing?

How will you know when you have enough information? You have enough when (1) you can answer all the questions that began the research project and (2) you begin noticing that sources are becoming redundant.[16] Too much information can frustrate your note-taking and processing efforts.

Stop when you reach the point at which additional effort provides little new information.

PROCESSING YOUR INFORMATION

Once you have selected your sources, it's time to start using what you've found. In some cases you may only need to read the material carefully and meet with your boss to discuss your findings—for example, when you're looking for the answer to a simple question. However, in most cases, you'll be asked to submit a written report or give an oral presentation on your findings. That means you'll need to go through your research and take some extensive notes.

Reading the Material and Taking Notes

Before you start taking notes, organize your research into a logical order. For instance, you might divide the material by subquestions and then divide it chronologically within each grouping. This approach will enable you to focus on a specific topic and read the most current information first. Afterward you can read earlier documents to fill in the history, gather background material, or find older statistics to analyze trends.

When you read a document to take notes, you need not read every word. Read the topic sentences first (generally the first sentence of paragraphs in a business article) to decide whether the paragraph may contain useful information. If it does, then read the entire paragraph.

Decide whether a document contains useful information before reading it carefully to take notes.

When your information is a computer printout or a photocopy, feel free to mark up these documents. Highlight key phrases, facts, or segments, and write comments in the margins. Then record your notes on cards or enter them directly into a computer.

Keeping Pace with Technology

Beware of the Mischievous Webmaster

Publishing information on the Internet is a snap. Just about anyone can write a webpage. So what can you do to avoid falling prey to the mischievous or careless webmaster? As with any print resource, you must carefully evaluate the material you find on the Internet, using the criteria discussed in this chapter. However, because not all Internet information is edited or checked by independent parties, take a closer look at the material's credibility, accuracy, and reasonableness.

Credibility

When evaluating the credibility of Internet information, consider the source:

- Is the publishing body or sponsor a company, organization, governmental body, or educational institution? Or is the material from a personal website?
- Is the sponsor or author recognized in the field? Does the sponsor or author appear qualified to address the topic at hand? Can the sponsor or author be contacted? Is bibliographic information given? Has the author published work in print format?
- Does the domain name or URL appear suspicious? For instance, is the name of the website spelled correctly (united.com rather than untied.com)? These days the distinctions among top-level domain names have blurred, but as Component Chapter B points out, they can still give you a clue about the author or source (com, org, net, gov, edu, or two-letter geographic code—jp for Japan, no for Norway, sz for Switzerland, etc.).
- Is the webpage part of the official website or is it a personal page created by someone who was given space on the web server in an unofficial capacity (designated by a tilde [~] in the URL).

Accuracy

When evaluating the accuracy of Internet information, take a closer look at the site's quality and currency.

- Is the webpage well organized? Is it easy to navigate? Is it full of examples of poor grammar? Are the graphics clear and helpful or distracting and confusing? Are numbers or statistics presented without providing an identifying source?
- Are the site's links kept up to date? Are they evaluated or annotated? Do they send you beyond the site to other reliable sources of information?
- Does the webpage include a publication date or a "last updated" date?

Reasonableness

When testing Internet material for reasonableness, check for balance and logic.

- Use information that is balanced, not selective or slanted. Be suspect of information that presents a one-sided view or that does not acknowledge opposing views.
- Do a reality check. Do you find it hard to believe the claim being made? Does the claim make sense? Does it seem too exaggerated to be true? For instance, if you read the statement "Half of all Americans have had their cars stolen," think about whether half of your friends have had their cars stolen.

To demonstrate just how easy it is to deceive or propagate ludicrous errors on the Internet, log on to the Mankato, Minnesota, website at lme.mankato.msus.edu/mankato/mankato.html. This site was created by some Internet educators to emphasize the importance of carefully checking Internet material. The site's homepage boasts a delightful spot where "the winter temperature in many Mankato neighborhoods has never dropped below a balmy 70 degrees." At a glace, the site seems professional and credible. But are you really going to pack a swimsuit if you're visiting Mankato in winter?

Career Applications

1. If your employee submits an informational report that lists websites as reference sources, how can you, the manager, validate the information in that report?
2. Why is it important to take extra care when relying on information from a website as opposed to relying on information from a newspaper or business journal?

The recording system that most students use (and many instructors recommend) is taking notes on three-by-five-inch index cards. Note cards are easy to use, carry, sort, and arrange. Until recently, people generally agreed that taking notes on a computer was slower and more cumbersome than using index cards. Computers simply didn't have the tools to make this task easy, and they tended to get in the way more than they helped. However, the portability of laptops and advances in software make it easier today to take notes by computer. Figure 10.5 shows a sample word-processing table used to record the same information traditionally recorded on a note card. By recording notes in electronic format instead of on handwritten cards, you can easily search

FIGURE 10.5 Sample Note Taking

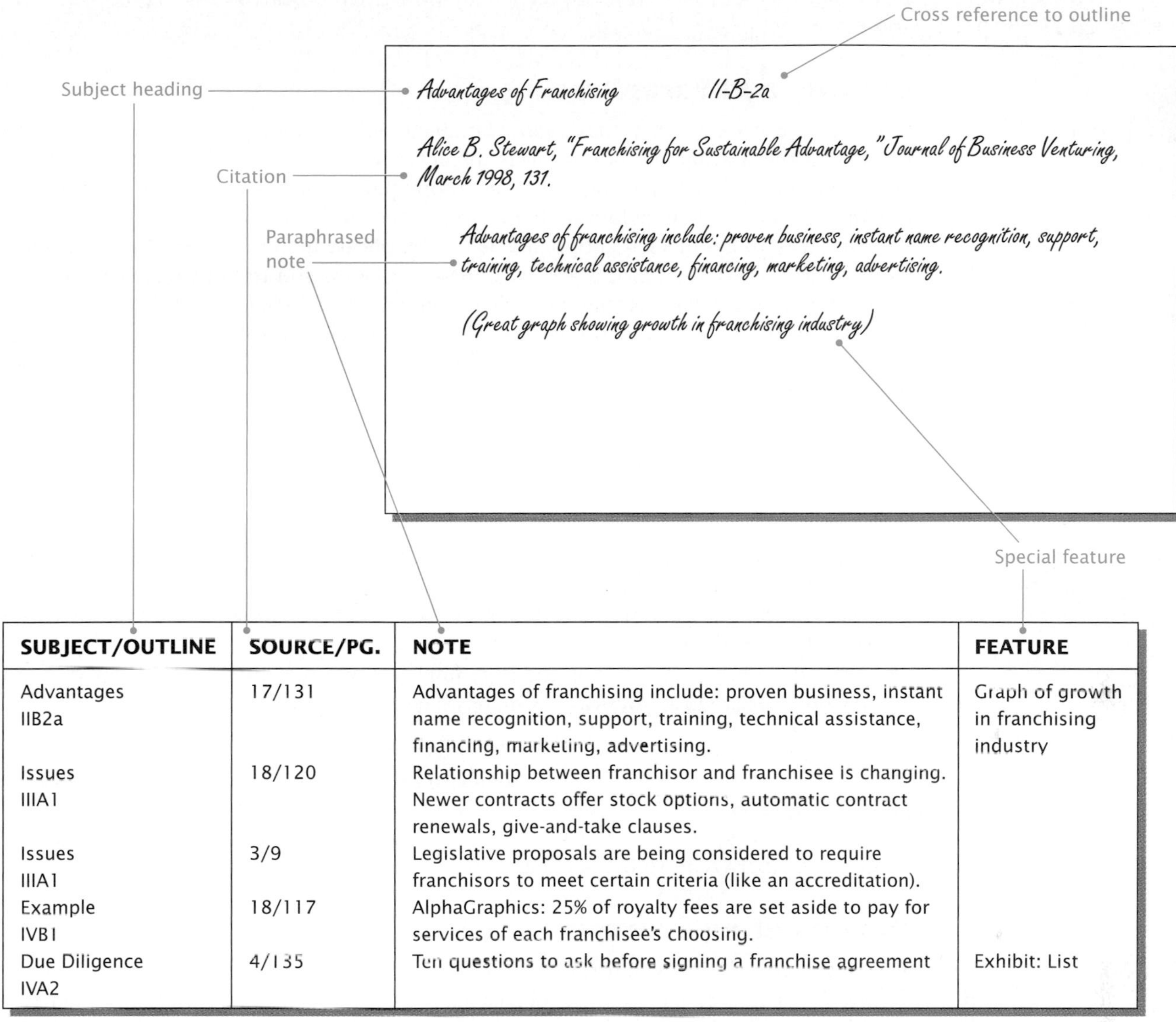

SUBJECT/OUTLINE	SOURCE/PG.	NOTE	FEATURE
Advantages IIB2a	17/131	Advantages of franchising include: proven business, instant name recognition, support, training, technical assistance, financing, marketing, advertising.	Graph of growth in franchising industry
Issues IIIA1	18/120	Relationship between franchisor and franchisee is changing. Newer contracts offer stock options, automatic contract renewals, give-and-take clauses.	
Issues IIIA1	3/9	Legislative proposals are being considered to require franchisors to meet certain criteria (like an accreditation).	
Example IVB1	18/117	AlphaGraphics: 25% of royalty fees are set aside to pay for services of each franchisee's choosing.	
Due Diligence IVA2	4/135	Ten questions to ask before signing a franchise agreement	Exhibit: List

Sources:

3: Alby Gallun, "Franchise Owners Must Play by the Rules," *Business Journal-Milwaukee,* 23 January 1998, 9.

4: Timothy Bates, "Survival Patterns Among Newcomers," *Journal of Business Venturing,* March 1998, 133–135.

17: Alice B. Stewart, "Franchising for Sustainable Advantage," *Journal of Business Venturing,* March 1998, 131.

18: Andrew E. Serwer, "Trouble in Franchise Nation," *Fortune,* 6 March 1995, 115–128.

for words (using the "find" function), sort the notes by column headings, and copy information directly into the document draft.

You may find that the best solution is using a combination of index cards (to capture information while you're reading it) and computer software (to manage the information once you've captured it or to take notes directly from the source). Whichever method you choose, be sure to take complete notes so that you can avoid backtracking to look up something you forgot.

When deciding whether to use note cards or computer software for taking notes, select whichever system works best for you.

On each note card write only one fact. Indicate whether the information is your own idea, a paraphrase of someone else's idea, or a direct quote (by using quotation marks, ellipses, and brackets as necessary). For your own reference and sorting purposes, write at the top of the card the general subject of the material (either a simple phrase or identifying numbers from your outline). Finally, carefully record bibliographic information so that you can cite the source later. If you are collecting several pieces of information from each source, you might prepare a bibliography card for

Each note card or computer entry should contain

- Only one fact
- A subject heading
- Complete source information or a cross-reference to bibliography cards

each source, number the source, and then use the numbers to cross-reference your note cards. Thus, notes taken from source 75 will be written on cards numbered 75.1, 75.2, and so on.

Quoting and Paraphrasing

Learning Objective 7

Discuss the difference between quoting and paraphrasing, and explain the appropriate uses of each

Express material in your own words unless quoting the original language will have a greater impact.

Use direct quotations when the original language will enhance your argument or when rewording the passage would lessen its impact. However, try not to quote sources at great length. Too much quoting creates a choppy patchwork of varying styles and gives the impression that you've lost control of your material.

One way to avoid such choppiness is to **paraphrase** material, or express it in your own words. When you paraphrase, you present information to your reader in a fresh, condensed manner that demonstrates your complete understanding of the material. In fact, paraphrasing may actually increase your comprehension of the source material, because when you recast a passage, you have to think carefully about its meaning—more carefully than if you merely copied it word for word.[17]

To paraphrase effectively, follow these tips:[18]

- Reread the original passage until you fully understand its meaning.
- Record your paraphrase on a note card or in an electronic format.
- Use business language and jargon that your audience is familiar with.
- Check your version with the original source to verify that you have not altered the meaning.
- Use quotation marks to identify any unique terms or phrases you have borrowed exactly from the source.
- Record the source (including the page number) on your note card so that you can give proper credit if you use this material in your report.

In short, good paraphrasing accomplishes three goals: (1) It's shorter than the original text, (2) it's presented in your own words, and (3) it does not alter or distort the meaning of the original text.[19]

Whether you paraphrase or use direct quotes, maintain your credibility and ethics by giving proper credit to the original source.

Documenting Sources and Giving Credit

Always give proper credit when you use someone else's material or ideas.

Whenever you quote or paraphrase, you are using someone else's words or ideas. Doing so without proper credit is **plagiarism**. You can avoid plagiarism by documenting the original source using one of the systems explained in Appendix II, "Documentation of Report Sources." Documenting your sources through footnotes, endnotes, or some similar system is necessary for books, articles, tables, charts, diagrams, song lyrics, scripted dialogue, letters, speeches—anything that you take from someone else. Even if you paraphrase the material, it's best to give credit to the person you obtained the original information from.

It's not necessary to give source credit for material that is general knowledge.

However, you do not have to cite a source for general knowledge or for specialized knowledge that's generally known among your readers. For example, everyone knows that Franklin Roosevelt was elected to the presidency of the United States four times. You can say so on your own authority, even if you've read an article in which the author says the same thing. Copyright law covers printed materials, audiovisual material, many forms of artistic expression, computer programs, maps, mailing lists, and even answering-machine messages. Copyright law does not protect

- Titles, names, short phrases, and slogans
- Familiar symbols or designs
- Lists of ingredients or contents
- Ideas, procedures, methods, systems, processes, concepts, principles, discoveries, or devices (although it does cover their description, explanation, or illustration)

A work is considered copyrighted as soon as it's put into fixed form, even if it hasn't been registered.[20]

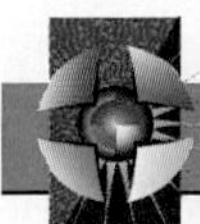

Focusing on Ethics

The Tangled Web of Internet Copyrights

Copyright laws restrict the copying of some kinds of materials and have existed since soon after Gutenberg invented the printing press. United States copyright law currently states that "original works of authorship fixed in a tangible medium of expression" created after January 1, 1978, are automatically copyrighted. It is illegal to copy such works without the author's permission. The law obviously applies to books, music, paintings, and other works that can be seen or heard, but how it applies to works in electronic form on computers and networks is much less clear.

Is it a copyright infringement to download a file from the Internet to your computer? Does making a file available on the Internet automatically place it in the public domain, giving anyone the right to copy and distribute it without restriction? Many cases involving alleged copyright violations are currently being heard in courts around the world. New laws involving Internet copyrights are being proposed daily. Many people are greatly interested in the revisions and interpretations of copyright laws concerning the Internet. Publishers and creators want strict controls on dissemination of their products, and Internet users do not want copyright controls to hamper the free flow of information on the web.

While the legal and ethical issues get sorted out, two techniques are being used to make it difficult to copy Internet files: encryption and watermarks. *Encryption* involves garbling the information so that a user must have a password or decoder to make the information usable. *Watermarks* are visible images that identify the owner of information. For example, Microsoft holds electronic rights to a great deal of artwork, and it uses watermarks to identify its images.

Because we have no clear definition of how copyright laws apply to electronic information, the safest approach to using any information from the Internet is to assume that it's copyrighted and to contact the author or owner for permission to use it. Keep in mind that ignorance is no excuse; you can be prosecuted even if you unknowingly violate a copyright. "Copyright law has no exemption for innocent infringement," according to Michael Grow, a Washington, D.C., attorney. And if you are putting information on the Internet, be aware that it is very easy for anyone to copy and reuse the information with or without your permission.

Career Applications

1. What should you do if you can't find the author or owner of some online information that you'd like to use in a report?
2. How might ethical and legal concerns slow the development of online libraries and other information resources?

Merely crediting the source is not always enough. According to the *fair use doctrine,* you can use other people's work only as long as you don't unfairly prevent them from benefiting as a result. For example, if you reproduce someone else's copyrighted questionnaire in a report you're writing, even if you identify the source thoroughly you may be preventing the author from selling a copy of that questionnaire to your readers.

The fair use doctrine offers guidelines for determining how copyrighted material may be used.

In general, avoid relying to such a great extent on someone else's work. However, when you can't avoid it, contact the copyright holder (usually the author or publisher) for permission to reprint. You'll usually be asked to pay a fee. (For a closer look at the permission needed for citing information from electronic sources, see "Focusing on Ethics: The Tangled Web of Internet Copyrights.")

ANALYZING YOUR DATA

By themselves, the data you've collected won't offer much meaning or insight. You'll need to search for relationships among the facts and the bits of evidence you've compiled. This analysis allows you to interpret your findings and thus answer the questions or solve the problem that instigated your report.

Analyze your results by calculating statistics, drawing reasonable and logical conclusions, and, if appropriate, developing a set of recommendations.

Much of the information you compile during the research phase will be in numerical form. However, Charley Shin can tell you that such statistical information in its raw state is of little practical value. It must be manipulated so that you and your readers can interpret its significance. Look at the data from various angles and try to detect patterns by fitting pieces together to form tentative conclusions. This process enables

TABLE 10.3 Three Types of Average: Mean, Median, and Mode

Salesperson	Sales	
Wilson	$3,000	
Green	5,000	
Carrick	6,000	
Wimper	7,000	Mean
Keeble	7,500	Median
Kemble	8,500	Mode
O'Toole	8,500	Mode
Mannix	8,500	Mode
Caruso	9,000	
Total	$63,000	

you to answer the questions you generated when defining the problem. As you proceed with your analysis, either verify or reject your conclusions.

The same set of data can be used to produce three kinds of averages: mean, median, and mode.

One useful way of looking at numerical data is to find the **average**, which is a number that represents a group of numbers. Three useful averages are shown in Table 10.3. The **mean** is the sum of all the items in the group divided by the number of items in that group. The **median** is the "middle of the road" average, or the midpoint of a series (with an equal number of items above and below). The **mode** is the number that occurs more often than any other in your sample. It's the best average for answering a question such as "What is the usual amount?"

Trend analysis involves examining data over time in order to detect patterns and relationships.

It's also helpful to look for a **trend**, a steady upward or downward movement in a pattern of events taking place over time. Trend analysis is common in business. By looking at data over a period of time, you can detect patterns and relationships that will help you answer important questions.

A correlation is a statistical relationship between two or more variables.

Once you have identified a trend, you'll want to look for a cause. To do so, you could look for a **correlation**, a statistical relationship between two or more variables. For example, if the salespeople with the largest accounts consistently produced higher sales, you might assume that those two factors were related in a predictable way. However, your conclusion might be wrong. Correlations are useful evidence, but they do not necessarily prove a cause-and-effect relationship. To be certain that factors are correlated, you might have to collect more evidence.

INTERPRETING YOUR FINDINGS

Learning Objective 8

Explain the difference between drawing a conclusion and developing a recommendation

Now your data are in a form that both you and your readers can understand. But you're not finished yet. Once you have thoroughly analyzed your information, your next step is to draw conclusions and, if requested, develop recommendations.

Drawing Conclusions

Conclusions are interpretations of the facts.

A **conclusion** is a logical interpretation of the facts in your report. Reaching good conclusions based on the evidence at hand is one of the most important skills you can develop in your business career. A sound conclusion

- **Must fulfill the original statement of purpose.** After all, drawing a conclusion is why you took on the project in the first place.
- **Must be based strictly on the information included in the rest of the report.** Consider all the information in your report. Don't ignore anything—even if it doesn't support your conclusion. Moreover, don't introduce any new information

in your conclusion. (After all, if something is that important, it should be in the body of your report.)

- **Must be logical.** A logical conclusion is one that follows accepted patterns of reasoning.

Even though conclusions need to be logical, they may not automatically flow from the evidence. Most business decisions require assumptions and judgment; relatively few are based strictly on the facts. Your personal values or the organization's values may also influence your conclusions; just be sure that you're aware of how these biases affect your judgment. Also, don't expect all team members to examine the evidence and arrive at the same conclusion. One of the reasons for bringing additional people into a decision is to gain their unique perspectives and experiences.

Check the logic that underlies your conclusions.

Developing Recommendations

Whereas a conclusion interprets the facts, a **recommendation** suggests what to do about the facts. The difference between a conclusion and a recommendation can be seen in the following example:

Recommendations are suggestions for action.

Conclusion	Recommendation
On the basis of its track record and current price, I conclude that this company is an attractive buy.	I recommend that we write a letter to the president offering to buy the company at a 10 percent premium over the market value of its stock.

When you've been asked to take the final step and translate your conclusions into recommendations, be sure to make the relationship between them clear. Remember, recommendations are inappropriate in a report when you're not expected to supply them. But when you do develop recommendations of your own, try not to let your assumptions and personal values influence them. To be credible, recommendations must be based on logical analysis and sound conclusions. They must also be practical and acceptable to your readers, the people who have to make the recommendations work. Finally, when making a recommendation, be certain that you have adequately described the steps that come next. Don't leave your readers scratching their heads and saying, "This all sounds good, but what do I do on Monday morning?"

Good recommendations are
- Practical
- Acceptable to readers
- Explained in enough detail for readers to take action

COMMUNICATION CHALLENGES AT GOSH ENTERPRISES

Charley Shin always keeps one eye on the consumer marketplace and one eye on his plans for expansion. He learned the importance of paying attention to the customer's perspective shortly after opening the first Charley's Steakery. The restaurant was named simply "Charley's"—until Shin realized that the name didn't communicate what kind of food customers could expect. When he spelled it out with a sign that said "Charley's Steakery," business increased by 50 percent.

That's why, in addition to the three-year growth plan, Shin wants to take another look at fast-food trends. Charley's Steakery made its reputation by serving fresh sandwiches with everything prepared to order—no frozen, microwaved entrees. This "fresh food" concept has been popular with customers since 1986. Is it still important to them? Some of his burger-selling competitors have returned to greasier, less healthy cuisine (boosting business tremendously, they claim), but Shin isn't so sure their numbers are giving an accurate picture; a double-digit increase in sales doesn't mean much if it's preceded by a huge plummet, as in the case of one competitor.

Individual Challenge: As part of Shin's marketing staff, you've been asked to begin setting up the study. First task: Develop a problem statement and state it as a question. Write your statement on paper and present it to the rest of your team.

Team Challenge: After the team members have presented their ideas and the problem statements have been agreed on, your team needs to develop subquestions to guide your research efforts. Finally, your team needs to select sources of secondary and primary information that they will consult to answer the subquestions. ■

SUMMARY OF LEARNING OBJECTIVES

1 Highlight six tasks you should complete when doing business research. When investigating business topics, you need to complete six basic tasks: (1) Understand your topic and assignment by gathering preliminary information and developing subquestions. (2) Find and access information by knowing what to look for and where to look. Gather secondary information in libraries, on the Internet, and in databases. Gather primary information from company documents, casual observations, formal experiments, surveys, or interviews. (3) Evaluate and finalize your sources by judging their relevance and credibility. (4) Process your information by reading the materials you've gathered, quoting and paraphrasing your sources, and giving credit to those sources. (5) Analyze your data by searching for relationships among the facts and evidence you've gathered. (6) Interpret your data by drawing conclusions and developing recommendations when appropriate.

2 Name seven types of secondary resources you might use to find business information. Popular secondary business resources include business books, electronic databases, newspapers, periodicals, directories, almanacs, and government publications.

3 Explain how to conduct an effective database search. To search databases effectively, you should select appropriate databases for your needs, use multiple search engines (if searching the Internet), translate concepts into key words and phrases, use short phrases rather than long ones, avoid stopwords and words contained in the name of the database, vary your search terms, specify a logical relationship between the keywords, use Boolean operators, use proximity operators, use wildcards, and evaluate your search results, refining your strategy if necessary.

4 Highlight five methods of collecting primary data. You can collect primary data by examining company documents such as sales reports, memos, financial statements, policy statements, brochures, newsletters, annual reports, and business correspondence. You can make observations and conduct experiments. You can conduct surveys by engaging in one-on-one interviews or distributing questionnaires. And you can conduct interviews.

5 Define information interviews, and list four types of interview questions. Interviews are planned conversations with a predetermined purpose that involve asking and answering questions. The interviewer seeks information that may broaden understanding or aid decision making. Interview questions are of four types: (1) open-ended questions (which invite the person being interviewed to offer an opinion), (2) direct open-ended questions (which suggest a response), (3) closed-ended questions (which require little more than yes-or-no answers), and (4) restatement questions (which mirror a respondent's previous answer and invite the person to expand on that answer).

6 Name nine criteria for evaluating the credibility of information. Information should come from a credible source that has a reputation for being honest and reliable; the source should also be unbiased. The purpose of the material should be known, and the author should be credible. The information should include references to sources (if obtained elsewhere), and it should be independently verifiable. The material should be current, and it should be complete. Finally, the information should seem logical.

7 Discuss the difference between quoting and paraphrasing, and explain the appropriate uses of each. Quoting is copying material word for word and is used when the original language would enhance the impact of the passage or when rewording it would alter its meaning. Paraphrasing is presenting material in your own words without altering or distorting its meaning; it is used in all occasions unless quoting is necessary. Whether you're quoting or paraphrasing, always give proper credit to the source.

8 Explain the difference between drawing a conclusion and developing a recommendation. A conclusion is the writer's analysis of what the findings mean (an interpretation of the facts), whereas a recommendation is the writer's opinion (based on reason and logic) about the course of action that should be taken.

TEST YOUR KNOWLEDGE

1. When might a businessperson need to conduct research?
2. How does primary information differ from secondary information?
3. What are the main advantages of electronic databases?
4. How does a search engine differ from a directory?
5. What four types of questions can be posed during an interview?
6. How will you know when you are finished with the research process?
7. What is paraphrasing, and what is its purpose?
8. What is the difference between the mean, median, and mode?
9. What are the characteristics of a sound conclusion?
10. How does a conclusion differ from a recommendation?

APPLY YOUR KNOWLEDGE

1. Why is browsing an important part of the research process?
2. Why must you be careful when citing information from a webpage?

3. Why do you need to evaluate your sources?
4. After an exhaustive study of an important problem, you have reached a conclusion that you believe your company's management will reject. What will you do? Explain your answer.
5. **Ethical Choices** If you want to make a specific recommendation following your research, should you include information that might support a different recommendation? Explain your answer.

PRACTICE YOUR KNOWLEDGE

Document for Analysis

Writing Effective Interview Questions

The following set of interview questions were prepared for a manager of Whirlpool Corporation. The goal of the interview was to learn some basic information about Whirlpool's meeting practices. Read the questions, then (1) critique them, as a whole, indicating what you like or dislike about this series of questions; and (2) select five questions and revise them to make them more effective.

1. What is your position in the company?
2. To whom do you report?
3. Do you attend or run many meetings?
4. Do your meetings start on time? Run late?
5. Do you distribute or receive a meeting agenda several days in advance of the meeting?
6. Do you like your job?
7. Do you travel a lot for your job?
8. Has your company cut back on travel expenditures? If so, how and why?
9. Does your company use videoconferencing as an alternative to travel?
10. Does your company own its own videoconferencing equipment?
11. Are videoconferences more or less effective than face-to-face meetings?
12. How long have you worked for Whirlpool?
13. Is Sears your largest retail customer?
14. How often does your management team meet with the managers of Sears?
15. Does your company produce only household appliances?
16. How do you keep your meetings on track?
17. Does someone prepare written minutes of meetings? Are the minutes distributed to meeting members?

Exercises

For live links to all websites discussed in this chapter, visit this text's website at www.prenhall.com/bovee. Just log on, select Chapter 10, and click on "Student Resources." Locate the name of the site or the URL related to the material in the text. For the "Exploring the Best of the Web" exercises, you'll also find navigational directions. Click on the live link to the site.

10.1 **Understanding Your Topic: Subquestions** Your boss has asked you to do some research on franchising. Actually, he's thinking about purchasing a few Subway franchises, and he needs some information. Visit www.amazon.com and review the site. On the home-page, perform a keyword search on "franchise." Explore some of the books by clicking on "read more about this title."
a. Use the information to develop a list of subquestions to help you narrow your focus.
b. Write down the names of three books you might purchase for your boss.
c. How can this website assist you with your research efforts?

10.2 **Finding Secondary Information** Using online, database, or printed sources, find the following information. Be sure to properly cite your source using the formats discussed in Appendix II (*Hint:* Start with Figure 10.2, Major Business Resources.)
a. Contact information for the American Management Association
b. Median weekly earnings of men and women by occupation
c. Current market share for Perrier water
d. Performance ratios for office supply retailers
e. Annual stock performance for Hewlett-Packard
f. Number of franchise outlets in the United States
g. Composition of the U.S. workforce by profession

10.3 **Finding Secondary Information** Businesspeople have to know where to look for secondary information when they conduct research. Prepare a list of the most important magazines and professional journals in the following fields of study:
a. Marketing/advertising
b. Insurance
c. Communications
d. Accounting

10.4 **Finding Information: Industry Information** Locate the NAICS codes for the following industries:
a. Hotels and motels
b. Breakfast cereals
c. Bottled water
d. Automatic vending machines

10.5 **Finding Information: Company Information** Select any public company and find the following information:
a. Names of the company's current officers
b. List of the company's products or services
c. Current issues in the company's industry
d. Outlook for the company's industry as a whole

10.6 **Finding Information: Search Strategy** You're getting ready to write a research paper on a topic of your choice. You decide to search for information using both the library databases and the Internet. Develop a search strategy.
a. What are some key words and phrases you might use?
b. Which Boolean operators would you use to narrow your search?
c. Which wildcard operators might you use?

10.7 **Finding Information: Search Techniques** Analyze any recent school or work assignment that required you to conduct research. How did you approach your investigation? Did you rely mostly on sources of primary information or mostly on sources of secondary information? Now that you have studied this chapter, can you identify two ways to improve the research techniques you used during that assignment? Briefly explain.

10.8 **Finding Information: Primary Information** Deciding how to collect primary data is an important part of the research process. Which one or more of the five methods of data collection (examining documents, making observations, surveying people, conducting experiments, and performing interviews) would you use if you were researching these questions?

a. Has the litter problem on campus been reduced since the cafeteria began offering fewer take-out choices this year than in past years?
b. Has the school attracted more transfer students since it waived the formal application process and allowed students at other colleges simply to send their transcripts and a one-page letter of application?
c. Have the number of traffic accidents at the school's main entrance been reduced since a traffic light was installed?
d. Has student satisfaction with the campus bookstore improved now that students can order their books over the Internet and pick them up at several campus locations?

10.9 **Finding Information: Surveys** You work for a movie studio that is producing a young director's first motion picture, the story of a group of unknown musicians finding work and making a reputation in a competitive industry. Unfortunately, some of your friends leave the first complete screening, saying that the 132-minute movie is simply too long. Others can't imagine any more editing cuts. Your boss wants to test the movie on a regular audience and ask viewers to complete a questionnaire that will help the director decide whether edits are needed and, if so, where. Design a questionnaire that you can use to solicit valid answers for a report to the director about how to handle the audience's reaction to the movie.

10.10 **Finding Information: Interviews** Plan to conduct an informational interview with a professional working in your chosen field of study. Plan the structure of the interview and create a set of interview questions. Conduct the interview. Using the information you gathered, write a memo to another student describing the tasks, advantages, and disadvantages of jobs in this field of study. (Your reader is a person who also plans to pursue a career in this field of study.)

10.11 **Finding Information: Interviews** You're conducting an information interview with a manager in another division of your company. Partway through the interview, the manager shows clear signs of impatience. How should you respond? What might you do differently to prevent this from happening in the future? Explain your answers.

10.12 **Teamwork: Evaluating Sources** Break into small groups and surf the Internet to find websites that provide business information such as company or industry news, trends, analysis, facts, or performance data. Using the criteria discussed under "Evaluating and Finalizing Your Sources" (see pages 324–325), evaluate the credibility of the information presented at these websites.

10.13 **Processing Information: Reading and Taking Notes** Select an article from a business journal such as *Business Week*, *Fortune*, or *Forbes*. Read the article and highlight the article's key points. Summarize the main idea of the article, paraphrasing the key points.

10.14 **Processing Information: Documenting Sources** Select five business articles from sources such as journals, books, newspapers, or websites. Develop a resource list using Appendix II as a guideline.

10.15 **Analyzing Data: Calculating the Mean** Your boss has asked you to analyze and report on your division's sales for the first nine months of this year. Using the following data from company invoices, calculate the mean for each quarter and all averages for the year to date. Then identify and discuss the quarterly sales trends.

January	$ 24,600	April	$ 21,200	July	$ 29,900
February	25,900	May	24,600	August	30,500
March	23,000	June	26,800	September	26,600

EXPAND YOUR KNOWLEDGE

Exploring the Best of the Web:

Check Out Materials at This Library 24 Hours a Day, *p. 314*

Visit the reference center of the Internet Public Library and explore the Business and Economics Reference section. Click on *Business Directories*.

1. Select five companies and use the links provided to find contact information (address, phone, website, officers' names, and so on) for each company. What kinds of contact information did you find at the company websites?
2. Gather information about the U.S. budget by using one of the site's directories: A Business Researcher's Interests. Why is using a directory such as this one an efficient way to obtain information?
3. Go back to the library's main reference center and click on Reference. Follow some of the reference links. How might these links help you when performing business research?

Exploring the Web on Your Own

Review these chapter-related websites on your own to improve your research skills.

1. Visit Microsoft's Complete Internet Guide at www.microsoft.com/insider/internet/default.htm and take the web tutorial to improve your online researching skills.
2. Brush up on your business research by following the links at the Basic Business Research Methods webpage, www.mapnp.org/library/research/research.htm.
3. Find out what makes a website work and learn more about website design, speed, navigational structure, and standards at Usable Web, http://usableWeb.com.

LEARN INTERACTIVELY

Interactive Study Guide

Visit "My Companion Website" at www.prenhall/bovee.com. For Chapter 10, take advantage of the interactive "Study Guide" to test your chapter knowledge. Get instant feedback on whether you need additional studying. Read the "Current Events" articles to get the latest on chapter topics, and complete the exercises—as specified by your instructor.

This site offers a variety of additional resources: The "Research Area" helps you locate a wealth of information to use in course assignments. You can even send a message to online research experts, who will help you find exactly the information you need. The "Study Hall" helps you succeed in this course. "Talk in the Hall" lets you leave messages and meet new friends online. If you have a question, you can "Ask the Tutor." And to get a better grade in this course, you can find more help at "Writing Skills," "Study Skills," and "Study Tips."

Grammar Diagnostic Tests

Review and reinforce your grammar and language skills by taking one of the four online diagnostic tests offered at our companion website, www.prenhall/bovee.com. The four tests cover a variety of topics, including spelling, capitals, punctuation, verbs, pronouns, adjectives, adverbs, sentence structure, sentence punctuation, clarity, word choice, style, organization skills, proofreading, and more. Submit your test and assess your competency. Then focus on improving areas where you are weak as you complete the exercises in this chapter.

Communicating Information Through Visuals

After studying this chapter, you will be able to

1 *Cite the advantages of preparing visuals before preparing text*

2 *Explain why business professionals use charts and other visuals*

3 *List several popular types of visuals and discuss when to use them*

4 *Discuss five principles of graphic design to keep in mind when preparing visuals*

5 *Name four qualities to look for before including a visual in a report or presentation*

COMMUNICATION CLOSE-UP AT BLACK ENTERTAINMENT TELEVISION

www.bet.com

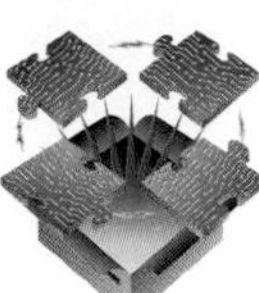

As the old saying goes, a picture is worth a thousand words. Curtis Symonds knows that this adage is especially true in the business world. He is executive vice president of affiliate sales and marketing for BET Holdings (parent company of Black Entertainment Television). Whether Symonds is writing a report for management or developing materials to market the company's jazz network, BET on Jazz, to cable television companies, he uses charts and visuals to help his audience grasp his most important ideas.

Symonds began working for the cable television industry in 1980. By 1984 he was the director of marketing for the ESPN sports network. Then in 1988 he joined BET Holdings, where he has remained ever since. During that time, Symonds has helped BET expand from its original television network to a media group consisting of four cable television networks, three magazines, several jazz-theme restaurants, and a national line of sportswear.

Succeeding in such a highly competitive marketplace depends on establishing a quick and lasting connection with the audience. Symonds engages his customers and holds their attention with his strategic use of visuals.

"You want to draw the person into the setting so that you can convey the information that most meets their needs," he says. For example, BET competes with many other networks for space on local cable channels, so Symonds provides solid evidence that BET offers viewers more of the cable programming they want, using tables and charts to present detailed data. "Research drives our business," he says. "We need to show that we understand the viewer in each specific local market."

To convince cable executives of the quality and appeal of BET's programs, Symonds not only turns research data into charts that depict the viewing habits of local customers but also uses the charts to demonstrate how the BET networks fit those viewing habits. He also uses charts to show how BET's programming has increased in popularity among various demographic groups. By presenting this type of information visually, Symonds enables cable companies to see how they might be able to profit from investing in the BET Network, BET on Jazz, BET Pay-Per-View, or BET Movies.

As much as Symonds relies on charts, he's careful not to use too many in his reports. Moreover, he's learned that understanding his audience is the key to developing effective visuals. In every situation, Symonds takes the time to consider his audience's needs and expectations before choosing to present his message in graphic format. "I want to make it as easy as possible for my readers," he says. "After all, they have other options."[1] ■

Using visual aids to help the audience grasp the most important ideas is one technique employees at Black Entertainment Television use to market the company.

PLANNING VISUALS

Learning Objective 1

Cite the advantages of preparing visuals before preparing text

Businesspeople such as BET's Curtis Symonds include charts and other visuals in their reports to convey important ideas. When preparing your own reports, you'll want to include visuals for the same reason. But which would you prepare first, visuals or text?

Suppose you've just completed the research for an important report or oral presentation, and you're about to begin the composition phase. Your first impulse might be to start with the introduction and proceed page by page until you've completed the text or script. Almost as an afterthought you might illustrate your words by throwing in a few visuals—tables, charts, graphs, schematic drawings, illustrations, photographs. Although fitting visuals to completed text makes some sense, many experienced businesspeople prefer to begin with the visuals.

Learning Objective 2

Explain why business professionals use charts and other visuals

Preparing your visuals first has three advantages. First, much of the fact finding and analytical work is already in tabular or graphic form, so sorting through and refining your visuals will help you decide exactly what you're going to say. Second, by starting with the visuals, you develop a graphic story line that can be used for your written report. Third, because your text will explain and refer to any tables, charts, and diagrams you include, you save time by having them ready before beginning to compose your text, particularly if you plan to use quite a few visuals.

Gain an Advantage with Visuals

Carefully prepared visuals can make your report or presentation more interesting. But even more important, pictures are an effective way to communicate with the diverse audiences that are common in today's business environment. Moreover, in the numbers-oriented world of work, people rely heavily on trend lines, distribution curves, and percentages. An upward curve means good news in any language. Finally, visuals attract and hold people's attention, helping your audience understand and remember your message.

Despite their value, Curtis Symonds recommends that you use visuals selectively and include only those elements that support your primary message. Use visuals to supplement the written or spoken word, not to replace it. Restrict

The mind favors information shown as pictures and quickly forgets information shown as words or numbers.

TABLE 11.1 When to Use Visuals

Purpose	*Application*
To clarify	Support text descriptions of "graphic" topics: quantitative or numerical information, explanations of trends, descriptions.
To simplify	Break complicated descriptions into components that can be depicted with conceptual models, flowcharts, organization charts, or diagrams.
To emphasize	Call attention to particularly important points by illustrating them with line, bar, and pie charts.
To summarize	Review major points in the narrative by providing a chart or table that sums up the data.
To reinforce	Present information in visual and written form to increase reader's retention.
To attract	Make material seem more interesting by decorating the cover or title page and by breaking up the text with visual aids.
To impress	Build credibility by putting ideas into visual form to convey the impression of authenticity and precision.
To unify	Depict the relationship among points—for example, with a flowchart.

When planning visuals

- Decide what you want to say
- Pick out the points that can best be made visually
- Judge whether you have too many or too few graphics

your use of visuals to situations in which they do the most good. Table 11.1 helps you identify those situations.

Identify Points Requiring Visual Support

Once you have selected the information that you will include in your report, you must identify which points to illustrate visually. Suppose you've been asked to compare your company's recent sales with those of a competitor. You have the following data on market share for the past month:

Sales Region	*Your Company's Share*	*Competitor's Share*
North	10%	25%
South	40	8
East	32	32
West	20	23

What message can you derive from this set of data? Some of the possibilities include the following:

- The two companies perform differently in different regions. Your company is strongest in the South, where your competitor is weakest.
- The two companies' performances are similar in the East and West.
- Both companies are uneven in their market share from region to region.

Analyze raw data to identify the points that support your main idea.

All these messages are true, and all of them might be useful. Your job is to analyze the information and decide how to present it.

Some of this information may lend itself to a prose presentation; other information may be expressed more easily in graphic form. For instance, whereas detailed facts and figures may be confusing and tedious in paragraph form, tables and charts can conveniently organize and display such detail with clarity. Some points may require a detailed description of physical relationships or procedures, in which case you might want to use flowcharts, drawings, or photographs to clarify the discussion. Or you may simply want to draw attention to a particular fact or detail by reinforcing the message visually.

Maintain a Balance Between Illustrations and Words

After you have identified which points require visual support, you must pare down your selection. Your goal is to achieve a reasonable balance between verbal and visual information. The ideal blend depends on the nature of your subject. Illustrating every point dilutes the effectiveness of your visuals. For example, telling your audience every paragraph or two to consult a table or chart is more likely to obscure than to illuminate the thread of your argument. Furthermore, readers tend to assume that the amount of space allocated to a topic indicates its relative importance. So by using visuals to illustrate a minor point, you may be sending a misleading message about its significance.

Avoid drafting a report with too many visuals.

When deciding on the mix of words and visuals, give some thought to your readers' needs and thought patterns. Some people ignore the visuals and focus on the words; others do the opposite. If you know that your audience prefers one form of communication over the other—or has special communication needs—you can adjust the balance accordingly. When General Mills redesigned its Hamburger Helper package, management decided to include both drawings and step-by-step photographs of the cooking directions. These visuals were particularly useful for audiences who speak English as their second language. The illustrations also provided additional help for people with limited cooking experience. "It's critically important that customers be able to follow the directions," says Craig Shulstad, a General Mills spokesperson, "because if they don't have a successful experience with the food, they won't buy the product again."[2]

Consider Your Production Schedule

Another factor to consider when deciding on the number and types of visuals to include in a report is your production schedule. If you're producing your report or presentation without the help of an art department or appropriate computer-graphics tools, you may want to restrict the number of visuals in your report. Creating charts, tables, and diagrams takes time, particularly if you're inexperienced. In addition, constructing visuals requires a good deal of both imagination and attention to detail.

Your timeline and access to resources govern the number of visuals you can create.

SELECTING THE RIGHT VISUAL FOR THE JOB

Learning Objective 3

List several popular types of visuals and discuss when to use them

Once you've selected which points to illustrate visually, your next step is to select the type of visual that will present your data most clearly and effectively to your audience. For instance, using the market-share data from our earlier example, how would you visually communicate the differences between your company's market share and your competitor's? A pie chart? A bar chart? Both could work in this case. Keep in mind that most types of visuals are not interchangeable. Some types of visuals depict certain kinds of data better than others:

Choose a type of graphic that best presents your message.

- To present detailed, exact values, use tables.
- To illustrate trends over time, use a line chart or a bar chart.
- To show frequency or distribution, use a pie chart, segmented bar chart, or area chart.
- To compare one item with another, use a bar chart.
- To compare one part with the whole, use a pie chart.
- To show correlations, use a line chart, a bar chart, or a scatter (dot) chart.

TABLE 11.2 Parts of a Table

		Multicolumn Head*		
Stub Head	***Subhead***	***Subhead***	***Single-column head***	***Single-column head***
Row head	XXX	XXX	XX	XX
Row head				
Subhead	XX	XXX	XX	X
Subhead	XX	XXX	XX	XX
Total	XXX	XXX	XX	XX

Source: (In the same format as a text footnote; see Appendix II.)
*Footnote (for explanation of elements in the table; a superscript number or small letter may be used instead of a asterisk or other symbol.)

- To show geographic relationships, use a map.
- To illustrate a process or a procedure, use a flowchart or a diagram.

Here's a closer look at each of these visuals.

Tables

Use tables to help your audience understand detailed information.

When you have to present detailed, specific information, choose a **table**, a systematic arrangement of data in columns and rows. Tables are ideal when the audience needs the information that would be either difficult or tedious to handle in the main text.

Most tables contain the standard parts illustrated in Table 11.2. Every table includes vertical columns and horizontal rows, with useful headings along the top and side. Tables projected onto a screen during an oral presentation should be limited to three column heads and six row heads; tables presented on paper may include from one or two heads to a dozen or more. If the table has too many columns to fit comfortably between the margins of the page, turn the paper horizontally and insert it in the report with the top toward the binding.

Although formal tables set apart from the text are necessary for complex information, you can present some data more simply within the text. You make the table, in essence, a part of the paragraph, typed in tabular format. Such text tables are usually introduced with a sentence that leads directly into the tabulated information. Here's an example:[3]

This table shows how FedEx stacks up against rival UPS:

Feature	***FedEx***	***UPS***
Sales (annual)	$17.5 billion	$27.2 billion
Daily packages delivered	4.5 million	13 million
Market share	25% of package-delivery market	55% of package-delivery market
Number of employees	149,000	344,000
Delivery equipment	43,500 trucks; 637 planes	150,000 trucks; 610 planes

Source: Adapted from Michael H. Mescon, Courtland L. Bovee, and John V. Thill, "Face-Off: FedEx vs. UPS," *Business Today* (Upper Saddle River, N.J.: Prentice Hall, 2001), 96

Many tables are strictly numerical, so when preparing such tables, be sure to

- Use common, understandable units, and clearly identify the units you're using: dollars, percentages, price per ton, or whatever.
- Express all items in a column in the same unit, and round off for simplicity.

- Label column headings clearly, and use a subhead if necessary.
- Separate columns or rows with lines or extra space to make the table easy to follow.
- Provide column or row totals or averages when relevant.
- Document the source of the data using the same format as a text footnote (see Appendix II).

Although numerical tables are more common, tables can also contain words. Word tables are particularly appropriate for presenting survey findings or for comparing various items against a specific standard.

Use word tables
- To summarize survey results
- To compare items with some standard

Line and Surface Charts

A **line chart** illustrates trends over time or plots the relationship of two variables. In line charts showing trends, the vertical, or *y*, axis shows the amount, and the horizontal, or *x*, axis shows the time or the quantity being measured. Ordinarily, both scales begin at zero and proceed in equal increments; however, in Figure 11.1 the vertical axis is broken to show that some of the increments have been left out. A broken axis is appropriate when the data are plotted far above zero, but be sure to clearly indicate the omission of data points.

Use line charts
- To indicate changes over time
- To plot the relationship of two variables

A simple line chart may be arranged in many ways. One of the most common is to plot several lines on the same chart for comparative purposes, as shown in Figure 11.2. Try to use no more than three lines on any given chart, particularly if the lines cross.

FIGURE 11.1 Line Chart with Broken Axis

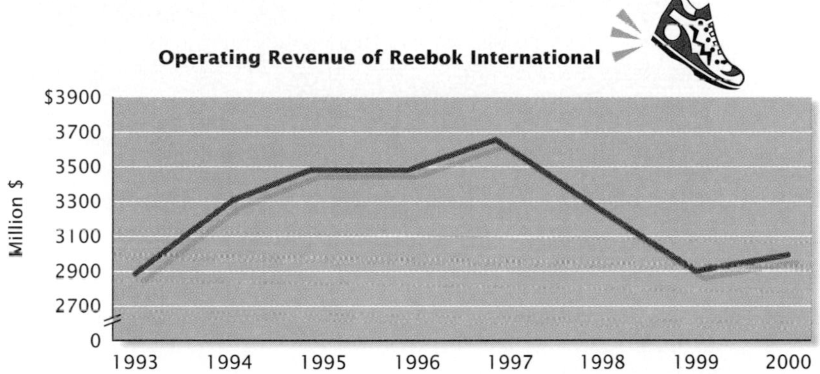

FIGURE 11.2 Line Chart with Multiple Lines

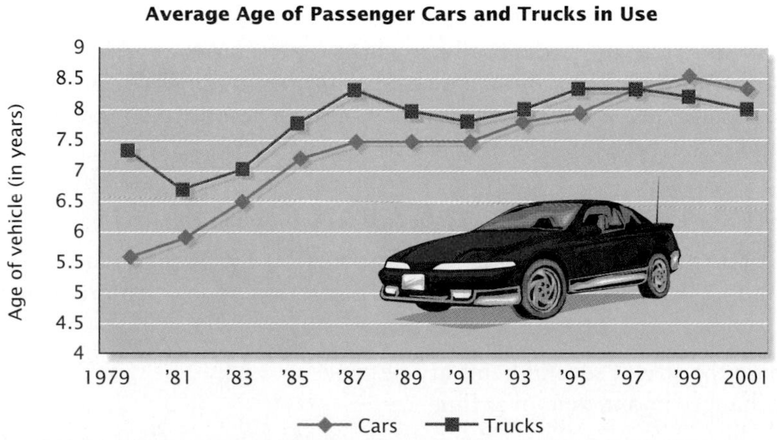

Average Age of Passenger Cars and Trucks in Use

Age of vehicle (in years)

9, 8.5, 8, 7.5, 7, 6.5, 6, 5.5, 5, 4.5, 4

1979 '81 '83 '85 '87 '89 '91 '93 '95 '97 '99 2001

Cars Trucks

FIGURE 11.3 Line Chart with Positive and Negative Values on Vertical Axis

Net Operating Income/Loss of Santa Monica Studios
$40
30
20
10
0
–10
–20
–30
–40
Million $
1993
'94
'95
'96
'97
'98
'99
2000

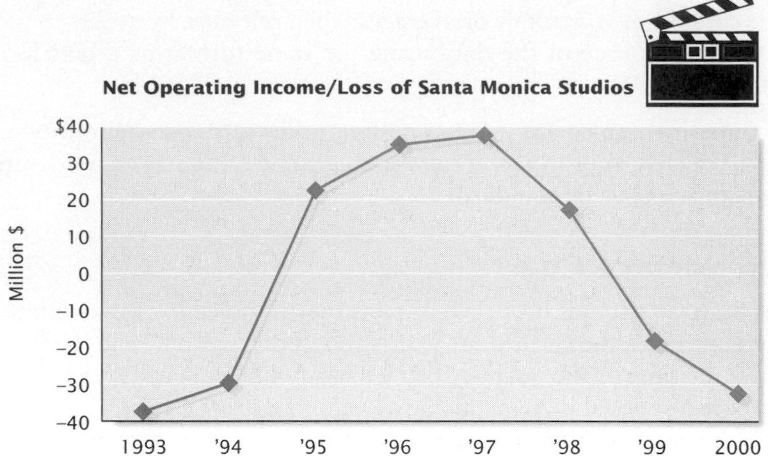

FIGURE 11.4 Surface Chart

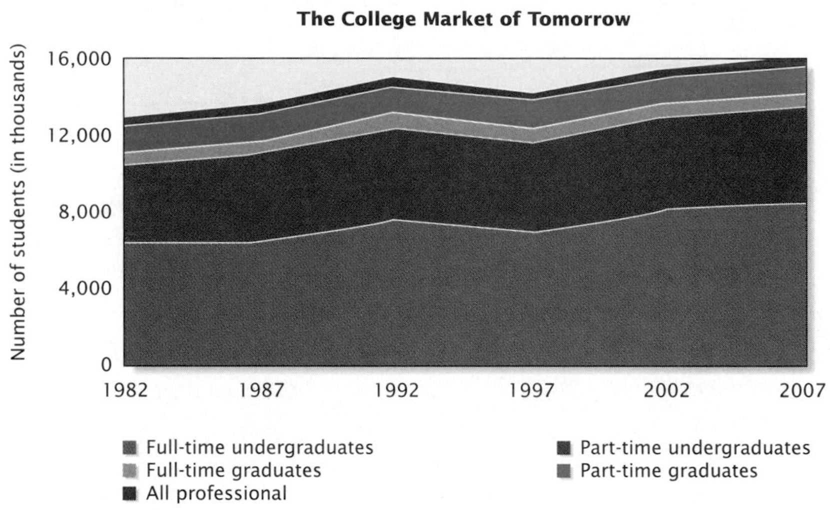

The College Market of Tomorrow
16,000
12,000
8,000
4,000
0
Number of students (in thousands)
1982
1987
1992
1997
2002
2007
Full-time undergraduates
Full-time graduates
All professional
Part-time undergraduates
Part-time graduates

Another variation of the simple line chart has a vertical axis with both positive and negative numbers (see Figure 11.3). This arrangement is handy when you have to illustrate losses.

A surface chart is a kind of line chart showing a cumulative effect.

A **surface chart**, also called an **area chart**, is a form of line chart with a cumulative effect; all the lines add up to the top line, which represents the total (see Figure 11.4). This form of chart helps you illustrate changes in the composition of something over time. When preparing a surface chart, put the most important segment against the baseline, and restrict the number of strata to four or five.

Bar Charts, Pictograms, and Gantt Charts

Bar charts, in which numbers are visually portrayed by rectangular bars, can take a variety of forms.

A **bar chart** portrays numbers by the height or length of its rectangular bars, making a series of numbers easy to read or understand. Bar charts are particularly valuable when you want to

- Compare the size of several items at one time
- Show changes in one item over time

- Indicate the composition of several items over time
- Show the relative size of components of a whole

As Figure 11.5 shows, bar charts can be singular (Where the College Students Are), grouped (Eating Occasions), deviation (Meadow Fresh Dairy), segmented (Targeted Talk), a combination of chart types (Commercial Superhighway—line and bar), and paired (Conference Attendance). Grouped bar charts compare more than one set of data (using a different color or pattern for each set). Segmented bar charts, also known as stacked bar charts, show how individual components contribute to a total number (using a different color or pattern for each component). Combination bar and line charts compare quantities that require different intervals. Paired bar charts show the correlations between two items. Deviation bar charts identify positive and negative values, or winners and losers.

Figure 11.5 shows that you can be creative with bar charts in many ways. You might align the bars either vertically or horizontally, or you might even use bar charts to show both positive and negative quantities. Be careful, however, to keep all the bars in the chart the same width; different widths could suggest a relative importance to the viewer. In addition, space the bars evenly and place them in a logical order, such as chronological or alphabetical. Keep in mind that most computer software (such as Microsoft Excel) will generate charts from data tables. The software will place the data in a chart based on the order that is used in the table. So plan ahead, and if you don't like the way the computer interprets your data graphically, go back to the data table and adjust the order there first.

You can also convert the bars into a line of symbols, with the number or length of symbols indicating the relative value of each item (see Figure 11.6 on page 346). A chart that uses symbols instead of words or numbers to portray data is known as a **pictogram**. The chief value of pictograms is their novelty and ability to convey a more literal, visual message. You can easily prepare pictograms by using software such as Excel and substituting a piece of clip art for the graphical bar. Although pictograms occasionally enhance a report, they tend to be less useful than other types of bar charts.

Pictograms use symbols instead of words or numbers to portray data.

Closely related to the bar chart is the **timeline chart**, which shows how much time is needed to complete each task in a given project. When you want to track progress toward completing a project, you can use a type of timeline chart known as a **Gantt chart** (named for management theorist Henry L. Gantt). The Gantt chart (see Figure 11.7 on page 346) shows the activities involved in designing the prototype and conducting the marketing research for product number 1575, which is running on schedule. The maroon bars indicate completed tasks; the blue bars indicate activities not yet completed; the black diamond is a milestone—in this case the prototype's due date.

Timeline charts show how much time is needed to complete a project's tasks.

Pie Charts

Like segmented bar charts and area charts, a **pie chart** shows how parts of a whole are distributed. Each segment represents a slice of a complete circle, or *pie*. As you can see in Figure 11.8 (on page 347), pie charts are an effective way to show percentages or to compare one segment with another. You can combine pie charts with tables to expand the usefulness of such visuals.

Use pie charts to show the relative sizes of the parts of a whole.

When composing pie charts, try to restrict the number of slices in the pie. Otherwise, the chart looks cluttered and is difficult to label. If necessary, lump the smallest pieces together in a "miscellaneous" category. Ideally, the largest or most important slice of the pie, the segment you want to emphasize, is placed at the twelve o'clock position; the rest are arranged clockwise either in order of size or in some other logical progression.

Use different colors or patterns to distinguish the various pieces. If you want to draw attention to the segment that is of the greatest interest to your readers, use a brighter color for that segment, draw an arrow to the segment, or explode it; that is, pull the segment away from the rest of the pie. In any case, label all the segments and indicate their value in either percentages or units of measure so that your readers will

FIGURE 11.5 The Versatile Bar Chart

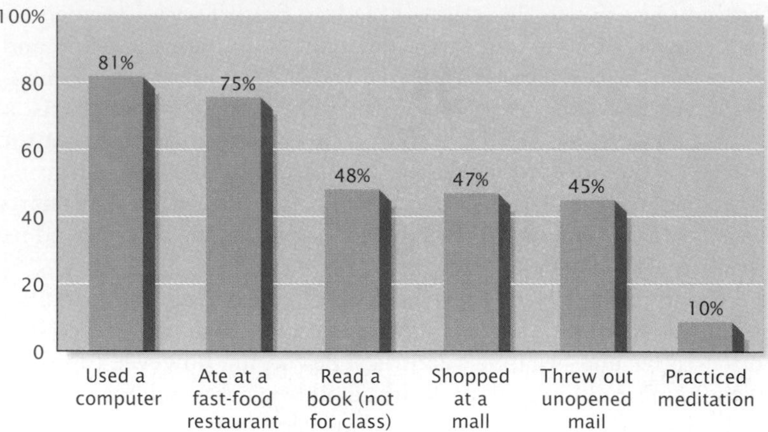

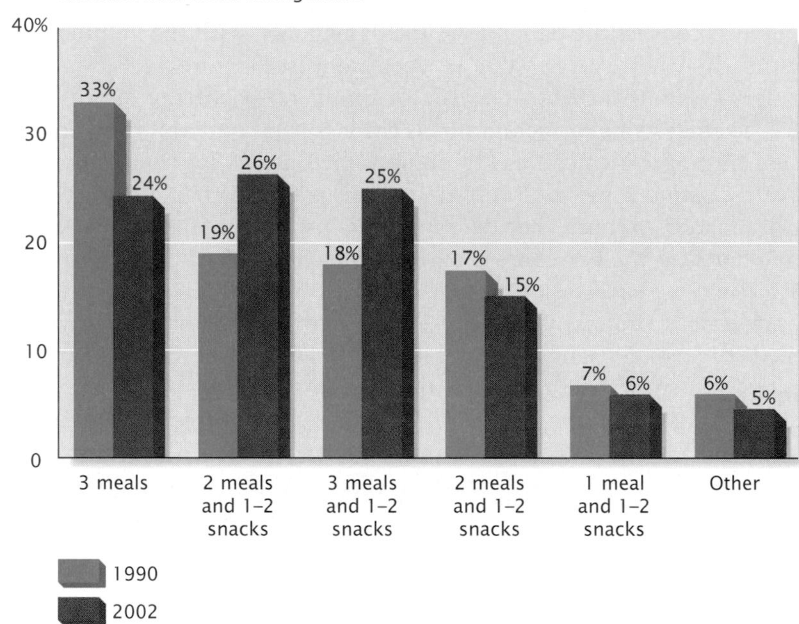

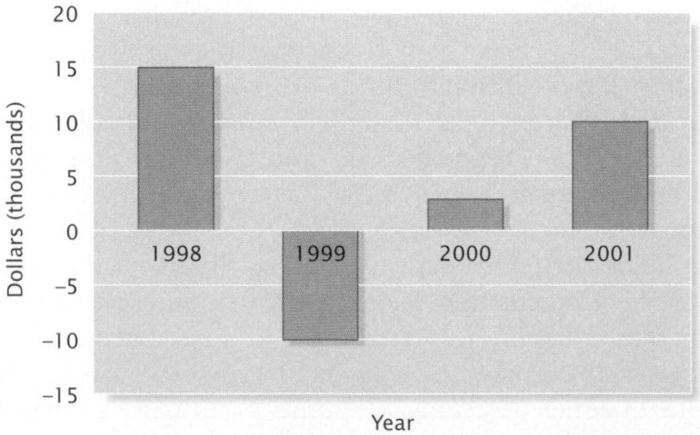

FIGURE 11.5 (Continued)

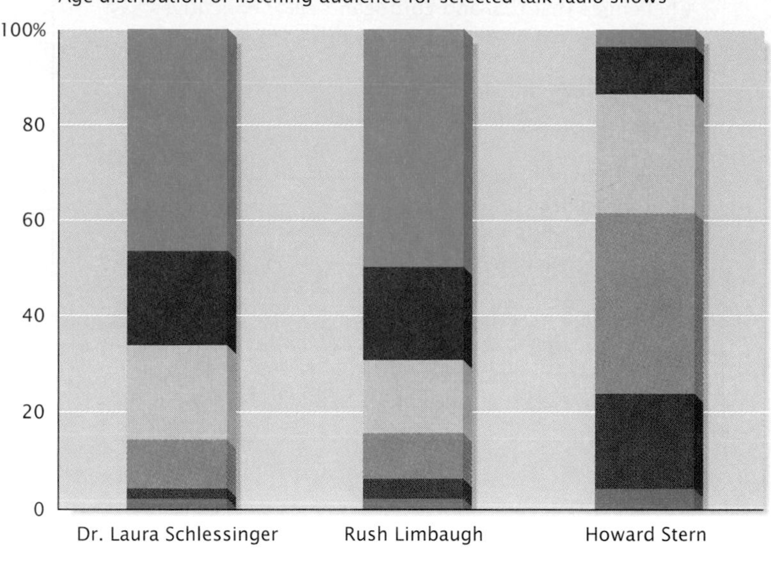

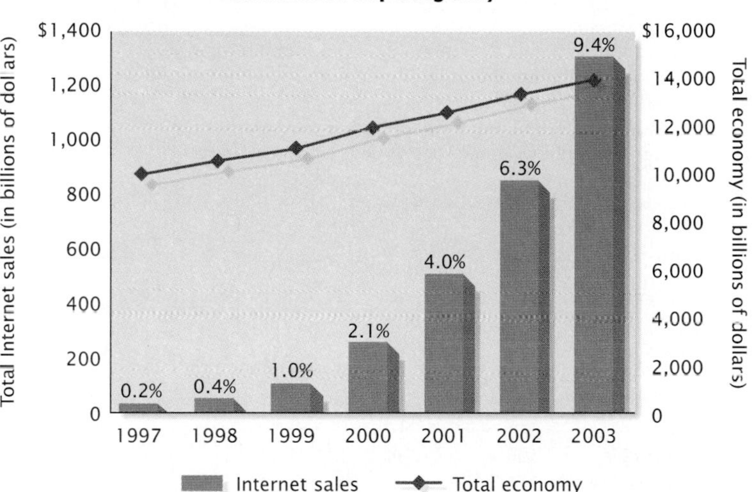

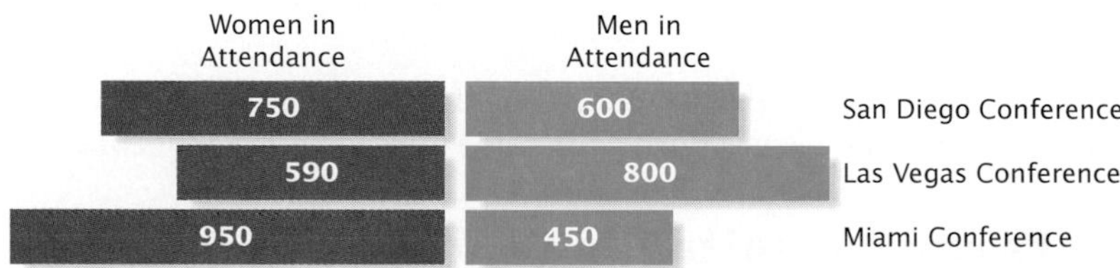

FIGURE 11.6 Pictogram

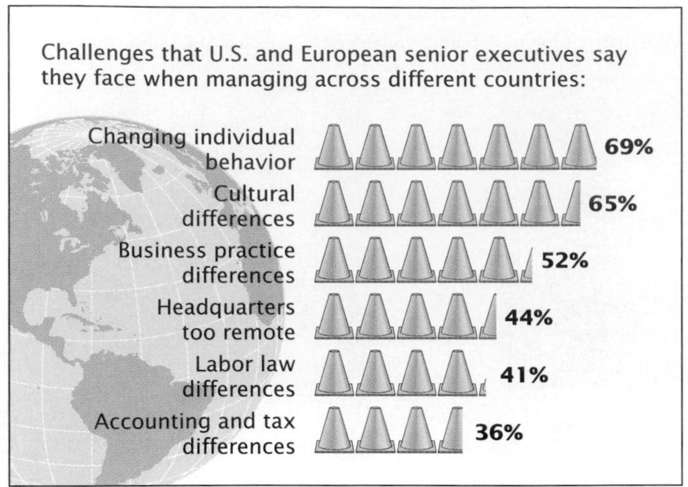

FIGURE 11.7 Gantt Chart

ID	Project Timeline for Product 1575	Start Date	End Date	Duration	Percent Complete	2001: June, July, August, September
1	**Design Phase**	**6/20/01**	**8/31/01**	**50d**	**90.00%**	
2	Design Project	6/20/01	7/31/01	30d	100.00	
3	Prototype Design	8/3/01	8/21/01	15d	100.00	
4	Test Prototype	8/24/01	8/28/01	5d	0.00	
5	Prototype Complete	8/31/01	8/31/01	0d	0.00	
6	**Marketing Research Phase**	**8/3/01**	**9/25/01**	**40d**	**25.00**	
7	Preliminary Research	8/3/01	8/7/01	5d	100.00	
8	Conduct Focus Groups	8/10/01	8/11/01	2d	100.00	
9	Interviews	8/12/01	8/14/01	3d	100.00	
10	Secondary Research	8/17/01	8/28/01	10d	0.00	
11	Create Business Plan	8/31/01	9/25/01	20d	0.00	

be able to judge the value of the wedges. Remember, the segments must add up to 100 percent if percentages are used or to the total number if numbers are used.

Flowcharts and Organization Charts

Use flowcharts
- To show a series of steps from beginning to end
- To show sequential relationships

If you need to show physical or conceptual relationships rather than numerical ones, you might want to use a flowchart or an organization chart. A **flowchart** illustrates a sequence of events from start to finish; it is indispensable when illustrating processes, procedures, and sequential relationships. The various elements in the process you want to portray may be represented by pictorial symbols or geometric shapes, as shown in Figure 11.9.

FIGURE 11.8 Pie Chart Combined with Table

Percentage of Time Spent Online by Age Group

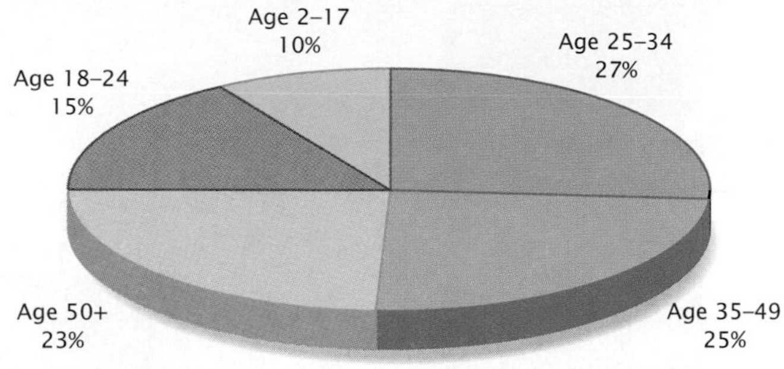

Age Group	Average Minutes per Month	Percent of Time by Age Group
Age 25–34	1642.4	27%
Age 35–49	1496.2	25%
Age 50+	1398.8	23%
Age 18–24	925.9	15%
Age 2–7	605.7	10%

FIGURE 11.9 Flowchart

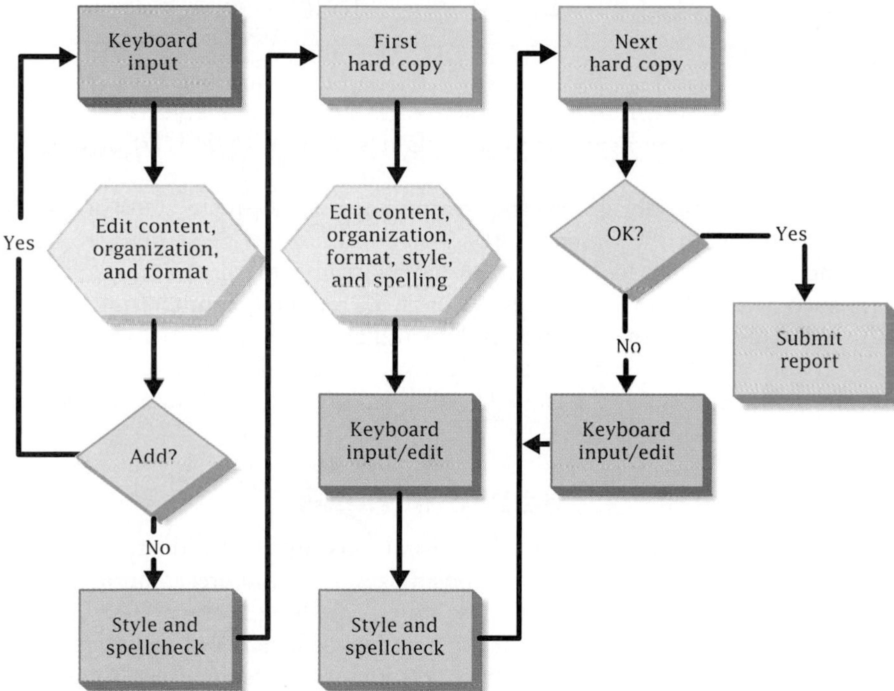

As the name implies, an **organization chart** illustrates the positions, units, or functions of an organization and the way they interrelate. An organization's normal communication channels are almost impossible to describe without the benefit of a chart like the one in Figure 11.10.

Use organization charts to depict the interrelationships among the parts of an organization.

Maps

For certain applications, maps are ideal. One of the most common uses is to show concentrations of something by geographic area. In your own reports, you might use

Use maps
- To represent statistics by geographic area
- To show location relationships

FIGURE 11.10 Organization Chart

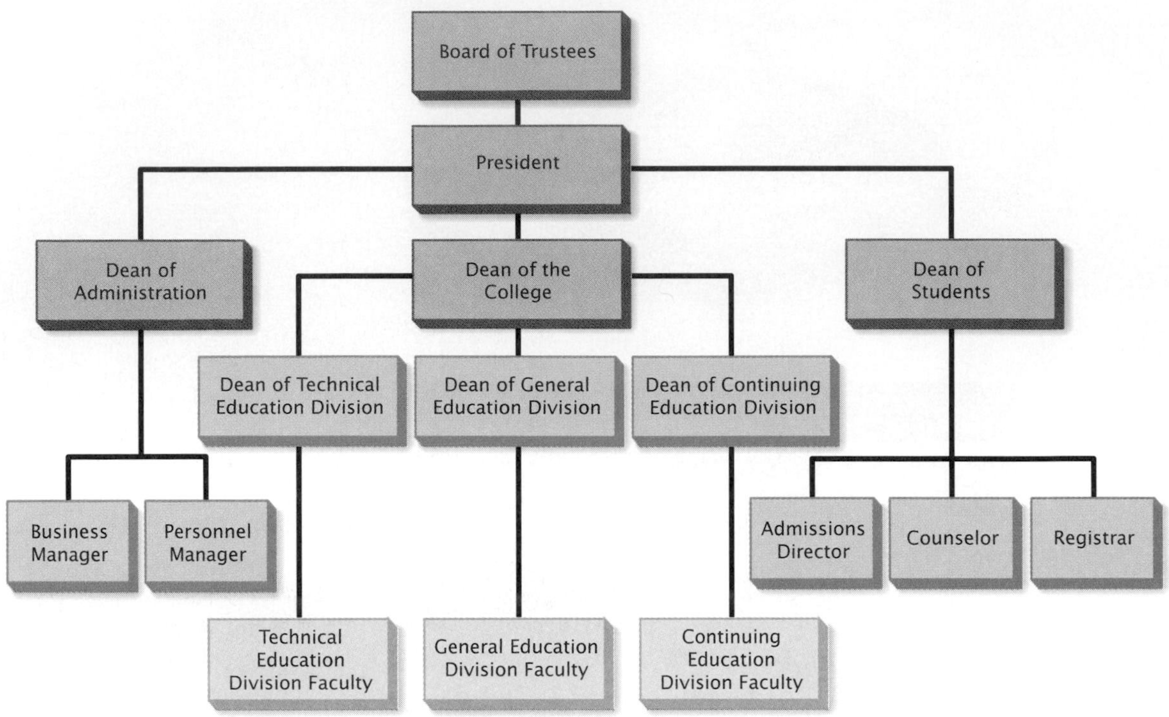

maps to show regional differences in such variables as your company's sales of a product, or you might indicate proposed plant sites and their relationship to key markets.

Most U.S. office supply stores carry blank maps of various regions of the world, including all or part of the United States. You can illustrate these maps to suit your needs, using dots, shading, color, labels, numbers, and symbols. In addition, popular software such as Excel and CorelDraw! come with regional, country, and world map templates. You just insert the columns of data and assign the data to a state or a country; the software will do the rest. Figure 11.11 was prepared using Excel's built-in map feature, the map template for the United States, and the projected state populations for 2025.

Drawings, Diagrams, and Photographs

Use drawings and diagrams to show
- How something looks or works
- How something is made or used

Although less commonly used than other visual aids, drawings, diagrams, and photographs can also be valuable elements in business reports and presentations. Drawings and diagrams are most often used to show how something looks or operates. Figure 11.12 was prepared using Visio software to explain the benefits of converged communication networks over traditional networks. Diagrams can be much clearer than words alone when it comes to giving your audience an idea of how an item looks or can be used. In industries such as engineering and architecture, computer-aided design (CAD) systems produce detailed diagrams and drawings. A variety of widely available software programs provide a file of symbols and pictures of various types that can be used (sparingly) to add a decorative touch to reports.

Use photographs
- For visual appeal
- To show exact appearance

Photographs have always been popular in certain types of business documents, such as annual reports, where their visual appeal is used to capture reader interest. As the technology for reproducing photographs improves and becomes less expensive, businesspeople are beginning to include photographs in more types of reports, even in analytical business reports for internal use. Digital cameras now make it easy to drop photographic images directly into a report or presentation. Furthermore, the collection

FIGURE 11.11 Map

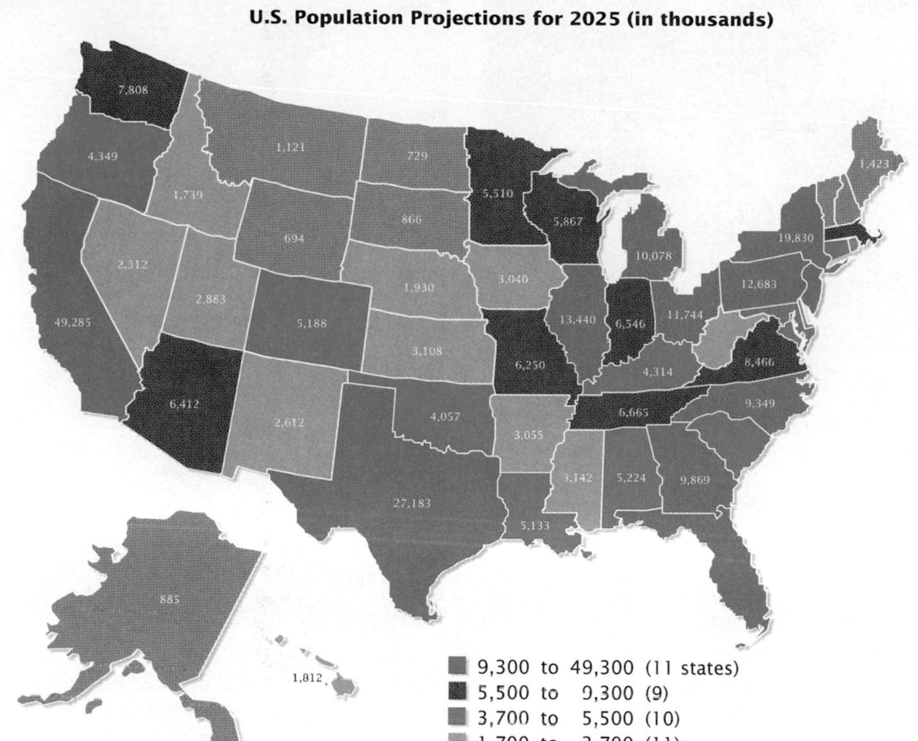

FIGURE 11.12 Diagram

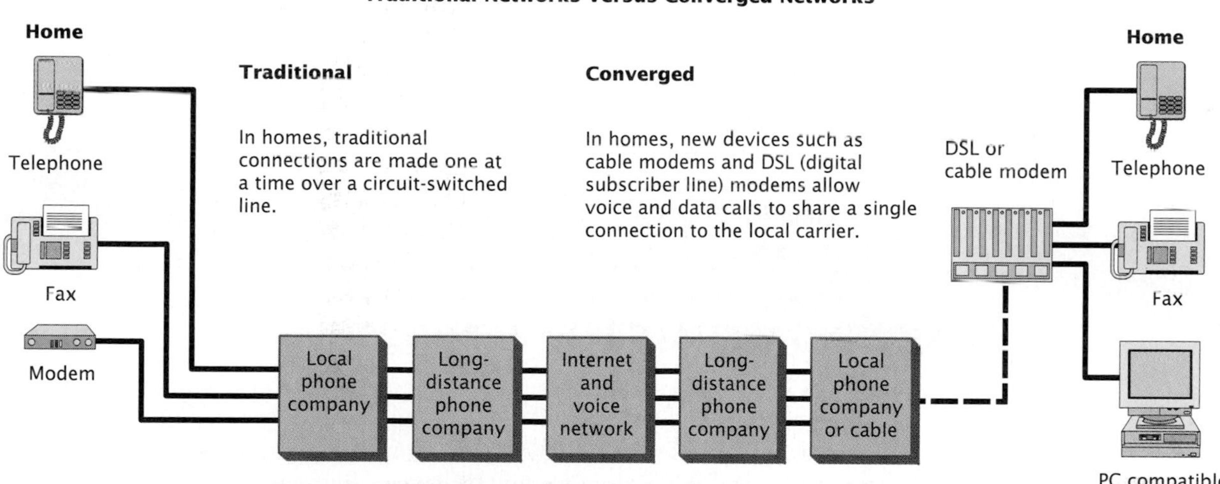

of available photographs that you can scan, import, crop, and clip grows daily. CD-ROMs provide an abundance of image libraries, and the Internet is another terrific resource for images. In most cases you can download pictures off the Internet for free; just be sure to give proper credit as you would for any material that you use from another source. To find specific photographs, images, or designs on the Internet, try the website AltaVista Photo Finder, image.altavista.com/cgi-bin/avncgi.

Nothing can demonstrate the exact appearance of a new facility, a piece of property or equipment, or a new product the way a photograph can. However, in some situations a photograph may show too much detail. This is one reason that repair manuals frequently use drawings instead of photos. With a drawing, you can select

With today's software you can digitally alter photos. In the photo on the right, the bakery has been given a complete name, the man's shirt has been changed to green, and a dog has been included. Is it ethical to change a photo without revealing the changes that were made to the original?

how much detail to show and focus the reader's attention on particular parts or places.

Technology makes it easier to use photographs in reports and presentations, but it also presents an important ethical concern. Software tools such as Photoshop and CorelDraw! make it easy for computer users to make dramatic changes to photos—without leaving a clue that they've been altered. Making small changes to photos has been possible for a long time (more than a few people have had blemishes airbrushed out of their yearbook photos), but computers make drastic changes easy and undetectable. You can remove people from photographs, put Person A's head on Person B's body, and make products look more attractive than they really are. As you do when using other technological tools, stop and ask yourself where the truth lies before you start making changes.[4]

DESIGNING VISUALS FOR REPORTS

Computer-graphics systems cut the time and cost involved in producing visuals.

Professional-looking graphics used to be extremely expensive and time-consuming to produce, but personal computer technology has changed all that. Graphics that used to cost hundreds of dollars and take several days to complete can now be done in minutes for little cost. Instead of relying on graphic designers, businesspeople are turning out their own professional-looking visual aids by turning to **computer graphics**: visuals created and produced using a computer program.

Creating Visuals with Computers

Presentation-graphics programs, drawing programs, painting programs, and spreadsheet programs can all be used to develop visuals.

With today's powerful computers, it's faster and easier than ever to produce good-looking visuals. You can create freehand drawings, manipulate existing images, and display numbers in graphic form using software programs such as CorelDraw!, PowerPoint, Photoshop, Painter, Excel, Lotus 1-2-3, and Visio—to name just a few.

Aside from speed, accuracy, and ease of use, another big advantage of using software to prepare visuals is the ability to save the results and use the visuals over and over again in various reports. If you spend a lot of time working with numbers, you'll find that a spreadsheet program such as Excel is particularly handy because it can serve as both an analytical tool and a communication tool. As you enter numerical data into the spreadsheet, you can use the software program to automatically calculate trend lines and growth curves. Later on, if you change the data or enter additional data, the program will automatically redraw the charts to reflect any changes. For example, if you track sales or profits by month, you can easily add the latest month's figures to your spreadsheet and create a new chart showing the cumulative pattern. (You'll want to save the new chart under a different file name so that you can preserve earlier charts.)

A computer-graphics system does more than draw charts; it also enhances your analytical capabilities.

For all the power and possibilities they offer, computer-graphics tools are not without some potential drawbacks. Using this equipment efficiently and effectively requires skills that many businesspeople lack, including the ability to use hardware and software and to make good design decisions. Many software products have become easier to use, but most continue to offer more and more options—type of chart, color and design of the background, typefaces, line weights, and so on. Most businesspeople lack the visual arts training to make informed design decisions; moreover, making all those choices takes time.

Fortunately, many graphics software programs can simplify the situation by making many of these decisions for you. Some products provide *templates* (prepared designs), clip art, and wizards (automated design generators). You simply fill in the blanks with the information you want, and the software makes all the design choices for you. However, be careful with templates. Even though they are designed by professional graphic artists, some are "overdesigned" and inappropriate for serious business uses, and some clutter the image with overly fancy borders and backgrounds that can distract the audience from the real message.

Before you take advantage of any computer-graphics tools, think about the kind of image you want to project. The style of your visuals communicates a subtle message about your relationship with the audience. A simple, hand-drawn diagram is fine for a working meeting but inappropriate for a formal presentation or report. On the other hand, elaborate, full-color visuals may be viewed as extravagant for an informal memo but may be entirely appropriate for a message to top management or influential outsiders. The image you want to project should determine the visual you create (see "Keeping Pace with Technology: Six Easy Ways to Create Eye-Catching Charts with Excel").

A visual's level of sophistication should match the communication situation.

Understanding Graphic Design Principles

Although you may not think of yourself as being the "artistic type," chances are you have a better sense of design than you realize. Most people seem to subconsciously recognize good design when they see it, even if they don't know how to achieve the same effects on their own.[5]

Best of the Web

Brush Up on Your Computer-Graphics Skills

Need some help using graphics software? Get started at the About.com graphics software website. Take the tutorials and learn how to manage fonts, images, and a variety of graphics-related tasks. View the illustrated demonstrations. Read the instructional articles. Learn how to use the most common file formats for graphics. Expand your knowledge of the basic principles of graphic design. And master some advanced color tips and theory. Don't leave without following the links to recommended books and magazines. Brushing up on design skills is a snap at this website.

graphicssoft.about.com

Keeping Pace with Technology

Six Easy Ways to Create Eye-Catching Charts with Excel

Excel's Chart Wizard is a convenient way to create good-looking charts. But if you want to produce eye-catching charts, edit the software's default selections by following these six tips:

- **Add some attention-getting text boxes.** Text boxes are an effective way to highlight key numbers or to explain anomalies in your data. To add text boxes, select the chart's plot area and just start typing. Excel automatically creates a text box. Once you've added the desired text box, you can move it anywhere on the chart and reformat it to your liking.
- **Modify the format of your titles and text.** The default font size for titles and other text objects on a chart is 10 points. Typically, 10-point chart titles are too small and 10-point legends are too large. To modify the font size, typeface, and type styles of your titles or text elements, select the element by clicking on it; then use the Format menu as you would with word-processing software. If you select the entire chart area, your formatting changes will apply to all text elements. To format a specific element such as the chart title or legend, click on that specific element. (Note: to change the text format of your axis points, you must double-click on an *x* or a *y* axis point.)
- **Adjust gridline settings.** Gridlines help readers see where data points cross category or value axes. Excel sets default gridlines at major axis points. To change the gridline intervals, click on any gridline to select the gridline chart element. Then choose Selected Gridlines from the Format menu and click on the Scale tab. Remove the checkmark in the major unit box, and reset the interval number. Experiment with several different settings and preview the results.
- **Add data labels to your values.** If you want category labels, worksheet values, or percentages to appear next to each point in a data series, check the "show value" button on the Chart Options screen under the Chart menu.
- **Add background color or change the color of a chart element.** The default background color for Excel charts is white. To change the color of the background or the color of a chart element, click on the chart's plot area or the individual element to select it, then right-click your mouse. Select a color under the "area" section of the dialog box. To choose a gradient or other fill effect, select the Fill Effects button and choose the Gradient, Texture, Pattern, or Picture tab.
- **Create a pictogram.** To change a bar chart into a pictogram, select the bars with your mouse and then right-click the mouse to access the Format Data Series dialog box. Select Fill Effects, the Picture tab, and Select Picture button. Search your hard drive or software disks for an appropriate picture or piece of clip art and insert. Click the Stack radio button in the Format dialog box and enter OK twice.

Career Applications

1. Use the Excel Wizard to create a line chart depicting annual sales for Sunshine Gardening Service. Enhance your chart by using the tips just discussed.
   Annual sales: 1995: $73,684; 1996: $65,028; 1997: $80,145; 1998: $81,478; 1999: $70,386; 2000: $90,608; 2001: $85,476.
2. Convert the Sunshine Gardening Service line chart to a bar chart. Create a pictogram.

Few of us have studied the "language" of line, mass, space, size, color, pattern, and texture. When arranged in certain ways, these elements of visual design are pleasing to the eye. More important for the business communicator, however, design elements have a meaning of their own. A thick line implies more power than a thin one; a deep-shaded color suggests strength; a solid mass seems substantial. To create effective visuals, become conscious of both the aesthetic and the symbolic aspects of graphic art so that you won't send the wrong message. Here are a few principles to be aware of:

The elements of design convey meaning in subtle ways.

Learning Objective 4

Discuss five principles of graphic design to keep in mind when preparing visuals

When designing visuals, observe the principles of continuity, contrast, emphasis, simplicity, and experience.

- **Continuity.** Readers view a series of visuals as a whole, assuming that design elements will be consistent from one page to the next. For instance, if your first chart shows results for Division A in blue, the audience will expect Division A to be shown in blue throughout the report or presentation. You'll confuse people if you make arbitrary changes in color, shape, size, texture, position, scale, or typeface.
- **Contrast.** Readers expect visual distinctions to match verbal ones. To emphasize differences, depict items in contrasting colors, such as red and blue, or black and white. But to emphasize similarities, make color difference more subtle. In a pie chart, you might show two similar items in two shades of blue and a dissimilar item in yellow. When using similar colors, consider using shaded colors (also called *graduated* or *variant* colors) to allow one color to dissolve into the next, giving it an airbrush effect in addition to dimension or depth. Keep in mind that accent colors draw attention to key elements, but they lose their effect if you overdo them.
- **Emphasis.** Readers assume that the most important point will receive the greatest visual emphasis. So present the key item on the chart in the most prominent way—through color, position, size, or whatever. Visually downplay less important items. Avoid using strong colors for unimportant data, and de-emphasize background features such as the grid lines on a chart.
- **Simplicity.** Limit the number of colors and design elements you use, and take care to avoid *chartjunk,* decorative elements that clutter documents (and confuse readers) without adding any relevant information.[6] Computers make it far too easy to add chartjunk, from clip art illustrations to three-dimensional bar charts that display only two dimensions of data. The two charts in Figure 11.13 show the same information, but the second one is cluttered with useless decoration. The three-dimensional bars don't show anything more than the simple two-dimensional bars in the first chart.
- **Experience.** Culture and education condition people to expect things to look a certain way, including visuals. For example, green may be associated with money in the United States, but not in countries whose currency is red or blue or yellow. A red cross on a white background stands for emergency medical care in many countries. But the cross is also a Christian symbol, so the International Red Cross uses a red crescent in Islamic countries.[7]

The use of color in visuals accelerates learning, retention, and recall by 55 percent to 78 percent, and it increases motivation and audience participation up to 80 percent.

The best time to think about the principles of good design is before preparing your visuals; making changes after the fact increases the amount of time required to produce them.

Fitting Visuals into the Text

Your approach to integrating text and visuals depends on the type of report you're preparing. If you're working on a glossy public relations document, handle the visuals as though they were illustrations in a magazine, positioning them to attract interest and tell a story of their own. However, in most business documents, the visuals clarify the

To tie visuals to the text
- Introduce them in the text
- Place them near the points they illustrate
- Choose a meaningful title and legend for each one

FIGURE 11.13 Simplify Graphics to Avoid Clutter and Confusion

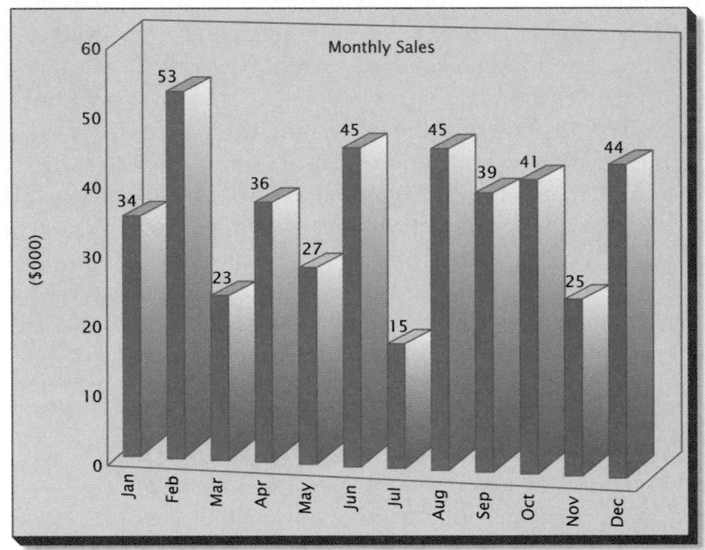

text, so tie them closely to the discussion. Integrate your visuals into text in a manner that is convenient for your audience and practical from a production standpoint.

Introduce Visuals in the Text

Every visual you use should be clearly referred to by number in the text of your report. Some report writers refer to all visuals as "exhibits" and number them consecutively throughout the report; many others number tables and figures separately (everything that isn't a table is regarded as a figure). In a very long report with numbered chapters (as in this book), illustrations may have a double number (separated by a period or a hyphen) representing the chapter number and the individual illustration number within that chapter.

In-text references tell readers why the illustration is important.

Help your readers understand the significance of visuals by referring to them before they appear in the text. The reference helps readers understand why the table or chart is important. The following examples show how you can make this connection in the text:

> Figure 1 summarizes the financial history of the motorcycle division over the past five years, with sales broken into four categories.

> Total sales were steady over this period, but the mix of sales by category changed dramatically (see Figure 2).
>
> The underlying reason for the remarkable growth in our sales of low-end fax machines is suggested by Table 4, which provides data on fax machine sales in the United States by region and model.

When describing the data shown in your visual aids, be sure to emphasize the main point you are trying to make. Don't make the mistake of simply repeating the data to be shown. Paragraphs like this are guaranteed to put the reader to sleep:

> Among women who replied to the survey, 17.4 percent earn less than $5 per hour; 26.4 percent earn $5–$7; 25.7 percent, $8–$12; 18.0 percent, $13–$24; 9.6 percent, $25–$49; and 2.9 percent, $50 and over.

The visual will provide these details; there is no need to repeat them in the text. Instead, use round numbers that sum up the message:

> Over two-thirds of the women who replied earn less than $12 per hour.

At Chapwell Marketing Resources, graphics play an important role not only in clients' projects but also in the company's own annual report. "It's worth the effort to learn how to incorporate effective visuals," says Ted Chapwell, founding partner (seated) along with Mark Wellington. "There's no better way to enhance a good report."

Place Visuals Near the Points They Illustrate

Try to position your visuals so that your audience won't have to flip back and forth too much between the visuals and the text. Ideally, it's best to place each visual right beside or right after the paragraph it illustrates so that readers can consult the explanation and the visual at the same time. Make sure each visual is clearly and correctly referred to in the text. If you have four or more visuals, prepare a separate list that can be placed with the table of contents at the front of the report. Some writers list tables separately from figures. The two lists should start on separate pages unless both lists will fit on the same page.

Most word-processing programs and desktop publishing systems let you create layouts with artwork and text on the same page. If you don't have these programs, or choose not to integrate your visuals with text, then put the visuals on separate pages and include them with the text after the report has been prepared. Having visuals on separate pages raises the question of where to put them. Some writers prefer to cluster them at the end of the report, either in a separate section or as an appendix. Others group them at the end of each chapter. Still others prefer to place them as close as possible to the paragraphs they illustrate. Although a case can be made for each approach, the best one is generally to place the page with the visual right after the page referring to it. This arrangement encourages readers to look at the visuals when you want them to, in the context you have prepared.

Place a visual as close as possible to its in-text reference to help readers understand the illustration's relevance.

Choose Titles and Legends with a Message

One of the best ways to tie your visuals to the text is to choose titles (or captions) and descriptions (or legends) that reinforce the point you want to make. This precaution is especially necessary when the visuals are widely separated from the text.

Titles and legends should
- Reinforce the point you want to make
- Be specific

When combined with labels and legends on the piece itself, the title of a visual aid should be complete enough to tell the reader what the content is. The title "Petroleum Tanks in the United States" is sufficient if it's the title of a line chart labeled "Year" along the horizontal axis and "Number (in thousands)" along the vertical axis. However, if the visual is a map overlaid with dots of different sizes, the title needs to explain a bit more: "Concentrations of Petroleum Tanks in the United States in 2002." A legend might then explain how many petroleum tanks each size of dot represents.

When you place a visual next to the text discussion that pertains to it, clear labeling and a good title are usually enough; the text can explain the visual's significance and details. However, when you place a visual elsewhere or when the illustration requires considerable explanation that would disrupt the flow of the text, you may need to add a legend to the visual. Legends are generally written as one or more complete sentences, and they do more than merely repeat what's already clear from the

Use a legend if an explanation of the illustration would disrupt the flow of the text.

title and figure labels. It's better to be too specific than too general when you're identifying the content of an illustration. As a check, ask yourself whether you've covered the who, what, when, where, why, and how of the illustration.

If you're using informative headings in your report, carry this style over into the titles and legends. Instead of using a **descriptive title**, which identifies the topic of the illustration, call attention to the conclusion that ought to be drawn from the data by using an **informative title**. Here's the difference:

Descriptive Title	Informative Title
Relationship Between Petroleum Demand and Refinery Capacity in the United States	Shrinking Refinery Capacity Results from Stagnant Petroleum Demand

Regardless of whether your titles and legends are informative or descriptive, phrase them consistently throughout the report. At the same time, be consistent in your format. If the title of the first visual is typed entirely in capital letters, type all the remaining titles that way as well. Although an employer may specify the placement of titles, as a general rule place all table titles at the top. Figure titles may be placed at the top or the bottom. When using legends, make them all roughly the same length. (For a review of the important points to remember when creating visuals, see this chapter's "Checklist: Creating Effective Visuals.")

Checking Over Visuals

Learning Objective 5

Name four qualities to look for before including a visual in a report or presentation

Any visuals that you have included are present to help your readers absorb, understand, and accept your message. Their appearance is crucial to your message's success, so be sure to check visuals for mistakes such as typographical errors, inconsistent color treatment, and misaligned elements. Also take a few extra minutes to make sure that your visuals are necessary, absolutely accurate, properly documented, and honest.

Is the Visual Necessary?

Avoid cluttering a report with too many visual aids; make sure each visual serves a specific purpose.

A few well-placed visuals can clarify and dramatize your message, but an avalanche of illustrations may bury it. Avoid the temptation to overload your reports with unnecessary tables, graphs, and charts. Remember that your audience is busy. Don't give people information they don't need simply because you want to impress them or because you've fallen in love with your computer's graphics capabilities.

✓ CHECKLIST: CREATING EFFECTIVE VISUALS

A. *Preparation*

1. Select the proper types of graphics for the data and for the objective of the message.
2. Be sure the visual contributes to overall understanding of the subject.
3. Depict data accurately.
4. Convey one message per chart.
5. Portray information honestly.
6. Give proper credit, if required, and follow proper bibliographic form.
7. Make sure that the material is appropriate for the intended audience.

B. *Design*

1. Make design elements consistent.
2. Make sure that design elements meet audience expectations.
3. Use color effectively.
4. Emphasize important points.
5. Make visuals simple and easy to understand.
6. Make headings, labels, titles, and legends clear, whether descriptive or informative.
7. Use space appropriately.
8. Clearly identify data units so that they are easily understandable.
9. Use typefaces and fonts that are clear and readable.
10. Use clip art sparingly.
11. Eliminate all unnecessary details.

C. *Layout*

1. Balance words and visuals.
2. Clearly reference illustrations in text.
3. Assign each illustration a number or letter.
4. Place visuals close to the points they illustrate.
5. Make sure that visuals appear balanced on the page.
6. Make captions short, precise, and informative.

Is the Visual Accurate?

Make sure that every number is correct. Verify that every line is plotted accurately and that every scale is drawn to reflect reality. Be sure that every bit of information included in a visual is consistent with what is said in the text. When you're proofreading, be sure to check each visual's source notes and content notes for accuracy.

Proof visuals as carefully as you proof text.

Is the Visual Properly Documented?

You may be the creator of the actual graphic design, but if you use someone else's data, you need to give credit by citing the source of any data you use in creating a visual. Identify the actual source of data (such as the name of the journal the information came from) or refer simply to the nature of the information (for example, "interviews with 50 soybean farmers"). If the data displayed in a visual are "primary" (you gathered the information for your own purposes), then say so. To avoid cluttering your graphic, you could use a shortened citation on the graphic itself and include a complete citation elsewhere in the report.

Cite the source of any data you use to create the visual.

Is the Visual Honest?

With visuals, you can have all the numbers right and still give your audience a false impression. Charts tend to oversimplify some numerical relationships. But deliberately leaving out important information is highly unethical (see "Focusing on Ethics: Visuals That Lie"). Don't leave out data points that don't fit your needs. And don't omit any outside influences on the data you're portraying.

The scale of a chart can also introduce distortion. As Figure 11.14 illustrates, you can transform modest results into dramatic ones by compressing the horizontal scale or by expanding the vertical scale. But when you do so, you abandon good business ethics and mislead your audience in the process. So choose a scale that conveys a realistic picture of what's happening. Likewise, maintain the same scale in successive charts comparing the same factors.

To prevent your charts and visuals from creating a false impression, be sure to

- Include all key data points
- Mention any important outside influence on the data
- Maintain a consistent scale of measurement

FIGURE 11.14 The Impact of Scale on the Slope of a Curve

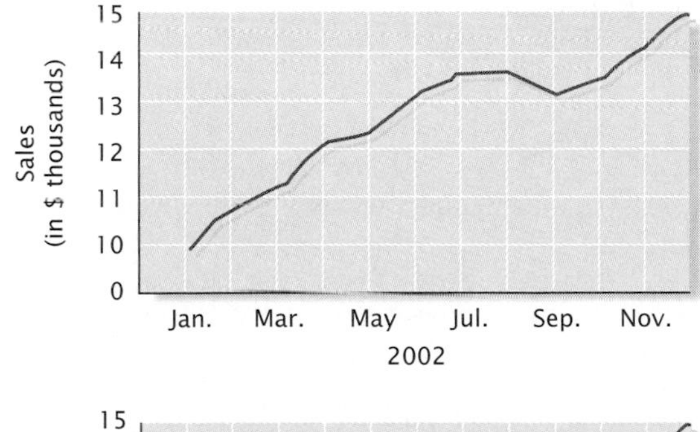

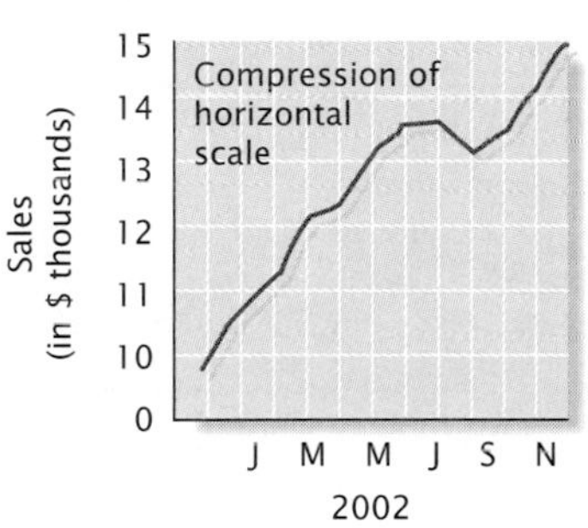

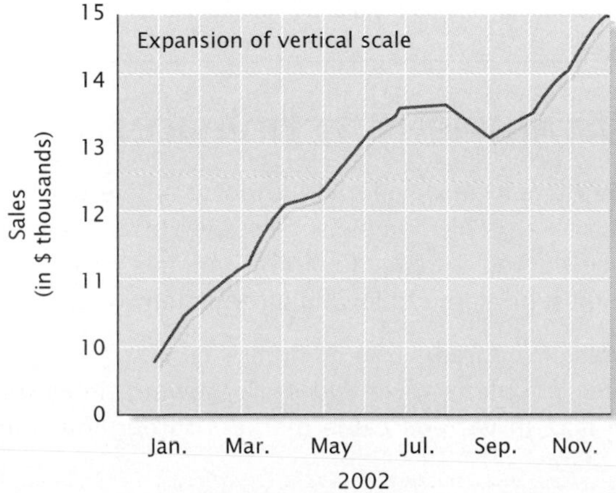

Focusing on Ethics

Visuals That Lie

The ease with which computers help people create visual displays of numerical information raises some important ethical issues. Here's a quick example of how easy it is to obscure information or otherwise mislead an audience (data in this example are all fictional). The line chart in Chart A shows the number of insecticide poisionings by age from 0 to 20. Chart B shows the same data, with one crucial difference: The vertical axis is scaled to fit the data. By expanding the axis way beyond the data, Chart A can create the impression that accident levels are far below the "maximum."

Chart C demonstrates another way graphs can "lie." By showing incidence levels for just four ages, the chart hides the facts that 4- and 5-year-olds suffered the most poisonings and that more 3-, 4-, and 5-year-olds died from poisioning than victims in any other age group. Six-year-olds *appear* to be the age hardest hit, but they aren't.

When it comes to presenting information, a good way to make ethical decisions is to ask what the audience needs to know in order to make an informed choice. If the audience needs the information, you need to show it.

Career Applications

1. How might your choice of a base unit affect your reader's perception of progress when viewing a Gantt chart?
2. Can you construct a pie chart from data that have been rounded up to equal more than 100 percent? Explain.

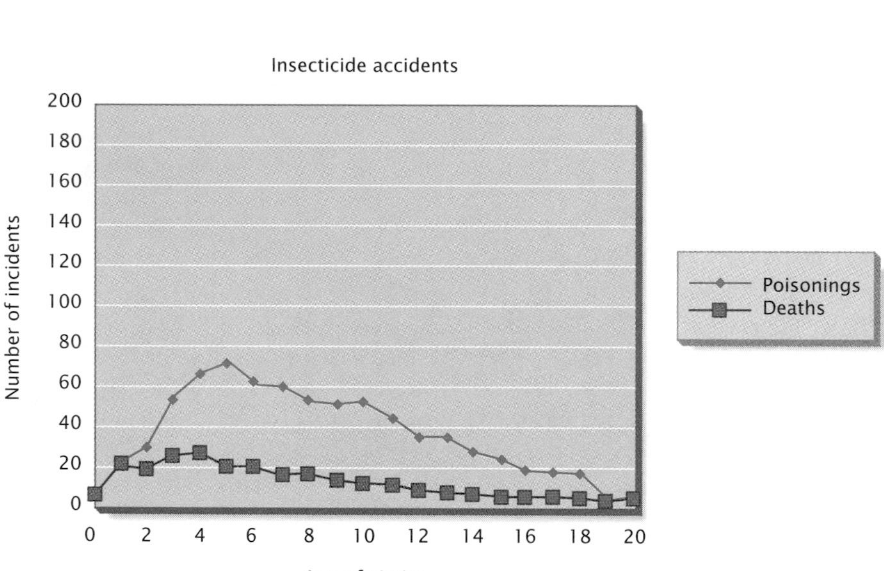

COMMUNICATION CHALLENGES AT BLACK ENTERTAINMENT TELEVISION

Jazz music is known around the world as a truly original American art form. Noticing a programming opportunity, BET Holdings developed a unique cable network called BET on Jazz. The network offers a wide range of jazz-related programming, including videos, documentaries, and talk shows. Recently, a major cable television service provider in the western United States approached BET about including BET on Jazz in its network offerings. Curtis Symonds has asked you to take the lead in developing an informative written report to be sent to cable company executives. The financial details will be worked out later. For now, Symonds wants you to focus on presenting the following information:

- The types of programs offered on BET on Jazz
- The most popular shows and peak viewing times for BET on Jazz in various cable markets throughout the United States

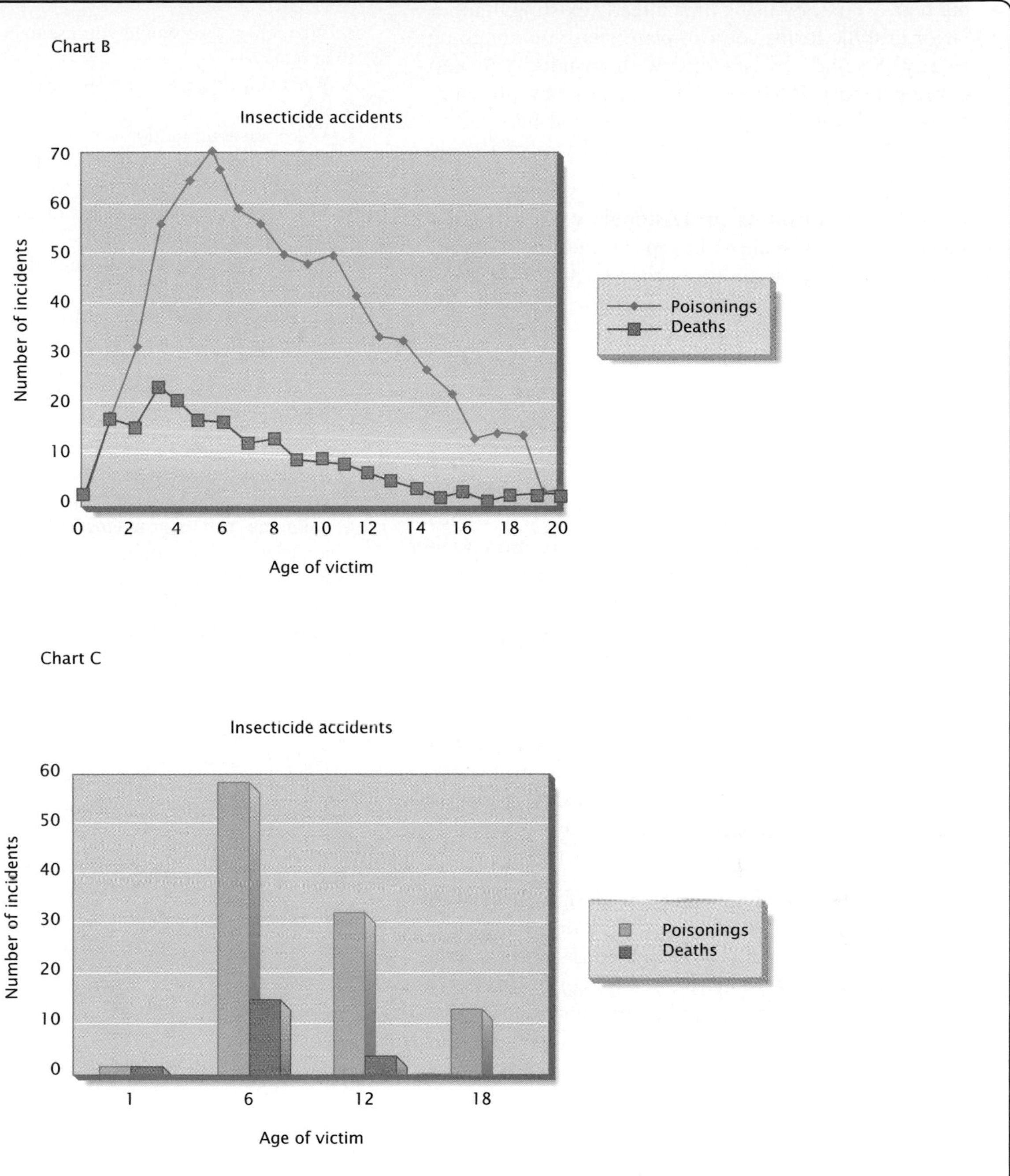

- The types of sponsors who advertise on BET on Jazz in local markets
- The annual growth of jazz music sales on the West Coast over the past 20 years
- The total estimated number of West Coast viewers for BET on Jazz
- The growth in popularity of music programming on cable television in the United States over the past 20 years

Individual Challenge: Select the best chart to depict each of these scenarios and construct the charts by making up any data you need.

Team Challenge: Working in small groups, and using the design principles highlighted in this chapter, critique the charts produced by each team member. Then working together, develop an introductory sentence to call out each visual before it appears in a written report.[8] ■

SUMMARY OF LEARNING OBJECTIVES

1 Cite the advantages of preparing visuals before preparing text. First, by using data already existing in tabular or graphic form, you can plan what you are going to say. Second, by starting with visuals, you can develop a story line for both written and oral presentations. Finally, it's easier to refer to your visuals and to explain them effectively in your text if you've already prepared them.

2 Explain why business professionals use charts and other visuals. Visuals make reports and presentations more interesting. In addition, they facilitate the communication and interpretation of numbers, trends, distributions, and percentages. Furthermore, they help people understand and remember a message. And finally, they help you draw attention to important points.

3 List several popular types of visuals and discuss when to use them. Tables communicate facts and detail in an easy-to-read format. Line charts illustrate trends over time or plot the relationships of two or more variables. Surface charts illustrate the cumulative effect of trends. Bar charts and pictograms portray numbers by the height or length of their rectangular bars and facilitate comparisons of size in addition to showing changes over time. Gantt charts track progress toward completing a project. Pie charts show percentages or how the parts of a whole are distributed. Flowcharts illustrate a sequence of events. Organization charts illustrate positions and functions in an organization. Maps show concentrations by geographic area. Drawings or diagrams show how something looks or operates.

4 Discuss five principles of graphic design to keep in mind when preparing visuals. When preparing visuals, you (1) use elements of design consistently so you don't confuse your audience; (2) use color effectively to show contrasting or similar information; (3) use design elements to draw attention to key elements and to visually downplay less important items; (4) avoid clutter; and (5) try to match design selections with audience expectations, such as green for U.S. currency.

5 Name four qualities to look for before including a visual in a report or presentation. Before finalizing a visual, ask yourself these four questions: (1) Is it necessary? In other words, does it help explain the material? (2) Is it accurate? (3) Does it give proper credit by citing the source of any data used to create the visual? (4) Is it honest? In other words, does it portray the data without distorting it or giving false impressions?

TEST YOUR KNOWLEDGE

1. What chart type would you use to compare one part with a whole?
2. What chart type would you use to present detailed, exact values?
3. What chart type would you use to compare one item with another?
4. What chart type would you use to illustrate trends over time?
5. When are combination bar and line charts used?
6. For what purposes are Gantt charts used?
7. How does a flowchart differ from an organization chart?
8. What are the advantages and disadvantages of using computers to create charts?
9. What is the purpose of adding titles and legends to visuals in reports?
10. How do you check a visual for accuracy?

APPLY YOUR KNOWLEDGE

1. What similarities do you see between visuals and nonverbal communication? Explain your answer.
2. You're writing a report to the director of human resources on implementing participative management throughout your company. You want to emphasize that since the new approaches were implemented six months ago, absenteeism and turnovers have been sharply reduced in all but two departments. How do you visually present your data in the most favorable light? Explain.
3. Besides telling readers why an illustration is important, why refer to it in the text of your document?
4. When you read a graph, how can you be sure that the visual impression you are receiving is an accurate reflection of reality? Please explain.
5. **Ethical Choices** What ethical issue is raised by the use of technology to alter photographs in reports?

PRACTICE YOUR KNOWLEDGE

Documents for Analysis

Document 11.A

Examine the pie charts in Figure 11.15 and point out any problems or errors you notice.

Document 11.B

Examine the line chart in Figure 11.16 and point out any problems or errors you notice.

Exercises

For live links to all websites discussed in this chapter, visit this text's website at www.prenhall.com/bovee. Just log on, select Chapter 11, and click on "Student Resources." Locate the name of the site or the URL related to the material in the text. For the "Exploring the Best of the Web" exercises, you'll also find navigational directions. Click on the live link to the site.

11.1 **Preparing Pie Charts** As a market researcher for a statewide chain of car dealerships, you're examining car and truck ownership and lease patterns among single drivers in various age groups. By discovering which age groups have the highest percentages of owners, you will

FIGURE 11.15 Pie Charts for Analysis

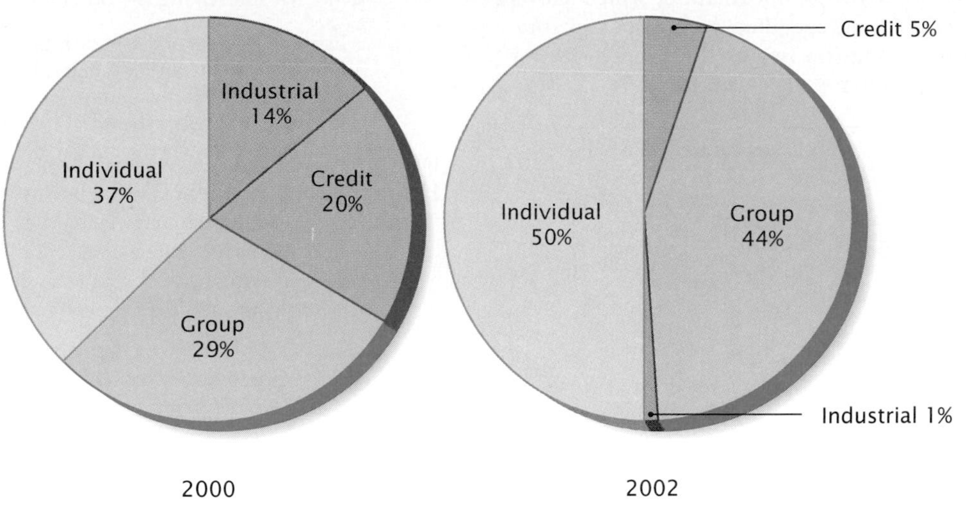

FIGURE 11.16 Line Chart for Analysis

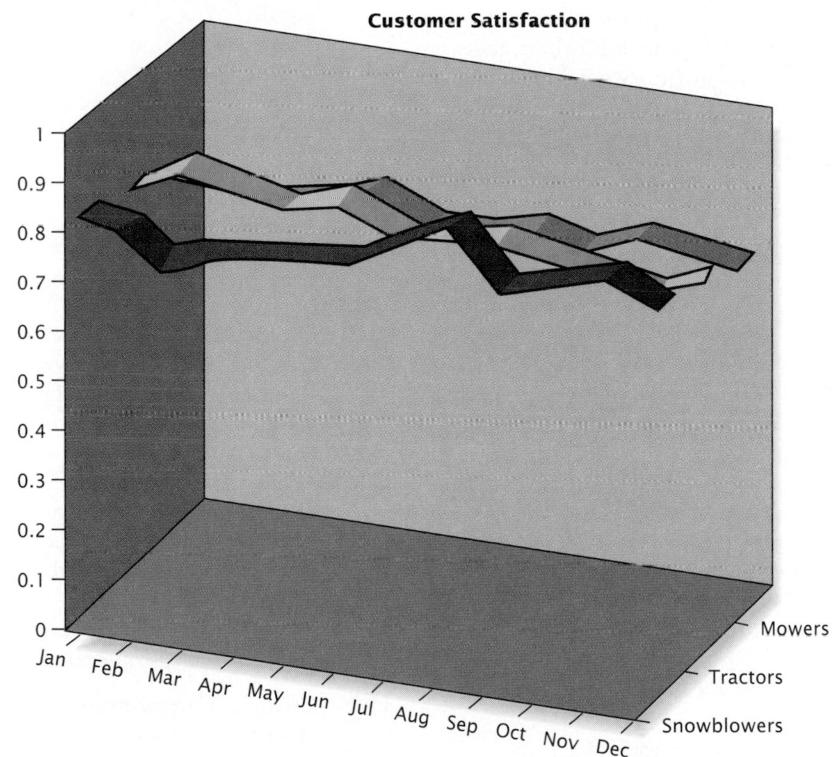

be better able to target advertising that promotes the leasing option. Using the following information, prepare a bar chart comparing the number of owners with the number of leasers in each age category. Be sure to label your chart, and include combined totals for owners and leasers ("total drivers"). Then prepare a pie chart showing the proportion of owners and leasers in the one age group that you think holds the most promise for leasing a new vehicle. Write a sentence that prepares your company's management for the information shown in the pie chart.

Age group	Number of owners (in 000s)	Number of leasers (in 000s)
18–24	1,830	795
25–29	1,812	1,483
30–34	1,683	1,413
35–44	1,303	1,932
45–54	1,211	1,894
55–64	1,784	1,435
65–74	3,200	1,142
75+	3,431	854

11.2 Preparing Pie Charts As director of new business development for a growing advertising agency, you're interested in how companies spend their advertising dollars. Create a pie chart based on the following information, which shows U.S. national advertising spending by media category. Summarize these findings (in two or three sentences) for publication in a report to top management.

Media type	Expenditure (in $ billions)
Internet	1.9
Outdoor	2.0
Radio	2.9
Yellow Pages	12.7
Magazines	16.6
Newspapers	21.2
Television	45.1
Direct mail, promotions, special events	112.9
Total Advertising[9]	215.3

11.3 Preparing Line Charts The pet food manufacturer you work for is interested in the results of a recent poll of U.S. pet-owning households. Look at the statistics that follow and decide on the most appropriate scale for a chart; then create a line chart of the trends in cat ownership. What conclusions do you draw from the trend you've charted? Draft a paragraph or two discussing the results of this poll and the potential consequences for the pet food business. Support your conclusions by referring readers to your chart.

> In 1985, 22 million U.S. households owned a cat. In 1990, 24 million households owned a cat. In 1995, 28 million households owned a cat. In 2000, 32 million households owned a cat.

11.4 Selecting the Right Visual You're preparing the annual report for FretCo Guitar Corporation. For each of the following types of information, select the right chart or visual to illustrate the text. Explain your choices.

- **a.** Data on annual sales for the past 20 years
- **b.** Comparison of FretCo sales, product by product (electric guitars, bass guitars, amplifiers, acoustic guitars), for this year and last year
- **c.** Explanation of how a FretCo acoustic guitar is manufactured
- **d.** Explanation of how the FretCo Guitar Corporation markets its guitars
- **e.** Data on sales of FretCo products in each of 12 countries
- **f.** Comparison of FretCo sales figures with sales figures for three competing guitar makers over the past 10 years

11.5 Preparing Bar Charts Team up with a classmate to design charts based on a comparison of the total tax burden of the U.S. taxpayer with that of people in other nations. One teammate should sketch a horizontal or vertical bar chart and the other should sketch a pictogram from the estimates that follow. Then exchange charts and analyze how well each conveys the situation of the U.S. taxpayer. Would the bar chart look best with vertical or horizontal bars? Why? What scale is best? How does the symbol used in the pictogram enhance or obscure the meaning or impact of the data? What suggestions can each student make for improving the other's visual aid?

> Estimates show that Swedish taxpayers spend 51 percent of their incomes on taxes, British taxpayers spend 48 percent, French taxpayers spend 37 percent, Japanese taxpayers spend 28 percent, and U.S. taxpayers spend 27 percent.

11.6 Selecting the Right Chart Here are last year's sales figures for the appliance and electronics megastore where you work. Construct charts based on these figures that will help you explain to the store's general manager seasonal variations in each department.

Store Sales in 2001 (in $ thousands)

Month	Home Electronics	Computers	Appliances
January	$68	$39	$36
February	72	34	34
March	75	41	30
April	54	41	28
May	56	42	44
June	49	33	48
July	54	31	43
August	66	58	39
September	62	58	36
October	66	44	33
November	83	48	29
December	91	62	24

11.7 Creating Maps You work for C & S Holdings, a company that operates coin-activated, self-service car washes. Research shows that the farther customers live from a car wash, the less likely they are to visit. You know that 50 percent of customers at each of your car washes live within a 4-mile radius of the location, 65 percent live within 6 miles, 80 percent live within 8 miles, and 90 percent live within 10 miles. B & T's owner wants to open two new car washes in your city and has asked you to prepare a report recommending locations. Using a map of your city, choose two possible locations for car washes and create a visual depicting the customer base surrounding each location.

11.8 Creating Organization Charts Create an organization chart for your school. You will probably need to consult your school library or administration office for documents listing the various offices and departments. Figure 11.10 can serve as a model for how to structure your chart.

11.9 Creating Line Charts Re-create the line chart in Figure 11.1 as a bar chart and as a pie chart. Which of these three formats does the best job of conveying the information? Are any of the formats definitely inappropriate for this information? Explain your answers.

11.10 Selecting the Right Chart With a team of three or four other students, brainstorm and then sketch at least three types of charts you can use to compare the populations of all 50 states in the United States. You can use any of the graphic ideas presented in this chapter, as well as any ideas or examples you find from other sources.

11.11 **Internet** One of the best places to see how data can be presented visually is in government statistical publications, which are often available on the Internet. For example, the International Trade Administration (ITA), a branch of the U.S. Department of Commerce, publishes monthly reports about U.S. trade with other countries. Visit the report page of its website at www.ita.doc.gov/td/industry/otea/ustrade.html and follow the link to the latest monthly trade update. Using what you learned in this chapter, evaluate the charts in the report. Do they present the data clearly? Are they missing any elements? What would you do to improve the charts? Print out a copy of the report to turn in with your answers, and indicate which charts you are evaluating.

11.12 **Ethical Choices** Create a bar or line chart using data you find online or in a business publication. Make of copy of your chart and alter the chart's scale. How does the altered chart distort the information? How might you detect whether a chart's scale has been altered?

EXPAND YOUR KNOWLEDGE

Exploring the Best of the Web:

Brush Up on Your Computer-Graphics Skills, p. 351

Need some help using graphics software? Get started at the About.com graphics software website and brush up on your computer-graphics skills.

1. What are the four basic file formats for graphics?
2. What are seven ways to create design contrast?
3. What kinds of tools are included in diagramming software?

Exploring the Web on Your Own

Review these chapter-related websites on your own to learn more about creating charts, diagrams, and other visuals for written and oral reports.

1. Become an Excel pro by reading the Tips and Tricks and How-to Articles at the Microsoft Excel homepage, www.microsoft.com/office/excel/default.htm. Click on Using Excel to get started.
2. Learn how to create effective diagrams at the Microsoft Visio website, www.microsoft.com/office/visio. Click on Using Visio to get started.
3. Check out the world's largest online encyclopedia of graphic symbols at Symbols.com, www.symbols.com.

LEARN INTERACTIVELY

Interactive Study Guide

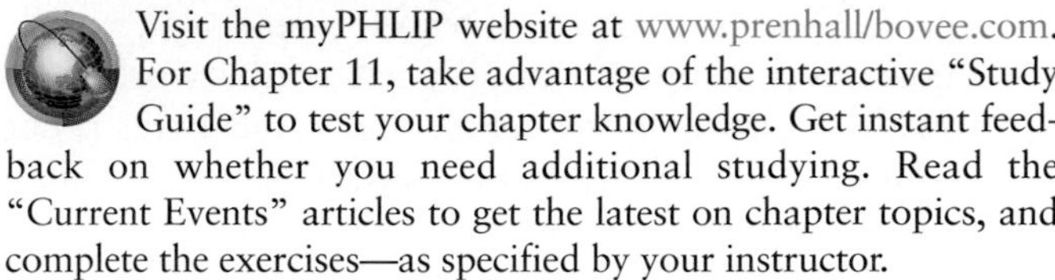

Visit the myPHLIP website at www.prenhall/bovee.com. For Chapter 11, take advantage of the interactive "Study Guide" to test your chapter knowledge. Get instant feedback on whether you need additional studying. Read the "Current Events" articles to get the latest on chapter topics, and complete the exercises—as specified by your instructor.

This site offers a variety of additional resources: The "Research Area" helps you locate a wealth of information to use in course assignments. You can even send a message to online research experts, who will help you find exactly the information you need. The "Study Hall" helps you succeed in this course. "Talk in the Hall" lets you leave messages and meet new friends online. If you have a question, you can "Ask the Tutor." And to get a better grade in this course, you can find more help at "Writing Skills," "Study Skills," and "Study Tips."

Grammar Diagnostic Tests

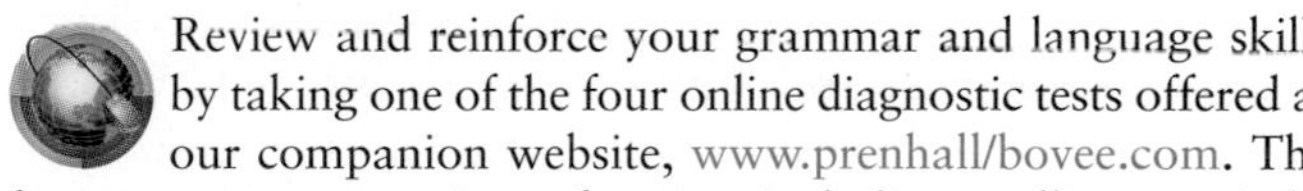

Review and reinforce your grammar and language skills by taking one of the four online diagnostic tests offered at our companion website, www.prenhall/bovee.com. The four tests cover a variety of topics, including spelling, capitals, punctuation, verbs, pronouns, adjectives, adverbs, sentence structure, sentence punctuation, clarity, word choice, style, organization skills, proofreading, and more. Submit your test and assess your competency. Then focus on improving areas where you are weak as you complete the exercises in this chapter.

Communicating Through the Internet and Other Technologies

COMMUNICATING IN THE INTERNET AGE

Technologies such as the Internet, e-mail, voice mail, and faxes allow people from all parts of the world to work together seamlessly by sending bits and bytes rocketing around the globe 24 hours a day. This global collaboration also enables companies to build their products, run their operations, and deliver their services better, faster, and cheaper. New technologies are changing not only the way we communicate but also the way we work. Some experts predict that these technologies will soon permeate every business practice, creating communication advances far more sophisticated than we can imagine today.[1]

When entering the business world, you'll be expected to know how to use the Internet and other technologies for effective workplace communication. In addition, you'll need to understand some of the communication challenges that companies face as a result of these new technologies. This component chapter discusses what businesses can do on the Internet and how they are using it, how businesspeople use other technologies to communicate, and how companies are handling communication challenges such as data security, employee productivity, and sabotage.

UNDERSTANDING THE INTERNET

As Chapter 1 demonstrates, it's difficult to study business communication without understanding the Internet.[2] The **Internet** is the world's largest computer network. Started in 1969 by the U.S. Department of Defense, the Internet is a voluntary, cooperative undertaking; no one individual, organization, or government owns it. The Internet is accessible to individuals, companies, colleges, government agencies, and other institutions all over the world. It links thousands of smaller computer networks and millions of individual computer users in homes, businesses, government offices, and schools worldwide. You can learn more about the Internet by taking the tour at www.learnthenet.com or www.netforbeginners.about.com/internet/netforbeginners.

To reach the Internet, you need a computer with a modem and an **Internet service provider (ISP)**—a company that provides access to the Internet. For a fee (either monthly or per use), you can dial into one of the ISP's host computers, which will link you to one of the networked computers in the Internet. You can dial into an ISP in a variety of ways. Although many people use a standard telephone line, others are willing to pay a bit more for the speed and convenience of a cable connection or a **digital subscriber line** (DSL), a high-speed phone line that carries both voice and data. In addition, you can connect on the go using either a handheld computer or a cell phone that is set up for wireless access.

The most widely used part of the Internet is the **World Wide Web**. Developed in 1990, the web enables users to search for, display, and save **multimedia** resources such as graphics, text, audio, and video files. This information is typically stored on a series of **webpages**, related files containing multimedia data that are made available on a **website**. You need a web **browser**—software such as Netscape Navigator or Microsoft's Internet Explorer—to read webpages.

The **homepage** of a website is the primary screen that users first access when visiting a site. Furthermore, each page in a website is identified by a unique address known as a **uniform resource locator** (URL). Consider http://www.yahoo.com, for example. The address begins with *http*, which is the abbreviation for **hypertext transfer protocol**, the communications protocol that allows you to navigate the web. The address continues with *www*, indicating that the site is located on the World Wide Web. The next part of the address is the registered **domain name** (in this case *yahoo.com*), a name unique to that site. The abbreviation following the period is the *top-level domain (TLD)*. The TLDs now available include the following:

company (com)
business (biz)
info (general information)
pro (professional)
museum (museum)
aero (aviation)
name (individual)
coop (cooperative)
educational (edu)
government (gov)
international (int)
military (mil)
network resources (net)
nonprofit organizations (org)
France (Fr) (There is a different code for each country.)

One convenient way to navigate the web is through **hyperlinks**, or *hotlinks*, which means you can click on words in **hypertext markup language** (HTML)—colored, underlined, or highlighted words—with your mouse and automatically jump to another webpage or website. Once you get to your new destination, you can **bookmark** the site by using a browser feature that places the site's URL in a file on your computer for future use. Then, whenever you are online and select the bookmark, you automatically go to that site's address. Another handy browser feature is the ability to navigate your trail backward or forward at any time by using the *back* and *forward* buttons or menus on your browser software. See the glossary at the end of this component chapter for more definitions of Internet-related terms.

How Businesses Are Using the Internet

The Internet is so easy to navigate that businesses are using it to make closer connections with organizations and customers all over the planet. In fact, the Internet has penetrated virtually every corner of the workplace. It's changing the way customers, suppliers, companies, and other stakeholders interact. Just as important, it's changing the way companies operate internally by allowing speedy, convenient exchanges of ideas and information—anytime, anywhere, across thousands of miles or across the street. Companies are using the Internet to

- Share text, photos, slides, videos, and other data within the organization
- Permit employees to **telecommute**, or work away from a conventional office, whether at home, on the road, or across the country[3]
- Recruit employees cost-effectively
- Locate information from external sources
- Find new business partners and attract new customers
- Locate and buy parts and materials from domestic and international suppliers
- Promote and sell goods and services to customers in any location
- Provide customers with service, technical support, and product information
- Collaborate with local, national, and international business partners
- Inform investors, industry analysts, and government regulators about business developments

All these uses of the Internet have one thing in common: They improve communication, which is the most important benefit that executives expect from the Internet, according to a recent survey by Booz-Allen & Hamilton and the Economist Intelligent Unit (see Figure B.1). So the question remains, how, exactly, does the Internet improve communication?

FIGURE B.1 Expected Internet Benefits

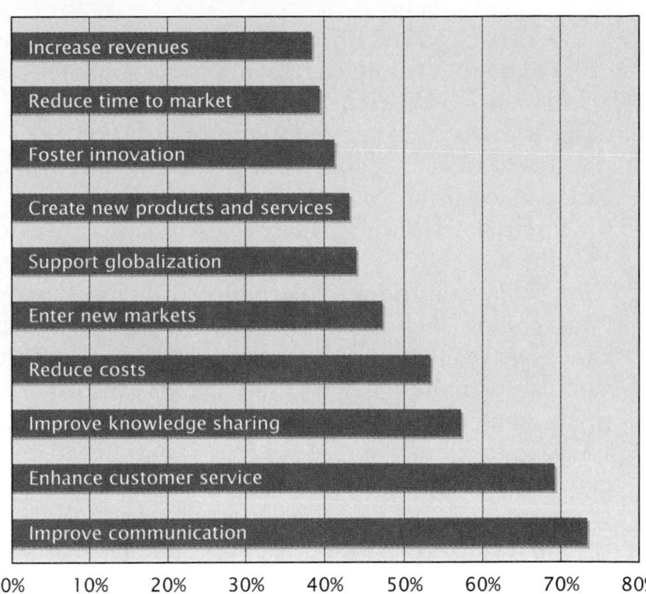

How the Internet Facilitates Communication

The Internet offers businesses a wide variety of choices for online communication:

- **E-mail.** Electronic mail (e-mail) enables users to create, send, and read written messages entirely on computer, as Chapter 4 points out. An e-mail document may be a simple text message, or it might include complex files or programs.
- **Discussion mailing lists.** Also known as *listservs*, **discussion mailing lists** are discussion groups to which you subscribe by sending a message to the list's e-mail address. From then on, copies of all messages posted by any other subscriber are sent to you via e-mail. It's like subscribing to an electronic newsletter to which everyone can contribute.
- **Newsgroups.** Consisting of posted messages and responses on a particular subject, **Usenet newsgroups** differ from discussion mailing lists in two ways. First, messages are posted at the newsgroup site, which you must access by using a news reader program. Second, messages posted to a newsgroup can be viewed by anyone. You can think of a newsgroup as a *place* you visit to read posted messages, whereas a discussion mailing list *delivers* posted messages to you.
- **Instant messaging and chat.** Many companies encourage the use of instant messaging and chat for work purposes, as Chapter 4 explains. Within a few years, more than 200 million employees will be using instant messaging for job-related communication.[4]
- **Videoconferencing.** As Chapter 2 points out, more businesses are using online videoconferencing

to replace face-to-face meetings with colleagues, customers, and suppliers.

- **Telnet.** This class of Internet application program allows you to communicate with other computers on a remote network, even if your computer is not a permanent part of that network. For instance, you would use **Telnet** to access your county library's electronic card catalog from your home computer.
- **Internet telephony.** Internet users can converse vocally over the web using **Internet telephony.** Converting traditional voice calls to digital signals and sending them over the Internet is much less expensive than calling over standard phone lines. It can also be more efficient, allowing an organization to accommodate more users on a single line at once. Internet telephony is growing so rapidly that it is expected to capture 4 percent of U.S. telephone company revenues.[5]
- **File transfers.** An internet service known as **file transfer protocol (FTP)** enables you to **download** files (transfer data from a server to your computer) and **upload** files (transfer data from your computer to another system).[6] FTP also allows you to attach formatted documents to your e-mail messages and download formatted files.[7] Sometimes users compress (or *zip*) large files—such as graphics files—to make them easier and faster to transfer. If you receive a zipped file, you must use special software (usually provided with your web browser) to decompress it before you can read it. The Internet also makes *peer-to-peer file sharing* possible. Using the Internet and software, people can exchange files directly (from user to user) without going through a central server.

Where are you? Your employees? Your clients? Doesn't matter. Thanks to the latest virtual-office technology, staying connected has never been easier.

Equitel, a division of Siemens Corp. in São Paulo, Brazil, uses videoconferencing to communicate and collaborate with its customers, suppliers, and employees who are thousands of miles apart.

In addition, companies can use intranets and extranets—two types of websites specifically designed for internal or external communication.

Intranets

Companies that want to set up special employee-only websites can use an **intranet**, a private internal corporate network. Intranets use the same technologies as the Internet and the World Wide Web, but the information provided and the access allowed are restricted to members of an organization (regardless of their actual location). Employees can use a password to log on to the corporate intranet and then move to public areas of the Internet; however, unauthorized people cruising the Internet cannot get into the internal corporate site.

More than half of companies with 500 employees or more have corporate intranets, although smaller companies are also boosting productivity through intranet technology. Three factors are fueling this intranet boom: (1) the desire to share global knowledge, (2) the need for greater access to company information, and (3) the web's ease of use and flexibility.[8] For example, Ford Motor Company uses its intranet to enable engineers and designers worldwide to collaborate in real time on the design of new car models. Every model has its own internal website to track design, production, quality control, and delivery processes. At IBM, employees can even log on to the corporate intranet to check their health insurance benefits.[9]

As these examples show, intranets can be used for numerous communication functions. In addition to sending e-mail, intranets can be used for filing electronic forms and reports, gaining access to company information from remote locations, and publishing electronic phone directories and company newsletters. Here are a few examples of the specific types of business information that companies are placing on their intranets:

- **Policy manuals.** The most current version is always available to all employees without having to reprint manuals when policies change.
- **Employee benefits information.** Employees can find out about benefits, reallocate the funds in their retirement and benefit plans, fill out electronic W-4 forms, view an electronic pay stub, and sign up for training programs.
- **Job openings.** Companies can post new positions and invite current employees to submit applications for transfer or promotion over the intranet.
- **Presentation materials used by marketing and sales departments.** Sales representatives can download marketing materials at customer sites all over the world. In addition, changes made by marketing representatives at company headquarters are immediately available to field salespeople.[10]
- **Company records and information.** Company directories, customer information, employee skills inventories, project status reports, company calendars and events, and many other records can be stored on an intranet so that they're accessible from anywhere in the world, using an Internet connection and a password.[11]

Providing such material on an intranet places crucial information at each employee's fingertips. Employees can find what they need quickly and easily, without digging through multiple filing cabinets or contacting various offices.

Extranets

Once a company has an intranet in place, adding external capabilities can result in substantial benefits, and the cost of doing so is minimal. An **extranet** is an external intranet that allows people to communicate and exchange data within a secure network.[12] Unlike intranets, which limit access to employees only, extranets allow qualified people from the outside—such as suppliers and customers—to enter the network using a password. Extranets can enhance communication with clients, suppliers, and colleagues, and they can save companies time and money.

Consider Boeing. Every year, the Chicago-based aerospace giant would ship a mountain of technical manuals, parts lists, and other maintenance documents to its 600 airline customers—enough paper to make a stack 130,000 feet tall—at an annual cost of millions of dollars. But now Boeing places all this information on an extranet so that customers can review the data, obtain product updates, and discuss maintenance issues in chat areas.[13]

Like Boeing, some executive search firms and employment agencies are allowing clients to tap into their extranets to search for job prospects. In addition, companies are inviting customers to use their extranets to check on the status of orders and shipping details. And doctors and hospitals are also using extranets to share best practices among their individual organizations. In the past they faxed this information to each other, but there was no guarantee that the right person would get the fax (or even know it existed) before the information became obsolete.

In short, besides saving paper, intranet and extranet technology can save a company time and money by

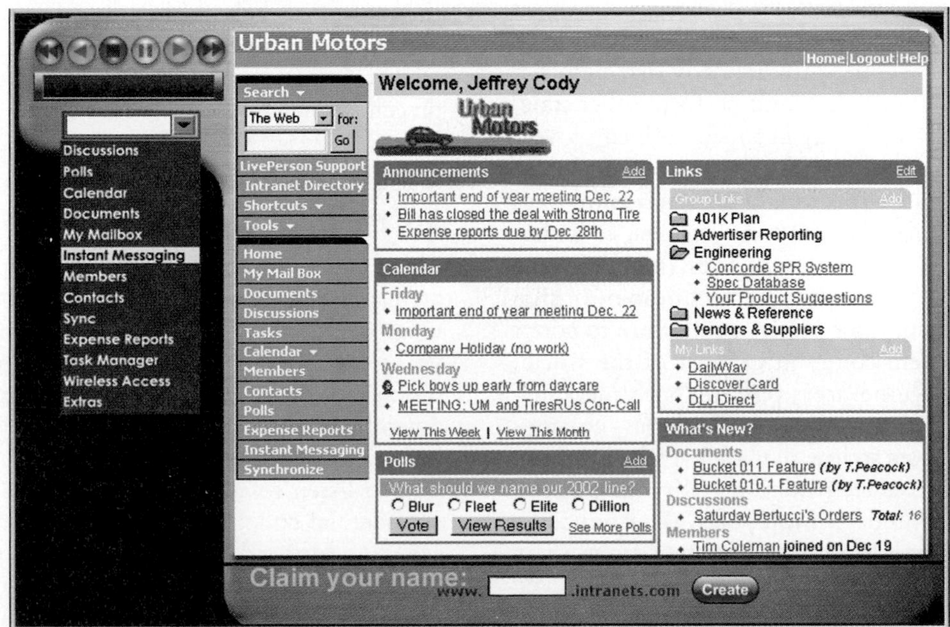

Jeff Cody logs into his company intranet to get the latest company announcements, event calendar, reports, directories, and more.

increasing employee communication and collaboration, reducing employee travel, eliminating unnecessary meetings, and making timely information more accessible.

EXPLORING INNOVATIONS IN OTHER COMMUNICATION TECHNOLOGIES

Although new technologies have clearly produced benefits in the workplace, some observers are concerned about the effect on employees' relationships with co-workers and clients. Today, phone calls, e-mail, faxes, pagers, and voice mail often take the place of face-to-face business meetings. Furthermore, as advanced technology permeates everyday life, many users are abandoning politeness and manners in their electronic communications. Improper etiquette can not only negatively affect your career but also strangle your company's success—especially when conducting business overseas.[14] Experts caution that before companies can expect employees to use powerful new communication tools wisely, they must train their employees to be responsible communicators.[15] Some of the innovations that employees must deal with include telephone systems, voice mail and speech-recognition software, and handheld computer devices.

Telephone Systems

Existing phone lines are still being used for communication. However, business phone systems have become less and less like home phones; in fact, many act like computers with phones attached. *Call-management* systems give companies better control over both the calls that come in and the calls that go out. For inbound calls, a *PBX (private branch exchange)* system can screen and route calls. Some are run by a human operator; others are nearly or completely computerized. For outbound calls, computers can track who called whom, automatically dial numbers from a list of potential contacts, and perform other time- and money-saving tasks. To stay in touch with employees who are on the go, a company can rely on cellular phones or use **pagers**, small radio receivers that signal employees to call someone—usually the office, a customer, or home.

Initially, the use of wireless phones in the United States was slowed by incompatible technologies, high infrastructure costs, high user prices, and failure to adopt the "caller pays" system common in most of the world. (Most U.S. wireless phone users pay for both incoming and outgoing calls.) Current advances in wireless communication are driving costs so low that some experts believe wireless phones will displace traditional wireline phones. This process is already under way. If you walk around any airport, you'll see people standing three feet from a pay phone talking on their cell phones.[16] Cell phones are even more commonplace in Europe, where carriers use a different technology than the U.S. standard. And cell phones are increasingly popular in China, where many people choose to avoid the long wait to have a wireline phone installed.[17]

FIGURE B.2 Make the Right Call: Tips for Cell Phone Etiquette

The latest cell phones can handle additional communication functions such as e-mail access and instant messaging, two-way text messaging, and web browsing.[18] Some also incorporate features such as appointment calendars, enabling businesspeople to get organized while they stay in touch. Although cell phones are extremely convenient, businesspeople should be aware of how and when to adjust their calling habits. (See Figure B.2 for tips on cell phone etiquette.)

Voice Mail and Speech-Recognition Software

The combination of phones and computers has also created an increased use of **voice mail** in the workplace. Much more than a glorified answering machine, voice mail lets you send, store, and retrieve verbal messages using any number of "mailboxes" on the system. Messages can be several minutes long, and you can review your recordings before sending them.

To listen to your voice-mail messages, you enter a confidential code; then you can play or delete your messages or forward them to other people on the system. Before recording your outgoing voice-mail message, organize your thoughts so that your message will be accurate and concise. Figure B.3 shows eight ideas for improving voice-mail communications.[19]

FIGURE B.3 Eight Ways to Improve Your Voice-Mail Communications

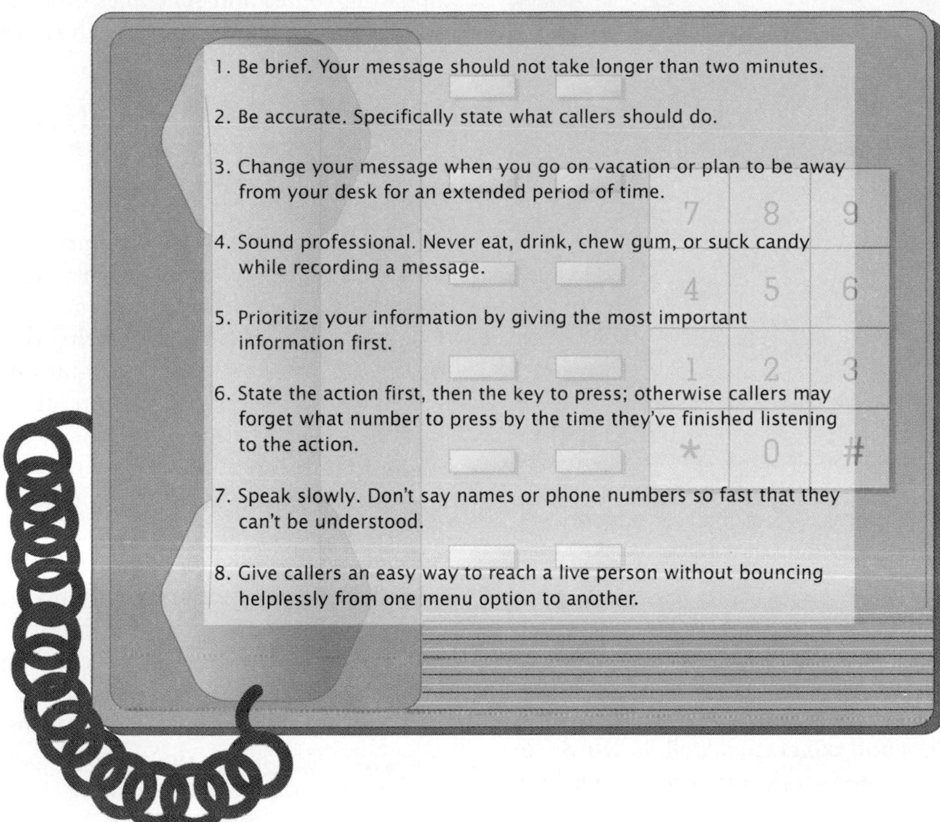

Voice mail solves the time-zone difficulties of cross-country and international communication. It can also reduce a substantial amount of interoffice paperwork. However, even though voice mail can make companies more productive, it's not universally loved. The biggest complaint comes from customers who try to reach a person by phone but must first listen to lengthy recordings and menus, only to be transferred to more recordings and menus.

In addition to voice mail, many companies are using speech-recognition software to provide callers with better customer service. After decades of painstaking research, software companies have created programs that recognize large numbers of words and natural language patterns. Businesses are using these programs to liberate call-in customers from the tedious "press one, press two" phone menus of voice mail. They are replacing Touch-Tone–activated menu systems with the voice of an operator that talks them through the choices or asks, "How can I help you?" But there's a catch—the operator isn't human.[20]

As you speak your request, these programs "listen" to your voice and break it into its phoneme blocks (tiny units of speech). Then they compare your voice blocks against a preloaded template and look for matches. If the system is not sure of the exact match, it responds with a message similar to "Did you say Susan Smith?" These systems disregard superfluous words and phrases such as "uhh," and many have a "barge through" feature that allows callers to begin speaking without waiting for the voice prompt to finish talking.[21]

Newer systems recognize tens of thousands of words and phrases in many languages—some with an accuracy of 97 percent. However, most speech-recognition systems perform their best under ideal conditions. Try to use it while other people in the room are speaking, and suddenly error rates shoot from a respectably low level all the way up to 50 percent—which means that every other word is wrong.[22]

Even so, companies such as UPS, Bell Canada, Coca-Cola New Zealand, American Express, United Airlines, and dozens of others are currently using these systems to reduce customer wait times without adding more operators or phone lines to handle high call volume. For instance, UPS uses speech-recognition software to respond to customers' inquiries on the whereabouts of their parcels. Bell Canada uses a system that can service 4 million directory-assistance calls a minute. And Coca-Cola New Zealand uses a speech-recognition system to solve a call-volume problem that used to leave both inbound and internal callers in perpetual telephone limbo. Today, Coca-Cola's callers are greeted with the message "Please say the full name of the party you wish to talk to or the name of the department you are looking for."[23]

To perfect the next generation of speech technology, scientists must build recognition systems that work accurately whatever the speaker's accent or whether the person

Advances in affordable telecommunications equipment have opened the way for small-business owners to become more active and more competitive away from their home bases.

is on a cell phone, on a land line, in the airport, or on a speaker phone. Furthermore, scientists recognize that before computers can truly grasp human language, they must be able to understand context as well as words. In other words, software "needs to know a lot about how the world works," says one researcher. Still, scientists are forging ahead to perfect speech-recognition technology so that humans won't have to mouse-click or keypunch their way through the oceans of data in gigantic corporate databases.[24]

Handheld Computer Devices

In recent years, more businesspeople and professionals are communicating on the fly, using pocket-sized, handheld devices made by Palm, Handspring, and other manufacturers. These compact **personal digital assistants**—also known as *PDAs* or *handheld computers*—store and organize data such as documents and contact information. With the right equipment, PDAs can become cell phones and Internet devices so that users can make phone calls, send instant messages, and upload or download data whenever and wherever they please. Some PDAs include miniature keyboards, while others use a form of handwriting recognition; cutting-edge models will soon operate on speech-recognition technology, such as a special chip made by IBM.[25] And some handhelds are geared specifically for e-mail functions, such as the small wireless devices made by BlackBerry.

Many organizations give their employees PDAs to expedite communication and improve internal productivity. For example, nurses in the Visiting Nurses Association of Orange County use PDAs to speed through their paperwork so that they can devote more time to patient care. Allegheny Power, which runs electrical and gas utilities in five states, has issued PDAs to its 300 meter readers. Now the utility can better direct its meter readers' activities by updating routes and schedules every day and highlighting special account needs along each route.[26]

HANDLING COMMUNICATION CHALLENGES IN THE INFORMATION AGE

As companies adopt new communication technologies and devices, many are facing new challenges. One of the most critical is information overload. As you saw in Chapter 1, organizations are being flooded by a rising tide of documents—so many that employees often can't discriminate between useful and useless information or between what is truly important and what is routine.

In response, companies are training employees to send fewer messages, to identify the most urgent ones, or even to avoid using e-mail for some part of every day. Cisco Systems has decided to limit the number of companywide e-mail messages that it distributes. At General Motors, assistants screen executives' incoming e-mail and add labels to indicate urgency: Red messages are the most important, whereas green ones are informational only.[27]

In addition to grappling with information overload, managers are also concerned about the challenges of maintaining data security, balancing employee productivity and privacy, and guarding against sabotage and theft.

Data Security

Before computers, companies typically conducted business mainly on paper, locking up sensitive documents and using security precautions when transporting important files. Furthermore, only a limited number of people had access to vital company data. But today companies are moving from paper-based systems to electronic data management, posing a real threat to corporate data security.[28] Global networks increase the possibility that crucial information located on an intranet or sent over the Internet will be altered or destroyed. Experts counted more than 40,000 attempts to penetrate corporate networks during one recent year—more than double the number reported during the previous year.[29] These infiltration attempts include **hacking** (breaking into a computer network such as an intranet to steal, delete, or change data) and **cracking** (entering a computer network for nondestructive reasons, such as to play a prank or show off).

Unfortunately, hacking and cracking are on the rise, as indicated by a 130 percent increase in complaints reported to the FBI. Another threat is **cyberterrorism**—orchestrated attacks on a company's information systems for political or economic purposes. Cyberterrorism is being taken even more seriously since the terrorist attacks on New York City and Washington, D.C., on September 11, 2001.[30]

To better police data security threats from domestic and international sources, the U.S. Justice Department has set up the National Infrastructure Protection Center

(NIPC) at the FBI. The FBI has also begun using a software program called Carnivore to screen e-mail messages for clues to crippling electronic and physical terrorist attacks. Although privacy advocates fear that Carnivore and other security measures are too intrusive and could lead to false accusations, government officials and many citizens are willing to give up some privacy for higher security against all types of terrorism.[31]

Security is also threatened when corporate networks lack proper safeguards, letting crooks steal or destroy sensitive data, which are far easier to duplicate and disseminate than are paper documents. Furthermore, a PC without the proper password protections can easily become a fountain of insider information. Even allowing people into a company's office or factory without carefully checking identification can open the door to theft of computers, passwords, and, ultimately, valuable data.

Companies can go beyond simple identification and password protection to prevent unauthorized computer access by using security software called a **firewall**, a special type of gateway that controls access to the company's local network. The firewall allows access only to users who present the proper password and system identification. In addition to firewalls, companies can protect data by (1) determining which employees should receive passwords to vital networks, (2) providing ongoing security enforcement and education, (3) conducting background checks on all new employees, (4) adopting a sound security policy (requiring employees to use passwords, turn computers off when not in use, encrypt sensitive e-mail, and apply stronger security measures to safeguard trade secrets), and (5) developing a plan for data recovery if disaster strikes.[32]

Employee Productivity and Privacy

Companies are increasingly concerned about employee productivity in the wired workplace, because so many employees are using office resources such as e-mail systems for personal business. According to a recent Ziff Davis survey, workers use the Internet for personal business more than they use any other company resource (see Figure B.4). Sending personal e-mail from work not only wastes company time and resources but also opens the company to lawsuits. Chevron, for example, paid $2.2 million to settle a sexual harassment lawsuit brought by female employees who complained about the distribution of offensive e-mail messages through the corporate network.[33]

To help prevent such problems, more employers are establishing policies governing online activities in the workplace. For instance, *The New York Times* strictly enforces its corporate policy forbidding personal e-mail. Not long ago, the company fired 23 out of 200 employees at its Norfolk, Virginia, facility for violating the rules.[34] Some companies have also begun monitoring on-the-job web access, e-mail, and voice-mail messages. According to an American Management Association survey, 74 percent of major U.S. companies keep tabs on workers by recording phone calls or voice mail and by checking employees' computer files and e-mail.[35]

Although employees worry about invasion of privacy, employers stress that since they own the computer resources—and pay for their employees' time—they have the legal right to know exactly what employees are doing at their keyboards. In fact, such surveillance is helping companies crack down on resource abuse: Just months after starting to monitor web usage, Xerox fired 40 employees for viewing inappropriate websites—primarily pornographic sites.[36]

Electronic traffic jams are another productivity problem that companies face. The Internet was originally designed like a single-lane highway with unlimited on-ramps and no traffic control. This unrestricted access has always been the Internet's strength, but it has become a weakness for users who need to move large amounts of

FIGURE B.4 Percentage of Employees Who Use Office Resources for Personal Business

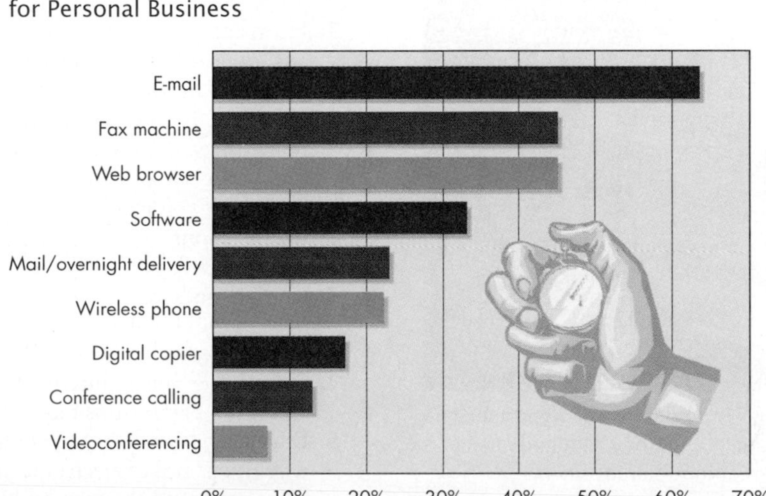

data more quickly. When traffic gets heavy, the Internet slows down, penalizing business users trying to move a lot of data. Now more than 185 universities and 70 corporations are collaborating to add a "high-speed" online toll lane. Dubbed Internet2, this fee-based network can be used by companies and individuals who need to move a lot of data (such as graphics and videoconferencing signals) hundreds of times faster than the original network can manage.[37]

Sabotage and Theft

Today, criminals are using technology to disrupt website and computer operations, steal credit card numbers from intranets and extranets, and cause other problems for companies, governments, and individuals. Among the most common forms of sabotage are viruses and worms. **Viruses** are programs that can change or delete files or programs. Embedded in legitimate software (without the manufacturer's knowledge) or in files passed from one computer to another, vicious viruses can quickly do tremendous damage. **Worms** are programs specifically designed to replicate over and over again. Spread by e-mail, these programs send more worms to everyone in the recipient's e-mail address book—taking up precious network space and snarling connections.

In a recent study, 85 percent of the firms surveyed said they had been victims of a virus. The resulting damage can be costly. Cleaning up the wreckage and protecting against additional viruses has forced companies to spend more than $12.1 billion annually on virus protection programs and other safeguards.[38]

Even so, cost is not the only concern. As worms and viruses spread, they can disrupt other interconnected government and company systems and slow Internet traffic. Even relatively simple sabotage, such as repeatedly trying to access an Internet address, can tie up a site or cause its equipment to crash—as eBay, E*Trade, Amazon.com, and other web-based businesses have learned.[39]

The FBI estimates that reported computer losses as a result of sabotage total $10 billion annually—and the biggest threat comes from within. Up to 60 percent of computer break-ins are perpetrated by employees. Other violators include laid-off workers, contractors, and consultants who destroy, alter, or expose critical data.[40] Furthermore, the situation could get worse. With the use of web-browsing cell phones, wireless communication devices, and other computerized and networked products and services, companies may find their systems even more vulnerable to sabotage and theft in the coming years.

E*Trade's CEO, Christos Cotsakos, understands the importance of implementing security policies and technology to guard against sabotage and other problems that might disrupt online operations.

TEST YOUR KNOWLEDGE

1. What do the different parts of a uniform resource locator (URL) stand for?
2. How do newsgroups differ from discussion mailing lists and e-mail?
3. What are some of the key benefits of intranets and extranets?
4. What types of organizations would benefit the most by adding speech-recognition software to their telephone systems?
5. Why would an employee with a laptop computer need or want a personal digital assistant?
6. Distinguish between hacking and cracking. Do you agree with the distinction between these activities?
7. What is a firewall, and why is it important?
8. What should a company include when formulating a policy about employees' online activities in the workplace?
9. What are the characteristics of Internet2, and why would a company prefer to use it?
10. Why are companies and government agencies concerned about viruses and worms?

APPLY YOUR KNOWLEDGE

1. How can a global corporation such as Coca-Cola take advantage of Internet technology to keep its people around the world in touch with each other?
2. You have been thinking about telecommuting from your home three days a week and going into the office on the remaining two days. You could easily do your work at home, but you'll need your boss's permission. Make a list of the questions your boss might ask about this arrangement. Then prepare your response for each question.
3. Under what circumstances might discussion mailing lists be more useful for sharing information within a company than instant messaging or e-mail?
4. Should there be an Internet2 for companies and individuals willing to pay for this technology? Why or why not?
5. **Ethical Choices** Do you think companies should monitor employees' use of electronic communication such as e-mail, voice mail, and the Internet? Explain your answer.

INTERNET GLOSSARY

bookmark A browser feature that places selected URLs in a file for quick access, allowing you to automatically return to the website by clicking on the site's name

browser Software, such as Netscape Navigator or Microsoft's Internet Explorer, that enables a computer to search for, display, and download the multimedia information that appears on the World Wide Web

cracking Entering a computer network for nondestructive reasons, such as to play a prank

cyberterrorism Orchestrated attacks on a company's information systems for political or economic purposes

digital subscribe line High-speed phone line that carries both voice and data

discussion mailing lists E-mail lists that allow people to discuss a common interest by posting messages that are received by everyone in the group

domain name The portion of an Internet address that identifies the host and indicates the type of organization it is

download Transmitting a file from one computer system to another; on the Internet, bringing data from the Internet into your computer

extranet Similar to an intranet, but extending the network to select people outside the organization

file transfer protocol (FTP) A software protocol that lets you copy or move files from a remote computer—called an FTP site—to your computer over the Internet; it is the Internet facility for downloading and uploading files

firewall Computer hardware and software that protects part or all of a private computer network attached to the Internet by preventing public Internet users from accessing it

hacking Breaking into a computer network to steal, delete, or change data

homepage The primary website for an organization or individual; the first hypertext document displayed on a website

hyperlink A highlighted word or image on a webpage or document that automatically allows people to move to another webpage or document when clicked on with a mouse

hypertext markup language (HTML) The software language used to create, present, and link pages on the World Wide Web

hypertext transfer protocol A communications protocol that allows people to navigate among documents or pages linked by hypertext and to download pages from the World Wide Web

Internet A worldwide collection of interconnected networks that enables users to share information electronically and provides digital access to a wide variety of services

Internet service provider (ISP) A company that provides access to the Internet, usually for a monthly fee, via telephone lines or cable; ISPs can be local companies or specialists such as America Online

Internet telephony Using the Internet to converse vocally

intranet A private network, set up within a corporation or organization, that operates over the Internet and may be used to link geographically remote sites

multimedia The combination of two or more of the following elements: graphics, text, sound, video, or computer programs

pagers Small radio receivers that signal users to call someone

personal digital assistant (PDA) Handheld computers that store and organize contact information, calendars, task lists, and other organizational and travel information

telecommute To work from home and communicate with company's main office via computer and communication devices

Telnet A way to access someone else's computer (the host computer) and to use it as if it were right at your desk

uniform resource locator (URL) Web address that gives the exact location of an Internet resource

upload To send a file from your computer to a server or host system

Usenet newsgroups One or more discussion groups on the Internet where people with similar interests can post articles and reply to messages

viruses Form of computer sabotage embedded in software or passed from one computer to the next that change or delete computer files or programs

voice mail A computerized telephone message recording system; an e-mail system that supports audio

webpages Related files containing multimedia data that are made available on a website

website A related collection of files on the World Wide Web

World Wide Web (Web) A hypertext-based system for finding and accessing Internet resources such as text, graphics, sound, and other multimedia resources

worms Form of computer sabotage sent by e-mail that reproduce, taking up network space and snarling connections

PART 5

Planning, Writing, and Completing Reports and Proposals

Planning Business Reports and Proposals

After studying this chapter, you will be able to

1 *Name five classifications of business reports*

2 *Describe four types of informational reports and provide examples of each*

3 *Describe two types of analytical reports and provide examples of each*

4 *Discuss how internal proposals differ from external proposals*

5 *Explain the function of a request for proposal (RFP)*

6 *Identify seven elements often included in a formal work plan*

7 *Clarify what it means to adapt your report to your audience*

8 *Cite the advantages and disadvantages of electronic reports*

COMMUNICATION CLOSE-UP AT DELL COMPUTER

www.dell.com

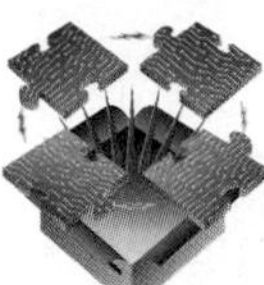

Since Michael Dell founded Dell Computer Corporation in 1984, the company has become the largest computer manufacturer in the United States and the fastest-growing computer-systems company in the world. But to maintain the company's leading edge in the computer industry, it must collect and analyze reams of information. As Michael Dell explains, "We have to stay on top of our customers' needs, and we have to monitor and understand the innovation in everything from semiconductors to liquid crystal displays." Of course, "information in its raw form doesn't present itself in neat and tidy packages," notes the founder. So Dell and his management team rely on well-planned reports that not only summarize and present carefully researched data but define problems, discuss pertinent issues, and analyze information.

For example, management uses reports to monitor such internal operations as average discount rates from suppliers and inventory turnover. "We track the order and delivery process, product reliability, and also service and support from the customer's point of view. We also evaluate suppliers on cost, delivery, availability of technology, and the ways in which they do business with us over the Internet," Dell explains. Moreover, Dell uses a "supplier report card to track an individual supplier's progress, as well to compare each supplier with other suppliers."

Reports also played a key role in Dell's e-commerce efforts. Before setting the goal of selling 50 percent of the company's products over dell.com, management gathered and analyzed information on overall market growth, the potential of online purchases, and the potential for the company's products. Based on these analytical reports, Dell introduced customers to the idea of ordering custom-built computers online—and quickly achieved its Internet sales goals. Today, through dell.com, company managers can track customer satisfaction levels, measure customer responses, monitor complaint resolutions, and prepare performance reports.

Dell relies on both informational and analytical reports to help determine the feasibility of entering new markets or offering new products. For instance, before expanding into a new country, management examines the company's market share, country-by-country and product-by-product, and evaluates the growth potential of the country under consideration."Because we glean data on all customers and products from countries around the world, we know what we ought to be able to achieve in terms of market penetration, sales force productivity, and other aspects of our business," says Michael Dell.

In addition to evaluating growth potential, management must also assess how new markets will affect the company's available pool of human resources. Dell's human resources employees produce reports that anticipate turnover, identify key job openings, and define training needs. Then management reviews the reports to make sure it can staff its human resources needs with qualified individuals.

Overall, Dell depends on more than 4,000 types of analytical and informational reports to keep operations running smoothly. "To say that we have become a data-driven company is almost an understatement," says Michael Dell. "Data is the engine that keeps

Managers at Dell Computer rely on market analyses and other types of informational reports to monitor company performance and evaluate the merits of expanding to international markets such as China.

us on track." And staying on track with accurate reports is one way Dell remains a leader in its industry.[1] ■

UNDERSTANDING BUSINESS REPORTS AND PROPOSALS

Like Michael Dell, most managers rely on reports to provide information and analyses so that they can make decisions and solve problems. As a businessperson, you will be expected to write and read all kinds of **reports**, written factual accounts that objectively communicate information about some aspect of the business. You need to know about how reports are classified and used in the workplace before you begin planning reports and proposals.

Business reports help companies make decisions and solve business problems.

A business report is any factual, objective document that serves a business purpose.

You may be surprised at the variety of messages that qualify as reports. The term covers everything from a fleeting image on a computer screen to preprinted forms to informal letters and memos to formal three-volume bound manuscripts. However, although business reports can serve hundreds of purposes, most reports are used for one of the six general purposes highlighted in Figure 12.1. Each of these purposes determines the type of report you use and the organizational structure of your message. For instance,

FIGURE 12.1 Six General Purposes of Reports

Informational Reports

1. Monitor and control operations
2. Implement policies and procedures
3. Comply with legal or regulatory requirements
4. Document work performed for clients

Analytical Reports

5. Guide decisions on particular issues
6. Get products, plans, or projects accepted by others

if management needs information about current inventory levels, you might create a report to monitor and control operations. If management needs to decide on the best way to finance a project, you might create a report to guide their decision. You might even follow in Toyota's footsteps and send them a detailed report before they meet. (See "Sharpening Your Career Skills: Reports Bring Toyota's Engineers Up to Speed.")

Learning Objective 1

Name five classifications of business reports

In addition to their purpose, reports are often classified by criteria such as who initiates them (source), how often they are needed (frequency), where they are being sent (target audience), how much detail they contain (length), and whether they are designed to simply educate or to present a decision and require action (intent):

Reports may be classified in several ways:

- Voluntary or authorized
- Routine or special
- Internal or external
- Short or long
- Informational or analytical

- **Source. Voluntary reports** are prepared on your own initiative. Thus, they usually require more detail and support than **authorized reports**, which are prepared at the request of someone else. When writing a voluntary report, you give more background on the subject, and you explain your purpose more carefully. An authorized report, on the other hand, is organized to respond to the reader's request.
- **Frequency. Routine** or **periodic reports** are submitted on a recurring basis (daily, weekly, monthly, quarterly, annually). Routine reports, such as sales or financial reports, are commonly prepared on preprinted or computerized forms (either of which the writer simply fills in), or they're organized in a standard way. Moreover, because they are routine, they require less introductory and transitional material than **special reports**, nonrecurring reports that typically present the results of specific, onetime studies or investigations.
- **Target audience. Internal reports** (designed for use within the organization) are generally less formal than **external reports** (sent to people outside the organization). Many internal reports, especially those under 10 pages, are written in memo format. On the other hand, external reports may be in letter format (if they are no longer than 5 pages) or in manuscript format (if they exceed 5 pages).
- **Length. Short reports** (generally 1 to 9 pages) differ from **long reports** (10 pages or more) in scope, research, and timetable. A long report examines a problem in detail and generally requires more extensive research and preparation time. In contrast, a short report may discuss just one part of the problem and may not require formal research. A *summary report* is a special kind of short report that gives a concise overview of a situation, publication(s), or document(s). Summaries highlight important details but refrain from including background material, examples, or specific details.

The purpose of informational reports is to explain, whereas analytical reports are meant to convince the audience that the conclusions and recommendations developed in the text are valid.

- **Intent. Informational reports** focus on facts and are intended mainly to explain something or to educate readers. In contrast, **analytical reports** are designed to solve a problem by convincing readers that the conclusions and recommendations reached are justified based on the data, analyses, and interpretations presented in such reports. Information in analytical reports plays a supporting role; it is a means to an end rather than an end in itself.

Informational reports provide a solid foundation for many managerial discussions. The most effective reports present information in a logical, concise format and make it easy for management to locate needed facts without reading through the entire report.

Keep in mind that a single report may have several classifications. For instance, a monthly sales report is generally an authorized, routine, internal, short, informational report, whereas a market analysis is generally an authorized, special, internal, long, analytical report. The remainder of this section takes a closer look at several types of informational and analytical reports and explains the purpose of each. Being familiar with these report types and purposes will help you plan your own reports more effectively.

Informational Reports

Informational reports present data and facts without analyses or recommendations. Common types of informational reports

Sharpening Your Career Skills

Reports Bring Toyota's Engineers Up to Speed

Toyota is renowned for its innovative and world-class manufacturing systems. So with more and more companies encouraging employees to use face-to-face communication instead of written reports and memos, why is Toyota doing just the opposite?

At Toyota's engineering department, written reports are the primary vehicle for getting things done. Whenever important issues require a meeting, engineering managers are required first to submit a written report to all concerned parties. The short, crisp report follows a standardized format: written on 11-by-17-inch paper (the largest faxable size), it analyzes the issue, develops a clear statement of a problem, provides key information, and highlights solutions and recommendations.

Recipients are expected to read and study the report and offer feedback to the sender, sometimes in the form of an additional report. Once the writer of the original report has received feedback from all interested parties, he or she writes a final version that summarizes everyone's input and highlights items of agreement and disagreement. Only then do the managers meet. But instead of spending time defining the issues and tossing out ideas that people have had little time to think about, they spend time addressing the few remaining items of concern, as highlighted in the reports, and hammering out implementation details.

Relying on preliminary reports accelerates the decision-making process and makes meetings more productive:

- **Participants are prepared.** Managers come to the meeting with a clear understanding of the key issues, facts, possible solutions, and roadblocks. Moreover, they have had ample time to voice their opinions and consider the viewpoints of others.
- **Input is widespread.** Because reports are accessible to all Toyota departments, managers gather companywide feedback regarding the issues and take into consideration the solutions or concerns posed by other departments.
- **Decision making is documented.** The reports document and summarize the analysis and decision making in a convenient form for future reference.

So while other organizations may grapple with meetings that stall or get thrown into reverse, Toyota uses written reports to make meetings and face-to-face interactions richer and more productive. In fact, writing reports is such an essential part of the job that Toyota provides formal training to help its managers master their report-writing skills. Written reports are just one way Toyota extends its world-class operation from the factory floor to the conference room.

Career Applications

1. Why are Toyota's engineering managers required to submit written reports to concerned parties before attending a meeting to discuss important issues?
2. What challenges might other companies face should they decide to implement a similar report policy?

include those for monitoring and controlling operations, statements of policies and procedures, compliance reports, and progress reports.

Learning Objective 2

Describe four types of informational reports and provide examples of each

Reports for Monitoring and Controlling Operations

Because managers cannot be everywhere at once, they rely on reports to find out what's happening to the operations under their control. These *monitor/control reports* focus on data, so they require special attention to accuracy, thoroughness, and honesty of content. They don't cover up the bad news and emphasize only the accomplishments, because such distortion defeats their purpose. The problems will show up anyway, so these reports are designed to get them out in the open before it is too late.

Monitor/control reports help managers find out what's happening in the operations under their control.

Monitor/control reports expose any problems that exist.

Three types of reports used for monitoring and controlling operations are plans, operating reports, and personal activity reports. In general, plans are written for both internal and external audiences. However, operating reports and personal activity reports are usually written for internal audiences only.

Plans One of the most widely used monitor/control reports is the **plan**, a written report that establishes guidelines for future action. Plans come in all shapes and sizes: *Strategic plans* document an organization's overall goals and the operational methods it will use to reach those goals. Such plans help guide internal operations and provide benchmarks for measuring progress toward goals.[2] *Business plans* are used by small

Plans help managers
- Coordinate the various activities of a business
- Guide the distribution of resources
- Motivate employees

Best of the Web

Pointers for Business Plans

What's involved in a business plan? BizPlanIt.Com offers tips and advice, consulting services, a free e-mail newsletter, and a sample virtual business plan. You'll find suggestions on what details and how much information to include in each section of a business plan. You can explore the site's numerous links to business-plan books and software, online magazines, educational programs, government resources, and women's and minority resources, and even find answers to your business-plan questions.

www.bizplanit.com

Sue Calloway, founder of S.C.R.U.B.S., submitted her business plan for whimsical hospital clothing to banks and outside investors so that she could obtain funding for her start-up operation.

businesses, divisions of larger businesses, and entrepreneurial start-ups to summarize the proposed business venture, to highlight a company's goals, to obtain financing, or to contract for managerial support services.[3] *Marketing plans* identify a firm's customers and explain how to serve them. Other plans include annual budgets, five-year plans, sales plans, recruiting plans, production plans, and so on. Internal audiences generally use such plans to (1) improve organizational coordination, (2) guide the distribution of money and material, and (3) motivate employees. Plans are also written for external audiences to obtain financing and other services.

Operating Reports **Operating reports** provide managers with detailed information from a management information system (MIS), which captures data about everything happening in the organization—sales, production, inventory, shipments, backlogs, costs, personnel, and so on. Such data are frequently computerized, so many operating reports submit data in their raw state via preprogrammed, computerized printouts. More extensive operating reports take the raw data and analyze it, format it, and at times organize it in paragraph form.

Periodic operating reports describe what has happened in a department or division during a particular period. *Corporate annual reports* are periodic reports that are formal and polished. *Monthly sales reports* are another example. The purpose of these recurring documents is to provide a picture of how things are going so that corporate managers will be up to date and can take corrective action if necessary.

The periodic report in Figure 12.2 was prepared by Roger Watson, real estate director for a San Francisco coffee retailer. "My manager needs to know that my department is making good decisions when we select new store locations," says Watson. However, Watson avoids burdening his boss with details about every potential site by making his report concise and presenting information in summary format.

Periodic operating reports are recurring monitor/control reports that keep managers informed about departments that report to them.

Personal activity reports describe the facts and decisions that emerge during conversations, trips, and business meetings.

Personal Activity Reports **Personal activity reports** describe what has occurred during a conference, convention, trip, or other activity. They're intended to report important information or decisions that emerged during the activity. These reports also help companies keep track of what's happening in the marketplace or with customers. *Sales-call reports* are one type of personal activity report that summarizes the events that occurred during an appointment with a customer. The report outlines the topics that were discussed and gives the salesperson's evaluation of the prospects for a sale, together with plans for follow-up action.

As owner and chief executive officer of Careers USA, a fast-growing personnel-placement service based in Philadelphia, Marilyn Ounjian reads sales-call reports to track her salespeople's effectiveness and to check sales trends in 21 offices spread

FIGURE 12.2 In-Depth Critique: Roger Watson's Periodic Operating Report

MEMO

TO: Joan Chen, V.P.
New Business Development
FROM: Roger Watson,
Real Estate Director

DATE: August 1, 2002

SUBJECT: July location scouting

During the last two weeks of July, I scouted four Denver locations for our coffee outlets. George Spindle recommended these sites in his business development report (which is on the intranet under "Regional reports" if you'd like to review it). All four sites are in existing office buildings.

Orients the reader but doesn't waste time with unnecessary explanations

HOW THE DENVER SITES COMPARE

Headings stand out to make report easier to read

Here's a quick look at the basic aspects of each site. Lease rates are comparable at all four locations, ranging from $34 to $38 a square foot.

Site	Space	Availability	Competition	Visibility
Lakewood	260 square feet	Now	Starbucks has begun construction 4 blocks north; no other stores within a 16-block radius	None; on the second of two retail floors in this building
Glendale	525 square feet; with additional 150 square feet in one year	January	2 Starbucks (2 blocks south and 8 blocks west); Chicago Blues (across street, but poor visibility)	
McNichols Arena	420 square feet	December	JavaLand 3 blocks east; Starbucks 4 blocks south	
University of Denver	Two options: 340 square feet, 655 square feet	Now for the smaller site; March for the larger	Five independents in the immediate area; Starbucks on campus (2 blocks west)	

Organizes summary information in the most time-saving format

SCOUTING PLANS FOR SEPTEMBER

Our schedule has been pretty tight for the last six months. Following are the plans for our efforts in September:

Denver: I'll contract Shure Research to conduct foot traffic counts at all four sites (we should have those numbers in 10 days). I've asked George's team to do a permits search to study future building plans in each location. I'll be talking with Melissa Hines next week about construction restrictions. (She's the Smith, Allen broker who helped us with the Grand Junction sites last year.)

Minneapolis: Jean-Luc Goddard wants us to review several sites he's had his eye on. I'll send Margie or visit them myself if my schedule permits.

Helps the reader maintain a timely overview of progress

across nine states. "I want to know what's happening now," she says. "Salespeople are on the front lines. If they're not growing, we're not growing."[4]

Other examples of personal activity reports are *expense reports, performance reviews, recruiting reports,* and any other document intended to keep management posted on the activities of individuals. Figure 12.3 is a rough draft of a personal activity report prepared by Carrie Andrews, the human resources manager of a small Indianapolis insurance firm. Her report summarizes the highlights of a seminar on legal issues. Figure 12.4 is the final, improved version of Andrews's report. Note how its content is more focused, organized, and readable.

Case Study: Juan Martinez's Annual Recruiting Report Juan Martinez is in charge of hiring for a Seattle-based software company. One of his responsibilities is to organize on-campus recruiting interviews. Every summer after company representatives

FIGURE 12.3 In-Depth Critique: Carrie Andrews's Personal Activity Report Draft

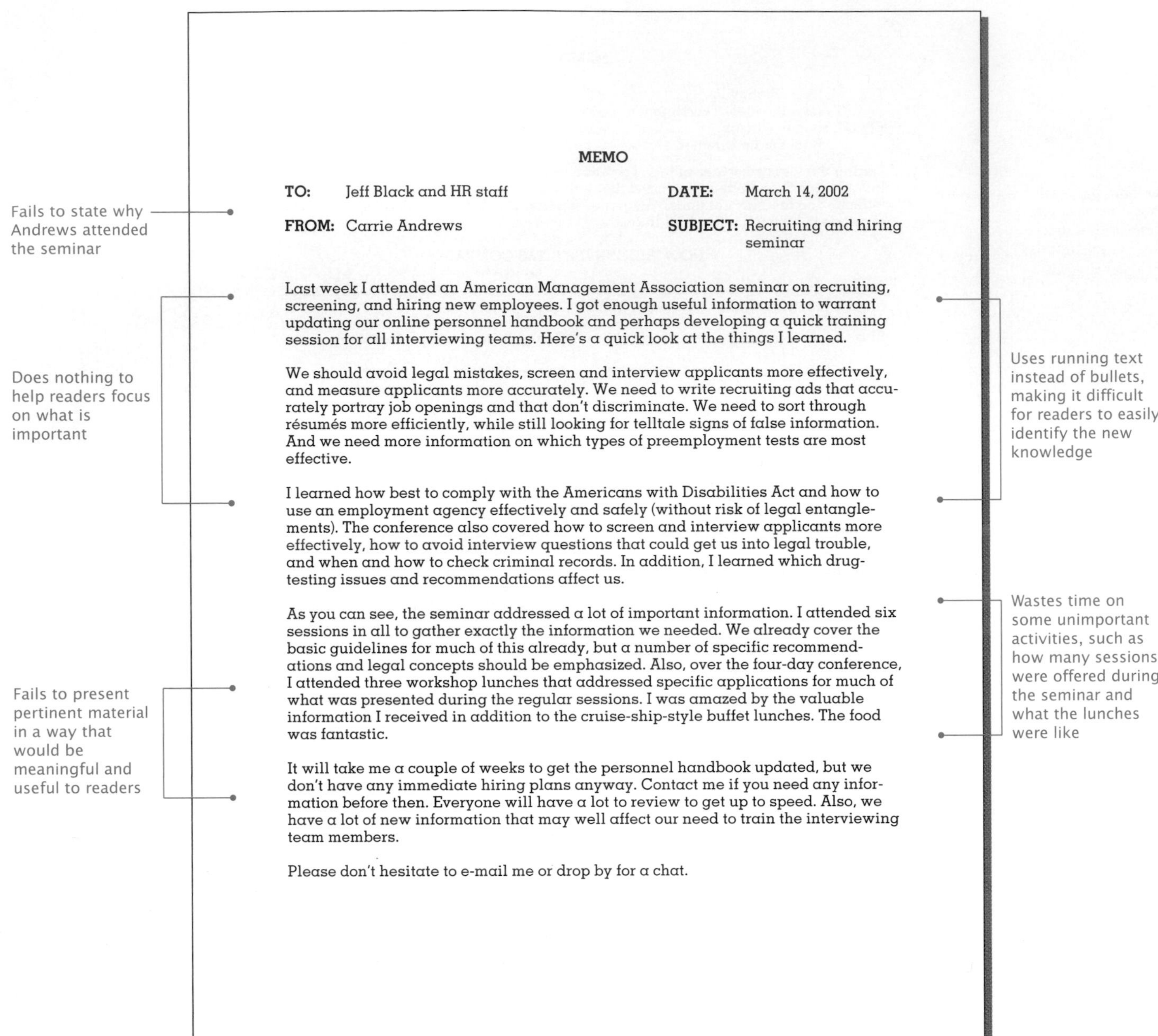

MEMO

TO: Jeff Black and HR staff
DATE: March 14, 2002
FROM: Carrie Andrews
SUBJECT: Recruiting and hiring seminar

Last week I attended an American Management Association seminar on recruiting, screening, and hiring new employees. I got enough useful information to warrant updating our online personnel handbook and perhaps developing a quick training session for all interviewing teams. Here's a quick look at the things I learned.

We should avoid legal mistakes, screen and interview applicants more effectively, and measure applicants more accurately. We need to write recruiting ads that accurately portray job openings and that don't discriminate. We need to sort through résumés more efficiently, while still looking for telltale signs of false information. And we need more information on which types of preemployment tests are most effective.

I learned how best to comply with the Americans with Disabilities Act and how to use an employment agency effectively and safely (without risk of legal entanglements). The conference also covered how to screen and interview applicants more effectively, how to avoid interview questions that could get us into legal trouble, and when and how to check criminal records. In addition, I learned which drug-testing issues and recommendations affect us.

As you can see, the seminar addressed a lot of important information. I attended six sessions in all to gather exactly the information we needed. We already cover the basic guidelines for much of this already, but a number of specific recommendations and legal concepts should be emphasized. Also, over the four-day conference, I attended three workshop lunches that addressed specific applications for much of what was presented during the regular sessions. I was amazed by the valuable information I received in addition to the cruise-ship-style buffet lunches. The food was fantastic.

It will take me a couple of weeks to get the personnel handbook updated, but we don't have any immediate hiring plans anyway. Contact me if you need any information before then. Everyone will have a lot to review to get up to speed. Also, we have a lot of new information that may well affect our need to train the interviewing team members.

Please don't hesitate to e-mail me or drop by for a chat.

have visited several colleges and universities to interview and recruit new employees, Martinez analyzes statistics about the interviews and prepares his annual report for the human resources director (see Figure 12.5 on page 384).

His report tracks how many students applied, were interviewed on campus, were flown to corporate headquarters for further interviews, and were eventually hired. The Seattle company has divisions in Europe and Asia, so Martinez also tracks language fluency. In addition, he includes recruiting costs (by college, company department, and new employee), so his report not only documents expenses but also helps the company decide which institutions are best for future recruiting. Because the director already knows the report's purpose and content, Martinez spends little time on extensive introductory material and organizes all the data in tables.

FIGURE 12.4 In-Depth Critique: Carrie Andrews's Personal Activity Report—Revised Version

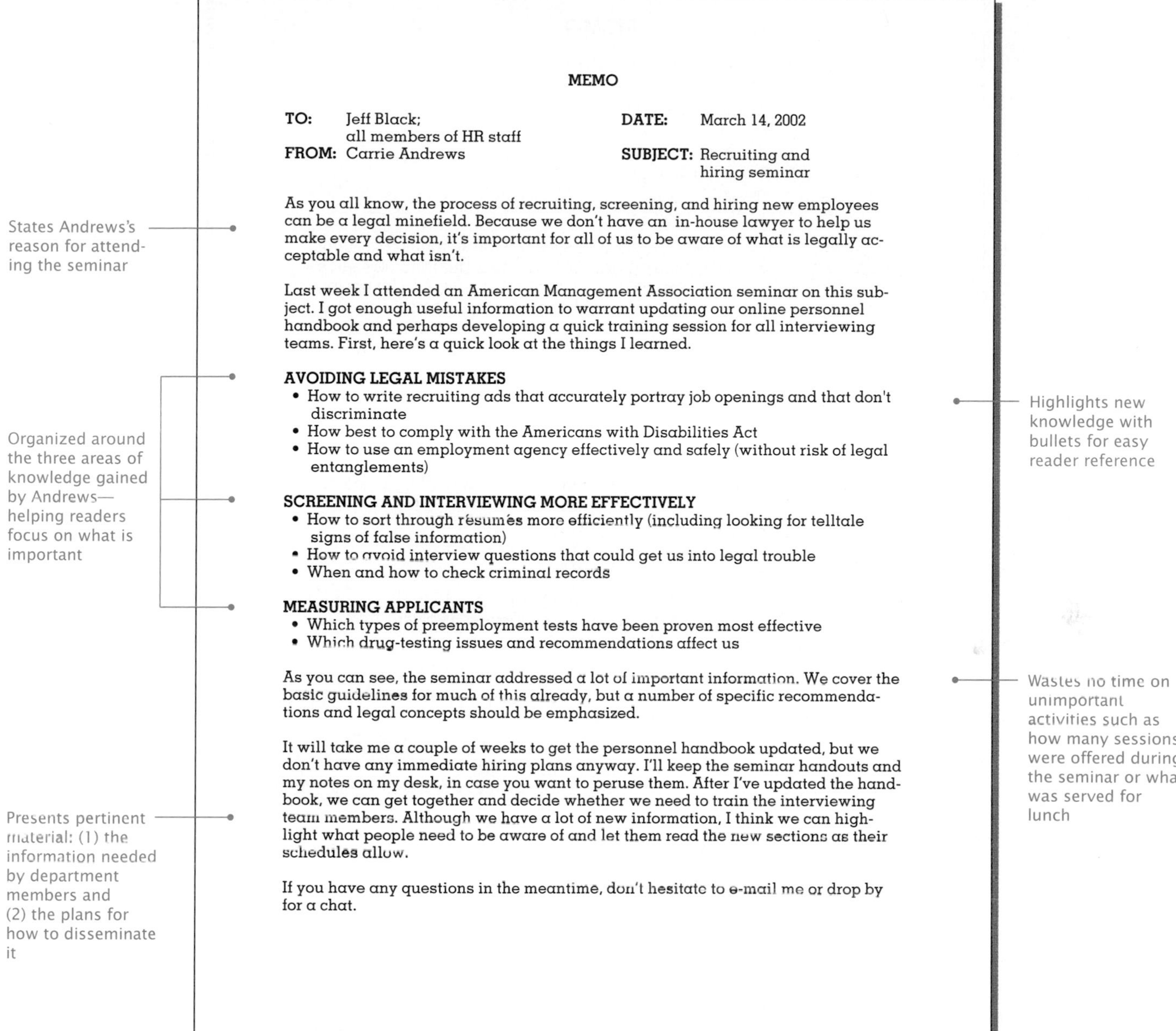

MEMO

TO: Jeff Black; all members of HR staff
FROM: Carrie Andrews
DATE: March 14, 2002
SUBJECT: Recruiting and hiring seminar

As you all know, the process of recruiting, screening, and hiring new employees can be a legal minefield. Because we don't have an in-house lawyer to help us make every decision, it's important for all of us to be aware of what is legally acceptable and what isn't.

Last week I attended an American Management Association seminar on this subject. I got enough useful information to warrant updating our online personnel handbook and perhaps developing a quick training session for all interviewing teams. First, here's a quick look at the things I learned.

AVOIDING LEGAL MISTAKES

- How to write recruiting ads that accurately portray job openings and that don't discriminate
- How best to comply with the Americans with Disabilities Act
- How to use an employment agency effectively and safely (without risk of legal entanglements)

SCREENING AND INTERVIEWING MORE EFFECTIVELY

- How to sort through résumés more efficiently (including looking for telltale signs of false information)
- How to avoid interview questions that could get us into legal trouble
- When and how to check criminal records

MEASURING APPLICANTS

- Which types of preemployment tests have been proven most effective
- Which drug-testing issues and recommendations affect us

As you can see, the seminar addressed a lot of important information. We cover the basic guidelines for much of this already, but a number of specific recommendations and legal concepts should be emphasized.

It will take me a couple of weeks to get the personnel handbook updated, but we don't have any immediate hiring plans anyway. I'll keep the seminar handouts and my notes on my desk, in case you want to peruse them. After I've updated the handbook, we can get together and decide whether we need to train the interviewing team members. Although we have a lot of new information, I think we can highlight what people need to be aware of and let them read the new sections as their schedules allow.

If you have any questions in the meantime, don't hesitate to e-mail me or drop by for a chat.

Reports for Implementing Policies and Procedures

Managers are unable to talk firsthand with everyone in an organization, so they rely on *policy and procedure reports.* Written reports are available to be read and reread by anyone with a question. These reports present their information in a straightforward matter. Even so, writers can have difficulty keeping the policies broad and the procedures simple. Highly respected retailer Nordstrom limited its policy manual to one sentence: "Use your best judgment at all times."[5] Some policy/procedure reports are preserved as lasting guidelines; others are onetime position papers.

Policy/procedure reports help managers communicate the company's standards.

Lasting Guidelines **Lasting guidelines** comprise the rules of an organization. For example, the production supervisor might develop guidelines for standardizing quality-control procedures, or the office manager might issue a memo explaining how to

Some policies and procedures provide lasting "recipes" for how things should be done.

FIGURE 12.5 In-Depth Critique: Juan Martinez's Recruiting Report (Excerpt)

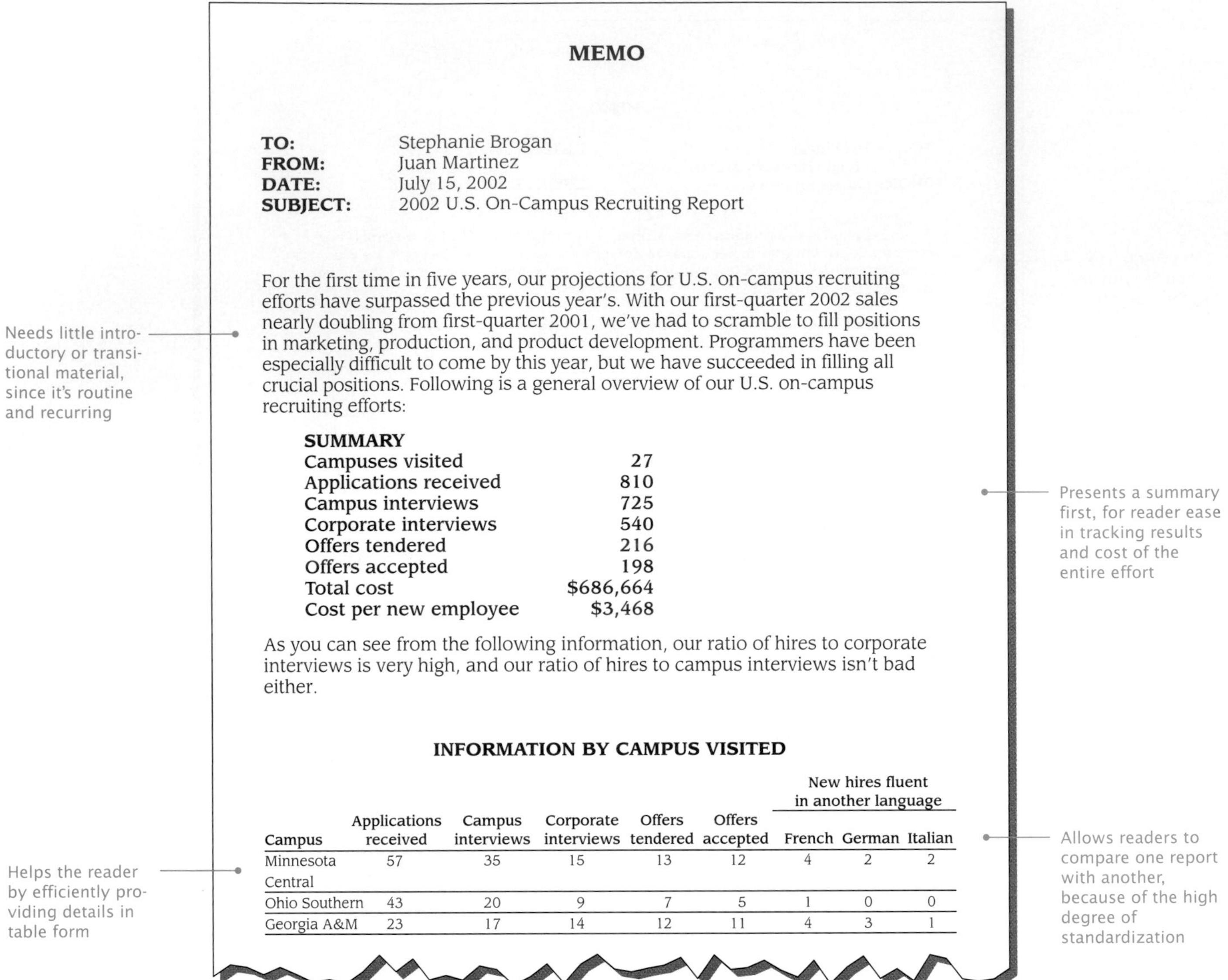

MEMO

TO: Stephanie Brogan
FROM: Juan Martinez
DATE: July 15, 2002
SUBJECT: 2002 U.S. On-Campus Recruiting Report

For the first time in five years, our projections for U.S. on-campus recruiting efforts have surpassed the previous year's. With our first-quarter 2002 sales nearly doubling from first-quarter 2001, we've had to scramble to fill positions in marketing, production, and product development. Programmers have been especially difficult to come by this year, but we have succeeded in filling all crucial positions. Following is a general overview of our U.S. on-campus recruiting efforts:

SUMMARY	
Campuses visited	**27**
Applications received	**810**
Campus interviews	**725**
Corporate interviews	**540**
Offers tendered	**216**
Offers accepted	**198**
Total cost	**$686,664**
Cost per new employee	**$3,468**

As you can see from the following information, our ratio of hires to corporate interviews is very high, and our ratio of hires to campus interviews isn't bad either.

INFORMATION BY CAMPUS VISITED

Campus	Applications received	Campus interviews	Corporate interviews	Offers tendered	Offers accepted	New hires fluent in another language: French	German	Italian
Minnesota Central	57	35	15	13	12	4	2	2
Ohio Southern	43	20	9	7	5	1	0	0
Georgia A&M	23	17	14	12	11	4	3	1

reserve the conference room for special meetings. Such policy/procedure reports then become part of the company's large body of lasting guidelines for doing things a certain way.

Other policies and procedures explain management's position on passing events.

Position Papers In contrast to lasting guidelines, **position papers** treat less-permanent issues. They explain management's views on particular nonrecurring issues or problems as they arise. For example, an office manager might write a report on the need for extra security precautions after a rash of burglaries in the area.

A building access policy is one example of a lasting guideline.

Case Study: William Lawson's Building Access Policy William Lawson is in charge of security for a medical research lab. Many of the scientists employed there work irregular hours—especially when a deadline approaches or when experiments need constant monitoring. Employees who must work nights or weekends were issued a key to the outside door. However, the company recently won several new government contracts and tripled its number of employees. With so many new faces, Lawson believed it was time to establish a more formal policy for building access. See Figure 12.6 for an excerpt from Lawson's policy report.

FIGURE 12.6 In-Depth Critique: William Lawson's Building Access Policy (Excerpt)

BUILDING ACCESS PROCEDURES

PURPOSE

The nature of our business demands a balance between free access to lab facilities and security for both equipment and information. One of the implications of our success in recent years is a dramatic increase in the number of employees, so much so that we can no longer rely on an informal approach to security. We've designed this new program to minimize the burden on employees while maximizing security. The program involves four elements:

- Photo ID badges for all employees
- A building access checkpoint
- A procedure for reporting unauthorized or suspicious entry
- Policies regarding personal guests and professional visitors

Employee ID Badges

To make personnel identification both easy and accurate, each employee will be issued a photo ID badge that must be worn at all times while in the building. The Human Resources Department will arrange photo sessions for all current employees. Badges for future new hires will be made during the new-employee orientation session.

Access Checkpoint

During normal working hours, 8:00 a.m. to 5:00 p.m. Monday through Friday, all employees will enter the building through the front door. Employees must show their photo ID badge to the receptionist before entering the lab.

For access after hours, all department heads will identify which employees need to enter the building outside normal working hours. A list of these employees will be kept at the receptionist's desk. After hours and on weekends the desk will be manned by a security guard. Each employee wanting to enter the building must show the guard a valid company ID card and must be included on the authorization list. If the employee is not on the list, the security guard will deny access.

Reporting Unauthorized or Suspicious Entry

We all stand to benefit from improved security, so the company considers it everyone's responsibility to watch for and report unauthorized or suspicious entry to the building.

Contains ample introductory and background information, since this is a special policy report

Establishes topics and emphasizes major points

Follows the format used in the company's policy and procedures manual

Emphasizes the important elements of the policy, as well as the steps in the procedure

Reports for Complying with Government Regulations

All *compliance reports* are written in response to regulations of one sort or another, most of them imposed by government agencies. The regulatory agency issues instructions on how to write the necessary reports. The important thing is to be honest, thorough, and accurate.

Compliance reports explain what a company is doing to conform to government regulations.

Annual Compliance Reports Perhaps the most common examples of governmental **annual compliance reports** are *income tax returns, annual reports* from corporations that have a pension plan, and *annual shareholder reports* for companies that sell their stock to the general public. The second half of annual shareholder reports must conform to information requirements laid out by the Securities and Exchange Commission (SEC), but the first half serves a public relations function, giving corporations a forum for educating and persuading readers about everything from corporate strategy to public misperceptions of company business. In fact, some companies show remarkable

Many compliance reports are prepared on an annual basis.

creativity and playfulness with their annual reports. Eskimo Pie produced a report in the shape of a popsicle, Comcast had a jigsaw puzzle for a front cover, and Oracle put its annual report on CD-ROM.[6]

Government agencies monitor and control their licensees by requiring interim compliance reports.

Interim Compliance Reports Many taxing and regulatory agencies monitor and control the compliance of their licensees by requiring **interim compliance reports**. Public corporations, for example, are required by the SEC to file *10Q quarterly reports*. Large employers are required to submit monthly and quarterly *employment tax reports* to the federal government and the state in which they operate. Licensed institutions such as nursing homes and child-care facilities are required to file a number of compliance reports similar to the one filed by Tai Chen.

Case Study: Tai Chen's Child-Care Facility Report Tai Chen operates a child-care facility in her home. To keep her state license current, she must submit regular reports on how her facility meets various state requirements. The report lists information such as the size of the facility, the number of bathrooms, whether the outdoor play area is fenced, and the number of staff members.

"I started my day-care center when I had my first child," Chen said. "That way I could stay home with my own children while still earning an income. Before I applied for my license, I had no idea how many regulations apply to child care and how much paperwork is involved." Figure 12.7 provides an excerpt from one of Chen's reports. It is straightforward and takes as little time as possible to prepare from the records that Chen keeps.

Reports for Documenting Progress

Reports documenting progress on a contract provide all the information the client needs.

Progress reports vary in importance and complexity. Some are a mere formality; others are a vital element in the client relationship. Whether you're writing a progress report for a client or for your boss, it's important to anticipate your reader's needs and to provide the required information clearly and tactfully.

Progress reports are generally submitted on a regular basis. They may be required monthly or weekly, or they may be keyed to phases of the project. In many cases these interim progress reports are followed by a final report at the conclusion of the contract.

Projects or jobs that take place over time must provide regular updates in the form of progress reports.

Interim Progress Reports **Interim progress reports** naturally vary in length, depending on the period covered and the complexity of the contract. They give others an idea of the work that has been accomplished to date. They are often keyed to the work plan that was established at the beginning of the contract or project. The writer states what tasks have been accomplished, identifies problems, outlines future steps, and summarizes important findings. If a strict deadline is involved, you can include a Gantt chart (see Figure 11.7 on page 346) to illustrate whether the project is on schedule.

At the end of the project, a final report provides a wrap-up of results.

Final Reports **Final reports** are generally more elaborate than interim reports and serve as a permanent record of what was accomplished. They focus on results rather than on progress. They deal with what was done, not with how it got done.

Case Study: Carlyce Johnson's Interim Progress Report Carlyce Johnson runs the office for her family's landscaping business. The jobs vary from replanting a few beds to installing thousands of square feet of new lawn and beds for businesses. Each customer must approve the design before installation can begin, and Johnson is responsible for monitoring and reporting progress on every job.

"Our landscaping jobs vary in length from part of a day to several months," explains Johnson. "Often the only report required is a short final report sent to the customer with our bill. For long jobs, I send weekly or monthly progress reports. These reports can vary from 1 to 20 pages, depending on the complexity of the

FIGURE 12.7 In-Depth Critique: Tai Chen's Compliance Report (Excerpt)

DEPARTMENT OF HEALTH AND SOCIAL SERVICES
ANNUAL COMPLIANCE REPORT

State law requires that all day-care facilities file this form by March 31 of each year. Failure to complete this form fully and accurately may result in loss of your day-care license. All questions on the form must be answered; if you need to speak with a licensing advisor before submitting the form, call the Department of Health and Social Services at 555-1754.

Needs no lengthy introduction because it is required and routine

FACILITY	
Type of facility:	Private home
Owner:	Tai and Hoa Chen
Type and age of building:	Brick, 14 years
Street address:	1625 Grandview
City:	Peterborough
Hours of operation:	7:00 a.m. to 6:00 p.m. Monday through Friday
Square footage of facility:	2,300 sq. ft total; 600 sq. ft used for child care
Play area provided:	600 sq. ft indoor playroom; 2,000 sq. ft fenced backyard
Number of bathrooms:	2.5 total, 1 opening directly off playroom
Location of emergency exits:	Door leads directly from room to fenced backyard
Number of children cared for:	Five
Age range:	2 to 9 years old
Meals provided:	Breakfast, lunch, snacks
STAFF	
Number of staff:	One
Education level:	B.A. in Elementary Education
Medical training:	Certified in first aid and CPR

Follows the format dictated by the regulatory agency's instructions

Emphasizes concise detail with impersonal legalistic language

Highly standardized because it is prepared for external readers who review many reports of the same type

installation." For an excerpt from one of Johnson's interim progress reports, see Figure 12.8.

Analytical Reports

In addition to informational reports, managers such as Michael Dell rely on the supporting information, analyses, and recommendations presented in analytical reports to make informed decisions. For instance, after studying a series of monthly sales-and-activity informational reports, Dell might review a special report analyzing why sales are declining so that he can develop new programs to help turn things around.

Analytical reports require a strong foundation of facts combined with good insight and excellent communication skills on the part of the writer. Typically, an analytical report ends by presenting a decision (or a solution) to a problem or by recommending a number of actions. The body of the report presents all the facts (both good and bad)

Learning Objective 3

Describe two types of analytical reports and provide examples of each

Reports that help managers make decisions about problems and opportunities are especially interesting to write.

FIGURE 12.8 In-Depth Critique: Carlyce Johnson's Interim Progress Report (Excerpt)

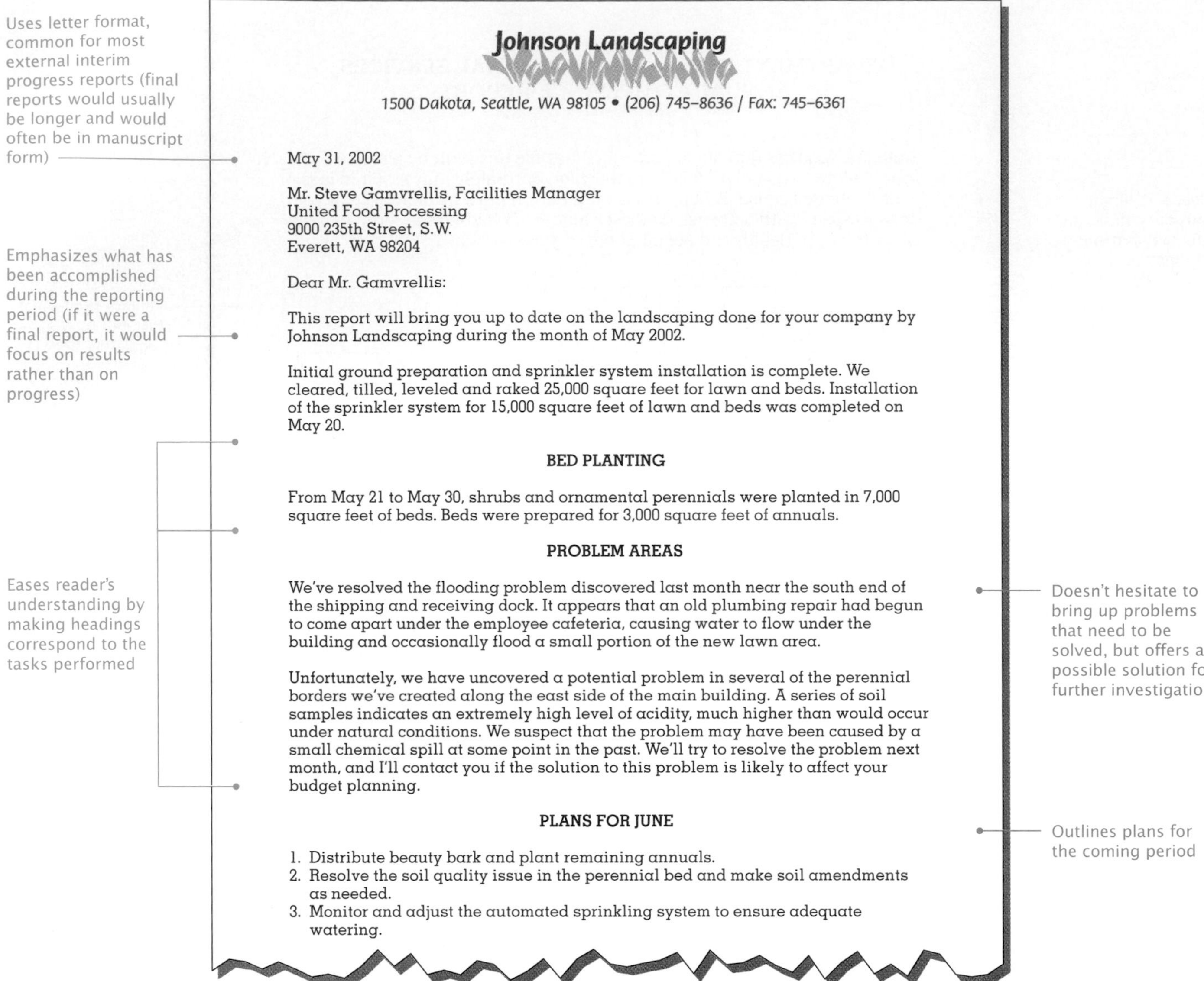

Johnson Landscaping

1500 Dakota, Seattle, WA 98105 • (206) 745-8636 / Fax: 745-6361

May 31, 2002

Mr. Steve Gamvrellis, Facilities Manager
United Food Processing
9000 235th Street, S.W.
Everett, WA 98204

Dear Mr. Gamvrellis:

This report will bring you up to date on the landscaping done for your company by Johnson Landscaping during the month of May 2002.

Initial ground preparation and sprinkler system installation is complete. We cleared, tilled, leveled and raked 25,000 square feet for lawn and beds. Installation of the sprinkler system for 15,000 square feet of lawn and beds was completed on May 20.

BED PLANTING

From May 21 to May 30, shrubs and ornamental perennials were planted in 7,000 square feet of beds. Beds were prepared for 3,000 square feet of annuals.

PROBLEM AREAS

We've resolved the flooding problem discovered last month near the south end of the shipping and receiving dock. It appears that an old plumbing repair had begun to come apart under the employee cafeteria, causing water to flow under the building and occasionally flood a small portion of the new lawn area.

Unfortunately, we have uncovered a potential problem in several of the perennial borders we've created along the east side of the main building. A series of soil samples indicates an extremely high level of acidity, much higher than would occur under natural conditions. We suspect that the problem may have been caused by a small chemical spill at some point in the past. We'll try to resolve the problem next month, and I'll contact you if the solution to this problem is likely to affect your budget planning.

PLANS FOR JUNE

1. Distribute beauty bark and plant remaining annuals.
2. Resolve the soil quality issue in the perennial bed and make soil amendments as needed.
3. Monitor and adjust the automated sprinkling system to ensure adequate watering.

and persuades readers to accept a stated decision, an action, or the recommendations detailed throughout the report. To persuade the reader, the writer carefully analyzes the facts and presents an argument in one of several ways, generally organizing ideas around conclusions, recommendations, or logical arguments. (Chapter 13 will discuss how to organize and present arguments in reports.)

Although the content of analytical reports may vary greatly, all of them tend to ask "should we or shouldn't we" questions: Should we expand into this market? Should we reorganize the research department? Should we invest in new equipment? Should we close this plant? Should we replace our computer system? Should we hire additional sales representatives? Two of the more common examples of analytical reports are problem-solving reports and proposals.

Problem-Solving Reports

Problem-solving reports provide management with background information and analysis of options.

When solving problems, managers need both basic information and detailed analysis to evaluate the possible solutions. *Problem-solving reports* provide such information and analyses. These reports typically require secondary or primary research on a number of topics, which include product demand, growth projections, competitor profiles, company strengths and weaknesses, and sales trends and forecasts. If the report is prepared on a computer, it might include a financial model that allows managers to compare various scenarios by plugging in different assumptions and projections.

Mindy and David Greenberg, owners of Chew-ets candies, studied a variety of analytical reports to help them decide on the merits of exporting their candies to countries in South America. Once the decision was made to expand globally, the two entrepreneurs acted fast and built a growing market—increasing company sales by 10 percent.

Troubleshooting Reports *Troubleshooting reports* are one type of problem-solving report. Whenever a problem exists, somebody has to investigate it and propose a solution. Regardless of the specific problem at hand, these troubleshooting reports deal with the same basic research questions: How did this problem arise, what's the extent of the damage, and what can we do about it? These reports usually start with some background information on the problem, then analyze alternative solutions, and finally recommend the best approach.

Feasibility and Justification Reports From time to time employees and managers write reports to evaluate the practicality and advisability of pursuing an optional course of action such as purchasing equipment, changing a procedure, hiring a consultant, entering into a venture with another company, or consolidating divisions. A **feasibility report** is a problem-solving report that studies proposed options to assess whether any or all of them are sound. The report answers such questions as: Will this action work? Is it profitable? Is one action better than the other? In some cases the report might conclude that a proposed action is not feasible because it is too costly to implement or because the advantages do not outweigh the disadvantages. If alternatives are presented, such as building a new facility or leasing an existing one, the report will evaluate each option and present a recommendation for the most attractive one.

Justification reports are similar to feasibility reports except for a timing difference. Justification reports are written after a course of action has been taken or after a decision has been made to justify the action or decision. For instance, if a company decides to build a new facility instead of leasing one, a justification report would provide the details and analysis to support or justify that decision.

Proposals

A **proposal** is a special type of analytical report designed to get products, plans, or projects accepted by others. Proposals are an important type of job-related writing because their acceptance can lead to significant operational improvements, new business, additional jobs, and safer working conditions. Proposals can be one or two pages, or they can be hundreds of pages if they involve large, complex jobs.

Proposals are reports written to get products, plans, or projects accepted by others.

Although the size and scope of a proposal can vary, these special types of reports analyze the audience's needs or a problem, present the solution to the problem, and persuade the audience that the solution presented is the best approach. Proposals are classified in two ways: (1) according to their target audience (internal versus external) and (2) according to their source (solicited versus unsolicited). In both cases, proposals are usually read by people in positions of authority.

Learning Objective 4

Discuss how internal proposals differ from external proposals

Internal Proposals **Internal proposals** are submitted to decision makers in one's own organization. They have two primary purposes: (1) to seek approval for a project or course of action (such as revising recruiting procedures, changing the company's training programs, reorganizing a department, engaging in a special study, or adopting a more efficient and effective way of doing something) or (2) to request additional resources (such as new or upgraded capital assets, human resources, or operating funds). Because most internal proposals advocate a change, you must take extra care to determine whether your audience will feel threatened by your plan.

Internal proposals are directed to decision makers in the organization.

Case Study: Shandel Cohen's Internal Proposal A good internal proposal explains why a project or course of action is needed, what it will involve, how much it will cost,

FIGURE 12.9 In-Depth Critique: Shandel Cohen's Internal Proposal

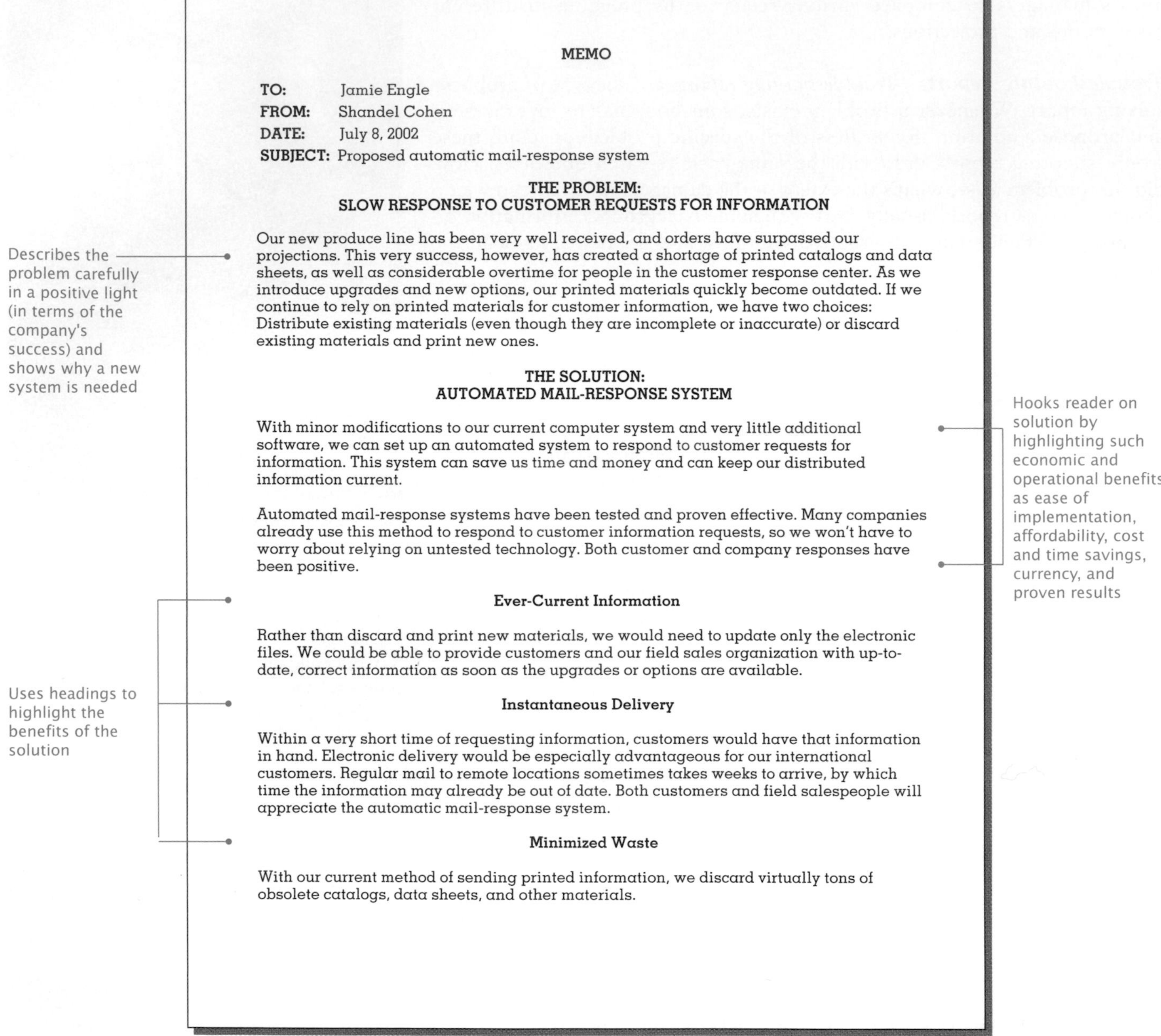

MEMO

TO: Jamie Engle
FROM: Shandel Cohen
DATE: July 8, 2002
SUBJECT: Proposed automatic mail-response system

THE PROBLEM:
SLOW RESPONSE TO CUSTOMER REQUESTS FOR INFORMATION

Our new produce line has been very well received, and orders have surpassed our projections. This very success, however, has created a shortage of printed catalogs and data sheets, as well as considerable overtime for people in the customer response center. As we introduce upgrades and new options, our printed materials quickly become outdated. If we continue to rely on printed materials for customer information, we have two choices: Distribute existing materials (even though they are incomplete or inaccurate) or discard existing materials and print new ones.

THE SOLUTION:
AUTOMATED MAIL-RESPONSE SYSTEM

With minor modifications to our current computer system and very little additional software, we can set up an automated system to respond to customer requests for information. This system can save us time and money and can keep our distributed information current.

Automated mail-response systems have been tested and proven effective. Many companies already use this method to respond to customer information requests, so we won't have to worry about relying on untested technology. Both customer and company responses have been positive.

Ever-Current Information

Rather than discard and print new materials, we would need to update only the electronic files. We could be able to provide customers and our field sales organization with up-to-date, correct information as soon as the upgrades or options are available.

Instantaneous Delivery

Within a very short time of requesting information, customers would have that information in hand. Electronic delivery would be especially advantageous for our international customers. Regular mail to remote locations sometimes takes weeks to arrive, by which time the information may already be out of date. Both customers and field salespeople will appreciate the automatic mail-response system.

Minimized Waste

With our current method of sending printed information, we discard virtually tons of obsolete catalogs, data sheets, and other materials.

(continued)

and how the company will benefit, as does Shandel Cohen's internal proposal for an automatic mail-response system (see Figure 12.9). It must also be completely unbiased.

Cohen manages the customer-response section of the marketing department at a Midwest personal computer manufacturer. Her section sends out product information requested by customers and the field sales force. Cohen has observed that the demand for information increases when a new product is released and diminishes as a product matures. This fluctuating demand causes drastic changes in her section's workload.

"Either we have more work than we can possibly handle," says Cohen, "or we don't have enough to keep us busy. But I don't want to get into a hiring-and-firing cycle." Cohen is also concerned about the amount of printed material that's discarded when products are upgraded or replaced.

FIGURE 12.9 (Continued)

2

By maintaining and distributing the information electronically, we would eliminate this waste. We would also free up a considerable amount of floor space and shelving that is required for storing printed materials.

Of course, some of our customers may still prefer to receive printed materials, or they may not have access to electronic mail. For these customers, we could simply print copies of the files when we receive requests.

Lower Overtime Costs

Besides savings in paper and space, we would also realize considerable savings in wages. Because of the increased interest in our new products, we must continue to work overtime or hire new people to meet the demand. An automatic mail-response system would eliminate this need, allowing us to deal with fluctuating interest without a fluctuating work-force.

Setup and Operating Costs

Carefully explains the costs of the proposal

The necessary equipment and software costs approximately $15,000. System maintenance and upgrades are estimated at $5,000 per year.

We expect the following annual savings from eliminating printed information:

$100,000	Printing costs
25,000	Storage costs
5,000	Postage
20,000	Wages
$150,000	Total savings

Justifies the cost by detailing projected annual savings

CONCLUSION

Closes by offering to answer any questions management may have— rather than trying to anticipate management's questions and including unnecessary detail

I will be happy to answer any questions you have about this system. I believe that such an automated mail-response system would greatly benefit our company, in terms of both cost and customer satisfaction. If you approve, we can have it installed and running in six weeks.

Cohen's internal proposal seeks management's approval to install an automatic mail-response system. Because the company manufactures computers, she knows that her boss won't object to a computer solution. Also, since profits are always a concern, her report emphasizes the financial benefits of her proposal. Her report describes the problem, her proposed solutions, the benefits to the company, and the projected costs.

External Proposals **External proposals** are submitted to decision makers outside of an organization, such as current or potential clients and government agencies. Like internal proposals, they solicit approval for projects or funds, but they have some important differences.

One difference is that external proposals are legally binding. Unlike internal proposals, external proposals form the basis of a contract if approval is granted, so they are prepared with extreme care. External proposals spell out precisely what your company will provide under specific terms and conditions. If you propose to sell 500 units at $250 each, you are bound to deliver at that price, come what may.

Another important difference is that external proposals often compete for a client's business. Although internal proposals may compete for company dollars, time, or resources, they don't compete for business; your company knows its own operation. However, the audience for your external proposal may

When writing proposals, Don Lessem understands the importance of showing potential investors how they can make money. Through his company, Dinosaur Productions, Lessem creates traveling dinosaur exhibits, such as *Dinosaurs of Jurasic Park/The Lost World* and *Discovering Dinosaurs*. For *The Lost World* exhibit, Lessem raised some $1.8 million from private investors. Since 1997, the exhibit has been traveling from museum to museum, making the company about $100,000 for each three-month stay.

External proposals are directed to outsiders, and if accepted, they become legally binding documents.

not know your company, so your proposal must convince readers that your organization is the best source of a product or service. When writing external proposals, you devote considerable space to explaining your experience, qualifications, facilities, and equipment. You must also show that you clearly understand your reader's problem or need.[7] Moreover, because external proposals are directed to outsiders, they tend to be more formal than internal proposals.

Learning Objective 5

Explain the function of a request for proposal (RFP)

A solicited proposal demonstrates that your organization is better qualified than competitors to handle a particular contract.

Solicited Proposals **Solicited proposals** are generally prepared at the request of external parties who need something done, but they may also be requested by such internal sources as management or the board of directors. Some external parties prepare an invitation to bid on their contract, called a *request for proposal* (RFP), which includes instructions that specify the exact type of work to be performed along with guidelines on how and when the company wants the work completed. You respond to RFPs by preparing a proposal that shows how you would meet the potential customer's needs. Say that the National Aeronautics and Space Administration (NASA) decides to develop a new satellite. The agency prepares an RFP that specifies exactly what the satellite should accomplish and sends it to several aerospace companies, inviting them to bid on the job.

To attract a large pool of qualified bidders, RFPs are sent to firms with good performance records in the field. They are also printed in trade publications and posted on the web. For example, the Commerce Business Daily, www.cos.com, lists the government's requests for equipment, supplies, and a variety of services. Regardless of how companies obtain an RFP, they must decide whether they're interested in the job and whether they have a reasonable chance of winning the contract. When the proposal effort actually begins, the company reviews the requirements, defines the scope of the work, determines the methods and procedures to be used, and estimates time requirements, personnel requirements, and costs. Then the proposal writers put it all on paper—exactly as specified in the RFP, following the exact format it requires and responding meticulously to every point it raises.[8]

Effective solicited proposals address each item listed in the RFP.

Unsolicited Proposals **Unsolicited proposals** are initiated by organizations attempting to obtain business or funding without a specific invitation from a potential client. They may also be initiated by employees or managers who wish to convince company insiders to adopt a program, policy, or idea. In other words, with an unsolicited proposal, the writer makes the first move.

An unsolicited proposal must first establish that a problem exists.

Unsolicited proposals also differ from solicited proposals in another important respect: Because the reader may not know about the problem you are addressing, the proposal must convince the reader that a problem exists and that you can solve it. Thus, unsolicited proposals generally spend considerable time explaining why the reader should take action and convincing the reader of the benefits of buying (or funding) something.

The form, length, and purpose of unsolicited proposals vary widely.

Unsolicited proposals vary widely in form, length, and purpose. For example, a university seeking funding for a specific research project might submit an unsolicited proposal to a large local corporation. To be convincing, the university's proposal would show how the research could benefit the corporation and would demonstrate that the university has the resources and expertise to conduct the research.[9] Or an entrepreneur seeking funding for a new venture might modify a business plan to create a proposal that shows potential investors the return they should expect in exchange for the use of their funds. Such a proposal would try to convince investors of the viability of the new business.

APPLYING THE THREE-STEP WRITING PROCESS TO BUSINESS REPORTS AND PROPOSALS

The three-step writing process applies to reports as well as to other business messages.

As with other business messages, when writing reports and proposals, you benefit from following the three-step writing process: (1) planning, (2) writing, and (3) completing business messages (see Figure 12.10). However, when preparing these longer messages,

FIGURE 12.10 The Three-Step Writing Process for Reports

Planning

Analyze
Study the situation and define the problem. Write the statement of purpose, select an appropriate report type, compose a preliminary outline, and develop a work plan.

Investigate
Gather primary and secondary information.

Adapt
Establish a good audience relationship and choose the right channel.

Writing

Organize
Decide on format, length, order, and structure.

Compose
Prepare final outline and draft introduction, body, and closing. Control your style through level of formality and tone. Establish a time perspective and provide supporting detail. Help readers find their way.

Completing

Revise
Evaluate content and review readability; edit and rewrite for conciseness and clarity.

Produce
Use effective design elements. Include prefatory and supplemental parts.

Proofread
Review text and visuals for errors in layout, spelling, and mechanics.

you may need to add some tasks to the familiar categories, or you may need to pay special attention to tasks you're already familiar with. For example, when planning a report, besides analyzing your purpose and your audience, you'll want to study the situation carefully to determine whether a report is called for and which type of report would be most appropriate. Because much of the writing process is covered in Chapters 4, 5, and 6, the following sections discuss only those parts that differ for reports and proposals.

This chapter focuses on Step 1, planning business reports and proposals. Step 2 is discussed in Chapter 13, "Writing Business Reports and Proposals," and Step 3 is the subject of Chapter 14, "Completing Formal Business Reports and Proposals."

The planning tasks for reports fall into the three familiar categories: analysis, investigation, and adaptation.

Analyzing the Situation

When planning a report, you will of course need to analyze your audience and purpose. But even before that, you'll want to analyze your particular situation to decide whether it merits writing a report in the first place. For instance, you may decide that your situation would best be handled by making a phone call, sending an e-mail, or conducting a meeting. If you do decide that writing a report is your best approach, you must determine whether to write an informational or an analytical report. For informational reports, you define the specific purpose of your report and select a report type that is appropriate for your purpose. For analytical reports, you must first define the problem your report will address before stating the purpose of your report and selecting an appropriate report type.

When writing reports, pay special attention to analysis tasks such as defining the problem and developing the statement of purpose.

Defining the Problem for Analytical Reports

In some cases, the problem your analytical report addresses may be defined by the person who authorizes the report. In other cases, you will have to define the problem you need to resolve. Be careful not to confuse a simple topic (campus parking) with a problem (the lack of enough campus parking). Moreover, if you're the only person who thinks a particular issue is a problem, your readers won't be very interested in your solution unless your report first convinces them that a problem does exist. This need for persuasion is especially important in unsolicited proposals.

The problem you need to resolve may be defined by your superior.

To help define the problem that your analytical report will address, answer these questions:

- What needs to be determined?
- Why is this issue important?
- Who is involved in the situation?
- Where is the trouble located?
- How did the situation originate?
- When did it start?

Not all these questions apply in every situation, but asking them helps you define the problem being addressed and limit the scope of your discussion.

Another way to help define the problem is to factor it.

Also try breaking down the "perceived" problem into a series of logical, connected questions that try to identify cause and effect. This process is sometimes called **problem factoring**. You probably subconsciously approach most problems this way. When your car won't start, what do you do? You use the available evidence to organize your investigation, to start a search for cause-and-effect relationships. For example, if the engine doesn't turn over at all, you might suspect a dead battery. If the engine does turn over but won't fire, you can conclude that the battery is okay but perhaps you're out of gas. When you speculate on the cause of a problem, you're forming a **hypothesis**, a potential explanation that needs to be tested. By subdividing a problem and forming hypotheses based on available evidence, you can tackle even the most complex situations.

Studies that focus on problem solving may be structured around hypotheses that the report writer plans to prove or disprove during the investigation.

Developing the Statement of Purpose

The statement of purpose defines the objective of your report.

Developing a statement of purpose will help you keep your report writing on task. In contrast to the problem statement, which defines *what* you are going to investigate, the **statement of purpose** defines *why* you are preparing the report (see Table 12.1).

The most useful way to phrase your purpose statement is to begin with an infinitive phrase. For instance, in an informational report, your statement of purpose can be as simple as these:

- To update clients on the progress of the research project (interim progress report)
- To develop goals and objectives for the coming year (strategic plan)

TABLE 12.1 Problem Statements Versus Purpose Statements

Problem Statement	***Statement of Purpose***
Our company's market share is steadily declining.	To explore different ways of selling our products and to recommend the ones that will most likely increase our market share.
Our current computer network system is inefficient and cannot be upgraded to meet our future needs.	To analyze various computer network systems and to recommend the system that will best meet our company's current and future needs.
We need $2 million to launch our new product.	To convince investors that our new business would be a sound investment so that we can obtain desired financing.
Our current operations are too decentralized and expensive.	To justify the closing of the Newark plant and the transfer of East Coast operations to a single Midwest location in order to save the company money.

- To identify customers and explain how the company will service them (marketing plan)
- To submit monthly sales statistics to management (periodic operating report)
- To summarize what occurred at the annual sales conference (personal activity report)
- To explain the building access procedures (policy implementation report)
- To submit required information to the SEC (compliance report)

Using an infinitive phrase (*to* plus a verb) encourages you to take control and decide where you're going before you begin. When you choose an infinitive phrase (*to inform, to confirm, to analyze, to persuade, to recommend*), you pin down your general goal in preparing the report.

The statement of purpose for analytical reports is often more comprehensive than for informational reports. Linda Moreno, the cost accounting manager for Electrovision, a high-tech company based in Los Gatos, California, was recently asked to find ways of reducing employee travel and entertainment costs (her complete report appears in Chapter 14). Because Moreno was supposed to suggest specific ways of reducing these costs, she phrased her statement of purpose accordingly:

Statements of purpose for analytical reports are often more complex than are those for informational reports.

> . . . to analyze the T&E [travel and entertainment] budget, evaluate the impact of recent changes in airfares and hotel costs, and suggest ways to tighten management's control over T&E expenses.

If Moreno had been assigned an informational report instead, she might have stated her purpose differently:

> To summarize Electrovision's spending on travel and entertainment.

You can see from these two examples how much influence the purpose statement has on the scope of your report. If Moreno's manager had expected her to suggest ways to reduce costs but Moreno had collected only cost data, her report would have failed to meet expectations. Because she was assigned an analytical report rather than an informational report, Moreno had to go beyond merely collecting data to drawing conclusions and making recommendations.

The purpose statement helps shape the scope of your report.

The more specific your purpose statement, the more useful it will be as a guide to planning your report. Furthermore, always double-check your statement of purpose with the person who authorized the report. Seeing the purpose written down in black and white, the authorizer may decide that the report needs to go in a different direction. Once your statement is confirmed, you can use it as the basis for your preliminary outline.

Prepare a written statement of your purpose; then review it with the person who authorized the study.

Developing a Preliminary Outline

Developing a preliminary outline gives you a visual diagram of the report, its important points, the order in which they will be discussed, and the detail to be included. You'll be using the preliminary outline to guide your research efforts and as a foundation for organizing and composing your report. Think of your preliminary report outline as a working draft that you'll revise and modify as you go along. For instance, you may rework your outline to take into account things you learn during your investigation, or you may decide to balance your discussion should you notice that it is too light in one area or too heavy in another.

Preliminary outlines establish the framework for your report.

Keep in mind that your preliminary outline will look different from the final outline you develop to write your report, as Chapter 13 points out. For instance, during your investigation, you might analyze five possible causes of a problem (listed in your preliminary outline) and discover that only two are relevant. In your report, you might not even introduce the three unrelated causes. Your final outline includes only the items you plan to discuss in your report (not any additional topics that you may have included on your preliminary outline).

The outline for investigation differs from the final outline of the report.

Chapter 5 presents two common outline formats that business writers use to guide their writing efforts: alphanumeric and decimal. Regardless of which format you use for your outlines, make sure that items of the same level are grammatically parallel.

TABLE 12.2 Types of Outline Headings

Descriptive (Topical) Outline	*Informative (Talking) Outline*	
	Question Form	*Summary Form*
I. Industry Characteristics	I. What is the nature of the industry?	I. Flour milling is a mature industry.
A. Annual sales	A. What are the annual sales?	A. Market is large.
B. Profitability	B. Is the industry profitable?	B. Profit margins are narrow.
C. Growth rate	C. What is the pattern of growth?	C. Growth is modest.
1. Sales	1. Sales growth?	1. Sales growth averages less than 3 percent a year.
2. Profit	2. Profit growth?	2. Growth in profits is flat.

Use parallel construction to show that your ideas are related, of similar importance, and on the same level of generality.

Parallel construction shows that the ideas are related, of similar importance, and on the same level of generality, as the following example demonstrates:

Why are we having trouble hiring secretaries?

I. Are salaries too low?
   a. What do we pay our secretaries?
   b. What do comparable companies pay their secretaries?
   c. How important is pay in influencing secretaries' job choices?
II. Is our location poor?
   a. Are we accessible by public transportation and major roads?
   b. Is the area physically attractive?
   c. Are housing costs affordable?
   d. Is crime a problem?
III. Is the supply of secretaries diminishing?
   a. How many secretaries were available five years ago as opposed to now?
   b. What was the demand for secretaries five years ago as opposed to now?

Informative outline headings are useful in guiding your work.

When wording outlines, choose between descriptive (topical) and informative (talking) headings. In some cases you may use these same headings for your final report. As Chapter 6 points out, descriptive headings label the subject that will be discussed, whereas informative headings (in either question or summary form) suggest more about the meaning of the issues (see Table 12.2). Although outlines with informative headings take a little longer to write, they're generally more useful in guiding your work and easier for others to review. If other people are going to comment on your outline, they may not have a clear idea of what you mean by the descriptive heading "Advertising." However, they will get the main idea if you use the informative heading "Did Ad Budget Cuts Cause Sales to Decline?"

With a purpose and a preliminary outline in place, you're ready to get to work. Writing a report can be a lengthy and encompassing task that involves primary and secondary research, preparation of visuals, and a number of other tasks. Preparing a work plan is one way to coordinate and monitor your efforts.

Preparing the Work Plan

In business, most reports have a firm deadline and finite resources. You not only have to produce quality reports, you have to do so quickly and efficiently. A carefully thought-out work plan is the best way to make sure you produce quality work on schedule. By identifying all the tasks that must be performed, you ensure that nothing is overlooked.

Whether you prepare an informal work plan for yourself or a detailed work plan for your team, be sure it identifies all the tasks that must be performed.

If you are preparing the work plan for yourself, it can be relatively informal: a simple list of the steps you plan to take and an estimate of their sequence and timing. If you're conducting a lengthy, formal study, however, you'll want to develop a detailed work plan that can guide the performance of many tasks over a span of time. Most proposals require a detailed work plan, which becomes the basis for a contract if the proposal is accepted. A formal work plan might include the following elements (especially the first two):

Learning Objective 6

Identify seven elements often included in a formal work plan

- **Statement of the problem.** The problem statement clarifies the challenge you face, helps you (and anyone working with you) stay focused on the core problem, and helps everyone avoid the distractions that are likely to arise during report preparation.
- **Statement of the purpose and scope of your investigation.** The purpose statement describes what you plan to accomplish with this report and thus the boundaries of your work. Stating which issues you will cover and which issues you won't cover is especially important with complex, lengthy investigations.
- **Discussion of tasks to be accomplished.** Be sure to indicate your sources of information, the research necessary, and any constraints (on time, money, personnel, or data). For simple reports, the list of tasks to be accomplished will be short and probably obvious. However, longer reports and complex investigations require an exhaustive list so that you can reserve time with customers, with executives, or for outside services such as pollsters or print shops.
- **Description of any products that will result from your investigation.** In many cases, the only product of your efforts will be the report itself. In other cases, you'll need to produce something beyond a report, perhaps a new marketing plan or even a tangible product. Make these expectations clear at the outset, and be sure to schedule enough time and resources to get the job done.
- **Review of project assignments, schedules, and resource requirements.** Indicate who will be responsible for what, when tasks will be completed, and how much the investigation will cost. If more than one person will be involved, you may also want to include a brief section on coordinating report writing and production. (Collaborative writing is discussed in detail in Chapter 2.)
- **Plans for following up after delivering the report.** Follow-up can be as simple as making sure people received the information they need or as complex as conducting additional research to evaluate the results of proposals included in your report. Even informal follow-up can help you improve your future reports and communicate that you care about your work's effectiveness and its impact on the organization.
- **Working outline.** Some work plans include a tentative outline of the report, as does the plan in Figure 12.11. This plan was developed for a report on whether to launch a company newsletter.

Investigating Information

Whether you're writing informational or analytical reports, you may need to gather data on specific companies, industries, trends, issues, products, events, or any number of topics. As discussed in Chapter 10, when researching long business messages, you'll need to complete all six tasks in the research process (see Figure 10.1 on page 308):

1. Identify the right questions to understand the topic and assignment
2. Find and access secondary and primary information
3. Evaluate and finalize your sources
4. Process your information
5. Analyze your data
6. Interpret your findings

These tasks need not be performed in this specific order. Also, the time you spend on each task depends on the sort of information you need and on the situation, your purpose, and your audience.

Adapting Your Report to Your Audience

Learning Objective 7

Clarify what it means to adapt your report to your audience

As with any business communication, you'll want to make sure that your report is audience-centered. To do that, you need to establish a good relationship with your

FIGURE 12.11 In-Depth Critique: Work Plan for a Formal Study

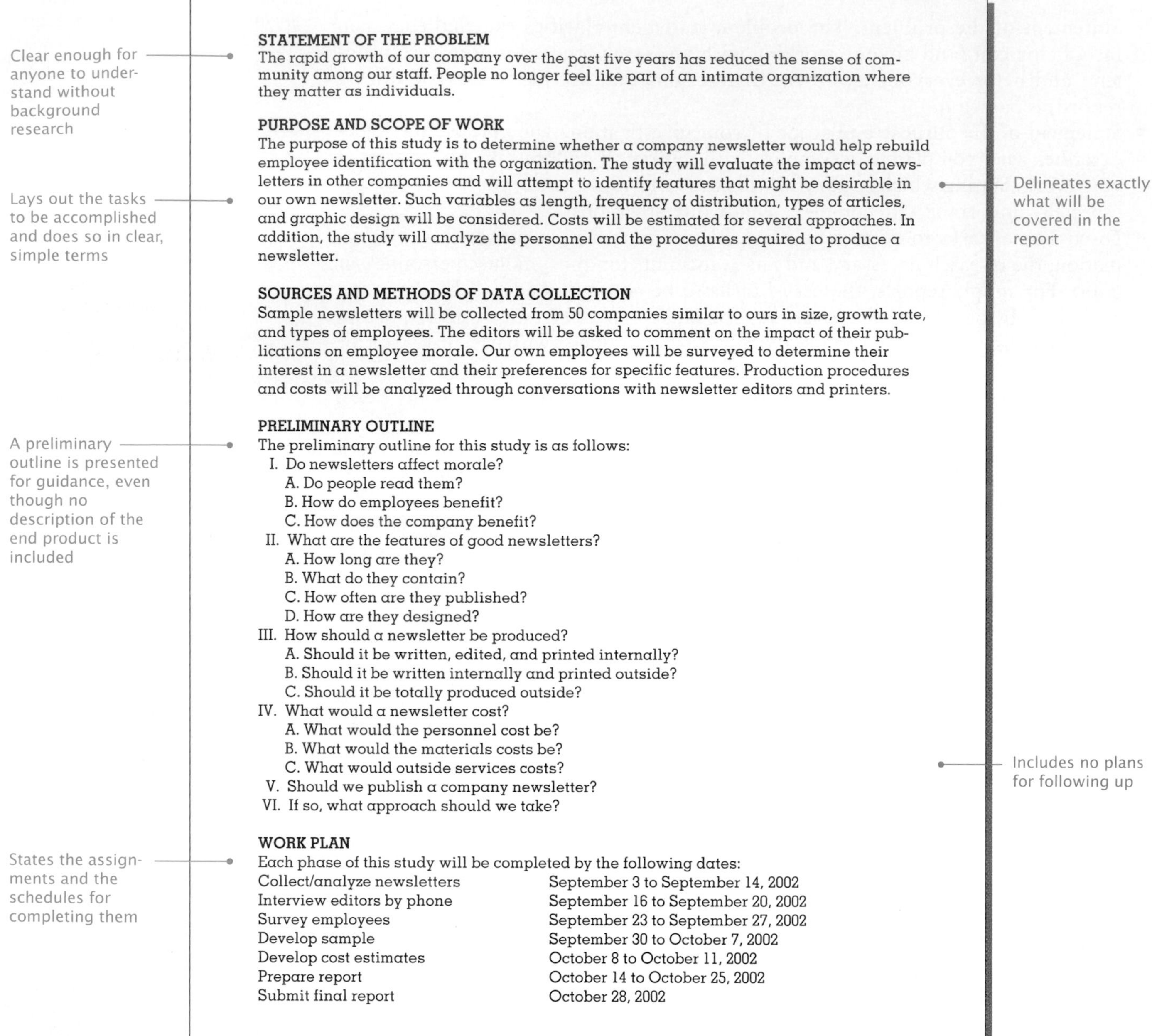

STATEMENT OF THE PROBLEM
The rapid growth of our company over the past five years has reduced the sense of community among our staff. People no longer feel like part of an intimate organization where they matter as individuals.

PURPOSE AND SCOPE OF WORK
The purpose of this study is to determine whether a company newsletter would help rebuild employee identification with the organization. The study will evaluate the impact of newsletters in other companies and will attempt to identify features that might be desirable in our own newsletter. Such variables as length, frequency of distribution, types of articles, and graphic design will be considered. Costs will be estimated for several approaches. In addition, the study will analyze the personnel and the procedures required to produce a newsletter.

SOURCES AND METHODS OF DATA COLLECTION
Sample newsletters will be collected from 50 companies similar to ours in size, growth rate, and types of employees. The editors will be asked to comment on the impact of their publications on employee morale. Our own employees will be surveyed to determine their interest in a newsletter and their preferences for specific features. Production procedures and costs will be analyzed through conversations with newsletter editors and printers.

PRELIMINARY OUTLINE
The preliminary outline for this study is as follows:

I. Do newsletters affect morale?
   A. Do people read them?
   B. How do employees benefit?
   C. How does the company benefit?
II. What are the features of good newsletters?
   A. How long are they?
   B. What do they contain?
   C. How often are they published?
   D. How are they designed?
III. How should a newsletter be produced?
   A. Should it be written, edited, and printed internally?
   B. Should it be written internally and printed outside?
   C. Should it be totally produced outside?
IV. What would a newsletter cost?
   A. What would the personnel cost be?
   B. What would the materials costs be?
   C. What would outside services costs?
V. Should we publish a company newsletter?
VI. If so, what approach should we take?

WORK PLAN
Each phase of this study will be completed by the following dates:

Collect/analyze newsletters	September 3 to September 14, 2002
Interview editors by phone	September 16 to September 20, 2002
Survey employees	September 23 to September 27, 2002
Develop sample	September 30 to October 7, 2002
Develop cost estimates	October 8 to October 11, 2002
Prepare report	October 14 to October 25, 2002
Submit final report	October 28, 2002

readers. You must also select a channel and medium that are appropriate to your readers and your purpose.

Establishing a Good Relationship with Your Audience

Establishing a good relationship with an audience is the same for reports as for other business messages.

Even though reports are meant to be factual, objective, and logical, they will succeed only if they focus on the audience. To help your audience accept what you're saying, remember the following advice:

- **Use the "you" attitude.** Show readers how your report answers *their* questions and solves *their* problems.
- **Emphasize the positive.** Even if your report recommends a negative action, remember to state the facts and make your recommendations positively. Instead of using a negative tone ("The only way we'll ever strengthen our cash position is to reduce

employee spending"), use a positive, forthright one ("Reducing employee spending will strengthen our cash position").

- **Establish your credibility.** One of the best ways to gain your audience's trust is to be thorough, research all sides of your topic, and document your findings with credible sources.
- **Be polite.** Earn your audience's respect by being courteous, kind, and tactful.
- **Use bias-free language.** Avoid unethical and embarrassing blunders in language related to gender, race, ethnicity, age, and disability.
- **Project the company's image.** Whether your report is intended for people inside or outside the company, be sure to plan how you will adapt your style and your language to reflect the image of your organization.

Selecting the Appropriate Channel and Medium

As with other business messages, you'll need to select the best format for conveying your report. In some cases a simple letter, memo, or e-mail message will do. At other times you'll need to write a formal report or discuss your findings in an oral presentation. You may even decide to prepare your report in an electronic format and post it on the company intranet.

For reports, channel and medium choice depends not only on audience and purpose but also on classification.

Written Reports Most reports are produced in writing for one of two reasons: (1) They contain complex information that needs to be presented in a logical and structured format, or (2) they are used for future reference. Chapter 4 discusses the benefits of using a written format.

Oral Reports In some cases you might want to deliver your report orally—perhaps as a presentation to managers, suppliers, or customers. Oral reports are most appropriate when you want immediate feedback, when there's an emotional component to your report, or when nonverbal communication is an important element of your message. Oral presentations can take the place of a written report, or they may accompany a written report. Chapter 15 discusses how to plan, write, and complete oral presentations. Chapter 16 explains how to create effective slides and overhead transparencies for your oral presentations.

Written reports can be accompanied with an oral presentation.

Electronic Reports The growing use of electronic communication in the workplace has made electronic reports an increasingly popular option. Electronic reports are stored on electronic media. They may be distributed on disk, attached to an e-mail, or posted on a website. Their electronic format makes it possible to include video, sound, and other multimedia effects in the report. Thousands of companies are using electronic reports to communicate with employees, customers, and suppliers (see "Keeping Pace with Technology: Minding Your Business with Online Reporting").[10]

Electronic reports are becoming increasingly popular.

When compared with their paper counterparts, electronic reports offer both advantages and disadvantages. The advantages include the following:

Learning Objective 8

Cite the advantages and disadvantages of electronic reports

- **Cost savings.** After the initial expenditure for hardware and software, electronic reports can save a significant amount of money in terms of paper, printing or photocopying, and distribution.
- **Space savings.** Electronic reports can be stored in far less space than paper reports: A basic CD-ROM can hold the equivalent of hundreds of pages of text, and higher-capacity CD-ROMs and other massive storage devices are on the way. This ease of storage can be a significant advantage for large businesses, businesses with heavy government reporting requirements, and businesses that must keep historical records for many years.
- **Faster distribution.** Electronic documents can reach their audiences in a few seconds, compared with the hours or days it can take to send paper documents to other locations. For example, the small pharmaceutical company Isis can compress its 40,000-page reports onto one CD-ROM, filing its reports with the U.S Food and Drug Administrations in one-third the usual time. Saving time increases the

Keeping Pace with Technology

Minding Your Business with Online Reporting

Mrs. Fields uses them. Mrs. Paul's uses them. However, you don't have to be in the cookie or fish business to work with electronic reports. More and more companies are adopting electronic reports over hard-copy reports to keep employees, managers, investors, and other stakeholders informed.

Computerized cash registers in Mrs. Fields cookie outlets are the heart of a sophisticated reporting system for monitoring and controlling operations. Rather than taking the time to write reports by hand, store managers enter data into the computer system by following report formats on their screen. Then they electronically transmit these reports to corporate headquarters in Park City, Utah. The computer system also serves as a two-way communication device, allowing store and corporate personnel to send messages back and forth in seconds. So Mrs. Fields corporate managers can quickly receive the information they need in order to track sales and productivity trends—and to spot potential problems—in more than 700 outlets around the world.

At Mrs. Paul's, a computerized reporting system allows production managers to continuously monitor and control the yield from the company's fish-processing operation. The system calculates the production yield using the weight of the fish before it's processed, the weight of any scraps, and the weight of the finished fish meals. If the reports show that the actual yield drops below the expected yield, the managers can immediately adjust the equipment to improve the yield. The production managers have instant access to electronic reports at each stage of the operation, so they can find and fix problems more quickly than if they had to wait for printed reports.

FedEx, the well-known package-shipping firm, uses extensive satellite and computer technologies to track the location of every package in the company's system. Customers can then access electronic reports to monitor the status of their shipments at any time. This tracking system not only helps the company serve its customers better, but it puts valuable information in the hands of customers with a click of the mouse. Like many companies, FedEx posts an electronic copy of its annual report and other corporate informational reports at its website.

As Mrs. Fields, Mrs. Pauls, FedEx, and other companies know, keeping customers, employees, investors, and other stakeholders informed with electronic reports is the only way to do business in the global workplace.

Career Applications

1. What advantages and disadvantages do you see in asking store managers at Mrs. Fields to file electronic troubleshooting reports immediately on the company's intranet?
2. What kinds of electronic reports might a company want to post on its website?

company's chances of being the first to introduce a new drug into the market—a critical advantage in the pharmaceutical industry.[11]

- **Multimedia features.** Sound and video can be integrated into some electronic reports, bringing text to life.
- **Easier maintenance.** The content of electronic reports can be easily changed, which makes such reports easier to correct, update, and customize for a user's individual needs. If a single figure changes in a sales report after you've distributed it, your options with a paper report are to reprint and redistribute the entire thing, send out a corrected page, or send a memo to all the recipients asking them to pencil in the correction by hand. But with an electronic report, you simply make the change and let everyone know via e-mail. This method ensures that the one copy of the report is kept current.[12]

For all their advantages, however, electronic reports are not a cure-all for business. Disadvantages of electronic reports include the following:

- **Hardware and software costs.** Naturally, you need some kind of computer equipment to create and distribute electronic documents. If those systems aren't already in place, their purchase, installation, and maintenance is an extra expense.
- **Computer system incompatibility.** As discussed in Component Chapter B, corporate intranets are helping businesspeople get around the computer compatibility problem, but those companies lacking intranets may find themselves with incompatible computer systems that preclude the use of electronic documents.

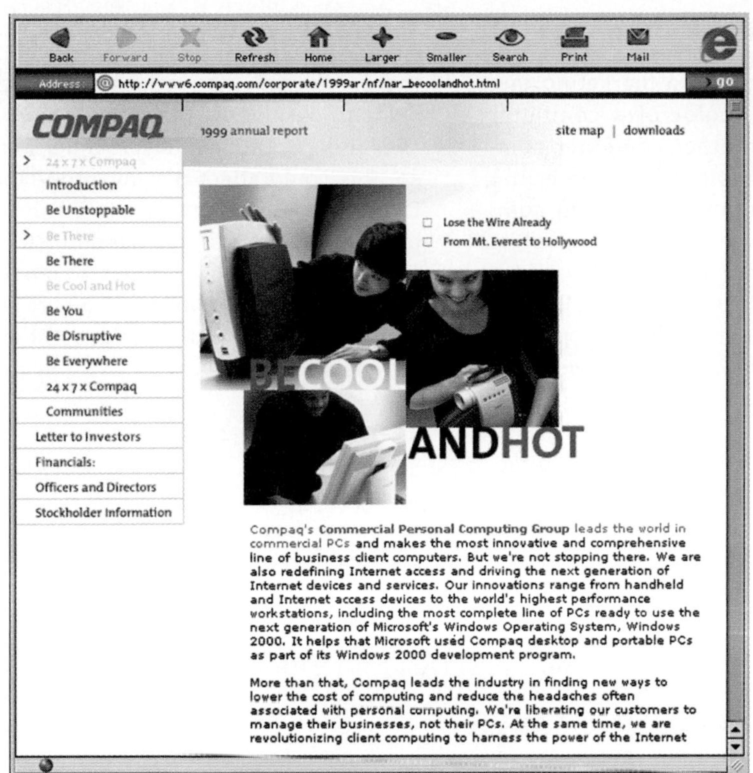

One big advantage of electronic reports is the ability to include a linked table of contents on each page and to highlight where readers are in the report. Readers can easily navigate the various sections of the Compaq online annual report by clicking on one of the headings.

- **Training needs.** Beyond the ability to read, receivers require little training in order to access most paper business reports. However, reading electronic reports can require training in using web browsers, accessing databases, or other skills.
- **Risks to data security and integrity.** Because information in electronic reports is not fixed on paper, it is vulnerable to tampering and inadvertent corruption. Even innocent computer errors can affect electronic reports and cause your carefully crafted document to end up as electronic rubbish.[13]

For additional discussion of communication challenges such as data security, sabotage, and theft, see Component Chapter B. This chapter's "Checklist: Planning Business Reports" reviews the tasks and concepts involved in planning business reports and proposals. Chapter 13 discusses the next step of the report-writing process: how to organize and compose reports and proposals. Chapter 14 concludes the three-step report-writing process by explaining how to assemble and format formal reports and proposals.

✓ CHECKLIST: PLANNING BUSINESS REPORTS

A. Analyzing the situation

1. Determine whether the situation merits writing a report.
2. Define the problem (for analytical reports) by answering questions, factoring the problem, and forming a hypothesis.
3. Develop a statement of purpose that specifically defines why you're preparing the report.
4. Select an appropriate report type.
5. Prepare a work plan to clarify the tasks to be accomplished; describe any products that result from the investigation; review all project assignments, schedules, and resource requirements; and plan for following up after the report has been delivered.
6. Develop a preliminary outline, using informative headings in parallel construction.

B. Investigating business reports

1. Find and access primary and secondary information.
2. Process your information.
3. Draw conclusions or develop recommendations if requested to do so.

C. Adapting business reports

1. Establish a good relationship with your audience, using the "you" attitude, emphasizing the positive, establishing your credibility, being polite, using bias-free language, and projecting the company image.
2. Select the appropriate channel and medium for your report, whether written, oral, or electronic.

COMMUNICATION CHALLENGES AT DELL COMPUTER

Michael Dell has authorized a marketing test to determine how the color of a computer affects sales. Although other computer companies have conducted similar research into the dynamics of consumer buying and computer color, Dell wants to know whether the buying habits of Dell customers differ from those of other computer manufacturers' customers. To conduct the test, Dell plans to offer computers with three distinct colors (red, purple, and blue) for a period of three months on its website, www.dell.com.

Individual Challenge: Michael Dell has asked you to recommend a reporting method for tracking sales of the red, purple, and blue computers. Dell explains, "Here's what we need to know: Does one color sell better than the other? Are there regional distinctions? In other words, do buyers respond positively to the same colors no matter where they live, or do West Coast buyers differ from East Coast buyers? If so, this could affect our inventory and our shipment costs. Don't worry about the psychology behind the choices of colors—we'll let marketing handle that." Prepare a short memo to Dell highlighting the kinds of reports the company needs for tracking sales patterns. Be sure to indicate who should write the reports and what kinds of information they should include.

Team Challenge: Your team must decide how to present your findings to Dell in your report. Using Chapter 11 as a guide, would you present your findings in a textual or visual format, or both? If your team decides to use visuals, which chart would best present computer sales by color by regions? ■

SUMMARY OF LEARNING OBJECTIVES

1 **Name five classifications of business reports.** Business reports can be classified according to their (1) source (whether they are voluntary or authorized); (2) frequency (whether they are routine or periodic); (3) target audience (whether they are designed for internal use or for external use by people outside the organization); (4) length (whether they are short or long); and (5) purpose (whether they focus on facts and are intended mainly to educate readers or whether they are designed to provide data analyses, interpretation, and a conclusion).

2 **Describe four types of informational reports and provide examples of each.** Typical informational reports include reports for monitoring and controlling operations, such as plans, operating reports, and personal activity reports; reports for implementing policies and procedures, such as lasting guidelines and position papers; compliance reports, such as annual reports to the SEC, income tax reports, and interim reports filed with regulatory agencies; and reports to document the progress of a project, which may be interim progress reports or final reports.

3 **Describe two types of analytical reports and provide examples of each.** Problem-solving reports are analytical reports that provide information and analyses to help managers make decisions and solve problems. Common problem-solving reports include troubleshooting reports, feasibility reports, and justification reports. Proposals are another type of analytical report. They are designed to get products, plans, or projects approved by others. Proposals typically present a solution to an identified problem and persuade the reader to adopt that solution in addition to hiring the submitting company to perform the work.

4 **Discuss how internal proposals differ from external proposals.** Internal proposals are sent to decision makers in your organization (1) to seek approval for a project or course of action, or (2) to request additional capital or human resources. External proposals are sent to decision makers outside an organization. Like internal proposals, they seek approval and request resources, but unlike internal proposals, they form the basis of a legally binding contract if the proposal is accepted. Moreover, external proposals compete for a client's business, so they must convince readers that the product or service being offered is the best one available.

5 **Explain the function of a request for proposal (RFP).** A request for proposal is an invitation to bid on a contract. It is used to attract and prequalify bidders by specifying the type of work to be performed, the guidelines and timeline for performing the work, and other project-related instructions.

6 **Identify seven elements often included in a formal work plan.** A formal work plan generally includes (1) a problem statement defining what you're going to investigate; (2) a statement of purpose defining *why* you are preparing the report; (3) the tasks to be accomplished and the sequence in which they should be performed; (4) a description of any product that will result from your study; (5) a review of responsibilities, assignments, schedules, and resource requirements; (6) plans for following up after delivering the report; and (7) a working outline.

7 Clarify what it means to adapt your report to your audience. As with other business messages, adapting a report to an audience involves establishing a good relationship and selecting the appropriate channel and medium. When preparing business reports, plan to use the "you" attitude, emphasize the positive, establish your own credibility, be polite, use bias-free language, and project the company's image. Then decide whether to convey your report in a letter, memo, or e-mail message or whether to emphasize formality with a report that's in the form of a manuscript or an oral presentation. For a certain audience, you may decide to convey your report in an electronic format.

8 Cite the advantages and disadvantages of electronic reports. The advantages of electronic reports include cost savings, space savings, faster distribution, multimedia capabilities, and easier maintenance. The disadvantages include the cost of additional hardware, software, and training; the potential for computer system incompatibility; and the possible threat to data security and integrity due to file tampering and inadvertent corruption.

TEST YOUR KNOWLEDGE

1. How can your written reports influence your professional success?
2. Why do routine reports require minimal introductory material?
3. How are reports for monitoring and controlling operations used?
4. What is the function of a strategic plan? Business plan? Marketing plan?
5. What functions do personal activity reports serve?
6. What functions do progress reports serve?
7. Why are written proposals important business documents?
8. What are the two primary purposes of internal proposals?
9. How do proposal writers use a RFP?
10. How can electronic reports save time and money?

APPLY YOUR KNOWLEDGE

1. Why are unsolicited proposals more challenging to write than solicited proposals?
2. What are the advantages and disadvantages of asking your employees to "fill in the blanks" on standardized reporting forms? Briefly explain.
3. If you want to make a specific recommendation in your report, should you include information that might support a different recommendation? Explain your answer.
4. If your report includes only factual information, is it objective? Please explain.
5. **Ethical Choices** If you were writing a troubleshooting report to help management decide how to reduce quality problems at a manufacturing plant, what ethical issues might you face? How might these ethical issues conflict with your need to report all the relevant facts and to offer evidence for your conclusions? Explain briefly.

PRACTICE YOUR KNOWLEDGE

Documents for Analysis

Document 12.A

The Securities and Exchange Commission (SEC) requires all public companies to file a comprehensive annual report (form 10-K) electronically. Many companies post links to these reports on their websites along with links to other company reports. Visit the website of Dell at www.dell.com and view the company's most recent annual reports: 10-K and Year in Review. (To view the reports, follow the links at the homepage to About Dell, Investor Relations, and Annual Reports.) Compare the style and format of the two reports. For which audience(s) is the Year in Review targeted? Who besides the SEC might be interested in the Annual Report 10-K? Which report do you find easier to read? More interesting? More detailed?

Exercises

For live links to all websites discussed in this chapter, visit this text's website at www.prenhall.com/bovee. Just log on and select Chapter 12, and click on "Student Resources." Locate the name of the site or the URL related to the material in the text. For the "Exploring the Best of the Web" exercises, you'll also find navigational directions. Click on the live link to the site.

12.1 **Understanding Business Reports and Proposals: How Companies Use Reports** Interview several people working in a career you might like to enter, and ask them about the types of written reports they receive and prepare. How do these reports tie in to the decision-making process? Who reads the reports they prepare? Summarize your findings in writing, give them to your instructor, and be prepared to discuss them with the class.

12.2 **Understanding Business Reports and Proposals: Report Classification** Using the information presented in this chapter, identify the type of report represented by each of the following examples. In addition, write a brief paragraph about each, explaining who the audience is likely to be, what type of data would be used, and whether conclusions and recommendations would be appropriate.

a. A statistical study of the pattern of violent crime in a large city during the last five years
b. A report prepared by a seed company demonstrating the benefits of its seed corn for farmers
c. A report prepared by an independent testing agency evaluating various types of cold remedies sold without prescription
d. A trip report submitted at the end of a week by a traveling salesperson
e. A report indicating how 45 acres of undeveloped land could be converted into an industrial park
f. An annual report to be sent to the shareholders of a large corporation
g. A report from a U.S. National Park wildlife officer to Washington, D.C., headquarters showing the status of the California condor (an endangered species)
h. A written report by a police officer who has just completed an arrest

12.3  **Internet** Follow the step-by-step hints and examples for writing a funding proposal at www.learnerassociates.net/proposal. Review the writing hints and the entire sample proposal online. What details did the author decide to include in appendixes? Why was this material placed in the appendixes and not the main body of the report? According to the author's tips, when is the best time to prepare a Project Overview?

12.4 **Informational Reports: Personal Activity Report** Imagine you're the manager of campus recruiting for Nortel, a Canadian telecommunications firm. Each of your four recruiters interviews up to 11 college seniors every day. What kind of personal activity report can you design to track the results of these interviews? List the areas you would want each recruiter to report on, and explain how each would help you manage the recruiting process (and the recruiters) more effectively.

12.5 **Informational Reports: Policy Report** You're the vice president of operations for a Florida fast-food chain. In the aftermath of a major hurricane, you're drafting a report on the emergency procedures to be followed by personnel in each restaurant when storm warnings are in effect. Answer who, what, when, where, why, and how, and then prepare a one-page draft of your report.

12.6 **Unsolicited Proposal** You're getting ready to launch a new lawn-care business that offers mowing, fertilizing, weeding, and other services. The lawn surrounding a nearby shopping center looks as if it could use better care, so you target that business for your first unsolicited proposal. To help prepare this proposal, write your answers to these questions:

a. What questions will you need to answer before you can write a proposal to solve the reader's problem? Be as specific as possible.
b. What customer benefits will you include in your proposal?
c. Will you use a letter or memo format for your proposal? Explain your answer.

12.7 **Teamwork: Unsolicited Proposal** Break into small groups and identify an operational problem occurring at your campus involving either registration, university housing, food services, parking, or library services. Then develop a workable solution to that problem. Finally, develop a list of pertinent facts that your team will need to gather to convince the reader that the problem exists and that your solution will work.

12.8 **Analyzing the Situation: Statement of Purpose** Sales at The Style Shop, a clothing store for men, have declined for the third month in a row. Your boss is not sure whether this decline is due to a weak economy or to another unknown reason. She has asked you to investigate the situation and to submit a report to her highlighting some possible reasons for the decline. Develop a statement of purpose for your report.

12.9 **Preparing the Work Plan** Using the situation described in Exercise 12.6, assume that you're the shopping center's facilities manager. You report to the general manager, who must approve any new contracts for lawn service. Before you contract for lawn care, you want to prepare a formal study of the current state of your lawn's health. The report will include conclusions and recommendations for your boss's consideration. Draft a work plan, including the problem statement, the statement of purpose and scope, a description of what will result from your investigation, the sources and methods of data collection, and a preliminary outline.

12.10 **Adapting Reports to the Audience** Review the following sample reports: Figure 12.6, William Lawson's Building Access Policy (Excerpt) and Figure 12.8, Carlyce Johnson's Interim Progress Report (Excerpt). Give concrete examples of how each of these reports establishes a good relationship with the audience. Consider such things as using the "you" attitude, emphasizing the positive, establishing credibility, being polite, using bias-free language, and projecting a good company image.

EXPAND YOUR KNOWLEDGE

Exploring the Best of the Web:

Pointers for Business Plans, p. 380

What are the components of a business plan? What do readers of a plan look for? What common mistakes should you avoid? For answers to these questions and to learn more about the function and content of business plans, log on to bizplanit.com.

1. Why is the executive summary such an important section of a business plan? What kind of information is contained in the executive summary?
2. What is the product/services section? What information should it contain? List some of the common errors to avoid when planning this part.
3. What type of business planning should you describe in the exit strategy section? Why?

Exploring the Web on Your Own

Review these chapter-related websites on your own to learn more about planning and using reports in the workplace.

1. If your report writing involves researching other companies, Wall Street Research network, www.wsrn.com, is one of the most comprehensive company information sites on the Internet.
2. Looking for a specific company? Try SuperPages at www.bigbook.com, where you'll find more than 16 million listings.
3. Searching for information on a company or industry? Internet Prospector, www.internet-prospector.org/company.html, is a good place to begin your online research.

LEARN INTERACTIVELY

Interactive Study Guide

Visit "My Companion Website" at www.prenhall/bovee.com. For Chapter 12, take advantage of the interactive "Study Guide" to test your chapter knowledge. Get instant feedback on whether you need additional studying. Read the "Current Events" articles to get the latest on chapter topics, and complete the exercises—as specified by your instructor.

This site offers a variety of additional resources: The "Research Area" helps you locate a wealth of information to use in course assignments. You can even send a message to online research experts, who will help you find exactly the information you need. The "Study Hall" helps you succeed in this course. "Talk in the Hall" lets you leave messages and meet new friends online. If you have a question, you can "Ask the Tutor." And to get a better grade in this course, you can find more help at "Writing Skills," "Study Skills," and "Study Tips."

Grammar Diagnostic Tests

Review and reinforce your grammar and language skills by taking one of the four online diagnostic tests offered at our companion website, www.prenhall/bovee.com. The four tests cover a variety of topics, including spelling, capitals, punctuation, verbs, pronouns, adjectives, adverbs, sentence structure, sentence punctuation, clarity, word choice, style, organization skills, proofreading, and more. Submit your test and assess your competency. Then focus on improving areas where you are weak as you complete the exercises in this chapter.

Writing Business Reports and Proposals

After studying this chapter, you will be able to

1. *Name four things you must decide on before drafting a business report or proposal*
2. *Describe the structure of informational reports*
3. *Describe the structure of analytical reports*
4. *Name five characteristics of effective report content*
5. *List the topics commonly covered in a report's introduction, body, and closing*
6. *Name six strategies to strengthen your proposal argument*
7. *List the topics commonly covered in a proposal's introduction, body, and closing*
8. *Briefly describe three tools that writers can use in long reports to help readers stay on track*

COMMUNICATION CLOSE-UP AT THE SAN DIEGO WILD ANIMAL PARK

www.sandiegozoo.org

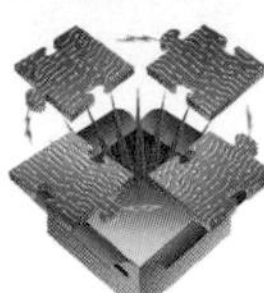

Whether encountering a cheetah, feeding a giraffe, or crossing a floating bridge to a "field biologist's research island," visitors to the San Diego Wild Animal Park aren't likely to be thinking about business proposals. But if it hadn't been for a dedicated team of five park employees and a particularly impressive proposal, the park's 30-acre "Heart of Africa" safari tour would not exist. Hardy tourists would not be trekking through the artificially created African forestland, savanna, wetlands, water holes, and islands to enjoy raging waterfalls, African plants, and lots of animals—grazing antelope, wattled cranes, sacred ibis, colobus monkeys, rhinos, wildebeests, gazelles, and some 250 other species of mammals and birds. If those determined park employees hadn't put their communication skills to work to sell a concept that was initially vetoed by the park's brainstorming committee, there would be no interpretive guides posing as "research scientists" and no demonstrations of radio telemetry tracking.

This is a communication success story. As education manager for the Wild Animal Park, Deirdre Ballou was part of the enthusiastic group that rescued the Heart of Africa concept from its early rejection. "We felt the idea was good and that if we carried it out a little bit more, we could try again," she explains. Ballou worked closely with the park's public relations manager and its curators of birds, mammals, and zoology. These five colleagues agreed among themselves to meet on their own time to develop a proposal that the rest of the committee just couldn't refuse. They would do their homework, they vowed, and then return with a comprehensive, clear, impressive, and persuasive proposal for the Heart of Africa project.

Ballou and her colleagues knuckled down, researched statistics published by zoo and museum professional organizations, and drew on their own experiences working both with the public and with the park's animal collections. They poured this information into their proposal, along with a discussion of the terrific educational opportunities at the research island, hoping to justify the hiring of interpretive staff to portray field researchers. Then, to capture the audience's interest, the team wrote an evocative scenario using "very creative words" to walk committee members through an imaginary tour of the team's vision for the Heart of Africa. They put the sizzle before the steak, as the old adage goes (also known as using the indirect approach). All contributed their expertise to the scenario, but the team's "best writer" did the honors, says Ballou.

"Committees and board members respect and will listen to people who have done their homework," Ballou says now, remembering the excitement of winning the committee's approval. Before long, she was out in the middle of a human-made lagoon in jeans and T-shirt, helping builders complete the final details in time for the Heart of Africa's official opening.

Ballou still routinely writes dozens of reports and proposals—funding proposals, budget and labor reports, and project status reports. And she still starts by asking: Will my audience be receptive? Have we met with them before? Are they expecting a formal presentation or a more casual approach? Then she chooses the right format, length, order,

Whether working on concepts such as the Heart of Africa project, raising funds, or educating sponsors and visitors, Deirdre Ballou often finds herself writing reports and proposals. Ballou pays special attention to the way she organizes and presents her ideas in her communications.

and tone to meet their expectations. But she also recalls with great fondness her participation on the team that saved the Heart of Africa and research island project. Who would have thought that preparing an ordinary business proposal could be so much fun—and so rewarding?[1] ■

ORGANIZING BUSINESS REPORTS AND PROPOSALS

Learning Objective 1

Name four things you must decide on before drafting a business report or proposal

Before you can compose a business report or proposal, you must organize the material you've collected, arranging it in a logical order that meets your audience's needs. Deirdre Ballou advises you to carefully choose the format, length, order, and structure for your report or proposal before drafting even the first word.

Deciding on Format and Length

The format and length decisions may not always be yours to make.

At times, the decision about format and length will be made for you by the person who requests the report. Such guidance is often the case with monitor/control reports, procedural reports, proposals, progress reports, and compliance reports. When selecting a format for your report, you have four options:

You may present a report in one of four formats: preprinted form, letter, memo, or manuscript.

- **Preprinted form.** Used for fill-in-the-blank reports. Most are relatively short (five or fewer pages) and deal with routine information, often mainly numerical. Use this format when it's requested by the person authorizing the report.
- **Letter.** Commonly used for reports of five or fewer pages that are directed to outsiders. These reports include all the normal parts of a letter, but they may also have headings, footnotes, tables, and figures.
- **Memo.** Commonly used for short (fewer than 10 pages) informal reports distributed within an organization. Like longer reports, they often have internal headings and sometimes include visual aids. Memos exceeding 10 pages are sometimes referred to as *memo reports* to distinguish them from their shorter cousins.
- **Manuscript.** Commonly used for reports that require a formal approach, whether a few pages or several hundred. As length increases, reports in manuscript format require more elements before the text (prefatory parts) and after (supplementary parts). Chapter 14 explains these elements in detail.

The more routine the report, the less flexibility you have in deciding format and length. Monthly status reports, for example, are usually pretty routine, so they will

Don't judge the quality or content of a report by its size. Like Smart Cars, smart, compact reports get you where you need to be—easily and conveniently.

have the same basic appearance and structure. Within that framework, however, there is room for flexibility, depending on the nature of the information being reported.

Periodic reports are usually written in memo format and don't need much of an introduction; a subject line on the memo is adequate. They should follow the same general format and organization from period to period. Personal activity reports are also written in memo format, but because they're nonrecurring documents, they require more introduction than periodic reports do.

The length of your report often depends on your subject and purpose, but it's also affected by your relationship with your audience. If your readers are relative strangers, skeptical, or hostile, or if your material is nonroutine or controversial, you usually have to explain your points in greater detail, which results in a longer document. You can afford to be brief if you are on familiar terms with your readers, if they are likely to agree with you, and if the information is routine or uncomplicated. Short reports are more common in business than long ones, and you'll probably write many more 5-page memos than 250-page formal reports.

Length depends on
- Your subject
- Your purpose
- Your relationship with your audience

When you do have some leeway in length and format, base your decisions on your readers' needs. As Wild Animal Park's Deirdre Ballou can attest, your goal is to tell your audience what they need to know in a format that is easy for them to use.

Choosing the Direct or Indirect Approach

The direct approach saves time and makes the report easier to understand by giving readers the main idea first.

What order is best for your audience and purpose? As Chapter 5 explains, when an audience is considered either receptive or open-minded, use the direct approach: Lead off with a summary of your key findings, conclusions, and recommendations. This "up-front" arrangement is by far the most popular and convenient for business reports. It saves time and makes the rest of the report easier to follow. For those who have questions or want more information, later parts of the report provide complete findings and supporting details. The direct approach also produces a more forceful report. You sound sure of yourself when you state your conclusions confidently at the outset.

The indirect approach helps overcome resistance by withholding the main idea until later in the report.

At times, however, confidence may be misconstrued as arrogance. If you're a junior member of a status-conscious organization or if your audience is skeptical or hostile, you may want to use the indirect approach: Introduce your complete findings and discuss all supporting details before presenting your conclusions and recommendations. The indirect approach gives you a chance to prove your points and gradually overcome your audience's reservations. By deferring the conclusions and recommendations, you imply that you've weighed the evidence objectively without prejudging the facts. You also imply that you're subordinating your judgment to that of the audience, whose members are capable of drawing their own conclusions when they have access to all the facts.

Consider length before choosing the direct or indirect approach.

Although the indirect approach has its advantages, some readers will always be in a hurry to get to "the answer" and will flip to the recommendations immediately, thus defeating your purpose. Therefore, consider length before choosing the direct or indirect approach. In general, the longer the message, the less effective an indirect approach is likely to be. Furthermore, an indirect argument is harder to follow than a direct one.

Businesspeople often combine the direct and indirect approaches.

Because both direct and indirect approaches have merit, businesspeople often combine them. They reveal their conclusions and recommendations as they go along, rather than putting them either first or last. Figure 13.1 presents the introductions from two reports with the same general outline. In the direct version, a series of state-

FIGURE 13.1 Direct Approach Versus Indirect Approach in an Introduction

THE DIRECT APPROACH

Since the company's founding 25 years ago, we have provided regular repair service for all our electric appliances. This service has been an important selling point as well as a source of pride for our employees. However, we are paying a high price for our image. Last year, we lost $500,000 on our repair business.

Because of your concern over these losses, you have asked me to study the pros and cons of discontinuing our repair service. With the help of John Hudson and Susan Lefkowitz, I have studied the issue for the past two weeks and have come to the conclusion that we have been embracing an expensive, impractical tradition.

By withdrawing from the electric appliance repair business, we can substantially improve our financial performance without damaging our reputation with customers. This conclusion is based on three basic points that are covered in the following pages:

- It is highly unlikely that we will ever be able to make a profit in the repair business.
- Sevice is no longer an important selling point with customers.
- Closing down the service operation will create few internal problems.

THE INDIRECT APPROACH

Since the company's founding 25 years ago, we have provided repair service for all our electric appliances. This service has been an important selling point as well as a source of pride for our employees. However, the repair business itself has consistently lost money.

Because of your concern over these losses, you have asked me to study the pros and cons of discontinuing our repair service. With the help of John Hudson and Susan Lefkowitz, I have studied the issue for the past two weeks. The following pages present my findings for your review. Three basic questions are addressed:

- What is the extent of our losses, and what can we do to turn the business around?
- Would withdrawal hurt our sales of electrical appliances?
- What would be the internal repercussions of closing down the repair business?

ments summarize the conclusion reached in relation to each main topic on the outline. In the indirect version, the same topics are introduced (in the same order) without drawing any conclusions about them. The conclusions appear within the body of the report instead. So is this second report direct or indirect? Business reports are often difficult to classify.

Regardless of the format, length, or order you use, you must still deal with the question of how your ideas will be subdivided and developed. Suppose you're writing a controversial report recommending that your company revise its policy on who reports to whom. You know that some of your readers will object to your ideas, so you decide to use indirect order. How do you develop your argument? Your job is to choose the most logical structure—the one that suits your topic and goals and that makes the most sense to your audience.

Structuring Informational Reports

Learning Objective 2

Describe the structure of informational reports

Informational reports are the easiest to organize because they provide nothing more than facts. When writing informational reports, reader reaction is not usually an issue. Most readers will presumably respond unemotionally to your material, so you can present it in the most direct fashion possible. What you do need to be concerned about, however, is reader comprehension. The information must be presented logically and accurately so that readers will understand exactly what you mean and be able to use your information in a practical way.

Reader reaction is rarely an issue in informational reports.

When writing an informational report, you can let the nature of whatever you're describing dictate your structure. For example, if you're describing a machine, each component can correspond to a part of your report. If you're describing an event, you can approach the discussion chronologically. And if you're explaining how to do something, you can describe the steps in a process. Informational reports use a **topical organization,** arranging material according to one of the following topics:

Topical organization is arranging material in order of importance, sequence, chronology, spatial relationships, location, or categories.

When choosing an approach for your reports, you must consider the preferences of international audiences—especially if you plan to post the report on your website, as Microsoft does.

- **Importance.** If you're reviewing five product lines, you might organize your study according to the sales for each product line, beginning with the line that produces the most revenue and proceeding to the one that produces the least.
- **Sequence.** If you're studying a process, discuss it step by step—1, 2, 3, and so on.
- **Chronology.** When investigating a chain of events, organize the study according to what happened in January, what happened in February, and so on.
- **Spatial orientation.** If you're explaining how a physical object works, describe it from left to right (or right to left in some cultures), top to bottom, outside to inside.
- **Geography.** If location is important, organize your study according to geography, perhaps by region of the United States or by area of a city.
- **Category.** If you're asked to review several distinct aspects of a subject, look at one category at a time, such as sales, profit, cost, or investment.

There are other bases for organization. Because some informational reports, especially compliance reports and internal reports, are prepared on preprinted forms, they are organized according to instructions supplied by the person requesting the information.

Learning Objective 3

Describe the structure of analytical reports

The structure of analytical reports depends on audience reaction.

Three popular ways to organize analytical reports:
- By conclusions
- By recommendations
- By logical arguments

Structuring Analytical Reports

It is more difficult to organize analytical reports that contain analyses and that are designed to lead the audience to specific conclusions and recommendations. Your choice of structural approach depends on the reaction you anticipate:

- **Receptive audiences.** When you expect your audience to agree with you, use a structure that focuses attention on conclusions and recommendations.
- **Skeptical audiences.** When you expect your audience to disagree with you or to be hostile, use a structure that focuses attention on the rationale behind your conclusions and recommendations.

TABLE 13.1 Common Ways to Structure Analytical Reports

Elements	Conclusions or Recommendations	Logical Argument: 2 + 2 = 4	Logical Argument: Scientific	Logical Argument: Yardstick
Readers	Are likely to accept	Are hostile or skeptical; need convincing	Need most convincing	Need most convincing
Order	Direct	Indirect	Indirect	Indirect
Writer credibility	High	Low	Low	Low
Advantages	Readers quickly grasp conclusions or recommendations	Readers follow writer's thinking process	Readers draw their own conclusions	Alternatives are all measured against same standards (criteria)
Drawbacks	Structure can make topic seem too simple	Structure can make report longer	Must discuss each alternative; very long	Must agree on criteria; can be boring; very long

The three most common structural approaches for analytical reports are (1) focusing on conclusions, (2) focusing on recommendations, and (3) focusing on logical argument (see Table 13.1).

When Jennifer Minorian, a partner at Blevitt and Blatt accounting firm, receives a report, she looks for the bottom line and skims the details to decide whether she needs to act promptly.

Focusing on Conclusions

When writing an analytical report for people from your own organization who have asked you to study something, you're writing for your most receptive readers. They may know from experience that you'll do a thorough job, and they may trust your judgment. If they're likely to accept your conclusions, you can structure your report around conclusions using a direct approach.

However, the direct approach does have some drawbacks. If your readers have reservations about either you or your material, strong statements at the beginning may intensify their resistance. Also, focusing on conclusions may make everything seem too simple. Your readers could criticize your report as being superficial: "Why didn't you consider this option?" or "Where did you get this number?" You're generally better off taking the direct approach in a report only when your credibility is high—when your readers trust you and are willing to accept your conclusions.

Analytical reports may be organized around conclusions and recommendations (direct approach) when the audience is receptive.

Cynthia Zolonka works on the human resources staff of a bank in Houston, Texas. Her company decided to have an outside firm handle its employee training, and a year after the outsourcing arrangement was established, Zolonka was asked to evaluate the results. She explains: "Moving our training programs to an outside supplier was a tough—and controversial—decision for the entire company. Some people were convinced outsourcing would never work; others thought it might save money but would hurt training quality. I took special care to do a thorough analysis of the data, and I supported my conclusion with objective answers, not personal opinions."

Figure 13.2 presents a preliminary outline of Zolonka's report. Her analysis shows that the outsourcing experiment was a success. She structured her report using a direct approach, as the outline illustrates.

When the reader is concerned with conclusions, use them as the main points.

You can use a similar structure whenever you're asked to analyze a problem or an opportunity. Readers who are interested mainly in your conclusions can grasp them quickly, and readers who want to know more about your analysis can look at the data you provide.

FIGURE 13.2 In-Depth Critique: Preliminary Outline of a Research Report Focusing on Conclusions

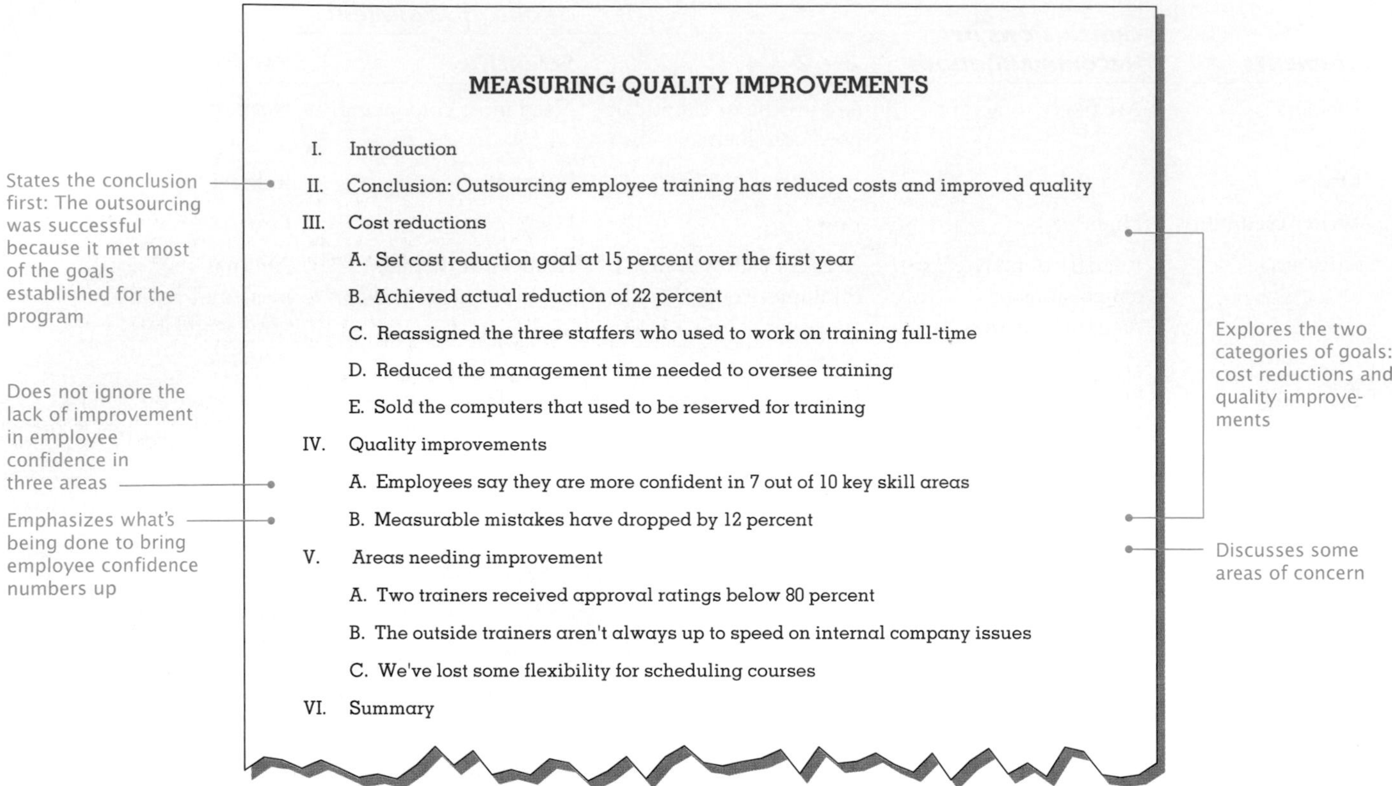

Focusing on Recommendations

When the reader is concerned about what action to take, use recommendations as the main points.

A slightly different approach is useful when your readers want to know what they ought to do (as opposed to what they ought to conclude). You'll often be asked to solve a problem rather than just study it. So the actions you want your readers to take become the main subdivisions of your report.

When structuring a report around recommendations, use the direct approach as you would for a report that focuses on conclusions. Then unfold your recommendations using a series of five steps:

1. Establish the need for action in the introduction, generally by briefly describing the problem or opportunity.
2. Introduce the benefit that can be achieved, without providing any details.
3. List the steps (recommendations) required to achieve the benefit, using action verbs for emphasis.
4. Explain each step more fully, giving details on procedures, costs, and benefits.
5. Summarize the recommendations.

After losing market share to competing retailers with websites, the board of directors of a Chicago-based retail chain asked Alycia Jenn, the business development manager, to suggest whether the company should set up a retailing site on the web and, if so, how to implement the site. As Jenn noted, "Setting up shop on the Internet is a big decision for our company. We don't have the big computer staffs that our larger competitors have, and our business development team is stretched rather thin already. On the other hand, I know that more and more people are shopping online, and we don't want to be left out if this mode of retailing really takes off. After studying the issue for

Sharpening Your Career Skills

Seven Errors in Logic That Can Undermine Your Reports

For your report to be effective, it must be logical. If you learn how to think logically, you'll also write more logically. Here are some common errors to avoid.

1. **Lack of objectivity.** Seeing only the facts that support your views and ignoring any contradictory information:

   "Although half the survey population expressed dissatisfaction with our current product, a sizable portion finds it satisfactory." *(You may be tempted to ignore the dissatisfied half instead of investigating the reasons for their dissatisfaction.)*

2. **Hasty generalizations.** Forming judgments on the basis of insufficient evidence or special cases:

   "Marketing strategy Z increased sales 13 percent in Atlanta supermarkets. Let's try it in Fairbanks." *(Atlanta and Fairbanks are probably vastly different markets.)*

3. **Hidden assumptions.** Hiding a questionable major premise:

   "We are marketing product X in trade journals because we marketed product Y in trade journals." *(Who says product X and product Y should be marketed the same way?)*

4. **Either-or scenarios.** Setting up two alternatives and not allowing for others:

   "We must open a new plant by spring, or we will go bankrupt." *(Surely there are other ways to avoid bankruptcy.)*

5. **False causal relationships.** Assuming that event A caused event B merely because A preceded B:

   "Sales increased 42 percent as soon as we hired the new sales director." *(Something besides the new sales director might have been responsible for increased sales.)*

6. **Begged questions.** Assuming as proven what you are seeking to prove:

   "We need a standard procedure so that we will have standard results." *(But why is standardization important?)*

7. **Personal attacks or appeals to popular prejudice.** Sinking people or ideas you don't like by chaining them to irrelevant but unpopular actions or ideas:

   "Ellen mishandled the budget last year, so she can't be expected to motivate her staff." *(Ellen's accounting ability may have nothing to do with her ability to motivate staff members.)* "It's un-American to impose government regulations." *(Regulations are unpopular, but they do exist in the United States.)*

Career Applications

1. Discuss some newsworthy business problem that arose from errors in logic. For example, Huffy tried to sell a combination mountain-and-racing bicycle through Kmart and other large stores that sold Huffy bicycles. Unfortunately, Huffy's logic was faulty. The company had no reason to assume that this special bike (priced higher than other Huffy models) could be sold by salespeople who weren't knowledgeable about bicycles. Huffy lost $5 million on the product.
2. Go through the "Letters to the Editor" columns in recent newspapers or newsmagazines. Examine the arguments made, and point out errors in logic.

several weeks, I concluded that we should go ahead with a site, but we had to be careful about how we implement it."

Jenn's memo appears in Figure 13.3. She uses her recommendations to structure her thoughts. Because the directors wouldn't be interested in a lot of technical detail, she keeps her discussion at a pretty high level. She also maintains a formal and respectful tone for this audience.

Focusing on Logical Arguments

Focusing on conclusions or recommendations is the most forceful and efficient way to structure an analytical report, but it isn't the best solution for every situation. As Deirdre Ballou knows, you can sometimes achieve better results by encouraging readers to weigh all the facts before you present your conclusions or recommendations.

FIGURE 13.3 In-Depth Critique: Sample Problem-Solving Report Focusing on Recommendations

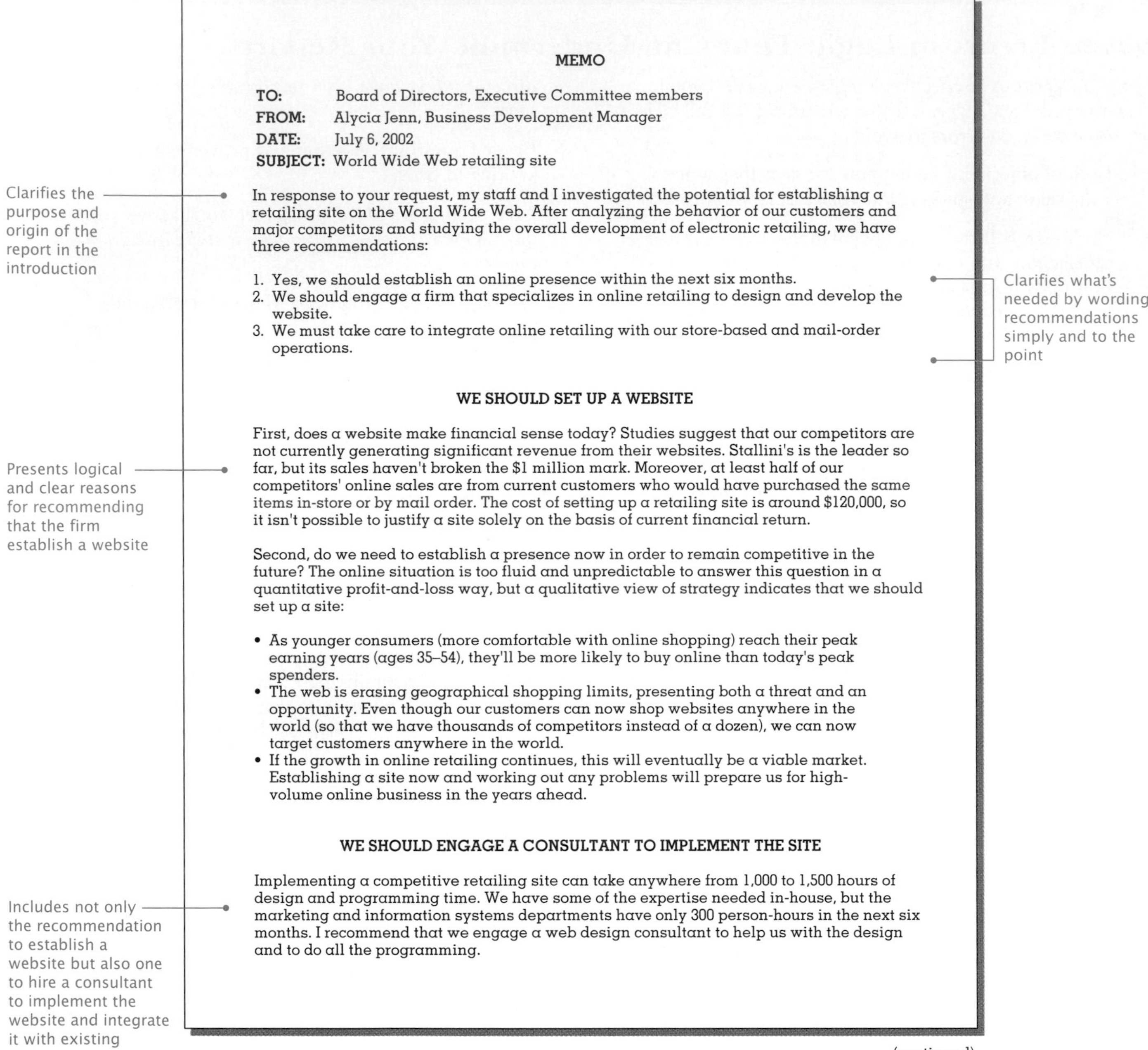

Clarifies the purpose and origin of the report in the introduction

Clarifies what's needed by wording recommendations simply and to the point

Presents logical and clear reasons for recommending that the firm establish a website

Includes not only the recommendation to establish a website but also one to hire a consultant to implement the website and integrate it with existing systems

MEMO

TO: Board of Directors, Executive Committee members
FROM: Alycia Jenn, Business Development Manager
DATE: July 6, 2002
SUBJECT: World Wide Web retailing site

In response to your request, my staff and I investigated the potential for establishing a retailing site on the World Wide Web. After analyzing the behavior of our customers and major competitors and studying the overall development of electronic retailing, we have three recommendations:

1. Yes, we should establish an online presence within the next six months.
2. We should engage a firm that specializes in online retailing to design and develop the website.
3. We must take care to integrate online retailing with our store-based and mail-order operations.

WE SHOULD SET UP A WEBSITE

First, does a website make financial sense today? Studies suggest that our competitors are not currently generating significant revenue from their websites. Stallini's is the leader so far, but its sales haven't broken the $1 million mark. Moreover, at least half of our competitors' online sales are from current customers who would have purchased the same items in-store or by mail order. The cost of setting up a retailing site is around $120,000, so it isn't possible to justify a site solely on the basis of current financial return.

Second, do we need to establish a presence now in order to remain competitive in the future? The online situation is too fluid and unpredictable to answer this question in a quantitative profit-and-loss way, but a qualitative view of strategy indicates that we should set up a site:

- As younger consumers (more comfortable with online shopping) reach their peak earning years (ages 35–54), they'll be more likely to buy online than today's peak spenders.
- The web is erasing geographical shopping limits, presenting both a threat and an opportunity. Even though our customers can now shop websites anywhere in the world (so that we have thousands of competitors instead of a dozen), we can now target customers anywhere in the world.
- If the growth in online retailing continues, this will eventually be a viable market. Establishing a site now and working out any problems will prepare us for high-volume online business in the years ahead.

WE SHOULD ENGAGE A CONSULTANT TO IMPLEMENT THE SITE

Implementing a competitive retailing site can take anywhere from 1,000 to 1,500 hours of design and programming time. We have some of the expertise needed in-house, but the marketing and information systems departments have only 300 person-hours in the next six months. I recommend that we engage a web design consultant to help us with the design and to do all the programming.

(continued)

Analytical reports may be organized around logical arguments (indirect approach) when the audience is unreceptive.

When your purpose is to collaborate with your audience and solve a problem or to persuade them to take a definite action, your structural approach must highlight logical arguments or focus the audience's attention on what needs to be done. When you want your audience to concentrate on why your ideas make sense, use a **logical organization:** Arrange your ideas around the reasoning behind your report's conclusions and recommendations. Organize your material to reflect the thinking process that will lead readers to your conclusions. (See "Sharpening Your Career Skills: Seven Errors in Logic That Can Undermine Your Reports" on page 413.)

Three basic structural approaches may be used to argue your case: the 2 + 2 = 4 approach, the scientific method, and the yardstick approach. These three approaches are not mutually exclusive. Essentially, you choose an approach that matches the rea-

FIGURE 13.3 (Continued)

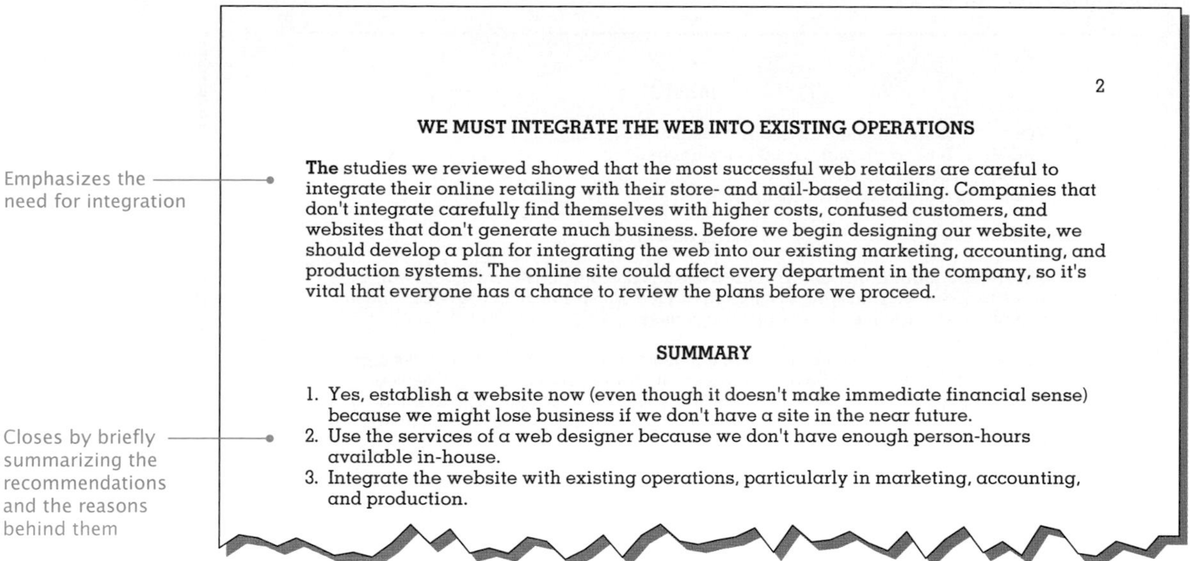

2

WE MUST INTEGRATE THE WEB INTO EXISTING OPERATIONS

The studies we reviewed showed that the most successful web retailers are careful to integrate their online retailing with their store- and mail-based retailing. Companies that don't integrate carefully find themselves with higher costs, confused customers, and websites that don't generate much business. Before we begin designing our website, we should develop a plan for integrating the web into our existing marketing, accounting, and production systems. The online site could affect every department in the company, so it's vital that everyone has a chance to review the plans before we proceed.

SUMMARY

1. Yes, establish a website now (even though it doesn't make immediate financial sense) because we might lose business if we don't have a site in the near future.
2. Use the services of a web designer because we don't have enough person-hours available in-house.
3. Integrate the website with existing operations, particularly in marketing, accounting, and production.

soning process you used to arrive at your conclusions. That way you can lead readers along the same mental pathways you used, in hopes they will follow you to the same conclusions.

In a long report, particularly, you may find it convenient to use differing organizational approaches for various sections. In general, however, simplicity of organization is a virtue. You need a clear, comprehensible argument in order to convince skeptical readers to accept your conclusions or recommendations.

Three organizational approaches are useful for convincing skeptical readers that your conclusions and recommendations are well founded: the 2 + 2 = 4 approach, the scientific method, and the yardstick approach.

The 2 + 2 = 4 Approach The 2 + 2 = 4 approach essentially convinces readers of your point of view by demonstrating that everything adds up. The main points in your outline are the main reasons behind your conclusions and recommendations. You support each reason with the evidence you collected during your analysis.

As national sales manager of a New Hampshire sporting goods company, Binh Phan was concerned about his company's ability to sell to its largest customers. His boss, the vice president of marketing, shared these concerns and asked Phan to analyze the situation and recommend a solution. As Phan says, "We sell sporting goods to retail chains across the country. Large nationwide chains with superstores modeled after Toys "Я" Us have been revolutionizing the industry, but we haven't had as much success with these big customers as we've had with smaller companies that operate strictly on a local or regional basis. With more and more of the industry in the hands of the large chains, we knew we had to fix the situation."

Phan's troubleshooting report appears in Figure 13.4. The main idea is that the company should establish separate sales teams for these major accounts, rather than continuing to service them through the company's four regional divisions. However, Phan knew his plan would be controversial because it required a big change in the company's organization and in the way sales reps are paid. His thinking had to be clear and easy to follow, so he used the 2 + 2 = 4 approach to focus on his reasons.

Because of its naturalness and versatility, the 2 + 2 = 4 approach is generally the most persuasive and efficient way to develop an analytical report for skeptical readers. When writing your own reports, try this structure first. You'll find that your arguments usually fall naturally into this pattern. However, not every problem or reporting situation can be handled with this organizational approach.

The 2 + 2 = 4 approach works well when you have many reasons for your point of view but no single reason is overwhelming.

FIGURE 13.4 In-Depth Critique: Sample Troubleshooting Report Using the 2 + 2 = 4 Approach

MEMO

TO: Robert Mendoza, Vice President of Marketing
FROM: Binh Phan, National Sales Manager
DATE: September 12, 2002
SUBJECT: Major accounts sales problems

INTRODUCTION

Begins by discussing report's purpose and scope, background, and methods of research—instead of summarizing recommendations

This report outlines the results of my investigation into the recent slowdown in sales to major accounts and the accompanying rise in sales- and service-related complaints from some of our largest customers.

As we discussed at last quarter's management retreat, major account sales dropped 12 percent over the last four quarters, whereas overall sales were up 7 percent. During the same time, we've all noticed an increase in both formal and informal complaints from larger customers regarding how confusing and complicated it has become to do business with us.

My investigation started with in-depth discussions with the four regional sales managers, first as a group and then individually. The tension I felt in the initial meeting eventually bubbled to the surface during my meetings with each manager. Staff members in each region are convinced that other regions are booking orders they don't deserve, with one region doing all the legwork only to see another region get credited with the sale and, naturally, the commission and quota credit.

I followed up the sales manager discussions with informal talks and e-mail exchanges with several sales reps from each region. Virtually everyone who is involved with our major national accounts has a story to share. No one is happy with the situation, and I sense that some reps are walking away from major customers because the process is so frustrating.

Main points are the very reasons for the recommendations

ORGANIZATIONAL ISSUES

Presents facts and observations in an objective tone, without revealing writer's point of view

When we divided the national sales force into four geographical regions last year, the idea was to focus our sales efforts and clarify responsibilities for each prospective and current customer. The regional managers have gotten to know their market territories very well, and sales have increased beyond even our most optimistic projections.

Unfortunately, while solving one problem, we seem to have created another. In the past 12 to 18 months, several regional customers have grown to national status. In addition, a few national retailers have taken on (or expressed interest in) our products. As a result, a significant portion of both our current sales and our future opportunities lie with these large national accounts.

I uncovered more than a dozen cases in which sales reps from two or more regions found themselves competing with each other by pursuing the same customer from different locations.

Moreover, the complaints from our major accounts about overlapping or nonexistent account coverage are a direct result of the regional organization. In some

(continued)

When organizing a report to reflect the scientific method, you discuss, one by one, hypothetical solutions to the problem.

The Scientific Method When you're trying to discover whether an explanation is true, whether an option will solve your problem, or which one of several solutions will work best, you're likely to find the scientific method useful. Every day, hundreds of managers ask themselves, "What's wrong with this operation, and what should we do about it?" They approach the problem by coming up with one or several possible solutions (hypotheses) and then conducting experiments or gathering information to find the most effective one.

Reports based on the scientific method begin with a statement of the problem and a brief description of the hypothetical solution or a list of possible solutions. The

FIGURE 13.4 (Continued)

2

cases, customers aren't sure which of our reps they're supposed to call with problems and orders. In others, no one has been in contact with them for several months.

An example should help illustrate the problem. AmeriSport, with retail outlets across the lower tier of the country, was being pitched by reps from our West, South, and East regions. Because we give our regional offices a lot of negotiating freedom, the three reps were offering the client different prices. But all of AmeriSport's buying decisions are made at their headquarters in Tampa, so all we did was confuse the customer.

The irony of this situation is that we're often giving our weakest selling and support efforts to the largest customers in the country.

COMMISSION ISSUES

The regional organization issues are compounded because of the way we assign commissions and quota credit. Salespeople in one region can invest a lot of time in pursuing a sale, only to have the customer place the order in another region. So some sales rep in the second region ends up with the commission on a sale that was partly or even entirely earned by someone in the first region.

Each main point is supported with concrete evidence

Also, sales reps sometimes don't pursue leads in their regions if they think that a rep in another region will get the commission. For example, Athletic Express, with outlets in 35 states spread across all four regions, finally got so frustrated with us that the company president called our headquarters. Athletic Express has been trying to place a large order for tennis and golf accessories, but none of our local reps seem interested in paying attention. I spoke with the rep responsible for Nashville, where the company is headquartered, and asked her why she wasn't working the account more actively. Her explanation was that last time she got involved with Athletic Express, the order was actually placed from their L.A. regional office, and she didn't get any commission after more than two weeks of selling time.

RECOMMENDATION

Saves recommendation for the fourth section, where writer adds up the reasons (2 + 2 = 4)

Our sales organization should reflect the nature of our customer base. To accomplish that goal, we need a group of reps who are free to pursue accounts across regional borders—and who are compensated fairly for their work. The most sensible answer is to establish a national accounts group. Any customers whose operations place them in more than one region would automatically be assigned to the national group.

The recommendation is a logical culmination of the main points that have been presented so carefully

Further, we need to modify our commission policy to reward people for team selling. I'll talk with the sales managers to work out the details, but in general, we'll need to split commissions whenever two or more reps help close a sale. This policy will also involve a "finder's fee" for a rep who pulls in leads at the regional level that are passed on to the national account team.

3

SUMMARY

The regional sales organization is working at the regional and local levels but not at the national level. We should establish a national accounts group to handle sales that cross regional boundaries.

Clearly and succinctly recaps the recommendation and the reasons for it

To make sure that the sales reps (at both the regional and national levels) are adequately motivated and fairly compensated, we need to devise a system of commission splitting and finders' fees. We'll then have one set of reps who are focused on the local and regional levels and another set who are pursuing national accounts. The two groups will have incentives to work together rather than against each other, as is now the case.

body of the report discusses each alternative in turn and offers evidence that will either confirm the alternative or rule it out. Because many problems have multiple causes and complex solutions, several alternatives may be relevant. The final section of the report summarizes the findings and indicates which solution or solutions are valid. The report concludes with recommendations for solving the problem or eliminating the causes.

A troubleshooting report using a variation of the scientific method was prepared by Fredrik Swensen, an executive with a Miami restaurant management firm (see the outline in Figure 13.5). The purpose of Swensen's report is to help his company decide which of four franchise operations to invest in. "We wanted to buy 45 or 50 more franchise outlets across the country," says Swensen, "so this was a major investment decision. Our company already owns several hundred fast-food franchises, so we have a good idea of how to evaluate which ones are right for us."

By analyzing each alternative, Swensen hoped to unify a divided audience. Your chances of bringing about a consensus are much better when you show the strengths and weaknesses of all the ideas. However, the main drawback is that many of the alternatives may turn out to be irrelevant or unproductive, but you still have to discuss them all. The more ideas you discuss, the more confused your readers may become and the more trouble they may have comparing pros and cons.

With the yardstick approach, the report is organized around criteria; the solution is the alternative that best meets the criteria.

The Yardstick Approach One way to reduce the confusion presented by having a lot of alternatives is to establish a yardstick for evaluating them. You begin by discussing the problem, as with the scientific method, but then you set up the conditions that must be met to solve the problem. These are the criteria against which you evaluate all possible solutions. The body of the report evaluates those alternatives in relation to the criteria. The main points of the outline are either the criteria themselves or the alternatives.

Yardstick reports are similar in some respects to those based on the scientific method, but in criteria-based reports, all the alternatives are reviewed against the same standards. Another distinction is that criteria-based reports can be used to prove the need for action: The current situation can be measured against the criteria and shown to be wanting.

Some proposals are best organized by using the client's criteria as the main points.

The yardstick approach is useful for certain kinds of proposals because the client who requests the proposal often provides a list of criteria the solution must meet. Say that your company has been asked to bid on a contract to install a computer for a large corporation. The client has listed the requirements (criteria) for the system, and you've developed a preliminary design to meet them. In the body of your proposal, you could use the client's list of requirements as the main headings and under each one explain how your preliminary design meets the requirement.

Figure 13.6 is an outline of a feasibility report that uses the yardstick approach. The report was provided by J. C. Hartley, a market analyst for a large Sacramento company that makes irrigation equipment for farms and ranches. "We've been so successful in the agricultural market that we're starting to run out of customers to sell to," says Hartley. "To keep the company growing, we needed to find another market. Two obvious choices to consider were commercial buildings and residences." Hartley says that she was determined to make careful recommendations because, "even though I don't make the final decision, the information and the professional opinions that I provide in my report weigh heavily in the decision process."

For the yardstick approach to work, readers must accept your criteria.

If there is any disagreement on the decision criteria, you'll spin your wheels if you try to push forward to a decision. In Hartley's case, the criteria had been agreed to before she began her investigation, so she included the criteria in her report to remind her readers and make it easy for them to evaluate the options available.

The yardstick approach has one other drawback: It can be a little boring. You may find yourself saying the same things over and over again: "Opportunity A has high growth potential, opportunity B has high growth potential, opportunity C has high

FIGURE 13.5 In-Depth Critique: Outline of a Troubleshooting Report Using the Scientific Method

Main Idea: We should purchase the 45 franchises currently for sale in the Burger World chain.

I. Statement of problem and purpose of this proposal
II. Scope of the investigation
III. Method used to compare the business opportunities
   A. Establish decision criteria
   B. Get input from consultants
   C. Gather secondary research
   D. Conduct market surveys for primary research
   E. Meet with franchisor management teams
   F. Analyze quantitative and qualitative data
   G. Prioritize and select the best opportunity
IV. Analysis of the four franchise operations
   A. Wacky Taco
      1. Description: Low-fat Mexican food; most locations in malls
      2. Pros: 58 units available within a year; consultants believe the concept has significant growth potential; operations easy to manage
      3. Cons: Company recently hit with employment discrimination lawsuit; franchise fees are 30 percent above average
      4. Conclusion: Priority = 3; lawsuit may be indicative of mismanagement; fees too high
   B. Thai in the Sky
      1. Description: Thai food served in New Age settings
      2. Pros: Healthy and interesting food, unusual theme concept; no franchised competition
      3. Cons: Complexity of food preparation; only 40 franchises available; franchisor's top management team replaced only six months ago
      4. Conclusion: Priority = 4; too risky and not enough units available
   C. Dog Tower
      1. Description: Gourmet hot dogs
      2. Pros: No nationwide competition; more than 60 franchises available within a year; easy to manage; fees lower than average
      3. Cons: Limited market appeal; many stores need updating
      4. Conclusion: Priority = 2; needs too much investment
   D. Burger World
      1. Description: Mainstream competitor to McDonald's and Burger King

Covers two major steps: (1) establishing the decision criteria and (2) testing each of four alternatives against those criteria

Assigns each of the four alternatives to an appropriate subdivision: description, pros, cons, and conclusion (priority)

      2. Pros: Aggressive franchisor willing to invest in national marketing; start-up costs are low; unique demographic target (teenagers and young adults; not a little kids' place)
      3. Cons: Fierce competition in burgers overall; some units in unproved locations
      4. Conclusion: Priority = 1; finances look good; research shows that teenagers will support a chain that doesn't cater to small children
V. Summary
VI. Appendixes
   A. Financial data
   B. Research results

Presents each alternative objectively—Swensen's task, even though the decision can never be black and white

FIGURE 13.6 In-Depth Critique: Outline of a Feasibility Report Using the Yardstick Approach

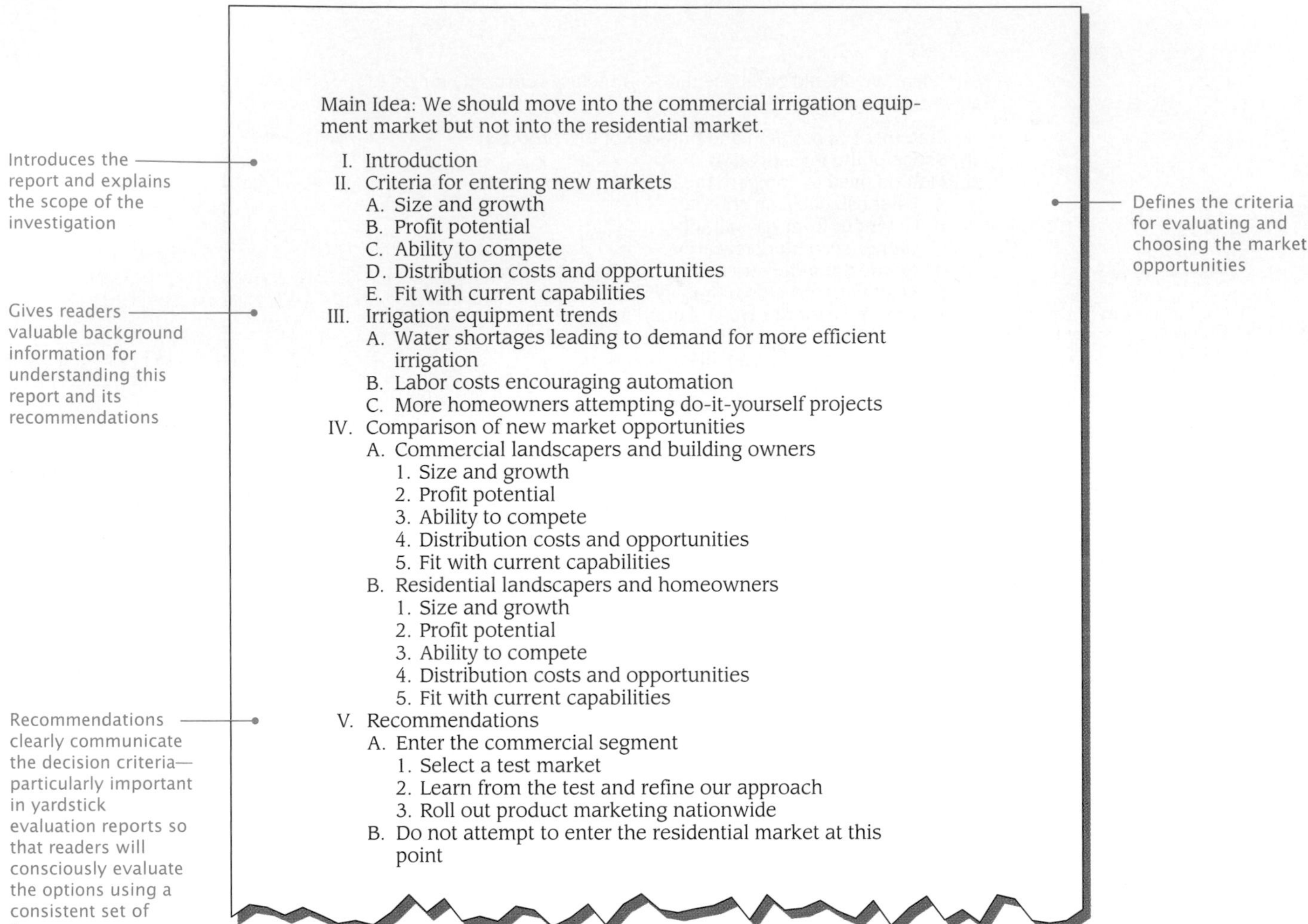

Main Idea: We should move into the commercial irrigation equipment market but not into the residential market.

I. Introduction
II. Criteria for entering new markets
 A. Size and growth
 B. Profit potential
 C. Ability to compete
 D. Distribution costs and opportunities
 E. Fit with current capabilities
III. Irrigation equipment trends
 A. Water shortages leading to demand for more efficient irrigation
 B. Labor costs encouraging automation
 C. More homeowners attempting do-it-yourself projects
IV. Comparison of new market opportunities
 A. Commercial landscapers and building owners
  1. Size and growth
  2. Profit potential
  3. Ability to compete
  4. Distribution costs and opportunities
  5. Fit with current capabilities
 B. Residential landscapers and homeowners
  1. Size and growth
  2. Profit potential
  3. Ability to compete
  4. Distribution costs and opportunities
  5. Fit with current capabilities
V. Recommendations
 A. Enter the commercial segment
  1. Select a test market
  2. Learn from the test and refine our approach
  3. Roll out product marketing nationwide
 B. Do not attempt to enter the residential market at this point

Tables are useful in the yardstick approach
- To avoid repetition
- To make the options easier to compare

growth potential," and so on. One way to minimize the repetition is to compare the options in tables and then highlight the more unusual or important aspects of each alternative in the text so that you get the best of both worlds. This approach allows you to compare all the alternatives against the same yardstick while calling attention to the most significant differences among them.

Structuring Business Proposals

The direct approach is common for solicited proposals.

As with reports, your choice of structural approach for proposals depends on whether you expect your audience to be receptive. In general, your audience may be more receptive with solicited proposals, since the problem and the solution have already been identified. The writer submits a proposal for the work specified in the RFP issued by the prospective client and structures the proposal using a direct approach, focusing on the recommendation.

The indirect approach may be a better choice for unsolicited proposals. When writing unsolicited proposals, you must first convince the audience that a problem exists and establish your credibility if you are unknown to the reader. To convince the reader that your recommendations are solid and logical, you unfold your solution to the problem using one of the logical arguments (2 + 2 = 4 approach, scientific method, or yardstick approach). As you unfold your solution, you have two goals: (1) to per-

A proposal is both a selling tool and a contractual commitment.

✓ CHECKLIST: ORGANIZING BUSINESS REPORTS AND PROPOSALS

A. Decide on format and length

1. For brief external reports, use letter format, including a title or a subject line that appears directly after the reader's address that clearly states the subject of the document.
2. For brief internal reports, use memo or manuscript format.
3. Follow company guidelines.
4. Choose a report length that matches your subject, your purpose, and your audience's expectations.

B. Select an organizational approach

1. Use direct order for informational reports to receptive readers, developing ideas around subtopics (chronologically, geographically, categorically).
2. Use direct order for analytical reports to receptive readers, developing points around conclusions or recommendations and placing conclusions and recommendations in the opening.
3. Use indirect order for analytical reports to skeptical or hostile readers, developing points around logical arguments.

C. Choose a structure that matches your needs

1. For informational reports, use one of six topical arrangements: importance, sequence, chronology, spatial orientations, geography, and category.
2. For analytical reports to receptive audiences, focus on conclusions or recommendations.
3. For analytical reports to skeptical audiences, focus on one of three logical arguments: 2 + 2 = 4 (to determine that everything adds up), the scientific method (to reveal the most effective solution), or the yardstick approach (to weigh possible solutions against criteria).
4. For solicited proposals, use the direct approach and focus on recommendations.
5. For unsolicited proposals, use the indirect approach and unfold recommendations, by focusing on logical argument.

suade readers to accept your idea and award you a contract, and (2) to spell out the terms of your proposal in the report's content.

For a review of the tasks involved in organizing business reports and proposals, see "Checklist: Organizing Business Reports and Proposals."

COMPOSING BUSINESS REPORTS AND PROPOSALS

Once you've decided on the proper organizational structure for your report or proposal, you're ready to begin composing your first draft. Effective writers begin the writing task by preparing a final outline. Aside from guiding you in the writing effort, a final outline forces you to reevaluate the information you have selected to include and the order in which you present it. For instance, you may decide to use an indirect approach instead of a direct one because now that you see your conclusions up front, you think it might be too forceful for your audience.

A final outline is a work in progress.

Preparing a final outline also gives you a chance to rephrase your outline points to set the tone of your report. If you want a hard-hitting, direct tone, use informative phrasing. If you prefer an objective, indirect tone, use descriptive phrasing. You may also want to use your outline points as section headings for longer reports, so be sure to use parallel construction when wording these points.

You can soften the force of controversial points by using descriptive (not informative) headings.

As you compose your report or proposal, use the writing process discussed in Chapter 5: Control your style and tone, select the best words, and create effective sentences and paragraphs. The remainder of this chapter discusses how to draft the content for your reports and proposals and provides some examples of the types of content commonly included in the introduction, body, and closing for each document type. It also presents some strategies for making your content more readable, such as using a proper degree of formality, sticking with a consistent time perspective, and providing structural clues to help readers navigate your document. Then in Chapter 14 we focus on revising, producing, and proofreading the content of your reports.

Drafting Reports and Proposals

As with other written business communications, the text of reports and proposals has three main sections: an introduction, a body, and a closing. The content and length of each section varies with the type and purpose of the document, the document's organizational structure, the length and depth of the material, the document's degree of formality, and the writer's relationship with the audience.

In the introduction, tell readers what to expect, tell them why your subject is important, and orient them toward your organizational approach.

The *introduction* is the first section in the text of any report or proposal. An effective introduction accomplishes at least four things:

- Puts the report or proposal in a broader context by tying it to a problem or an assignment
- Introduces the subject or purpose of the report or proposal and indicates why the subject is important
- Previews the main ideas and the order in which they'll be covered
- Establishes the tone of the document and the writer's relationship with the audience

The body contains the substance of your report or proposal.

The *body* is the middle section in the text of your report or proposal. It consists of the major divisions or chapters (with various levels of headings for long documents). These divisions present, analyze, and interpret the information gathered during your investigation, and they support the recommendations or conclusions discussed in your document. The body contains the "proof," the detailed information necessary to support your conclusions and recommendations. Look back at Figure 13.3 (see pages 414–415). Alycia Jenn uses the body of her report to support her recommendation for establishing a retail website.

Reemphasize your main ideas in the ending.

The *closing* is the final section in the text of your report or proposal. It has four important functions:

- Emphasizes the main points of the message
- Summarizes the benefits to the reader if the document suggests a change or some other course of action
- Refers back to all the pieces and reminds readers how those pieces fit together
- Brings all the action items together in one place and gives the details about who should do what, when, where, and how

The final section of a report or proposal is important because it leaves a strong lasting impression.

Research shows that the final section of a report or proposal leaves a strong lasting impression. The closing gives you one last chance to make sure that your report says what you intended.[2]

Report Content

Learning Objective 4

Name five characteristics of effective report content

Effective reports are:
- Accurate
- Complete
- Balanced
- Logical
- Properly documented

The content and quality of your reports will likely influence your professional success, because they show how well you think, gather and analyze data, draw conclusions, and develop and support your recommendations. Your credibility and future success is on the line with every business report you write. You'll create more successful reports if your content is

- **Accurate.** Information presented in a report must be factually correct and error-free. When writing reports, be sure to double-check your facts and references in addition to checking for typos.
- **Complete.** To help colleagues or supervisors make a decision, include all the information necessary for readers to understand the situation, problem, or proposal. Support all key assertions using illustrations, explanations, and facts.[3] But remember, time is precious, so tell your readers what they need to know—no more, no less—and present the information in a way that is geared to their needs.
- **Balanced.** Present all sides of the issue fairly and equitably, and include all the essential information. Even though you want to be as brief as possible, your

Best of the Web

Research Before You Report

Research your competition at Corporate Information and find out what you need to know before you write your next report or proposal. This website has links to over 350,000 company profiles, data on 30 industries in 65 countries, and current economic information for over 100 countries. You'll also find research reports analyzing sales, dividends, earnings, and profit ratios on some 15,000 companies, current foreign exchange rates, and the definitions of commonly used global company extensions such as GmbH, SA, de CV, and more.

www.corporateinformation.com

readers need a minimum amount of information before they can grasp the issue being presented. Omitting relevant information or facts can make your report biased.

- **Structured clearly and logically.** Clear sentence structure and good transitions are essential.[4] Save your readers time by making sure your sentences appear uncluttered, contain well-chosen words, and proceed logically. To help your readers move from one point to the next, make your transitions just as clear and logical. For a successful report, identify the ideas that belong together, and organize them in a way that's easy to understand.[5]
- **Documented properly.** If you use primary and secondary sources for your report or proposal, be sure to properly document and give credit to your sources, as Chapter 10 explains.

Keeping these points in mind will help you draft the most effective introduction, body, and closing for your report.

Learning Objective 5

List the topics commonly covered in a report's introduction, body, and closing

Report Introduction The following topics are commonly covered in a report introduction. Some of these items may be combined, and some may not be discussed at all. You need only include those elements that will help your readers understand and accept your report:

- **Authorization.** When, how, and by whom the report was authorized; who wrote it; and when it was submitted. This material is especially important when no letter of transmittal is included.
- **Problem/purpose.** The reason for the report's existence and what is to be accomplished as a result of the report's being written.
- **Scope.** What is and what isn't going to be covered in the report. The scope indicates the report's size and complexity.
- **Background.** The historical conditions or factors that led up to the report. This section enables readers to understand how the problem developed and what has been done about it so far.
- **Sources and methods.** The primary and secondary sources of information used. This section explains how samples were selected, how questionnaires were constructed (which should be included in an appendix with any cover letters), what follow-up was done, and so on. This section builds reader confidence in the work and in the sources and methods used.
- **Definitions.** A brief statement introducing a list of terms and their definitions. This section is unnecessary if readers are familiar with the terms you've used in your report. However, if you have any question about reader knowledge, define any terms that might be misinterpreted. Terms may also be defined in the body, explanatory notes, or glossary.
- **Limitations.** Factors beyond your control that affect report quality, such as a budget too small to do needed work, a schedule to short to do needed research, and unreliable or unavailable data. This section includes doubts about any aspect of

your report. Such candor may lead readers to question results, but it also helps them assess those results, and it builds your report's integrity. Even so, limitations do not excuse a poor study or a bad report.

- **Report organization.** The organization of the report (what topics are covered and in what order), along with a rationale for following this plan. This section is a road map that helps readers understand what's coming at each turn of the report and why.

In a relatively brief report, these topics may be discussed in only a paragraph or two. Here's an example of a brief indirect opening, taken from the introduction of a memo on why a new line of luggage has failed to sell well. The writer's ultimate goal is to recommend a shift in marketing strategy.

> The performance of the Venturer line can be improved. In the two years since its introduction, this product line has achieved a sales volume lower than we expected, resulting in a drain on the company's overall earnings. The purpose of this report is to review the luggage-buying habits of consumers in all markets where the Venturer line is sold, so that we can determine where to put our marketing emphasis.

This paragraph quickly introduces the subject (disappointing sales), tells why the problem is important (drain on earnings), and indicates the main points to be addressed in the body of the report (review of markets where the Venturer line is sold), without revealing what the conclusions and recommendations will be. In a major formal report, the discussion of these topics may span several pages. For examples of the type of information commonly included in report introductions, review Figure 13.3 (on pages 414–415) and Figure 13.4 (on pages 416–417).

Restrict the body to those details necessary to prove your conclusions and recommendations.

Report Body One of the decisions you need to make when writing the body of your report is how much detail to include. Here again, your decision depends on many variables, including the needs of your audience. Some audiences and situations require detailed coverage; others lend themselves to shorter treatment. Provide only enough detail in the body to support your conclusions and recommendations; put additional detail in tables, charts, and appendixes.

Among the topics commonly covered in a report body are

- Explanations of a problem or opportunity
- Facts, statistical evidence, and trends
- Results of studies or investigations
- Discussion and analyses of potential courses of action
- Advantages, disadvantages, costs, and benefits of a particular course of action
- Procedures and steps for a process
- Methods and approaches
- Criteria for evaluating alternatives and options
- Conclusions and recommendations
- Supporting reasons for conclusions or recommendations

For analytical reports using the direct organizational approach, you'll generally state your conclusions or recommendations up front and use the body of your report to provide your evidence and support, as Alycia Jenn does in Figure 13.3 (see pages 414–415). If you're using the indirect organizational approach, you'll likely use the body to discuss your logic and reserve your conclusions or recommendations until the very end. You may even refrain from stating them until the closing of your report.

The length and depth of your closing will depend on your organizational approach.

Report Closing Your choice of a direct or indirect order, among other variables, determines the content and length of your report closing. If your report is organized in the direct order, end with a summary of key points (except in short memos), and list them in order, as they appear in the report body. If appropriate, briefly restate your conclusions or recommendations as Alycia Jenn does in her closing summary (see Figure 13.3 on pages 414–415). If your report is organized in the indirect order, your conclusions or recommendations may be presented for the first time at the end, as in Robert Mendoza's report (see Figure 13.4 on pages 416–417). Just remember that new facts are never presented in a report's conclusion or recommendation.

If your report is intended to lead to action, use the ending to spell out exactly what should happen next. Readers may agree with everything you say in your report but still fail to take any action if you're vague about what should happen next. Your readers must understand what's expected of them and must have some appreciation of the difficulties that are likely to arise. Providing a schedule and specific task assignments is helpful because concrete plans have a way of commanding action.

Use the closing to tell your readers what's expected of them.

In a short report, the ending may be only a paragraph or two. However, a long report may have separate sections for conclusions, recommendations, and actions. Using separate sections helps your reader locate this material. It also gives you a final opportunity to emphasize this important content. Keep in mind that it's fine to combine the conclusions and recommendations under one heading, because it is often difficult to present a conclusion without implying a recommendation.

The ending of a short report may only be a paragraph or two.

If you have multiple conclusions, recommendations, or actions, you may want to number and list them. An appropriate lead-in to such a list might be, "The findings of this study lead to the following conclusions." A statement that could be used for a list of recommendations might be, "Based on the conclusions of this study, the following recommendations are made." A statement that could be used for actions might be, "In order to accomplish our goals on time, the following actions must be completed before the end of the year."

Number or list multiple recommendations or actions.

Proposal Content

Like reports, proposals have an introduction, a body, and a closing. The content for each section is governed by many variables—the key variable being the source of your proposal. If your proposal is unsolicited, you have some latitude in the scope and organization of the proposal's content. However, the scope and organization of a solicited proposal are often governed by the request for proposal. Most RFPs spell out precisely what you should cover and in what order so that all bids will be similar in form. This uniformity enables the client to evaluate the competing proposals in a systematic way. In many organizations a team of evaluators splits up the proposals and looks at various sections. An engineer might review the technical portions of all the proposals submitted, and an accountant might review the cost estimates.

Unsolicited proposals have different content than solicited proposals.

A proposal is a persuasive message.

Learning Objective 6

Name six strategies to strengthen your proposal argument

The general purpose of any proposal is to persuade the readers to do something, such as purchase goods or services, fund a project, or implement a program. Thus, your writing approach for a proposal is similar to that used for persuasive sales messages (see Chapter 9). Your proposal must sell your audience on your ideas, product, service, methods, and company. Just as with any persuasive message, you use the AIDA plan to gain attention, build interest, create desire, and motive action. Here are some additional strategies to strengthen your argument:[6]

- **Demonstrate your knowledge.** Everything you write should show your reader that you have the knowledge and experience to solve the problem.
- **Provide concrete examples.** Even if you offer a dynamic plan, your readers may question everything you say. All your enthusiasm and good intentions will not substitute for the hard facts readers will demand. Avoid vague, unsupported generalizations such as "We are losing money on this program." Instead, provide quantifiable details such as the amount of money being lost, how, why, and so on. Explain how much money your proposed solution will save. Spell out your plan and give details on how the job

When Karla Brown applied to the Small Business Association (SBA) for a microloan, she was facing stiff competition for the agency's limited resources. So Brown wrote a proposal using the AIDA plan and successfully persuaded the SBA to lend her $19,000 to start her business, Ashmont Flowers Plus.

Concrete examples and facts help persuade readers.

will be done. Such concrete examples persuade readers; unsupported generalizations don't.

- **Research the competition.** Use trade publications and the Internet to become familiar with your competitors' product lines, services, and prices. This strategy is especially important if you are competing against others for a job.

Consider your audience's capabilities and limitations.

- **Prove that your proposal is workable.** Your proposal must be appropriate and feasible for the audience. It should be consistent with the audience's capabilities. For instance, it would be foolish to recommend a plan of action that requires three times the number of employees or that doubles the budget.
- **Adopt a "you" attitude.** Relate your product, service, or personnel to the reader's exact needs either as stated in the RFP for a solicited proposal or as discovered through your own investigation for an unsolicited proposal.
- **Package your proposal attractively.** Make sure your proposal is letter perfect, inviting, and readable. Readers will judge the type of work you perform by your submitted proposal. If it contains errors, omissions, or inconsistencies, they will likely withhold approval.

Be careful with how much information you include in your proposal.

Keep in mind that when writing proposals, you have one additional challenge: You must disclose enough information to win the job without giving away your ideas so that your services aren't needed.

Learning Objective 7

List the topics commonly covered in a proposal's introduction, body, and closing

In the introduction, establish the need for action and summarize the key benefits of your proposal.

Proposal Introduction The introduction presents and summarizes the problem you want to solve and your solutions. It orients the readers to the remainder of the text. If your proposal is solicited, its introduction should refer to the RFP; if unsolicited, its introduction should mention any factors that led you to submit your proposal. You might mention mutual acquaintances, or you might refer to previous conversations you've had with readers. The following topics are commonly covered in a proposal introduction:

- **Background or statement of the problem.** Briefly reviews the reader's situation and establishes a need for action. Readers may not perceive a problem or opportunity the same way you do. In unsolicited proposals, you must convince them that a problem or opportunity exists before you can convince them to accept your solution. In a way that is meaningful to your reader, discuss the current situation and explain how things could be better.
- **Solution.** Briefly describes the change you propose and highlights your key selling points and their benefits, showing how your proposal will solve the reader's problem. In long proposals, the heading for this section might also be "Preliminary Analysis," "Overview of Approach," or some other wording that will identify this section as a summary of your solution.
- **Scope.** States the boundaries of the proposal—what you will and will not do. This brief section may also be labeled "Delimitations."
- **Report organization.** Orients the reader to the remainder of the proposal and calls attention to the major divisions of thought.

In short proposals, your discussion of these elements will be brief—perhaps only a sentence or two for each topic. For long, formal proposals, each of these topics may warrant separate subheadings and several paragraphs of discussion.

Proposal Body The proposal's body has the same purpose as the body of other reports: It gives complete details on the proposed solution and specifies what the anticipated results will be. In addition to providing facts and evidence to support your conclusions, an effective body covers this information:

In the approach section, demonstrate the superiority of your ideas, products, or services.

- **Proposed approach.** May also be titled "Technical Proposal," "Research Design," "Issues for Analysis," or "Work Statement." This section describes what you have to offer: your concept, product, or service. To convince readers that your proposal has merit, focus on the strengths of your offer in relation to reader needs. Stress the benefits of your product or service that are relevant to your readers' needs, and point out any advantages that you have over your competitors—such as warranties or extended service options.

- **Work plan.** Describes how you'll accomplish what must be done (unless you'll provide a standard, off-the-shelf item). Explain the steps you'll take, their timing, the methods or resources you'll use, and the person(s) responsible. Specifically include when the work will begin, how it will be divided into stages, when you will finish, and whether any follow-up is involved. If possible, include a timeline or Gantt chart highlighting any critical dates. For solicited proposals, make sure your dates match those specified in the RFP. Remember, if your proposal is accepted, the work plan is contractually binding, so don't promise to deliver more than you can realistically achieve within a given period.

Use the work plan to describe the tasks to be completed under the terms of the contract.

- **Statement of qualifications.** Describes your organization's experience, personnel, and facilities—all in relation to reader needs. If you work for a large company that frequently submits proposals, you might borrow much of this section intact from previous proposals. However, be sure to tailor any boilerplate material to suit the situation. The qualifications section can be an important selling point, and it deserves to be handled carefully. Document your qualifications by including a list of client references.

In the qualifications section, demonstrate that you have the personnel, facilities, and experience to do a competent job.

- **Costs.** Has few words and many numbers but can make or break your proposal. A high price can lose the bid; however, a low price could doom you to losing money on the project. Estimating costs is difficult, so prove that your costs are realistic—break them down in detail so that readers can see how you got your numbers: so much for labor, so much for materials, so much for transportation, travel, training, and other useful categories.

The more detailed your cost proposal is, the more credibility your estimates will have.

In an informal proposal, discussion of some or all of these elements may be grouped together and presented in a letter format, as the proposal in Figure 13.7 does. In a formal proposal, the discussion of these elements will be quite long and thorough. The format may resemble long reports with multiple parts, as Chapter 14 discusses.

Proposal Closing The final section of a proposal generally summarizes the key points of the proposal, emphasizes the benefits that the readers will realize from your solution, summarizes the merits of your approach, reemphasizes why you and your firm are the ones to do the work, and asks for a decision from the client. This is your last opportunity to persuade readers to accept your proposal. In both formal and informal proposals, make this section relatively brief, assertive, and confident.

The proposal closing is your final chance to win the reader's business.

Choosing the Proper Degree of Formality

Whether you're writing content for a report or a proposal, you must choose an appropriate degree of formality. Your choice is closely related to the document's format, length, and organization. If you know your readers reasonably well and if your report is likely to meet with their approval, you can generally adopt a fairly informal tone. You can speak to readers in the first person, referring to yourself as *I* and to your readers as *you*. This personal approach is often used in brief memo or letter reports, although there are many exceptions.

For informal reports, adopt a personal style, using the pronouns *I* and *you*.

Longer reports, especially those dealing with controversial or complex information, are traditionally written using a more formal tone. You'll also write more formally when your report will be sent to other parts of the organization or to customers or suppliers. Communicating with people in other cultures often calls for more formality, for two reasons. First, the business environment outside the United States tends to be more formal in general, and that formality must be reflected in your communication style. Second, the things you do to make a document informal, such as using humor and idiomatic language, are the hardest to transfer from culture to culture. Reducing formality in cross-cultural reports and proposals increases the risks of offending people and miscommunicating information.

Certain audiences and situations require a more formal style.

FIGURE 13.7 In-Depth Critique: Solicited Proposal in Letter Format

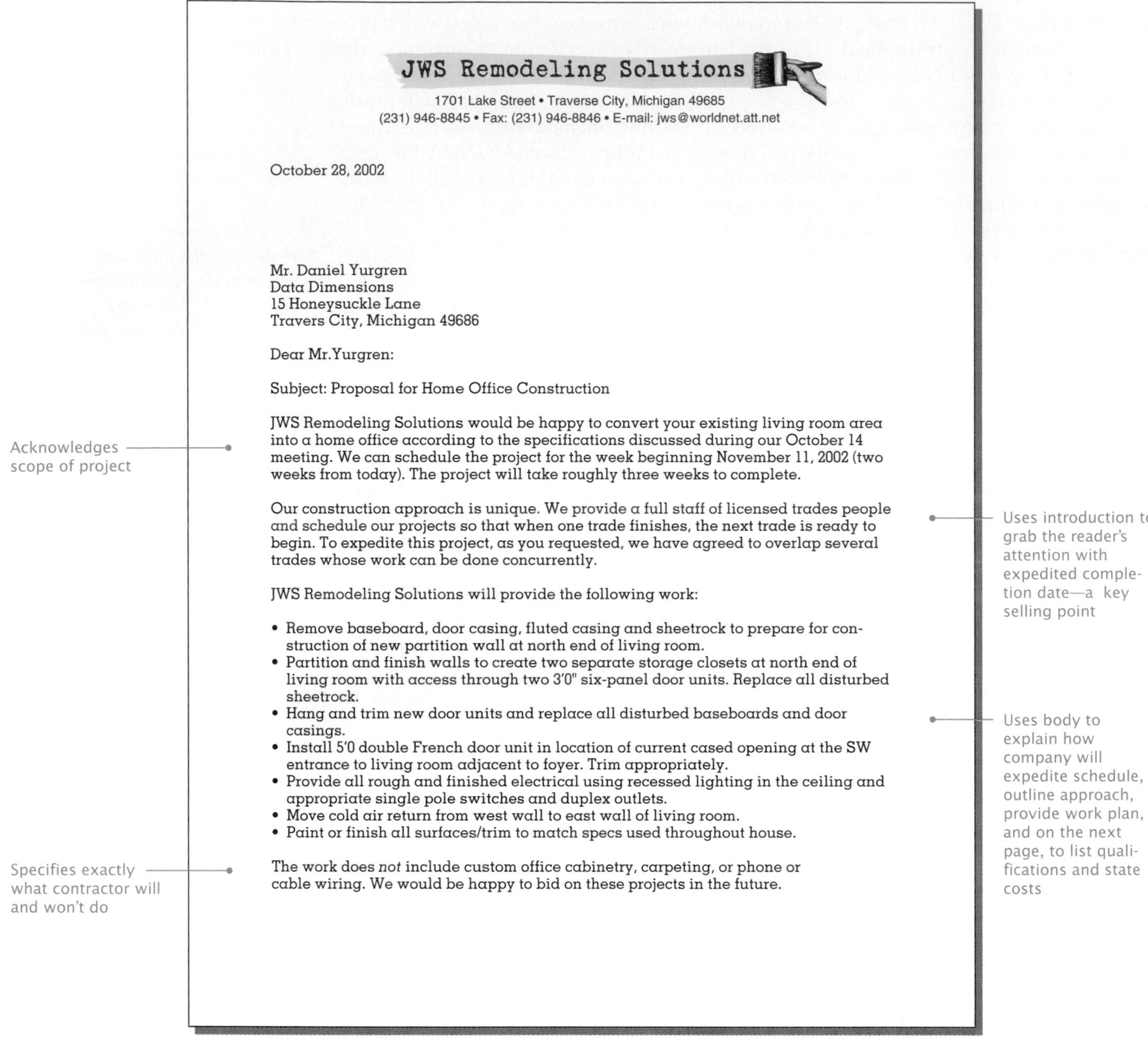

JWS Remodeling Solutions
1701 Lake Street • Traverse City, Michigan 49685
(231) 946-8845 • Fax: (231) 946-8846 • E-mail: jws@worldnet.att.net

October 28, 2002

Mr. Daniel Yurgren
Data Dimensions
15 Honeysuckle Lane
Travers City, Michigan 49686

Dear Mr.Yurgren:

Subject: Proposal for Home Office Construction

JWS Remodeling Solutions would be happy to convert your existing living room area into a home office according to the specifications discussed during our October 14 meeting. We can schedule the project for the week beginning November 11, 2002 (two weeks from today). The project will take roughly three weeks to complete.

Our construction approach is unique. We provide a full staff of licensed trades people and schedule our projects so that when one trade finishes, the next trade is ready to begin. To expedite this project, as you requested, we have agreed to overlap several trades whose work can be done concurrently.

JWS Remodeling Solutions will provide the following work:

- Remove baseboard, door casing, fluted casing and sheetrock to prepare for construction of new partition wall at north end of living room.
- Partition and finish walls to create two separate storage closets at north end of living room with access through two 3'0" six-panel door units. Replace all disturbed sheetrock.
- Hang and trim new door units and replace all disturbed baseboards and door casings.
- Install 5'0 double French door unit in location of current cased opening at the SW entrance to living room adjacent to foyer. Trim appropriately.
- Provide all rough and finished electrical using recessed lighting in the ceiling and appropriate single pole switches and duplex outlets.
- Move cold air return from west wall to east wall of living room.
- Paint or finish all surfaces/trim to match specs used throughout house.

The work does *not* include custom office cabinetry, carpeting, or phone or cable wiring. We would be happy to bid on these projects in the future.

(continued)

You achieve a formal tone by using the impersonal style, eliminating all references to *I* (including *we, us,* and *our*) and *you*. The style is borrowed from journalism, which stresses the reporter's objectivity. However, be careful that avoiding personal pronouns doesn't lead to overuse of phrases such as *there is* and *it is*, which are both dull and wordy. Also, avoiding personal pronouns makes it easier to slip into the passive voice. Instead of saying "I think we should buy TramCo," you might end up saying "It is recommended that the company buy TramCo."

Being formal means putting your readers at a distance and establishing an objective, businesslike relationship.

When you write in a formal style, you impose a certain distance between you and your readers. You remain businesslike, unemotional, and objective. You eliminate your own opinions and perceptions and retain only the provable facts (see "Focusing on

FIGURE 13.7 (Continued)

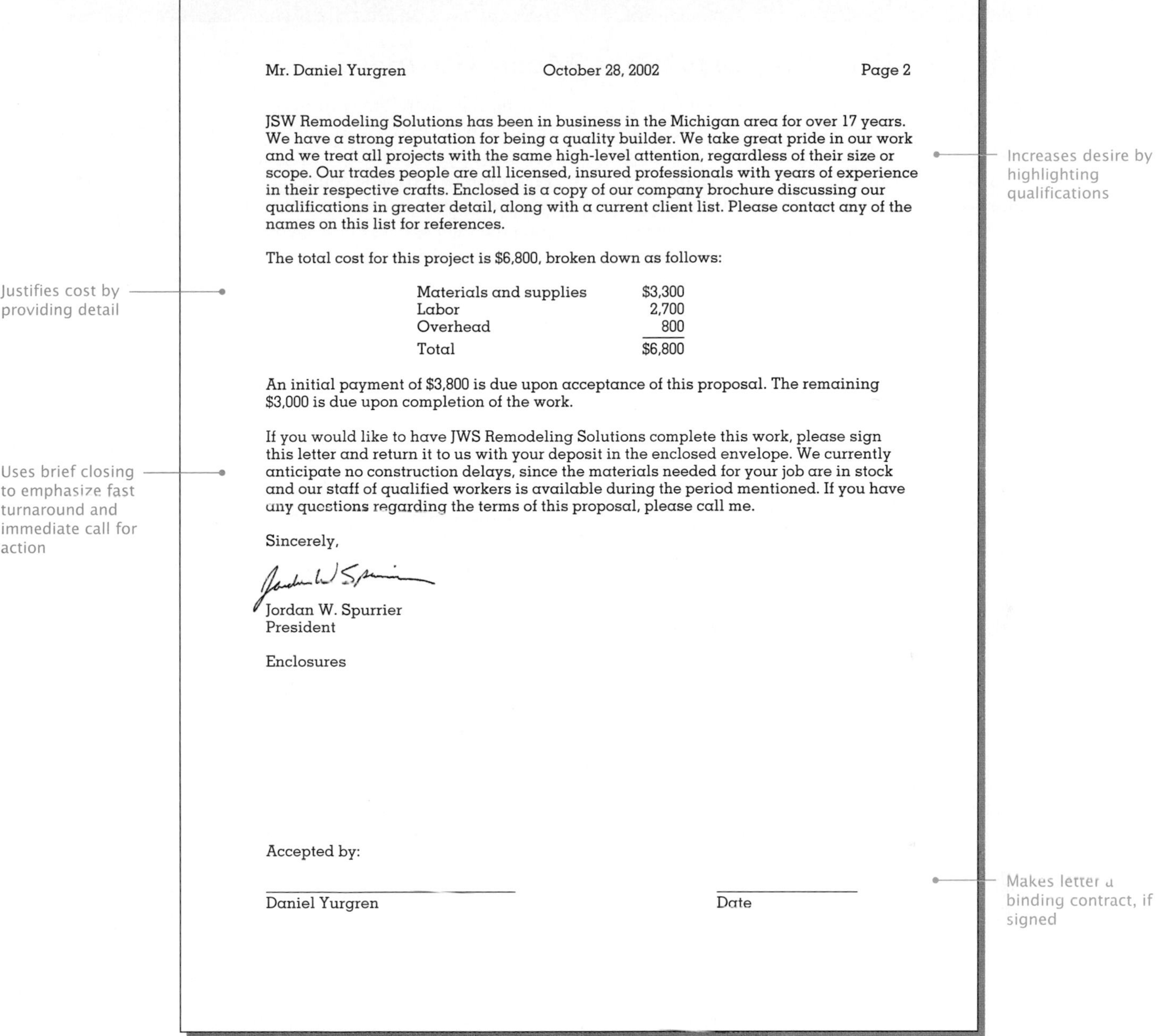

Mr. Daniel Yurgren October 28, 2002 Page 2

JSW Remodeling Solutions has been in business in the Michigan area for over 17 years. We have a strong reputation for being a quality builder. We take great pride in our work and we treat all projects with the same high-level attention, regardless of their size or scope. Our trades people are all licensed, insured professionals with years of experience in their respective crafts. Enclosed is a copy of our company brochure discussing our qualifications in greater detail, along with a current client list. Please contact any of the names on this list for references.

The total cost for this project is $6,800, broken down as follows:

Materials and supplies	$3,300
Labor	2,700
Overhead	800
Total	$6,800

An initial payment of $3,800 is due upon acceptance of this proposal. The remaining $3,000 is due upon completion of the work.

If you would like to have JWS Remodeling Solutions complete this work, please sign this letter and return it to us with your deposit in the enclosed envelope. We currently anticipate no construction delays, since the materials needed for your job are in stock and our staff of qualified workers is available during the period mentioned. If you have any questions regarding the terms of this proposal, please call me.

Sincerely,

Jordan W. Spurrier
President

Enclosures

Accepted by:

Daniel Yurgren Date

Ethics: Top Tips for Writing Reports That Mean Business"). You use no jokes, no similes or metaphors, and very few colorful adjectives or adverbs. You can easily destroy your credibility by exaggerating and using overblown language. Consider the following example:

You are not being objective if you
- Use exaggerated language
- Omit crucial evidence

The catastrophic collapse in sales, precipitated by cutthroat pricing on the part of predatory and unscrupulous rivals, has jeopardized the very survival of the once-soaring hot-air balloon division.

Although this sentence contains no personal references, the colorful adjectives make its objectivity highly questionable.

Your selection of a formal style does not guarantee objectivity of content. Your selection of facts is just as important as the way you phrase them, if not more so. If you

Focusing on Ethics

Top Tips for Writing Reports That Mean Business

Put nothing in writing that you're unwilling to say in public, and write nothing that may embarrass or jeopardize your employer. Does this directive mean you should cover up problems? Of course not. However, when you're dealing with sensitive information, be discreet. Present the information in such a way that it will help readers solve a problem. Avoid personal gripes, criticisms, alibis, attempts to blame other people, sugarcoated data, and unsolicited opinions.

To be useful, the information must be accurate, complete, and honest. Of course, being honest is not always a simple matter. Everyone sees reality a little differently, and individuals describe what they see in their own way. To restrict the distortions introduced by differences in perception, follow these guidelines:

- **Describe facts or events in concrete terms.** Indicate quantities whenever you can. Say, "Sales have increased 17 percent," or "Sales have increased from $40,000 to $43,000 in the past two months." Don't say, "Sales have skyrocketed."
- **Report all relevant facts.** Regardless of whether these facts support your theories or please your readers, they must be included. Omitting the details that undermine your position may be convenient, but it is misleading and inaccurate.
- **Put the facts in perspective.** Taken out of context, the most concrete facts are misleading. If you say, "Stock values have doubled in three weeks," you offer an incomplete picture. Instead, say, "Stock values have doubled in three weeks, rising from $2 to $4 per share."
- **Give plenty of evidence for your conclusions.** Statements such as "We have to reorganize the sales force or we'll lose market share" may or may not be true. Readers have no way of knowing unless you provide enough data to support your claim.
- **Present only verifiable conclusions.** Check facts, and use reliable sources. Don't draw conclusions too quickly (one rep may say that customers are unhappy, but that doesn't mean they all are). And don't assume that one event caused another (sales may have dipped right after you switched ad agencies, but that doesn't mean the new agency is at fault—the general state of the economy may be responsible).
- **Keep your personal biases in check.** Even if you feel strongly about your topic, keep those feelings from influencing your choice of words. Don't say, "Locating a plant in Kraymore is a terrible idea because the people there are mostly students who would rather play than work and who don't have the ability to operate our machines." Such language not only offends but also obscures the facts and provokes emotional responses.

Career Applications

1. When would you use vague language instead of concrete detail? Would this action be unethical or merely one form of emphasizing the positive?
2. Recent budget cuts have endangered the day-care program at your local branch of a national company. You're writing a report for headquarters about the grave impact on employees. Describe the situation in a single sentence that reveals nothing about your personal feelings but that clearly shows your position.

omit crucial evidence, you're not being objective, even though you're using an impersonal style.

The impersonal style is a well-entrenched tradition in many businesses.

Despite its drawbacks, the impersonal style is a well-entrenched tradition in many business organizations. You can often tell what tone is appropriate for your readers by looking at other reports of a similar type in your company. If all the other reports on file are impersonal, you should probably adopt the same tone yourself, unless you're confident that your readers prefer a more personal style. However, most organizations expect an unobtrusive, impersonal writing style for business reports.

Establishing a Consistent Time Perspective

Be consistent in the verb tense you use.

In what time frame will your report exist? Will you write in the past or present tense? The person who wrote this paragraph never decided:

> Of those interviewed, 25 percent report that they are dissatisfied with their present brand. The wealthiest participants complained most frequently, but all income categories are interested in trying a new brand. Only 5 percent of the interviewees say they had no interest in alternative products.

By flipping from tense to tense when describing the same research results, you only confuse your readers. Is the shift significant, they wonder, or are you just being sloppy? Such confusion can be eliminated by using tense consistently.

Also be careful to observe the chronological sequence of events in your report. If you're describing the history or development of something, start at the beginning and cover each event in the order of its occurrence. If you're explaining the steps in a process, take each step in proper sequence.

Follow a proper chronological sequence in your report.

Learning Objective 8

Briefly describe three tools that writers can use in long reports to help readers stay on track

Helping Readers Find Their Way

Your readers' perspective differs from yours, so without help from you, they may not see your overall organization and may not understand how all the pieces fit together.

As you begin to compose the text for your report, remember that readers have no concept of how the various pieces of your report relate to one another. Because you have done the work, you have a sense of your document's wholeness and can see how each page fits into the overall structure. But readers see the report one page at a time. Report experts such as Deirdre Ballou know that good writers give their readers a preview or road map of a report's structure, clarifying how the various parts are related. If you fail to provide readers with these clues to the structure of your report, they'll read aimlessly and miss important points, much like drivers trying to find their way through a strange city without a map. Providing structural directions is especially important for people from other cultures and countries, whose language skills and business expectations may differ from yours.

In a short report, readers are in little danger of getting lost. As the length of a report increases, however, so do readers' opportunities for becoming confused and losing track of the relationships among ideas. If you want readers to understand and accept your message, help them avoid confusion. Three tools are particularly useful for giving readers a sense of the overall structure of your document and for keeping them on track as they read along: headings, smooth transitions, and previews and reviews.

At this Fuji photo film factory packing area, workers understand the importance of having a smooth flow of goods. When writing reports, you must do the same. Make sure your reports are easy to follow by using previews and reviews, headings, smooth transitions, and other techniques.

Headings

Headings are brief titles that cue readers about the content of the section that follows. They improve a document's readability and are especially useful markers for clarifying the framework of a report. They visually indicate shifts from one idea to the next, and when *subheadings* (lower-level headings) and headings are both used, they help readers see the relationship between subordinate and main ideas. In addition, busy readers can quickly understand the gist of a document simply by scanning the headings. Look back at Chapter 6 to review how to write effective headings. Keep in mind that many companies specify a format for headings; if yours does, use that format. Otherwise, you can use the scheme shown in Figure 13.8.

Use headings to give readers the gist of your report.

Transitions

Chapter 5 defines transitions as words or phrases that tie ideas together and show how one thought is related to another. Good report writers use transitions to help readers move from one section of a report to the next. Depending on the length of the report, such transitions can be words, sentences, or complete paragraphs that serve as previews of the next section of a report or reviews of the ideas presented in the section just ending. Here's an example:

Use transitions consisting of a single word, a few words, or a whole paragraph to provide additional structural clues.

> Given our declining profits, we have three alternatives. As the previous section indicates, we can raise our selling prices of existing products, increase our offering by adding new products, or reduce our manufacturing costs. Each of these alternatives has advantages and disadvantages, which are discussed in the following section.

When writing transitions, be sure to list your topics in the order they are discussed.

FIGURE 13.8 Heading Format for Reports

TITLE

The title is centered at the top of the page in all capital letters, usually, boldfaced (or underlined if typewritten), often in a large font (type size), and often using a sans serif typeface. When the title runs to more than one line, the lines are usually double-spaced and arranged as an inverted pyramid (longer line on the top).

FIRST-LEVEL HEADING

A first-level heading indicates what the following section is about, perhaps by describing the subdivisions. All first-level headings are grammatically parallel, with the possible exception of such headings as "Introduction," "Conclusions," and "Recommendations." Some text appears between every two headings, regardless of their levels. Still boldfaced and sans serif, the font may be smaller than that used in the title but still larger than the typeface used in the text and still in all capital letters.

Second-Level Heading

Like first-level headings, second-level headings indicate what the following material is about. All second-level headings within a section are grammatically parallel. Still boldfaced and sans serif, the font may either remain the same or shrink to the size used in the text, and the style is now initial capitals with lower case. Never use only one second-level heading under a first-level heading. (The same is true for every other level of heading.)

Third-Level Heading

A third-level heading is worded to reflect the content of the material that follows. All third-level headings beneath a second-level heading should be grammatically parallel.

Fourth-Level Heading. Like all the other levels of heading, fourth-level headings reflect the subject that will be developed. All fourth-level headings within a subsection are parallel.

Fifth-level headings are generally the lowest level of heading used. However, you can indicate further breakdowns in your ideas by using a list:

1. *The first item in a list.* You may indent the entire item in block format to set it off visually. Numbers are optional.
2. *The second item in a list.* All lists have at least two items. An introductory phrase or sentence may be italicized for emphasis, as shown here.

Previews and Reviews

Throughout your report, introduce topics with previews, and summarize them with reviews.

You may have heard the old saying, "Tell 'em what you're going to tell 'em, tell 'em, then tell 'em what you just told 'em." Using a *preview section* to introduce an important topic helps readers get ready for new information. Previews are particularly helpful when the information is complex or unexpected. You don't want readers to get halfway into a section before figuring out what it's all about.

Review sections come after a body of material and summarize the information for your readers. Reviews help readers absorb details while keeping track of the big picture. Long reports and reports dealing with complex subjects can often benefit from multiple review sections, and not just a single review at the very end.

Swimming is a good analogy for using preview and review sections. Before you jump into the water, you look around, get your bearings, and get an idea of what you're about to dive into. A preview section serves the same purpose for your reader. After you dive in and swim for a few moments, you come back up for air. You look around and get your bearings again. Whenever you've had your readers "swimming in details" for any length of time, bring them back to the surface with a review section so that they can get their bearings again.

Previews and reviews can be written in a sentence format or in bulleted lists. Both are effective, but bullets can increase your document's readability by adding white space to the document design. Consider the following preview, which was written using both formats:

Use bulleted lists to set off important ideas and enhance your document's readability and design.

Sentence Format	Bulleted List
The next section discusses the advantages of advertising on the Internet. Among them are currency, global reach, affordability, and interactivity.	As the next section shows, advertising on the Internet has four advantages: ■ Currency ■ Global reach ■ Affordability ■ Interactivity

In long reports, bulleted lists may be worded to match actual paragraph headings. For a more in-depth discussion of how to write effective bullets and lists, see the section in Chapter 6 titled "Use Lists and Bullets for Emphasis and Clarity." To review the tasks discussed in this section, see this chapter's "Checklist: Composing Business Reports and Proposals."

✓ CHECKLIST: COMPOSING BUSINESS REPORTS AND PROPOSALS

A. Prepare a final writing outline

1. Use the outline to revise the order and content of information as needed.
2. Use informative headings for a hard-hitting, direct tone.
3. Use descriptive headings for an objective, indirect tone.
4. Use parallel construction.

B. Draft content for report introduction, body, and closing

1. Cover these topics in the introduction: authorization, purpose, scope, background, sources of information and methods of research, definitions, restrictions (in conducting the study), organization of the report, and recommendations or conclusion (if using the direct approach).
2. Use the body to present information. If writing an analytical report, use the body to develop points around conclusions, recommendations, or logical argument.
3. For direct-order reports, use the closing to summarize major findings in discussion order and to emphasize main points. For indirect-order reports, end with conclusions, recommendations, and a summary of key points.

C. Draft content for proposal introduction, body, and closing

1. Include these items in the introduction: purpose, background, solution, scope, and organization. Refer to RFP if proposal is solicited.
2. Use the body to give such details as proposed approach, work plan (steps, methods, timeline), qualifications, and costs. Persuasively explain audience benefits.
3. Use the closing to summarize key points and main benefits. Persuade readers to accept the proposal, and conclude with a call to action.

D. Choose proper degree of formality

1. Use an informal style (*I* and *you*) for letter and memo reports (unless your company prefers impersonal third person).
2. Use an impersonal style for more formal short reports in manuscript format.

E. Maintain a consistent time frame

1. Write in either the present or the past tense, using other tenses only to indicate prior or future events.
2. Don't flip from tense to tense.
3. Observe the chronological sequence of events.

F. Help readers find their way

1. Provide headings to improve readability, clarify framework, and indicate shifts in discussion.
2. Use transitions to tie ideas together and help readers move from one topic to the next.
3. Provide previews to prepare readers for new information.
4. Provide reviews to summarize information and help readers see the big picture.

COMMUNICATION CHALLENGES AT THE SAN DIEGO WILD ANIMAL PARK

Deirdre Ballou often helps the Zoological Society of San Diego's development department solicit funding for the nonprofit organization. Educational projects are a favorite among corporate sponsors, so Ballou's expertise is invaluable. For the past three years, one corporation has underwritten an annual Educators' Event at the Wild Animal Park (WAP), which allows Ballou and staff to host and inform groups of teachers about the unique educational opportunities the park offers. For example, imagine trying to get schoolkids excited about keeping a detailed information log. Then picture them visiting the park's simulated research station and learning about logs from a guide portraying a real scientist who is tracking and recording the behavior of colobus monkeys that inhabit a nearby island.

Although some sponsors want only the facts about a project (proposal followed by preliminary, interim, and final reports), Ballou knows that this particular company likes colorful proposals and reports, describing everything from the menu served at the event to what the weather was like. But they also want to see a proposed time line and budget spreadsheets. For this year's event, Ballou is planning a behind-the-scenes tour led by WAP animal experts, culminating in a visit to the research island, where interpretive guides will demonstrate how they entertain and inform visitors with their lab equipment, charts, maps, logs, microscopes, centrifuges, water purification equipment, discovery scopes, and radio telemetry tracking—not to mention their hand-reared animals. An aardvark is a permanent resident of the island, and 10 other creatures—including a pygmy falcon, a lilac-breasted roller, a leopard tortoise, a springhaas (of the rodent family), and a fennec fox—are brought to the station throughout each day for demonstrations.

Individual Challenge: Ballou is meeting again with company representatives, and she wants to take along a preliminary proposal for this year's Educators' Event. Use what you've learned in this chapter to suggest an outline for Ballou's preliminary proposal. Make up any details you need to make your outline authentic. Suggest a length, format, organization, and level of formality.

Team Challenge: Ballou will also need to convince park management that hiring extra interpretive guides for a new exhibit is a necessity. Trouble is, because of their special knowledge and training, their hourly rate is higher than that of other park personnel, and keeping labor costs low is a primary concern for the general manager. Brainstorm ideas for solving Ballou's dilemma. How should she broach the subject and convince the general manager that the cost is justified? Make detailed notes explaining and justifying your recommended strategy.[7] ■

SUMMARY OF LEARNING OBJECTIVES

1 Name four things you must decide on before drafting a business report or proposal. Before composing a business report or proposal, you must select one of four format options—preprinted form, letter, memo, manuscript—taking into consideration company guidelines. You must also decide on the length, which will be guided by the subject and purpose of your report and your relationship with the audience. Third, you must choose between a direct and an indirect approach—weighing the advantages and disadvantages of each. Finally, you must decide on your report's structure: how your ideas will be subdivided and developed.

2 Describe the structure of informational reports. Because reader reaction is rarely an issue for informational reports, structure is dictated by the nature of your topic. Of utmost concern is reader comprehension, so informational reports must be both logical and accurate. Topical organization allows you to structure your report in six common arrangements. When basing your structure on importance, cover the most important facts first and the least important last. When using sequence, cover a process step-by-step. When basing your structure on chronology, cover facts as a chain of events occurring in time. When using spatial orientation, detail physical aspects from right to left, left to right, top to bottom, or outside to inside. To base your structure on geography, cover facts by location. And to use category as your structural basis, cover facts as distinct aspects that can be classified into groups.

3 Describe the structure of analytical reports. Because the structure of analytical reports depends on anticipated audience reaction, use either a structure that focuses attention on conclusions and recommendations (for receptive audiences) or one that focuses attention on the rationale behind your conclusions and recommendations (for skeptical or hostile audiences). Focusing directly on conclusions or recommendations can intensify resistance or even make your solution seem too simple. When you want your audience to focus on why your ideas will work, you need to draw attention to the logic of your argument. There are three popular approaches to a logical organization. The 2 + 2 = 4 approach demonstrates that everything in your report adds up. The scientific method reveals the most effective solution, or hypothesis, by showing evidence that either proves or disproves each alternative. The yardstick approach establishes conditions, or criteria, against which all possible solutions are measured.

4 **Name five characteristics of effective report content.** Effective report content is accurate if it is factually correct and error-free. It is complete if it includes all necessary information and supports all key assertions. It is balanced if it presents all sides of an argument. It is clear and logical if it is well-written and organized logically. It is properly documented if credit is given to all primary and secondary sources of information used.

5 **List the topics commonly covered in a report's introduction, body, and closing.** The introduction highlights who authorized the report, the purpose and scope of a report, necessary background material, the sources or methods used to gather information, important definitions, any limitations, and the order in which the various topics are covered. The body discusses such details as problems, opportunities, facts, evidence, trends, results of studies or investigations, analysis of potential courses of action, process procedures and steps, methods and approaches, evaluation criteria for options, conclusions, recommendations, and supporting reasons. The closing summarizes key points, restates conclusions and recommendations, and lists action items.

6 **Name six strategies to strengthen your proposal argument.** To strengthen your argument, you should demonstrate your knowledge, provide concrete examples, research the competition, prove that your proposal is workable, adopt a "you" attitude, and make your document attractive and error-free.

7 **List the topics commonly covered in a proposal's introduction, body, and closing.** The introduction discusses the background or existing problem, the solution to the problem, the scope of the proposal, and the order in which information is presented in the document. The body discusses the proposed approach and benefits to the reader, the work plan, the organization's qualifications, and the costs of the proposal. The closing briefly summarizes the key points, the merits and benefits of the proposed approach, and the submitting firm's competencies.

8 **Briefly describe three tools that writers can use in long reports to help readers stay on track.** Effective reports help readers navigate the document by using these three tools: (1) Headings set off important ideas and provide the reader with clues as to the report's framework and shifts in discussion; (2) transitions tie ideas together and keep readers moving along; (3) previews and reviews prepare readers for new information and summarize previously discussed information.

TEST YOUR KNOWLEDGE

1. What are your options for selecting a report format?
2. What are your options for structuring an informational report?
3. What are your options for structuring an analytical report?
4. What steps should you follow when structuring a report around recommendations?
5. How does topical organization differ from logical organization?
6. What is the function of a report introduction?
7. What information might you include in the closing of a report?
8. What information might you include in the introduction of a proposal?
9. Why is the work plan a key component of a proposal?
10. What tools can you use to help readers follow the structure and flow of information in a long report?

APPLY YOUR KNOWLEDGE

1. Should a report always explain the writer's method of gathering evidence or solving a problem? Why or why not?
2. Would you use the direct or indirect approach to document inventory shortages at your manufacturing plant? To propose an employee stock-option plan? Why?
3. What tense is better for most business reports, past or present? Explain.
4. If you were writing an analytical report about your company's advertising policies, where would you include your recommendations—in the beginning of the report or at the end? Why?
5. **Ethical Choices** If a company receives a solicited formal proposal, is it ethical for the company to adopt the recommendations discussed in the proposal even though the company does not to hire the submitting firm?

Practice Your Knowledge

Document for Analysis

Read Figure 13.9, a solicited memo proposal; then (1) analyze the strengths and weaknesses of this document and (2) revise the document so that it follows this chapter's guidelines.

Exercises

For live links to all websites discussed in this chapter, visit this text's website at www.prenhall.com/bovee. Just log on and select Chapter 12, and click on "Student Resources." Locate the name of the site or the URL related to the material in the text. For the "Exploring the Best of the Web" exercises, you'll also find navigational directions. Click on the live link to the site.

13.1 **Organizing Reports: Choosing the Direct or Indirect Approach** Of the organizational approaches introduced in the chapter, which is best suited for writing a report that answers the following questions? Briefly explain why. (Note, you will write one report for each question item.)

a. In which market segment—root beer, cola, or lemon-lime—should Fizz Drinks, Inc., introduce a new soft drink to take advantage of its enlarged research and development budget?

FIGURE 13.9 Solicited Memo Proposal

MEMO

TO: Ken Estes, Northern Illinois Concrete
FROM: Kris Beiersdorf
DATE: April 19, 2002
PROJECT: IDOT Letting Item #83 Contract No. 79371 DuPage County

Memco Consruction proposes to furnish all labor, material, equipment, and supervision to provide Engineered Fill—Class II and IV for the following unit prices.

Engineered Fill – Class II and IV

Description	Unit	Quantity	Unit Price	Total
Mobilization*	Lump Sum	1	$4,500.00	$4,500.00
Engineered Fill Class II	Cubic Yards	1,267	$33.00	$41,811.00
Engineered Fill Class IV	Cubic Yards	1,394	$38.00	$52,972.00

* Mobilization includes one move-in. Additional move-ins to be billed at $1,100.00 each.

The following items clarify and qualify the scope of our subcontracting work:

1. All forms, earthwork, clearing, etc. to be provided and maintained by others at no cost to Memco Construction.
2. General Contractor shall provide location for staging, stockpiling material, equipment, and storage at the job site.
3. Memco Construction shall be paid strictly based upon the amount of material actually used on the job.
4. All prep work, including geotechnical fabrics, geomembrane liners, etc. to be done by others at no cost to Memco Construction.
5. Water is to be available at project site at no charge to Memco Construction.
6. Dewatering to be done by others at no cost to Memco Construction.
7. Traffic control setup, devices, maintenance, and flagmen are to be provided by others at no cost to Memco Construction.
8. Memco Construction LLC may withdraw this bid if we do not receive a written confirmation that we are the apparent low sub-bidder within 10 days of your receipt of this proposal.
9. Our F.E.I.N. is 36-4478095.
10. Bond is not included in above prices. Bond is available for an additional 1 percent.

If you have any questions, please contact me at the phone number listed below.

Kris Beiersdorf
Memco Construction
187 W. Euclid Avenue, Glenview, IL 60025
Office: (847) 352-9742, ext. 30
Fax: (847) 352-6595
E-mail: Kbeiersdorf@memco.com
www.memco.com

b. Should Major Manufacturing, Inc., close down operations of its antiquated Bellville, Arkansas, plant despite the adverse economic impact on the town that has grown up around the plant?

c. Should you and your partner adopt a new accounting method to make your financial statements look better to potential investors?

d. Should Grand Canyon Chemicals buy disposable test tubes to reduce labor costs associated with cleaning and sterilizing reusable test tubes?

e. What are some reasons for the recent data loss at the college computer center, and how can we avoid similar problems in the future?

13.2 Choosing the Direct or Indirect Approach Look through recent issues (print or online) of *Business Week, Fortune*, or other business publications for an article that describes how an executive's conclusions about his or her company's current situation or future opportunities led to changes in policy, plans, or products. Construct an outline of the material, using (a) direct order and (b) indirect order. Which approach do you think the executive would use when reporting these conclusions to stockholders? When reporting to other senior managers? Explain your answers.

13.3 Organizing Reports: Deciding on Format Go to the library or visit the Internet site www.annualreportservice.com

and review the annual reports recently released by two corporations in the same industry. Analyze each report and be prepared to discuss the following questions in class:

a. What organizational differences, if any, do you see in the way each corporation discusses its annual performance? Are the data presented clearly so that shareholders can draw conclusions about how well the company performed?
b. What goals, challenges, and plans do top managers emphasize in their discussion of results?
c. How do the format and organization of each report enhance or detract from the information being presented?

13.4 **Organizing Reports: Structuring Informational Reports** Assume that your college president has received many student complaints about campus parking problems. You are appointed the chair a student committee organized to investigate the problems and recommend solutions. The president gives you the file labeled "Parking: Complaints from Students," and you jot down the essence of the complaints as you inspect the contents. Your notes look like this:

- Inadequate student spaces at critical hours
- Poor night lighting near the computer center
- Inadequate attempts to keep resident neighbors from occupying spaces
- Dim marking lines
- Motorcycles taking up full spaces
- Discourteous security officers
- Spaces (usually empty) reserved for college officials
- Relatively high parking fees
- Full fees charged to night students even though they use the lots only during low-demand periods
- Vandalism to cars and a sense of personal danger
- Inadequate total space
- Resident harassment of students parking on the street in front of neighboring houses

Prepare an outline for an informational report to be submitted to committee members. Use a topical organization that categorizes this information.

13.5 **Organizing Reports: Structuring Analytical Reports** Three years ago, your company (a carpet manufacturer) modernized its Georgia plant in anticipation of increasing demand for carpets. Because of the depressed housing market, the increase in demand for new carpets has been slow to materialize. As a result, the company has excess capacity at both its Georgia and California plants. On the basis of your research, you have recommended that the company close the California plant. The company president, J. P. Lawrence, has asked you to prepare a justification report to support your recommendation. Here are the facts you gathered by interviewing the respective plant managers:

Operational Statistics

- Georgia plant: This plant has newer equipment, productivity is higher, employs 100 nonunion production workers, and ships $12 million in carpets a year. Hourly base wage is $16.
- California plant: California plant employs 80 union production workers and ships $8 million in carpets a year. Hourly base wage is $20.

Financial Implications

- Savings by closing California plant: (1) Increase productivity by 17% ; (2) reduce labor costs by 20% (total labor savings would be $1 million per year; see assumptions); (3) annual local tax savings of $120,000 (Georgia has a more favorable tax climate).
- Sale of Pomona, California, land: Purchased in 1952 for $200,000. Current market value $2.5 million. Net profit (after capital gains tax) over $1 million.
- Sale of plant and equipment: Fully depreciated. Any proceeds a windfall.
- Costs of closing California plant: One-time deductible charge of $250,000 (relocation costs of $100,000 and severance payments totaling $150,000).

Assumptions

- Transfer 5 workers from California to Georgia.
- Hire 45 new workers in Georgia.
- Lay off 75 workers in California.
- Georgia plant would require a total of 150 workers to produce the combined volume of both plants.

a. Which approach (focus on conclusions, recommendations, or logical arguments) will you use to structure your report to the president? Why?
b. Suppose this report were to be circulated to plant managers and supervisors instead. What changes, if any, might you make in your approach?
c. List some conclusions that you might draw from the above information to use in your report.
d. Using the structure you selected for your report to the president, draft a final report outline with first- and second-level informative headings.

13.6 **Composing Reports: Report Content** You are writing an analytical report on the U.S. sales of your newest product. Of the following topics, identify those that should be covered in the report's introduction, body, and closing. Briefly explain your decisions:

a. Regional breakdowns of sales across the country
b. Date the product was released in the marketplace
c. Sales figures from competitors selling similar products worldwide
d. Predictions of how the struggling U.S. economy will affect sales over the next six months
e. Method used for obtaining the above predictions
f. The impact of similar products being sold in the United States by Japanese competitors
g. Your recommendation as to whether the company should sell this product internationally
h. Actions that must be completed by year end if the company decides to sell this product internationally

13.7 **Composing Business Reports** Your boss, Len Chow (vice president of corporate planning), has asked you to research opportunities in the cosmetics industry and to prepare a report that presents your findings and your recommendation for where you think the company should focus its marketing efforts. Here's a copy of your note cards (data were created for this exercise):

Sub: Demand ref:1.1 Industry grew through 1970s, 1980s, and early 1990s fueled by per capita consumption
Sub: Competition ref:1.2 700 companies currently in cosmetics industry
Sub: Niches ref:1.3 Focusing on special niches avoids head-on competition with industry leaders
Sub: Competition ref: 1.4 Industry dominated by market leaders: Revlon, Procter & Gamble, Avon, Gillette
Sub: Demand ref: 1.5 Industry no longer recession-proof: Past year, sales sluggish; consumer spending is down; most affected were mid- to high-priced brands; consumers traded down to less expensive lines
Sub: Competition ref: 1.6 Smaller companies (Neutrogena, Mary Kay, Soft Soap, and Noxell) survive by: specializing in niches, differentiating product line, focusing on market segment
Sub: Demand ref: 1.7 Consumption of cosmetics relatively flat for past five years
Sub: Competition ref: 1.8 Prices are constant while promotion budgets are increasing
Sub: Niches ref: 1.9 Men: 50% of adult population; account for one-fifth of cosmetic sales; market leaders have attempted this market but failed
Sub: Demand ref: 1.10 Cosmetic industry is near maturity but some segments may vary. Total market currently produces annual retail sales of $14.5 billion: Cosmetics/lotions/fragrances—$5.635 billion; Personal hygiene products—$4.375 billion; Hair-care products—$3.435 billion; shaving products—$1.055 billion
Sub: Niches ref: 1.11 Ethnic groups: Some firms specialize in products for African Americans; few firms oriented toward Hispanic, Asian, or Native Americans, which tend to be concentrated geographically
Sub: Demand ref: 1.12 Average annual expenditure per person for cosmetics is $58
Sub: Competition ref: 1.13 Competition is intensifying and dominant companies are putting pressure on smaller ones
Sub: Demand ref: 1.14 First quarter of current year, demand is beginning to revive; trend expected to continue well into next year
Sub: Niches ref: 1.15 Senior citizens: large growing segment of population; account for 6% of cosmetic sales; specialized needs for hair and skin not being met; interested in appearance
Sub: Demand ref: 1.16 Demographic trends: (1) Gradual maturing of baby-boomer generation will fuel growth by consuming greater quantities of shaving cream, hair-coloring agents, and skin creams; (2) population is increasing in the South and Southwest, where some brands have strong distribution

List the main idea of your message (your recommendation), the major points (your conclusions), and supporting evidence. Then construct a final report outline with first- and second-level informative headings focusing on your conclusions. Because Chow requested this report, you can feel free to use the direct approach. Finish by writing a draft of your memo report to Chow.

13.8 Composing Reports Find an article in a business newspaper or journal (in print or online) that recommends a solution to a problem. Identify the problem, the recommended solution(s), and the supporting evidence provided by the author to justify his or her recommendation(s). Did the author cite any formal or informal studies as evidence? What facts or statistics did the author include? Did the author cite any criteria for evaluating possible options? If so, what were they?

13.9 Composing Reports: Navigational Clues Review a long business article in a journal or newspaper. Highlight examples of how the article uses heading, transitions, and previews and reviews to help the readers find their way.

13.10 Ethical Choices Your boss has asked you to prepare a feasibility report to determine whether the company should advertise its custom-crafted cabinetry in the weekly neighborhood newspaper. Based on your primary research, you think they should. As you draft the introduction to your report, however, you discover that the survey administered to the neighborhood newspaper subscribers was flawed. Several of the questions were poorly written and misleading. You used the survey results, among other findings, to justify your recommendation. The report is due in three days. What actions might you want to take, if any, before you complete your report?

EXPAND YOUR KNOWLDEGE

Exploring the Best of the Web:

Research Before You Report, p. 423

Research your competition at Corporate Information and find out what you need to know before you write your next report or proposal.

1. Select an industry of your choice from one of the listed countries and follow the links to reports, analyses, and data on that industry. What specific types of information did you find on the industry? How might you use this information when writing a report or proposal?
2. Read the online research reports for a company of your choice. What types of specific information are available in these reports? How might you use this information when writing a report or proposal?
3. What do the company extensions GmbH, KK, LLC, OHG, SA, and SNC mean?

Exploring the Web on Your Own

Review these chapter-related websites to learn more about writing reports and proposals.

1. Researching Companies Online, home.sprintmail.com/~debflanagan/index.html, has some good advice for finding company and industry information on the web. Take the tutorial.
2. Learn how to find specific information on the web and validate what you find at Internet Search FAQ, www.purefiction.com. Click on links, then click on "Using the Internet for Research FAQ."
3. The Spire Project, www.spireproject.com/, claims to have a better way to find information on the web. Check it out.

LEARN INTERACTIVELY

Interactive Study Guide

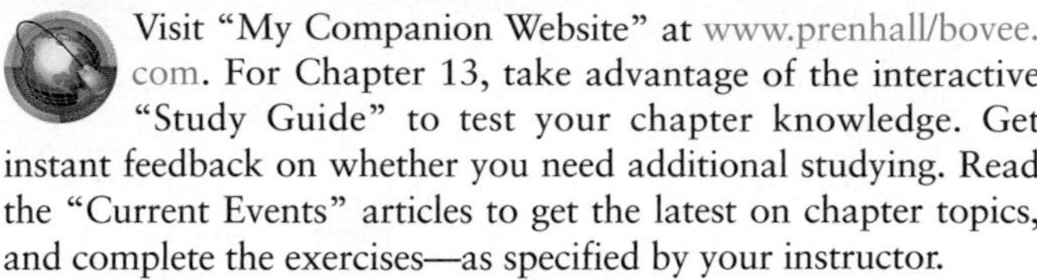

Visit "My Companion Website" at www.prenhall/bovee.com. For Chapter 13, take advantage of the interactive "Study Guide" to test your chapter knowledge. Get instant feedback on whether you need additional studying. Read the "Current Events" articles to get the latest on chapter topics, and complete the exercises—as specified by your instructor.

This site offers a variety of additional resources: The "Research Area" helps you locate a wealth of information to use in course assignments. You can even send a message to online research experts, who will help you find exactly the information you need. The "Study Hall" helps you succeed in this course. "Talk in the Hall" lets you leave messages and meet new friends online. If you have a question, you can "Ask the Tutor." And to get a better grade in this course, you can find more help at "Writing Skills," "Study Skills," and "Study Tips."

Grammar Diagnostic Tests

Review and reinforce your grammar and language skills by taking one of the four online diagnostic tests offered at our companion website, www.prenhall/bovee.com. The four tests cover a variety of topics, including spelling, capitals, punctuation, verbs, pronouns, adjectives, adverbs, sentence structure, sentence punctuation, clarity, word choice, style, organization skills, proofreading, and more. Submit your test and assess your competency. Then focus on improving areas where you are weak as you complete the exercises in this chapter.

CASES

INFORMAL INFORMATIONAL REPORTS

1. My progress to date: Interim progress report on your academic career As you know, the bureaucratic process involved in getting a degree or certificate is nearly as challenging as any course you could take.

Your task: Prepare an interim progress report detailing the steps you've taken toward completing your graduation or certification requirements. After examining the requirements listed in your college catalog, indicate a realistic schedule for completing those that remain. In addition to course requirements, include steps such as completing the residency requirement, filing necessary papers, and paying necessary fees. Use memo format for your report, and address it to anyone who is helping or encouraging you through school.

2. Gavel to gavel: Personal activity report of a meeting Meetings, conferences, and conventions abound in the academic world, and you have probably attended your share.

Your task: Prepare a personal activity report on a meeting, convention, or conference that you recently attended. Use memo format, and direct the report to other students in your field who were not able to attend.

3. Check that price tag: Informational report on trends in college costs Are tuition costs going up, going down, or remaining the same? Your college's administration has asked you to compare your college's tuition costs with those of a nearby college and determine which has risen

more quickly. Research the trend by checking your college's annual tuition costs for each of the most recent four years. Then research the four-year tuition trends for a neighboring college. For both colleges, calculate the percentage change in tuition costs from year to year and between the first and fourth year.

Your task: Prepare an informal report (using the letter format) presenting your findings and conclusions to the president of your college. Include graphics to explain and support your conclusions.

4. Get a move on it: Lasting guidelines for moving into college dormitories Moving into a college dormitory is one experience you weren't quite prepared for. In addition to lugging your earthly belongings up four flights of stairs in 90-degree heat, channeling electrical cords to the one room outlet tucked in the corner of the room, lofting your beds, and negotiating with your roommate over who gets the bigger closet, you had to hug your parents goodbye in the parking lot in front of the entire freshman class—or so it seemed. Now that you are a pro, you've offered to write some lasting guidelines for future freshmen so they know what is expected of them on moving day.

Your task: Prepare an informational report for future freshmen classes outlining the rules and procedures to follow when moving into a college dorm. Lay out the rules such as starting time, handling trash and empty boxes, items permitted and not permitted in dorm rooms, common courtesies, and so on. Be sure to mention what the policy is for removing furniture from the room, lofting beds, and overloading electrical circuits. Of course, any recommendations on how to handle disputes with roommates would be helpful. So would some brief advice on how to cope with anxious parents. Direct your memo report to the college dean.

INFORMAL ANALYTICAL REPORTS

5. My next career move: Feasibility report organized around recommendations If you've ever given yourself a really good talking-to, you'll be quite comfortable with this project.

Your task: Write a memo report directed to yourself and signed with a fictitious name. Indicate a possible job that your college education will qualify you for, mention the advantages of the position in terms of your long-range goals, and then outline the actions you must take to get the job.

6. Staying the course: Unsolicited proposal using the 2 + 2 = 4 approach Think of a course you would love to see added to the core curriculum at your school. Conversely, if you would like to see a course offered as an elective rather than being required, write your e-mail report accordingly.

Your task: Write a short e-mail proposal using the 2 + 2 = 4 approach. Prepare your proposal to be submitted to the academic dean by e-mail. Be sure to include all the reasons supporting your idea.

7. Planning my program: Problem-solving report using the scientific method Assume that you will have time for only one course next term.

Your task: List the pros and cons of four or five courses that interest you, and use the scientific method to settle on the course that is best for you to take at this time. Write your report in memo format, addressing it to your academic adviser.

8. "Would you carry it?" Unsolicited sales proposal recommending a product to a retail outlet Select a product you are familiar with, and imagine that you are the manufacturer trying to get a local retail outlet to carry it. Use the Internet and other resources to gather information about the product.

Your task: Write an unsolicited sales proposal in letter format to the owner (or manager) of the store, proposing that the item be stocked. Use the information you gathered to describe some of the product's features and benefits to the store. Then make up some reasonable figures, highlighting what the item costs, what it can be sold for, and what services your company provides (return of unsold items, free replacement of unsatisfactory items, necessary repairs, and so on).

9. Restaurant review: Troubleshooting report on a restaurant's food and operations Visit any restaurant, possibly your school cafeteria. The workers and fellow customers will assume that you are an ordinary customer, but you are really a spy for the owner.

Your task: After your visit, write a short memo to the owner, explaining (a) what you did and what you observed, (b) any violations of policy that you observed, and (c) your recommendations for improvement. The first part of your report (what you did and what you observed) will be the longest. Include a description of the premises, inside and out.

Tell how long it took for each step of ordering and receiving your meal. Describe the service and food thoroughly. You are interested in both the good and bad aspects of the establishment's décor, service, and food. For the second section (violations of policy), use some common sense. If all the servers but one have their hair covered, you may assume that policy requires hair to be covered; a dirty window or restroom obviously violates policy. The last section (recommendations for improvement) involves professional judgment. What management actions will improve the restaurant?

10. On the books: Troubleshooting report on improving the campus bookstore Imagine that you are a consultant hired to improve the profits of your campus bookstore.

Your task: Visit the bookstore and look critically at its operations. Then draft a memo to the bookstore manager, offering recommendations that would make the store more profitable, perhaps suggesting products it should carry, hours that it should remain open, or added services that it should make available to students. Be sure to support your recommendations.

11. Press 1 for efficiency: Unsolicited proposal on a telephone interviewing system How can a firm be thorough yet efficient when considering dozens of applicants for each position? One tool that just may help is IntelliView, a 10-minute question-and-answer session conducted by Touch-Tone telephone. The company recruiter dials up the IntelliView computer and then leaves the room. The candidate punches in answers to roughly 100 questions about work attitudes and other issues. In a few minutes, the recruiter can call Pinkerton, which offers the service, and find out the results. On the basis of what the IntelliView interview revealed, the recruiter can delve more deeply into certain areas and, ultimately, have more information on which to base the hiring decision.

Your task: As a recruiter for Curtis Box and Crate, you think that IntelliView might help your firm. Write a brief memo to Wallace Jefferson, the director of human resources, in which you suggest a test of the IntelliView system. Your memo should tell your boss why you believe your firm should test the system before making a long-term commitment.[8]

12. Day and night: Problem-solving report on stocking a 24-hour convenience store When a store is open all day, every day, when's the best time to restock the shelves? That's the challenge at Store 24, a retail chain that never closes. Imagine you're the assistant manager of a Store 24 branch that just opened near your campus. You want to set up a restocking schedule that won't conflict with prime shopping hours. Think about the number of customers you're likely to serve in the morning, afternoon, evening, and overnight hours. Consider, too, how many employees you might have during these four periods.

Your task: Using the scientific approach, write a problem-solving report in letter form to the store manager (Isabel Chu) and the regional manager (Eric Angstrom), who must agree on a solution to this problem. Discuss the pros and cons of each of the four periods, and include your recommendation for restocking the shelves.

Completing Business Reports and Proposals

After studying this chapter, you will be able to

1 *List the three tasks involved in completing business reports and proposals, and briefly explain what's involved in revising them*

2 *Describe the 10 prefatory parts of a formal report*

3 *Explain the difference between a synopsis and an executive summary*

4 *Describe the three supplementary parts of a formal report*

COMMUNICATION CLOSE-UP AT CORPORATE DYNAMICS

www.corpdyn.com

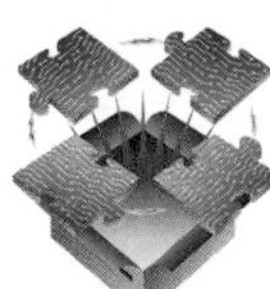

In business, the phrase "dog and pony show" is sometimes used to describe a report or presentation that looks attractive on the surface but lacks substance. As president of Corporate Dynamics, Mark Landiak developed a sales proposal for one potential client by capitalizing on that expression: He put a tiny image of a toy dog and pony on the report cover and titled the report "Corporate Dynamics: Not Your Typical Dog and Pony Show." This creative strategy "worked like a charm," says Landiak. "It made the client laugh, and it made us really stand out."

In fact, standing out, or differentiation, is what Corporate Dynamics is all about. Founded in 1989 by Landiak, this Chicago-based company provides clients, both large and small, with innovative training and consulting in sales, customer service, and management applications. Landiak's team begins by holding one- to two-day "workout sessions" with senior managers from various parts of the client company. The group discusses the challenges the firm is facing, as well as the company's goals and specific needs. Then Landiak's team further researches these issues, including details on the client's market, competitors, and so on.

After weeks—even months—of analysis, Corporate Dynamics sums up its findings in a formal report or proposal. Such reports generally detail the client's current position, describe any problems being faced or situations requiring change, state future objectives, point out barriers to success, and recommend strategies for productive organizational change. All the information is useful—especially the final recommendation, which often suggests training from Landiak and his staff of experts. Landiak knows, however, that to convince clients to use his company's services, he must provide a compelling argument—the key to a successful report.

Corporate Dynamics's reports can be as short as 5 pages or as long as 30, depending on the client's needs and the issues involved. Report formats also vary. Many clients have their own reporting styles, and Landiak tries to imitate them so that his reports feel familiar and are thus easier for clients to read. He even asks managers for a report template to work from.

In addition, Landiak is careful to use language that is familiar to his audience. "One client may call a goal a *strategic imperative,*" he explains, "while another may call it a *critical issue.* You have to align yourself with the clients' terminology and use their jargon rather than creating a new vocabulary." Even so, Landiak stresses the importance of avoiding too much technical language or detail. "If you dance around the issue, you will lose your audience," says Landiak. So Landiak and his team strive to make their reports straightforward and concise. "A lot of people make the mistake of including too much ancillary material," he says. "If you put in extraneous information, the reader will turn to the back looking for the bottom line." How does Landiak find the right balance between too much information and just enough? With a lot of effort.

At Corporate Dynamics, no one wants to bury all that effort in a report that is unclear or sloppy. "Someone has to be willing to go the extra mile to produce a good report," says

Mark Landiak builds corporate success strategies for his clients one page at a time. By gathering critical data from clients during joint "workout sessions," Landiak identifies critical issues and makes sure that each issue is adequately addressed in his final report to the client.

Landiak. Going the extra mile means paying close attention to detail and proofreading carefully to ensure that the final product is as clear as it can be. "Report writing is an extension of you, your organization, and the job you will do," says Landiak. "If a report is average, the image you project to the client is average."[1] ■

REVISING REPORTS AND PROPOSALS

Experienced business communicators such as Mark Landiak realize that writing a report or proposal is a demanding and time-consuming task. They also know that the process of writing a report or proposal doesn't end with a first draft. As Chapter 5 points out, when you compose a first draft, you simply try to get your ideas on paper with some semblance of organization, and you save strengthening, tightening, and polishing for later. Once you have finished your first draft, you perform three tasks to complete your report: revise, produce, and proofread.

Learning Objective 1

List the three tasks involved in completing business reports and proposals, and briefly explain what's involved in revising them

The revision process is basically the same for reports as for any business message, but it may take longer, depending on the length of your report or proposal. You evaluate the report's organization, style, and tone, making sure that you've said what you want to say and that you've said it in the most logical order and in a way that responds to your audience's needs. You improve the report's readability by varying sentence length, keeping paragraphs short, using lists and bullets, and adding headings and subheadings. And you revise the content of your report so that it is clear and concise.

PRODUCING FORMAL REPORTS AND PROPOSALS

Once you are satisfied with your changes, you produce your report by incorporating the design elements discussed in Chapter 6. Headings, captions, typographical devices (such as capital letters, italics, and boldface type), margins, line justifications, and white space are just some of the techniques and tools you can use to present your material effectively. Also useful are visual aids and preview and review statements to frame sections of your text. Many organizations have format guidelines that make your decisions easier, but the goal is always to focus readers' attention on major points and on the flow of ideas.

In organizations that produce many reports and proposals, the preparation process involves teamwork.

How the final version of your report or proposal is actually produced depends on the nature of your organization. The traditional approach was usually a team effort, with secretaries or other support personnel handling the typing, formatting, and other tasks. For important, high-visibility reports, a graphics department would help with charts, drawings, covers, and other visual elements.

Personal computers can handle many of the mechanical aspects of report preparation.

However, as personal computers have become commonplace in the business office, more and more employees are expected to handle most or even all the formatting and production of their own reports. The good news is that computer tools are now generally easy enough for the average businessperson to use productively. A software "suite" such as Microsoft Office makes it easy to produce reports that incorporate graphics, tables, spreadsheet data, and database records. Even advanced report features such as photography are relatively simple these days, with the advent of low-cost color desktop scanners and inexpensive color printers with near-photo-quality output.

Noel Forgeard, CEO of Airbus, is ramping up Airbus to produce the world's largest aircraft (the A380), holding 600 passengers. To set priorities and focus on his goals, Forgeard must read a lot of reports. He expects a report's introduction to (1) give him perspective on where the report fits into the overall picture, (2) clearly state its purpose, (3) preview the contents, and (4) establish a tone that defines its relationship with its readers.

The bad news is that continually improving computer tools increases your audience's expectations. People are influenced by packaging, so a handsomely bound report with full-color graphics will impress your audience more than a plain, typewritten-style report containing the same information. The bar is raised even higher when your report must compete with electronic reports filled with multimedia effects and hypertext links. In some cases, sending a custom-made CD-ROM containing your new business proposal might be your best option.

Be sure to schedule enough time to turn out a document that looks professional.

No matter which tools you use, make sure you have scheduled enough time for formatting and production. When working on reports or any other business document, remember Murphy's law (which says that if something can go wrong, it will). Corrupted disk files, printing problems, and other glitches can consume hours. If you are preparing a long, formal report, you will need extra time to prepare and assemble all the various prefatory and supplementary parts. The more formal your report, the more components you'll include.

Components of a Formal Report

A formal report's manuscript format and impersonal tone convey an impression of professionalism. A formal report can be either short (fewer than 10 pages) or long (10 pages or more). It can be informational or analytical, direct or indirect. It may be targeted to readers inside or outside the organization. What sets it apart from other reports is its polish.

The three basic divisions of a formal report:

- Prefatory parts
- Text
- Supplementary parts

The parts included in a report depend on the type of report you are writing, the requirements of your audience, the organization you're working for, and the length of your report. At Corporate Dynamics, Mark Landiak pays close attention to his readers' needs, whether his readers are employees, customers, or members of the community. From the style of the report to the language used, Landiak targets his readers' preferences and familiarity, including only the parts that are appropriate for each audience. The components listed in Figure 14.1 fall into three categories, depending on where they are found in a report: prefatory parts, text of the report, and supplementary parts. For an illustration of how the various parts fit together, see Linda Moreno's Electrovision report in the "In-Depth Critique: Analyzing a Formal Report" on pages 446–464.

Think carefully about page breaks.

Many of the components in a formal report start on a new page, but not always. Inserting page breaks consumes more paper and adds to the bulk of your report (which may be a significant financial concern if you plan to distribute many copies). On the other hand, starting a section on a new page helps your readers navigate the report and recognize transitions between major sections or features.

When a particular section is designed to stand apart, it generally starts on a new page, and the material after it also starts on a new page. Most prefatory parts (such as the table of contents) should be placed on their own pages. However, the various

FIGURE 14.1 Parts of a Formal Report

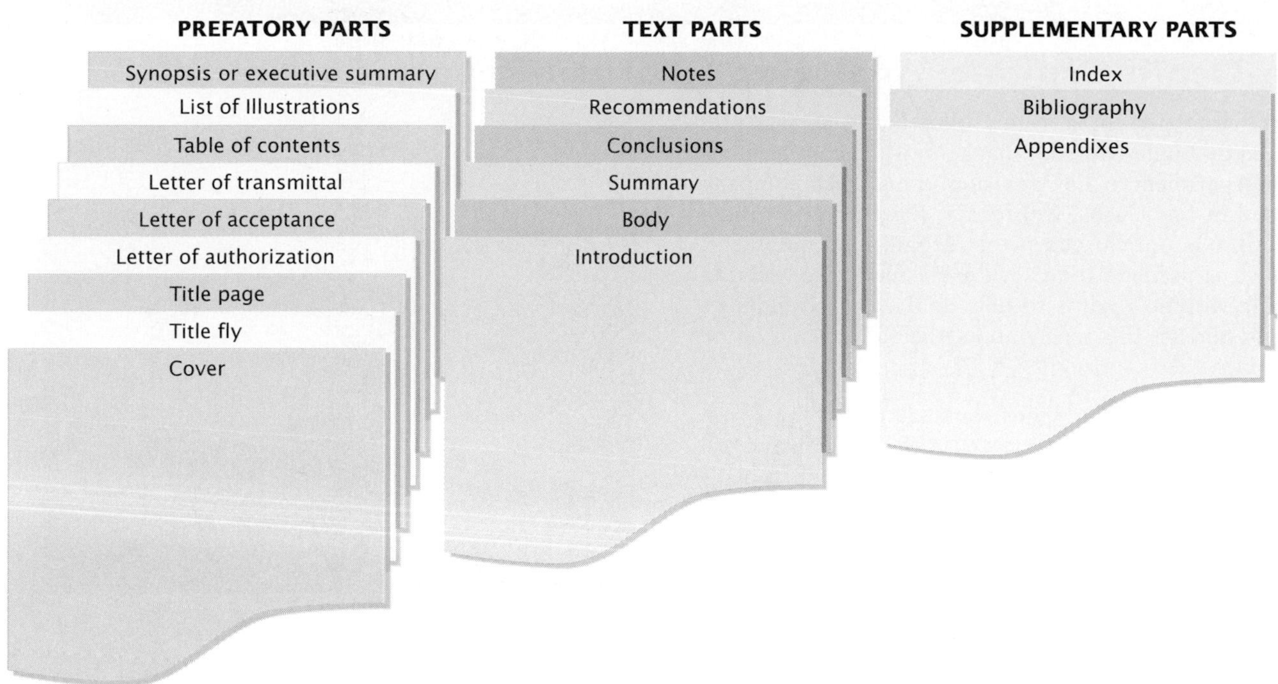

parts in the report text are often run together and seldom stand alone. If your introduction is only a paragraph long, don't bother with a page break before moving into the body of your report. If the introduction runs longer than a page, however, a page break can signal the reader that a major shift is about to occur in the flow of the report.

You can use this textbook as a model for deciding where to put page breaks. Each chapter starts on a new page, which provides a clear break between chapters. On the other hand, the opening vignettes flow right into the chapter without a page break.

Prefatory Parts

Learning Objective 2

Describe the 10 prefatory parts of a formal report

Prefatory parts are front-end materials that provide key preliminary information so that readers can decide whether to and how to read the report.[2] Although these parts are placed before the text of the report, you may not want to write them until after you've written the text. Many of these parts—such as the table of contents, list of illustrations, and executive summary—are easier to prepare after the text has been completed, because they directly reflect the contents. Other parts can be prepared at almost any time.

Prefatory parts may be written after the text has been completed.

Cover Many companies have standard covers for reports, made of heavy paper and imprinted with the company's name and logo. Report titles are either printed on these covers or attached with gummed labels. If your company has no standard covers, you can usually find something suitable in a good stationery store. Look for a cover that is attractive, convenient, and appropriate to the subject matter. Also, make sure it can be labeled with the report title, the writer's name (optional), and the submission date (also optional).

Think carefully about the title you put on the cover. A business report is not a mystery novel, so give your readers all the information they need: the who, what, when, where, why, and how of the subject. At the same time, try to be reasonably concise. You don't want to intimidate your audience with a title that's too long or awkward. You can reduce the length of your title by eliminating phrases such as *A Report of, A Study of,* or *A Survey of.* (*continued on page 465*)

Choose a report title that is informative but not too long.

Report Writer's Notebook

In-Depth Critique: Analyzing a Formal Report

The report presented in the following pages was prepared by Linda Moreno, manager of the cost accounting department at Electrovision, a high-tech company based in Los Gatos, California. Electrovision's main product is optical character recognition equipment, which is used by the U.S. Postal Service for sorting mail. Moreno's job is to help analyze the company's costs. She has this to say about the background of the report:

> For the past three or four years, Electrovision has been on a roll. Our A-12 optical character reader was a real breakthrough, and the post office grabbed up as many as we could make. Our sales and profits kept climbing, and morale was fantastic. Everybody seemed to think that the good times would last forever. Unfortunately, everybody was wrong. When the Postal Service announced that it was postponing all new equipment purchases because of cuts in its budget, we woke up to the fact that we are essentially a one-product company with one customer. At that point, management started scrambling around looking for ways to cut costs until we could diversify our business a bit.
>
> The vice president of operations, Dennis McWilliams, asked me to help identify cost-cutting opportunities in travel and entertainment. On the basis of his personal observations, he felt that Electrovision was overly generous in its travel policies and that we might be able to save a significant amount by controlling these costs more carefully. My investigation confirmed his suspicion.
>
> I was reasonably confident that my report would be well received. I've worked with Dennis for several years and know what he likes: plenty of facts, clearly stated conclusions, and specific recommendations for what should be done next. I also knew that my report would be passed on to other Electrovision executives, so I wanted to create a good impression. I wanted the report to be accurate and thorough, visually appealing, readable, and appropriate in tone.

When writing the analytical report that follows, Moreno used an organization based on conclusions and recommendations, presented in direct order. The first two sections of the report correspond to Moreno's two main conclusions: that Electrovision's travel and entertainment costs are too high and that cuts are essential. The third section presents recommendations for achieving better control over travel and entertainment expenses. As you review the report, analyze both the mechanical aspects and the way Moreno presents her ideas. Be prepared to discuss the way the various components convey and reinforce the main message.

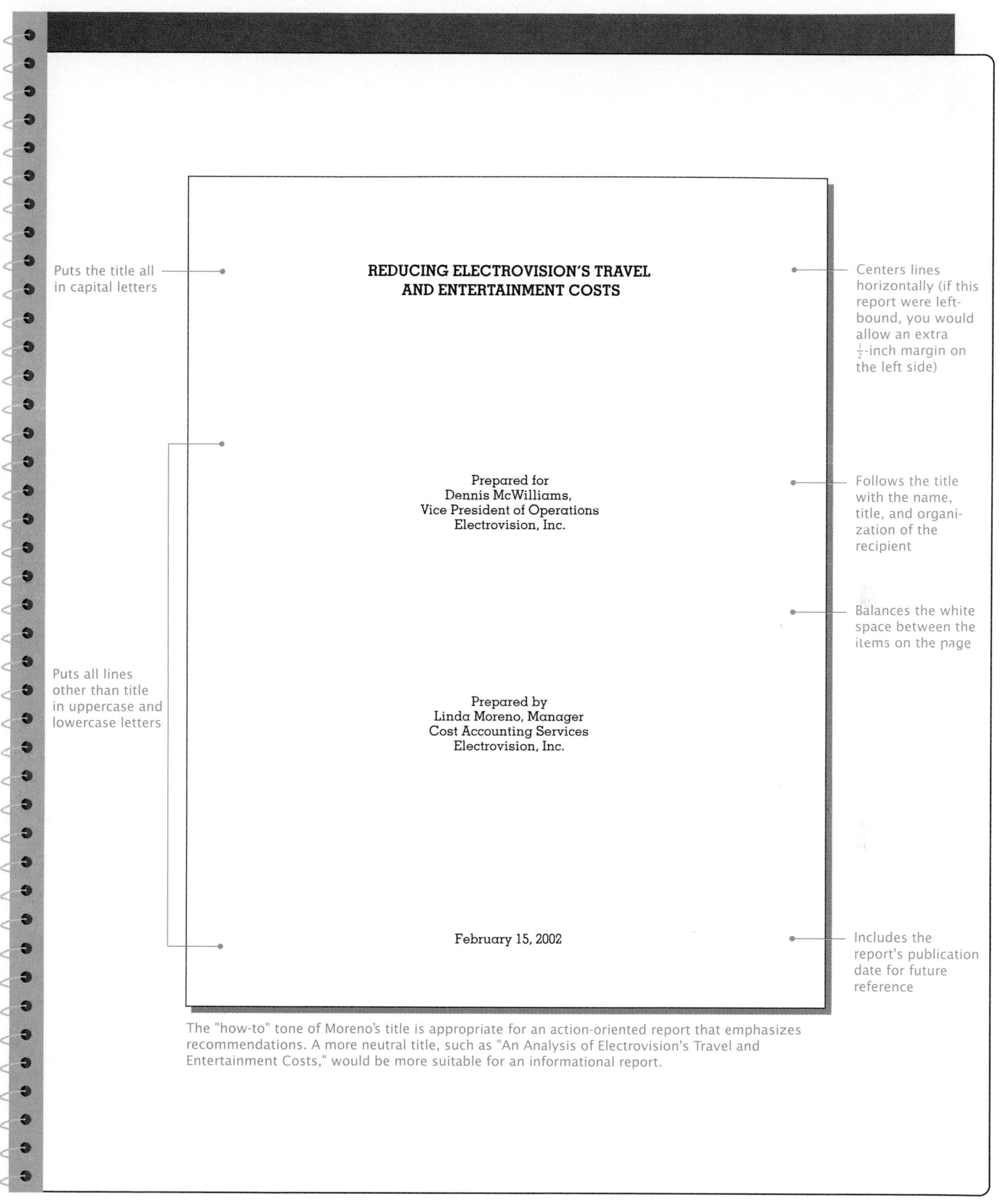

The "how-to" tone of Moreno's title is appropriate for an action-oriented report that emphasizes recommendations. A more neutral title, such as "An Analysis of Electrovision's Travel and Entertainment Costs," would be more suitable for an informational report.

MEMORANDUM

Uses memo format for transmitting this internal report; otherwise, letter format would be used for transmitting external reports

TO: Dennis McWilliams, Vice President of Operations

FROM: Linda Moreno, Manager of Cost Accounting Services

DATE: February 15, 2002

SUBJECT: Reducing Electrovision's Travel and Entertainment Costs

Here is the report you requested January 30 on Electrovision's travel and entertainment costs.

Presents the main conclusion right away (because Moreno expects a positive response)

Your suspicion was right. We are spending far too much on business travel. Our unwritten policy has been "anything goes," leaving us with no real control over T&E expenses. Although this hands-off approach may have been understandable when Electrovision's profits were high, we can no longer afford the luxury of going first class.

Uses an informal, conversational style

The solutions to the problem seem rather clear. We need to have someone with centralized responsibility for travel and entertainment costs, a clear statement of policy, an effective control system, and a business-oriented travel service that can optimize our travel arrangements. We should also investigate alternatives to travel, such as videoconferencing. Perhaps more important, we need to change our attitude. Instead of viewing travel funds as a bottomless supply of money, all traveling employees need to act as though they were paying the bills themselves.

Getting people to economize is not going to be easy. In the course of researching this issue, I've found that our employees are exceedingly attached to their first-class travel privileges. I think they would almost prefer a cut in pay to a loss in travel status. We'll need a lot of top management involvement to sell people on the need for moderation. One thing is clear: People will be very bitter if we create a two-class system in which top executives get special privileges while the rest of the employees make the sacrifices.

Acknowledges help that has been received

I'm grateful to Mary Lehman and Connie McIlvain for their help in rounding up and sorting through five years' worth of expense reports. Their efforts were truly Herculean.

Closes with thanks and an offer to discuss results (when appropriate, you could also include an offer to help with future projects)

Thanks for giving me the opportunity to work on this assignment. It's been a real education. If you have any questions about the report, please give me a call.

In this report, Moreno decided to write a brief memo of transmittal and include a separate executive summary. Short reports (fewer than 10 pages) often combine the synopsis or executive summary with the memo or letter of transmittal.

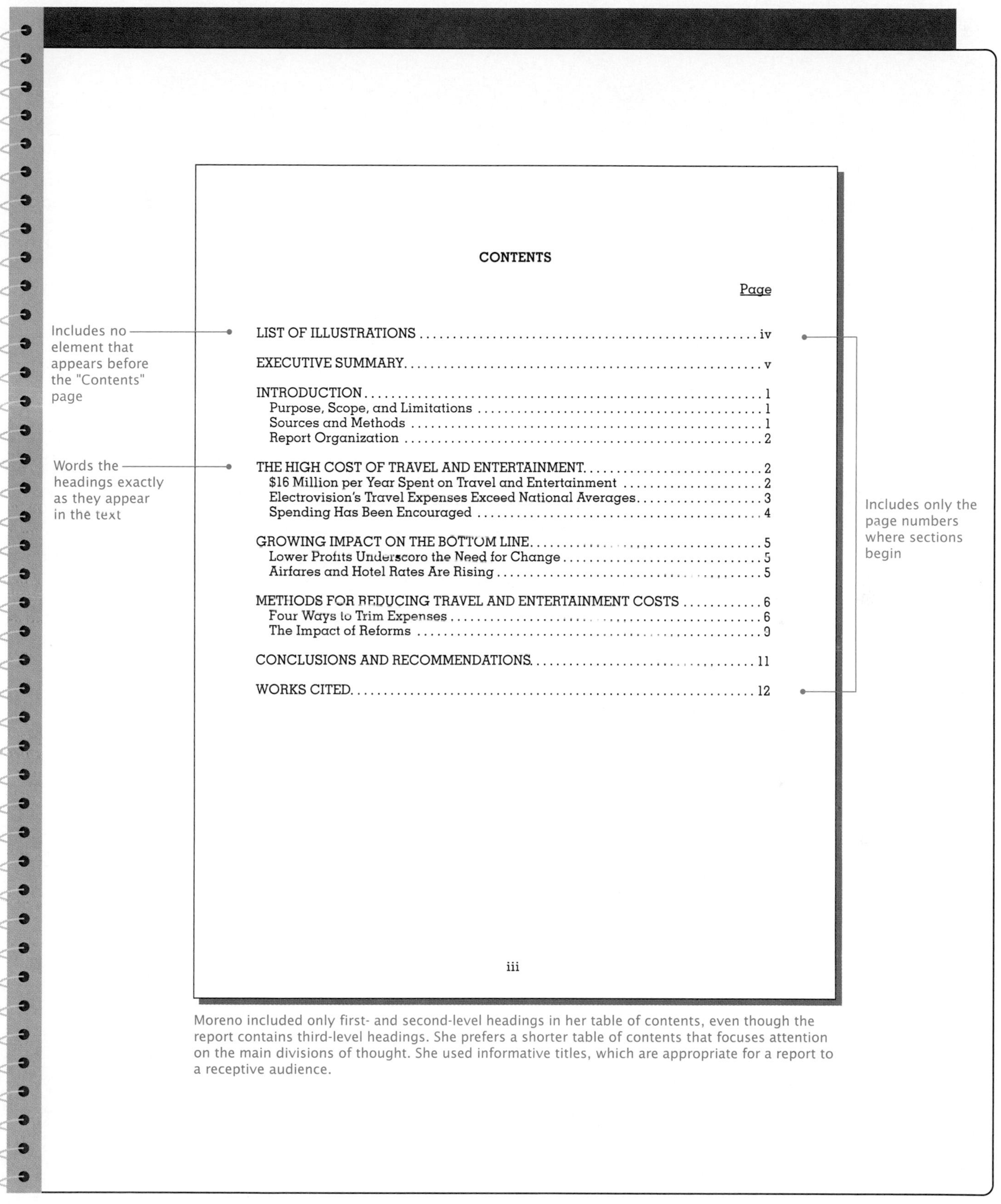

Includes no element that appears before the "Contents" page

Words the headings exactly as they appear in the text

Includes only the page numbers where sections begin

CONTENTS

Page

iii

Moreno included only first- and second-level headings in her table of contents, even though the report contains third-level headings. She prefers a shorter table of contents that focuses attention on the main divisions of thought. She used informative titles, which are appropriate for a report to a receptive audience.

Numbers figures consecutively throughout the report

LIST OF ILLUSTRATIONS

Numbers the contents pages with lowercase roman numerals centered at the bottom margin

iv

Because figures and tables were numbered separately in the text, Moreno listed them separately here. If all were labeled as exhibits, a single list of illustrations would have been appropriate.

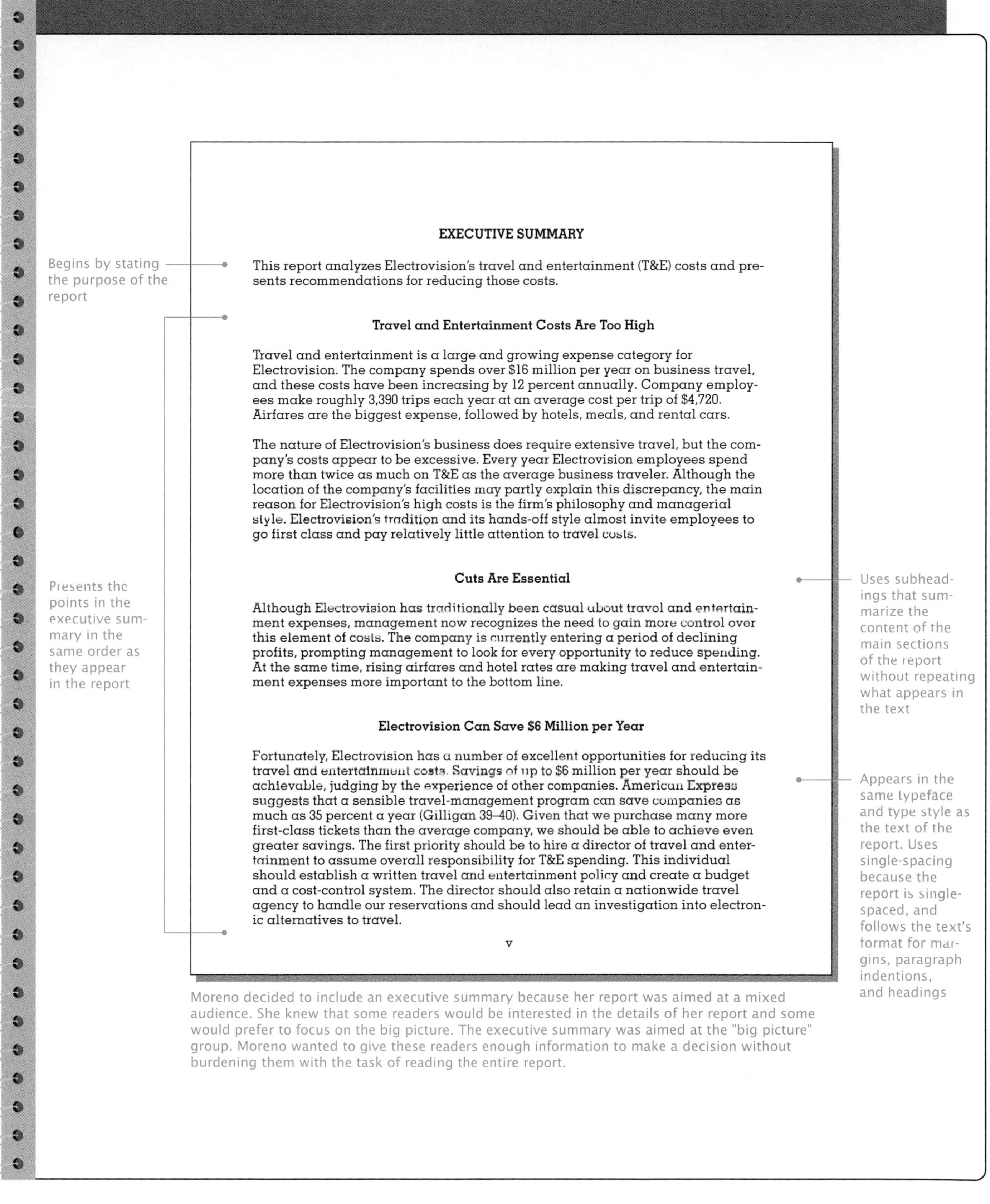

EXECUTIVE SUMMARY

This report analyzes Electrovision's travel and entertainment (T&E) costs and presents recommendations for reducing those costs.

Travel and Entertainment Costs Are Too High

Travel and entertainment is a large and growing expense category for Electrovision. The company spends over $16 million per year on business travel, and these costs have been increasing by 12 percent annually. Company employees make roughly 3,390 trips each year at an average cost per trip of $4,720. Airfares are the biggest expense, followed by hotels, meals, and rental cars.

The nature of Electrovision's business does require extensive travel, but the company's costs appear to be excessive. Every year Electrovision employees spend more than twice as much on T&E as the average business traveler. Although the location of the company's facilities may partly explain this discrepancy, the main reason for Electrovision's high costs is the firm's philosophy and managerial style. Electrovision's tradition and its hands-off style almost invite employees to go first class and pay relatively little attention to travel costs.

Cuts Are Essential

Although Electrovision has traditionally been casual about travel and entertainment expenses, management now recognizes the need to gain more control over this element of costs. The company is currently entering a period of declining profits, prompting management to look for every opportunity to reduce spending. At the same time, rising airfares and hotel rates are making travel and entertainment expenses more important to the bottom line.

Electrovision Can Save $6 Million per Year

Fortunately, Electrovision has a number of excellent opportunities for reducing its travel and entertainment costs. Savings of up to $6 million per year should be achievable, judging by the experience of other companies. American Express suggests that a sensible travel-management program can save companies as much as 35 percent a year (Gilligan 39–40). Given that we purchase many more first-class tickets than the average company, we should be able to achieve even greater savings. The first priority should be to hire a director of travel and entertainment to assume overall responsibility for T&E spending. This individual should establish a written travel and entertainment policy and create a budget and a cost-control system. The director should also retain a nationwide travel agency to handle our reservations and should lead an investigation into electronic alternatives to travel.

v

Moreno decided to include an executive summary because her report was aimed at a mixed audience. She knew that some readers would be interested in the details of her report and some would prefer to focus on the big picture. The executive summary was aimed at the "big picture" group. Moreno wanted to give these readers enough information to make a decision without burdening them with the task of reading the entire report.

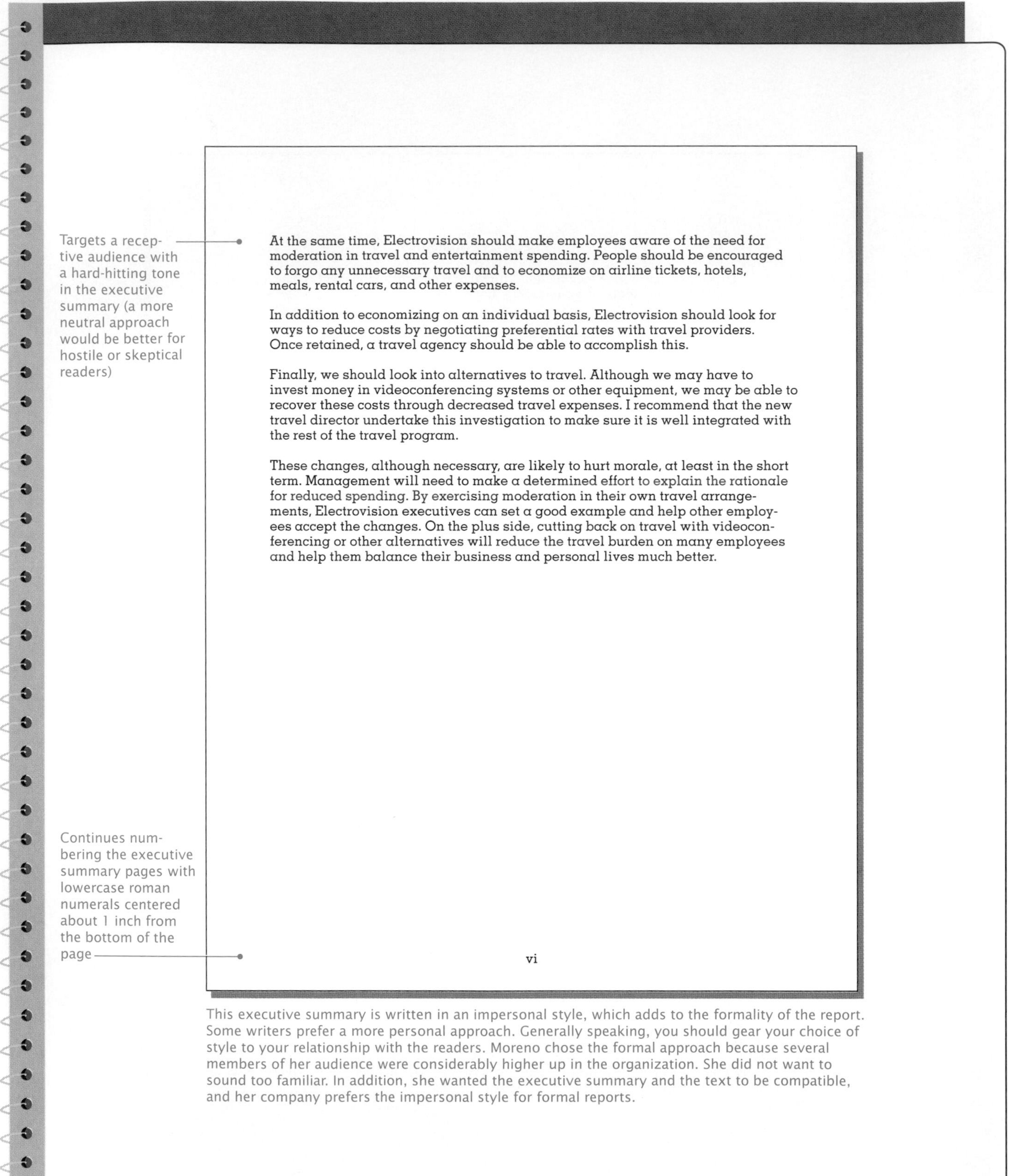

Targets a receptive audience with a hard-hitting tone in the executive summary (a more neutral approach would be better for hostile or skeptical readers)

At the same time, Electrovision should make employees aware of the need for moderation in travel and entertainment spending. People should be encouraged to forgo any unnecessary travel and to economize on airline tickets, hotels, meals, rental cars, and other expenses.

In addition to economizing on an individual basis, Electrovision should look for ways to reduce costs by negotiating preferential rates with travel providers. Once retained, a travel agency should be able to accomplish this.

Finally, we should look into alternatives to travel. Although we may have to invest money in videoconferencing systems or other equipment, we may be able to recover these costs through decreased travel expenses. I recommend that the new travel director undertake this investigation to make sure it is well integrated with the rest of the travel program.

These changes, although necessary, are likely to hurt morale, at least in the short term. Management will need to make a determined effort to explain the rationale for reduced spending. By exercising moderation in their own travel arrangements, Electrovision executives can set a good example and help other employees accept the changes. On the plus side, cutting back on travel with videoconferencing or other alternatives will reduce the travel burden on many employees and help them balance their business and personal lives much better.

Continues numbering the executive summary pages with lowercase roman numerals centered about 1 inch from the bottom of the page

vi

This executive summary is written in an impersonal style, which adds to the formality of the report. Some writers prefer a more personal approach. Generally speaking, you should gear your choice of style to your relationship with the readers. Moreno chose the formal approach because several members of her audience were considerably higher up in the organization. She did not want to sound too familiar. In addition, she wanted the executive summary and the text to be compatible, and her company prefers the impersonal style for formal reports.

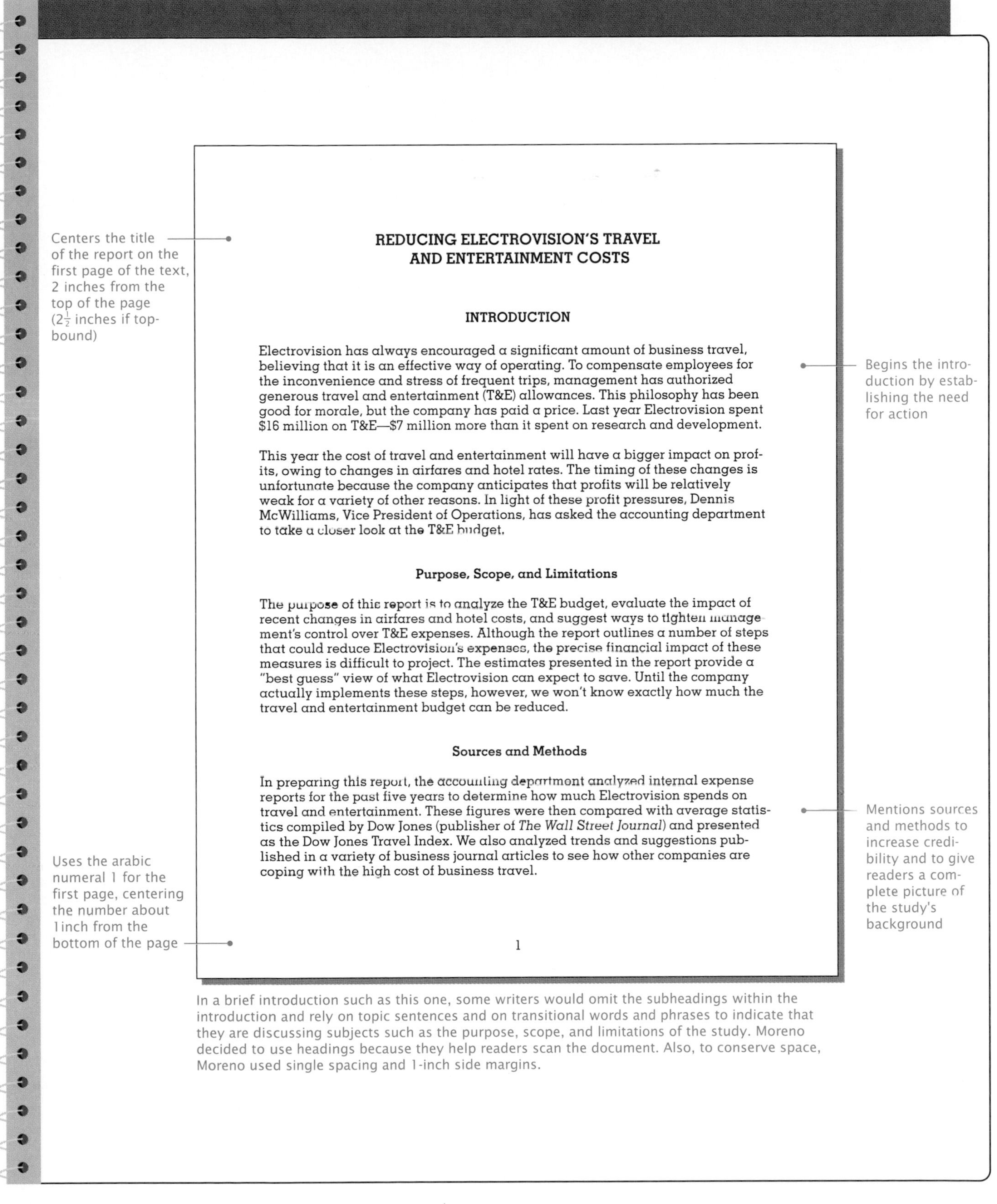

Centers the title of the report on the first page of the text, 2 inches from the top of the page ($2\frac{1}{2}$ inches if top-bound)

REDUCING ELECTROVISION'S TRAVEL AND ENTERTAINMENT COSTS

INTRODUCTION

Electrovision has always encouraged a significant amount of business travel, believing that it is an effective way of operating. To compensate employees for the inconvenience and stress of frequent trips, management has authorized generous travel and entertainment (T&E) allowances. This philosophy has been good for morale, but the company has paid a price. Last year Electrovision spent $16 million on T&E—$7 million more than it spent on research and development.

Begins the introduction by establishing the need for action

This year the cost of travel and entertainment will have a bigger impact on profits, owing to changes in airfares and hotel rates. The timing of these changes is unfortunate because the company anticipates that profits will be relatively weak for a variety of other reasons. In light of these profit pressures, Dennis McWilliams, Vice President of Operations, has asked the accounting department to take a closer look at the T&E budget.

Purpose, Scope, and Limitations

The purpose of this report is to analyze the T&E budget, evaluate the impact of recent changes in airfares and hotel costs, and suggest ways to tighten management's control over T&E expenses. Although the report outlines a number of steps that could reduce Electrovision's expenses, the precise financial impact of these measures is difficult to project. The estimates presented in the report provide a "best guess" view of what Electrovision can expect to save. Until the company actually implements these steps, however, we won't know exactly how much the travel and entertainment budget can be reduced.

Sources and Methods

In preparing this report, the accounting department analyzed internal expense reports for the past five years to determine how much Electrovision spends on travel and entertainment. These figures were then compared with average statistics compiled by Dow Jones (publisher of *The Wall Street Journal*) and presented as the Dow Jones Travel Index. We also analyzed trends and suggestions published in a variety of business journal articles to see how other companies are coping with the high cost of business travel.

Mentions sources and methods to increase credibility and to give readers a complete picture of the study's background

Uses the arabic numeral 1 for the first page, centering the number about 1 inch from the bottom of the page

1

In a brief introduction such as this one, some writers would omit the subheadings within the introduction and rely on topic sentences and on transitional words and phrases to indicate that they are discussing subjects such as the purpose, scope, and limitations of the study. Moreno decided to use headings because they help readers scan the document. Also, to conserve space, Moreno used single spacing and 1-inch side margins.

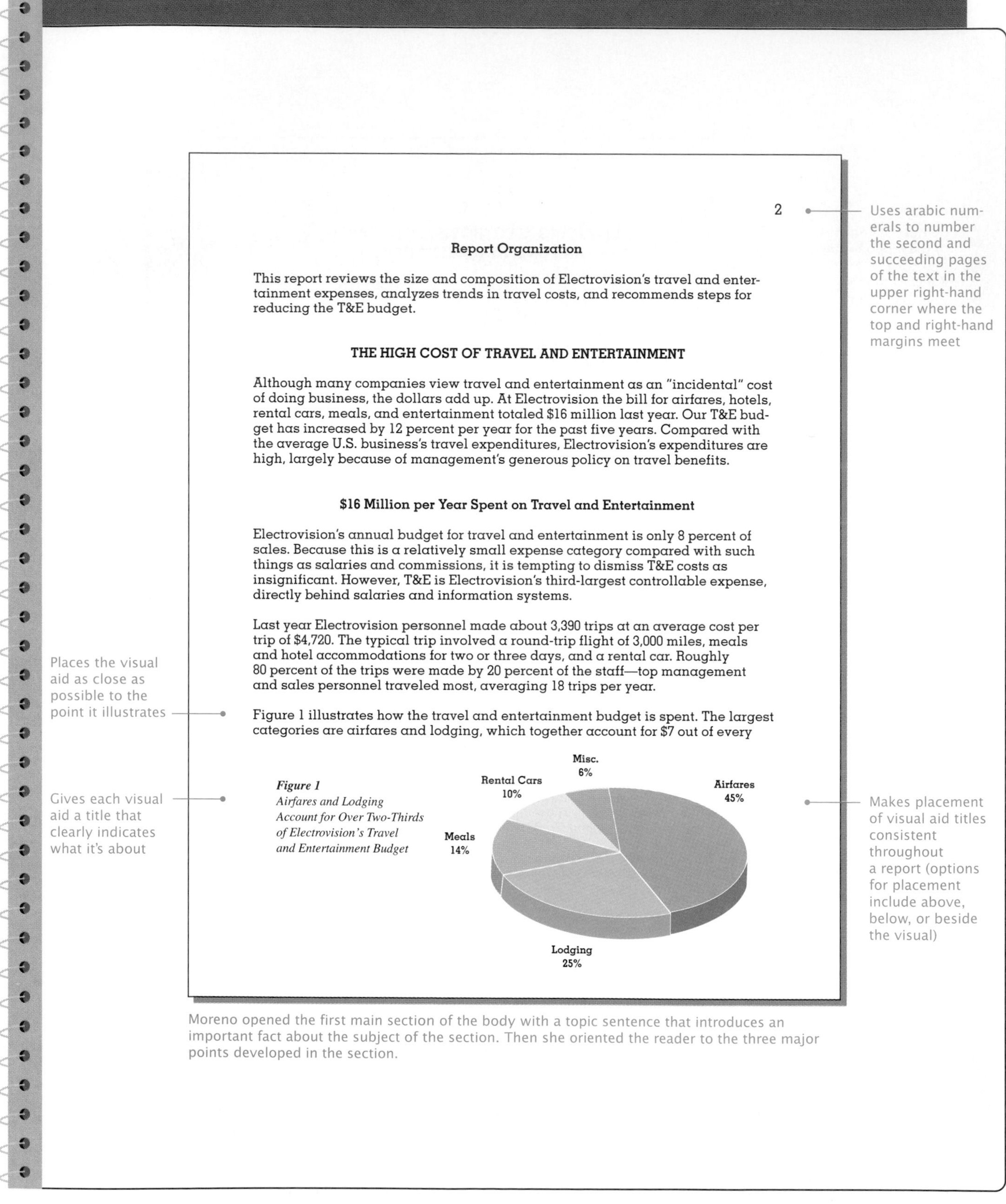

2

Uses arabic numerals to number the second and succeeding pages of the text in the upper right-hand corner where the top and right-hand margins meet

Report Organization

This report reviews the size and composition of Electrovision's travel and entertainment expenses, analyzes trends in travel costs, and recommends steps for reducing the T&E budget.

THE HIGH COST OF TRAVEL AND ENTERTAINMENT

Although many companies view travel and entertainment as an "incidental" cost of doing business, the dollars add up. At Electrovision the bill for airfares, hotels, rental cars, meals, and entertainment totaled $16 million last year. Our T&E budget has increased by 12 percent per year for the past five years. Compared with the average U.S. business's travel expenditures, Electrovision's expenditures are high, largely because of management's generous policy on travel benefits.

$16 Million per Year Spent on Travel and Entertainment

Electrovision's annual budget for travel and entertainment is only 8 percent of sales. Because this is a relatively small expense category compared with such things as salaries and commissions, it is tempting to dismiss T&E costs as insignificant. However, T&E is Electrovision's third-largest controllable expense, directly behind salaries and information systems.

Last year Electrovision personnel made about 3,390 trips at an average cost per trip of $4,720. The typical trip involved a round-trip flight of 3,000 miles, meals and hotel accommodations for two or three days, and a rental car. Roughly 80 percent of the trips were made by 20 percent of the staff—top management and sales personnel traveled most, averaging 18 trips per year.

Places the visual aid as close as possible to the point it illustrates

Figure 1 illustrates how the travel and entertainment budget is spent. The largest categories are airfares and lodging, which together account for $7 out of every

Gives each visual aid a title that clearly indicates what it's about

Figure 1
Airfares and Lodging Account for Over Two-Thirds of Electrovision's Travel and Entertainment Budget

Makes placement of visual aid titles consistent throughout a report (options for placement include above, below, or beside the visual)

Moreno opened the first main section of the body with a topic sentence that introduces an important fact about the subject of the section. Then she oriented the reader to the three major points developed in the section.

3

$10 that employees spend on travel and entertainment. This spending breakdown has been relatively steady for the past five years and is consistent with the distribution of expenses experienced by other companies.

Although the composition of the T&E budget has been consistent, its size has not. As mentioned earlier, these expenditures have increased by about 12 percent per year for the past five years, roughly twice the rate of the company's growth in sales (see Figure 2). This rate of growth makes T&E Electrovision's fastest-growing expense item.

Introduces visual aids before they appear and indicates what readers should notice about the data

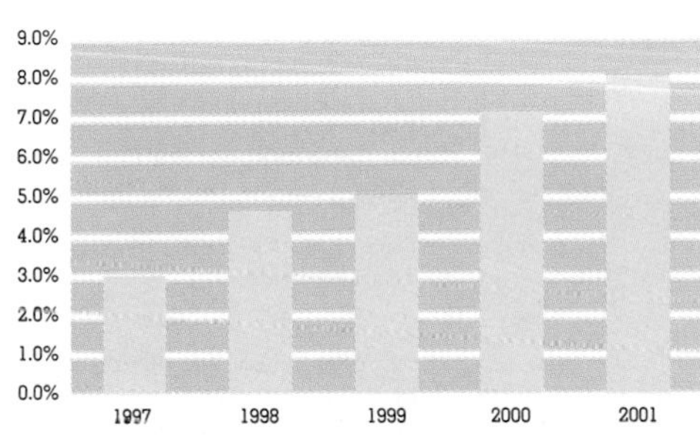

Figure 2
Travel and Entertainment Expenses Have Increased as a Percentage of Sales

Numbers the visual aids consecutively and refers to them in the text by their numbers (if your report is a book-length document, you may number the visual aids by chapter; for example, Figure 4-2 would be the second figure in the fourth chapter)

Electrovision's Travel Expenses Exceed National Averages

Much of our travel budget is justified. Two major factors contribute to Electrovision's high travel and entertainment budget:

- With our headquarters on the West Coast and our major customer on the East Coast, we naturally spend a lot on cross-country flights.
- A great deal of travel takes place between our headquarters here on the West Coast and the manufacturing operations in Detroit, Boston, and Dallas. Corporate managers and division personnel make frequent trips to coordinate these disparate operations.

However, even though a good portion of Electrovision's travel budget is justifiable, our travelers spend considerably more on travel and entertainment than the average business traveler (see Figure 3).

Moreno originally drew the bar chart in Figure 2 as a line chart, showing both sales and T&E expenses in absolute dollars. However, the comparison was difficult to interpret because sales were so much greater than T&E expenses. Switching to a bar chart expressed in percentage terms made the main idea much easier to grasp.

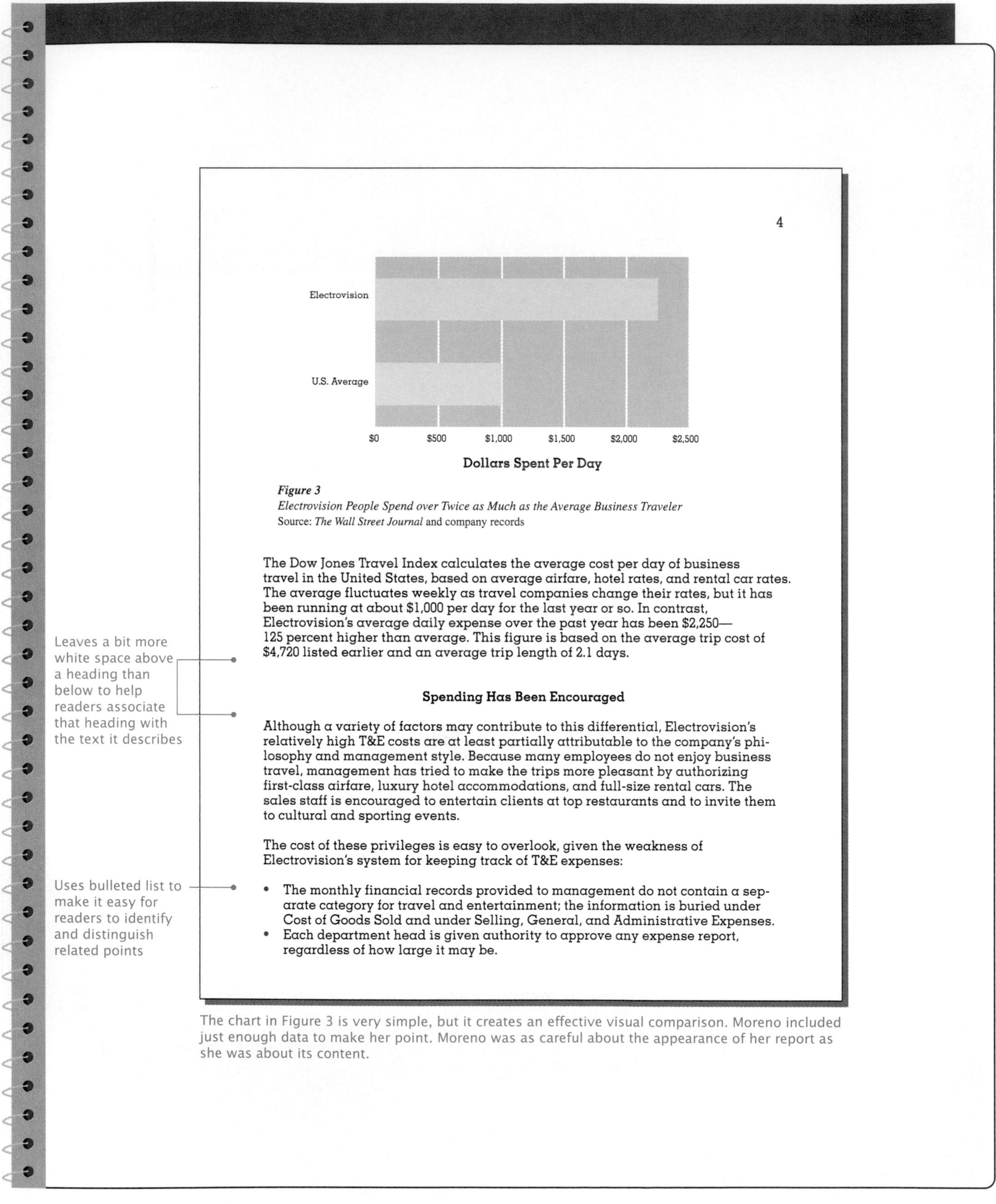

Figure 3
Electrovision People Spend over Twice as Much as the Average Business Traveler
Source: *The Wall Street Journal* and company records

The Dow Jones Travel Index calculates the average cost per day of business travel in the United States, based on average airfare, hotel rates, and rental car rates. The average fluctuates weekly as travel companies change their rates, but it has been running at about $1,000 per day for the last year or so. In contrast, Electrovision's average daily expense over the past year has been $2,250—125 percent higher than average. This figure is based on the average trip cost of $4,720 listed earlier and an average trip length of 2.1 days.

Leaves a bit more white space above a heading than below to help readers associate that heading with the text it describes

Spending Has Been Encouraged

Although a variety of factors may contribute to this differential, Electrovision's relatively high T&E costs are at least partially attributable to the company's philosophy and management style. Because many employees do not enjoy business travel, management has tried to make the trips more pleasant by authorizing first-class airfare, luxury hotel accommodations, and full-size rental cars. The sales staff is encouraged to entertain clients at top restaurants and to invite them to cultural and sporting events.

The cost of these privileges is easy to overlook, given the weakness of Electrovision's system for keeping track of T&E expenses:

Uses bulleted list to make it easy for readers to identify and distinguish related points

- The monthly financial records provided to management do not contain a separate category for travel and entertainment; the information is buried under Cost of Goods Sold and under Selling, General, and Administrative Expenses.
- Each department head is given authority to approve any expense report, regardless of how large it may be.

The chart in Figure 3 is very simple, but it creates an effective visual comparison. Moreno included just enough data to make her point. Moreno was as careful about the appearance of her report as she was about its content.

5

- Receipts are not required for expenditures of less than $100.
- Individuals are allowed to make their own travel arrangements.
- No one is charged with the responsibility for controlling the company's total spending on travel and entertainment.

Uses informative headings to focus reader attention on the main points (such headings are appropriate when a report is in direct order and intended for a receptive audience; however, descriptive headings are more effective when a report is in indirect order and readers are less receptive)

GROWING IMPACT ON THE BOTTOM LINE

During the past three years, the company's healthy profits have resulted in relatively little pressure to push for tighter controls over all aspects of the business. However, as we all know, the situation is changing. We're projecting flat to declining profits for the next two years, a situation that has prompted all of us to search for ways to cut costs. At the same time, rising airfares and hotel rates have increased the impact of T&E expenses on the company's financial results.

Lower Profits Underscore the Need for Change

The next two years promise to be difficult for Electrovision. After several years of steady increases in spending, the Postal Service is tightening procurement policies for automated mail-handling equipment. Funding for the A-12 optical character reader has been canceled. As a consequence, the marketing department expects sales to drop by 15 percent. Although Electrovision is negotiating several promising R&D contracts with nongovernment clients, the marketing department does not foresee any major procurements for the next two to three years.

At the same time, Electrovision is facing cost increases on several fronts. As we've known for several months, the new production facility now under construction in Salt Lake City is behind schedule and over budget. Labor contracts in Boston and Dallas expire within the next six months, and plant managers there anticipate that significant salary and benefits concessions may be necessary to avoid strikes. Moreover, marketing and advertising costs are expected to increase as we attempt to strengthen these activities to better cope with competitive pressures. Given the expected decline in revenues and increase in costs, the Executive Committee's prediction that profits will fall by 12 percent in the coming fiscal year does not seem overly pessimistic.

Airfares and Hotel Rates Are Rising

Business travelers have grown accustomed to frequent fare wars and discounting in the travel industry in recent years. Excess capacity and aggressive price competition, particularly in the airline business, made travel a relative bargain.

However, that situation has changed, as weaker competitors have been forced out and the remaining players have grown stronger and smarter. Airlines and

Because airfares represent Electrovision's biggest T&E expense, Moreno included a subsection that deals with the possible impact of trends in the airline industry. Airfares are rising, so it is especially important to gain more control over employees' air travel arrangements.

hotels are better at managing inventory and keeping occupancy rates high, and high occupancy translates into higher prices because suppliers have less reason to compete on price. Last year saw some of the steepest rate hikes in years. Business airfares (tickets most likely to be purchased by business travelers) jumped over 40 percent in many markets. The trend is expected to continue, with rates increasing another 5 to 10 percent overall (Phillips 331; "Travel Costs Under Pressure" 30; Dahl B6).

Documents the facts to add weight to Moreno's argument

Given the fact that airfare and hotel costs account for 70 percent of Electrovision's T&E budget, the trend toward higher prices in these two categories will have serious consequences on the company's expenses unless management takes action to control these costs.

METHODS FOR REDUCING TRAVEL AND ENTERTAINMENT COSTS

By implementing a number of reforms, management can expect to reduce Electrovision's T&E budget by as much as 40 percent. This estimate is based on the general assessment made by American Express (Gilligan 130–40) and the fact that we have an opportunity to significantly reduce air travel costs by reducing or eliminating first-class travel. However, these measures are likely to be unpopular with employees. To gain acceptance for such changes, management will need to sell employees on the need for moderation in travel and entertainment allowances.

Gives recommendations an objective flavor by pointing out both the benefits and the risks of taking action

Four Ways to Trim Expenses

By researching what other companies are doing to curb travel and entertainment expenses, the accounting department has identified four prominent opportunities that should enable Electrovision to save about $6 million annually in travel-related costs.

Institute Tighter Spending Controls

A single individual should be appointed director of travel and entertainment to spearhead the effort to gain control of the T&E budget. More than a third of all U.S. companies now employ travel managers in an effort to keep costs in line ("Businesses Use Savvy Managers" 4). The director should be familiar with the travel industry and should be well versed in both accounting and information technology. The director should also report to the vice president of operations. The director's first priorities should be to establish a written travel and entertainment policy and to implement a system for controlling travel and entertainment costs.

Moreno created a forceful tone by using action verbs in the third-level subheadings of this section. This approach is appropriate to the nature of the study and the attitude of the audience. However, in a status-conscious organization, the imperative verbs might sound a bit too presumptuous coming from a junior member of the staff.

Breaks up text with bulleted lists, which not only call attention to important points but also add visual interest (you can also use visual aids, headings, and direct quotations to break up large, solid blocks of print)

7

Electrovision currently has no written policy on travel and entertainment, a step widely recommended by air travel experts (Smith D4). Creating a policy would clarify management's position and serve as a vehicle for communicating the need for moderation. At a minimum, the policy should include the following provisions:

- All travel and entertainment should be strictly related to business and should be approved in advance.
- Except under special circumstances to be approved on a case-by-case basis, employees should travel by coach and stay in mid-range business hotels.
- The travel and entertainment policy should apply equally to employees at all levels in the organization. No special benefits should be allowed for top executives.

To implement the new policy, Electrovision will need to create a system for controlling travel and entertainment expenses. Each department should prepare an annual T&E budget as part of its operating plan. These budgets should be presented in detail so that management can evaluate how travel and entertainment dollars will be spent and recommend appropriate cuts.

To help management monitor performance relative to these budgets, the director of travel should prepare monthly financial statements showing actual travel and entertainment expenditures by department. The system for capturing this information should be computerized and should be capable of identifying individuals who consistently exceed approved spending levels. The recommended average should range between $2,000 and $2,500 per month for each professional employee, depending on the individual's role in the company. Because they make frequent trips, sales and top management personnel can be expected to have relatively high travel expenses.

Specifies the steps required to implement recommendations

The director of travel should also be responsible for retaining a business-oriented travel service that will schedule all employee business trips and look for the best travel deals, particularly in airfares. In addition to centralizing Electrovision's reservation and ticketing activities, the agency will negotiate reduced group rates with hotels and rental car agencies. The agency selected should have offices nationwide so that all Electrovision facilities can channel their reservations through the same company. By consolidating its travel planning in this way, Electrovision can increase its control over costs and achieve economies of scale. This is particularly important in light of the dizzying array of often wildly different airfares available between some cities. It's not uncommon to find dozens of fares along commonly traveled routes (Rowe 30).

The director should also work with the agency to explore low-cost alternatives, such as buying tickets from airfare consolidators (the air travel equivalent of factory outlet malls). In addition, the director can help coordinate travel across the company to secure group discounts whenever possible (Barker 31; Miller B6).

Moreno decided to single-space her report to create a formal, finished look; however, double-spacing can make the text of a long report somewhat easier to read and provide more space for readers to write comments.

Reduce Unnecessary Travel and Entertainment

One of the easiest ways to reduce expenses is to reduce the amount of traveling and entertaining that occurs. An analysis of last year's expenditures suggests that as much as 30 percent of Electrovision's travel and entertainment is discretionary. The professional staff spent $2.8 million attending seminars and conferences last year. Although some of these gatherings are undoubtedly beneficial, the company could save money by sending fewer representatives to each function and by eliminating some of the less valuable seminars.

Similarly, Electrovision could economize on trips between headquarters and divisions by reducing the frequency of such visits and by sending fewer people on each trip. Although there is often no substitute for face-to-face meetings, management could try to resolve more internal issues through telephone, electronic, and written communication.

Electrovision can also reduce spending by urging employees to economize. Instead of flying first class, employees can fly tourist class or take advantage of discount fares. Instead of taking clients to dinner, Electrovision personnel can hold breakfast meetings, which tend to be less costly. Rather than ordering a $50 bottle of wine, employees can select a less-expensive bottle or dispense with alcohol entirely. People can book rooms at moderately priced hotels and drive smaller rental cars. In general, employees should be urged to spend the company's money as though it were their own.

Obtain Lowest Rates from Travel Providers

Apart from urging individual employees to economize, Electrovision can also save money by searching for the lowest available airfares, hotel rates, and rental car fees. Currently, few Electrovision employees have the time or specialized knowledge to seek out travel bargains. When they need to travel, they make the most convenient and most comfortable arrangements. However, if Electrovision contracts with a professional travel service, the company will have access to professionals who can more efficiently obtain the lower rates from travel providers.

Judging by the experience of other companies, Electrovision may be able to trim as much as 30 to 40 percent from the travel budget by looking for bargains in airfares and negotiating group rates with hotels and rental car companies. Electrovision should be able to achieve these economies by analyzing its travel patterns, identifying frequently visited locations, and selecting a few hotels that are willing to reduce rates in exchange for guaranteed business. At the same time, the company should be able to save up to 40 percent on rental car charges by negotiating a corporate rate.

Note how Moreno made the transition from section to section. The first sentence under the second heading on this page refers to the subject of the previous paragraph and signals a shift in thought.

The possibilities for economizing are promising, but it's worth noting that making the best arrangements is a complicated undertaking, requiring many trade-offs such as the following:

- The best fares might not always be the lowest. Indirect flights are often less expensive than direct flights, but they take longer and may end up costing more in lost work time.
- The cheapest tickets may have to be booked 30 days in advance, often impossible for us.
- Discount tickets may be nonrefundable, which is a real drawback if the trip has to be canceled at the last minute.

Electrovision is currently ill-equipped to make these and other trade-offs. However, by employing a business-oriented travel service, the company will have access to computerized systems that can optimize its choices.

Replace Travel with Technological Alternatives

Points out possible difficulties to show that all angles have been considered and to build reader confidence in the writer's judgment

We might be able to replace a significant portion of our interdivisional travel with electronic meetings that utilize videoconferencing, real-time document sharing on PC screens, and other alternatives. Naturally, we don't want to reduce employee or team effectiveness, but many companies are using these new tools to cut costs and reduce wear and tear on employees.

Rather than make specific recommendations in this report, I suggest that the new travel director conduct an in-depth study of the company's travel patterns as part of an overall cost-containment effort. A thorough analysis of why employees travel and what they accomplish will highlight any opportunities for replacing face-to-face meetings. Part of this study should include limited-scope tests of various communication systems as a way of measuring their impact on both workplace effectiveness and overall costs.

The Impact of Reforms

By implementing tighter controls, reducing unnecessary expenses, negotiating more favorable rates, and exploring "electronic travel," Electrovision should be able to reduce its travel and entertainment budget significantly. As Table 1 illustrates, the combined savings should be in the neighborhood of $6 million, although the precise figures are somewhat difficult to project.

Note how Moreno calls attention in the last paragraph to items in the following table without repeating the information in the table.

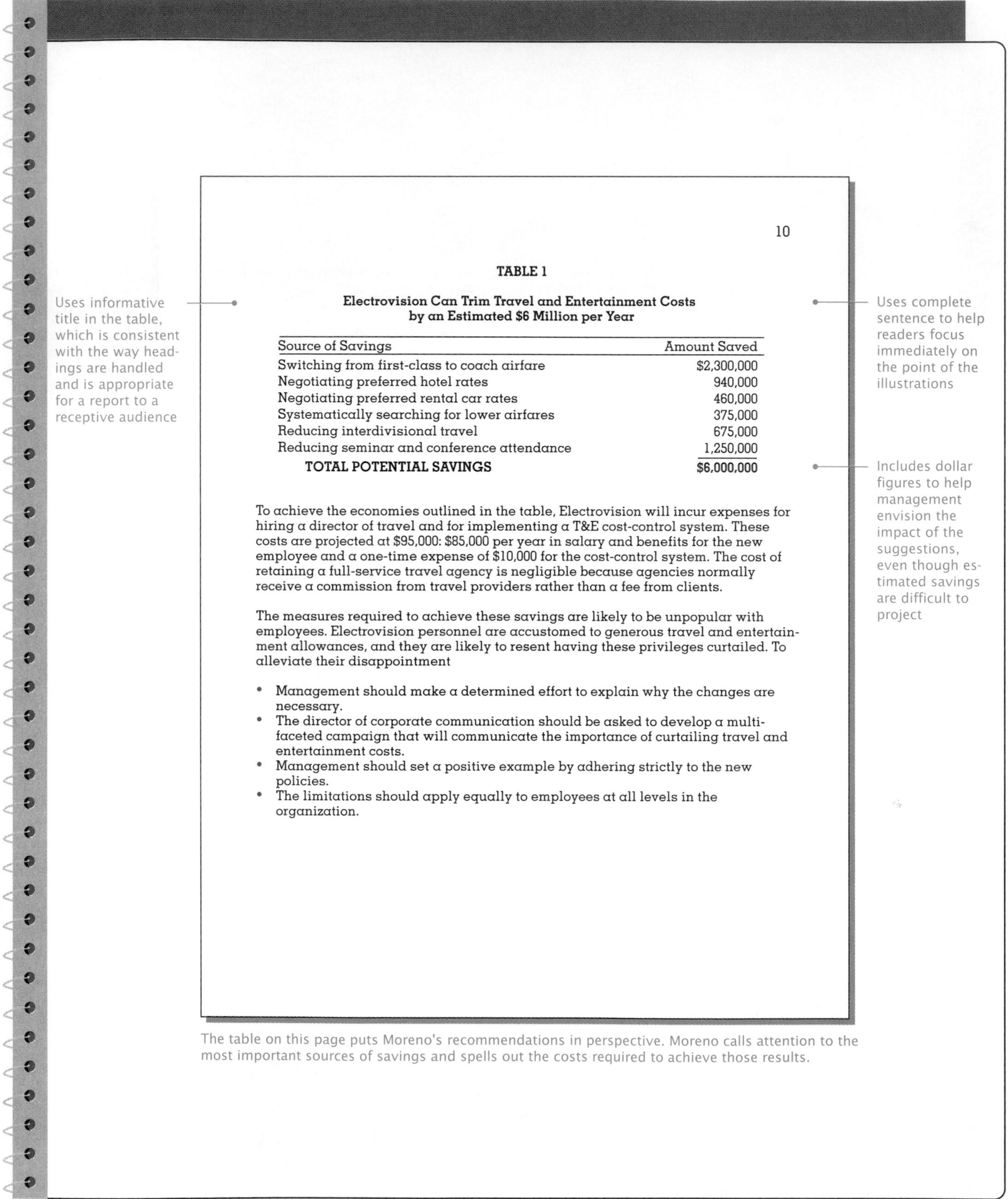

10

TABLE 1

Electrovision Can Trim Travel and Entertainment Costs by an Estimated $6 Million per Year

Source of Savings	Amount Saved
Switching from first-class to coach airfare	$2,300,000
Negotiating preferred hotel rates	940,000
Negotiating preferred rental car rates	460,000
Systematically searching for lower airfares	375,000
Reducing interdivisional travel	675,000
Reducing seminar and conference attendance	1,250,000
TOTAL POTENTIAL SAVINGS	**$6,000,000**

To achieve the economies outlined in the table, Electrovision will incur expenses for hiring a director of travel and for implementing a T&E cost-control system. These costs are projected at $95,000: $85,000 per year in salary and benefits for the new employee and a one-time expense of $10,000 for the cost-control system. The cost of retaining a full-service travel agency is negligible because agencies normally receive a commission from travel providers rather than a fee from clients.

The measures required to achieve these savings are likely to be unpopular with employees. Electrovision personnel are accustomed to generous travel and entertainment allowances, and they are likely to resent having these privileges curtailed. To alleviate their disappointment

- Management should make a determined effort to explain why the changes are necessary.
- The director of corporate communication should be asked to develop a multifaceted campaign that will communicate the importance of curtailing travel and entertainment costs.
- Management should set a positive example by adhering strictly to the new policies.
- The limitations should apply equally to employees at all levels in the organization.

Uses informative title in the table, which is consistent with the way headings are handled and is appropriate for a report to a receptive audience

Uses complete sentence to help readers focus immediately on the point of the illustrations

Includes dollar figures to help management envision the impact of the suggestions, even though estimated savings are difficult to project

The table on this page puts Moreno's recommendations in perspective. Moreno calls attention to the most important sources of savings and spells out the costs required to achieve those results.

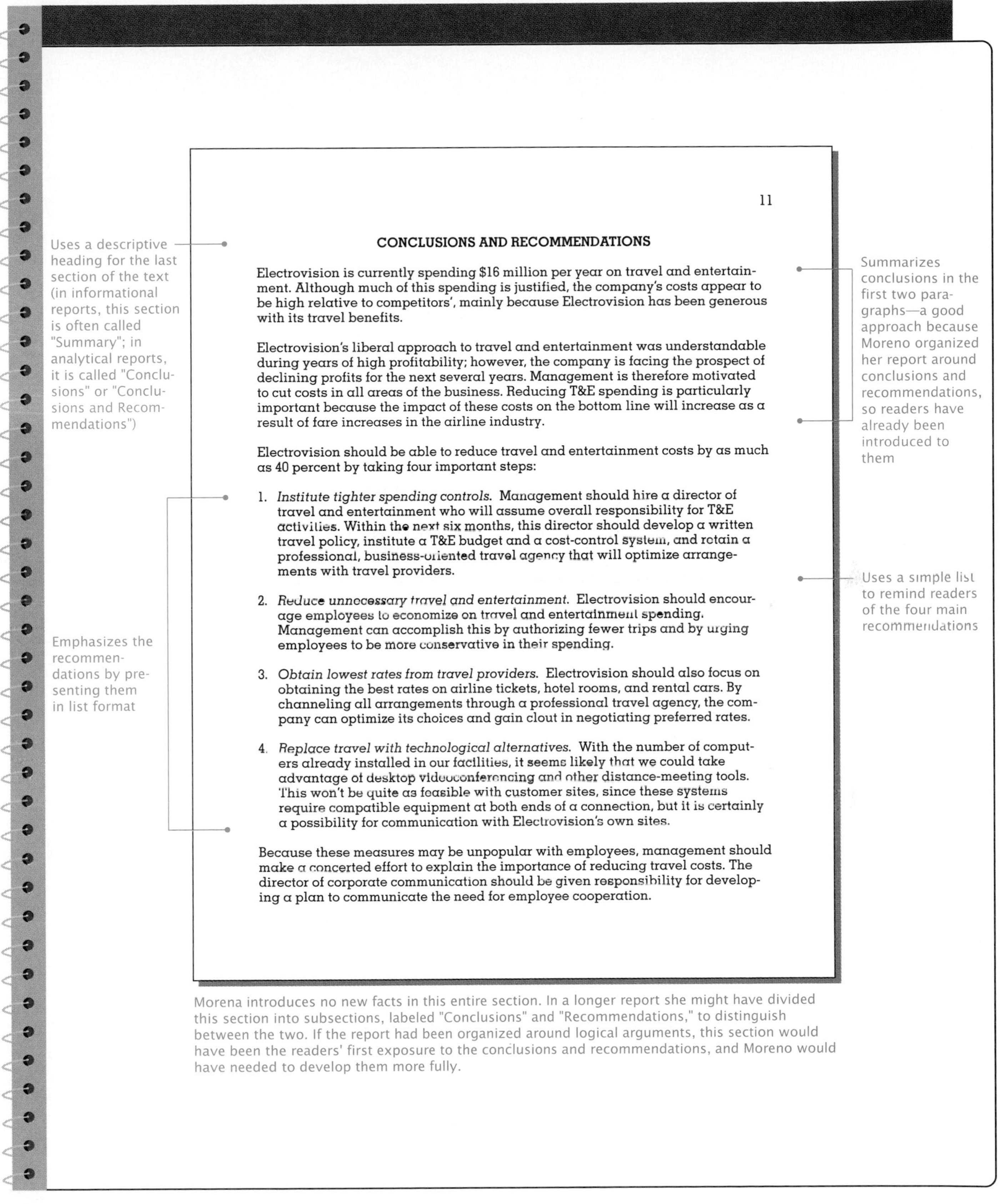

11

CONCLUSIONS AND RECOMMENDATIONS

Electrovision is currently spending $16 million per year on travel and entertainment. Although much of this spending is justified, the company's costs appear to be high relative to competitors', mainly because Electrovision has been generous with its travel benefits.

Electrovision's liberal approach to travel and entertainment was understandable during years of high profitability; however, the company is facing the prospect of declining profits for the next several years. Management is therefore motivated to cut costs in all areas of the business. Reducing T&E spending is particularly important because the impact of these costs on the bottom line will increase as a result of fare increases in the airline industry.

Electrovision should be able to reduce travel and entertainment costs by as much as 40 percent by taking four important steps:

1. *Institute tighter spending controls.* Management should hire a director of travel and entertainment who will assume overall responsibility for T&E activities. Within the next six months, this director should develop a written travel policy, institute a T&E budget and a cost-control system, and retain a professional, business-oriented travel agency that will optimize arrangements with travel providers.
2. *Reduce unnecessary travel and entertainment.* Electrovision should encourage employees to economize on travel and entertainment spending. Management can accomplish this by authorizing fewer trips and by urging employees to be more conservative in their spending.
3. *Obtain lowest rates from travel providers.* Electrovision should also focus on obtaining the best rates on airline tickets, hotel rooms, and rental cars. By channeling all arrangements through a professional travel agency, the company can optimize its choices and gain clout in negotiating preferred rates.
4. *Replace travel with technological alternatives.* With the number of computers already installed in our facilities, it seems likely that we could take advantage of desktop videoconferencing and other distance-meeting tools. This won't be quite as feasible with customer sites, since these systems require compatible equipment at both ends of a connection, but it is certainly a possibility for communication with Electrovision's own sites.

Because these measures may be unpopular with employees, management should make a concerted effort to explain the importance of reducing travel costs. The director of corporate communication should be given responsibility for developing a plan to communicate the need for employee cooperation.

Uses a descriptive heading for the last section of the text (in informational reports, this section is often called "Summary"; in analytical reports, it is called "Conclusions" or "Conclusions and Recommendations")

Summarizes conclusions in the first two paragraphs—a good approach because Moreno organized her report around conclusions and recommendations, so readers have already been introduced to them

Emphasizes the recommendations by presenting them in list format

Uses a simple list to remind readers of the four main recommendations

Morena introduces no new facts in this entire section. In a longer report she might have divided this section into subsections, labeled "Conclusions" and "Recommendations," to distinguish between the two. If the report had been organized around logical arguments, this section would have been the readers' first exposure to the conclusions and recommendations, and Moreno would have needed to develop them more fully.

Lists references alphabetically by the author's last name, and when the author is unknown, by the title of the reference (see Appendix II for additional details on preparing reference lists)

12

WORKS CITED

Barker, Julie. "How to Rein in Group Travel Costs." *Successful Meetings* Feb. 2001: 31.

"Businesses Use Savvy Managers to Keep Travel Costs Down." *Christian Science Monitor* 17 July 2000: 4.

Dahl, Jonathan. "1998: The Year Travel Costs Took Off." *Wall Street Journal* 29 Dec. 2000: B6.

Gilligan, Edward P. "Trimming Your T&E Is Easier Than You Think." *Managing Office Technology* Nov. 2001: 39–40.

Miller, Lisa. "Attention, Airline Ticket Shoppers." *Wall Street Journal* 7 July 2001: B6.

Phillips, Edward H. "Airlines Post Record Traffic." *Aviation Week & Space Technology* 8 Jan. 2002: 331.

Rowe, Irene Vlitos. "Global Solution for Cutting Travel Costs." *European* 12 Oct. 2000: 30.

Smith, Carol. "Rising, Erratic Air Fares Make Company Policy Vital." *Los Angeles Times* 2 Nov. 2001: D4.

"Travel Costs Under Pressure." *Purchasing* 15 Feb. 2001: 30.

Moreno's list of references follows the style recommended in *The MLA Style Manual.*

Title Fly and Title Page The **title fly** is a plain sheet of paper with only the title of the report on it. You don't really need one, but it adds a touch of formality.

The **title page** includes four blocks of information, as shown in Moreno's Electrovision report: (1) the title of the report; (2) the name, title, and address of the person, group, or organization that authorized the report (usually the intended audience); (3) the name, title, and address of the person, group, or organization that prepared the report; and (4) the date on which the report was submitted. On some title pages the second block of information is preceded by the words *Prepared for* or *Submitted to*, and the third block of information is preceded by *Prepared by* or *Submitted by*. In some cases the title page serves as the cover of the report, especially if the report is relatively short and is intended solely for internal use.

The title page usually includes four blocks of information.

Letter of Authorization and Letter of Acceptance If you received written authorization to prepare the report, you may want to include that letter or memo in your report (and you may sometimes even include the letter or memo of acceptance). The **letter of authorization** (or *memo of authorization*) is a document requesting that a report be prepared. It normally follows the direct-request plan described in Chapter 5, and it typically specifies the problem, scope, time and money restrictions, special instructions, and due date.

A letter of authorization usually follows the direct-request plan.

The **letter of acceptance** (or *memo of acceptance*) acknowledges the assignment to conduct the study and to prepare the report. Following the good-news plan, the acceptance confirms time and money restrictions and other pertinent details. This document is rarely included in reports.

Use the good-news plan for a letter of acceptance.

Letter of Transmittal The **letter of transmittal** (or *memo of transmittal*) conveys your report to your audience. (In a book, this section is called the preface.) The letter of transmittal says what you'd say if you were handing the report directly to the person who authorized it, so the style is less formal than the rest of the report. For example, the letter would use personal pronouns (*you, I, we*) and conversational language. Moreno's Electrovision report includes a one-page transmittal memo from Moreno to her boss (the person who requested the report).

Use a less formal style for the letter of transmittal than for the report itself.

The transmittal letter usually appears right before the table of contents. If your report will be widely distributed, however, you may decide to include the letter of transmittal only in selected copies so that you can make certain comments to a specific audience. If your report discusses layoffs or other issues that affect people in the organization, you might want to discuss your recommendations privately in a letter of transmittal to top management. If your audience is likely to be skeptical of or even hostile to something in your report, the transmittal letter is a good opportunity to acknowledge their concerns and explain how the report addresses the issues they care about.

The letter of transmittal follows the routine and good-news plans described in Chapter 7. Begin with the main idea, officially conveying the report to the readers and summarizing its purpose. Such a letter typically begins with a statement such as "Here is the report you asked me to prepare on . . ." The rest includes information about the scope of the report, the methods used to complete the study, and the limitations that became apparent. In the middle section of the letter, you may also highlight important points or sections of the report, make comments on side issues, give suggestions for follow-up studies, and offer any details that will help readers understand and use the report. You may also wish to acknowledge help given by others. The concluding paragraph is a note of thanks for having been given the report assignment, an expression of willingness to discuss the report, and an offer to assist with future projects.

Use the good-news plan for a letter of transmittal.

If the report does not have a synopsis, the letter of transmittal may summarize the major findings, conclusions, and recommendations. This material would be placed after the opening of the letter.

The synopsis of short reports is often included in the letter of transmittal.

The table of contents outlines the text and lists prefatory and supplementary parts.

Table of Contents The table of contents (titled simply "Contents") indicates in outline form the coverage, sequence, and relative importance of the information in the report. The headings used in the text of the report are the basis for the table of contents. Depending on the length and complexity of the report, your contents page may show only the top two or three levels of headings or only first-level headings. The exclusion of some levels of headings may frustrate readers who want to know where to find every subject you cover. On the other hand, a simpler table of contents helps readers focus on the major points. No matter how many levels you include, make sure readers can easily distinguish between them (see Figure 13.8 on page 432 for examples of various levels of headings).

The table of contents is prepared after the other parts of the report have been typed, so that the beginning page numbers for each heading can be shown. The headings should be worded exactly as they are in the text of the report. Also listed on the contents page are the prefatory parts (only those that follow the contents page) and the supplementary parts. If you have fewer than four visual aids, you may wish to list them in the table of contents, too; but if you have four or more visual aids, create a separate list of illustrations.

Be sure the headings in the table of contents match up perfectly with the headings in the text.

List of Illustrations For simplicity's sake, some reports refer to all visual aids as illustrations or exhibits. In other reports, as in Moreno's Electrovision report, tables are labeled separately from other types of visual aids, which are called figures. Regardless of the system used to label visual aids, the list of illustrations gives their titles and page numbers.

If you have enough space on a single page, include the list of illustrations directly beneath the table of contents. Otherwise, put the list on the page after the contents page. When tables and figures are numbered separately, they should also be listed separately. The two lists can appear on the same page if they fit; otherwise, start each list on a separate page.

Put the lists of figures and tables on separate pages if they won't fit on one page with the table of contents.

Learning Objective 3

Explain the difference between a synopsis and an executive summary

Synopsis or Executive Summary A **synopsis** is a brief overview (one page or less) of a report's most important points, designed to give readers a quick preview of the contents. It's often included in long informational reports dealing with technical, professional, or academic subjects and can also be called an **abstract**. Because it's a concise representation of the whole report, it may be distributed separately to a wide audience; then interested readers can request a copy of the entire report.

The phrasing of a synopsis can be either informative or descriptive, depending on whether the report is in direct or indirect order. In an informative synopsis, you present the main points of the report in the order in which they appear in the text. A descriptive synopsis, on the other hand, simply tells what the report is about, using only moderately greater detail than the table of contents; the actual findings of the report are omitted. Here are examples of statements from each type:

Use a descriptive synopsis for a skeptical or hostile audience, an informative synopsis for most other situations.

Informative Synopsis	Descriptive Synopsis
Sales of super-premium ice cream make up 11 percent of the total ice cream market.	This report contains information about super-premium ice cream and its share of the market.

The way you handle a synopsis reflects the approach you use in the text. If you're using an indirect approach in your report, you're better off with a descriptive synopsis. An informative synopsis, with its focus on conclusions and key points, may be too confrontational if you have a skeptical audience. You don't want to spoil the effect by providing a controversial beginning. No matter which type of synopsis you use, be sure to present an accurate picture of the report's contents.[3]

Many business report writers prefer to include an **executive summary** instead of a synopsis or an abstract. Whereas a synopsis is a prose table of contents that outlines the main points of the report, an executive summary is a fully developed "mini" ver-

Put enough information in an executive summary so that an executive can make a decision without reading the entire report.

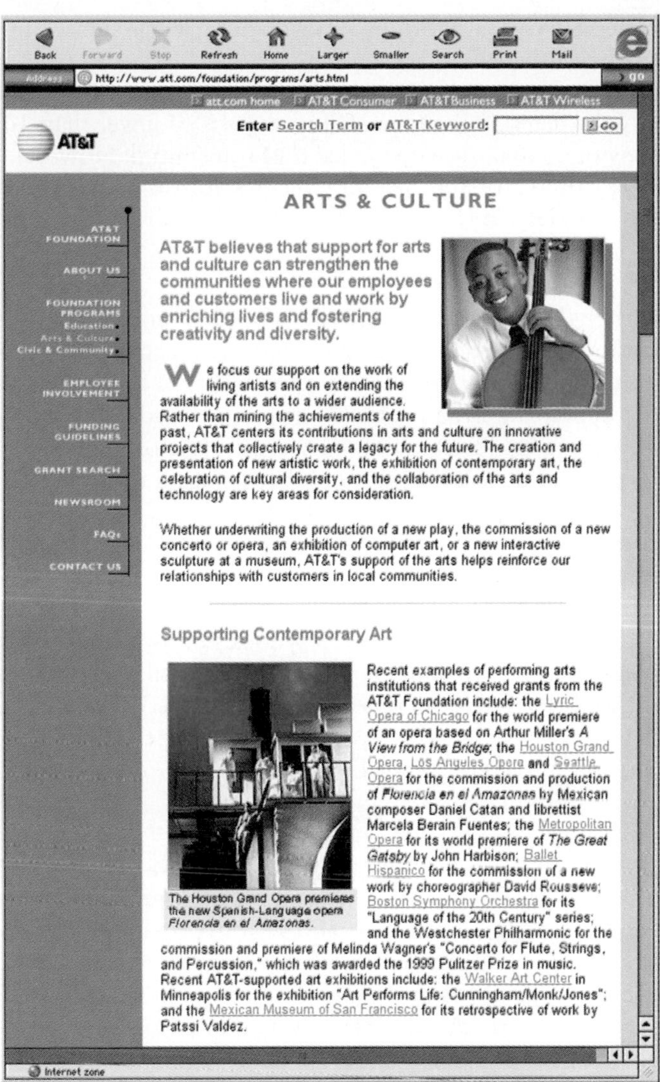

This AT&T online report uses a synopsis to give readers a brief overview of the main points covered. Those who want more information can click on hotlinks and go directly to the appropriate report section.

sion of the report itself. Executive summaries are more comprehensive than a synopsis; many contain headings, well-developed transitions, and even visual aids. A good executive summary opens a window into the body of the report and allows the reader to quickly see how well you have managed your message. It is often organized in the same way as the report, using a direct or an indirect approach, depending on the audience's receptivity. However, executive summaries can also deviate from the sequence of material in the remainder of the report.

Executive summaries are intended for readers who lack the time or motivation to study the complete text. As a general rule, keep the length of an executive summary proportionate to the length of the report. A brief business report may have only a one-page or shorter executive summary. Longer business reports may have a two- or three-page summary. Anything longer, however, might cease to be a summary.[4]

Linda Moreno's Electrovision report provides one example of an executive summary. After reading the summary, audience members know the essentials of the report and are in a position to make a decision. Later, when time permits, they may read certain parts of the report to obtain additional detail. However, from daily newspapers to websites, businesspeople are getting swamped with more and more data and information. They are looking for ways to cut through all the clutter, and reading executive summaries is a popular shortcut. Because you can usually assume that many of your readers will not read the main text of your report, make sure you cover all your important points (along with significant supporting information) in the executive summary.

Many reports require neither a synopsis nor an executive summary. Length is usually the determining factor. Most reports of fewer than 10 pages either omit such a preview or combine it with the letter of transmittal. However, if your report is over 30 pages long, you'll probably include either a synopsis or an executive summary as a convenience for readers. Which one you'll provide depends on the traditions of your organization.

Text of the Report

Three main text parts of a report are
- Introduction
- Body
- Closing

Although reports may contain a variety of components, the heart of a report is always composed of three main parts: an introduction, a body, and closing. As Chapter 13 points out, the length and content of each of these parts varies with the length and type of report, the organizational structure, and the reader's familiarity with the topic. Following is a brief review of the three major parts of the report text. See Chapter 13 for a more detailed discussion of composing these parts.

An introduction has a number of functions and covers a wide variety of topics.

Introduction A good introduction helps the reader follow and comprehend the information that follows. It invites the audience to continue reading by telling them what the report is about, why the audience should be concerned, and how the report is organized. If your report has a synopsis or an executive summary, avoid redundancy by balancing the introduction with the material in your summary as Linda Moreno does in her Electrovision report. For example, Moreno's executive summary is fairly detailed, so she makes her introduction relatively brief. If you believe that your introduction must repeat information that has already been covered in one of the prefatory parts, simply use different wording.

Too much data can bore readers.

Body This section contains the information that supports your conclusions and recommendations as well as your analysis, logic, and interpretation of the information. See the body of Linda Moreno's Electrovision report for an example of the types of supporting detail commonly included in this section. Pay close attention to her effective use of visuals. Most inexperienced writers have a tendency to include too much data in their reports or place too much data in paragraph format instead of using tables and charts. Such treatment increases the chance of boring or losing the audience. If you find yourself with too much information, include only the essential supporting data in the body, use visuals, and place any additional information in an appendix.

A report's organizational structure will determine the length of the closing.

Closing You want the closing of your report to summarize the main idea of your report, highlight your conclusions or recommendations, and list any courses of action you expect the reader to take. In a long report, this section may be labeled "Summary," or "Conclusions and Recommendations." As Chapter 13 points out, if you have organized your report in a direct pattern, your closing should be relatively brief, like Linda Moreno's. If you have organized your report indirectly, you may be using this section to present your recommendations and conclusions for the first time, in which case this section could be relatively extensive.

Learning Objective 4

Describe the three supplementary parts of a formal report

Supplementary Parts

Supplementary parts follow the text of the report and provide information for readers who seek more detailed discussion. Supplements are more common in long reports than in short ones, and typically include the appendixes, bibliography, and index.

Put into an appendix materials that are
- Bulky or lengthy
- Not directly relevant to the text

Appendixes An **appendix** contains materials related to the report but not included in the text because they're too lengthy or bulky or because they lack direct relevance. However, as Mark Landiak warns, be sure not to include too much ancillary material. Keep your reports straightforward and concise. Well-designed appendixes provide enough but not too much additional information for those readers who want it.

Frequently included in appendixes are sample questionnaires and cover letters, sample forms, computer printouts, statistical formulas, financial statements and spreadsheets, copies of important documents, and complex illustrations; a glossary may be put in an appendix or may stand as a separate supplementary part. The best place to include visual aids is in the text body nearest the point of discussion, but if any visuals are too large to fit on one page or are only indirectly relevant to your report, they too may be put in an appendix. In fact, some organizations specify that all visual aids be placed in an appendix.

Put visuals in the body of the report nearest the point of discussion.

Each type of material deserves a separate appendix. Identify the appendixes by labeling them—for example, "Appendix A: Questionnaire," "Appendix B: Computer Printout of Raw Data," and so on. All appendixes should be mentioned in the text and listed in the table of contents.

Bibliography You have an ethical and a legal obligation to give other people credit for their work. A **bibliography** is a list of secondary sources consulted when preparing the report. In her Electrovision report, Linda Moreno labeled her bibliography "Works Cited" because she listed only the works that were mentioned in the report. You might call this section "Sources" or "References" if it includes works consulted but not mentioned in your report. Linda Moreno's Electrovision report uses the author-date system. An alternative is to use numbered footnotes (bottom of the page) or endnotes (end of the report). For more information on citing sources, see Appendix II, "Documentation of Report Sources."

List your secondary sources in the bibliography.

In addition to providing a bibliography, some authors prefer to cite references in the report text. Acknowledging your sources in the body of your report demonstrates that you have thoroughly researched your topic. Furthermore, mentioning the names of well-known or important authorities on the subject helps build credibility for your message. It's often a good idea to mention a credible source's name several times if you need to persuade your audience. On the other hand, you don't want to make your report read like an academic treatise, dragging along from citation to citation. The source references should be handled as conveniently and inconspicuously as possible. One approach, especially for internal reports, is simply to mention a source in the text:

Give credit where credit is due.

> According to Dr. Lewis Morgan of Northwestern Hospital, hip replacement operations account for 7 percent of all surgery performed on women age 65 and over.

However, if your report will be distributed to outsiders, include additional information on where you obtained the data. Most college students are familiar with citation methods suggested by the Modern Language Association (MLA) or the American Psychological Association (APA). *The Chicago Manual of Style* is a reference often used by typesetters and publishers. All of these sources encourage the use of in-text citations (inserting the author's last name and a year of publication or a page number directly into the text).

Best of the Web

Preview Before You Produce

A good way to get ideas for the best style, organization, and format of a report is by looking at copies of professional business reports. To find samples of various types of reports, you can use a metasearch engine such as Ixquick Metasearch. Ixquick searches many engines simultaneously; in addition to searching in English, you can conduct your search in five other languages. See what Ixquick produces when you enter the phrase *business reports*. Choose from various titles or descriptions to compare different kinds of reports. This research could result in your preparing better reports and proposals.

www.ixquick.com

FIGURE 14.2 Parts of a Formal Proposal

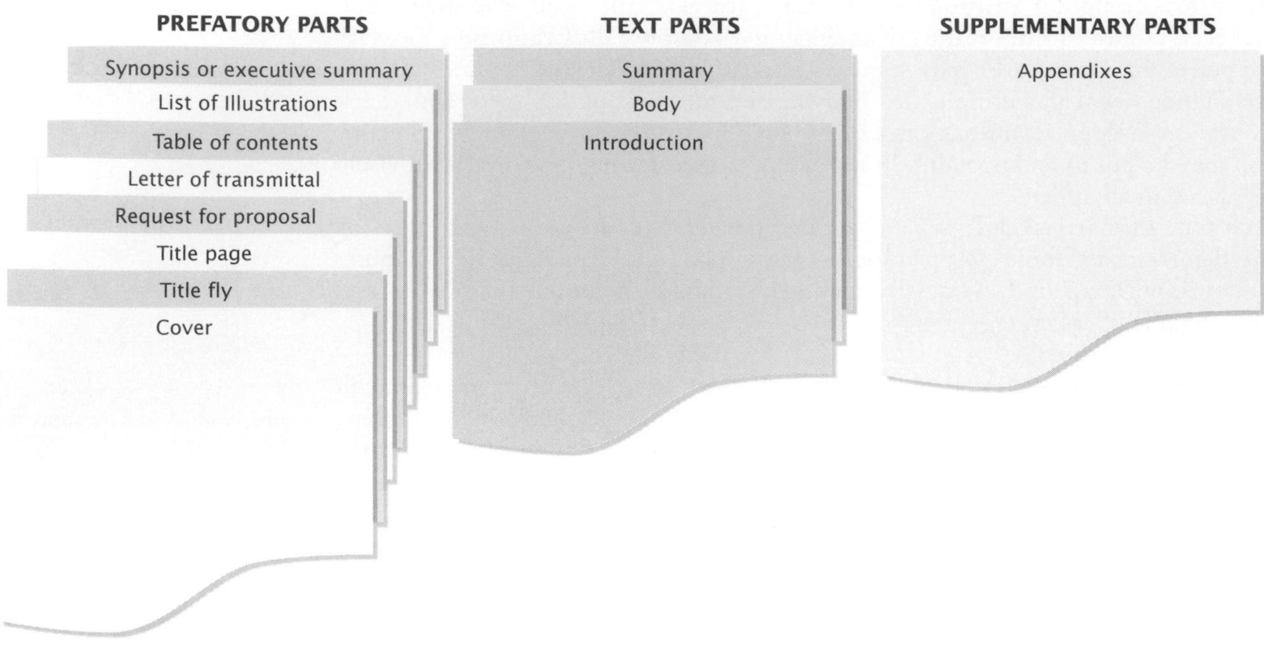

Senior Vice President June Yee Felix solicited proposals from consultants and research firms when she needed to start a service for online bill payment at Chase Manhattan's Bank. The RFP stated her criteria and detailed requirements for selecting a service provider.

Index An **index** is an alphabetical list of names, places, and subjects mentioned in the report, along with the pages on which they occur (see the index for this book). An index is rarely included in unpublished reports.

Components of a Formal Proposal

As discussed in Chapter 13, certain analytical reports are called proposals, which include bids to perform work under a contract and pleas for financial support from outsiders. Such bids and pleas are almost always formal. As Mark Landiak knows only too well, the goal of a proposal is to impress readers with your professionalism and to make your service and your company stand out. This goal is best achieved through a structured and deliberate approach.

Formal proposals contain many of the same components as other formal reports (see Figure 14.2). The difference lies mostly in the text, although a few of the prefatory parts are also different. With the exception of an occasional appendix, most proposals have few supplementary parts.

Prefatory Parts

The cover, title fly, title page, table of contents, and list of illustrations are handled the same as in other formal reports. However, other prefatory parts are handled quite differently, such as the copy of the RFP, the synopsis or executive summary, and the letter of transmittal.

Formal proposals contain most of the same prefatory parts as other formal reports.

Copy of the RFP Instead of having a letter of authorization, a formal proposal may have a copy of the request for proposal (RFP), which is a letter or memo soliciting a proposal or a bid for a particular project. If the RFP includes detailed specifications, it may be too long to bind into the proposal; in that case, you may want to include only the introductory portion of the RFP. Another option is to omit the RFP and simply refer to it in your letter of transmittal.

Use a copy of the request for proposal in place of the letter of authorization.

Synopsis or Executive Summary Although you may include a synopsis or an executive summary for your reader's convenience when your proposal is quite long, these components are often less useful in a formal proposal than they are in a formal report. If your proposal is unsolicited, your transmittal letter will already have caught the reader's interest, making a synopsis or an executive summary pointless. It may also be pointless if your proposal is solicited, because the reader is already committed to studying your proposal to find out how you intend to satisfy the terms of a contract. The introduction to a solicited proposal would provide an adequate preview of the contents. However, in some cases, an executive summary can serve you well.

Most proposals do not require a synopsis or an executive summary.

Bruce Rogow was a junior engineering major at San Diego State University when he was first struck by the idea of leading a team of students to design, build, and race a solar car at the World Solar Challenge Race across the Australian outback. The race itself would be the least of Rogow's challenges: First he had to convince students and faculty of the project's benefits; then he had to keep them motivated (and working long, hard hours) while he tackled administrative and engineering roadblocks that even he couldn't predict.

Bruce Rogow with *Suntrakker* in Australia. Rogow wrote his business plan proposal to raise financial and team support for designing, building, and racing *Suntrakker*. The project involved 35 students, who raised $145,000. Their solar car finished 42nd out of 52 cars in Australia's World Solar Challenge race.

Ultimately, the SDSU Solar Car Project succeeded, and it drew involvement from various academic departments, dozens of student volunteers, several corporate benefactors, and many news organizations. Rogow challenged science, engineering, and computer students to design and test *Suntrakker* (as the car was named). But he also challenged SDSU's business students to come up with a proposal that would help him raise the support *Suntrakker* required.

"We needed to raise $145,000," Rogow recalls. "And since we had no faculty support in the beginning, we had to have something that would give us credibility. The proposal gave us much more than that."

Three students from an entrepreneurship class agreed to work with Rogow on a proposal that eventually filled over 70 pages. "The proposal mapped out every detail of our project, from start to finish, and made us look at things we had not considered. It also earned us respect from the faculty and was responsible for a $5,000 donation from our local power company." Rogow now believes that the proposal made the difference between "thriving and just surviving."

With the students' combined skills and Rogow's determined leadership, *Suntrakker* gave an impressive showing in Australia. The futuristic-looking solar car now tours schools as part of a university recruiting program. Moreover, both a book and a documentary film (*Warriors of the Sun*) have been produced about the project.

Figure 14.3 shows an excerpt from the executive summary that Rogow included in his unsolicited proposal. The proposal presents the benefits up front and the financial information at the close. Detailed and thorough, it includes sections describing the vehicle, the management team, and even "Critical Risks." Appendixes include an organization chart, résumé, design schematics, letters of support, lists of volunteers and contributors, and a telemarketing script.

Letter of Transmittal The way you handle the letter of transmittal depends on whether the proposal is solicited or unsolicited. If the proposal is solicited, the transmittal letter follows the pattern for good-news messages, highlighting those aspects of your proposal that may give you a competitive advantage. If the proposal is unsolicited, the transmittal letter follows the pattern for persuasive messages (see Chapter 9). The letter must persuade the reader that you have something worthwhile to offer, something that justifies the time required to read the entire proposal. Because the transmittal letter may be all that the client reads, it must be especially convincing.

Use the good-news pattern for the letter of transmittal if the proposal is solicited; use the persuasive plan if the proposal is unsolicited.

FIGURE 14.3 In-Depth Critique: Bruce Rogow's Proposal (Executive Summary Excerpt)

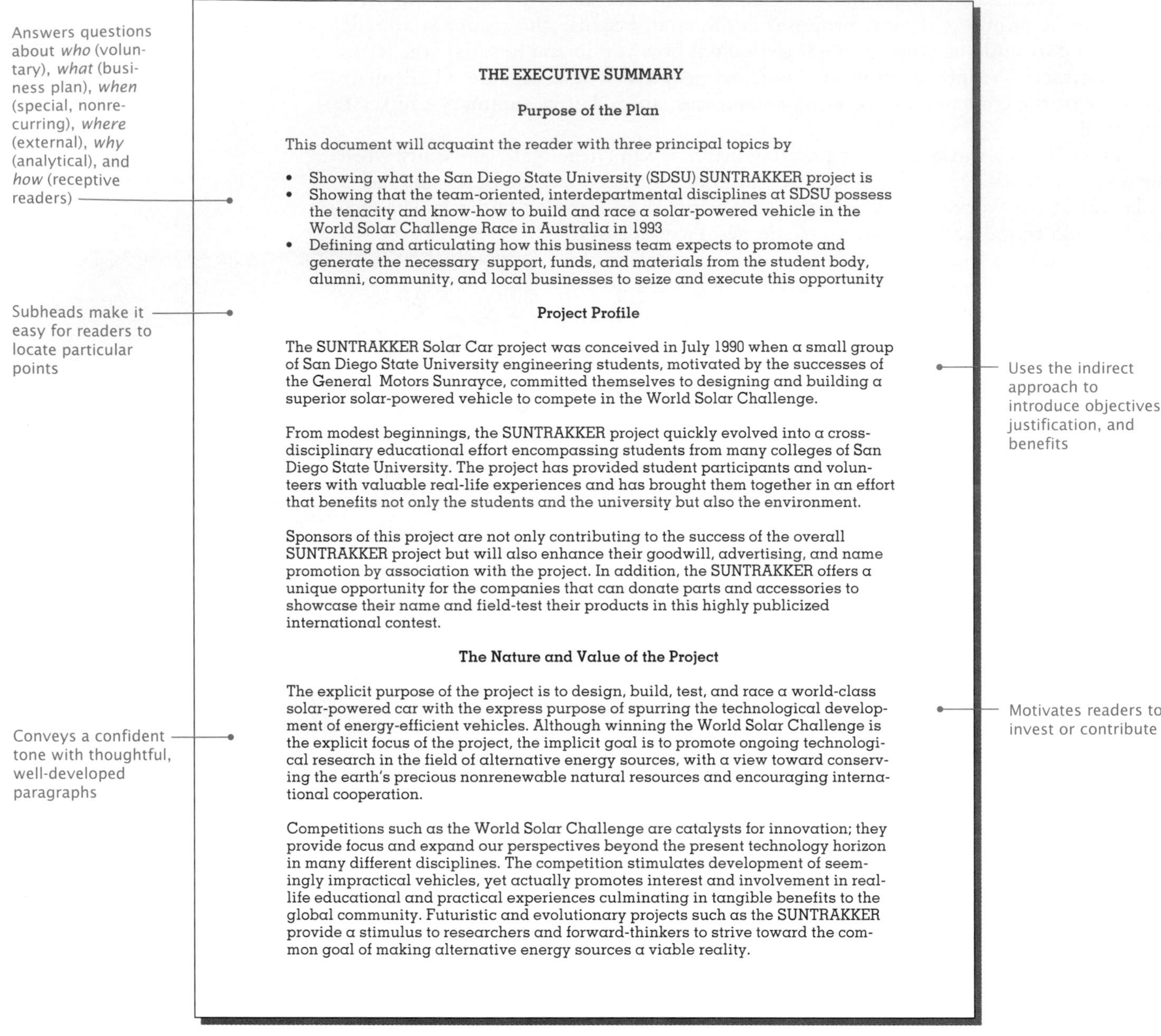

THE EXECUTIVE SUMMARY

Purpose of the Plan

This document will acquaint the reader with three principal topics by

- Showing what the San Diego State University (SDSU) SUNTRAKKER project is
- Showing that the team-oriented, interdepartmental disciplines at SDSU possess the tenacity and know-how to build and race a solar-powered vehicle in the World Solar Challenge Race in Australia in 1993
- Defining and articulating how this business team expects to promote and generate the necessary support, funds, and materials from the student body, alumni, community, and local businesses to seize and execute this opportunity

Project Profile

The SUNTRAKKER Solar Car project was conceived in July 1990 when a small group of San Diego State University engineering students, motivated by the successes of the General Motors Sunrayce, committed themselves to designing and building a superior solar-powered vehicle to compete in the World Solar Challenge.

From modest beginnings, the SUNTRAKKER project quickly evolved into a cross-disciplinary educational effort encompassing students from many colleges of San Diego State University. The project has provided student participants and volunteers with valuable real-life experiences and has brought them together in an effort that benefits not only the students and the university but also the environment.

Sponsors of this project are not only contributing to the success of the overall SUNTRAKKER project but will also enhance their goodwill, advertising, and name promotion by association with the project. In addition, the SUNTRAKKER offers a unique opportunity for the companies that can donate parts and accessories to showcase their name and field-test their products in this highly publicized international contest.

The Nature and Value of the Project

The explicit purpose of the project is to design, build, test, and race a world-class solar-powered car with the express purpose of spurring the technological development of energy-efficient vehicles. Although winning the World Solar Challenge is the explicit focus of the project, the implicit goal is to promote ongoing technological research in the field of alternative energy sources, with a view toward conserving the earth's precious nonrenewable natural resources and encouraging international cooperation.

Competitions such as the World Solar Challenge are catalysts for innovation; they provide focus and expand our perspectives beyond the present technology horizon in many different disciplines. The competition stimulates development of seemingly impractical vehicles, yet actually promotes interest and involvement in real-life educational and practical experiences culminating in tangible benefits to the global community. Futuristic and evolutionary projects such as the SUNTRAKKER provide a stimulus to researchers and forward-thinkers to strive toward the common goal of making alternative energy sources a viable reality.

(continued)

Text of the Proposal

Content may be different for solicited and unsolicited proposals.

Just as with reports, the text of a proposal is composed of three main parts: an introduction, body, and conclusion. The content and depth of each part depend on whether the proposal is solicited or unsolicited, formal or informal. See Chapter 13 for a more detailed discussion of the topics covered in each part. Here's a brief review:[5]

- **Introduction.** This section presents and summarizes the problem you intend to solve and your solution to that problem, including any benefits the reader will receive from the solution.
- **Body.** This section explains the complete details of the solution: how the job will be done, how it will be broken into tasks, what method will be used to do it

FIGURE 14.3 (Continued)

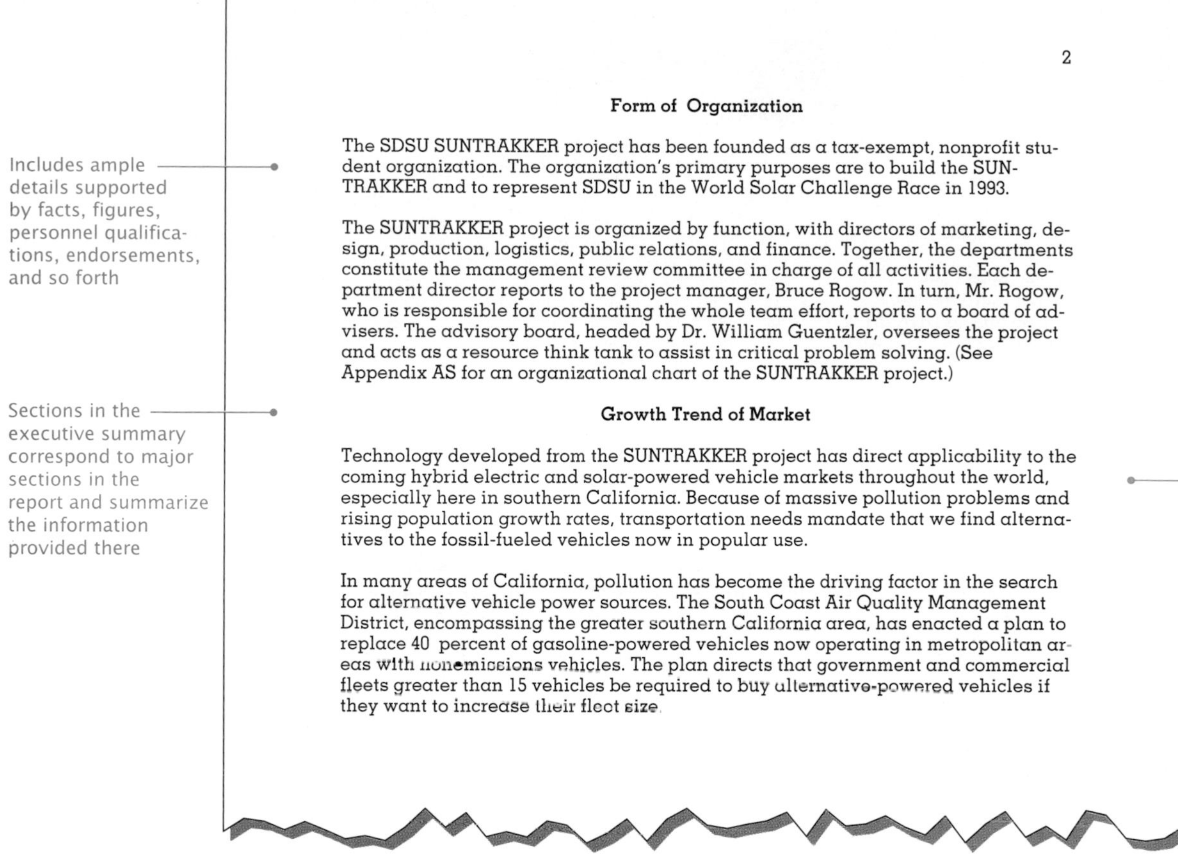

2

Form of Organization

The SDSU SUNTRAKKER project has been founded as a tax-exempt, nonprofit student organization. The organization's primary purposes are to build the SUNTRAKKER and to represent SDSU in the World Solar Challenge Race in 1993.

The SUNTRAKKER project is organized by function, with directors of marketing, design, production, logistics, public relations, and finance. Together, the departments constitute the management review committee in charge of all activities. Each department director reports to the project manager, Bruce Rogow. In turn, Mr. Rogow, who is responsible for coordinating the whole team effort, reports to a board of advisers. The advisory board, headed by Dr. William Guentzler, oversees the project and acts as a resource think tank to assist in critical problem solving. (See Appendix AS for an organizational chart of the SUNTRAKKER project.)

Growth Trend of Market

Technology developed from the SUNTRAKKER project has direct applicability to the coming hybrid electric and solar-powered vehicle markets throughout the world, especially here in southern California. Because of massive pollution problems and rising population growth rates, transportation needs mandate that we find alternatives to the fossil-fueled vehicles now in popular use.

In many areas of California, pollution has become the driving factor in the search for alternative vehicle power sources. The South Coast Air Quality Management District, encompassing the greater southern California area, has enacted a plan to replace 40 percent of gasoline-powered vehicles now operating in metropolitan areas with nonemissions vehicles. The plan directs that government and commercial fleets greater than 15 vehicles be required to buy alternative-powered vehicles if they want to increase their fleet size.

(including the required equipment, material, and personnel), when the work will begin and end, how much the entire job will cost (including a detailed breakdown), and why your company is qualified.
- **Closing.** This section emphasizes the benefits that readers will realize from your solution, and it urges readers to act.

Figure 14.4 is an informal proposal submitted by Dixon O'Donnell, vice president of O'Donnell & Associates, a geotechnical engineering firm that conducts a variety of environmental testing services. The company is bidding on the mass grading and utility work specified by AGI Builders. As you review this document, pay close attention to the specific items addressed in the proposal's introduction, body, and closing. See Chapter 13 for a more detailed discussion of the topics covered in each of these parts.

PROOFREADING FORMAL REPORTS AND PROPOSALS

Once you have assembled all the various components of your report or proposal, revised the entire document's content for clarity and conciseness, and designed the document to please readers, you have essentially produced your document in its final form. Now you need to review it thoroughly one last time, looking for inconsistencies, errors, and missing components. For

During the proofreading stage, you have one final opportunity to strengthen your report or proposal. Just as with kickboxing or any aerobic exercise, your extra efforts will pay off.

FIGURE 14.4 In-Depth Critique: Dixon O'Donnell's Informal Solicited Proposal

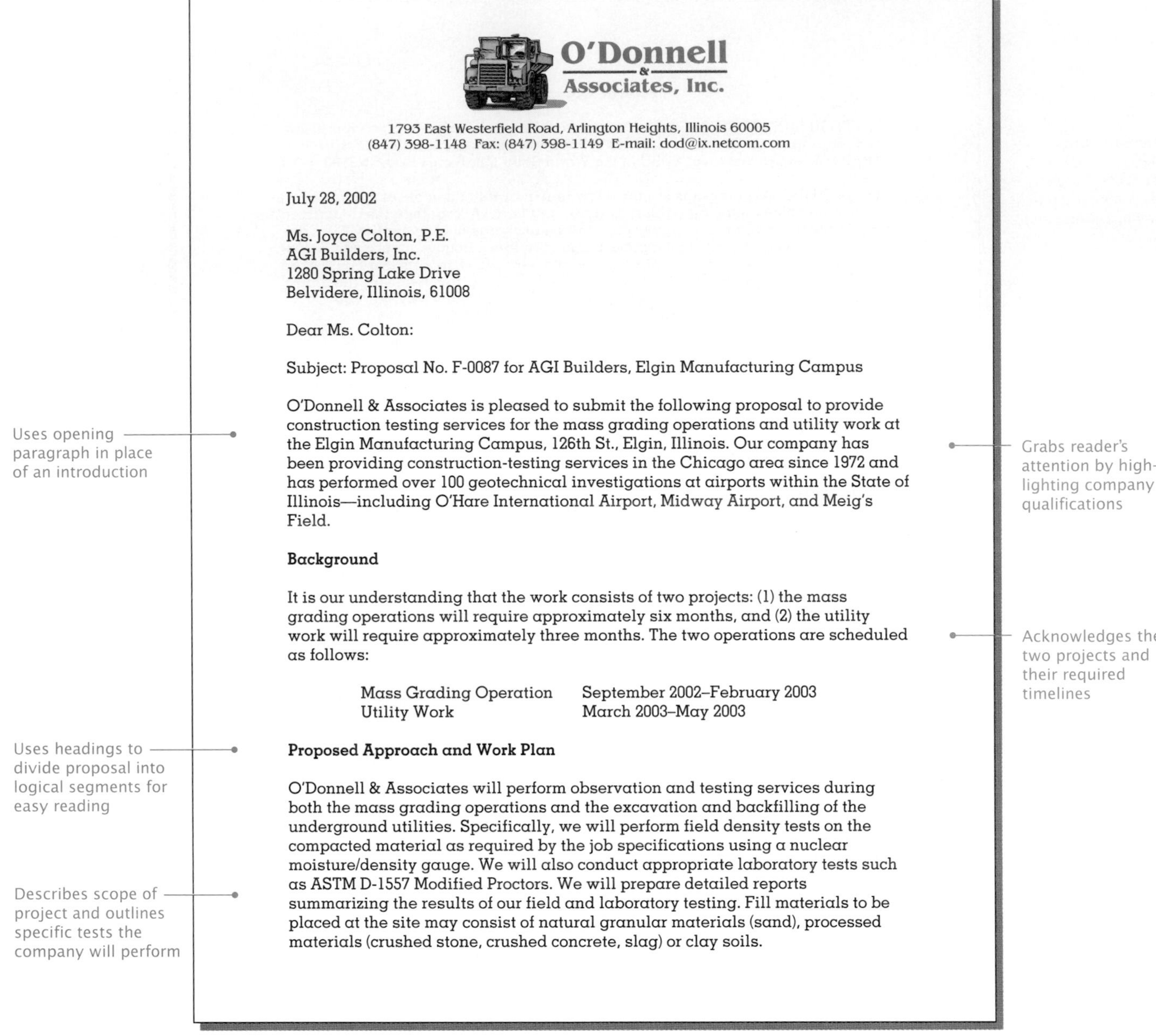

O'Donnell & Associates, Inc.

1793 East Westerfield Road, Arlington Heights, Illinois 60005
(847) 398-1148 Fax: (847) 398-1149 E-mail: dod@ix.netcom.com

July 28, 2002

Ms. Joyce Colton, P.E.
AGI Builders, Inc.
1280 Spring Lake Drive
Belvidere, Illinois, 61008

Dear Ms. Colton:

Subject: Proposal No. F-0087 for AGI Builders, Elgin Manufacturing Campus

O'Donnell & Associates is pleased to submit the following proposal to provide construction testing services for the mass grading operations and utility work at the Elgin Manufacturing Campus, 126th St., Elgin, Illinois. Our company has been providing construction-testing services in the Chicago area since 1972 and has performed over 100 geotechnical investigations at airports within the State of Illinois—including O'Hare International Airport, Midway Airport, and Meig's Field.

Background

It is our understanding that the work consists of two projects: (1) the mass grading operations will require approximately six months, and (2) the utility work will require approximately three months. The two operations are scheduled as follows:

Mass Grading Operation	September 2002–February 2003
Utility Work	March 2003–May 2003

Proposed Approach and Work Plan

O'Donnell & Associates will perform observation and testing services during both the mass grading operations and the excavation and backfilling of the underground utilities. Specifically, we will perform field density tests on the compacted material as required by the job specifications using a nuclear moisture/density gauge. We will also conduct appropriate laboratory tests such as ASTM D-1557 Modified Proctors. We will prepare detailed reports summarizing the results of our field and laboratory testing. Fill materials to be placed at the site may consist of natural granular materials (sand), processed materials (crushed stone, crushed concrete, slag) or clay soils.

(continued)

Don't forget to proofread everything one last time.

Keep the report's purpose in mind as you write the report, and make sure nothing has been left out or overlooked.

instance, if you changed a heading in the report's text part, make sure that you also changed the corresponding heading in the table of contents and in all references to that heading in your report.

Proofreading the textual part of your report is pretty much the same as proofreading any business message—you check for typos, spelling errors, and mistakes in punctuation. However, reports often have elements that may not be included in other messages, so don't forget to proof your visual aids thoroughly, as Chapter 11 points out, and make sure they are positioned correctly. If you need specific tips on proofreading documents, look back at Chapter 6 for some reminders on what to look for when proofreading text and how to proofread like a pro. For instance, you'll want to make sure that nothing has been left out or overlooked and that every word contributes to your report's purpose.

FIGURE 14.4 (Continued)

O'Donnell & Associates, Inc. July 28, 2002 Page 2

Explains who will be responsible for the various tasks

O'Donnell & Associates will provide qualified personnel to perform the necessary testing. Mr. Kevin Patel will be the lead field technician responsible for the project. A copy of Mr. Patel's résumé is included with this proposal for your review. Kevin will coordinate field activities with your job site superintendent and make sure that appropriate personnel are assigned to the job site. Overall project management will be the responsibility of Mr. Joseph Proesel. Project engineering services will be performed under the direction of Mr. Dixon O'Donnell, P.E. All field personnel assigned to the site will be familiar with and abide by the Project Site Health and Safety Plan prepared by Carlson Environmental, Inc., dated April 2002.

Encloses résumé rather than list qualifications in the document

Qualifications

O'Donnell & Associates has been providing quality professional services since 1972 in the areas of

- Geotechnical engineering
- Materials testing and inspection
- Pavement evaluation
- Environmental services
- Engineering and technical support (CADD) services

Grabs attention by mentioning distinguishing qualifications

The company provides Phase I and Phase II environmental site assessments, preparation of LUST site closure reports, installation of groundwater monitoring wells, and testing of soil/groundwater samples of environmental contaminants. Geotechnical services include all phases of soil mechanics and foundation engineering including foundation and lateral load analysis, slope stability analysis, site preparation recommendations, seepage analysis, pavement design, and settlement analysis.

O'Donnell & Associates materials testing laboratory is certified by AASHTO Accreditation Program for the testing of Soils, Aggregate, Hot Mix Asphalt and Portland Cement Concrete. A copy of our laboratory certification is included with this proposal. In addition to in-house training, field and laboratory technicians participate in a variety of certification programs, including those sponsored by American Concrete Institute (ACI) and Illinois Department of Transportation (IDOT).

Gains credibility by describing certifications

Costs

On the basis of our understanding of the scope of the work, we estimate the total cost of the two projects to be $100,260.00, as follows:

(continued)

Once you've completed your formal report and sent it off to your audience, you'll naturally expect a positive response, and quite often you'll get one—but not always. You may get halfhearted praise or no action on your conclusions and recommendations. Even worse, you may get some serious criticism. Try to learn from these experiences. Sometimes you won't get any response at all. If you don't hear from your readers within a week or two, you might want to ask politely whether the report arrived. In hope of stimulating a response, you might ask a question about the report, such as "How do you think accounting will react to the proposed budget increase?" You might also offer to answer any questions or provide additional information. To review the ideas presented in this chapter, consult this chapter's "Checklist: Producing Formal Reports and Proposals" on page 478.

Ask for feedback, and learn from your mistakes.

FIGURE 14.4 (Continued)

O'Donnell & Associates, Inc. July 28, 2002 Page 3

Builds interest by describing all services provided by the company

Itemizes costs by project and gives supporting detail

Table of Cost Estimates

Cost Estimate: Mass Grading	Units	Rate ($)	Total Cost ($)
Field Inspection			
Labor	1,320 hours	$38.50	$ 50, 820.00
Nuclear Moisture Density Meter	132 days	35.00	4,620.00
Vehicle Expense	132 days	45.00	5,940.00
Laboratory Testing			
Proctor Density Tests (ASTM D-1557)	4 tests	130.00	520.00
Engineering/Project Management			
Principal Engineer	16 hours	110.00	1,760.00
Project Manager	20 hours	80.00	1,600.00
Administrative Assistant	12 hours	50.00	600.00
Subtotal			***$ 65,860.00***
Cost Estimate: Utility Work	**Units**	**Rate ($)**	**Total Cost ($)**
Field Inspection			
Labor	660 hours	$ 38.50	$ 25,410.00
Nuclear Moisture Density Meter	66 days	5.00	2,310.00
Vehicle Expense	66 days	45.00	2,970.00
Laboratory Testing			
Proctor Density Tests (ASTM D-1557)	2 tests	130.00	260.00
Engineering/Project Management			
Principal Engineer	10 hours	110.00	1,100.00
Project Manager	20 hours	80.00	1,600.00
Administrative Assistant	15 hours	50.00	750.00
Subtotal			***34,400.00***
Total Project Costs			**$100,260.00**

This estimate assumes full-time inspection services. However, our services may also be performed on an as-requested basis, and actual charges will reflect time associated with the project. We have attached our standard fee schedule for your review. Overtime rates are for hours in excess of 8.0 hours per day, before 7:00 a.m., after 5:00 p.m., and on holidays and weekends.

Provides alternative option in case full-time service costs exceed client's budget

(continued)

COMMUNICATION CHALLENGES AT CORPORATE DYNAMICS

Corporate Dynamics is competing against six other consulting firms for a large contract to analyze and recommend improvements to the customer service department of a major industrial materials manufacturer. Landiak wants to make sure that Corporate Dynamics's sales proposal stands out, so he sent his team out to survey the marketplace and interview a few of the potential client's customers. After all, Landiak knows that one way to capture a client's attention is to use customer quotations in a report that discusses opportunities, challenges, and how Corporate Dynamics can help.

Individual Challenge: Landiak's team came back with a lot of useful information about the potential client. Although many of the comments from customers were positive, the team also received some negative feedback, including "The customer service representatives never seem to be able to

FIGURE 14.4 (Continued)

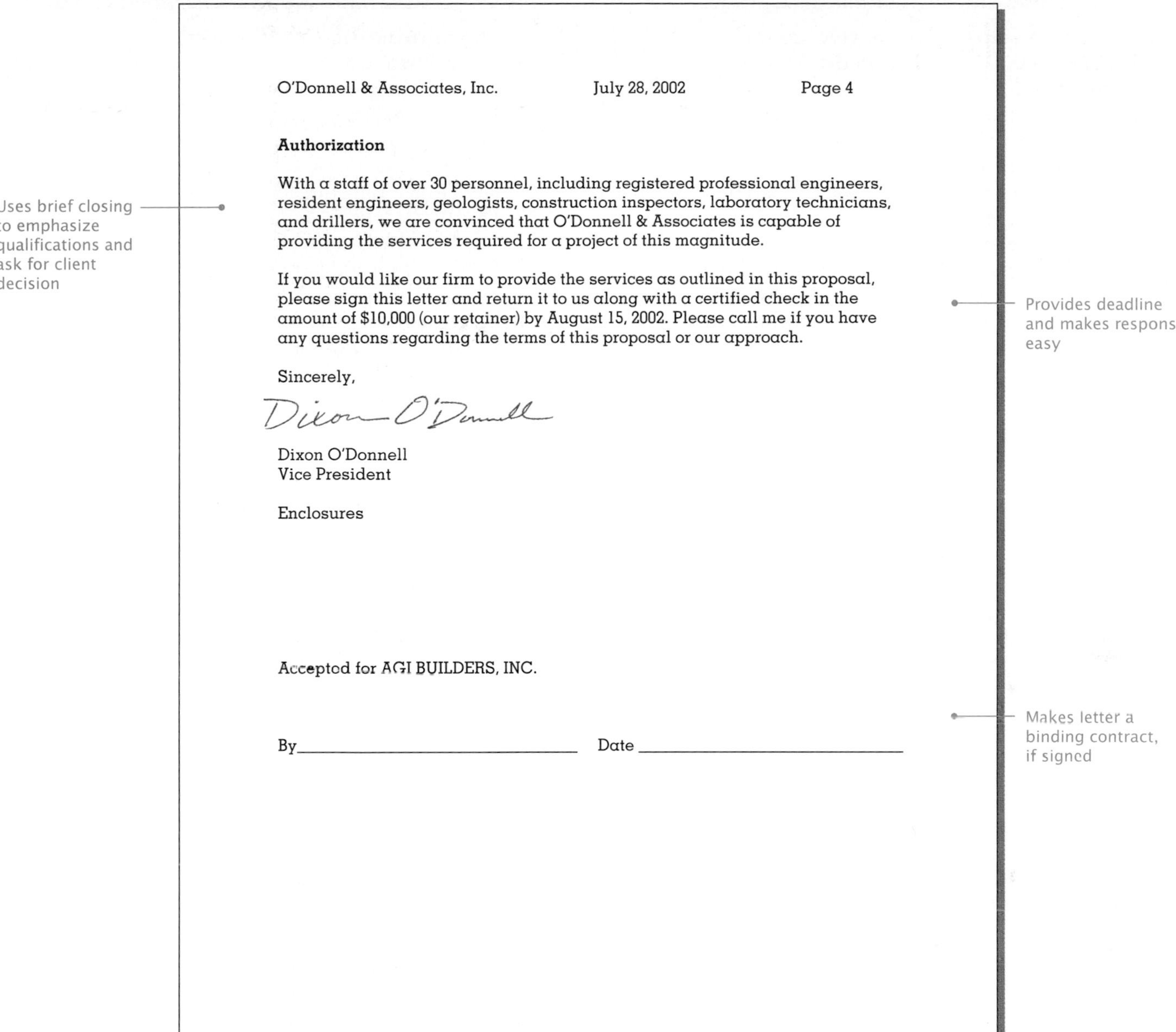

O'Donnell & Associates, Inc. July 28, 2002 Page 4

Authorization

With a staff of over 30 personnel, including registered professional engineers, resident engineers, geologists, construction inspectors, laboratory technicians, and drillers, we are convinced that O'Donnell & Associates is capable of providing the services required for a project of this magnitude.

If you would like our firm to provide the services as outlined in this proposal, please sign this letter and return it to us along with a certified check in the amount of $10,000 (our retainer) by August 15, 2002. Please call me if you have any questions regarding the terms of this proposal or our approach.

Sincerely,

Dixon O'Donnell

Dixon O'Donnell
Vice President

Enclosures

Accepted for AGI BUILDERS, INC.

By__________________________ Date __________________________

answer my questions," "The sales representative doesn't call on me as often as some of the competitors' representatives do," and "I don't carry the company's products because my customers never ask for them." Although these may seem like problems, Landiak wants to present them as opportunities for positive change. He has asked you, a member of his team, to draft a transmittal letter that will set a positive tone, explaining how and why the team obtained this customer information. This is your opportunity to say what you'd say if you were handing the report directly to the client.

Team Challenge: Landiak has assigned your team the job of organizing and formatting a proposal to this potential client. Because Corporate Dynamics is competing with six other firms for the contract, you must concentrate on making your proposal stand out. Your first step is to decide what components to include in the proposal. For example, what types of visuals might you include? Will you include appendixes? If so, what kind of material would be suitable for appendixes? Will you include an executive summary? Why or why not? Would it be more effective for your team to put your conclusions at the beginning or at the end of your report? Why?[6] ■

✓ CHECKLIST: PRODUCING FORMAL REPORTS AND PROPOSALS

A. Prepare a sturdy, attractive cover
1. Label the cover clearly with the title of the document.
2. Use a title that tells the audience exactly what the document is about.

B. Prepare title page
1. List title; recipient's name, title, affiliation; author's name, title, affiliation; date of submission.
2. Balance the information in blocks on the page.

C. Include copy of letter of authorization or request for proposal, if appropriate

D. Prepare letter or memo of transmittal
1. Include only in some copies if it contains sensitive information suitable for some but not all readers.
2. Convey the document officially to the readers.
3. Refer to authorization and discuss purpose, scope, background, source and methods, and limitations.
4. Acknowledge everyone who was especially helpful in preparing the document.
5. Close with thanks, offer to be of further assistance, and suggest future projects, if appropriate.

E. Prepare table of contents
1. Include all first- and second-level headings (and perhaps all third-level headings).
2. Give the page number of each heading.
3. Word all headings exactly as they appear in the text.
4. Include the synopsis (if there is one) and supplementary parts.
5. Number table of contents and all prefatory pages with lowercase roman numerals (bottom center).

F. Prepare list of illustrations if you have four or more visual aids
1. Put the list in the same format as the table of contents.
2. Identify visuals either directly under table of contents or on a separate page under its own heading.

G. Develop synopsis or executive summary (for long, formal documents)
1. Tailor the synopsis or executive summary to the document's length and tone.
2. Condense the document's main points, using either the informative or the descriptive approach.
3. Present the points in a synopsis in the same order as they appear in the document. An executive summary can deviate from the order of points appearing in the report.

H. Prepare introduction to text
1. Leave a two-inch margin at the top of the page, and center the title of the document.
2. In a long document, type the first-level heading "Introduction" three lines below title.
3. In a short document, omit "Introduction" heading and begin typing three lines below title.
4. Discuss the authorization (unless already covered in letter of transmittal), purpose, scope, background, sources and methods, definitions, limitations, and text organization.

I. Prepare body of document
1. For left-bound documents, number all pages with arabic numerals in the upper right-hand corner (except for the first page, where the number is centered one inch from the bottom).
2. For top-bound documents, number all pages with arabic numerals centered one inch from the bottom.

J. Prepare conclusion of document
1. Wrap up the text of reports and proposals with a summary.
2. If appropriate, include conclusions and recommendations.

K. Prepare appendixes, if necessary
1. Give each appendix a title.
2. For multiple appendixes, number or letter them consecutively in the order the text refers to them.

L. Prepare reference list (bibliography), if necessary
1. Use a consistent format.
2. Place on a separate page of report.

M. Review document thoroughly, double-check for inconsistencies and errors
1. Verify that all material quoted or paraphrased from secondary sources is documented.
2. Check that all visual aids are numbered consistently throughout the report and placed close to their textual explanation.
3. Check all page-number references.
4. Make sure that terminology is appropriate.
5. Verify that abbreviations, names, and addresses are correct.
6. Check that headings use a consistent format; limit headings to three levels when possible.
7. Place additional information in appendix.
8. Format appropriately: Single-space text; double-space between paragraphs; leave a space between headings.

SUMMARY OF LEARNING OBJECTIVES

1 **List the three tasks involved in completing business reports and proposals, and briefly explain what's involved in revising them.** To complete business reports and proposals, you need to revise, produce, and proofread the document just as you would with any other business message. Revising reports and proposals involves evaluating content, style, organization, and tone; reviewing for readability; and editing for clarity and conciseness.

2 **Describe the 10 prefatory parts of a formal report.** Depending on readers' preferences and familiarity, formal reports may include as many as 9 of the 10 possible prefatory parts: (1) The cover includes at least the report's title and maybe the writer's name and submission date. (2) The title fly is a blank sheet of paper that adds a touch of formality. (3) The title page includes the report title; the name, title, and address of the person or group that authorized the report; the name, title, and address of the person or group that prepared the report; and the date of submission. (4) The letter (or memo) of authorization is the document requesting a report be written. (5) The letter (or memo) of acceptance acknowledges the assignment and is rarely included in reports. (6) The letter (or memo) of transmittal conveys the report to the audience and may appear in only selected copies of the report. (7) The table of contents lists report headings in outline form with page numbers. (8) The list of illustrations gives the titles and page numbers of visual aids. (9) A synopsis (or abstract) is a brief (one page or less) review of the report's most important points. (10) The executive summary is a fully developed "mini" version of the report that may contain headings and even visual aids. The executive summary would replace the synopsis, since both components would never be included in the same report.

3 **Explain the difference between a synopsis and an executive summary.** A synopsis is a brief overview of the entire report and may either highlight the main points as they appear in the text or simply tell the reader what the report is about. It is designed to entice the audience to read the report, but is not intended to replace the report. By contrast, an executive summary is more comprehensive than a synopsis. It may contain headings, visual aids, and enough information to help busy executives make quick decisions. Although executive summaries are not designed to replace the report, in some cases it may be the only thing that a busy executive reads carefully.

4 **Describe the three supplementary parts of a formal report.** Formal reports may include an appendix, a bibliography, and an index. The appendix contains a variety of additional information that is useful but not critical to the report. Some of this material may be too detailed or bulky to be included in the report body. A bibliography is a list of secondary sources consulted when preparing the report; it may or may not be mentioned in the report body. An index is an alphabetical list of names, places, and subjects mentioned in the report along with their corresponding pages. Indexes are more commonly found in textbooks than in business reports.

TEST YOUR KNOWLEDGE

1. What are the tasks involved in revising a report or proposal?
2. When should you start a report section on a new page?
3. What information is included on the title page of a report?
4. What is the difference between a letter of authorization and a letter of acceptance?
5. What is a letter of transmittal, and where is it positioned within a report?
6. When are executive summaries useful?
7. What are three supplementary parts often included in formal reports?
8. What types of material does an appendix contain?
9. Why do some writers cite references in the report text?
10. What is the equivalent of a letter of authorization for a proposal?

APPLY YOUR KNOWLEDGE

1. How does improved technology influence the production of reports?
2. Under what circumstances would you include more than one index in a lengthy report?
3. If you were submitting a solicited proposal to build an indoor pool, would you include as references the names and addresses of other clients for whom you recently built similar pools? Would you include these references in an unsolicited proposal? Where in either proposal would you include these references? Why?
4. If you included a bibliography in your report, would you also need to include in-text citations? Please explain.
5. **Ethical Choices** How would you report on a confidential survey in which employees rated their managers' capabilities? Both employees and managers expect to see the results. Would you give the same report to employees and managers? What components would you include or exclude for each audience? Explain your choices.

PRACTICE YOUR KNOWLEDGE

Document for Analysis

Visit the U.S. Department of Justice reports page at www.ins.usdoj.gov/graphics/aboutins/repsstudies/addition.html. Read the brief description of the department's "Triennial Comprehensive Report on Immigration" and follow the link to the executive summary. Using the information in this chapter, analyze the executive summary and offer specific suggestions for revising it.

Exercises

For live links to all websites discussed in this chapter, visit this text's website at www.prenhall.com/bovee. Just log on and select Chapter 14, and click on "Student Resources." Locate the name of the site or the URL related to the material in the text. For the "Exploring the Best of the Web" exercises, you'll also find navigational directions. Click on the live link to the site.

14.1 **Teamwork** You and a classmate are helping Linda Moreno prepare her report on Electrovision's travel and entertainment costs (see "Report Writer's Notebook," beginning on page 446.) This time, however, the report is to be informational rather than analytical, so it will not include recommendations. Review the existing report and determine what changes would be needed to make it an informational report. Be as specific as possible. For example, if your team decides the report needs a new title, what title would you use? Now draft a transmittal memo for Moreno to use in conveying this informational report to Dennis McWilliams, Electrovision's vice president of operations.

14.2 **Producing Reports: Letter of Transmittal** You are president of the Friends of the Library, a nonprofit group that raises funds and provides volunteers to support your local library. Every February, you send a report of the previous year's activities and accomplishments to the County Arts Council, which provides an annual grant of $1,000 toward your group's summer reading festival. Now it's February 6, and you've completed your formal report. Here are the highlights:

- Back-to-school book sale raised $2,000.
- Holiday craft fair raised $1,100.
- Promotion and prizes for summer reading festival cost $1,450.
- Materials for children's program featuring local author cost $125.
- New reference databases for library's career center cost $850.
- Bookmarks promoting library's website cost $200.

Write a letter of transmittal to Erica Maki, the council's director. Because she is expecting this report, you can use the direct approach. Be sure to express gratitude for the council's ongoing financial support.

14.3 **Internet** Government reports vary in purpose and structure. Read through the Department of Education's report on how population growth is affecting school enrollment, posted online at www.ed.gov/pubs/bbecho00/index.html. What is the purpose of this document? Does the title communicate this purpose? What type of report is this, and what is the report's structure? Which prefatory and supplementary parts are included? Now analyze the visuals. What types are included in this report? Are they all necessary? Are the titles and legends sufficiently informative? How does this report take advantage of the online medium to enhance readability?

14.4 **Ethical Choices: Team Challenge** You submitted what you thought was a masterful report to your boss over three weeks ago. The report analyzes current department productivity and recommends several steps that you think will improve employee output without increasing individual workloads. Brilliant, you thought. But you haven't heard a word from your boss. Did you overstep your boundaries by making recommendations that might imply that she has not been doing a good job? Did you overwhelm her with your ideas? You'd like some feedback. In your last e-mail to her, you asked if she had read your report. So far you've received no reply. Then yesterday, you overhead the company vice president talk about some productivity changes in your department. The changes were ones that you had recommended in your report. Now you're worried that your boss submitted your report to senior management and will take full credit for your terrific ideas. What, if anything, should you do? Should you confront your boss about this? Should you ask to meet with the company vice president? Discuss this situation among your teammates and develop a solution to this sticky situation. Present your solution to the class, explaining the rationale behind your decision.

EXPAND YOUR KNOWLEDGE

Exploring the Best of the Web:

Preview Before You Produce, p. 469

One way to learn how to write more skillfully and effectively is by reading other writers' work. Look at different examples of professional business reports, and skim their contents to reinforce what you've learned in this chapter about structure, style, and organization. Let ixquick.com work for you. Log on and enter the phrase *business reports* in the search window, then choose a report and review it.

1. What is the purpose of the report you read? Who is its target audience? Explain why the structure and style of the report make it easy or difficult to follow the main idea.
2. What type of report did you read? Briefly describe the main message. Is the information well organized? If you answer "yes," explain how you can use the report as a guide for a report you might write. If you answer "no," explain why the report is not helpful.
3. Drawing on what you know about the qualities of a good business report, review a report and describe what features contribute to its readability.

Exploring the Web on Your Own

Review these chapter-related websites to learn more about writing reports and proposals.

1. Plan your way to profit by learning how to write effective business plans at Learn2 Write a Business Plan, www.learn2.com/06/0603/0603.asp.
2. Looking for the perfect transitional word? Cues and Transitions for the Reader, at www.mapnp.org/library/writing/cuestran.htm, has some recommendations to help you.
3. Develop a better business plan by following the advice at the Small Business Association website, www.sba.gov/starting/indexbusplans.html.

LEARN INTERACTIVELY

Interactive Study Guide

Visit "My Companion Website" at www.prenhall/bovee.com. For Chapter 14, take advantage of the interactive "Study Guide" to test your chapter knowledge. Get instant feedback on whether you need additional studying. Read the "Current Events" articles to get the latest on chapter topics, and complete the exercises—as specified by your instructor.

This site offers a variety of additional resources: The "Research Area" helps you locate a wealth of information to use in course assignments. You can even send a message to online research experts, who will help you find exactly the information you need. The "Study Hall" helps you succeed in this course. "Talk in the Hall" lets you leave messages and meet new friends online. If you have a question, you can "Ask the Tutor." And to get a better grade in this course, you can find more help at "Writing Skills," "Study Skills," and "Study Tips."

Grammar Diagnostic Tests

Review and reinforce your grammar and language skills by taking one of the four online diagnostic tests offered at our companion website, www.prenhall/bovee.com. The four tests cover a variety of topics, including spelling, capitals, punctuation, verbs, pronouns, adjectives, adverbs, sentence structure, sentence punctuation, clarity, word choice, style, organization skills, proofreading, and more. Submit your test and assess your competency. Then focus on improving areas where you are weak as you complete the exercises in this chapter.

CASES

SHORT FORMAL REPORTS REQUIRING NO ADDITIONAL RESEARCH

1. Giving it the online try: Report analyzing the advantages and disadvantages of corporate online learning As the newest member of the corporate training division of Paper Products, Inc., you have been asked to investigate and analyze the merits of establishing Internet courses (e-learning) for the company's employees. The president of your company thinks e-learning might be a good employee benefit as well as a terrific way for employees to learn new skills that they can use on the job. You've already done your research and here's a copy of your notes:

Online courses open up new horizons for working adults, who often find it difficult to juggle conventional classes with jobs and families.
Adults over 25 now represent nearly half of higher-ed students; most are employed and want more education to advance their careers.
Some experts believe that online learning will never be as good as face-to-face instruction.
Online learning requires no commute and is appealing for employees who travel regularly.
Enrollment in courses offered online by postsecondary institutions is expected to increase from 2 million students in 2001 to 5 million students in 2006.
E-learning is a cost-effective way to get better-educated employees.
Corporate spending on e-learning is expected to more than quadruple by 2005, to $18 billion.
At IBM, some 200,000 employees received education or training online last year, and 75 percent of the company's Basic Blue course for new managers is online. E-learning cut IBM's training bill by $350 million last year—mostly because online courses don't require travel.
There are no national statistics, but a recent report from the *Chronicle of Higher Education* found that institutions are seeing dropout rates that range from 20 to 50 percent for online learners. The research does not adequately explain why the dropout rates for e-learners are higher.
A recent study of corporate online learners reported that employees want the following things from their online courses: college credit or a certificate; active correspondence with an online facilitator who has frequent virtual office hours; access to 24-hour, seven-day-a-week technical support; and the ability to start a course anytime.

Corporate e-learners said that their top reason for dropping a course was lack of time. Many had trouble completing courses from their desktops because of frequent distractions caused by co-workers. Some said they could only access courses through the company's intranet, so they couldn't finish their assignments from home.
Besides lack of time, corporate e-learners cited the following as e-learning disadvantages: lack of management oversight; lack of motivation; problems with technology; lack of student support; individual learning preferences; poorly designed courses; substandard/inexperienced instructors.
A recent study by GE Capital found that finishing a corporate online course was dependent on whether managers gave reinforcement on attendance, how important employees were made to feel, and whether employee progress in the course was tracked.
Sun Microsystems found that interactivity can be a critical success factor for online courses. Company studies showed that only 25 percent of employees finish classes that are strictly self-paced. But 75 percent finish when give similar assignments and access to tutors through e-mail, phone, or threaded discussion.
Too often companies dump courses on their employees and wonder why they don't finish them.
Company managers must supervise e-learning just as they would any other important initiative.
For online learning to work, companies must develop a culture that takes online learning just as seriously as classroom training.
For many e-learners, studying at home is optimal. Whenever possible, companies should offer courses through the Internet or provide intranet access at home. Having employees studying on their own time will more than cover any added costs.

Corporate e-learning has flared into a $2.3 billion market, making it one of the fastest-growing segments of the education industry.
Rather than fly trainers to 7,000 dealerships, General Motors University now uses interactive satellite broadcasts to teach salespeople the best way to highlight features on the new Buick.
Fast and cheap, e-training can shave companies' training costs while it saves employees travel time.
Pharmaceutical companies such as Merck are conducting live, interactive classes over the web, allowing sales reps to learn about the latest product information at home rather than fly them to a conference center.
McDonald's trainers can log into Hamburger University to learn such skills as how to assemble a made-to-order burger or properly place the drink on a tray.
One obstacle to the spread of online corporate training is the mismatch between what employees really need—customized courses that are tailored to a firm's products and its unique corporate culture—and what employers can afford.
80 percent of companies prefer developing their own online training courses in-house. But creating even one customized e-course can take months, involve armies of experts, and cost anywhere from $25,000 to $50,000. Thus, most companies either stick with classroom training or buy generic courses on such topics as how to give performance appraisals, understanding basic business ethics, and so on. Employers can choose from a wide selection of noncustomized electronic courses.
For online learning to be effective, content must be broken into short "chunks" with lots of pop quizzes, online discussion groups, and other interactive features that let students demonstrate what they've learned. For instance, Circuit City's tutorial on digital camcorders consists of three 20-minute segments. Each contains audio demonstrations of how to handle customer product queries, tests on terminology, and "try-its" that propel trainees back onto the floor to practice what they've learned.

Your task: Write a short (3–5 page) memo report to the director of human resources, Kerry Simmons, presenting the advantages and disadvantages of e-learning and making a recommendation as to whether Paper Products, Inc., should invest time and money in training its employees this way. Be sure to organize your information so that it is clear, concise, and logically presented. Simmons likes to read the "bottom line" first, so be direct: Present your recommendation up front and support your recommendation with your findings.[7]

2. Climbing the ladder: Report summarizing data about corporate opportunities for women As the assistant director of human resources for a large financial services firm, you hear the concerns of many different employees. Lately, increasing numbers of female employees have been complaining about being passed up for promotions and management positions. They feel that male employees receive preferential treatment, even though many females are more highly qualified.

Table 14.1 indicates the results of a research study conducted by your staff. The study displays several key statistics pertaining to the male and female employees working for your company. Table 14.2 depicts how executives in Fortune 1000 companies perceive the barriers to female advancement, and Table 14.3 shows why female executives feel that women should be given more opportunities in the corporate world. These studies may help shed light on what could be viewed as a pattern of sex discrimination by your company. Because your company believes in equitable treatment for all employees, regardless of their gender, you believe your boss will be interested in this information.

Your task: Write a short report to the director of human resources, interpreting and summarizing the information in these tables. Suggest a possible course of action to remedy the situation at your company.[8]

3. Do it yourself: Report using statistical data to analyze industry trends Auto parts stores get a lot of their business from do-it-yourselfers, people who repair their cars themselves. Auto parts retailers would like to see the number of do-it-yourselfers increase. Auto mechanics, on the other hand, would prefer that drivers bring their cars into a repair shop when something goes wrong. As assistant to Rob Ebbin, a market analyst for the Automotive Parts and Accessories Association (APAA), you don't necessarily have a preference.

TABLE 14.1 Statistics for Male and Female Managers

Employee Statistics	*Female Managers*	*Male Managers*
Average number of years with the company	12.3	9.5
Average number of years of management experience	7.2	6.9
Percentage who have an MBA or other advanced degree	74%	63%
Average annual salary	$76,000	$84,000
Average number of times promoted	4.2	4.4

TABLE 14.2 Why Female Executives Don't Advance into Corporate Leadership Positions

Reason Cited	According to Female Executives	According to Male CEOs
Male stereotyping preconceptions	52%	25%
Exclusion from informal networks	49	15
Lack of general management/ line experience	47	82
Inhospitable corporate culture	35	18
Women not in pipeline long enough	29	64

TABLE 14.3 Why Female Executives Think Companies Should Increase the Number of Female Senior Managers

Reason	Agree	Srongly Agree
Women are large part of management talent pool	29%	69%
Women contribute unique perspective	32	61
Women are large part of consumer base	45	36
Companies have social responsibility	41	10
Shareholders want more executive women	41	7
Customers want more executive women	34	7
Lawsuits are increasing	40	5

After all, both do-it-yourselfers and professional mechanics have to buy auto parts. However, the APAA has asked you to summarize the results of some recent surveys aimed at better understanding the do-it-yourselfer segment of the auto parts market (see Table 14.4 and Figures 14.5–14.8). The report will be available to all association members.

Your task: Write a report to your boss that summarizes the survey results, pointing out some basic trends that would be of interest to both auto parts retailers and auto mechanics. Is the

TABLE 14.4 Top Five Reasons Do-It-Yourselfers Perform Car Maintenance Tasks

Reason	Percent
Saves money	67
Something I can do for myself	21
Saves time	12
Can make sure it's done right	10
Easy to do	9

FIGURE 14.5 Percentage of U.S. Car Owners Who Purchased Selected Auto Parts in the Past Year

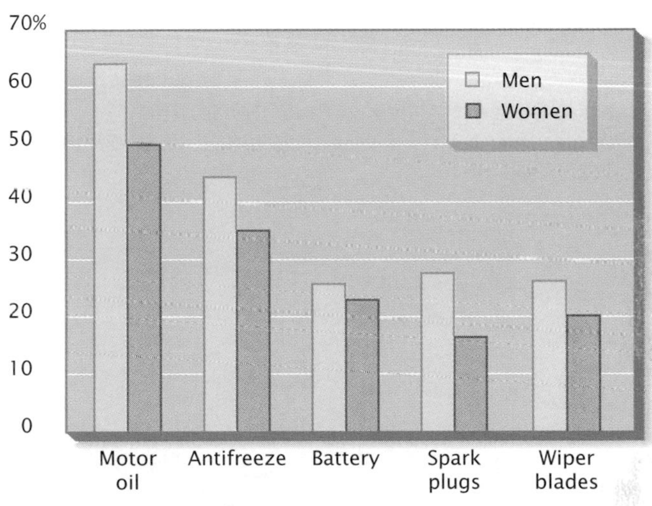

FIGURE 14.6 Percentage of Car Owners Who Perform Selected Maintenance Tasks Themselves, by Gender and Age (Note: Maintenance tasks include changing, adding, or installing any of the following: oil, oil filter, battery, antifreeze, spark plugs.)

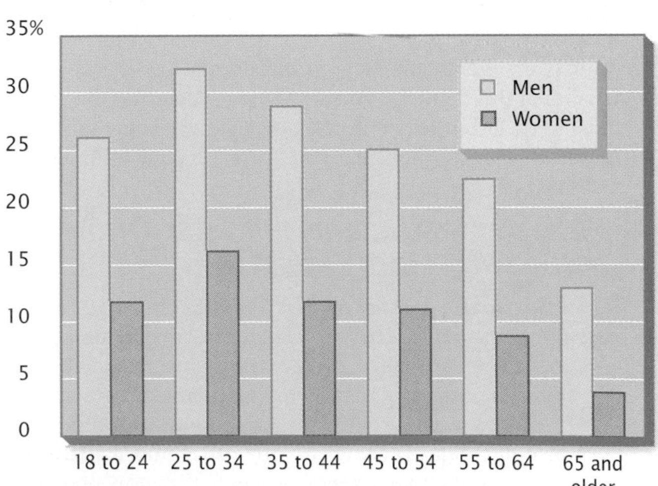

FIGURE 14.7 Median Age of Cars and Trucks in Operation in the United States, 1970–2000

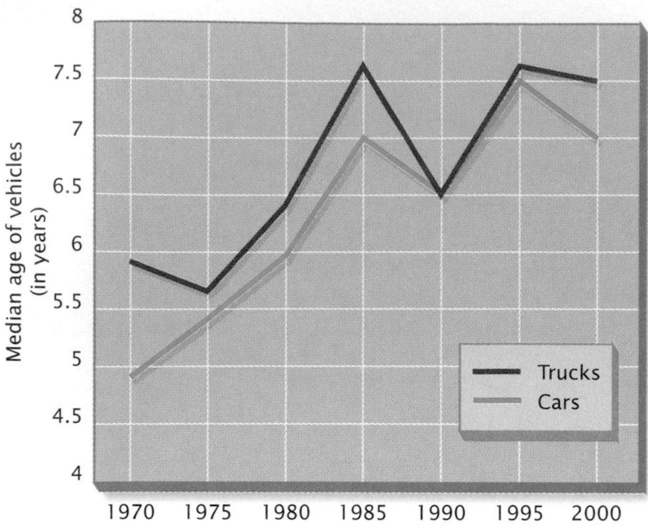

FIGURE 14.8 Billions of U.S. Dollars Spent on Replacement Parts and Service Repair, 1980–2000 (in 2000 Dollars)

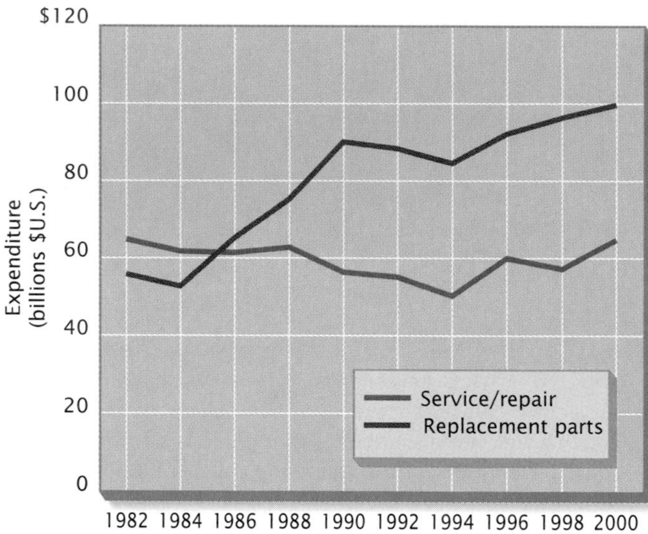

do-it-yourselfer segment growing? What are the key characteristics of this market segment? What products do they purchase most frequently? Be sure to acknowledge the source of any data in the tables and figures that you discuss in your summary.[9]

SHORT FORMAL REPORTS REQUIRING ADDITIONAL RESEARCH

4. Picking the better path: Research report assisting a client in a career choice You are employed by Open Options, a career-counseling firm, where your main function is to help clients make career choices. Today a client with the same name as yours (a truly curious coincidence!) came to your office and asked for help deciding between two careers—careers that you yourself had been interested in (an even greater coincidence!).

Your task: Do some research on the two careers and then prepare a short report that your client can study. Your report should compare at least five major areas, such as salary, working conditions, and education required. Interview the client to understand her or his personal preferences regarding each of the five areas. For example, what is the minimum salary the client will accept? By comparing the client's preferences with the research material you collect, such as salary data, you will have a basis for concluding which of the two careers is best. The report should end with a career recommendation. (Note: One good place for career-related information is the Occupational Outlook Handbook, published by the U.S. Bureau of Labor Statistics, available in print and online at stats.bls.gov/oco/ocoiab.htm.)

5. Selling overseas: Research report on the prospects for marketing a product in another country Select (a) a product and (b) a country. The product might be a novelty item that you own (an inexpensive but accurate watch or clock, a desk organizer, or a coin bank). The country should be one that you are not currently familiar with. Imagine that you are with the international sales department of the company that manufactures and sells the novelty item and that you are proposing to make it available in the country you have selected.

The first step is to learn as much as possible about the country where you plan to market the product. Check almanacs, encyclopedias, the Internet, and library databases for the most recent information, paying particular attention to descriptions of the social life of the inhabitants, their economic conditions, and cultural traditions that would encourage or discourage use of the product.

Your task: Write a short report that describes the product you plan to market abroad, briefly describes the country you have selected, indicates the types of people in this country who would find the product attractive, explains how the product would be transported into the country (or possibly manufactured there if materials and labor are available), recommends a location for a regional sales center, and suggests how the product should be sold. Your report is to be submitted to the chief operating officer of the company, whose name you can either make up or find in a corporate directory. The report should include your conclusions (how the product will do in this new environment) and your recommendations for marketing (steps the company should take immediately and those it should develop later).

6. The new way to advertise: Report summarizing Internet demographics The number of Internet users continues to grow rapidly in the United States and around the world. For marketers, the Internet represents a veritable goldmine of potential customers. Unlike traditional print and broadcast media, an Internet site can be seen around the world at any time. The trick, however, is to get your target customers to take the time to visit your page.

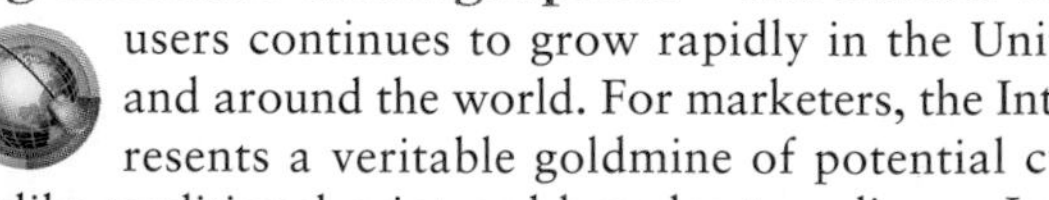

As marketing strategist for a specialty foods mail-order company, you have been toying with the idea of going online for quite some time. Your company, Martha's Kitchen, has been selling its cakes, cheeses, fruit, and candy in printed catalogs for a little over a decade and has built up a loyal clientele. Most of your customers are affluent adults age 30 and over, and 75 percent of them are women. Of course, large portions of your sales come during the holidays.

As more and more customers ask about ordering on the Internet, you feel compelled to establish an Internet presence. Nevertheless, you have heard conflicting reports about whether companies actually make any money by selling over the Internet. Moreover, developing a top-notch website will likely cost a lot of money. How can you sort through the hype to find real answers?

Your task: Write a short formal report to the director of marketing, explaining whether Martha's Kitchen should develop an Internet presence. You will need some solid figures about the demographics of Internet users, their surfing habits, the types of products they purchase online, and growth trends in online commerce. The following are good online resources to help you get started:

- The Internet Economy Indicators, www.internetindicators.com
- Ecommerce Times, www.ecommercetimes.com
- Business 2.0, www.business2.com
- ZD Net, www.zdnet.com (click on Tech Update)

These sites also contain links to other sites with additional useful information. As background, you may also find it helpful to look at some competitors' sites, such as Harry and David, www.harryanddavid.com, and Norm Thompson, www.normthompson.com.

On the basis of your findings, how do you think an Internet site will improve the company's bottom line? Use your imagination to fill in the details about the company.

LONG FORMAL REPORTS REQUIRING NO ADDITIONAL RESEARCH

7. Selling to Online America: Report analyzing the who, what, when, where, and why of U.S. online shoppers You are the administrative manager to Jerry Ordonez, the vice president of new business at First Horizon bank. Recently Ordonez has been flooded with requests to finance electronic commerce initiatives from both start-up e-tailers (those who will operate an online business for the first time) and existing retail stores that want to expand their physical-store sales by selling goods online. All loan applicants are claiming that the potential for online sales is very attractive. All claim to understand the online consumer quite well. Trouble is, Ordonez has received marketing reports with conflicting data: online sales projections, profiles of the online consumer, what the online consumer wants—none of it adds up. "Where did they get these data from?" he wonders. "I can't take their word for this. There's too much money at stake, so I did my own research—using reliable sources," he adds as he hands you a file. When you glance inside the file, you find Ordonez's research notes and statistics:

- Typical Internet users frequent an average of 10 websites per month, down from 15 websites one year ago, but they're visiting more pages per site, digging deeper rather than wider.
- Typical Internet users spend only 50 seconds at each webpage.
- 56 percent of the U.S. population (about 154 million people) accessed the Internet in November of this year—a 30 percent increase over the same month of the previous year. Newer research shows that 64 million U.S. adults go online *every* month.
- 56 percent of U.S. companies sell their products online, and this number is expected to rise.
- More than 60 percent of U.S. online consumers made at least one purchase on the web within a 90-day period this year.
- Average Internet user age is 39 years and rising.
- Small businesses that use the Internet to sell goods have grown 46 percent faster than those that do not.
- Many online shoppers behave like they do at the local mall: buying from the same merchants.
- Almost half of all U.S. adults with Internet access now purchase goods and services online.
- Offline, Americans tend to shop lightly during the week and then invade stores on the weekends. The opposite occurs online: Shoppers buy throughout the week, peaking on Wednesday, before fading on the weekend.
- Seasonal shopping patterns are different online. Traditional brick-and-mortar stores record the lion's share of their sales during the Christmas season, but most e-tailers operate at a steady pace throughout the year: less of a high in December, less of a low in January.
- Despite studies showing that the Internet gap is shrinking between ethnic groups, differences remain, as suggested by Table 14.5.
- Women continue to purchase online at a slightly higher rate than men (73 percent versus 71 percent).
- American teenagers actually spend about 30 percent less time on the web than adults.
- Airline tickets is the largest category of goods purchased on line. Other top categories of items purchased online are listed in Table 14.6.
- Consumers spent $101 billion online in 2001, $59.7 billion online in 2000, and $30.1 billion in 1999. Consumer online spending is expected to reach $167 billion in 2002, $250 billion in 2003, and $428 billion by 2004.

TABLE 14.5 Online Behavior by Ethnic Group for 10 Key Activities

Activity	*Whites*	*Blacks*	*Hispanics*
E-mail	93%	88%	87%
Get product information	73	71	73
Get travel information	65	64	63
Get weather information	63	53	55
Surf just for fun	61	73	69
Get news	59	62	58
Do research for school	54	65	59
Do research for work	49	48	51
Buy a product	48	35	42
Buy a travel product	29	28	29

TABLE 14.6 Top 15 Items Purchased Online Monthly

Item	Dollars (in thousands)	Percent
Airline tickets	$746,170	21.60
Hotel reservations	445,186	12.89
Other	365,567	10.58
Computer hardware	335,784	9.72
Apparel	224,743	6.50
Consumer electronics	191,878	5.55
Car rental	188,620	5.46
Toys/videogames	162,449	4.70
Books	151,561	4.39
Health and beauty	121,444	3.52
Music	118,318	3.42
Software	112,759	3.26
Videos	109,814	3.18
Sporting goods	92,005	2.66
Food/beverages	88,680	2.57
Total	**$3,454,978**	**100.00%**

- Online consumers want satisfactory fulfillments: They want to receive the correct ordered items in a timely way, and they want an efficient and simple way to make returns, if necessary. A recent survey of online buyers found that 83 percent would like to be able to return purchases at offline stores, 59 percent would like to buy products online and pick them up at an offline store; one survey found that 71 percent of online consumers value convenience when making a purchase online, compared with 29 percent who value price savings.
- As an alternative to crowded shopping malls, buying online provides speed, simplicity, and comparison shopping capabilities.
- A survey of online purchasers reports that the following percentage of respondents said these factors influenced their online buying decision: shipping fees (92 percent), prices (92 percent), product availability (86 percent), special promotions or incentives (76 percent), product selection (69 percent), order tracking (66 percent), clearly identified delivery time (65 percent), return policy (63 percent), ease of using website (62 percent), website performance/speed (51 percent).
- More than 60 percent of online shoppers abandon their shopping carts before reaching the credit card transaction.
- A report cited these reasons that online consumers abandon their shopping carts: high shipping prices (72 percent), comparison shopping or browsing (61 percent), changed mind (56 percent), saving items for later purchase (51 percent), total cost of items is too high (43 percent), checkout process is too long (41 percent), checkout requires too much personal information (35 percent), site requires registration before purchase (34 percent), site is unstable or unreliable (31 percent), checkout process is confusing (27 percent).
- A survey showed that 47 percent of online consumers said that having a physical store makes a difference in where they shop, and 53 percent said it doesn't matter.
- A survey showed that online shoppers prefer the following promotions: savings/discount (67 percent), free shipping (25 percent), free gift with purchase (8 percent).

Your task: Use Jerry Ordonez's research to write a formal informational report profiling today's online consumer. Organize and present your information using three to four categories and use headings so that Ordonez can easily compare your profile to those submitted by loan applicants. Don't worry about citing the information sources; Ordonez did the research and he is confident that he selected only reliable sources. Ordonez complimented you on your use of tables and charts in the last report you submitted to him, so he's probably expecting more of the same.[10]

8. Software in a hard market: Report on selling software in China Breaking into the U.S. software market can be tough, especially when your product competes with well-known brands in established categories. As marketing director for a small (22 employees) developer of financial management software, you are keenly aware of how difficult it is to take on domestic market leaders such as Quicken and Microsoft Money. Fortunately, you also know that greater opportunities may exist for you in international markets.

Your company is considering marketing its product in China, where consumers are less brand-loyal and more likely to try new products. The Chinese economy has boomed over the past decade, growing at a rate of 9 percent per year. Research also indicates that a growing percentage of China's 1.2 billion consumers make more money today than ever before. In addition, software sales in China totaled $1.35 bil-

TABLE 14.7 Profile of China's Consumers

Market Segment	*Nouveau Riche (Baofahu)*	*Yuppies (Dushi Yapishi)*	*Salary Men (Bongxin Jieceng)*	*Working Poor (Qionglaogong)*
Size	200,000	60 million	330 million	800 million
Geographic location	Coastal urban areas	Major urban areas	Urban areas	Rural areas, small towns, urban areas
Average annual household income ($U.S.)	Over $5,000	$1,800–$5,000	$1,150–$1,799	Less than $1,150
Age	30–65	25–45	18–60	15–65
Highest level of education	Various levels	College	High school	Elementary school
Type of employment	Commercial/ entrepreneurial, entertainment, government	Managerial, professional, technical	Low-skilled office work, factory work, teaching	Manual labor, farming, migrant work
Lifestyle characteristics	Wheeling and dealing, wining and dining	Frequent travel and dining out	8-to-5 daily workweek, limited budget, few purchases	Struggling to make ends meet
Consumer readiness	High	Moderate	Low	Minimal
Innovativeness	Trendsetters	Opinion leaders	Emulators	Laggards
Risk aversion	Low	Moderate	High	Very high

lion in 2000, representing a 23 percent jump over the previous year, and analysts expect the growth to continue. Because your product can be used for both business and home financial management, China looks like a ripe market.

Of course, the Chinese market also has its problems. For one thing, competition is fierce. One Chinese firm, User Friend, markets an accounting software package that commands 40 percent of the market. Furthermore, economic growth slowed this past year to about 7 percent, and studies show that consumers are feeling a sense of uncertainty as a result of volatility in Asian markets. Consumer saving this year is up 17 percent over last year, while retail sales growth has slowed from almost 40 percent to just under 10 percent.

Another concern is avoiding software piracy. China has a reputation for being lax about enforcing patent and copyright laws. According to a recent study by the Business Software Alliance and the Software Publisher's Association, 96 percent of all software units in use in China are pirated.

On the other hand, the new financial concerns of Chinese consumers might actually present an opportunity for your company. After all, you are marketing software to help consumers and businesses manage their money more wisely. Moreover, Chinese domestic demand is expected to increase. And, according to reliable sources, China will guide investment from foreign companies into such areas as electronic information, biotechnology, new materials, chemical industry, and construction materials—all of which could boost demand for financial software.

Your task: Write an analytical report on the current market conditions in China. Make a recommendation as to whether your company should attempt to sell its financial management software in China. You have already gathered a lot of data from a variety of sources (see Tables 14.7–14.10 and Figures 14.9–14.11). Now you must interpret the data and make clear recommendations. Identify your target customer and make projections about how much software you think the company can sell over the next three years. Assuming that the product sells for the equivalent of $45, how much revenue do you expect the Chinese market to generate for your company?[11]

TABLE 14.8 Selected Responses to a Survey of 800 Urban Consumers in China

Purchase Practices of Respondents	*Percent*
Plan to buy or replace a personal computer in the next 3 years	26
Always look for new products when they shop	75
Try to cut down on expenses wherever they can	68
Saving more than they did a year ago	58
Try to buy Chinese brands whenever they can	71

TABLE 14.9 Key China Economic Sectors as Percentage of GDP

Sector	1976	1986	1996	1997	2000
Agriculture	33.2%	27.1%	20.2%	19.7%	15.0%
Industry (all)	42.3	44.0	49.0	50.8	50.0
Services	24.5	28.9	30.8	29.5	35.0

TABLE 14.10 Additional Economic Indicators for China

Economic Indicators	1976	1986	1996	1997	2000
Gross domestic product (GDP) ($U.S. billions)	148.8	295.7	825.0	935.0	1,075.0
Exports of goods and services ($U.S. millions)	7,383	29,583	171,700	207,800	232,000
Imports of goods and services ($U.S. millions)	7,125	37,472	154,100	162,700	197,000

FIGURE 14.9 Percentage of Population That Uses Selected Durable Products, Beijing, Shanghai, Chengdu, and Guangzhou (Major Urban Centers), 2000

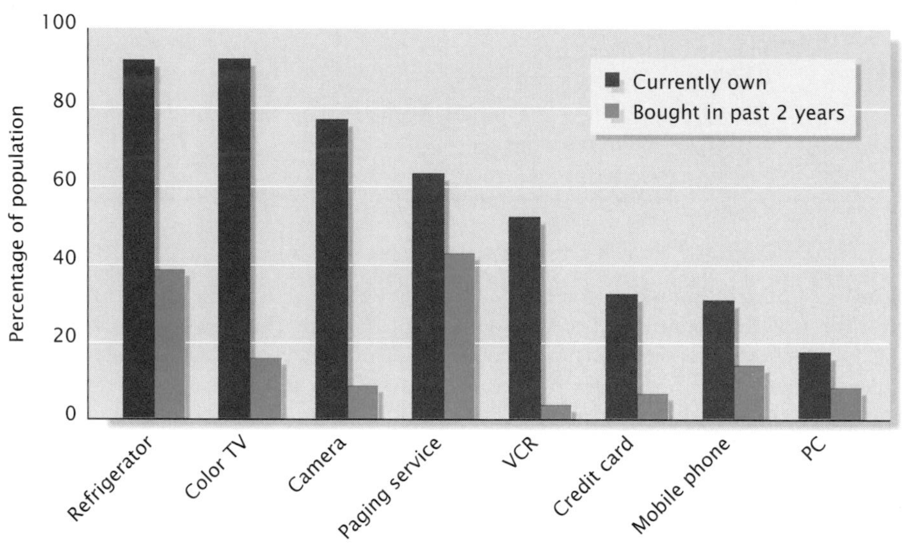

FIGURE 14.10 China's Retail-Sales Growth Rate

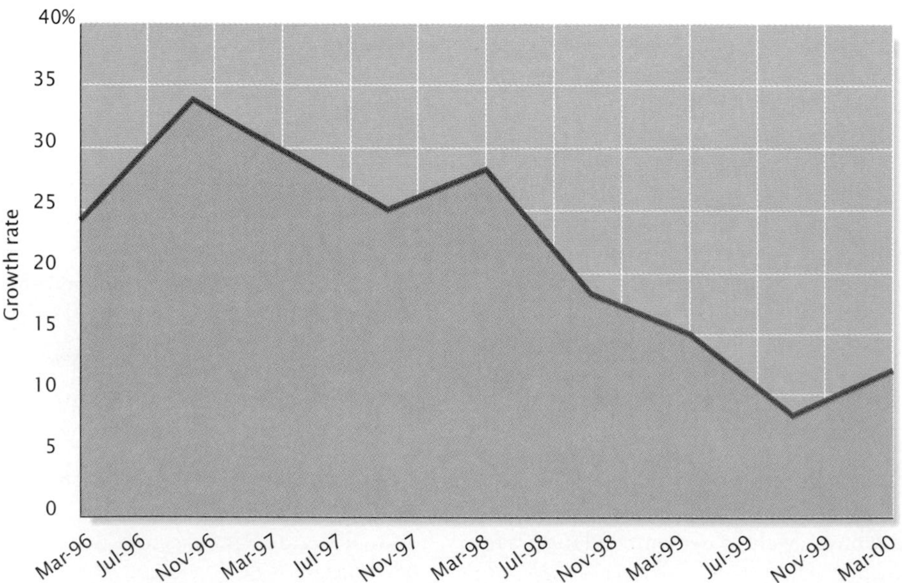

FIGURE 14.11 Software Market in China, 2000 (Total Software Sales $1.35 Billion)

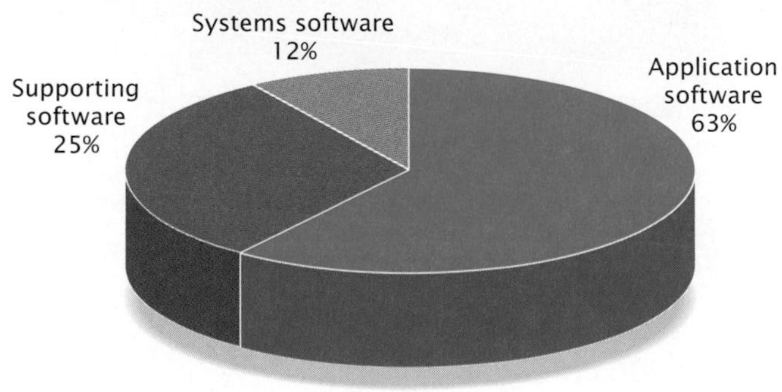

LONG FORMAL REPORTS REQUIRING ADDITIONAL RESEARCH

9. Face-off: Informational report comparing and contrasting two companies in the same industry Your boss, Dana Hansell, has been searching for some solid companies to personally invest in for the long term. After reviewing security analysts' reports and financial statements for several candidates, Hansell has narrowed the list to these leading industry competitors:

- Boeing; Airbus (aerospace and airline industry)
- Gateway; Dell (computers and software industry)
- Merrill Lynch; Schwab (finance, banking, and insurance industry)
- Barnes and Noble; Amazon.com (book industry—retail and wholesale)
- UPS; FedEx (Trucking and freight industry)

According to Hansell, all of these candidates have about the same financial outlook for the future, so she is not interested in obtaining more financial performance detail. Instead, your boss is looking for more substantive information, such as:

- Fundamental philosophical differences in management styles, launching and handling products and services, marketing products and services, and approach to e-commerce that sets one rival company apart from the other
- Future challenges that each competitor faces
- Important decisions made by the two competitors and how those decisions affected their company
- Fundamental differences in each company's vision of their industry's future (for instance, do they both agree on what consumers want, what products to deliver, and so on?)
- Specific competitive advantages held by each rival
- Past challenges each competitor has faced and how each met those challenges
- Strategic moves made by one rival that might affect the other
- Company success stories
- Brief company background information (Hansell already has some from the brokers' reports)
- Brief comparative statistics such as annual sales, market share, number of employees, number of stores, types of equipment, number of customers, sources of revenue, and so on

Hansell has heard that you are the department's most proficient researcher and an effective writer. You have been assigned the task of preparing a formal, long informational report for her. You need not make a recommendation or come to any conclusions; Hansell will do that based on the informational content of your report.

Your task: Select two industry competitors from the above list (or another list provided by your instructor) and write a long formal informational report comparing and contrasting how the two companies are addressing the topics outlined by Hansell. Of course, not every topic will apply to each company, and some will be more important than others—depending on the companies you select. Hansell will invest in only one of the two companies in your report. (Note: Because these topics require considerable research, your instructor may choose to make this a team project.)

10. Is there any justice? Report critiquing legislation Plenty of people complain about their state legislators, but few are specific about their complaints. Here's your chance.

Your task: Write a long formal report about a law that you believe should not have been enacted or should be enacted. Be objective. Write the report using specific facts to support your beliefs. Reach conclusions and offer your recommendation at the end of the report. As a final step, send a copy of the report to an appropriate state official or legislator.

11. Travel opportunities: Report comparing two destinations You are planning to take a two-week trip abroad sometime within the next year. Because there are a couple of destinations that appeal to you, you are going to have to do some research before you can make a decision.

Your task: Prepare a lengthy comparative study of two countries that you would like to visit. Begin by making a list of important questions you will need to answer. Do you want a relaxing vacation or an educational experience? What types of services will you require? What will your transportation needs be? Where will you have the least difficulty with the language? Using resources in your library, the Internet, and perhaps travel agencies, analyze the suitability of these two destinations with respect to your own travel criteria. At the end of the report, recommend the better country to visit this year.

12. Secondary sources: Report based on library research Perhaps one of the following questions has been on your mind.

a. Which is the best college at which to pursue a graduate degree in business?
b. How can you organize a student group to make your campus safer at night?
c. Which of three companies that you would like to work for has the most responsible environmental policies?
d. What market factors led to the development of a product that you use frequently, and how are those factors different today?
e. Which three U.S. companies have had the best stock price performance over the past 30 years and why?
f. What are the best small-business opportunities available today?

Your task: Answer one of those questions, using secondary sources for information. Be sure to document your sources in the correct form. Give conclusions and recommendations in your report.

13. Doing business abroad: Report summarizing the social and business customs of a foreign country Your company would like to sell its products overseas. Before they begin negotiating on the international horizon, however, management must have a clear understanding of the social and business customs of the countries where they intend to do business.

Your task: Choose a non-English-speaking country and write a long formal report summarizing the country's social and business customs. Review Chapter 3 and use that chapter's "Checklist: Doing Business Abroad" as a guide for the types of information you should include in your report.

FORMAL PROPOSALS

14. Brewing up sales: Proposal to supply coffee to Peter's Doughnuts You are the president of Lighthouse Roasters, a small but growing coffee-roasting company. The company has made a name for itself by offering fresh, dark-roasted gourmet coffees. However, unlike Starbucks and other competitors, Lighthouse Roasters does not operate its own stores. Instead, it sells roasted gourmet coffee beans to retailers such as restaurants, bakeries, and latte carts. These retailers then use the Lighthouse beans to make their coffee beverages.

Lighthouse's total cost to produce a pound of roasted gourmet coffee is $2.75. The company wholesales its roasted gourmet beans for an average price of $4.50 per pound. Competitors that sell nongourmet-variety coffees typically charge about $3.00 per pound. However, the average price of a gourmet coffee beverage is $1.50, about $.50 more than beverages made with regular coffee (including both brewed coffee and espresso drinks). Each pound of coffee yields about 40 beverages.

Peter's Doughnuts, which owns 76 doughnut shops across 13 states, has seen its sales decline in recent months after Starbucks began opening stores in Peter's markets. Starbucks not only sells gourmet coffee, it carries a selection of pastries that offer alternatives to doughnuts. Peter's management figures that by offering gourmet coffee, it will win back customers who like doughnuts but who also want darker-roasted coffees. Therefore, Peter's has invited you to submit a proposal to be its exclusive supplier of coffee. Peter's anticipates that it will need 400 pounds of coffee a month during the colder months (October–March) and 300 pounds during the warmer months (April–September). The company has said it wants to pay no more than $3.75 per pound for Lighthouse coffee.

Your task: Using your imagination to supply the details, write a proposal describing your plan to supply the coffee. Considering your costs, will you meet Peter's pricing demands, or will you attempt to gain a higher price?

15. Creative marketing: Proposal to sell educational/advertising materials to schools Reaching children poses significant challenges to marketers because children typically don't listen to the radio or read magazines or newspapers. They do watch television, but television ads can be expensive. However, marketers have a new opportunity to get their messages out to children, thanks to Jeff Lederman. His company, Planet Report, targets youngsters by placing ads where they are most likely to be noticed—in the classroom. The ads are part of teaching materials that Planet Report distributes free to schools. These materials usually take the form of posters displaying information about current events. Each month, the company sends teachers a new poster containing tidbits of current news items and facts about science, politics, and culture. Along with this information are attractive ads for Disney movies, ABC television programs, Vans sneakers, and other products that appeal to young consumers. Lederman and an employee create two versions of each poster, one aimed at high school students and the other at elementary or middle school students. Teachers who use the posters also receive prepared questions they can use to test the students on the information in the posters. Besides questions about the factual information on the posters, the tests contain questions about the ads. Planet Report also distributes bookmarks with ads printed on them that teachers can give out as prizes or awards.

At a time when schools are facing tough financial constraints, Planet Report's strategy can be a real win-win situation. "Teachers get something they can use and a marketing purpose is served," says Lederman. Many teachers like the posters because they encourage students to read and learn. As one teacher who uses the posters says, "Whatever we can get that encourages voluntary reading is a plus."

However, not everyone supports the idea. Critics say that ads don't belong in the classroom. They complain that the posters distract students from their studies and encourage a commercial culture. Moreover, including test questions on the commercial content of the posters may cause confusion about what is most important for students to learn. One fourth-grade teacher points out that his students rarely miss questions about the ads, but they are likely to forget some of the other information.

Your task: Write a proposal that Jeff Lederman can use to convince school administrators to adopt Planet Report's posters in their schools. Provide details such as how the posters will benefit students. Keep in mind that not everyone supports the idea of advertising in schools, even if it is linked to effective learning materials. How will you address the concerns of your critics and convince your audience that your product is good for both students and schools?[12]

16. Put me in, Coach: Proposal to provide executive coaching services In today's fast-paced business world, companies are spending increasing sums of money on employee training and development. As part of this trend, many companies are turning to executive coaches to help make their managers more effective and productive. Coaches work with employees both one-on-one and in groups. They may provide guidance on how to communicate more effectively, build stronger leadership abilities, work with teams, develop career goals that mesh with company goals, embrace change, and develop the additional skills they need to move up the corporate ladder. Many companies offer coaching as a perk to managers. Some, such as financial services giant Chase Manhattan, even tie coaching to employee performance reviews. What's more, companies are willing to pay anywhere between $75 and $400 an hour for a coach's services.

Jean Isberg is an executive coach who has been increasing her clientele steadily for almost a decade. Isberg, a former sales executive in the information technology field, made a career change in the early 1990s by opening her own sales training business. After a while, she noticed that she was most effective at helping her clients understand themselves and their role in their organizations. Following her talents, Isberg began to coach executives about how to be more effective in their lives and in their work. Soon she began to focus exclusively on coaching female executives, and she named her company Executive Coaching for Women.

Isberg meets with her clients over a nine-week period in sessions lasting 60 to 90 minutes. She also gives reading, writing, and thinking exercises to be completed between sessions. And once each quarter, clients are invited to participate in group review sessions. Isberg tells her clients that to reach their career goals, they must know what they really want, make sure they have the training necessary to make their goals realistic, let others know they are capable, and let others help them achieve success.

Isberg operates her business from her home, renting office and conference space for meetings as needed. But low overhead doesn't necessarily mean a low price; Isberg's services start at $3,000.

Until now, Isberg has counseled clients on a one-on-one basis, with the client paying the cost herself. However, one of Isberg's clients, the vice president of marketing and sales at international telecommunications company Cable & Wireless USA, is so pleased with the coaching she received that she has asked Isberg to submit a proposal to provide coaching services to the company's top female managers. The client believes that many of these managers have yet to realize their full potential in their work and that with Isberg's help, they will become far more effective managers. However, Isberg will need a top-notch proposal in order to get the rest of the company's top brass to buy in and foot the bill. Isberg has delegated the task of drafting the proposal to you, her business development coordinator.

Your task: Jean Isberg has given you the important information about her skills and about the clients she is seeking. Now she needs you to draft a proposal that will land her the Cable & Wireless contract. Give special consideration to how you can help Isberg distinguish herself from other executive coaches the company has dealt with. Use your imagination to fill in the details.[13]

PART 6

Designing and Delivering Oral Presentations

CHAPTER 15

Planning, Writing, and Completing Oral Presentations

CHAPTER 16

Enhancing Your Oral Presentations with Electronic Slides and Overhead Transparencies

Planning, Writing, and Completing Oral Presentations

After studying this chapter, you will be able to

1 *Explain how planning oral presentations differs from planning written documents*

2 *Describe the five tasks that go into organizing oral presentations*

3 *Delineate the tasks involved in developing the three main parts of your oral presentation*

4 *Highlight four delivery methods for oral presentations*

5 *List nine ways to overcome your anxiety and feel more confident*

6 *Discuss six ways effective speakers maintain control during the question-and-answer period*

COMMUNICATION CLOSE-UP AT ANDERSON BUSINESS RESOURCES

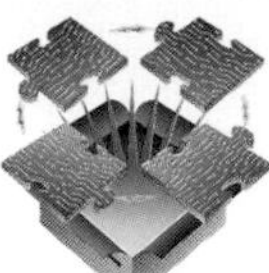

When Leanne Anderson prepares an oral presentation, she doesn't worry about whether her audience is going to like her. Instead, she focuses on whether she will offer useful information to her audience. As the owner of Anderson Business Resources, she helps businesspeople become better public speakers by training them to focus on their audience's needs.

Anderson believes that knowing your audience is the most important element of a successful speech. "If you don't know whom you are talking to," she says, "the content becomes much less important and your message won't be heard." Anderson learned this lesson firsthand when delivering a presentation in Cairo about improving corporate image. "I spent too much time on domestically oriented topics," she recalls, "so my message wasn't global enough for that audience." Anderson admits that doing her homework in advance would have made her a more effective speaker. By understanding the members of your audience, "you can create examples specifically for them, personalize your message, avoid sensitive topics, and appeal to the most important issues on their minds."

Of course, it also helps to know who is speaking before or after you, what their topic is, and what their style is like. Anderson learned this lesson when she had the difficult task of delivering a speech immediately after a talk by presidential candidate Ross Perot. He was a tough act to follow, and Anderson was not prepared. Now she tries to find out as much as possible about the message and style of anyone speaking before or after her. This preparation allows her to tailor her own presentation so that it's fresh and interesting for the audience. "If you follow a great speaker and you don't have that same punch," she advises, "don't compete—be different."

One way to be different, advises Anderson, is to use anecdotes, stories, quotations, and statistics to distinguish yourself and hold the audience's attention. Another way is to get the audience to participate in a presentation by asking questions or soliciting opinions. Writing well-organized material that is clear, concise, and focused is another good way to make your presentation stand out from others. So Anderson advocates being a ruthless editor.

"Most of us fall in love with our own words, and our presentations get too long and complicated," says Anderson, who advises speakers to eliminate anything that is not absolutely necessary. She recommends that you organize your speech by creating a storyboard, much as advertisers do when developing a commercial. Then examine each part of the speech to determine whether and how it is related to the core message. If it's irrelevant, cut it. "Economy of language is the real key to good communication," she says. "That means choosing the best way of saying something to get the desired result."

In fact, getting results is one of the many reasons Anderson's clients seek her advice. She tells them: "Fine-tune your public speaking skills . . . Don't wing it. Practice at least eight times by yourself and in front of others who will be honest with you. The more you practice, the more confident and relaxed you will be." And to make a really lasting impression, Anderson encourages clients to inject their personality into the speech. "Have some fun with it," she says. "Stop concentrating on 'Will they like me?' and instead focus on 'What will they gain from hearing me?'"[1] ■

Being yourself, having fun, and letting your personality shine through are some of the ways speakers can make a lasting impression on their audience, advises Leanne Anderson.

THE THREE-STEP ORAL PRESENTATION PROCESS

Like Leanne Anderson, chances are you'll have the opportunity to deliver a number of oral presentations throughout your career. You may not speak before large audiences of employees or the media, but you'll certainly be expected to present ideas to your colleagues, make sales presentations to potential customers, or engage in other kinds of spoken communication. For instance, if you're in the human resources department, you may give orientation briefings to new employees or explain company policies, procedures, and benefits at assemblies. If you're a department supervisor, you may conduct training programs. Or, if you're a problem solver or consultant, you may give analytical presentations on the merits of various proposals.

The content and style of speeches and presentations vary, depending on your purpose.

Regardless of your job or the purpose of your presentation, you will be more effective if you adopt an oral presentation process that follows these three steps (see Figure 15.1):

1. Plan your presentation.
2. Write your presentation.
3. Complete your presentation.

The three-step oral presentation process is quite similar to the three-step writing process.

FIGURE 15.1 The Three-Step Oral Presentation Process

Planning

Analyze
Study your purpose, lay out your schedule, and profile your audience.

Investigate
Gather needed information through formal or informal research methods.

Adapt
Adapt your presentation to occasion and audience; then establish a good relationship with your audience.

Writing

Organize
Define your main idea, limit the scope, choose your approach, prepare your outline, and decide on style.

Compose
Compose your presentation, ensuring that the introduction, body, close, and question-and-answer period all accomplish the necessary tasks for an oral medium.

Completing

Revise
Edit presentation for content, conciseness, and clarity.

Produce
Review everything for typos, improper grammar, and mechanical errors.

Proofread
Practice your presentation, check the location, overcome your anxiety, and field questions responsibly.

STEP 1: PLANNING ORAL PRESENTATIONS

Learning Objective 1

Explain how planning oral presentations differs from planning written documents

Preparing oral presentations requires some special communication techniques to ensure your audience hears what you say.

Planning oral presentations is much like planning any other business message: It requires analyzing your purpose and your audience, investigating necessary information, and adapting your message to the occasion and your audience so that you can establish a good relationship. However, because presentations are delivered orally under relatively public circumstances, they require a few special communication techniques. For one thing, a presentation is a onetime event; your audience cannot leaf back through printed pages to review something you said earlier. You must make sure that audience members will hear what you say and remember it. To do so, you must capture their attention immediately and keep them interested. Otherwise, you'll lose them, and chances are you won't get them back. So when you prepare your presentation, begin by defining your purpose clearly and thinking of ways to engage your audience.

You usually give an oral presentation for one of four purposes.

The four basic purposes for giving a presentation are to inform, to persuade, to motivate, and to entertain. Here are sample statements of purpose for business presentations:

- To inform the accounting department of the new remote data-access policy
- To explain to the executive committee the financial ramifications of OmniGroup's takeover offer
- To persuade potential customers that our bank offers the best commercial banking services for their needs
- To motivate the sales force to increase product sales by 10 percent

The purpose of your oral presentation will govern the content you include and the style in which you present the content.

Most of your presentations or speeches will be informative, requiring a straightforward statement of the facts. If you're involved in a marketing or sales position, however, you'll probably be writing and delivering quite a few persuasive presentations and speeches using the organizational and writing techniques discussed in Chapter 9. Motivational speeches tend to be more specialized, so many companies bring in outside professional speakers to handle this type of presentation. Entertainment speeches are

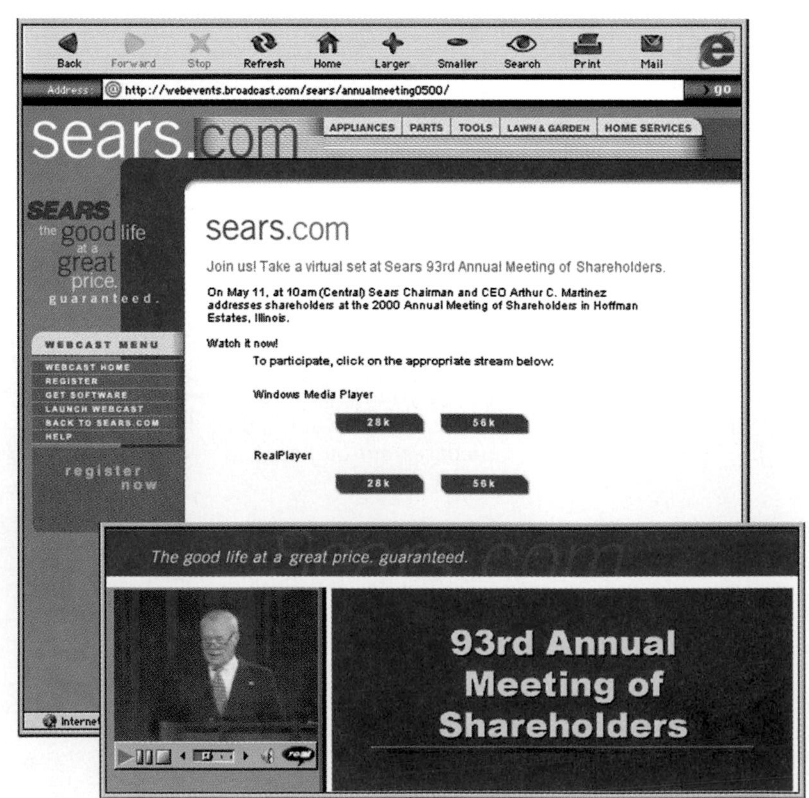

Companies such as Sears, Avon, Nike, and America Online use webcast speeches to make live announcements of financial news, new products, and management changes, as shown on the Yahoo! Broadcast site. Unlike ordinary speeches that address a particular audience at a particular time and place, webcast speeches can be viewed and listened to long after the speaker has left the podium.

Communicating Across Cultures

Five Tips for Making Presentations Around the World

In any successful oral presentation, getting your message across to an audience requires clear communication. But how can you communicate successfully with members of an international audience—especially if their fluency in your language ranges from expert to novice?

1. **Speak slowly and distinctly.** The most common complaint of international audiences is that English speakers talk too fast. If you speak too rapidly, your less fluent listeners will be lost. Articulate every word carefully. Emphasize consonants for clarity, and pause frequently so that the audience will have time to absorb each key point.
2. **Repeat key words and phrases.** When audiences are less familiar with your language, they need to hear important information more than once. In addition, they may not be familiar with synonyms, so refer to key points in the same way throughout your presentation. If you introduce the concept of *benefits,* for example, continue to use the same word. Don't refer to *advantages* later on.
3. **Aim for clarity.** Keep your message simple. Eliminate complex sentence structure, abbreviations, and acronyms. Avoid two-word verbs such as *look over* and *check out.* Such verbs are confusing because the definition of each separate word differs from the meaning of the two words combined. For clearer communication, use one specific term (substitute *review* for *look over; examine* for *check out; write* for *jot down; visit* for *drop by*). Stay away from cultural idioms, such as *once in a blue moon,* which may be unfamiliar to an international audience.
4. **Communicate with body language.** Establish a relationship with your audience through strong eye contact. And don't forget to smile! Smiles are universally recognized facial expressions. Moreover, multilingual audiences pay close attention to a speaker's body language to get clues about the meanings of unfamiliar words. For example, prepositions can often be confusing to multilingual listeners, so use gestures to illustrate the meaning of words such as *up, down,* or *under.*
5. **Support your oral message with visual aids.** For most audiences, visual messages support and clarify spoken words. As Chapter 16 discusses in detail, handouts, flip charts, overheads, and electronic slides can help you describe your key points. To eliminate problems with rapid speech, unclear pronunciations, or strange accents, prepare captions both in English and in your audience's native language. Avoid confusion about quantities by presenting numbers in graphs or pie charts and by converting financial figures into local currency.

Career Applications

1. As marketing director for an international corporation, you will be making a presentation to the company's marketing representatives in Germany. How will you communicate company goals and sales projections clearly?
2. Make a list of 10 two-word verbs. How does the meaning of each separate word differ from the definition of the combined words? Replace each two-word verb with a single, specific word that will be clearer to an international audience.

perhaps the rarest in the business world; they are usually limited to after-dinner speeches and to speeches at conventions or retreats.

Regardless of your purpose, you will be more effective if you keep your audience interested in your message. To do so, you must understand who your audience members are and what they need. If you're involved in selecting the audience or speaking to a group of peers at work, you'll certainly have information about their characteristics. But in many cases, you'll be speaking to a group of people you know little about, so you'll want to investigate their needs and characteristics before showing up to speak. You can ask your host or some other contact person for help with audience analysis, and you can supplement that information with some educated estimates of your own.

Gear the content, organization, and style of your message to your audience's size, background, attitudes, and interests.

As Leanne Anderson points out, analyzing your audience is particularly important when addressing people from other cultures (see "Communicating Across Cultures: Five Tips for Making Presentations Around the World"). For a reminder of how to analyze an audience, review Chapter 4's "Develop an Audience Profile" and this chapter's "Checklist: Audience Analysis." For even more insight into audience evaluation (including emotional and cultural issues), consult a good public-speaking textbook.

✓ CHECKLIST: AUDIENCE ANALYSIS

A. Determine audience size and composition
1. Estimate how many people will attend.
2. Consider whether they have some political, religious, professional, or other affiliation in common.
3. Analyze the mix of men and women, age ranges, socioeconomic and ethnic groups, occupations, and geographic regions represented.

B. Predict the audience's probable reaction
1. Analyze why audience members are attending the presentation.
2. Determine the audience's general attitude toward the topic: interested, moderately interested, unconcerned, open-minded, or hostile.
3. Analyze the mood that people will be in when you speak to them.
4. Find out what kind of backup information will most impress the audience: technical data, historical information, financial data, demonstrations, samples, and so on.
5. Consider whether the audience has any biases that might work against you.
6. Anticipate possible objections or questions.

C. Gauge the audience's level of understanding
1. Analyze whether everybody has the same background and experience.
2. Determine what the audience already knows about the subject.
3. Decide what background information the audience will need to better understand the subject.
4. Consider whether the audience is familiar with your vocabulary.
5. Analyze what the audience expects from you.
6. Think about the mix of general concepts and specific details you will need to present.

STEP 2: WRITING ORAL PRESENTATIONS

You may never actually write out a presentation word for word. But that doesn't mean that developing its content will be any easier or quicker than preparing a written document. Speaking intelligently about a topic may actually involve more work and more time than preparing a written document about the same topic.

Organizing Your Oral Presentation

Learning Objective 2

Describe the five tasks that go into organizing oral presentations

What you know about your audience affects your main idea, scope, approach, outline, and style.

Every facet of organizing your oral presentation is driven by what you know about your audience. For example, if you're organizing a sales presentation, focus on how much your product will benefit the people in your audience, not on how great the product is. If you're explaining a change in medical benefits for company employees, address the concerns your audience is likely to have, such as cost and quality of care. You should organize an oral message just as you would a written message, by focusing on your audience as you define your main idea, limit your scope, choose your approach, prepare your outline, and decide on the most effective style for your presentation.

Define the Main Idea

The main idea points out how the audience can benefit from your message.

What is the one message you want audience members to walk away with? What do you want them to do after listening to you? Look for a one-sentence generalization that links your subject and purpose to your audience's frame of reference, much as an advertising slogan points out how a product can benefit consumers. Here are some examples:

- Convince audience that reorganizing the data-processing department will improve customer service and reduce employee turnover
- Convince audience that we should build a new plant in Texas to eliminate manufacturing bottlenecks and improve production quality
- Address audience's concerns regarding a new employee health-care plan by showing how the plan will reduce costs and improve the quality of care

Using the "you" attitude makes your material relevant to your audience and helps keep their attention.

Each of these statements puts a particular slant on the subject, one that directly relates to the audience's interests. This sort of "you" attitude helps keep your audience's attention and convinces people that your points are relevant. For example, a group of new employees will be much more responsive to your discussion of plant

Best of the Web

Speak with Flair

The Virtual Presentation Assistant offers abundant resources with related links to other websites that contain useful articles, reviews, or supplemental materials for planning presentations. You can also connect to popular media and library pages with worldwide research information. You'll find examples of presentation types, suggestions for selecting and focusing your topic, tips on audience analysis, delivery, use of visual aids, and various other guidelines to help you prepare and deliver an effective oral presentation. If you need inspiration, check out this site.

www.ukans.edu/cwis/units/coms2/vpa/vpa.htm

safety procedures if you focus on how the procedures can save lives rather than on how the rules conform to Occupational Safety and Health Administration guidelines.

Limit Your Scope

Effective presentations not only focus on the audience's needs but also tailor the material to the time allowed, which is often strictly regulated. You can use your outline to estimate how much time your presentation will take. The average speaker can deliver about 125 to 150 words per minute (or roughly 7,500 to 9,000 words per hour), which corresponds to between 20 and 25 double-spaced, typed pages of text per hour. The average paragraph is about 125 to 150 words, so most of us can speak at a rate of about one paragraph per minute.

In one minute, the average speaker can deliver about one paragraph, or 125 to 150 words.

Say you want to make three basic points. In a 10-minute presentation, you could take about 2 minutes to explain each point, using roughly two paragraphs for each. If you devoted a minute each to the introduction and the conclusion, you would have 2 minutes left to interact with the audience. If you had an hour, however, you could spend the first 5 minutes introducing the presentation, establishing rapport with the audience, providing background information, and giving an overview of your topic. In the next 30 to 40 minutes, you could explain each of the three points, spending about 10 to 13 minutes on each (the equivalent of 5 or 6 typewritten pages). Your conclusion might take another 3 to 5 minutes. The remaining 10 to 20 minutes would then be available for responding to questions and comments from the audience.

Fit your oral presentation to the time allotted.

Which is better, the 10-minute speech or the hour-long presentation? If your speech doesn't have to fit into a specified time slot, the answer depends on your subject, your audience's attitude and knowledge, and the relationship you have with your audience. For a simple, easily accepted message, 10 minutes may be enough. On the other hand, if your subject is complex or your audience is skeptical, you'll probably need more time. Don't squeeze a complex presentation into a period that is too brief, and don't spend any more time than necessary on a simple talk.

Choose Your Approach

With a well-defined main idea to guide you and a clear idea about the scope of your presentation, you can begin to arrange your message. If you have 10 minutes or less to deliver your message, organize your presentation much as you would a letter or a brief memo: Use the direct approach if the subject involves routine information or good news, and use the indirect approach if the subject involves bad news or persuasion. Plan your introduction to arouse interest and to give a preview of what's to come. For the body of the presentation, be prepared to explain the who, what, when, where, why, and how of your subject. In the final paragraph or two, review the points you've made, and close with a statement that will help your audience remember the subject of your talk.

Structure a short oral presentation like a letter or a memo.

Longer presentations are organized like reports. If the purpose is to entertain, motivate, or inform, use direct order and a structure imposed naturally by the subject: importance, sequence, chronology, spatial orientation, geography, or category (as

Organize longer speeches and presentations like formal reports.

FIGURE 15.2 In-Depth Critique: Sample Outline for a 30-Minute Presentation

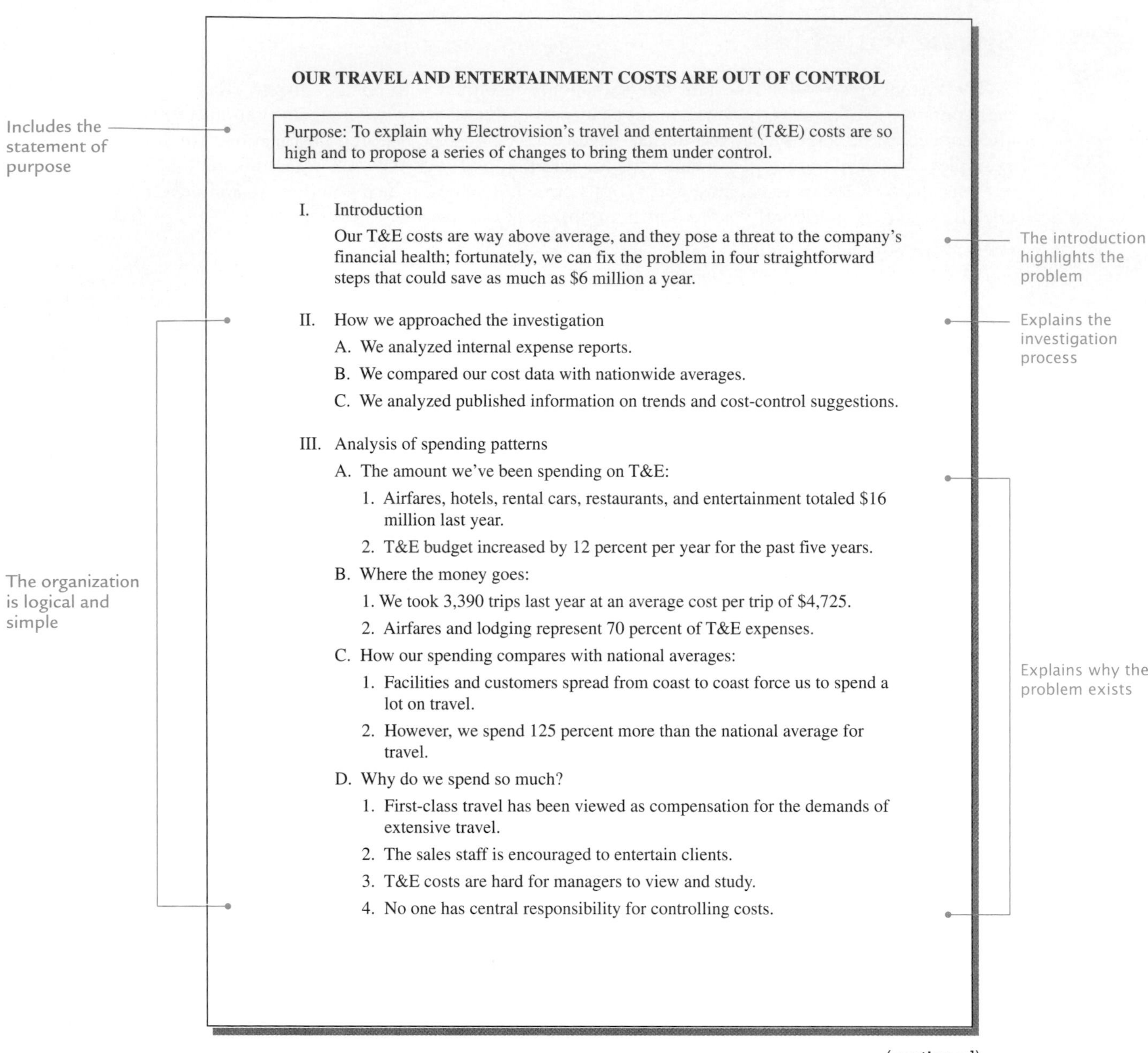

OUR TRAVEL AND ENTERTAINMENT COSTS ARE OUT OF CONTROL

Purpose: To explain why Electrovision's travel and entertainment (T&E) costs are so high and to propose a series of changes to bring them under control.

I. Introduction

Our T&E costs are way above average, and they pose a threat to the company's financial health; fortunately, we can fix the problem in four straightforward steps that could save as much as $6 million a year.

II. How we approached the investigation
   - A. We analyzed internal expense reports.
   - B. We compared our cost data with nationwide averages.
   - C. We analyzed published information on trends and cost-control suggestions.

III. Analysis of spending patterns
   - A. The amount we've been spending on T&E:
     1. Airfares, hotels, rental cars, restaurants, and entertainment totaled $16 million last year.
     2. T&E budget increased by 12 percent per year for the past five years.
   - B. Where the money goes:
     1. We took 3,390 trips last year at an average cost per trip of $4,725.
     2. Airfares and lodging represent 70 percent of T&E expenses.
   - C. How our spending compares with national averages:
     1. Facilities and customers spread from coast to coast force us to spend a lot on travel.
     2. However, we spend 125 percent more than the national average for travel.
   - D. Why do we spend so much?
     1. First-class travel has been viewed as compensation for the demands of extensive travel.
     2. The sales staff is encouraged to entertain clients.
     3. T&E costs are hard for managers to view and study.
     4. No one has central responsibility for controlling costs.

(continued)

discussed in Chapter 13). If your purpose is to analyze, persuade, or collaborate, organize your material around conclusions and recommendations or around a logical argument. Use direct order if the audience is receptive and indirect if you expect resistance. Figure 15.2 is an outline for a 30-minute analytical presentation. It is organized around conclusions and presented in direct order. This outline is based on Chapter 14's Electrovision report, written by Linda Moreno.

You may have to adjust your organization in response to feedback from your audience, especially if your purpose is to collaborate. You can plan ahead by thinking of several organizational possibilities (based on "what if" assumptions about your audience's reactions). If someone says something that undercuts your planned approach, you can switch smoothly to another one.

Use a clear, direct organization to accommodate your listeners' limitations.

Regardless of the length of your presentation, bear in mind that simplicity of organization is especially valuable in oral communication. If listeners lose the thread of your comments, they'll have a hard time catching up and following the remainder of your message. They can't review a paragraph or flip pages back and forth as they can

FIGURE 15.2 (Continued)

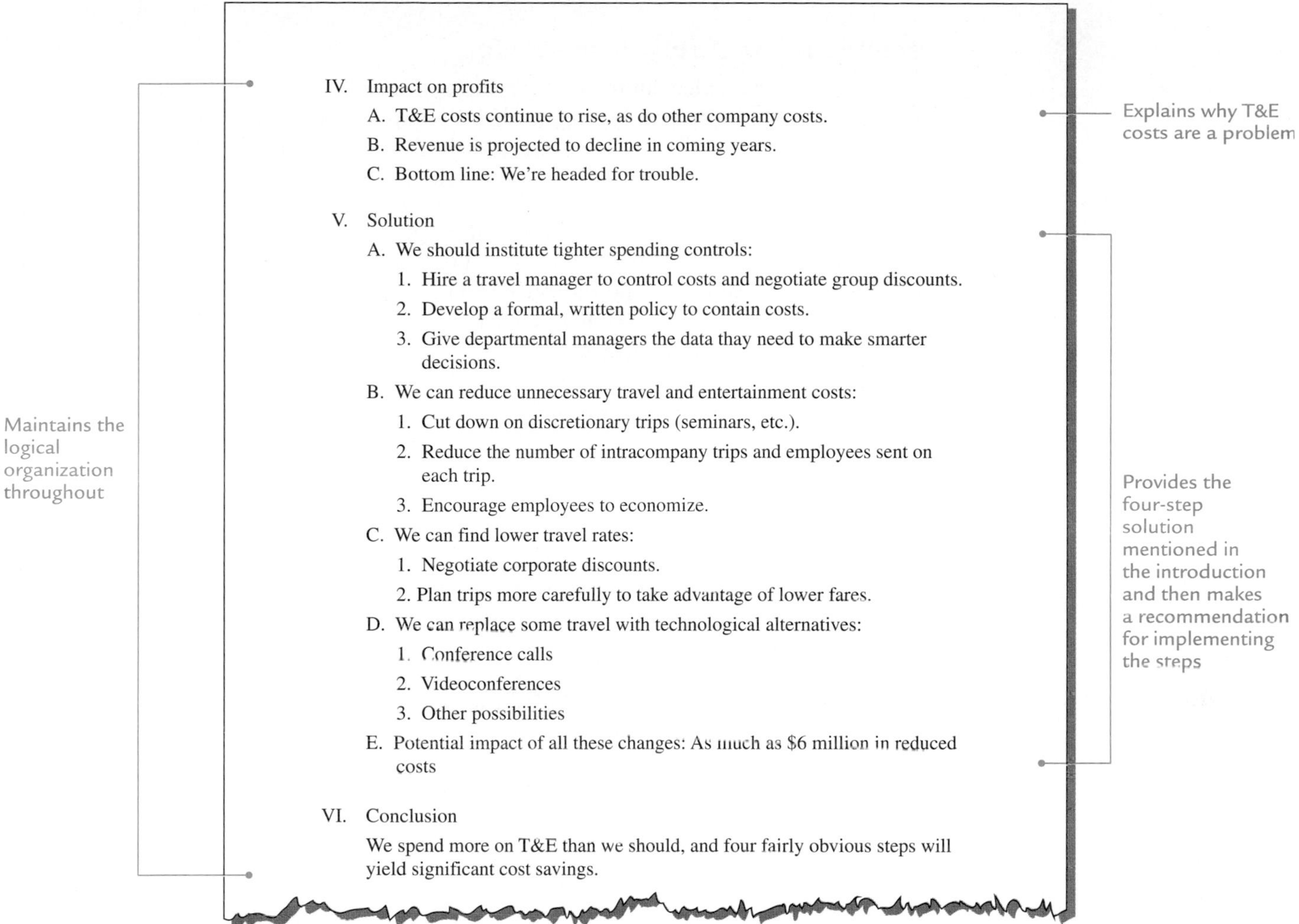
IV. Impact on profits

A. T&E costs continue to rise, as do other company costs.

B. Revenue is projected to decline in coming years.

C. Bottom line: We're headed for trouble.

V. Solution

A. We should institute tighter spending controls:

1. Hire a travel manager to control costs and negotiate group discounts.
2. Develop a formal, written policy to contain costs.
3. Give departmental managers the data thay need to make smarter decisions.

B. We can reduce unnecessary travel and entertainment costs:

1. Cut down on discretionary trips (seminars, etc.).
2. Reduce the number of intracompany trips and employees sent on each trip.
3. Encourage employees to economize.

C. We can find lower travel rates:

1. Negotiate corporate discounts.
2. Plan trips more carefully to take advantage of lower fares.

D. We can replace some travel with technological alternatives:

1. Conference calls
2. Videoconferences
3. Other possibilities

E. Potential impact of all these changes: As much as $6 million in reduced costs

VI. Conclusion

We spend more on T&E than we should, and four fairly obvious steps will yield significant cost savings.

when reading. So look for the most obvious and natural way to organize your ideas, using a direct order of presentation whenever possible. Explain at the beginning how you've organized your material, and try to limit the number of main points to three or four—even when the speech or presentation is rather long.

To keep the audience's attention, be sure to include only the most useful, interesting, and relevant supporting evidence. Leanne Anderson advises that you ask yourself whether this evidence is related to your core message. If it isn't, take it out. In addition, at the end of each section, reorient the audience by summarizing the point you've just made and explaining how it fits into your overall framework.

Prepare Your Outline

A carefully prepared outline can be more than just the starting point for composing a speech or presentation—it will help you stay on task. You can use your outline to make sure your message accomplishes its purpose to help you keep your presentation both audience-centered and within the allotted time. If you plan to deliver your presentation from notes rather than from a written text, your outline can also become your final "script."

Outlines can help you compose your presentation and stay on task.

When your outline will serve as your speaking notes, the headings should be complete sentences or lengthy phrases, rather than one- or two-word topic headings. In addition, you can include notes that indicate where visual aids will be used. You might also want to write out the transitional sentences you'll use to connect main points. Or you may even want to jot down notes about using a certain tone or body language.

When you use your outline as speaking notes, you'll make some special alterations.

Cues such as *pause here, speak slowly,* and *give extra emphasis* can be helpful when it comes to practicing and delivering your presentation.[2]

Decide on an Appropriate Style

Another important element in your preparation is style. Will you present a formal presentation in an impressive setting, with professionally produced visual aids? Or will you lead a casual, roll-up-your-sleeves working session? Choose your style to fit the occasion. Your audience's size, your subject, your purpose, your budget, and the time available for preparation all influence your style.

Use a casual style for small groups; use a formal style for large groups and important events.

If you're speaking to a relatively small group, you can use a casual style that encourages audience participation. A small conference room, with your audience seated around a table, may be appropriate. Use simple visual aids, and invite your audience to interject comments. Deliver your remarks in a conversational tone, using notes to jog your memory if necessary.

If you're addressing a large audience and the event is an important one, you'll want to establish a more formal atmosphere. A formal style is well suited to announcements about mergers or acquisitions, new products, financial results, and other business milestones. During formal presentations, speakers are often located on a stage or platform, standing behind a lectern and using a microphone so that their remarks can be heard throughout the room. These presentations are often accompanied by slides and other visual aids showcasing major products, technological breakthroughs, and other information that the speakers want audience members to remember.

Keep in mind that whether you're delivering a formal or an informal presentation, you should always choose your words carefully. If you try to impress your audience with obscure or unfamiliar vocabulary, your message will be lost. Make sure you can define all the words you use. And keep things simple. If you repeatedly stumble over a word as you rehearse, use a different one.[3]

In both formal and informal presentations, keep things simple.

Developing Your Oral Presentation

How formal presentations differ from formal reports:

- More interaction with the audience
- Use of nonverbal cues to express meaning
- Less control of content
- Greater need to help the audience stay on track

Developing a major presentation is much like writing a formal report, with one important difference: You need to adjust your technique to an oral communication channel, which presents both opportunities and challenges. The major opportunity lies in the interaction that is possible between you and your audience. When you speak before a group, you can receive information as well as transmit it, which means you can adjust both your content and your delivery as you go along to clarify information or to be more compelling. Instead of simply expressing your ideas, you can draw ideas from your audience and then reach a mutually acceptable conclusion. Another opportunity is your ability to use nonverbal cues to reinforce your message. Audiences will receive much richer stimuli during a speech than they can while reading a written report.

The major challenge of using an oral communication channel is being able to control what happens. As you develop each part of your presentation, think about how you will deliver the information. The more you expect to interact with your audience, the less control you'll have. Moreover, because listeners cannot refer back and forth to what has been or will be said, you must work harder to help them stay on track. Halfway through your presentation, a comment from someone in the audience might force you to shift topics. If you can anticipate such shifts, you'll have a chance to prepare for them as you develop each part of your oral presentation: the introduction, body, and close.

Learning Objective 3

Delineate the tasks involved in developing the three main parts of your oral presentation

Introduction

The introduction must capture attention, inspire confidence, and preview the contents.

A good introduction arouses the audience's interest in your topic, establishes your credibility, and prepares the audience for what will follow. That's a lot to pack in the first few minutes of your presentation. So, of the total time you allocate to writing your oral presentation, plan on spending a disproportionate amount on developing your introduction.

Arousing Audience Interest Some subjects are naturally more interesting than others. If you will be discussing a matter of profound significance that will personally affect the members of your audience, chances are they'll listen regardless of how you begin. All you really have to do is announce your topic ("Today I'll be explaining the reorganization of our company").

To capture attention, connect your topic to your listeners' needs and interests.

Other subjects call for more imagination. How do you get people to listen if you're explaining your pension program to a group of new clerical employees, none of whom will be full participants for another five years and most of whom will probably leave the company within two? The best approach to dealing with an uninterested audience is to appeal to human nature and encourage people to take the subject personally. Show them how they'll be affected as individuals. For example, you might begin addressing the new clerical employees like this:

> If somebody offered to give you $200,000 in exchange for $5 per week, would you be interested? That's the amount you can expect to collect during your retirement years if you choose to contribute to the voluntary pension plan. During the next two weeks, you will have to decide whether you want to participate. Although retirement is many years away for most of you, it is an important financial decision. During the next 20 minutes, I hope to give you the information you need to make that decision intelligently.

Another way to arouse the audience's interest is to draw out ideas and encourage comments from the audience throughout your presentation. Of course, this technique works better with a small group of co-workers than it does when you're addressing a large audience—particularly if the members of that large audience are hostile or unknown to you. During a presentation to a large group or one that covers controversial material, responding to questions and comments can interrupt the flow of information, weaken your argument, and reduce your control of the situation. In such situations, it's best to ask people to hold their questions until after you have concluded your remarks. Just be sure to allow ample time for audience questions at the end of your presentation, as this chapter discusses later.

Table 15.1 suggests several techniques you can use to arouse audience interest and keep listeners involved. Regardless of which technique you choose, always make sure that the introduction matches the tone of your presentation. If the occasion is supposed to be fun, you may begin with something light; but if you're talking business to a group of executives, don't waste their time with cute openings. Avoid jokes and personal anecdotes when you're discussing a serious problem. If you're giving a routine oral

Match the introduction to the tone of your presentation.

TABLE 15.1 Five Ways to Get Attention and Keep It

Use humor	Even though the subject of most business presentations is serious, including a light comment now and then can perk up the audience. Just be sure the humor is relevant to the presentation and not offensive to the audience.
Tell a story	Slice-of-life stories are naturally interesting and can be compelling. Be sure your story illustrates an important point.
Pass around a sample	Psychologists say that you can get people to remember your points by appealing to their senses. The best way to do so is to pass around a sample. If your company is in the textile business, let the audience handle some of your fabrics. If you sell chocolates, give everybody a taste.
Ask a question	Asking questions will get the audience actively involved in your presentation and, at the same time, will give you information about them and their needs.
State a startling statistic	People love details. If you can interject an interesting statistic, you can often wake up your audience.

Movie stars and recognized product spokespersons such as George Foreman may have instant credibility, but if you're like most public speakers, you will have to establish your credibility in a short period of time. Use your introduction to highlight a few personal accomplishments that your audience will value and respect.

report, don't be overly dramatic. Most of all, be natural. Nothing turns off the average audience faster than a trite, staged beginning.

Building Your Credibility One of the chief drawbacks of overblown openings is that they damage a speaker's credibility, and building credibility is probably even more important than arousing interest. A speaker with high credibility is more persuasive than one with low credibility. Use your introduction to establish your credentials—and quickly; people will decide within a few minutes whether you're worth listening to.[4]

You have only a few minutes to establish your credibility.

You want your audience to like you as a person and to respect your opinion. But to establish this sort of credibility, you need to lay the groundwork while you're developing your speech. If you're speaking to a familiar, open-minded audience, establishing your credibility is relatively easy. The difficulty comes when you try to earn the confidence of strangers, especially those predisposed to be skeptical or antagonistic.

To build credibility, you can let someone else introduce you or you can introduce yourself—explaining (without boasting) why you are qualified to speak on the subject.

One way to build credibility is to let someone else introduce you. That person can present your credentials so that you won't appear boastful. However, make sure that the person introducing you doesn't exaggerate your qualifications—some members of the audience are likely to bristle if you're billed as being the world's greatest authority on your subject.

If you're introducing yourself, plan to keep your comments simple. At the same time, don't be afraid to mention your accomplishments. Your listeners will be curious about your qualifications, so tell them briefly who you are and why you're there. Generally, you need mention only a few aspects of your background: your position in an organization, your profession, and the name of your company. You might plan to say something like this:

> I'm Karen Whitney, a market research analyst with Information Resources Corporation. For the past five years, I've specialized in studying high-technology markets. Your director of engineering, John LaBarre, has asked me to talk to you about recent trends in computer-aided design so that you'll have a better idea of how to direct your research efforts.

This speaker establishes credibility by tying her credentials to the purpose of her presentation. By mentioning her company's name, her specialization and position, and the name of the audience's boss, she lets her listeners know immediately that she is qualified to tell them something they need to know. She connects her background to their concerns.

Let the audience know what lies ahead.

Previewing Your Presentation In addition to arousing audience interest and building your credibility, a good introduction gives your audience a preview of what's ahead, helping them understand the structure and content of your message. A reader can get an idea of the structure and content of a report by looking at the table of contents and scanning the headings. In an oral presentation, however, the speaker provides that framework with a preview. Without cues from the speaker, the audience may be unable to figure out how the main points of the message fit together.

Your preview should summarize the main idea of your presentation, identify the supporting points, and indicate the order in which you'll develop those points. Tell your listeners in so many words, "This is the subject, and these are the points I will cover." Once you've established the framework, you can be confident that the audience will understand how the individual facts and figures are related to your main idea as you move into the body of your presentation.

Body

The bulk of your speech or presentation is devoted to a discussion of the three or four main points in your outline. Use the same organizational patterns you'd use in a letter, memo, or report, but keep things simple. As Leanne Anderson can tell you, your goals are to make sure that (1) the organization of your presentation is clear and (2) your presentation holds the audience's attention.

Limit the body to three or four main points.

Connecting Your Ideas To show how ideas are related, a written report uses typographical and formatting clues: headings, paragraph indentions, white space, and lists. An oral presentation, however, must rely on words to link various parts and ideas.

Help your audience follow your presentation by using clear transitions between sentences and paragraphs, as well as between major sections.

For the small links between sentences and paragraphs, use one or two transitional words: *therefore, because, in addition, in contrast, moreover, for example, consequently, nevertheless,* or *finally.* To link major sections of a presentation, use complete sentences or paragraphs, such as "Now that we've reviewed the problem, let's take a look at some solutions." Every time you shift topics, be sure to stress the connection between ideas. Summarize what's been said, then preview what's to come.

The longer your presentation, the more important your transitions become. If you will be presenting many ideas, audience members may have trouble absorbing them and seeing the relationships among them. Your listeners need clear transitions to guide them to the most important points. Furthermore, they need transitions to pick up any ideas they may have missed. So by repeating key ideas in your transitions, you can compensate for lapses in your audience's attention. When you actually give your presentation, you might also want to call attention to the transitions by using gestures, changing your tone of voice, or introducing a visual aid, as Chapter 16 points out.

Emphasize your transitions by repeating key ideas, using gestures, changing your tone of voice, or introducing a visual aid.

Holding Your Audience's Attention To communicate your points effectively, you must do more than connect your ideas with clear transitions—you also have to hold your audience's attention. Here are a few helpful tips for engaging an audience:

Make a special effort to capture wandering attention.

- **Relate your subject to your audience's needs.** People are interested in things that affect them personally. Plan to present every point in light of your audience's needs and values.
- **Anticipate your audience's questions.** Try to anticipate as many questions as you can, and address these questions in the body of your presentation. You'll also want to prepare and reserve additional material to use during the question-and-answer period should the audience ask for greater detail.
- **Use clear, vivid language.** People become bored quickly when they don't understand the speaker. If your presentation will involve abstract ideas, plan to show how those abstractions connect with everyday life. Use familiar words, short sentences, and concrete examples.
- **Explain the relationship between your subject and familiar ideas.** Plan to show how your subject is related to ideas that audience members already understand, so that you give people a way to categorize and remember your points.[5]

When attempting to hold an audience's attention, public speakers sometimes face distractions in the background. It takes a focused speaker to overcome such physical interruptions and get his or her message across.

As Leanne Anderson suggests, asking for opinions or pausing occasionally for questions or comments is another good way to involve audience members and hold their attention. Audience feedback helps you determine whether your listeners understand a key point before you launch into another section. Feedback also gives your audience a chance to switch for a time from listening to participating. Plan your pauses, even going so far as to note them in your outline so that you won't forget to pause once you're on stage.

Close

The close should leave a strong and lasting impression.

The close of a speech or presentation is almost as important as the beginning, because audience attention peaks at this point. Plan to devote about 10 percent of your total time to the ending. When developing your conclusion, begin by telling listeners that you're about to finish, so that they'll make one final effort to listen intently. Don't be afraid to sound obvious. Consider saying something such as "In conclusion" or "To sum it all up." You want people to know that this is the home stretch.

Summarize the main idea, and restate the main points.

Restating Your Main Points Once you've decided how to announce your close, plan on repeating your main idea. Be sure to emphasize what you want your audience to do or think, and state the key motivating factor. Finally, reinforce your theme by repeating the three or four main supporting points. A few sentences are generally enough to refresh people's memories. One speaker ended a presentation on the company's executive compensation program by repeating his four specific recommendations and then concluding with a memorable statement that would motivate his audience to take action:

> We can all be proud of the way our company has grown. If we want to continue that growth, however, we will have to adjust our executive compensation program to reflect competitive practices. If we don't, our best people will look for opportunities elsewhere.
>
> In summary, our survey has shown that we need to do four things to improve executive compensation:
>
> - Increase the overall level of compensation
> - Install a cash bonus program
> - Offer a variety of stock-based incentives
> - Improve our health insurance and pension benefits
>
> By making these improvements, we can help our company cross the threshold of growth into the major leagues.

Be certain that everyone agrees on the outcome and understands what should happen next.

Describing the Next Steps Some presentations require the audience to reach a decision or agree to take specific action. In such cases the close provides a clear wrap-up. If the audience agrees on an issue covered in the presentation, plan to review the consensus in a sentence or two. If they don't agree, make the lack of consensus clear by saying something like "We seem to have some fundamental disagreement on this question." Then you'll be ready to suggest a method of resolving the differences.

If you expect any action to occur as a result of your speech, you must explain who is responsible for doing what. One effective technique is to list the action items, with an estimated completion date and the name of the person responsible. You can present this list in a visual aid and ask each person on the list to agree to accomplish his or her assigned task by the target date. This public commitment to action is the best insurance that something will happen.

If the required action is likely to be difficult, make sure that everyone understands the problems involved. You don't want people to leave the presentation thinking their tasks will be easy, only to discover later that the jobs are quite demanding. You'll want everyone to have a realistic attitude and to be prepared to handle whatever arises. So when planning your presentation, use the close to alert people to potential difficulties or pitfalls.

Make your final words memorable.

Ending on a Strong Note Make sure that your final remarks are encouraging and memorable. After summarizing the key points of your presentation, conclude with a quote, a call to action, or some encouraging words. For instance, you might stress the benefits of action or express confidence in the listeners' ability to accomplish the work ahead. An alternative is to end with a question or a statement that will leave your audience thinking.

At the completion of your presentation, your audience should feel satisfied. The close is not the place to introduce new ideas or to alter the mood of the presentation. Even if parts of your presentation are downbeat, you want to close on a positive note. Avoid using a staged finale—keep it natural. As with everything else in your oral presentation, plan your closing remarks carefully. You don't want to wind up on stage with nothing to say but "Well, I guess that's it."

STEP 3: COMPLETING ORAL PRESENTATIONS

To complete your oral presentation, you will need to evaluate the content of your message and edit your remarks for clarity and conciseness as you would for any business message. As Chapter 16 discusses, you may also need to develop visual aids for your presentation and coordinate them with your delivery. Besides these tasks, four additional areas require your special attention: mastering the art of delivery, preparing to speak, overcoming anxiety, and handling questions responsively.

Mastering the Art of Delivery

Learning Objective 4

Highlight four delivery methods for oral presentations

Once you've planned, written, and developed visuals for your presentation, you're ready to begin practicing your delivery. You have a variety of delivery methods to choose from, some of which are easier to handle than others:

Not all methods of delivery are ideal.

- **Memorizing.** Unless you're a trained actor, avoid memorizing your speech, especially a long one. You're likely to forget your lines, and your speech will sound stilted. Besides, you'll often need to address audience questions during your speech, so you must be flexible enough to adjust your speech as you go. However, memorizing a quotation, an opening paragraph, or a few concluding remarks can bolster your confidence and strengthen your delivery.
- **Reading.** If you're delivering a technical or complex presentation, you may want to read it. Policy statements by government officials are sometimes read because the wording may be critical. If you choose to read your speech, practice enough so that you can still maintain eye contact with your audience. Triple-spaced copy, wide margins, and large type will help. You might even want to include stage cues, such as *pause, raise hands, lower voice.*
- **Speaking from notes.** Making a presentation with the help of an outline, note cards, or visual aids is probably the most effective and easiest delivery mode. This approach gives you something to refer to and still allows for eye contact and interaction with the audience. If your listeners look puzzled, you can expand on a point or rephrase it. (Generally, note cards are preferable to sheets of paper, because nervousness is easier to see in shaking sheets of paper.)
- **Impromptu speaking.** You might have to give an impromptu, or unrehearsed, speech if you're called on to speak unexpectedly or if you've agreed to speak but neglected to prepare your remarks. Avoid speaking unprepared unless you've spoken countless times on the same topic or are an extremely good public speaker. When you're asked to speak "off the cuff," take a moment to think through what you'll say. Then avoid the temptation to ramble.

Speaking from notes is generally the best way to handle delivery.

Practicing your oral presentation with a co-worker or a friend is a terrific way to polish your public-speaking skills in a relaxed setting.

Regardless of which delivery mode you use, be sure that you're thoroughly familiar with your subject. Knowing what you're talking about is the best way to build your self-confidence.

Practice indeed makes perfect, especially if you haven't had much experience with public speaking. If you rehearse in front

Before you speak:
- Practice
- Prepare the location
- Consider cultural differences

of a mirror, try to visualize the room filled with listeners. Put your talk on tape to check the sound of your voice, as well as your timing, phrasing, and emphasis. If possible, rehearse on videotape to see yourself as your audience will.

Preparing to Speak

In addition to knowing your material and practicing your delivery, you can build confidence in other ways. First, know that your location is ready and that you will have everything you'll need. Second, make sure you're prepared to address audiences from other cultures.

Whenever you can, check the location for your presentation in advance. Check the seating arrangements to make sure they're appropriate for your needs. If you want audience members to sit at tables, be sure tables are available. Check the room for any outlets you'll need for a projector or microphone. Locate light switches and dimmers. If you need a flip-chart easel or a chalkboard, be sure it's on hand. Check for chalk, an eraser, a pointer, extension cords, and any other small but crucial items you might need.

If you're addressing an audience that doesn't speak your language, consider using an interpreter. Working with an interpreter does constrain your presentation somewhat—you must speak slowly enough for the interpreter to keep up with you but not so slowly that the rest of your audience loses interest. Send your interpreter a copy of your speech and any visual aids as far in advance as possible.

Any time you deliver an oral presentation to people from other cultures, you may need to adapt the content of your presentation. It is also important to take into account any cultural differences in appearance, mannerisms, and other customs. Your interpreter will be able to suggest appropriate changes for a specific audience or particular occasion.

Overcoming Anxiety

Learning Objective 5

List nine ways to overcome your anxiety and feel more confident

If you're nervous about facing an audience and experience stage fright, you're not alone. Even speakers with years of experience feel some anxiety about getting up in front of an audience (see "Sharpening Your Career Skills: Nerves—The Secret Weapon of Polished Presenters"). Although you might not be able to make your nervous feelings disappear, you can learn to cope with your anxiety.

Feeling More Confident

Several techniques can help you become a more confident speaker.

Nervousness shows that you care about your audience, your topic, and the occasion. If your palms get wet or your mouth goes dry, don't think of nerves, think of excitement. Such stimulation can give you the extra energy you need to make your presentation sparkle. Here are some ways to harness your nervous energy to become a more confident speaker:[6]

- **Prepare more material than necessary.** Combined with a genuine interest in your topic, extra knowledge will reduce your anxiety.
- **Rehearse.** The more familiar you are with your material, the less panic you'll feel.
- **Think positively.** See yourself as polished and professional, and your audience will too.
- **Visualize your success.** Use the few minutes before you actually begin speaking to tell yourself you're on and you're ready.
- **Take a few deep breaths.** Before you begin to speak, remember that your audience is silently wishing you success.
- **Be ready.** Have your first sentence memorized and on the tip of your tongue.
- **Be comfortable.** If your throat is dry, drink some water.
- **Don't panic.** If you feel that you're losing your audience during your speech, try to pull them back by involving them in the action; ask for their opinions or pause for questions.
- **Keep going.** Things usually get better as you go.

Sharpening Your Career Skills

Nerves: The Secret Weapon of Polished Presenters

What do Barbra Streisand, Liza Minnelli, and Donny Osmond have in common? These professional performers and many others admit to being nervous about public speaking. If the pros can feel fear, it's no wonder beginners are sometimes scared speechless. Survey after survey has confirmed that public speaking is the number one fear in the United States—so if you're anxious about stepping in front of an audience, you're not alone.

Nervousness might make your hands tremble, your knees knock, your mouth feel dry, or your stomach churn. As bad as these symptoms can be, remember that nerves are a good indicator of your concern for the occasion, the topic, and the audience. If you didn't care, you wouldn't be anxious. A speaker who cares is more likely to seek out every method of communicating with the audience.

Remember also that you'll feel a little less nervous with every oral presentation. Once you see how the audience responds to your first attempt, you'll realize that you did better than you feared you would. Audience members can't see the butterflies fluttering; they're too busy paying attention and responding to your ideas. People in the audience want you to succeed; they're interested in learning from you or being inspired by your words, not in straining to hear the sound of your knees knocking together.

You can harness your nerves by focusing on what you want to accomplish. In the words of actress Carol Channing, "I don't call it nervousness—I prefer to call it concentration." Like Channing, you can concentrate your efforts on making that all-important connection with your audience. But don't make the mistake of expecting perfection. Put that nervous energy into planning, preparing, and practicing, and you'll be better equipped to face your audience the first time and every time.

Career Applications

1. Think of any lectures or presentations you've recently attended. Have you ever noticed a speaker's level of anxiety? Were any of the speakers successful in overcoming this fear? As an informed observer, describe the ways in which a particular speaker visibly conquered his or her nervousness. If that speaker failed, what techniques might have helped?
2. As a member of the audience, what can you do to help a speaker overcome his or her nervousness? Briefly explain.

Perhaps the best way to overcome stage fright and feel more confident is to concentrate on your message and on your audience, not on yourself. When you're busy thinking about your subject and observing your audience's response, you tend to forget your fears.

The best technique for overcoming your anxiety is to concentrate on your listeners and on their needs, rather than focusing on yourself.

Appearing More Confident

As you deliver your presentation, try to be aware of the nonverbal signals you're transmitting. Regardless of how you feel inside, your effectiveness greatly depends on how you look and sound.

Well-delivered presentations start with your first minute at the podium, so don't rush. As you approach the speaker's lectern, walk slowly, breathe deeply, and stand up straight. Face your audience, adjust the microphone, count to three slowly, then survey the room. When you find a friendly face, make eye contact and smile. Count to three again, and then begin your presentation.[7] If you are nervous, this slow, controlled beginning will help you establish rapport and appear more confident.

Don't rush the opening.

Once your presentation is under way, be particularly careful to maintain eye contact with your audience. Pick out several people positioned around the room, and shift your gaze from one to another. Looking directly at your listeners will make you appear sincere, confident, and trustworthy. It also helps you get an idea of the impression you're creating.

Use eye contact, posture, gestures, and voice to convey an aura of mastery and to keep your audience's attention.

Your posture is also important in projecting more confidence. Stand tall, with your weight on both feet and your shoulders back. Avoid gripping the lectern. In fact, you might step out from behind the lectern to help your audience feel more comfortable with you and to express your own comfort and confidence in what you're saying. Use your hands to emphasize your remarks with appropriate gestures. Meanwhile, vary your facial expressions to make the message more dynamic.

During meetings at Tellme.com, polished speakers use question-and-answer sessions to reinforce their ideas and credibility.

Finally, think about the sound of your voice. Studies indicate that people who speak with lower vocal tones at a slightly faster than average rate are perceived as being more credible.[8] Speak in a normal, conversational tone but with enough volume for everyone to hear you. Try to sound poised and confident, varying your pitch and speaking rate to add emphasis. Don't ramble. Use silence instead of meaningless filler words such as *um, you know, okay,* and *like.* Silence adds dramatic punch and gives the audience time to think about the message. Remember, speak clearly and crisply, articulating all the syllables, and sound enthusiastic about what you're saying.

Handling Questions Responsively

The question-and-answer period is one of the most important parts of an oral presentation. Questions give you a chance to obtain important information, to emphasize your main idea and supporting points, and to build enthusiasm for your point of view. Without questions, you might just as well write a report. If you don't expect to interact with the audience, you're wasting the chief advantage of an oral format. In addition to giving you valuable feedback, this period gives you a chance to emphasize points you made earlier, work in material that didn't fit into the formal presentation, and identify and try to overcome audience resistance.

Be ready with answers so that you can
- Emphasize your most important points
- Refer to material that didn't fit in the formal presentation
- Overcome audience resistance

Many speakers do well delivering their oral presentation only to falter during the question-and-answer period. But since you've already spent time anticipating these questions, you are ready with answers. Some experts recommend that you hold back some dramatic statistics as ammunition for the question-and-answer session.[9] If your message is unpopular, you should also be prepared for hostile questions. Treat them as legitimate requests for information. Maintaining your professionalism will improve your credibility.

Learning Objective 6

Discuss six ways effective speakers maintain control during the question-and-answer period

Focus on the Questioner

Use body language to emphasize the fact that you're listening to the questioner.

When someone poses a question, focus your attention on that individual. Pay attention to body language and facial expression to help determine what the person really means. Nod your head to acknowledge the question; then repeat it aloud to confirm your understanding and to ensure that the entire audience has heard it. If the question is vague or confusing, ask for clarification; then give a simple, direct answer. If you're asked to choose between two alternatives, don't feel you must do so. Offer your own choice instead, if that makes more sense.[10]

Respond Appropriately

Keep your answers short and to the point.

Be sure to answer the question you're asked. Don't sidestep it, ignore it, or laugh it off. Furthermore, don't say more than you need to if you want to have enough time to cover all the questions. If giving an adequate answer would take too long, simply say, "I'm sorry, we don't have time to get into that issue right now, but if you'll see me after the presentation, I'll be happy to discuss it with you." If you don't know the answer, don't pretend that you do. Instead, say something like "I don't have those figures. I'll get them for you as quickly as possible." Remember, you don't have to answer every question that is asked.

Maintain Control

Maintain control by stating some ground rules in the beginning of the question-and-answer session.

Try to maintain control during the question-and-answer session by establishing some ground rules up front. Announce a time limit or question limit per person before you begin. Establishing limits will protect you from getting into a heated exchange with one member of the audience and from allowing one or two people to monopolize the question period. Give as many audience members as possible a chance to participate by calling on people from different parts of the room. If the same person keeps angling for attention, restate the question limit or say something like "Several other people have questions; I'll get back to you if time permits."

If audience members try to turn a question into an opportunity to mount their own soapboxes, it's up to you to stay in control. You might ask people to identify themselves before they ask questions. People are more likely to behave themselves when everyone present knows their name.[11] You might admit that you and the questioner have differing opinions and, before calling on someone else, offer to get back to the questioner once you've done more research. Or you might simply respond with a brief answer, avoiding a lengthy debate or additional questions.[12] Finally, you might thank the person for the comments and then remind everyone that you were looking for specific questions.

Survive the Hot Seat

Respond unemotionally to tough questions.

If a question ever puts you on the hot seat, remember to be honest, but keep your cool. Look the person in the eye, answer the question as well as you can, and try not to show your feelings. Don't get into an argument. Questioners who challenge your ideas, logic, or facts may be trying to push you into overreacting. Defuse hostility by paraphrasing the question and asking the questioner to confirm that you've understood it correctly. Break long, complicated questions into parts that you can answer simply. State your response honestly, accurately, and factually; then move on to the next question. Avoid postures or gestures that might seem antagonistic. Maintain a businesslike tone of voice and a pleasant expression.[13] Don't indulge in put-downs—they may backfire and make the audience more sympathetic to the questioner.

Motivate Questions

Help audience members ask you questions.

In case your audience is too timid or hostile to ask questions, you might plant some of your own. If a friend or the meeting organizer gets the ball rolling, other people in the audience will probably join in. You might ask a question yourself: "Would you like to know more about . . ." If someone in the audience answers, act as if the question came from that person in the first place. When all else fails, say something like "I know from experience that most questions are asked after the question period. So I'll be around afterward to talk."[14]

Conclude Your Presentation

Finish up on time—even if people are eager to continue.

When the time allotted for your presentation is up, call a halt to the question-and-answer session, even if more people want to talk. Prepare the audience for the end by saying, "Our time is almost up. Let's have one more question." After you've made your reply, summarize the main idea of the presentation and thank people for their attention. Conclude the way you opened: by looking around the room and making eye contact. Then gather your notes and leave the podium, shoulders straight, head up. (This chapter's "Checklist: Oral Presentations" is a reminder of the tasks involved in oral communication.)

COMMUNICATION CHALLENGES AT ANDERSON BUSINESS RESOURCES

Leanne Anderson's expertise as a business consultant and speaker have earned her professional success as well as a busy schedule. Anderson likes to prepare her own oral presentations as much as possible. Nonetheless, she sometimes enlists others to help her analyze her audience, organize her message, write content, and check facts.

Anderson was recently asked to speak at an upcoming conference for small-business owners on the topic of how to deliver an effective presentation. This event is a great opportunity for her to network with owners of growing companies who could become clients for Anderson Business Resources. Although she is excited by the opportunity, Anderson has already committed to

✓ CHECKLIST: ORAL PRESENTATIONS

A. Planning your oral presentation

1. Define your purpose.
2. Analyze your audience.

B. Writing the oral presentation

1. Define your main idea.
2. Limit your scope.
3. Choose an appropriate approach.
4. Prepare your outline.
5. Decide on an appropriate style.
6. Prepare the introduction: Begin with an attention-getter, build credibility, preview the main points.
7. Prepare the body by explaining who, what, when, where, why, and how.
8. Tell listeners what's in it for them.
9. Connect your ideas with transitions (use bridge words, ask questions, repeat key ideas).
10. Reinforce your transitions with physical gestures.
11. In longer presentations, include previews and summaries of major points as you go along.
12. Include only necessary material.
13. Prepare the close: Review the main points, make a memorable statement, describe the next steps, assign responsibilities, and end on a strong note.
14. Prepare for the question-and-answer period: Figure out how to control the situation, and anticipate questions and objections.

C. Delivering the oral presentation

1. Practice delivery elements: (1) Establish eye contact, (2) speak clearly, (3) speak distinctly (not too fast), (4) make sure everyone can hear, (5) speak in your own natural style, (6) stand up straight, (7) use gestures naturally and appropriately, (8) stress the important words and phrases.
2. Check out the room ahead of time, and make sure the equipment works.
3. Control your anxiety and use your nervousness as a tool.
4. Keep your eyes focused on your audience.
5. Encourage questions.
6. Respond to questions without getting sidetracked.
7. Show sufficient knowledge to maintain credibility.
8. Keep control of your audience and the situation.
9. Maintain control of your feelings despite criticism.
10. Use answers to refocus on your theme or message.

other speaking engagements around the same time as the conference. It looks as if she will need some help preparing for this one.

Individual Challenge: Anderson has asked you, an intern at Anderson Business Resources, to help her prepare for her oral presentation for the small-business conference. What must you do to prepare for the presentation? What will you need to learn about the audience? What is the main idea that the presentation should convey? What can Anderson do to establish credibility with this audience? Based on the knowledge you've gained from this book, develop a rough outline for the presentation. (Anderson is an expert on this topic, so your outline should not be overly detailed. Your main concern should be to outline the primary topics that she should address in a half-hour presentation.)

Team Challenge: In groups of three or more, discuss some of the techniques that Anderson could use to grab and hold her audience's attention during the presentation. Try to come to a consensus about which techniques would be most effective, given the audience and the subject. Then develop some specific ideas for how Anderson might execute the technique (for example, think of some stories, anecdotes, or facts that she could use to relate the material to her audience). Next, discuss some of the questions that might arise from the audience. Share your questions as a class and discuss possible answers as well as techniques for handling especially difficult questions.[15] ■

SUMMARY OF LEARNING OBJECTIVES

1 Explain how planning oral presentations differs from planning written documents. Unlike a written document, an oral presentation is a onetime event, so audience members cannot browse through the speaker's comments to verify something said earlier. Thus, when planning an oral presentation, you must take extra care to define the purpose of your presentation (to inform, explain, persuade, or motivate) and relate your purpose to your audience's interests. You must also think of ways to immediately capture the audience's attention and keep them interested throughout your presentation.

2 Describe the five tasks that go into organizing oral presentations. When you organize an oral presentation, you need to complete five tasks: (1) When you define the main idea, you create a one-sentence generalization that first states the one message you want your audience to walk away with and then relates that message to your audience's needs. (2) When you limit your scope, you make sure that your speech or presentation fits into the time allowed for it and that the time allowed is enough for the complexity of your subject. (3) When you choose your approach, you arrange your speech in the order that is most appropriate for your audience's receptivity and for the purpose and duration of your speech. (4) When you prepare an outline of your speech, you use it to compose your speech, to stay on task as you proceed, to make sure your speech accomplishes your purpose, and sometimes to serve as speaking notes. (5) When you decide on an appropriate style, you match the occasion of your speech—anything from a formal presentation before a large audience to a casual working session around a conference table.

3 **Delineate the tasks involved in developing the three main parts of your oral presentation.** As you develop each part of your oral presentation, you must make sure that you accomplish specific tasks. In the introduction, you must arouse audience interest, build your credibility, and preview your presentation. In the body, you must connect your ideas and hold your audience's attention. In the close, you must restate your main points, describe the next steps, and end on a strong note.

4 **Highlight four delivery methods for oral presentations.** You can deliver an oral presentation using one of these four methods: (1) memorizing, which is especially difficult unless you are a trained performer; (2) reading, which is appropriate for policy statements and acceptable for complex presentations; (3) speaking from notes, which is the preferred delivery method for most business presentations; and (4) impromptu speaking, which should be avoided unless you are extremely knowledgeable about your topic and a gifted public speaker.

5 **List nine ways to overcome your anxiety and feel more confident.** To overcome anxiety and feel more confident as a speaker, prepare more material than necessary so that the extra knowledge will reduce your nervousness. Rehearse your oral presentation to become as familiar as possible with your topic. Think positively and see yourself as a polished professional. Right before speaking, visualize your success and tell yourself you're ready. Take a few deep breaths and remember that your audience actually wants you to succeed. Be ready by memorizing your first sentence. Be comfortable by sipping some water. If you feel you're losing your audience, don't panic; instead, pull them back by asking for their opinions or questions and involving them in the action. Keep going no matter what, because you'll get better as you go.

6 **Discuss six ways effective speakers maintain control during the question-and-answer period.** Effective speakers keep the question-and-answer period under control by (1) focusing on the question and paying attention to their body language; (2) responding accurately and concisely to the question and not avoiding it; (3) maintaining control by sticking to an announced time limit; (4) keeping their cool by avoiding arguments, by simplifying questions, and by defusing hostility; (5) motivating questions by either asking the audience a question first or relying on friends and acquaintances to initiate the first question; and (6) concluding on time.

TEST YOUR KNOWLEDGE

1. What must you think about when planning an oral presentation?
2. What are the four basic purposes for giving an oral presentation?
3. Why do you have to limit your scope when planning a presentation?
4. Why is simplicity of organization important in oral communication?
5. How can outlines help you with the writing and delivery of an oral presentation?
6. What three goals should you accomplish during the introduction of an oral presentation?
7. How can a speaker get and keep the audience's attention?
8. How does the delivery method of impromptu speaking differ from the delivery method of speaking from notes?
9. As a speaker, what nonverbal signals can you send to appear more confident?
10. What can speakers do to maintain control during the question-and-answer period of a presentation?

APPLY YOUR KNOWLEDGE

1. Would you rather (a) deliver an oral presentation to an outside audience, (b) be interviewed for a news story, or (c) make a presentation to a departmental meeting? Why? How do the communication skills differ among those situations? Explain.
2. How might the audience's attitude affect the amount of audience interaction during or after a presentation? Explain your answer.
3. If you were giving an oral presentation on the performance of a company product, what three attention-getters might you use to enliven your talk?
4. From the speaker's perspective, what are the advantages and disadvantages of responding to questions from the audience throughout an oral presentation, rather than just afterward? From the listener's perspective, which approach would you prefer? Why?
5. **Ethical Choices** What ethical concerns are raised by an oral presentation that encourages audience members to take illegal or questionable actions?

PRACTICE YOUR KNOWLEDGE

Document for Analysis

Pick a speech from *Vital Speeches of the Day*, a publication containing recent speeches on timely and topical subjects. As an alternative, select a speech from an online source such as the speech archives of NASA (www.nasa.gov) or AT&T (www.att.com/speeches). Examine both the introduction and the close; then analyze how these two sections work together to emphasize the main idea. What action does the speaker want the audience to take?

Next, identify the transitional sentences or phrases that clarify the speech's structure for the listener, especially those that help the speaker shift between supporting points. Using these transitions as clues, list the main message and supporting points; then indicate how each transitional phrase links the current supporting point to the succeeding one. Finally, prepare a brief (two- to three-minute) oral presentation summarizing your analysis for your class.

Exercises

For live links to all websites discussed in this chapter, visit this text's website at www.prenhall.com/bovee. Just log on and select Chapter 15, and click on "Student Resources." Locate the name of the site or the URL related to the material in the text. For the "Exploring the Best of the Web" exercises, you'll also find navigational directions. Click on the live link to the site.

15.1 **Internet** For many years, Toastmasters has been dedicated to helping its members give speeches. Instruction, good speakers as models, and practice sessions aim to teach members to convey information in lively and informative ways. Visit the Toastmasters website at www.toastmasters.org and carefully review the linked pages about listening, speaking, voice, and body. Evaluate the information and outline a three-minute presentation to your class, telling why Toastmasters and its website would or would not help you and your classmates write and deliver an effective speech.

15.2 **Mastering Delivery: Analysis** Attend a presentation at your school or in your town, or watch a speech on television. Categorize the speech as one that motivates or entertains, one that informs or analyzes, or one that persuades or urges collaboration. Then compare the speaker's delivery with this chapter's "Checklist: Oral Presentations." Write a two-page report analyzing the speaker's performance and suggesting improvements.

15.3 **Mastering Delivery: Nonverbal Signals** Observe and analyze the delivery of a speaker in a school, work, or other setting. What type of delivery did the speaker use? Was this delivery appropriate for the occasion? What nonverbal signals did the speaker use to emphasize key points? Were these signals effective? Which nonverbal signals would you suggest to further enhance the delivery of this oral presentation—and why?

15.4 **Ethical Choices** Think again about the oral presentation you observed and analyzed in 15.3. How could the speaker have used nonverbal signals to unethically manipulate the audience's attitudes or actions?

15.5 **Teamwork** You've been asked to give an informative 10-minute talk on vacation opportunities in your home state. Draft your introduction, which should last no more than 2 minutes. Then pair off with a classmate and analyze each other's introductions. How well do these two introductions arouse the audience's interest, build credibility, and preview the presentation? Suggest how these introductions might be improved.

15.6 **Completing Oral Presentations: Self-Assessment** How good are you at planning, writing, and delivering oral presentations? Rate yourself on each of the following elements of the oral presentation process. Then examine your ratings to identify where you are strongest and where you can improve, using the tips in this chapter.

Element of Presentation Process	Always	Frequently	Occasionally	Never
1. I start by defining my purpose.	________	________	________	________
2. I analyze my audience before writing an oral presentation.	________	________	________	________
3. I match my presentation length to the allotted time.	________	________	________	________
4. I begin my oral presentations with an attention-getting introduction.	________	________	________	________
5. I look for ways to build credibility as a speaker.	________	________	________	________
6. I cover only a few main points in the body of my presentation.	________	________	________	________
7. I use transitions to help listeners follow my ideas.	________	________	________	________
8. I review main points and describe next steps in the close.	________	________	________	________
9. I practice my presentation beforehand.	________	________	________	________
10. I prepare in advance for questions and objections.	________	________	________	________
11. I conclude oral presentations by summarizing my main idea.	________	________	________	________

EXPAND YOUR KNOWLEDGE

Exploring the Best of the Web:

Speak with Flair, p. 499

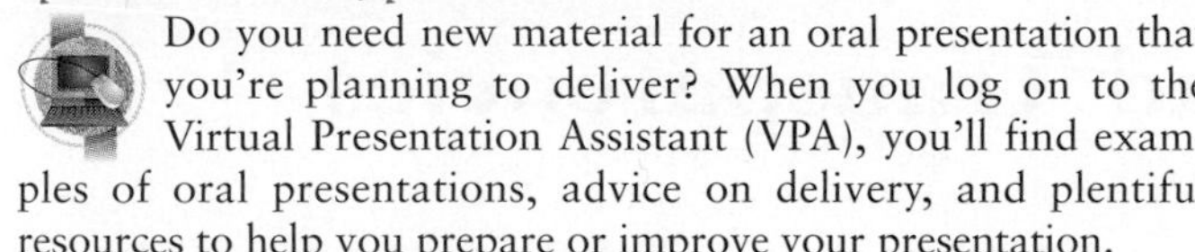

Do you need new material for an oral presentation that you're planning to deliver? When you log on to the Virtual Presentation Assistant (VPA), you'll find examples of oral presentations, advice on delivery, and plentiful resources to help you prepare or improve your presentation.

1. Suppose you have been asked to prepare an oral presentation on a business issue currently in the news. How could you use what you've discovered at the VPA site to help you select a topic? How could you use this site to find additional information or supplementary materials related to your topic?
2. According to this website, what factors should you consider when analyzing your audience?
3. What topics or information will entice you to return to this site or its links? (If you don't find the Virtual Presentation Assistant useful, explain why.)

Exploring the Web on Your Own

Review these chapter-related websites on your own to enhance your oral presentation skills and knowledge.

1. Take the free Public Speaker's Online Tutorials and read some online articles about public speaking at the Gove-Siebold website, www.govesiebold.com.
2. Visit the Advanced Public Speaking Institute, at www.public-speaking.org, and learn how to be the best public speaker you can be.
3. Learn to prepare, write, and polish your oral presentations at Learn2 Write a Speech, www.learn2.com/06/0694/0694.asp.

LEARN INTERACTIVELY

Interactive Study Guide

Visit "My Companion Website" at www.prenhall.com/bovée. For Chapter 15, take advantage of the interactive "Study Guide" to test your chapter knowledge. Get instant feedback on whether you need additional studying. Read the "Current Events" articles to get the latest on chapter topics, and complete the exercises—as specified by your instructor.

This site offers a variety of additional resources: The "Research Area" helps you locate a wealth of information to use in course assignments. You can even send a message to online research experts, who will help you find exactly the information you need. The "Study Hall" helps you succeed in this course. "Talk in the Hall" lets you leave messages and meet new friends online. If you have a question, you can "Ask the Tutor." And to get a better grade in this course, you can find more help at "Writing Skills," "Study Skills," and "Study Tips."

Grammar Diagnostic Tests

Review and reinforce your grammar and language skills by taking one of the four online diagnostic tests offered at our companion website, www.prenhall/bovee.com. The four tests cover a variety of topics, including spelling, capitals, punctuation, verbs, pronouns, adjectives, adverbs, sentence structure, sentence punctuation, clarity, word choice, style, organization skills, proofreading, and more. Submit your test and assess your competency. Then focus on improving areas where you are weak as you complete the exercises in this chapter.

Enhancing Your Oral Presentations with Electronic Slide Shows and Overhead Transparencies

After studying this chapter, you will be able to

1 *Explain how visual aids enhance oral presentations, and list several popular types of visual aids*

2 *Highlight the advantages and disadvantages of using overhead transparencies as visual aids*

3 *Highlight the advantages and disadvantages of using electronic presentations as visual aids*

4 *Explain how color can improve the effectiveness of your slides*

5 *Discuss the benefits of using transitions and builds in electronic presentations*

6 *List seven characteristics of effective slides*

7 *Describe three types of structural slides and highlight the function of each slide*

COMMUNICATION CLOSE-UP AT ALLBEE GREEN

www.allbeegreen.com

When corporations need electronic presentations for trade shows, press conferences, new product launches, or other live events, they frequently call on the talents of Kevan Allbee and David Green. Co-owners of Allbee Green in Orem, Utah, the two men help clients develop visual aids for oral presentations—from simple slide shows for small audiences to elaborate electronic productions with live music and theatrical touches. Regardless of the size of the audience or the complexity of the visual effects, Allbee and Green know that creating effective slides for oral presentations begins with careful planning.

"Planning is everything," says Kevan Allbee. "In fact, planning *is* the work." First, he defines his objectives for the presentation, asking such questions as, "What do I want my audience to do? Who is the audience, and what do they need to know? What solutions will I present? What stories or demonstrations can I use to illustrate these issues?" He also considers the amount of time allotted for the presentation, the size of the audience, the time of day, and the location for the presentation.

After objectives are clearly defined, Allbee prepares the script for the presentation. "Always, always, always write the script before creating the graphics," he advises. "First, know what you're going to say, then build the script. Like a good play or movie script, it should have a 'plot'—a strong message flow, good transitions between points, and a compelling conclusion."

Once the script is written, Allbee carefully plans the content and appearance of each slide. "Each slide should be a delightful guidepost along the trail of your presentation—not the whole brochure. Slides should highlight key points, illustrate concepts, and help create interest in the words being spoken. They work best when the objectives are to show, tell, and motivate," he explains.

Although most of Allbee's clients provide design guidelines for the use of such elements as company logos, colors, and fonts, it's up to Allbee to make sure that the slides have a consistent layout and a sophisticated feel. To design effective slides, Allbee limits headlines to three to five words and uses a maximum of six bullet points per slide. He also tries to make effective use of white space and to select fonts that are appropriate for the presentation. "Each font has a personality," he notes. "Some fonts are business casual, some black tie. Be sure the fonts match the audience and the speaker's objectives."

Allbee limits the use of illustrations in presentations, not wanting to distract from the message with excessive clip art or photos. He also makes sure that he doesn't cram too much information on each slide. Trying to illustrate every word or concept results in "a presentation that is impossible for anyone to remember or internalize," he notes. "Leave the details in your manuals and brochures. When your audience tunes you out to read your slide, that slide is counterproductive."

To help his clients perfect their delivery, Allbee advises presenters to know their audience and their material. "Never focus on what you want the audience to *know*. Instead, think about what you want the audience to *do* at the end of the presentation," he

Kevin Allbee and David Green remind clients that technology and visual aids are presentation tools. Good presenting still requires fundamental speaking skills and techniques.

says. "Great speakers know how to relate with the audience's points of interest or concern, then deliver the solution, and move the audience toward action. The audience's action after the presentation is the ultimate difference between effective or ineffective presentations."[1] ■

USING VISUAL AIDS IN ORAL PRESENTATIONS

The ability to create and deliver an effective presentation is a vital skill in today's workplace. Chapter 15 presents a three-step process for designing and delivering oral presentations, focusing on how to organize and develop content for oral presentations and how to deliver that content effectively. But, as Kevan Allbee and David Green know, good content and a smooth delivery are not enough. Audiences will also expect you to use visual aids in your oral presentations.

Visual aids help the audience remember important points.

Visual aids can improve the quality and impact of your oral presentation by creating interest, illustrating points that are difficult to explain in words alone, adding variety, and increasing the audience's ability to absorb and remember information. Studies of behavioral research have shown that visual aids can improve learning by up to 400 percent because humans can process visuals 60,000 times faster than text.[2]

As a speaker, you'll find that visual aids can help you remember the details of the message (no small feat in a lengthy presentation) and improve your professional image: Speakers who use presentation visuals generally appear better prepared and more knowledgeable than speakers who do not use visuals aids.

Learning Objective 1

Explain how visual aids enhance oral presentations, and list several popular types of visual aids

Today's speakers can select from a variety of visual aids to enhance oral presentations. Among the most popular types of visual aids are overhead transparencies, electronic presentations, chalkboards and whiteboards, flip charts, and 35-millimeter slides:

Overheads are the most common types of visual aids.

- **Overhead transparencies.** Overhead transparencies have been the standard visual aid for decades. An **overhead transparency** is a piece of clear plastic with writing or some other image on it. Transparencies are shown by placing them on an overhead projector that projects the image or writing on a screen. Transparencies can be created using word processing, page layout, or electronic slide presentation software and can even be prepared by hand. Because their content and design elements are similar to electronic slides, we sometimes refer to transparencies as slides for purposes of this chapter.

An effective electronic presentation can significantly boost the retention level of audience members.

- **Electronic presentations.** The availability of affordable software and new technology has made electronic presentations the visual aid of choice in most business situations. An **electronic presentation** or *slide show* consists of a series of **electronic slides** composed using popular computer software such as Microsoft PowerPoint, Lotus Freelance Graphics, or Corel Draw. The software allows you to incorporate photos, sound, video, graphics, animation, and other movement into the slides, enabling you to capture and engage your audience like no other visual aid. With special projection equipment, a personal computer can be turned into a large-screen "intelligent chalkboard" that allows you to create and modify your electronic slides as the presentation unfolds. For live presentations, an increasing number of businesses now use LCD (liquid crystal display) projectors or display panels. These products grab the images from your computer screen and display them on the same projection screens used for viewing overhead transparencies.[3]

An electronic presentation is a series of computerized slides.

- **Chalkboards and whiteboards.** Chalkboards and whiteboards are effective tools for recording points made during small-group brainstorming sessions. Because these visual aids are produced on the spot, they offer flexibility. However, they're too informal for some situations.

Chalkboards and whiteboards are informal.

- **Flip charts.** Large sheets of paper attached at the top like a tablet can be propped on an easel so that you can flip the pages as you speak, with each chart illustrating or clarifying a point. You might have a few lines from your outline on one, a graph or diagram on another, and so on. By using felt-tip markers of various colors, you can also record ideas generated during a discussion.

Unlike boards, flip charts can be prepared in advance.

- **35-millimeter slides.** The content of 35-millimeter slides may be text, graphics, or pictures. If you're trying to create a polished, professional atmosphere, you might find this approach worthwhile, particularly if you'll be addressing a crowd and don't mind speaking in a darkened room. If you choose this visual aid, remember, you will need to coordinate your slides with your speech and appoint someone to operate the projector.

35-millimeter slides generally require someone else to operate the projector.

- **Other visual aids.** In technical or scientific presentations, a sample of a product or material allows the audience to experience your subject directly. Models built to scale are convenient representations of an object. Audiotapes are often used to supplement a slide show or to present a precisely worded and timed message. Filmstrips and movies can capture the audience's attention with color and movement. Television and videotapes are good for showing demonstrations, interviews, and other events. In addition, filmstrips, movies, television, and videotapes can be used as stand-alone vehicles (independent of a speaker) to communicate with dispersed audiences at various times.

Other visual aids include product samples, models, audiotapes, filmstrips, and videotapes.

The two most popular types of visual aids are overhead transparencies and electronic presentations—the focus of this chapter. Even though these two visual aids differ in the features they offer and in the way they are delivered, both consist of a collection of slides that must be well written and well designed to be effective. Once the slides are created, they are either printed on clear plastic sheets for overhead transparencies or stored electronically and further embellished with multimedia effects for electronic presentations.

Overhead transparencies and electronic presentations consist of a series of slides.

PLANNING EFFECTIVE SLIDES FOR ORAL PRESENTATIONS

Just as Kevan Allbee suggests, effective slides are the result of careful planning. Overhead transparencies and electronic slides are no different from the text of your presentation; that is, they send a message to your audience. Thus, you need to analyze both your purpose in creating the slides and the audience who will be viewing them. Because slides tend to condense information, your attention to purpose is crucial. Be sure you know exactly what it is you want each slide to say. And just as important, be aware of your audience's needs. What do audience members need to understand from each slide? How will your design affect audience members? What cultural preferences should you consider?

Once you have completely analyzed each slide, make sure you have all the information you need to include visually. Gather the details carefully, and document your sources fairly and thoroughly. If you're presenting a chart to illustrate a point in your presentation, you want to guarantee that it is not only accurate but complete.

Finally, to adapt your message to your audience and establish a good relationship, be careful to choose the correct form of slide for your presentation. Both overhead transparencies and electronic slides have advantages and disadvantages.

Advantages and Disadvantages of Overhead Transparencies

Learning Objective 2

Highlight the advantages and disadvantages of using overhead transparencies as visual aids

Many businesspeople prefer to use overhead transparencies in oral presentations, for a number of reasons. They are inexpensive, easy to create, and simple to use. You can prepare high-quality overheads using a computer and a high-resolution color inkjet or laser printer. Moreover, they require little extra equipment to show: Most conference rooms or classrooms have overhead projectors and a table large enough to stack transparencies. And, because transparency images can be projected in full daylight, speakers can maintain eye contact with the audience. They can also use special markers to write on transparencies as they present information.

Simplicity, availability, and affordability are key advantages of overhead transparencies.

In spite of these advantages, transparencies have a number of drawbacks. First, because they are in a permanent printed format, they must be replaced if their content changes. You cannot erase or change a word, color, or graph on a transparency as you would on an electronic slide. Second, each time you add or remove an overhead from the sequence, you must manually renumber the batch. Third, transparencies are fragile: They chip, flake, scratch, and tear easily. You can protect transparencies with cardboard or plastic frames or with transparent sleeves, but these protectors are costly and are bulky to store or transport. Fourth, overhead projectors can be noisy and a challenge to talk over. Finally, transparencies must be aligned carefully on the overhead projector (one at a time). This requirement limits the presenter's ability to move freely about the room.

Overhead transparencies are fragile, difficult to modify, and clumsy to use.

Advantages and Disadvantages of Electronic Presentations

Learning Objective 3

Highlight the advantages and disadvantages of using electronic presentations as visual aids

The biggest advantage of electronic presentations is their computerized format, which makes real-time manipulation of data easy to perform. You can change a graphic, add a bulleted phrase, and even alter the sequence of your slides with a simple click of the mouse. You can add animation, video clips, sound, hypertext, and other multimedia effects to slides—turning them into dazzling professional presentations. You can even preprogram and automate the release of text and graphical elements. Furthermore, electronic presentations are easy to store, transport, and customize for different audiences.

Electronic slides offer more features and benefits than overhead transparencies.

Electronic presentations are not without disadvantages, however. First, electronic slides require more expensive display equipment than overhead transparencies—especially if you are presenting to large audiences. This equipment can be complicated to use and may not be available in all situations. Second, most people spend too much time focusing on the technical components of an electronic presentation—they pay more attention to the animation and special effects of their slide shows than they do to the content of their message. Third, inexperienced presenters tend to pack too many special effects in their electronic slides, creating a visual feast of pictures and graphics that dazzle the audience but blur the key message. People may walk away

Most people pay too much attention to the technical components of an electronic presentation.

Team members generally plan, write, and edit group oral presentations together.

saying, "I really liked the graphics and motion—I wonder what software program the speaker used," but have no idea of the points the speaker was trying to make.

CREATING EFFECTIVE SLIDES FOR ORAL PRESENTATIONS

As Kevan Allbee knows, most people place a higher priority on the design of their slides than they do on the written content. As a result, they work on their slides in reverse order: they select a background design and create special effects (if developing an electronic presentation) before writing the content of their slides. Design is an important element indeed, but as Allbee points out, it is secondary to a well-organized, well-developed, audience-centered message. Once you've planned what a slide is going to say, organize the content as you would for any written message. Then write and polish the written content before focusing on the slide's design elements.

Slides are most effective when they are simple.

When creating slides, keep in mind that simplicity is the key to effectiveness. Slides that are too complex or poorly written will confuse the audience. People can't read and listen at the same time, so your slides must be simple enough for the audience to understand within a moment or two. Therefore, your primary focus when creating text or graphic slides is to keep content and graphics simple and readable, select design elements that enhance your message without overshadowing it, be consistent in your design selections, and use special effects selectively.

Writing Readable Content

Text visuals help listeners follow the flow of ideas.

Text visuals help the audience follow the flow of ideas. They are simplified outlines of your presentation and are used to summarize and preview your message or to signal major shifts in thought. One of the biggest mistakes you can make when writing text visuals is to overload them with too much information. People do so for two reasons: (1) They believe that every word or concept they wish to convey should be illustrated by a slide, and (2) they use their slides as speaker's notes—focusing on their own needs instead of the needs of their audience.

Use text visuals to highlight your spoken words, not as a substitute for them.

Slides with excessive text take the audience's eyes off the speaker.

Text slides are not intended to display your entire script or highlight each point you make.[4] They are not your notes. Effective text slides supplement your words. They highlight key points of your message, illustrate concepts, and help create interest in your oral message, but they are not the presentation itself. Slides with too much text, long sentences, or wordy bullets are difficult to read from a distance and difficult to understand. They confuse and distract the audience, and they diminish your credibility as a speaker.[5] If you overload your slides with content, members of the audience will assume that you are afraid to look at them and interact with them.

When writing content for text slides, keep your message short and simple:

- Limit each slide to one thought, concept, or idea.
- Limit the content to about 40 words—with no more than six lines of text containing about six or seven words per line.
- Write short bulleted phrases rather than long sentences or paragraph-length blocks of text.
- Phrase list items in grammatical form and use telegraphic wording ("Profits Soar," for example) without being cryptic ("Profits").
- Make your slides easy to read by using the active voice.
- Include short informative titles.

Figure 16.1 is a good example of text slides that have been revised according to these principles to make their content more readable.

FIGURE 16.1 Writing Readable Content

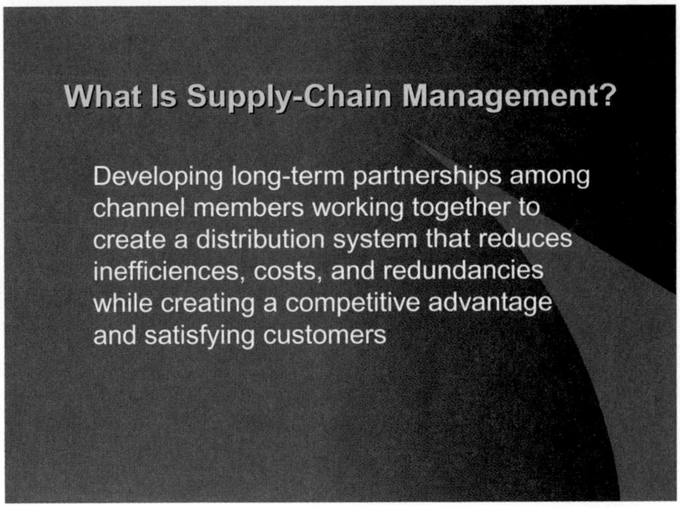

What Is Supply-Chain Management?

Developing long-term partnerships among channel members working together to create a distribution system that reduces inefficiences, costs, and redundancies while creating a competitive advantage and satisfying customers

Figure 16.1a—Inappropriate paragraph style

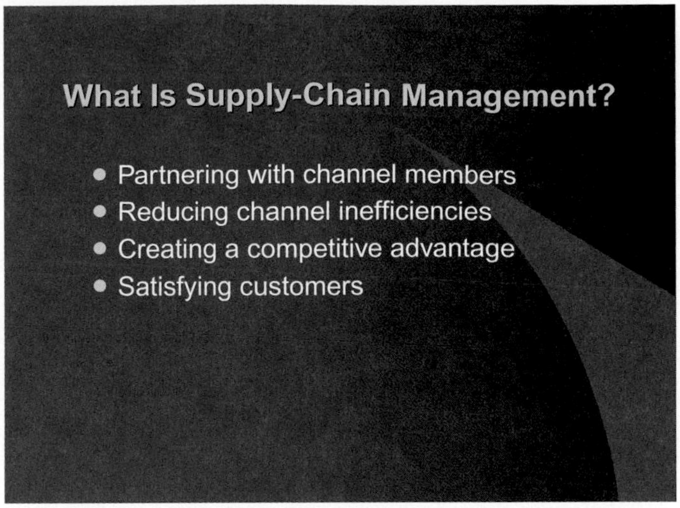

What Is Supply-Chain Management?

- Partnering with channel members
- Reducing channel inefficiencies
- Creating a competitive advantage
- Satisfying customers

Figure 16.1b—Appropriate bulleted phrases

The definition provided in Figure 16.1a was taken from a persuasive report written by the speaker. The paragraph style is inappropriate for slides and difficult to read. Figure 16.1b restates the definition in short phrases that highlight the key point of the definition. The speaker will explain these points while showing the slide.

Figure 16.1c—Wordy bullets

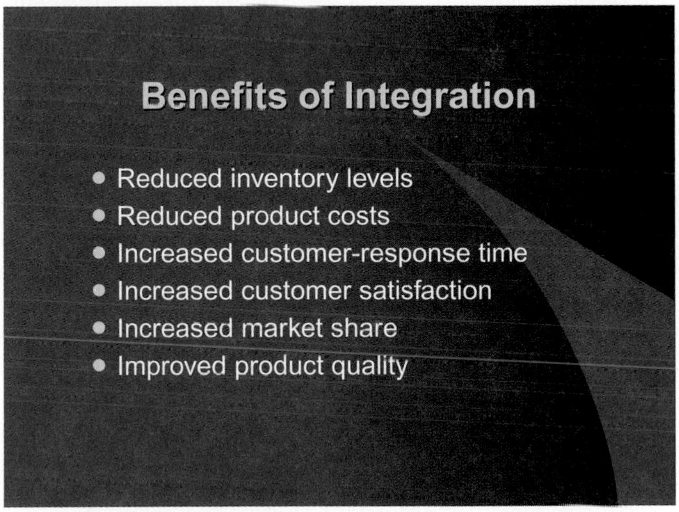

Benefits of Integration

- Reduced inventory levels
- Reduced product costs
- Increased customer-response time
- Increased customer satisfaction
- Increased market share
- Improved product quality

Figure 16.1d—Concise bullets

Although Figure 16.1c falls within acceptable word-count guidelines, unnecessary words still make the slide difficult to read. Figure 16.1d is an improved version of Figure 16.1c: The sentences are converted to short, parallel phrases and the slide's title is condensed.

Modifying Graphics for Slides

The old saying "A picture is worth a thousand words" is especially true when it comes to creating effective slides. As Figure 16.2 shows, graphic visuals can be an effective way to clarify a concept, show a process, or highlight important information. They can help the audience absorb information in a short time in addition to increasing audience interest and retention.

Use graphic visuals to
- Clarify a concept
- Show a process
- Highlight key information

Chapter 12 discusses how to create effective graphics such as charts, diagrams, maps, drawings, and tables for written documents. When using such graphics in oral presentations, your first task is to simplify them. When slides contain excessive graphic

FIGURE 16.2 Converting Text into Graphics

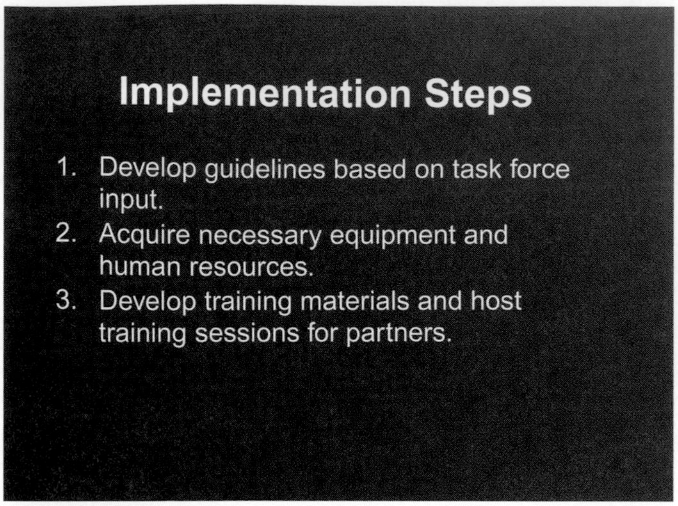

Implementation Steps
1. Develop guidelines based on task force input.
2. Acquire necessary equipment and human resources.
3. Develop training materials and host training sessions for partners.

Figure 16.2a—Steps in written format

Implementation Steps
Step 1
Develop guidelines
Step 2
Acquire resources
Step 3
Train partners

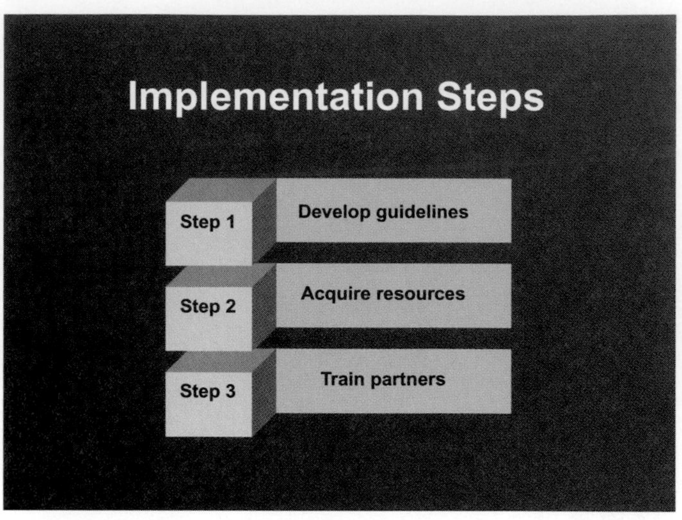

Figure 16.2b—Steps in graphic format

These two slides relay the same information; however, Figure 16.2b shortens the steps and converts them into a simple but effective graphic. As a result, the message in Figure 16.2b is easier to read, easier to understand, and more powerful than the message in Figure 16.2a. The speaker will explain the steps as the slide is presented.

Graphics used in oral presentations should be simplified versions of those used in written reports.

detail, they are difficult to read on screen. You can create effective visuals by following these guidelines:

- **Reduce the detail.** Eliminate anything that is not absolutely essential to the message. Show only key numbers on a chart. If people need to see only trends, then show only the trend line and not the numbers. If necessary, break information into more than one graphic illustration.
- **Avoid repeating text.** Don't repeat the same word five times. Minimize repetition by including the word in a title, subtitle, label, or legend.
- **Shorten numbers.** On graphs, use 02 for the year 2002; round off numbers such as \$12,500.72 to \$12 or \$12.5, and then label the axis to indicate thousands.
- **Limit data.** Don't put more than five lines or five sets of bars on one chart.
- **Highlight key points.** Use arrows, boldface type, and color to direct your audience's eyes to the main point of a visual. Summarize the intent of the graphic in one clear phrase or sentence, such as "Earnings have increased by 15 percent."
- **Adjust the size and design.** Modify the size of the graphic to accommodate the size of a slide. Leave plenty of white space (area with no text or graphics) so that the audience members can view and interpret content from a distance. Use colors that stand out from the slide's background, and choose a font that's clear and easy to read.

Figure 16.3 is an example of how to modify a graph using these guidelines. The graph in Figure 16.3a was included in the annual sales report for Bressler Toyota car dealership. Figure 16.3b is a modified version of the same graph used by the company's general manager during an oral presentation.

Selecting Design Elements

Poor design can overshadow effective slide content.

Once you've composed the text and graphic elements of your slides, you're ready to focus on their design. Nothing detracts from good content more than poorly designed slides. By paying attention to a few design basics, however, you can transform a dull presentation into one that is both dynamic and readable.

Chapter 11 highlights five principles of effective design: continuity, contrast, emphasis, simplicity, and experience (see page 353). Pay close attention to these principles as you select the color, background design, artwork, fonts, and typestyles for your slides. Then once you have selected the best design elements for your slides, stick with them throughout your presentation.

FIGURE 16.3 Modifying Graphs for Slides

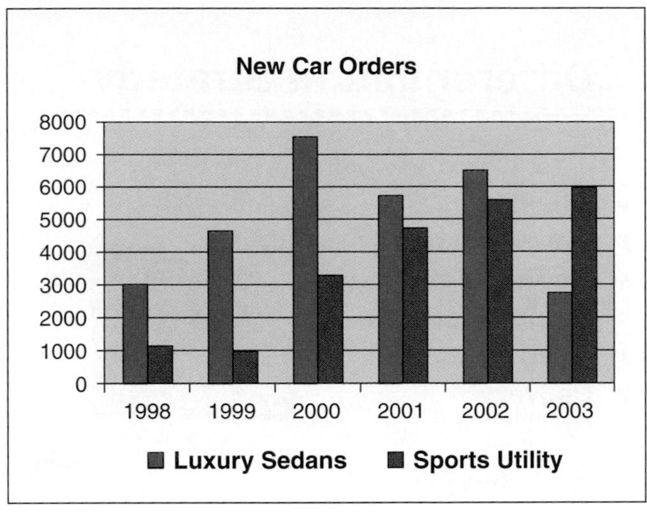

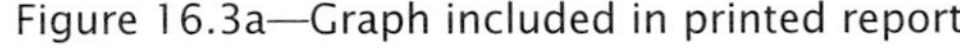
Figure 16.3a—Graph included in printed report

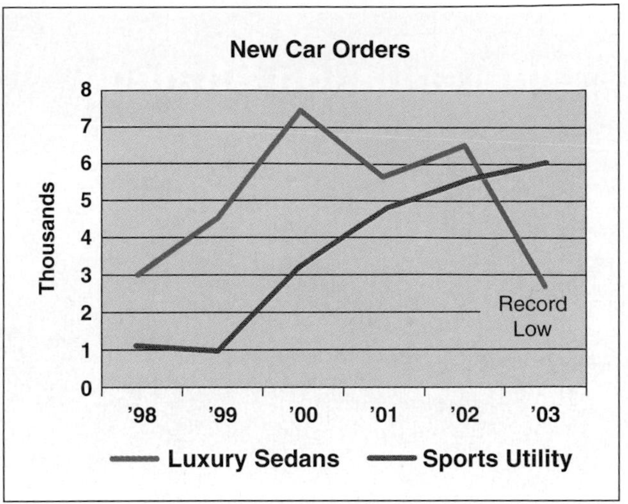

Figure 16.3b—Graph simplified for overhead

The graph shown in Figure 16.3a has too much detail for a visual aid. It was copied from the 2003 annual sales report for Bressler Toyota car dealership, where it filled an entire page. Scaled down to fit a slide format, Figure 16.3a crams too much data into too little space. Figure 16.3b simplifies the graph for an overhead transparency by shortening the numbers, adding a title to the Y axis, changing the format from bars to trend lines, and highlighting a key segment of the graph with the words "record low."

Color

Learning Objective 4

Explain how color can Improve the effectiveness of your slides

Color can increase the appeal and impact of your slides.

Color is a critical design element. It grabs the viewer's attention, emphasizes important ideas, creates contrast, and isolates slide elements. Color can make your slides more attractive, lively, and professional. It can also play a key role in the overall acceptance of your message. Research shows that color visuals can account for 60 percent of an audience's acceptance or rejection of an idea. Color can increase willingness to read by up to 80 percent, and it can enhance learning and improve retention by more than 75 percent.[6]

Your color choice can also stimulate different emotions, as Table 16.1 suggests. For instance, if you wish to excite your audience, add some warm colors such as red and orange to your slides. If you wish to achieve a more relaxed and receptive environment, blue would be a better choice.[7] Remember, color may have a different meaning for certain cultures (see Chapter 3). So if you are creating slides for international audiences, be sensitive to cultural differences.

TABLE 16.1 Color and Emotion

Color	*Emotional Associations*	*Best Use*
	Peaceful, soothing, tranquil, cool, trusting	Background for electronic business presentations (usually dark blue); safe and conservative
	Neutral, innocent, purity, wisdom	Font color of choice for most electronic business presentations with a dark background
	Warm, bright, cheerful, enthusiasm	Text bullets and subheadings with a dark background
	Losses in business, passion, danger, action, pain	Promote action or stimulate audience; seldom used as a background
	Money, growth, assertive, prosperity, envy, relaxation	Highlight and accent color

FIGURE 16.4 Adjusting Color for Lighting Differences

Figure 16.4a—electronic slide

Figure 16.4b—overhead transparency

Figure 16.4a uses a dark background with light text suitable for projecting in a dark room. Figure 16.4b reverses the colors, using a light background with dark text suitable for projecting in a well-lit room.

Use contrasting colors on slides to increase readability.

When selecting color, limit your choices to a few complementary ones, and keep in mind that some colors work better together than others. Contrasting colors, for example, increase readability. So when selecting color for backgrounds, titles, and text, avoid choosing colors that are close in hue: yellow text on a white background, brown on green, blue on black, blue on purple, and so on.[8] Because most electronic presentations are shown in a dark room, use dark colors such as blue for the background, a midrange of brightness for illustrations, and light colors for text. If you are showing overhead transparencies in well-lit rooms, reverse the colors: Use light colors for the background and dark colors for text (see Figure 16.4). When changing colors from slide to slide, don't switch back and forth from very dark to very bright, because it will be jarring to the audience's eyes.[9]

Reverse background and text colors for overhead transparencies.

Background Designs and Clip Art

Your choice of background design sends a message to the audience.

A good background design is the key to a positive first impression. Your design choice can silently persuade the audience to pay attention, or it can encourage them to look the other way. To ensure effective slides, many companies hire professional graphic artists to develop a custom background design to be used in all company slides. Custom designs generally include a company logo, company colors, and other distinguishing design elements.

If you are not using a custom company background design, you have several options. Popular software programs such as Microsoft's PowerPoint come with a collection of professionally developed background designs. Some are nicely done and are effective for business presentations; others are too busy or too colorful to be used in business settings. You can also purchase collections of slide backgrounds over the Internet or obtain them from other software packages. Or you can create your own. Regardless of your source, when selecting a background for slides, avoid ones dominated by heavy color, busy patterns, or strong graphics—all three of which would compete with your text. Choose a background design that is simple, is appropriate for the subject, and will appeal to the audience. As Kevan Allbee recommends, you don't want to use a blue-jean background when the audience is wearing pin-striped suits.

Select a background design that fits with your message and your audience.

Your selection of clip art is just as important as your selection of a background design. Inappropriate, improperly sized, or too much clip art detracts from a slide's

FIGURE 16.5 Using Clip Art Effectively

Figure 16.5a

Figure 16.5b

Both of these slides use clip art effectively. In Figure 16.5a, the small target placed in the title adds impact and helps explain the purpose of the slide. The body of the slide has no room for additional clip art without its crowding and competing with the text. Figure 16.5b uses a similar piece of clip art to emphasize the theme of the slide. The clip art is larger and placed to the side of the text to fill the void. Although the company usually includes its logo (a small cake) at the bottom right corner of its slides, the logo has been removed so that it doesn't compete with the clip art.

message. So don't throw in art simply because you like it or have it. Instead, use art to help explain the main idea of your message and draw attention to key parts of your slide. Furthermore, make sure the art fits the slide's overall design, and place it carefully so that it doesn't compete with text and other design elements (see Figure 16.5).

Use clip art selectively.

Fonts and Type Styles

The selection of fonts offered by most software programs is immense. However, even though decorative fonts appear attractive, few of them project well on screen. That's because print on screen has a much lower resolution than print on a page. When selecting fonts and type styles for slides, follow these guidelines:

Decorative fonts and italicized type are hard to read on slides.

- Avoid script or decorative fonts.
- Limit your fonts to one or two per slide (if two fonts are used, reserve one for headings and the other for bulleted items).
- Use boldface type for electronic slides so that letters won't look washed out.
- Avoid italicized type because it is difficult to read when projected.
- Use both uppercase and lowercase letters, with extra white space between lines of text.

Keep in mind that bigger is not always better when it comes to type size. Large type can force text from one line to two and diminish the slide's white space. A good rule of thumb is to use between 24- and 36-point type for electronic presentations, reserving the larger size for titles and the smaller size for bullet items. Headings of the same level of importance should use the same font, type size, and color. Once you have selected your fonts and type styles, test them for readability by viewing sample slides from a distance (see Figure 16.6).

Test your font and typeface selections by viewing slides from the back of a room.

Achieving Design Consistency

Graphic elements such as borders, backgrounds, and a company logo should repeat on every visual. Consistency of design not only makes your slides easier to read but gives

Be consistent in designing slides.

FIGURE 16.6 Selecting Readable Fonts and Type Styles

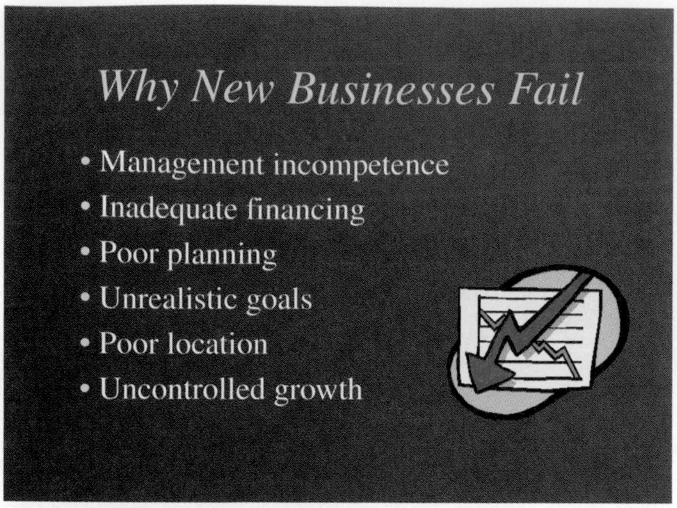

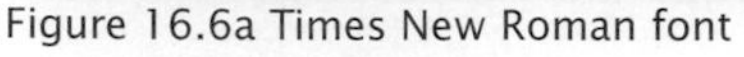

Figure 16.6a Times New Roman font

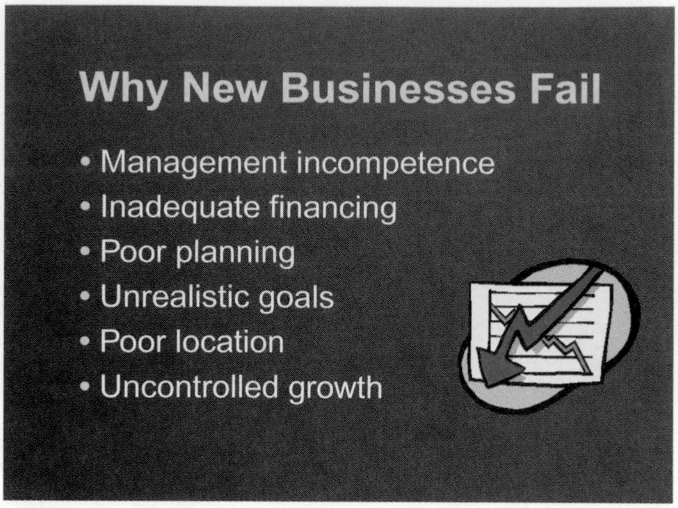

Figure 16.6b Arial font

Times New Roman is a standard font for many print documents; however, as Figure 16.6a demonstrates, the serifs at the end of each letter make it difficult to read on screen, and so does the italicized type. As Figure 16.6b shows, sans serif fonts such as Arial are a better choice for slides; they are cleaner and easier to read from a distance.

Slide master stores design elements and helps ensure consistency among your slides.

your presentation a clean, professional look. Fortunately, most electronic presentation software programs can help you with this challenge. When you program your design selections into the software's special **slide master**, the saved design elements are included on all the new slides you insert in your presentation (see Figure 16.7). The slide master can be used whether you are designing overhead transparencies or an electronic slide show.

Layout templates are easy to use.

Another good way to achieve design consistency is to use the layout templates that are included with most presentation software packages. As Figure 16.8 shows, each layout contains placeholders for specific slide elements such as a title, graphic art, or bulleted text. The templates use a landscape orientation, which minimizes the amount of text that wraps to the next line. When possible, place bulleted text toward the top of the slide, where it is easier to read from a distance.

Adding Animation and Special Effects

You can add sound, animation, and video to electronic slides.

Electronic slide shows can make use of a number of special effects, including sound, animation, and video (for links to special-effect online resources and PowerPoint tips, see "Sharpening Your Career Skills: Ordinary or Extraordinary? Using the Web to Produce Better Presentations"). You can even automate your program to move from one slide to the next without the speaker's intervention. Automation is especially useful for running electronic presentations on television monitors in large places such as conventions and trade shows, where the slide show is, in effect, the only information present. Automation and special effects are not possible with static overhead transparencies.

Don't overdo special effects.

The biggest challenge is the tendency to use too many of these features. Excessive special effects overwhelm and distract audiences. Used sparingly, however, special effects can add punch to an oral presentation. So before you add animation or special effects to your presentation, ask yourself, Will the special effect support and enhance the message? If not, don't use it.

Learning Objective 5

Discuss the benefits of using transitions and builds in electronic presentations

Transitions and Builds

Transitions control how one electronic slide replaces another on screen. When used effectively, transitions can make your presentation flow smoothly from slide to slide so

FIGURE 16.7 PowerPoint Slide Master

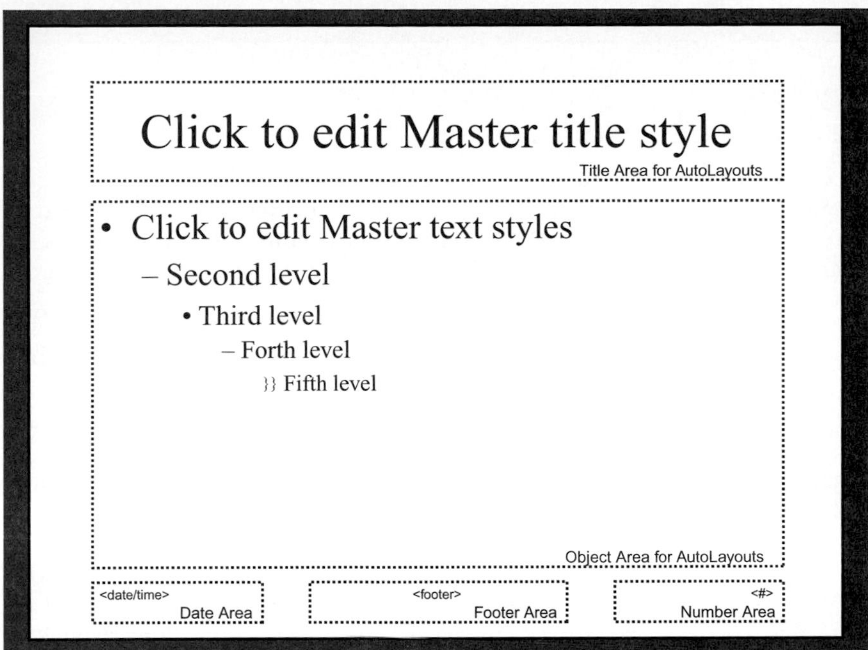

Whenever you want to change all the slides in a presentation (except title slides) in exactly the same way, use slide master.

FIGURE 16.8 PowerPoint's Predefined Layouts

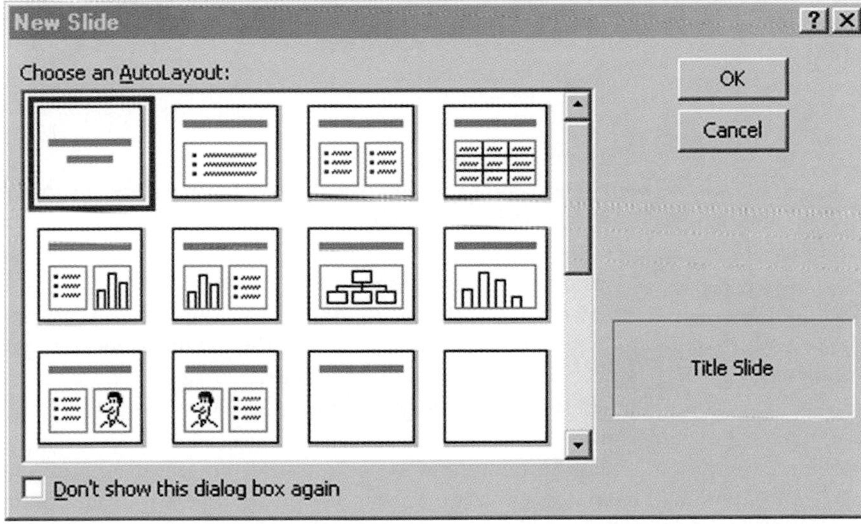

When designing a new slide for a presentation, beginning with one of PowerPoint's preformatted layouts can save you time and improve the consistency of your presentation.

that you keep the audience's attention. Most electronic software packages include a number of effective transition effects. Table 16.2 lists the ones most commonly used.

Use transitions between electronic slides to soften your approach.

Similar to transitions, **builds** control the release of text, graphics, and other elements on slides. With builds you can make your bullet points appear one at a time rather than having all of them appear on a slide at once (making it difficult to focus on a single point). This controlled release of information helps draw the audience's attention to the point being discussed and prevents the audience from reading ahead.

"Builds" help the audience focus on one bullet point at a time.

The most basic build effects are flys and dissolves. You can choose the direction your bullets fly in, or you can choose a motion effect similar to those available in slide

Sharpening Your Career Skills

Ordinary or Extraordinary? Using the Web to Produce Better Presentations

Looking for some PowerPoint tutorials? Need expert advice on mastering the software's advanced features? Searching for the perfect photo, sound bite, or video clip to enhance your presentation? One good place to begin your journey for such information is the web. Follow these links to a wealth of online resources and transform your electronic presentations from ordinary slide shows to extraordinary events.

The Best PowerPoint Tutorials

Microsoft: www.microsoft.com/education/?ID=PptTutorial
Indiana University—Purdue University, Indianapolis: www.iupui.edu/~webtrain/tutorials/powerpoint2000_basics.html
University of Maryland: www.education.umd.edu/blt/tcp/resetpp.html
University of Alberta: www.quasar.ualberta.ca/edit202/tutorial/PowerPoint/PowerPoint

To locate a complete list of tutorials on the web, go to www.queryserver.com, enter the term "PowerPoint Tutorial," and press "search."

Articles

For more than 150 how-to articles on PowerPoint, with more being added every day, go to www.computertim.com.

Newsgroup and Forum

The PowerPoint newsgroup can be found at microsoft.public.powerpoint. A PowerPoint forum is at www.zdnet.com/community.

Artistic Tips and Photography

For tips on how to use Adobe Photoshop techniques for producing better slides, and for a search engine for locating stock photographs, go to www.creativepro.com. For free fonts and graphics, go to www.thefreesite.com.

Sound Libraries

For voices from movies and for speeches by prominent individuals, go to www.dailywav.com or www.wavcentral.com. For other free sounds, including music, go to www.thefreesite.com.

Software

For a vast library of free utilities and shareware to energize your presentations with 3D effects, to animate title slides, to add attractive backgrounds, to add unusual fonts, and to convert presentations into streaming web broadcasts, go to www.download.com.

Design and Color Selection

For learning the basics of good design, tips about layout, advice about font selection, and how to choose appropriate colors, go to http://powerpoint.35mmslides.com/goodbad.html. For a site that offers comprehensive treatment on the psychology of color usage, color and the brain, color in design, and color and computers, go to www.colormatters.com.

Using New Technologies with PowerPoint

To brighten up your slides, learn how to create your own Flash movie and insert it into PowerPoint. For eight Flash lessons in all, and a free trial version of Flash, go to www.techtv.com/dash/animationtipis. Another Flash tutorial is at www.flashgeek.com/tutorials/index.htm.

With Online Presenter, you can easily present and control your presentation from any PC to anyone in the world. With EmailPresenter, you can deliver your fully loaded presentation with speed and security. With PowerConverter, you can convert your presentation into Flash format for easy posting to your website. Learn about these technologies at www.presentationpro.com.

For an online tutorial using PowerPoint slides on how to create a streaming audio presentation with synchronized slides, go to www.online.uillinois.edu/lynnward/realmedia/realmedia/index.htm, which features RealMedia technology. For HotFoot technology to create a synchronized presentation, go to www.aspstreet.com/tools/print.taf/id,639.

Other Free Materials

For PowerPoint tips and tricks, for art, for technical support, and for software updates, go to www.microsoft.com/office/powerpoint.

Effective presentations have more to do with your audience's visual preferences than with your own. Read how George Fox University increased the persuasiveness of presentations by using audience-focused imagery. The same site offers free design templates. Go to www.presentersuniversity.com.

For learning how to make clearer presentations, animate graphics, simulate templates, post a presentation, change colors and textures, master layout techniques, and do a host of other things, go to www.zdnet.com/help/specials/powerpoint/stories/1103.html. You can also "Ask an Expert" at this site.

Career Applications

1. Visit several of the recommended websites to take a tutorial or read some expert advice. How did the material offered at these sites help you improve your electronic slides?
2. For what kinds of presentations might the advanced artistic and animation features discussed at these websites be appropriate?

TABLE 16.2 Types of Transition Effects

Transition	*Effect*
Blind	The new slide is unveiled in a series of horizontal or vertical rows, similar to the effect of opening window blinds.
Box	The new slide "grows" from the middle of the previous slide, or grows inward from the edges of the screen.
Checkerboard	The new slide appears over the previous slide as a series of boxes.
Dissolve	The new slide is unveiled using an advanced case of checker-boards with numerous small boxes or other graphic elements.
Wipe	The new slide replaces the previous slide from left to right, top to bottom, or diagonally.
Fade	The first slide fades to black before the next slide is revealed.
Paintbrush	The new slide is "painted" on top of the preceding slide in a series of "strokes."
Split	The new slide expands horizontally or vertically from the center of the screen.

transitions. Builds can also alter the intensity of the text's color for one bullet as you discuss it while fading the text of others into the background.

Once you've assigned builds to your slides, use a mouse to control the motion. For instance, click the mouse and the slide's title appears. Click again, and the first bullet point appears. Keep clicking to display each programmed element of your slide. You can even build graphs section by section. Say, for example, you have a graph that illustrates how sales have taken off in the past year. You could show the whole graph all at one time and emphasize the spike in the final number verbally, or you could have the bars fly onto the graph one at a time, building up to the spike in the final quarter.

As with design elements, use the same transitions and builds throughout your presentation. Don't introduce text that builds left to right on one slide and from top to bottom on the next. To ensure consistency among your slides, program any transitions and build elements into the slide master (as you would design elements).

Use the same transitions and builds throughout your presentation.

Hyperlinks

Hyperlinks allow you to build interactivity into electronic slides by coding text, graphics, or pictures with hypertext markup language. When you click on a slide's hyperlink with a mouse, you are taken to a different slide in your presentation, to other files on a computer, or even to a webpage. Hyperlinks are a great tool for illustrating fine details without having to incorporate each detail into a slide. You can also use hyperlinks to customize one electronic presentation for several audiences. You simply create extra slides for each audience, "hide" them from the regular lineup by invoking a special "hidden" command when building the presentation, and activate them by clicking on the hyperlinks embedded in your slides.

Hyperlinks add flexibility to an electronic slide presentation.

Hyperlinked slides are especially helpful during the question-and-answer period of the presentation. For instance, when viewing the slides about holiday promotion plans (see Figure 16.9), marketing managers would probably want to see more information than operational managers would. Or, as another example, international customers may need information about overseas shipping policies, whereas local customers would not. You can even use hyperlinks to call up a set of "just-in-case" slides to use if an audience needs more help understanding a difficult concept.

Hyperlinked slides are especially useful during question-and-answer periods.

FIGURE 16.9 Building Slides with Hyperlinks

Figure 16.9a

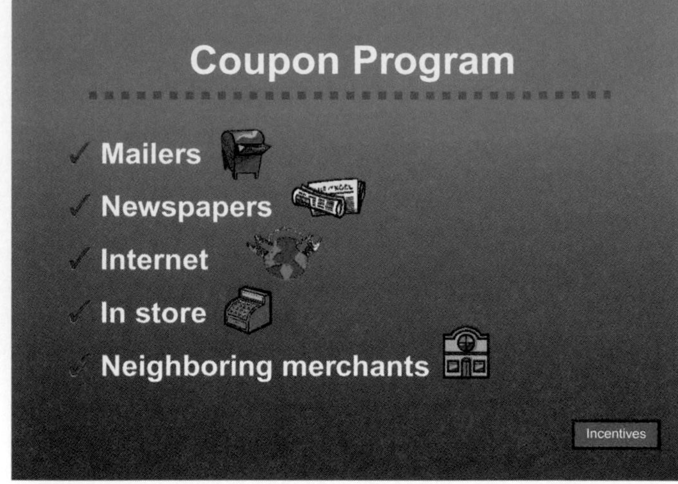

Figure 16.9b

Both of these slides contain multiple hyperlinks. By clicking on the words that appear on the gifts in Figure 16.9a, the speaker advances to a new slide explaining the details of that particular program. For instance, if the speaker clicks on coupons, the slide show will advance to Figure 16.9b. Each of the bullets in Figure 16.9b also contains a hyperlink. By clicking on the mailbox icon, the speaker will advance to a series of slides discussing how mailers work and how much the program costs. One slide will even provide a sample copy of a typical coupon. To return to Figure 16.9a, the speaker clicks on *Incentives* in the lower right corner.

COMPLETING EFFECTIVE SLIDES FOR ORAL PRESENTATIONS

Learning Objective 6

List seven characteristics of effective slides

Review and revise your slides as you would any written message.

Just as you would review any written message for content, style, tone, readability, clarity, and conciseness, you must also do the same for slides and transparencies. As you look over your presentation for the final time, make sure that all visuals are

- **Readable.** Are the font sizes large enough? Too large? Can they be seen from the back of the room? Does the font color stand out from the background?
- **Consistent.** Are colors and design elements used consistently?
- **Simple.** Should some information be illustrated by a chart, diagram, or picture? Should some information be eliminated or moved to handouts or backup slides? Should some slides be eliminated altogether?
- **Audience-centered.** Are design elements such as clip art and color appropriate for the audience?
- **Clear.** Is the main point of a slide obvious? Easy to understand? Can the audience grasp the main point in five to eight seconds?
- **Mechanically correct.** Is text written in concise phrases? Are the phrases parallel?
- **Focused.** Does each slide cover only one thought, concept, or idea? Does the slide grab the viewer's attention in the right place and support the key points of the message? Are arrows, symbols, or other techniques used to draw the audience's attention to the key sections of a chart or diagram?

Effective slides do not distract the audience or upstage the speaker.

Remember, you want the audience to listen to you, not study the slides. So unless you keep things simple, your slides will be counterproductive.

Slider sorter view makes it easier to check your slides for consistency and logical organization.

Electronic presentation software can help you during the editing and revision process. As Figure 16.10 shows, the *slide sorter view* lets you see a file's entire batch of slides at once, making it relatively easy to add and delete slides, reposition slides, and check slides for design consistency. You can also use this view to preview animation and transition effects and experiment with design elements. For instance, if you wish to experiment with a different background design or different font, select a new design

FIGURE 16.10 Slide Sorter View

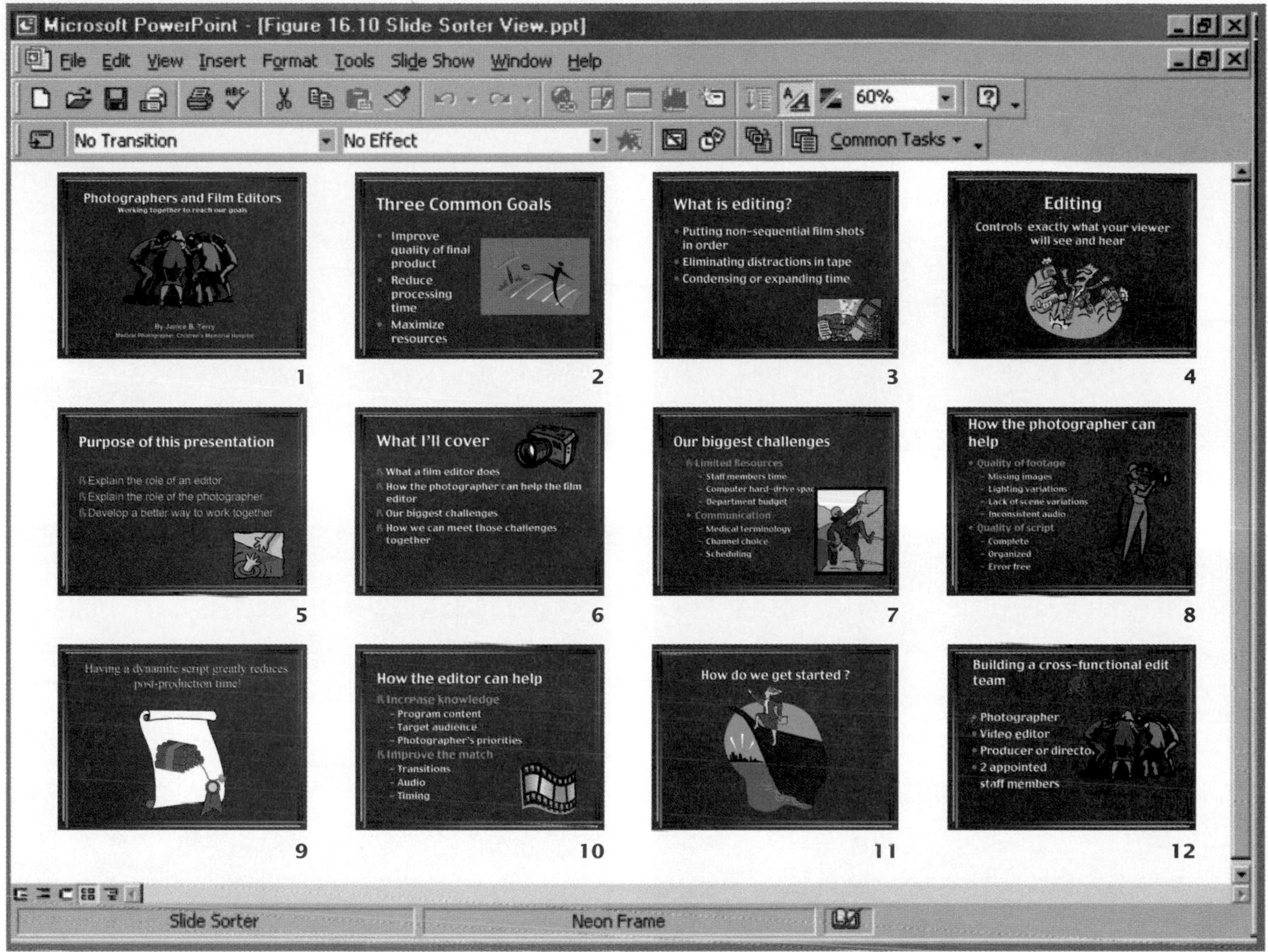

Examining thumbnails of slides on one screen is the best way to check the overall design of your final product. Note how each slide in this group looks uncluttered (not overburdened with text) and uses consistent colors and design elements.

element and preview it in your slides. If you choose to keep the new design, execute the "apply all" command to update all existing slides and to change the slide master, which applies the design changes to any new slides you create. Of course, it's always a good idea to rename and save a copy of your file before making such irreversible changes.

Developing a Clear Structure for Oral Presentations

Poorly structured oral presentations are like books without chapters—they can leave the audience wondering where they are and where they are headed. Three types of structural slides can help you keep the audience on track. Used properly, they tell the audience what you're talking about, why, and in what order:

Learning Objective 7

Describe three types of structural slides and highlight the function of each slide

- A **cover slide** is your opportunity to make a good first impression on the audience. As Figure 16.11 shows, a cover slide is the equivalent of a report's title page and should contain these elements: the title of your presentation (and optional subtitle), the presenter's name and affiliation (if appropriate), and an image that grabs the audience's attention and invites them to start looking at the screen.

A cover slide serves the same function as the cover page of a report.

- **Introduction slides**, such as the ones illustrated in Figures 16.11, define the topic of the presentation, clarify the topic, and inform the audience why you are speaking

FIGURE 16.11 Cover and Introduction Slides

Figure 16.11a Cover slide

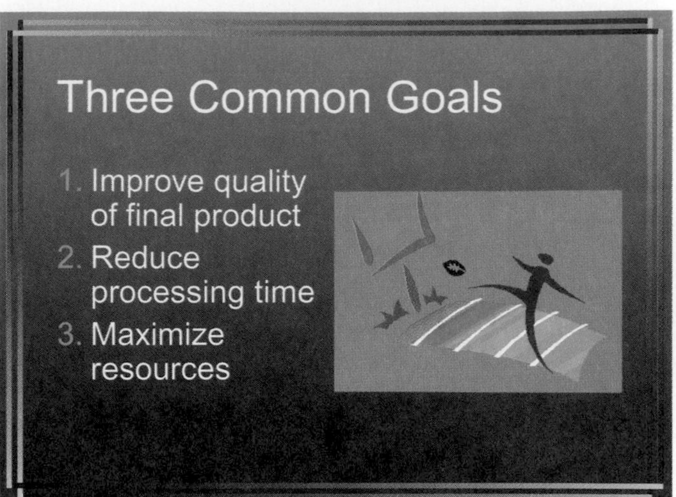

Figure 16.11b Introduction slide—clarify topic

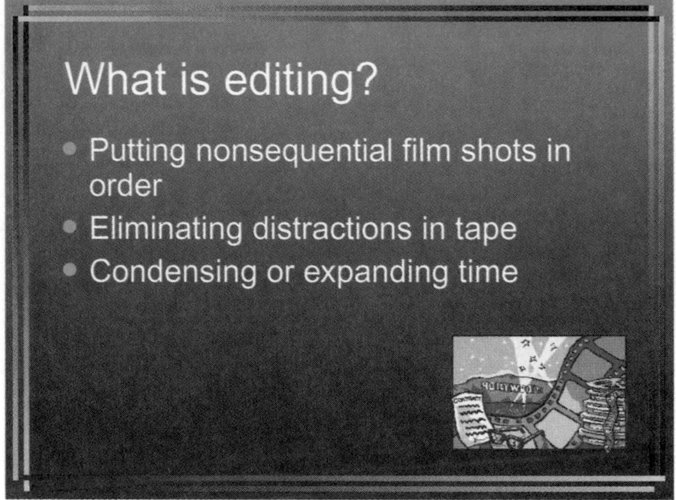

Figure 16.11c Introduction slide—clarify topic

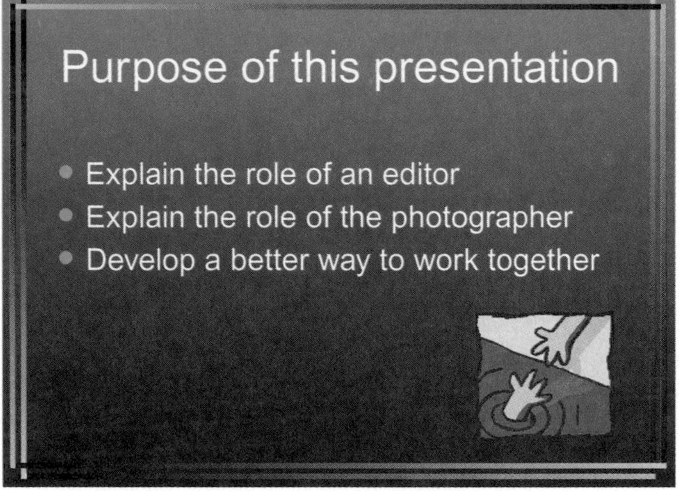

Figure 16.11d Introduction slide—explain purpose

Effective presentations begin with an inviting cover slide, followed by several introduction slides that define key terms, clarify the topic, and explain the purpose of the presentation.

Use introduction slides to
- Define and clarify your topic
- Explain the purpose of your presentation

Blueprint slides provide structural signposts and help the audience navigate your presentation.

on this topic in addition to what expectations, if any, you may have for the audience. Are you going to ask them to make a decision? Take some action? Or are you simply explaining a new company policy?[10]

- A **blueprint slide** serves as your agenda chart and provides a road map of your presentation, telling the audience where you're going and where you've been. Used in the beginning of a presentation, it lists three or four major points your presentation will cover. Used later in the presentation, **moving blueprint slides** serve as a signpost; they signal to the audience that you are moving from one major part of the presentation to another (see Figure 16.12). Moving blueprint slides can also be used at the end of the presentation to summarize and review the presentation's key points.

Figure 16.13 illustrates the placement of cover, introduction, and blueprint slides in a typical oral presentation. Notice how the blueprint slide reappears or moves throughout the presentation.

FIGURE 16.12 Blueprint Slides

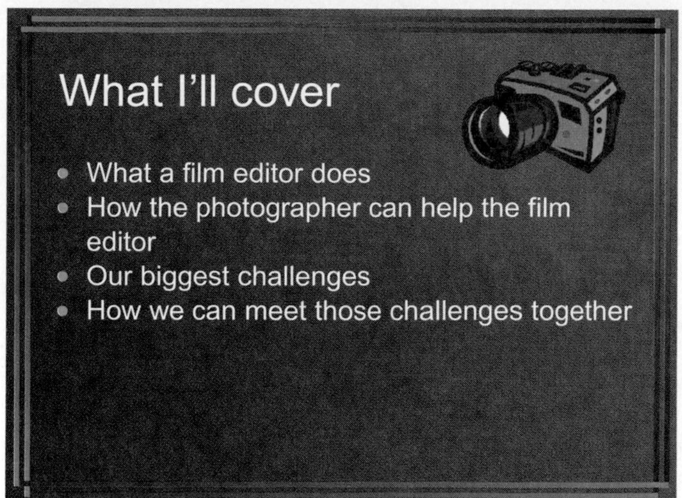

Figure 16.12a Blueprint slide

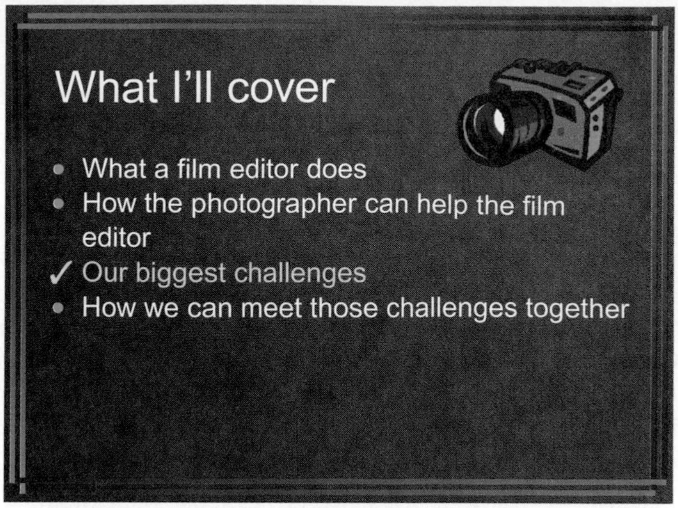

Figure 16.12b Moving blueprint slide

A blueprint slide, such as Figure 16.12a, is introduced at the beginning of the presentation to define its structure. It is reintroduced each time the speaker moves to a new topic. For instance, the yellow checkmark and text in Figure 16.12b highlights the speaker's next topic. This slide is called a moving blueprint because the next time it is introduced, the yellow checkmark will appear before the fourth bullet point, whose text will also change to yellow. Blueprint slides share the same design elements as other slides in the presentation, but they can have a slightly different background design or use a different color to distinguish them from other slides in the presentation.

Creating Effective Handouts

Handouts are a terrific way to offer your audience additional material without overloading your slides with information. Candidates for good handout material include the following:[11]

Good handouts keep the audience informed without overwhelming them with information.

- **Complex charts and diagrams.** Charts and tables that are too unwieldy for the screen or that demand thorough analysis make good handouts. One common approach is to create a stripped-down version of a chart or graphic for the presentation slide and include a more detailed version in your handout.
- **Company reports.** In most cases lengthy research reports promise information overload and are inappropriate for handouts. But photocopies of specific pages that highlight or underline relevant text are welcome material.
- **Magazine articles.** Magazine articles make good handout materials. They are easy to photocopy and they are already formatted in an easy-to-read layout. However,

FIGURE 16.13 Structure of a Typical Presentation

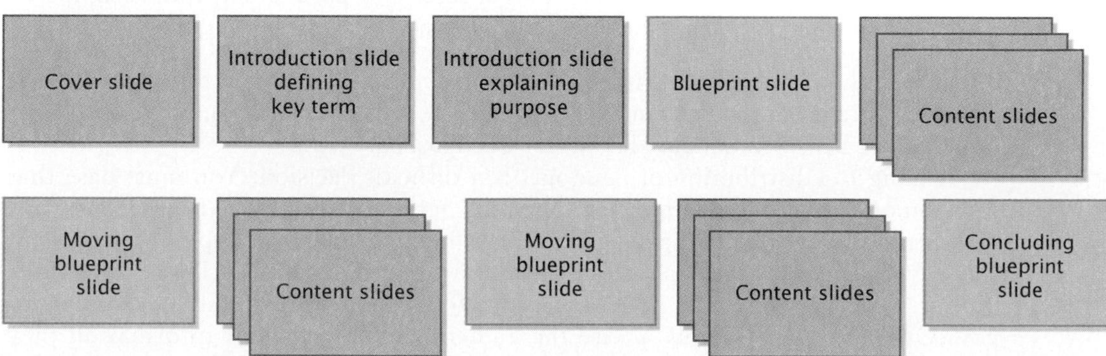

By following a structure similar to the one depicted in this diagram, you can help the audience follow your material.

Sharpening Your Career Skills

Handouts That Won't Get Trashed

Good handouts extend your message and serve as a valuable resource. They are the only insurance that people will remember your talk tomorrow, next week, or next month. People listen at or below a 25 percent efficiency rate, remember only about half of what's said during a 10-minute conversation, and forget half of that within 48 hours. A well-prepared handout is the best way to jog someone's memory and to make sure the hard work you put into your presentation is not wasted. To help you create handouts that won't get trashed, here are some guidelines.

Plan, Plan, Plan

One way to create effective handouts is to plan them simultaneously with your presentation material. By planning both together, you allow one to inform the other, so that by the end of the preparation process, you have a well-researched presentation and an even better researched packet of handout materials. The added bonus of planning the two together is that you will deliver a more informed presentation. Gathering additional information for your handouts will increase your knowledge of your subject.

Draw the Line

How do you determine which material is best suited for handouts? One approach is the draw-the-line technique. Think of handouts as a place to store information overflow. Draw a line down the middle of a sheet of paper and label one column "presentation" and the other "handouts." Then separate primary information from secondary information, assigning primary information (need to know) to the "presentation" column and secondary information (nice to know) to the "handout" column.

Be Selective

When adding material to the handout column, be selective. Some experts suggest that you limit the quantity of handouts to 10 pages. This is a good guideline, but it depends on which 10 pages you decide to include. So once you've assembled material for your handouts, weed out once more. Eliminate duplicate material and minimize information overkill. Include information that directly supports the goal of your presentation. If a one-page handout will do the job, don't feel you have to provide more. If you choose to include more than 10 pages, color-code your documents to help the audience differentiate between important and extra material. Finally, organize your handouts logically, add a title page, and bind them for a professional look.

Career Applications

1. When preparing your presentation and handouts, how can you draw the line between "need-to-know" and "nice-to-know" information?
2. Why is it important to plan your presentation and handouts simultaneously?

be sure to create quality copies. Nothing is more frustrating than an illegible handout.

- **Case studies.** Summaries of case studies along with references and contact information make good supplemental reading material.
- **Websites.** Lists of websites related to your topic are useful. In addition to the URL address, annotate each item with a one- or two-sentence summary of each site's content.
- **Copies of presentation slides.** In many cases, audiences like to have small print versions of slides used by the speaker (about three to a page) along with accompanying comments and blank lines for note taking.

Other good handout materials include brochures, pictures, outlines, and a copy of the presentation agenda. For tips on creating effective handout material, see "Sharpening Your Career Skills: Handouts That Won't Get Trashed."

Handouts can be both useful and distracting.

Timing the distribution of handouts is a difficult decision. You must base that decision on the content of your handouts, the nature of your presentation, and your personal preference. Some speakers distribute handout materials—perhaps copies of slides, with space for taking notes—before the presentation begins. The downside of doing so is that it allows your audience to read ahead instead of listening to you. Other speakers simply advise the audience of the types of information they are including in handouts but delay distributing anything until they have finished speaking.

FIGURE 16.14 Speaker's Notes

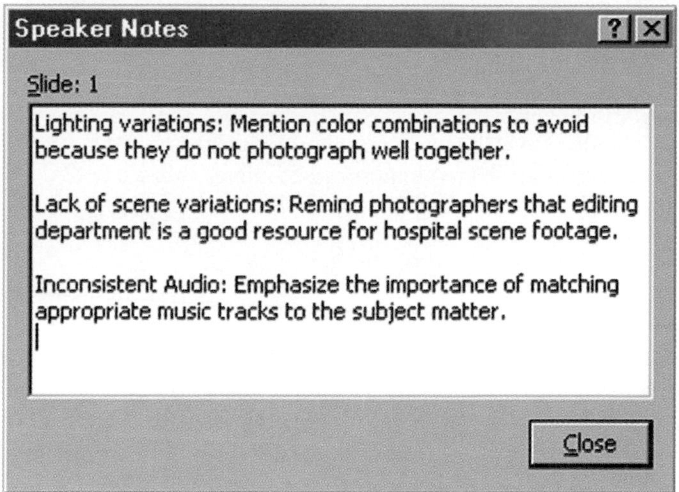

Figure 16.14a Speaker's notes

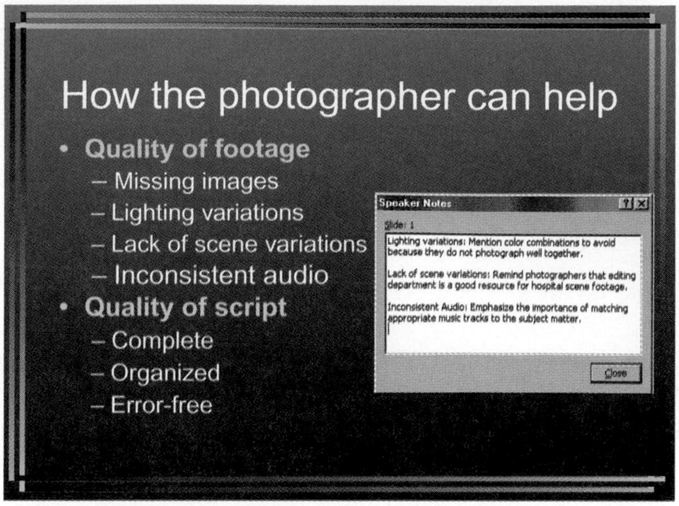

How the photographer can help

- Quality of footage
  - Missing images
  - Lighting variations
  - Lack of scene variations
  - Inconsistent audio
- Quality of script
  - Complete
  - Organized
  - Error-free

Figure 16.14b Corresponding slide

Speaker's notes, such as the ones displayed in Figure 16.14a, are an added benefit of using electronic presentations. The notes are displayed only on the presenter's screen while the corresponding slide, Figure 16.14b, is presented to the audience.

Practicing Your Delivery

Don't read your slides to the audience.

As Kevan Allbee and David Green know, the most common mistake people make when delivering a presentation is reading their slides. When speakers read bulleted points to the audience word for word, they lose contact with the audience and lose voice inflection. As a result, the listeners become bored and eventually stop paying attention. Moreover, people who read slides insult the audience's intelligence. Audiences expect speakers to add valuable information that is not included on slides. To do so, however, speakers must know enough about the subject of their presentation to elaborate on each bullet point. They must do their research and practice.

Learn as much as you can about the subject of your presentation.

When practicing your presentation, run through it about five times using your electronic slides or overhead transparencies. Your credibility is dramatically enhanced when you move seamlessly through your presentation. Practicing helps keep you on track, helps you maintain a conversational tone with your audience, and boosts your confidence and composure.

Don't be too dependent on your slides or notes when speaking.

Use speaker's notes to jog your memory.

As you practice, try not to be so dependent on your slides that you're unable to function without them. Some people are quite capable of delivering a perfect presentation without notes. But for those who require notes, electronic software gives you an added advantage. Speaker's notes (as shown in Figure 16.14) are a helpful tool included with most popular electronic presentation software packages. You can display these notes along with a scaled-down version of your slide on a computer screen so that only you can see the notes. Speaker's notes are not intended to be read word for word. Instead, use them to list important facts or to remind yourself of supporting comments you should make as you present the slide. For instance, you might input such notes as "Don't forget to explain the impact of last year's bad weather on sales."

Practicing in front of a live audience is the best way to perfect your presentation.

Practicing in front of a mirror is always a good idea, especially if your primary concern is the mechanics of the presentation. But if you're concerned about the content of your presentation and the effectiveness of your slides, nothing beats practicing in front of people who are willing to stop you when they don't understand your message or when they need you to clarify a point on your slide.

As you practice, keep in mind that using overhead transparencies and electronic slides effectively during oral presentations requires three extra steps: First, you must learn how to use the software to create your slides or transparencies and you must

Best of the Web

Look Smart in Your Electronic Presentations

Visit the presentation center at 3M and follow the expert advice on creating and delivering effective oral presentations. Find out why a bad presentation can kill even the best idea. Did you pick the right colors? Is your presentation too long? Too wordy? Find out why a strong template is the key to positive first impressions. Review the five tips for better presentation. Download some templates and look smart. Log on and learn the secrets from the pros. You'll be glad you did.

www.3m.com/meetingnetwork/presentations/

learn how to operate the technology to deliver your visuals. You must also know how to fix minor technological glitches, since you will likely encounter some during a presentation. Second, you must introduce your visuals and practice coordinating your visuals with your talk so that the result is as seamless as a professionally staged production. Third, you must limit the number of slides so that you can deliver your presentation in the allotted time frame.

Technology can and will fail.

Introducing Slides

All visual aids must be properly introduced. Too many speakers show a visual aid first and then introduce it. Effective speakers do the reverse. They verbally introduce the next visual aid before they show it by stating their transition out loud:

Introduce your slides before you show them.

> "We can get started with this new program by introducing these policies . . ."
> "The next segment of my presentation discusses . . ."
> "The three most significant issues facing our company are . . ."

Practice placing overhead transparencies on a projector so that it becomes second nature.

Effective speakers also avoid referring to the slides in their transitional comments. For instance, they don't say, "The next slide illustrates . . ." Instead, they match their words to the slide and let the audience make the proper connection.

You are not tied to the projector or front of the room with electronic slides.

If you are using overhead transparencies, the best approach is to introduce the next overhead as you remove the old one and position the new one on the projector. Immediately cover all but the first bulleted phrase with a sheet of paper to prevent the audience from reading ahead. Then step aside to give the audience about five seconds to look it over before you start discussing it. As you advance through your discussion, you can move the paper down the transparency to uncover the next bullet, waiting a few seconds for the audience to find your point of reference. When you are finished using the transparency, it's often a good idea to cover it until you're ready to introduce a new slide. Keep in mind that placing overhead transparencies on a projector takes a bit more time than clicking a mouse to advance electronic slides, so you may be introducing a new topic while the old one is still displayed. Don't be concerned. The audience will probably have little interest in reading the old transparency once your comments move forward.[12]

It takes practice to learn how to focus on the audience and interact with them while using electronic slides and overhead transparencies.

If you are using electronic slides, the best approach is to introduce the slide before you show it and then give the audience a few seconds to view the title and design elements. With electronic slides, you have more control over the release of information than you do if you're using overhead transparencies. For instance, you can release bulleted points or sections of a graph as you discuss them. This control gives you more flexibility to move about the room than you have with overheads. Take advantage of this benefit. Moving around can increase audience involvement and enhance your impact. You may even want to invest in a mouse with an extended cord or a battery-operated remote mouse to maximize your freedom to walk around.

If you're using a pointer, keep in mind that it's a tool meant to guide the audience to a specific part of a visual. It is not a riding crop, conductor's baton, leg scratcher, or walking stick. Use the pointer only at the time you need it, then fold it and remove it from sight. If you are using a laser pointer that puts a focused dot of light on the desired part of your visual, don't overdo it. A laser pointer is an excellent tool if used judiciously, but in the hands of the overzealous presenter, it can become a distraction.[13]

Not sure whether a slide is effective? Ask a friend or co-worker. A second pair of eyes can be your best critic.

Limiting the Number of Slides

Even if you produce an outstanding set of slides, they'll do you no good if you can't complete your presentation in the allotted time. Having too many visuals can detract from your message. It forces you to either rush through a presentation or skip slides—some of which may be critical to your message.

So how do you gauge the correct number of slides to include? That depends on the length of your presentation and the complexity of the subject matter. If you are using electronic slides, you must also factor in the time it takes for the special effects. As a general guideline, try to average one slide for every 90 seconds you speak. For a 30-minute presentation, you would create about 20 slides.[14] Of course, you may spend more time discussing some slides than others, so the best way to find the "right" number is to time your presentation as you practice.

You can keep track of the amount of time you spend on each slide and on the presentation as a whole by using the timing function included in most electronic presentation software. This information can help you identify slides that take too long to discuss, either because they are too complex or because they cover too much information. For example, if you find yourself spending five minutes explaining a single slide, you may want to simplify the slide, split it into two slides, or even omit the slide and its related discussion altogether. Similarly, if you discover that you're taking only a few seconds to discuss a slide, it may be a clue that the slide is too elementary.[15]

Limit the number of slides to a few good ones.

As you time your presentation, keep in mind that it is much better to cover less information in a relaxed style than to cover too much information in a hurried and disorganized state. No one likes to listen to someone who keeps saying, "I just don't have enough time."[16] Build enough time in your presentation for a smile, an anecdote, or further illustration of a point. Remember, audiences won't be angry if you let them out early, but they might be upset if you keep them late.

Audiences like speakers who run on time, smile, and let them out early.

COMMUNICATION CHALLENGES AT ALLBEE GREEN

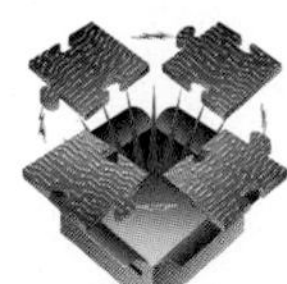

As creative partner of Allbee Green, Kevan Allbee is responsible for developing electronic presentations for major corporations. But whether he is developing an elaborate event with live music and theatrical effects for a trade show or a simple slide show for a small group, Allbee carefully plans the content of the presentation before designing the slides. First, he defines the objectives of the presentation and determines what he wants the audience to do at the end of the presentation. Then he writes the script, working toward the goal of motivating the audience to act on the information in the presentation. Finally, he develops slides by carefully selecting images to add interest and by composing short phrases for the slides to emphasize the major points in his script.

Team Challenge: Review the points in this chapter on developing electronic presentations. With several of your classmates, develop an outline of the chapter material for a presentation on "How to Develop an Effective Electronic Presentation." Assume that your audience will be a group of college students and that the information will be presented in a classroom setting. What will be the objectives of your presentation? What points should you include? Which points in the chapter, if any, should you eliminate? How will you introduce the topic? How will you end the presentation?

Individual Challenge: Using the outline prepared as a team challenge, develop the content for each slide. Determine whether you will illustrate your presentation with photos or clip art, and compose the wording for each slide that you plan to use. Write effective titles, subheadings, and bulleted phrases by following the guidelines in this chapter. ■

SUMMARY OF LEARNING OBJECTIVES

1 **Explain how visual aids enhance oral presentations, and list several popular types of visual aids.** Visual aids create interest, illustrate and clarify important points, add variety, and help the listener absorb the information being presented. Popular visual aids include overhead transparencies, electronic presentations, chalkboards and whiteboards, flipcharts, 35-millimeter slides, product samples, models, audiotapes, filmstrips, and videotapes.

2 **Highlight the advantages and disadvantages of using overhead transparencies as visual aids.** Overhead transparencies are inexpensive, easy to create, and simple to use. They can be viewed in full light, allowing presenters to maintain full eye contact with their audience. The biggest disadvantage of overhead transparencies is their permanent printed format. Transparencies must be replaced if their content changes. Moreover, they are fragile and can be bulky to store and transport. Furthermore, because transparencies must be manually placed on overhead projectors, they limit the speaker's ability to move about the room.

3 **Highlight the advantages and disadvantages of using electronic presentations as visual aids.** The biggest advantage of electronic presentations is their computerized format, which permits real-time modifications and the ability to add automated features and special effects. Unlike transparencies, electronic presentations are easy to store and transport. Two drawbacks of using electronic presentations are the tendency to overdo animation effects and the need for computers and expensive display equipment to show electronic slides to large audiences.

4 **Explain how color can improve the effectiveness of your slides.** Color creates contrast, grabs the viewer's attention, emphasizes key ideas, and draws attention to slide elements. It can influence the overall acceptance of a message, increase learning, improve retention, and stimulate emotions.

5 **Discuss the benefits of using transitions and builds in electronic presentations.** If used properly, transitions and builds can enhance an electronic presentation by softening the movement between slides, controlling the release of information, guiding audience attention to key points, increasing audience interest in the presentation, and adding consistency to slides.

6 **List seven characteristics of effective slides.** Effective slides are readable by all members in the audience, consistent, simple, audience-centered, clear, mechanically correct, and focused.

7 **Describe three types of structural slides and highlight the function of each slide.** Three types of structural slides are (1) a cover slide, which provides basic information about the presentation and is the equivalent of a report's title page; (2) introductory slides, which define and clarify the presentation topic and explain the purpose of the presentation; and (3) blueprint slides, which list the main segments to be addressed during the presentation and guide the audience from one segment to the next.

TEST YOUR KNOWLEDGE

1. When creating slides for oral presentations, which should you do first: select the background design for your slides or write your bulleted phrases? Explain your answer.
2. What is the recommended number of fonts you should use per slide?
3. How can hyperlinks be used in electronic slides?
4. How does *slide sorter view* facilitate the editing process for an electronic presentation?
5. How is a blueprint slide used in an oral presentation?
6. When should you distribute handouts? Why?
7. What kinds of items should you include in speaker's notes?
8. What is the advantage of practicing an oral presentation with visual aids before a live audience?
9. When should you introduce slides?
10. On average, how many slides should you create for a 20-minute presentation?

APPLY YOUR KNOWLEDGE

1. Why do most people include too much information on their slides?
2. How might you modify a graph appearing in a printed document to make it appropriate for a slide?
3. What should you strive for when selecting background designs, fonts, and type styles for your slides?
4. How can you use slide master to enhance the effectiveness of your slides?
5. **Ethical Choices** How can you use design elements and special effects to persuade an audience? Is it ethical to do so?

PRACTICE YOUR KNOWLEDGE

Documents for Analysis

Document 16.A

Examine the slide in Figure 16.15 and point out any problems you notice. How would you correct these problems?

Document 16.B

The graph in Figure 16.16 was copied from E-Z Net's annual report. Examine the graph and decide how to modify it for an electronic presentation using the guidelines discussed in this chapter.

Exercises

For live links to all websites discussed in this chapter, visit this text's website at www.prenhall.com/bovee. Just log on and select Chapter 16, and click on "Student Resources." Locate the name of the site or the URL related to the material in the text. For "Exploring the Best of the Web" exercises, you'll also find navigational directions. Click on the live link to the site.

FIGURE 16.15 Piece of Cake Bakery Electronic Slide #8

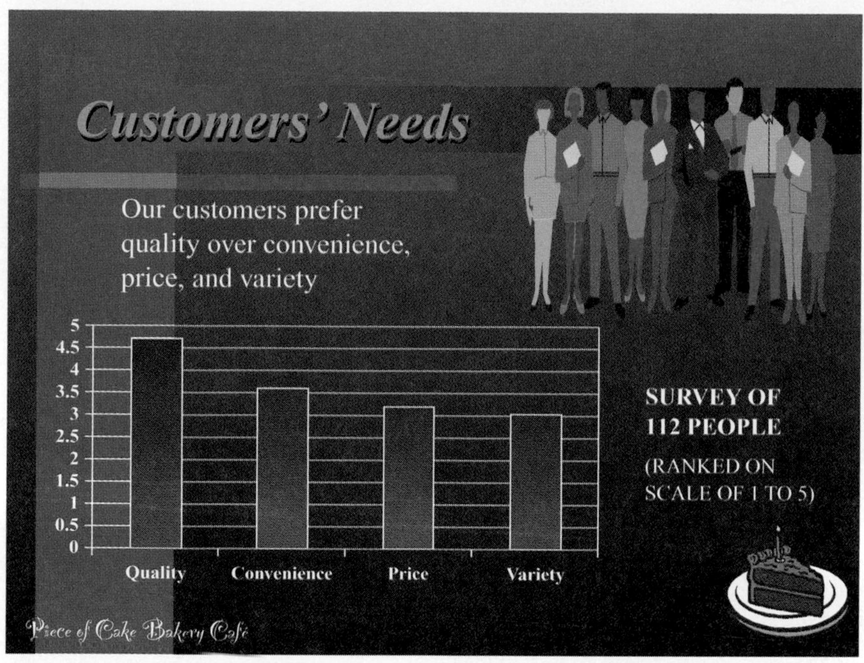

FIGURE 16.16 Contribution of Internet Sales to Total Economy

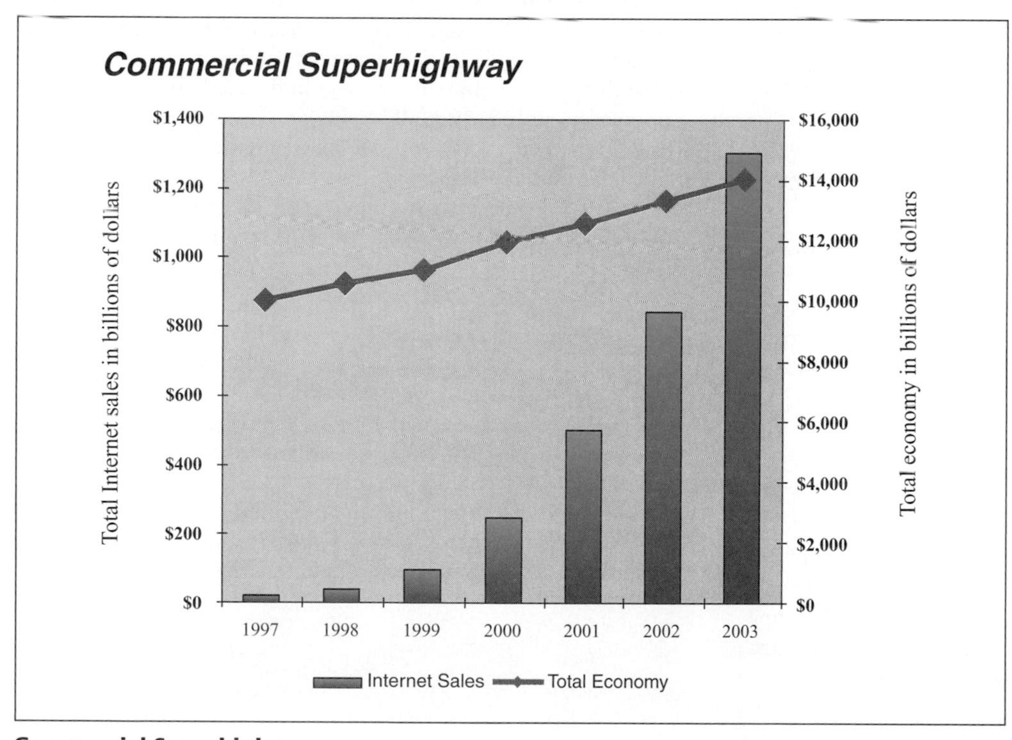

Commercial Superhighway

Year	1997	1998	1999	2000	2001	2002	2003
Internet Sales	$20	$42	$100	$250	$500	$840	$1,300
Total Economy (in billions of dollars)	$10,000	$10,500	$11,000	$11,900	$12,500	$13,300	$14,000

16.1 **Creating Effective Slides: Content** Look through recent issues (print or online) of *Business Week, Fortune,* or other business publications for articles discussing issues a specific company or industry is facing. Using the articles and the guidelines discussed in this chapter, create three to five text or graphic slides summarizing these issues. Then create a cover slide and a blueprint slide for your presentation. If you don't have access to computer presentation software or a word processor, you can draw the slides on plain paper.

16.2 **Creating Effective Slides: Content and Design** You've been asked to give an informative 10-minute talk to a group of conventioneers on great things to see and do while visiting your hometown. To keep them interested, you've decided to whip up a couple of slides for your oral presentation. Write the content for three or four slides (including a cover slide). Then think about the design elements for your slides. Which colors, clip art, and other design elements will you use to enhance your slides?

16.3 **Completing Electronic Presentation: Slide Sorter View** PowerPoint comes with several prefabricated presentation templates. Use the software's AutoContent Wizard to create a short presentation by selecting a presentation type and supplying information for the slide templates (feel free to make up material). Then use the *slide sorter view* to critique the content, layout, and design elements of your presentation. Edit and revise the slides to improve their overall effectiveness. Finally, add a few builds and transitions for some special effects.

16.4 **Creating Effective Slides: Design Elements** Most word-processing software packages include a large selection of fonts. Review the fonts available to you and select three to five fonts suitable for electronic slides or overhead transparencies. Explain the criteria you use for your selections.

16.5 **Internet** Creating hyperlinks to live websites can perk up an electronic presentation, but it also means being prepared for the unexpected. What are some of the obstacles you might encounter when creating live Internet links? How can you prepare in advance to overcome such obstacles?

EXPAND YOUR KNOWLEDGE

Exploring the Best of the Web:

Look Smart in Your Electronic Presentations, p. 536

Fine-tune your electronic presentations using the expert advice from 3M's presentation center. Read the 18 tips for making your next presentation less stressful and learn how to prevent presentation paralysis and look smart.

1. What three questions should you answer for a successful presentation?
2. What common PowerPoint pitfalls should you avoid?
3. What are the two common causes of presentation paralysis?

Exploring the Web on Your Own

Review these chapter-related websites on your own to learn more about creating effective slides for oral presentations.

1. Save time with PowerPoint tips and tricks at the Microsoft PowerPoint homepage, www.microsoft.com/office/powerpoint.
2. Take the online tutorial at the KU Medical Center, www.kumc.edu/SAH/OTEd/jradel/effective.html, and learn how to design effective visual aids.
3. Develop better presentations with the helpful advice at Presenters Online, www.presentersonline.com.

LEARN INTERACTIVELY

Interactive Study Guide

Visit "My Companion Website" at www.prenhall.com/bovee. For Chapter 16, take advantage of the interactive "Study Guide" to test your chapter knowledge. Get instant feedback on whether you need additional studying. Read the "Current Events" articles to get the latest on chapter topics, and complete the exercises—as specified by your instructor.

This site offers a variety of additional resources: The "Research Area" helps you locate a wealth of information to use in course assignments. You can even send a message to online research experts, who will help you find exactly the information you need. The "Study Hall" helps you succeed in this course. "Talk in the Hall" lets you leave messages and meet new friends online. If you have a question, you can "Ask the Tutor." And to get a better grade in this course, you can find more help at "Writing Skills," "Study Skills," and "Study Tips."

Grammar Diagnostic Tests

Review and reinforce your grammar and language skills by taking one of the four online diagnostic tests offered at our companion website, www.prenhall/bovee.com. The four tests cover a variety of topics, including spelling, capitals, punctuation, verbs, pronouns, adjectives, adverbs, sentence structure, sentence punctuation, clarity, word choice, style, organization skills, proofreading, and more. Submit your test and assess your competency. Then focus on improving areas where you are weak as you complete the exercises in this chapter.

PART 7

Writing Employment Messages and Interviewing for Jobs

Writing Résumés and Application Letters

After studying this chapter, you will be able to

1 *Discuss how today's changing workplace is affecting the employment-search process from both the employer's and the candidate's perspective*

2 *Explain three things you can do before you graduate and while you're job hunting that will make you more valuable to employers*

3 *Discuss how to choose the appropriate résumé organization, and list the advantages or disadvantages of the three options*

4 *List the major sections of a traditional résumé*

5 *Describe what you can do to adapt your résumé to a scannable format*

6 *Define the purpose of application letters, and explain how to apply the AIDA organizational approach to them*

COMMUNICATION CLOSE-UP AT RECREATIONAL EQUIPMENT INCORPORATED (REI)

www.rei.com

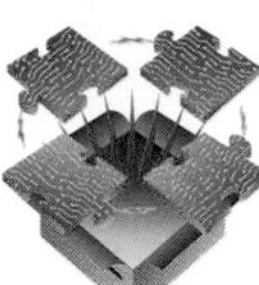

What does it take to land a job interview with a company listed by *Fortune* magazine as one of the 100 best places to work in the United States? Just ask Doug Halm, employment manager with Recreational Equipment Incorporated (REI), a national outdoor gear and clothing cooperative. Halm receives over 400 résumés each month. His job is to determine whether the person represented by the résumé would be a good candidate for REI. This task isn't an easy one, but after 18 years in human resources management, Halm is quite skilled at it.

"Experience is the most important thing," says Halm. "I try to see what a person's knowledge, skills, and experience are and whether they fit the job." He advises, "In your résumé and application letter, you want to create a picture of what you really did and what you accomplished." One applicant included a "PAR sheet," which outlines problems, actions, and results. The candidate identified problems she had encountered in previous jobs, explained actions she pursued to solve the problems, and documented her results. This strategy got Halm's attention with solid substantive content.

Halm also looks for well-roundedness. "Show that you can handle responsibility, such as your previous positions in clubs or social groups. In an interactive culture like REI, someone who is a leader, who worked after school, and who understands teamwork may do better than someone who got good grades but didn't do these things." Halm stresses that knowing your audience and adopting the "you" attitude are just as important in your résumé and application letter as they are in any other type of business communication.

Of course, even if you have all these attributes, you won't get a call from Halm if your résumé doesn't look professional. "The résumé should be laid out well and visually appealing. That means lots of white space, boldface headings, bullet points, and a font size that is easy to read," notes Halm. Spelling errors, poor organization, and sloppy grammar are just a few of the mistakes that can cast a dark cloud over an otherwise attractive résumé. When Halm received an application from a qualified candidate who misspelled a number of words, he wasn't very forgiving: "The person hired for this position will make important decisions, represent the company, write proposals, and develop marketing strategies—and he can't even get his own résumé right?" Halm's advice: "Proofread with a fine-tooth comb. And ask other people to review your résumé, preferably professionals or someone who has a good eye."

Halm advises candidates to think of a résumé as a personal marketing document. It should get someone's attention without carrying things to the extremes. Of course, even the best résumé can't say all there is to know about a person's qualifications. "The application letter lets you personalize the résumé and bring yourself alive in the recruiter's mind," explains Halm. "It gives you the chance to say why you want the job and why you would be good for the job. It fills in the blanks and it answers questions that your résumé might create."[1] ■

When a position opens at an REI store, Doug Halm looks for candidates with specific skills in addition to a passion for outdoor activities.

BUILDING TOWARD A CAREER

As Doug Halm will tell you, getting the job that's right for you takes more than sending out a few résumés and application letters. Before entering the workplace, you need to learn as much as you can about your capabilities and the job marketplace.

Understanding Today's Changing Workplace

Numerous forces are changing today's workplace.

Anyone seeking employment must realize that the workplace today is not the same as it was even a decade ago.[2] Chapter 1 discusses how the workplace is being influenced by globalization, advancing technology, information overload, growing diversity, and team-based organizations. In addition, the attitudes and expectations of both employers and employees are being affected by forces such as ongoing deregulation, increased activism among shareholders, continued corporate downsizing and cost-cutting initiatives, persistent mergers and acquisitions, growing dependency on flexible employment techniques such as outsourcing, and increasing entrepreneurism (people starting their own business or buying a franchise).[3]

How the Changing Workplace Affects Hiring Practices

Learning Objective 1

Discuss how today's changing workplace is affecting the employment-search process from both the employer's and the candidate's perspective

Today, employment is viewed as more flexible, with much less focus on lifelong employment.

In the face of all these changes, employment is more flexible than in the past. Today, rather than looking for lifelong employees, many employers hire temporary workers and consultants on a project-by-project basis. At the same time, rather than staying with one employer for their entire career, growing numbers of employees are at ease in moving from company to company. In a recent poll, only 39 percent of workers say they intend to hold the same job five years from now; 31 percent say they plan to leave their current work; and 29 percent say they do not know.[4]

The forces of change also affect where people find work. Fewer jobs are being created by large companies. One expert predicts that soon 80 percent of the labor force will be working for firms employing fewer than 200 people. Moreover, self-employment seems to be an increasingly attractive option for many former employees.[5]

What Today's Employers Seek in Job Applicants

Employers seek people who
- Can adapt to new situations
- Are unafraid of change
- Continue to learn on the job
- Are sensitive to cultural differences.

Employers such as Doug Halm are looking for people who are able and willing to adapt to diverse situations, who thrive in an ever-changing workplace, and who continue to learn throughout their careers. Companies want team players with strong work records, leaders who are versatile, and employees with diversified skills and varied job experience.[6] In addition, most employers expect college graduates to be sensitive to intercultural differences and to have a sound understanding of international affairs.[7] In fact, in some cases, your chances of being hired are better if you've studied abroad or learned another language.

Adapting to the Changing Workplace

Do you have what employers are looking for? Before you limit your employment search to a particular industry or job, it's a good idea to analyze what you have to offer and what you hope to get from your work. This advance preparation allows you to identify employers who are likely to want you and vice versa.

What Do You Have to Offer?

What you have to offer:
- Functional skills
- Education and experience
- Personality traits

Get started by jotting down 10 achievements you're proud of, such as learning to ski, taking a prize-winning photo, tutoring a child, or editing your school paper. Think carefully about what specific skills these achievements demanded. For example, leadership skills, speaking ability, and artistic talent may have helped you coordinate a winning presentation to your school's administration. As you analyze your achievements, you'll begin to recognize a pattern of skills. Which of them might be valuable to potential employers?

Next, look at your educational preparation, work experience, and extracurricular activities. What do your knowledge and experience qualify you to do? What have you learned from volunteer work or class projects that could benefit you on the job? Have you held any offices, won any awards or scholarships, mastered a second language?

Take stock of your personal characteristics. Are you aggressive, a born leader? Or would you rather follow? Are you outgoing, articulate, great with people? Or do you prefer working alone? Make a list of what you believe are your four or five most important qualities. Ask a relative or friend to rate your traits as well.

Your campus placement office can help you determine your interests, characteristics, and capabilities.

If you're having difficulty figuring out your interests, characteristics, or capabilities, consult your college placement office. Many campuses administer a variety of tests to help you identify interests, aptitudes, and personality traits. These tests won't reveal your "perfect" job, but they'll help you focus on the types of work best suited to your personality.

What Do You Want to Do?

Knowing what you *can* do is one thing. Knowing what you *want* to do is another. Don't lose sight of your own values. Discover the things that will bring you satisfaction and happiness on the job.

Envision the ideal "day at the office." What would you enjoy doing every day?

- **What would you like to do every day?** Talk to people in various occupations about their typical workday. You might consult relatives, local businesses, or former graduates (through your school's alumni relations office). Read about various occupations. Start with your college library or placement office.
- **How would you like to work?** Consider how much independence you want on the job, how much variety you like, and whether you prefer to work with products, machines, people, ideas, figures, or some combination thereof. Do you like physical work, mental work, or a mix? Constant change or a predictable role?

How much do you want to earn, and how high do you hope to climb?

- **What specific compensation do you expect?** What do you hope to earn in your first year? What kind of pay increase do you expect each year? What's your ultimate earnings goal? Would you be comfortable getting paid on commission, or do you prefer a steady paycheck? Are you willing to settle for less money in order to do something you really love?
- **Can you establish some general career goals?** Consider where you'd like to start, where you'd like to go from there, and the ultimate position you'd like to attain. How soon after joining the company would you like to receive your first promotion? Your next one? What additional training or preparation will you need to achieve them?

- **What size company would you prefer?** Do you like the idea of working for a small, entrepreneurial operation? Or would you prefer a large corporation?
- **What type of operation is appealing to you?** Would you prefer to work for a profit-making company or a nonprofit organization? Are you attracted to service businesses or manufacturing operations? Do you want regular, predictable hours, or do you thrive on flexible, varied hours? Would you enjoy a seasonally varied job such as education (which may give you summers off) or retailing (with its selling cycles)?

What type of industry and organization do you want to work in?

- **What location would you like?** Would you like to work in a city, a suburb, a small town, an industrial area, or an uptown setting? Do you favor a particular part of the country? A country abroad? Do you like working indoors or outdoors?
- **What facilities do you envision?** Is it important to you to work in an attractive place, or will simple, functional quarters suffice? Do you need a quiet office to work effectively, or can you concentrate in a noisy, open setting? Is access to public transportation or freeways important?
- **What sort of corporate culture are you most comfortable with?** Would you be happy in a formal hierarchy with clear reporting relationships? Or do you prefer less structure? Are you looking for a paternalistic firm or one that fosters individualism? Do you like a competitive environment? One that rewards teamwork? What qualities do you want in a boss?

What type of corporate culture best suits you?

How Can You Make Yourself More Valuable to Employers?

While you're figuring out what you can offer an employer and what you want from a job, you can take positive steps toward building your career. There is a lot you can do before you graduate from college and while you are seeking employment. The following suggestions will help potential employers recognize the value of hiring you:

Learning Objective 2

Explain three things you can do before you graduate and while you're job hunting that will make you more valuable to employers

Your chances of getting a job are increased by career-building efforts.

- **Keep an employment portfolio.** Get a three-ring notebook and a package of plastic sleeves that open at the top. Collect anything that shows your ability to perform (classroom or work evaluations, certificates, awards, papers you've written). Your portfolio is a great resource for writing your résumé, and it gives employers tangible evidence of your professionalism.
- **Take interim assignments.** As you search for a permanent job, consider temporary or freelance work. Also gain a competitive edge by participating in an internship program. These temporary assignments not only help you gain valuable experience and relevant contacts but also provide you with important references and with items for your portfolio.[8]
- **Work on polishing and updating your skills.** Whenever possible, join networks of professional colleagues and friends who can help you keep up with your occupation and industry. While waiting for responses to your résumé, take a computer course or seek out other educational or life experiences that would be hard to get while working full-time.

Even after an employer hires you, continue improving your skills to distinguish yourself from your peers and to make yourself more valuable to current and potential employers. Becoming a lifelong learner will help you reach your personal goals in the workplace:[9]

Your career-building efforts don't stop after you are hired.

- Work hard to acquire as much technical knowledge as you can, to build broad-based experience, and to develop a high level of social skills.
- Learn to accept change (that way you can adapt if your "perfect" traditional career path eludes your grasp).
- Regularly read publications such as *The Wall Street Journal, Business Week,* and *U.S. News & World Report* (you can never have too much timely information about the economy, new technologies that affect work, "hot" new industries, and other workplace trends).
- Learn to see each job as an opportunity to learn more and to expand your knowledge, experience, and social skills.

FIGURE 17.1 The Employment Search

- Take on as much responsibility as you can outside your job description (that means listening to and learning from others, as well as being willing to actively pursue new or better skills).
- Jump into change with a positive attitude and a nose for opportunity (if you don't understand the changes in your organization, don't complain about it; find out what is going on).
- Share what you know with others (don't hoard knowledge in the hope of becoming indispensable).
- Understand the big picture (knowing your own job inside and out just isn't enough any more).
- Understand that what counts isn't only who you know but also what you know and who knows you.

Seeking Employment in the Changing Workplace

The search for employment is a process.

Even armed with knowledge about today's workplace and what you can do to adapt to it, you still need to learn about the process of seeking employment. Look at Figure 17.1 for an idea of what an employment search entails. The first two tasks are discussed in this chapter; the rest are discussed in Chapter 18. The more you know about this process, the more successful you'll be in your job search. Plus, it's important to keep in mind that employers and job candidates approach the process differently.

Understanding Employers' Approach to the Employment Process

Employers find job candidates through

- Employee referrals
- On-campus interviews
- Placement agencies
- Unsolicited résumés
- Advertisements

When searching for the job you want, you can save considerable time and effort by understanding how employers approach the recruiting process (see Figure 17.2). Generally, employers prefer to look for candidates within their organizations. When hiring outside the company, they rely heavily on referrals from people they know and trust. In fact, personal contacts appear to be the prime source of jobs, regardless of whether a candidate has just graduated from college or has been out of school for several years.[10] Companies will often pay handsome referral bonuses to their employees for recommending a candidate who is hired and who stays for a designated period.[11]

Many employers send representatives to college campuses to interview students for job openings. These interviews are usually coordinated by the campus placement office, which keeps files of college records, data sheets, and recommendation letters for all students registered for the service. In addition, many employers accept unsolicited résumés. Growing companies like to maintain a steady influx of potential employees.

FIGURE 17.2 How Organizations Prefer to Find New Employees

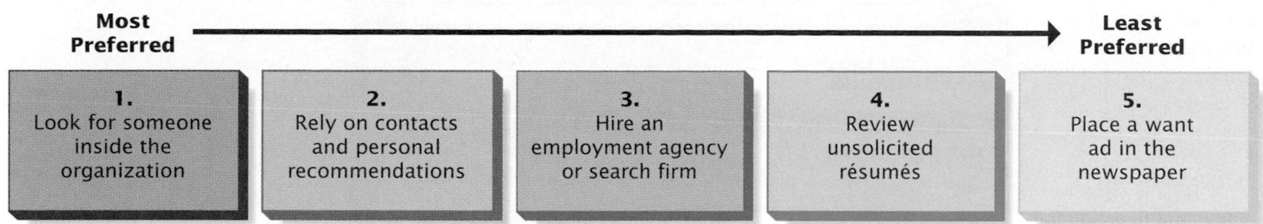

In tight labor markets, companies probably have jobs for any good candidate they happen upon.[12] Most employers keep unsolicited résumés on file or in a database.

Employers also recruit candidates through employment agencies, state employment services, temporary staffing services, and the employment bureaus operated by some trade associations. Moreover, they post jobs through classified and display ads in newspapers, trade magazines, and campus publications. Some CEOs are even using nontraditional recruiting media, such as radio and television.[13] Many companies have begun advertising positions on the Internet.

Organizing Your Approach to the Employment Process

Don't worry if you don't have personal contacts in organizations you would like to work for. Your approach to the employment process is to gather as much information as you can, narrowing it as you go until you know precisely the companies you want to approach. Begin by finding out where the job opportunities are, which industries are strong, which parts of the country are booming, and which specific job categories offer the best prospects for the future. From there you can investigate individual organizations, doing your best to learn as much about them as possible.

Find out where the job opportunities are.

Stay Abreast of Business and Financial News If you don't already do so, subscribe to a major newspaper (print or online editions) and scan the business pages every day. Watch some of the television programs that focus on business, such as *Wall Street Week*. You can find information about the future of specific jobs in the *Dictionary of Occupational Titles* (U.S. Employment Service), the employment publications of Science Research Associates, and the *Occupational Outlook Handbook* (U.S. Bureau of Labor Statistics). This last reference is available in print and online at www.bls.gov/oco/.

Research Specific Companies Chapter 10 discusses how to find information on individual industries and companies and provides a list of popular business resources. Begin your job search by reviewing those sources, as well as professional and trade journals in the fields that interest you. Once you've identified a promising industry and career field, compile a list of specific organizations that appeal to you (perhaps by consulting directories of employers at your college library, at your career center, or on the Internet). The web offers an amazing amount of company and employment information, both general and specific. In addition to gaining detailed information about your prospective employers, you can use the web to look for and respond to job openings:

Make a list of desirable employers.

- **Learn about the organization.** Find out whether a company maintains a website. Those that do generally include a company profile, press releases, financial information, and information on employment opportunities. You'll find information about an organization's mission, products, annual reports, and employee benefits. You can also e-mail organizations and ask for annual reports, descriptive brochures, or newsletters.
- **Look for job openings.** An increasing number of large and small companies are posting job openings on the Internet. You can locate company sites by knowing the URL (web address), using links from other sites, or using a search engine such as AltaVista, Lycos, or Google. You can also find jobs at websites that list openings from multiple companies. See "Keeping Pace with Technology: Netting a Job on

The web offers valuable information about companies and job openings.

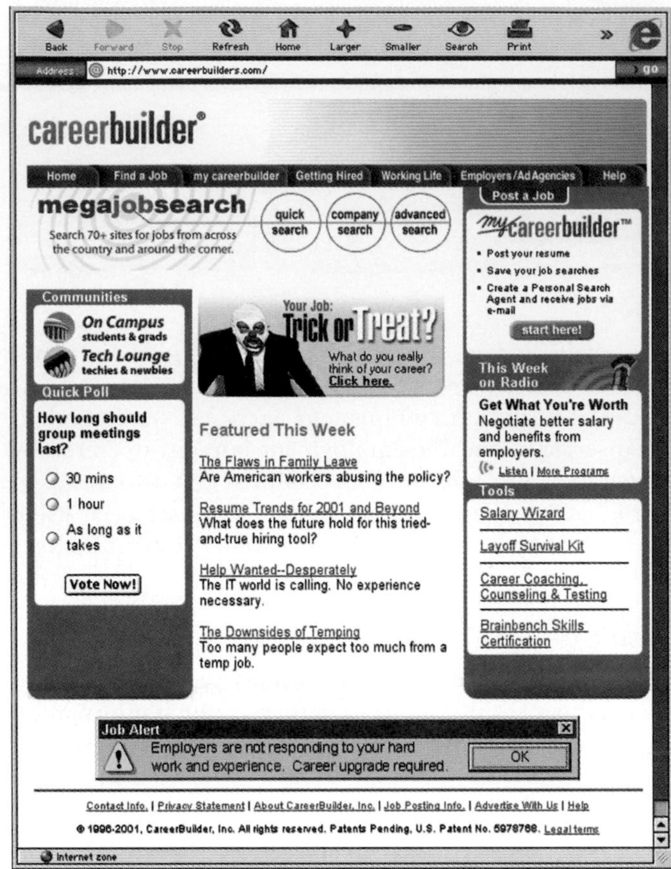

CareerBuilder is just one of the many websites that job seekers turn to for career advice, as well as for employer information and company job postings.

the Web" for a list of popular online indexes (or job boards), many of which allow you to search by region, industry, job title, company, skills, or requirements.

- **Respond to job openings.** You can respond directly to job postings without going through recruiters, post tailor-made résumés (that match the qualifications required by a particular position), send résumés quickly and cheaply through e-mail, and send focused cover letters directly to the executives doing the hiring. Most campus placement offices are retooling to help you take advantage of web opportunities.

Despite the web's obvious advantages, you must use other job-seeking tools to be successful.

Keep in mind that because e-mailing résumés is so easy, companies are getting thousands of electronic résumés a day. Thus, in some cases you may want to try a more personal touch such as a printed letter or phone call.[14] Moreover, at least 10 million U.S. employers don't even think of the Internet when it's time to hire. So in addition to using the web to look for job openings, you'll still want to use other techniques for finding employment, such as looking in local and major newspapers, signing up for campus interviews, networking, and finding career counseling.

Networking can help you learn about specific companies, learn more about your field, and find potential employers.

Network You have any number of options for networking with people who work at the organizations you're interested in or who work in a field you would like to investigate. You may be able to network with executives in your field by joining or participating in student business organizations, especially those with ties to real-world organizations such as the American Marketing Association or the American Management Association. You might try visiting some organizations, contacting their personnel departments, and talking with key employees.

Using the web, you can locate and communicate with potential employers through numerous types of discussion groups dedicated to your field. Usenet newsgroups provide an electronic bulletin board so that members can leave and retrieve messages whenever they visit. Listservs (Internet mailing lists) send each message to every mem-

Keeping Pace with Technology

Netting a Job on the Web

Can the web provide the answer to all your employment dreams? Perhaps . . . or perhaps not. As the web grows, the employment information it provides is constantly expanding. And you're fortunate, because you don't have to start from scratch like some intrepid adventurer. For helpful hints and useful web addresses, you can turn to books such as *What Color Is Your Parachute?* by Richard Nelson Bolles. Other places to check out online include the following:*

- **America's Career InfoNet** (www.acinet.org). Good place to begin. Offers information on typical wages and employment trends. Gives education, knowledge, and skills requirements for most occupations. Includes links to multiple career resources on the Internet.
- **The Monster Board** (www.monster.com). Posts more than 25,000 openings and 300,000 résumés. Heavily marketed, it brings a flood of employers (many with under 500 employees).
- **America's Job Bank** (www.ajb.dni.us). State agencies post an average of 5,000 new openings each day on this government site. Companies contribute another 3,000.
- **HotJobs.Com** (www.hotjobs.com). A member-based site that charges companies a hefty fee to post openings or search through résumés. Job seekers can create a personal page to manage their search and collect statistics on how many companies have retrieved their résumé.
- **NationJob Network** (www.nationjob.com). Posts more than 15,000 jobs nationwide, with an emphasis on those in the Midwest.
- **Headhunter** (www.headhunter.net). More then 70,000 jobs updated daily on this site. Includes a career resources center.
- **4Work** (www.4work.com). One of the few sites that includes listings of internships and volunteer opportunities.
- **Net-Temps** (www.net-temps.com). Maintained by career consultants; offers several thousand updated listings and real-time seminars. Network forums help you develop new contacts and job leads. Includes chat room for online interviews.
- **CareerBuilder** (www.careerbuilder.com). Offers a network of career services, job-search information, and tips on how to succeed once you're hired. Includes a database of 20,000 openings.
- **MonsterTrak** (www.monstertrak.com). Has formed partnerships with 750 campuses nationwide and serves as a virtual career center for students and alumni. Many entry-level postings.
- **Yahoo! Classifieds** (classifieds.yahoo.com). Offers extensive listing of companies by city, in addition to a wealth of job-related information at the parent website, www.yahoo.com. Click on Business & Economy/Jobs/Company Job Listings.

*Direct links to these websites can be accessed at the Riley Guide (www.dbm.com/jobguide).

Career Applications

1. Surfing the web can chew up a disproportionate amount of your job-seeking time. Explain how you can limit the amount of time you spend on the web and still make it work for you.
2. When posting your résumé on the web, you're revealing a lot of information about yourself that could be used by people other than employers (salespeople, people competing for similar positions, con artists). What sort of information might you leave off your web résumé that would certainly appear on a traditional résumé?

ber's e-mail address. Commercial systems (Prodigy, America Online, etc.) have their own discussion groups (and make a profit from the time users spend accessing their services). Once you locate a potential contact, you can use e-mail to request information about the company or inquire about job openings.

Find Career Counseling College placement offices offer individual counseling, credential services, job fairs, on-campus interviews, and job listings. They can give you advice on résumé-writing software and provide workshops in job-search techniques, résumé preparation, interview techniques, and more.[15] You can also find job counseling online. You might begin your self-assessment, for example, with the Keirsey Temperament Sorter, an online personality test at www.advisorteam.com/userkitsintro.asp. For excellent job-seeking pointers and counseling, visit college- and university-run online career centers. Commercial career centers range from award winning to depressing, so seek out those whose advice is both useful and sensible.

Career counseling is available on and off the Internet.

Cisco Systems participates in college job fairs as one way to recruit new employees.

PREPARING RÉSUMÉS

While looking for employment, you'll need to send out messages such as résumés, application letters, job inquiries, and follow-up letters. Whenever you send out such employment messages, you have an opportunity to showcase your communication skills—skills valued highly by the majority of employers. So write these messages carefully by following the three-step writing process (see Figure 17.3). To distinguish you from all the other people looking for work, you need to start with a well-written résumé. In fact, your success in finding a job will depend on how carefully you plan, write, and complete your résumé.

Planning Your Résumé

Your résumé must be more than a simple list of jobs you've held. As with other business messages, planning a résumé means analyzing your purpose and your audience.

Analyze Your Purpose and Audience

Your résumé is a structured, written summary of your educational and employment background and shows your qualifications for a job.

The purpose of the résumé is to get you an interview.

To create interest, learn what you can about your audience's needs.

A **résumé** is a structured, written summary of a person's education, employment background, and job qualifications. Although many people have misconceptions about résumés (see Table 17.1), the fact is that a résumé is a form of advertising. It is intended to stimulate an employer's interest in you—in meeting you and learning more about you. A successful résumé inspires a prospective employer to invite you to interview with the company. Thus, your purpose in writing your résumé is to create interest—*not* to tell readers everything about you. In fact, it may be best to only hint at some things and leave the reader wanting more. The potential employer will then have even more reason to contact you.[16]

Since you've already completed a good deal of research on specific companies, you should know quite a bit about the organizations you'll be applying to. But take some time now to learn what you can about the individuals who may be reading your résumé. If you're applying to a Fortune 500 company, you may have to make some educated guesses about the people in the human resources department and what their needs might be. But in smaller companies, you may be able to learn the name of the

FIGURE 17.3 Three-Step Writing Process for Employment Messages

Planning

Analyze
Study your purpose and your audience to tailor your message for maximum effect.

Investigate
Gather relevant information about you and about the employer you're targeting.

Adapt
Establish a good relationship by highlighting those skills and qualifications that match each employer.

Writing

Organize
Use the AIDA approach in letters and choose the most appropriate résumé format to highlight your strongest points.

Compose
Make your letters friendly, businesslike, and slightly more formal than usual. For résumés, use action verbs and make your style direct, brief, and crisp.

Completing

Revise
Evaluate content, revising for both clarity and conciseness.

Produce
Ensure a clean, sharp look whether your message is printed, e-mail, or online.

Proofread
Look carefully for errors in spelling and mechanics that can detract from your professionalism.

TABLE 17.1 Fallacies and Facts About Résumés

Fallacy	*Fact*
⊗ The purpose of a résumé is to list all your skills and abilities.	☑ The purpose of a résumé is to kindle employer interest and generate an interview.
⊗ A good résumé will get you the job you want.	☑ All a résumé can do is get you in the door.
⊗ Your résumé will be read carefully and thoroughly by an interested employer.	☑ Your résumé probably has less than 45 seconds to make an impression.
⊗ The more good information you present about yourself in your résumé, the better.	☑ Too much information on a résumé may actually kill the reader's appetite to know more.
⊗ If you want a really good résumé, have it prepared by a résumé service.	☑ Prepare your own résumé—unless the position is especially high-level or specialized. Even then, you should check carefully before using a service.

recruiter or manager you'll be addressing. Either way, try to put yourself in your audience's position so that you'll be able to tailor your résumé to satisfy your audience's needs.

Investigate Pertinent Information

To provide all the information your audience will need, gather every scrap of pertinent personal history you can think of, including all the specific dates, duties, and accomplishments of any previous jobs you've held. Collect every piece of relevant educational experience that adds to your qualifications, such as formal degrees, skills certificates, academic awards, or scholarships. Also, gather any relevant information about personal endeavors: dates of your membership in an association, offices you may have held in a club or professional organization, any presentations you might have given to a community group. You'll want to have every bit of this information at your fingertips before you begin composing your résumé.

Gather every piece of relevant information before trying to write your résumé.

Adapt Your Résumé to Your Audience

Because your résumé will have little time to make an impression, be sure to adopt a "you" attitude and think about your résumé from the employer's perspective. Ask yourself: What key qualifications will this employer be looking for? Which of these qualifications are your greatest strengths? What quality would set you apart from other candidates in the eyes of a potential employer? What are three or four of your greatest accomplishments, and what resulted from these accomplishments?

A good résumé is flexible and can be customized for various situations and employers. If you're applying for a marketing job at an international company such as Hewlett-Packard, the first skill on your list might be your ability to speak French. However, if you're applying for a sales position at Frito-Lay, the first skill on your list will probably be your summer job building product displays at a local grocery store. It's perfectly fine to have several résumés, each tailored for a different type of position or company.

Tailor your résumé to fit diverse situations and employers.

It's up to you to combine your experiences into a straightforward message that communicates what you can do for your potential employer.[17] Think in terms of an image or a theme you'd like to project. Are you academically gifted? A campus leader? A well-rounded person? A creative genius? A technical wizard? Don't exaggerate, and don't alter the past or claim skills you don't have. However, don't dwell on negatives, either. By knowing yourself and your audience, you'll focus successfully on the strengths needed by potential employers.

Writing Your Résumé

To write a successful résumé, you need to convey seven qualities that employers seek. You want to show that you (1) think in terms of results, (2) know how to get things done, (3) are well rounded, (4) show signs of progress, (5) have personal standards of excellence, (6) are flexible and willing to try new things, and (7) possess strong communication skills. As you organize and compose your résumé, think about how you can convey those seven qualities.

Organize Your Résumé Around Your Strengths

Learning Objective 3

Discuss how to choose the appropriate résumé organization, and list the advantages or disadvantages of the three options

Know how to handle common résumé problems.

Although you may want to include a little information in all categories, emphasize the information that has a bearing on your career objective, and minimize or exclude any that is irrelevant or counterproductive. To interest potential employers in your résumé, call attention to your best features and downplay your weaknesses—but be sure you do so without distorting or misrepresenting the facts.[18] Do you have something in your history that might trigger an employer's red flag? Following are some common problems and some quick suggestions for overcoming them:[19]

- **Frequent job changes.** Group all contract and temporary jobs under one heading if they're similar.
- **Gaps in work history.** Mention relevant experience and education gained during time gaps, such as volunteer or community work. If gaps are due to personal problems such as drug or alcohol abuse or mental illness, offer honest but general explanations about your absences ("I had serious health concerns and had to take time off to fully recover").
- **Inexperience.** Do related volunteer work. List relevant course work and internships. Offer hiring incentives such as "willing to work nights and weekends."
- **Overqualification.** Tone down your résumé, focusing exclusively on pertinent experience and skills.
- **Long-term employment with one company.** Itemize each position held at the firm to show "interior mobility" and increased responsibilities. Don't include obsolete skills and job titles.
- **Job termination for cause.** Be honest with interviewers. Show you're a hard-working employee and counter their concerns with proof such as recommendations and examples of completed projects.
- **Criminal record.** Consider sending out a "broadcast letter" about your skills and experience, rather than a résumé and cover letter. Prepare answers to questions that interviewers will probably pose ("You may wonder whether I will be a trustworthy employee. I'd like to offer you a list of references from previous bosses and co-workers who will attest to my integrity. I learned some hard lessons during that difficult time in my life, and now I'm fully rehabilitated").

Select an organizational pattern that focuses attention on your strengths.

To focus attention on your strongest points, adopt the appropriate organizational approach—make your résumé chronological, functional, or a combination of the two. The "right" choice depends on your background and your goals.

The Chronological Résumé In a **chronological résumé**, the work-experience section dominates and is placed in the most prominent slot, immediately after the name and address and the objective. You develop this section by listing your jobs sequentially in reverse order, beginning with the most recent position and working backward toward earlier jobs. Under each listing, describe your responsibilities and accomplishments, giving the most space to the most recent positions. If you're just graduating from college, you can vary this chronological approach by putting your educational

FIGURE 17.4 In-Depth Critique: Ineffective Chronological Résumé

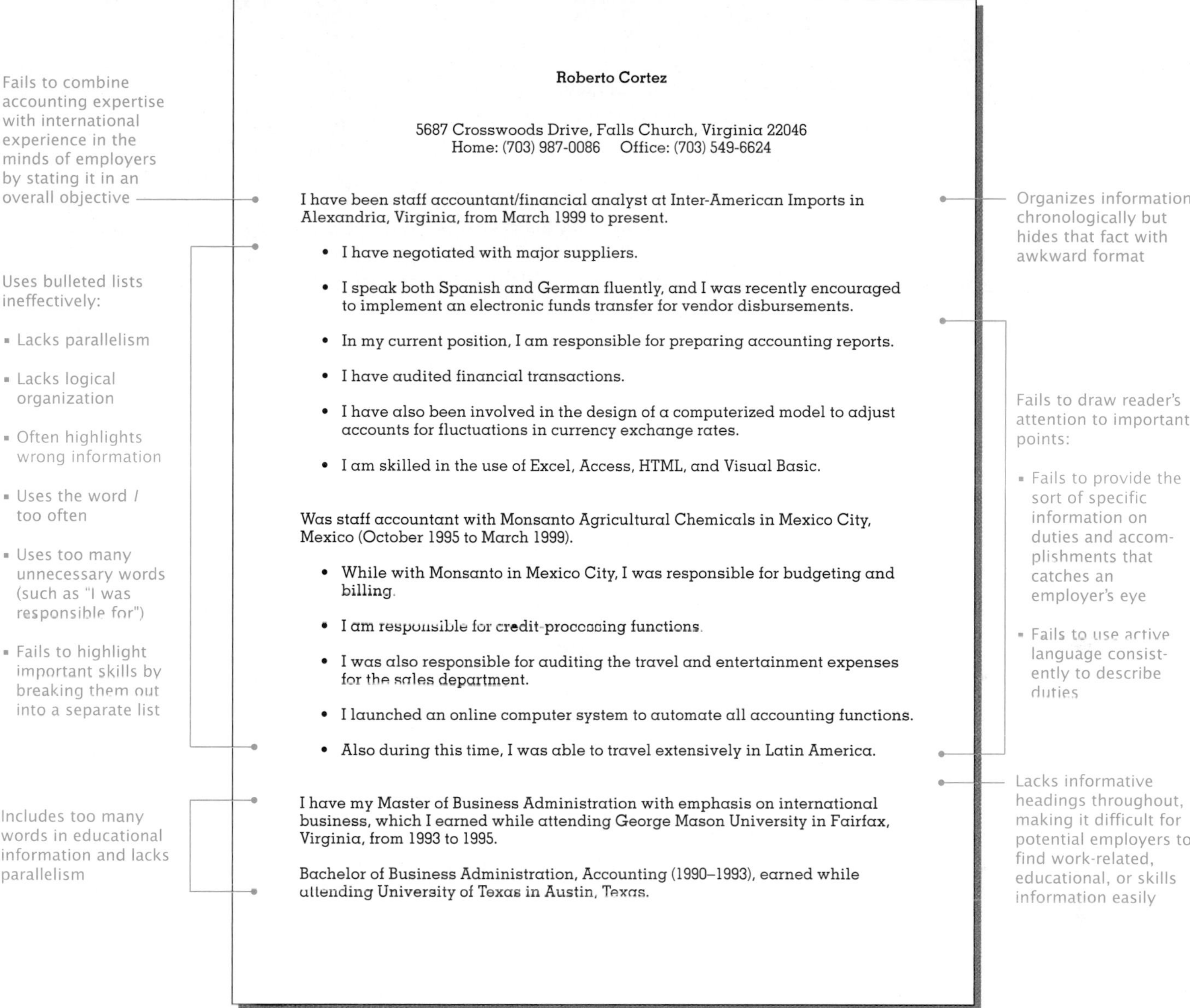

Roberto Cortez

5687 Crosswoods Drive, Falls Church, Virginia 22046
Home: (703) 987-0086 Office: (703) 549-6624

I have been staff accountant/financial analyst at Inter-American Imports in Alexandria, Virginia, from March 1999 to present.

- I have negotiated with major suppliers.
- I speak both Spanish and German fluently, and I was recently encouraged to implement an electronic funds transfer for vendor disbursements.
- In my current position, I am responsible for preparing accounting reports.
- I have audited financial transactions.
- I have also been involved in the design of a computerized model to adjust accounts for fluctuations in currency exchange rates.
- I am skilled in the use of Excel, Access, HTML, and Visual Basic.

Was staff accountant with Monsanto Agricultural Chemicals in Mexico City, Mexico (October 1995 to March 1999).

- While with Monsanto in Mexico City, I was responsible for budgeting and billing.
- I am responsible for credit-processing functions.
- I was also responsible for auditing the travel and entertainment expenses for the sales department.
- I launched an online computer system to automate all accounting functions.
- Also during this time, I was able to travel extensively in Latin America.

I have my Master of Business Administration with emphasis on international business, which I earned while attending George Mason University in Fairfax, Virginia, from 1993 to 1995.

Bachelor of Business Administration, Accounting (1990–1993), earned while attending University of Texas in Austin, Texas.

qualifications before your experience, thereby focusing attention on your academic credentials.

The chronological approach is the most common way to organize a résumé, and many employers prefer it. This approach has three key advantages: (1) Employers are familiar with it and can easily find information, (2) it highlights growth and career progression, and (3) it highlights employment continuity and stability.[20] As vice president with Korn/Ferry International, Robert Nesbit speaks for many recruiters: "Unless you have a really compelling reason, don't use any but the standard chronological format. Your résumé should not read like a treasure map, full of minute clues to the whereabouts of your jobs and experience. I want to be able to grasp quickly where a candidate has worked, how long, and in what capacities."[21]

Most recruiters prefer the chronological plan: a historical summary of your education and work experience.

The chronological approach is especially appropriate if you have a strong employment history and are aiming for a job that builds on your current career path. This is the case for Roberto Cortez. Compare the ineffective and effective versions of Cortez's résumé in Figures 17.4 and 17.5.

Planning

Analyze
Decide how best to combine accounting expertise with international experience.

Investigate
Gather data from contacts and research.

Adapt
Point out specific achievements to interest potential employers.

Writing

Organize
A chronological résumé will best emphasize years of work experience.

Compose
The style is direct, brief, and crisp, using action verbs to focus on employment history, professional achievements, and international abilities.

Completing

Revise
Make content clear and concise.

Produce
Give traditional résumé a clean, sharp look with dates set off in margin.

Proofread
Review for spelling and mechanical errors.

FIGURE 17.5 In-Depth Critique: Effective Chronological Résumé

ROBERTO CORTEZ
5687 Crosswoods Drive
Falls Church, Virginia 22046
Home: (703) 987-0086 Office: (703) 549-6624

OBJECTIVE

Accounting management position requiring a knowledge of international finance

EXPERIENCE

March 1999 to present — **Staff Accountant/Financial Analyst,** Inter-American Imports (Alexandria, Virginia)
- Prepare accounting reports for wholesale giftware importer ($15 million annual sales)
- Audit financial transactions with suppliers in 12 Latin American countries
- Created a computerized model to adjust accounts for fluctuations in currency exchange rates
- Negotiated joint-venture agreements with major suppliers in Mexico and Colombia
- Implemented electronic funds transfer for vendor dispursements, improving cash flow and eliminating payables clerk position

October 1995 to March 1999 — **Staff Accountant,** Monsanto Agricultural Chemicals (Mexico City, Mexico)
- Handled budgeting, billing, and credit-processing functions for the Mexico City branch
- Audited travel/entertainment expenses for Monsanto's 30-member Latin American sales force
- Assisted in launching an online computer system to automate all accounting functions

EDUCATION

1993 to 1995 — Master of Business Administration with emphasis on international business
George Mason University (Fairfax, Virginia)

1990 to 1993 — Bachelor of Business Administration, Accounting, University of Texas, Austin

INTERCULTURAL AND TECHNICAL SKILLS

- Fluent in Spanish and German
- Traveled extensively in Latin America
- Excel • Access • HTML • Visual Basic

Combines accounting expertise with international experience in the minds of employers by stating it in an overall objective

Organizes information chronologically and emphasizes that organization with format

Makes each description concise, easy to read, and informative:

- Avoids the word *I* throughout
- Uses no unnecessary words

Highlights important skills by breaking them out into a list in a separate section

Draws reader's attention to important points:

- Provides the sort of specific information on duties and accomplishments that catches an employer's eye
- Highlights duties and work achievements in bulleted lists
- Uses active language to describe duties

Includes informative headings throughout, making it easy for potential employers to find work-related, educational, or skills information

FIGURE 17.6 In-Depth Critique: Functional Résumé

Glenda S. Johns

Home: 457 Mountain View Road
Clear Lake, Iowa 50428
(515) 633-5971

College: 1254 Main Street
Council Bluffs, Iowa 51505
(712) 438-5254

OBJECTIVE

Retailing position that utilizes my experience

RELEVANT SKILLS

Describes relevant skills first because Johns is a recent graduate

- Personal Selling/Retailing
  - Led housewares department in employee sales for spring 2000
  - Created end-cap and shelf displays for special housewares promotions
  - Sold the most benefit tickets during college fund-raising drive for local community center
- Public Interaction
  - Commended by housewares manager for resolving customer complaints amicably
  - Performed in summer theater productions in Clear Lake, Iowa
- Managing
  - Trained part-time housewares employees in cash register operation and customer service
  - Reworked housewares employee schedules as assistant manager
  - Organized summer activities for children 6–12 years old for city of Clear Lake, Iowa—including reading programs, sports activities, and field trips

Uses action verbs to enhance résumé effectiveness

EDUCATION

- Associate in Arts, Retailing Mid-Management (3.81 GPA / 4.0 scale), Iowa Western Community College, June 2000
- In addition to required retailing, buying, marketing, and merchandising courses, completed electives in visual merchandising, business information systems, principles of management, and business math

WORK EXPERIENCE

Describes but does not emphasize Johns's sketchy work history

- Assistant manager, housewares, at Jefferson's Department Store during off-campus work experience program, Council Bluffs, Iowa (fall 1999–spring 2000)
- Sales clerk, housewares, at Jefferson's Department Store during off-campus work experience program, Council Bluffs, Iowa (fall 1998–spring 1999)
- Assistant director, Summer Recreation Program, Clear Lake, Iowa (summer 1998)
- Actress, Cobblestone Players, Clear Lake, Iowa (summer 1997)

LEADERSHIP EXPERIENCE

- Student Co-Chair for Clear Lake Women's Auxiliary Board Fashion Show 2000 (raised $45,000)
- President of Phi Kappa Phi Sorority 1999
- Student representive (high school) to Clear Lake Chamber of Commerce (2 years)

Calls attention to leadership abilities and experience by listing her leadership positions in a separate section

The Functional Résumé A **functional résumé** emphasizes a list of skills and accomplishments, identifying employers and academic experience in subordinate sections. This pattern stresses individual areas of competence, so it's useful for people who are just entering the job market, want to redirect their careers, or have little continuous career-related experience. The functional approach also has three advantages: (1) Without having to read through job descriptions, employers can see what you can do for them, (2) you can emphasize earlier job experience, and (3) you can de-emphasize any lack of career progress or lengthy unemployment.

A functional résumé focuses attention on your areas of competence.

Figure 17.6 illustrates how Glenda Johns uses the functional approach to showcase her qualifications for a career in retail. Although she has not held any paid, full-time positions in retail sales, Johns has participated in work-experience programs, and she knows a good deal about the profession from research and from talking with people in the industry. She organized her résumé in a way that demonstrates her ability to handle

FIGURE 17.7 In-Depth Critique: Combination Résumé

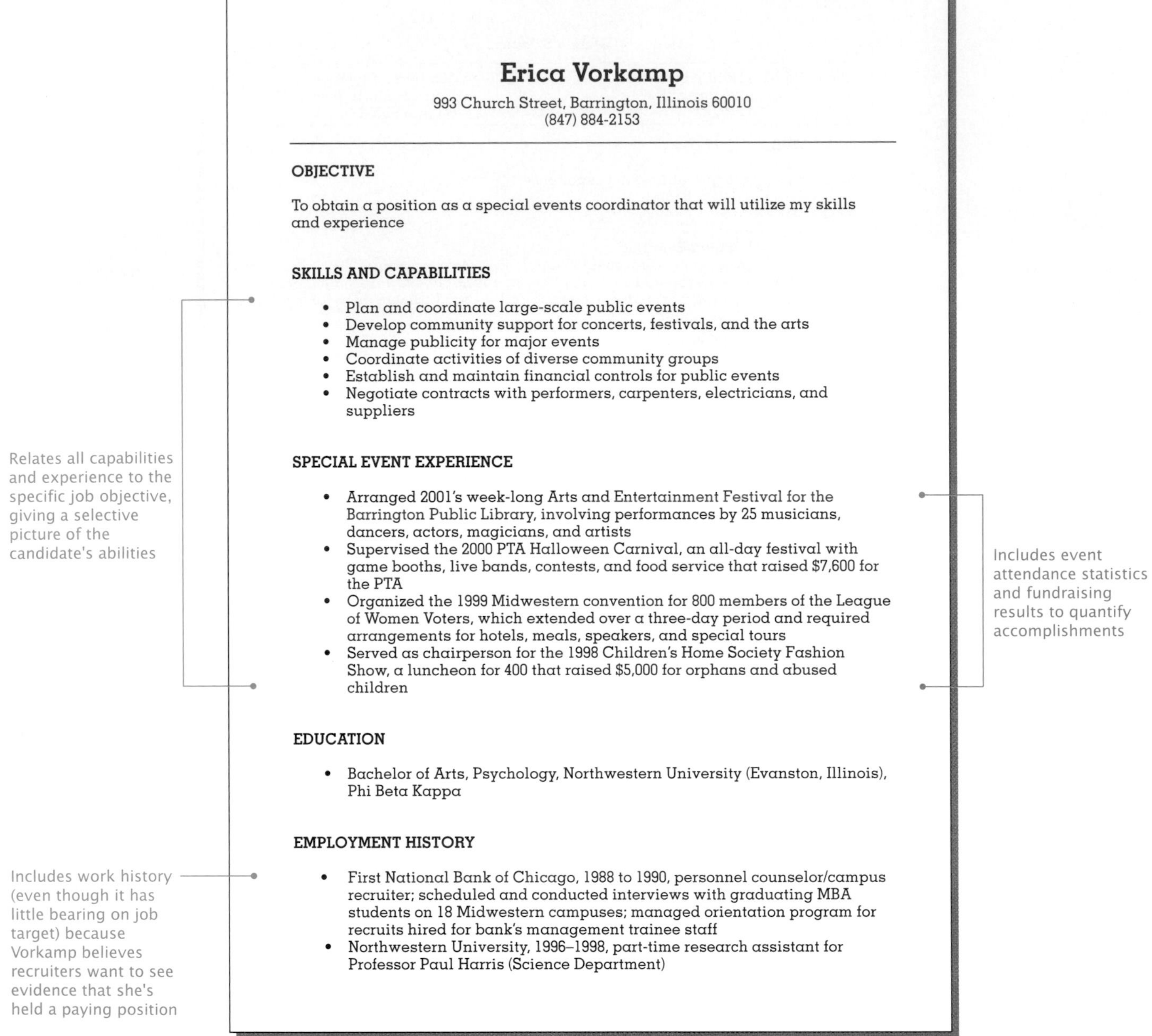

Erica Vorkamp

993 Church Street, Barrington, Illinois 60010
(847) 884-2153

OBJECTIVE

To obtain a position as a special events coordinator that will utilize my skills and experience

SKILLS AND CAPABILITIES

- Plan and coordinate large-scale public events
- Develop community support for concerts, festivals, and the arts
- Manage publicity for major events
- Coordinate activities of diverse community groups
- Establish and maintain financial controls for public events
- Negotiate contracts with performers, carpenters, electricians, and suppliers

SPECIAL EVENT EXPERIENCE

- Arranged 2001's week-long Arts and Entertainment Festival for the Barrington Public Library, involving performances by 25 musicians, dancers, actors, magicians, and artists
- Supervised the 2000 PTA Halloween Carnival, an all-day festival with game booths, live bands, contests, and food service that raised $7,600 for the PTA
- Organized the 1999 Midwestern convention for 800 members of the League of Women Voters, which extended over a three-day period and required arrangements for hotels, meals, speakers, and special tours
- Served as chairperson for the 1998 Children's Home Society Fashion Show, a luncheon for 400 that raised $5,000 for orphans and abused children

EDUCATION

- Bachelor of Arts, Psychology, Northwestern University (Evanston, Illinois), Phi Beta Kappa

EMPLOYMENT HISTORY

- First National Bank of Chicago, 1988 to 1990, personnel counselor/campus recruiter; scheduled and conducted interviews with graduating MBA students on 18 Midwestern campuses; managed orientation program for recruits hired for bank's management trainee staff
- Northwestern University, 1996–1998, part-time research assistant for Professor Paul Harris (Science Department)

Relates all capabilities and experience to the specific job objective, giving a selective picture of the candidate's abilities

Includes event attendance statistics and fundraising results to quantify accomplishments

Includes work history (even though it has little bearing on job target) because Vorkamp believes recruiters want to see evidence that she's held a paying position

such a position. Bear in mind, however, that many seasoned employment professionals are suspicious of this résumé style. They assume that candidates who use it are trying to hide something.[22]

A combination résumé is a hybrid of the chronological and functional résumés.

The Combination Résumé A **combination résumé** includes the best features of the chronological and functional approaches. Nevertheless, it is not commonly used, and it has two major disadvantages: (1) It tends to be longer, and (2) it can be repetitious if you have to list your accomplishments and skills in both the functional section and the chronological job descriptions.[23] When Erica Vorkamp developed her résumé, she chose not to use a chronological pattern, which would focus attention on her lack of recent work experience. As Figure 17.7 shows, she used a combination approach to emphasize her abilities, skills, and accomplishments while also including a complete job history.

Compose Your Résumé to Impress

To save your readers time and to state your information as forcefully as possible, write your résumé using a simple and direct style. Use short, crisp phrases instead of whole sentences, and focus on what your reader needs to know. Avoid using the word *I*. Instead, start your phrases with impressive action verbs such as these:[24]

To capture attention quickly, leave out the word *I*, and begin your phrases with strong action verbs.

accomplished	coordinated	initiated	participated	set up
achieved	created	installed	performed	simplified
administered	demonstrated	introduced	planned	sparked
approved	developed	investigated	presented	streamlined
arranged	directed	joined	proposed	strengthened
assisted	established	launched	raised	succeeded
assumed	explored	maintained	recommended	supervised
budgeted	forecasted	managed	reduced	systematized
chaired	generated	motivated	reorganized	targeted
changed	identified	operated	resolved	trained
compiled	implemented	organized	saved	transformed
completed	improved	oversaw	served	upgraded

For instance, you might say, "Coached a Little League team to the regional play-offs" or "Managed a fast-food restaurant and four employees." Here are some additional examples of how to phrase your accomplishments using active statements that show results:

Avoid Weak Statements	Use Active Statements That Show Results
Responsible for developing a new filing system	Developed a new filing system that reduced paperwork by 50 percent
I was in charge of customer complaints and all ordering problems	Handled all customer complaints and resolved all product order discrepancies
Won a trip to Europe for opening the most new customer accounts in my department	Generated the highest number of new customer accounts in my department
Member of special campus task force to resolve student problems with existing cafeteria assignments	Assisted in implementing new campus dining program allowing students to eat at any college dorm

Learning Objective 4

List the major sections of a traditional résumé

In addition to listing your accomplishments, include your name and address, academic credentials, employment history, activities and achievements, and relevant personal data.

The opening section shows at a glance

- Who you are
- How to reach you

Name and Address The first thing an employer needs to know is who you are and where you can be reached: your name, address, and phone number (as well as your e-mail address or URL, if you have one). If you have contact information at school and at home, you can include both. Similarly, if you have a work phone and a home phone, list both and indicate which is which. Many résumé headings are nothing more than the name and address centered at the top of the page. You don't really need to include the word *résumé*. Just make sure the reader can tell in an instant who you are and how to communicate with you.

Stating your objective or summarizing your qualifications helps the recruiter categorize you.

Career Objective or Summary of Qualifications Experts disagree about the need to state a career objective on your résumé. Some argue that your objective is obvious from your qualifications. Some also maintain that such a statement only limits you as a candidate (especially if you want to be considered for a variety of openings) because it labels you as being interested in only one thing. Other experts argue that employers will try to categorize you anyway, so you might as well make sure they attach the right label. Remember, your goal is to generate interest immediately. If you decide to state your objective, make it effective by being as specific as possible about what you want:

A software sales position in a growing company requiring international experience

Advertising assistance with print media emphasis requiring strong customer-contact skills

If you have different types of qualifications (such as a certificate in secretarial science and two years' experience in retail sales), prepare separate résumés, each with a different objective. If your immediate objective differs from your ultimate one, combine the two in a single statement:

A marketing position with an opportunity for eventual managerial status

Proposal writer, with the ultimate goal of becoming a contracts administrator

Instead of stating your objective, you might summarize your qualifications in a brief statement that highlights your strongest points, particularly if you have had a good deal of varied experience. Use a short, simple phrase:

Summary of qualifications: Ten years of experience in commission selling with track record of generating new customer leads through creative advertising and community leadership positions

The career objective or summary may be the only section read fully by the employer, so if you include either one, make it strong, concise, and convincing.

If education is your strongest selling point, discuss it thoroughly and highlight it visually.

Education If you're still in school, education is probably your strongest selling point. Present your educational background in depth, choosing facts that support your "theme." Give this section a heading such as "Education," "Professional College Training," or "Academic Preparation." Then, starting with the school you most recently attended, list the name and location of each one, the term of your enrollment (in months and years), your major and minor fields of study, significant skills and abilities you've developed in your course work, and the degrees or certificates you've earned. If you're working on an uncompleted degree, include in parentheses the expected date of completion. Showcase your qualifications by listing courses that have directly equipped you for the job you are seeking, and indicate any scholarships, awards, or academic honors you've received.

The education section also includes off-campus training sponsored by business or government. Include any relevant seminars or workshops you've attended, as well as the certificates or other documents you've received. Mention high school or military training only if the associated achievements are pertinent to your career goals. Whether you list your grades depends on the job you want and the quality of your grades. If you choose to show a grade-point average, be sure to mention the scale, especially if a five-point scale is used instead of a four-point scale.

Education is usually given less emphasis in a résumé after you've worked in your chosen field for a year or more. If work experience is your strongest qualification, save the section on education for later in the résumé and provide less detail.

Work Experience, Skills, and Accomplishments Like the education section, the work-experience section focuses on your overall theme. Tailor your description to highlight the relationship between your previous responsibilities and your target field. Call attention to skills you've developed and your progression from jobs of lesser to greater responsibility.

When describing your work experience, list your jobs in chronological order, with the current or last one first. Include any part-time, summer, or intern positions, even if unrelated to your current career objective. Employers will see that you have the ability to get and hold a job—an important qualification in itself. If you have worked your way through school, say so. Employers interpret this as a sign of character.

Each listing includes the name and location of the employer. If readers are unlikely to recognize the organization, briefly describe what it does. When you want to keep the name of your current employer confidential, identify the firm by industry only ("a large film-processing laboratory") or use the name but request confidentiality in the application letter or in an underlined note ("Résumé submitted in confidence") at the top or bottom of the résumé. If an organization's name or location has since changed, state the current name and location and then "formerly . . ."

The work experience section lists all the related jobs you've had:

- Name and location of employer
- What the organization does (if not clear from its name)
- Your functional title
- How long you worked there
- Your duties and responsibilities
- Your significant achievements or contributions

Before or after each job listing, state your functional title, such as "clerk typist" or "salesperson." If you were a dishwasher, say so. Don't try to make your role seem more important by glamorizing your job title, functions, or achievements. Employers are checking on candidates' backgrounds more than they used to, so inaccuracies are likely to be exposed sooner or later (see "Focusing on Ethics: Résumé Deception: Risky or Fatal?"). Also state how long you worked on each job, from month/year to month/year. Use the phrase "to present" to denote current employment. If a job was part-time, say so.

Devote the most space to the jobs that are related to your target position. If you were personally responsible for something significant, be sure to mention it ("Devised a new collection system that accelerated payment of overdue receivables"). Facts about your skills and accomplishments are the most important information you can give a prospective employer, so quantify them whenever possible:

Quantify your accomplishments whenever possible.

Designed a new ad that increased sales by 9 percent

Raised $2,500 in 15 days for cancer research

You may also include a section describing other aspects of your background that pertain to your career objective. If you were applying for a position with a multinational organization, you would mention your command of another language or your travel experience. Other skills you might mention include the ability to operate a computer, word processor, or other specialized equipment. You might title a special section "Computer Skills" or "Language Skills" and place it near your education or work-experience section.

Include miscellaneous facts that are related to your career objective:

- Command of other languages
- Computer expertise
- Date you can start working

If samples of your work might increase your chances of getting the job, insert a line at the end of your résumé offering to supply them on request. You may put "References available upon request" at the end of your résumé, but doing so is not necessary; the availability of references is usually assumed. Don't include actual names of references. List your references on a separate sheet and take them to your interview.

Activities and Achievements Your résumé should also describe any volunteer activities that demonstrate your abilities. List projects that require leadership, organization, teamwork, and cooperation. Emphasize career-related activities such as "member of the Student Marketing Association." List skills you learned in these activities, and explain how these skills are related to the job you're applying for. Include speaking, writing, or tutoring experience; participation in athletics or creative projects; fundraising or community-service activities; and offices held in academic or professional organizations. (However, mention of political or religious organizations may be a red flag to someone with differing views, so use your judgment.)

Nonpaid activities may provide evidence of work-related skills.

Note any awards you've received. Again, quantify your achievements whenever possible. Instead of saying that you addressed various student groups, state how many and the approximate audience sizes. If your activities have been extensive, you may

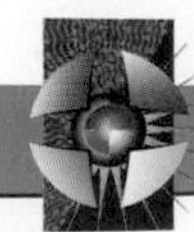

Focusing on Ethics

Résumé Deception: Risky or Fatal?

In an effort to put your best foot forward, you may be tempted to waltz around a few points that could raise questions about your résumé. As you weigh the alternatives, you may say to yourself, "Everybody else is probably shading the facts to make their résumés look good. I'd be a fool not to do the same."

Although statistics on the prevalence of résumé inflation are difficult to gather, according to an analysis of more than 1.8 million background checks last year, roughly one in four résumés has a lie in it. Other estimates are as high as 40 percent of all résumés either omitting potentially damaging information or exaggerating the candidate's accomplishments. The majority of recruiters agree that distortion is common.

The most frequent forms of deception include the following:

- **Claiming nonexistent educational credits.** Candidates may state (or imply) that they earned a degree when, in fact, they never attended the school or attended but did not complete the regular program. A typical claim might read, "Majored in business administration at Wayne State University."
- **Inflating grade-point averages.** Students who feel pressured to impress employers with their academic performance may claim a higher GPA than they actually achieved.
- **Stretching dates of employment to cover gaps.** Many candidates try to camouflage gaps in their work history by giving vague dates of employment. For example, a candidate who left a company in January 1992 and joined another in December 1993 might cover up by showing that the first job ended in 1992 and the next began in 1993.
- **Claiming to be self-employed.** Another common way people cover a period of unemployment is by saying that they were "self-employed" or a "consultant." The candidate claims to have operated an independent business during the period in question.
- **Claiming to have worked for companies that are out of business.** Candidates who need to fill a gap in their work record sometimes say they worked for a firm that has gone out of business. Checking such claims is difficult because the people who were involved in the disbanded business are hard to track down.
- **Omitting jobs that might cause embarrassment.** Being fired from one or two jobs is understandable when corporate mergers and downsizing are commonplace. However, a candidate who has lost several jobs in quick succession may seem a poor employee to recruiters. To cover a string of job losses, candidates may decide to leave out a few positions and stretch the dates of employment for the jobs held before and after.
- **Exaggerating expertise or experience.** Candidates often inflate their accomplishments by using verbs somewhat loosely. Words such as *supervised, managed, increased, improved,* and *created* imply that the candidate was personally responsible for results that, in reality, were the outcome of a group effort.

---

want to group them into divisions such as "College Activities," "Community Service," "Professional Associations," "Seminars and Workshops," and "Speaking Activities." An alternative is to divide them into two categories: "Service Activities" and "Achievements, Awards, and Honors."

Provide only the personal data that will help you get the job.

Personal Data Experts advise you to leave personal interests off your résumé—unless including them enhances the employer's understanding of why you would be the best candidate for the job.[25] For instance, candidates applying for a bodyguard position with Pinkerton's security division may want to list martial arts achievements among their personal interests. Someone applying to REI may want to list outdoor activities. According to REI's Doug Halm, such information helps show how a candidate will fit in with the organization's culture.

Some information is best excluded from your résumé. Civil rights laws prohibit employers from discriminating on the basis of gender, marital or family status, age (although only persons aged 40 to 70 are protected), race, religion, national origin, and physical or mental disability. So be sure to exclude any items that could encourage discrimination. Experts also recommend excluding salary information, reasons for leaving jobs, names of previous supervisors, your Social Security number, and other identification codes. Save these items for the interview, and offer them only if the employer specifically requests them.

DO	DON'T
☑ **Tell the truth** If you lie, you will almost certainly get caught, and the damage to your career could be significant.	☒ **Fabricate** Fake academic degrees and nonexistent jobs are checked first and will cost you the job, before or after you're hired.
☑ **Make your story positive** Most blemishes on your record can be framed in a positive way.	☒ **Make blatant omissions** Failing to disclose a job that didn't work out is almost as bad as making one up.
☑ **Sanitize your record** Clear up unresolved issues such as tax liens and lawsuits.	☒ **Exaggerate successes** Be ready to prove any claim about your accomplishments.
☑ **Think small** Candidates with criminal histories or other career impediments should focus on smaller companies, which are less likely to conduct background checks.	☒ **Go overboard** There's usually no need to disclose career or personal history that's more than 15 years old. If asked directly, answer truthfully—but with a minimum of elaboration.

Think twice before trying one of these ploys yourself. If you misrepresent your background and your résumé raises suspicion, you will probably get caught, and your reputation will be damaged. A deceptive résumé can "seriously impact your ability to be employed and advance your career," says Kathi Vanyo, a managing consultant with Drake Beam Morin.

Experienced recruiters are familiar with the games that candidates play to enhance their image. Many employers fire people who lied on their résumés, and companies today are hiring highly skilled investigators who can access much-improved databases to seek the truth. Middle managers are facing detailed investigations of court records, academic credentials, previous employers, and even former associates.

Sure, it's fine to present your strongest, most impressive qualifications and to minimize your weaknesses. But don't exaggerate, alter the past, or claim to have skills you don't have. Just how far can you go to make your résumé strong and positive?

Career Applications

1. You quit your summer job as a door-to-door encyclopedia sales representative. Describe how you might handle that period on your résumé. Should you omit it? Can you mention it without revealing why you quit?
2. Consider one or two positions you've held (whether in a club, in a volunteer organization, or with a business). Write a realistic description of your responsibilities that doesn't inflate them but presents them in a positive light.

If military service is relevant to the position, you may list it in this section (or under "Education" or "Work Experience"). List the date of induction, the branch of service, where you served, the highest rank you achieved, any accomplishments related to your career goals, and the date you were discharged.

Completing Your Résumé

The last step in the three-step writing process is no less important than the other two. As with any other business message, you need to revise your résumé, produce it in an appropriate form, and proofread it for any errors.

Revise Your Résumé

The key to writing a successful résumé is to adopt the "you" attitude and focus on your audience. Think about what the prospective employer needs, and then tailor your résumé accordingly. Employers such as Doug Halm read thousands of résumés every year, and they complain about the following common problems:

The "perfect" résumé responds to the reader's needs and preferences and avoids some common faults.

- **Too long.** The résumé is not concise, relevant, and to the point.
- **Too short or sketchy.** The résumé does not give enough information for a proper evaluation of the applicant.

- **Hard to read.** A lack of "white space" and of devices such as indentions and boldfacing makes the reader's job more difficult.
- **Wordy.** Descriptions are verbose, with numerous words used for what could be said more simply.
- **Too slick.** The résumé appears to have been written by someone other than the applicant, which raises the question of whether the qualifications have been exaggerated.
- **Amateurish.** The applicant appears to have little understanding of the business world or of a particular industry, as revealed by including the wrong information or presenting it awkwardly.
- **Poorly reproduced.** The print is faint and difficult to read.
- **Misspelled and ungrammatical throughout.** Recruiters conclude that candidates who make spelling and grammar mistakes lack good verbal skills, which are important on the job.
- **Boastful.** The overconfident tone makes the reader wonder whether the applicant's self-evaluation is realistic.
- **Dishonest.** The applicant claims to have expertise or work experience that he or she does not possess.
- **Gimmicky.** The words, structure, decoration, or material used in the résumé depart so far from the usual as to make the résumé ineffective.

Guard against making these mistakes in your own résumé, and compare your final version with the suggestions in this chapter's "Checklist: Writing Résumés."

Produce Your Traditional Résumé

The key characteristics of a good résumé are
- Neatness
- Simplicity
- Accuracy
- Honesty

With less than a minute to make a good impression, your résumé needs to look sharp and grab a recruiter's interest in the first few lines. A typical recruiter devotes 45 seconds to each résumé before tossing it into either the "maybe" or the "reject" pile.[26] Most recruiters scan a résumé rather than read it from top to bottom. If yours doesn't stand out, chances are the recruiter won't look at it long enough to judge your qualifications.

To give your printed résumé the best appearance possible, use a clean typeface on high-grade, letter-size bond paper (in white or some light earth tone). Your stationery and envelope should match. Leave ample margins all around, and make sure that any corrections are unnoticeable. Avoid italic typefaces, which are difficult to read, and use a quality printer.

Try to keep your résumé to one page. If you have a great deal of experience and are applying for a higher-level position, you may need to prepare a somewhat longer résumé. The important thing is to have enough space to present a persuasive, but accurate, portrait of your skills and accomplishments.

Lay out your résumé to make information easy to grasp.[27] Break up the text with headings that call attention to various aspects of your background, such as work experience and education. Underline or capitalize key points, or set them off in the left margin. Use lists to itemize your most important qualifications, and leave plenty of white space, even if doing so forces you to use two pages rather than one.

Under Jeff Taylor's guidance, Monster.com now lists more than 10 million résumés on its recruitment website.

Converting Your Traditional Résumé to a Scannable Format You need to format your résumé in at least two and maybe three ways: (1) as a traditional printed document such as the one just discussed, (2) as a plain-text (or ASCII) document that can be scanned from a hard copy or submitted electronically, and (3) as an HTML-coded document that can be uploaded to the Internet to post on a webpage (should you choose to).

Overwhelmed by the number of résumés they receive, most Fortune 1000 companies encourage applicants to submit electronic (scannable) résumés. By scanning these résumés into their electronic database, companies can quickly narrow the field of applicants. However, good scanning systems cost up to

✓ CHECKLIST: WRITING RÉSUMÉS

A. Organizational approach

1. Use the chronological approach unless you have a weak employment history.
2. Use the functional approach if you are new to the job market, want to redirect your career, or have gaps in your employment history.
3. Use the combined approach to maximize the advantages of both chronological and functional résumés, but only when neither of the other two formats will work.

B. Format and style

1. Use short noun phrases and action verbs, not whole sentences.
2. Use facts, not opinions.
3. Adopt a "you" attitude.
4. Omit personal pronouns (especially *I*).
5. Omit the date of preparation, desired salary, and work schedule.
6. Use parallelism when listing multiple items.
7. Use positive language and simple words.
8. Use white space, quality paper, and quality printing.

C. Opening

1. Include contact information (name, address).
2. Include a career objective or a skills summary if desired.
3. Make your career objective specific and interesting.
4. Prepare two separate résumés if you can perform two unrelated types of work.
5. In a skills summary, present your strongest qualifications first.

D. Education

1. List the name and location of every postsecondary school you've attended (with dates, and with degrees/certificates obtained).
2. Indicate your college major (and minor).
3. Indicate numerical scale (4.0 or 5.0) if you include your grade-point average.
4. List other experiences (seminars, workshops), with dates and certificates obtained.

E. Work experience, skills, and accomplishments

1. List all relevant work experience (paid employment, volunteer work, internships).
2. List full-time and part-time jobs.
3. Provide name and location of each employer (with dates of employment).
4. List job title and describe responsibilities.
5. Note on-the-job accomplishments and skills; quantify them whenever possible.

F. Activities and achievements

1. List all relevant offices and leadership positions.
2. List projects you have undertaken.
3. Show abilities such as writing or speaking, and list publications and community service.
4. List other information, such as your proficiency in languages other than English.
5. Mention ability to operate special equipment, including technical, computer, and software skills.

G. Personal data

1. Omit personal details that might be seen as negative or used to discriminate against you.
2. Leave personal interests off unless they are relevant to the position being sought.
3. List a reference only with permission to do so.

H. Modifications for an electronic résumé

1. Eliminate graphics, boldface, underlines, italics, small print, tabs, and all format codes.
2. Save the file in plain-text (ASCII) format.
3. Add blank spaces, align text, and use asterisks for bullets.
4. Add a "Keyword Summary," listing nouns to define skills, experience, education, and professional attributes.
5. Mirror the job description when possible.
6. Add job-related jargon, but don't overdo it.

I. Modifications for an online résumé

1. Provide your URL and e-mail address.
2. Use a keyword hyperlink to an ASCII version so that employers can download it.
3. Use a keyword hyperlink to a fully formatted résumé that can be read online and printed.

$100,000, so companies with fewer than 100 employees seldom use them.[28] If you're unsure whether an employer accepts scannable résumés, call and ask, or visit the company's website.

Learning Objective 5

Describe what you can do to adapt your résumé to a scannable format

Reformatting your traditional résumé is helpful if it will be scanned or if you will be posting it on the Internet or submitting it via e-mail.

Scannable résumés should convey the same information as traditional résumés, but the format and style must be changed to one that is computer friendly, because scannable résumés are not intended to be read by humans. To understand why the format is different for scannable résumés, here's a closer look at how résumé scanning works.

During the scanning process, special hardware and software are used to convert a paper résumé into an image on the employer's computer. Optical character recognition (OCR) software creates an electronic text document from the original by examining

FIGURE 17.8 Understanding the Scanning Process

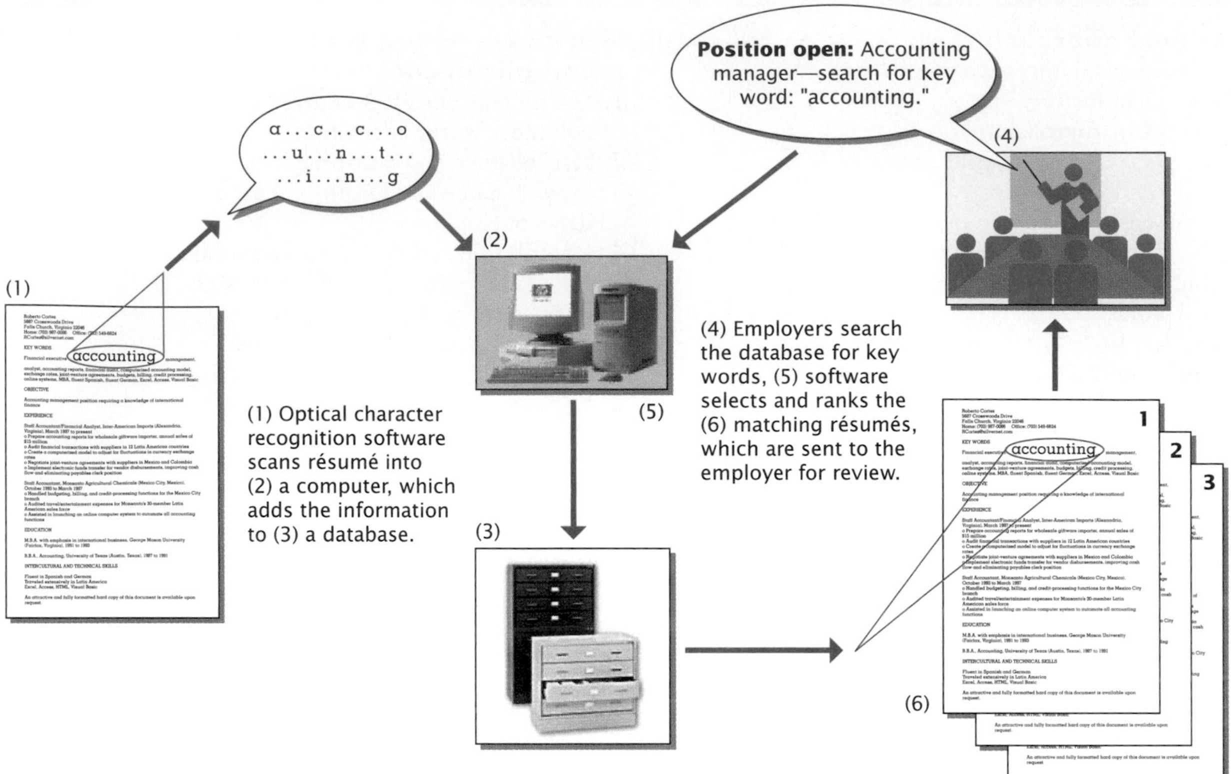

A system with special software and hardware reads your scannable résumé and stores it in a database that can be searched by employers.

and reproducing every letter or number. This electronic document is then downloaded into a company database, which can be searched and sorted by keywords, criteria, or almost anything the employer wants (see Figure 17.8). For example, a manager may want to hire a marketing representative who is fluent in Spanish, has five years' sales experience, has a background in new product marketing, and is experienced in cold calling. The employer enters these keywords (plus others) into the database program and performs a sort function on all the résumés in the database. The computer then provides a list of candidates whose résumés include these keywords. Next to the candidate's name is a percentage indicating how closely the résumé reflects the employer's requirements.[29]

To make your traditional résumé a scannable one, format it as plain-text (ASCII) document, improve its look, and modify its content slightly by providing a list of keywords and by balancing common language with current jargon.[30]

ASCII is a plain-text language that can be read by any computer, regardless of the word-processing software.

Prepare Your Résumé in ASCII Format ASCII is a common plain-text language that allows your résumé to be read by any scanner and accessed by any computer, regardless of the word-processing software you used to prepare the document. All word-processing programs allow you to save files as plain text. To convert your résumé to an ASCII plain-text file:

To make your scanable résumé computer friendly,

- Eliminate graphics
- Eliminate formatting codes
- Use a scannable typeface between 10 and 14 points

- Remove all formatting (boldfacing, underlining, italics, centering, bullets, graphic lines, etc.) and all formatting codes such a tab settings or tables.
- Remove shadows and reverse print (white letters on black background).
- Remove graphics and boxes.
- Use scannable typefaces (such as Helvetica, Futura, Optima, Univers, Times New Roman, Palatino, New Century Schoolbook, and Courier).
- Use a font size of 10 to 14 points.
- Remove multicolumn formats that resemble newspapers or newsletters.
- Save your document under a different name by using your word processor's "save as" option and selecting "text only with line breaks."

Best of the Web

Post an Online Résumé

At CareerBuilder, you'll find sample résumés, tips on preparing different types of résumés (including scannable ones), links to additional articles, and expert advice on creating résumés that bring positive results. After you've polished your résumé-writing skills, you can search for jobs online using the site's numerous links to national and international industry-specific websites. You can access the information at CareerBuilder to develop your résumé and then post it with prospective employers—all free of charge. Take advantage of what this site offers, and get ideas for writing or improving a new résumé.

www.careerbuilder.com

Improve the Look of Your Scannable Résumé Résumés in ASCII format (without special formatting) look ugly in comparison to traditional résumés. Use the following formatting techniques (which are acceptable for scannable résumés) to enhance the résumé's overall look and effectiveness:[31]

- Align text by adding some blank spaces (rather than tabs).
- Create headings and separate paragraphs by adding a few blank lines.
- Indicate bullets with an asterisk or the lowercase letter *o*.
- Use white space so that scanners and computers can tell when one topic ends and another begins.
- Do condense the spacing between letters.
- Use all capital letters for section headings as long as the letters do not touch each other.
- Put your name at the top of each page on its own line (with no text appearing above or beside your name).
- Use the standard address format below your name.
- List each phone number on its own line.
- Use white or light-colored $8^{1}/_{2}$-by-11-inch paper, printing on one side only.

Because scannable résumés are designed to be read by computers, it's fine to submit multiple pages—but don't get carried away. To increase your chances of a quality scan, do not fold or staple the résumé and do not send a photocopy. Provide a printed original, if possible.

Provide a List of Keywords When converting your résumé to a scannable format, emphasize certain keywords to help potential employers select your résumé from the thousands they scan. Employers generally search for nouns (since verbs tend to be generic rather than specific to a particular position or skill). To maximize the number of matches (or hits), include a keyword summary of 20 to 30 words and phrases that define your skills, experience, education, professional affiliations, and so on. Place this list right after your name and address. Here's an example of a possible keyword summary for an accountant:

Keywords help potential employers sort through an entire database of résumés.

Keyword Summary

Accountant, Corporate Controller, Fortune 1000, Receivables, Payables, Inventory, Cash Flow, Financial Analysis, Payroll Experience, Corporate Taxes, Activity-Based Accounting, Problem Solving, Computer Skills, Excel, Access, Networks, HTML, Peachtree, Quick Books, BA Indiana University--Accounting, CPA, Dean's List, Articulate, Team Player, Flexible, Willing to Travel, Fluent Spanish.

One way to identify which keywords to include in your electronic summary is to underline all the skills listed in ads for the types of jobs you're interested in. Make sure these ads match your qualifications and experience. Some job candidates try to beat the system by listing every conceivable skill and by guessing which words the computer is likely

FIGURE 17.9 In-Depth Critique: Electronic Résumé

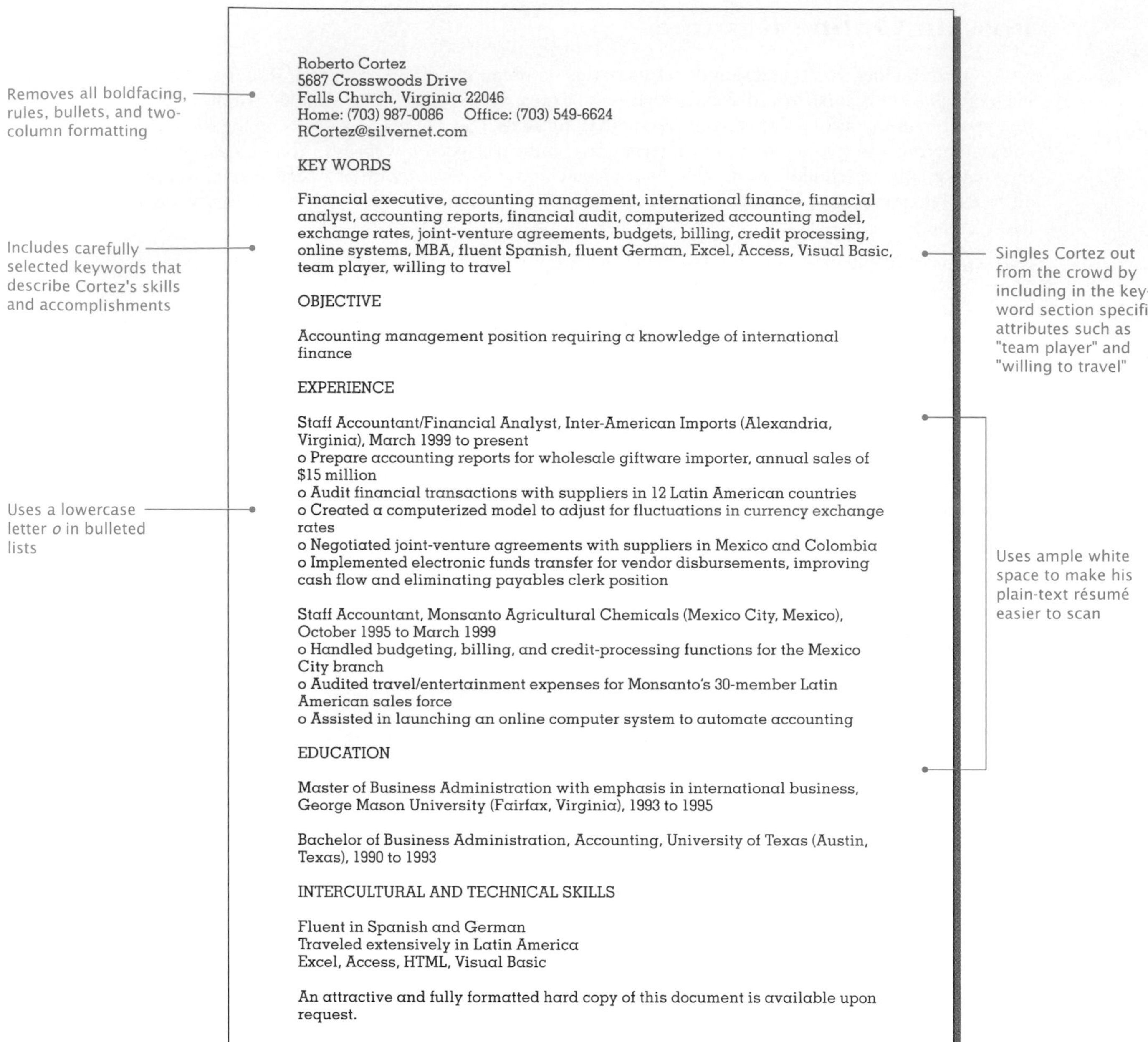

Roberto Cortez
5687 Crosswoods Drive
Falls Church, Virginia 22046
Home: (703) 987-0086 Office: (703) 549-6624
RCortez@silvernet.com

KEY WORDS

Financial executive, accounting management, international finance, financial analyst, accounting reports, financial audit, computerized accounting model, exchange rates, joint-venture agreements, budgets, billing, credit processing, online systems, MBA, fluent Spanish, fluent German, Excel, Access, Visual Basic, team player, willing to travel

OBJECTIVE

Accounting management position requiring a knowledge of international finance

EXPERIENCE

Staff Accountant/Financial Analyst, Inter-American Imports (Alexandria, Virginia), March 1999 to present
o Prepare accounting reports for wholesale giftware importer, annual sales of $15 million
o Audit financial transactions with suppliers in 12 Latin American countries
o Created a computerized model to adjust for fluctuations in currency exchange rates
o Negotiated joint-venture agreements with suppliers in Mexico and Colombia
o Implemented electronic funds transfer for vendor disbursements, improving cash flow and eliminating payables clerk position

Staff Accountant, Monsanto Agricultural Chemicals (Mexico City, Mexico), October 1995 to March 1999
o Handled budgeting, billing, and credit-processing functions for the Mexico City branch
o Audited travel/entertainment expenses for Monsanto's 30-member Latin American sales force
o Assisted in launching an online computer system to automate accounting

EDUCATION

Master of Business Administration with emphasis in international business, George Mason University (Fairfax, Virginia), 1993 to 1995

Bachelor of Business Administration, Accounting, University of Texas (Austin, Texas), 1990 to 1993

INTERCULTURAL AND TECHNICAL SKILLS

Fluent in Spanish and German
Traveled extensively in Latin America
Excel, Access, HTML, Visual Basic

An attractive and fully formatted hard copy of this document is available upon request.

to be looking for. But that strategy seldom works. The computer may be looking for a Harvard Business School graduate who once worked at Netscape and now lives in Arizona. If you went to Yale, worked at Yahoo!, and live in Maine, you're out of luck.[32]

Use words your employer will understand by including some jargon specific to your field.

Balance Common Language with Current Jargon Another way to maximize hits on your résumé is to use words that potential employers will understand (for example, use *keyboard*, not *input device*). Also, use abbreviations sparingly (except for common ones such as BA or MBA). At the same time, learn and use the important buzzwords in your field. Look for current jargon in the want ads of major newspapers such as *The Wall Street Journal* and in other résumés in your field that are posted online. Be careful to check and recheck the spelling, capitalization, and punctuation of any jargon you include, and use only those words you see most often.

Roberto Cortez created an electronic résumé by changing his formatting and adding a list of keywords. However, the information remains essentially the same and appears in the same order, as you can see in Figure 17.9. Now his target employers can scan his résumé into a database, and Cortez can submit his résumé via e-mail or post it on the Internet.

E-mail is the best way to transmit your plain-text résumé.

Submitting Scannable Résumés If an employer gives you an option of submitting a scannable résumé by mail, by fax, or by e-mail, choose e-mail. E-mail puts your résumé directly into the employer's database, bypassing the scanning process. If you send your résumé in a paper format by regular mail or by fax, you run the risk that an OCR scanning program will create an error when reading it. In fact, increasing numbers of job applicants are submitting both a traditional and a scannable résumé, explaining in their cover letter that the scannable résumé is for downloading into a database if the company desires.[33]

When submitting your résumé by e-mail, don't attach it as a separate document. Most human resources departments won't accept attached files (they're concerned about computer viruses). Instead, paste your résumé into the body of your e-mail message. Whenever you know a reference number or a job ad number, include it in your e-mail subject line.

If you're posting your scannable résumé to an employer's online résumé builder, copy and paste the appropriate sections from your electronic file directly into the employer's form. This method avoids rekeying and eliminates errors.

If you fax your scannable résumé, set your machine to "fine" mode (to ensure a high-quality printout on the receiving end). If you're mailing your résumé, you may want to send both a well-designed traditional résumé and a scannable one. Simply attach Post-it notes, labeling one "visual résumé" and the other "scannable résumé."

One advantage of posting your résumé on your website is the opportunity to use hyperlinks.

Building an Online Résumé If you wish to post your résumé on your webpage, provide employers with your URL; most recruiters won't take the time to use search engines to find your site.[34] As you design your website résumé, think of important keywords to use as hyperlinks—words that will grab an employer's attention and make the recruiter want to click on that hyperlink to learn more about you. You can make links to papers you've written, recommendations, and sound or video clips. Don't distract potential employers from your credentials by using hyperlinks to organizations or other websites.

Keep your résumé up to date.

To post your résumé with an index service, you must convert it to an electronic format (see page 562). Transmit it by mail, fax, modem, or e-mail. Once your résumé is in the service's database, it is sent to employers who match the keywords you've listed.

When posting your résumé online, do not use photos, and avoid providing information that reveals your age, gender, race, marital status, or religion. Because a website is a public access area, you should also leave out the names of references and previous employers. Either mention that references are available on request, or say nothing. Also, instead of naming companies, simply refer to "a large accounting firm" or "a wholesale giftware importer." Finally, include an ASCII version of your résumé on your webpage so that prospective employers can download it into their company's database.

Proofread Your Résumé

Doug Halm cautions that your résumé is a concrete example of how you will prepare material on the job. So in every format, remember to pay close attention to mechanics and details. Check all headings and lists for parallelism, and be sure that your grammar, spelling, and punctuation are correct.

Once your résumé is complete, update it continuously. As already mentioned, employment is becoming much more flexible these days, so it's likely you'll want to change employers. Besides, you'll also need your résumé to apply for membership in professional organizations and to work toward a promotion. Keeping your résumé updated is a good idea.

JobDirect.com is a leading job-search site for college and entry-level professional positions, with résumé matching and daily e-mails to students.

PREPARING OTHER TYPES OF EMPLOYMENT MESSAGES

Although your résumé will take the greatest amount of time and effort, you'll also need to prepare other employment messages, including application letters, job-inquiry letters, application forms, and follow-up notes.

Application Letters

Whenever you submit your résumé, accompany it with a cover, or application, letter to let readers know what you're sending, why you're sending it, and how they can benefit from reading it. Because your application letter is in your own style (rather than the choppy, shorthand style of your résumé), it gives you a chance to show your communication skills and some personality.

Application letters are intended to interest readers enough to read your résumé.

Always send your résumé and application letter together, because each has a unique job to perform. The purpose of your résumé is to get employers interested enough to contact you for an interview. The purpose of your application letter is to get employers interested enough to read your résumé.

Learning Objective 6

Define the purpose of application letters, and explain how to apply the AIDA organizational approach to them

Before drafting a letter, learn something about the organization you're applying to; then focus on your audience so that you can show you've done your homework. Imagine yourself in the recruiter's situation, and show how your background and talents will solve a particular problem or fill a specific need the company has. The more you can learn about the organization, the better you'll be able to capture the reader's attention and convey your interest in the company.[35] During your research, find out the name, title, and department of the person you're writing to. Reaching and addressing the right person is the most effective way to gain attention. Avoid phrases such as "To Whom It May Concern" and "Dear Sir."

When putting yourself in your reader's shoes, remember that this person's in-box is probably overflowing with résumés and cover letters. So respect your reader's time. Steer clear of gimmicks, which almost never work, and include nothing in your cover letter that already appears in your résumé. Keep your letter straightforward, fact-based, short, upbeat, and professional. Some quick tips for cover letters include the following:[36]

- **Be specific.** Avoid general objectives. Be as clear as possible about the kind of opportunity and industry you're looking for.
- **Include salary.** If you've been working in your field, include your current salary, but make sure your reader understands that this information is not a demand but intended to inform and assist.
- **Make e-mail covers even shorter.** When sending a cover letter by e-mail, make it a bit shorter than traditional application letters. Remember, e-mail readers want the gist very quickly.
- **Aim for high quality.** Meticulously check your spelling, mechanics, and grammar. Recruiters are complaining about the declining quality of written communication, including cover letters.

REI's Doug Halm believes that a good application letter should be no longer than three paragraphs. It should maintain a friendly yet conversational tone. "The letter is a sales piece," Halm advises. "Look at the job advertisement and highlight the specific points the company is looking for. Show that you know the job."

You write a solicited application letter in response to an announced job opening.

If you're sending a **solicited application letter**—in response to an announced job opening—you'll usually know what qualifications the organization is seeking. You'll also have more competition because hundreds of other job seekers will have seen the listing and may be sending applications too. The letter in Figure 17.10 was written in response to a help-wanted ad. Kenneth Sawyer highlights his chief qualifications and mirrors the requirements specified in the ad. He actually grabs attention by focusing on the phrase "proven skills" used in the ad: He elaborates on his own proven skills throughout the letter and even mentions the term in the closing paragraph.

FIGURE 17.10 In-Depth Critique: Sample Solicited Application Letter

2893 Jack Pine Road
Chapel Hill, NC 27514
February 2, 2002

Ms. Angela Clair
Director of Administration
Cummings and Welbane, Inc.
770 Campus Point Drive
Chapel Hill, NC 27514

Dear Ms. Clair:

In the January 31 issue of the *Chapel Hill Post*, your ad mentioned "proven skills." I believe I have what you are looking for in an administrative assistant. In addition to experience in a variety of office settings, I am familiar with the computer software used in your office.

States the reason for writing and links the writer's experience to stated qualifications

I recently completed a three-course sequence at Hamilton College on Microsoft Word and PowerPoint. I learned how to apply those programs to speed up letter- and report-writing tasks. A workshop on "Writing and Editing with the Unix Processor" gave me experience with other valuable applications such as composing and formatting sales letters, financial reports, and presentation slides.

Explains an achievement mentioned in the résumé and refers the reader to the enclosure

Discusses how specific skills apply to the job sought, showing that Sawyer understands the job's responsibilities

These skills have been invaluable to me as assistant to the chief nutritionist at our campus cafeteria (please refer to my résumé). I'm particularly proud of the order-confirmation system I designed, which has sharply reduced the problems of late shipments and depleted inventories.

Because "proven skills" are best explained in person, I would appreciate an interview with you. Please phone me any afternoon between 3 and 5 p.m. at (919) 220-6139 to let me know the day and time most convenient for you.

Asks for an interview and facilitates action

Sincerely,

Kenneth Sawyer

Kenneth Sawyer

Enclosure: Résumé

In some respects, an **unsolicited letter**—sent to an organization that has not announced an opening—stands a better chance of being read and receiving individualized attention. In her unsolicited application letter in Figure 17.11, Glenda Johns manages to give a snapshot of her qualifications and skills without repeating what is said in her résumé (which appears in Figure 17.6). She gains attention by focusing on the needs of the employer.

You write an unsolicited application letter to an organization that has not announced a job opening.

Both solicited and unsolicited letters present your qualifications similarly. The main difference is in the opening paragraph. In a solicited letter, you need no special attention-getter because you have been invited to apply. In an unsolicited letter, you need to start by capturing the reader's attention and interest.

Getting Attention

Like your résumé, your application letter is a form of advertising, so organize it as you would a sales letter: Use the AIDA approach, focus on your audience, and emphasize reader benefits (as discussed in Chapter 9). Make sure your style projects confidence. To sell a potential employer on your merits, you must believe in them and sound as though you do.

Follow the AIDA approach when writing your application letter: attention, interest, desire, action.

FIGURE 17.11 In-Depth Critique: Sample Unsolicited Application Letter

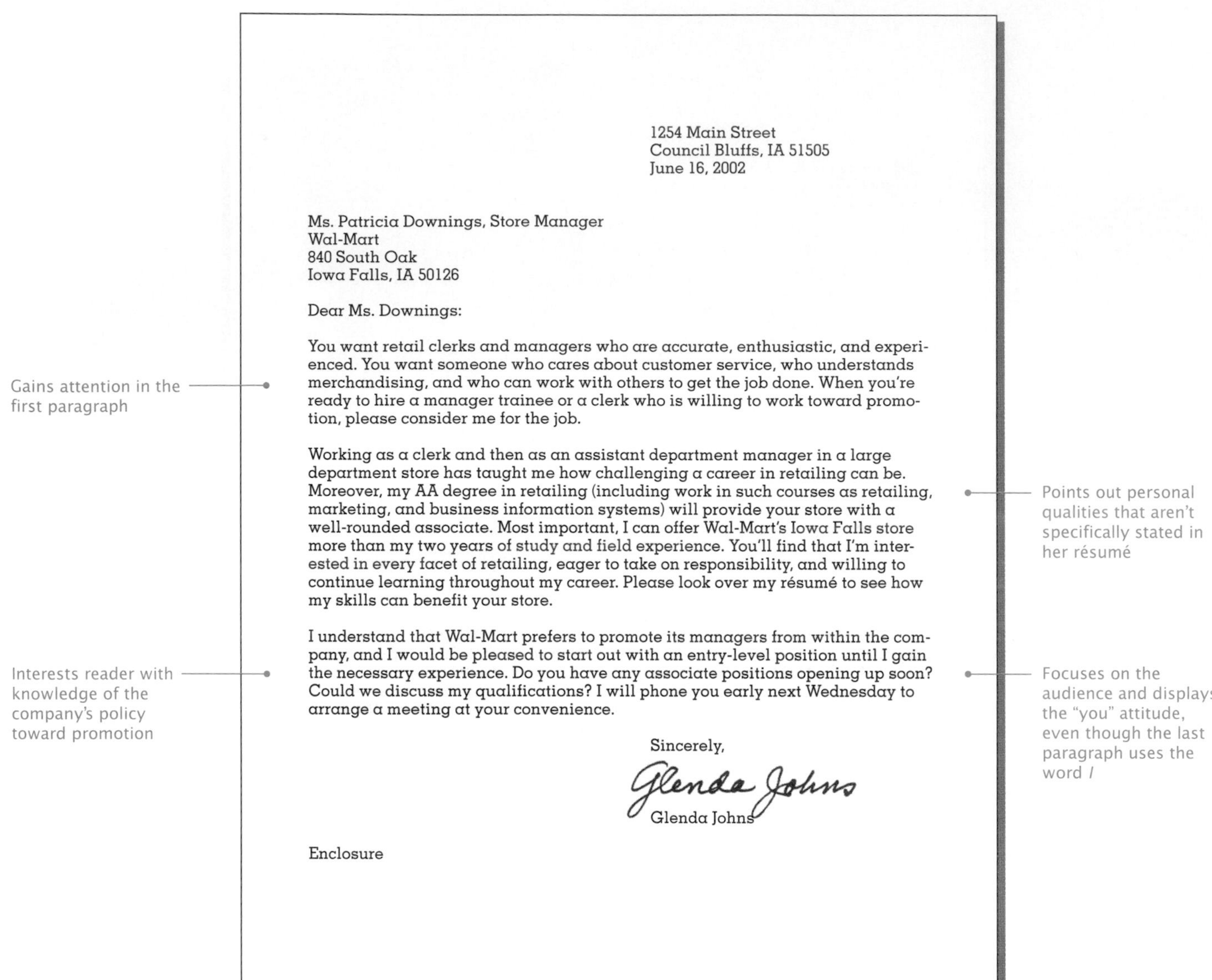

1254 Main Street
Council Bluffs, IA 51505
June 16, 2002

Ms. Patricia Downings, Store Manager
Wal-Mart
840 South Oak
Iowa Falls, IA 50126

Dear Ms. Downings:

You want retail clerks and managers who are accurate, enthusiastic, and experienced. You want someone who cares about customer service, who understands merchandising, and who can work with others to get the job done. When you're ready to hire a manager trainee or a clerk who is willing to work toward promotion, please consider me for the job.

Working as a clerk and then as an assistant department manager in a large department store has taught me how challenging a career in retailing can be. Moreover, my AA degree in retailing (including work in such courses as retailing, marketing, and business information systems) will provide your store with a well-rounded associate. Most important, I can offer Wal-Mart's Iowa Falls store more than my two years of study and field experience. You'll find that I'm interested in every facet of retailing, eager to take on responsibility, and willing to continue learning throughout my career. Please look over my résumé to see how my skills can benefit your store.

I understand that Wal-Mart prefers to promote its managers from within the company, and I would be pleased to start out with an entry-level position until I gain the necessary experience. Do you have any associate positions opening up soon? Could we discuss my qualifications? I will phone you early next Wednesday to arrange a meeting at your convenience.

Sincerely,

Glenda Johns

Glenda Johns

Enclosure

The opening of an application letter captures attention, gives the reason you're writing, and states which job you're applying for.

Open a solicited application letter by mentioning how you found out about the position.

The middle section of an application letter
- Summarizes your relevant qualifications
- Emphasizes your accomplishments
- Suggests desirable personal qualities
- Justifies salary requirements
- Refers to your résumé

The opening paragraph of your application letter must also state your reason for writing and the position you are applying for. Table 17.2 highlights some important ways to spark interest and grab attention in your opening paragraph. All these openings demonstrate the "you" attitude, and many indicate how the applicant can serve the employer. You can give your reason in one of these ways:

Please consider my application for an entry-level position in technical writing. Your firm advertised a fleet sales position (on September 23, 2002, in the *Baltimore Sun*). With my 16 months of new-car sales experience, won't you consider me for that position?

Another way to state your reason for writing is to use a title at the opening of your letter:

Subject: Application for bookkeeper position

Building Interest and Increasing Desire

The middle section of your application letter presents your strongest selling points in terms of their potential benefit to the organization, thereby building interest in you and creating a desire to interview you. If you already mentioned your selling points in the

TABLE 17.2 Tips for Getting Attention in Application Letters

Tip	*Example*
Unsolicited Application Letters	
• Show how your strongest skills will benefit the organization. A 20-year-old in her third year of college might begin like this:	When you need a secretary in your export division who can take shorthand at 125 words a minute and transcribe notes at 70—in English, Spanish, or Portuguese—call me.
• Describe your understanding of the job's requirements and then show how well your qualifications fit them	Your annual report states that Mobil Corporation runs employee-training programs about workforce diversity. The difficulties involved in running such programs can be significant, as I learned while tutoring inner-city high school students last summer. My 12 pupils were enrolled in vocational training programs and came from diverse ethnic and racial backgrounds. The one thing they had in common was a lack of familiarity with the typical employer's expectations. To help them learn the "rules of the game," I developed exercises that cast them in various roles: boss, customer, new recruit, and coworker. Of the 12 students, 10 subsequently found full-time jobs and have called or written to tell me how much they gained from the workshop.
• Mention the name of a person known to and highly regarded by the reader	When Janice McHugh of your franchise sales division spoke to our business communication class last week, she said you often need promising new marketing graduates at this time of year.
• Refer to publicized company activities, achievements, changes, or new procedures	Today's issue of the *Detroit News* reports that you may need the expertise of computer programmers versed in robotics when your Lansing tire plant automates this spring.
• Use a question to demonstrate your understanding of the organization's needs	Can your fast-growing market research division use an interviewer with 1½ years of field survey experience, a B.A. in public relations, and a real desire to succeed? If so, please consider me for the position.
• Use a catchphrase opening if the job requires ingenuity and imagination	*Haut monde*—whether said in French, Italian, or Arabic, it still means "high society." As an interior designer for your Beverly Hills showroom, not only could I serve and sell to your distinguished clientele, but I could do it in all these languages. I speak, read, and write them fluently.
Solicited Application Letters	
• Identify the publication in which the ad ran; then describe what you have to offer	Your ad in the April issue of *Travel & Leisure* for a cruise-line social director caught my eye. My eight years of experience as a social director in the travel industry would allow me to serve your new Caribbean cruise division well.

opening, don't repeat them. Simply give supporting evidence. Be careful not to repeat the facts presented in your résumé; simply interpret those facts for the reader. Otherwise, spell out a few of your key qualifications, and back up your assertions with some convincing evidence of your ability to perform:

> **Poor:** I completed three college courses in business communication, earning an A in each course, and have worked for the past year at Imperial Construction.
>
> **Improved:** Using the skills gained from three semesters of college training in business communication, I developed a collection system for Imperial Construction that reduced its 2001 bad-debt losses by 3.7 percent, or $9,902, over those of 2000. Instead of using timeworn terminology, the new system's collection letters offered discount incentives for speedy payment.
>
> **Improved:** Experience in customer relations and college courses in public relations have taught me how to handle the problem-solving tasks that arise in a leading retail clothing firm like yours. Such important tasks include identifying and resolving customer complaints, writing letters that build good customer relations, and above all, promoting the organization's positive image.

When writing a solicited letter responding to an advertisement, be sure to discuss each requirement specified in the ad. If you are deficient in any of these requirements, stress other solid selling points to help strengthen your overall presentation.

The middle of your application letter also demonstrates a few significant job-related qualities, such as your diligence or your ability to work hard, learn quickly, handle responsibility, or get along with people:

> While attending college full-time, I trained 3 hours a day with the varsity track team. In addition, I worked part-time during the school year and up to 60 hours a week each summer in order to be totally self-supporting while in college. I can offer your organization the same level of effort and perseverance.

Another matter you might bring up in this section is your salary requirements—but *only* if the organization has asked you to state them. Unless you know approximately what the job pays, suggest a salary range, or indicate that the salary is negotiable or open. You might consult the latest government "Area Wage Survey" at the library to get an idea of the salary range for various job classifications and geographic areas. If you do state a target salary, tie it to the benefits you would bring to the organization (much as you would handle price in a sales letter):

> For the past two years, I have been helping a company similar to yours organize its database. I would therefore like to receive a salary in the same range (the mid-20s) for helping your company set up a more efficient customer database.

Toward the end of this section, refer the reader to your résumé by citing a specific fact or general point covered there:

> You will find my people skills an asset. As you can see in the attached résumé, I've been working part-time with a local publisher since my sophomore year, and during that time, I have successfully resolved more than a few "client crises."

Motivating Action

Close by asking for an interview and making the interview easy to arrange.

The final paragraph of your application letter has two important functions: to ask the reader for a specific action and to make a reply easy. In almost all cases, the action you request is an interview. Don't demand it, however; try to sound natural and appreciative. Offer to come to the employer's office at a convenient time or, if the firm is some distance away, to meet with its nearest representative. Make the request easy to fulfill by stating your phone number and the best time to reach you—or, if you wish to be in control, by mentioning that you will follow up with a phone call in a few days. Refer again to your strongest selling point and, if desired, your date of availability:

> After you have reviewed my qualifications, could we discuss the possibility of putting my marketing skills to work for your company? Because I will be on spring break the week of March 8, I would like to arrange a time to talk then. I will call in late February to schedule a convenient time when we could discuss employment opportunities at your company.

Once you have edited and proofread your application letter, mail it and your résumé promptly, especially if they have been solicited.

Adapting Style and Approach to Culture

You may need to vary your approach according to your reader's culture.

The AIDA approach isn't appropriate for job seekers in every culture. If you're applying for a job abroad or want to work with a subsidiary of an organization based in another country, you may need to adjust your tone. Blatant self-promotion is considered bad form in some cultures. Other cultures stress group performance over individual contributions. As for format, recruiters in some countries (including France) prefer

✓ CHECKLIST: WRITING APPLICATION LETTERS

A. Attention (opening paragraph)

1. Open the letter by capturing the reader's attention in a businesslike way.
2. Use a summary, name, source, question, news, personalized, or creative opening.
3. State that you are applying for a job, and identify the position or the type of work you seek.

B. Interest and desire, or evidence of qualifications (next several paragraphs)

1. Present your key qualifications for the job, highlighting what is on your résumé: job-related education and training; relevant work experience; and related activities, interests, and qualities.
2. Adopt a mature, businesslike tone.
3. Eliminate boasting and exaggeration.
4. Back up your claims by citing specific achievements in educational, work, and outside settings.
5. Demonstrate your knowledge of the organization by citing its operations or trends in the industry.
6. Link your education, experience, and personal qualities to the job requirements.
7. Relate aspects of your training or work experience to those of the target position.
8. Outline your educational preparation for the job.
9. Provide evidence that you can learn quickly, work hard, handle responsibility, and get along with others.
10. Show that you possess personal qualities and work attitudes that are desirable for job performance.
11. If asked to state salary requirements in your letter, state current salary or a desired salary range, and link it to the benefits of hiring you.
12. Refer the reader to the enclosed résumé.

C. Action (closing paragraph)

1. Request an interview at the reader's convenience.
2. Request a screening interview with the nearest regional representative, if company headquarters is some distance away.
3. Make it easy to comply with your request by providing your phone number (with area code) and stating the best time to reach you, or mention a time when you will be calling to set up an interview.
4. Express your appreciation for an opportunity to have an interview.
5. Repeat your strongest qualification, to reinforce your claim that you can contribute to the organization.

handwritten letters to printed or typed ones—another good reason to research a company carefully before drafting your application letter.

For U.S. and Canadian companies, let your letter reflect your personal style. Be yourself, but be businesslike too; avoid sounding cute. Don't use slang or a gimmicky layout. The only time to be unusually creative in content or format is when the job you're seeking requires imagination, such as a position in advertising. Compare your own letters with the tasks in this chapter's "Checklist: Writing Application Letters."

Job-Inquiry Letters

Before considering you for a position, some organizations require you to fill out and submit an **application form**, a standardized data sheet that simplifies the comparison of applicants' qualifications. To request such a form, send a job-inquiry letter and include enough information about yourself in the letter to show that you have at least some of the requirements for the position you are seeking:

Use a job-inquiry letter to request an application form, which is a standardized data sheet that simplifies comparison of applicants' credentials.

> Please send me an application form for work as an interior designer in your home furnishings department. For my certificate in design, I took courses in retail merchandising and customer relations. I have also had part-time sales experience at Capwell's department store.

Instead of writing a letter of this kind, you may want to drop in at the office you're applying to. You probably won't be able to talk to anyone other than the receptionist or a human resources assistant, but you can pick up the form, get an impression of the organization, and demonstrate your initiative and energy.

Organizations will use your application form as a convenient one-page source for information about your qualifications. So try to be thorough and accurate when filling it out. Have your résumé with you to remind you of important information, and if you

Your care in filling out application forms suggests to the employer that you will be thorough and careful in your work.

can't remember something and have no record of it, provide the closest estimate possible. If you cannot provide some information because you have no such background (military experience, for example), write "Not applicable." When filling out applications, use a pen (unless specifically requested to use a pencil) and print legibly.

Application forms rarely give you enough space or ask you the right questions to reflect your skills and abilities accurately. Nevertheless, show your cooperation by doing your best to fill out the form completely. If you get an interview, you'll have an opportunity to fill in the gaps. You might also ask whether you might submit a résumé and an application letter along with the application.

Application Follow-Ups

Use a follow-up letter to let the employer know you're still interested in the job.

If your application letter and résumé fail to bring a response within a month or so, follow up with a second letter to keep your file active. This follow-up letter also gives you a chance to update your original application with any recent job-related information:

> Since applying to you on May 3 for an executive secretary position, I have completed a course in office management at South River Community College. I received straight A's in the course. I now am a proficient user of MS Word, including macros and other complex functions.
>
> Please keep my application in your active file, and let me know when you need a skilled executive secretary.

Even if you've received a letter acknowledging your application and saying that it will be kept on file, don't hesitate to send a follow-up letter three months later to show that you are still interested:

> Three months have elapsed since I applied to you for an underwriting position, but I want to let you know that I am still very interested in joining your company.
>
> I recently completed a four-week temporary work assignment at a large local insurance agency. I learned several new verification techniques and gained experience in using the online computer system. This experience could increase my value to your underwriting department.
>
> Please keep my application in your active file, and let me know when a position opens for a capable underwriter.

Unless you state otherwise, the human resources office is likely to assume that you've already found a job and are no longer interested in the organization. Moreover, requirements change. A follow-up letter can demonstrate that you're sincerely interested in working for the organization, that you're persistent in pursuing your goals, and that you're upgrading your skills to make yourself a better employee. And it might just get you an interview.

COMMUNICATION CHALLENGES AT RECREATION EQUIPMENT INCORPORATED (REI)

REI receives hundreds of unsolicited résumés each month. Doug Halm has recently revised the procedures for screening all résumés. Instead of reviewing them at REI's headquarters, Halm's staff now sorts the résumés and sends them directly to the human resources departments in the functional units that have specific openings. This procedure enables the people who actually do the hiring to evaluate the résumés. Although this method has several advantages, Halm is concerned about one possible problem: inconsistency in the evaluation process.

Individual Challenge: To ensure that all REI units use similar criteria to screen résumés, Halm wants to develop a guideline for evaluating the résumés of graduating students. The guideline will help REI's managers identify people who have good work habits, strong communication skills, commitment to teamwork, leadership potential, and a love for the outdoors. However, Halm wants to avoid imposing any rigid screening criteria that might arbitrarily eliminate promising candidates. He has asked you to develop the guideline and a one-page memo explaining how to use it. After you have done so, test the guideline by evaluating the résumés of three fellow students.

Team Challenge: Halm is planning a workshop on writing application letters for a Career Day at a nearby college. He wants to present letters that effectively portray limited work experiences in a positive light. He asks a group of you to draft letters that describe useful work skills and habits learned when (1) one applicant worked part-time as a supermarket cashier, (2) a second applicant worked as a camp counselor, and (3) a third applicant typed envelopes for a mailing service. Explain what employers may find relevant about the skills and habits described in each letter.[37] ■

SUMMARY OF LEARNING OBJECTIVES

1 **Discuss how today's changing workplace is affecting the employment-search process from both the employer's and the candidate's perspective.** Both employers and employees view employment as being more flexible than in the past. Employers hire temporary workers and consultants on a project-by-project basis, while employees are moving from company to company. Since fewer jobs are being created by large companies, more people are going to work for organizations with fewer than 200 people. Also, self-employment is increasing.

2 **Explain three things you can do before you graduate and while you're job hunting that will make you more valuable to employers.** To build toward a successful career, take the following actions: (1) Keep an employment portfolio of anything that shows your ability to perform, so that you can use it when writing your résumé and show it to employers as tangible evidence of your professionalism. (2) Take interim assignments (such as freelance work or internships) to gain valuable experience, relevant contacts, and important references. (3) Work on polishing and updating your skills by joining professional networks, taking a computer course, or seeking out other educational or life experiences.

3 **Discuss how to choose the appropriate résumé organization, and list the advantages or disadvantages of the three options.** Each organizational approach emphasizes different strengths. If you have a lot of employment experience, you would choose the chronological approach because it focuses on your work history. The advantages of the chronological résumé are (1) it helps employers easily locate necessary information, (2) it highlights your professional growth and career progress, and (3) it emphasizes continuity and stability in your employment background. The functional approach focuses on particular skills and competencies you've developed. The advantages of the functional résumé are (1) it helps employers easily see what you can do for them, (2) it allows you to emphasize earlier job experience, and (3) it lets you downplay any lengthy periods of unemployment or a lack of career progress. The combination approach uses the best features of the other two, but it has two disadvantages: (1) It tends to be longer, and (2) it can be repetitious if you must list accomplishments and skills in the functional section as well as in the individual job descriptions.

4 **List the major sections of a traditional résumé.** Your résumé must include three sections: (1) your name and address, (2) your education background (with related skills and accomplishments), and (3) your work experience (with related skills and accomplishments). Options include listing your career objective or a summary of qualifications, describing related activities and achievements, and perhaps (although not necessarily recommended) providing relevant personal data.

5 **Describe what you can do to adapt your résumé to a scannable format.** Begin by eliminating all fancy printing, graphics, and formatting such as boldface, italics, and tabs. Save the résumé as a plain-text (ASCII) document, adding some blank spaces, blank lines, and asterisks to make it more readable. Finally, provide a list of keywords (nouns) that define your skills, experience, and education. Make sure it also includes important jargon that is characteristic of the language in your field.

6 **Define the purpose of application letters, and explain how to apply the AIDA organizational approach to them.** The purpose of an application letter is to convince readers to look at your résumé. This makes application letters a type of sales letter, so you'll want to use the AIDA organizational approach. Get attention in the opening paragraph by showing how your work skills could benefit the organization, by explaining how your qualifications fit the job, or by demonstrating an understanding of the organization's needs. Build interest and desire by showing how you can meet the job requirements, and be sure to refer your reader to your résumé near the end of this section. Finally, motivate action by making your request easy to fulfill and by including all necessary contact information.

TEST YOUR KNOWLEDGE

1. What is the purpose of maintaining an employment portfolio?
2. In what ways can job seekers use the Internet during their career and employment search?
3. What is a résumé, and why is it important to adopt a "you" attitude when preparing one?
4. How does a chronological résumé differ from a functional résumé, and when is each appropriate?
5. What elements are commonly included in a résumé?
6. What are some of the most common problems with résumés?
7. Why is it important to provide a keyword summary in a scannable or electronic résumé?
8. What advantages do résumés sent by e-mail have over résumés sent by fax or by mail?
9. How does a solicited application letter differ from an unsolicited letter?
10. How does the AIDA approach apply to an application letter?

APPLY YOUR KNOWLEDGE

1. According to experts in the job placement field, the average job seeker relies too heavily on the résumé and not enough on other elements of the job search. Which elements do you think are most important? Please explain.
2. One of the disadvantages of résumé scanning is that some qualified applicants will be missed because the technology isn't perfect. However, more companies are using this approach. Do you think that résumé scanning is a good idea? Please explain.
3. Stating your career objective on a résumé or application might limit your opportunities by labeling you too narrowly. Not stating your objective, however, might lead an employer to categorize you incorrectly. Which outcome is riskier? Do summaries of qualifications overcome such drawbacks? If so, how? Explain briefly.
4. When writing a solicited application letter and describing the skills requested in the employer's ad, how can you avoid using *I* too often? Explain and give examples.
5. **Ethical Choices** Between your sophomore and junior year, you quit school for a year to earn the money to finish college. You worked as a clerk in a finance company, checking references on loan applications, typing, and filing. Your manager made a lot of the fact that he had never attended college. He seemed to resent you for pursuing your education, but he never criticized your work, so you thought you were doing okay. After you'd been working there for six months, he fired you, saying that you failed to be thorough enough in your credit checks. You were actually glad to leave, and you found another job right away at a bank doing similar duties. Now that you've graduated from college, you're writing your résumé. Will you include the finance company job in your work history? Please explain.

PRACTICE YOUR KNOWLEDGE

Documents for Analysis

Read the following documents; then (1) analyze the strengths or weaknesses of each document and (2) revise each document so that it follows the guidelines presented in this chapter.

Document 17.A: Writing a Résumé

Sylvia Manchester
765 Belle Fleur Blvd.
New Orleans, LA 70113
(504) 312-9504
smanchester@rcnmail.com

PERSONAL: Single, excellent health, 5′8″, 116 lbs.; hobbies include cooking, dancing, and reading.

JOB OBJECTIVE: To obtain a responsible position in marketing or sales with a good company.

Education: BA degree in biology, University of Louisiana. Graduated with a 3.0 average. Member of the varsity cheerleading squad. President of Panhellenic League. Homecoming queen.

WORK EXPERIENCE

<u>Fisher Scientific Instruments, 2000 to present, field sales representative.</u> Responsible for calling on customers and explaining the features of Fisher's line of laboratory instruments. Also responsible for writing sales letters, attending trade shows, and preparing weekly sales reports.

<u>Fisher Scientific Instruments, 1997–99, customer service representative.</u> Was responsible for handling incoming phone calls from customers who had questions about delivery, quality, or operation of Fisher's line of laboratory instruments. Also handled miscellaneous correspondence with customers.

<u>Medical Electronics, Inc., 1994–97, administrative assistant to the vice president of marketing.</u> In addition to handling typical secretarial chores for the vice president of marketing, I was in charge of compiling the monthly sales reports, using figures provided by members of the field sales force. I also was given responsibility for doing various market research activities.

<u>New Orleans Convention and Visitors Bureau, 1991–94, summers, tour guide.</u> During the summers of my college years, I led tours of New Orleans for tourists visiting the city. My duties included greeting conventioneers and their spouses at hotels, explaining the history and features of the city during an all-day sight-seeing tour, and answering questions about New Orleans and its attractions. During my fourth summer with the bureau, I was asked to help train the new tour guides. I prepared a handbook that provided interesting facts about the various tourist attractions, as well as answers to the most commonly asked tourist questions. The Bureau was so impressed with the handbook they had it printed up so that it could be given as a gift to visitors.

<u>University of Louisiana, 1991–94, part-time clerk in admissions office.</u> While I was a student in college, I worked 15 hours a week in the admissions office. My duties included filing, processing applications, and handling correspondence with high school students and administrators.

Document 17.B: Writing an Application Letter

I'm writing to let you know about my availability for the brand manager job you advertised. As you can see from my enclosed résumé, my background is perfect for the position.

Even though I don't have any real job experience, my grades have been outstanding considering that I went to a top-ranked business school.

I did many things during my undergraduate years to prepare me for this job:

- Earned a 3.4 out of a 4.0 with a 3.8 in my business courses
- Elected representative to the student governing association
- Selected to receive the Lamar Franklin Award
- Worked to earn a portion of my tuition

I am sending my résumé to all the top firms, but I like yours better than any of the rest. Your reputation is tops in the industry, and I want to be associated with a business that can pridefully say it's the best.

If you wish for me to come in for an interview, I can come on a Friday afternoon or anytime on weekends when I don't have classes. Again, thanks for considering me for your brand manager position.

Document 17.C: Writing Application Follow-Up Messages

Did you receive my résumé? I sent it to you at least two months ago and haven't heard anything. I know you keep résumés on file, but I just want to be sure that you keep me in mind. I heard you are hiring health-care managers and certainly would like to be considered for one of those positions.

Since I last wrote you, I've worked in a variety of positions that have helped prepare me for management. To wit, I've become lunch manager at the restaurant where I work, which involved a raise in pay. I now manage a waitstaff of 12 girls and take the lunch receipts to the bank every day.

Of course, I'd much rather be working at a real job, and that's why I'm writing again. Is there anything else you would like to know about me or my background? I would really like to know more about your company. Is there any literature you could send me? If so, I would really appreciate it.

I think one reason I haven't been hired yet is that I don't want to leave Atlanta. So I hope when you think of me, it's for a position that wouldn't require moving. Thanks again for considering my application.

Exercises

For live links to all websites discussed in this chapter, visit this text's website at www.prenhall.com/bovee. Just log on and select Chapter 17, and click on "Student Resources." Locate the name of the site or the URL related to the material in the text. For "Exploring the Best of the Web" exercises, you'll also find navigational directions. Click on the live link to the site.

17.1 Work-Related Preferences: Self-Assessment What work-related activities and situations do you prefer? Evaluate your preferences in each of the following areas. Use the results as a good start for guiding your job search.

Activity or Situation	Strongly Agree	Agree	Disagree	No Preference
1. I want to work independently.	______	______	______	______
2. I want variety in my work.	______	______	______	______
3. I want to work with people.	______	______	______	______
4. I want to work with products or machines.	______	______	______	______
5. I want physical work.	______	______	______	______
6. I want mental work.	______	______	______	______
7. I want to work for a large organization.	______	______	______	______
8. I want to work for a nonprofit organization.	______	______	______	______
9. I want to work for a small family business.	______	______	______	______
10. I want to work for a service business.	______	______	______	______
11. I want regular, predictable work hours.	______	______	______	______
12. I want to work in a city location.	______	______	______	______
13. I want to work in a small town or suburb.	______	______	______	______
14. I want to work in another country.	______	______	______	______
15. I want to work outdoors.	______	______	______	______
16. I want to work in a structured environment.	______	______	______	______

17.2 **Internet** Based on the preferences you identified in the self-assessment (Exercise 17.1) and the academic, professional, and personal qualities you have to offer, perform an Internet search for an appropriate career, using any of the websites listed in "Keeping Pace with Technology: Netting a Job on the Web." Draft a brief report indicating how the careers you select and job openings you find match your strengths and preferences.

17.3 **Teamwork** Working with another student, change the following statements to make them more effective for a traditional résumé by using action verbs.

a. Have some experience with database design.
b. Assigned to a project to analyze the cost accounting methods for a large manufacturer.
c. I was part of a team that developed a new inventory control system.
d. Am responsible for preparing the quarterly department budget.
e. Was a manager of a department with seven employees working for me.
f. Was responsible for developing a spreadsheet to analyze monthly sales by department.
g. Put in place a new program for ordering supplies.

17.4 **Résumé Preparation: Work Accomplishments** Using your team's answers to Exercise 17.3, make the statements stronger by quantifying them (make up any numbers you need).

17.5 **Ethical Choices** Assume that you achieved all the tasks shown in Exercise 17.3 not as an individual employee, but as part of a work team. In your résumé, must you mention other team members? Explain your answer.

17.6 **Résumé Preparation: Electronic Version** Using your revised version of Document for Analysis 17.A (on page 576), prepare a fully formatted print résumé. What formatting changes would Sylvia Manchester need to make if she were sending her résumé electronically? Develop a keyword summary and make all the changes needed to complete this electronic résumé.

EXPAND YOUR KNOWLEDGE

Exploring the Best of the Web:

Post an Online Résumé, p. 565

Your résumé is like a letter of introduction: It should make a good first impression. It must be organized, error-free, and in an appropriate format. In today's electronic business world, you should know how to prepare a résumé to post on the Internet or to send by e-mail. Learn this and more by logging on to CareerBuilder.

1. Before writing a new résumé, make a list of action verbs that describe your skills and experience.
2. Describe the advantages and disadvantages of chronological and functional résumé formats. Do you think a combination résumé would be an appropriate format for your new résumé? Explain why or why not.
3. List some of the tips you learned for preparing an electronic résumé.

Exploring the Web on Your Own

Review these chapter-related websites on your own to learn more about writing résumés and cover letters.

1. To find out what happens when résumés are scanned, log on to Proven Résumés, www.provenresumes.com/reswkshps/electronic/scnres.html.
2. Learn how to produce cover letters with brilliance, flair, and speed at So You Wanna Write a Cover Letter?, www.soyouwanna.com/site/syws/coverletter/coverletter.html.
3. Take measures to ensure that your e-mail résumé arrives intact by following the helpful advice at Learn2 Email Your Résumé, www.learn2.com/04/0437/0437.asp.

LEARN INTERACTIVELY

Interactive Study Guide

Visit "My Companion Website" at www.prenhall.com/bovee. For Chapter 17, take advantage of the interactive "Study Guide" to test your chapter knowledge. Get instant feedback on whether you need additional studying. Read the "Current Events" articles to get the latest on chapter topics, and complete the exercises—as specified by your instructor.

This site offers a variety of additional resources: The "Research Area" helps you locate a wealth of information to use in course assignments. You can even send a message to online research experts, who will help you find exactly the information you need. The "Study Hall" helps you succeed in this course. "Talk in the Hall" lets you leave messages and meet new friends online. If you have a question, you can "Ask the Tutor." And to get a better grade in this course, you can find more help at "Writing Skills," "Study Skills," and "Study Tips."

Grammar Diagnostic Tests

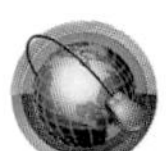

Review and reinforce your grammar and language skills by taking one of the four online diagnostic tests offered at our companion website, www.prenhall/bovee.com. The four tests cover a variety of topics, including spelling, capitals, punctuation, verbs, pronouns, adjectives, adverbs, sentence structure, sentence punctuation, clarity, word choice, style, organization skills, proofreading, and more. Submit your test and assess your competency. Then focus on improving areas where you are weak as you complete the exercises in this chapter.

CASES

BUILDING TOWARD A BETTER CAREER

1. Taking stock and taking aim: Application package for the right job Think about yourself. What are some things that come easily to you? What do you enjoy doing? In what part of the country would you like to live? Do you like to work indoors? Outdoors? A combination of the two? How much do you like to travel? Would you like to spend considerable time on the road? Do you like to work closely with others or more independently? What conditions make a job unpleasant? Do you delegate responsibility easily, or do you like to do things yourself? Are you better with words or numbers? Better at speaking or writing? Do you like to work under fixed deadlines? How important is job security to you? Do you want your supervisor to state clearly what is expected of you, or do you like the freedom to make many of your own decisions?

Your task: After answering these questions, gather information about possible jobs that suit your profile by consulting reference materials (from your college library or placement center) and by searching the Internet (using some of the search strategies discussed in Chapter 10). Next, choose a location, a company, and a job that interests you. With guidance from your instructor, decide whether to apply for a job you're qualified for now or one you'll be qualified for with additional education. Then, as directed by your instructor, write one or more of the following: (a) a job-inquiry letter, (b) a résumé, (c) a letter of application, (d) a follow-up letter to your application letter.

2. Scanning the possibilities: Résumé for the Internet In your search for a position, you discover Career Magazine, a website that lists hundreds of companies advertising on the Internet. Your chances of getting an interview with a leading company will be enhanced if you submit your résumé and cover letter electronically. On the web, explore www.careermag.com.

Your task: Prepare a scannable résumé that could be submitted to one of the companies advertising at the Career Magazine website. Print out the résumé for your instructor.

3. Online application: Electronic cover letter introducing a résumé *Motley Fool* (www.fool.com) is a "Generation X" online magazine accessed via the web. Although its founders and writers are extremely creative and motivated, they lack business experience and need a fellow "X'er" to help them manage the business. Among articles in a recent edition was one titled "The Soul of the Dead," about the influence of the Grateful Dead on more than one generation of concert-goers. Other articles deal with lifestyle issues, pop movies, music, and "trends for an old-young generation."

Your task: Write an e-mail message that will serve as your cover letter and address your message to Louis Corrigan, Managing Editor. Try to limit your message to one screen (about 23 lines). You'll need a creative "hook" and a reassuring approach that identifies you as the right person to help *Motley Fool* become financially viable.

WRITING A RÉSUMÉ AND AN APPLICATION LETTER

4. "Help wanted": Application for a job listed in the classified section Among the jobs listed in today's *Chicago Tribune* (435 N. Michigan Avenue, Chicago, IL 60641) are the following:

Accounting Assistant

Established leader in the vacation ownership industry has immediate opening in its Northbrook corp. accounting dept. for an Accounting Assistant. Responsibilities include: bank reconciliation, preparation of deposits, AP, and cash receipt posting. Join our fast-growing company and enjoy our great benefits package. Flex work hours, medical, dental insurance. Fax résumé to Lisa: 847-564-3876.

Administrative Assistant

Fast-paced Wood Dale office seeks professional with strong computer skills. Proficient in MS Word & Excel, PowerPoint a plus. Must be detail oriented, able to handle multiple tasks, and possess strong communication skills. Excellent benefits, salary, and work environment. Fax résumé to 630-350-8649.

Customer Service

A nationally known computer software developer has an exciting opportunity in customer service and inside sales support in its fast-paced downtown Chicago office. You'll help resolve customer problems over the phone, provide information, assist in account management, and administer orders. If you're friendly, self-motivated, energetic, and have 2 years of experience, excellent problem-solving skills, organizational, communication, and PC skills, and communicate well over the phone, send résumé to J. Haber, 233 North Lake Shore Drive, Chicago, IL 60641.

Sales-Account Manager

MidCity Baking Company is seeking an Account Manager to sell and coordinate our programs to major accounts in the Chicago market. The candidate should possess strong analytical and selling skills and demonstrate computer proficiency. Previous sales experience with major account level assignment desired. A degree in business or equivalent experience preferred. For confidential consideration please mail résumé to Steven Crane, Director of Sales, MidCity Baking Company, 133 N. Railroad Avenue, Northlake IL 60614.

Your task: Send a résumé and an application letter to one of these potential employers.

WRITING OTHER TYPES OF EMPLOYMENT MESSAGES

5. Crashing the last frontier: Letter of inquiry about jobs in Alaska Your friend can't understand why you would want to move to Alaska. So you explain: "What really decided it for me was that I'd never seen the northern lights."

"But what about the bears? The 60-degree-below winters? The permafrost?" asks your friend.

"No problem. Anchorage doesn't get much colder than Buffalo does. It is just windier and wetter. Anyhow, I want to live near Fairbanks, which is near the gold-mining area—and the university is there. Fairbanks has lots of small businesses, like a frontier town in the West about 150 years ago. I think it still has homesteading tracts for people who want to do their own building and are willing to stay for a certain number of years."

"Your plans seem a little hasty," your friend warns. "Maybe you should write for information before you just take off. How do you know you could get a job?"

Your task: Take your friend's advice and write to the Chamber of Commerce, Fairbanks, AK 99701. Ask what types of employment are available to someone with your education and experience, and ask who specifically is hiring year-round employees.

Interviewing for Employment and Following Up

After studying this chapter, you will be able to

1 *Describe the typical sequence of interviews*

2 *Describe briefly what employers look for during an employment interview*

3 *List six tasks you need to complete to prepare for a successful job interview*

4 *Explain the three stages of a successful employment interview*

5 *Name six common employment messages that follow an interview, and state briefly when you would use each one*

COMMUNICATION CLOSE-UP AT MICROSOFT

www.microsoft.com

To get a job at Microsoft—the world's largest software company—"you have to be able to think on your feet," explains college recruiting manager Jodi DeLeon. You can expect technical questions even in the 30-minute screening interviews, where you'll be asked problem-solving questions designed to help you demonstrate whatever your résumé says you do best.

"We're not trying to intimidate or scare people at all," DeLeon explains. "We just want to find out as much as we can." For example, DeLeon might ask students applying for a marketing position how they would penetrate their school with more Microsoft products, at both the student and administration levels. However, she's not looking for a particular answer.

"I look at how they focus their thoughts. I look at the steps they take to get from the beginning to the end. I look at all the resources they pull in, the implications they think about. Do they ask me questions? Do they need to?" She's been most impressed by candidates who have walked her through an idea using pen and paper or who have jumped up to sketch on a chalkboard. Such responses can't be faked.

Good interviewers know when you're being genuine or just spouting off some pat, memorized response. Don't try to impress anyone by saying, "Excel? Oh, I know everything about Excel." You could be in big trouble if your claim isn't true. DeLeon says, "It's fine if you know Excel and admit, 'I think Excel is great, but it would be a lot easier if it had X, Y, or Z.' That's the kind of thing that the Microsoft person has to think about every day. Students shouldn't be afraid to say things like that."

When evaluating candidates, DeLeon asks how they set priorities for all the various projects they're currently working on. That's where demonstrating an ability to juggle school with extracurricular activities can help. She also looks at a student's drive and ambition, resourcefulness, and analytical ability. Good grades help, of course, but she's more interested in how well a person listens to and thinks through what she says.

Although companies differ, Microsoft doesn't consider it "cool" to dress like the interviewer, who may be in jeans and T-shirt. "Dress professionally," DeLeon advises. She adds that thank-you notes help, and follow-up phone calls (made after, not before, a promised answer date) are essential to demonstrate your continued interest in the job. However, avoid attention-getting gimmicks. DeLeon recalls one résumé that was sent in a pizza—and the candidate didn't stop there. "She just went above and beyond good judgment to get her foot in the door here," says DeLeon. After the pizza came fortune cookies with the applicant's qualifications in them, and then balloons. DeLeon finally had to write and ask her to stop.

The best way to prepare for an interview, suggests DeLeon, is to think about the job itself. "Ask yourself, what have I done in my life that is related to some aspect of this job?" That question may never actually be asked during the interview, but your understanding of the answer will shine through every statement you make. Most important, she adds, be yourself.[1] ■

Microsoft conducts on-campus interviews and participates in job fairs. Company representatives look for enthusiasm and an ability to think logically. Students who do well in screening interviews are flown to headquarters in Redmond, Washington, for the next round of interviews.

UNDERSTANDING THE INTERVIEWING PROCESS

Like Microsoft's Jodi DeLeon, most recruiters have a list of qualities and accomplishments they are looking for in job candidates. An **employment interview** is a formal meeting during which both employer and applicant ask questions and exchange information. These meetings have a dual purpose: (1) The organization's main objective is to find the best person available for the job by determining whether the applicant and the organization are a good match, and (2) the applicant's main objective is to find the job best suited to his or her goals and capabilities. While recruiters such as those at Microsoft are trying to decide whether you are right for them, you must decide whether Microsoft or any other company is right for you.

An employment interview is a formal meeting in which both employer and applicant ask questions and exchange information to learn more about each other.

Microsoft and other large organizations that hire hundreds of new employees every year take a more systematic approach to the recruiting and interviewing process than small local businesses that hire only a few new people each year. You'll need to adjust your job search according to the company's size and hiring practices. Table 18.1 contrasts the recruiting procedures of large companies with those of smaller companies and provides tips for increasing your chances of getting an interview with either type of employer. In general, the easiest way to connect with a big company is through your campus placement office; the most efficient way to approach a smaller business is by contacting the company directly.

As CEO of SAS (Statistical Analysis Software), Jim Goodnight recruits loyal employees by creating a corporate culture that respects them and their need for balancing their work with their personal lives.

Regardless of which path you choose, interviewing takes time, so start seeking jobs well in advance of the date you want to start work. Some students begin their job search as much as nine months before graduation. During downturns in the economy, early planning is even more crucial. Many employers become more selective and many corporations reduce their campus visits and campus hiring programs, so more of the job-search burden falls on you. As you plan your

TABLE 18.1 Recruiting Procedures of Big Companies Versus Small Companies: The Best Way to Get Your Foot in the Door

	Big Companies	*Small Companies*
Number and type of applicants sought	Consistently hire thousands of new emloyees each year; have relatively specific hiring criteria, depending on the position; tend to be highly selective	Hire a handful of new people each year, but requirements fluctuate widely depending on ups and downs in the business; may have specific requirements but are often looking for flexibility, versatility; are often somewhat more open-minded than big corporations about candidate's background
Person or department in charge of recruiting	Handled by human resources or personnel department	Companies at large end of the small-company scale (500 employees) may have a specialized human resources department, but many depend on line managers to staff their own functions; in really small companies, the founder/top manager makes all hiring decisions
General recruiting and interviewing style	Governed by formal policies and procedures; typically involves series of several interviews on campus and at company facility; approach is generally systematic, well planned, and well financed	Conducted informally on an as-needed basis without a standard procedure; hiring decision may be made after first interview or may drag on for several months; company generally lacks budget/motive for conducting elaborate recruiting programs
Where/how they advertise	Use national and local newspapers, trade journals, campus placement offices, word of mouth, online job banks, company websites	Rely heavily on word of mouth and local newspapers; may post openings at local colleges or at a few colleges whose graduates have specific qualifications
Use of employment agencies, search firms	Roughly 60 percent use employment agencies, whereas 40 percent use executive search firms; however, new college graduates are generally recruited directly without help of intermediaries	Agency use varies widely among small companies; cost may be a factor
Responsiveness to unsolicited résumés	Receive hundreds of unsolicited résumés, which typically get less attention than résumés obtained through department's own planned recruiting program; most companies will scan unsolicited résumés into a database if they maintain one; best to send résumé directly to line manager or potential co-worker in department where you want to work	Receive relatively few unsolicited résumés, so they pay close attention to them; however, given limited hiring needs, chances are slim that your résumé will arrive when company has a corresponding opening
Reliance on campus recruiting	Roughly 80 percent rely heavily on campus recruiting programs to fill entry-level professional, technical, and managerial positions; however, most limit their recruiting to a relatively small number of campuses	Companies at large end of small-company scale (500 employees) may have limited campus recruiting programs; the smaller the company, the less likely it is to recruit in this manner, and the fewer schools it is likely to visit
Best way for candidate to approach company	Use campus placement office to schedule interviews with companies that recruit on your campus; if these interviews are by invitation only, send a letter and résumé to company asking to be included on its schedule; if company does not recruit on your campus, call the person in charge of college recruiting, explain your situation, and ask for advice on best way to get an interview	Check with campus placement office; try to make direct personal contact with owner/manager or department head; get names and addresses from chamber of commerce, business directories, or local economic development agency; send résumé and application letter; follow up with phone call

job-search strategy, keep in mind that it can take an average of 10 interviews to get one job offer. Thus, if you hope to have several offers to choose from, expect to go through 20 or 30 interviews during your job search.[2]

In a typical job search, you can expect to have many interviews before you accept a job offer.

The Typical Sequence of Interviews

Learning Objective 1

Describe the typical sequence of interviews

Not all organizations interview potential candidates the same way. At Southwest Airlines, for example, a candidate undergoes a rigorous interview process that can take as long as six weeks.[3] However, most employers interview an applicant two or three times before deciding to make a job offer. Applicants often face a sequence of interviews, each with a different purpose. First is the preliminary *screening stage,* which is generally held on campus and which helps employers screen out unqualified applicants. Those candidates who best meet the organization's requirements are invited to visit company offices for further evaluation. Interviews at the screening stage are fairly structured, so applicants are often asked roughly the same questions. Many companies use standardized evaluation sheets to "grade" the applicants so that all the candidates will be measured against the same criteria. In some cases, technology has transformed the initial, get-to-know-you interview, allowing employers to screen candidates by phone, video interview, or computer.[4]

Most organizations interview an applicant several times before extending a job offer:

- Screening stage
- Selection stage
- Final stage

Your best approach to an interview at the screening stage is to follow the interviewer's lead. Keep your responses short and to the point. Time is limited, so talking too much can be a big mistake. However, to give the interviewer a way to differentiate you from other candidates and to demonstrate your strengths and qualifications, try to emphasize the "theme" you used in developing your résumé.

During the screening stage of interviews, try to differentiate yourself from other candidates.

The next stage of interviews helps the organization narrow the field a little further. Typically, if you're invited to visit a company, you will talk with several people: a member of the human resources department, one or two potential colleagues, and your potential supervisor. You might face a panel of several interviewers who ask you questions during a single session. By noting how you listen, think, and express yourself, they can decide how likely you are to get along with colleagues. Your best approach during this *selection stage* of interviews is to show interest in the job, relate your skills and experience to the organization's needs, listen attentively, ask insightful questions, and display enthusiasm.

During the selection stage of interviews, you may interview with several people, perhaps even all at once.

If the interviewers agree that you're a good candidate, you may receive a job offer, either on the spot or a few days later by phone or mail. In other cases, you may be invited back for a final evaluation by a higher-ranking executive who has the authority to make the hiring decision and to decide on your compensation. An underlying objective of the *final stage* is often to sell you on the advantages of joining the organization.

During the final stage, the interviewer may try to sell you on working for the firm.

Types of Interviews

Organizations use various types of interviews to discover as much as possible about applicants. A **structured interview** is generally used in the screening stage. Here the employer controls the interview by asking a series of prepared questions in a set order. Working from a checklist, the interviewer asks candidates each question, staying within an allotted time period. All answers are noted. Although useful in gathering facts, the structured interview is generally regarded as a poor measure of an applicant's personal qualities. Nevertheless, some companies use structured interviews to create uniformity in their hiring process.[5]

A structural interview is controlled by the interviewer to gather facts.

By contrast, the **open-ended interview** is less formal and unstructured, with a relaxed format. The interviewer poses broad, open-ended questions and encourages the applicant to talk freely. This type of interview is good for bringing out an applicant's personality and is used to test professional judgment. However, some candidates reveal too much, rambling on about personal or family problems that have nothing to do with their qualifications for employment, their ability to get along with co-workers, or any personal interests that could benefit their performance on the job. So be careful. You need to strike a delicate balance between being friendly and remembering that you're in a business situation.

In an open-ended interview, the recruiter encourages the candidate to speak freely.

Some organizations perform **group interviews**, meeting with several candidates simultaneously to see how they interact. This type of interview is useful for judging

Group interviews help recruiters see how candidates interact with one another.

interpersonal skills. For example, the Walt Disney Company uses group interviews when hiring people for its theme parks. During a 45-minute session, the Disney recruiter watches how three candidates relate to one another. Do they smile? Are they supportive of one another's comments? Do they try to score points at each other's expense?[6]

Stress interviews help recruiters see how you handle yourself under pressure.

Perhaps the most unnerving type of interview is the **stress interview**, which is set up to see how well a candidate handles stressful situations (an important qualification for certain jobs). During a stress interview, you might be asked pointed questions designed to irk or unsettle you. You might be subjected to long periods of silence, criticisms of your appearance, deliberate interruptions, and abrupt or even hostile reactions by the interviewer.

Video interviews require some special preparation.

As employers try to cut travel costs, the **video interview** is becoming more popular. Many large companies use videoconferencing systems to screen middle-management candidates or to interview new recruits at universities. Experts recommend that candidates prepare a bit differently for a video interview than for an in-person meeting:[7]

- Ask for a preliminary phone conversation to establish rapport with the interviewer.
- Arrive early enough to get used to the equipment and setting.
- During the interview, speak clearly but not more slowly than normal.
- Sit straight.
- Look up but not down.
- Try to show some animation, but not too much (since it will appear blurry to the interviewer).

In situational interviews, candidates must explain how they would handle a specific set of circumstances.

Another modern twist is the **situational interview**, in which an interviewer describes a situation and asks, "How would you handle this?" Many companies have learned that no correlation exists between how well people answer interview questions in a traditional interview and how well they perform on the job. So companies such as Kraft Foods, Delta Air Lines, AT&T, and Procter & Gamble rely on situational interviews. Proponents of this approach claim that interviewing is about the job, not about a candidate's five-year goals, weaknesses or strengths, challenging experiences, or greatest accomplishment. So the situational interview is a hands-on, at-work meeting between an employer who needs a job done and a worker who must be fully prepared to do the work.[8]

Regardless of the type of interview you may face, a personal interview is vital because your résumé can't show whether you're lively and outgoing or subdued and low key, able to take direction or able to take charge. Each job requires a different mix of personality traits. The interviewer's task is to find out whether you will be effective on the job.

What Employers Look For

Having the right personality traits for the job is important in today's workplace. Southwest Airlines recruiters know exactly what they're looking for in a potential employee. A sense of humor tops the list because they believe that people who don't take themselves too seriously are better able to cope with the stress of airline work. Southwest also wants employees who are self-motivated, enthusiastic, not afraid to make decisions, willing to take risks, intelligent, good communicators, and considerate of others.[9]

Current research shows that employees with certain personality traits tend to be more successful at their job. As a result, many employers today seek candidates with a high "emotional intelligence," or EQ (emotional quotient). People with a high EQ generally possess these desirable attributes: self-awareness, good impulse control, persistence, confidence, self-motivation, and empathy, as well as the abilities to persuade, articulate a mission, interpret the mood of a group, and communicate with people in terms they understand (see Figure 18.1).

Learning Objective 2

Describe briefly what employers look for during an employment interview

When it comes down to it, every job has basic qualifications. Employers first look for two things: evidence that a candidate will fit in with the organization and proof that the person can handle a specific job.

Compatibility with the organization is judged on the basis of personal background, attitudes, and style.

A Good Fit with the Organization

Interviewers try to decide whether a candidate will be compatible with the other people in the organization. Some interviewers believe that personal background is an indica-

FIGURE 18.1 What's Your EQ?

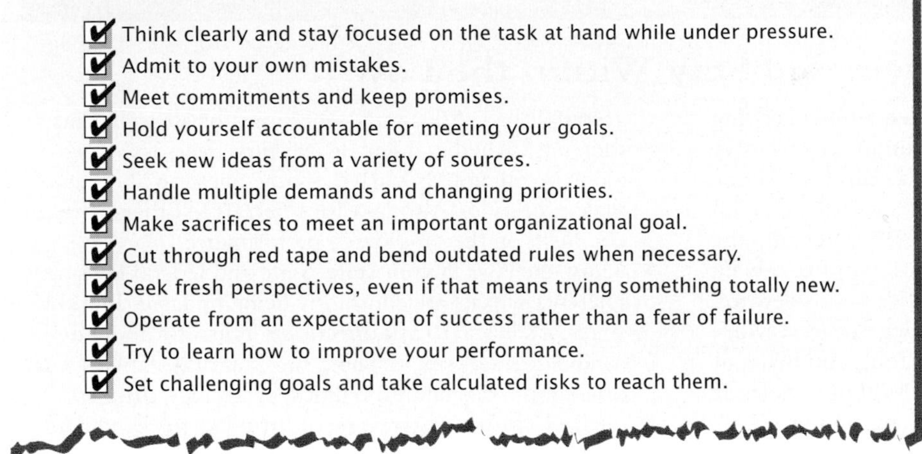

tion of how well the candidate will fit in, so they might ask about your interests, hobbies, awareness of world events, and so forth. You can expand your potential along these lines by reading widely, making an effort to meet new people, and participating in discussion groups, seminars, and workshops.

Some interviewers may also consider a candidate's personal style. You're likely to impress an employer by being open, enthusiastic, and interested. Some interviewers also look for courtesy, sincerity, willingness to learn, and a style that is positive and self-confident. All of these qualities help a new employee adapt to a new workplace and new responsibilities.

Impress employers by being open, enthusiastic, and interested.

Qualifications for the Job

When you're invited to interview for a position, the interviewer may already have some idea of whether you have the right qualifications, based on a review of your résumé. But during the interview, you'll be asked to describe your education and previous jobs in more depth so that the interviewer can determine how well your skills match the requirements. In many cases, the interviewer will be seeking someone with the flexibility to apply diverse skills in several areas.[10]

Suitability for the specific job is judged on the basis of
- Academic preparation
- Work experience
- Job-related personality traits

When describing your skills, be honest. If you don't know how to do something, say so. Given the high cost of hiring unsuitable employees, more and more companies are performing background checks (see Figure 18.2 and "Sharpening Your Career

FIGURE 18.2 Checking Out New Hires

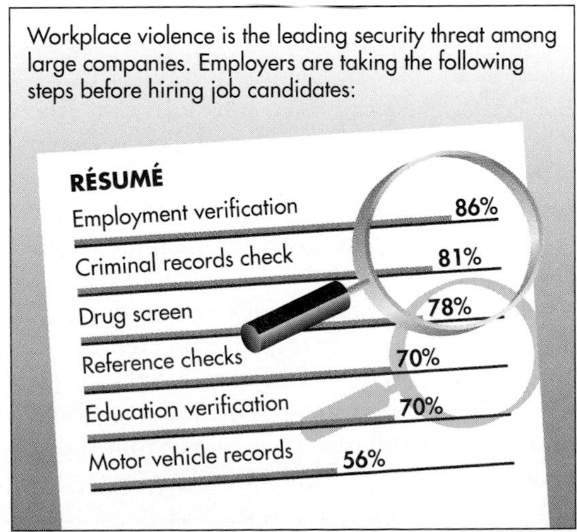

Sharpening Your Career Skills

How to Check References and Stay Within the Law

Employers who hire people without adequately checking their backgrounds face not only the possibility of expensive hiring mistakes but also legal action if problems arise. Some chilling examples include the building janitor with an unchecked criminal record who murdered a tenant, the school bus driver with an unchecked record of drunk-driving arrests, and the "chemist" whose difficulties on his new job were finally explained by his forged college degree. More commonly, reference checks can reveal long employment gaps, inflated accomplishments, false claims about academic degrees, and potential interpersonal problems on the job.

Even though companies realize how much they need to share relevant information on employees, many executives are uncomfortable about committing their remarks to paper. Here's some advice from the most successful reference checkers.

- **Get applicants involved.** Ask candidates to provide a list of references to check. Have them sign a waiver releasing their references from legal liability for their statements, and ask each candidate to contact references beforehand to encourage them to speak freely.
- **Take your time, and don't delegate.** Take about two hours per candidate. Call early in the morning or after five, when executives are likely to answer the phone themselves.
- **Prepare your questions carefully.** Whether writing or calling, pose open-ended, job-related questions about *how* a candidate performed, not just what was accomplished. Ask similar questions for all applicants (don't ask whether a female executive fears traveling alone if you wouldn't ask the same question about a male executive). Also, ask for referrals to others who can comment on the candidate's performance.
- **Know the laws in your state.** State and federal laws on reference checks are constantly being updated. In most states, it's illegal to ask directly or indirectly about a candidate's age, sex, religion, race, marital status, sexual orientation, disabilities, politics, pregnancy, drug use, medical history, or arrest records (unless the candidate will be working with minors). But it's legal in most states to contact police departments and former employers to ask about arrest records or whether a person has ever been *convicted* of a crime. Also, you can (and should) contact schools, or have applicants request to have course transcripts mailed directly to you.

Career Applications

1. Think about who you would supply as references on an employment application. Now assume a potential employer's perspective, and prepare the questions you'd want those references to answer about you and your work.
2. You've interviewed a job candidate who has all the right answers and seems to have the right qualifications, but your intuition tells you something isn't quite right. What checking would you do to confirm or quell your concerns?

Skills: How to Check References and Stay Within the Law"). In addition to background checks, many employers administer preemployment tests.[11] Such tests verify candidates' skills and determine whether applicants are suited to the job and whether they'll be worth the expense of hiring and training.

Preemployment Testing

Preemployment tests attempt to provide objective, quantitative information about a candidate's skills, attitudes, and habits.

Three types of preemployment tests frequently administered by companies are job-skills tests, psychological tests, and drug tests. Job-skills tests, the most common type, are designed to assess competency or specific abilities needed to perform a job. Psychological tests usually take the form of questionnaires. These tests can be used to assess overall intellectual ability, attitudes toward work, interests, managerial potential, or personality characteristics—including dependability, commitment, honesty, and motivation.

Approximately 45 percent of all companies now require applicants to undergo drug and alcohol testing, and this percentage is expected to rise for two reasons:[12] (1) Companies seek to avoid the increased costs and reduced productivity associated with drug abuse in the workplace (estimated to cost industry some $100 billion a year), and (2) studies show that substance abusers have two to four times as many accidents as other employees and that drug use can be linked to 40 percent of industrial fatalities.[13]

Statistics such as these are enough to worry any employer, particularly given the threat of being held liable for negligent hiring practices if an employee harms an innocent party on the job.

Tests have their critics. Some employers prefer not to go to the extra expense of administering them or feel that educated judgment works just as well. Some applicants question the validity of honesty and drug tests or consider them an invasion of privacy. However, when used in conjunction with other evidence, such as reference checks, employment tests attempt to provide an objective, quantitative measure of an applicant's qualifications. To protect candidates' interests, employment tests must meet strict criteria of fairness set forth by the Equal Employment Opportunity Commission (EEOC).

Just as written messages need planning, employment interviews need preparation.

PREPARING FOR A JOB INTERVIEW

Learning Objective 3

List six tasks you need to complete to prepare for a successful job interview

For a successful interview, preparation is mandatory. As Jodi DeLeon points out, the best way to prepare for a job interview is to think about the job itself and prepare. It's perfectly normal to feel a little anxious before an interview. But good preparation will help you perform well. Be sure to consider any cultural differences when preparing for interviews, and base your approach on what your audience expects. The advice in this chapter is most appropriate for companies and employers in the United States and Canada. Before the interview, learn about the organization, think ahead about questions, bolster your confidence, polish your interview style, plan to look good, and be ready when you arrive.

In his efforts to find work, Mark Calimlim gets help from the Career Center at Syracuse University.

Learn About the Organization

When planning your employment search, you probably already researched the companies you sent your résumé to. But now that you've been invited for an interview, you'll want to fine-tune your research and brush up on the facts you've collected (see Table 18.2). You can review Chapter 10 for ideas on where to look for information.

Today's companies expect serious candidates to demonstrate an understanding of the company's operations, its market, and its strategic and tactical problems.[14] Learning about the organization and the job enables you to show the interviewer just how you will meet the organization's particular needs. With a little research, for instance, you would discover that Microsoft plans on investing heavily in the technical and marketing support of software developers as well as making things simpler for all users and system administrators.[15] Knowing these facts might help you pinpoint aspects

Best of the Web

Planning for a Successful Interview

How can you practice for a job interview? What are some questions that you might be asked, and how should you respond? What questions are you not obligated to answer? Job-interview.net provides mock interviews based on actual job openings. It provides job descriptions, questions and answers for specific careers and jobs, and links to company guides and annual reports. You'll find a step-by-step plan that outlines key job requirements, lists practice interview questions, and helps you put together practice interviews. The site offers tips on the keywords to look for in a job description, which will help you narrow your search and anticipate the questions you might be asked on your first or next job interview.

www.job-interview.net

TABLE 18.2 Finding Out About the Organization and the Job

Where to Look for Information	
• *Annual report*	Summarizes operations; describes products, lists events, names key personnel
• *In-house magazine or newspaper*	Reveals information about company operations, events, personnel
• *Product brochure or publicity release*	Gives insight into firm's operations and values (obtain from public relations office)
• *Stock research report*	Helps assess stability and growth prospects (obtain online or from stockbroker)
• *Newspaper's business or financial pages*	Contain news items about organizations, current performance figures
• *Periodicals indexes*	Contain descriptive listings of magazine/newspaper articles about firms (obtain from library)
• *Better Business Bureau and Chamber of Commerce*	Distribute information about some local organizations
• *Former and current employees*	Have insight into job and work environment
• *College placement office*	Collects information on organizations that recruit and on job qualifications and salaries
What to Find Out About the Organization	
• *Full Name*	How the firm is officially known (e.g., 3M is Minnesota Mining & Manufacturing Company)
• *Location*	Where the organization's headquarters, branch offices, and plants are
• *Age*	How long the organization has been in business
• *Products*	What goods and services the organization produces and sells
• *Industry position*	What the organization's current market share, financial position, and profit picture are
• *Earnings*	What the trends in the firm's stock prices and dividends are (if firm is publicly held)
• *Growth*	How the firm's earnings/holdings have changed in recent years and prospects for expansion
• *Organization*	What subsidiaries, divisions, and departments make up the whole
What to Find Out About the Job	
• *Job title*	What you will be called
• *Job functions*	What the main tasks of the job are
• *Job qualifications*	What knowledge and skills the job requires
• *Career path*	What chances for ready advancement exist
• *Salary range*	What the firm typically offers and what is reasonable in this industry and geographic area
• *Travel opportunities*	How often, long, and far you'll be allowed (or required) to travel
• *Relocation opportunities*	Where you might be allowed (or required) to move and how often

Be prepared to relate your qualifications to the organization's needs.

of your background (such as the ability to simplify processes) that would appeal to Microsoft's recruiters.

Think Ahead About Questions

Planning ahead for the interviewer's questions will help you handle them more confidently and intelligently. (See "Sharpening Your Career Skills: Interview Strategies: Answering the 16 Toughest Questions.") Moreover, you will want to prepare intelligent questions of your own.

Sharpening Your Career Skills

Interview Strategies: Answering the 16 Toughest Questions

The answers to challenging interview questions can reveal a lot about a candidate. You can expect to face several such questions during every interview. If you're prepared with thoughtful answers that are related to your specific situation, you're bound to make a good impression. Here are 16 tough questions and guidelines for planning answers that put your qualities in the best light.

1. **What was the toughest decision you ever had to make?** Be prepared with a good example, explaining why the decision was difficult and how you decided.
2. **Why do you want to work for this organization?** Show that you've done your homework, and cite some things going on in the company that appeal to you.
3. **Why should we employ you?** Emphasize your academic strengths, job skills, and enthusiasm for the firm. Tie specific skills to the employer's needs, and give examples of how you can learn and become productive quickly. Cite past activities to prove you can work with others as part of a team.
4. **If we hire you, what changes would you make?** No one can know what to change in a position before settling in and learning about the job and company operations. State that you would take a good hard look at everything the company is doing before making recommendations.
5. **Can we offer you a career path?** Reply that you believe so, but you need to know more about the normal progression within the organization.
6. **What are your greatest strengths?** Answer sincerely by summarizing your strong points: "I can see what must be done and then do it" or "I'm willing to make decisions" or "I work well with others."
7. **What are your greatest weaknesses?** Describe a weakness so that it sounds like a virtue—honestly revealing something about yourself while showing how it works to an employer's advantage. If you sometimes drive yourself too hard, explain that it has helped when you've had to meet deadlines.
8. **What didn't you like about previous jobs you've held?** State what you didn't like and discuss what the experience taught you. Avoid making slighting references to former employers.
9. **How do you spend your leisure time?** Rather than focusing on just one, mention a cross section of interests—active and quiet, social and solitary.
10. **Are there any weaknesses in your education or experience?** Take stock of your weaknesses before the interview, and practice discussing them in a positive light. You'll see they're minor when discussed along with the positive qualities you have to offer.
11. **Where do you want to be five years from now?** This question tests (1) whether you're merely using this job as a stopover until something better comes along and (2) whether you've given thought to your long-term goals. Saying that you'd like to be company president is unrealistic, and yet few employers want people who are content to sit still. Your answer should reflect your long-term goals and the organization's advancement opportunities.
12. **What are your salary expectations?** If you're asked this at the outset, say, "Why don't we discuss salary after you decide whether I'm right for the job?" If the interviewer asks this after showing real interest in you, speak up. Do your homework, but if you need a clue about salary levels, say, "Can you discuss the salary range with me?"
13. **What would you do if ...** This question tests your resourcefulness. For example: "What would you do if your computer broke down during an audit?" Your answer is less important than your approach to the problem—and a calm approach is best.
14. **What type of position are you interested in?** Job titles and responsibilities vary from firm to firm. So state your skills ("I'm good with numbers") and the positions that require those skills ("accounts payable").
15. **Tell me something about yourself.** Answer that you'll be happy to talk about yourself, and ask what the interviewer wants to know. If this point is clarified, respond. If it isn't, explain how your skills can contribute to the job and the organization. This is a great chance to sell yourself.
16. **Do you have any questions about the organization or the job?** Employers like candidates who are interested in the organization. Convey your interest and enthusiasm.

Be sure that your answers are sincere, truthful, and positive. Take a moment to compose your thoughts before responding, so that your answers are to the point.

Career Applications

1. What makes an effective answer to an interviewer's question? Consider some of the ways answers can vary: specific versus general, assertive versus passive, informal versus formal.
2. Think of four additional questions that pertain specifically to your résumé. Practice your answers.

Planning for the Employer's Questions

Employers usually gear their interview questions to specific organizational needs. You can expect to be asked about your skills, achievements, and goals, as well as about your attitude toward work and school, your relationships with others (work supervisors, colleagues, and fellow students), and occasionally your hobbies and interests. Candidates might be asked to collaborate on a decision or to develop a group presentation. Trained observers evaluate the candidates' performance using predetermined criteria and then advise management on how well each person is likely to handle the challenges normally faced on the job.[16]

Practice answering interview questions.

For a look at the types of questions often asked, see Table 18.3. Jot down a brief answer to each one. Then read over the answers until you feel comfortable with each of them. Although practicing your answers will help you feel prepared and confident, you don't want to memorize responses or sound overrehearsed. You might also give a list of interview questions to a friend or relative and have that person ask you various questions at random. This method helps you learn to articulate answers and to look at the person as you answer.

Planning Questions of Your Own

The questions you ask in an interview are just as important as the answers you provide. By asking intelligent questions, you demonstrate your understanding of the organization, and you can steer the discussion into those areas that allow you to present your qualifications to best advantage. Before the interview, prepare a list of about a dozen questions you need answered in order to evaluate the organization and the job.

You are responsible for deciding whether the work and the organization are compatible with your goals and values.

Don't limit your questions to those you think will impress the interviewer, or you won't get the information you'll need to make a wise decision if and when you're offered the job. Here's a list of some things you might want to find out:

- **Are these my kind of people?** Observe the interviewer, and if you can, arrange to talk with other employees.
- **Can I do this work?** Compare your qualifications with the requirements described by the interviewer.
- **Will I enjoy the work?** Know yourself and what's important to you. Will you find the work challenging? Will it give you feelings of accomplishment, of satisfaction, and of making a real contribution?
- **Is the job what I want?** You may never find a job that fulfills all your wants, but the position you accept should satisfy at least your primary ones. Will it make use of your best capabilities? Does it offer a career path to the long-term goals you've set?
- **Does the job pay what I'm worth?** By comparing jobs and salaries before you're interviewed, you'll know what's reasonable for someone with your skills in your industry.
- **What kind of person would I be working for?** If the interviewer is your prospective boss, watch how others interact with that person, tactfully query other employees, or pose a careful question or two during the interview. If your prospective boss is someone else, ask for that person's name, job title, and responsibilities. Try to learn all you can.
- **What sort of future can I expect with this organization?** How healthy is the organization? Can you look forward to advancement? Does the organization offer insurance, pension, vacation, or other benefits?

Types of questions to ask during an interview:
- Warm-up
- Open-ended
- Indirect

Rather than bombarding the interviewer with these questions the minute you walk in the room, use a mix of formats to elicit this information. Start with a warm-up question to help break the ice. You might ask a Microsoft recruiter, "What departments usually hire new graduates?" After that, you might build rapport by asking an open-ended question that draws out the interviewer's opinion ("How do you think Internet sales will affect Microsoft's continued growth?"). Indirect questions can elicit useful

TABLE 18.3 Twenty-Five Common Interview Questions

Questions About College	
1.	What courses in college did you like most? Least? Why?
2.	Do you think your extracurricular activities in college were worth the time you spent on them? Why or why not?
3.	When did you choose your college major? Did you ever change your major? If so, why?
4.	Do you feel you did the best scholastic work you are capable of?
5.	Which of your college years was the toughest? Why?
Questions About Employers and Jobs	
6.	What jobs have you held? Why did you leave?
7.	What percentage of your college expenses did you earn? How?
8.	Why did you choose your particular field of work?
9.	What are the disadvantages of your chosen field?
10.	Have you served in the military? What rank did you achieve? What jobs did you perform?
11.	What do you think about how this industry operates today?
12.	Why do you think you would like this particular type of job?
Questions About Personal Attitudes and Preferences	
13.	Do you prefer to work in any specific geographic location? If so, why?
14.	How much money do you hope to be earning in 5 years? In 10 years?
15.	What do you think determines a person's progress in a good organization?
16.	What personal characteristics do you feel are necessary for success in your chosen field?
17.	Tell me a story.
18.	Do you like to travel?
19.	Do you think grades should be considered by employers? Why or why not?
Questions About Work Habits	
20.	Do you prefer working with others or by yourself?
21.	What type of boss do you prefer?
22.	Have you ever had any difficulty getting along with colleagues or supervisors? With instructors? With other students?
23.	Would you prefer to work in a large or a small organization? Why?
24.	How do you feel about overtime work?
25.	What have you done that shows initiative and willingness to work?

information and show that you've prepared for the interview ("I'd really like to know more about Microsoft's plans for expanding its corporate presence on the web" or "That recent *Business Week* article about the company was very interesting"). Any questions you ask should be in your own words so that you don't sound like every other candidate. For a list of other good questions you might use as a starting point, see Table 18.4.

Write your list of questions on a notepad and take it to the interview. If you need to, jot down brief notes during the meeting, and be sure to record answers in more detail afterward. Having a list of questions should impress the interviewer with your organization and thoroughness. It will also show that you're there to evaluate the organization and the job as well as to sell yourself.

Impress the interviewer with your ability to organize and be thorough by bringing a list of questions to the job interview.

TABLE 18.4 Fifteen Questions to Ask the Interviewer

Questions About the Job	Questions About the Organization
What are the job's major responsibilities?	What are the organization's major strengths? Weaknesses?
What qualities do you want in the person who fills this position?	Who are your organization's major competitors, and what are their strengths and weaknesses?
Do you want to know more about my related training?	What makes your organization different from others in the industry?
What is the first problem that needs the attention of the person you hire?	What are your organization's major markets?
Would relocation be required now or in the future?	Does the organization have any plans for new products? Acquisitions?
Why is this job now vacant?	How would you define your organization's managerial philosophy?
What can you tell me about the person I would report to?	What additional training does your organization provide?
	Do employees have an opportunity to continue their education with help from the organization?

Bolster Your Confidence

If you feel shy or self-conscious, remember that recruiters are human too.

By building your confidence, you'll make a better impression. The best way to counteract any apprehension is to remove its source. You may feel shy or self-conscious because you think you have some flaw that will prompt others to reject you. Bear in mind, however, that you're much more conscious of your limitations than other people are.

If some aspect of your appearance or background makes you uneasy, correct it or offset it by exercising positive traits such as warmth, wit, intelligence, or charm. Instead of dwelling on your weaknesses, focus on your strengths so that you can emphasize them to an interviewer. Make a list of your good points and compare them with what you see as your shortcomings.

Remember that you're not alone. All the other candidates for the job are just as nervous as you are. Even the interviewer may be nervous.

Polish Your Interview Style

Confidence helps you walk into an interview, but once you're there, you want to give the interviewer an impression of poise, good manners, and good judgment. Some job seekers hire professional coaches and image consultants to create just the right impression. Charging anywhere from $125 to $500 an hour, these professionals spend a majority of their time teaching clients how to assess communication styles, and to do so they use role-playing, videotaping, and audiotaping.[17] You can use these techniques too.

Staging mock interviews with a friend is a good way to hone your style.

You can develop an adept style by staging mock interviews with a friend. After each practice session, try to identify opportunities for improvement. Have your friend critique your performance, using the list of interview faults shown in Figure 18.3. You can tape-record or videotape these mock interviews and then evaluate them yourself. The taping process can be intimidating, but it helps you work out any problems before you begin actual job interviews.

Nonverbal behavior has a significant effect on the interviewer's opinion of you.

As you stage your mock interviews, pay particular attention to your nonverbal behavior. In the United States, you are more likely to have a successful interview if you

FIGURE 18.3 Marks Against Applicants (in General Order of Importance)

WHAT EMPLOYERS DON'T LIKE TO SEE IN CANDIDATES

- Poor personal appearance
- Overbearing, overaggressive, conceited demeanor; a "superiority complex"; "know it all" attitude
- Inability to express ideas clearly; poor voice, diction, grammar
- Lack of knowledge or experience
- Poor preparation for the interview
- Lack of interest in the job
- Lack of planning for career; lack of purpose, goals
- Lack of enthusiasm; passive and indifferent demeanor
- Lack of confidence and poise; appearance of being nervous and ill at ease
- Insufficient evidence of achievement
- Failure to participate in extracurricular activities
- Overemphasis on money; interest only in the best dollar offer
- Poor scholastic record; just got by
- Unwillingness to start at the bottom; expecting too much too soon
- Tendency to make excuses
- Evasive answers; hedges on unfavorable factors in record
- Lack of tact
- Lack of maturity
- Lack of courtesy; ill-mannered
- Condemnation of past employers
- Lack of social skills
- Marked dislike for schoolwork
- Lack of vitality
- Failure to look interviewer in the eye
- Limp, weak handshake

maintain eye contact, smile frequently, sit in an attentive position, and use frequent hand gestures. These nonverbal signals convince the interviewer that you're alert, assertive, dependable, confident, responsible, and energetic.[18] Some companies based in the United States are owned and managed by people from other cultures, so during your research, find out about the company's cultural background and preferences regarding nonverbal behavior.

The way you speak is almost as important as what you say.

The sound of your voice can also have a major impact on your success in a job interview.[19] You can work with a tape recorder to overcome voice problems. If you tend to speak too rapidly, practice speaking more slowly. If your voice sounds too loud or too soft, practice adjusting it. Work on eliminating speech mannerisms such as *you know, like,* and *um*, which might make you sound inarticulate.

Plan to Look Good

To look like a winner
- Dress conservatively
- Be well groomed
- Smile when appropriate

Physical appearance is important because clothing and grooming reveal something about a candidate's personality and professionalism. When it comes to clothing, the best policy is to dress conservatively. Wear the best-quality businesslike clothing you can, preferably in a dark, solid color. Avoid flamboyant styles, colors, and prints. Even in companies where interviewers may dress casually, it's important to show good judgment by dressing (and acting) in a professional manner. Some candidates are asking interviewers ahead of time what they should wear. One human resources executive tells job seekers to dress business casual because dressing in a suit, for example, looks awkward at his company.[20]

When Patricia Washington interviews potential employees, she looks for people who communicate well. Part of good communication is being prepared with résumés and work samples; another part is knowing how to look. Applicants show more than their job skills—they also demonstrate their ability to communicate and their concern for a professional appearance.

Good grooming makes any style of clothing look better. Make sure your clothes are clean and unwrinkled, your shoes unscuffed and well shined, your hair neatly styled and combed, your fingernails clean, and your breath fresh. If possible, check your appearance in a mirror before entering the room for the interview. Finally, remember that one of the best ways to look good is to smile at appropriate moments.

Be Ready When You Arrive

Plan to take a small notebook, a pen, a list of the questions you want to ask, two copies of your résumé (protected in a folder), an outline of what you have learned about the organization, and any past correspondence about the position. You may also want to take a small calendar, a transcript of your college grades, a list of references, and a portfolio containing samples of your work, performance reviews, and certificates of achievement. In an era when many people exaggerate their qualifications, visible proof of your abilities carries a lot of weight.[21]

Be sure you know when and where the interview will be held. The worst way to start any interview is to be late. Check the route you will take, even if it means phoning the interviewer's secretary to ask. Find out how much time it takes to get there; then plan to arrive early. Allow a little extra time in case you run into a problem on the way.

Once you arrive, relax. You may have to wait a little while, so bring along something to read (the less frivolous or controversial, the better). If company literature is available, read it while you wait. In any case, be polite to the interviewer's assistant. If the opportunity presents itself, ask a few questions about the organization or express enthusiasm for the job. Refrain from smoking before the interview (nonsmokers can smell smoke on the clothing of interviewees), and avoid chewing gum in the waiting room. Anything you do or say while you wait may well get back to the interviewer, so make sure your best qualities show from the moment you enter the premises. That way you'll be ready for the interview itself once it actually begins.

Be prepared for the interview by
- Taking proof of your accomplishments
- Arriving on time
- Waiting graciously

INTERVIEWING FOR SUCCESS

How you handle a particular interview depends on where you stand in the interview process. If you're being interviewed for the first time, your main objective is to differentiate yourself from the many other candidates who are also being screened. Without resorting to gimmicks, call attention to one key aspect of your background so that the recruiter can say, "Oh yes, I remember Jones—the one who sold used Toyotas in Detroit." Just be sure the trait you accentuate is relevant to the job in question. In addition, you'll want to be prepared in case an employer expects you to demonstrate a particular skill (perhaps problem solving) during the screening interview.

Present a memorable "headline" during an interview at the screening stage.

If you progress to the initial selection interview, broaden your sales pitch. Instead of telegraphing the "headline," give the interviewer the whole story. Touch briefly on all your strengths, but explain three or four of your best qualifications in depth. At the same time, probe for information that will help you evaluate the position objectively. As important as it is to get an offer, it's also important to learn whether the job is right for you.

Cover all your strengths during an interview at the selection stage.

If you're asked back for a final visit, your chances of being offered a position are quite good. At this point, you'll talk to a person who has the authority to make an offer and negotiate terms. This individual may have already concluded that your background is right for the job and may be more concerned with sizing up your personality. Both you and the employer need to find out whether there is a good psychological fit. Be honest about your motivations and values. If the interview goes well, your objective should be to clinch the deal on the best possible terms.

Emphasize your personality during a final interview.

Regardless of where you are in the interview process, every interview will proceed through three stages: the warm-up, the question-and-answer session, and the close.

Learning Objective 4

Explain the three stages of a successful employment interview

The Warm-Up

Of the three stages, the warm-up is the most important, even though it may account for only a small fraction of the time you spend in the interview. Psychologists say that 50 percent of an interviewer's decision is made within the first 30 to 60 seconds, and another 25 percent is made within 15 minutes. If you get off to a bad start, it's extremely difficult to turn the interview around.[22]

The first minute of the interview is crucial.

Body language is important at this point. Because you won't have time to say much in the first minute or two, you must sell yourself nonverbally. Begin by using the interviewer's name if you're sure you can pronounce it correctly. If the interviewer extends a hand, respond with a firm but gentle handshake, and wait until you're asked to be seated. Let the interviewer start the discussion, and listen for cues that tell you what he or she is interested in knowing about you as a potential employee.

The Question-and-Answer Stage

Questions and answers will consume the greatest part of the interview. The interviewer will ask you about your qualifications and discuss many of the points mentioned in your résumé. You'll also be asking questions of your own.

Dealing with Questions

Let the interviewer lead the conversation, and never answer a question before he or she has finished asking it. Surprisingly, the last few words of the question might alter how you respond. As questions are asked, tailor your answers to make a favorable impression. Don't limit yourself to yes-or-no answers. If you're asked a difficult question, be sure you pause to think before responding.

Tailor your answers to emphasize your strengths.

If you periodically ask a question or two from the list you've prepared, you'll not only learn something but also demonstrate your interest. Probe for what the company is looking for in its new employees so that you can show how you meet the firm's needs. Also try to zero in on any reservations the interviewer might have about you so that you can dispel them.

Listening to the Interviewer

Paying attention when the interviewer speaks can be as important as giving good answers or asking good questions. The recruiters at Microsoft agree that listening should make up about half the time you spend in an interview. For tips on becoming a better listener, see Chapter 2.

Paying attention to both verbal and nonverbal messages can help you turn the question-and-answer stage to your advantage.

The interviewer's facial expressions, eye movements, gestures, and posture may tell you the real meaning of what is being said. Be especially aware of how your comments are received. Does the interviewer nod in agreement or smile to show approval? If so, you're making progress. If not, you might want to introduce another topic or modify your approach.

Fielding Discriminatory Questions

Employers cannot legally discriminate against a job candidate on the basis of race, color, gender, age (from 40 to 70), marital status, religion, national origin, or disability. In general, the following topics should not be directly or indirectly introduced by an interviewer:[23]

Some questions should not be asked by interviewers.

- Your religious affiliation or organizations and lodges you belong to
- Your national origin, age, marital status, or former name
- Your spouse, spouse's employment or salary, dependents, children, or child-care arrangements

TABLE 18.5 Interview Questions That May and May Not Be Asked

You may ask this . . .	*But not this*
What is your name?	What was your maiden name?
Are you over 18?	When were you born?
Did you graduate from high school?	When did you graduate from high school?
[No questions about race are allowed.]	What is your race?
Can you perform [specific tasks]?	Do you have physical or mental disabilities?
	Do you have a drug or alcohol problem?
	Are you taking any prescription drugs?
Would you be able to meet the job's requirement to frequently work weekends?	Would working on weekends conflict with your religion?
Do you have the legal right to work in the United States?	What country are you a citizen of?
Have you ever been convicted of a felony?	Have you ever been arrested?
This job requires that you speak Spanish. Do you?	What language did you speak in your home when you were growing up?

- Your height, weight, gender, pregnancy, or any health conditions or disabilities that are not reasonably related to job performance
- Arrests or criminal convictions that are not related to job performance

Although federal law does not specifically prohibit questions that touch on these areas, the Equal Employment Opportunity Commission (EEOC) considers such questions with "extreme disfavor." Table 18.5 compares specific questions that may and may not be asked during an employment interview.

Think about how you might respond if you are asked to answer unlawful interview questions.

How to Respond If your interviewer asks these personal questions, how you respond depends on how badly you want the job, how you feel about revealing the information asked for, what you think the interviewer will do with the information, and whether you want to work for a company that asks such questions. If you don't want the job, you can tell the interviewer that you think a particular question is unethical or simply refuse to answer—responses that will leave an unfavorable impression.[24] If you do want the job, you might (1) ask how the question is related to your qualifications, (2) explain that the information is personal, (3) respond to what you think is the interviewer's real concern, or (4) answer both the question and the concern. If you answer an unethical or unlawful question, you run the risk that your answer may hurt your chances, so think carefully before answering.[25]

Where to File a Complaint When a business can show that the safety of its employees or customers is at stake, it may be allowed to ask questions that would seem discriminatory in another context. Despite this exception, if you believe an interviewer's questions are unreasonable, unrelated to the job, or an attempt to discriminate, you may complain to the EEOC or to the state agency that regulates fair employment practices. To report discrimination on the basis of age or physical disability, contact the employer's equal opportunity officer or the U.S. Department of Labor. If you file a complaint, be prepared to spend a lot of time and effort on it—and keep in mind that you may not win.[26]

The Close

Like the opening, the end of the interview is more important than its duration would indicate. In the last few minutes, you need to evaluate how well you've done. You also need to correct any misconceptions the interviewer might have.

Concluding Gracefully

Conclude the interview with courtesy and enthusiasm.

You can generally tell when the interviewer is trying to conclude the session. He or she may ask whether you have any more questions, sum up the discussion, change position, or indicate with a gesture that the interview is over. When you get the signal, respond promptly, but don't rush. Be sure to thank the interviewer for the opportunity and express an interest in the organization. If you can do so comfortably, try to pin down what will happen next, but don't press for an immediate decision.

If this is your second or third visit to the organization, the interview may culminate with an offer of employment. You have two options: Accept it or request time to think it over. The best course is usually to wait. If no job offer is made, the interviewer may not have reached a decision yet, but you may tactfully ask when you can expect to know the decision.

Discussing Salary

Be realistic in your salary expectations and diplomatic in your negotiations.

If you do receive an offer during the interview, you'll naturally want to discuss salary. However, let the interviewer raise the subject. If asked your salary requirements, say that you would expect to receive the standard salary for the job in question. If you have added qualifications, point them out: "With my 18 months of experience in the field, I would expect to start in the middle of the normal salary range." Some applicants find the Internet a terrific resource for salary information.

Negotiating salary can be tricky.

When to Negotiate If you don't like the offer, you might try to negotiate, provided you're in a good bargaining position and the organization has the flexibility to accommodate you. You'll be in a fairly strong position if your skills are in short supply and you have several other offers. It also helps if you're the favorite candidate and the organization is booming. However, many organizations are relatively rigid in their salary practices, particularly at the entry level. In the United States and some European countries, it is perfectly acceptable to ask, "Is there any room for negotiation?"

Negotiating benefits may be one way to get more value from an employment package.

What to Negotiate Even if you can't bargain for more money, you may be able to win some concessions on benefits and perquisites. The value of negotiating can be significant because benefits often cost the employer 25 to 45 percent of your salary. In other words, if you're offered an annual salary of $20,000, you'll ordinarily get an additional $5,000 to $9,000 in benefits: life, health, and disability insurance; pension and savings plans; vacation time; or even tuition reimbursement.[27]

If you can trade one benefit for another, you may be able to enhance the value of the total package. For example, life insurance may be relatively unimportant to you if you're single, whereas extra vacation time might be very valuable indeed. Don't inquire about benefits, however, until you know you have a job offer.

Interview Notes

Keep a written record of your job interviews.

If yours is a typical job search, you'll have many interviews before you accept an offer. For that reason, keeping a notebook or binder of interview notes can help you refresh your memory of each conversation. As soon as the interview ends, jot down the names and titles of the people you met. Briefly summarize the interviewer's answers to your questions. Then quickly evaluate your performance during the interview, listing what you handled well and what you didn't. Going over these notes can help you improve

✓ CHECKLIST: SUCCEEDING WITH JOB INTERVIEWS

A. Preparation

1. Determine the requirements and general salary range of the job.
2. Research the organization's products, structure, financial standing, and prospects for growth.
3. Determine the interviewer's name, title, and status in the firm.
4. Prepare (but don't over-rehearse) answers for the questions you are likely to be asked.
5. Develop relevant questions to ask.
6. Dress in a businesslike manner, regardless of the mode of dress preferred within the organization.
7. Take a briefcase or portfolio—with pen, paper, list of questions, two résumés, work samples.
8. Double-check the location and time of the interview, mapping out the route beforehand.
9. Plan to arrive 10 to 15 minutes early; allow 10 to 15 minutes for possible problems en route.

B. Initial stages of the interview

1. Greet the interviewer by name, with a smile and direct eye contact.
2. Offer a firm (not crushing) handshake if the interviewer extends a hand.
3. Take a seat only after the interviewer invites you to be seated or has taken his or her own seat.
4. Listen for cues about what the questions are trying to reveal about you and your qualifications.
5. Assume a calm and poised attitude (avoiding gum chewing, smoking, and other signs of nerves).

C. Body of the interview

1. Display a genuine (not artificial) smile, when appropriate.
2. Convey interest and enthusiasm.
3. Listen attentively so that you can give intelligent responses (taking few notes).
4. Relate your knowledge and skills to the position and stress your positive qualities.
5. Keep responses brief, clear, and to the point.
6. Avoid exaggeration, and convey honesty and sincerity.
7. Avoid slighting references to former employers.
8. Avoid alcoholic drinks if you are interviewed over lunch or dinner.

D. Salary discussions

1. Let the interviewer initiate the discussion of salary, but put it off until late in the interview if possible.
2. If asked, state that you would like to receive the standard salary for the position.

E. Closing stages of the interview

1. Watch for signs that the interview is about to end.
2. Tactfully ask when you will be advised of the decision on your application.
3. If you're offered the job, either accept or ask for time to consider the offer.
4. With a warm smile and a handshake, thank the interviewer for meeting with you.

your performance in the future.[28] In addition to improving your performance during interviews, interview notes will help you keep track of any follow-up messages you'll need to send. Whenever you need to review important tips, consult this chapter's "Checklist: Succeeding with Job Interviews."

FOLLOWING UP AFTER THE INTERVIEW

Touching base with the prospective employer after the interview, either by phone or in writing, shows that you really want the job and are determined to get it. As Microsoft's DeLeon points out, following up brings your name to the interviewer's attention once again and reminds him or her that you're waiting for the decision.

Learning Objective 5

Name six common employment messages that follow an interview, and state briefly when you would use each one

Six types of follow-up messages:

- Thank-you message
- Inquiry
- Request for a time extension
- Letter of acceptance
- Letter declining a job offer
- Letter of resignation

The two most common forms of follow-up are the thank-you message and the inquiry. These messages are often handled by letter, but an e-mail or a phone call can be just as effective, particularly if the employer seems to favor a casual, personal style. Other types of follow-up messages are sent only in certain cases—letters requesting a time extension, letters of acceptance, letters declining a job offer, and letters of resignation. These four types of employment messages are best handled in writing to document any official actions relating to your employment.

Thank-You Message

Express your thanks within two days after the interview, even if you feel you have little chance for the job. Acknowledge the interviewer's time and courtesy, and be sure to restate the specific job you're applying for. Convey your continued interest, then ask politely for a decision.

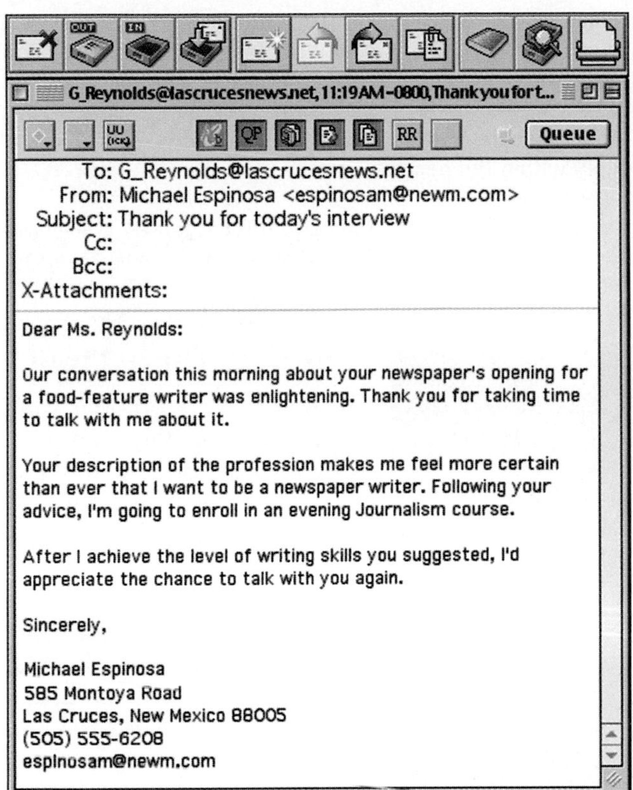
To: G_Reynolds@lascrucesnews.net
From: Michael Espinosa <espinosam@newm.com>
Subject: Thank you for today's interview
Cc:
Bcc:
X-Attachments:

Dear Ms. Reynolds:

Our conversation this morning about your newspaper's opening for a food-feature writer was enlightening. Thank you for taking time to talk with me about it.

Your description of the profession makes me feel more certain than ever that I want to be a newspaper writer. Following your advice, I'm going to enroll in an evening Journalism course.

After I achieve the level of writing skills you suggested, I'd appreciate the chance to talk with you again.

Sincerely,

Michael Espinosa
585 Montoya Road
Las Cruces, New Mexico 88005
(505) 555-6208
espinosam@newm.com

When Michael Espinosa followed up after a recent job interview, he sent his thank-you message by e-mail the same day. He included his e-mail address in the signature block at the close of the letter in case the interviewer wanted to contact him electronically.

Keep your thank-you message brief (less than five minutes for a phone call or only one page for a letter), and organize it like a routine message. Demonstrate the "you" attitude, and sound positive without sounding overconfident. The following sample thank-you letter shows how to achieve all this in three brief paragraphs:

A note or phone call thanking the interviewer

- Is organized like a routine message
- Closes with a request for a decision or future consideration

After talking with you yesterday, touring your sets, and watching the television commercials being filmed, I remain enthusiastic about the possibility of joining your staff as a television/film production assistant. Thanks for taking so much time to show me around.

Reminds the interviewer of the reasons for meeting and graciously acknowledges the consideration shown to the applicant

During our meeting, I said that I would prefer not to relocate, but I've reconsidered the matter. I would be pleased to relocate wherever you need my skills in set decoration and prop design.

Indicates the writer's flexibility and commitment to the job if hired

Reminds the recruiter of special qualifications

Now that you've explained the details of your operation, I feel quite strongly that I can make a contribution to the sorts of productions you're lining up. You can also count on me to be an energetic employee and a positive addition to your crew. Please let me know your decision as soon as possible.

Closes on a confident you-oriented note

Ends with a request for decision.

Even if the interviewer has said that you are unqualified for the job, a thank-you message may keep the door open.

Letter of Inquiry

If you're not advised of the interviewer's decision by the promised date or within two weeks, you might make an inquiry. A letter of inquiry is particularly appropriate if you've received a job offer from a second firm and don't want to accept it before you have an answer from the first. The following letter illustrates the general plan for a direct request; the writer assumes that a simple oversight, and not outright rejection, is the reason for the delay:

An inquiry about a hiring decision follows the plan for a direct request.

Identifies the position and introduces the main idea

When we talked on April 7 about the fashion coordinator position in your Park Avenue showroom, you said you would let me know your decision before May 1. I would still like the position, so I'm eager to know what conclusion you've reached.

Places the reason for the request second

To complicate matters, another firm has now offered me a position and has asked that I reply within the next two weeks.

Makes a courteous request for specific action last, while clearly stating a preference for this organization

Because your company seems to offer a greater challenge, I would appreciate knowing about your decision by Thursday, May 12. If you need more information before then, please let me know.

Geoffrey Collins understands that inquiring about interview results electronically can be faster than sending a letter. But he is careful to make sure that the potential employer is open to electronic communication.

Request for a Time Extension

If you receive a job offer while other interviews are still pending, you'll probably want more time to decide, so write to the offering organization and ask for a time extension. Employers understand that candidates often interview with several companies. They want you to be sure you're making the right decision, so most are happy to accommodate you with a reasonable extension.

Preface your request with a friendly opening. Ask for more time, stressing your enthusiasm for the organization. Conclude by allowing for a quick decision if your request for additional time is denied. Ask for a prompt reply confirming the time extension if the organization grants it. This type of letter is, in essence, a direct request. However, because the recipient may be disappointed, be sure to temper your request for an extension with statements indicating your continued interest. The letter in Figure 18.4 is a good example.

Letter of Acceptance

A letter of acceptance follows the good-news plan.

When you receive a job offer that you want to accept, reply within five days. Begin by accepting the position and expressing thanks. Identify the job that you're accepting. In the next paragraph, cover any necessary details. Conclude by saying that you look forward to reporting for work. As always, a good-news letter should convey your enthusiasm and eagerness to cooperate:

Confirms the specific terms of the offer with a good-news statement at the beginning

I'm delighted to accept the graphic design position in your advertising department at the salary of $1,575 a month.

Covers miscellaneous details in the middle

Enclosed are the health insurance forms you asked me to complete and sign. I've already given notice to my current employer and will be able to start work on Monday, January 18.

Closes with another reference to the good news and a look toward the future

The prospect of joining your firm is exciting. Thank you for giving me this opportunity for what I'm sure will be a challenging future.

Written acceptance of a job offer is legally binding.

Be aware that a job offer and a written acceptance of that offer constitute a legally binding contract, for both you and the employer. Before you write an acceptance letter, be sure you want the job.

Letter Declining a Job Offer

A letter declining a job offer follows the bad-news plan.

After all your interviews, you may find that you need to write a letter declining a job offer. The bad-news plan is ideally suited to this type of letter. Open warmly, state the reasons for refusing the offer, decline the offer explicitly, and close on a pleasant note, expressing gratitude. By taking the time to write a sincere, tactful letter, you leave the door open for future contact.

FIGURE 18.4 In-Depth Critique: Request for a Time Extension

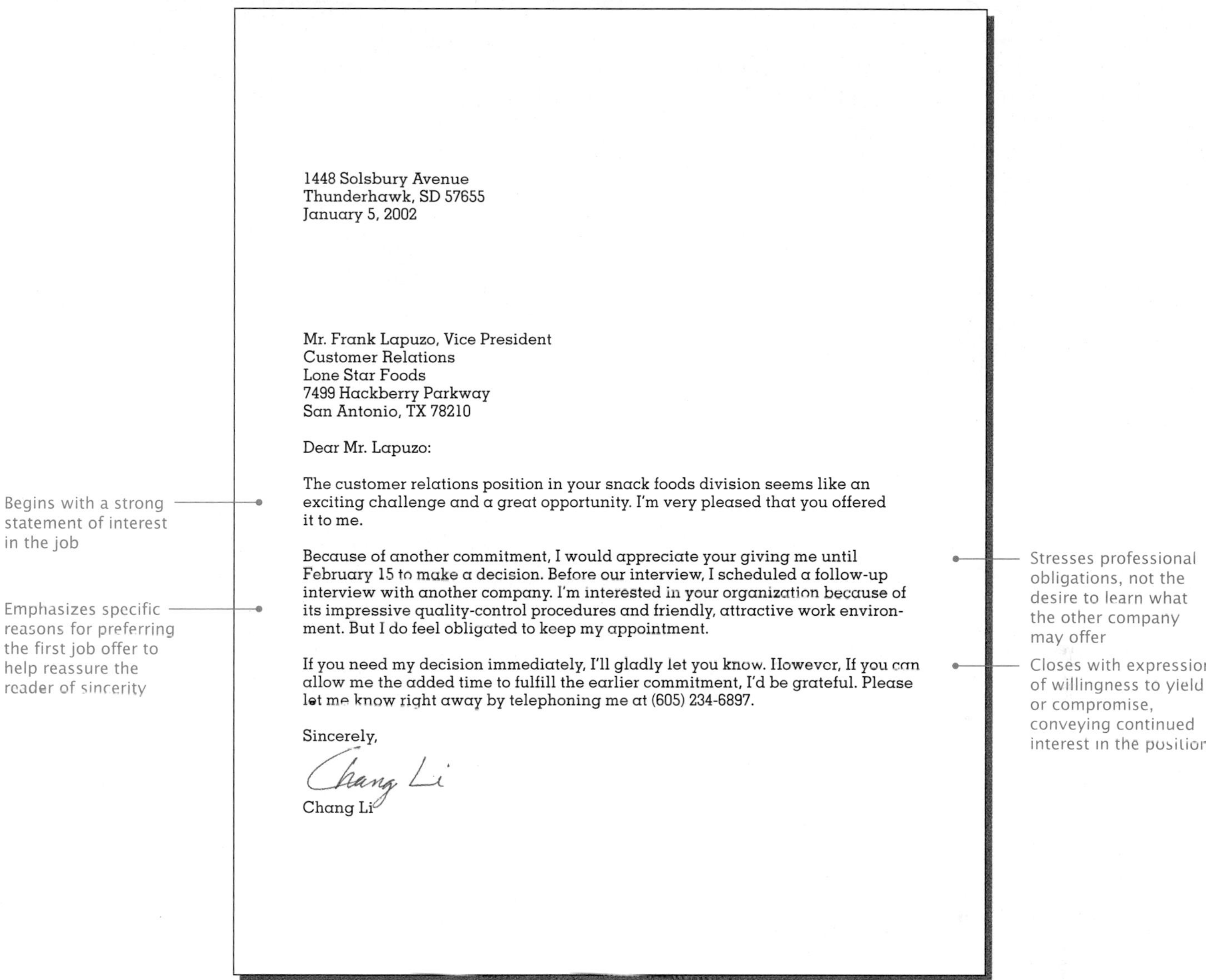

1448 Solsbury Avenue
Thunderhawk, SD 57655
January 5, 2002

Mr. Frank Lapuzo, Vice President
Customer Relations
Lone Star Foods
7499 Hackberry Parkway
San Antonio, TX 78210

Dear Mr. Lapuzo:

The customer relations position in your snack foods division seems like an exciting challenge and a great opportunity. I'm very pleased that you offered it to me.

Because of another commitment, I would appreciate your giving me until February 15 to make a decision. Before our interview, I scheduled a follow-up interview with another company. I'm interested in your organization because of its impressive quality-control procedures and friendly, attractive work environment. But I do feel obligated to keep my appointment.

If you need my decision immediately, I'll gladly let you know. However, If you can allow me the added time to fulfill the earlier commitment, I'd be grateful. Please let me know right away by telephoning me at (605) 234-6897.

Sincerely,

Chang Li

One of the most interesting interviews I have ever had was the one last month at your Durham textile plant. I'm flattered that you would offer me the computer analyst position that we talked about.

Makes the opening paragraph a buffer

During my job search, I applied to five highly rated firms like your own, each one a leader in its field. Both your company and another offered me a position. Because my desire to work abroad can more readily be satisfied by the other company, I have accepted that job offer.

Precedes the bad news with tactfully phrased reasons for the applicant's unfavorable decision, and leaves the door open

I deeply appreciate the hour you spent talking with me. Thank you again for your consideration and kindness.

Lets the reader down gently with a sincere and cordial ending

Letter of Resignation

If you get a job offer and are currently employed, you can maintain good relations with your current employer by writing a letter of resignation to your immediate supervisor. Follow the bad-news plan, and make the letter sound positive, regardless of how you feel. Say something favorable about the organization, the people you work with, or what you've learned on the job. Then state your intention to leave and give the date of your last day on the job. Be sure you give your current employer at least two weeks' notice.

A letter of resignation also follows the bad-news plan.

✓ CHECKLIST: WRITING FOLLOW-UP MESSAGES

A. Thank-you messages

1. Write a thank-you letter within two days of the interview (keeping it to one page).
2. If you have no alternative, thank the interviewer by phone (in less than five minutes).
3. In the opening, express thanks and identify the job and the time and place of the interview.
4. Use the middle section for supporting details.
5. Express your enthusiasm about the organization and the job.
6. Add any new facts that may help your chances.
7. Try to repair any negative impressions you may have left during the interview.
8. Use an action ending.

B. Inquiries

1. Make an inquiry—by letter, phone, or e-mail—if you aren't informed of the decision by the promised date.
2. Follow the plan for direct requests: main idea, necessary details, specific request.

C. Requests for a time extension

1. Request an extension if you have pending interviews and need time to decide about an offer.
2. Open with an expression of warmth.
3. In the middle, explain why you need more time and express continued interest in the company.
4. In the close, promise a quick decision if your request is denied, and ask for a confirmation if your request is granted.

D. Letters accepting a job offer

1. Send this message within five days of receiving the offer.
2. State clearly that you accept the offer, identify the job you're accepting, and include vital details.
3. Conclude with a statement that you look forward to reporting for work.

E. Letters rejecting a job offer

1. Open a letter of rejection warmly.
2. Explain why you are refusing the offer, and express your appreciation.
3. End on a sincere, positive note.

F. Letters of resignation

1. Send a letter of resignation to your current employer as soon as possible.
2. Begin with an appreciative buffer.
3. In the middle section, state your reasons for leaving, and actually state that you are resigning.
4. Close cordially.

Uses on appreciative opening to serve as a buffer

My sincere thanks to you and to all the other Emblem Corporation employees for helping me learn so much about serving the public these past 11 months. You have given me untold help and encouragement.

States reasons before the bad news itself, using tactful phrasing to help keep the relationship friendly, should the writer later want letters of recommendation

You may recall that when you first interviewed me, my goal was to become a customer relations supervisor. Because that opportunity has been offered to me by another organization, I am submitting my resignation. I will miss all of you, but I want to take advantage of this opportunity.

Discusses necessary details in an extra paragraph

I would like to terminate my work here two weeks from today but can arrange to work an additional week if you want me to train a replacement.

Tempers any disappointment with a cordial close

My sincere thanks and best wishes to all of you.

Compare your messages with the suggestions in this chapter's "Checklist: Writing Follow-up Messages."

COMMUNICATION CHALLENGES AT MICROSOFT

Cooking up new questions for interviews has become a favorite pastime at Microsoft (right up there with lunchtime Frisbee games). Says Jodi DeLeon, "You'll often walk down the hall and see a group of technical people bouncing ideas off each other." The challenge is to attract the best and brightest from the nation's campuses while making sure these candidates will fit in at Microsoft.

DeLeon believes it's important for every applicant to leave the screening interview with a positive feeling toward Microsoft. "They may not get a job here, but they may turn out to be a major consumer of our products." So she advises

Microsoft interviewers to be fair and considerate, giving equal time to everyone and allowing candidates time to add information about their qualifications and to ask questions.

Individual Challenge: Microsoft needs communication assistants in the busy Office Products division. Once hired, the new employees will help handle public relations for Microsoft Office, Word, Excel, PowerPoint, Access, and Outlook. The best candidates will know how to organize and write letters, memos, press releases, and possibly advertising copy, but they'll also be innovative in their thinking. DeLeon has come up with a problem-solving question for the campus interviews that she wants to test on you: What are some of the ways you might use written or spoken communications to promote Microsoft's Office software to teachers and administrators? Write your answer just as you would explain it in an interview, drawing on everything you've learned so far in this course.

Team Challenge: To test your answers, divide your group so that one member role-plays the job candidate being interviewed by the others. Start by posing the problem-solving question. Then, if time allows, ask a few follow-up questions to determine more about the "applicant's" knowledge of good communication principles. Take turns until each of you plays the role of job candidate. This will give you some practice thinking on your feet and a chance to experience the interviewer's perspective.[29] ■

SUMMARY OF LEARNING OBJECTIVES

1 **Describe the typical sequence of interviews.** The typical sequence of interviews involves three stages. During the first or *screening stage,* employers administer fairly structured interviews to eliminate unqualified applicants. During the second or *selection stage,* the pool of applicants is narrowed considerably. The employer administers a series of structured and unstructured interviews to find the best candidates for the job. Those candidates who advance to the third or *final stage* of the sequence have a good chance of receiving a job offer. During this stage, candidates meet with executives who have the authority to offer the job and set compensation. The underlying objective of this final stage is to select the final candidate(s) and convince the candidate(s) to accept a job offer.

2 **Describe briefly what employers look for during an employment interview.** Employers look for two things during an employment interview. First, they seek evidence that an applicant will be compatible with the other people in the organization. Whether interviewers focus on personal background or personal style, they are interested in finding someone who will easily adapt to a new workplace and new responsibilities. Second, employers seek evidence that an applicant is qualified for the position. Even though interviewers have already reviewed your résumé, they want to see how well your skills match their requirements and perhaps even get a sense of your ability to be flexible and apply diverse skills in more than one area. Sometimes, interviewers will use preemployment tests to help them gather the evidence they need to make a decision.

3 **List six tasks you need to complete to prepare for a successful job interview.** To prepare for a successful job interview, begin by (1) refining the research you did when planning your résumé. Knowing as much as you can about the company and its needs helps you highlight the aspects of your background and qualifications that will appeal to the organization. (2) Next, think ahead about questions—both those you'll need to answer and those you'll want to ask. (3) Bolster your confidence by focusing on your strengths to overcome any apprehension. (4) Polish your style by staging mock interviews and paying close attention to nonverbal behaviors, including voice problems. (5) Plan to look your best with businesslike clothing and good grooming. And (6) arrive on time and ready to begin.

4 **Explain the three stages of a successful employment interview.** All employment interviews have three stages. The warm-up stage is the most important, because first impressions greatly influence an interviewer's decision. The question-and-answer stage is the longest, during which you will answer and ask questions. Listening carefully and watching the interviewer's nonverbal clues help you determine how the interview is going. The close is also important because you need to evaluate your performance to see whether the interviewer has any misconceptions that you must correct.

5 **Name six common employment messages that follow an interview, and state briefly when you would use each one.** The two most common types of follow-up messages are usually in letter form but can also be effective by phone or e-mail. You send the *thank-you* message within two days after your interview to show appreciation, express your continued interest in the job, and politely ask for a decision. You send an *inquiry* if you haven't received the interviewer's decision by the date promised or within two weeks of the interview—especially if you've received a job offer from another firm. The remaining four employment messages are best sent in letter form, to document any official action. You request a *time extension* if you receive a job offer while other interviews are pending and you want more time to complete those interviews before making a decision. You send a *letter of acceptance* within five days of receiving a job offer that you want to take. You send a *letter declining a job offer* when you want to refuse an offer tactfully and leave the door open for future contact. You send a *letter of resignation* when you receive a job offer that you want to accept while you are currently employed.

TEST YOUR KNOWLEDGE

1. How does a structured interview differ from an open-ended interview and a situational interview?
2. What typically occurs during a stress interview?
3. Why do employers conduct preemployment testing?
4. Why are the questions you ask during an interview as important as the answers you give to the interviewer's questions?
5. What are the three stages of every interview, and which is the most important?
6. How should you respond if an interviewer at a company where you want to work asks you a question that seems too personal or unethical?
7. What should you say in a thank-you message after an interview?
8. What is the purpose of sending a letter of inquiry after an interview?
9. What is the legal significance of a letter of acceptance?
10. What organization plan is appropriate for a letter of resignation? Why?

APPLY YOUR KNOWLEDGE

1. How can you distinguish yourself from other candidates in a screening interview and still keep your responses short and to the point? Explain.
2. What can you do to make a favorable impression when you discover that an open-ended interview has turned into a stress interview? Briefly explain your answer.
3. If you want to switch jobs because you can't work with your supervisor, how can you explain this situation to a prospective employer? Give an example.
4. During a group interview you notice that one of the other candidates is trying to monopolize the conversation. He's always the first to answer, his answer is the longest, and he even interrupts the other candidates while they are talking. The interviewer doesn't seem to be concerned about his behavior, but you are. You would like to have more time to speak so that the interviewer could get to know you better. What should you do?
5. **Ethical Choices** Why is it important to distinguish unethical or illegal interview questions from acceptable questions? Explain.

PRACTICE YOUR KNOWLEDGE

Documents for Analysis

Read the following documents; then (1) analyze the strengths or weaknesses of each document and (2) revise each document so that it follows this chapter's guidelines.

Document 18.A: Thank-You Message

Thank you for the really marvelous opportunity to meet you and your colleagues at Starret Engine Company. I really enjoyed touring your facilities and talking with all the people there. You have quite a crew! Some of the other companies I have visited have been so rigid and uptight that I can't imagine how I would fit in. It's a relief to run into a group of people who seem to enjoy their work as much as all of you do.

I know that you must be looking at many other candidates for this job, and I know that some of them will probably be more experienced than I am. But I do want to emphasize that my two-year hitch in the Navy involved a good deal of engineering work. I don't think I mentioned all my shipboard responsibilities during the interview.

Please give me a call within the next week to let me know your decision. You can usually find me at my dormitory in the evening after dinner (phone: 877-9080).

Document 18.B: Letter of Inquiry

I have recently received a very attractive job offer from the Warrington Company. But before I let them know one way or another, I would like to consider any offer that your firm may extend. I was quite impressed with your company during my recent interview, and I am still very interested in a career there.

I don't mean to pressure you, but Warrington has asked for my decision within 10 days. Could you let me know by Tuesday whether you plan to offer me a position? That would give me enough time to compare the two offers.

Document 18.C: Letter Declining a Job Offer

I'm writing to say that I must decline your job offer. Another company has made me a more generous offer, and I have decided to accept. However, if things don't work out for me there, I will let you know. I sincerely appreciate your interest in me.

Exercises

For live links to all websites discussed in this chapter, visit this text's website at www.prenhall.com/bovee. Just log on and select Chapter 18, and click on "Student Resources." Locate the name of the site or the URL related to the material in the text. For "Exploring the Best of the Web" exercises, you'll also find navigational directions. Click on the live link to the site.

18.1  **Internet** Select a large company (one that you can easily find information on) where you might like to work. Use Internet sources to gather some preliminary research on the company.

a. What did you learn about this organization that would help you during an interview there?
b. What Internet sources did you use to obtain this information?
c. Armed with this information, what aspects of your background do you think might appeal to this company's recruiters?
d. If you choose to apply for a job with this company, what keywords would you include on your résumé, and why?

18.2 **Teamwork** Divide the class into two groups. Half the class will be recruiters for a large chain of national department stores looking to fill manager trainee positions (there are 15 openings). The other half of the class will be candidates for the job. The company is specifically looking for candidates who demonstrate these three qualities: initiative, dependability, and willingness to assume responsibility.
a. Have each recruiter select and interview an applicant for 10 minutes.
b. Have all the recruiters discuss how they assessed the applicant in each of the three desired qualities. What questions did they ask or what did they use as an indicator to determine whether the candidate possessed the quality?
c. Have all the applicants discuss what they said to convince the recruiters that they possessed each of these qualities.

18.3 **Interviews: Understanding Qualifications** Write a short memo to your instructor, discussing what you believe are your greatest strengths and weaknesses from an employment perspective. Next, explain how these strengths and weaknesses would be viewed by interviewers evaluating your qualifications.

18.4 **Interviews: Being Prepared** Prepare written answers to 10 of the questions listed in Table 18.3, "Twenty-Five Common Interview Questions" (see page 591).

18.5 **Ethical Choices** You have decided to accept a new position with a competitor of your company. Write a letter of resignation to your supervisor, announcing your decision.
a. Will you notify your employer that you are joining a competing firm? Please explain.
b. Will you use the direct or the indirect approach? Please explain.
c. Will you send your letter by e-mail, send it by regular mail, or place it on your supervisor's desk?

EXPAND YOUR KNOWLEDGE

Exploring the Best of the Web:

Planning for a Successful Interview, p. 587

If you have not interviewed recently (or ever) for a job, do you have an idea of the kind of questions you might be asked? How can you prepare for an interview so that you'll appear knowledgeable about the job and confident in your skills? At Job-interview.net you'll get advice and ideas to make your next interview successful.

1. What are some problem questions you might be asked during a job interview? How would you handle these questions?
2. Choose a job title from the list, and read more about it. What did you learn that could help during an actual interview for the job you selected?
3. Developing an "interview game plan" ahead of time helps you make a strong, positive impression during an interview. What are some of the things you can practice to help make everything you do during an interview seem to come naturally?

Exploring the Web on Your Own

Review these chapter-related websites on your own to learn more about interviewing for jobs.

1. Get over 2,000 pages of career advice at Monster.com, www.monster.com, and talk to career experts in your choice of industry or profession.
2. Learn how to prepare for and handle yourself with care during a job interview at So You Wanna Ace A Job Interview, www.soyouwanna.com/site/syws/aceinterview/aceinterview.html.
3. Follow the steps at Learn2, www.learn2.com/09/0957/0957.asp, and be prepared for your next job interview.

LEARN INTERACTIVELY

Interactive Study Guide

Visit the "My Companion Website" at www.prenhall.com/bovee. For Chapter 18, take advantage of the interactive "Study Guide" to test your chapter knowledge. Get instant feedback on whether you need additional studying. Read the "Current Events" articles to get the latest on chapter topics, and complete the exercises—as specified by your instructor.

This site offers a variety of additional resources: The "Research Area" helps you locate a wealth of information to use in course assignments. You can even send a message to online research experts, who will help you find exactly the information you need. The "Study Hall" helps you succeed in this course. "Talk in the Hall" lets you leave messages and meet new friends online. If you have a question, you can "Ask the Tutor." And to get a better grade in this course, you can find more help at "Writing Skills," "Study Skills," and "Study Tips."

Grammar Diagnostic Tests

Review and reinforce your grammar and language skills by taking one of the four online diagnostic tests offered at our companion website, www.prenhall/bovee.com. The four tests cover a variety of topics, including spelling, capitals, punctuation, verbs, pronouns, adjectives, adverbs, sentence structure, sentence punctuation, clarity, word choice, style, organization skills, proofreading, and more. Submit your test and assess your competency. Then focus on improving areas where you are weak as you complete the exercises in this chapter.

CASES

INTERVIEWING WITH POTENTIAL EMPLOYERS

1. Interviewers and interviewees: Classroom exercise in interviewing Interviewing is clearly an interactive process involving at least two people. The best way to practice for interviews is to work with others.

Your task: You and all other members of your class are to write letters of application for an entry-level or management-trainee position requiring a pleasant personality and intelligence but a minimum of specialized education or experience. Sign your letter with a fictitious name that conceals your identity. Next, polish (or prepare) a résumé that accurately identifies you and your educational and professional accomplishments.

Now, three members of the class who volunteer as interviewers divide up all the anonymously written application letters. Then each interviewer selects a candidate who seems the most pleasant and convincing in his or her letter. At this time the selected candidates identify themselves and give the interviewers their résumés.

Each interviewer then interviews his or her chosen candidate in front of the class, seeking to understand how the items on the résumé qualify the candidate for the job. At the end of the interviews, the class may decide who gets the job and discuss why this candidate was successful. Afterward, retrieve your letter, sign it with the right name, and submit it to the instructor for credit.

2. Internet interview: Exercise in interviewing Using the Web 100 site at www.web100.com, locate the homepage of a company you would like to work for. Then identify a position within the company for which you would like to apply. Study the company, using any of the online business resources discussed in Chapter 10, and prepare for an interview with that company.

Your task: Working with a classmate, take turns interviewing each other for your chosen positions. Interviewers should take notes during the interview. Once the interview is complete, critique each other's performance (interviewers should critique how well candidates prepared for the interview and answered the questions; interviewees should critique the quality of the questions asked). Write a follow-up letter thanking your interviewer and submit the letter to your instructor.

FOLLOWING UP AFTER THE INTERVIEW

3. A slight error in timing: Letter asking for delay of an employment decision You botched your timing and applied for your third-choice job before going after what you really wanted. What you want to do is work in retail marketing with Neiman Marcus in Dallas; what you have been offered is a similar job with Longhorn Leather and Lumber, 55 dry and dusty miles away in Commerce, just south of the Oklahoma panhandle.

You review your notes. Your Longhorn interview was three weeks ago with the human resources manager, R. P. Bronson, a congenial person who has just written to offer you the position. The store's address is 27 Sam Rayburn Drive, Commerce, TX 75428. Mr. Bronson notes that he can hold the position open for 10 days. You have an interview scheduled with Neiman Marcus next week, but it is unlikely that you will know the store's decision within this 10-day period.

Your task: Write to R. P. Bronson, requesting a reasonable delay in your consideration of his job offer.

4. Job hunt: Set of employment-related letters to a single company Where would you like to work? Pick a real or an imagined company, and assume that a month ago you sent your résumé and application letter. Not long afterward, you were invited to come for an interview, which seemed to go very well.

Your task: Use your imagination to write the following: (a) a thank-you letter for the interview, (b) a note of inquiry, (c) a request for more time to decide, (d) a letter of acceptance, and (e) a letter declining the job offer.

Appendix I

Format and Layout of Business Documents

An effective letter, memo, or report does more than store words on paper. It communicates with the right person, makes the right impression, and tells the recipient who wrote it and when it was written. It may even carry responses back to the sender, if only to relate how and by whom it was received and processed.

Over the centuries, certain conventions have developed for the format and layout of business documents. Conventions vary from country to country, and even within the United States few hard-and-fast rules exist. Many organizations develop variations of standard styles to suit their own needs, adopting the style that's best for the types of messages they send and for the kinds of audiences that receive them. The conventions described here are more common than others. Whether you handle all your own communication on your computer or rely on someone else to handle it for you, your knowledge of the proper form for your documents and of how to make them attractive to your readers is crucial.

FIRST IMPRESSIONS

A letter or other written document is often the first (and sometimes only) contact you have with an external audience. Within an organization, memos and other documents represent you to supervisors, colleagues, and employees. So it's important that all your documents look neat, present a professional image, and are easy to read. Your audience's first impressions come from the paper you use, the way you customize it, and the general appearance of your document. These elements tell readers a lot about you and about your company's professionalism.

Paper

From your own experience, you know that a flimsy, see-through piece of paper gives a much less favorable impression than a richly textured piece. Paper quality is measured in two ways. The first is weight, specifically the weight of four reams (each a 500-sheet package) of letter-size paper. The quality most commonly used by U.S. business organizations is 20-pound paper, but 16- and 24-pound versions are also used. The second measure of quality is the percentage of cotton in the paper. Cotton doesn't yellow over time the way wood pulp does, and it's both strong and soft. Paper with a 25 percent cotton content is an appropriate quality for letters and outside reports. For memos and other internal documents, lighter-weight paper and paper with a lower cotton content may be used. Also, airmail-weight paper may be more cost-effective for international correspondence, but make sure it isn't too flimsy.[1]

In the United States the standard size of paper for business documents is $8^1/2$ by 11 inches. Standard legal documents are $8^1/2$ by 14 inches. Executives sometimes have heavier 7-by-10-inch paper on hand (with matching envelopes) for such personal messages as congratulations and recommendations.[2] They may also have a box of correspondence note cards imprinted with their initials and a box of plain folded notes for condolences or for acknowledging formal invitations.

Stationery may vary in color. White is standard for business purposes, although neutral colors such as gray and ivory are sometimes used. Memos are sometimes produced on pastel-colored paper so that internal correspondence can be more easily distinguished from external. Memos are also sometimes printed or typed on various colors of paper for routing to separate departments. Light-colored papers are distinctive and often appropriate; bright or dark colors make reading difficult and may appear too frivolous.

Customization

For letters to outsiders, U.S. businesses commonly use letterhead stationery, which may be either professionally printed or designed in-house using word-processing templates and graphics. The letterhead includes the company's name and address, usually at the top of the page but sometimes along the left side or even at the bottom of the page. Other information may be included in the letterhead as well: the company's telephone number, fax number, cable address, website address, product lines, date of establishment, officers and directors, slogan, and symbol (logo). The idea is to give the recipient pertinent reference data and a good idea not only of what the company does but also of the company's image.[3] Nevertheless, the letterhead should be as simple as possible; too much information gives the page a cluttered look, cuts into the space needed for the letter, and may become outdated before all the letterhead has been used. If you correspond frequently with people abroad, be sure your letterhead is intelligible to foreigners, and make sure it includes the name of your country as well as your cable, telex, e-mail address, or fax information.

In the United States, company letterhead is always used for the first page of a letter. Successive pages are usually plain sheets of paper that match the letterhead in color and quality, although some companies use a specially printed second-page letterhead bearing only the company's name. Other countries have other conventions. For example, Latin American companies use a cover page with their printed seal in the center.

Many companies also design and print standardized forms for memos and for reports that are written frequently and always require the same sort of information (such as sales reports and expense reports). These forms may be printed in sets for use with carbon paper or in carbonless copy sets that produce multiple copies automatically with the original. More and more, organizations are using computers to generate their standardized forms. These electronic forms can save money and time.[4]

Appearance

Most business documents are produced using either a letter-quality (not a dot matrix) printer or a typewriter. Some short informal memos are handwritten, and it's appropriate to handwrite a note of condolence to a close business associate. Envelopes are handwritten, printed, or typed to match a document. However, even a letter on the best-quality paper with the best-designed letterhead may look unprofessional if it's poorly produced.

Margins and Line Length

Companies in the United States make sure that documents (especially external ones) are centered on the page, with margins of at least an inch all around (unlike documents produced in Latin America, which use much wider margins and thus look much longer). Using word-processing or desktop-publishing software, you can achieve this balanced appearance simply by defining the format parameters. If you are using a typewriter, such balance can be achieved either by establishing a standard line length or by establishing a "picture frame." The most common line length is about six inches.

Lines aren't usually right-hand justified, because the resulting text can be hard to read, even with proportional spacing, and because the document generally looks too much like a form letter. Varying line length makes the document look more personal and interesting. The larger, pica type will give you 60 characters in a line; the smaller, elite type will give you 72 characters in a line. The number of lines between elements of the document (such as between the date line and inside address in a letter) can be adjusted to ensure that a short document fills the page vertically or that a longer document extends to at least three lines of body on the last page.

Spacing

Another important aspect of a professional-looking document is the proper spacing after punctuation. For example, U.S. conventions include leaving one space after commas and semicolons and leaving two spaces after periods at the ends of sentences and after colons (unless your typeface is proportional, which requires only one space). Each letter in a person's initials is followed by a period and a single space. Abbreviations for organizations, such as P.T.A., may or may not have periods, but they never have internal spaces.

Special Symbols

When using a computer, use appropriate symbols to give your document a professional look. Computers allow you to use case fractions (½) instead of typed fractions (1/2). They provide professional symbols for copyright (©), registered trademark (®), cents (¢), British pound (£), paragraph (¶), and many others. Plus, they make it particularly easy to select from a variety of bullet symbols to use in lists (•, ◆, ■, ❑, ✓, ☑, ☒).

Instead of two hyphens, computers allow you to use the em-dash symbol to emphasize words, phrases, and clauses more strongly than a comma or parentheses would. For example, use em dashes to set off material that is a sudden turn of thought ("This quarter's loss—nearly $2 million—could mean bankruptcy."). Instead of a single hyphen, computers allow you to use the en-dash symbol for inclusive numbers or for showing duration ("Read pages 75–87 and then include that material in the November–December report.") When using a typewriter that has no special characters for dashes, use a hyphen for the en dash and two hyphens (with no space before, between, or after) for the em dash. Other details of this sort are provided in your company's style book or in most secretarial handbooks.

Corrections

Finally, messy corrections are dreadfully obvious and unacceptable in business documents. Be sure that any letter, report, or memo requiring a lot of corrections is reprinted or retyped. Word-processing software and self-correcting typewriters can produce correction-free documents at the push of a button.

LETTERS

For a long time, letters have begun with some kind of phrase in greeting and have ended with some sort of polite expression before the writer's signature. Books printed in the sixteenth century prescribed letter formats for writers to follow. Styles have changed some since then, but all business letters still have certain elements in common. Several of these elements appear in every letter; others appear only when desirable or appropriate. In addi-

FIGURE I.1 Standard Letter Parts

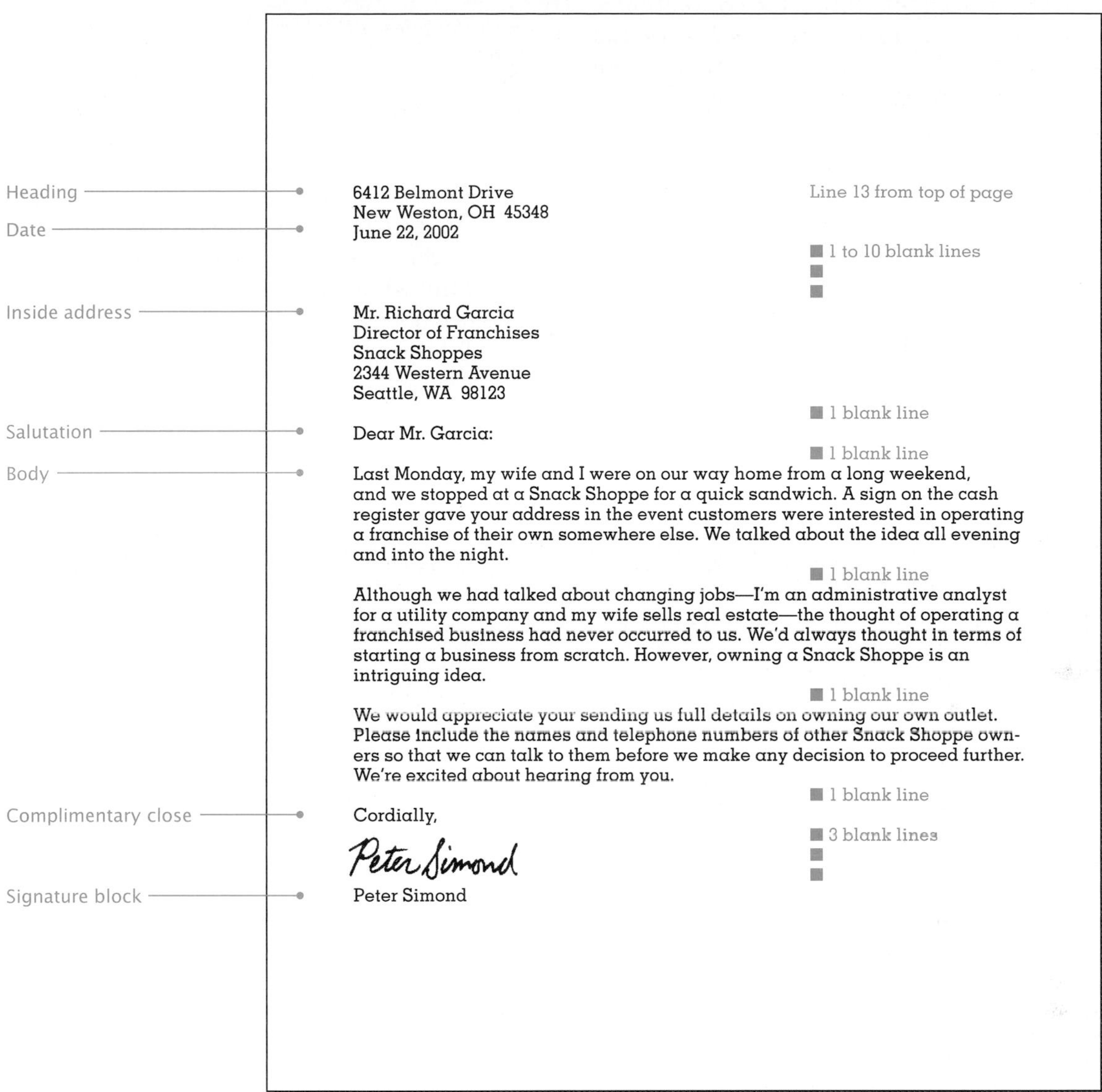

6412 Belmont Drive
New Weston, OH 45348
June 22, 2002

Mr. Richard Garcia
Director of Franchises
Snack Shoppes
2344 Western Avenue
Seattle, WA 98123

Dear Mr. Garcia:

Last Monday, my wife and I were on our way home from a long weekend, and we stopped at a Snack Shoppe for a quick sandwich. A sign on the cash register gave your address in the event customers were interested in operating a franchise of their own somewhere else. We talked about the idea all evening and into the night.

Although we had talked about changing jobs—I'm an administrative analyst for a utility company and my wife sells real estate—the thought of operating a franchised business had never occurred to us. We'd always thought in terms of starting a business from scratch. However, owning a Snack Shoppe is an intriguing idea.

We would appreciate your sending us full details on owning our own outlet. Please include the names and telephone numbers of other Snack Shoppe owners so that we can talk to them before we make any decision to proceed further. We're excited about hearing from you.

Cordially,

Peter Simond

Peter Simond

tion, these letter parts are usually arranged in one of three basic formats.

Standard Letter Parts

All business letters typically include seven elements, in the following order: (1) heading, (2) date, (3) inside address, (4) salutation, (5) body, (6) complimentary close, and (7) signature block. The letter in Figure I.1 shows the placement of these standard letter parts. The writer of this personal business letter had no letterhead available but correctly included a heading.

Heading

Letterhead (the usual heading) shows the organization's name, full address, and (almost always) telephone number. Executive letterhead also bears the name of an individual within the organization. Computers allow you to design your own letterhead (either one to use for all correspondence or a new one for each piece of correspondence). If letterhead stationery is not available, the heading includes a return address (but no name) and starts 13 lines from the top of the page, which leaves a two-inch top margin.

Date

If you're using letterhead, place the date at least one blank line beneath the lowest part of the letterhead. Without letterhead, place the date immediately below the return address. The standard method for writing the date in the United States is to use the full name of the month (no abbreviations), followed by the day (in numerals, without *st, nd, rd,* or *th*), a comma, and then the year: July 14, 2002 (7/14/02). The U.S. government and some U.S. industries place the day (in numerals) first, followed by the month (unabbreviated), followed by the year—with no comma: 14 July 2002 (14/7/02). This convention is similar to the one used in Europe, except that European convention replaces the U.S. solidus (diagonal line) with periods when the date appears all in numerals: 14 July 2002 (14.7.2002). The international standard places the year first, followed by the month and the day, separated by commas in the all-numeral form: 2002 July 14 (2002,7,14). To maintain the utmost clarity, always spell out the name of the month in dates for international correspondence.[5]

When communicating internationally, you may also experience some confusion over time. Some companies in the United States refer to morning (A.M.) and afternoon (P.M.), dividing a 24-hour day into 12-hour blocks so that they refer to four o'clock in the morning (4:00 A.M.) or four o'clock in the afternoon (4:00 P.M.). The U.S. military and European companies refer to one 24-hour period, so that 0400 hours (4:00 A.M.) is always in the morning and 1600 hours (4:00 P.M.) is always in the afternoon.[6] Make sure your references to time are as clear as possible, and be sure you clearly understand your audience's time references.

Inside Address

The inside address identifies the recipient of the letter. For U.S. correspondence, begin the inside address one or more lines below the date, depending on how long the letter is. Precede the addressee's name with a courtesy title, such as *Dr., Mr.,* or *Ms.* The accepted courtesy title for women in business is *Ms.,* although a woman known to prefer the title *Miss* or *Mrs.* is always accommodated. If you don't know whether a person is a man or a woman (and you have no way of finding out), do not use a courtesy title. For example, *Terry Smith* could be either a man or a woman. The first line of the inside address would be just *Terry Smith,* and the salutation would be *Dear Terry Smith.* The same is true if you know only a person's initials, as in *S. J. Adams.*

Spell out and capitalize titles that precede a person's name, such as *Professor* or *General* (see Table I.1 for the proper forms of address). The person's organizational title, such as *Director,* may be included on this first line (if it is short) or on the line below; the name of a department may follow. In addresses and signature lines, don't forget to capitalize any professional title that follows a person's name:

Mr. Ray Johnson, Dean

Ms. Patricia T. Higgins
Assistant Vice President

However, professional titles not appearing in an address or signature line are capitalized only when they directly precede the name:

President Kenneth Johanson will deliver the speech.

Maria Morales, president of ABC Enterprises, will deliver the speech.

The Honorable Helen Masters, senator from Arizona, will deliver the speech.

If the name of a specific person is unavailable, you may address the letter to the department or to a specific position within the department. Also, be sure to spell out company names in full, unless the company itself uses abbreviations in its official name.

Other address information includes the treatment of buildings, house numbers, and compass directions. Capitalize the names of buildings, and if you specify a location within a building (suite, room, and so on), capitalize it and use a comma to separate it from the building name:

Empire State Building, Suite 1073

Use numerals for all house or building numbers, except the number *one:*

One Trinity Lane
637 Adams Avenue, Apt. 7

Spell out compass directions that fall within a street address, but abbreviate compass directions that follow the street address:

1074 West Connover Street
783 Main Street, N.E., Apt. 27

Apartment, suite, and room numbers always appear in numerals (as in the above examples). The following example shows all the information that might be included in the inside address and its proper order for U.S. correspondence:

Ms. Linda Coolidge, Vice President
Corporate Planning Department
Midwest Airlines
Kowalski Building, Suite 21-A
7279 Bristol Avenue
Toledo, OH 43617

Canadian addresses are similar, except that the name of the province is usually spelled out:

Dr. H. C. Armstrong
Research and Development
Commonwealth Mining Consortium
The Chelton Building, Suite 301
585 Second Street SW
Calgary, Alberta T2P 2P5
CANADA

TABLE I.1 Forms of Address

Person	In Address	In Salutation
	Personal Titles	
Man	Mr. [first & last name]	Dear Mr. [last name]:
Woman (marital status unknown)	Ms. [first & last name]	Dear Ms. [last name]:
Woman (single)	Ms. or Miss [first & last name]	Dear Ms. *or* Miss [last name]:
Woman (married)	Ms. or Mrs. [wife's first & last name] or Mrs. [husband's first & last name]	Dear Ms. *or* Mrs. [last name]:
Woman (widowed)	Ms. or Mrs. [wife's first name & last name]	Dear Ms. *or* Mrs. [last name]:
Woman (separated or divorced)	Ms. or Mrs. [first & last name]	Dear Ms. *or* Mrs. [last name]:
Two men (or more)	Mr. [first & last name] and Mr. [first & last name]	Dear Mr. [last name] and Mr. [last name] *or* Messrs. [last name] and [last name]:
Two women (or more)	Ms. [first & last name] and Ms. [first & last name]	Dear Ms. [last name] and Ms. [last name] *or* Mses. [last name] and [last name]:
	or Mrs. [first & last name] and Mrs. [first & last name]	Dear Mrs. [last namc] and Mrs. [last name]: *or* Dear Mesdames [last name] and [last name] *or* Mesdames:
	Miss [first & last name] Mrs. [first & last name]	Dear Miss [last name] and Mrs. [last name]:
One woman and one man	Ms. [first & last name] and Mr. [first & last name]	Dear Ms. [last name] and Mr. [last name]:
Couple (married)	Mr. and Mrs. [husband's first & last name]	Dear Mr. and Mrs. [last name]:
Couple (married with different last names)	[title] [first & last name of husband] [title] [first & last name of wife]	Dear [title] [husband's last name] and [title] [first & last name]:
Couple (marricd professionals with same title and same last name)	[title in plural form] [husband's first name] and [wife's first name]	Dear [title in plural form] [last name]:
Couple (married professionals with different titles and same last name)	[title] [first & last name of husband [title] [first & last name of wife]	Dear [title] and [title] [last name]:

(continued)

When addressing correspondence for other countries, follow the format and information that appear in the company's letterhead.[7] Be especially careful about the format of international correspondence so that everything is as clear as possible.[8] The order and layout of address information vary from country to country, so follow the conventions of the country of the recipient. When you're sending mail from the United States, however, be sure that the name of the destination country appears on the last line of the address in capital letters. Also, use the English version of the country name so that your mail is routed from the United States to the right country. Then, to be sure your mail is routed correctly within the destination country, use the foreign spelling of the city name (using the characters and diacritical marks that would be commonly used in the region). For example, the following address uses *Köln* instead of *Cologne*:

H. R. Veith, Director	Addressee
Eisfieren Glaswerk	Company Name
Blaubachstrabe 13	Street address
Postfach 10 80 07	Post office box
D-5000 Köln I	District, city
GERMANY	Country

TABLE I.1 (Continued)

Person	***In Address***	***In Salutation***
	Professional Titles	
President of a college or university (doctor)	Dr. [first & last name], President	Dear Dr. [last name]:
Dean of a school of college	Dean [first & last name] *or* Dr., Mr., Mrs., *or* Miss [first & last name] Dean of (title)	Dear Dean [last name]: Dear Dr., Mr., Ms., Mrs., *or* Miss [last name]:
Professor	Professor [first & last name]	Dear Professor [last name]:
Physician	[first & last name], M.D.	Dear Dr. [last name]:
Lawyer	Mr., Ms., Mrs., *or* Miss [first & last name]	Dear Mr., Ms., Mrs., *or* Miss [last name]:
Service personnel	[full rank, first & last name, abbreviation of service designation] (add *Retired* if applicable)	Dear [rank] [last name]:
Company or corporation	[name of organization]	Ladies and Gentlemen *or* Gentlemen and Ladies
	Governmental Titles	
President of the United States	The President	Dear Mr. *or* Madam President:
Senator of the United States	Honorable [first & last name]	Dear Senator [last name]:
Cabinet member Postmaster General Attorney General	Honorable [first & last name]	Dear Mr. *or* Madam Secretary: Dear Mr. *or* Madam Postmaster General: Dear Mr. *or* Madam Attorney General:
Mayor	Honorable [first & last name] Mayor of [name of city]	Dear Mayor [last name]:
Judge	The Honorable	Dear Judge [last name]:
	Religious Titles	
Priest	The Reverend [first & last name], [initials of order, if any]	Reverend Sir: (formal) *or* Dear Father [last name]: (informal)
Rabbi	Rabbi Rabbi [first & last name]	Dear Rabbi [last name]:
Minister	The Reverend [first & last name] [title, if any]	Dear Reverend [last name]:

Additional addresses might look similar to the following:

Mr. Toru Hasegawa
7-35 Kitashinagawa
6 Chrome—141 Shinagawa-ku
Tokyo
JAPAN

Cairo
Cleopatra
165 El Corniche Road
Mrs. Ahmed Abbas Zaki
EGYPT

Crédit Lyonnais
c/o Claude Rubinowicz
19, Boulevard des Italiens
75002 Paris
FRANCE

Sr. Ari Matos Cardoso
Superintendent of Human Resources and Personnel
Av. República do Chile, 65
Centro-Rio de Janeiro, RJ
CEP 20035
BRAZIL

Be sure to get organizational titles correct when addressing international correspondence. Job designations vary around the world. In England, for example, a managing director is often what a U.S. company would call its chief executive officer or president, and a British deputy is the equivalent of a vice president. In France, responsibilities are assigned to individuals without regard to title or organizational structure, and in China the title *project manager* has meaning, but the title *sales manager* may not. To make matters worse, businesspeople in some countries sign correspondence without their names typed below. In Germany, for example, the belief is that employees represent the company, so it's inappropriate to emphasize personal names.[9] Use the examples in Table I.2 as guidelines when addressing correspondence to countries outside the United States.

Salutation

In the salutation of your letter, follow the first line of the inside address. That is, if the first line is a person's name, the salutation is *Dear Mr.* or *Ms.* [*Name*]. Base the formality of the salutation on your relationship with the addressee. If in conversation you would say "Mary," your letter's salutation should be *Dear Mary,* followed by a colon. In letters to people you don't know well enough to address personally, include the courtesy title and last name, followed by a colon. Presuming to write *Dear Lewis* instead of *Dear Professor Chang* demonstrates a disrespectful familiarity that a stranger will probably resent. If the first line is a position title such as *Director of Personnel,* then use *Dear Director*; if the addressee is unknown, use a polite description, such as *Dear Alumnus, Dear SPCA Supporter,* or *Dear Voter.* If the first line is plural (a department or company), then use *Ladies and Gentlemen* (look again at Table I.1). When you do not know whether you're writing to an individual or a group (for example, when writing a reference or a letter of recommendation), use *To whom it may concern.*

In the United States some letter writers use a "salutopening" on the salutation line. A salutopening omits *Dear* but includes the first few words of the opening paragraph along with the recipient's name. After this line, the sentence continues a double space below as part of the body of the letter, as in these examples:

Thank you, Mr. Brown,	Salutopening
for your prompt payment of your bill.	Body
Congratulations, Ms. Lake!	Salutopening
Your promotion is well deserved.	Body

Don't overlook an especially important point with personalized salutations: Whether they're informal or formal, make sure names are spelled right. A misspelled name is glaring evidence of carelessness, and it belies the personal interest you're trying to express.

Body

The body of the letter is your message. Almost all letters are single-spaced, with double spacing (one blank line) before and after the salutation or salutopening, between paragraphs, and before the complimentary close. The body may include indented lists, entire paragraphs indented for emphasis, and even subheadings. If it does, all similar elements should be treated in the same way. Your department or company may select a format to use for all letters.

Complimentary Close

The complimentary close begins on the second line below the body of the letter. Alternatives for wording are available, but currently the trend seems to be toward using one-word closes, such as *Sincerely* and *Cordially.* In any case, the complimentary close reflects the relationship between you and the person you're writing to. Avoid cute closes, such as *Yours for bigger profits.* If your audience doesn't know you well, your sense of humor may be misunderstood.

Signature Block

Leave three blank lines for a written signature below the complimentary close, then include the sender's name (unless it appears in the letterhead). The person's title may appear on the same line as the name or on the line below:

Cordially,

Raymond Dunnigan
Director of Personnel

TABLE I.2 International Address and Salutations

Country	Postal Address	Address Elements	Salutations
Argentina	Sr. Juan Pérez Editorial Internacional S.A. Av. Sarmiento 1337, 8° P. C C1035AAB BUENOS AIRES - CF ARGENTINA	S.A. = Sociedad Anónima (corporation) Av. Sarmiento (name of street) 1337 (building number) 8° = 8th. P = Piso (floor) C (room or suite) C1035AAB (postcode + city) CF = Capital Federal (federal capital)	Sr. = Señor (Mr.) Sra. = Señora (Mrs.) Srta. = Señorita (Miss) Don't use given names except with with people you know well.
Australia	Mr. Roger Lewis International Publishing Pty.Ltd. 166 Kent Street, Level 9 GPO Box 3542 SYDNEY NSW 2001 AUSTRALIA	Pty.Ltd. = Proprietory Limited (corp.) 166 (building number) Kent Street (name of street) Level (floor) GPO Box (post office box) city + state (abbrev.) + postcode	Mr. and Mrs. used on first contact. Ms. not common (avoid use). Business is informal—use given name freely.
Austria	Herrn Dipl.-Ing. J.Gerdenitsch International Verlag Ges.m.b.H. Glockengasse 159 1010 WIEN AUSTRIA	Herrn = To Mr. (separate line) Dipl.-Ing. (engineering degree) Ges.m.b.H. (a corporation) Glockengasse (street name) 159 (building number) 1010 (postcode + city) WIEN (Vienna)	Herr (Mr.) Frau (Mrs.) Fräulein (Miss) obsolete in business, so do not use. Given names are almost never used in business.
Brazil	Ilmo. Sr. Gilberto Rabello Ribeiro Editores Internacionais S.A. Rua da Ajuda, 228-6° Andar Caixa Postal 2574 20040-000 RIO DE JANEIRO - RJ BRAZIL	Ilmo. = Ilustrissimo (honorific) Ilma. = Ilustrissima (hon.female) S.A. = Sociedade Anônima (corporation) Rua = street, da Ajuda (street name) 228 (building number) 6° = 6th. Andar (floor) Caixa Postal (P.O. box) 20040-000 (postcode + city) - RJ (state abbrev.)	Sr. = Senhor (Mr.) Sra. = Senhora (Mrs.) Srta. = Senhorita (Miss) Family name at end, e.g., Senhor Ribeiro (Rabello is mother's family—as in Portugal) Given names readily used in business.
China	Xia Zhiyi International Publishing Ltd. 14 Jianguolu Chaoyangqu BEIJING 100025 CHINA	Ltd. (limited liability corporation) 14 (building number) Jianguolu (street name), lu (street) Chaoyangqu (district name) (city + postcode)	Family name (single syllable) first. Given name (2 syllables) second, sometimes reversed. Use Mr. or Ms. at all times (Mr. Xia).
France	Monsieur LEFÈVRE Alain Éditions Internationales S.A. Siège Social Immeuble Le Bonaparte 64-68, av. Galliéni B.P. 154 75942 PARIS CEDEX 19 FRANCE	S.A. = Société Anonyme Siège Social (head office) Immeuble (building + name) 64-68 (building occupies 64, 66, 68) av. = avenue (no initial capital) B.P. = Boîte Postale (P.O. box) 75942 (postcode) CEDEX (postcode for P.O. box)	Monsieur (Mr.) Madame (Mrs.) Mademoiselle (Miss) Best not to abbreviate. Family name is sometimes in all caps with given name following.
Germany	Herrn Gerhardt Schneider International Verlag GmbH Schillerstraße 159 44147 DORTMUND GERMANY	Herrn = To Herr (on a separate line) GmbH (inc.—incorporated) -straße (street—'ß' often written 'ss') 159 (building number) 44147 (postcode + city)	Herr (Mr.) Frau (Mrs.) Fräulein (Miss) obsolete in business. Business is formal: (1) do not use given names unless invited, and (2) use academic titles precisely.

(continued)

TABLE I.2 (Continued)

Country	*Postal Address*	*Address Elements*	*Salutations*
India	Sr. Shyam Lal Gupta International Publishing (Pvt.) Ltd. 1820 Rehaja Centre 214, Darussalam Road Andheri East BOMBAY - 400049 INDIA	(Pvt.) (privately owned) Ltd. (limited liability corporation) 1820 (possibly office #20 on 18th floor) Rehaja Centre (building name) 214 (building number) Andheri East (suburb name) (city + *hyphen* + postcode)	Shri (Mr.), Shrimati (Mrs.) but English is common business language, so use Mr., Mrs., Miss. Given names are used only by family and close friends.
Italy	Egr. Sig. Giacomo Mariotti Edizioni Internazionali S.p.A. Via Terenzio, 21 20138 MILANO ITALY	Egr. = Egregio (honorific) Sig. = Signor (not nec. a separate line) S.p.A. = Società per Azioni (corp.) Via (street) 21 (building number) 20138 (postcode + city)	Sig. = Signore (Mr.) Sig.ra = Signora (Mrs.) Sig.a (Ms) Women in business are addressed as Signora. Use given name only when invited.
Japan	Mr. Taro Tanaka Kokusai Shuppan K.K. 10-23, 5-chome, Minamiazabu Minato-ku TOKYO 106 JAPAN	K.K. = Kabushiki Kaisha (corporation) 10 (lot number) 23 (building number) 5-chome (area #5) Minamiazabu (neighborhood name) Minato-ku (city district) (city + postcode)	Given names not used in business. Use family name + job title. Or use family name + "-san" (Tanaka-san) or more respectfully, add "-sama" or "-dono."
Korea	Mr. KIM Chang-ik International Publishers Ltd. Room 206, Korea Building 33-4 Nonhyon-dong Kangnam-ku SEOUL 135-010 KOREA	English company names common Ltd. (a corporation) 206 (office number inside the building) 33-4 (area 4 of subdivision 33) -dong (city neighborhood name) -ku (subdivision of city) (city + postcode)	Family name is normally first but sometimes placed after given name. A two-part name is the given name. Use Mr. or Mrs in letters, but use job title in speech.
Mexico	Sr. Francisco Pérez Martínez Editores Internacionales S.A. Independencia No.322 Col. Juárez 06050 MEXICO D.F.	S.A. = Sociedad Anónima (corporation) Independencia (street name) No. = Número (number) 322 (building number) Col. = Colonia (city district) Juárez (locality name) 06050 (postcode + city) D.F. = Distrito Federal(federal capital)	Sr. = Señor (Mr.) Sra. = Señora (Mrs.) Srta. = Señorita (Miss) Family name in middle: e.g., Sr. Pérez (Martínez is mother's family). Given names are used in business.
South Africa	Mr. Mandla Ntuli International Publishing (Pty.)Ltd. Private Bag X2581 JOHANNESBURG 2000 SOUTH AFRICA	Pty. = Proprietory (privately owned) Ltd. (a corporation) Private Bag (P.O. Box) (city + postcode) or (postcode + city)	Mnr = Meneer (Mr.) Mev. = Mevrou (Mrs.) Mejuffrou (Miss) is not used in business. Business is becoming less formal, so the use of given names is possible.
United Kingdom	Mr. N. J. Lancaster International Publishing Ltd. Kingsbury House 12 Kingsbury Road EDGEWARE Middlesex HA8 9XG ENGLAND	N. J. (initials of given names) Ltd. (limited liability corporation) Kingsbury House (building name) 12 (building number) Kingsbury Road (name of street/road) EDGEWARE (city—all caps) Middlesex (county—not all caps) HA8 9XG (postcode—after 6 spaces, or on a separate line)	Mr. and Ms. used mostly. Mrs. and Miss sometimes used in North and by older women. Given names—called Christian names—are used in business after some time. Wait to be invited.

FIGURE I.2 Additional Letter Parts

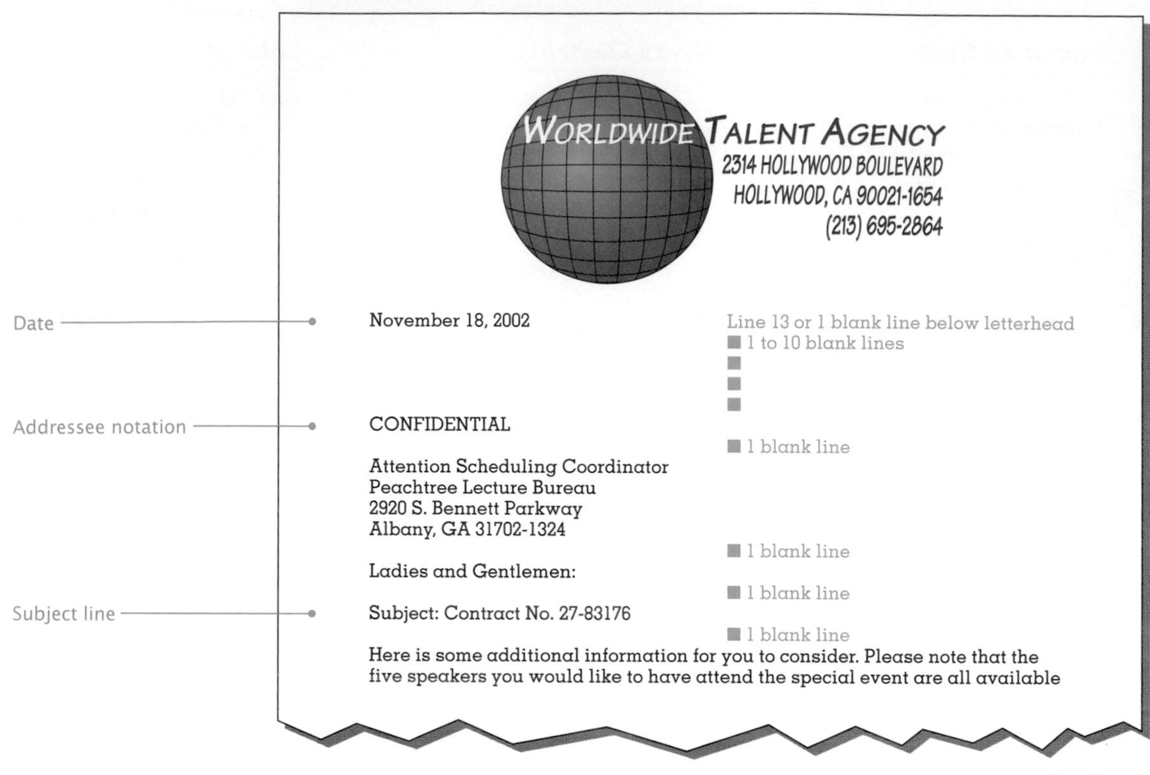

(continued)

Your letterhead indicates that you're representing your company. However, if your letter is on plain paper or runs to a second page, you may want to emphasize that you're speaking legally for the company. The accepted way of doing so is to place the company's name in capital letters a double space below the complimentary close and then include the sender's name and title four lines below that:

Sincerely,

WENTWORTH INDUSTRIES

(Mrs.) Helen B. Taylor
President

If your name could be taken for either a man's or a woman's, a courtesy title indicating gender should be included, with or without parentheses. Also, women who prefer a particular courtesy title should include it:

Mrs. Nancy Winters
(Miss) Juana Flores
Ms. Pat Li
(Mr.) Jamie Saunders

Additional Letter Parts

Letters vary greatly in subject matter and thus in the identifying information they need and the format they adopt. The following elements may be used in any combination, depending on the requirements of the particular letter, but generally in this order:

1. Addressee notation
2. Attention line
3. Subject line
4. Second-page heading
5. Company name
6. Reference initials
7. Enclosure notation
8. Copy notation
9. Mailing notation
10. Postscript

The letter in Figure I.2 shows how these additional parts should be arranged.

Addressee Notation

Letters that have a restricted readership or that must be handled in a special way should include such addressee notations as *Personal, Confidential,* or *Please Forward.* This sort of notation appears a double space above the inside address, in all capital letters.

Attention Line

Although an attention line is not commonly used today, you may find it useful if you know only the last name of the person you're writing to. An attention line can also be

FIGURE I.2 (Continued)

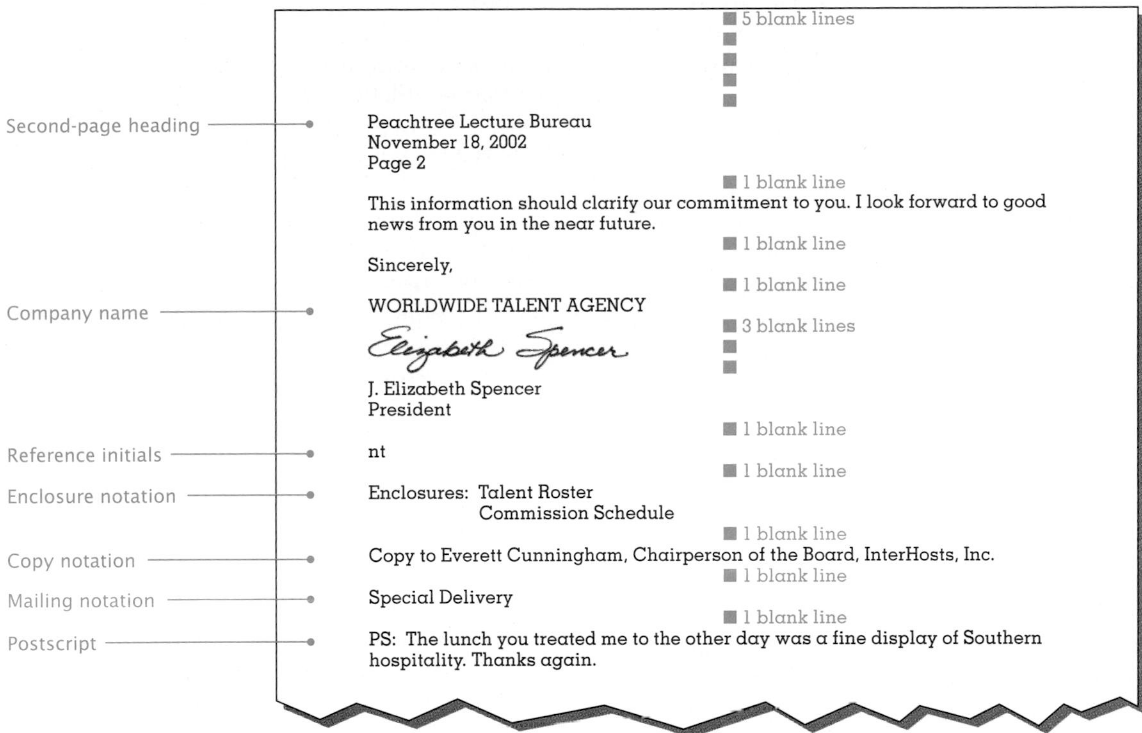

Peachtree Lecture Bureau
November 18, 2002
Page 2

This information should clarify our commitment to you. I look forward to good news from you in the near future.

Sincerely,

WORLDWIDE TALENT AGENCY

J. Elizabeth Spencer
President

nt

Enclosures: Talent Roster
Commission Schedule

Copy to Everett Cunningham, Chairperson of the Board, InterHosts, Inc.

Special Delivery

PS: The lunch you treated me to the other day was a fine display of Southern hospitality. Thanks again.

used to direct a letter to a position title or department. An attention line may take any of the following forms or variants of them: *Attention Dr. McHenry*, *Attention Director of Marketing*, or *Attention Marketing Department*. You may place the attention line on the first line and use the company name as the second line of the inside address.[10] The address on the envelope should always match the style of the inside address.

Subject Line

The subject line lets the recipient know at a glance what the letter is about; it also indicates where to file the letter for future reference. It usually appears below the salutation—against the left margin, indented as the paragraphs in the body of the letter, or centered on the line. Sometimes the subject line is placed above the salutation or at the very top of the page. The subject line may take a variety of forms, including the following:

Subject: RainMaster Sprinklers
About your February 2, 2002, order
FALL 1998 SALES MEETING
Reference Order No. 27920

Sometimes the subject line (or the last line of a long subject "line") is underscored. Some writers omit the word *Subject* and put the other information all in capitals to distinguish it from the other letter parts. Organizations such as insurance and financial institutions, attorneys, and government offices may use the words *Re:* or *In re:* (meaning "concerning" or "in the matter of") rather than using the word *Subject.*

Second-Page Heading

If the letter is long and an additional page is required, use a second-page heading. Some companies have second-page letterhead, with the company name and address on one line and in a smaller typeface than on the regular letterhead. In any case, the second-page heading bears the name that appears in the first line of the inside address (the person or organization receiving the letter), the page number, and the date of the letter; you can also include a reference number. All the following are acceptable:

Ms. Melissa Baker
May 10, 1998
Page 2

Ms. Melissa Baker, May 10, 2002, Page 2

Ms. Melissa Baker -2- May 10, 2002

Triple-space (leave two blank lines) between the second-page heading and the body. If a paragraph must be continued on a second page, make sure at least two lines of that paragraph appear on the first page and on the second page. Also, the closing lines of a business letter must never appear alone on a continued page. At least two lines of the body must precede the complimentary close or signature lines. And finally, don't hyphenate the last word on a page.

Company Name

If you include the company's name in the signature block, put it all in capital letters a double space below the complimentary close. You usually include the company's name in the signature block only when the writer is serving as the company's official spokesperson or when letterhead has not been used.

Reference Initials

Because it can happen in business that one person may dictate or write a letter and another person may produce it, reference initials are used to show who helped prepare the letter. Reference initials appear at the left margin, a double space below the last line of the signature block. When the writer's name has been included in the signature block, only the preparer's initials are necessary. If only the department appears in the signature block, both sets of initials should appear, usually in one of the following forms:

RSR/sm
RSR:sm
RSR:SM

The first set of initials is the writer's; the second set is the preparer's.

Sometimes the writer and the signer of a letter are different people. In that case, at least the file copy of a letter should bear both their initials as well as those of the typist: *JFS/RSR/sm* (signer, writer, preparer). When businesspeople keyboard their own letters, reference initials are not included, so such initials are becoming more and more rare.

Enclosure Notation

Enclosure notations also appear at the bottom of a letter, one or two lines below the reference initials. Some common forms:

Enclosure
Enclosures (2)
Enclosures: Résumé
Photograph
Attachment

Copy Notation

Copy notations may follow reference initials or enclosure notations. They indicate who's receiving a *courtesy copy (cc)*. Some companies indicate copies made on a photocopier *(pc)*, or they simply use *copy (c)*. Recipients are listed in order of rank or (rank being equal) in alphabetical order. Among the forms used:

cc: David Wentworth
pc: Martha Littlefield
Copy to Hans Vogel
c: Joseph Martinez

In addition to the name of an individual, copy notations may include any combination of that person's courtesy title, position, department, company, and complete address, along with notations about any enclosures being sent with the copies.

On occasion, copies are sent to benefit readers other than the person who receives the original letter. In that case, place the notation *bc, bcc,* or *bpc* (for "blind copy," "blind courtesy copy," or "blind photocopy") with the name where the copy notation would normally appear—but only on the copy, not on the original.

Mailing Notation

You may place a mailing notation (such as *Special Delivery* or *Registered Mail*) at the bottom of the letter, after reference initials or enclosure notations (whichever one is last) and before copy notations. Or you may place it at the top of the letter, either above the inside address on the left-hand side or just below the date on the right-hand side. For greater visibility, mailing notations may appear in capital letters.

Postscript

Letters may also bear postscripts: afterthoughts to the letter, messages that require emphasis, or personal notes. The postscript is usually the last thing on any letter and may be preceded by *P.S., PS., PS:,* or nothing at all. A second afterthought would be designated *P.P.S.,* meaning "post postscript."

Postscripts usually indicate poor planning, so generally avoid them. However, they're commonly used in sales letters, not as an afterthought but as a punch line to remind the reader of a benefit for taking advantage of the offer.

LETTER FORMATS

Although the basic letter parts have remained the same for centuries, ways of arranging them do change. Sometimes a company adopts a certain format as its policy; sometimes the individual letter writer or preparer is allowed to choose the format most appropriate for a given letter or to settle on a personal preference. In the United States, three major letter formats are commonly used:

- **Block format.** Each letter part begins at the left margin. The main advantage is quick and efficient preparation (see Figure I.3).

FIGURE I.3 Block Letter Format

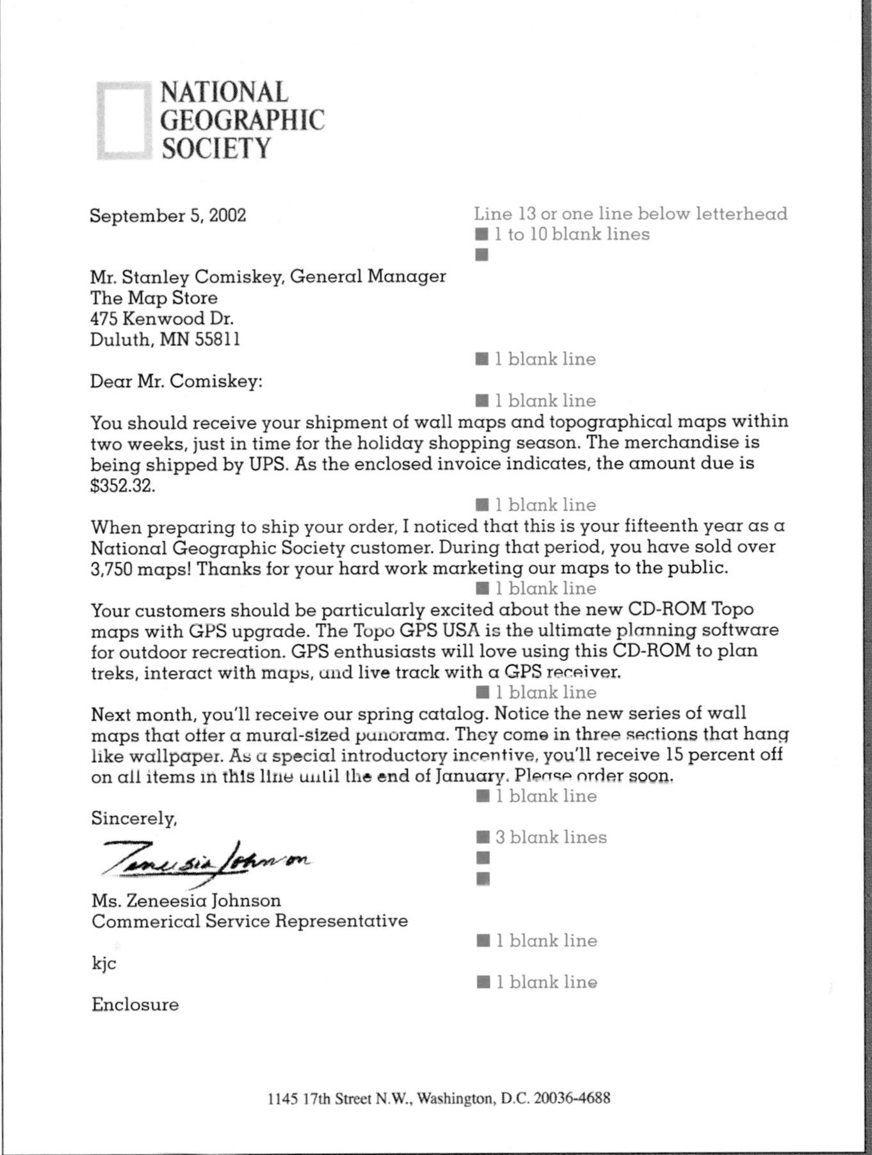

NATIONAL
GEOGRAPHIC
SOCIETY

September 5, 2002 — Line 13 or one line below letterhead
■ 1 to 10 blank lines
■

Mr. Stanley Comiskey, General Manager
The Map Store
475 Kenwood Dr.
Duluth, MN 55811
■ 1 blank line

Dear Mr. Comiskey:
■ 1 blank line

You should receive your shipment of wall maps and topographical maps within two weeks, just in time for the holiday shopping season. The merchandise is being shipped by UPS. As the enclosed invoice indicates, the amount due is $352.32.
■ 1 blank line

When preparing to ship your order, I noticed that this is your fifteenth year as a National Geographic Society customer. During that period, you have sold over 3,750 maps! Thanks for your hard work marketing our maps to the public.
■ 1 blank line

Your customers should be particularly excited about the new CD-ROM Topo maps with GPS upgrade. The Topo GPS USA is the ultimate planning software for outdoor recreation. GPS enthusiasts will love using this CD-ROM to plan treks, interact with maps, and live track with a GPS receiver.
■ 1 blank line

Next month, you'll receive our spring catalog. Notice the new series of wall maps that offer a mural-sized panorama. They come in three sections that hang like wallpaper. As a special introductory incentive, you'll receive 15 percent off on all items in this line until the end of January. Please order soon.
■ 1 blank line

Sincerely,
■ 3 blank lines
■
■

Ms. Zeneesia Johnson
Commerical Service Representative
■ 1 blank line

kjc
■ 1 blank line

Enclosure

1145 17th Street N.W., Washington, D.C. 20036-4688

- **Modified block format.** Same as block format, except the date, complimentary close, and signature block start near the center of the page (see Figure I.4). The modified block format does permit indentions as an option. This format mixes preparation speed with traditional placement of some letter parts. It also looks more balanced on the page than the block format does.
- **Simplified format.** Instead of using a salutation, this format often works the audience's name into the first line or two of the body and often includes a subject line in capital letters (see Figure I.5). It also omits the complimentary close, so you sign your name after the body of the letter, followed by the printed (or typewritten) name (customarily in all capital letters). The advantages include convenience when you don't know your audience's name. However, some people object to this format because it seems mechanical and impersonal (a drawback that may be overcome with a warm writing style). In this format, the elimination of certain letter parts changes some of the spacing between lines.

These formats differ in the way paragraphs are indented, in the way letter parts are placed, and in some punctuation. However, the elements are always separated by at least one blank line, and the printed (or typewritten) name is always separated from the line above by at least three blank lines to allow space for a signature. If paragraphs are indented, the indention is normally five spaces.

FIGURE I.4 Modified Block Letter

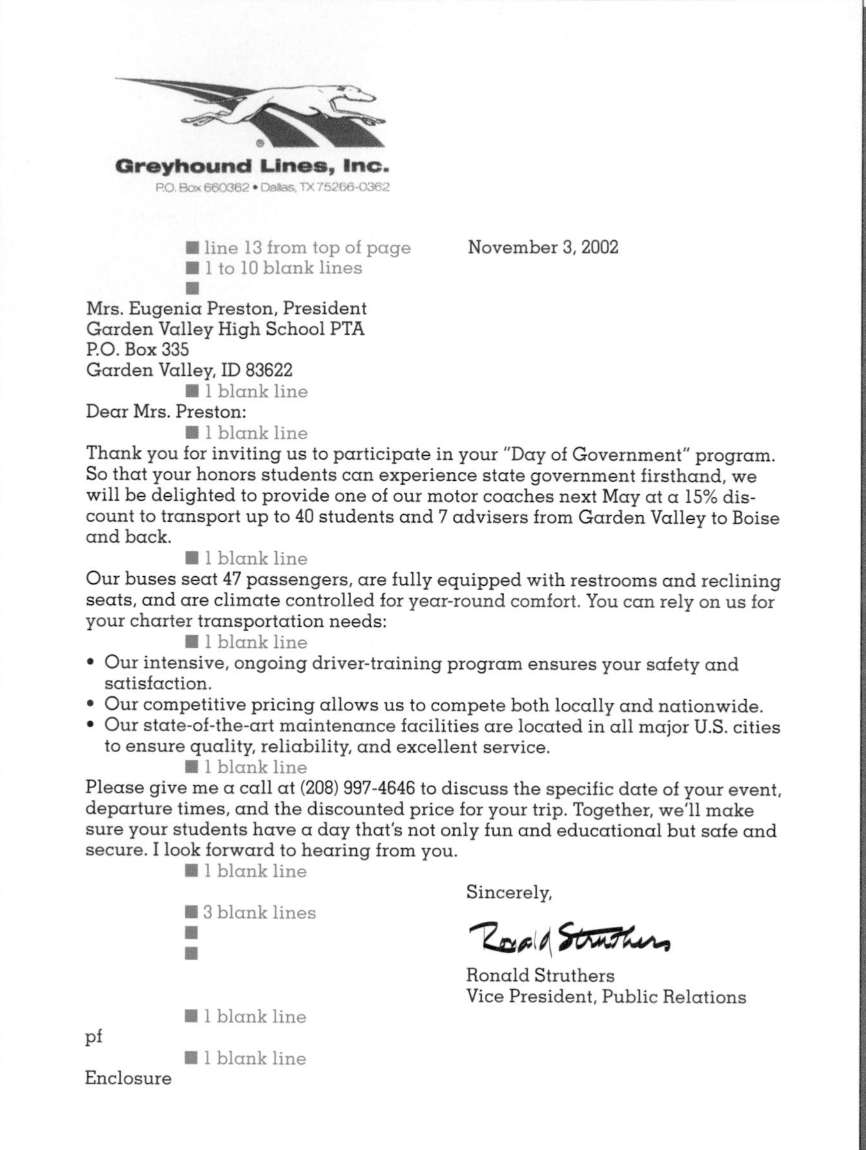

November 3, 2002

Mrs. Eugenia Preston, President
Garden Valley High School PTA
P.O. Box 335
Garden Valley, ID 83622

Dear Mrs. Preston:

Thank you for inviting us to participate in your "Day of Government" program. So that your honors students can experience state government firsthand, we will be delighted to provide one of our motor coaches next May at a 15% discount to transport up to 40 students and 7 advisers from Garden Valley to Boise and back.

Our buses seat 47 passengers, are fully equipped with restrooms and reclining seats, and are climate controlled for year-round comfort. You can rely on us for your charter transportation needs:

- Our intensive, ongoing driver-training program ensures your safety and satisfaction.
- Our competitive pricing allows us to compete both locally and nationwide.
- Our state-of-the-art maintenance facilities are located in all major U.S. cities to ensure quality, reliability, and excellent service.

Please give me a call at (208) 997-4646 to discuss the specific date of your event, departure times, and the discounted price for your trip. Together, we'll make sure your students have a day that's not only fun and educational but safe and secure. I look forward to hearing from you.

Sincerely,

Ronald Struthers
Vice President, Public Relations

pf

Enclosure

The most common formats for intercultural business letters are the block style and the modified block style. Use either the U.S. or the European format for dates. For the salutation, use *Dear [Title/Last name]*. Close the letter with *Sincerely* or *Cordially,* and sign it.

In addition to these three letter formats, letters may also be classified according to the style of punctuation they use. *Standard,* or *mixed, punctuation* uses a colon after the salutation (a comma if the letter is social or personal) and a comma after the complimentary close. *Open punctuation* uses no colon or comma after the salutation or the complimentary close. Although the most popular style in business communication is mixed punctuation, either style of punctuation may be used with block or modified block letter formats. Because the simplified letter format has no salutation or complimentary close, the style of punctuation is irrelevant.

ENVELOPES

The quality of the envelope is just as important for first impressions as the quality of the stationery. In fact, letterhead and envelopes should be of the same paper stock, have the same color ink, and be imprinted with the same address and logo. Most envelopes used by U.S. businesses are No. 10 envelopes ($9^1/2$ inches long), which are sized to contain an $8^1/2$-by-11-inch piece of paper folded in thirds. Some occasions call for a smaller, No. $6^3/4$, envelope or for envelopes proportioned to fit special stationery. Figure I.6 shows the two most common sizes.

FIGURE I.5 Simplified Letter Format

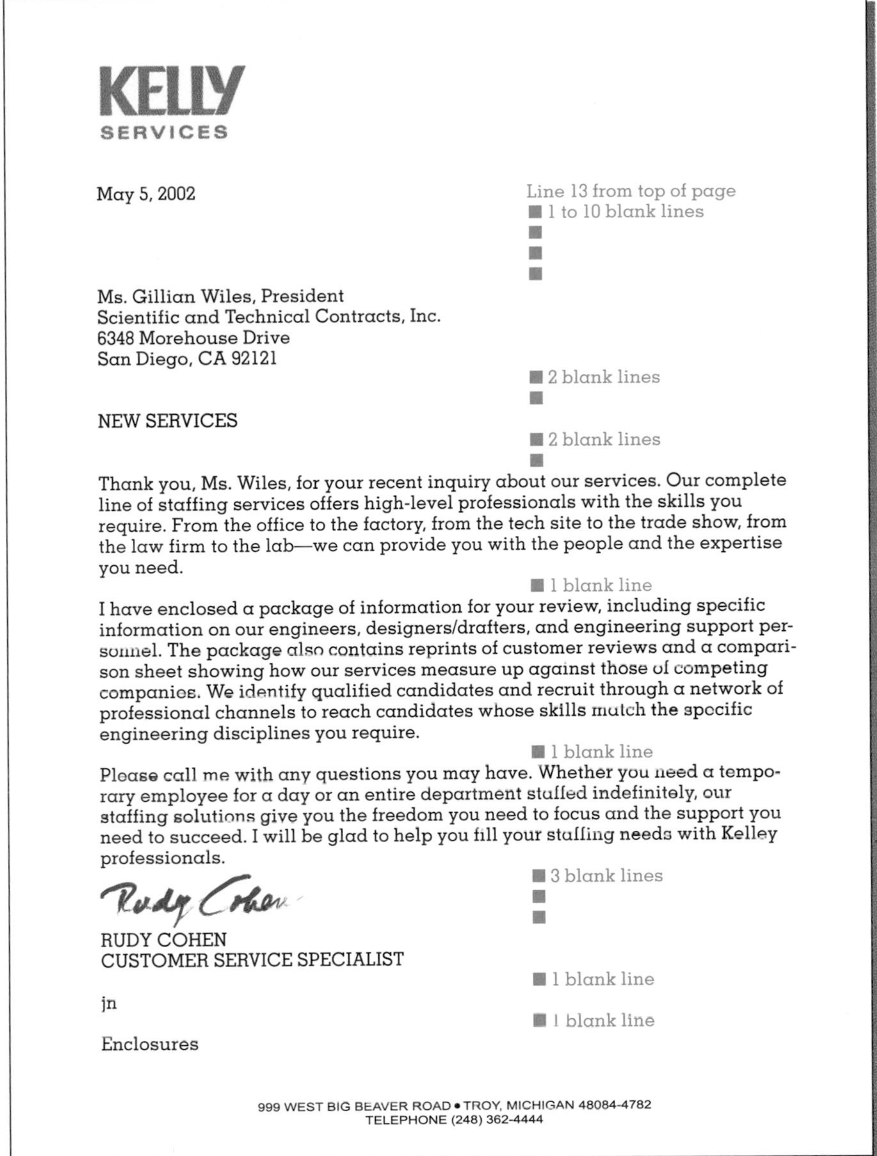

KELLY SERVICES

May 5, 2002

Ms. Gillian Wiles, President
Scientific and Technical Contracts, Inc.
6348 Morehouse Drive
San Diego, CA 92121

NEW SERVICES

Thank you, Ms. Wiles, for your recent inquiry about our services. Our complete line of staffing services offers high-level professionals with the skills you require. From the office to the factory, from the tech site to the trade show, from the law firm to the lab—we can provide you with the people and the expertise you need.

I have enclosed a package of information for your review, including specific information on our engineers, designers/drafters, and engineering support personnel. The package also contains reprints of customer reviews and a comparison sheet showing how our services measure up against those of competing companies. We identify qualified candidates and recruit through a network of professional channels to reach candidates whose skills match the specific engineering disciplines you require.

Please call me with any questions you may have. Whether you need a temporary employee for a day or an entire department staffed indefinitely, our staffing solutions give you the freedom you need to focus and the support you need to succeed. I will be glad to help you fill your staffing needs with Kelley professionals.

RUDY COHEN
CUSTOMER SERVICE SPECIALIST

jn

Enclosures

999 WEST BIG BEAVER ROAD • TROY, MICHIGAN 48084-4782
TELEPHONE (248) 362-4444

Addressing the Envelope

No matter what size the envelope, the address is always single-spaced and in block form—that is, with all lines aligned on the left. The address on the envelope is in the same style as the inside address and presents the same information. The order to follow is from the smallest division to the largest:

1. Name and title of recipient
2. Name of department or subgroup
3. Name of organization
4. Name of building
5. Street address and suite number, or post office box number
6. City, state, or province, and ZIP code or Postal Code
7. Name of country (if the letter is being sent abroad)

Because the U.S. Postal Service uses optical scanners to sort mail, envelopes for quantity mailings, in particular, should be addressed in the prescribed format. As in the mailing address on the No. 10 envelope in Figure I.6, everything is in capital letters, no punctuation is included, and all mailing instructions of interest to the post office are placed above the address area. Canada Post requires a similar format, except that only the city is all in capitals and the Postal Code is placed on the line below the name of the city. The post office scanners read addresses from the bottom up, so if a letter is to be sent to a post office box rather than to a street address, the street address

FIGURE I.6 Prescribed Envelope Format

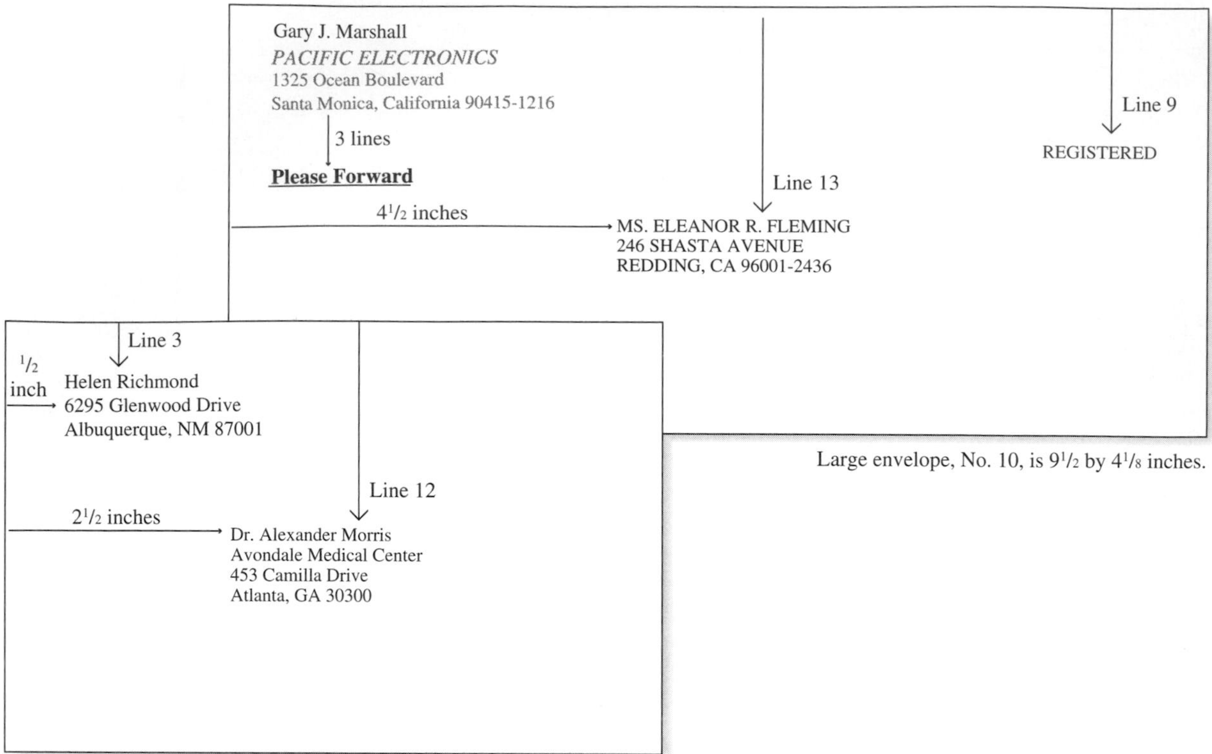

Large envelope, No. 10, is 9½ by 4⅛ inches.

Small envelope, No. 6¾, is 6½ by 3⅝ inches.

should appear on the line above the box number. Figure I.6 also shows the proper spacing for addresses and return addresses.

The U.S. Postal Service and the Canada Post Corporation have published lists of two-letter mailing abbreviations for states, provinces, and territories (see Table I.3), to be used without periods or commas. Nevertheless, some executives prefer that state and province names be spelled out in full and that a comma be used to separate the city and state or province names. Thus the use of a comma between the name of the city and the state or province name is an unresolved issue. Most commonly, the comma is included; sometimes, however, the comma is eliminated to conform with post office standards.

Quantity mailings follow post office requirements. For letters that aren't mailed in quantity, a reasonable compromise is to use traditional punctuation and uppercase and lowercase letters for names and street addresses but two-letter state or province abbreviations, as shown here:

Mr. Kevin Kennedy
2107 E. Packer Drive
Amarillo, TX 79108

For all out-of-office correspondence, use the ZIP codes and Postal Codes that have been assigned to speed mail delivery. The U.S. Postal Service has divided the United States and its territories into 10 zones, each represented by a digit from 0 to 9; this digit comes first in the ZIP code. The second and third digits represent smaller geographical areas within a state, and the last two digits identify a "local delivery area." Canadian Postal Codes are alphanumeric, with a three-character "area code" and a three-character "local code" separated by a single space (K2P 5A5). ZIP codes and Postal Codes should be separated from state and province names by one space. As an alternative, a Canadian Postal Code may be put on the bottom line of the address all by itself.

The U.S. Postal Service has added ZIP + 4 codes, which add a hyphen and four more numbers to the standard ZIP codes. The first two of the new numbers may identify an area as small as a single large building, and the last two digits may identify one floor in a large building or even a specific department of an organization. The ZIP + 4 codes are especially useful for business correspondence. The Canada Post Corporation achieves the same result with special postal codes assigned to buildings and organizations that receive a large volume of mail.

Folding to Fit

The way a letter is folded also contributes to the recipient's overall impression of your organization's professionalism. When sending a standard-size piece of paper in a No. 10 envelope, fold it in thirds, with the bottom folded up first and the top folded down over it (see Figure I.7);

TABLE I.3 Two-Letter Mailing Abbreviations for the United States and Canada

State/ Territory/ Province	Abbreviation	State/ Territory/ Province	Abbreviation	State/ Territory/ Province	Abbreviation
UNITED STATES					
Alabama	AL	Michigan	MI	Utah	UT
Alaska	AK	Minnesota	MN	Vermont	VT
Arizona	AZ	Mississippi	MS	Virginia	VA
Arkansas	AR	Missouri	MO	Virgin Islands	VI
American Samoa	AS	Montana	MT	Washington	WA
California	CA	Nebraska	NE	West Virginia	WV
Canal Zone	CZ	Nevada	NV	Wisconsin	WI
Colorado	CO	New Hampshire	NH	Wyoming	WY
Connecticut	CT	New Jersey	NJ		
Delaware	DE	New Mexico	NM	CANADA	
District of Columbia	DC	New York	NY	Alberta	AB
Florida	FL	North Carolina	NC	British Columbia	BC
Georgia	GA	North Dakota	ND	Labrador	LB
Guam	GU	Northern Mariana	CM	Manitoba	MB
Hawaii	HI	Ohio	OH	New Brunswick	NB
Idaho	ID	Oklahoma	OK	Newfoundland	NF
Illinois	IL	Oregon	OR	Northwest Territories	NT
Indiana	IN	Pennsylvania	PA	Nova Scotia	NS
Iowa	IA	Puerto Rico	PR	Ontario	ON
Kansas	KS	Rhode Island	RI	Prince Edward Island	PE
Kentucky	KY	South Carolina	SC	Quebec	PQ
Louisiana	LA	South Dakota	SD	Saskatchewan	SK
Maine	ME	Tennessee	TN	Yukon Territory	YT
Maryland	MD	Trust Territories	TT		
Massachusetts	MA	Texas	TX		

FIGURE I.7 Letter Folds for Standard-Size Letterhead

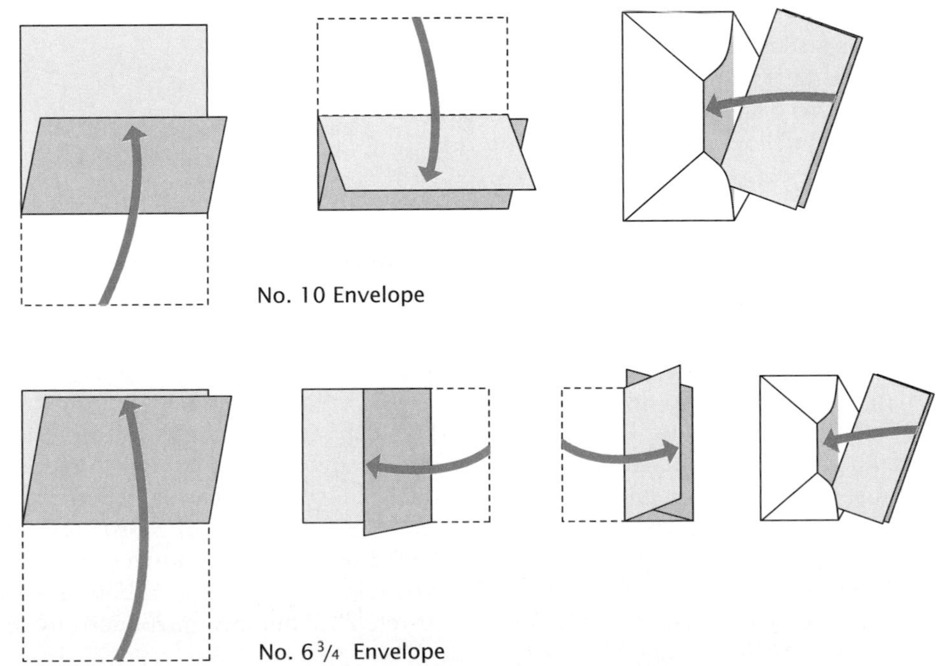

the open end should be at the top of the envelope and facing out. Fit smaller stationery neatly into the appropriate envelope simply by folding it in half or in thirds. When sending a standard-size letterhead in a No. 6$^{3}/_{4}$ envelope, fold it in half from top to bottom and then in thirds from side to side.

International Mail

When sending mail internationally, remember that postal service differs from country to country. For example, street addresses are uncommon in India, and the mail there is unreliable.[11] It's usually a good idea to send international correspondence by airmail and to ask that responses be sent that way as well. Also, remember to check the postage; rates for sending mail to most other countries aren't the same as the rates for sending mail within your own country.

Three main categories of international mail are the following:

- **LC mail.** An abbreviation of the French *Lettres et Cartes* ("letters and cards"), this category consists of letters, letter packages, aerograms, and postcards.
- **AO mail.** An abbreviation of the French *Autres Objets* ("other articles"), this category includes regular printed matter, books and sheet music, matter for the blind, small packets, and publishers' periodicals (second class).
- **CP mail.** An abbreviation of the French *Colis Postaux* ("parcel post"), this category resembles fourth-class mail, including packages of merchandise or any other articles not required to be mailed at letter postage rates.

The U.S. Postal Service also offers Express Mail International Service (EMS), a high-speed mail service to many countries; International Priority Airmail (IPA), an international service that's as fast as or faster than regular airmail service; International Surface Air Lift (ISAL), a service providing quicker delivery and lower cost for all kinds of printed matter; Bulk Letter Service to Canada, an economical airmail service for letters weighing 1 ounce or less; VALUEPOST/CANADA, a reduced postage rate for bulk mailings; International Electronic Post (INTELPOST), a service offering same- or next-day delivery of fax documents; International Postal Money Orders, a service for transferring funds to other countries; and several optional special services.

To prepare your mail for international delivery, follow the instructions in the U.S. Postal Service Publication 51, *International Postal Rates and Fees.* Be sure to note instructions for the address, return address, and size limits. Envelopes and wrappers must be clearly marked to show their classification (letter, small packet, printed matter, airmail). All registered letters, letter packages, and parcel post packages must be securely sealed. Printed matter may be sealed only if postage is paid by permit imprint, postage meter, precanceled stamps, or second-class imprint. Otherwise, prepare contents so that they're protected but in such a way that they won't hinder inspection. Finally, because international mail is subject to customs examination in the country of destination, the contents and value of packages and heavy envelopes must be declared on special forms.

MEMOS

Interoffice memos aren't distributed outside the organization, so they may not need the best-quality paper. However, they still convey important information, so clarity, careful arrangement, and neatness are important. Like those for letters, the guidelines for formatting memos help recipients understand at a glance what they've received and from whom.

Many organizations have memo forms preprinted, with labeled spaces for the recipient's name (or sometimes a checklist of all departments in an organization or all persons in a department), the sender's name, the date, and the subject (see Figure I.8). If such forms don't exist, you can use a memo template (which comes with word-processing software and provides margin settings, headings, and special formats), or you can use plain paper.

When preparing a memo, include a title such as *MEMO* or *INTEROFFICE CORRESPONDENCE* (all in capitals) centered at the top of the page or aligned with the left margin. Also at the top, include the words *To, From, Date,* and *Subject*—followed by the appropriate information—with a blank line between, as shown here:

MEMO

TO:

DATE:

FROM:

SUBJECT:

Sometimes the heading is organized like this:

MEMO

TO:	DATE:
FROM:	SUBJECT:

You can arrange these four pieces of information in almost any order. The date sometimes appears without the heading *Date.* The subject may be presented with the letters *Re:* (in place of *SUBJECT:*) or may even be presented without any heading (but put it in capital letters so that it stands out clearly). You may want to include a file or reference number, introduced by the word *File.*

FIGURE I.8 Preprinted Memo Form

MEMO

TO:			
DEPT:		FROM:	
DATE:		TELEPHONE:	
SUBJECT:		For your ☐ APPROVAL ☐ INFORMATION ☐ COMMENT	

The following guidelines will help you effectively format specific memo elements:

- **Addressees.** If you send a memo to a long list of people, include the notation *See distribution list* or *See below* in the *To* position at the top; then list the names at the end of the memo. Arranging such a list alphabetically is usually the most diplomatic course, although high-ranking officials may deserve more prominent placement. You can also address memos to groups of people—*All Sales Representatives, Production Group, Assistant Vice Presidents.*
- **Courtesy titles.** You don't need to use courtesy titles anywhere in a memo; first initials and last names, first names, or even initials alone are often sufficient. As a general rule, however, use a courtesy title if you would use one in face-to-face encounters with the person.
- **Subject line.** The subject line of a memo helps busy colleagues quickly find out what your memo is about. Although the subject "line" may overflow onto a second line, it's most helpful when it's short (but still informative).
- **Body.** Start the body of the memo on the second or third line below the heading. Like the body of a letter, it's usually single-spaced with blank lines between paragraphs. Indenting paragraphs is optional. Handle lists, important passages, and subheadings as you do in letters. If the memo is very short, you may double-space it.
- **Second page.** If the memo carries over to a second page, head the second page just as you head the second page of a letter.
- **Writer's initials.** Unlike a letter, a memo doesn't require a complimentary close or a signature, because your name is already prominent at the top. However, you may initial the memo—either beside the name appearing at the top of the memo or at the bottom of the memo—or you may even sign your name at the bottom, particularly if the memo deals with money or confidential matters.
- **Other elements.** Treat elements such as reference initials, enclosure notations, and copy notations just as you would in a letter.

Memos may be delivered by hand, by the post office (when the recipient doesn't work at the same location as the memo writer), or through interoffice mail. Interoffice mail may require the use of special reusable envelopes that have spaces for the recipient's name and department or room number; the name of the previous recipient is simply crossed out. If a regular envelope is used, the words *Interoffice Mail* appear where the stamp normally goes, so that it won't accidentally be stamped and mailed with the rest of the office correspondence.

Informal, routine, or brief reports for distribution within a company are often presented in memo form (see Chapter 13). Don't include report parts such as a table of contents and appendixes, but write the body of the memo report just as carefully as you'd write a formal report.

E-MAIL

Because e-mail messages can act both as memos (carrying information within your company) and as letters (carrying information outside your company and around the world), their format depends on your audience and purpose. You may choose to have your e-mail resemble a formal letter or a detailed report, or you may decide to keep things as simple as an interoffice memo. A modified memo format is appropriate for most e-mail messages.[12] All e-mail programs include two major elements: the header and the body (see Figure I.9).

Header

The e-mail header depends on the particular program you use. Some programs even allow you to choose between a shorter and a longer version. However, most headers contain similar information.

The *To:* line contains your audience's e-mail address. The most common e-mail addresses are Internet addresses, like the following:

- NMAA.BETSY@C.SI.EDU [Smithsonian Institute's National Museum of American Art]
- webwsj@dowjones.com [*Wall Street Journal*'s homepage]

FIGURE I.9 A Typical E-Mail Message

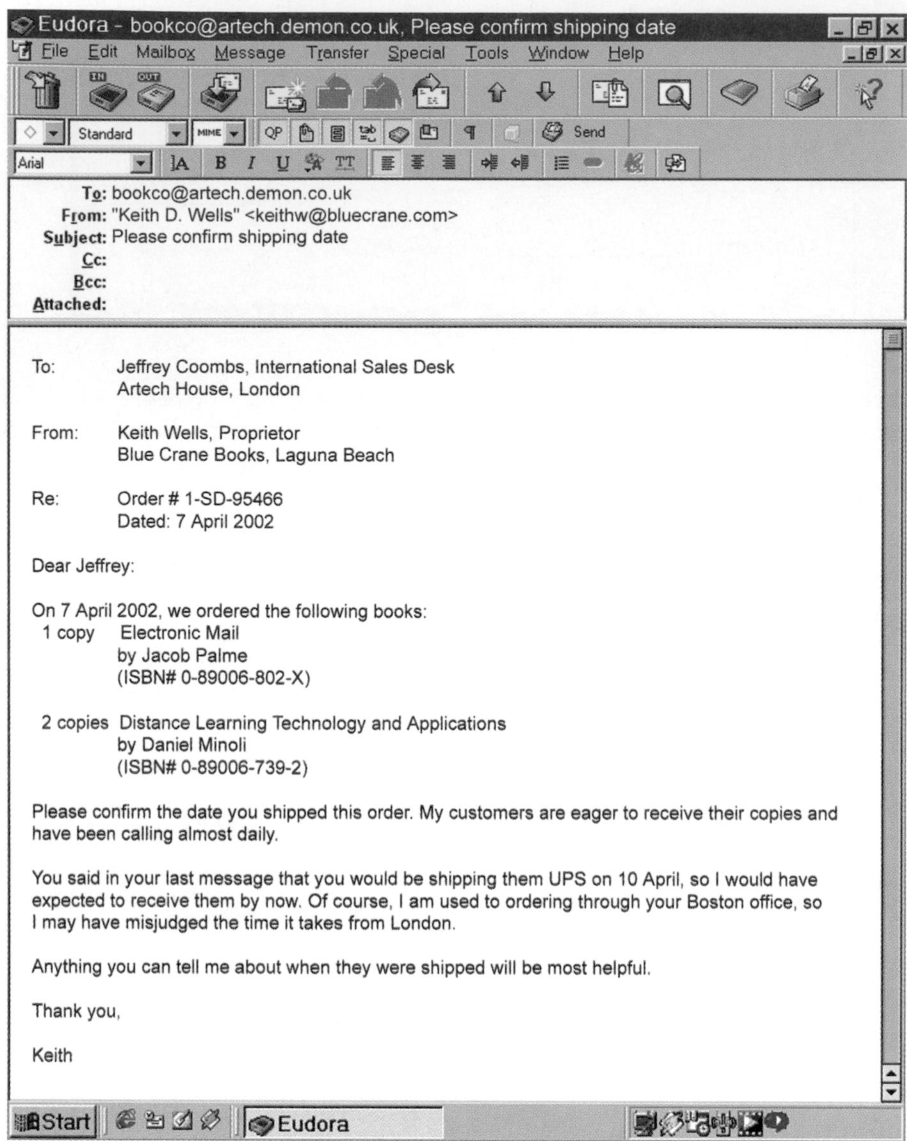

Eudora - bookco@artech.demon.co.uk, Please confirm shipping date

To: bookco@artech.demon.co.uk
From: "Keith D. Wells" <keithw@bluecrane.com>
Subject: Please confirm shipping date
Cc:
Bcc:
Attached:

To: Jeffrey Coombs, International Sales Desk
Artech House, London

From: Keith Wells, Proprietor
Blue Crane Books, Laguna Beach

Re: Order # 1-SD-95466
Dated: 7 April 2002

Dear Jeffrey:

On 7 April 2002, we ordered the following books:
1 copy Electronic Mail
by Jacob Palme
(ISBN# 0-89006-802-X)

2 copies Distance Learning Technology and Applications
by Daniel Minoli
(ISBN# 0-89006-739-2)

Please confirm the date you shipped this order. My customers are eager to receive their copies and have been calling almost daily.

You said in your last message that you would be shipping them UPS on 10 April, so I would have expected to receive them by now. Of course, I am used to ordering through your Boston office, so I may have misjudged the time it takes from London.

Anything you can tell me about when they were shipped will be most helpful.

Thank you,

Keith

- mailto: cc131@iway.fr [Chamber of Commerce and Industry in Toulouse, France]

On the Internet, everything on the left side of the @ symbol is the user name; everything on the right side describes the computer where that user has an account. This machine name usually ends with a country code (such as *fr* for France, *dk* for Denmark, *hk* for Hong Kong, *ca* for Canada). But within the United States, the country code is replaced with a top-level domain (TLD), which generally indicates the type of organization that operates that particular website:[13]

.com business and commercial users
.edu educational institutions
.gov nonmilitary government and related groups
.mil military-related groups
.net network providers
.org organizations and nonprofit groups

To keep up with increasing demand for unique website addresses, new TLDs (*biz, pro, coop, info, museums, aero,* and more) have recently been added.

Most e-mail programs also allow you to send mail to an entire group of people all at once. First, you create a distribution list. Then you type the name of the list in the *To:* line instead of typing the addresses of every person in the group.[14]

The *From:* line contains your e-mail address. The *Date:* line contains the day of the week, date (day, month, year), time, and time zone. The *Subject:* line describes the content of the message and presents an opportunity for you to build interest in your message. The *cc:* line allows you to send copies of a message to more than one person at a time. It also allows everyone on the list to see who else received the same message. The *Bcc:* line lets you send copies to people without the other recipients knowing—a practice considered unethical by some.[15] The *Attachments:* line contains the name(s) of the file(s) you attach to your e-mail message. The file can be a word-processing document, a digital image, an audio or video message, a spreadsheet, or a software program.[16]

Other lines containing more detailed information can be listed in your e-mail's header, including *Message-Id* (the exact location of this e-mail message on the sender's system), *X-mailer:* (the version of the e-mail program being used), and *Content type:* (a description of what kind of text and character set is contained in the message). Also, the *Received:* lines include information about each of the systems your e-mail passed through en route to your mailbox.[17] Most e-mail programs now allow you the choice of hiding or revealing this sort of detailed information.

Body

You might consider your mail program's header to be something like letterhead, because the rest of the space below the header is for the body of your message. In the *To:* and *From:* lines, some headers actually print out the names of the sender and the receiver (in addition to the e-mail addresses). Other headers do not. If your mail program includes only the e-mail addresses, you might consider including your own memo-type header, as in Figure I.9. The writer even included a subject line in his memo-type header that is more specific than the one in the mail program header. Although some may applaud the clarity such a second header provides, others may criticize the space it takes. Your decision depends on how formal you want to be.

Do include a greeting in your e-mail. As pointed out in Chapter 5, greetings personalize your message. Leave one line space above and below your greeting to set it off from the rest of your message. Again, depending on the level of formality you want, you may choose to end your greeting with a colon (most formal), a comma (conversational), or even two hyphens (informal).

Your message begins one blank line space below your greeting. Just as in memos and letters, skip one line space between paragraphs and include headings, numbered lists, bulleted lists, and embedded lists when appropriate. Limit your line lengths to a maximum of 80 characters by inserting a hard return at the end of each line.

One blank line space below your message, include a simple closing, often just one word. A blank line space below that, include your signature. Whether you type your name or use a signature file, including your signature personalizes your message.

TIME-SAVING MESSAGES

If there's a way to speed up the communication process, the organization stands to gain. Telephones and electronic mail systems are quick, as are mailgrams, telegrams, faxes, and the like. In addition, organizations have developed special formats to reduce the amount of time spent writing and typing short messages:

- **Fax cover sheets.** When faxing messages, you may use a fax cover sheet, which includes the recipient's name, company, fax number, and city; the sender's name, complete address, fax number, and telephone number; the number of pages being sent; a phone number to call if the faxed transmission isn't successful; and enough space for any brief message.[18] The format for this information varies widely. When a document is self-explanatory, a cover sheet may be unnecessary, so be sure not to waste paper or transmission time.
- **Memo-letters.** Printed with a heading somewhat like a memo's, memo-letters provide a space for an inside address so that the message may be sent outside the company (see Figure I.10). When the memo is folded properly, the address shows through a window in the envelope, thereby eliminating the need to address the envelope separately. Memo-letters often include a space for a reply message so that the recipient doesn't have to print out or type a whole new letter in response; carbonless copy sets allow sender and recipient to keep on file a copy of the entire correspondence. Although convenient, memo-letters are much less formal than business letters for outside correspondence.
- **Short-note reply technique.** Popular in many organizations, this technique can be used even without a special form. The recipient of a memo (or sometimes a letter) simply handwrites a response on the original document, makes a copy for the files, and sends the annotated original back to the person who wrote it.
- **Letterhead postcards.** Ideal for short, impersonal messages, letterhead postcards are preprinted with a list of responses so that the "writer" merely checks the appropriate response(s) and slips the postcard into the mail. Organizations such as mail-order companies and government agencies use these time-saving devices to communicate frequently with individuals by mail.

The important thing to realize about these and all other message formats is that they've developed over time to meet the need for clear communication and to speed responses to the needs of customers, suppliers, and associates.

REPORTS

You can enhance your report's effectiveness by paying careful attention to its appearance and layout. Follow whatever guidelines your organization prefers, but remember to be neat and consistent throughout. If it's up to you to decide formatting questions, the following conventions may help you decide how to handle margins, headings, spacing and indention, and page numbers.

Margins

All margins on a report page are at least 1 inch wide. Margins of 1 inch are customary for double-spaced pages,

FIGURE I.10 Memo-Letter

MEMO

TO: Green Ridge Gifts
1786 Century Road
Nashua, NH 03060
USA

FROM: Whiteside Import/Export, Ltd.
1601 Ronson Drive
Toronto, Ontario M9W 3E3
CANADA

SUBJECT: Order for Royal Dorchester china completer sets

DATE: October 11, 2002

MESSAGE:

The six Wellington pattern completer sets that you ordered by telephone October 9 are on their way and should reach your shop by October 18.

The three Mayfield pattern completer sets are coming from the factory, however, and will not arrive here until October 26 or 27. That means you will get them around November 2 or 3.

Do you still want the Mayfield sets? Would you like us to bill you for the Wellington sets only so that you can pay for the Mayfield order separately? Please add your reply below, retain the yellow copy for your records, and send us the white and pink copies.

SIGNED: Barbara Hutchins

REPLY: PLEASE SEND THE MAYFIELD SETS AS SOON AS POSSIBLE. YOU MAY BILL FOR BOTH MAYFIELD AND WELLINGTON SETS.

DATE: OCT. 15, 2002

SIGNED:

and margins of between $1^1/4$ and $1^1/2$ inches are customary for single-spaced pages. The top, left, and right margins are usually the same, but the bottom margins can be $1^1/2$ times as deep as the others. Some special pages also have deeper top margins. Set top margins as deep as 2 inches for pages that contain major titles: prefatory parts such as the table of contents or the executive summary, supplementary parts such as the reference notes or bibliography, and textual parts such as the first page of the text or the first page of each chapter.

If you're going to bind your report at the left or at the top, add half an inch to the margin on the bound edge (see Figure I.11). Because of the space taken by the binding on left-bound reports, make the center point of the page a quarter inch to the right of the center of the paper. Be sure that centered headings are centered between the margins, not centered on the paper. Computers can do this for you automatically. Other guidelines for formatting a report can be found in the sample in Chapter 14.

Headings

Headings of various levels provide visual clues to a report's organization. Figure 13.8, on page xxx, illustrates one good system for showing these levels, but many variations exist. No matter which system you use, be sure to be consistent.

Spacing and Indentions

The spacing and indention of most elements of a report are relatively easy. If your report is double-spaced (perhaps to ease comprehension of technical material), indent all paragraphs five character spaces (or about $^1/2$ inch). In single-spaced reports, you can block the paragraphs (no indentions), leaving one blank line between them.

FIGURE I.11 Margins for Formal Reports

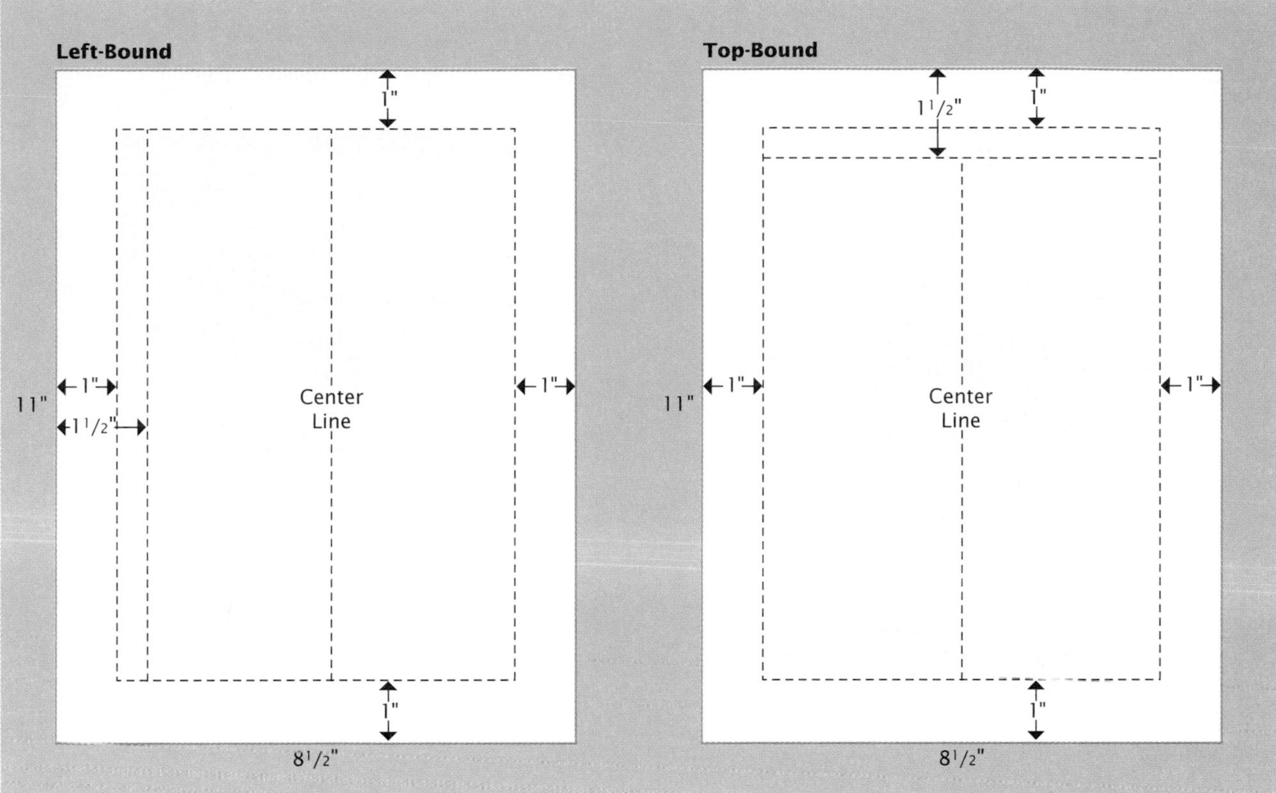

When using a typewriter, properly spacing the material on the title page is more complicated. For reports that will be bound on the left, start a quarter inch to the right of center. From that point, backspace once for each two letters in the line so that the line will appear centered once the report is bound.

To correctly place lines of type on the title page, first count the number of lines in each block of copy, including blank lines. Subtract the total from 66 (the total number of lines on an 11-inch page) to get the number of unused lines. To allocate these unused lines equally among the spaces between the blocks of copy, divide the number of unused lines by the number of blank areas (always one more than the number of blocks of copy). The result is the number of blank lines to devote to each section. A computer with a good word-processing program will do these calculations for you at the click of a mouse. As the title page of the sample report in Chapter 14 shows, the title page should look well balanced.

Page Numbers

Remember that every page in the report is counted but that not all pages have numbers shown on them. The first page of the report, normally the title page, is not numbered. All other pages in the prefatory section are numbered with a lowercase roman numeral, beginning with ii and continuing with iii, iv, v, and so on. The unadorned (no dashes, no period) page number is centered at the bottom margin.

Number the first page of the text of the report with the unadorned arabic numeral 1, centered at the bottom margin (double- or triple-spaced below the text). In left-bound reports, number the following pages (including the supplementary parts) consecutively with unadorned arabic numerals (2, 3, and so on), placed at the top right-hand margin (double- or triple-spaced above the text). For top-bound reports and for special pages having 2-inch top margins, center these page numbers at the bottom margin.

Appendix II

Documentation of Report Sources

Documenting a report is too important a task to undertake haphazardly. By providing information about your sources, you improve your own credibility as well as the credibility of the facts and opinions you present. Documentation gives readers the means for checking your findings and pursuing the subject further. Also, documenting your report is the accepted way to give credit to the people whose work you have drawn from.

What style should you use to document your report? Experts recommend various forms, depending on your field or discipline. Moreover, your employer or client may use a form different from those the experts suggest. Don't let this discrepancy confuse you. If your employer specifies a form, use it; the standardized form is easier for colleagues to understand. However, if the choice of form is left to you, adopt one of the styles described here. Whatever style you choose, be consistent within any given report, using the same order, punctuation, and format from one reference citation or bibliography entry to the next.

A wide variety of style manuals provide detailed information on documentation:

- American Psychological Association. *Publication Manual of the American Psychological Association.* 5th ed. Washington, D.C.: American Psychological Association, 2001. Details the author-date system, which is preferred in the social sciences and often in the natural sciences as well.
- *The Chicago Manual of Style.* 14th ed. Chicago: University of Chicago Press, 1993. Often referred to only as *Chicago* and widely used in the publishing industry; provides detailed treatment of documentation in Chapters 15, 16, and 17.
- Gibaldi, Joseph. *MLA Style Manual and Guide to Scholarly Publishing.* 2d ed. New York: Modern Language Association, 1998. Serves as the basis for the note and bibliography style used in much academic writing and is recommended in many college textbooks on writing term papers; provides a lot of examples in the humanities.
- Harnack, Andrew, and Eugene Kleppinger. *Online! A Reference Guide to Using Internet Sources—2000.* New York: St. Martin's Press, 2000. Offers an approach to style for citing online references.

Although many schemes have been proposed for organizing the information in source notes, all of them break the information into parts: (1) information about the author (name), (2) information about the work (title, edition, volume number), (3) information about the publication (place, publisher), (4) information about the date, and (5) information on relevant page ranges.

In the following sections, we summarize the major conventions for documenting sources in three styles: *The Chicago Manual of Style* (Chicago), the *Publication Manual of the American Psychological Association* (APA), and the *MLA Style Manual* (MLA).

CHICAGO STYLE

The Chicago Manual of Style recommends two types of documentation systems. The *documentary-note,* or *humanities,* style gives bibliographic citations in notes—either footnotes (when printed at the bottom of a page) or endnotes (when printed at the end of the report). The humanities system is often used in literature, history, and the arts. The other system strongly recommended by Chicago is the *author-date* system, which cites the author's last name and the date of publication in the text, usually in parentheses, reserving full documentation for the reference list (or bibliography). For the purpose of comparing styles, we will concentrate on the humanities system, which is described in detail in Chicago.

In-Text Citation—Chicago Style

To document report sources in text, the humanities system relies on superscripts—arabic numerals placed just above the line of type at the end of the reference:

Toward the end of his speech, Myers sounded a note of caution, saying that even though the economy is expected to grow, it could easily slow a bit.[10]

The superscript lets the reader know how to look for source information in either a footnote or an endnote (see Figure II.1). Some readers prefer footnotes so that they can simply glance at the bottom of the page for information. Others prefer endnotes so that they can read the text without a clutter of notes on the page. Also, endnotes relieve the writer from worrying about how long each note will be and how much space it will take away from the page. Both footnotes and endnotes are handled automatically by today's word-processing software.

For the reader's convenience, you can use footnotes for **content notes** (which may supplement your main text with asides about a particular issue or event, provide a cross-reference to another section of your report,

FIGURE II.1 Sample Endnotes—Chicago Style

NOTES

Journal article with volume and issue numbers	1. James Assira, "Are They Speaking English in Japan?" *Journal of Business Communication* 36, no. 4 (Fall 2001): 72.
Brochure	2. BestTemp Staffing Services, *An Employer's Guide to Staffing Services.* 2d ed. (Denver: BestTemp Information Center, 1999), 31.
Newspaper article, no author	3. "Buying Asian Supplies on the Net," *Los Angeles Times.* 12 February 1999. sec. D, p. 3.
Annual report	4. Eurotec, *2000 Annual Report* (New York: Eurotec, Inc., 2000), 48.
Magazine article	5. Holly Graves, "Prospecting Online," *Business Week,* 17 November 2001, 43–45.
Television broadcast	6. Daniel Han, "Trade Wars Heating Up Around the Globe." *CNN Headline News* (Atlanta: CNN, 5 March 2001).
Internet, World Wide Web	7. "Intel—Company Capsule," Hoover's Online [cited 8 March 2002], 3 screens, available at www.hoovers.com/capsules/13787.html.
Book, component parts	8. Sonja Kuntz, "Moving Beyond Benefits," in *Our Changing Workforce,* ed. Randolf Jacobson (New York: Citadel Press, 2000), 213–27.
Dissertation or thesis	9. George H. Morales, "The Economic Pressures on Industrialized Nations in a Global Economy" (Ph.D. diss., University of San Diego, 2000).
Paper presented at a meeting	10. Charles Myers, "HMOs in Today's Environment" (paper presented at the Conference on Medical Insurance Solution, Chicago, Ill., August 2000), 16–17.
Online magazine article	11. Preston Norwalk, "Training Managers to Help Employees Accept Change," in *Business Line* [online] (San Francisco, 2001 [updated 17 September 2001; cited 3 October 2001]); available from www.busline.com/news.
CD-ROM encyclopedia article,one author	12. Robert Parkings, "George Eastman," *The Concise Columbia Encyclopedia* (New York: Columbia University Press, 1997) [CD-ROM].
Newspaper article, one author	13. Evelyn Standish, "Global Market Crushes OPEC's Delicate Balance of Interests," *Wall Street Journal,* 19 January 2001, sec. A, p. 1.
Interview	14. Georgia Stainer, general manager, Day Cable and Communications, interview by author, Topeka, Kansas, 2 March 1999.
Book, two authors	15. Miriam Toller and Jay Fielding, *Global Business for Smaller Companies* (Rocklin, Calif: Prima Publishing, 2000), 102–03.
Government publication	16. U.S. Department of Defense, *Stretching Research Dollars: Survival Advice for Universities and Government Labs* (Washington, D.C.: GPO, 1999), 126.

or direct the reader to a related source). Then you can use endnotes for **source notes** (which document direct quotations, paraphrased passages, and visual aids). Consider which type of note is most common in your report, then choose whether to present these notes all as endnotes or all as footnotes. Regardless of the method you choose for referencing textual information in your report, both content notes and source notes for visual aids are placed on the same page as the visual aids.

Bibliography—Chicago Style

The humanities system may or may not be accompanied by a bibliography (because the notes give all the necessary bibliographic information). However, endnotes are arranged in order of appearance in the text, so an alphabetical bibliography can be valuable to your readers. The bibliography may be titled *Bibliography, Reference List, Sources, Works Cited* (if you include only those sources you actually cited in your report), or *Works Consulted* (if you include uncited sources as well). This list of sources may also serve as a reading list for those who want to pursue the subject of your report further, so you may want to annotate each entry—that is, comment on the subject matter and viewpoint of the source, as well as on its usefulness to readers. Annotations may be written in either complete or incomplete sentences. (See the annotated list of style

FIGURE II.2 Sample Bibliography—Chicago Style

BIBLIOGRAPHY

Journal article with volume and issue numbers	Assira, James. “Are They Speaking English in Japan?” *Journal of Business Communication* 36, no. 4 (Fall 2002): 72.
Brochure	BestTemp Staffing Services. *An Employer's Guide to Staffing Services.* 2d ed. Denver: BestTemp Information Center, 1999.
Newspaper article, no author	“Buying Asian Supplies on the Net.” *Los Angeles Times,* 12 February 1999, sec. D., p. 3.
Annual report	Eurotec, 2000 *Annual Report.* New York: Eurotec, Inc., 2000.
Magazine article	Graves, Holly. “Prospecting Online.” *Business Week,* 17 November 2001, 43–45.
Television broadcast	Han, Daniel. “Trade Wars Heating Up Around the Globe.” *CNN Headline News.* Atlanta: CNN, 5 March 2001.
Internet, World Wide Web	“Intel—Company Capsule.” *Hoover's Online* [cited 8 March 2002]. 3 screens. Available online from World Wide Web at www.hoovers.com/capsules/13787.html.
Book, component parts	Kuntz, Sonja. “Moving Beyond Benefits.” In *Our Changing Workforce,* edited by Randolf Jacobson, 213–27. New York: Citadel Press, 2000.
Dissertation or thesis	Morales, George H. “The Economic Pressures on Industrialized Nations in a Global Economy” Ph.D. diss., University of San Diego, 2000.
Paper presented at a meeting	Myers, Charles. “HMOs in Today's Environment.” Paper presented at the Conference on Medical Insurance Solutions, Chicago, Ill., August 2000.
Online magazine article	Norwalk, Preston. “Training Managers to Help Employees Accept Change.” In *Business Line* [online]. San Francisco, 2002 [updated 17 September 2001; cited 3 October 2001]. Available from www.busline.com/news.
CD-ROM encyclopedia article, one author	Parkings, Robert. “George Eastman.” *The Concise Columbia Encyclopedia.* New York: Columbia University Press, 1997. [CD-ROM].
Newspaper article, one author	Standish, Evelyn. “Global Market Crushes OPEC's Delicate Balance of Interests.” *Wall Street Journal,* 19 January 2001, sec. A, p. 1.
Interview	Stainer, Georgia, general manager, Day Cable and Communications. Interview by author. Topeka, Kansas, 2 March 1999.
Book, two authors	Toller, Miriam, and Jay Fielding, *Global Business for Smaller Companies.* Rocklin, Calif.: Prima Publishing, 2000.
Government publication	U.S. Department of Defense. *Stretching Research Dollars: Survival Advice for Universities and Government Labs.* Washington, D.C.: GPO, 2001.

manuals early in this component chapter.) A bibliography may also be more manageable if you subdivide it into categories (a classified bibliography), either by type of reference (such as books, articles, and unpublished material) or by subject matter (such as government regulation, market forces, and so on). Following are the major conventions for developing a bibliography according to Chicago style (see Figure II.2):

- Alphabetize entries by the last name of the lead author (listing last name first). The names of second and succeeding authors are listed in normal order. Entries without an author name are alphabetized by the first important word in the title.
- Format entries as hanging indents (indent second and succeeding lines three to five spaces).
- Arrange entries in the following general order: (1) author name, (2) title information, (3) publication information, (4) date, (5) periodical page range.
- Use quotation marks around the titles of articles from magazines, newspapers, and journals—capitalizing the first and last words, as well as all other important words.
- Use italics to set off the names of books, newspapers, journals, and other complete publications—capitalizing the first and last words, as well as all other important words.

- For journal articles, include the volume number and the issue number (if necessary). Include the year of publication inside parentheses and follow with a colon and the page range of the article: *Journal of Business Communication* 36, no. 4 (2001): 72. (In this source, the volume is 36, the number is 4, and the page is 72.)
- Use brackets to identify all electronic references: [Online database] or [CD-ROM].
- Explain how electronic references can be reached: Available from www.busline.com/news.
- Give the citation date for online references: [cited 23 August 2001.]

APA STYLE

The American Psychological Association (APA) recommends the author-date system of documentation, which is popular in the physical, natural, and social sciences. When using this system, you simply insert the author's last name and the year of publication within parentheses following the text discussion of the material cited. Include a page number if you use a direct quote. This approach briefly identifies the source so that readers can locate complete information in the alphabetical reference list at the end of the report. The author-date system is both brief and clear, saving readers time and effort.

In-Text Citation—APA Style

To document report sources in text using the APA style, insert the author's surname and the date of publication at the end of a statement. Enclose this information in parentheses. If the author's name is referred to in the text itself, it can be omitted from parenthetical material.

Some experts recommend both translation and back-translation when dealing with any non-English-speaking culture (Assira, 2001).

Toller and Fielding (2000) make a strong case for small companies succeeding in global business.

Personal communications and interviews conducted by the author would not be listed in the reference list at all. Such citations would appear in the text only.

Increasing the role of cable companies is high on the list of Georgia Stainer, general manager at Day Cable and Communications (personal communication, March 2, 2001).

List of References—APA Style

The APA style recommends listing only those works actually cited in the text (so you would not include works for background or for further reading). Report writers must choose their references judiciously. Following are the major conventions for developing a reference list according to APA style (see Figure II.3):

- Format entries as hanging indents.
- List all author names in reversed order (last name first), and use only initials for the first and middle names.
- Arrange entries in the following general order: (1) author name, (2) date, (3) title information, (4) publication information, (5) periodical page range.
- Follow the author name with the date of publication in parentheses.
- List titles of articles from magazines, newspapers, and journals without underlines or quotation marks. Capitalize only the first word of the title, any proper nouns, and the first word to follow an internal colon.
- Italicize titles of books, capitalizing only the first word, any proper nouns, and the first word to follow a colon.
- Italicize names of magazines, newspapers, journals, and other complete publications—capitalizing all the important words.
- For journal articles, include the volume number (in italic) and, if necessary, the issue number (in parentheses). Finally, include the page range of the article: *Journal of Business Communication, 36*(4), 72. (In this example, the volume is 36, the number is 4, and the page number is 72.)
- Include personal communications (such as letters, memos, e-mail, conversations) only in text, not in reference lists.
- Electronic references include author, date of publication, title of article or work, name of publication (if one), volume, date of retrieval (month, day, year), and the source.
- For electronic references, indicate the actual year of publication, and the exact date of retrieval.
- For electronic references, specify the URL; leave periods off the ends of URLs.

MLA STYLE

The style recommended by the Modern Language Association of America is used widely in the humanities, especially in the study of language and literature. Like APA style, MLA style uses brief parenthetical citations in the text. However, instead of including author name and year, MLA citations include author name and page reference.

In-Text Citation—MLA Style

To document report sources in text using MLA style, insert the author's last name and a page reference inside parentheses following the cited material: (Matthews 63). If the author's name is mentioned in the text reference, the name can be omitted from the parenthetical citation: (63). The citation indicates that the reference came from page 63 of a work by Matthews. With the author's name, readers can find complete publication information in the alphabetically arranged list of works cited that comes at the end of the report.

FIGURE II.3 Sample References—APA Style

	REFERENCES
Journal article with volume and issue numbers	Assira, J. (2001) Are they speaking English in Japan? *Journal of Business Communication* 36(4), 72.
Brochure	BestTemp Staffing Services. (1999). *An employer's guide to staffing services*. (2d ed.) [Brochure]. Denver: BestTemp Information Center.
Newspaper article, no author	Buying Asian supplies on the net. (1999, February 12). *Los Angeles Times,* p. D3.
Annual report	Eurotec (2000). *2000 annual report.* New York: Author.
Magazine article	Graves, H. (2001, November 17). Prospecting online. *Business Week,* 43–45.
Television broadcast	Han, D. (2001, March 5). Trade wars heating up around the globe. *CNN Headline News* [television broadcast]. Atlanta, GA: CNN.
Internet, World Wide Web	Intel—company capsule. (2001). *Hoover's Online.* Retrieved March 8, 2002 from http://www.hoovers.com/capsules/13787.html
Book, component parts	Kuntz, S. (2000). Moving beyond benefits. In Randolph Jacobson (Ed.), *Our changing workforce* (pp. 213-227). New York: Citadel Press.
Dissertation or thesis	Morales, G. H. (2000). The economic pressures on industrialized nations in a global economy. Unpublished doctoral dissertation, University of San Diego.
Paper presented at a meeting	Myers, C. (2000, August). *HMOs in today's environment.* Paper presented at the Conference on Medical Insurance Solutions, Chicago, IL.
Online magazine article	Norwalk, P. (2001, July 17). Training managers to help employees accept change. *Business Line.* [On-line]. Retrieved March 8, 2002 from http://www.busline.com/news
CD-ROM encyclopedia article, one author	Parkings, R. (1997) George Eastman. *The concise Columbia encyclopedia.* [CD-ROM]. New York: Columbia University Press.
Newspaper article, one author	Standish, E. (2001, January 19). Global market crushes OPEC's delicate balance of interests. *Wall Street Journal,* p. A1.
Interview	*Cited in text only, not in the list of references.*
Book, two authors	Toller, M., & Fielding J. (2000). *Global business for smaller companies.* Rocklin, CA: Prima Publishing.
Government publication	U.S. Department of Defense. (2001). *Stretching research dollars: Survival advice for universities and government labs.* Washington, DC: U.S. Government Printing Office, 1999.

Some experts recommend both translation and back-translation when dealing with any non-English-speaking culture (Assira 72).

Toller and Fielding make a strong case for small companies succeeding in global business (102–03).

List of Works Cited—MLA Style

The *MLA Style Manual* recommends preparing your list of works cited first so that you will know what information to give in the parenthetical citation (for example, whether to add a short title if you're citing more than one work by the same author, or whether to give an initial or first name if you're citing two authors who have the same last name). Your list of works cited appears at the end of your report, contains all the works that you cite in your text, and lists them in alphabetical order. Following are the major conventions for developing a reference list according to MLA style (see Figure II.4):

- Format entries as hanging indents (that is, indent second and succeeding lines by three to five character spaces).
- Arrange entries in the following general order: (1) author name, (2) title information, (3) publication information, (4) date, (5) periodical page range.
- List the lead author's name in reverse order (last name first), using either full first names or initials. List second and succeeding author names in normal order.

FIGURE II.4 Sample References—MLA Style

WORKS CITED

Journal article with volume and issue numbers	Assira, James. "Are They Speaking English in Japan?" *Journal of Business Communication* 36.4 (2001): 72.
Brochure	BestTemp Staffing Services. *An Employer's Guide to Staffing Services.* 2d ed. Denver: BestTemp Information Center, 1999.
Newspaper article, no author	"Buying Asian Supplies on the Net." *Los Angeles Times* 12 Feb. 1999: D3.
Annual report	Eurotec. *2000 Annual Report.* New York: Eurotec, Inc., 2000.
Magazine article	Graves, Holly. "Prospecting Online." *Business Week* 17 November 2001: 43–45.
Television broadcast	Han, Daniel. "Trade Wars Heating Up Around the Globe." *CNN Headline News.* CNN Atlanta. 5 Mar. 2001.
Internet, World Wide Web	"Intel—Company Capsule." *Hoover's Online* 2001. Hoover's Company Information. 8 Mar. 2002 <http://www.hoovers.com/capsules/13787.html>.
Book, component parts	Kuntz, Sonja. "Moving Beyond Benefits." *Our Changing Workforce,* Ed. Randolf Jacobson. New York: Citadel Press, 2000. 213–27.
Dissertation or thesis	Morales, George H. "The Economic Pressures on Industrialized Nations in a Global Economy" Diss. U of San Diego, 2000. DAI 52 (2000): 5436C–37C.
Paper presented at a meeting	Myers, Charles. "HMOs in Today's Environment." Conference on Medical Insurance Solutions. Chicago. 13 August 2000.
Online magazine article	Norwalk, Preston. "Training Managers to Help Employees Accept Change." *Business Line* 17 July 2001 <http://www.busline.com/news>.
CD-ROM encyclopedia article, one author	Parkings, Robert. "George Eastman." *The Concise Columbia Encyclopedia.* CD-ROM. New York: Columbia UP, 1997.
Interview	Stainer, Georgia, general manager, Day Cable and Communications. Telephone interview. Topeka. 2 Mar. 1999.
Newspaper article, one author	Standish, Evelyn. "Global Market Crushes OPEC's Delicate Balance of Interests." *Wall Street Journal* 19 Jan. 2001: A1.
Book, two authors	Toller, Miriam, and Jay Fielding. *Global Business for Smaller Companies.* Rocklin, Calif: Prima Publishing, 2000.
Government publication	United States. Department of Defense. *Stretching Research Dollars: Survival Advice for Universities and Government Labs.* Washington: GPO, 2001.

- Use quotation marks around the titles of articles from magazines, newspapers, and journals—capitalize all important words.
- Italicize the names of books, newspapers, journals and other complete publications, capitalizing all main words in the title.
- For journal articles, include the volume number and the issue number (if necessary). Include the year of publication inside parentheses and follow with a colon and the page range of the article: *Journal of Business Communication* 36.4 (2001): 72. (In this source, the volume is 36, the number is 4, and the page is 72.)
- Electronic sources are less fixed than print sources, and they may not be readily accessible to readers. So citations for electronic sources must provide more information. Always try to be as comprehensive as possible, citing whatever information is available.
- The date for electronic sources should contain both the date assigned in the source and the date accessed by the researcher.
- The URL for electronic sources must be as accurate and complete as possible, from access-mode identifier (http, ftp, gopher, telnet) to all relevant directory and file names. Be sure to enclose this path inside angle brackets: <http://www.hoovers.com/capsules/13787.html>.

Appendix III

Fundamentals of Grammar and Usage

Grammar is nothing more than the way words are combined into sentences, and usage is the way words are used by a network of people—in this case, the community of businesspeople who use English. You'll find it easier to get along in this community if you know the accepted standards of grammar and usage. What follows is a review of the basics of grammar and usage—things you've probably learned but may have forgotten. Without a firm grasp of these basics, you risk not only being misunderstood but also damaging your company's image, losing money for your company, and possibly even losing your job.

1.0 GRAMMAR

The sentence below looks innocent, but is it really?

> We sell tuxedos as well as rent.

You might sell rent, but it's highly unlikely. Whatever you're selling, some people will ignore your message because of a blunder like this. The following sentence has a similar problem:

> Vice President Eldon Neale told his chief engineer that he would no longer be with Avix, Inc., as of June 30.

Is Eldon or the engineer leaving? No matter which side the facts are on, the sentence can be read the other way. You may have a hard time convincing either person that your simple mistake was not a move in a game of office politics. Now look at this sentence:

> The year before we budgeted more for advertising sales were up.

Confused? Perhaps this is what you meant:

> The year before, we budgeted more for advertising. Sales were up.

Maybe you meant this:

> The year before we budgeted more for advertising, sales were up.

The meaning of language falls into bundles called sentences. A listener or reader can take only so much meaning before filing a sentence away and getting ready for the next one. So, as a writer, you have to know what a sentence is. You need to know where one ends and the next one begins.

If you want to know what a thing is, you have to find out what goes into it, what its ingredients are. Luckily, the basic ingredients of an English sentence are simple. They're called the parts of speech, and the content-bearing ones are nouns, pronouns, verbs, adjectives, and adverbs. They combine with a few functional parts of speech to convey meaning. Meaning is also transmitted by punctuation, mechanics, and vocabulary.

1.1 Nouns

A noun names a person, place, or thing. Anything you can see or detect with one of your other senses has a noun to name it. Some things you can't see or sense are also nouns—ions, for example, or space. So are things that exist as ideas, such as accuracy and height. (You can see that something is accurate or that a building is tall, but you can't see the idea of accuracy or the idea of height.) These names for ideas are known as abstract nouns. The simplest nouns are the names of things you can see or touch: car, building, cloud, brick.

1.1.1 Proper Nouns and Common Nouns

So far, all the examples of nouns have been common nouns, referring to general classes of things. The word *building* refers to a whole class of structures. Common nouns such as *building* are not capitalized.

If you want to talk about one particular building, however, you might refer to the Glazier Building. The name is capitalized, indicating that *Glazier Building* is a proper noun.

Here are three sets of common and proper nouns for comparison:

Common	Proper
city	Kansas City
company	Blaisden Company
store	Books Galore

1.1.2 Plural Nouns

Nouns can be either singular or plural. The usual way to make a plural noun is to add *s* to the singular form of the word:

Singular	Plural
rock	rocks
picture	pictures
song	songs

Many nouns have other ways of forming the plural. Letters, numbers, and words used as words are sometimes made plural by adding an apostrophe and an *s*. Very often, *'s* is used with abbreviations that have periods, lowercase letters that stand alone, and capital letters that might be confused with words when made into plurals:

> Spell out all *St.*'s and *Ave.*'s.
>
> He divided the page with a row of *x*'s.
>
> Sarah will register the *A*'s through the *G*'s at the convention.

In other cases, however, the apostrophe may be left out:

> They'll review their ABCs.
>
> The stock market climbed through most of the 1980s.
>
> Circle all *the*s in the paragraph.

In some of these examples, the letters used as letters and words used as words are *italicized* (discussed later).

Other nouns, such as those below, are so-called irregular nouns; they form the plural in some way other than simply adding *s:*

Singular	Plural
tax	taxes
specialty	specialties
cargo	cargoes
shelf	shelves
child	children
woman	women
tooth	teeth
mouse	mice
parenthesis	parentheses
son-in-law	sons-in-law
editor-in-chief	editors-in-chief

Rather than memorize a lot of rules about forming plurals, use a dictionary. If the dictionary says nothing about the plural of a word, it's formed the usual way: by adding *s*. If the plural is formed in some irregular way, the dictionary often shows the plural spelling.

1.1.3 Possessive Nouns

A noun becomes possessive when it's used to show the ownership of something. Then you add *'s* to the word:

> the man's car   the woman's apartment

However, ownership does not need to be legal:

> the secretary's desk   the company's assets

Also, ownership may be nothing more than an automatic association:

> a day's work   the job's prestige

An exception to the rule about adding *'s* to make a noun possessive occurs when the word is singular and already has two "s" sounds at the end. In cases like the following, an apostrophe is all that's needed:

> crisis' dimensions   Mr. Moses' application

When the noun has only one "s" sound at the end, however, retain the *'s*:

> Chris's book   Carolyn Nuss's office

With hyphenated nouns (compound nouns), add *'s* to the last word:

Hyphenated Noun	Possessive Noun
mother-in-law	mother-in-law's
mayor-elect	mayor-elect's

To form the possessive of plural nouns, just begin by following the same rule as with singular nouns: add *'s*. However, if the plural noun already ends in an *s* (as most do), drop the one you've added, leaving only the apostrophe:

> the clients' complaints   employees' benefits

1.2 Pronouns

A pronoun is a word that stands for a noun; it saves repeating the noun:

> Drivers have some choice of weeks for vacation, but *they* must notify this office of *their* preference by March 1.

The pronouns *they* and *their* stand in for the noun *drivers*. The noun that a pronoun stands for is called the antecedent of the pronoun; *drivers* is the antecedent of *they* and *their.*

When the antecedent is plural, the pronoun that stands in for it has to be plural; *they* and *their* are plural pronouns because *drivers* is plural. Likewise, when the antecedent is singular, the pronoun has to be singular:

> We thought the *contract* had expired, but we soon learned that *it* had not.

1.2.1 Multiple Antecedents

Sometimes a pronoun has a double (or even a triple) antecedent:

> *Kathryn Boettcher* and *Luis Gutierrez* went beyond *their* sales quotas for January.

If taken alone, *Kathryn Boettcher* is a singular antecedent. So is *Luis Gutierrez*. However, when together, they are the plural antecedent of a pronoun, so the pronoun has to be plural. Thus the pronoun is *their* instead of *her* or *his.*

1.2.2 Unclear Antecedents

In some sentences the pronoun's antecedent is unclear:

> Sandy Wright sent Jane Brougham *her* production figures for the previous year. *She* thought they were too low.

To which person does the pronoun *her* refer? Someone who knew Sandy and Jane and knew their business relationship might be able to figure out the antecedent for *her*. Even with such an advantage, however, a reader might receive the wrong meaning. Also, it would be nearly impossible for any reader to know which name is the antecedent of *she*.

The best way to clarify an ambiguous pronoun is usually to rewrite the sentence, repeating nouns when needed for clarity:

> Sandy Wright sent her production figures for the previous year to Jane Brougham. *Jane* thought they were too low.

The noun needs to be repeated only when the antecedent is unclear.

1.2.3 Gender-Neutral Pronouns

The pronouns that stand for males are *he, his,* and *him*. The pronouns that stand for females are *she, hers,* and *her*. However, you'll often be faced with the problem of choosing a pronoun for a noun that refers to both females and males:

> Each manager must make up (his, her, his or her, its, their) own mind about stocking this item and about the quantity that (he, she, he or she, it, they) can sell.

This sentence calls for a pronoun that's neither masculine nor feminine. The issue of gender-neutral pronouns responds to efforts to treat females and males evenhandedly. Here are some possible ways to deal with this issue:

> Each manager must make up *his* . . .

(Not all managers are men.)

> Each manager must make up *her* . . .

(Not all managers are women.)

> Each manager must make up *his or her* . . .

(This solution is acceptable but becomes awkward when repeated more than once or twice in a document.)

> Each manager must make up *her* . . . Every manager will receive *his* . . . A manager may send *her* . . .

(A manager's gender does not alternate like a windshield wiper!)

> Each manager must make up *their* . . .

(The pronoun can't be plural when the antecedent is singular.)

> Each manager must make up *its* . . .

(*It* never refers to people.)

The best solution is to make the noun plural or to revise the passage altogether:

> Managers must make up *their* minds . . .
> Each manager must decide whether . . .

When making these kinds of changes, be careful not to change the original meaning.

1.2.4 Case of Pronouns

The case of a pronoun tells whether it's acting or acted on:

> *She sells* an average of five packages each week.

In this sentence *she* is doing the selling. Because *she* is acting, *she* is said to be in the nominative case. Now consider what happens when the pronoun is acted on:

> After six months Ms. Browning promoted *her*.

In this sentence the pronoun *her* is acted on. The pronoun *her* is thus said to be in the objective case.

Contrast the nominative and objective pronouns in this list:

Nominative	Objective
I	me
we	us
he	him
she	her
they	them
who	whom
whoever	whomever

Objective pronouns may be used as either the object of a verb (such as *promoted*) or the object of a preposition (such as *with*):

> Rob worked with *them* until the order was filled.

In this example *them* is the object of the preposition *with* because Rob acted on—worked with—them.

Here's a sample sentence with three pronouns, the first one nominative, the second the object of a verb, and the third the object of a preposition:

> *He* paid *us* as soon as the check came from *them*.

He is nominative; *us* is objective because it's the object of the verb *paid*; *them* is objective because it's the object of the preposition *from*.

Every writer sometimes wonders whether to use *who* or *whom:*

> (Who, Whom) will you hire?

Because this sentence is a question, it's difficult to see that *whom* is the object of the verb *hire*. You can figure out which pronoun to use if you rearrange the question and temporarily try *she* and *her* in place of *who* and *whom:* "Will you hire *she*?" or "Will you hire *her*?" *Her* and *whom* are both objective, so the correct choice is "*Whom* will you hire?" Here's a different example:

> (Who, Whom) logged so much travel time?

Turning the question into a statement, you get:

> *He* logged so much travel time.

Therefore, the correct statement is:

> *Who* logged so much travel time?

1.2.5 Possessive Pronouns

Possessive pronouns are like possessive nouns in the way they work: They show ownership or automatic association.

her job their preferences
his account its equipment

However, possessive pronouns are different from possessive nouns in the way they are written. That is, possessive pronouns never have an apostrophe.

Possessive Noun	Possessive Pronoun
the woman's estate	her estate
Roger Franklin's plans	his plans
the shareholders' feelings	their feelings
the vacuum cleaner's attachments	its attachments

The word *its* is the possessive of *it*. Like all other possessive pronouns, its doesn't have an apostrophe. Some people confuse *its* with *it's,* the contraction of *it is.* Contractions are discussed later.

1.3 Verbs

A verb describes an action:

They all *quit* in disgust.

It may also describe a state of being:

Working conditions *were* substandard.

The English language is full of action verbs. Here are a few you'll often run across in the business world:

verify	perform	fulfill
hire	succeed	send
leave	improve	receive
accept	develop	pay

You could undoubtedly list many more.

The most common verb describing a state of being instead of an action is *to be* and all its forms:

I *am, was,* or *will be;* you *are, were,* or *will be*

Other verbs also describe a state of being:

It *seemed* a good plan at the time.

She *sounds* impressive at a meeting.

These verbs link what comes before them in the sentence with what comes after; no action is involved. (See Section 1.7.5 for a fuller discussion of linking verbs.)

1.3.1 Verb Tenses

English has three simple verb tenses: present, past, and future.

Present: Our branches in Hawaii *stock* other items.
Past: We *stocked* Purquil pens for a short time.
Future: Rotex Tire Stores *will stock* your line of tires when you begin a program of effective national advertising.

With most verbs (the regular ones), the past tense ends in *ed;* the future tense always has *will* or *shall* in front of it. But the present tense is more complex:

First Person	Second Person	Third Person
Singular		
I stock	you stock	he/she/it stocks
Plural		
we stock	you stock	they stock

The basic form, *stock,* takes an additional *s* when *he, she,* or *it* precedes it. (See section 1.3.4 for more on subject-verb agreement.)

In addition to the three simple tenses, there are three perfect tenses using forms of the helping verb *have.* The present perfect tense uses the past participle (regularly the past tense) of the main verb, *stocked,* and adds the present-tense *have* or *has* to the front of it:

(I, we, you, they) *have stocked.*

(He, she, it) *has stocked.*

The past perfect tense uses the past participle of the main verb, *stocked,* and adds the past-tense *had* to the front of it:

(I, you, he, she, it, we, they) *had stocked.*

The future perfect tense also uses the past participle of the main verb, *stocked,* but adds the future-tense *will have:*

(I, you, he, she, it, we, they) *will have stocked.*

Keep verbs in the same tense when the actions occur at the same time:

When the payroll checks *came* in, everyone *showed* up for work.

We *have found* that everyone *has pitched* in to help.

When the actions occur at different times, you may change tense accordingly:

The shipment *came* last Wednesday, so if another one *comes* in today, please *return* it.

The new employee *had been* ill at ease, but now she *has become* a full-fledged member of the team.

1.3.2 Irregular Verbs

Many verbs don't follow in every detail the patterns already described. The most irregular of these verbs is *to be:*

Tense	Singular	Plural
Present:	I *am*	we *are*
	you *are*	you *are*
	he, she, it *is*	they *are*
Past:	I *was*	we *were*
	you *were*	you *were*
	he, she, it *was*	they *were*

The future tense of *to be* is formed in the same way that the future tense of a regular verb is formed.

The perfect tenses of *to be* are also formed as they would be for a regular verb, except that the past participle is a special form, *been,* instead of just the past tense:

Present perfect: you have been
Past perfect: you had been
Future perfect: you will have been

Here's a sampling of other irregular verbs:

Present	Past	Past Participle
begin	began	begun
shrink	shrank	shrunk
know	knew	known
rise	rose	risen
become	became	become
go	went	gone
do	did	done

Dictionaries list the various forms of other irregular verbs.

1.3.3 Transitive and Intransitive Verbs

Many people are confused by three particular sets of verbs:

lie/lay sit/set rise/raise

Using these verbs correctly is much easier when you learn the difference between transitive and intransitive verbs.

Transitive verbs convey their action to an object; they "transfer" their action to an object. Intransitive verbs do not. Here are some sample uses of transitive and intransitive verbs:

Intransitive	Transitive
We should include in our new offices a place to *lie* down for a nap.	The workers will be here on Monday to *lay* new carpeting.
Even the way an interviewee *sits* is important.	That crate is full of stemware, so *set* it down carefully.
Salaries at Compu-Link, Inc., *rise* swiftly.	They *raise* their level of production every year.

The workers *lay* carpeting, you *set* down the crate, they *raise* production; each action is transferred to something. In the intransitive sentences, one *lies* down, an interviewee *sits,* and salaries *rise* without (at least grammatically) affecting anything else. Intransitive sentences are complete with only a subject and a verb; transitive sentences are not complete unless they also include an object, or something to transfer the action to.

Tenses are a confusing element of the *lie/lay* problem:

Present	Past	Past Participle
I lie	I lay	I have lain
I lay (something down)	I laid (something down)	I have laid (something down)

The past tense of *lie* and the present tense of *lay* look and sound alike, even though they're different verbs.

1.3.4 Subject-Verb Agreement

Whether regular or irregular, every verb must agree with its subject, both in person (first, second, or third) and in number (single or plural).

First Person	Second Person	Third Person
Singular		
I *am*; I *write*	you *are*; you *write*	he/she/it *is*; he/she/it *writes*
Plural		
we *are*; we *write*	you *are*; you *write*	they *are*; they *write*

In a simple sentence, making a verb agree with its subject is a straightforward task:

Hector Ruiz *is* a strong competitor. (third-person singular)

We *write* to you every month. (first-person plural)

Confusion sometimes arises when sentences are a bit more complicated. For example, be sure to avoid agreement problems when words come between the subject and verb (in the following examples, the verb appears in italics, and its subject is underlined):

The analysis of existing documents *takes* a full week.

Even though *documents* is a plural, the verb is in the singular form. That's because the subject of the sentence is *analysis,* a singular noun. When determining agreement, the phrase *of existing documents* can be disregarded. Here is another example:

The answers for this exercise *are* in the study guide.

Take away the phrase *for this exercise,* and you are left with the plural subject *answers.* Therefore, the verb takes the plural form.

Verb agreement is also complicated when the subject is not a specific noun or pronoun and when the subject may be considered either singular or plural. In such cases, you have to analyze the surrounding sentence to determine which verb form to use:

The staff *is* quartered in the warehouse.

The staff *are* at their desks in the warehouse.

The computers and the staff *are* in the warehouse.

Neither the staff nor the computers *are* in the warehouse.

Every computer *is* in the warehouse.

Many a computer *is* in the warehouse.

Did you notice that words such as *every* use the singular verb form? In addition, when a *neither/nor* phrase combines singular and plural nouns, the verb takes the form that matches the noun closest to it.

In the business world, some subjects require extra attention. Company names, for example, are considered singular and therefore take a singular verb in most cases—even if they contain plural words:

Stater Brothers *offers* convenient grocery shopping.

In addition, quantities are sometimes considered singular and sometimes plural. If a quantity refers to a total amount, it takes a singular verb; if a quantity refers to individual, countable units, it takes a plural verb:

Three hours *is* a long time.
The eight dollars we collected for the fund *are* tacked on the bulletin board.

Fractions may also be singular or plural, depending on the noun that accompanies them:

One-third of the warehouse *is* devoted to this product line.
One-third of the products *are* defective.

For a related discussion, see Section 1.7.2, "Longer Sentences," later in this Handbook.

1.3.5 Voice of Verbs

Verbs have two voices, active and passive:

Active: The buyer paid a large amount.
Passive: A large amount was paid by the buyer.

The passive voice uses a form of the verb *to be.*

Also, the passive-voice sentence uses eight words, whereas the active-voice sentence uses only six words to say the same thing. The words *was* and *by* are unnecessary to convey the meaning of the sentence. In fact, extra words usually clog meaning. So be sure to opt for the active voice when you have a choice.

At times, however, you have no choice:

Several items *have been taken,* but so far we don't know who took them.

The passive voice becomes necessary when you don't know (or don't want to say) who performed the action; the active voice is bolder and more direct.

1.3.6 Mood of Verbs

You have three moods to choose from, depending on your intentions. Most of the time you use the indicative mood to make a statement or to ask a question:

The secretary *mailed* a letter to each supplier.

Did the secretary *mail* a letter to each supplier?

When you wish to command or request, use the imperative mood:

Please *mail* a letter to each supplier.

Sometimes, especially in business, a courteous request is stated like a question; in that case, however, no question mark is required:

Would you *mail* a letter to each supplier.

The subjunctive mood, most often used in formal writing or in presenting bad news, expresses a possibility or a recommendation. The subjunctive is usually signaled by a word such as *if* or *that.* In these examples, the subjunctive mood uses special verb forms:

If the secretary *were to mail* a letter to each supplier, we might save some money.

I suggested that the secretary *mail* a letter to each supplier.

Although the subjunctive mood is not used as often as it once was, it's still found in such expressions as *Come what may* and *If I were you.* In general, it is used to convey an idea that is contrary to fact: If iron *were* lighter than air.

1.4 Adjectives

An adjective modifies (tells something about) a noun or pronoun:

an *efficient* staff	a *heavy* price
brisk trade	*poor* you

Each of these phrases says more about the noun or pronoun than the noun or pronoun would say alone.

Adjectives always tell us something we wouldn't know without them. So you don't need to use adjectives when the noun alone, or a different noun, will give the meaning:

a *company* employee

(An employee ordinarily works for a company.)

a *crate-type* container

(Crate gives the entire meaning.)

At times, adjectives pile up in a series:

It was a *long* and *active* workday.

Such strings of adjectives are acceptable as long as they all convey a different part of the phrase's meaning.

Verbs in the *ing* (present participle) form can be used as adjectives:

A *boring* job can sometimes turn into a *fascinating* career.

So can the past participle of verbs:

A freshly *painted* house is a *sold* house.

Adjectives modify nouns more often than they modify pronouns. When adjectives do modify pronouns, however, the sentence usually has a linking verb:

They were *attentive*. It looked *appropriate*.
He seems *interested*. You are *skillful*.

1.4.1 Comparative Degree

Most adjectives can take three forms: simple, comparative, and superlative. The simple form modifies a single noun or pronoun. Use the comparative form when comparing two items. When comparing three or more items, use the superlative form.

Simple	Comparative	Superlative
hard	harder	hardest
safe	safer	safest
dry	drier	driest

The comparative form adds *er* to the simple form, and the superlative form adds *est*. (The *y* at the end of a word changes to *i* before the *er* or *est* is added.)

A small number of adjectives are irregular, including these:

Simple	Comparative	Superlative
good	better	best
bad	worse	worst
little	less	least

When the simple form of an adjective is two or more syllables, you usually add *more* to form the comparative and *most* to form the superlative:

Simple	Comparative	Superlative
useful	more useful	most useful
exhausting	more exhausting	most exhausting
expensive	more expensive	most expensive

The most common exceptions are two-syllable adjectives that end in *y*:

Simple	Comparative	Superlative
happy	happier	happiest
costly	costlier	costliest

If you choose this option, change the *y* to *i*, and tack *er* or *est* onto the end.

Some adjectives cannot be used to make comparisons because they themselves indicate the extreme. For example, if something is perfect, nothing can be more perfect. If something is unique or ultimate, nothing can be more unique or more ultimate.

1.4.2 Hyphenated Adjectives

Many adjectives used in the business world are actually combinations of words: *well-written* report, *last-minute* effort, *fifth-floor* suite, *well-built* engine. As you can see, they are hyphenated when they come before the noun they modify. However, when they come after the noun they modify, they are not hyphenated. In the following example, the adjectives appear in italics and the nouns they modify are underlined:

The <u>report</u> is *well written* because of our team's *last-minute* <u>efforts</u>.

Hyphens are not used when part of the combination is a word ending in *ly* (because that word is usually not an adjective). Hyphens are also omitted from word combinations that are used frequently:

We live in a *rapidly shrinking* world.
Our *highly motivated* employees will be well paid.
Please consider renewing your *credit card* account.
Send those figures to our *data processing* department.
Our new intern is a *high school* student.

1.5 Adverbs

An adverb modifies a verb, an adjective, or another adverb:

Modifying a verb:	Our marketing department works *efficiently*.
Modifying an adjective:	She was not dependable, although she was *highly* intelligent.
Modifying another adverb:	His territory was *too* broadly diversified, so he moved *extremely* cautiously.

Most of the adverbs mentioned are adjectives turned into adverbs by adding *ly*, which is how many adverbs are formed:

Adjective	Adverb
efficient	efficiently
high	highly
extreme	extremely
special	specially
official	officially
separate	separately

Some adverbs are made by dropping or changing the final letter of the adjective and then adding *ly:*

Adjective	Adverb
due	duly
busy	busily

Other adverbs don't end in *ly* at all. Here are a few examples of this type:

often	fast	too
soon	very	so

Some adverbs are difficult to distinguish from adjectives. For example, in the following sentences, is the underlined word an adverb or an adjective?

> They worked <u>well</u>.
> The baby is <u>well</u>.

In the first sentence, *well* is an adverb modifying the verb worked. In the second sentence, *well* is an adjective modifying the noun *baby.* To choose correctly between adverbs and adjectives, remember that verbs of being link a noun to an adjective describing the noun. In contrast, you would use an adverb to describe an action verb.

Adjective	Adverb
He is a *good* worker. (What kind of worker is he?)	He works *well.* (How does he work?)
It is a *real* computer. (What kind of computer is it?)	It *really* is a computer. (To what extent is it a computer?)
The traffic is *slow.* (What quality does the traffic have?)	The traffic moves *slowly.* (How does the traffic move?)

1.5.1 Negative Adverbs

Negative adverbs (such as *neither, no, not, scarcely,* and *seldom*) are powerful words and therefore do not need any help in conveying a negative thought. In fact, using double negatives gives a strong impression of illiteracy, so you would be well advised to avoid sentences like these:

> I don't want no mistakes.
>
> (Correct: "I don't want any mistakes" or "I want no mistakes.")
>
> They couldn't hardly read the light type.
>
> (Correct: "They could hardly read the report" or "They couldn't read the report.")
>
> They scarcely noticed neither one.
>
> (Correct: "They scarcely noticed either one" or "They noticed neither one.")

1.5.2 Comparative Degree

Like adjectives, adverbs can be used to compare items. Generally, the basic adverb is combined with *more* or *most,* just as long adjectives are. However, some adverbs have one-word comparative forms:

One Item	Two Items	Three Items
quickly	more quickly	most quickly
sincerely	less sincerely	least sincerely
fast	faster	fastest
well	better	best

1.6 Other Parts of Speech

Nouns, pronouns, verbs, adjectives, and adverbs carry most of the meaning in a sentence. Four other parts of speech link them together in sentences: prepositions, conjunctions, articles, and interjections.

1.6.1 Prepositions

Prepositions are words like these:

of	to	for	with
at	by	from	about

Some prepositions consist of more than one word—like these:

> because of   in addition to   out of   except for

And some prepositions are closely linked with a verb. When using phrases like *look up* and *wipe out,* keep the phrase intact and do not insert anything between the verb and the preposition.

Prepositions most often begin prepositional phrases, which function like adjectives and adverbs by telling more about a pronoun, noun, or verb:

of a type	*by* Friday
to the point	*with* characteristic flair

To prevent misreading, prepositional phrases should be placed near the element they modify:

> *Of all our technicians,* <u>she</u> is the best trained.
>
> They couldn't see the <u>merit</u> *in my proposal.*
>
> Someone left a <u>folder</u> *on my desk.*

It was once considered totally unacceptable to put a preposition at the end of a sentence. Now you may:

> I couldn't tell what they were interested in.
>
> What did she attribute it to?

However, be careful not to place prepositions at the end of sentences when doing so is unnecessary. In fact, avoid using any unnecessary preposition. In the following examples, the prepositions in parentheses should be omitted:

> All (of) the staff members were present.
>
> I almost fell off (of) my chair with surprise.

Where was Mr. Steuben going (to)?

They couldn't help (from) wondering.

The opposite problem is failing to include a preposition when you should. Consider the two sentences that follow:

Sales were over $100,000 for Linda and Bill.

Sales were over $100,000 for Linda and for Bill.

The first sentence indicates that Linda and Bill had combined sales over $100,000; the second, that Linda and Bill each had sales over $100,000, for a combined total in excess of $200,000. The preposition *for* is critical here.

Prepositions are also required in sentences like this one:

Which type of personal computer do you prefer?

Certain prepositions are used with certain words. When the same preposition can be used for two or more words in a sentence without affecting the meaning, only the last preposition is required:

We are familiar (*with*) and satisfied *with* your company's products.

But when different prepositions are normally used with the words, all the prepositions must be included:

We are familiar *with* and interested *in* your company's products.

Here is an incomplete list of prepositions used in a particular way with particular words:

among/between: *Among* is used to refer to three or more (*Circulate the memo among the staff*); *between* is used to refer to two (*Put the copy machine between Judy and Dan*).
as if/like: *As if* is used before a clause (*It seems as if we should be doing something*); *like* is used before a noun or pronoun (*He seems like a nice guy*).
have/of: *Have* is a verb used in verb phrases (*They should have checked first*); *of* is a preposition and is never used in such cases.
in/into: *In* is used to refer to a static position (*The file is in the cabinet*); *into* is used to refer to movement toward a position (*Put the file into the cabinet*).

And here is an incomplete list of some prepositions that have come to be used with certain words:

according to
agree to (a proposal)
agree with (a person)
buy from
capable of
comply with
conform to
differ from (things)
differ with (person)
different from
get from (receive)
get off (dismount)
in accordance with
in search of
independent of
interior to
plan to
prefer to
prior to
reason with
responsible for
similar to
talk to (without interaction)
talk with (with interaction)
wait for (person or thing)
wait on (like a waiter)

1.6.2 Conjunctions

Conjunctions connect the parts of a sentence: words, phrases, and clauses. You are probably most familiar with coordinating conjunctions such as the following:

and	for	or	yet
but	nor	so	

Conjunctions may be used to connect clauses (which have both a subject and a predicate) with other clauses, to connect clauses with phrases (which do not have both a subject and a predicate), and to connect words with words:

We sell designer clothing *and* linens.

(Words with words)

Their products are expensive *but* still appeal to value-conscious consumers.

(Clauses with phrases)

I will call her on the phone today, *or* I will visit her office tomorrow.

(Clauses with clauses)

Some conjunctions are used in pairs:

Both . . . and	neither. . . nor	whether . . . or
Either . . . or	not only . . . but also	

With paired conjunctions, you must be careful to construct each phrase in the same way.

They *not only* are out of racquets *but also* are out of balls.

They are *not only* out of racquets *but also* out of balls.

They are out of *not only* racquets *but also* balls.

In other words, the construction that follows each part of the pair must be parallel, containing the same verbs, prepositions, and so on. The same need for parallelism exists when using conjunctions to join the other parts of speech:

He is listed in *either* your roster *or* my roster.

He is listed *neither* in your roster *nor* on the master list.

They *both* gave *and* received notice.

A certain type of conjunction is used to join clauses that are unequal—that is, to join a main clause to one that is subordinate or dependent. Here is a partial list of conjunctions used to introduce dependent clauses:

although	before	once	unless
as soon as	even though	so that	until
because	if	that	when

Using conjunctions is also discussed in sections 1.7.3 and 1.7.4.

1.6.3 Articles and Interjections

Only three articles exist in English: *the*, *a*, and *an*. These words are used, like adjectives, to specify which item you are talking about.

Interjections are words that express no solid information, only emotion:

Wow!	Well, well!
Oh, no!	Good!

Such purely emotional language has its place in private life and advertising copy, but it only weakens the effect of most business writing.

1.7 Sentences

Sentences are constructed with the major building blocks, the parts of speech.

Money talks.

This two-word sentence consists of a noun (*money*) and a verb (*talks*). When used in this way, the noun works as the first requirement for a sentence, the subject, and the verb works as the second requirement, the predicate. Now look at this sentence:

They merged.

The subject in this case is a pronoun (*they*), and the predicate is a verb (*merged*). This is a sentence because it has a subject and a predicate. Here is yet another kind of sentence:

The plans are ready.

This sentence has a more complicated subject, the noun *plans* and the article *the*; the complete predicate is a state-of-being verb (*are*) and an adjective (*ready*).

Without these two parts, the subject (who or what does something) and the predicate (the doing of it), no collection of words is a sentence.

1.7.1 Commands

In commands, the subject (always *you*) is only understood, not stated:

(You) Move your desk to the better office.

(You) Please try to finish by six o'clock.

1.7.2 Longer Sentences

More complicated sentences have more complicated subjects and predicates, but they still have a simple subject and a predicate verb. In the following examples, the subject is underlined once, the predicate verb twice:

Marex and Contron enjoy higher earnings each quarter.

(*Marex* [and] *Contron* do something; *enjoy* is what they do.)

My interview, coming minutes after my freeway accident, did not impress or move anyone.

(*Interview* is what did something. What did it do? It *did* [not] *impress* [or] *move.*)

In terms of usable space, a steel warehouse, with its extremely long span of roof unsupported by pillars, makes more sense.

(*Warehouse* is what *makes.*)

These three sentences demonstrate several things. First, in all three sentences, the simple subject and predicate verb are the "bare bones" of the sentence, the parts that carry the core idea of the sentence. When trying to find the subject and predicate verb, disregard all prepositional phrases, modifiers, conjunctions, and articles.

Second, in the third sentence the verb is singular (*makes*) because the subject is singular (*warehouse*). Even though the plural noun *pillars* is closer to the verb, *warehouse* is the subject. So *warehouse* determines whether the verb is singular or plural. Subject and predicate must agree.

Third, the subject in the first sentence is compound (*Marex* [and] *Contron*). A compound subject, when connected by *and,* requires a plural verb (*enjoy*). Also in the second sentence, compound predicates are possible (*did* [not] *impress* [or] *move*).

Fourth, the second sentence incorporates a group of words—*coming minutes after my freeway accident*—containing a form of a verb (*coming*) and a noun (*accident*). Yet this group of words is not a complete sentence for two reasons:

- *Accident* is not the subject of *coming*. Not all nouns are subjects.
- A verb that ends in *ing* can never be the predicate of a sentence (unless preceded by a form of *to be,* as in *was coming*). Not all verbs are predicates.

Because they don't contain a subject and a predicate, the words *coming minutes after my freeway accident* (called a phrase) can't be written as a sentence. That is, the phrase cannot stand alone; it cannot begin with a capital letter and end with a period. So a phrase must always be just one part of a sentence.

Sometimes a sentence incorporates two or more groups of words that do contain a subject and a predicate; these word groups are called clauses:

My interview, because it came minutes after my freeway accident, did not impress or move anyone.

The independent clause is the portion of the sentence that could stand alone without revision:

My interview did not impress or move anyone.

The other part of the sentence could stand alone only by removing *because:*

(because) It came minutes after my freeway accident.

This part of the sentence is known as a dependent clause; although it has a subject and a predicate (just as an independent clause does), it's linked to the main part of the sentence by a word (*because*) showing its dependence.

In summary, the two types of clauses—dependent and independent—both have a subject and a predicate. Dependent clauses, however, do not bear the main meaning of the sentence and are therefore linked to an independent clause. Nor can phrases stand alone, because they lack both a subject and a predicate. Only independent clauses can be written as sentences without revision.

1.7.3 Sentence Fragments

An incomplete sentence (a phrase or a dependent clause) that is written as though it were a complete sentence is called a fragment. Consider the following sentence fragments:

> Marilyn Sanders, having had pilferage problems in her store for the past year. Refuses to accept the results of our investigation.

This serious error can easily be corrected by putting the two fragments together:

> Marilyn Sanders, having had pilferage problems in her store for the past year, refuses to accept the results of our investigation.

Not all fragments can be corrected so easily. Here's more information on Sanders's pilferage problem.

> Employees a part of it. No authority or discipline.

Only the writer knows the intended meaning of those two phrases. Perhaps the employees are taking part in the pilferage. If so, the sentence should read:

> Some employees are part of the pilferage problem.

On the other hand, it's possible that some employees are helping with the investigation. Then the sentence would read:

> Some employees are taking part in our investigation.

It's just as likely, however, that the employees are not only taking part in the pilferage but are also being analyzed:

> Those employees who are part of the pilferage problem will accept no authority or discipline.

Even more meanings could be read into these fragments. Because fragments can mean so many things, they mean nothing. No well-written memo, letter, or report ever demands the reader to be an imaginative genius.

One more type of fragment exists, the kind represented by a dependent clause. Note what *because* does to change what was once a unified sentence:

> Our stock of sprinklers is depleted.
> Because our stock of sprinklers is depleted.

Although the second version contains a subject and a predicate, adding *because* makes it a fragment. Words such as *because* form a special group of words called subordinating conjunctions. Here's a partial list:

since	though	whenever
although	if	unless
while	even if	after

When a word of this type begins a clause, the clause is dependent and cannot stand alone as a sentence. However, if a dependent clause is combined with an independent clause, it can convey a complete meaning. The independent clause may come before or after the dependent clause:

> We are unable to fill your order because our stock of sprinklers is depleted.

> Because our stock of sprinklers is depleted, we are unable to fill your order.

Another remedy for a fragment that is a dependent clause is to remove the subordinating conjunction. That solution leaves a simple but complete sentence:

> Our stock of sprinklers is depleted.

The actual details of a transaction will determine the best way to remedy a fragment problem.

The ban on fragments has one exception. Some advertising copy contains sentence fragments, written knowingly to convey a certain rhythm. However, advertising is the only area of business in which fragments are acceptable.

1.7.4 Fused Sentences and Comma Splices

Just as there can be too little in a group of words to make it a sentence, there can also be too much:

> All our mail is run through a postage meter every afternoon someone picks it up.

This example contains two sentences, not one, but the two have been blended so that it's hard to tell where one ends and the next begins. Is the mail run through a meter every afternoon? If so, the sentences should read:

> All our mail is run through a postage meter every afternoon. Someone picks it up.

Perhaps the mail is run through a meter at some other time (morning, for example) and is picked up every afternoon:

> All our mail is run through a postage meter. Every afternoon someone picks it up.

The order of words is the same in all three cases; sentence division makes all the difference. Either of the last two cases is grammatically correct. The choice depends on the facts of the situation.

Sometimes these so-called fused sentences have a more obvious point of separation:

> Several large orders arrived within a few days of one another, too many came in for us to process by the end of the month.

Here the comma has been put between two independent clauses in an attempt to link them. When a lowly comma separates two complete sentences, the result is called a comma splice. A comma splice can be remedied in one of three ways:

- Replace the comma with a period and capitalize the next word: ". . . one another. Too many . . ."

- Replace the comma with a semicolon and do not capitalize the next word: " . . . one another; too many . . ." This remedy works only when the two sentences have closely related meanings.
- Change one of the sentences so that it becomes a phrase or a dependent clause. This remedy often produces the best writing, but it takes more work.

The third alternative can be carried out in several ways. One is to begin the blended sentence with a subordinating conjunction:

> Whenever several large orders arrived within a few days of one another, too many came in for us to process by the end of the month.

Another way is to remove part of the subject or the predicate verb from one of the independent clauses, thereby creating a phrase:

> Several large orders arrived within a few days of one another, too many for us to process by the end of the month.

Finally, you can change one of the predicate verbs to its *ing* form:

> Several large orders arrived within a few days of one another, too many coming in for us to process by the end of the month.

At other times a simple coordinating conjunction (such as *or, and,* or *but*) can separate fused sentences:

> You can fire them, or you can make better use of their abilities.
>
> Margaret drew up the designs, and Matt carried them out.
>
> We will have three strong months, but after that sales will taper off.

Be careful using coordinating conjunctions: Use them only to join simple sentences that express similar ideas.

Also, because they say relatively little about the relationship between the two clauses they join, avoid using coordinating conjunctions too often: *and* is merely an addition sign; *but* is just a turn signal; *or* only points to an alternative. Subordinating conjunctions such as *because* and *whenever* tell the reader a lot more.

1.7.5 Sentences with Linking Verbs

Linking verbs were discussed briefly in the section on verbs (Section 1.3). Here you can see more fully the way they function in a sentence. The following is a model of any sentence with a linking verb:

> A (*verb*) B.

Although words such as *seems* and *feels* can also be linking verbs, let's assume that the verb is a form of *to be:*

> A *is* B.

In such a sentence, A and B are always nouns, pronouns, or adjectives. When one is a noun and the other is a pronoun, or when both are nouns, the sentence says that one is the same as the other:

> She is president.
> Rachel is president.

When one is an adjective, it modifies or describes the other:

> She is forceful.

Remember that when one is an adjective, it modifies the other as any adjective modifies a noun or pronoun, except that a linking verb stands between the adjective and the word it modifies.

1.7.6 Misplaced Modifiers

The position of a modifier in a sentence is important. The movement of *only* changes the meaning in the following sentences:

> Only we are obliged to supply those items specified in your contract.
>
> We are obliged only to supply those items specified in your contract.
>
> We are obliged to supply only those items specified in your contract.
>
> We are obliged to supply those items specified only in your contract.

In any particular set of circumstances, only one of those sentences would be accurate. The others would very likely cause problems. To prevent misunderstanding, place modifiers such as *only* as close as possible to the noun or verb they modify.

For similar reasons, whole phrases that are modifiers must be placed near the right noun or verb. Mistakes in placement create ludicrous meanings:

> Antia Information Systems has bought new computer chairs for the programmers *with more comfortable seats.*

The anatomy of programmers is not normally a concern of business writers. Obviously, the comfort of the chairs was the issue:

> Antia Information Systems has bought new computer chairs *with more comfortable seats* for the programmers.

Here is another example:

> I asked him to file all the letters in the cabinet that had been answered.

In this ridiculous sentence the cabinet has been answered, even though no cabinet in history is known to have asked a question.

That had been answered is too far from *letters* and too close to *cabinet.* Here's an improvement:

> I asked him to file in the cabinet all the letters that had been answered.

In some cases, instead of moving the modifying phrase closer to the word it modifies, the best solution is to move the word closer to the modifying phrase.

2.0 PUNCTUATION

On the highway, signs tell you when to slow down or stop, where to turn, when to merge. In similar fashion, punctuation helps readers negotiate your prose. The proper use of punctuation keeps readers from losing track of your meaning.

2.1 Periods

Use a period (1) to end any sentence that is not a question, (2) with certain abbreviations, and (3) between dollars and cents in an amount of money.

2.2 Question Marks

Use a question mark after any direct question that requests an answer:

> Are you planning to enclose a check, or shall we bill you?

Don't use a question mark with commands phrased as questions for the sake of politeness:

> Will you send us a check today.

2.3 Exclamation Points

Use exclamation points after highly emotional language. Because business writing almost never calls for emotional language, you will seldom use exclamation points.

2.4 Semicolons

Semicolons have three main uses. One is to separate two closely related independent clauses:

> The outline for the report is due within a week; the report itself is due at the end of the month.

A semicolon should also be used instead of a comma when the items in a series have commas within them:

> Our previous meetings were on November 11, 1998; February 20, 1999; and April 28, 2000.

Finally, a semicolon should be used to separate independent clauses when the second one begins with a word such as *however, therefore,* or *nevertheless* or a phrase such as *for example* or *in that case:*

> Our supplier has been out of part D712 for 10 weeks; however, we have found another source that can ship the part right away.

> His test scores were quite low; on the other hand, he has a lot of relevant experience.

Section 4.4 has more information on using transitional words and phrases.

2.5 Colons

Use a colon after the salutation in a business letter. You also use a colon at the end of a sentence or phrase introducing a list or (sometimes) a quotation:

> Our study included the three most critical problems: insufficient capital, incompetent management, and inappropriate location.

In some introductory sentences, phrases such as *the following* or *that is* are implied by using a colon.

A colon should not be used when the list, quotation, or idea is a direct object or part of the introductory sentence:

> We are able to supply
> staples
> wood screws
> nails
> toggle bolts

> This shipment includes 9 videotapes, 12 CDs, and 14 cassette tapes.

Another way you can use a colon is to separate the main clause and another sentence element when the second explains, illustrates, or amplifies the first:

> Management was unprepared for the union rep's demands: this fact alone accounts for their arguing well into the night.

However, in contemporary usage, such clauses are frequently separated by a semicolon.

2.6 Commas

Commas have many uses; the most common is to separate items in a series:

> He took the job, learned it well, worked hard, and succeeded.

> Put paper, pencils, and paper clips on the requisition list.

Company style often dictates omitting the final comma in a series. However, if you have a choice, use the final comma; it's often necessary to prevent misunderstanding.

A second place to use a comma is between independent clauses that are joined by a coordinating conjunction (*and, but,* or *or*) unless one or both are very short:

> She spoke to the sales staff, and he spoke to the production staff.

> I was advised to proceed and I did.

A third use for the comma is to separate a dependent clause at the beginning of a sentence from an independent clause:

> Because of our lead in the market, we may be able to risk introducing a new product.

However, a dependent clause at the end of a sentence is separated from the independent clause by a comma only when the dependent clause is unnecessary to the main meaning of the sentence:

> We may be able to introduce a new product, although it may involve some risk.

A fourth use for the comma is after an introductory phrase or word:

> Starting with this amount of capital, we can survive in the red for one year.
>
> Through more careful planning, we may be able to serve more people.
>
> Yes, you may proceed as originally planned.

However, with short introductory prepositional phrases and some one-syllable words (such as *hence* and *thus*), the comma is often omitted:

> Before January 1 we must complete the inventory.
>
> Thus we may not need to hire anyone.
>
> In short the move to Tulsa was a good idea.

Fifth, commas are used to surround nonrestrictive phrases or words (expressions that can be removed from the sentence without changing the meaning):

> The new owners, the Kowacks, are pleased with their purchase.

Sixth, commas are used between adjectives modifying the same noun (coordinate adjectives):

> She left Monday for a long, difficult recruiting trip.

To test the appropriateness of such a comma, try reversing the order of the adjectives: *a difficult, long recruiting trip*. If the order cannot be reversed, leave out the comma (*a good old friend* isn't the same as *an old good friend*). A comma is also not used when one of the adjectives is part of the noun. Compare these two phrases:

> a distinguished, well-known figure
>
> a distinguished public figure

The adjective-noun combination of *public* and *figure* has been used together so often that it has come to be considered a single thing: *public figure*. So no comma is required.

Seventh, commas should precede *Inc.*, *Ltd.*, and the like:

> Cloverdell, Inc. Beamer, Ltd.

In a sentence, a comma also follows such abbreviations:

> Belle Brown, Ph.D., is the new tenant.

Eighth, commas are used both before and after the year in sentences that include month, day, and year:

> It will be sent by December 15, 2002, from our Cincinnati plant.

Some companies write dates in another form: 15 December 2002. No commas should be used in that case. Nor is a comma needed when only the month and year are present (December 2002).

Ninth, a comma may be used after an informal salutation in a letter to a personal friend. (In business letters, however, the salutation is followed by a colon.)

Tenth, a comma is used to separate a quotation from the rest of the sentence:

> Your warranty reads, "These conditions remain in effect for one year from date of purchase."

However, the comma is left out when the quotation as a whole is built into the structure of the sentence:

> He hurried off with an angry "Look where you're going."

Finally, a comma should be used whenever it's needed to avoid confusion or an unintended meaning. Compare the following:

> Ever since they have planned new ventures more carefully.
>
> Ever since, they have planned new ventures more carefully.

2.7 Dashes

Use a dash to surround a comment that is a sudden turn in thought:

> Membership in the IBSA—it's expensive but worth it—may be obtained by applying to our New York office.

A dash can also be used to emphasize a parenthetical word or phrase:

> Third-quarter profits—in excess of $2 million—are up sharply.

Finally, use dashes to set off a phrase that contains commas:

> All our offices—Milwaukee, New Orleans, and Phoenix—have sent representatives.

Don't confuse a dash with a hyphen. A dash separates and emphasizes words, phrases, and clauses more strongly than a comma or parentheses can; a hyphen ties two words so tightly that they almost become one word.

On computer, use the em dash symbol. When typing a dash in e-mail or on a typewriter, type two hyphens with no space before, between, or after.

2.8 Hyphens

Hyphens are mainly used in three ways. The first is to separate the parts of compound words beginning with such prefixes as *self-*, *ex-*, *quasi-*, and *all-*:

> self-assured quasi-official
> ex-wife all-important

However, hyphens are usually left out and the words closed up in words that have such prefixes as *pro*, *anti*, *non*, *un*, *inter*, and *extra*:

> prolabor nonunion
> antifascist interdepartmental

Exceptions occur when (1) the prefix occurs before a proper noun or (2) the vowel at the end of the prefix is the same as the first letter of the root word:

> pro-Republican anti-American
> anti-inflammatory extra-atmospheric

When in doubt, consult your dictionary.

Hyphens are also used in some compound adjectives, which are adjectives made up of two or more words. Specifically, you should use hyphens in compound adjectives that come before the noun:

an interest-bearing account   well-informed executives

However, you need not hyphenate when the adjective follows a linking verb:

This account is interest bearing.

Their executives are well informed.

You can shorten sentences that list similar hyphenated words by dropping the common part from all but the last word:

Check the costs of first-, second-, and third-class postage.

Finally, hyphens may be used to divide words at the end of a typed line. Such hyphenation is best avoided, but when you have to divide words at the end of a line, do so correctly (see Section 3.4). A dictionary will show how words are divided into syllables.

2.9 Apostrophes

Use an apostrophe in the possessive form of a noun (but not in a pronoun):

On *his* desk was a reply to Bette *Ainsley's* application for the *manager's* position.

Apostrophes are also used in place of the missing letter(s) of a contraction:

Whole Words	Contraction
we will	we'll
do not	don't
they are	they're

2.10 Quotation Marks

Use quotation marks to surround words that are repeated exactly as they were said or written:

The collection letter ended by saying, "This is your third and final notice."

Remember: (1) When the quoted material is a complete sentence, the first word is capitalized. (2) The final comma or period goes inside the closing quotation marks.

Quotation marks are also used to set off the title of a newspaper story, magazine article, or book chapter:

You should read "Legal Aspects of the Collection Letter" in *Today's Credit.*

The book title is shown here in italics. When typewritten, the title is underlined. The same treatment is proper for newspaper and magazine titles. (Appendix II explains documentation style in more detail.)

Quotation marks may also be used to indicate special treatment for words or phrases, such as terms that you're using in an unusual or ironic way:

Our management "team" spends more time squabbling than working to solve company problems.

When using quotation marks, take care to insert both sets—the closing marks as well as the opening ones.

Although periods and commas always go inside any quotation marks, colons and semicolons go outside them. A question mark goes inside the quotation marks only if the quotation is a question:

All that day we wondered, "Is he with us?"

If the quotation is not a question but the entire sentence is, the question mark goes outside:

What did she mean by "You will hear from me"?

2.11 Parentheses

Use parentheses to surround comments that are entirely incidental:

Our figures do not match yours, although (if my calculations are correct) they are closer than we thought.

Parentheses are also used in legal documents to surround figures in arabic numerals that follow the same amount in words:

Remittance will be One Thousand Two Hundred Dollars ($1,200).

Be careful to put punctuation (period, comma, and so on) outside the parentheses unless it is part of the statement in parentheses.

2.12 Ellipses

Use ellipsis points, or three spaced dots, to indicate that material has been left out of a direct quotation. Use them only in direct quotations and only at the point where material was left out. In the following example, the first sentence is quoted in the second:

The Dow Jones Industrial Average, which skidded 38.17 points in the previous five sessions, gained 4.61 to end at 2213.84.

According to the *Honolulu Star Bulletin,* "The Dow Jones Industrial Average . . . gained 4.61" on June 10.

The number of dots in ellipses is not optional; always use three. Occasionally, the points of ellipsis come at the end of a sentence, where they seem to grow a fourth dot. Don't be fooled: The first dot is the period that ends the sentence.

2.13 Underscores and Italics

Usually a line typed underneath a word or phrase either provides emphasis or indicates the title of a book, magazine, or newspaper. If possible, use italics instead of an underscore. Italics (or underlining) should also be used for defining terms and for discussing words as words:

> In this report *net sales* refers to after-tax sales dollars.

> The word *building* is a common noun and should not be capitalized.

3.0 MECHANICS

The most obvious and least tolerable mistakes that a business writer makes are probably those related to grammar and punctuation. However, a number of small details, known as writing mechanics, demonstrate the writer's polish and reflect on the company's professionalism.

3.1 Capitals

You should capitalize words that begin sentences:

> *Before* hanging up, he said, "*We'll* meet here on Wednesday at noon."

A quotation that is a complete sentence should also begin with a capitalized word.

Capitalize the names of particular persons, places, and things (proper nouns):

> We sent Ms. Larson an application form, informing her that not all applicants are interviewed.

> Let's consider opening a branch in the West, perhaps at the west end of Tucson, Arizona.

> As office buildings go, the Kinney Building is a pleasant setting for TDG Office Equipment.

Ms. Larson's name is capitalized because she is a particular applicant, whereas the general term *applicant* is left uncapitalized. Likewise, *West* is capitalized when it refers to a particular place but not when it means a direction. In the same way, *office* and *building* are not capitalized when they are general terms (common nouns), but they are capitalized when they are part of the title of a particular office or building (proper nouns).

Titles within families, governments, or companies may also be capitalized:

> When Uncle David offered me a job, I had to decline because I wouldn't be comfortable working for one of my uncles.

> We've never had a president quite like President Sweeney.

In addition, always capitalize the first word of the salutation and complimentary close of a letter:

> *Dear* Mr. Andrews: *Yours* very truly,

Finally, capitalize the first word after a colon when it begins a complete sentence:

> Follow this rule: When in doubt, leave it out.

Otherwise, the first word after a colon should not be capitalized (see Section 2.5).

3.2 Abbreviations

Abbreviations are used heavily in tables, charts, lists, and forms. They're used sparingly in prose paragraphs, however. Here are some abbreviations often used in business writing:

Abbreviation	Full Term
b/l	bill of lading
ca.	circa (about)
dol., dols.	dollar, dollars
etc.	et cetera (and so on)
FDIC	Federal Deposit Insurance Corporation
Inc.	Incorporated
L.f.	Ledger folio
Ltd.	Limited
mgr.	manager
NSF or N/S	not sufficient funds
P&L or P/L	profit and loss
reg.	regular
whsle.	wholesale

Because *etc.* contains a word meaning "and," never write *and etc.*

3.3 Numbers

Numbers may be correctly handled many ways in business writing, so follow company style. In the absence of a set style, however, generally spell out all numbers from one to nine and use arabic numerals for the rest.

There are some exceptions to this general rule. First, never begin a sentence with a numeral:

> *Twenty* of us produced *641* units per week in the first *12* weeks of the year.

Second, use numerals for the numbers one through nine if they're in the same list as larger numbers:

> Our weekly quota rose from *9* to *15* to *27*.

Third, use numerals for percentages, time of day (except with *o'clock*), dates, and (in general) dollar amounts.

> Our division is responsible for *7* percent of total sales.

> The meeting is scheduled for *8:30* A.M. on August *2*.

> Add *$3* for postage and handling.

Use a comma in numbers with four digits (*1,257*), unless the company specifies another style.

When writing dollar amounts, use a decimal point only if cents are included. In lists of two or more dollar amounts, use the decimal point either for all or for none:

> He sent two checks, one for *$67.92* and one for *$90.00*.

3.4 Word Division

In general, avoid dividing words at the ends of lines. When you must, follow these rules:

- Don't divide one-syllable words (such as *since, walked,* and *thought*); abbreviations (*mgr.*); contractions (*doesn't*); or numbers expressed in numerals (*117,500*).
- Divide words between syllables, as specified in a dictionary or word-division manual.
- Make sure that at least three letters of the divided word are moved to the second line: *sin-cerely* instead of *sincere-ly.*
- Do not end a page or more than three consecutive lines with hyphens.
- Leave syllables consisting of a single vowel at the end of the first line (*impedi-ment* instead of *imped-iment*), except when the single vowel is part of a suffix such as *-able, -ible, -ical,* or *-ity* (*re-spons-ible* instead of *re-sponsi-ble*).
- Divide between double letters (*tomor-row*), except when the root word ends in double letters (*call-ing* instead of *cal-ling*).
- Wherever possible, divide hyphenated words at the hyphen only: Instead of *anti-inde-pendence,* use *anti-independence.*

4.0 VOCABULARY

Using the right word in the right place is a crucial skill in business communication. However, many pitfalls await the unwary.

4.1 Frequently Confused Words

Because the following sets of words sound similar, be careful not to use one when you mean to use the other:

Word	Meaning
accede	to comply with
exceed	to go beyond
accept	to take
except	to exclude
access	admittance
excess	too much
advice	suggestion
advise	to suggest
affect	to influence
effect	the result
allot	to distribute
a lot	much or many
all ready	completely prepared
already	completed earlier
born	given birth to
borne	carried
capital	money; chief city
capitol	a government building
cite	to quote
sight	a view
site	a location
complement	complete amount; to go well with
compliment	to flatter
corespondent	party in a divorce suit
correspondent	letter writer
council	a panel of people
counsel	advice; a lawyer
defer	to put off until later
differ	to be different
device	a mechanism
devise	to plan
die	to stop living; a tool
dye	to color
discreet	careful
discrete	separate
envelop	to surround
envelope	a covering for a letter
forth	forward
fourth	number four
holey	full of holes
holy	sacred
wholly	completely
human	of people
humane	kindly
incidence	frequency
incidents	events
instance	example
instants	moments
interstate	between states
intrastate	within a state
later	afterward
latter	the second of two

lead	a metal
led	guided
lean	to rest at an angle
lien	a claim
levee	embankment
levy	tax
loath	reluctant
loathe	to hate
loose	free; not tight
lose	to mislay
material	substance
materiel	equipment
miner	mineworker
minor	underage person
moral	virtuous; a lesson
morale	sense of well-being
ordinance	law
ordnance	weapons
overdo	to do in excess
overdue	past due
peace	lack of conflict
piece	a fragment
pedal	a foot lever
peddle	to sell
persecute	to torment
prosecute	to sue
personal	private
personnel	employees
precedence	priority
precedents	previous events
principal	sum of money; chief; main
principle	general rule
rap	to knock
wrap	to cover
residence	home
residents	inhabitants
right	correct
rite	ceremony
write	to form words on a surface
role	a part to play
roll	to tumble; a list
root	part of a plant
rout	to defeat
route	a traveler's way
shear	to cut
sheer	thin, steep
stationary	immovable
stationery	paper
than	as compared with
then	at that time
their	belonging to them
there	in that place
they're	they are
to	a preposition
too	excessively; also
two	the number
waive	to set aside
wave	a swell of water; a gesture
weather	atmospheric conditions
whether	if

In the preceding list, only enough of each word's meaning is given to help you distinguish between the words in each group. Several meanings are left out entirely. For more complete definitions, consult a dictionary.

4.2 Frequently Misused Words

The following words tend to be misused for reasons other than their sound. Reference books (including the *Random House College Dictionary,* revised edition; Follett's *Modern American Usage;* and Fowler's *Modern English Usage*) can help you with similar questions of usage.

a lot: When the writer means "many," *a lot* is always two separate words, never one.

correspond with: Use this phrase when you are talking about exchanging letters. Use *correspond to* when you mean "similar to." Use either *correspond with* or *correspond to* when you mean "relate to."

disinterested: This word means "fair, unbiased, having no favorites, impartial." If you mean "bored" or "not interested," use *uninterested.*

etc.: This is the abbreviated form of a Latin phrase, *et cetera.* It means "and so on" or "and so forth." The current tendency among business writers is to use English rather than Latin.

imply/infer: Both refer to hints. Their great difference lies in who is acting. The writer implies; the reader infers, sees between the lines.

lay: This is a transitive verb. Never use it for the intransitive *lie.* (See Section 1.3.3.)

less: Use *less* for uncountable quantities (such as amounts of water, air, sugar, and oil). Use *fewer* for countable quantities (such as numbers of jars, saws, words, pages, and humans). The same distinction applies to *much* and *little* (uncountable) versus *many* and *few* (countable).

like: Use *like* only when the word that follows is just a noun or a pronoun. Use *as* or *as if* when a phrase or clause follows:

> She looks *like* him.
> She did just *as* he had expected.
> It seems *as if* she had plenty of time.

many/much: See *less.*

regardless: The *less* ending is the negative part. No word needs two negative parts, so it is illiterate to add *ir* (a negative prefix) at the beginning.

to me/personally: Use these phrases only when personal reactions, apart from company policy, are being stated (not often the case in business writing).

try: Always follow with *to,* never *and.*

verbal: People in the business community who are careful with language frown on those who use verbal to mean "spoken" or "oral." Many others do say "verbal agreement." Strictly speaking, *verbal* means "of words" and therefore includes both spoken and written words. Be guided in this matter by company usage.

4.3 Frequently Misspelled Words

All of us, even the world's best spellers, sometimes have to check a dictionary for the spelling of some words. People who have never memorized the spelling of commonly used words must look up so many that they grow exasperated and give up on spelling words correctly.

Don't expect perfection, and don't surrender. If you can memorize the spelling of just the words listed here, you'll need the dictionary far less often and you'll write with more confidence.

absence
absorption
accessible
accommodate
accumulate
achieve
advantageous
affiliated
aggressive
alignment
aluminum
ambience
analyze
apparent
appropriate
argument
asphalt
assistant
asterisk
auditor

bankruptcy
believable
brilliant
bulletin

calendar
campaign
category
ceiling
changeable
clientele
collateral
committee
comparative
competitor
concede
congratulations
connoisseur
consensus
convenient
convertible
corroborate
criticism

definitely
description
desirable
dilemma
disappear
disappoint
disbursement
discrepancy
dissatisfied
dissipate

eligible
embarrassing
endorsement
exaggerate
exceed
exhaust
existence
extraordinary

fallacy
familiar
flexible
fluctuation
forty

gesture
grievous

haphazard
harassment
holiday

illegible
immigrant
incidentally
indelible
independent
indispensable
insistent
intermediary
irresistible

jewelry
judgment
judicial

labeling
legitimate
leisure
license
litigation

maintenance
mathematics
mediocre
minimum

necessary
negligence
negotiable

newsstand
noticeable

occurrence
omission

parallel
pastime
peaceable
permanent
perseverance
persistent
personnel
persuade
possesses
precede
predictable
preferred
privilege
procedure
proceed
pronunciation
psychology
pursue

questionnaire

receive
recommend
repetition
rescind
rhythmical
ridiculous

salable
secretary
seize
separate
sincerely
succeed
suddenness
superintendent
supersede
surprise

tangible
tariff
technique
tenant
truly

unanimous
until

vacillate
vacuum
vicious

4.4 Transitional Words and Phrases

The following sentences don't communicate as well as they might because they lack a transitional word or phrase:

> Production delays are inevitable. Our current lag time in filling orders is one month.

A semicolon between the two sentences would signal a close relationship between their meanings, but it wouldn't even hint at what that relationship is. Here are the sentences, now linked by means of a semicolon, with a space for a transitional word or phrase:

> Production delays are inevitable; ________, our current lag time in filling orders is one month.

Now read the sentence with *nevertheless* in the blank space. Now try *therefore, incidentally, in fact,* and *at any rate* in the blank. Each substitution changes the meaning of the sentence.

Here are some transitional words (called conjunctive adverbs) that will help you write more clearly:

accordingly	furthermore	moreover
anyway	however	otherwise
besides	incidentally	still
consequently	likewise	therefore
finally	meanwhile	

The following transitional phrases are used in the same way:

as a result	in other words
at any rate	in the second place
for example	on the other hand
in fact	to the contrary

When one of these words or phrases joins two independent clauses, it should be preceded by a semicolon and followed by a comma, as shown here:

> The consultant recommended a complete reorganization; moreover, she suggested that we drop several products.

Appendix IV

Tips for Effective E-Mail

Electronic communication is so quick and easy that it's often the most popular way to contact people. Sending e-mail almost guarantees you'll reach your audience. Many businesspeople travel with their laptop computers and check their e-mail no matter where they are.

Indeed, e-mail has revolutionized the way we work. It helps us respond to customers and co-workers faster. It allows us to communicate at our own convenience—even when that's at 2:00 A.M. or from 2,000 miles away. E-mail can also save valuable time by enabling the frontline staff to communicate with executives without going through the formal chain of command.

However, for all its advantages, e-mail has specific limitations. Keep in mind that nothing beats face-to-face communication. Electronic communication may be faster and more convenient, but the best way to build a relationship with someone is in person. E-mail cannot convey emotion or tone the way a face-to-face conversation or even a phone call can. And when you want to send a special message or make a personal impression, consider using traditional paper and pen. Your message may arrive several days later, but the greater impact makes the effort worthwhile.

The fact is that ineffective e-mail can cause outright confusion and loss of productivity. For instance, executives who rely too heavily on e-mail and avoid personal meetings can lower morale and make employees feel neglected. The best business communicators know the basics of e-mail: They know how to communicate quickly and courteously. They know how to refrain from putting anything in writing that could come back to haunt them. And they know how important it is to proofread e-mail messages before sending them. The following tips will help you communicate better by e-mail.

FOLLOW YOUR ORGANIZATION'S GUIDELINES

Organizations need their employees to use e-mail in a responsible, businesslike manner. Thus, many companies actually train employees in the use of e-mail. At the least, most organizations develop guidelines for effective e-mail use. These guidelines set a positive framework for the use of e-mail by making known organizational expectations and policies. They may even help employees reduce unnecessary communications and confusion by defining appropriate e-mail content and use.

Typical e-mail guidelines include the following instructions:

- **Stick to appropriate content.** In most organizations, e-mail is used for sharing information such as goals, schedules, research, company news, and the like. Electronic messages are not the place for delivering tragic news or for disciplining people. Such messages should be reserved for personal meetings.
- **Avoid sending personal messages at work.** In countless incidents, employees have been dismissed because they sent personal e-mail—messages that criticized their company, discussed starting a new business, or mentioned a new position with another company. Moreover, many companies archive all e-mail for at least two years, so personal e-mails may live for a long time.
- **Follow the chain of command.** E-mail makes it possible for any employee to communicate directly with any other employee, even the CEO. But don't abuse this convenience. When corresponding with superiors, for instance, don't send a complaint via e-mail straight to the "top" just because e-mail makes it easy to do so. Your e-mail is more effective if you follow the organizational hierarchy.
- **Compose offline.** When you are composing an important e-mail message, consider drafting your letter in a word processor and then cutting and pasting your letter into the body of your e-mail. This way, you can spend the time necessary to compose just the message you want but without using up network resources or incurring significant Internet connect charges.

RESPECT YOUR READERS

Common courtesy is an important consideration when sending e-mail. Because e-mail creates a false sense of intimacy, audience focus is as important in e-mail as in every other type of business communication. Your writing reflects both your personality and your professionalism, so to be among the best communicators, always think about how your messages affect your various audiences. To be truly respectful and considerate, you must take extra care to ensure that your message reaches the proper audience, that it addresses your readers in the terms they expect, that it doesn't waste their time, and that it doesn't impose on them with insensitive material.

- **Send only necessary messages.** One of the things that makes e-mail different from other types of business communication is volume. In a survey of 17 companies across 10 industries, 72 percent of respondents said they spend one to two hours daily just handling e-mail. Ten percent of those e-mails are unnecessary and unwanted. So it's important to do your best not to add to this information overload.[1]
- **Know who your audience is.** As you consider what to say, also think about who actually needs to hear it. Then before clicking the Send button, double-check your addressees to make sure you've included everyone necessary and no one else. An oversight could prevent an urgent message from reaching intended recipients or, worse yet, could cause your message to be sent to unintended recipients.
- **Know your audience's culture.** In addition to knowing the names and addresses of your readers, make sure you know their culture and language before you begin to write. If necessary, have your message translated into the language(s) best understood by your audience.
- **Be clear about time.** When sending international e-mail messages, be sure to use a 24-hour, military time format. For example, instead of saying "6:00 P.M.," say "18:00." Also, be sure to indicate the appropriate time zone, such as Eastern Standard Time (EST) or Pacific Standard Time (PST).
- **Respect your audience's schedule.** By sending an e-mail message, you're taking up other people's time. For example, you might identify messages that require no response by including words such as "for your information only" in your subject line or opening comments. And be sure not to send jokes, chain letters, or derogatory comments.
- **Don't flame.** An e-mail message that contains insensitive, insulting, or critical comments is called a flame. If you're upset about something or angry with someone, compose yourself before composing your e-mail. If you're fuming, give yourself 48 hours to cool off before writing your e-mail message. If you do write an emotionally charged message, leave it in your outbox or drafts folder for at least a day. Ask yourself, "Would I say this face-to-face?" Remember that a live person is on the receiving end of your communication.
- **Use the priority feature with care.** Many e-mail packages allow you to assign a priority to your message, such as *high, normal,* or *low.* Such priority simply helps readers decide how quickly to read and respond to messages. However, if every message you send is "high priority," readers will begin to disregard the label and question the importance of all your messages. So make sure the priority assigned to your message matches its urgency.

CREATE THE RIGHT TONE

Be friendly; smile as you write—your tone shows in your message. It may be tempting to toss around the sort of cyberspeak prevalent on the Internet, but be careful. Business e-mail differs from personal e-mail—it's closer to a business letter than a phone call or face-to-face meeting. So leave off the "cute" stuff, and by all means avoid sarcasm.

- **Don't use offbeat acronyms.** Acronyms such as BCNU (be seeing you), FWIW (for what it's worth) and IMHO (in my humble opinion) annoy people rather than amuse them. Although such acronyms may seem to be a shortcut for the writer, they are not easily interpreted by those unfamiliar with them—especially non-native English speakers. To be considerate and as clear as possible, reserve cyber shorthand for strictly personal messages away from work.
- **Steer clear of smileys and other gimmicks.** Rely on the strength of your writing—not on smileys or other typeface gimmicks—to communicate your intended message in the appropriate tone. Overusing smileys and other cyber gimmicks reflects poorly on you any way you look at it. People who are unfamiliar with these notations will not understand them, and more experienced readers will label you an e-mail novice.
- **Avoid using exclamation points.** Many e-mail writers mistakenly believe that they can inject life into their electronic writing—and elicit reader interest—by slapping an exclamation point on every important sentence. Don't fall into this trap. Just as you would in other types of business communication, put power into your writing by selecting descriptive words and crafting well-written sentences. Use exclamation points sparingly, if at all.

CULTIVATE GOOD COMMUNICATION SKILLS

As with other types of business communication, e-mail that contains disorganized ideas, intimidating layout, or grammatically incorrect sentences is a reflection on your organization. Clients often evaluate a company's capability and dependability based on its written communications, including e-mail. Poor writing suggests to customers and other outsiders that your product or service may be poor as well. Moreover, poor writing limits personal promotions within an organization. Your entire relationship with co-workers or customers may rest solely on your e-mail exchanges. You could complete a $40 million project without ever meeting your co-workers or customers face-to-face. So reflect a positive company image and a responsible personal image by making your e-mail messages simple, clear, and accurate.

- **Keep subject lines truthful.** Despite the instant nature of e-mail, it is still necessary to compose a document that keeps the reader's attention. E-mail subject lines can be effective attention-grabbers. However, be careful that you don't stretch the truth. A reader may fall for a misleading subject line once, but that reader may ignore or delete your next message before reading it.
- **Limit the scope of e-mail messages.** Each e-mail message should have only one purpose. If you find yourself with two or three purposes, write separate e-mails. This narrow scope not only helps your readers focus on your message but also facilitates filing and forwarding. Addressing only one topic in each message makes relevant e-mail easier to find later on. Multiple-topic messages are difficult to retrieve when you need them for reference.
- **Craft tight, meaningful messages.** Cover only what is necessary. Identify the issue, add the relevant facts, suggest a resolution, mention possible obstacles, present a timetable for response, and ask for agreement.
- **Write short e-mail messages.** Keep your e-mail messages short whenever possible. Many recipients delete e-mails that exceed three or four paragraphs. Short, direct messages have a much better chance of being understood and acted on than long, roundabout ones. However, be careful not to edit your e-mail messages so much that your readers cannot understand them. Make sure you include all relevant information, especially if you're sending a question to someone you don't know.
- **Rely on short sentences.** Long sentences are particularly hard to read on screen. They tend to bury ideas and confuse readers. Whenever possible, break up long sentences into short, concise ones. If you need to write longer sentences now and then, make sure they are logically and clearly written.
- **Aim for clarity over hype.** Writing e-mail messages is no different from writing other business correspondence. They must be clear and concise, and they must be inoffensive to the reader. For example, if you use a signature file or other identifier at the bottom of your e-mail messages to provide your contact information, refrain from including marketing hype thinly disguised as a signature block.

MAINTAIN AN INTELLIGIBLE APPEARANCE

Clarity is the goal of e-mail, so your first step toward ease of reading is to avoid a cluttered appearance. Before your readers can even try to grasp your message, they must be able to physically read it. The easier it is for your audience to decipher your message, the easier it will be to communicate your ideas.

- **Use an appropriate typeface.** Few things are harder to read than e-mail composed with unusual type. Whenever your subject is business-related, create a polished, professional look by using a standard typeface such as Times New Roman, Courier, or Arial. Moreover, keep font size between 10 and 12 points, as most readers are comfortable reading text within that range.
- **Don't yell.** A message written in all uppercase letters is considered yelling and is more difficult to read than one written in standard style. Audiences are used to reading a mixture of uppercase and lowercase letters. When you draft e-mail in uppercase letters, you run the risk of slowing down and annoying readers.
- **Don't whisper either.** A message written in all lowercase letters is considered whispering and is just as difficult to read as a message written using all uppercase letters. In addition, using all lowercase implies insecurity or meekness on your part.
- **Use white space.** Just as you would in other business messages, include plenty of white space in e-mail messages. Avoid using large amounts of text, separate paragraphs with a blank line, and use bullets and headings for clarity and ease of reading.
- **Avoid double-spacing.** Although double-spacing between paragraphs aids readability, never double-space your entire e-mail message. Readers need to grasp sentences, paragraphs, and lists as single units. Double-spacing on the screen makes that more difficult to do.

MAKE RESPONSIBLE REPLIES

E-mail makes it extremely easy to reply to messages—almost too easy. Whenever you use the automatic reply feature, take every precaution. You definitely want to avoid sending replies to the wrong recipients, overloading recipients with unnecessary messages, confusing readers with inappropriate subject lines, and revealing more than you intend about just who is receiving a copy of your message.

- **Be sure you hit the right reply button.** When you receive an e-mail message, it may be addressed to you alone, it may be addressed to dozens of other recipients, it may be "copied" to others, or it may be "blind copied" to recipients that you don't even know about. So when you reply, make sure you hit the correct reply button. Don't carelessly hit the "reply to all" button.
- **When you choose to "reply to all," do so wisely.** Even though the original e-mail sender may think it's a good idea to update everyone on the team, not all

team members may need to see every recipient's reply. No one wants to receive e-mail messages that are irrelevant or unnecessary. And if colleagues receive such messages from you, it won't be long before they simply ignore your messages altogether.

- **Modify subject lines.** When you hit the "reply" or "forward" button on an e-mail message, the same subject line appears on the new document. This "thread" becomes a convenience for the first few responses, but too many messages with the same subject line can become confusing. Typically, after a few volleys, change the subject line to keep it informative and focused on the specific topic of the latest message.
- **Understand the use of the cc and bcc fields.** When you add addresses to the cc (courtesy copy) field, a copy of your message will go to each person, and each recipient will be able to see who else received a copy. When you add addresses to the bcc (blind courtesy copy) field, a copy of your message will also go to each person; however, to add a degree of privacy, no recipient will be able to see who else received a copy of your message.

TAKE TIME TO RESPOND CAREFULLY

E-mail's speed is its greatest benefit and can also be its greatest drawback—it prompts such quick responses that we often forget to organize our thoughts or proofread what we've written. However, sending quick e-mail messages full of punctuation, grammar, and spelling errors taxes the reader's patience and lessens credibility. In the battle for audience attention, carefully written e-mail comes out on top.

When you respond to your e-mail, heed these suggestions:

- **Slow down.** Take a moment to ask yourself, "What am I trying to say?" Jot down the points you want to make, and arrange them logically. Only then should you begin keyboarding your message. Every word matters. Your best bet is to treat every e-mail as if it's a résumé that you're submitting for an important job opening. Even though the fast pace of technology encourages instantaneous responses, take your time and proceed at your own comfortable pace. The other party will wait.
- **Reread your message.** Avoid sending important e-mail messages immediately after you write them. Ideally, reread them the next morning and make changes. When busy entrepreneurs reread what they wrote the day before, they almost always ask themselves, "What was I thinking?"
- **Edit e-mail carefully.** Once you've finished composing your message, spare yourself embarrassment and extra work by double-checking your e-mail message before sending it. Use a spell checker to avoid misspellings that can undermine your document's integrity. But don't stop there. Proofread every sentence for content and fluency, and correct your punctuation and grammar. Finally, make sure your message is complete and that promised documents are attached.
- **Correct misspelled names.** Receiving an e-mail message with your name spelled incorrectly is insulting. When executives misspell the names of their employees, they are often perceived as snobbish and insensitive. When employees misspell the names of their superiors, they are often perceived as incompetent. Typos are common in e-mail, so in addition to catching other spelling errors, make sure all proper names are spelled correctly.
- **Avoid knee-jerk reactions.** Take your time when responding to others' questions, solicitations of opinions, requests, and recommendations. Too often, people open, read, and reply to e-mail without thinking. Plan your response as carefully as you would plan any memo or letter. Speed is a potentially negative habit.

HANDLE ATTACHMENTS APPROPRIATELY

One of the handiest features of e-mail is the ability to attach files to your message. Attachments range from short, less-than-one-page documents to 200-page formal reports with photos and charts. No matter what form your attachments take, consider your recipient's time, convenience, and vulnerability to viruses.

- **Ask permission to send lengthy attachments.** Consider that recipients may not have the time to wait while long attachments are downloading or may not have the capacity to receive large files. Some of these people may not even need to look at the attached file for more than a few seconds. So don't burden them with attachments they don't want. Also consider that many businesspeople check their e-mail while traveling and that your long attachment could choke their mailbox, blocking them from receiving other messages.
- **Use compressed files.** Even if you obtain permission to send a large attachment, and especially if your attachment contains graphics or presentations, compress it so that it takes up as few resources as possible. There are great tools for doing this. For example, PC users can download WinZip and Netzip from the Internet, while Mac users can download Stuffit Expander.
- **Include summaries.** When you need to convey a lot of information in an attachment, include a synopsis or executive summary in the body of your e-mail message. This way, recipients seeking additional information can decide whether to review or print out the attached file.

- **Mention the file name.** When sending e-mail attachments, be sure to identify the file name in your e-mail message so that your recipients can locate your attachment. Create a file name that is a shortened explanation of the contents. Identification becomes particularly important when you attach more than one document to a single e-mail message.
- **Don't forget to attach your attachment.** If you forget to attach your attachment, your recipient must send you a separate message requesting the file. To avoid wasting your audience's time, remember to attach your file first before composing your message.
- **Be aware of viruses.** Many people will not open e-mail messages with attached files for fear that they may contain viruses. Always make sure that the attachments you send are virus-free. As an alternative, you can cut and paste the contents of your file directly into your e-mail message. Just be sure that your message doesn't become too long. Remember that some recipients delete anything over three or four paragraphs.

MANAGE FILES EFFECTIVELY

Just as you would keep memos and letters to preserve a paper trail of decisions, suggestions, and the like, you'll want to keep your e-mail messages to preserve an electronic trail. So that you can find everything you need when you need it, take extra care to keep your e-mail filing system in order. It may become more important than your paper files.

- **Make backups.** Be sure to back up or even print out a hard copy of important e-mail messages. Many systems automatically delete files that are more than one month old.
- **Think thin.** When setting up your file folders, aim for a flat structure. Name your folders so that they collect fewer documents. That way, you'll be able to browse through them more quickly to locate a single document.
- **Keep secret your password or personal identification number (PIN).** Once you share your password with others, you lose control over new and previously stored messages. Do not write down your username and password in the same place. And don't carry your password in your wallet or purse.

DON'T LET INCOMING MAIL RUN YOUR LIFE

Many people have become almost chained to their desks or laptops by the e-mail popping onto their screen. Their compulsion stems from confusion between the urgent and the important. Few e-mails actually require an immediate response. Technology is a tool that should work for you, not the reverse.

- **Don't overcheck your e-mail.** Check your e-mail frequently, but don't overdo it. Instead of being constantly distracted, let the e-mails pile up, and check them only a few times a day. You can stay informed of what's happening without breaking your concentration on more important tasks.
- **Avoid checking e-mail while on vacation.** Do check your e-mail while you are away from the office. Your colleagues will thank you. But if possible, refrain from checking while on vacation. Everyone needs a little time away from the office now and again. Most systems enable you to change your e-mail message to state your travel plans and provide alternate contacts during your absence.
- **Use appropriate filters.** You don't need to read and respond to every e-mail. Many e-mail systems contain filters that you can set up to prevent information overload by screening out unimportant or less-than-critical messages.
- **Apply order.** Adopt a last-in, first-out order when reading e-mail. If you read and respond to e-mail messages in chronological order, you'll often find yourself responding to questions or issues that have been resolved in later messages. By reading the last e-mail first, you may discover that it summarizes all the issues from the previous e-mails. This procedure could save you from having to read several prior e-mails. However, if you read the latest e-mail and find you need more detail, then go back and review the prior e-mails to get the full picture.

The tips in this appendix should help you send, receive, and use e-mail messages effectively.[2]

Appendix V

Correction Symbols

Instructors often use these short, easy-to-remember correction symbols and abbreviations when evaluating students' writing. You can use them too, to understand your instructor's suggestions and to revise and proofread your own letters, memos, and reports. Refer to Appendix III for information on grammar and usage.

CONTENT AND STYLE

Acc	Accuracy. Check to be sure information is correct.
ACE	Avoid copying examples.
ACP	Avoid copying problems.
Adp	Adapt. Tailor message to reader.
App	Follow proper organization approach. (Refer to Chapter 5.)
Assign	Assignment. Review instructions for assignment.
AV	Active verb. Substitute active for passive.
Awk	Awkward phrasing. Rewrite.
BC	Be consistent.
BMS	Be more sincere.
Chop	Choppy sentences. Use longer sentences and more transitional phrases.
Con	Condense. Use fewer words.
CT	Conversational tone. Avoid using overly formal language.
Depers	Depersonalize. Avoid attributing credit or blame to any individual or group.
Dev	Develop. Provide greater detail.
Dir	Direct. Use direct approach; get to the point.
Emph	Emphasize. Develop this point more fully.
EW	Explanation weak. Check logic; provide more proof.
Fl	Flattery. Avoid compliments that are insincere.
FS	Figure of speech. Find a more accurate expression.
GNF	Good news first. Use direct order.
GRF	Give reasons first. Use indirect order.
GW	Goodwill. Put more emphasis on expressions of goodwill.
H/E	Honesty/ethics. Revise statement to reflect good business practices.
Imp	Imply. Avoid being direct.
Inc	Incomplete. Develop further.
Jar	Jargon. Use less specialized language.
Log	Logic. Check development of argument.
Neg	Negative. Use more positive approach or expression.
Obv	Obvious. Do not state point in such detail.
OC	Overconfident. Adopt humbler language.
OM	Omission.
Org	Organization. Strengthen outline.
OS	Off the subject. Close with point on main subject.
Par	Parallel. Use same structure.
Pom	Pompous. Rephrase in down-to-earth terms.
PV	Point of view. Make statement from reader's perspective rather than your own.
RB	Reader benefit. Explain what reader stands to gain.
Red	Redundant. Reduce number of times this point is made.
Ref	Reference. Cite source of information.
Rep	Repetitive. Provide different expression.
RS	Resale. Reassure reader that he or she has made a good choice.
SA	Service attitude. Put more emphasis on helping reader.
Sin	Sincerity. Avoid sounding glib or uncaring.
SL	Stereotyped language. Focus on individual's characteristics instead of on false generalizations.
Spec	Specific. Provide more specific statement.
SPM	Sales promotion material. Tell reader about related goods or services.

Stet	Let stand in original form.
Sub	Subordinate. Make this point less important.
SX	Sexist. Avoid language that contributes to gender stereotypes.
Tone	Tone needs improvement.
Trans	Transition. Show connection between points.
UAE	Use action ending. Close by stating what reader should do next.
UAS	Use appropriate salutation.
UAV	Use active voice.
Unc	Unclear. Rewrite to clarify meaning.
UPV	Use passive voice.
USS	Use shorter sentences.
V	Variety. Use different expression or sentence pattern.
W	Wordy. Eliminate unnecessary words.
WC	Word choice. Find a more appropriate word.
YA	"You" attitude. Rewrite to emphasize reader's needs.

GRAMMAR, USAGE, AND MECHANICS

Ab	Abbreviation. Avoid abbreviations in most cases; use correct abbreviation.
Adj	Adjective. Use adjective instead.
Adv	Adverb. Use adverb instead.
Agr	Agreement. Make subject and verb or noun and pronoun agree.
Ap	Appearance. Improve appearance.
Apos	Apostrophe. Check use of apostrophe.
Art	Article. Use correct article.
BC	Be consistent.
Cap	Capitalize.
Case	Use cases correctly.
CoAdj	Coordinate adjective. Insert comma between coordinate adjectives; delete comma between adjective and compound noun.
CS	Comma splice. Use period or semicolon to separate clauses.
DM	Dangling modifier. Rewrite so that modifier clearly relates to subject of sentence.
Exp	Expletive. Avoid expletive beginnings, such as it is, there are, there is, this is, and these are.
F	Format. Improve layout of document.
Frag	Fragment. Rewrite as complete sentence.
Gram	Grammar. Correct grammatical error.
HCA	Hyphenate compound adjective.
lc	Lowercase. Do not use capital letter.
M	Margins. Improve frame around document.
MM	Misplaced modifier. Place modifier close to word it modifies.
NRC	Nonrestrictive clause (or phrase). Separate from rest of sentence with commas.
P	Punctuation. Use correct punctuation.
Par	Parallel. Use same structure.
PH	Place higher. Move document up on page.
PL	Place lower. Move document down on page.
Prep	Preposition. Use correct preposition.
RC	Restrictive clause (or phrase). Remove commas that separate clause from rest of sentence.
RO	Run-on sentence. Separate two sentences with comma and coordinating conjunction or with semicolon.
SC	Series comma. Add comma before *and*.
SI	Split infinitive. Do not separate *to* from rest of verb.
Sp	Spelling error. Consult dictionary.
Stet	Let stand in original form.
S-V	Subject-verb pair. Do not separate with comma.
Syl	Syllabification. Divide word between syllables.
WD	Word division. Check dictionary for proper end-of-line hyphenation.
WW	Wrong word. Replace with another word.

PROOFREADING MARKS

Symbol	Meaning	Symbol Used in Context	Corrected Copy
	Align horizontally	meaningful re sult	meaningful result
	Align vertically	1. Power cable 2. Keyboard	1. Power cable 2. Keyboard
.....	Stet (don't delete)	the staff talked openly	the staff talked openly
	Capitalize	Pepsico, Inc.	PepsiCo, Inc.
	Close up space	self- confidence	self-confidence
	Delete	harrassment and abuse	harassment
STET	Restore to original	none of the STET	none of the
∧	Insert	tirquoise shirts (u; and white)	turquoise and white shirts
	Insert comma	a, b and c	a, b, and c
	Insert period	Harrigan et al	Harrigan et al.
/	Lowercase	TULSA, South of here	Tulsa, south of here
	Move left	Attention: Security	Attention: Security
	Move right	February 2, 2000	February 2, 2000
	Move down	Sincerely,	Sincerely,
	Move up	THIRD-QUARTER SALES	THIRD-QUARTER SALES
	Center	Awards Banquet	Awards Banquet
	Start new line	Marla Fenton, Manager, Distri- bution	Marla Fenton Manager, Distribution
	Run lines together	Manager, Distribution	Manager, Distribution
¶	Start new paragraph	¶ The solution is easy to determine but difficult to implement in a competitive environment like the one we now face.	The solution is easy to determine but difficult to implement in a competitive environment like the one we now face.
#	Insert space	realestate testcase	real estate test case
	Spell out	COD	cash on delivery
SP	Spell out	SP Assn. of Biochem. Engrs.	Association of Biochemical Engineers
	Transpose	airy, light, casaul tone	light, airy, casual tone

References

Chapter 1

1. Adapted from Karen Lake, "Chatting Back to Your Customers" <strategyweek.com> (accessed 7 May 2001). <strategyweek.com/rs.nsf/StrategyArticles/Robert+LoCascio?OpenDocument>; Mary Wagner, "The Long Road to Online Checkout," *Internet World*, April 2001 (accessed 7 May 2001), <www.internetretailer.com/article.asp?id=3416>; Karen J. Bannan, "Burning Up the Wires," *PSINet eBusiness,* Winter 2001, 48–51; Bruce Horovitz, "Site Untangles E-Customer Service Mess," *USA Today,* 23 November 1999 (accessed 7 May 2001), <www.usatoday.com/life/cyber/tech/review/crg256.htm>; "LivePerson Reels in $19 Million," *Red Herring*, 10 August 1999 (accessed 7 May 2001), <www.redherring.com/index.asp?/layout+story&channel=40000004&doc_id=380011438>; Connie Guglielmo, "LivePerson Puts a Pulse into Web Interaction," *ZDNet,* 21 June 1999 (accessed 7 May 2001), <www.zdnet.com/intweek/stories/news/0,4164,407708,00.html>; Vanessa Geneva Melter, "Closing the Sale with Interactive Chat," *ShopGuide News*, 7 June 1999 (accessed 7 May 2001), <www.shopguide.com/news/article_report2_06-07-99.asp>; Jennifer Gilbert, "LivePerson Focuses on the Human Touch," *Advertising Age*, 1 June 1999 (accessed 7 May 2001); <adage.com/interactive/articles/19990601/article2.html>; Craig Bicknell, "Somebody Freakin' Talk to Me!" *Wired,* 1 June 1999 (accessed 7 May 2001), <www.wired.com/news/business/0,1367,19965,00.html>.
2. Raymond M. Olderman, *10 Minute Guide to Business Communication* (New York: Simon & Schuster, 1997), 1–2.
3. Stephanie Armour, "Failure to Communicate Costly for Companies," *USA Today,* 30 September 1998, 1A; Ted Pollock, "Nine Ways to Improve Your Communication," *Supervision,* February 1999, 24–26.
4. Philip C. Kolin, *Successful Writing at Work,* 6th ed. (Boston: Houghton Mifflin, 2001), 17–23.
5. Paula Jacobs, "Strong Writing Skills Essential for Success, Even in IT," *InfoWorld,* 6 July 1998, 86.
6. David Givens, "You Animal! How to Win Friends and Influence *Homo sapiens*," *The Toastmaster,* August 1986, 9.
7. Stuart Berg Flexner, "From Gadzooks' to Nice, the Language Keeps Changing," *U.S. News & World Report,* 18 February 1985, 59.
8. "Interpersonal Skills Are Key in Office of the Future," *TMA Journal,* July–August 1999, 53.
9. Michael H. Mescon, Courtland L. Bovée, and John V. Thill, *Business Today,* 9th ed. (Upper Saddle River, N.J.: Prentice Hall, 1999), 214.
10. Lillian H. Chaney and Jeanette S. Martin, *Intercultural Business Communications* (Upper Saddle River, N.J.: Prentice Hall, 2000), 1–2.
11. Chaney and Martin, *Intercultural Business Communications,* 1–2.
12. Timothy Aeppel, "A 3Com Factory Hires a Lot of Immigrants, Gets Mix of Languages," *Wall Street Journal,* 30 March 1999, A1, A12.
13. James M. Citrin and Thomas J. Neff, "Digital Leadership," *Strategy and Business,* First Quarter 2000, 42–50; Gary L. Neilson, Bruce A. Pasternack, and Albert J. Viscio, "Up the E-Organization," *Strategy and Business,* First Quarter 2000, 52–61.
14. "How to Improve Communications," *Control Engineering* 45, no. 12 (September 1998): 23.
15. Donald O. Wilson, "Diagonal Communication Links with Organizations," *Journal of Business Communication* 29, no. 2 (Spring 1992): 129–143.
16. Carol Hymowitz, "Spread the Word: Gossip Is Good," *Wall Street Journal,* 4 November 1988, B1; Donald B. Simmons, "The Nature of the Organizational Grapevine," *Supervisory Management,* November 1985, 40.
17. J. David Johnson, William A. Donohoe, Charles K. Atkin, and Sally Johnson, "Differences Between Formal and Informal Communication Channels," *Journal of Business Communication* 31, no. 2 (1994): 111–122.
18. "Presumed Guilty: Managing When Your Company's Name Is Mud," *Working Woman,* November 1991, 31; Judy A. Smith, "Crisis Communications: The War on Two Fronts," *Industry Week,* 20 May 1996, 136.
19. Timothy Aeppel, Clare Ansberry, Milo Geyelin, and Robert L. Simison, "Road Signs: How Ford, Firestone Let the Warnings Slide By as Debacle Developed," *Wall Street Journal,* 6 September 2000, A1; Joann Muller, David Welch, Jeff Green, Lorraine Woellert, and Nicole St. Pierre, "A Crisis of Confidence," *Business Week,* 18 September 2000, 40–42.
20. Robert Manor, "One 'Stone' Too Many for Bridgestone?" *Chicago Tribune,* 6 June 2001, sec. 3, 1, 4.
21. Some material adapted from Courtland L. Bovée, John V. Thill, Marian Burk Wood, and George P. Dovel, *Management* (New York: McGraw-Hill, 1993), 537–538.
22. Gillian Flynn, "Pillsbury's Recipe Is Candid Talk," *Workforce*, February 1998, 56–57+.
23. Bruce W. Speck, "Writing Professional Codes of Ethics to Introduce Ethics in Business Writing," *Bulletin of the Association for Business Communication* 53, no. 3 (September 1990): 21–26; H. W. Love, "Communication, Accountability and Professional Discourse: The Interaction of Language Values and Ethical Values," *Journal of Business Ethics* 11 (1992): 883–892; Kathryn C. Rentz and Mary Beth Debs, "Language and Corporate Values: Teaching Ethics in Business Writing Courses," *Journal of Business Communication* 24, no. 3 (Summer 1987): 37–48.
24. Gerry McGovern, "Less Is More," *Publish,* March–April 2001, 24.

25. Don Clark, "Managing the Mountain," *Wall Street Journal,* 21 June 1999, R4.
26. Michael Taylor, "Intranets—A New Technology Changes All the Rules," *Telecommunications,* January 1997, 39–10.
27. Samuel Greengard, "Surviving Internet Speed," *Workforce,* April 2001, 28–43.
28. Jay Stuller, "Overload," *Across the Board,* April 1996, 16–22.
29. J. Michael Sproule, *Communication Today* (Glenview, Ill.: Scott Foresman, 1981), 329.
30. Carol Hymowitz, "If the Walls Had Ears You Wouldn't Have Any Less Privacy," *Wall Street Journal,* 19 May 1998, B1.
31. Kenneth Hein, "Hungry for Feedback," *Incentive,* September 1997, 9+.
32. John A. Byrne, "Jack," *Business Week,* 8 June 1998, 92–111.
33. A. Thomas Young, "Ethics in Business: Business of Ethics," *Vital Speeches,* 15 September 1992, 725–730.
34. Philip C. Kolin, *Successful Writing at Work,* 6th ed. (Boston: Houghton Mifflin, 2001), 24–30.
35. David Grier, "Confronting Ethical Dilemmas: The View from Inside—A Practitioner's Perspective," *Vital Speeches,* 1 December 1989, 100–104.
36. Joseph L. Badaracco Jr., "Business Ethics: Four Spheres of Executive Responsibility," *California Management Review,* Spring 1992, 64–79; Kenneth Blanchard and Norman Vincent Peale, *The Power of Ethical Management* (1989; reprint, New York: Fawcett Crest, 1991), 7–17.
37. Blanchard and Peale, *The Power of Ethical Management,* 7–17; Badaracco, "Business Ethics: Four Spheres of Executive Responsibility," 64–79.
38. Jules Harcourt, "Developing Ethical Messages: A Unit of Instruction for the Basic Business Communication Course," *Bulletin of the Association for Business Communication* 53, no. 3 (September 1990): 17–20; John D. Pettit, Bobby Vaught, and Kathy J. Pulley, "The Role of Communication in Organizations," *Journal of Business Communication* 27, no. 3 (Summer 1990): 233–249; Kenneth R. Andrews, "Ethics in Practice," *Harvard Business Review,* September–October 1989, 99–104; Priscilla S. Rogers and John M. Swales, "We the People? An Analysis of the Dana Corporation Policies Document," *Journal of Business Communication* 27, no. 3 (Summer 1990): 293–313; Larry Reynolds, "The Ethics Audit," *Business Ethics,* July–August 1991, 120–122.
39. "When Rumors Disrupt Your Staff," *Working Woman,* October 1992, 36

Chapter 2

1. Adapted from the SEI Investment website (accessed 2 May 2001) <www2.seic.com>; Rich Blake, "Makeover Artist," *Institutional Investor,* April 2001, 32–42; Andy Gotlieb, "Secret Is Out on SEI," *Philadelphia Business Journal,* 19 January 2001, 15; Cathy Olofson, "Banking on the Web: SEI Investments," *Fast Company,* 1 December 2000, 366; Aaron Lucchetti, "Monthly Mutual Funds Review: SEI Is Building Its Assets; It's Just Hard to Say How," *Wall Street Journal,* 6 December 1999, M8; Anna Muoio, "Updating the Agenda: A Second Look at the 1998 Agenda Role Models," *Fast Company,* 1 April 1999, 184; "Doing the Work That Needs Doing: Conversations with the Leaders," *Training & Development,* January 1999, 56–60; Scott Kirsner, "Total Teamwork—SEI Investments," *Fast Company,* April 1998, 130; Scott Kirsner, "Their Teamwork Agenda," *Fast Company,* April 1998, 132.
2. Michael H. Mescon, Courtland L. Bovée, and John V. Thill, *Business Today* (Upper Saddle River, N.J.: Prentice Hall, 1999), 203.
3. Richard L. Daft, *Management,* 4th ed. (Fort Worth: Dryden, 1997), 338.
4. "Teamwork Translates into High Performance," *HR Focus,* July 1998, 7.
5. Ellen Neuborne, "Companies Save, But Workers Pay," *USA Today,* 25 February 1997, B2; Charles L. Parnell, "Teamwork: Not a New Idea, But It's Transforming the Workplace," *Vital Speeches of the Day,* 1 November 1996, 46.
6. Neuborne, "Companies Save, But Workers Pay," B1; Daft, *Management,* 594–595; Stephen P. Robbins and David A. De Cenzo, *Fundamentals of Management,* 2d ed. (Upper Saddle River, N.J.: Prentice Hall, 1998), 336–338.
7. Richard Moderow, "Teamwork Is the Key to Cutting Costs," *Modern Healthcare,* 29 April 1996, 138.
8. Stephen P. Robbins, *Essentials of Organizational Behavior,* 6th ed. (Upper Saddle River, N.J.: Prentice Hall, 2000), 109.
9. Heath Row, "The Joys of Togetherness," *Webmaster,* June 1997, 44–48.
10. Deborah L. Duarte and Nancy Tennant Snyder, *Mastering Virtual Teams* (San Francisco: Jossey-Bass Publishers, 1999), 23.
11. Daft, *Management,* 612–615.
12. Robbins, *Essentials of Organizational Behavior,* 98.
13. Mike Verespej, "Drucker Sours on Teams," *Industry Week,* 6 April 1998, 16+.
14. B. Aubrey Fisher, *Small Group Decision Making: Communication and the Group Process,* 2d ed. (New York: McGraw-Hill, 1980), 145–149; Robbins and De Cenzo, *Fundamentals of Management,* 334–335; Daft, *Management,* 602–603.
15. Lynda McDermott, Bill Waite, and Nolan Brawley, "Executive Teamwork," *Executive Excellence,* May 1999, 15.
16. Larry Cole and Michael Cole, "Why Is the Teamwork Buzz Word Not Working?" *Communication World,* February/March 1999, 29; Patricia Buhler, "Managing in the 90s: Creating Flexibility in Today's Workplace," *Supervision,* January 1997, 24+; Allison W. Amason, Allen C. Hochwarter, Wayne A. Thompson, and Kenneth R. Harrison, "Conflict: An Important Dimension in Successful Management Teams," *Organizational Dynamics,* Autumn 1995, 20+.
17. "Team Players," *Executive Excellence,* May 1999, 18.
18. Daft, *Management,* 609–612.
19. Thomas K. Capozzoli, "Conflict Resolution—A Key Ingredient in Successful Teams," *Supervision,* November 1999, 14–16.

20. Janis Graham, "Sharpen Your Negotiating Skills," *Sylvia Porter's Personal Finance,* December 1985, 54–58.
21. Amason, Hochwarter, Thompson, and Harrison, "Conflict."
22. Jesse S. Nirenberg, *Getting Through to People* (Paramus, N.J.: Prentice Hall, 1973), 134–142.
23. Nirenberg, *Getting Through to People.*
24. Nirenberg, *Getting Through to People.*
25. Jon Hanke, "Presenting as a Team," *Presentations,* January 1998, 74–82.
26. William P. Galle, Jr., Beverly H. Nelson, Donna W. Luse, and Maurice F. Villere, *Business Communication: A Technology-Based Approach* (Chicago: Irwin, 1996), 260.
27. Mary Beth Debs, "Recent Research on Collaborative Writing in Industry," *Technical Communication* (November 1991), 476–484.
28. Ruth G. Newman, "Communication: Collaborative Writing with Purpose and Style," *Personnel Journal,* April 1988, 37–38; Galle, Nelson, Luse, and Villere, *Business Communication,* 256.
29. Joel Haness, "How to Critique a Document," *IEEE Transactions on Professional Communication* PC-26, no. 1 (March 1983): 15–17.
30. Charles E. Risch, "Critiquing Written Material," *Manage* 35, no. 4 (1983): 4–6.
31. Risch, "Critiquing Written Material."
32. Brenda Park Sundo, "Are You Noticing Too Many Yawns?" *Workforce,* April 1998, 16–17.
33. "Better Meetings Benefit Everyone: How to Make Yours More Productive," *Working Communicator Bonus Report,* July 1998, 1.
34. Ken Blanchard, "Meetings Can Be Effective," *Supervisory Management,* October 1992, 5.
35. William C. Waddell and Thomas A. Rosko, "Conducting an Effective Off-Site Meeting," *Management Review,* February 1993, 40–44.
36. "Better Meetings Benefit Everyone."
37. Kathy E. Gill, "Board Primer: Parliamentary Procedure," *Association Management,* 1993, L-39.
38. Kristen Bell DeTienne, *Guide to Electronic Communication* (Upper Saddle River, N.J.: Prentice Hall, 2001), 78–79.
39. Bob Lamons, "Good Listeners Are Better Communicators," *Marketing News,* 11 September 1995, 13+; Phillip Morgan and H. Kent Baker, "Building a Professional Image: Improving Listening Behavior," *Supervisory Management,* November 1985, 35–36.
40. Robyn D. Clarke, "Do You Hear What I Hear?" *Black Enterprise,* May 1998, 129; Dot Yandle, "Listening to Understand," *Pryor Report Management Newsletter Supplement* 15, no. 8 (August 1998): 13.
41. Augusta M. Simon, "Effective Listening: Barriers to Listening in a Diverse Business Environment," *Bulletin of the Association for Business Communication* 54, no. 3 (September 1991): 73–74.
42. Clarke, "Do You Hear What I Hear?"
43. "An Added Joy of E-Mail: Fewer Face-to-Face Meetings," *Wall Street Journal,* 14 July 1998, A1.
44. "Listening: Hearing Better at Meetings," *Communication Briefings* 18, no. 11 (September 1999): 2.
45. J. Michael Sproule, *Communication Today* (Glenview, Ill.: Scott, Foresman, 1981), 69.
46. Sproule, *Communication Today.*
47. Sproule, *Communication Today.*
48. Sherwyn P. Morreale and Courtland L. Bovée, *Excellence in Public Speaking* (Orlando, Fla.: Harcourt Brace, 1998), 72–76; Lyman K. Steil, Larry L. Barker, and Kittie W. Watson, *Effective Listening: Key to Your Success* (Reading, Mass.: Addison-Wesley, 1983), 21–22.
49. Patrick J. Collins, *Say It with Power and Confidence* (Upper Saddle River, N.J.: Prentice Hall, 1997), 40–45.
50. Collins, *Say It with Power and Confidence,* 40–45.
51. David Lewis, *The Secret Language of Success* (New York: Carroll & Graf, 1989), 67, 170.
52. Nido Qubein, *Communicate Like a Pro* (New York: Berkeley Books, 1986), 97.
53. Dale G. Leathers, *Successful Nonverbal Communication: Principles and Applications* (New York: Macmillan, 1986), 19.
54. Gerald H. Graham, Jeanne Unrue, and Paul Jennings, "The Impact of Nonverbal Communication in Organizations: A Survey of Perceptions," *Journal of Business Communication* 28, no. 1 (Winter 1991): 45–62.
55. Graham, Unrue, and Jennings, "The Impact of Nonverbal Communication in Organizations."

Chapter 3

1. Michiru Tamanai, director of training, and Kayomi Kaneda, training administrator, Sheraton Hotels Hawaii, personal communication, August 1998.
2. N. Hed Seelye and Alan Seelye-James, *Culture Clash* (Chicago: NTC Business Books, 1995), xv, xviii.
3. Michael H. Mescon, Courtland L. Bovée, and John V. Thill, *Business Today,* 10th ed. (Upper Saddle River, N.J.: Prentice Hall, 2002), 69.
4. Sari Kalin, "The Importance of Being Multiculturally Correct," *Computerworld,* 6 October 1997, G16–G17; Lawrence M. Fisher, "REI Climbs Online," *Strategy and Business,* First Quarter 2000, 116–129.
5. Rona Gindin, "Dealing with a Multicultural Workforce," *Nation's Restaurant News,* September/October 1998, 31, 83; Howard Gleckman, "A Rich Stew in the Melting Pot," *Business Week,* 31 August 1998, 76+; Toby B. Gooley, "A World of Difference," *Logistics Management and Distribution Report,* June 2000, 51–55; William H. Miller, "Beneath the Surface," *Industry Week,* 20 September 1999, 13–16.
6. Joan Crockett, "Winning Competitive Advantage Through a Diverse Workforce," *HRFocus,* May 1999, 9–10.
7. Lillian H. Chaney and Jeanette S. Martin, *Intercultural Business Communication* (Upper Saddle River, N.J.: Prentice Hall, 2000), 6.
8. Philip R. Harris and Robert T. Moran, *Managing Cultural Differences,* 3d ed. (Houston: Gulf, 1991), 394–397, 429–430.
9. Chaney and Martin, *Intercultural Business Communication,* 9.
10. Larry A. Samovar and Richard E. Porter, "Basic Principles of Intercultural Communication," in *Intercultural*

Communication: A Reader, 6th ed., edited by Larry A. Samovar and Richard E. Porter (Belmont, Calif.: Wadsworth, 1991), 12.

11. Lalita Khosla, "You Say Tomato," *Forbes Best of the Web,* 21 May 2001, 36.

12. Gus Tyler, "Tokyo Signs the Paychecks," *New York Times Book Review,* 12 August 1990, 7.

13. Chaney and Martin, *Intercultural Business Communication,* 159.

14. Otto Kreisher, "Annapolis Has a New Attitude Toward Sexual Harassment," *San Diego Union,* 30 July 1990, A-6.

15. Linda Beamer, "Teaching English Business Writing to Chinese-Speaking Business Students," *Bulletin of the Association for Business Communication* 57, no. 1 (1994): 12–18.

16. Edward T. Hall, "Context and Meaning," in *Intercultural Communication,* edited by Samovar and Porter, 46–55.

17. Beamer, "Teaching English Business Writing to Chinese-Speaking Business Students."

18. Charley H. Dodd, *Dynamics of Intercultural Communication,* 3d ed. (Dubuque, Iowa: Brown, 1991), 69–70.

19. Chaney and Martin, *Intercultural Business Communication,* 206–211.

20. James Wilfong and Toni Seger, *Taking Your Business Global* (Franklin Lakes, N.J.: Career Press, 1997), 277–278.

21. Harris and Moran, *Managing Cultural Differences,* 260.

22. Skip Kaltenheuser, "Bribery Is Being Outlawed Virtually Worldwide," *Business Ethics,* May–June 1998, 11; Thomas Omestad, "Bye-bye to Bribes," *U.S. News & World Report,* 22 December 1997, 39, 42–44.

23. Kaltenheuser, "Bribery Is Being Outlawed Virtually Worldwide"; Omestad, "Bye-bye to Bribes."

24. Guo-Ming Chen and William J. Starosta, *Foundations of Intercultural Communication* (Boston: Allyn & Bacon, 1998), 288–289.

25. Sharon Ruhly, *Intercultural Communication,* 2d ed., MODCOM (Modules in Speech Communication) (Chicago: Science Research Associates, 1982), 14.

26. Mary A. DeVries, *Internationally Yours* (New York: Houghton Mifflin, 1994), 194.

27. Robert O. Joy, "Cultural and Procedural Differences That Influence Business Strategies and Operations in the People's Republic of China," *SAM Advanced Management Journal,* Summer 1989, 29–33.

28. Chaney and Martin, *Intercultural Business Communication,* 122–123.

29. Chaney and Martin, *Intercultural Business Communication,* 110–111.

30. Laray M. Barna, "Stumbling Blocks in Intercultural Communication," in *Intercultural Communication,* edited by Samovar and Porter, 345–352; Jean A. Mausehund, Susan A. Timm, and Albert S. King, "Diversity Training: Effects of an Intervention Treatment on Nonverbal Awareness," *Business Communication Quarterly* 38, no. 1 (1995): 27–30.

31. Jane E. Lasky, "Make the Right Gesture on a Trip to Asia," *The Secured Lender,* November/December 2000, 80–84.

32. Chen and Starosta, *Foundations of Intercultural Communication,* 39–40.

33. Richard W. Brislin, "Prejudice in Intercultural Communication," in *Intercultural Communication,* edited by Samovar and Porter, 366–370.

34. James S. O'Rourke IV, "International Business Communication: Building a Course from the Ground Up," *Bulletin of the Association for Business Communication* 56, no. 4 (1993): 22–27.

35. Jensen J. Zhao and Calvin Parks, "Self-Assessment of Communication Behavior: An Experiential Learning Exercise for Intercultural Business Success," *Business Communication Quarterly* 58, no. 1 (1995): 20–26; Dodd, *Dynamics of Intercultural Communication,* 142–143, 297–299; Stephen P. Robbins, *Organizational Behavior,* 6th ed. (Paramus, N.J.: Prentice Hall, 1993), 345.

36. "Less Yiddish, More Tagalog," *U.S. News & World Report,* 10 May 1993, 16; Gary Levin, "Marketers Learning New Languages for Ads," *Advertising Age,* 10 May 1993, 33.

37. Chaney and Martin, *Intercultural Business Communication,* 130.

38. Bob Nelson, "Motivating Workers Worldwide," *Global Workforce,* November 1998, 25–27.

39. Justin Fox, "The Triumph of English," *Fortune,* 18 September 2000, 209–212.

40. David A. Victor, *International Business Communication* (New York: HarperCollins, 1992), 36.

41. Suzanne Daley, "Pilots Just Say Non to English-Only," *New York Times,* 23 May 2000, A4.

42. Stephen Dolainski, "Are Expats Getting Lost in the Translation?" *Workforce,* February 1997, 32–39.

43. Doreen Mangan, "What's New in Language Translation: A Tool for Examining Foreign Patents and Research," *New York Times,* 19 November 1989, sec. 3, 15.

44. Wilfong and Seger, *Taking Your Business Global,* 232.

45. Vern Terpstra, *The Cultural Environment of International Business* (Cincinnati: South-Western, 1979), 19.

46. Mona Casady and Lynn Wasson, "Written Communication Skills of International Business Persons," *Bulletin of the Association for Business Communication* 57, no. 4 (1994): 36–40.

47. Michiru Tamanai, director of training, and Kayomi Kaneda, training administrator, Sheraton Hotels Hawaii, personal communication, August 1998.

48. Michael Copeland, specialist, international training, personal communication, January 1990.

Chapter 4

1. Adapted from Home Depot's Web site (accessed 8 March 2000), <www.homedepot.com>; Bernie Marcus and Arthur Blank with Bob Andelman, *Built from Scratch* (New York: Random House, 1999) 105, 110, 125, 135–137, 142, 149, 155–161, 178, 205, 216, 240–241, 255–258, 280, 287–289, 313; Carlton P. McNamara, "Making Human Capital More Productive," *Business and Economic Review,* October– December 1999, 10–13; Sarah Rose, "Building a Powerhouse," *Money,* December 1999, 62–64; Chris Roush, *Inside Home Depot* (New York: McGraw-Hill, 1999) 5–6, 12, 29, 31–35; 89, 101–108, 115, 141, 213–215, 221; Robert S. Salomon,

Jr., "Reinventing Retail," *Forbes*, 19 October 1998, 171; Bruce Upin, "Profit in a Big Orange Box," *Forbes*, 24 January 2000, 122–127.

2. Sanford Kaye, "Writing Under Pressure," *Soundview Executive Book Summaries* 10, no. 12, part 2 (December 1988): 1–8.

3. Peter Bracher, "Process, Pedagogy, and Business Writing," *Journal of Business Communication* 24, no. 1 (Winter 1987): 43–50.

4. Mahalingam Subbiah, "Adding a New Dimension to the Teaching of Audience Analysis: Cultural Awareness," *IEEE Transactions on Professional Communication* 35, no. 1 (March 1992): 14–19; Ronald E. Dulek, John S. Fielden, and John S. Hill, "International Communication: An Executive Primer," *Business Horizons*, January–February 1991, 20–25; Dwight W. Stevenson, "Audience Analysis Across Cultures," *Journal of Technical Writing and Communication* 13, no. 4 (1983): 319–330.

5. Iris I. Varner, "Internationalizing Business Communication Courses," *Bulletin of the Association for Business Communication* 50, no. 4 (December 1987): 7–11.

6. Laurey Berk and Phillip G. Clampitt, "Finding the Right Path in the Communication Maze," *IABC Communication World*, October 1991, 28–32.

7. Berk and Clampitt, "Finding the Right Path in the Communication Maze."

8. Berk and Clampitt, "Finding the Right Path in the Communication Maze."

9. Raymond M. Olderman, *10 Minute Guide to Business Communication* (New York: Alpha Books, 1997), 19–20.

10. Mohan R. Limaye and David A. Victor, "Cross-Cultural Business Communication Research: State of the Art and Hypotheses for the 1990s," *Journal of Business Communication* 28, no. 3 (Summer 1991): 277–299.

11. Berk and Clampitt, "Finding the Right Path in the Communication Maze."

12. Berk and Clampitt, "Finding the Right Path in the Communication Maze."

13. Mike Bransby, "Voice Mail Makes a Difference," *Journal of Business Strategy*, January–February 1990, 7–10.

14. J. D. Biersdorfer, "To Nail the Sale, E-Mail's Too Slow," *New York Times*, 13 June 2001, 3; Heather Newman, "Instant Messaging a Communications Revolution," *San Diego Union-Tribune*, 12 June 2001, 4.

15. Tim McCollum, "The Net Result of Computer Links," *Nation's Business*, March 1998, 55–58.

16. Elizabeth Blackburn and Kelly Belanger, "You-Attitude and Positive Emphasis: Testing Received Wisdom in Business Communication," *Bulletin of the Association for Business Communication* 56, no. 2 (June 1993): 1–9.

17. Annette N. Shelby and N. Lamar Reinsch, Jr., "Positive Emphasis and You Attitude: An Empirical Study," *Journal of Business Communication* 32, no. 4 (1995): 303–322.

18. Judy E. Pickens, "Terms of Equality: A Guide to Bias-Free Language," *Personnel Journal*, August 1985, 24.

19. Lisa Taylor, "Communicating About People with Disabilities: Does the Language We Use Make a Difference?" *Bulletin of the Association for Business Communication* 53, no. 3 (September 1990): 65–67

Chapter 5

1. Julie Galle, writer/producer, weather.com, personal communication, 27 June 2001; Chuck Salter, "Weathering the Storm," *Fast Company*, December 2000, 186–200; Keith Flamer, "Eye of the Storm," *Broadcasting & Cable*, 25 September 2000, 84–86.

2. Carol S. Mull, "Orchestrate Your Ideas," *The Toastmaster*, February 1987, 19.

3. Susan Hall and Theresa Tiggeman, "Getting the Big Picture: Writing to Learn in a Finance Class," *Business Communication Quarterly* 58, no. 1 (1995): 12–15.

4. Bruce B. MacMillan, "How to Write to Top Management," *Business Marketing*, March 1985, 138.

5. Ernest Thompson, "Some Effects of Message Structure on Listener's Comprehension," *Speech Monographs* 34 (March 1967): 51–57.

6. Based on the Pyramid Model developed by Barbara Minto of McKinsey & Company, management consultants.

7. Philip Subanks, "Messages, Models, and the Messy World of Memos," *Bulletin of the Association for Business Communication* 57, no. 1 (1994): 33–34.

8. Mary A. DeVries, *Internationally Yours* (Boston: Houghton Mifflin, 1994), 61.

9. Susan Benjamin, *Words at Work* (Reading, Mass.: Addison-Wesley, 1997), 136–137.

10. Randolph H. Hudson, Gertrude M. McGuire, and Bernard J. Selzler, *Business Writing: Concepts and Applications* (Los Angeles: Roxbury, 1983), 79–82.

11. William M. Bulkeley, "Software Writers Try to Speak a Language Users Understand," *Wall Street Journal*, 30 June 1992, B6.

12. Peter Crow, "Plain English: What Counts Besides Readability?" *Journal of Business Communication* 25, no. 1 (Winter 1988): 87–95.

13. Alinda Drury, "Evaluating Readability," *IEEE Transactions on Professional Communication* PC-28 (December 1985): 12.

14. Portions of this section are adapted from Courtland L. Bovée, *Techniques of Writing Business Letters, Memos, and Reports* (Sherman Oaks, Calif.: Banner Books International, 1978), 13–90.

15. Robert Hartwell Fiske, *Thesaurus of Alternatives to Worn-out Words and Phrases* (Cincinnati: Writer's Digest Books, 1994), 171.

16. Iris I. Varner, "Internationalizing Business Communication Courses," *Bulletin of the Association for Business Communication* 50, no. 4 (December 1987): 7–11.

17. David Angell and Brent Heslop, *The Elements of E-Mail Style* (Reading, Mass.: Addison-Wesley, 1994), 20.

18. Renee B. Horowitz and Marian G. Barchilon, "Stylistic Guidelines for E-Mail," *IEEE Transactions on Professional Communication* 37, no. 4 (December 1994): 207–212; Angell and Heslop, *The Elements of E-Mail Style*, 22.

19. Jill H. Ellsworth and Matthew V. Ellsworth, *The Internet Business Book* (New York: Wiley, 1994), 91.

20. Lance Cohen, "How to Improve Your E-Mail Messages," <galaxy.einet/galaxy/Business-and-Commerce/Management/ Communications/How_to_Improve_Your Email.html>.

21. Angell and Heslop, *The Elements of E-Mail Style*, 18–19.

22. Horowitz and Barchilon, "Stylistic Guidelines for E-Mail"; Cohen, "How to Improve Your E-Mail Messages."

23. Milton Moskowitz, Michael Katz, and Robert Levering, eds., *Everybody's Business: An Almanac* (San Francisco: Harper & Row, 1980), 131.

24. Randolph H. Hudson, Gertrude M. McGuire, and Bernard J. Selzler, *Business Writing: Concepts and Applications* (Los Angeles: Roxbury, 1983), 27.

Chapter 6

1. Adrianne Proeller, corporate communications manager, Turner Broadcasting System, personal communication, March 1997.

2. Susan Benjamin, *Words at Work* (Reading, Mass.: Addison-Wesley, 1997), 71.

3. Cynthia Crossen, "If You Can Read This, You Most Likely Are a High School Grad," *Wall Street Journal,* 1 December 2000, A1, A11; Kevin T. Stevens, Kathleen C. Stevens, and William P. Stevens, "Measuring the Readability of Business Writing: The Cloze Procedure Versus Readability Formulas," *Journal of Business Communication* 29, no. 4 (1992): 367–382; Alinda Drury, "Evaluating Readability," *IEEE Transactions on Professional Communication* PC-28 (December 1985): 11.

4. Iris I. Varner, "Internationalizing Business Communication Courses," *Bulletin of the Association for Business Communication* 50, no. 4 (December 1987): 7–11.

5. Mary A. DeVries, *Internationally Yours* (Boston: Houghton Mifflin, 1994), 168; Benjamin, *Words at Work*, 61, 140–141.

6. William Zinsser, *On Writing Well*, 5th ed. (New York: HarperCollins, 1994), 9.

7. "Message Lost in Some Memos," *USA Today,* 25 March 1987, 1A.

8. Zinsser, *On Writing Well,* 7, 17.

9. DeVries, *Internationally Yours,* 160.

10. Zinsser, *On Writing Well,* 126.

11. William Wresch, Donald Pattow, and James Gifford, *Writing for the Twenty-First Century: Computers and Research Writing* (New York: McGraw-Hill, 1988), 192–211; Melissa E. Barth, *Strategies for Writing with the Computer* (New York: McGraw-Hill, 1988), 108–109, 140, 172–177.

12. Patsy Nichols, "Desktop Packaging," *Bulletin of the Association for Business Communication* 54, no. 1 (March 1991): 43–45; Raymond W. Beswick, "Designing Documents for Legibility," *Bulletin of the Association for Business Communication* 50, no. 4 (December 1987): 34–35.

13. "A Misspelling Proves Costly," *New York Times,* 23 November 1991, 29.

14. Eric J. Adams, "The Fax of Global Business," *World Trade,* August–September 1991, 34–39.

15. Adrianne Proeller, corporate communications manager, Turner Broadcasting System, personal communication, March 1993.

16. Benjamin, *Words at Work,* 121.

Component Chapter A

1. Reid Goldsborough, "Words for the Wise," *Link-Up,* September–October 1999, 25–26.

2. John Morkes and Jakob Nielsen, "How to Write for the Web" (accessed 23 April 2000), <www.useit.com/papers/webwriting/writing.html>.

3. Jakob Nielsen, "Reading on the Web" (accessed 23 April 2000), <www.useit.com/alertbox/9710a.html>.

4. Nielsen, "Reading on the Web."

5. Goldsborough, "Words for the Wise."

6. Jakob Nielsen, "Failure of Corporate Websites" (accessed online 23 April 2000), <www.useit.com/alertbox/981018. html>.

7. Shel Holtz, "Writing for the Wired World," *International Association of Business Communicators,* 1999, 6–9.

8. Holtz, "Writing for the Wired World," 95.

9. Holtz, "Writing for the Wired World," 28–29.

10. Holtz, "Writing for the Wired World," 72–73.

11. Holtz, "Writing for the Wired World," 95.

12. "Web Writing: How to Avoid Pitfalls," *Investor Relations Business,* 1 November 1999, 15.

13. Michael Lerner, "Building Worldwide Websites," IBM website (accessed 23 April 2000), <www.4.ibm.com/software/developer/library/web-localization.html>.

14. Lerner, "Building Worldwide Websites."

15. Goldsborough, "Words for the Wise."

16. Morkes and Nielsen, "How to Write for the Web."

17. Holstead, "Three Steps to Web-Smart Editing."

18. Holtz, "Writing for the Wired World," 11–15.

19. Steve Outing, "Some Advice on Writing, Web-Style," E&P Online (accessed 23 April 2000), <www.mediainfo.com/ephome/news/newshtm/stop/st061899.htm>.

20. Good Documents website (accessed 15 July 2001), www.gooddocuments.com/techniques/techniqueshome.htm.

21. Jakob Nielsen, "Microcontent: How to Write Headlines, Page Titles, and Subject Lines" (accessed 23 April 2000), <www.useit.com/alertbox/980906.html>.

22. Jakob Nielsen, P.J. Schemenaur, and Jonathan Fox, "Writing for the Web," Sun Microsystems website (accessed 23 April 2000), <www.sun.com/980713/webwriting>.

23. Holtz, "Writing for the Wired World," 111.

24. Amy Gahran, "Writing for the Web and Creating Effective Online Content," Webword.com (accessed 31 May 2000), <www.webword.com/interviews/gahran.html>.

Chapter 7

1. Becky Bumgardner, senior corporate writer, Unum Provident Corporation, personal communication, 10 August 2001.

2. Daniel P. Finkelman and Anthony R. Goland, "Customers Once Can Be Customers for Life," *Information Strategy: The Executive's Journal*, Summer 1990, 5–9.

3. Susan Stobaugh, "Watch Your Language," *Inc.*, May 1985, 156.

4. *Techniques for Communicators* (Chicago: Lawrence Ragan Communication, 1995), 34, 36.

5. John A. Byrne, "Jack," *Business Week,* 8 June 1998, 91–112.

6. Donna Larcen, "Authors Share the Words of Condolence," *Los Angeles Times,* 20 December 1991, E11.

7. Adapted from Floorgraphics website (accessed 18 June 2001), <www.floorgraphics.com>; John Grossman, "It's an Ad, Ad, Ad, Ad World," *Inc.*, March 2000, 23–26; David Wellman, "*Floor Toons*," *Supermarket Business*, 15 November 1999, 47; "Floorshow," *Dallas Morning News*, 4 September 1998, 11D.

8. Adapted from George Anders, "Voyage to the New Economy," *Fast Company* 36:142 (accessed 11 July 2000), <wysiwyg://22/http://fastcompany.com/online/36/migration2.html>; Pamela Kruger, "Stop the Insanity!" *Fast Company* 36: 240 (accessed 11 July 2000), <wysiwyg://12/http://www.fastcompany.com/online/36/stopinsanity.html>; Anna Muoio, "Should I Go .Com?" *Fast Company* 36:164 (accessed 11 July 2000), <wysiwyg://46/http://www.fastcompany.com/online/36/stein.html>.

9. Adapted from Subway website, www.subway.com; Robert Maynard, "Choosing a Franchise," *Nation's Business*, October 1996, 54–55.

10. Adapted from Jamba Juice website (accessed 19 July 2001), <jamabacareers.com/benefits.html>; Brenda Paik Sunoo, "Blending a Successful Workforce," *Workforce,* March 2000, 44–48; Michael Adams, "Kirk Perron: Jamba Juice," *Restaurant Business*, 15 March 1999, 38; "Live in a Blender," *Restaurant Business*, 1 December 2000, 48–50; David Goll, "Jamba Juices Up 24-Hour Fitness Clubs," *Fast Bay Business Times*, 30 June 2000, 6.

11. Adapted from Michael Mescon, Courtland Bovée, and John Thill, *Business Today,* 10th ed. (Upper Saddle River, NJ: Prentice Hall, 2002), 220.

12. Adapted from Tom Lowry, "Thieves Swipe Credit with Card Readers," *USA Today*, 28 June 1999, 1B; Elaine Shannon, "A New Credit-Card Scam," *Time*, 5 June 2000, 54–55; Linda Punch, "Card Fraud: Down but Not Out," *Credit Card Management*, June 1999, 30–42.

13. Adapted from Jane Costello, "Check Your Insurance Before Renting an SUV," *Wall Street Journal*, 13 June 2001 (accessed 14 June 2001),<interactive.wsj.com/articles/SB991402678854239871.htm>.

14. Adapted from Calvin Sims, "Reporter Disciplined for Reading His Co-workers' Electronic Mail," *New York Times*, 6 December 1993, A8.

15. Adapted from Barbara Carton, "Farmers Begin Harvesting Satellite Data to Boost Yields," *Wall Street Journal*, 11 July 1996, B4.

16. Adapted from LifeSketch.com website (accessed 24 July 2000), <www.lifesketch.com>.

17. Adapted from Michael Mescon, Courtland Bovée, and John Thill, *Business Today,* 10th ed. (Upper Saddle River, N.J.: Prentice Hall, 2002), 258–259; Anne Marie Squeo, "Boeing Plans to Build Smaller, Faster Jet," *Wall Street Journal*, 30 March 2001, A3, A8.

18. Adapted from Dylan Tweney, "The Defogger: Slim Down That Homepage," *Business 2.0*, 13 July 2001 (accessed 1 August 2001), <www.business2.com/articles/web/0,1653,16483,FF.html>.

19. "Entrepreneurs Across America," *Entrepreneur Magazine Online* (accessed 12 June 1997), <www.entrepreneurmag.com/entmag/50states5.hts#top>.

20. Adapted from Bernard Weinraub, "New Harry Potter Book Becoming a Publishing Phenomenon," *New York Times*, 3 July 2000 (accessed 12 July 2000), <www.nytimes.com/library/books/070300potter-parties.html>; Laura Miller, "Pottermania at Midnight," *Salon.com*, 8 July 2000 (accessed 12 July 2000), <www.salon.com/books/features/2000/07/08/potter/; David D. Kirkpatrick, "Harry Potter Magic Halts Bedtime for Youngsters," *New York Times*, 9 July 2000 (accessed 12 July 2000), <www.nytimes.com/library/books/070900potter-goblet.html>; David D. Kirkpatrick, "Vanishing Off the Shelves," *New York Times,* 10 July 2000 (accessed 10 July 2000), <www.nytimes.com/library/books/071000rowling-goblet.html>.

21. Joseph Weber, "From Soup to Nuts and Back to Soup," *Business Week,* 5 November 1990, 114, 116; Biography of Zoe Coulson from *Marquis Who's Who* (accessed 24 May 1992), <www.marquiswhoswho.com>.

22. Adapted from Carol Vinzant, "They Want You Back," *Fortune*, 2 October 2000, 271–272; Stephanie Armour, "Companies Recruiting Former Employees," *USA Today*, 2 February 2000, B1.

23. Adapted from John Noble Wilford, "An Old Observatory Finds a New Life," *New York Times*, 3 July 2001 (accessed on 03 July 2001), <www.nytimes.com/2001/07/03/science/03WILS.html>.

Chapter 8

1. Jeffrey R. Caponigro, president and CEO, Caponigro Public Relations, Inc., personal communication, 17 July 2001; Jeffrey R. Caponigro, *The Crisis Counselor* (Southfield, Mich.: Barker Business Books, 1998), 151–221.

2. Mark H. McCormack, *On Communicating* (Los Angeles: Dove Books, 1998), 87.

3. Curtis Sittenfeld, "Good Ways to Deliver Bad News," *Fast Company,* April 1999, 58–60.

4. Ram Subramanian, Robert G. Insley, and Rodney D. Blackwell, "Performance and Readability: A Comparison of Annual Reports of Profitable and Unprofitable Corporations," *Journal of Business Communication* 30, no. 2 (1993): 49–61.

5. *Techniques for Communicators* (Chicago: Lawrence Ragan Communication, 1995), 18.

6. Iris I. Varner, "A Comparison of American and French Business Correspondence," *Journal of Business Communication* 24, no. 4 (Fall 1988): 55–65.

7. Susan Jenkins and John Hinds, "Business Letter Writing: English, French, and Japanese," *TESOL Quarterly* 21, no. 2 (June 1987): 327–349; Saburo Haneda and Hiosuke Shima, "Japanese Communication Behavior As Reflected in Letter Writing," *Journal of Business Communication* 19, no. 1 (1982): 19–32.

8. James Calvert Scott and Diana J. Green, "British Perspectives on Organizing Bad-News Letters: Organizational Patterns Used by Major U.K. Companies," *Bulletin of the Association for Business Communication* 55, no. 1 (March 1992): 17–19.

9. Maura Dolan and Stuart Silverstein, "Court Broadens Liability for Job References," *Los Angeles Times,* 28 January 1997, A1, A11; Frances A. McMorris, "Ex-Bosses Face Less Peril Giving Honest Job References," *Wall Street Journal,* 8 July 1996, B1, B8.

10. Thomas S. Brice and Marie Waung, "Applicant Rejection Letters: Are Businesses Sending the Wrong Message?" *Business Horizons,* March–April 1995, 59–62.
11. Gwendolyn N. Smith, Rebecca F. Nolan, and Yong Dai, "Job-Refusal Letters: Readers' Affective Responses to Direct and Indirect Organizational Plans," *Business Communication Quarterly* 59, no. 1 (1996): 67–73; Brice and Waung, "Applicant Rejection Letters."
12. Korey A. Wilson, "Put Rejection Up-Front," *Black Enterprise,* November 1999, 69.
13. Judi Brownell, "The Performance Appraisal Interviews: A Multipurpose Communication Assignment," *Bulletin of the Association for Business Communication* 57, no. 2 (1994): 11–21.
14. Brownell, "The Performance Appraisal Interviews."
15. Stephanie Gruner, "Feedback from Everyone," *Inc.,* February 1997, 102–103.
16. Howard M. Bloom, "Performance Evaluations," *New England Business,* December 1991, 14.
17. David I. Rosen, "Appraisals Can Make—or Break—Your Court Case," *Personnel Journal,* November 1992, 113.
18. Patricia A. McLagan, "Advice for Bad-News Bearers: How to Tell Employees They're Not Hacking It and Get Results," *Industry Week,* 15 February 1993, 42; Michael Lee Smith, "Give Feedback, Not Criticism," *Supervisory Management,* 1993, 4; "A Checklist for Conducting Problem Performer Appraisals," *Supervisory Management,* December 1993, 7–9.
19. Jane R. Goodson, Gail W. McGee, and Anson Seers, "Giving Appropriate Performance Feedback to Managers: An Empirical Test of Content and Outcomes," *Journal of Business Communication* 29, no. 4 (1992): 329–342.
20. Craig Cox, "On the Firing Line," *Business Ethics,* May–June 1992, 33–34.
21. Cox, "On the Firing Line."
22. Adapted from Michal H. Mescon, Courtland L. Bovée, and John V. Thill, *Business Today,* 10th ed. (Upper Saddle River, N.J.: Prentice Hall, 2002), 369; Bruce Upbin, "Profit in a Big Orange Box," *Forbes*, 165, no. 2, 24 January 2000, (accessed 2 August 2001) <http://www.forbes.com/forbes/2000/0124/6502122a.html>.
23. Adapted from Courtney Barry, "10 Months, 10 Minutes, $10 Million," *New York Times,* 7 June 2000, H3; Courtney Barry, "After a Spring of Hope, a Dot-Com's Autumn of Reckoning," *New York Times,* 13 December 2000, H16.
24. Adapted from Craftopia.com print advertisement, 31 July 2000; Craftopia.com website (accessed 24 August 2000), <www.craftopia.com/shop/promo/martha3.asp>; Claire Furia Smith, "West Chester Start-up Tries to Become a Crafters' Utopia," *Philadelphia Inquirer,* 26 June 2000 (accessed 24 August 2000), <www.craftopia.com/shop/features/about_us_mc_6_26_00_ inquirer.asp>; Laura M. Naughton, "Crafting a Niche," *Daily Local News,* 8 March 2000 (accessed 24 August 2000), <www.craftopia.com/shop/features/about_us_mc_3_8_00_dailylocal.asp>.
25. Adapted from Wolf Blitzer, "More Employers Taking Advantages of New Cyber-Surveillance Software," CNN.com website, 10 July 2000 (accessed 11 July 2000), <www.cnn.com/2000/US/07/10/workplace.eprivacy/index.html>.
26. Adapted from Dan McSwain, "Consumers Could Owe $1.4B for Cuts," *North County Times,* 20 August 2000, A1; R. J. Ignelzi, "Now, Bill Can Be Clearer Than Mud But That Won't Ease Baseline Frustration," *San Diego Union-Tribune,* 15 August 2000, E-1 (accessed 29 August 2000), <www.uniontrib.com/news/utarchives/cgi/idoc.cgi?589762+unix++www.uniontrib.com..80+Union−Tribune+Union-Tribune+Library+Library++%28sdge%29>; Craig D. Rose, "Power Industry Politics: Ominous Signs Point to Higher Electricity Bills," *San Diego Union-Tribune,* 22 July 2000, A-1 (accessed on 29 August 2000), <www.uniontrib.com/news/utarchives/cgi/idoc.cgi?585891+unix++www.uniontrib.com..80+Union-Tribune+Union-Tribune+Library+Library++%28sdge%29>.
27. Adapted from Union Bank of California teleservices, personal communication, 16 August 2001.
28. Adapted from the Disclosure Project website (accessed 20 August 2001), <www.disclosureproject.org>; Katelynn Raymer and David Ruppe, "UFOs, Aliens and Secrets," ABCNews.com, 10 May 2001 (accessed 20 August 2001), <http://more.abcnews.go.com/sections/scitech/DailyNews/ufo010509.html>; Rachael Myer, "UFO Probe Sought," *Las Vegas Review-Journal*, 11 May 2001 (accessed 20 August 2001), <www.lvrj.com/cgi-bin/printable.cgi?/lvrj_home/2001/May-11-Fri-2001/news/16064080.html>.
29. Adapted from "Motorola to Cut Arizona Jobs," CNNfn website, 15 August 2001 (accessed 15 August 2001), <http://cnnfn.cnn.com/2001/18/15/companies/motorola>; Barnaby J. Feder, "Motorola Says It Expects Loss in Third Quarter," *New York Times,* 13 July 2001, C4; David Barboza, "Motorola Cuts 3% of Its Jobs as Chip Demand Cools Off," *New York Times,* 10 February 2001, C2; Dave Carpenter, "Motorola to Lop Another 4,000," *Chicago Sun-Times*, 13 July 2001, 49; Roger O. Crockett, "Motorola Can't Seem to Get Out of Its Own Way," *Business Week*, 22 January 2001, 72; Roger O. Crockett, "A New Company Called Motorola," *Business Week,* 17 April 2000, 86–92.
30. Adapted from Martha Brannigan, Susan Carey, and Scott McCartney, "First Class Mutiny: Fed Up with Airlines, Business Travelers Start to Fight Back," *Wall Street Journal,* 28 August 2001, A1, A4; "Survey Shows U.S. Corporations Cutting Overall Travel Spending; Lowering Costs Through Online Booking," *PR Newswire,* 30 July 2001; Andrew Edgecliffe-Johnson, "U.S. Airlines in Business Tailspin," *Financial Times* (London), 29 June 2001, 27; Joe Sharkey, "Corporate Rebound Expected by Fall," *Minneapolis Star Tribune,* 25 June 2001, 2D; Jon E. Hilsenrath, "Managers & Managing: Drop in U.S. Corporate Travel Spurs Cuts in Airfares, Hotel Rates," *Wall Street Journal Europe,* 20 June 2001, 24; Melanie Trottman, "Corporate Travel: Feeling the Pinch—Companies Scrutinize the Cost of Plane Tickets, Hotels, Expense-Account Dinners," *Wall Street Journal,* 8 May 2001, B1.
31. Adapted from Mescon, Bovée, and Thill, *Business Today,* 424-425; "Webvan Checks Out," *San Francisco Chronicle,* 13 July 2001, A22; Linda Himelstein with

Gerry Khermouch, "Webvan Left the Basics on the Shelf," *Business Week,* 23 July 2001, 43; Roger Blackwell, "Manager's Journal: Why Webvan Went Bust," *Wall Street Journal,* 16 July 2001, A22; Devon Spurgeon, "Traditional Grocers Feel Vindicated by Webvan's Failure," *Wall Street Journal,* 11 July 2001; Tim Wilson, "Webvan to Sell Tech at Auction," *Internetweek,* 16 July 2001, P11, P42.

32. Pascal Zachary, "Sun Microsystems Apologizes in Letter for Late Payments," *Wall Street Journal,* 11 October 1989, B4.

33. Peter Fritsch, "It's Lighter Than Glass and Hurts Less When Thrown, But Can Plastic Stack Up?" *Wall Street Journal,* 24 July 1996, B1.

34. Adapted from Associated Press, "Children's Painkiller Recalled," CNN.com/Health website, 16 August 2001 (accessed 22 August 2001), <www.cnn.com/2001/HEALTH/parenting/08/16/kids.drug.recalled.ap/index.html>; Perrigo Company website (accessed 29 August 2001), <www.perrigo.com>.

35. Adapted from Julie Vallese, "Motorized Scooter Injuries on the Rise," CNN.com website, 22 August 2001 (accessed 22 August 2001), <www.cnn.com/2001/US/08/22/scooter.advisory/index.html>; The Sports Authority website (accessed 28 August 2001), www.thesportsauthority.com.

36. Adapted from Dan Goodin, "Graduating Students Weigh New Job Incentive: Money to Stay Away," *Wall Street Journal,* 4 May 2001, B1; Mark Larson, "Intel Offering Buy-outs to Workers, College Recruits," *Sacramento Business Journal,* 4 May 2001, 1; Barbara Clements, "The Workplace: This Year's College Grads Will Face a More Challenging Job Hunt," *Tacoma,* (Wash.) *News Tribune,* 7 May 2001, D1.

37. Adapted from Ty Holland, "Vision Quest," *TV Guide,* 22 July 2000, 3.

38. Adapted from "Medical Plan Cost Shifting," *Controller's Report,* May 2001, 7; "Benefits Highlights 2001," San Diego Gas & Electric (A Sempra Energy company) employee benefits brochure.

39. Adapted from Associated Press, "Employers Restricting Use of Cell Phones in Cars," CNN.com website, 27 August 2001 (accessed 27 August 2001), <www.cnn.com/2001/TECH/08/27/cellphones.cars.ap/index.html>; Julie Vallese, "Study: All Cell Phones Distract Drivers," CNN.com website, 16 August 2001 (accessed 7 September 2001), <www.cnn.com/2001/US/08/16/cell.phone.driving/index.html>.

Chapter 9

1. Jeanne Anderson, sales director, Language Line Services, AT&T, personal communication, December 1992.

2. Jay A. Conger, "The Necessary Art of Persuasion," *Harvard Business Review,* May–June 1998, 84–95; Jeanette W. Gilsdorf, "Write Me Your Best Case for . . ." *Bulletin of the Association for Business Communication* 54, no. 1 (March 1991): 7–12.

3. "Vital Skill for Today's Managers: Persuading, Not Ordering Others," *Soundview Executive Book Summaries,* September 1998, 1.

4. Anne Fisher, "Success Secret: A High Emotional IQ," *Fortune,* 16 October 1998, 293–298.

5. Mary Cross, "Aristotle and Business Writing: Why We Need to Teach Persuasion," *Bulletin of the Association for Business Communication* 54, no. 1 (March 1991): 3–6.

6. Abraham H. Maslow, *Motivation and Personality* (New York: Harper & Row, 1954), 12, 19.

7. Robert T. Moran, "Tips on Making Speeches to International Audiences," *International Management,* April 1980, 58–59.

8. Conger, "The Necessary Art of Persuasion."

9. Gilsdorf, "Write Me Your Best Case for . . ."

10. Raymond M. Olderman, *10-Minute Guide to Business Communication* (New York: Macmillan Spectrum/Alpha Books, 1997), 57–61.

11. Gilsdorf, "Write Me Your Best Case for . . ."

12. John D. Ramage and John C. Bean, *Writing Arguments: A Rhetoric with Readings,* 3d ed. (Boston: Allyn & Bacon, 1995), 430–442.

13. Conger, "The Necessary Art of Persuasion."

14. Dianna Booher, *Communicate with Confidence* (New York: McGraw-Hill, 1994), 110.

15. Tamra B. Orr, "Persuasion Without Pressure," *Toastmaster,* January 1994, 19–22; William Friend, "Winning Techniques of Great Persuaders," *Association Management,* February 1985, 82–86; Patricia Buhler, "How to Ask for—and Get—What You Want!" *Supervision*, February 1990, 11–13.

16. Booher, *Communicate with Confidence*, 102.

17. Conger, "The Necessary Art of Persuasion."

18. Robert L. Hemmings, "Think Before You Write," *Fund Raising Management,* February 1990, 23–24.

19. Teri Lammers, "The Elements of Perfect Pitch," *Inc.,* March 1992, 53–55.

20. Kimberly Paterson, "The Writing Process—Sales Letters That Work," *Rough Notes*, April 1998, 59–60.

21. William North Jayme, quoted in Albert Haas Jr., "How to Sell Almost Anything by Direct Mail," *Across the Board,* November 1986, 50.

22. Paterson, "The Writing Process."

23. Hemmings, "Think Before You Write."

24. Hemmings, "Think Before You Write."

25. Conrad Squires, "How to Write a Strong Letter, Part Two: Choosing a Theme," *Fund Raising Management,* November 1991, 65–66.

26. Conrad Squires, "Getting the Compassion out of the Box," *Fund Raising Management,* September 1992, 55, 60.

27. Squires, "Getting the Compassion out of the Box."

28. Constance L. Clark, "25 Steps to Better Direct Mail Fundraising," *Nonprofit World,* July–August 1989, 11–13; Squires, "How to Write a Strong Letter."

29. Squires, "How to Write a Strong Letter."

30. Clark, "25 Steps to Better Direct Mail Fundraising."

31. Conrad Squires, "Why Some Letters Outpull Others," *Fund Raising Management,* January 1991, 67, 72.

32. Squires, "Why Some Letters Outpull Others"; Clark, "25 Steps to Better Direct Mail Fundraising"; Jerry Huntsinger, "My First 29 1/2 Years in Direct-Mail Fund Raising: What I've Learned," *Fund Raising Management,* January 1992, 40–43.

33. Jeanne Anderson, sales director, Language Line Services, AT&T, personal communication, December 1992.

34. Kevin M. Savetz, "Preventive Medicine for the Computer User," *Multimedia Online* 2, no. 2 (June 1996): 58–60.

35. Adapted from Hotel del Coronado website (accessed 7 September 2001), <www.hoteldel.com>; International Shark Attack Files, Florida Museum of Natural History website (accessed 2 September 2001), <www.flmnh.ufl.edu/fish/Sharks/Statistics/statsus.htm>; "Sharks Attack Three Off Florida's East Coast," 20 August 2001 (accessed 21 August 2001), <www.cnn.com/2001/US/08/19/shark.attack/index.html>; "Year of Shark 'Hype,' Says Expert," CNN.com, September 2001 (accessed 4 September 2001), <www.cnn.com/2001/US/09/03/shark.perspective>; "Boy Dies After Shark Attack," CNN.com, 2 September 2001 (accessed 2 September 2001), <www.cnn.com/2001/US/09/04/shark.attack/index.html>; "Labor Day Shark Attack Survivor Hanging On," CNN.com, 5 September 2001 (accessed 5 September 2001), <www.cnn.com/2001/US/09/02/shark.attack/index.html>; Thurston Hatcher, "Florida Panel Embraces Ban on Shark Feeding," CNN.com, 7 September 2001 (accessed 7 September 2001), <www.cnn.com/2001/US/09/06/shark.feeding/index.html>.

36. Adapted from Caryne Brown, "How to Make Your Ex-Boss Your Client," *Black Enterprise*, April 1994, 92; Time Swanson and Claude Brodesser, "Hollywood Slipping into Slo-Mo," ABCNews.com, 24 September 2001 (accessed 24 September 2001), <www.abcnews.go.com/wire/Entertainment/reuters20010924_68.html> Miramax Films website (accessed 24 September 2001), <www.miramax.com>.

37. Adapted from Michael Mescon, Courtland Bovée, and John Thill, *Business Today*, 10th ed. (Upper Saddle River, N.J.: Prentice Hall, 2002), 272–274; Jason Roberson, "Rush-Hour Rebellion," *Dallas Business Journal*, 22 June 2001, 31; Carole Hawkins, "Ready, Set, Go Home," *Black Enterprise*, August 2001, 118–124; Wayne Tompkins, "Telecommuting in Transition," *Louisville (Ky.) Courier-Journal*, 9 July 2001, 1C.

38. Adapted from Mescon, Bovée, and Thill, *Business Today*, 269; Peter Baker, "Work: Have Fun. And That's an Order," *The Observer* (London), 3 January 1999, 11; "The Power of Laughter," Oprah.com (accessed 29 September 2001), <www.oprah.com/living/lifemake/experts/tracy/expert_tracy_laughter.html>.

39. Adapted from Mescon, Bovée, and Thill, *Business Today*, 306–307; John R. Hall, "Recruiting via the Internet," *Air Conditioning, Heating & Refrigeration News*, 9 April 2001, 26; Kim Peters, "Five Keys to Effective E-cruiting," *Ivey Business Journal* (London), January–February 2001, 8–10; C. Glenn Pearce and Tracy L. Tuten, "Internet Recruiting in the Banking Industry," *Business Communication Quarterly*, March 2001, 9–18; Christopher Caggiano, "The Truth About Internet Recruiting," *Inc*, December 1999, 156.

40. Adapted from Julian E. Barnes, "Fast-Food Giveaway Toys Face Rising Recalls," *New York Times*, 16 August 2001, A1; Shirley Leung, "Burger King Recalls 2.6 Million Kids Meal Toys," *Wall Street Journal*, 1 August 2001, B2.

41. Adapted from advertisement, *Atlantic Monthly*, January 2000, 119; Endless Pools, Inc., website (accessed 31 August 2000), <www.endlesspools.com/>.

42. Adapted from "Tobacco Smoke and the Nonsmoker," Americans for Nonsmokers' Rights, 1988, revised 1994; "Nuisance/Real Property" case citation and abstract, "*Contract Management Services, Inc., et al. v. Kuykendahl Joint, Inc., and Kamen Management, Inc.*, Dist. Ct. Harris County (TX), 61st Jud. Dist., No. 93-006228 (1993)," Tobacco Control Resource Center, 1998, 39.

43. Adapted from Bruce Haring, "Trouble Getting up to Speed," *USA Today*, 27 December 1999, D3, D2; Mike Rogoway, "AT&T Seeks to Improve Internet Connections," *Vancouver (Wash.) Columbian*, 9 March 2001, E1.

44. Adapted from Michael S. James, "No Expiration on Recall Risk," ABCNews.com, 31 August 2001 (accessed 31 August 2001), <http://abcnews.go.com/sections/living/DailyNews/meat_recall010830.html>; James F. Balch, M.D., and Phyllis A. Balch, C.N.C, *Prescription for Nutritional Healing*, 2d ed. (Garden City Park, N.Y.: Avery Publishing Group, 1997), 277–282.

45. Adapted from CNET Shopper.com (accessed 1 October 2001), <http://shopper.cnet.com/shopping/0-1257.html?tag=sh>.

46. Adapted from Gateway website (accessed 2 October 2001), <www.gateway.com>; Gateway customer service sales representative, 1-800-GATEWAY, personal interview, 10 October 2001.

47. Adapted from Quotesmith.com website, Investor Overview and FAQ (accessed 31 August 2000), <investor.quotesmith.com/ireye/ir_site.zhtml?ticker=QUOT&script=2100>.

48. Mescon, Bovée, and Thill, *Business Today*, 211; ScrubaDub website (accessed 2 October 2001), <www.scrubadub.com>.

49. Adapted from the American Red Cross website (accessed 3 October 2001), <www.redcross.org>; American Red Cross San Diego Chapter website (accessed 3 October 2001), <www.sdarc.org/blood.htm>.

Chapter 10

1. Charles Shin, founder, Charley's Steakery, personal communication, June 1996.

2. Information for this section was obtained from "Finding Industry Information" (accessed 3 November 1998), <www.pitt.edu/~buslibry/industries.htm.>; Thomas P. Bergman, Stephen M. Garrison, and Gregory M. Scott, *The Business Student Writer's Manual and Guide to the Internet* (Upper Saddle River, N.J.: Prentice Hall, 1998), 67–80; Ernest L. Maier, Anthony J. Faria, Peter Kaatrude, and Elizabeth Wood, *The Business Library and How to Use It* (Detroit: Omnigraphics, 1996), 53–76; Sherwyn P. Morreale and Courtland L. Bovée, *Excellence in Public Speaking* (Fort Worth: Harcourt Brace College Publishers, 1998), 166–171.

3. Jason Zien, "Measuring the Internet," *About.com*, 13 July 1999 (accessed 17 July 1999), <internet.about.com/library/weekly/1999/aa071399a.htm>; "FAST Aims

for Largest Index," *Search Engine Watch,* 4 May 1999 (accessed 17 July 1999), <searchenginewatch.internet.com/sereport/99/05-fast.htm>.

4. Thomas E. Weber, "Web's Vastness Foils Even Best Search Engines," *Wall Street Journal,* 3 April 1998, B1, B7; Matt Lake, "Desperately Seeking Susan OR Suzie NOT Sushi," *New York Times,* 3 September 1998, D1, D7; "How Search Engines Work" (accessed 18 January 1998), <www.searchenginewatch.com/work.htm>.

5. "How Search Engines Work."

6. Thomas A. Stewart, "Internet Portals: No One-Stop Shop," *Fortune,* 7 December 1998, 235–236; James Coates, "Netscape, AOL May Form an Alliance," *Chicago Tribune,* 19 November 1998, sec. 3, 1, 3.

7. Maier, Faria, Kaatrude, and Wood, *The Business Library and How to Use It,* 84–97; Lake, "Desperately Seeking Susan OR Suzie NOT Sushi."

8. Leslie Ann Forrester, "Push Technology," *Legal Assistant Today,* May–June 1998, 36–37.

9. Andy Eddy, "Whither Push Technology," *Network World,* 3 August 1998, 27–30; Michael Marriott, "Happy Birthday, Your Team Won, Your Stock Crashed," *New York Times,* 17 September 1998, D1, D8.

10. Andrew Brown and Imran Kahn, "Internet Innovations Workshop '96: Internet Agents" (accessed 24 November 1998), <www.cs.toronto.edu/~andy/IIW>.

11. "How to Design and Conduct a Study," *Credit Union Magazine,* October 1983, 36–46.

12. Erin White, "Market Research on the Internet Has Its Drawbacks," *Wall Street Journal,* 2 March 2000, B4.

13. Morreale and Bovée, *Excellence in Public Speaking,* 177.

14. Morreale and Bovée, *Excellence in Public Speaking,* 178–180.

15. Morreale and Bovée, *Excellence in Public Speaking,* 182.

16. Robert E. Cason, *Writing for the Business World* (Upper Saddle River, N.J.: Prentice Hall, 1997), 102.

17. Bergman, Garrison, and Scott, *The Business Student Writer's Manual and Guide to the Internet,* 65.

18. "How to Paraphrase Effectively: 6 Steps to Follow," Researchpaper.com (accessed 26 October 1998), <www.researchpaper.com/writing_center/30.html>.

19. Cason, *Writing for the Business World,* 71–72.

20. Dorothy Geisler, "How to Avoid Copyright Lawsuits," *IABC Communication World,* June 1984, 34–37.

Chapter 11

1. Curtis Symonds, executive vice president of affiliate sales and marketing, BET Holdings Group, personal communication, 23 July 1998; Karen Gutloff, "Show and Sell," *Black Enterprise,* July 1998, 106.

2. Stephanie McKinnon, "Pictures, Signs and Symbols Prove to Be Powerful Tools," *Gannett Suburban Newspapers,* 27 September 1992, 12.

3. The information in this example was adapted from Michael H. Mescon, Courtland L. Boveé, and John Thill, "Face-Off: FedEx vs. UPS," *Business Today* (Upper Saddle River, N.J: Prentice Hall, 2001), 96.

4. Sheri Rosen, "What Is Truth?" *IABC Communication World,* March 1995, 40.

5. Maureen Jones, "Getting Good Graphs," *PC Magazine,* 23 July 1985, 217.

6. Edward R. Tufte, *The Visual Display of Quantitative Information* (Cheshire, Conn.: Graphic Press, 1983), 113.

7. Courtland L. Bovée, Michael J. Houston, and John V. Thill, *Marketing,* 2d ed. (New York: McGraw-Hill, 1995), 250.

8. Curtis Symonds, personal communication, 23 July 1998.

9. "Leading National Advertisers," *Advertising Age,* 25 September 2000, S4.

Component Chapter B

1. Samuel Greengard, "How Technology Will Change the Workplace," *Workforce,* January 1998, 78–84.

2. Information for this section was taken in part from Michael Mescon, Courtland Bovée, and John Thill, *Business Today,* 10th ed. (Upper Saddle River, N.J.: Prentice Hall, 2002), 30–41.

3. Paul Franson, *High Tech, High Hope* (New York: Wiley, 1998), 252.

4. Maria Godoy, "Instant Messaging Goes to Work," *ABCNews.com* (accessed 20 August 2001), <www.abcnews.go.com>.

5. Anne Zieger, "Enterprise Computing: IP Telephony Gets Real," *InfoWorld,* 5 January 1998, 20; Laura Kujubu, "Telcos Answer Wake-Up Call from Internet," *InfoWorld,* 15 December 1997, 19.

6. David Morse, ed., *CyberDictionary: Your Guide to the Wired World* (Santa Monica, Calif: Knowledge Exchange, 1996), 113.

7. Morse, *CyberDictionary,* 233.

8. Michael Taylor, "Intranets—A New Technology Changes All the Rules," *Telecommunication,* January 1997, 39–40.

9. Stephanie Armour, "Workers Just Click to Enroll for Benefits," *USA Today,* 8 November 2000, B1; Charlene Marmer Solomon, "Sharing Information Across Borders and Time Zones," *Global Workforce,* March 1998, 13–18; Eryn Brown, "Nine Ways to Win on the Web," *Fortune,* 24 May 1999, 112.

10. Taylor, "Intranets."

11. Amy Cortese, "Here Comes the Intranet," *Business Week,* 26 February 1996, 76–84.

12. John R. L. Rizza, "Extranets: The Internet Gets Down to Business," *Entrepreneurial Edge* 3 (1998): 76–78; Samuel Greengard, "Extranets Linking Employees with Your Vendors," *Workforce,* November 1997, 28–34.

13. Andy Reinhardt, "The Paperless Manual," *Business Week e.Biz,* 18 September 2000, EB92.

14. Shari Caudron, "Virtual Manners," *Industry Week,* 6 July 1998, 52–53; Phil Waga, "Advanced Technology Sends Manners Back to the Stone Age," *Gannett Suburban Newspapers,* 1 August 1997, S09.

15. William R. Pape, "Becoming a Virtual Company," *Inc. Technology* 4 (1995): 29, 31.

16. Lisa Bransten, "Staying in Touch," *Wall Street Journal,* 16 November 1998, R14.

17. "Mobile Phones in China: A Billion Voices Calling?" *Economist,* 1 September 2001, 54.

18. Jennifer Tanaka, "Teen Talkathon," *Newsweek,* November 5, 2001, 40J.
19. Mike Bransby, "Voice Mail Makes a Difference," *Journal of Business Strategy,* January–February 1990, 7–10.
20. Neil Gross, Paul C. Judge, Otis Port, and Stephen H. Wildstrom, "Let's Talk," *Business Week,* 23 February 1998, 61–76.
21. Derrek Schartz, "Can We Talk?" *Communication News,* April 1998, 24+.
22. Gross, Judge, Port, and Wildstrom, "Let's Talk"; Michael J. Himowitz, "Dictating to Your PC," *Fortune,* New York, 9 November 1998, 240+.
23. Gross, Judge, Port, and Wildstrom, "Let's Talk"; Schartz, "Can We Talk?"
24. Gross, Judge, Port, and Wildstrom, "Let's Talk."
25. "Talking to Your Computer," *CNNMoney.com* (accessed 31 October 2001), <money.cnn.com/2001/10/31/technology/v_leading_edge>.
26. "Nurses, Physicians Increase PDA Usage," *Health Management Technology,* October 2001, 10; Mitch Wagner, "One System for Meter Readers—Allegheny Power Streamlines by Consolidating on Windows CE," *InternetWeek,* 1 October 2001, 23+.
27. Rebecca Blumenstein, "For Your Eyes Only," *Wall Street Journal,* June 21, 1999, R10, R19.
28. Samuel Greengard, "How Secure Is Your Data?" *Workforce,* May 1998, 52–60; Nikhil Hutheesing and Philip E. Ross, "Hackerphobia," *Forbes,* 23 March 1998, 150–154.
29. Dan Luzadder, "Corporate Security Gets Urgent," *Interactive Week* (accessed 23 October 2001), <techupdate.zdnet.com/techupdate/stories/main/0,14179,2819412,00.html>.
30. Robert D. Hof, "Tech's Reliability Gap," *BusinessWeek e.Biz,* 29 October 2001, EB 32
31. Steve Patterson, "Congress to Weigh Privacy Right vs. Security Need; Legislation May Mean Intrusiveness," *Florida Times Union,* 24 September 2001, A-1.
32. "Corporate Security Gets Urgent: 10 Tips for Creating a Network Security Policy," *Interactive Week* (accessed 23 October 2001), <techupdate.zdnet.com/techupdate/stories/main/0,14179,2819412-9,00.html>.
33. Keith Naughton, "CyberSlacking," *Business Week,* 29 November 1999, 62–65; Jennifer Tanaka, "Getting Personal," *Newsweek,* 22 November 1999, 101–103; Susan Gregory Thomas, "Getting to Know You.com," *U.S. News & World Report,* 15 November 1999, 102–110; G. Beato, "Traffic Cops," *Business 2.0,* November 1999, 51–54.
34. Christa Degnan, "Firings Renew Debate over E-Mail Policies," *PC Week Online* (accessed 6 December 1999), <www.zdnet.com>.
35. Jeff Howe, "Big Boss Is Watching," *Yahoo! Internet Life,* October 2000, 105–107.
36. Elisa Deardorff, "With Voice Mail, You Never Know Who's Listening," *Chicago Tribune,* 1 June 1998, B1, B8; "40 Fired for Sex-Site Abuse," *CNN America* (accessed 6 October 1999), <cnnfn.com/1999/10/06/companies/xerox>.
37. Sam Ames, "Tech Partners Keep Faith in Internet2," *ZDNet News* (accessed 4 October 2001), <www.zdnet.com>; Robyn Meredity, "Building 'Internet 2,'" *New York Times,* 2 February 1998, C3.
38. Richard Behar, "Fear Along the Firewall," *Fortune,* 15 October 2001, 145–148; Brian Fonseca, "Study: Viruses Cost $12B in '99," *InfoWorld.com,* 17 January 2000 (accessed 5 November 2001), <www.computerworld.com>.
39. David S. Bernstein, "We've Been Hacked," *Inc. Tech 2000,* no. 3, 106+.
40. Del Jones, "Businesses Battle over Intellectual Property," *USA Today,* 2 August 2000, 1B, 2B; Greengard, "How Secure Is Your Data?"

Chapter 12

1. Adapted from Dell Computer Corporation's website (accessed 1 September 2001), <www.dell.com>; Michael Dell with Catherine Fredman, *Direct from Dell (*New York: HarperCollins Publishers, 1999) 8–15, 36–38, 66–80, 92–101, 133, 144–145, 175–182, 186, 196–197, 208; Daniel Roth, "Dell's Big New Act," *Fortune*, 6 December 1999, 152–156; Louise Fickel, "Know Your Customer," *CIO*, 15 August 1999, 62–72; Neel Chowdhury, "Dell Cracks China," *Fortune*, 21 June 1999, 120–124; "Interview: E-commerce Drives Dell Computer's Success," *IT Cost Management Strategies*, June 1999, 4–6; Carla Johnson, "Moving at the Speed of Dell," *HRMagazine*, April 1999, 50–56.
2. Dan Steinhoff and John F. Burgess, *Small Business Management Fundamentals,* 5th ed. (New York: McGraw-Hill, 1989), 37.
3. Joan F. Vesper and Karl H. Vesper, "Writing a Business Plan: The Total Term Assignment," *Bulletin of the Association for Business Communication* 56, no. 2 (June 1993): 29–32.
4. Elizabeth Conlin, "The Daily Sales Report," *Inc.,* January 1991, 73–75.
5. Tom Peters, "Don't Send Memos!" *Washington Monthly,* November 1987, 13.
6. Eric D. Randall, "Firms Serve Annual Reports with a Twist," *USA Today*, 17 May 1994, 6B; Patrick Flanagan, "Make Your Annual Report Work Harder," *Management Review*, October 1993, 52–58.
7. Tom Sant, *Persuasive Business Proposals* (New York: American Management Association, 1992), summarized in *Soundview Executive Book Summaries* 14, no. 10, pt. 2 (October 1992): 3.
8. Iris Varner, *Contemporary Business Report Writing,* 2d ed. (Chicago: Dryden Press, 1991), 170.
9. Varner, *Contemporary Business Report Writing*, 178.
10. Susan L. Leach, "SEC Takes Next Leap into Computer Age," *Christian Science Monitor*, 7 June 1994, 8.
11. Michael H. Mescon, Courtland L. Bovée, and John V. Thill, *Business Today,* 9th ed. (Upper Saddle River, N.J.: Prentice Hall, 1999), 135.
12. Scott Steinacher, "Putting the Power Back in Reports," *InfoWorld,* 24 January 2000, 69–70.
13. Stephan Manes, "E-Mail Troubles? You Have No Idea!" *PC World*, July 1996, 39.

Chapter 13

1. Dierdre Ballou, education manager, San Diego Wild Animal Park, personal communication, July 1997.

2. A. S. C. Ehrenberg, "Report Writing—Six Simple Rules for Better Business Documents," *Admap,* June 1992, 39–42.

3. Michael Netzley and Craig Snow, *Guide to Report Writing* (Upper Saddle River, N.J.: Prentice Hall, 2001), 15.

4. Claudia Mon Pere McIsaac, "Improving Student Summaries Through Sequencing," *Bulletin of the Association for Business Communication* (September 1987): 17–20.

5. David A. Hayes, "Helping Students GRASP the Knack of Writing Summaries," *Journal of Reading* (November 1989): 96–101.

6. Philip C. Kolin, *Successful Writing at Work,* 6th ed. (Boston: Houghton Mifflin, 2001), 552–555.

7. Dierdre Ballou, education manager, San Diego Wild Animal Park, personal communication, July 1997.

8. Adapted from Bob Smith, "The Evolution of Pinkerton," *Management Review,* September 1993, 54–58.

Chapter 14

1. Mark Landiak, president, Corporate Dynamics, personal communication, 20 August 1998.

2. Michael Netzley and Craig Snow, *Guide to Report Writing* (Upper Saddle River, N.J.: Prentice Hall, 2001), 57.

3. Oswald M. T. Ratteray, "Hit the Mark with Better Summaries," *Supervisory Management,* September 1989, 43–45.

4. Netzley and Snow, *Guide to Report Writing,* 43.

5. Alice Reid, "A Practical Guide For Writing Proposals" (accessed 31 May 2001), <members.dca.net/areid/proposal.htm>.

6. Mark Landiak, president, Corporate Dynamics, personal communication, 20 August 1998.

7. Adapted from William C. Symonds, "Giving It the Old Online Try," *Business Week,* 3 December 2001, 76–80; Karen Frankola, "Why Online Learners Drop Out," *Workforce,* October 2001, 52–60; Mary Lord, "They're Online and on the Job; Managers and Hamburger Flippers Are Being E-Trained at Work," *U.S. News & World Report,* 15 October 2001, 72–77.

8. Bickley Townsend, "Room at the Top," *American Demographics,* July 1996, 28–37.

9. Alison Stein Wellner, "Keeping Old Cars on the Road," *American Demographics,* July 1997, 53–58.

10. Adapted from Michael J. Weiss, "Online America," *American Demographics,* March 2001, 53–60; "E-Commerce Shows Signs of Waking from Summer Slumber," *CyberAtlas,* 23 August 2001 (accessed 14 December 2001), <http://cyberatlas.internet.com/markets/retailing/artcle/0,6061_871621,00.html>; "E-Commerce Survives an Enigmatic September," *CyberAtlas,* 16 October 2001 (accessed 14 December, 2001), <http://cyberatlas.internet.com/markets/retailing/article/0,6061_904451,00.html>; "Despite Customer Service Woes, Online Retailing Keeps Growing," *CyberAtlas,* 21 March 2001 (accessed 14 December, 2001), <http://cyberatlas.internet.com/markets/retailing/article/0,6061_719771,00.html>; "E-Commerce Should Hold Its Own This Holiday Season," *CyberAtlas,* 15 October 2001 (accessed 14 December 2001), <http://cyberatlas.internet.com/markets/retailing/article/0,6061_903401,00.html>; "Lump of Coal for E-Commerce Predictions," *CyberAtlas,* 5 November 2001 (accessed 14 December 2001), <http://cyberatlas.internet.com/markets/retailing/article/0,6061_916681,00.html>; "Online Shoppers Want a Real Store, Too," USA Today Snapshot, *USA Today,* 18 July 2001, B1; "Online Shoppers Prefer Discounts," USA Today Snapshot, *USA Today,* 16 January 2001, B1.

11. Adapted from Bruce Einhorn, Chester Dawson, Irene Kunii, Dexter Roberts, and Peter Engardio, "Asia's Future China," *Business Week,* October 29, 2001, 48–52; "WTO Membership to Boost China's GDP Growth," *Xinhua News Agency,* 11 December 2001, 1+; Gina Fraone, "China's Challenge," *Electronic Business* 24, no. 12 (1998), 24; Trish Saywell, "Preparing for Take-Off," *Far Eastern Economic Review* 161, no. 48 (1998), 38; Colin Bates, "The Many China Markets," *China Business Review* 25, no. 5 (1998): 26–29; U.S. Department of Commerce, *Big Emerging Markets Information Resource Page,* 28 August 1998 (accessed 1 December 1998), <www.ita.doc.gov/bems/index.html>; Trish Saywell, "Curious in China," *Far Eastern Economic Review* 161, no. 28 (1998): 74–76; Catherine Gelb, "Installing a Software Sector," *China Business Review* 24, no. 5 (1997): 28–36; Geng Cui, "The Different Faces of the Chinese Consumer," *China Business Review* 24, no. 4 (1997): 34–38.

12. Denis Gellene, "Marketers Target Schools by Offering Facts and Features," *Los Angeles Times,* 4 June 1998, D1.

13. Sandra Evans, "First Come Goals, Then Guts and Glory," *Washington Post,* 5 October 1998, F10; Lisa Lee Freeman, "Getting Ahead May Mean Getting a Coach," *Investor's Business Daily,* 2 December 1997, A1; Anita Bruzzese, "Considering Taking a New Job?" *Gannett News Service,* 14 August 1997, S12.

Chapter 15

1. Leanne Anderson, founder of Anderson Business Resources, personal communications, 24 April 1997 and 23 July 1998; Leanne Anderson, "Speak Up," *Entrepreneur,* March 1997, 92–95.

2. Sherwyn P. Morreale and Courtland L. Bovée, *Excellence in Public Speaking* (Fort Worth: Harcourt Brace, 1998), 309.

3. "Choose and Use Your Words Deliberately," *Soundview Executive Book Summaries,* 20, no. 6, pt. 2 (June 1998): 3.

4. Walter Kiechel III, "How to Give a Speech," *Fortune,* 8 June 1987, 180.

5. *Communication and Leadership Program* (Santa Ana, Calif.: Toastmasters International, 1980), 44, 45.

6. Morreale and Bovée, *Excellence in Public Speaking,* 24–25.

7. Judy Linscott, "Getting On and Off the Podium," *Savvy,* October 1985, 44.

8. Iris R. Johnson, "Before You Approach the Podium," *MW,* January–February 1989, 7.

9. Sandra Moyer, "Braving No Woman's Land," *The Toastmaster,* August 1986, 13.

10. "Control the Question-and-Answer Session," *Soundview Executive Book Summaries* 20, no. 6, pt. 2 (June 1998): 4.

11. "Control the Question-and-Answer Session."
12. Teresa Brady, "Fielding Abrasive Questions During Presentations," *Supervisory Management,* February 1993, 6.
13. Robert L. Montgomery, "Listening on Your Feet," *The Toastmaster,* July 1987, 14–15.
14. Adapted from Ronald L. Applebaum and Karl W. E. Anatol, *Effective Oral Communication: For Business and the Professions* (Chicago: Science Research Associates, 1982), 240–244.
15. Anderson, personal communications; Anderson, "Speak Up."

Chapter 16

1. Kevan Allbee, creative partner, Allbee Green, personal communication, 13 July 2001; Kevan J. Allbee, David L. Green, and Kari Woolf, "Pre-Show Business," *Presentations,* May 2001, 50–54.
2. "Polishing Your Presentation," 3M Meeting Network (accessed 8 June 2001), <www.mmm.com/meetingnetwork/readingroom/meetingguide_pres.html>
3. Kathleen K. Weigner, "Visual Persuasion," *Forbes,* 16 September 1991, 176; Kathleen K. Weigner, "Showtime!" *Forbes,* 13 May 1991, 118.
4. Claudyne Wilder and David Fine, *Point, Click & Wow* (San Francisco: Jossey-Bass Pfeiffer, 1996), 50.
5. Allbee, personal communication.
6. Margo Halverson, "Choosing the Right Colors for Your Next Presentation," 3M Meeting Network (accessed 8 June 2001), <www.mmm.com/meetingnetwork/readingroom/meetingguide_right_color.html>.
7. Carol Klinger and Joel G. Siegel, "Computer Multimedia Presentations," *CPA Journal,* June 1996, 46.
8. Jon Hanke, "Five Tips for Better Visuals," 3M Meeting Network (accessed 8 June 2001), <www.mmm.com/meetingnetwork/presentations/pmag_better_visuals.html>.
9. Hanke, "Five Tips for Better Visuals."
10. Edward P. Bailey, *Writing and Speaking at Work* (Upper Saddle River, N.J.: Prentice Hall, 1999), 138–145.
11. Ted Simons, "Handouts That Won't Get Trashed," *Presentations,* February 1999, 47–50.
12. Bailey, *Writing and Speaking at Work,* 177–178.
13. Patrick J. Collins, *Say It with Power and Confidence* (Upper Saddle River, N.J.: Prentice Hall, 1997), 122–124.
14. Allbee, personal communication, 13 July 2001.
15. Ed Bott and Woody Leonard, *Special Edition—Using Microsoft Office 2000* (Indianapolis: Que Corporation, 1999), 907.
16. Mary Munter, *Guide to Managerial Communication* 5th ed. (Upper Saddle River, N.J.: Prentice Hall, 2000), 59.

Chapter 17

1. Doug Halm, manager, human resources, Recreational Equipment Incorporated, personal communication, August 1998.
2. Camille DeBell, "Ninety Years in the World of Work in America," *Career Development Quarterly* 50, no.1 (September 2001): 77–88.
3. John A. Challenger, "The Changing Workforce: Workplace Rules in the New Millenium," *Vital Speeches of the Day* 67, no. 23 (15 September 2001): 721–8.
4. Marvin J. Cetron and Owen Davies, "Trends Now Changing the World: Technology, the Workplace, Management, and Institutions," *Futurist* 35, no. 2 (March/April 2001): 27–42.
5. Cetron and Davies, "Trends Now Changing the World."
6. Amanda Bennett, "GE Redesigns Rungs of Career Ladder," *Wall Street Journal,* 15 March 1993, B1, B3.
7. Robin White Goode, "International and Foreign Language Skills Have an Edge," *Black Enterprise,* May 1995, 53.
8. Nancy M. Somerick, "Managing a Communication Internship Program," *Bulletin of the Association for Business Communication* 56, no. 3 (1993): 10–20.
9. Joan Lloyd, "Changing Workplace Requires You to Alter Your Career Outlook," *Milwaukee Journal Sentinel,* 4 July 1999, 1; DeBell, "Ninety Years in the World of Work in America."
10. Robert J. Gerberg, *Robert Gerberg's Job Changing System,* summarized by Macmillan Book Clubs, Inc., in the "Macmillan Executive Summary Program," April 1987, 4.
11. Christoper Caggiano, "Recruiting Secrets," *Inc.,* October 1998, 29–42; Donna Fenn, "The Right Fit," *Inc. 500,* 1997, 104+.
12. Caggiano, "Recruiting Secrets," 29–42.
13. Caggiano, "Recruiting Secrets," 29–42.
14. Stephanie Armour, "Employers: Enough Already with the E-Résumés," *USA Today,* 15 July 1999, 1B.
15. Cheryl L. Noll, "Collaborating with the Career Planning and Placement Center in the Job-Search Project," *Business Communication Quarterly* 58, no. 3 (1995): 53–55.
16. Rockport Institute, "How to Write a Masterpiece of a Résumé" (accessed 16 October 1998), <www.rockportinstitute.com/résumés.html>.
17. Sal Divita, "If You're Thinking Résumé, Think Creatively," Marketing News, 14 September 1992, 29.
18. Pam Stanley-Weigand, "Organizing the Writing of Your Resume," Bulletin of the *Association for Business Communication* 54, no. 3 (September 1991): 11–12.
19. Susan Vaughn, "Answer the Hard Questions Before Asked," *Los Angeles Times,* 29 July 2001, W1–W2.
20. Richard H. Beatty and Nicholas C. Burkholder, *The Executive Career Guide for MBAs* (New York: Wiley, 1996), 133.
21. Adapted from Burdette E. Bostwick, *How to Find the Job You've Always Wanted* (New York: Wiley, 1982), 69–70.
22. Beatty and Burkholder, *The Executive Career Guide for MBAs,* 151.
23. Rockport Institute, "How to Write a Masterpiece of a Résumé."
24. Rockport Institute, "How to Write a Masterpiece of a Résumé."
25. Rockport Institute, "How to Write a Masterpiece of a Résumé."
26. Beverly Culwell-Block and Jean Anna Sellers, "Résumé Content and Format—Do the Authorities Agree?" *Bulletin of the Association for Business Communication* 57, no. 4 (1994): 27–30.

27. Janice Tovey, "Using Visual Theory in the Creation of Résumés: A Bibliography," *Bulletin of the Association for Business Communication* 54, no. 3 (September 1991): 97–99.

28. Regina Pontow, "Electronic Résumé Writing Tips" (accessed 18 October 1998), <www.provenresumes.com/reswkshps/electronic/scnres.html>.

29. Ellen Joe Pollock, "Sir: Your Application for a Job Is Rejected; Sincerely, Hal 9000," *Wall Street Journal,* 30 July 1998, A1, A12.

30. Bronwyn Fryer, "Job Hunting the Electronic Way," *Working Woman,* March 1995, 59–60, 78; Joyce Lane Kennedy and Thomas J. Morrow, *Electronic Resume Revolution,* 2d ed. (New York: Wiley, 1995), 30–33; Mary Goodwin, Deborah Cohn, and Donna Spivey, *Netjobs: Use the Internet to Land Your Dream Job* (New York: Michael Wolff, 1996), 149–150; Zane K. Quible, "Electronic Résumés: Their Time Is Coming," *Business Communication Quarterly* 58, no. 3 (1995): 5–9; Alfred Glossbrenner and Emily Glossbrenner, *Finding a Job on the Internet* (New York: McGraw-Hill, 1995), 194–197; Pam Dixon and Silvia Tiersten, *Be Your Own Headhunter Online* (New York: Random House, 1995), 80–83.

31. Quible, "The Electronic Resume: An Important New Job-Search Tool."

32. Pollock, "Sir: Your Application for a Job Is Rejected."

33. Quible, "The Electronic Resume: An Important New Job-Search Tool."

34. Pontow, "Electronic Résumé Writing Tips."

35. William J. Banis, "The Art of Writing Job-Search Letters," *CPC Annual,* 36th ed., no. 2 (1992): 42–50.

36. Toni Logan, "The Perfect Cover Story," *Kinko's Impress* 2 (2000): 32, 34.

37. Halm, personal communication.

Chapter 18

1. Jodi DeLeon, college recruiting manager, Microsoft Corporation, personal communication, May 1993; Microsoft webpage (accessed October 1998), <www.microsoft.com>.

2. Sylvia Porter, "Your Money: How to Prepare for Job Interviews," *San Francisco Chronicle,* 3 November 1981, 54.

3. George Donnelly, "Recruiting, Retention & Returns," *cfonet,* March 2000 (accessed 10 April 2000), <www.cfonet.com/html/Articles/CFO/2000/00Marecr.html>.

4. Stephanie Armour, "The New Interview Etiquette," *USA Today,* 23 November 1999, B1, B2.

5. Samuel Greengard, "Are You Well Armed to Screen Applicants?" *Personnel Journal,* December 1995, 84–95.

6. Charlene Marmer Solomon, "How Does Disney Do It?" *Personnel Journal,* December 1989, 53.

7. Marcia Vickers, "Don't Touch That Dial: Why Should I Hire You?" *New York Times,* 13 April 1997, F11.

8. Nancy K. Austin, "Goodbye Gimmicks," *Incentive,* May 1996, 241.

9. "Southwest Is Picky," *Soundview Executive Book Summaries,* September 1998, 5.

10. Joel Russell, "Finding Solid Ground," *Hispanic Business,* February 1992, 42–44, 46.

11. Michael P. Cronin, "This Is a Test," *Inc.,* August 1993, 64–68.

12. Tyler D. Hartwell, Paul D. Steele, and Nathaniel F. Rodman, "Workplace Alcohol-Testing Programs: Prevalence and Trends," *Monthly Labor Review,* June 1998, 27–34.

13. "Substance Abuse in the Workplace," *HR Focus,* February 1997, 1, 4+.

14. Austin, "Goodbye Gimmicks."

15. Microsoft 1997 Annual Report (accessed 23 October 1998), <www.microsoft.com>.

16. Peter Rea, Julie Rea, and Charles Moonmaw, "Training: Use Assessment Centers in Skill Development," *Personnel Journal,* April 1990, 126–131; Greengard, "Are You Well Armed to Screen Applicants?"

17. Anne Field, "Coach, Help Me Out with This Interview," *Business Week,* 22 October 2001, 134E2, 134E4.

18. Robert Gifford, Cheuk Fan Ng, and Margaret Wilkinson, "Nonverbal Cues in the Employment Interview: Links Between Applicant Qualities and Interviewer Judgments," *Journal of Applied Psychology* 70, no. 4 (1985): 729.

19. Dale G. Leathers, *Successful Nonverbal Communication* (New York: Macmillan, 1986), 225.

20. Armour, "The New Interview Etiquette."

21. Shirley J. Shepherd, "How to Get That Job in 60 Minutes or Less," *Working Woman,* March 1986, 119.

22. Shepherd, "How to Get That Job in 60 Minutes or Less," 118.

23. H. Anthony Medley, *Sweaty Palms: The Neglected Art of Being Interviewed* (Berkeley, Calif.: Ten Speed Press, 1993), 179.

24. Gerald L. Wilson, "Preparing Students for Responding to Illegal Selection Interview Questions," *Bulletin of the Association for Business Communication* 54, no. 2 (1991): 44–49.

25. Jeff Springston and Joann Keyton, "Interview Response Training," *Bulletin of the Association for Business Communication* 54, no. 3 (1991): 28–30; Gerald L. Wilson, "An Analysis of Instructional Strategies for Responding to Illegal Selection Interview Questions," *Bulletin of the Association for Business Communication* 54, no. 3 (1991): 31–35.

26. Stephen J. Pullum, "Illegal Questions in the Selection Process: Going Beyond Contemporary Business and Professional Communication Textbooks," *Bulletin of the Association for Business Communication* 54, no. 3 (1991): 36–43; Alicia Kitsuse, "Have You Ever Been Arrested?" *Across the Board,* November 1992, 46–49; Christina L. Greathouse, "Ten Common Hiring Mistakes," *Industry Week,* 20 January 1992, 22–23, 26.

27. Marilyn Moats Kennedy, "Are You Getting Paid What You're Worth?" *New Woman,* November 1984, 110.

28. Harold H. Hellwig, "Job Interviewing: Process and Practice," *Bulletin of the Association for Business Communication* 55, no. 2 (1992): 8–14.

29. Jodi DeLeon, college recruiting manager, Microsoft Corporation, personal communication, May 1993.

Appendix I

1. Mary A. De Vries, *Internationally Yours* (Boston: Houghton Mifflin, 1994), 9.
2. Patricia A. Dreyfus, "Paper That's Letter Perfect," *Money,* May 1985, 184.
3. "When Image Counts, Letterhead Says It All," *Stamford (Conn.) Advocate and Greenwich Times,* 10 January 1993, F4.
4. Mel Mandell, "Electronic Forms Are Cheap and Speedy," *D&B Reports,* July–August 1993, 44–45.
5. Linda Driskill, *Business and Managerial Communication: New Perspectives* (Orlando, Fla.: Harcourt Brace Jovanovich, 1992), 470.
6. Driskill, *Business and Managerial Communication,* 470.
7. Lennie Copeland and Lewis Griggs, *Going International: How to Make Friends and Deal Effectively in the Global Marketplace,* 2d ed. (New York: Random House, 1985), 24–27.
8. De Vries, *Internationally Yours,* 8.
9. Copeland and Griggs, *Going International,* 24–27.
10. U.S. Postal Service, *Postal Addressing Standards* (Washington, D.C.: GPO, 1992).
11. Copeland and Griggs, *Going International,* 24–27.
12. Renee B. Horowitz and Marian G. Barchilon, "Stylistic Guidelines for E-Mail," *IEEE Transactions on Professional Communications,* 37, no. 4 (1994): 207–212.
13. Jill H. Ellsworth and Matthew V. Ellsworth, *The Internet Business Book* (New York: Wiley, 1994), 93.
14. William Eager, *Using the Internet* (Indianapolis: Que Corporation, 1994), 11.
15. Eager, *Using the Internet,* 10.
16. William Eager, Larry Donahue, David Forsyth, Kenneth Mitton, and Martin Waterhouse, *Net.Search* (Indianapolis: Que Corporation, 1995), 221.
17. Rosalind Resnick and Dave Taylor, *Internet Business Guide* (Indianapolis: Sams.net Publishing, 1995), 117.
18. James L. Clark and Lyn R. Clark, *How 7: A Handbook for Office Workers,* 7th ed. (Cincinnati: South-Western, 1995), 431–432.

Appendix IV

1. Dianna Booher, *E-Writing* (New York: Pocket Books, 2001), 6.
2. Eve Milrod and Arthur VanDam, *Mastering Communication Through Technology* (Woodmere, N.Y.: Career Advance Center, Inc., 2001), 13–14, 20–22, 24–29, 30–32, 37, 39, 40, 43; Nancy Flynn and Tom Flynn, *Writing Effective E-Mail* (Menlo Park, Calif.: Crisp Publications, 1998), 3, 5–6, 10, 14–15, 17, 29, 47, 55, 61, 62, 71; Booher, *E-Writing,* ix, 2, 6–7, 16, 19, 23, 25–27, 30, 33, 36, 39, 41–42, 49; Morey Stettner, "The Right Way to Write: Composing Clear, Crisp Memos and E-Mail," *The Edward Lowe Report,* June 2000, 2; Karen Kalis, "Make Your E-Mail More Effective," *Supervision* 62, no. 9 (September 2001): 23–25; T. L. Aardsma, "Improve Your E-Mail Etiquette," *Inside the Internet* 8, no. 7 (July 2001): 6–9; Andrea C. Poe, "Don't Touch That 'Send' Button!" *HRMagazine* 46, no. 7 (July 2001): 74–80.

Acknowledgments

Text

7 (Business Writing: A Craft Under Siege?) Adapted from John Hendren, "Personal Business: Defending English from Assault on the Job," *New York Times*, 4 February 2001, 3, 14; Jennifer Lee, "In China, Computer Use Erodes Traditional Handwriting, Stirring a Cultural Debate," *New York Times,* 1 February 2001, C3; David W. Orr, "Verbicide," *American Educator,* Winter 2000–2001, 26–29, 48; Diane E. Lewis, "Writing Still Counts," *Boston Globe,* 26 December 1999, F4. **21 (Ethical Boundaries: Where Would You Draw the Line?)** Adapted from Ben Stein, "An Employer's Bill of Rights," *Business Month,* April 1990, 55; Thomas A. Young, "Ethics in Business: Business of Ethics," *Vital Speeches,* 15 September 1992, 725–730; "Business Ethics: What Are Your Personal Standards?" *Working Woman,* February 1990, 61–62; Kyle Herger, "One Communicator's Gold Star Is Another's Scarlet Letter," *IABC Communication World,* September 1989, 34–36; Barbara D. Langham, "Ethics: Where Do You Stand?" *IABC Communication World,* May 1989, 21–22, 24–25; Frank Yanacek, "A Question of Ethics," *Transportation and Distribution,* December 1988, 48–50. **42 (What You Should Know About Videoconferencing vs. Face-to-Face Meetings)** Adapted from "Air Travel Fears to Drive Videoconferencing Market," *Electronic Commerce News*, 15 October 2001, 1+; "Amid Terrorism Fears, More Businesses Are Conducting Virtual Meetings," *Palm Beach Post*, 14 October 2001, 4F; Charles E. Ramirez, "Videoconference Demand Up: More Companies Seek Services After Attacks," *Detroit News*, 10 October 2001, 1; Fred O. Williams, "Reluctant Travelers; Videoconferencing Gets Boost from Businesses," *Buffalo News*, 7 October 2001, B11; Wayne Tompkins, "Face-to-Face Meetings Are Less Likely for Now," *Courier-Journal*, 1 October 2001, 5C; Benny Evangelista, "Meetings via Video: More Businesses Skipping Travel, Tuning Into Videoconferencing, *San Francisco Chronicle*, 1 October 2001, E1; James R. Healey, "Business Travelers Keep Their Feet on the Ground: Videoconferencing, Telecommuting Replace Good Old Face-to-Face," *USA Today*, 26 September 2001, B1; Thomas E. Weber, "E-World: After Terror Attacks, Companies Rethink In-Person Meetings," *Wall Street Journal*, 24 September 2001, B1. **45 (Checklist: Improving Your Listening Skills)** *Source:* Robert A. Luke, Jr., "Improving Your Listening Ability," *Supervisory Management,* June 1992, 7; Madelyn Burley-Allen, "Listening for Excellence in Communication," *The Dynamics of Behavior Newsletter* 2, no. 2 (Summer 1992): 1; Bob Lamons, "Good Listeners Are Better Communicators," *Marketing News,* 11 September 1995, 13+. **47 (Actions Speak Louder than Words All Around the World)** Adapted from David A. Victor, *International Business Communication* (New York: HarperCollins, 1992); David Wallace, "Mind Your Manners," *World Trade,* October 1992, 52, 54–55; Hannele Duvfa, "Innocents Abroad: The Politics of Cross-Cultural Communication," *Communication and Discourse Across Cultures and Languages,* 1991, 73–89; M. Katherine Glover, "Do's and Taboos: Cultural Aspects of International Business," *Business America,* 13 August 1990, 2–6; C. Barnum and N. Woniansky, "Taking Cues from Body Language," *Management Review,* June 1989, 59–60. **48 (Checklist: Improving Nonverbal Communication Skills)** *Source:* Gerald H. Graham, Jeanne Unrue, and Paul Jennings, "The Impact of Nonverbal Communication in Organizations: A Survey of Perceptions," *Journal of Business Communication* 28, no. 1 (Winter 1991): 45–62; Dianna Booher, *Communicate with Confidence* (New York: McGraw-Hill, 1994), 363–370. **57 (Test Your Intercultural Knowledge)** Adapted from David A. Ricks, "International Business Blunders: An Update," *Business & Economic Review,* January–March 1988, 25; Valerie Frazee, "Keeping Up on Chinese Culture," *Global Workforce,* October 1996, 16–17; Valerie Frazee, "Establishing Relations in Germany," *Global Workforce,* April 1997, 16–17; James Wilfong and Toni Seger, *Taking Your Business Global* (Franklin Lakes, N.J.: Career Press, 1997), 282. **69 (Communicating with a Global Audience on the Web)** Adapted from Laura Morelli, "Writing for a Global Audience on the Web," *Marketing News*, 17 August 1998, 16; Yuri and Anna Radzievsky, "Successful Global Web Sites Look Through Eyes of the Audience," *Advertising Age's Business Marketing,* January 1998, 17; Sari Kalin, "The Importance of Being Multiculturally Correct," *Computerworld*, 6 October 1997, G16–G17; and B.G. Yovovich, "Making Sense of All the Web's Numbers," *Editor & Publisher*, November 1998, 30–31; David Wilford, "Are We All Speaking the Same Language?" *The Times,* (London), 20 April 2000, 4. **91(Caution! E-Mail Can Bite)** Adapted from John J. DiGilio, "Electronic Mail: From Computer to Courtroom," *Information Management Journal,* April 2000, 32–44; Mary Beth Currie and Daniel Black, "E-merging Issues in the Electronic Workplace," *Ivey Business Journal,* January–February 2001, 18–29; Mike Elgan, "The Trouble with E-Mail," *Windows Magazine,* November 1998, 31; Jerry Adler, "When E-Mail Bites Back," *Newsweek,* 23 November 1998, 45–46; Amy Harmon, "Corporate Delete Keys Busy as E-Mail Turns Up in Court," *New York Times,* 12 November 1998, A1, C2. **95 (Spin Cycle: Deciphering Corporate Doublespeak)** Adapted from William Lutz, "Life Under the Chief Doublespeak Officer," *USA Today,* 17 October 1996, 15A. **122 (No Need to Explain It—Just Say It in Plain English)** Adapted from Toddi Gutner, "At Last, the Readable Prospectus," *Business Week,* 13 April 1998, 11; Philip Maher, "One for the Writers," *Investment Dealers' Digest,* 17 November 1997, 4+; Ronald G. Shafer, "Government Bureaucrats to Learn a New Language: Simple English," *Wall Street Journal,* 2 June 1998, B1; Peder Zane, "For Investors, an Initial Public Offering of English," *New York Times,* 25 August 1996, 7; Dan Seligman, "The Gobbledygook Profession," *Forbes,* 7 September 1998, 174–175; Michael Weiss and James Hildebrandt, "Art of Clear Writing Lost in Sea of Legalese," *San Antonio Business Journal,*

28 October 1996 (accessed September 1998), <www.amcity.com/sanantonio/stories/ 102896/editorial2.html>. **153 (Warding Off Digital Disaster)** Adapted from Marcia Stepanek, "From Digits to Dust," *Business Week,* 20 April 1998, 128–130; Stephan H. Wildstrom, "Don't Be a Crash Dummy," *Business Week,* 13 April 1998, 15; Gary Sutton, "Backing Up Onsite—or Online: 25 Smart Ways to Protect Your PC from Data Disaster," *Computer Technology Review,* February 1998, 38, 42+; Deborah Branscum and Jennifer Lach, "E-Mail Scare," *Newsweek,* 10 August 1998, 10; Brooks Talley, "Killing Viruses Dead," *InfoWorld,* 10 August 1998, 1, 66+; Stan Miastkowski, "Virus Killers," *PC World Online,* 1 March 1998; Philip Elmer-DeWitt, Scott Brown, and Thomas McCarroll, "Invasion of the Data Snatchers," *Time,* 26 September 1998, 62+; James E. Hunton, "Facts and Fables About Computer Viruses," *Journal of Accountancy,* May 1998, 39–42. **161 (How to Proofread Like a Pro)** Adapted from Philip C. Kolin, *Successful Writing at Work*, 2d ed., 102. Used with permission of D. C. Heath & Company; Dennis Hensley, "A Way with Words: Proofreading Can Save Cash and Careers," *Dallas Magazine,* May 1986, 57–58. Reprinted with permission. **171** (Figure A.1) www.orbitz.com. **172** (Figure A.2) www.sas.com/corporate/community. **173** (Figure A.3) www.burpee.com/Burpee/ GardenSchool/ school1/ class1/c1p1.asp?uid=. **174** (Figure A.4) http://se.yahoo.com/. **176** (Figure A.5) www.usatoday.com/money/autos/2001-07-19-tires-no.htm. **177** (Figure A.6) www.vanguard.com. **177** (Figure A.7) www.att/com/foundation. **178** (Figure A.8) www.breadworld.com/sitecontent. **179** (Figure A.9) www.southwest.com. **180** (Figure A.10) www.cnn.com. **187 (How Direct Is Too Direct?)** Source: Adapted from Mary A. DeVries, *Internationally Yours* (Boston: Houghton Mifflin, 1994), 195; Myron W. Lustig and Jolene Koester, *Intercultural Competence* (New York: HarperCollins, 1993), 66–72; Mary Munter, "Cross-Cultural Communication for Managers," *Business Horizons,* May–June 1993, 69–78; David A. Victor, *International Business Communication* (New York: HarperCollins, 1992), 137–168; Larry A. Samovar and Richard E. Porter, *Intercultural Communication: A Reader,* 6th ed. (Belmont, Calif.: Wadsworth, 1991), 109–110; Larry A. Samovar and Richard E. Porter, *Communication Between Cultures* (Belmont, Calif.: Wadsworth, 1991), 235–244; Carley H. Dodd, *Dynamics of Intercultural Communication,* 3d ed. (Dubuque, Iowa: Wm. C. Brown, 1989), 69–73. **206 (Recommendation Letters: What's Right to Write?)** Source: Adapted from Maura Dolan and Stuart Silverstein, "Court Broadens Liability for Job References," *Los Angeles Times,* 28 January 1997, A1, A11; David A. Price, "Good References Pave Road to Court," *USA Today,* 13 February 1997, 11A; Frances A. McMorris, "Ex-Bosses Face Less Peril Giving Honest Job References," *Wall Street Journal,* 8 July 1996, B1, B8; Dawn Gunsch, "Gray Matters: Centralize Control of Giving References," *Personnel Journal,* September 1992, 114, 116–117; Betty Southard Murphy, Wayne E. Barlow, and D. Diane Hatch, "Manager's Newsfront: Job Reference Liability of Employees," *Personnel Journal,* September 1991, 22, 26; Ross H. Fishman, "When Silence Is Golden," *Nation's Business,* July 1991, 48–49. **245 (Should Employers Use E-Mail to Deliver Negative Employment Messages?)** Adapted from Stephanie Armour, "E-Mail Lets Companies Deliver Bad News From Afar," *USA Today,* 20 February 2001, B1; Cheryl Maday, "How to Break Bad News," *Psychology Today,* November–December 1999, 18; Nancy Flynn and Tom Flynn, *Writing Effective E-Mail* (Menlo Park, Calif: Crisp Learning, 1998), 4. **248 (Mastering the Art of Constructive Criticism)** Adapted from Les Giblin, *How to Have Confidence and Power in Dealing with People* (New York: Prentice Hall, 1956), 132–133. **285 (What You May Legally Say in a Sales Letter)** Ronald A. Anderson, Ivan Fox, David P. Twomey, and Marianne M. Jennings, *Business Law and the Legal Environment* (Cincinnati: West Educational Publishing, 1999), 229–230, 237–240, 247, 524–526, 567; Sales Letter Tips (accessed 26 June 2000)<www.smartbiz.com/sbs/arts/sbs47.htm>; Instant Sales Letters (accessed 26 June 2000), <instantsalesletters.com>. **326 (Beware of the Mischievous Webmaster)** Adapted from Alastair Smith, "Criteria for Evaluation of Internet Information Resources" (accessed 28 October 2001), <www.vuw.ac.nz/~agsmith/evaln/index.htm>; "ICYouSee: T is for Thinking," Ithaca Library (accessed 28 October 2001), <www.ithaca.edu/library/Training/hott.html>; La Jean Humphries, "Teaching Users to Evaluate Internet Sites: Sources on Sources," *Searcher,* May 2000, 68–70; "Evaluating Information Found on the Internet" (accessed 28 October 2001), <milton.mse.jhu.edu/research/education/net.html>; Robert Harris, "Evaluating Internet Research Sources," *Virtual Salt* (accessed 28 October 2001), <www.virtualsalt.com/evalu8it.htm>. **329 (The Tangled Web of Internet Copyrights)** Adapted from Janet S. Parrack, "Get the 411 on Copyright and the Internet," *Reading Today,* April–May 2001, 7; *The Internet Unleashed,* 2d ed. (Indianapolis: Sams.net Publishing, 1995), 1056; Alice Bredin, "The Hard Drive: Analog Laws Can't Keep Up with Digital Technology," *Newsday*, 30 April 1995, 2; Ron Coleman, "Copycats on the Superhighway," *ABA Journal* 81 (1 July 1995): 68. **352 (Six Easy Ways to Create Eye-Catching Charts with Excel)** Adapted from Ed Bott and Woody Leonhard, *Special Edition Using Microsoft Office 2000* (Indianapolis: Que Corporation, 1999), 549–556; Microsoft Office website (accessed 14 November 2001),<office.microsoft.com/assistance/2002/articles/xllrgAboutFormattingCharts.aspx>; Julie Hill, "The Charting Game," *Presentations,* March 2001, 50–54; "Conditionally Change Bar Colors in a Chart to Highlight Successes," *Inside Microsoft Excel,* December 2000, 9–11. **358 (Visuals That Lie)** Adapted from A. S. C. Ehrenberg, "The Problem of Numeracy," *Admap,* February 1992, 37–40; Mary S. Auvil and Kenneth W. Auvil, *Introduction to Business Graphics: Concepts and Applications* (Cincinnati: South-Western, 1992), 40, 192–193; Peter H. Selby, *Using Graphs and Tables: A Self-Teaching Guide* (New York: Wiley, 1979), 8–9. **379 (Reports Bring Toyota's Engineers Up to Speed)** Adapted from Durward K. Sobek II, Jeffrey K. Liker, and Allen C. Ward, "Another Look at How Toyota Integrates Product Development," *Harvard Business Review*, July–August 1998, 36–49; Trevor Hopper and Nathan Joseph, "The Dissection of Dinosaur: Experiments in Control at Toyota," *Management Accounting,* May 1995, 34+; Ronald M. Becker, "Learning to Think Lean: Lean Manufacturing and the Toyota Production System," *Automotive Manufacturing and Production,* June 2001, 64–65. **400 (Minding Your Business with Online Reporting)** Adapted from Scott Steinacher, "Putting the Power Back in Reports," *InfoWorld,* 24 January 2000, 69–70; Federal Express website (accessed 25 November 2001) <www.fedex.com>; Jack Schember, "Mrs. Fields' Secret Weapon," *Personnel Journal,* September 1991, 56–58; Paul Kondstadt, "Ship 54—

Where Are You?" *CIO,* May 1990, 80–81, 84, 86; Bruce G. Posner and Bo Burlingham, "The Hottest Entrepreneur in America," *Inc.,* January 1988, 44–48. **413 (Seven Errors in Logic That Can Undermine Your Reports)** Adapted from Christopher Power, "Flops," *Business Week,* 16 August 1993, 79; Mary Munter, *Guide to Managerial Communication,* 2d ed. (Upper Saddle River, N.J.: Prentice Hall, 1982), 31. Adapted by permission of Prentice Hall, Inc., Upper Saddle River, N.J. **430 (Top Tips for Writing Reports That Mean Business)** Adapted from Joan Minninger, *The Perfect Memo* (New York: Doubleday, 1990), 169–170. Copyright ©1990 by Joan Minninger. Used by permission of Doubleday, a division of Bantam Doubleday Dell Publishing Group, Inc. **497 (Five Tips for Making Presentations Around the World)** Adapted from Patricia L. Kurtz, *The Global Speaker* (New York: AMACOM, 1995), 35–47, 56–68, 75–82, 87–100; David A. Victor, *International Business Communication* (New York: HarperCollins Publishers, 1992), 39–45; Lalita Khosla, "You Say Tomato," *Forbes,* 21 May 2001, 36; Stephen Dolainski, "Are Expats Getting Lost in the Translation?" *Workforce,* February 1997, 32–39. **509 (Nerves: The Secret Weapon of Polished Presenters)** Adapted from Sherwyn P. Morreale and Courtland L. Bovée, *Excellence in Public Speaking* (Fort Worth: Harcourt Brace, 1998), 7; Leon Fletcher, "A Remedy for Stage Fright," *The Toastmaster,* June 1994, 8–10; Greg Dahl, "Fear of Fear," *The Toastmaster,* June 1994, 10–11; "A Survival Guide to Public Speaking," *Training & Development Journal,* September 1990, 15–16, 18 25. **534 (Handouts That Won't Get Trashed)** Source: Ted Simons, "Handouts That Won't Get Trashed," *Presentations,* February 1999, 47–50; David Green, personal communication, 13 July 2001; "Help 'Em Remember With Handouts," Idea Café: Handouts for Your Business Presentations (accessed 4 October 2001),<http://www.ideacafe.com/fridge/spotlight/spothandouts.html>; Bob Lamons, "Good Listeners Are Better Communicators," *Marketing News,* 11 September 1995, 13+; Phillip Morgan and H. Kent Baker, "Building a Professional Image: Improving Listening Behavior," *Supervisory Management,* November 1985, 35–36. **549 (Netting a Job on the Web)** Adapted from Richard N. Bolles, "Career Strategizing or, What Color Is Your Web Parachute?" *Yahoo! Internet Life,* May 1998, 116, 121; Tara Weingarten, "The All-Day, All-Night, Global, No-Trouble Job Search," *Newsweek,* 6 April 1998, 17; Michele Himmelberg, "Internet an Important Tool in Employment Search," *San Diego Union-Tribune,* 7 September 1998, D2; Gina Imperato, "35 Ways to Land a Job Online," *Fast Company,* August 1998, 192–197; Roberta Maynard, "Casting the Net for Job Seekers," *Nation's Business,* March 1997, 28–29. **560 (Résumé Deception: Risky or Fatal?)** Adapted from Anne Field, "Coach, Help Me Out with This Interview," *Business Week,* 22 October 2001, 134E4, 134E6; Joan E. Rigdon, "Deceptive Résumés Can Be Door-Openers but Can Become an Employee's Undoing," *Wall Street Journal,* 17 June 1992, B1; Diane Cole, "Ethics: Companies Crack Down on Dishonesty," *Managing Your Career,* Spring 1991, 8–11; Nancy Marx Better, "Résumé Liars," *Savvy,* December 1990–January 1991, 26–29. **586 (How to Check References and Stay Within the Law)** Adapted from James Krohe, Jr., "Why Traditional Screening Doesn't Work," *Across the Board,* December 1997, 22+; Frances A. McMorris, "Ex-Bosses Face Less Peril Giving Honest Job References," *Wall Street Journal,* 8 July 1996, B1, B8; Michael Kinsman, "Firm's Cost Cutting Left This Job-Seeker out in the Cold," *San Diego Union-Tribune,* 21 June 1996, C1; Samuel Greengard, "Are You Well Armed to Screen Applicants?" *Personnel Journal,* December 1995, 84–95; "Employers Find It More Difficult to Check References," *Personnel Journal,* May 1993, 20; Tim Weiner, "Fearing Suits, Companies Avoid Giving Job References," *New York Times,* 8 May 1993, 17, 29; David B. Kern, "Handling Reference Requests on Fired Employees," *Supervisory Management,* January 1993, 6; Paul W. Barada, "Check References with Care," *Nation's Business,* May 1993, 54, 56; Max Messmer, "Nothing but the Truth," *Small Business Reports,* March 1993, 11–14; "Managing People: Reference-Checking Tips," *Inc.,* November 1992, 38; James W. Fenton, Jr., and Kay W. Lawrimore, "Employment Reference Checking, Firm Size, and Defamation Liability," *Journal of Small Business Management,* October 1992, 88–95; George D. Webster, "Background and Reference Checks," *Agency Sales Magazine,* October 1992, 26–28; Emily Leinfuss, "Reference Checks: The Truth Be Known," *Computerworld,* 22 April 1991, 88; Lois Vander Waerdt, "Take Nothing for Granted," *Management World,* March–April 1990, 5–10; Arthur Bragg, "Checking References," *Sales & Marketing Management,* November 1990, 68, 70, 73; James Braham, "Hiring Mr. Wrong," *Industry Week,* 7 March 1988, 31–34; Robert Half, "Reference Checking: A Critical Part of the Hiring Process," *Journal of Accountancy,* August 1988, 130–134. **589 (Interview Strategies: Answering the 16 Toughest Questions)** Adapted from "Career Strategies," *Black Enterprise,* February 1986, 122. Copyright © 1986, Black Enterprise Magazine, The Earl Graves Publishing Company, Inc., New York, NY. All rights reserved.

Figures and Tables

32 (Table 2.1) Adapted from J. Michael Sproule, *Communication Today* (Glenview, Ill.: Scott, Foresman, 1981), by permission of J. Michael Sproule. Copyright J. Michael Sproule. **43** (Table 2.2) Copyright, Dr. Lyman K. Steil, president, Communication Development, Inc., St. Paul, Minn. Prepared for the Sperry Corporation. Reprinted with permission of Dr. Steil and Unisys Corporation. **46** (Figure 2.2) Adapted from S. E. Taylor, L. A. Peplan, and D. O. Sears, *Social Psychology,* 9th ed. (Upper Saddle River, N.J.: Prentice Hall, 1997) 98. Photographs by Paul Ekman, Ph.D. Used with permission. **54** (Figure 3.1) Global Has Its Barriers, *USA Today,* 3 May 2000, B1. **58** (Table 3.1) Mary O'Hara-Devereaux and Robert Johansen, *Global Work: Bridging Distance, Culture, and Time* (San Francisco: Jossey-Bass, 1994), 55, 59. **60** (Figure 3.2) Lillian H. Chaney and Jeanette S. Martin, *Intercultural Business Communication,* 2d edition (Upper Saddle River, N.J.: Prentice Hall, 2000), 50. **66** (Table 3.2) Guo-Ming Chen and William J. Starosta, *Foundations of Intercultural Communication* (Boston: Allyn and Bacon, 1998), 66. **192** (Figure 7.2) Courtesy Ace Hardware. **200** (Figure 7.5) Courtesy Herman Miller. **205** (Figure 7.7) Courtesy Discover Communications. **207** (Figure 7.8) Courtesy Target. **266** (Figure 9.1) Adapted from Abraham H. Maslow, *Motivation and Personality* (New York: Harper & Row, 1954), 12, 19, Copyright © 1970 by Abraham H. Maslow. Reprinted by permission of HarperCollins Publishers. **282** (Figure 9.6) Courtesy Qantas Airlines. **308** (Figure 10.1) Partially adapted from Michael Eisenberg and Robert Berkowitz, "Big Six" Model, Copyright 1998. big6.syr.edu/

body.html, accessed 6 November 1998. **310–311** (Figure 10.2) Adapted from "Finding Industry Information" [accessed 3 November 1998] www.pitt.edu/~buslibry/industries.htm; Thomas P. Bergman, Stephen M. Garrison, and Gregory M. Scott, *The Business Student Writer's Manual and Guide to the Internet* (Paramus, N.J., Prentice Hall, 1998), 67–80; Ernest L. Maier, Anthony J. Faria, Peter Kaatrude, and Elizabeth Wood, *The Business Library and How to Use It* (Detroit: Omnigraphics, 1996), 53–76. **341** (Figure 11.1) *Standard & Poor's Industry Surveys—Footware,* 1 December 1998, 26; Hoovers Capsules online [accessed 11 November 2001], www.hoovers.com/co/capsule. **342** (Figure 11.4) *American Demographics,* March 1998, 42. **344–345** (Figure 11.5) *American Demographics,* March 1998, 47/*American Demographics,* January 1998, 58/*American Demographics,* February 1998, 52/ *Wall Street Journal,* 7 December 1998, R4. **346** (Figure 11.6) "Going Global Has Its Barriers," *USA Today,* 3 May 2000, B1. **347** (Figure 11.8) Brad Reagan, "Sounding Off," *Wall Street Journal,* 29 October 2001, R4. **347** (Figure 11.9) Iris I. Varner, *Contemporary Business Report Writing,* 2d ed. (Chicago: Dryden Press, 1991), 75. **349** (Figure 11.11) www.census.gov/statab/ranks/pg05.txt. **349** (Figure 11.12) "How the Networks Deliver the Goods," *Business Week,* 6 April 1998, 91–92. **365** (Figure B.1) Charles V. Callahan and Bruce A. Pasternack, "Corporate Strategy in the Digital Age," *Strategy and Business,* Second Quarter, www.strategy-business.com/research/99202:page2.html. **368** (Figure B.2) Adapted from Jeffrey Gitomer, "Sales Moves: A Lesson in Cell Phone Etiquette," *Baltimore Business Journal,* January 21, 2000, baltimore.bcentral.com/baltimore/stories/2000/01/24/smallb2.html. **369** (Figure B.3) Adapted from "Ten Steps to Caller-Friendly Voice Mail," *Managing Office Technology,* January 1995, 25. **371** (Figure B.4) John Galvin, "Cheating, Lying, Stealing," SmartBusinessMag.com, June 2000, 86–99. **482** (Table 14.1) Catalyst, New York, cited in Bickley Townsend, "Room at the Top," *American Demographics,* July 1996, 31. **483** (Table 14.2) Catalyst, New York, cited in Bickley Townsend, "Room at the Top," *American Demographics,* July 1996, 31. **483** (Table 14.3) Catalyst, New York, cited in Bickley Townsend, "Room at the Top," *American Demographics,* July 1996, 33. **483** (Table 14.4) Automotive Parts & Accessories Association, Bethesda, Md., cited in Alison Stein Wellner, "Keeping Old Cars on the Road," *American Demographics,* July 1997, 54–57. **483** (Figure 14.5) Automotive Parts & Accessories Association, Bethesda, Md., cited in Alison Stein Wellner, "Keeping Old Cars on the Road," *American Demographics,* July 1997, 54–57. **483** (Figure 14.6) Automotive Parts & Accessories Association, Bethesda, Md., cited in Alison Stein Wellner, "Keeping Old Cars on the Road," *American Demographics,* July 1997, 54–58. **484** (Figure 14.7) Adapted from Automotive Parts & Accessories Association, Bethesda, Md., cited in Alison Stein Wellner, "Keeping Old Cars on the Road," *American Demographics,* July 1997, 54–58. **484** (Figure 14.8) Adapted from Automotive Parts & Accessories Association, Bethesda, Md., cited in Alison Stein Wellner, "Keeping Old Cars on the Road," *American Demographics,* July 1997, 54–58. **485** (Table 14.5) Adapted from multiple sources listed for Case #7, Selling to Online America. **486** (Table 14.6) Adapted from multiple sources listed for Case #7, Selling to Online America. **487** (Table 14.7) Geng Cui, "The Different Faces of the Chinese Consumer," *China Business Review* 24, no. 4 (1997): 34–38. **487** (Table 14.8) Adapted from multiple sources listed for Case #8, Software in a Hard Market. **488** (Table 14.9) *CIA-The World Factbook-China,* [accessed 16 December 2001] www.odci.gov/cia/publications/factbook/geos/ch.html; U.S. Department of Commerce, *Big Emerging Markets Information Resource Page,* 28 August 1998 [accessed 1 December 1998] www.ita.doc.gov/bems/index.html. **488** (Table 14.10) *CIA-The World Factbook-China,* [accessed 16 December 2001], www.odci.gov/cia/publications/factbook/geos/ch.html; "WTO Membership to Boost China's Growth," *Xinhua News Agency,* 12 December 2001, 1+; U.S. Department of Commerce, *Big Emerging Markets Information Resource Page,* 28 August 1998 [accessed 1 December 1998] www.ita.doc.gov/bems/index.html. **489** (Figure 14.9) Adapted from multiple sources listed for Case #8 Software in a Hard Market. **489** (Figure 14.10) Adapted from multiple sources listed for Case #8 Software in a Hard Market. **489** (Figure 14.11) Adapted from multiple sources listed for Case #8 Software in a Hard Market. **495** (Figure 15.1) Adapted from Eric J. Adams, "Management Focus: User-Friendly Presentation Software," *World Trade,* March 1995, 92. **503** (Table 15.1) Adapted from Eric J. Adams, Management Focus: User-Friendly Presentation Software, *World Trade,* March 1995, 92. **523** (Table 16.1) Adapted from Claudyne Wilder and David Fine, *Point, Click & Wow* (San Francisco: Jossey-Bass Pfeiffer, 1996), 63. **527** (Figure 16.7) Microsoft PowerPoint2000 software. **528** (Figure 16.8) Microsoft PowerPoint2000 software. **529** (Table 16.2) Roger C. Parker, "10 Tips for Using Slideshow Transitions More Effectively," *3M Meeting Network* (accessed 8 June 2001), www.mmm.com/meetingnetwork/presentations/pmag_slideshowtransitions.html. **547** (Figure 17.2) Adapted from Richard Nelson Bolles, *What Color Is Your Parachute?* (Berkeley, Calif.: Ten Speed Press, 1997), 67. **585** (Figure 18.1) Adapted from Anne Fisher, "Success Secret: A High Emotional IQ," *Fortune,* 26 October 1998, 293–298; Laura Lyne McMurchie, "Careers Can Rise and Fall with an EQ," *Computing Canada,* September 1998, 18, 21. **585** (Figure 18.2) USA Today Snapshot "Checking Out New Hires," *USA Today,* 18 May 2000, B1. **591** (Table 18.3) Adapted from *The Northwestern Endicott Report* (Evanston, Ill.: Northwestern University Placement Center). **592** (Table 18.4) Adapted from H. Lee Rust, *Job Search: The Completion Manual for Jobseekers* (New York: American Management Association, 1979), 56. **593** (Figure 18.3) Adapted from *The Northwestern Endicott Report* (Evanston: Ill.: Northwestern University Placement Center). **596** (Table 18.5) "Dangerous Questions," *Nation's Business,* May 1999, 22.

Photo Credits

1 Corbis/Stock Market/George B. Diebold **9** PhotoEdit/Spencer Grant **10** Lonely Planet Images/Photo 20-20/Jay Daniel **14** CORBIS **19** Danny Turner Photography **29** Corbis/Stock Market/Chuck Savage **33** Barbel Schmidt Photography **34** Andy Freeberg Photography **35** Andy Freeberg Photography **42** AP/Wide World Photos/Cliff Schiappa/AP/Wide World Photos **46** Paul Ekman, Ph.D., Professor of Psychology **53** ITT Sheraton Hotel Hawaii **56** Brian Coats Photography **61** Stock Boston/Ilene Perlman **61** Getty Images, Inc./Ron Chapple **67** PhotoEdit/D. Young-Wolff **77** Corbis/Stock Market/John Gillmoure/TSM-25166 **79** Corbis/Sygma/Gary I. Rothstein **82** Jamaican Jerk Hut Foods, Inc. **83** Mark Richards

93 William Mercer McLeod **101** Ward-Williams Inc./Chip Williams/© 2000 Chip Williams **107** Weather Channel/Photo courtesy of Weather.com **111** AP/Wide World Photos/Lynsey Addario **113** Barry Staver **117** Churchill & Klehr Photography **125** Black Star/Robin Nelson **141** Omni-Photo Communications, Inc./Grace Davies **147** Corbis/Stock Market/Ariel Skelley **151** Starbucks Coffee Company **156** William Mercer McLeod **158** John R. Fulton, Jr. **164** Caldwell Photography **183** Index Stock Imagery, Inc./Carol and Mike Werner **185** Photo Network/Mark Sherman **186** Philip Saltonstall **191** Jyoti Cuisine India/Joe McGinn/Jyoti Cuisine India **199** Rahn & Associates Photographic Inc. **210** The Image Works/Jeff Greenberg **216** Bill Cramer Photography **218** PhotoEdit/Amy C. Etra **219** Corbis/Stock Market/LWA-Dann Tardif **223** The Blue Marble **227** Caponigro Public Realations, Inc. **229** AP/Wide World Photos/Paul Sakuma/AP/Wide World Photos **230** New York Times Pictures/Ozier Muhammad **243** Corbis/Sygma/Frederic Neema **256** AP/Wide World Photos/Suzanne Plunkett **257** PhotoEdit/Michael Newman **261** AP/Wide World Photos/James Walker **265** AT&T Archives/Property of AT&T Archives, reprinted with permission of AT&T **273** Pictor, New York **283** Michael L. Abramson Photography/Michael L. Abramson **287** Ferguson and Katzman Photography, Inc./Mark Katzman **305** Corbis/Stock Market/William Whitehurst **305** Corbis/Stock Market/Bill Westheimer **307** Charley Shin **313** PhotoEdit/Mary Kate Denny **320** PhotoEdit/Dana White **322** PhotoEdit/Michael Newman **337** Getty Images Inc./Frank Herholdt **337** Corbis/Stock Market/Jose L Pelaez, Inc. **350** Getty Images, Inc./PhotoDisc, Inc./John A. Rizzo **352** Comstock Royalty Free Division **353** Getty Images Inc./Tim Brown/Stone **355** Getty Images Inc./Steve Niedorf **366** The Image Works/John Maier, Jr. **366** Corbis/Stock Market/Ariel Skelley **370** Getty Images, Inc./Jon Riley **372** New York Times Pictures/Ann Dowie **375** Masterfile Corporation/Sarah Jones **377** Contact Press Images Inc./Greg Girard **378** SuperStock, Inc. **380** T. Michael Keza Photography **389** James Wasserman Photography **391** William Polo/Copyright Photo By Bill Polo **407** Photo Researchers, Inc./Porterfield/Chickering **408** Getty Images, Inc/Reuters/Michael Dalder/Archive Photos **411** International Stock Photography Ltd./Johnny Stockshooter **425** Richard Howard Photography **431** The Image Works/Steven Rubin **440** AP/Wide World Photos/Charles Rex Arbogast **441** Churchill & Klehr Photography **443** Corporate Dynamics **444** Brad Trent Photography/© 2001 Brad Trent **470** Peter Gregoire/Peter Gregoire **471** Bruce Rogow/Raymond Guardiano **473** Corbis/SABA Press Photos, Inc./Jason Grow **486** International Stock Photography Ltd./Miwako Ikeda **490** Frank Oberle Photography **493** Masterfile Corporation/Ken Davies **495** Getty Images, Inc./Michael Krasowitz **504** Karin Leitza/Karen Leitza **505** Barbel Schmidt Photography **507** Corbis/Stock Market/Jon Feingersh **510** Mark Richards **517** Picture Perfect USA, Inc./J & D Begg/Ace **518** SuperStock, Inc. **520** Corbis/Stock Market/Paul Barton **536** Corbis/Stock Market/Jim Erickson **537** Getty Images, Inc./Michael Krasowitz **541** Index Stock Imagery, Inc./Terry Why **543** REI Recreational Equipment Inc. **550** PhotoEdit/Mark Richards **562** Mark Wilson Photographer **567** Bo Parker **581** SAS Institute, Inc. **581** Randy Wells Wide World/Randy Wells **587** Syracuse University/Syracuse University, School of Management, Career Center **594** The Image Works/Bob Daemmrich **600** Getty Images, Inc./Dan Bosler

Organization/Brand/ Company Index

Subject Index

Z

Notes

Notes

Notes

Notes

Notes

Notes

Notes

Notes

Notes

Notes

TAKE AN INSIDE LOOK AT BUSINESS COMMUNICATION TODAY!

EXPLORE OUR "COMMUNICATION CLOSE-UPS" AND "COMMUNICATION CHALLENGES" AT THESE EXCITING COMPANIES

SEE OUR INSTRUCTIVE BOXED FEATURES CENTERING ON FOUR THEMES

Keeping Pace with Technology

Focusing on Ethics

Communicating Across Cultures

Sharpening Your Career Skills